HISTORICAL ATLAS

WILLIAM R. SHEPHERD

Late Professor of History, Columbia University

Eighth Edition, 1956

This edition contains all maps of the Seventh Revised and Enlarged Edition and a special supplement of historical maps for the period since 1929 prepared by C. S. Hammond & Company

Published by
The Colonial Offset Co., Inc.
Pikesville, Maryland

Sole Distributors
Barnes & Noble, Inc.
New York, N. Y.

Eighth Edition, 1956

Library of Congress Card Catalogue No. Map 56-4

To T. S.
my life's companion
who induced me to go forth
and see the world

Printed in the United States of America

PREFACE TO THE EIGHTH EDITION

Long a classic in its field, the Shepherd Atlas was out of print for many years, but remained in constant demand. Since the plates, originally made in Germany, were destroyed, this edition was printed by offset lithography. A special supplementary section of historical maps for the period since 1929 was prepared for the new edition by C. S. Hammond & Company.

In his preface to the Seventh Edition, 1929, the author expressed appreciation to Professor Charles H. Haskins, Harvard University; Professor Charles M. Andrews, Yale University; his colleagues, Professors Austin P. Evans, William Linn Westermann and Harry J. Carman, Columbia University; Mr. Harry W. Martin, Horace Mann Boy's School, New York; Dr. Isaiah Bowman and Mr. W. L. G. Joerg, the American Geographical Society; Principal C. Grant Robertson, Birmingham University; Honorary Professor T. F. Tout, Manchester University; Mr. L. Cecil Jane, Aberystwyth College, University of Wales; and the officials of the Library of the British Museum, in particular Mr. F. D. Sladen, Superintendent of the Reading Room.

For suggestions helpful in the preparation of the Eighth Edition, the publisher wishes to thank Mr. James M. Darley, Chief Cartographer of the National Geographic Society; Professor Walther Kirchner, University of Delaware; Professor John A. Krout, Vice President and Provost, Columbia University; Professor Bert James Loewenberg, Sarah Lawrence College; Professor Thomas C. Mendenhall, Yale University; Professor Marshall Smelser, University of Notre Dame.

ACKNOWLEDGMENT

Among the works consulted in the preparation of the Atlas the following have been especially serviceable:

R. Altamira y Crevea, Historia de España y de la civilización española. (4 vols. Madrid, 1909—1911)

E. Ambrosius ed., Andrees Allgemeiner Handatlas. (8th ed. 2d imp. Leipzig, 1924)

F. M. Anderson and A. S. Hershey, Handbook for the diplomatic history of Europe, Asia and Africa, 1870—1914. (Washington, 1918)

K. Andree, Geographie des Welthandels. (3 vols. Frankfort, 1910—1913)

Archiv für Eisenbahnwesen. (Berlin, 1878 . . . .)

E. M. Avery, A history of the United States and its people. (7 vols. Cleveland, 1904—1910)

J. G. Bartholomew, An Atlas of economic geography. (London, 1914)

J. G. Bartholomew ed., The Times survey atlas of the world. (London, 1922)

C. R. Beazley, The dawn of modern geography. (3 vols. London, 1897—1906)

E. Bonvalot, Le Tiers État d'après la charte de Beaumont-en-Argonne et ses filiales. (Paris, 1884)

I. Bowman, The new world. (Yonkers, 1926)

J. H. Breasted, A history of Egypt from the earliest times to the Persian conquest. (2d ed. New York, 1909)

J. Brunhes, Human Geography. (New York, 1920)

—, La géographie de l'histoire. (Paris, 1921)

J. Buchan ed., A history of the great war. (4 vols. New York, 1922)

The Cambridge ancient history. (6 vols. Cambridge, 1923 . . . .)

The Cambridge history of British foreign policy, 1783—1919. (3 vols. Cambridge, 1922—1923)

The Cambridge medieval history (5 vols. Cambridge, 1911 . . . .)

The Cambridge modern history (13 vols. Cambridge, 1902—1912).

The Cambridge modern history atlas. (2d ed. Cambridge, 1924)

A del Cantillo, Tratados, convenios y declaraciones de paz y de comercio. (Madrid, 1843)

H. M. Chadwick, The origin of the English nation. (Cambridge, 1907)

C. U. J. Chevalier, Répertoire des sources historiques du moyen-âge; Pt. II: topo-bibliographie. (2 vols. Paris, 1894—1903)

The Colonial Office list. (London, 1862 . . . .)

J. S. Corbett, Drake and the Tudor navy. (2 vols. London, 1899)

H. W. C. Davis, England under the Normans and Angevins. (London, 1915)

E. Debes ed., Neuer Handatlas über alle Teile der Erde. (4th ed. 2d imp. Leipzig, 1914)

L. Dominian, The frontiers of language and nationality in Europe. (New York, 1917)

G. Droysen, Allgemeiner historischer Handatlas. (Leipzig, 1886)

E. M. Earle, Turkey, the great powers and the Bagdad railway. (New York, 1923)

C. Errera, L'epoca delle grandi scoperte geografiche. (Milan, 1902)

Europäischer Geschichtskalender. (Munich, 1860 . . .)

H. J. Fleure, Human geography in western Europe. (2d ed. London, 1919)

—, The treaty settlement of Europe. (London, 1921)

E. Florez, España sagrada. (51 vols. Madrid, 1747—1879)

Foreign Affairs. (New York, 1922)

E. A. Freeman, Historical geography of Europe. (2 vols. 3d ed. London, 1903)

A García Cubas, Cuadro geográfico, estadístico, descriptivo e histórico de los Estados Unidos Mexicanos. (Mexico, 1884)

The Geographical Journal. (London, 1893 . . . .)

The Geographical Review (New York, 1916 . . . .)

W. Götz, Die Verkehrswege im Dienste des Welthandels. (Stuttgart, 1888)

—, Historische Geographie: Beispiele und Grundlinien. (Leipzig, 1904)

A. B. Hart ed., The American nation: a history from original sources by associated scholars. (28 vols. New York, 1904—1918)

C. H. Haskins and R. H. Lord, Some problems of the peace conference. (Cambridge, Mass., 1920)

F. J. Haverfield, The Roman occupation of Britain. (Oxford, 1924)

A. J. Herbertson and O. J. R. Howarth eds., The Oxford survey of the British Empire. (6 vols. Oxford, 1914)

E. Hertslet ed., China treaties (3d ed. London, 1908)

—, The map of Africa by treaty (3d ed. 3 vols. London, 1909)

—, The map of Europe by treaty. (4 vols. London, 1875, 1891)

K. Heussi and H. Mulert, Atlas zur Kirchengeschichte. (Tübingen, 1905)

W. v. Heyd, Histoire du commerce du Levant au moyen-âge. (2 vols. Leipzig, 1885—1886)

ACKNOWLEDGMENT

A. Himly, Histoire de la formation territoriale des états de l'Europe centrale. (2 vols. Paris, 1876)

T. H. Holdich, Boundaries in Europe and the Near East. (London, 1918)

L. Hugues, Cronologia delle scoperte e delle esplorazioni geografiche dall' anno 1492 a tutto il secolo XIX. (Milan, 1903)

C. Huelsen, The Roman forum. (2d ed. Rome, 1909)

W. W. Hunter, History of British India. (2 vols. London, 1899—1900)

P. Huvelin, Essai historique sur le droit des marchés et des foires. (Paris, 1897)

The imperial gazetteer of India. 3d ed. 26 vols. Oxford, 1907—1909)

C. Joppen, Historical atlas of India. (London, 1914)

J. S. Keltie, The partition of Africa. (2d ed. London, 1895)

H. and R. Kiepert, Formae orbis antiqui. (Berlin, 1901 . . . .)

C. G. de Koch and M. S. F. Schoell, Histoire abrégée des traités de paix entre les puissances de l'Europe depuis la paix de Westphalie. (15 vols. Paris, 1817—1818)

C. Kretschmer, Die Entdeckung Amerikas in ihrer Bedeutung für die Geschichte des Weltbildes. (Berlin, 1892)

C. de Lannoy and H. van der Linden, Histoire de l'expansion coloniale des peuples européens. (2 vols. Brussels, 1907—1911)

J. N. Larned ed., History for ready reference. (7 vols. Springfield, 1913)

E. Lavisse, Histoire de France depuis les origines jusqu'à la révolution. (9 vols. Paris, 1900 to 1911)

Lippincott's new gazetteer. (Philadelphia, 1916)

W. J. Loftie, London. (3d ed. London, 1892)

A. Longnon, Atlas historique de la France. (Paris, 1907)

C. Lucas ed., A historical geography of the British colonies. (12 vols. Oxford, 1905 to 1925)

K. von Martens and F. de Cussy, Recueil manuel et pratique de traités, conventions et autres actes diplomatiques. (7 vols. Leipzig, 1846 to 1857)

L. de Mas-Latrie, Trésor de chronologie d'histoire et de géographie pour l'étude et l'emploi des documents du moyen-âge. (Paris, 1889)

E. Mc Clure, Historical church atlas. (London, 1897)

H. R. Mill, The international geography. (New York, 1909)

C. F. R. de Montalambert, The monks of the west from Saint Benedict to Saint Bernard. (6 vols. New York, 1896)

R. Muir and G. Philip, Philips' New historical atlas for students. (5th ed. London, 1923)

J. Murdoch and I. Yamagata, A history of Japan. (2 vols. Yokohama, 1903, 1910)

D. P. Myers, Manual of collection of treaties. (Cambridge, Mass., 1922)

H. Nissen, Italische Landeskunde. (2 vols. Berlin, 1883—1902)

A. E. Nordenskiöld, Facsimile atlas to the early history of cartography. (London, 1889)

A. Oakes and R. B. Mowat eds., The great European treaties of the nineteenth century. (Oxford, 1918)

C. W. C. Oman, England before the Norman conquest. (5th ed. London, 1921)

E. L. Oxenham, Historical atlas of the Chinese Empire. (London, 1898)

P. Pelet, Atlas des colonies françaises. (Paris 1900—1902)

A. Petermanns Mitteilungen aus Justus Perthes' geographischer Anstalt über wichtige neue Erforschungen auf dem Gesamtgebiete der Geographie. (Gotha, 1855 . . . .)

O. F. Peschel, Geschichte des Zeitalters der Entdeckungen. (Stuttgart, 1858)

H. Pirenne, Medieval cities. (Princeton, 1925)

E. Porritt, The unreformed House of Commons. (2 vols. Cambridge, 1903)

R. L. Poole ed., Historical atlas of modern Europe. (Oxford, 1896—1902)

B. Poten ed., Handwörterbuch der Militärwissenschaften. (5 vols. Leipzig, 1877—1880)

F. W. Putzgers Historischer Schul-Atlas (48th ed. Leipzig, 1928)

H. Rashdall, The universities of Europe in the middle ages. (2 vols. Oxford, 1895)

O. Reclus, Atlas de la plus grande France. (Paris, 1913)

F. P. W. von Richthofen, China: Ergebnisse eigener Reisen und darauf gegründeter Studien. (5 vols. Berlin, 1877—1912)

E. K. A. Riehm, Handwörterbuch des biblischen Altertums. (2 vols. Leipzig, 1898)

W. Z. Ripley, The races of Europe. (New York, 1910)

C. G. Robertson and J. G. Bartholomew, An historical atlas of modern Europe from 1789 to 1922. (2d ed. London, 1924)

C. G. Robertson and J. G. Bartholomew, Historical and modern atlas of the British Empire (with supplement, London, 1905, 1924)

H. T. Robinson, Colonial chronology. (London, 1892)

Royal Asiatic Society of Great Britain and Ireland, Journal. (London, 1834 . . . .)

—, Transactions. (London, 1827 . . . .)

Royal Colonial Institute, Proceedings. (London, 1869 . . . .)

Royal Geographical Society, Journal. (London, 1831 . . . .)

S. Ruge, Die Entwicklung der Kartographie von Amerika bis 1570. (Gotha, 1892)

F. Schrader, Atlas de géographie historique. (Paris, 1911)

F. Seebohm, The English village community. (4th ed. London, 1905)

E. C. Semple, American history and its geographic conditions. (New York, 1903)

W. H. Siebert, The underground railroad from slavery to freedom. (New York, 1898)

W. Sievers, Süd- und Mittelamerika. (3d ed. Leipzig, 1914)

G. A. Smith and J. G. Bartholomew, Atlas of the historical geography of the Holy Land. (London, 1915)

C. von Spruner and T. Menke, Handatlas für die Geschichte des Mittelalters und der neueren Zeit. (Gotha, 1871—1880)

C. von Spruner, Historisch-geographischer Handatlas zur Geschichte Asiens, Afrikas, Amerikas und Australiens. (Gotha, 1855)

The statesman's year-book. (London, 1864 . . . .)

Stielers Handatlas. (Gotha, 1925)

A. M. H. J. Stokvis, Manuel d'histoire, de généalogie et de chronologie de tous les états du globe . . . (3 vols. Leyden, 1888—1893)

A. Supan, Die territoriale Entwicklung der europäischen Kolonien. (Gotha, 1906)

P. Teleki, Atlas zur Geschichte der Kartographie der japanischen Inseln. (Budapest, 1909)

H. W. V. Temperley, ed., A history of the peace conference of Paris. (5 vols. London, 1920 to 1921)

L. Thorndike, The history of medieval Europe. (New York, 1917)

M. Torrente, Historia de la revolución hispanoamericana. (3 vols. Madrid, 1829—1830)

The treaties of peace. (2 vols. New York, 1924)

U. S. Bureau of the Census, Statistical atlas of the United States. (Washington, 1903, 1914, 1925)

P. Vidal de la Blache, Histoire et géographie: atlas général Vidal-Lablache. (Paris, 1922)

P. Vinogradoff, The growth of the manor (rev. ed. London, 1911)

—, Villainage in England. (Oxford, 1892)

L. Vivien de Saint-Martin, Atlas universel de géographie (rev. ed. Paris, 1923)

E. A. Walker, Historical atlas of South Africa. (London, 1922)

World atlas of commercial geology: Pt. I, Distribution of mineral production. (Washington, 1921)

World missionary atlas. (London, 1925)

J. K. Wright, Geographical lore at the time of the crusades. (New York, 1924)

H. Yule, Cathay and the way thither (new ed. 4 vols. London, 1915—1916)

A. Zimmermann, Die europäischen Kolonien. (5 vols. Berlin, 1896—1903)

New York, March 1928

W. R. S.

CONTENTS

	PAGE
Physical Map of Europe, Western Asia and Northern Africa	2. 3
Mycenean Greece and the Orient, 2100—1300 B. C. Inset: Reference Map of the Nile Delta.	4
The Assyrian Empire and the Region about the Eastern Mediterranean, 850—625 B. C.	5
Reference Map of Ancient Palestine Insets: Plan of Jerusalem. Dominions of David and Solomon (1025—953 B. C.). Palestine under the later Kings (953—722 B. C.). Palestine under Joshua and the Judges (1250—1125 B. C.).	6. 7
The Orient 600—500 B. C. The Oriental Empires about 600 B. C. The Persian Empire about 500 B. C.	8
The Beginnings of Historic Greece, 700—600 B. C.	8
Vicinity of Troy. The Shores of the Propontis. Plan of Olympia	9
Reference Map of Ancient Greece. Northern Part	10. 11
Greek and Phoenician Settlements in the Mediterranean Basin, about 550 B. C.	12
Greece at the Time of the War with Persia, 500—479 B. C. The Athenian Empire at its Height (about 450 B. C.)	13
Reference Map of Ancient Greece. Southern Part Inset: Crete.	14. 15
Reference Map of Attica. Plan of Thermopylæ, 480 B. C. Inset: Harbors of Athens.	16
Greece at the Beginning of the Peloponnesian War (431 B. C.). Greece under Theban Headship (362 B. C.)	17
The Macedonian Empire, 336—323 B. C. Insets: The Ætolian and Achaian Leagues. Plan of Tyre.	18. 19
Kingdoms of the Diadochi After the Battle of Ipsus (301 B. C.). At the Beginning of the Struggle with Rome (about 200 B. C.).	18. 19
Reference Map of Asia Minor under the Greeks and Romans	20
Plan of Imperial Rome	22
Plan of Athens Inset: Plan of the Acropolis of Athens.	23
Plan of Republican Rome	23
Republican Forum. Imperial Forums	24
Reference Map of Ancient Italy. Northern Part	26. 27
The Growth of Roman Power in Italy to 218 B. C.	29
Reference Map of Ancient Italy. Southern Part Insets: Vicinity of Naples. Plan of Syracuse.	30. 31
Rome and Carthage at the Beginning of the Second Punic War, 218 B. C.	32
The Growth of Roman Power in Asia Minor I, after the Treaty of Apamea, 188 B. C.; II, before the outbreak of the Mithradatic Wars, 90 B. C.; III, as organized by Pompey, 63 B. C.	33
Territorial Expansion of Rome Insets: Plan of Carthage. Vicinity of Rome. Plan of Alexandria.	34. 35

CONTENTS

	PAGE
Reference Map of the Európean Provinces of the Roman Empire Insets: Gaul in the Time of Cæsar. The Rhine Country in Roman Times. Country about the Lower Danube in Roman Times.	38. 39
The Roman Empire about 395	42. 43
Economic Map of the Ancient World	44
Migrations and Conquests, 150—1066	45
Development of Christianity to 1300	46. 47
The Roman and Hunnic Empires about 450	48
Physical Map of the British Isles	49
The Germanic Kingdoms and the East Roman Empire in 486	50
Roman Britain about 410. Britain about 600	51
The Germanic Kingdoms and the East Roman Empire, 526—600 The Germanic Kingdoms and the East Roman Empire in 526. Europe and the East Roman Empire, 533—600.	52
The Califate in 750	53
Growth of Frankish Power, 481—814	53
The Carolingian and Byzantine Empires and the Califate about 814 Inset: Northern Austrasia about 814.	54. 55
Disruption of the Carolingian Empire, 843—888	56
The Peoples of Europe about 900	57
Europe and the Byzantine Empire about 1000	58. 59
England in the Eighth and Ninth Centuries England in the Eighth Century. England in the Ninth Century.	60
France about 1035	61
Central Europe, 919—1125	62. 63
Italy about 1050 Inset: The Patrimony of St. Peter.	64
Danish Dominions, 1016—1241	64
England 1087—1154	65
Europe and the Mediterranean Lands about 1097 Inset: Europe and the Mediterranean Lands by Religions about 1097.	66. 67
Asia Minor and the States of the Crusaders in Syria, about 1140 Insets: Palestine. Plan of Jerusalem about 1187.	68
France, 1154—1184 Inset: Domain, Fiefs and Suzerains of the Count of Champagne in the Twelfth Century.	69
Europe and the Mediterranean Lands about 1190 Inset: Guelf, Hohenstaufen and Ascanian Domains in Germany about 1176.	70. 71
The Holy Roman Empire under the Hohenstaufen, 1138—1254	72
The Mediterranean Lands after 1204	73
The British Isles, 1200—1450. Plan of London about 1300. Vicinity of London, 1200—1600	74. 75
France in 1328 Inset: The Chief Wool-raising Districts of England and Wool-manufacturing Towns of Flanders, Artois and Brabant.	76
Europe, 1360—1400	77
Central Europe in 1378 Inset: Dominions of Ottocar of Bohemia.	78. 79
Spread of German Settlements to the Eastward, 800—1400 Inset: The March of Lusatia.	80
The Great Schism, 1378—1417	81
France in 1453	81
Spain, 910—1492 Spain in 910. Spain in 1037. Spain in 1150. Spain, 1212—1492.	82. 83
England and France, 1455—1494	84
Decline of the March of Brandenburg under the Houses of Wittelsbach and Luxemburg, 1320—1415	85
The Wettin Lands, 1221—1485 Inset: Temporary break-up of the Wettin Lands about 1300.	85
Central Europe about 1477	86. 87

CONTENTS

	PAGE
Decline of German Power in the Baltic Region, 1380—1560	88
The Byzantine Empire, 1265—1355	89
I. The Byzantine Empire in 1265. II. The Byzantine Empire and the Ottoman Turks in 1355.	
Italy about 1494	90
Insets: The Milanese under the Visconti, 1339 - 1402. The Republic of Florence, 1300—1494.	
The Swiss Confederation, 1291—1513	91
The Mongol Dominions, 1227—1405	92
The Ottoman Empire, 1451—1481. Constantinople	93
Ecclesiastical Map of Western Europe in the Middle Ages	94. 95
Inset: Vicinity of Naples.	
Plan of Rome in the Middle Ages	96
The Roman Suburbicarian (Cardinal) Bishoprics about the 12th Century	96
Ecclesiastical Map of the British Isles in the Middle Ages	97
Mediaeval Commerce (Europe)	98. 99
Insets: England. Hanseatic League in Northern Germany.	
Rural Deaneries	100
Part of the bishopric of Winchester showing rural deaneries and religious houses during the Middle Ages.	
Mediaeval Universities	100
Ground-Plan of a Monastery (St. Gall, Switzerland)	101
Mediaeval Industry (Western Europe)	102. 103
Plan of a Mediaeval Manor	104
Enfranchisment of Mediaeval Towns	104A
Expansion of the Charter of Beaumont-en-Argonne, 1182—1300.	
Mediaeval Commerce (Asia)	104B. 104C
Inset: India.	
Europe in 1490	104D
The West Indies and Central America, 1492—1525	105
Inset: Watling's Island.	
The Conquest of Mexico, 1519—1521	106
The Expansion of Europe, 1340—1600	107—110
The Conquest of Peru, 1531-1533	111
The Portuguese Colonial Dominions in India and the Malay Archipelago, 1498—1580	112
The Imperial Circles about 1512	113
Central Europe about 1547	114. 115
Insets: Principality of Orange. Wettin Lands, 1485—1554.	
The Religious Situation in Europe about 1560	116
The Religious Situation in Central Europe about 1560. The Religious Situation in Europe about 1560.	
The Netherlands, 1559—1609	117
Europe about 1560	118. 119
The Religious Situation in Central Europe about 1618	120
Sweden about 1658	120
Principal Seats of War in Europe, 1618—1660	121
Treaty Adjustments, 1648—1660	121
1. Treaty of Westphalia, 1648. 2. Treaty of the Pyrenees, 1659; Peace of Roeskilde-Oliva, 1658, 1660.	
Central Europe about 1648	122. 123
Europe in 1648	124
Principal Seats of War in Europe, 1672—1699	125
Treaty Adjustments, 1668—1699	125
Treaties of Aix-la-Chapelle, Nimwegen, St. Germain, Ryswick, Carlowitz.	
Extension of the French Frontiers, 1601—1789	126
England an Ireland, 1485—1688	127
England and Wales, 1485—1688. Ireland, 1550—1653. Ecclesiastical England, 1534—1547.	
Scotland, 1488—1688	128
The Ottoman Empire, 1481—1683	128A
The Expansion of Europe, 1600—1700	128B. 128C
Insets: Partition of Guiana and the West Indies. India. The Establishment of Dutch Power in the Malay Archipelago, 1602—1641. Guinea Coast.	

CONTENTS

	PAGE
Principal Seats of War in Europe, 1700—1721	129
Europe about 1740 Inset: The Growth of Savoy, 1418—1748.	130. 131
Principal Seats of War, 1740—1763 Inset: Spain. West Africa. West Indies. Canada. India.	132
Treaty Adjustments, 1713—1763 Treaties of Utrecht, Rastatt, Baden, Stockholm, Frederiksborg, Nystad, Passarowitz, Vienna, Belgrade, Breslau, Dresden, Aix-la-Chapelle, Paris, Hubertusburg. Insets: Acadia and Newfoundland. Eastern North America.	133
Central Europe about 1786	134. 135
The Expansion of Europe, 1700—1763 Insets: The West Indies, 1700—1763. Cook's Voyages in the Southern Pacific.	136
India, 1700—1792	137
The Growth of Russia in Europe, 1300—1796	138. 139
Typical German States before and since the French Revolution	
I. Baden. Insets: County of Sponheim. Lordship of Grävenstein. Baden since 1801.	142
II. Wurtemberg Insets: County of Horburg and Lordship of Reichenweier. Principality-County of Montbéliard. Wurtemberg since 1495.	143
France in 1789 The "Gouvernements". The Generalities or Intendancies. The Salt tax and the Customs. Laws and Courts.	146. 147
Ecclesiastical Map of France, 1789 and 1802	148
France in 1791	148
Plans of Versailles and Paris in 1789	149
Napoleon's Campaign in Egypt, 1798	150
Northern Italy, 1796 (for the campaigns of 1796—1805)	150
Germany and Italy in 1803	151
Germany and Italy in 1806	151
Treaty Adjustments, 1810—1812 Insets: India. Cape Colony.	152
Principal Seats of War, 1788—1815 Insets: India. Egypt. Napoleon's Campaign in Russia, 1812.	153
Central Europe in 1812 Inset: Europe in 1812.	154. 155
The Waterloo Campaign. Europe in 1815 Plan of the Waterloo Campaign, June 16—18, 1815. Europe in 1815.	156
Treaty Adjustments, 1814, 1815 Inset: Fortresses along the French Frontier.	157
Central Europe, 1815—1866	158. 159
The German Zollverein (Customs Union) 1828—1872 1828—1834. After 1834.	160
Germany, 1866—1919	161
Italy, 1815—1924	161
Industrial England since 1750	162
England and Wales in 1832	163
The Ottoman Empire, 1683—1913 Insets: Southwestern Crimea, 1854. Plan of Sevastopol, 1854—1855.	164
Peoples of Southeastern Europe and Asia Minor in 1913	165
Europe, 1871—1914	166. 167
Peoples of Austria-Hungary in 1914	168
The World at War, 1914—1918	168A
Principal Seats of War, 1914—1918	168B
The Western European Front, 1914—1918	168C
Treaty Adjustments, 1919—1926	168D

CONTENTS

PAGE

Treaty Adjustments 1919—1926. The Rhineland 168E

Europe in 1928 168F. 168G

Peoples of Central Europe in 1928 168H
Inset: South Tyrol.

The Near East since 1913. I. 168J. 168K

The Near East. II. 168L
Proposed Partitions of the Ottoman Empire, 1915, 1916. The Dardanelles. Partitions of Thrace. 1878—1923. The Religious Situation.

The Growth of European and Japanese Dominions in Asia since 1801 170. 171
Inset: Vicinity of Peking.

Australia and New Zealand since 1788 172

The Partition of Africa 174. 175
Insets: The Suez Canal and Lower Egypt. The Boer Republics till 1902. The Spanish Zone in Morocco.

Distribution of European Languages 176

European, African and Asiatic Migration 177

The World in 1929 179—182

Localities in Western Europe, connected with American History 184

Localities in England, connected with American History 185

Physical Map of North America 186. 187

The Indians in the United States to 1905 188

Reference Map of the New England Colonies, 1607—1760 189
Insets: Rhode Island. Vicinity of Boston. Vicinity of New York.

European Exploration and Settlement in the United States, 1513—1776 190. 191
Inset: Principal English Grants, 1606—1665.

Reference Map of the Middle Colonies, 1607—1760 192
Inset: Settlements on the Delaware River.

Reference Map of the Southern Colonies, 1607—1760 193
Inset: Settlements on the James River. The Georgian Coast.

PAGE

The British Colonies in North America, 1763—1775 194
Inset: Middle Colonies.

Campaigns of the American Revolution, 1775—1781 195
Insets: Vicinity of Boston (1775—1776). The West and South, 1778—1781.

The United States, 1783—1803 196
Insets: The State of Franklin, 1784—1788. Early Distribution of the Public Lands (Ohio).

Territorial Expansion of the United States since 1803 198. 199
Insets: Alaska. Hawaii. Guam. Samoa Islands. Wake Island. Midway Island. Virgin Islands. Porto Rico. The Philippine Islands.

Campaigns of the War of 1812 200
Campaigns of the War of 1812. The Southwest. Vicinity of Washington in 1814.

Campaigns of the Mexican War, 1846—1847 201
Inset: Route from Vera Cruz to Mexico.

The Organization of Territories in the United States since 1803 202. 203
I. 1803—1810. II. 1810—1835. III. 1835—1855. IV. Since 1855.

Slavery and the Staple Agricultural Products in the Southern States, 1790—1860 204

Slavery and Emancipation in the United States, 1777—1865 206. 207
Inset: The Region South of the Great Lakes.

Seat of the Civil War, 1861—1865 204
Inset: Vicinity of Gettysburg.

Westward Development of the United States 210. 211

Canada and Newfoundland 212
Inset: The Arbitration Boundary between Canada and Alaska.

Mexico, Central America and the West Indies 213
Inset: Central Mexico.

South America 214. 215
Inset: South America about 1790.

Hispanic America, 1828—1929 216
Inset: The Chilean — Peruvian — Bolivian Frontier.

CONTENTS

Maps, since 1929, prepared by C. S. Hammond & Company

Europe, 1930-1939 218

The Far East, 1930-1941 218

European Theater of War
1939-1945 219

Far Eastern Theater of War
1939-1945 219

The World at War, 1939-1945 ...... 220. 221

The World of the United Nations
and the Cold War, 1945-1955 .... 222. 223

Retreat of Colonialism in the
Postwar Period 224. 225

Europe in 1955 226

Scale 1:30000000
Miles.
Areas above 5000 feet
" " 1600 "
" " 600 "
" below " "
" " sea-level
Desert
ICELAND
Hecla
ARCTIC
North Cape
Lofoten Is.
Arctic Circle
Faroe Is.
Shetland Is.
Orkney Is.
The Hebrides
BRITISH ISLES
ATLANTIC OCEAN
Grampian Mts.
Central Plain
IRISH SEA
Pennine Chain
Welsh Mts.
Central Plain
Lands End
NORTH SEA
JUTLAND PENINSULA
SCANDINAVIAN HIGHLANDS
SCANDINAVIAN PENINSULA
GULF OF BOTHNIA
LAKE REGION
GULF OF FINLAND
BALTIC SEA
English Channel
Strait of Dover
GREAT LOWLAND
Elbe R.
Oder R.
Vistula R.
Marshes of the Pripet
Seine R.
Rhine R.
Loire R.
PLAIN OF FRANCE
Erzgebirge
Plain of Bohemia
Danube R.
C.Finisterre
BAY OF BISCAY
Cantabrian Mts.
PYRENEES
Mt. Blanc
Mte Rosa
THE ALPS
Plain of Lombardy
Po R.
Hungarian Plain
CARPATHIAN MTS.
Dniester R.
Pruth R.
IBERIAN PENINSULA
Spanish Plateau
Douro R.
Ebro R.
Tagus R.
Sierra Morena
Guadalquivir R.
Sierra Nevada
C.St.Vincent
Madeira Is.
Strait of Gibraltar
C. Spartel
Balearic Is.
Corsica
SARDINIA
APENNINES
ITALIAN PENINSULA
ADRIATIC SEA
Mt. Vesuvius
Wallachian Plain
Danube R.
BALKAN MTS.
BALKAN PENINSULA
GRECIAN PENINSULA
MOREA PENINSULA
AEGEAN SEA
Isthmus of Corinth
MEDITERRANEAN SEA
Strait of Messina
SICILY
Mt. Etna
Malta
Crete
CANARY IS.
THE TELL
ATLAS MOUNTAINS
ALGERIAN PLATEAUS
Oasis of Wargla
ALGERIAN SAHARA
Oases of Tuat
Barka Plateau
LIBYAN DESERT
Oases of Fezzan
Oases of Kufra
SAHARA
TIBESTI HIGHLANDS
Oasis of Kawar
Niger River
L. CHAD
Longitude West of Greenwich 0 Longitude East of Greenwich

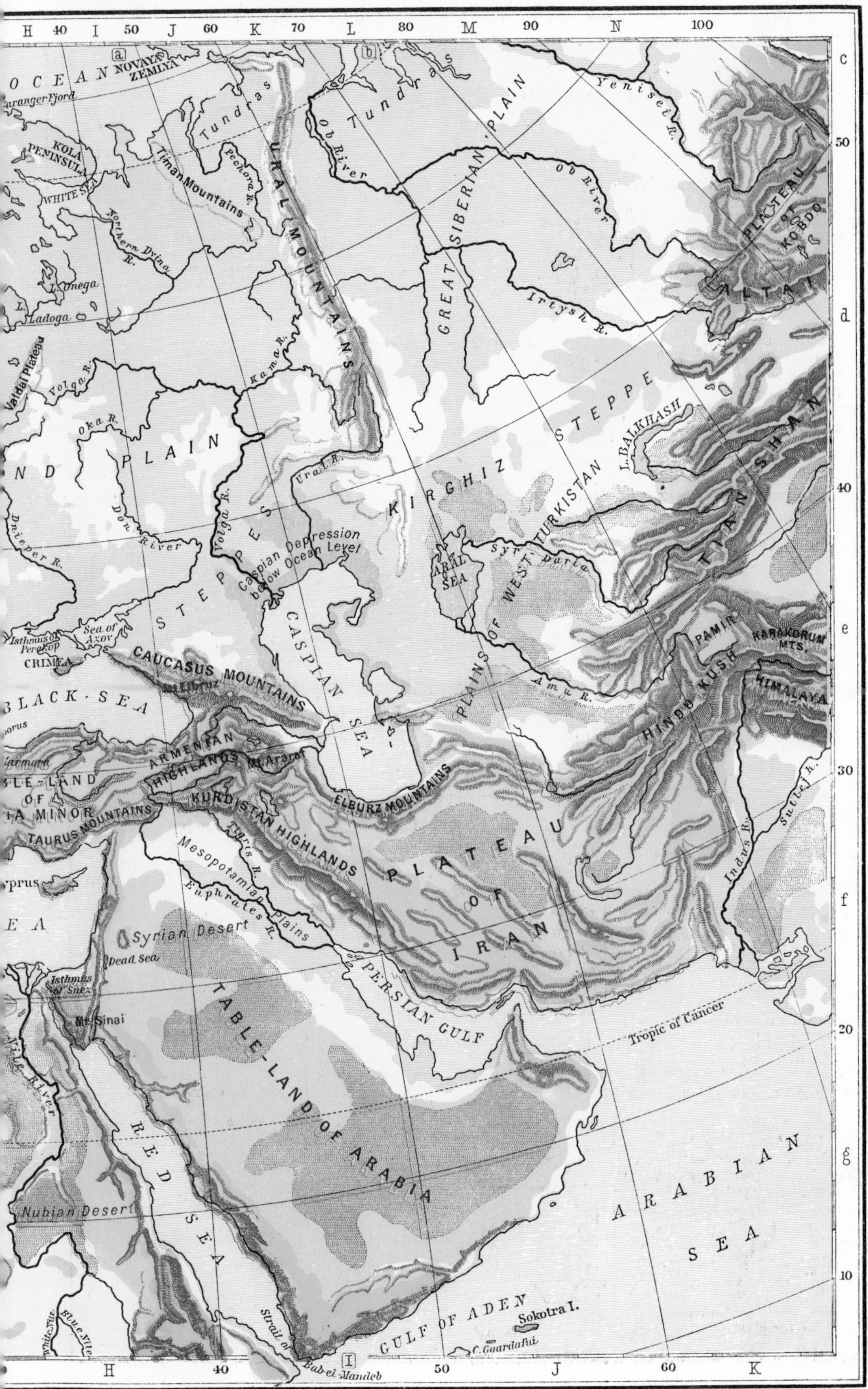
OCEAN
NOVAYA ZEMLYA
Varanger Fjord
KOLA PENINSULA
WHITE SEA
Northern Dvina R.
L. Onega
L. Ladoga
Valdai Plateau
Timan Mountains
Pechora R.
Tundras
URAL MOUNTAINS
Ob River
Tundras
GREAT SIBERIAN PLAIN
Yenisei R.
Ob River
Irtysh R.
PLATEAU of KOBDO
ALTAI
Volga R.
Kama R.
Oka R.
PLAIN
Don River
Dnieper R.
Volga R.
Ural R.
KIRGHIZ STEPPE
L. BALKHASH
TIAN SHAN
STEPPES
Caspian Depression below Ocean Level
ARAL SEA
Syr Daria
PLAINS OF WEST TURKISTAN
Sea of Azov
Isthmus of Perekop
CRIMEA
CAUCASUS MOUNTAINS
Mt. Elbruz
BLACK SEA
CASPIAN SEA
PAMIR
KARAKORUM MTS.
HIMALAYA
HINDU KUSH
Amu R.
ARMENIAN HIGHLANDS
Mt. Ararat
ELBURZ MOUNTAINS
KURDISTAN HIGHLANDS
TAURUS MOUNTAINS
A MINOR
Cyprus
Tigris R.
Mesopotamian Plains
Euphrates R.
PLATEAU OF IRAN
Indus R.
Sutlej R.
Syrian Desert
Dead Sea
Isthmus of Suez
Mt. Sinai
PERSIAN GULF
Tropic of Cancer
TABLE-LAND OF ARABIA
Nile River
RED SEA
Nubian Desert
ARABIAN SEA
GULF OF ADEN
Sokotra I.
C. Guardafui
Strait of Bab-el-Mandeb
White Nile
Blue Nile
H 40 I 50 J 60 K 70 L 80 M 90 N 100
H 40 50 J 60 K
c d e f g
50 40 30 20 10

Mycenean Greece and The Orient, 2100—1300 B.C.

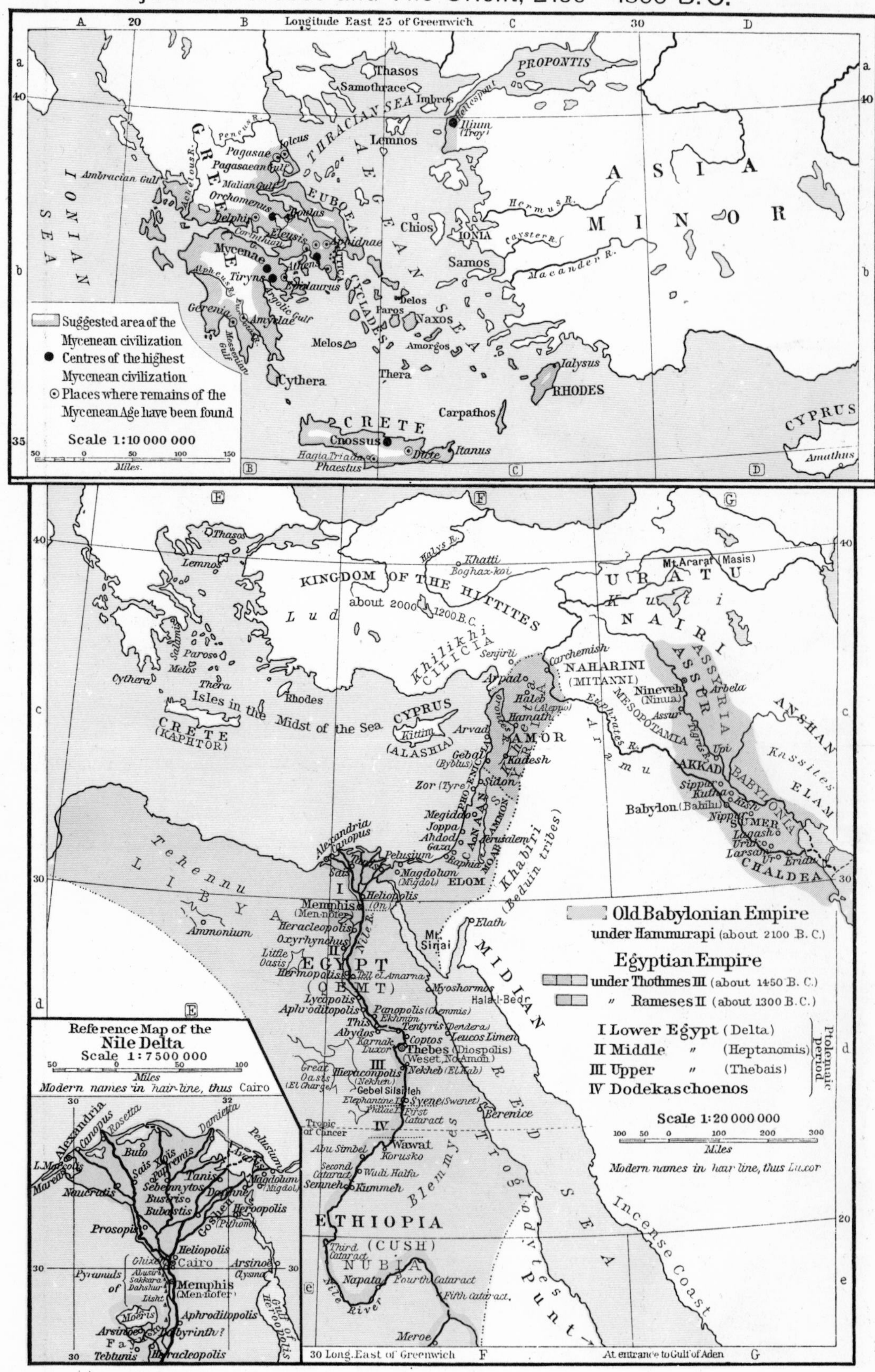

The Assyrian Empire and the Region about the Eastern Mediterranean, 850—625 B.C. 5

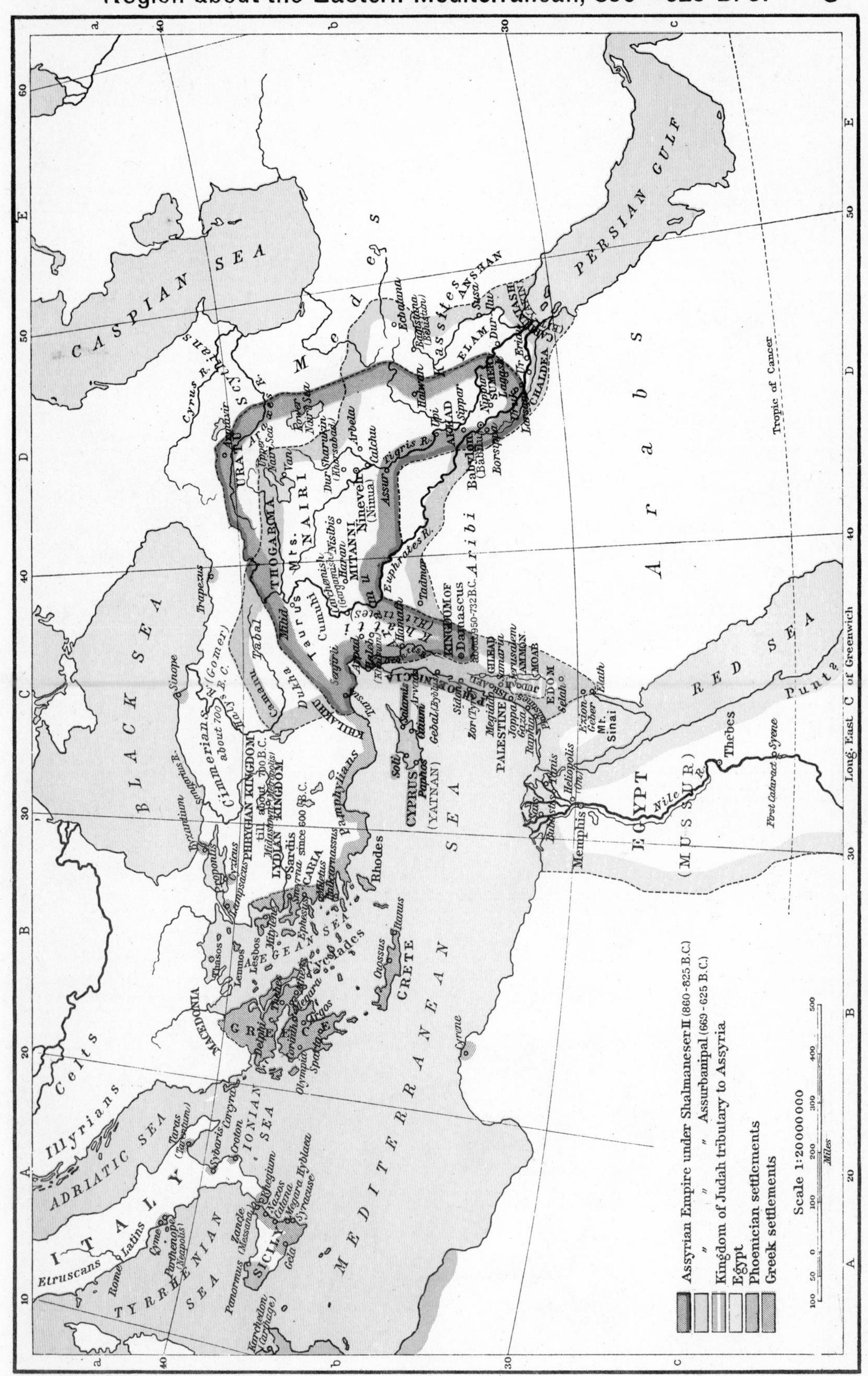

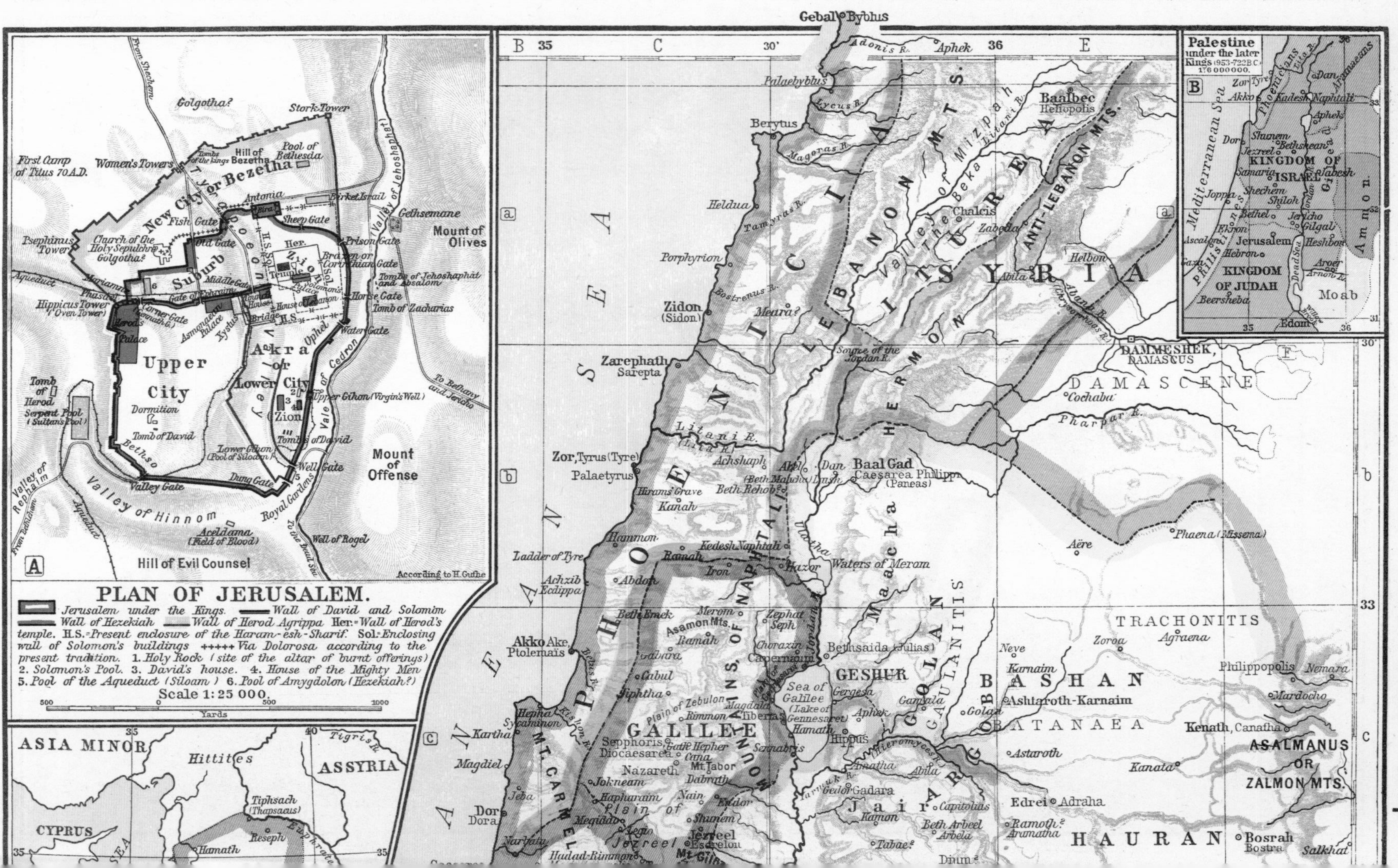

PLAN OF JERUSALEM.
Jerusalem under the Kings. Wall of David and Solomon
Wall of Hezekiah Wall of Herod Agrippa Her.=Wall of Herod's temple. H.S.=Present enclosure of the Haram-esh-Sharif. Sol.=Enclosing wall of Solomon's buildings +++++ Via Dolorosa according to the present tradition. 1. Holy Rock (site of the altar of burnt offerings) 2. Solomon's Pool. 3. David's house. 4. House of the Mighty Men 5. Pool of the Aqueduct (Siloam) 6. Pool of Amygdolon (Hezekiah?)
Scale 1:25 000.
Yards
According to H. Guthe
Upper City
Mount of Olives
Mount of Offense
Hill of Evil Counsel
Palestine under the later Kings (953-722 B.C.) 1:6 000 000.
KINGDOM OF ISRAEL
KINGDOM OF JUDAH
Mediterranean Sea
ANTI-LEBANON MTS.
LEBANON MTS.
HERMON
ITURAEA
SYRIA
PHOENICIA
DAMASCENE
TRACHONITIS
BASHAN
BATANAEA
GAULANITIS
GALILEE
MT. CARMEL
HAURAN
ASALMANUS OR ZALMON MTS.
ASIA MINOR
ASSYRIA
CYPRUS

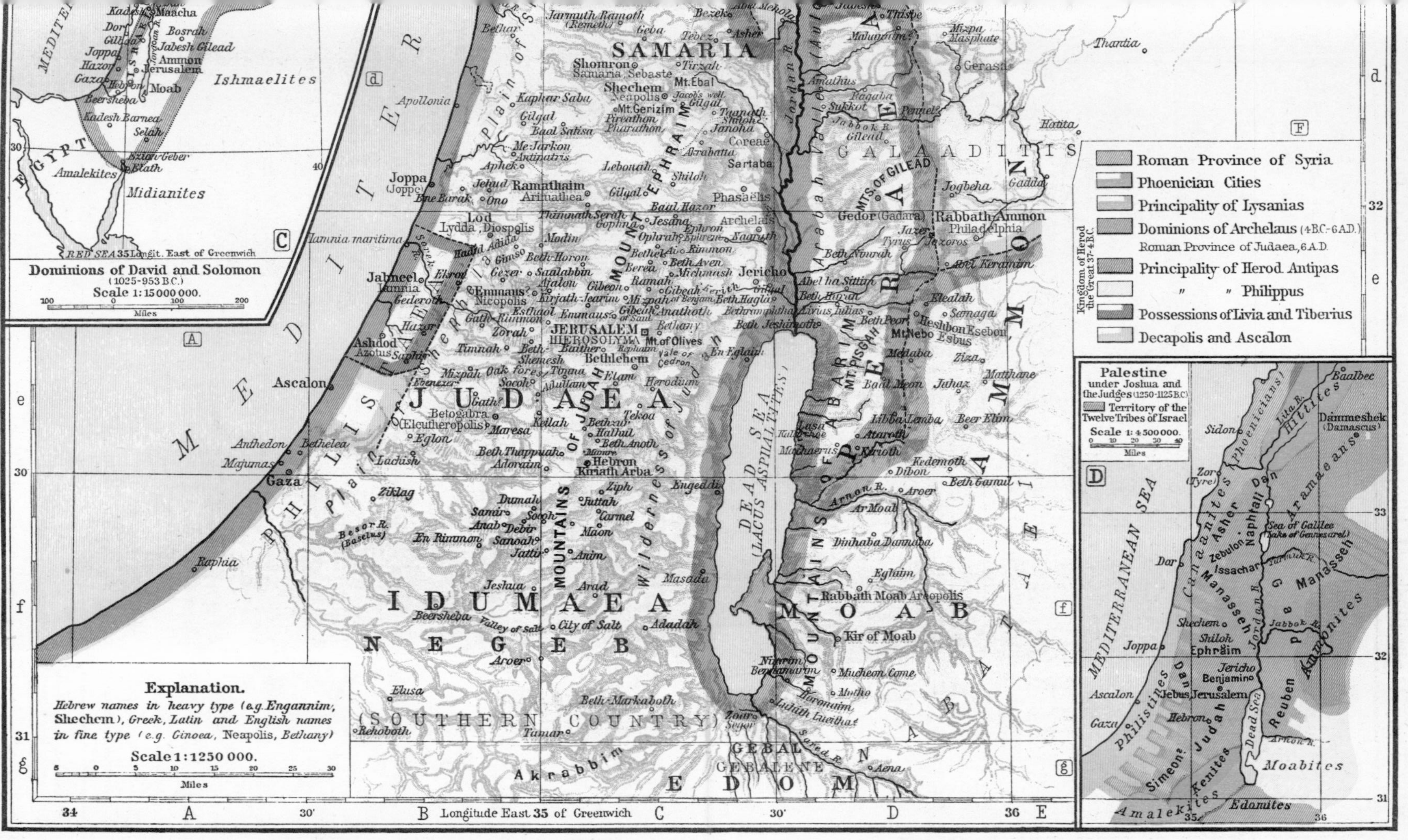
Roman Province of Syria
Phoenician Cities
Principality of Lysanias
Dominions of Archelaus (4 B.C.–6 A.D.)
Roman Province of Judaea, 6 A.D.
Principality of Herod Antipas
" " Philippus
Possessions of Livia and Tiberius
Decapolis and Ascalon
Kingdom of Herod the Great 37–4 B.C.
Palestine under Joshua and the Judges (1250–1125 B.C.)
Territory of the Twelve Tribes of Israel
Scale 1 : 4 500 000.
Dominions of David and Solomon (1025–953 B.C.)
Scale 1 : 15 000 000.
Explanation.
Hebrew names in heavy type (e.g. Engannim, Shechem), Greek, Latin and English names in fine type (e.g. Ginoea, Neapolis, Bethany)
Scale 1 : 1 250 000.
Longitude East 35 of Greenwich

The Orient, 600—500 B. C.
8 The Beginnings of Historic Greece, 700—600 B. C.

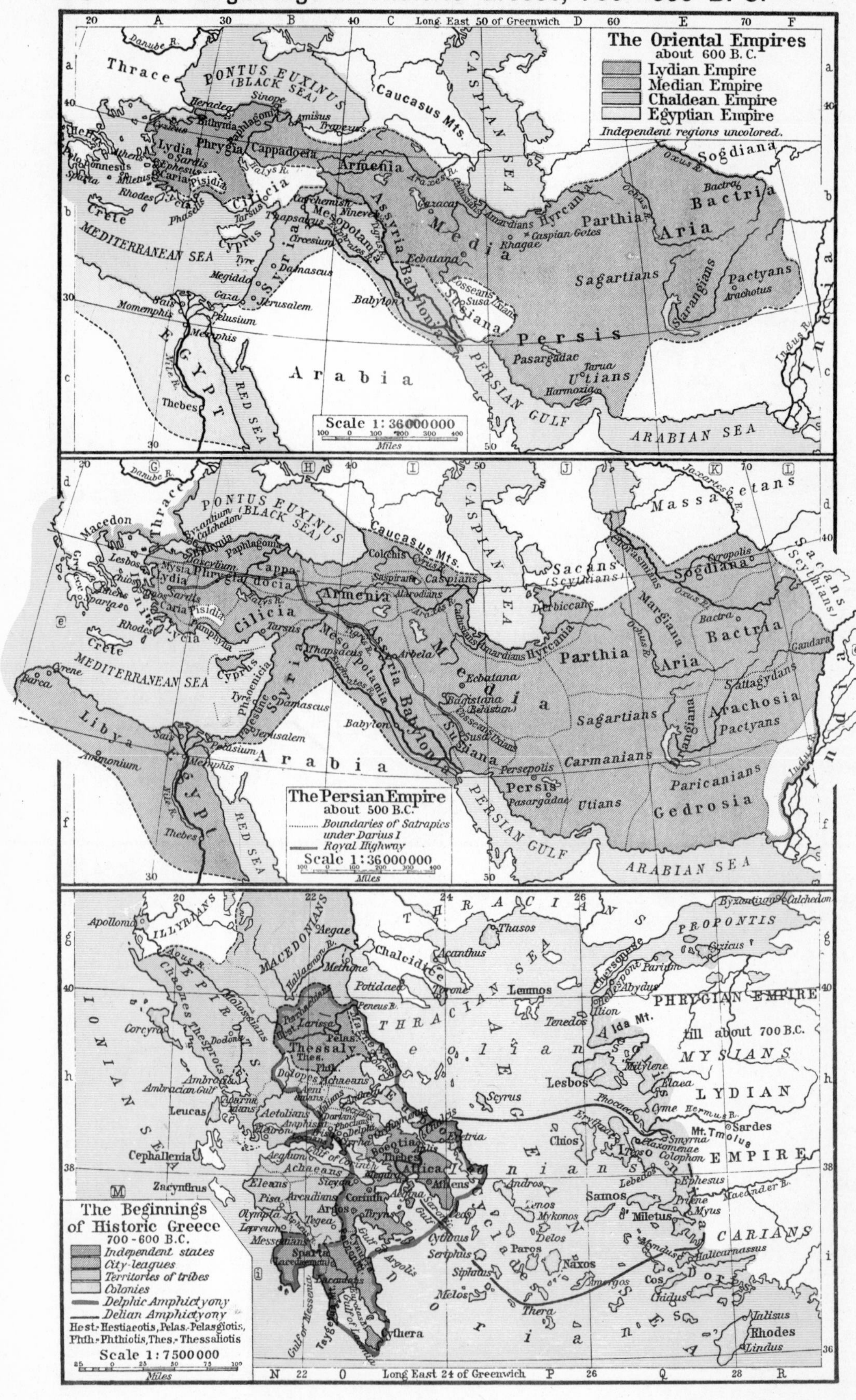

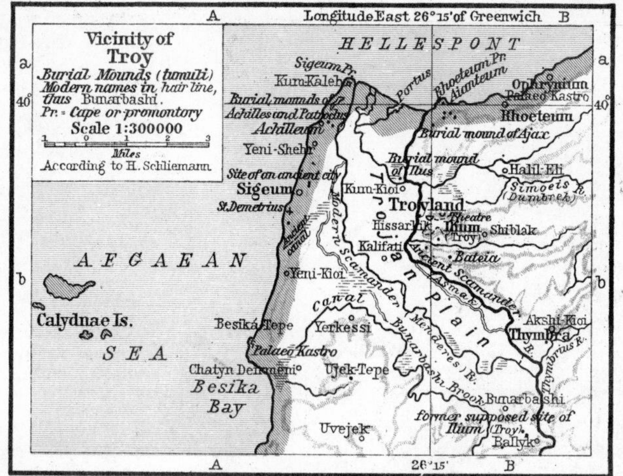
Vicinity of Troy
Burial Mounds (tumuli)
Modern names in hair line, thus Bunarbashi.
Pr. = Cape or promontory
Scale 1:300000
Miles
According to H. Schliemann
Longitude East 26°15' of Greenwich
HELLESPONT
AEGAEAN
SEA
Calydnae Is.
Besika Bay
Sigeum Pr.
Kum Kaleh
Burial mounds of Achilles and Patroclus
Achilleum
Yeni-Shehr
Site of an ancient city
Sigeum
St. Demetrius
Portus
Rhoeteum Pr.
Aianteum
Ophrynium
Palaeo Kastro
Rhoeteum
Burial mound of Ajax
Burial mound of Ilus
Halil-Eli
Simoeis R.
(Dumbrek)
Kum-Kioi
Troyland
Hissarlik
Theatre
Ilium
(Troy)
Shiblak
Kalifatli
Bateia
Yeni-Kioi
Ancient Scamander
Modern Scamander
canal
Trojan plain
Akshi-Kioi
Thymbra
Thymbrius R.
Besika Tepe
Yerkessi
Palaeo Kastro
Chatyn Demenemi
Ujek-Tepe
Bunarbashi Brook
Bunarbashi
former supposed site of Ilium (Troy)
Ballyk
Uvejek
26°15'

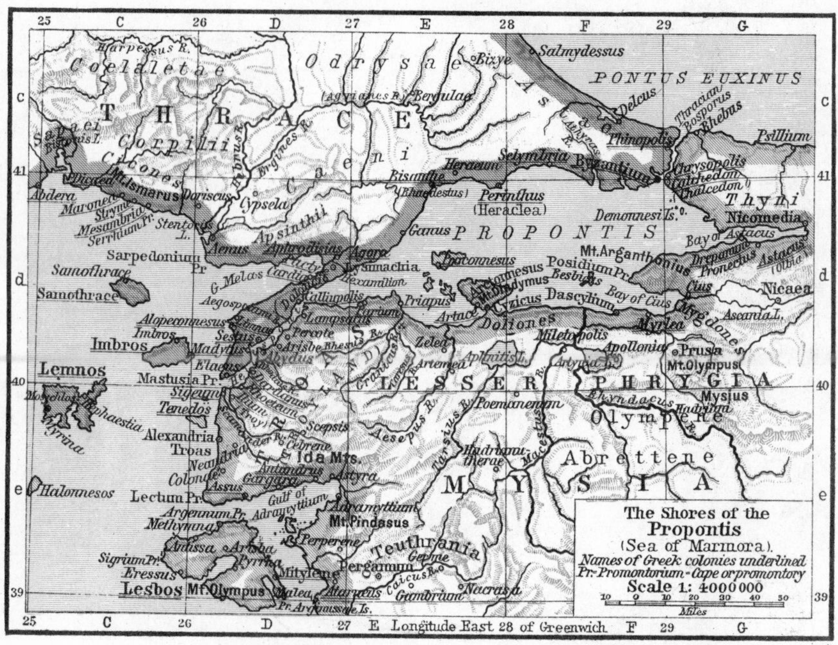
The Shores of the Propontis
(Sea of Marmora).
Names of Greek colonies underlined
Pr. = Promontorium = Cape or promontory
Scale 1: 4000000
Miles
Longitude East 28 of Greenwich
THRACE
PONTUS EUXINUS
PROPONTIS
Salmydessus
Odrysae
Coelaletae
Corpilii
Cicones
Apsinthii
Caeni
Byzantium
Selymbria
Perinthus
(Heraclea)
Chalcedon
Chrysopolis
Thyni
Nicomedia
Nicaea
Mt. Arganthonius
Cyzicus
Dascylium
Doliones
Miletopolis
Apollonia
Prusa
Mt. Olympus
PHRYGIA
LESSER PHRYGIA
Olympene
Abrettene
MYSIA
Teuthrania
Pergamum
Adramyttium
Mt. Pindasus
Ida Mts.
Lampsacus
Abydus
Sestus
Lysimachia
Cardia
Aenus
Abdera
Maronea
Samothrace
Imbros
Lemnos
Tenedos
Alexandria Troas
Sigeum
Lectum Pr.
Assus
Lesbos
Mt. Olympus
Methymna
Mytilene
Halonnesos
Sarpedonium Pr.
Mastusia Pr.

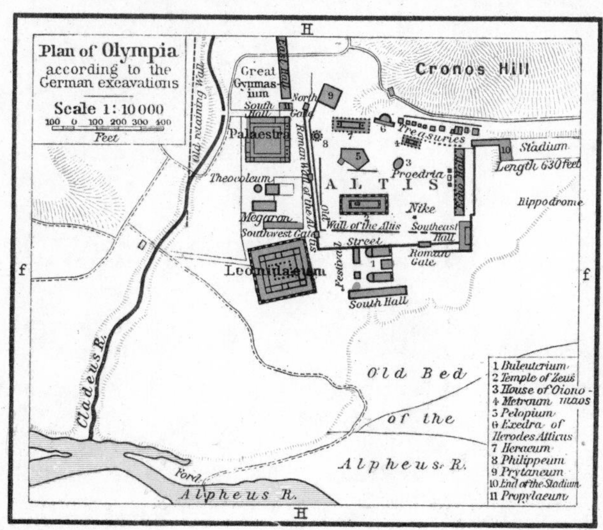
Plan of Olympia
according to the German excavations
Scale 1: 10000
Feet
Cronos Hill
Great Gymnasium
South Hall
North Gate
Palaestra
Theocoleum
Megaron
Southwest Gate
Leonidaeum
Treasuries
ALTIS
Proedria
Nike
Wall of the Altis
Southeast Hall
Street
Roman Gate
Festival Street
South Hall
Stadium
Length 630 feet
Hippodrome
Cladeus R.
Old Bed of the Alpheus R.
Alpheus R.
Ford
1 Buleuterium
2 Temple of Zeus
3 House of Oionomaos
4 Metroum
5 Pelopium
6 Exedra of Herodes Atticus
7 Heraeum
8 Philippeum
9 Prytaneum
10 End of the Stadium
11 Propylaeum

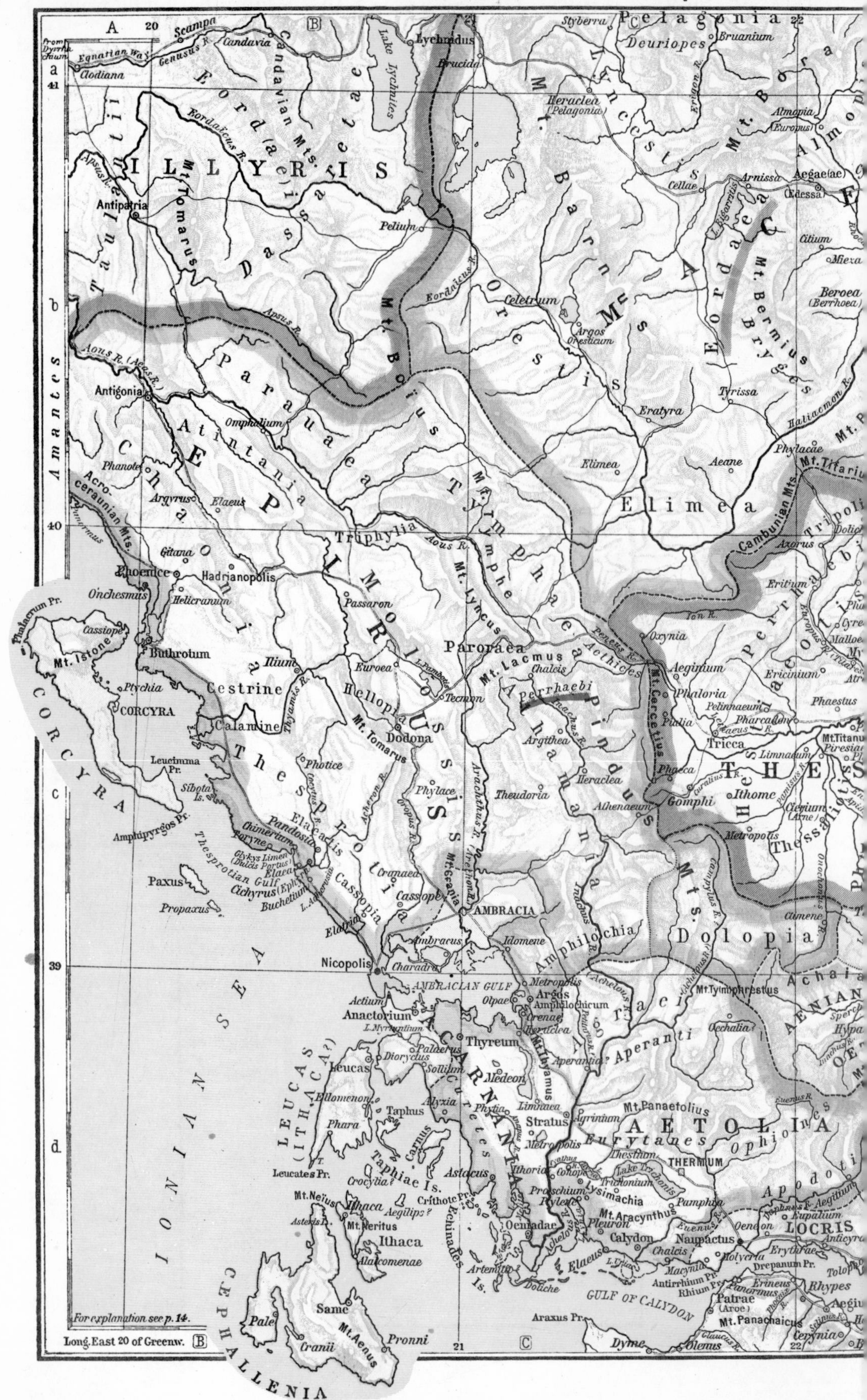
ILLYRIS
EPIRUS
MOLOSSIS
Thesprotia
Chaonia
Paravaea
Atintania
Dassaretae
Eordaea
Orestis
Elimea
Lyncestis
Pelagonia
Deuriopes
Bruanium
Eordaea
Almopia
Athamania
Perrhaebi
Dolopia
Amphilochia
ACARNANIA
AETOLIA
Eurytanes
Ophiones
Apodoti
Aperanti
Agraei
Dolopia
Achaia
AENIANES
THESSALIOTIS
LOCRIS
Hellopia
Cestrine
Cassopia
Parauaea
Triphylia
Paroraea
Amantes
Taulanti
CORCYRA
CEPHALLENIA
LEUCAS (ITHACA?)
IONIAN SEA
AMBRACIAN GULF
GULF OF CALYDON
Thesprotian Gulf
Egnatian Way
Scampa
Candavia
Candavian Mts.
Genusus R.
Clodiana
Lychnidus
Lake Lychnites
Brucida
Styberra
Heraclea (Pelagonia)
Erigon R.
Mt. Barnus
Mt. Bora
Almopia
Europus
Cellae
Arnissa
Aegae(ae)
Edessa
L. Begorritis
Mt. Bermius
Brygi
Citium
Mieza
Beroea (Berrhoea)
Tyrissa
Haliacmon R.
Eratyra
Aeane
Phylacae
Mt. Titarius
Cambunian Mts.
Tripolis
Azorus
Doliche
Eritium
Ion R.
Oxynia
Aeginium
Phaloria
Pelinnaeum
Pharcadon
Tricca
Limnaeum
Ericinium
Phaestus
Mt. Titanus
Pamisus R.
Ithome
Gomphi
Metropolis
Cierium (Arne)
Onochonus R.
Cimene
Mt. Tymphrestus
Oechalia
Sperchius
Hypata
Inachus R.
Mt. Panaetolius
Euenus R.
Aegitium
Daphnus R.
Eupalium
Anticyra
Erythrae
Tolophon
Naupactus
Molycria
Drepanum Pr.
Antirrhium Pr.
Rhium Pr.
Panormus
Erineus
Rhypes
Aegium
Patrae (Aroe)
Phoenix R.
Selinus R.
Mt. Panachaicus
Ceryneia
Glaucus R.
Olenus
Dyme
Araxus Pr.
Oeneon
Chalcis
Macynia
Calydon
Pleuron
Mt. Aracynthus
Pamphia
Lysimachia
Lake Trichonis
Trichonium
Thermum
Thestieum
Proschium
Pylene
Conope
Ithoria
Metropolis
Agrinium
Stratus
Limnaea
Achelous R.
Oeniadae
Artemita
Echinades Is.
Doliche
L. Uria
Elaeus
Astacus
Crithote Pr.
Alyzia
Palaerus
Sollium
Medeon
Thyreum
Phytia
Curetes
Mt. Thyamus
Anactorium
Actium
L. Myrtuntium
Argos Amphilochicum
Olpae
Crenae
Heraclea
Metropolis
Limnaea
Idomene
Ambracus
Charadra
Nicopolis
AMBRACIA
Mt. Crania
Arachthus R.
Cassope
Cranaea
Elatria
Bucheti(um)
Cichyrus (Ephyra)
Elaea
Glykys Limen (Dulcis Portus)
Pandosia
Toryne
Chimerium
Elaeatis
L. Acherusia
Acheron R.
Oropus R.
Cocytus R.
Photice
Phylace
Dodona
Mt. Tomarus
Thyamis R.
Ilium
Euroea
L. Pambotis
Tecmon
Passaron
Mt. Lacmus
Chalcis
Aethices
Peneus R.
Mt. Cercetius
Argithea
Inachus R.
Heraclea
Theudoria
Athenaeum
Pindus Mts.
Mt. Lyncus
Aous R.
Mt. Tymphe
Tymphaea
Mt. Boius
Eordaicus R.
Celetrum
Argos Oresticum
Pelium
Apsus R.
Eordaicus R.
Mt. Tomarus
Antipatria
Apsus R.
Aous R. (Aeas R.)
Antigonia
Omphalium
Phanote
Argyrus
Elaeus
Panormus
Acroceraunian Mts.
Gitana
Phoenice
Hadrianopolis
Onchesmus
Helicranum
Buthrotum
Calamine
Sibota Is.
Thalacrum Pr.
Cassiope
Mt. Istone
Ptychia
CORCYRA
Leucimma Pr.
Amphipyrgos Pr.
Paxus
Propaxus
Leucas
Ellomenon
Phara
Taphus
Carnus
Taphiae Is.
Leucates Pr.
Crocylia?
Aegilips?
Mt. Neïus
Ithaca
Asteris I.
Mt. Neritus
Ithaca
Alalcomenae
Same
Pale
Cranii
Mt. Aenus
Pronni
Dioryctus
For explanation see p. 14.
Long. East 20 of Greenw.
A
B
C
a
b
c
d
20
21
22
39
40
41
From Dyrrh. Daum

Greek and Phoenician Settlements in the Mediterranean Basin, about 550 B. C.

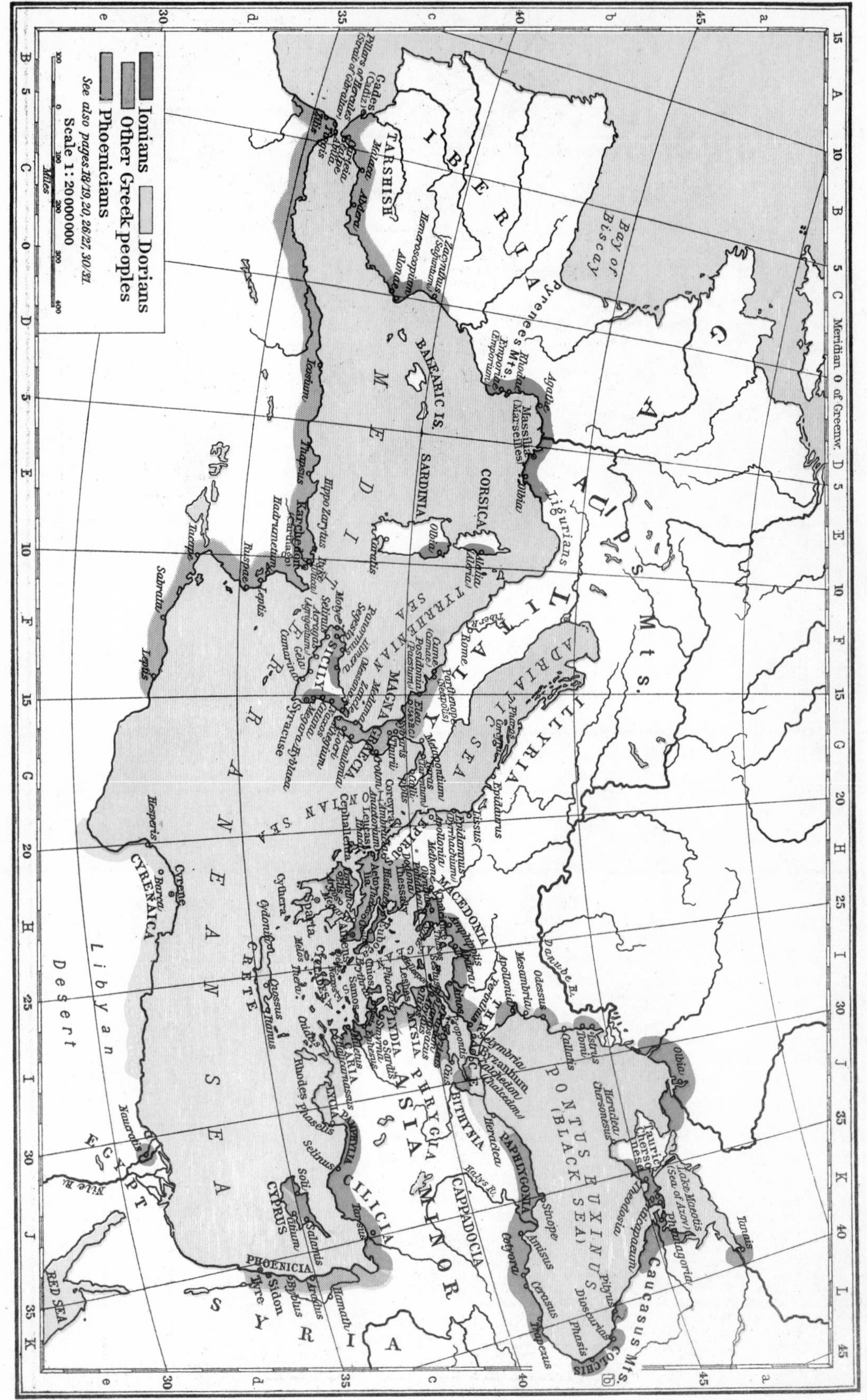

Greece at the Time of the War with Persia. The Athenian Empire at its Height.

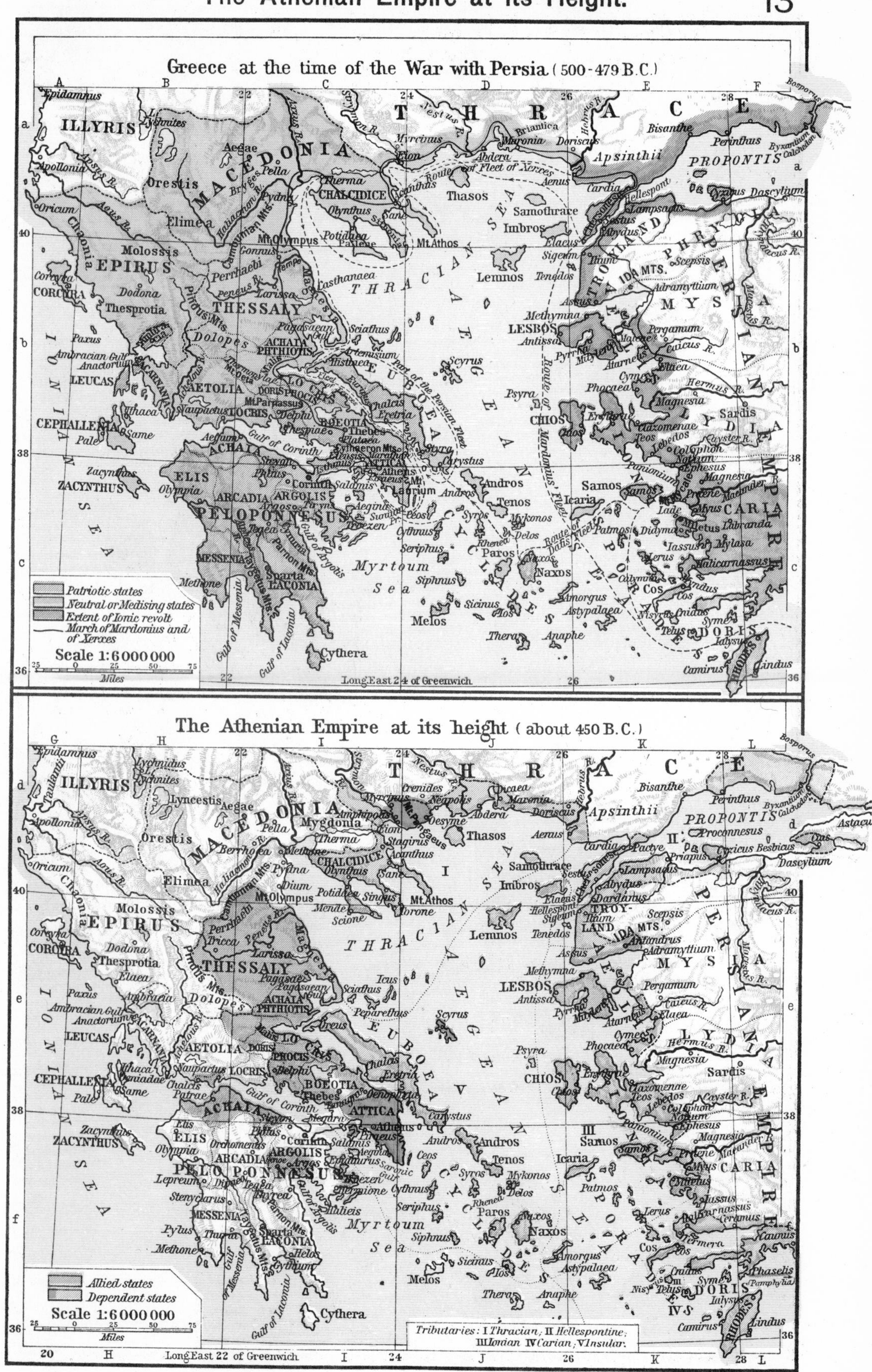

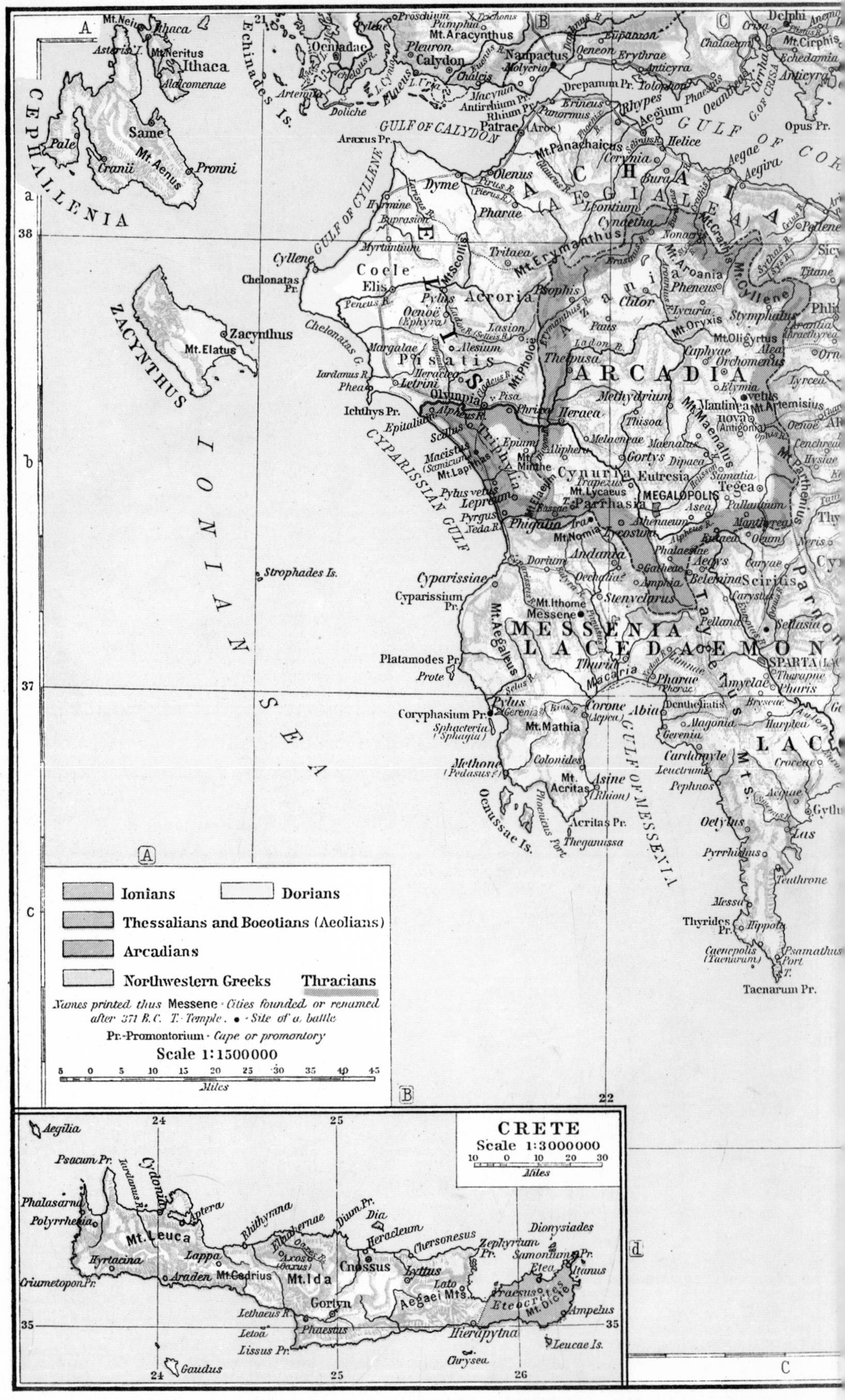
Ionians
Dorians
Thessalians and Boeotians (Aeolians)
Arcadians
Northwestern Greeks
Thracians
Names printed thus Messene - Cities founded or renamed after 371 B.C. T.- Temple. • - Site of a battle
Pr.-Promontorium - Cape or promontory
Scale 1:1500000
5 0 5 10 15 20 25 30 35 40 45
Miles
CEPHALLENIA
Ithaca
Same
Mt. Aenus
Pronni
Cranii
Pale
ZACYNTHUS
Zacynthus
Mt. Elatus
IONIAN SEA
Strophades Is.
Echinades Is.
GULF OF CALYDON
GULF OF CYLLENE
CYPARISSIAN GULF
GULF OF MESSENIA
GULF OF CORINTH
Oeniadae
Calydon
Pleuron
Naupactus
Delphi
Crisa
Mt. Cirphis
Anticyra
Patrae
Aegium
Helice
Dyme
Olenus
Pharae
Cyllene
Chelonatas Pr.
Coele Elis
Elis
Acroria
Pisatis
Olympia
Pisa
Letrini
Ichthys Pr.
Scillus
Triphylia
Lepreum
Phigalia
Mt. Erymanthus
Psophis
Cleitor
Pheneus
Mt. Cyllene
Stymphalus
ARCADIA
Orchomenus
Mantinea
Heraea
Methydrium
Gortys
Tegea
MEGALOPOLIS
Parrhasia
Cynuria
Mt. Lycaeus
Andania
Cyparissiae
Cyparissium Pr.
Mt. Ithome
Messene
Stenyclarus
MESSENIA
LACEDAEMON
SPARTA
Sellasia
Amyclae
Pylus
Coryphasium Pr.
Sphacteria
Methone
Corone
Asine
Mt. Mathia
Mt. Acritas
Acritas Pr.
Oenussae Is.
Platamodes Pr.
Prote
Cardamyle
Leuctrum
Oetylus
Teuthrone
Messa
Thyrides Pr.
Caenepolis (Taenarum)
Psamathus Port
Taenarum Pr.
CRETE
Scale 1:3000000
10 0 10 20 30
Miles
Aegilia
Psacum Pr.
Cydonia
Phalasarna
Polyrrhenia
Aptera
Mt. Leuca
Lappa
Hyrtacina
Criumetopon Pr.
Araden
Mt. Cedrius
Mt. Ida
Rhithymna
Eleutherna
Axos
Dium Pr.
Dia
Heracleum
Cnossus
Lyttus
Chersonesus
Gortyn
Phaestus
Aegaei Mts.
Hierapytna
Praesus
Eteocretes
Mt. Dicte
Itanus
Ampelus
Samonium Pr.
Dionysiades
Leucae Is.
Chrysea
Lethaeus R.
Lissus Pr.
Gaudus

AEGEAN SEA
MYRTOUM SEA
CRETAN SEA
SARONIC GULF
GULF OF ARGOLIS
BOEOTIA
ATTICA
EUBOEA
MEGARIS
CYCLADES
ANDROS
TENOS
CEOS
SYROS
CYTHNUS
SERIPHUS
SIPHNUS
PAROS
MELOS
CRETE
ATHENS
THEBES
MEGARA
CHALCIS
AEGINA
Eretria
Marathon
Piraeus
Eleusis
Salamis
Troezen
Epidaurus
Hermione
Hydrea
Gyarus
Rhenea
Delos
Cimolus
Polyaegus
Sicinus
Pholegandrus
Cythera
Aegilia
Cydonia
Belbina
Helena
Sunium Pr.
Caphereus Pr.
Geraestus
Carystus
Styra
Mt. Ocha
Malea Pr.
Epidelium Pr.
Zarax
Epidaurus Limera
Mt. Tityrus
Psacum Pr.
Corycum Pr.
Phalasarna
Myrtilis Bay
Longitude East 23 of Greenwich
D
E
25
F
a
b
c
d
38
37
36

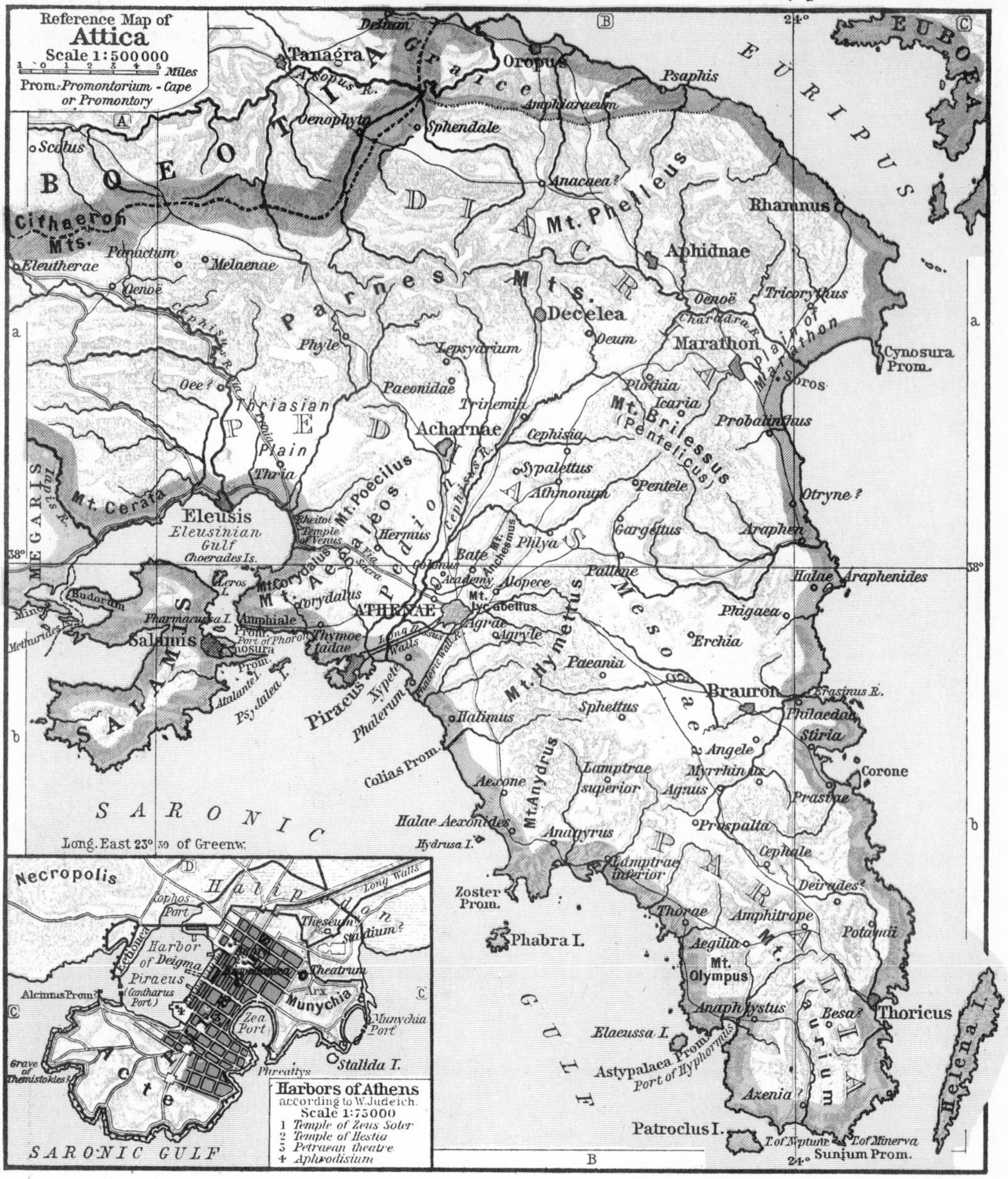

Reference Map of **Attica**
Scale 1:500000
Miles
Prom.=Promontorium - Cape or Promontory

Long. East 23° 30 of Greenw.

Harbors of Athens
according to W. Judeich.
Scale 1:75000
1 Temple of Zeus Soter
2 Temple of Hestia
3 Peiraean theatre
4 Aphrodisium

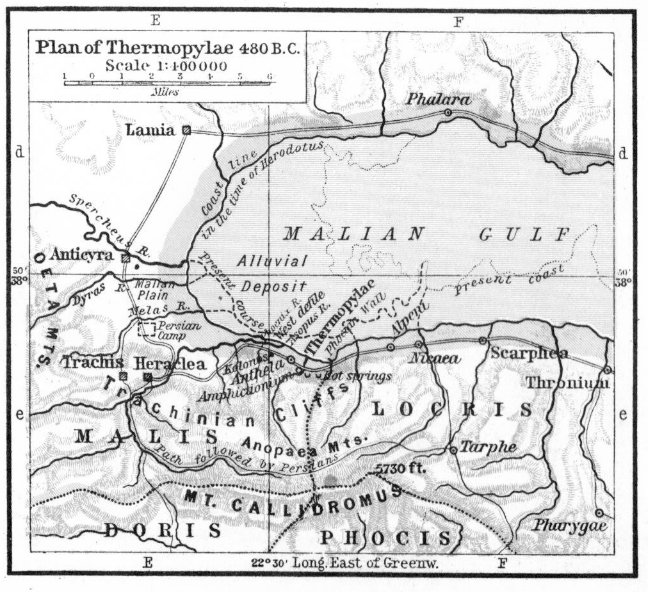

Greece at the Beginning of the Peloponnesian War.
Greece under Theban Headship.

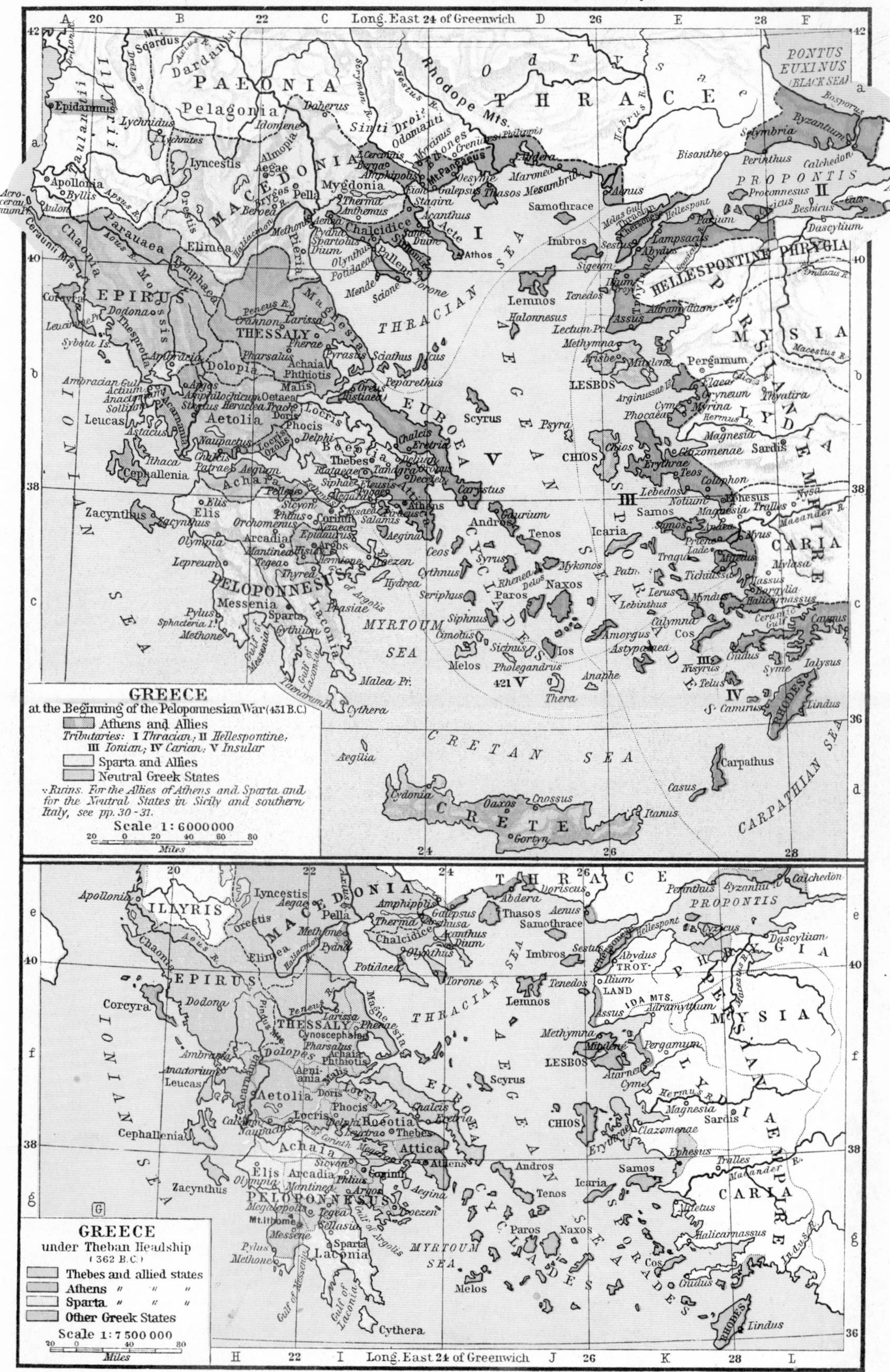

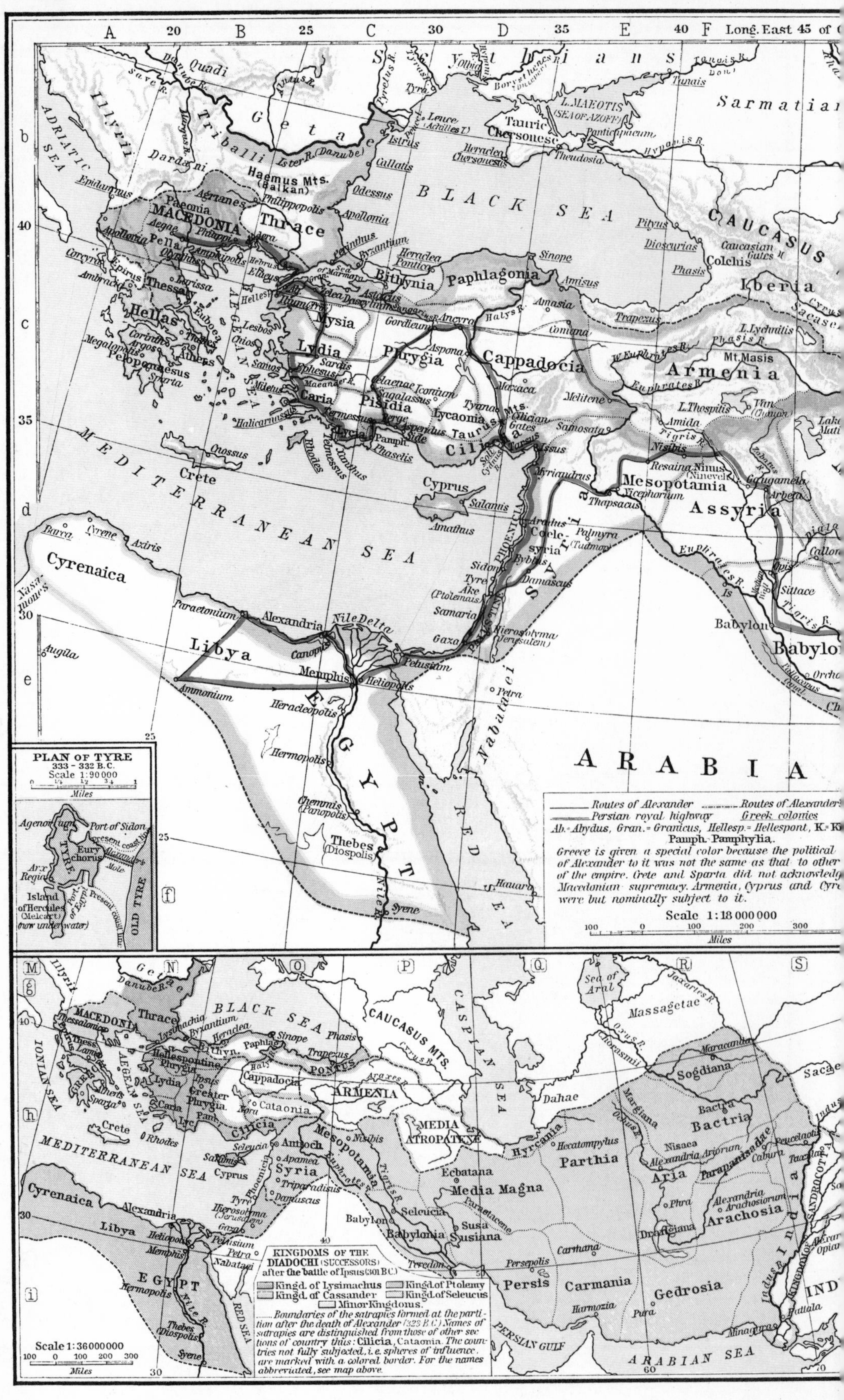
PLAN OF TYRE
333 - 332 B.C.
Scale 1:90 000
Miles
Agenorium
Port of Sidon
present coast line
TYRE
Eury chorus
Alexander's Mole
Arx Regia
Island of Hercules (Melcart) (now under water)
Port of Egypt
Present coast line
OLD TYRE
Routes of Alexander
Routes of Alexander's
Persian royal highway
Greek colonies
Ab.=Abydus, Gran.=Granicus, Hellesp.=Hellespont, K.=K
Pamph.=Pamphylia.
Greece is given a special color because the political
of Alexander to it was not the same as that to other
of the empire. Crete and Sparta did not acknowledg
Macedonian supremacy. Armenia, Cyprus and Cyre
were but nominally subject to it.
Scale 1:18 000 000
Miles
MEDITERRANEAN SEA
BLACK SEA
ARABIA
EGYPT
MACEDONIA
Thrace
Hellas
Cyrenaica
Libya
Alexandria
Mesopotamia
Assyria
Armenia
Cappadocia
Phrygia
Cilicia
Cyprus
Crete
KINGDOMS OF THE DIADOCHI (SUCCESSORS) after the battle of Ipsus (301 B.C.)
Kingd. of Lysimachus
Kingd. of Ptolemy
Kingd. of Cassander
Kingd. of Seleucus
Minor Kingdoms.
Boundaries of the satrapies formed at the partition after the death of Alexander (323 B.C.) Names of satrapies are distinguished from those of other sections of country thus: Cilicia, Catаonia. The countries not fully subjected, i.e. spheres of influence, are marked with a colored border. For the names abbreviated, see map above.
Scale 1:36 000 000
Miles
CASPIAN SEA
PERSIAN GULF
ARABIAN SEA
Parthia
Bactria
Sogdiana
Media Magna
Persis
Carmania
Gedrosia
Arachosia
Aria
Babylonia
Susiana

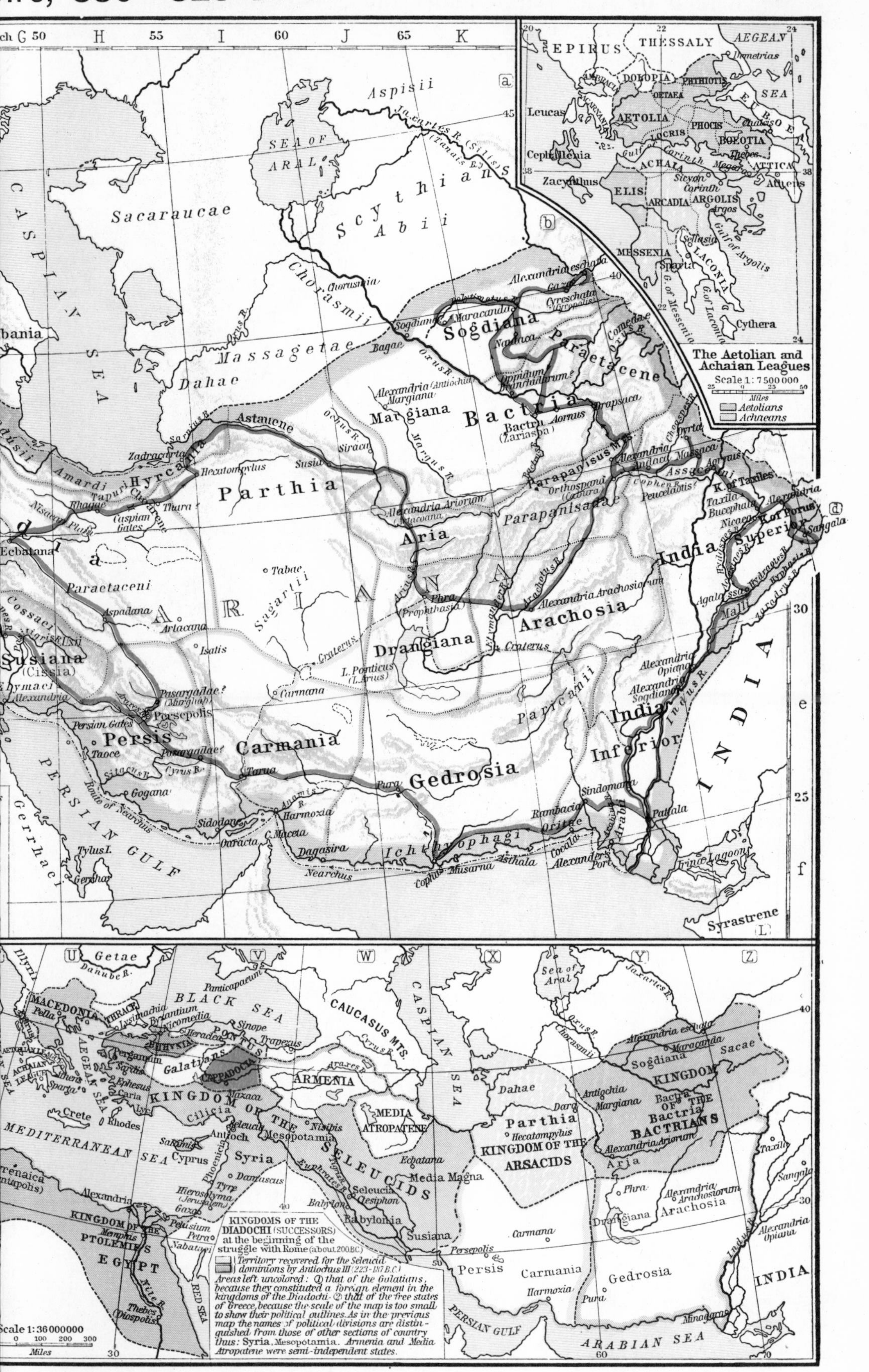
Aspisii
SEA OF ARAL
Jaxartes R. (Tanais R.) (Silis)
Scythians
Abii
Sacaraucae
CASPIAN SEA
Chorasmii
Chorasmia
Massagetae
Dahae
Sogdiana
Maracanda
Alexandria eschata
Cyreschata
Paraetacene
Bactria
Bactra (Zariaspa)
Aornus
Drapsaca
Margiana
Alexandria (Antiochia) Margiana
Oxus R.
Astauene
Hyrcania
Zadracarta
Amardi
Tapuri
Rhagae
Caspian Gates
Hecatompylus
Susia
Parthia
Alexandria Ariorum
Artacoana
Aria
Parapanisadae
Parapanisus Mts.
Orthospana
Cophen R.
Peucelaotis
Assaceni
Massaca
Taxila
K. of Taxiles
K. of Porus
Bucephala
Nicaea
Sangala
India Superior
Ecbatana
Paraetaceni
Tabae
Sagartii
ARIANA
Phra
(Prophthasia)
Drangiana
Arachosia
Alexandria Arachosiorum
Craterus
L. Ponticus (L. Arius)
Isatis
Aspadana
Artacana
Cossaei
Susiana (Cissia)
Elymaei
Alexandria
Pasargadae (Marginah)
Persepolis
Persian Gates
Persis
Taoce
Pasargadae?
Carmania
Carmana
Gedrosia
Pura
Paricanii
India Inferior
Alexandria Opiana
Alexandria Sogdiana
Indus R.
INDIA
Malli
Sindomana
Rambacia
Oritae
Patala
Arabii
Alexanders Port
Cocala
Ichthyophagi
Harmoxia
Anamis R.
Gogana
Sidodone
Oaracta
C. Maceta
Dagasira
Nearchus
Cophas
Musarna
Asthala
Irinae Lagoon
Syrastrene
PERSIAN GULF
Gerrhaei
Gerrha
Tylus I.
Route of Nearchus
EPIRUS
THESSALY
AEGEAN SEA
Demetrias
DOLOPIA
PHTHIOTIS
OETAEA
AETOLIA
PHOCIS
LOCRIS
BOEOTIA
Chalcis
EUBOEA
Leucas
ACARNANIA
Cephallenia
Zacynthus
ACHAIA
Gulf of Corinth
Megara
ATTICA
Athens
Thebes
Sicyon
Corinth
ELIS
ARCADIA
ARGOLIS
Argos
Gulf of Argolis
MESSENIA
Sparta
LACONIA
G. of Messenia
G. of Laconia
Cythera
Sellasia
The Aetolian and Achaian Leagues
Scale 1: 7 500 000
Miles
Aetolians
Achaeans
Getae
Danube R.
MACEDONIA
Pella
THRACE
Lysimachia
Byzantium
Nicomedia
Heraclea
Panticapaeum
BLACK SEA
Sinope
PONTUS
Trapezus
BITHYNIA
Pergamum
Galatians
CAPPADOCIA
CAUCASUS MTS.
Cyrus R.
Araxes R.
ARMENIA
AEGEAN SEA
Sardis
Ephesus
Caria
Rhodes
Crete
KINGDOM OF THE SELEUCIDS
Mazaca
Cilicia
Seleucia
Nisibis
Mesopotamia
MEDIA ATROPATENE
Antioch
Salamis
Cyprus
Syria
Phoenicia
Tyre
Damascus
Hierosolyma (Jerusalem)
Gaza
Euphrates R.
Tigris R.
Ecbatana
Media Magna
Seleucia
Ctesiphon
Babylon
Babylonia
Susiana
MEDITERRANEAN SEA
Cyrenaica (Pentapolis)
Alexandria
KINGDOM OF THE PTOLEMIES
Memphis
Pelusium
Petra
Nabataei
EGYPT
Nile R.
Thebes (Diospolis)
RED SEA
Scale 1:36 000000
Miles
Sea of Aral
Jaxartes R.
Oxus R.
Chorasmii
Sacae
Sogdiana
Alexandria eschata
Maracanda
KINGDOM OF THE BACTRIANS
Bactra
Dahae
Parthia
Hecatompylus
KINGDOM OF THE ARSACIDS
Antiochia Margiana
Dara
Alexandria Ariorum
Aria
Phra
Drangiana
Alexandria Arachosiorum
Arachosia
Taxila
Sangala
Alexandria Opiana
Indus R.
INDIA
Carmana
Persepolis
Persis
Carmania
Harmozia
Pura
Gedrosia
Minnagara
PERSIAN GULF
ARABIAN SEA
KINGDOMS OF THE DIADOCHI (SUCCESSORS) at the beginning of the struggle with Rome (about 200 B.C.)
Territory recovered for the Seleucid dominions by Antiochus III (223-187 B.C.)
Areas left uncolored: ① that of the Galatians, because they constituted a foreign element in the kingdoms of the Diadochi; ② that of the free states of Greece, because the scale of the map is too small to show their political outlines. As in the previous map the names of political divisions are distinguished from those of other sections of country thus: Syria, Mesopotamia. Armenia and Media Atropatene were semi-independent states.

20 Reference Map of Asia Minor under the Greeks and Romans.

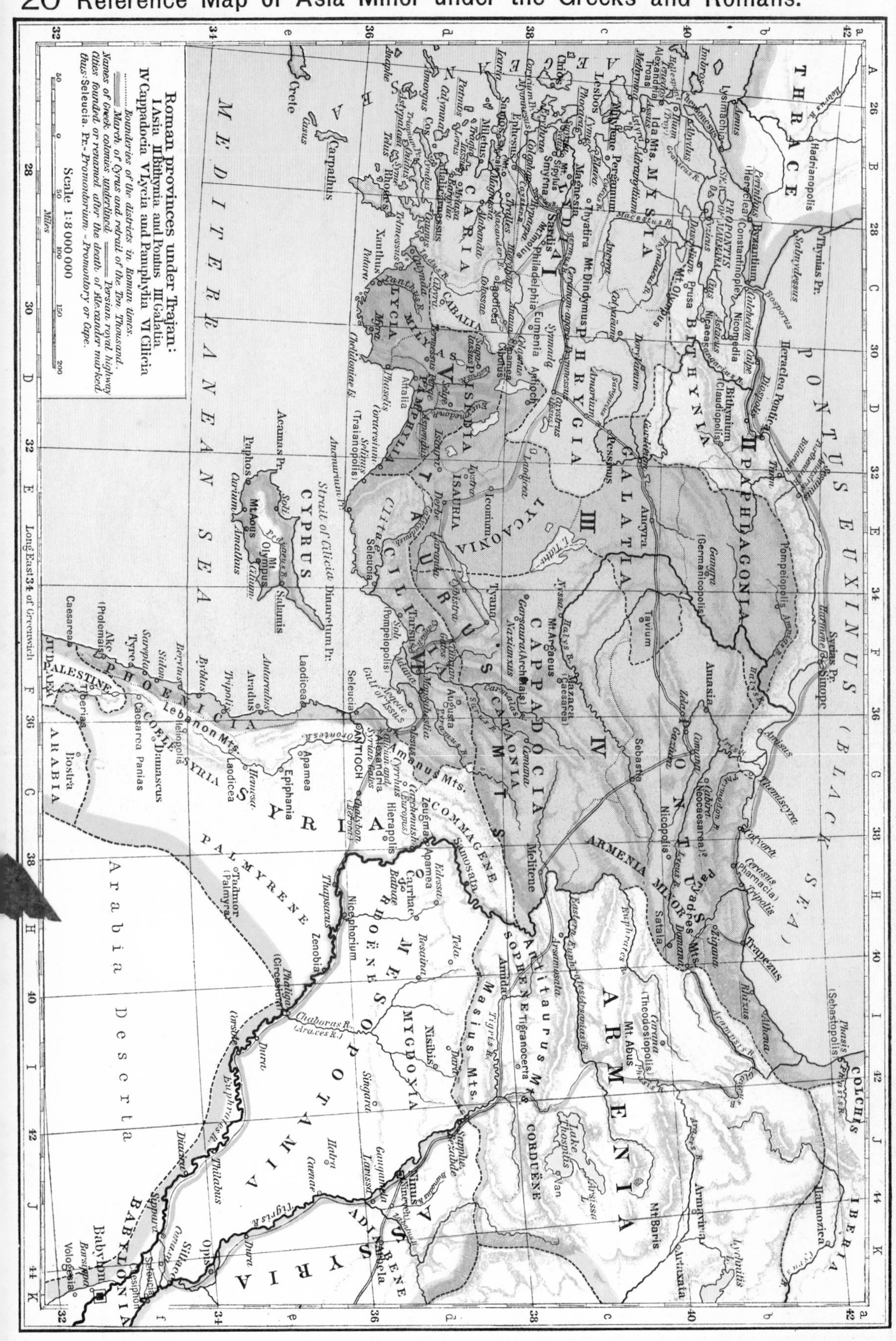

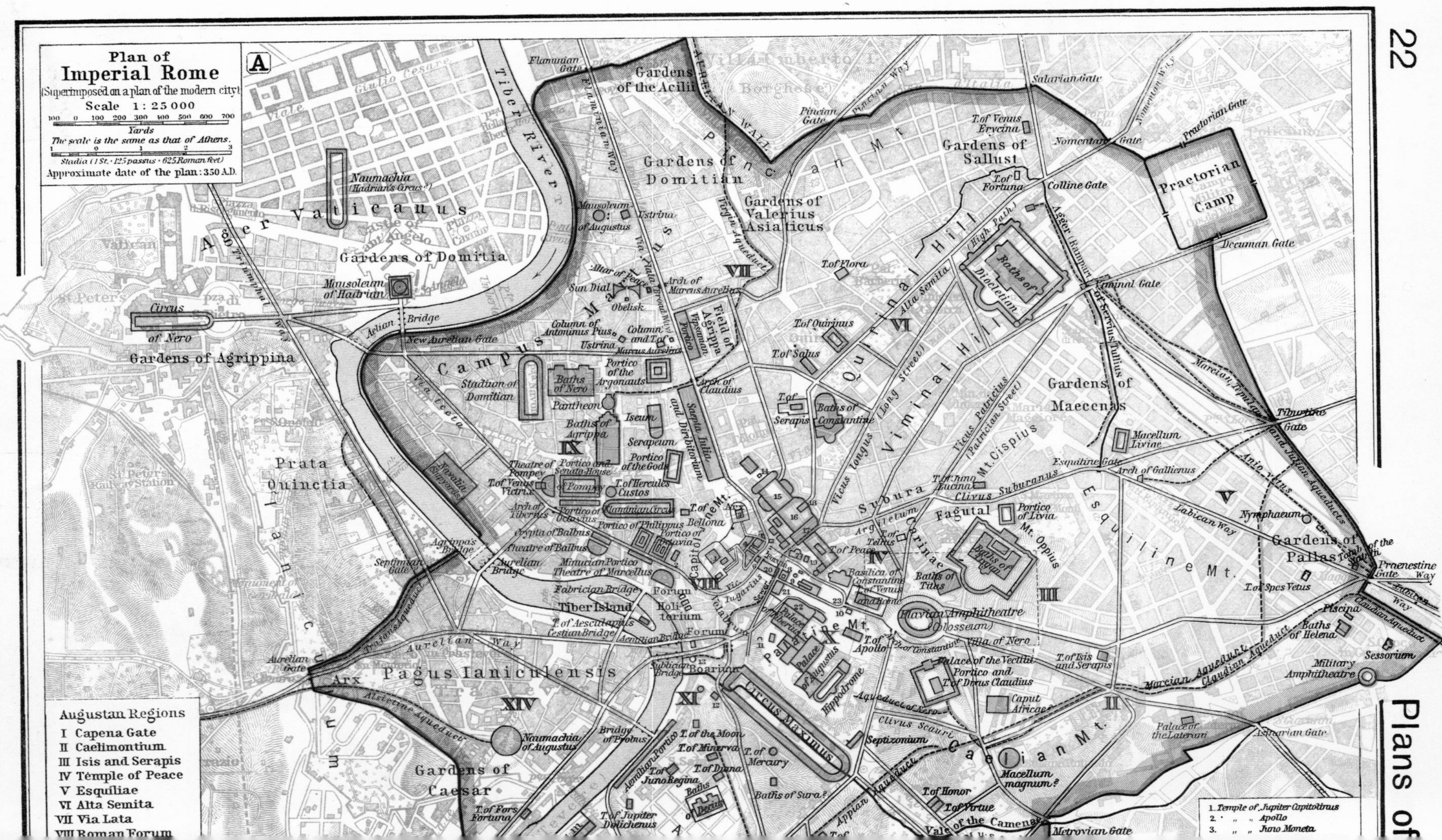

A
Plan of
Imperial Rome
(Superimposed on a plan of the modern city)
Scale 1 : 25 000
100 0 100 200 300 400 500 600 700
Yards
The scale is the same as that of Athens.
Stadia (1 St.: 125 passus: 625 Roman feet)
Approximate date of the plan: 350 A.D.
Augustan Regions
I Capena Gate
II Caelimontium
III Isis and Serapis
IV Temple of Peace
V Esquiliae
VI Alta Semita
VII Via Lata
VIII Roman Forum
1. Temple of Jupiter Capitolinus
2. " " Apollo
3. " " Juno Moneta
Praetorian Camp
Praetorian Gate
Decuman Gate
Nomentan Way
Nomentan Gate
Salarian Gate
Colline Gate
Viminal Gate
Tiburtine Gate
Praenestine Gate
Way
Sessorium
Military Amphitheatre
Baths of Helena
Piscina
Claudian Aqueduct
Marcian Aqueduct
Gardens of Pallas
T. of Spes Vetus
Nymphaeum
Anio vetus
Labican Way
Marcian, Tepulan and Julian Aqueducts
Gardens of Sallust
T. of Venus Erycina
T. of Fortuna
Baths of Diocletian
Agger (Rampart) of Servius Tullius
(High Path)
Gardens of Maecenas
Macellum Liviae
Arch of Gallienus
Esquiline Gate
Esquiline Mt.
Portico of Livia
Mt. Oppius
Baths of Trajan
Flavian Amphitheatre (Colosseum)
Baths of Titus
Villa of Nero
Carinae
Subura
Clivus Suburanus
Fagutal
Mt. Cispius
Vicus longus (Long Street)
Vicus Patricius (Patrician Street)
Viminal Hill
Quirinal Hill
Alta Semita
T. of Flora
T. of Quirinus
T. of Salus
Baths of Constantine
T. of Serapis
Gardens of Valerius Asiaticus
Gardens of Domitian
Pincian Gate
Pincian Way
Pincian Mt.
Aurelian Wall
Virgin Aqueduct
Gardens of the Acilii
Field of Agrippa
Vipsanian Portico
Arch of Claudius
Arch of Marcus Aurelius
Saepta Julia and Diribitorium
Via Lata (Broad Way)
Flaminian Way
Flaminian Gate
Mausoleum of Augustus
Ustrina
Altar of Peace
Obelisk
Sun Dial
Column of Antoninus Pius
Column and T. of Marcus Aurelius
Portico of the Argonauts
Iseum
Serapeum
Portico of the Gods
Pantheon
Baths of Agrippa
Baths of Nero
Campus Martius
Stadium of Domitian
Theatre of Pompey
Portico and Senate House of Pompey
T. of Venus Victrix
T. of Hercules Custos
Theatre of Balbus
Crypta of Balbus
Theatre of Marcellus
Minucian Portico
Portico of Octavia
Portico of Philippus
T. of Bellona
Flaminian Circus
Arch of Tiberius
Navalia (Shipyards)
Via Tecta
Tiber River
Tiber Island
Fabrician Bridge
Cestian Bridge
T. of Aesculapius
Aemilian Bridge
Sublician Bridge
Forum Holitorium
Forum Boarium
Velabrum
Capitol
T. of Peace
Basilica of Constantine
T. of Venus and Rome
Palatine Mt.
Palace of Tiberius
Palace of Augustus
T. of Apollo
Arch of Constantine
Hippodrome
Circus Maximus
Aqueduct of Nero
Palace of the Vectilii
Portico and T. of Divus Claudius
Caput Africae
T. of Isis and Serapis
Septizonium
Clivus Scauri
Caelian Mt.
Macellum magnum?
Palace of the Laterani
Asinarian Gate
Metrovian Gate
Appian Aqueduct
T. of Honor
T. of Virtue
Vale of the Camenae
Baths of Sura?
T. of Mercury
T. of Diana
T. of the Moon
T. of Minerva
T. of Juno Regina
Baths of Decius
Aemilian Portico
T. of Jupiter Dolichenus
Bridge of Probus
Naumachia of Augustus
T. of Fors Fortuna
Gardens of Caesar
Pagus Ianiculensis
Arx
Aurelian Gate
Aurelian Way
Alsietine Aqueduct
Trajan's Aqueduct
Septimian Gate
Agrippa's Bridge
Aurelian Bridge
Prata Quinctia
Aelian Bridge
New Aurelian Gate
Mausoleum of Hadrian
Naumachia (Hadrian's Circus?)
Gardens of Domitia
Ager Vaticanus
Triumphal Way
Circus of Nero
Gardens of Agrippina

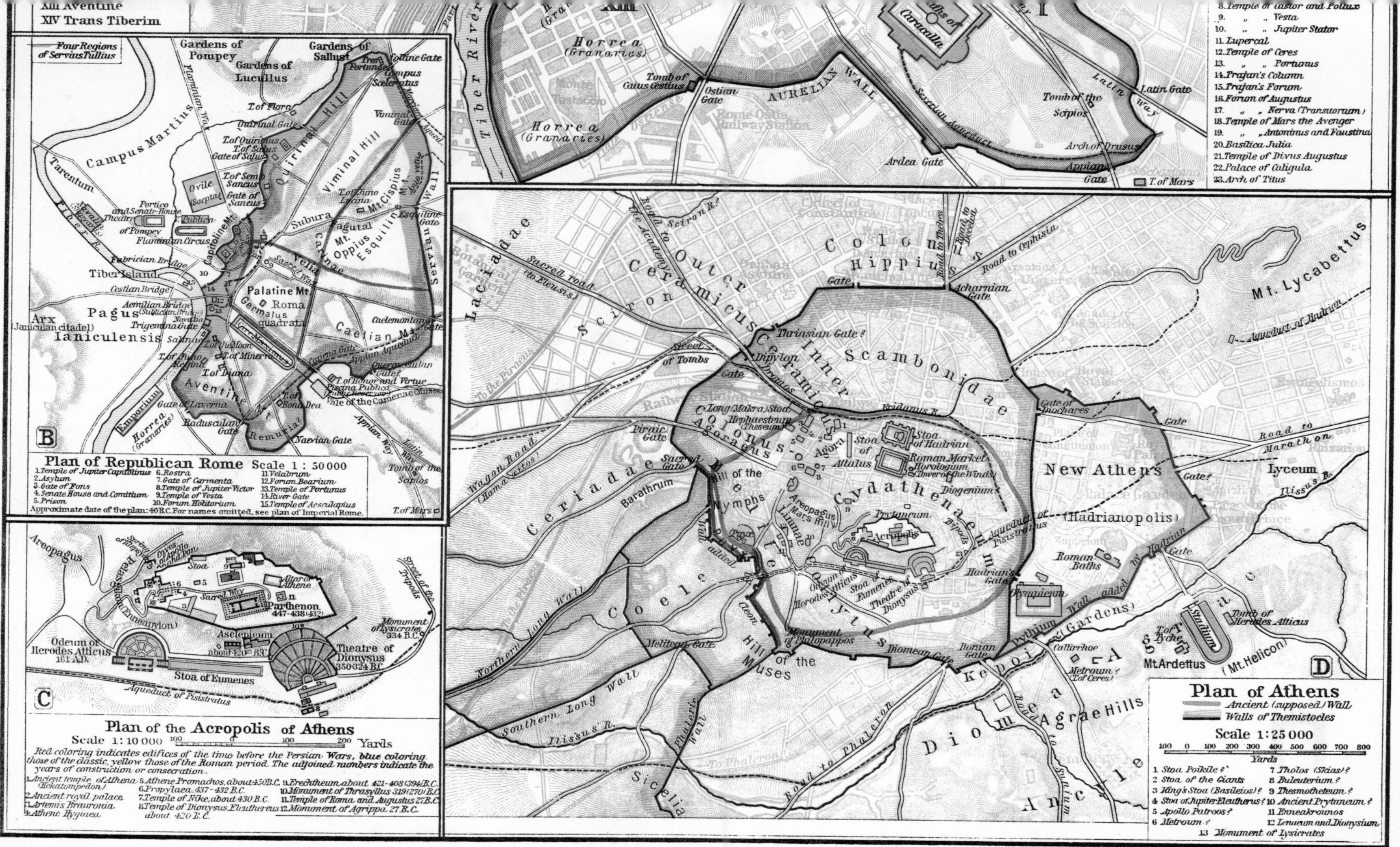

8. Temple of Castor and Pollux
9. " " Vesta
10. " " Jupiter Stator
11. Lupercal
12. Temple of Ceres
13. " " Portunus
14. Trajan's Column
15. Trajan's Forum
16. Forum of Augustus
17. " " Nerva (Transitorium)
18. Temple of Mars the Avenger
19. " " Antoninus and Faustina
20. Basilica Julia
21. Temple of Divus Augustus
22. Palace of Caligula
23. Arch of Titus
XIII Aventine
XIV Trans Tiberim
AURELIAN WALL
Tiber River
Horrea (Granaries)
Tomb of Caius Cestius
Ostian Gate
Latin Gate
Latin Way
Tomb of the Scipios
Arch of Drusus
Appian Gate
Ardea Gate
T. of Mars
Four Regions of Servius Tullius
Gardens of Pompey
Gardens of Lucullus
Gardens of Sallust
Campus Martius
Tarentum
Quirinal Hill
Viminal Hill
Capitoline Mt.
Palatine Mt.
Roma quadrata
Caelian Mt.
Aventine Mt.
Subura
Esquiline
Tiber Island
Pagus Ianiculensis
Arx (Janiculan citadel)
Emporium
B
Plan of Republican Rome Scale 1 : 50 000
1. Temple of Jupiter Capitolinus
2. Asylum
3. Gate of Fons
4. Senate House and Comitium
5. Prison
6. Rostra
7. Gate of Carmenta
8. Temple of Jupiter Victor
9. Temple of Vesta
10. Forum Holitorium
11. Velabrum
12. Forum Boarium
13. Temple of Portunus
14. River Gate
15. Temple of Aesculapius
Approximate date of the plan: 40 B.C. For names omitted, see plan of Imperial Rome.
Areopagus
Parthenon 447-438 (432)
Asclepieum
Odeum of Herodes Atticus 161 A.D.
Theatre of Dionysus 350-324 B.C.
Monument of Lysicrates 334 B.C.
Stoa of Eumenes
Aqueduct of Pisistratus
Street of the Tripods
C
Plan of the Acropolis of Athens
Scale 1:10 000 Yards
Red coloring indicates edifices of the time before the Persian Wars, blue coloring those of the classic, yellow those of the Roman period. The adjoined numbers indicate the years of construction or consecration.
1. Ancient temple of Athena (Hekatompedon)
2. Ancient royal palace
3. Artemis Brauronia
4. Athene Hygaea
5. Athene Promachos, about 450 B.C.
6. Propylaea, 437-432 B.C.
7. Temple of Nike, about 430 B.C.
8. Temple of Dionysus Eleutherus about 420 B.C.
9. Erechtheum about 421-408 (394) B.C.
10. Monument of Thrasyllus 319 (270) B.C.
11. Temple of Roma and Augustus 27 B.C.
12. Monument of Agrippa 27 B.C.
Laciadae
Outer Ceramicus
Sciron
Colonus Hippius
Inner Ceramicus
Scambonidae
Mt. Lycabettus
Aqueduct of Hadrian
Dipylon
Agora
Stoa of Hadrian
Roman Market
Acropolis
Cydathenaeum
Ceriadae
Koile
Hill of the Muses
Hill of the Nymphs
New Athens (Hadrianopolis)
Lyceum
Olympieum
Stadium
Mt. Ardettus
Agrae Hills
Diomea
D
Plan of Athens
Ancient (supposed) Wall
Walls of Themistocles
Scale 1:25 000
Yards
1 Stoa Poikile?
2 Stoa of the Giants
3 King's Stoa (Basileios)?
4 Stoa of Jupiter Eleutherus?
5 Apollo Patroos?
6 Metroum?
7 Tholos (Skias)?
8 Buleuterium?
9 Thesmotheteum?
10 Ancient Prytaneum?
11 Enneakrounos
12 Lenaeum and Dionysium
13 Monument of Lysicrates

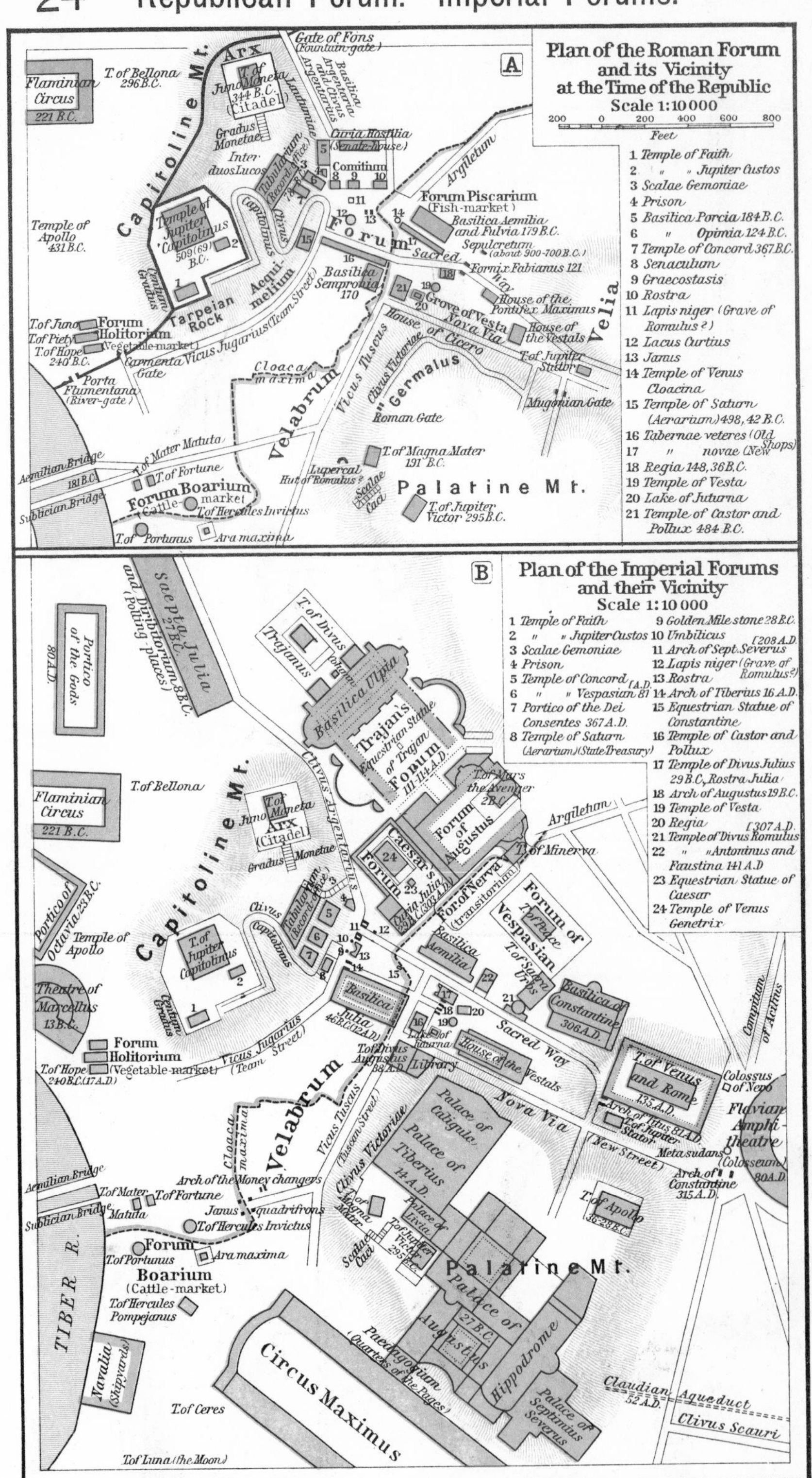

The dates given are those of the construction or consecration of the buildings.

Helvetii
RAETIA
Mt. Adula
[St. Gothard]
Suanetes
Cunus aureus
[St. Bernardino]
[Splügen]
[Julier]
[Septimer]
[Maloja]
[Stilfser Joch]
Noviodunum
Lousonna
Viviscus
Lake Lemanus (Geneva)
Penneloci
Nantuates
Seduni
Rhone R.
Uberi
Genava
Tarnaiae
Sedunum
Pennine Valley
[Simplon]
PENNINE ALPS
Lepontii
RAETIAN ALPS
Clavenna
Bergalei
Summo lacu
Venonetes
Bilitio
Octodurus
Veragri
Oscela
Allobroges
Alpis Poenina
[Gr. St. Bernard]
Verbanus
Larius
Orumbovii
Camunni
Leuceras
Mt. Brennus
GAUL
Alpis Graia
[Lit. St. Bernard]
GRAIAN ALPS
Augusta Praetoria
Salassi
Vitricium
Obilunnum
Axima
Darantasia
Ceutrones
Atrectian Alps
TRANSPADANE GAUL
Insubres
Comum
Bergomum
Brixia
Sabini
Eporedia
Victumulae
Novaria
Mediolanium
(Milan)
Modicia
Pons Aureoli
Cenomani
Libici
Vercellae
Campi Raudii
Rigomagus
Laevi
Laus Pompeia
Ticinum
(Papia)
Marici
Cremona
Graioceli
[Mt. Cenis]
Quadratae
Taurini
Segusio
Ocelum
Industria
Cuttiae
Scingomagus
Augusta Taurinorum
(Taurasia)
Laumellum
Mt. Matrona
[Mt. Genèvre]
Brigantio
Forum Fulvii
Hasta
Iria
Postumian Way
Camillomagus
Clastidium
Placentia
Retovium
Dertona
Anamari
Florentiola
Aemilian Way
Fidentia
Brixellum
Parma
Tannetum
Caturiges
Caburrum
Forum Vibii
Pollentia
Alba Pompeia
Julian Augustan Way
LIGURIA
Bobium
Castrum
Veleia
Veleiates
CISPADANE
Regium Lepidi
Mt. Vesulus
COTTIAN ALPS
Eburodunum
Cottius
Forum Germanorum
Augusta Bagiennorum
Carrea Potentia
Aquae Statiellae
Crixia
Libarna
Mt. Ioventio
[P.d. Grovi]
APENNINES
[La Cisa]
Mt. Bardonis
Mt. Caenia
Stura R.
Pedo
Ceba
Calanicum
Savo
Vada Sabatia
Genua
(Genoa)
Ingauni
Portus Delphini
Segesta
Monilia
Bodetia
Apuani
Albingaunum
Berritini
Varus R.
MARITIME ALPS
Intimilii
Luna
Salinae
Vedianti
Cemenelum
Portus Maurici
Albintimilium
Portus Veneris
Taberna frigida
Forum Clodii
Fossae Papirianae
Luca
Pisae
Arnus R.
Vintium
Deciates
Monoecus
Nicaea
Antipolis
Oxybii
Tropaeum Augusti
Portus Herculis Monoeci
Horrea
Forum Iulii
Athenopolis
Sambracitan Gulf
Valvata
Portus Pisanus
GULF OF GENOA
Urgo
(Gorgon)
Ad Fines
Vada Volaterrana
Volaterrae
Aegilos
(Capraria)
Sacrum Pr.
Centurinum
Aquae Populoniae
Populonium
Falesia
Argous Portus
Portus Traianus
Ilva (Aethalia)
Planasia
Oglasa
Tilox Pr.
Attium Pr.
Ropicum
Mantinum
Viriballum Pr.
Mariana
CORSICA
Rhium Pr.
Urcinium
Mt. Aureus
Alalia
(Aleria)
TYRRHENIAN
Scale 1:2 500 000
Miles
Greek colonies
Phoenician colonies
Roman colonies before the civil wars (See also p. 29)
Of the two northern boundaries of Italy and of Etruria, the more southerly is that of the period before Augustus, and the more northerly that of the period after Augustus.
Modern names of passes thus [Julier]
Pr.-Promontorium - Cape or promontory
Long. East 10 of Greenwich

NORICUM
CARNIC ALPS
TRIDENTINE ALPS
JULIAN VENETIAN ALPS
Mt. Caruanca
PANNONIA
Latovici
ALPS
DALMATIA
ILLYRICUM
VENETIA
Carni
Venetia
ISTRIA
GULF OF TERGESTE
GULF OF FLANONA
ADRIATIC SEA
Liburni
GAUL
Ager Gallicus
Senones
UMBRIA
PICENUM
Praetutii
Vestini
Aequi
Paeligni
Marsi
Hernici
Caraceni
Frentani
ETRURIA
SEA
Mt. Fiscellus
Mt. Tetrica
Aguontum
Teurnia
Sebatum
Littamum
Loncium
Santicum
Virunum
Iuenna
Colatio
Celeia
Atrans
Emona
Nauportus
Longaticum
Acervo
Neviodunum
Praetorium Latovicorum
Metulum
Tergeste
Aquileia
Concordia
Opitergium
Altinum
Tarvisium
Vicetia
Patavium
Ateste
Atria
Hostilia
Ravenna
Ariminum
Pisaurum
Sena Gallica
Ancona
Firmum
Asculum
Hadria
Corfinium
Perusia
Arretium
Florentia
Faesulae
Cortona
Clusium
Volsinii
Tarquinii
Caere
Veii
ROME
Ostia
Tibur
Praeneste
Tusculum
Alba Fucens
Amiternum
Reate
Spoletium
Interamna
Narnia
Falerii
Pola
Polaticum Pr.
Parentium
Neapolis
Senia
Iader
Asseria
Tarsatica
Flanona
Portunata
Celadussae Is.
Mentorides Is.
Lissa
Absorus
Crexi
Histonium
Buca
Teate
Ortona
Aternum
Bovianum vetus
Teruentum
Aufidena
Sulmo
Marruvium
Lake Fucinus
Castrum novum
Centumcellae
Cosa
Saturnia
Visentium
Volci
Tuscana
Nepete
Sutrium
Ocriculum
Tuder
Ameria
Iguvium
Tifernum Tiberinum
Urbinum
Sentinum
Camerinum
Nuceria
Asisium
Hispellum
Fulginiae
Trebiae
Nursia
Tridentum
Feltria
Bellunum
Tiber R.
Po R.
Savus R.
Dravus R.
Rubicon R.

The Growth of Roman Power in Italy to 218 B.C.

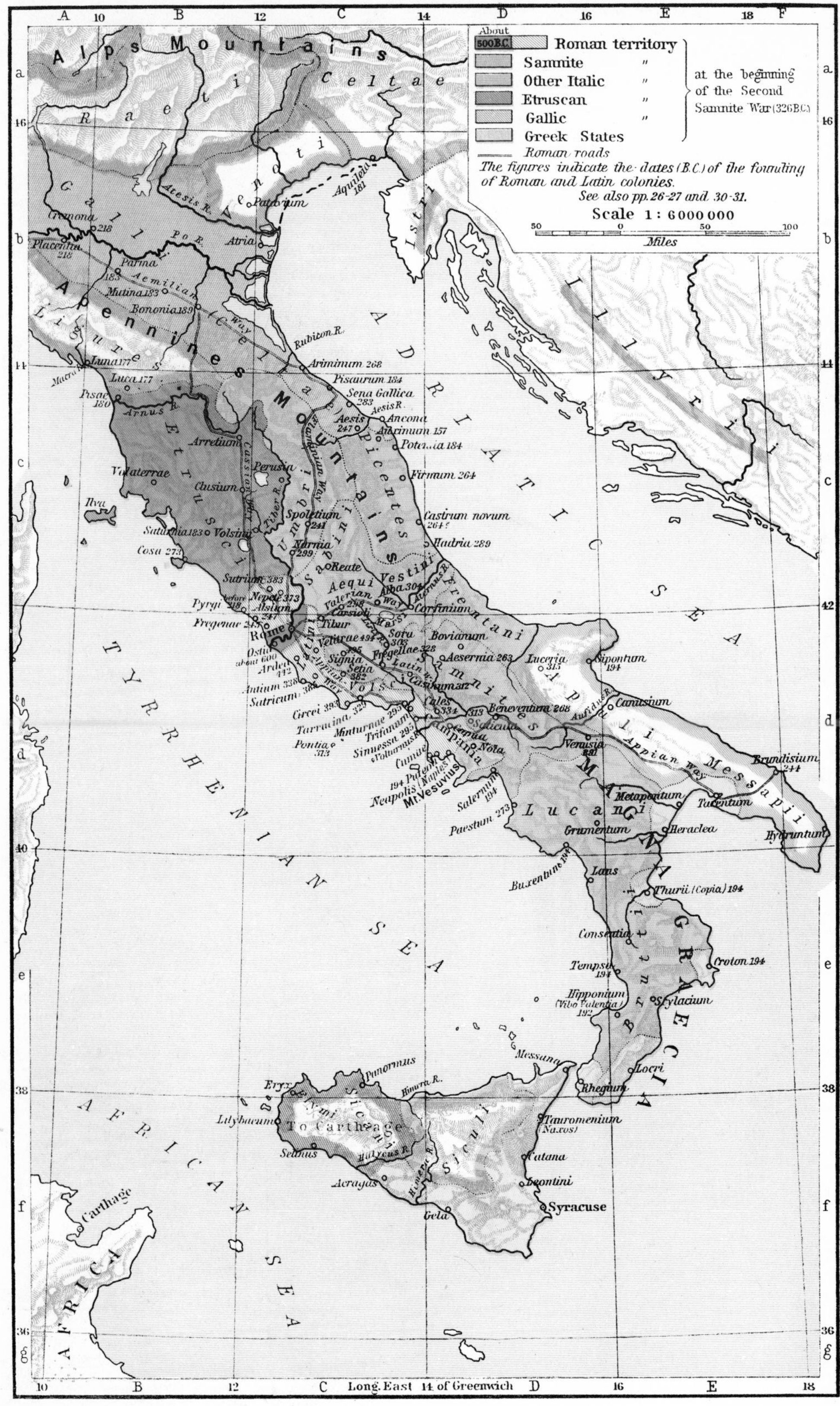

ROME
Ostia
Tusculum
Praeneste
Marsi
Hernici
LATIUM
Antium
Astura
Circaeum Pr.
Tarracina
Aurunci
Minturnae
Sinuessa
Volturnum
Liternum
Cumae
Pithecussae Is.
Aenaria
Mt. Epopeus
Prochyta
Pr. of Misenum
Neapolis (Naples)
BAY OF NAPLES
Herculaneum
Mt. VESUVIUS
Pompeii
Stabiae
Surrentum
Pr. of Minerva
Capreae
Nuceria Alfaterna
Salernum
Picentini
BAY OF PAESTUM
Paestum (Posidonia)
Posidium Pr.
Velia (Elea)
Palinurus Pr.
Buxentum Pr.
CAMPANIA
Capua
Nola
Beneventum
Caudium
Bovianum
Aesernia
Luceria
Samnium
Pentri
Frentani
Palmaria
Sinonia
Pontia
Pontiae Is.
Pandateria
TYRRHENIAN SEA
Ustica (Osteodes)
Liparacae (Aeoliae or Vulcaniae) Is.
Phoenicussa
Didyme
Ericussa
Euonymus
Lipara
Hiera, Thermessa (Vulcan I.)
SICILY
Aegates (Aegusae) Is.
Phorbantia
Hiera (Maritima)
Aegusa
Motye
Lilybaeum
Eryx
Drepanum
Segesta (Egesta)
Elymi
Halicyae
Entella
Sicani
Mazara
Selinus
Triocala
Thermae Selinuntiae
Gemelli Hills
Heraclea Minoa (Macara)
Halycus R.
Agrigentum (Acragas)
Mt. Ecnomus
Phintias
Gela
Camarina
Hyccara
Mt. Ercte
Panormus (Palermo)
Solus (Soluntum)
Thermae Himeraeae
Himera
Cephaloedium
Halaesa
Caleacte
Agathyrnum
Haluntium
Tyndaris
Mylae
Messana
Mts. of Neptune
NEBRODES MTS.
MT. ETNA
Tauromenium
Naxus
Henna
Morgantina
Catana
HERAEAN MOUNTAINS
Leontini
Megara Hybl.
Thapsus
Taurus Pr.
Helorus
Pachynus Pr.
A
B
C
D
a
b
c
d
e
41
40
39
38
37
12
13
14
15
Longitude East 13 of Greenwich

ADRIATIC SEA
GULF OF TARENTUM
IONIAN SEA
MAGNA GRAECIA
APULIA
CALABRIA
BRUTTIUM
ILLYRICUM
Barium
Neapolis
Gnatia (Egnatia)
Brundisium
Tarentum (Taras)
(Col. Neptunia)
Metapontum
Heraclea
Siris
Hydruntum
Callipolis
Sybaris
Thurii (Col. Copia)
Croton
Lacinium Pr.
Scolacium (Scylacium)
GULF OF SCYLACIUM
Caulonia
Locri Epizephyrii
Zephyrium Pr.
Dyrrhachium (Epidamnus)
Apollonia
Aulon
Oricum
Vicinity of Naples
Phlegraean Fields
Mt. Gaurus
Cyme, Cumae
Naples
Palaeopolis
Forum Vulcani (Solfatara)
Dicaearchia, Puteoli
Baiae
Nesis
Pausilypum
Scale 1:300000
Present area of Naples
Modern names in hair line
Plan of Syracuse
At the time of the Peloponnesian War (431-404 B.C.)
Extension under Dionysius I (405-367 B.C.)
ACHRADINA
TYCHA
EPIPOLAE
NEAPOLIS
ORTYGIA (NASOS)
Great Harbor
Little Harbor
PLEMMYRIUM
Scale 1:200000
1 Arethusa Spring
2 Temple of Athene
3 " " Artemis
4 Citadel of Dionysius
5 Pentapylum
6 Forum
7 Stone quarries (Latomiae)
8 Roman amphitheatre
9 Greek theatre
10 Heracleum
11 Hexapylum
12 Temple of Demeter and Persephone
Neapolis Allies of Athens
Syracuse " " Sparta
Croton Neutral States
during the Peloponnesian War (431-404 B.C.)
For scale and explanation, see p. 26-27.

Rome and Carthage at the Beginning of the Second Punic War, 218 B. C.

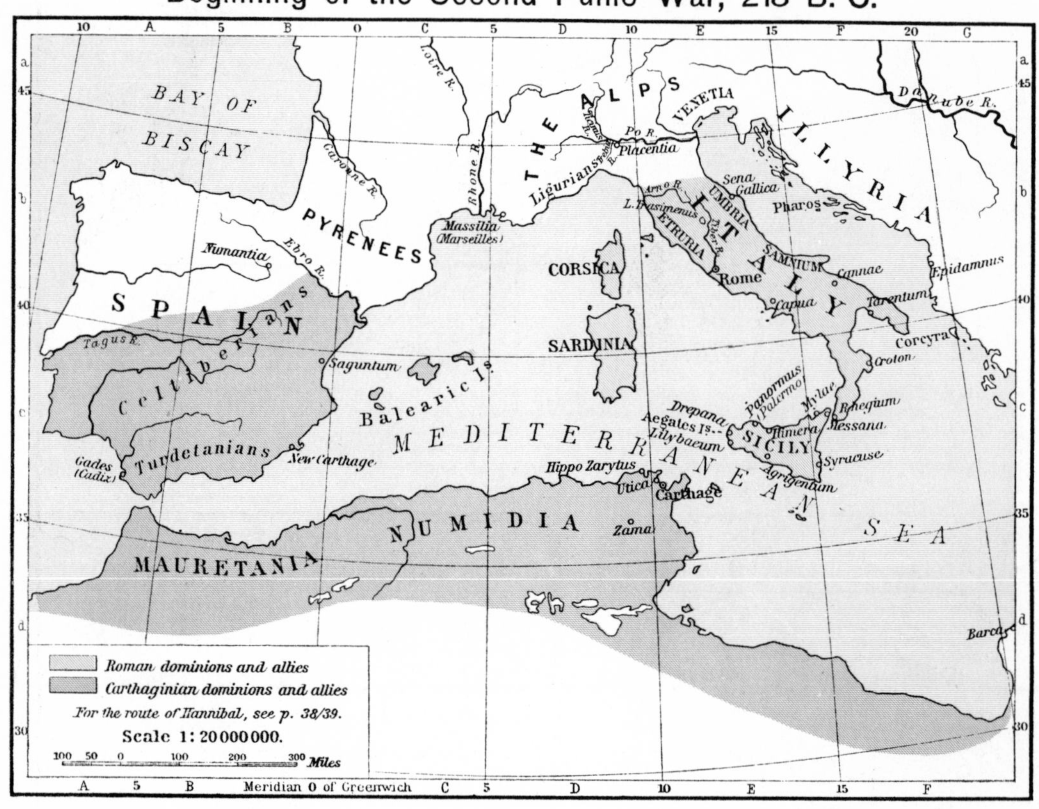

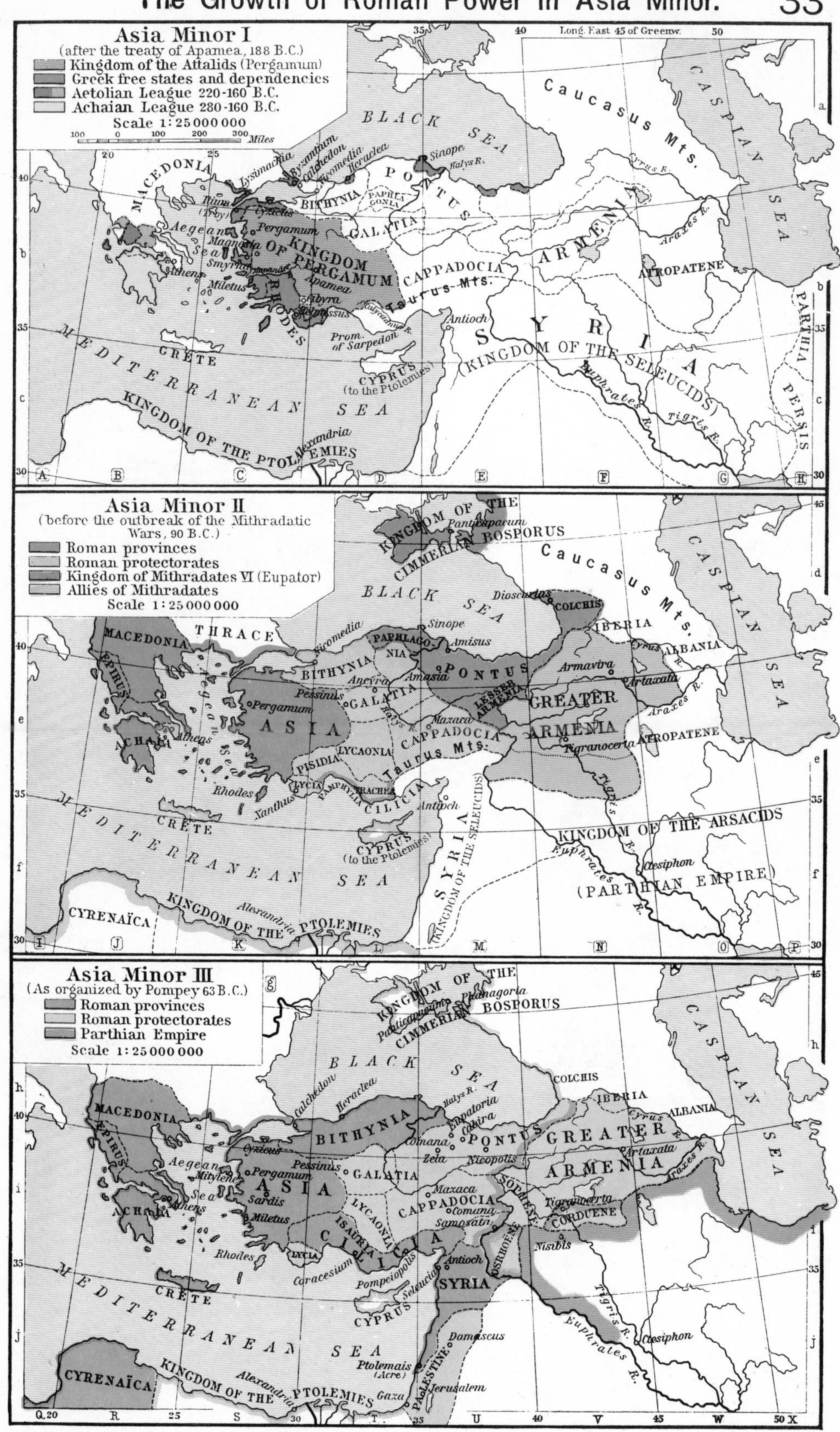
Asia Minor I
(after the treaty of Apamea, 188 B.C.)
Kingdom of the Attalids (Pergamum)
Greek free states and dependencies
Aetolian League 220-160 B.C.
Achaian League 280-160 B.C.
Scale 1: 25 000 000
Miles
BLACK SEA
Caucasus Mts.
CASPIAN SEA
MACEDONIA
Byzantium
Chalcedon
Nicomedia
Heraclea
Sinope
Halys R.
PONTUS
PAPHLAGONIA
BITHYNIA
GALATIA
Aegean Sea
Pergamum
KINGDOM OF PERGAMUM
Athens
Miletus
Apamea
RHODES
CAPPADOCIA
Taurus Mts.
ARMENIA
Araxes R.
ATROPATENE
PARTHIA
PERSIS
Antioch
SYRIA
(KINGDOM OF THE SELEUCIDS)
Euphrates R.
Tigris R.
Prom. of Sarpedon
CRETE
CYPRUS (to the Ptolemies)
MEDITERRANEAN SEA
KINGDOM OF THE PTOLEMIES
Alexandria
Asia Minor II
(before the outbreak of the Mithradatic Wars, 90 B.C.)
Roman provinces
Roman protectorates
Kingdom of Mithradates VI (Eupator)
Allies of Mithradates
Scale 1: 25 000 000
KINGDOM OF THE CIMMERIAN BOSPORUS
Panticapaeum
Caucasus Mts.
CASPIAN SEA
BLACK SEA
Dioscurias
COLCHIS
IBERIA
ALBANIA
THRACE
MACEDONIA
EPIRUS
ACHAIA
Athens
Nicomedia
Sinope
Amisus
PAPHLAGONIA
BITHYNIA
Ancyra
Amasia
PONTUS
Armavira
Artaxata
Pessinus
GALATIA
LESSER ARMENIA
GREATER ARMENIA
Pergamum
ASIA
Mazaca
CAPPADOCIA
LYCAONIA
PISIDIA
Taurus Mts.
Tigranocerta
ATROPATENE
Rhodes
LYCIA
PAMPHYLIA
TRACHEA
CILICIA
Xanthus
Antioch
CRETE
CYPRUS (to the Ptolemies)
SYRIA (KINGDOM OF THE SELEUCIDS)
KINGDOM OF THE ARSACIDS
(PARTHIAN EMPIRE)
Ctesiphon
Euphrates R.
Tigris R.
MEDITERRANEAN SEA
CYRENAÏCA
KINGDOM OF THE PTOLEMIES
Alexandria
Asia Minor III
(As organized by Pompey 63 B.C.)
Roman provinces
Roman protectorates
Parthian Empire
Scale 1: 25 000 000
KINGDOM OF THE CIMMERIAN BOSPORUS
Phanagoria
Panticapaeum
CASPIAN SEA
BLACK SEA
COLCHIS
IBERIA
ALBANIA
Chalcedon
Heraclea
Halys R.
Eupatoria
Cabira
MACEDONIA
EPIRUS
BITHYNIA
Comana
PONTUS
GREATER ARMENIA
Artaxata
Cyzicus
Zela
Nicopolis
Aegean Sea
Mitylene
Pergamum
Pessinus
GALATIA
ASIA
Sardis
Athens
ACHAIA
Miletus
Mazaca
CAPPADOCIA
Comana
Samosata
SOPHENE
Tigranocerta
CORDUENE
LYCAONIA
ISAURIA
CILICIA
LYCIA
Rhodes
Nisibis
OSRHOENE
Coracesium
Pompeiopolis
Seleucia
Antioch
SYRIA
CRETE
CYPRUS
Tigris R.
Ctesiphon
Euphrates R.
Damascus
MEDITERRANEAN SEA
Ptolemais (Acre)
PALESTINE
Jerusalem
CYRENAÏCA
KINGDOM OF THE PTOLEMIES
Alexandria
Gaza

Plan of Carthage
Scale 1:300000
Miles
1. Trade harbor
2. War harbor (Cothon)
3. Forum
4. Byrsa (Citadel)
5. Temple of Esmin (Aesculapius)
6. Amphitheatre
7. Circus
8. Theatre.
Megara
Magalia
i.e. New city
Old city
Scipio's camp
Scipio's mole
STAGNUM TUNETICUM
(BAY OF TUNIS)
Taenia
Plan of Alexandria
according to Puchstein
Scale 1:100000
Mile
Lochias
Pharos (lighthouse)
Myrmex
GREAT HARBOR
Pharos I.
Heptastadium
PORTUS EUNOSTUS (OLD PORT)
Posidium
Theatre
Jewish Quarter
Gate of the Sun (Canopic Gate)
Regia
Museum
Bruchium
Dromos
Rhakotis
Gate of the Moon
LAKE MAREOTIS
1. Palace harbor
2. Antirrhodus I.
3. Timonium
4. Harbor of Cibotus
5. Ancient } mouth of the
6. Present } Nile canal
7. Serapeum and Pompey's Pillar
8. Temple of Neptune
9. Nile canal
Present shore.
Abbreviations:
P. A. Pennine Alps
M.A. Maritime Alps
K.C. Kingdom of Cottius
Scale 1:20000000
Miles
Meridian 0 of Greenw.
ATLANTIC OCEAN
NORTH SEA
BAY OF BISCAY
ENGLISH CHANNEL
IBERIAN SEA
TYRRHENIAN SEA
ADRIATIC SEA
MEDITERRANEAN SEA
HIBERNIA (IRELAND)
CALEDONIA (SCOTLAND)
BRITAIN
Wall of Antoninus or Severus
Hadrian's Wall
Orcades Is. (Orkneys)
Ebudae Is. (Hebrides)
Thule I.?
Cassiterides Is.?
Eburacum (York)
Londinium (London)
GAUL
LUGUDUNENSIS
AQUITANIA
BELGICA
NARBONENSIS
GERMANIA INFERIOR
GERMANIA SUPERIOR
GERMANIA
SPAIN
TARRACONENSIS
LUSITANIA
FARTHER BAETICA
ITALY
CORSICA
SARDINIA
SICILY
BALEARIC IS.
RAETIA
NORICUM
VINDELICIA
MAURETANIA TINGITANA
MAURETANIA CAESARIENSIS
NUMIDIA
PROCONSULAR AFRICA
GAETULIA
SCATINAVIA (SCANDINAVIA)
CIMBRIC CHERSONESE (DENMARK)
Mt. Saevo
Sitones
Suiones
Goths
Garamantes
SYRTIS MINOR
Carthage
Rome
Lutetia
Massilia (Marseilles)
Mediolanum (Milan)

Vicinity of Rome
Scale 1:1000000
Miles
Main roads and branch roads
Aqueducts. (A)
1. Milvian Bridge
2. Virgin Aqueduct
3. Appian Aqueduct
4. Ferentinian Grove
5. T. of Jupiter Latiaris
6. Trajan's Aqueduct
7. Hadrian's Villa.
ROME
Ager Romanus
Ager Solonius
Ostia
Port of Augustus
Port of Claudius
Port of Trajan
Veii
Caere
Alsium
Fregenae
Fidenae
Tibur
Praeneste
Tusculum
Alba Longa
Aricia
Lanuvium
Lavinium
Ardea
Velitrae
Signia
Cora
Norba
Anagnia
Gabii
Carsioli
SARMATIA
Huns
Alans
Budini
Roxolani
Vonedae
Navari
Aestui
Fenni
Aorsi
Utii
Siracae
DACIA
107-275 A.D.
Getae
LOWER MOESIA
THRACE
MACEDONIA
ACHAIA
BLACK SEA
KINGDOM OF THE CIMMERIAN BOSPORUS
Tauric Chersonese
CASPIAN SEA
Caucasus Mts.
COLCHIS
IBERIA
ALBANIA
ARMENIA
115-117 A.D.
MEDIA ATROPATENE
BITHYNIA
PAPHLAGONIA
PONTUS
GALATIA
CAPPADOCIA
ASIA
LYCIA
PAMPHYLIA
CILICIA
MESOPOTAMIA
ASSYRIA
EMPIRE OF THE PARTHIANS
BABYLONIA
SYRIA
CYPRUS
CRETE
PALESTINE
ARABIA
EGYPT
CYRENAICA
MARMARICA
Alexandria
Antioch
Byzantium (Constantinople)
Damascus
Ctesiphon
Babylon
RED SEA
Roman territory at the beginning of the 1st. Punic War (264 B.C.)
Acquired as a result of the 1st. Punic War (238 B.C.)
Acquired up to the end of the 2nd. Punic War (201 B.C.)
" up to 133 B.C.
" up to the death of Caesar (44 B.C.)
" " " " " " Augustus (14 A.D.)
" " " " " " Marcus Aurelius (180 A.D.)
Boundaries of the Roman provinces before the time of Diocletian
Imperial } Provinces
Senatorial }
Colored border indicates countries semi-independent. Unless accompanied by the letters A.D., the figures given are those of the date of acquisition B.C. The shifting of imperial and senatorial provinces from one control to the other is not indicated, except by an occasional double underlining, thus CYPRUS
...d capitals of the four divisions under Diocletian, 284-305 A.D.

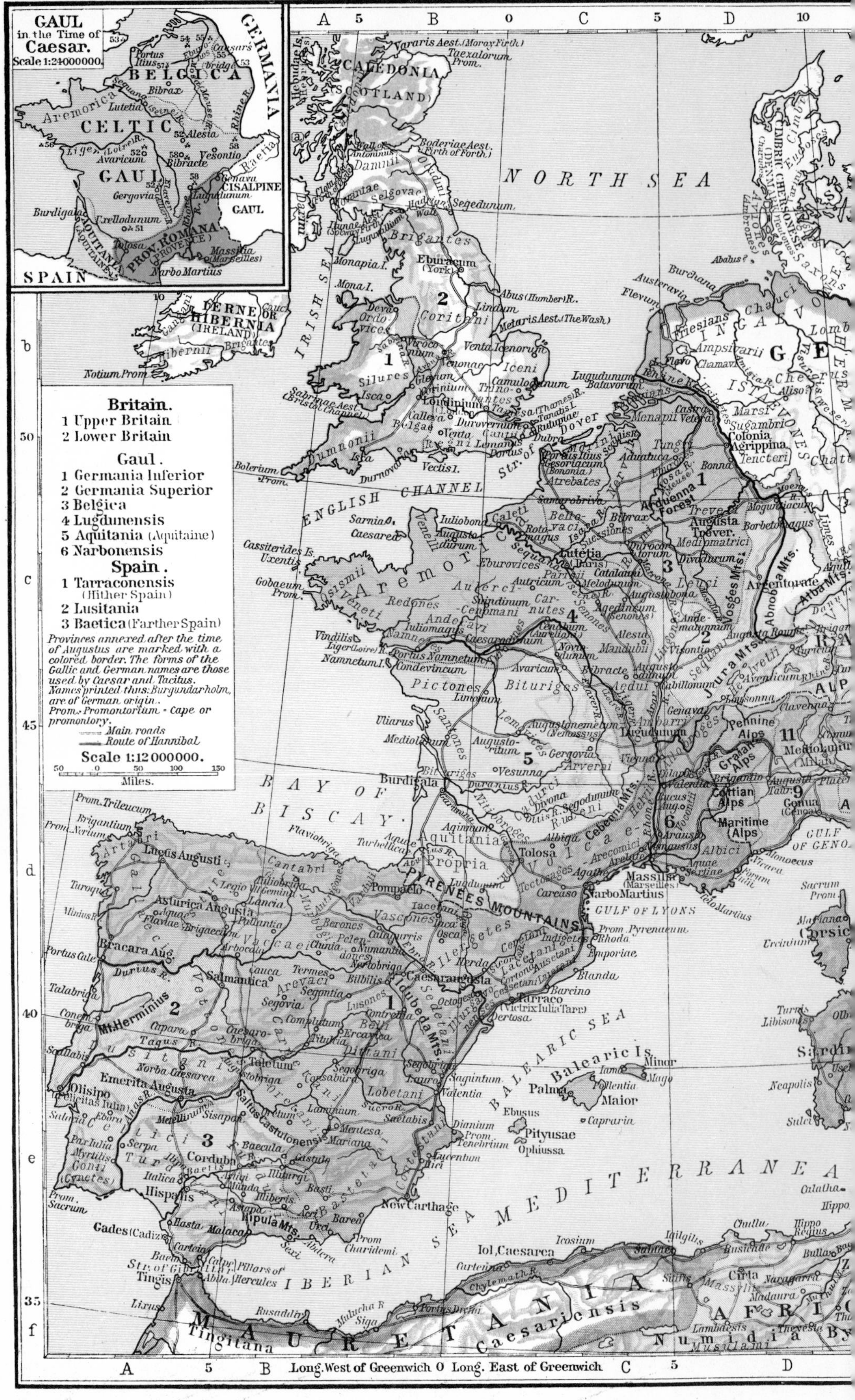
GAUL
in the Time of
Caesar.
Scale 1:24000000.
BELGICA
CELTIC
GAUL
GERMANIA
CISALPINE
GAUL
PROV. ROMANA
(PROVENCE)
AQUITANIA
(AQUITAINE)
SPAIN
Britain.
1 Upper Britain
2 Lower Britain
Gaul.
1 Germania Inferior
2 Germania Superior
3 Belgica
4 Lugdunensis
5 Aquitania (Aquitaine)
6 Narbonensis
Spain.
1 Tarraconensis (Hither Spain)
2 Lusitania
3 Baetica (Farther Spain)
Provinces annexed after the time of Augustus are marked with a colored border. The forms of the Gallic and German names are those used by Caesar and Tacitus.
Names printed thus: Burgundarholm, are of German origin.
Prom. = Promontorium = Cape or promontory.
Main roads
Route of Hannibal
Scale 1:12 000000.
50 0 50 100 150
Miles.
CALEDONIA
(SCOTLAND)
NORTH SEA
IRISH SEA
HIBERNIA
(IRELAND)
ENGLISH CHANNEL
Str. of Dover
BAY OF BISCAY
PYRENEES MOUNTAINS
GULF OF LYONS
BALEARIC SEA
Balearic Is.
IBERIAN SEA
MEDITERRANEAN
MAURETANIA
Tingitana
Caesariensis
Numidia
Long. West of Greenwich 0 Long. East of Greenwich

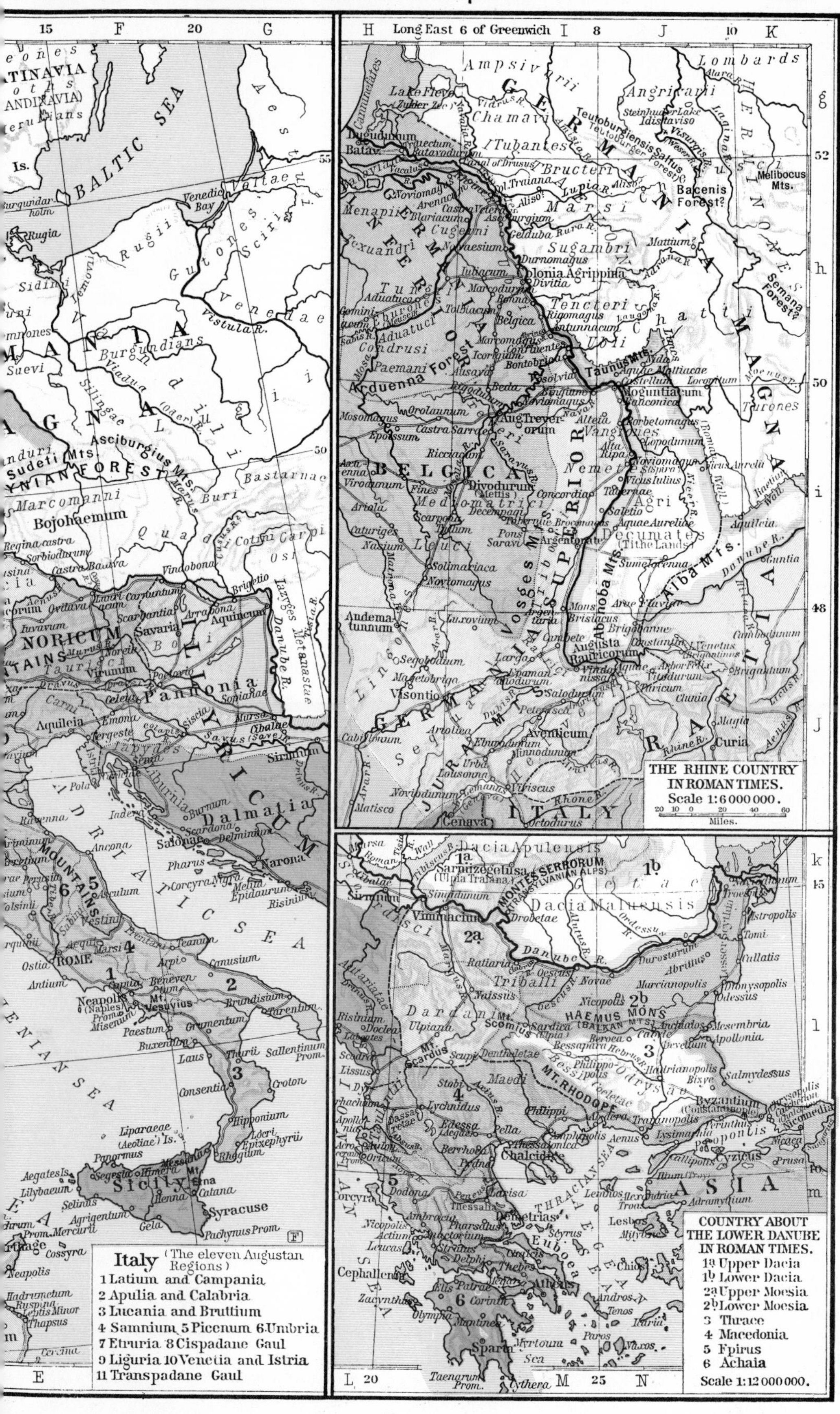
Long East 6 of Greenwich
THE RHINE COUNTRY IN ROMAN TIMES.
Scale 1: 6 000 000.
Miles.
COUNTRY ABOUT THE LOWER DANUBE IN ROMAN TIMES.
1a Upper Dacia
1b Lower Dacia
2a Upper Moesia
2b Lower Moesia
3 Thrace
4 Macedonia
5 Epirus
6 Achaia
Scale 1: 12 000 000.
Italy (The eleven Augustan Regions)
1 Latium and Campania
2 Apulia and Calabria
3 Lucania and Bruttium
4 Samnium 5 Picenum 6 Umbria
7 Etruria 8 Cispadane Gaul
9 Liguria 10 Venetia and Istria
11 Transpadane Gaul
BALTIC SEA
ADRIATIC SEA
GERMANIA MAGNA
GERMANIA INFERIOR
GERMANIA SUPERIOR
BELGICA
RAETIA
NORICUM
Pannonia
ILLYRICUM
Dalmatia
Dacia Apulensis
Dacia Maluensis
HAEMUS MONS (BALKAN MTS.)
MT. RHODOPE
AEGEAN SEA
ASIA
Sicily
ROME
ITALY
JURA MTS.
Vosges Mts.
Alba Mts.
Danube R.
Rhine R.

The Roman

ATLANTIC OCEAN
NORTH SEA
ENGLISH CHANNEL
BAY OF BISCAY
HIBERNIA
CALEDONIA
Wall of Hadrian
York
Lincoln
St. Albans
Colchester
London
Caerleon upon Usk
D. OF BRITAIN
Frisians
Saxons
Franks
Thuringians
Burgundians
Lombards
Jutes
DENMARK
Angles
Alamanni
Elbe R.
Oder R.
Cologne
Tongres
Trèves
Mayence
Worms
Strasburg
Ratisbon
Passau
Augsburg
Vienna
Soissons
Rouen
Reims
Châlons
Verdun
Metz
Toul
Paris
Sens
Nantes
Tours
Loire R.
Poitiers
Bourges
Besançon
Vindonissa
Geneva
Lyons
Vienne
Bordeaux
Toulouse
Narbonne
Arles
Marseilles
Nicaea
D. OF GAUL
PYRENEES
Braga
Leon
Astorga
Duero R.
Calahorra
Ebro R.
Saragossa
Avila
Toledo
Tagus R.
Merida
Evora
Guadiana R.
Cordova
Castulo
Italica
Sevilla
Faro
Cadiz
Malaga
Elvira
Baza
Cartagena
Urci
Gerona
Barcelona
Tarragona
Balearic Is
WEST ROMAN EMPIRE
Milan
Turin
Po R.
Bergamo
Brescia
Verona
Aquileia
Bologna
Ravenna
Genoa
Pisa
Florence
APENNINES
ROME
Ostia
Naples
Brindisi
Taranto
Messina
Palermo
Sicily
Syracuse
Corsica
Sardinia
Cagliari
D. OF THE CITY OF ROME
MARE TYRRHENUM
ADRIATIC SEA
Salona
Siscia
Laibach
ITALY
MEDITERRANEAN
Caesarea Mauretaniae
Tipasa
Sitifis
Cirta
Hippo Regius
Tagaste
Carthage
Sicca
Bagae
Hadrumetum
Thapsus
Sufes
Ruspe
Vita
P. OF AFRICA
Leptis magna
DIOCESE
PREFECTURE
AFRICA
Mauretanians
ATLAS
Limits of the Roman Empire
Boundaries of dioceses
Boundaries of provinces
Seat of a patriarchate
Seat of a metropolitanate (archbishopric)
Seat of a bishopric
D.- DIOCESE; P.- PROCONSULATE
Scale 1:20000000
Miles
Long. West of Greenwich 0 Long. East of Greenwich
For Roman
given here

Provinces
PREFECTURE OF GAUL
DIOCESE OF SPAIN
1. Baetica, 2. Lusitania, 3. Galicia,
4. Tarraconensis, 5. Carthaginiensis,
6. Mauretania Tingitana
7. Balearic Isles.
DIOCESE OF GAUL
1. Viennensis, 2. Lugdunensis,
3.4, Germania I. II,
5.6, Belgica I. II,
7. Maritime Alps,
8. Pennine and Graian Alps,
9. Maxima Sequanorum,
10.11, Aquitaine I. II,
12. Novempopulana,
13.14, Narbonnensis I. II,
DIOCESE OF BRITAIN
1. Maxima Caesariensis, 2. Valentia,
3.4, Britain I. II,
5. Flavia Caesariensis.
PREFECTURE OF ITALY
DIOCESE OF AFRICA
1. Byzacium, 2. Numidia,
3. Tripolitana,
4. Mauretania Sitifensis
5. Mauretania Caesariensis
DIOCESE OF THE CITY OF ROME
1. Campania, 2. Tuscany and Umbria,
3 Picenum Suburbicarium, 4. Sicily,
5. Apulia and Calabria,
6. Bruttia and Lucania,
7. Samnium, 8. Sardinia,
9. Corsica, 10. Valeria.
DIOCESE OF ITALY
1. Venetia and Istria,
2. Aemilia, 3. Liguria,
4. Flaminia and Picenum Annonarium, 5. Cottian Alps,
6.7, Raetia I. II, 8. Pannonia II,
9. Savia, 10. Pannonia I, 11. Dalmatia,
12. Noricum mediterraneum,
13. Noricum ripense,
14. Valeria ripensis
PROCONSULATE OF AFRICA
PREFECTURE OF ILLYRICUM
DIOCESE OF MACEDONIA
1. Macedonia, 2. Crete, 3. Thessaly,
4. Epirus vetus, 5. Epirus nova,
6. Macedonia Salutaris.
DIOCESE OF DACIA
1. Dacia mediterranea, 2. Moesia I,
3. Praevalitana, 4. Dardania,
5. Dacia ripensis.
PROCONSULATE OF ACHAIA
PREFECTURE OF THE EAST
DIOCESE OF EGYPT
1. Upper Libya, 2. Lower Libya,
3. Thebais, 4. Egypt, 5. Arcadia,
6. Augustamnica.
DIOCESE OF THE EAST
1. Palestine I, 2. Phoenicia,
3. Syria I, 4. Cilicia I,
5. Cyprus, 6. Palestine II,
7. Palestine Salutaris,
8. Phoenicia Libani,
9. Eufratensis, 10. Syria Salutaris,
11. Osrhoëne, 12. Mesopotamia,
13. Cilicia II, 14. Isauria,
15. Arabia.
DIOCESE OF PONTUS
1. Bithynia, 2. Galatia,
3. Paphlagonia, 4. Honorias,
5. Galatia Salutaris,
6.7, Cappadocia I. II,
8. Helenopontus,
9. Pontus Polemoniacus.
10.11, Armenia I. II,
DIOCESE OF ASIA
1. Pamphylia, 2. Lydia,
3. Caria, 4. Lycia,
5. Lycaonia, 6. Pisidia,
7. Phrygia Pacatiana,
8. Phrygia Salutaris.
DIOCESE OF THRACE
1. Europe, 2. Thrace,
3. Haemimontium,
4. Rhodope, 5. Moesia II,
6. Scythia.
PROCONSULATE OF ASIA
Slavs
East Goths
Alans
Dnieper R.
Dniester R.
Don R.
Volga R.
CARPATHIAN MTS.
CASPIAN SEA
BLACK SEA
CAUCASUS MOUNTAINS
ARMENIA
EAST ROMAN EMPIRE
PREFECTURE OF THE EAST
DOMINION OF THE SASSANIDS
Cherson
Theodosia
Bosporus
Pityus
Phasis
Koura R.
Sinope
CONSTANTINOPLE
Tomi
Dorostorium
Marcianopolis
Anchialus
Adrianople
Heraclea
Nicomedia
Claudiopolis
Amasia
Neocaesarea
Gangra
Sebaste
Nicaea
Ancyra
Pessinus
Cyzicus
Thessalonica
Philippopolis
Sardica
Larissa
Lemnos
Lesbos
Chios
Sardis
Ephesus
Laodicea
Synnada
Iconium
Perge
Caesarea
Tyana
Anazarbus
Melitene
Amida
Nisibis
Edessa
Hierapolis
Mosul
Arbela
Tarsus
Seleucia
Antioch
Apamea
Palmyra
Emesa
Damascus
Constantia
Cyprus
Paphos
Myra
Rhodes
Melos
Thera
Cnossus
Crete
Sidon
Tyre
Scythopolis
Caesarea
Bostra
Jerusalem
Pelusium
Alexandria
Cabasa
Leontopolis
Petra
Arabia Petraea
Ammonium
Oxyrhynchus
Antinoë
Nile R.
Cyrene
Darnis
Ctesiphon
Seleucia
Babylon
Tigris R.
Euphrates R.
RED SEA
To D. of Macedonia

Economic Map of the Ancient World.

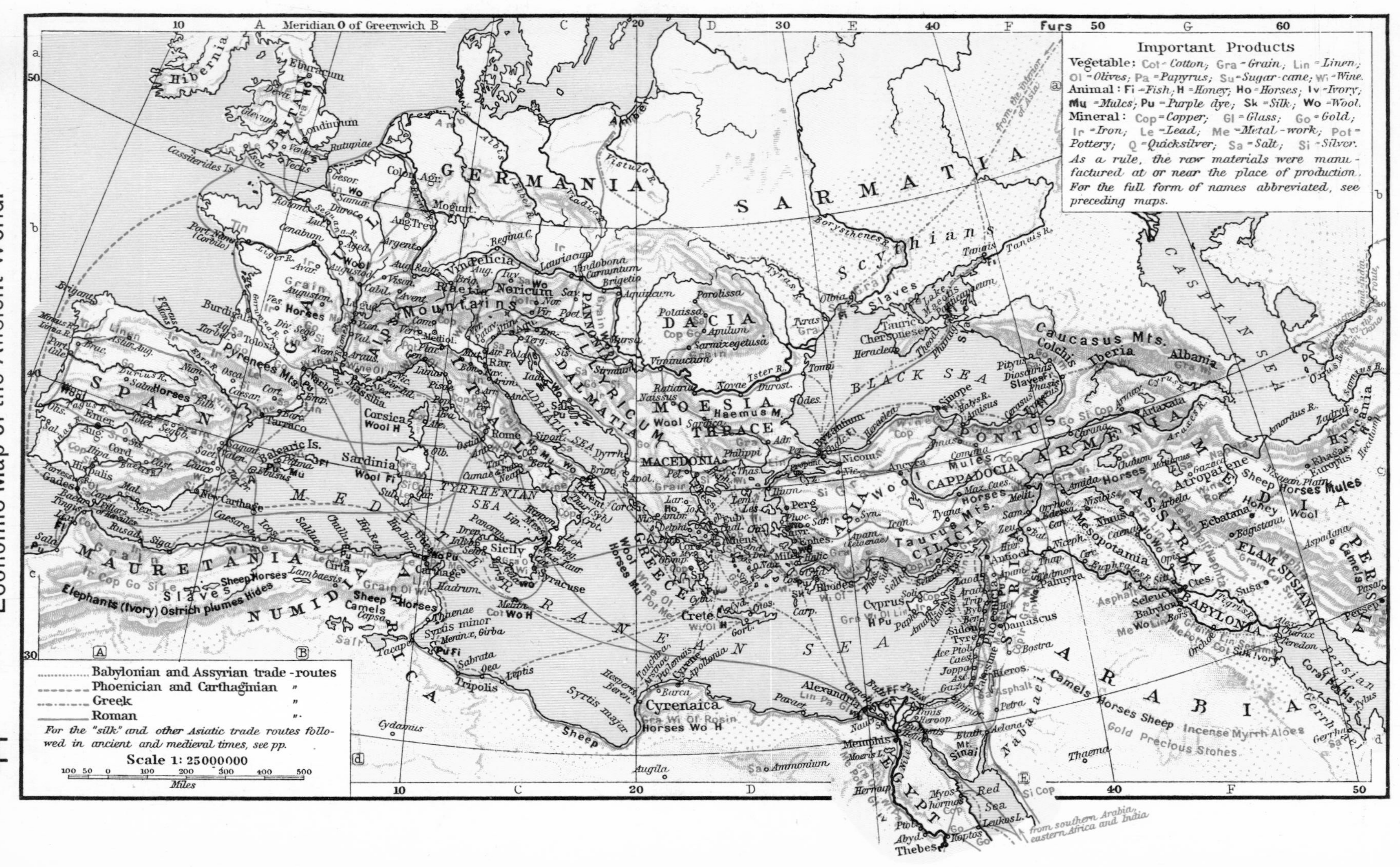

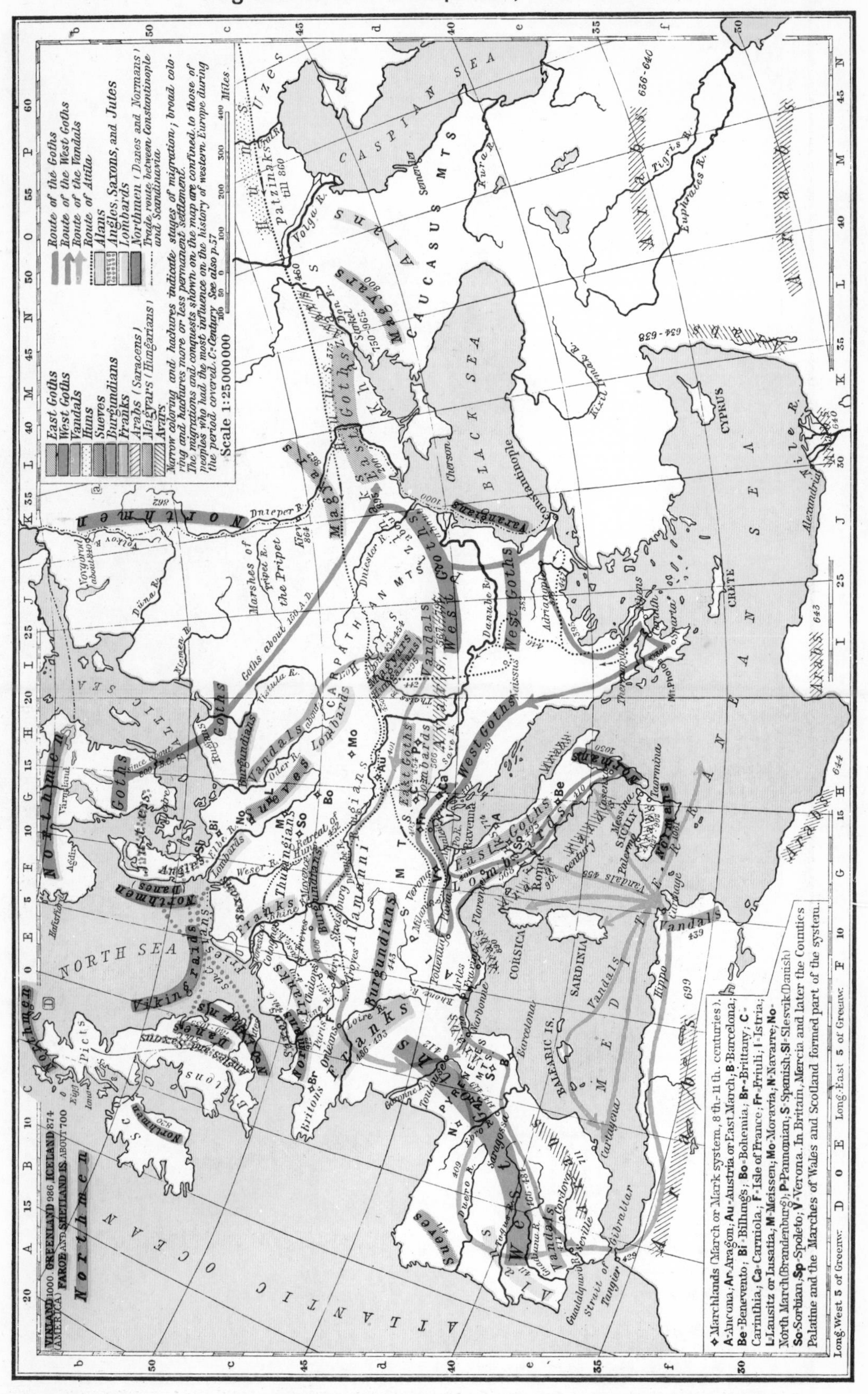
East Goths
West Goths
Vandals
Huns
Sueves
Burgundians
Franks
Arabs (Saracens)
Magyars (Hungarians)
Avars
Route of the Goths
Route of the West Goths
Route of the Vandals
Route of Attila
Alans
Angles, Saxons, and Jutes
Lombards
Northmen (Danes and Normans)
Trade route between Constantinople and Scandinavia
Narrow coloring and hachures indicate stages of migration; broad coloring and hachures more or less permanent settlement.
The migrations and conquests shown on the map are confined to those of peoples who had the most influence on the history of western Europe during the period covered. C=Century. See also p.57
Scale 1:25 000 000
✣ Marchlands (March or Mark system, 8 th.-11 th. centuries). A=Ancona; Ar=Aragon; Au=Austria or East March; B=Barcelona; Be=Benevento; Bi=Billungs; Bo=Bohemia; Br=Brittany; C=Carinthia; Ca=Carniola; F=Isle of France; Fr=Friuli; I=Istria; L=Lausitz or Lusatia; M=Meissen; Mo=Moravia; N=Navarre; No=North March (Brandenburg); P=Pannonian; S=Spanish; Sl=Slesvik (Danish) So=Sorbian; Sp=Spoleto; V=Verona. In Britain, Mercia and later the Counties Palatine and the Marches of Wales and Scotland formed part of the system.

ATLANTIC OCEAN
NORTH SEA
IRELAND
Christianity introduced by St. Patrick 440-493
Iona
Christianity introduced from Ireland by St. Columba 563
Roman Britain partially Christianized in 3d Century. Christianity subsequently uprooted in England by Anglo-Saxon invasions of 5th and 6th Centuries
STRATHCLYDE
NORTHUMBRIA
Lindisfarne
Whitby
York
Bangor
WALES
MERCIA
EAST ANGLIA
WESSEX
ESSEX
SUSSEX
KENT
Canterbury
London
CORNWALL
Augustine 597
English Channel
Frisians
Saxons
Danes
Norwegians
Swedes
GOTHIA
Ribe
Hamburg
Abotrites
Wends
Pomeranians
BOHEMIA
Czechs
MORAVIA
PANNONIA
ILLYRICUM
Prague
Cologne
Treves
Mainz
Fulda
Magdeburg
Thuringians
Bavarians
Alamanni
Franks
Rouen
Amiens
Soissons
Reims
Paris
Nantes
Tours
Christianity introduced in 496
Poitiers
Limoges
GAUL
Burgundians
Lyons
Vienne
Bordeaux
Bay of Biscay
Agen
Eauze
Toulouse
Narbonne
Arles
Orange
Marseilles
Nice
Pyrenees
Sueves
Arians in the 5th Century Catholics in 550
Leon
Astorga
Duero R.
Ebro R.
Tagus R.
SPAIN
Visigoths
Arians in the 5th Century Catholics in 589
Lisbon
Evora
Merida
Toledo
Saragossa
Gerona
Barcelona
Tarragona
Cordova
Guadalquivir R.
Faro
Cadiz
Strait of Gibraltar
Malaga
Cartagena
Lombards
Arians in 5th Century Catholics in 7th Century
Milan
Verona
Aquileia
Trieste
Pavia
Bologna
Ravenna
Rimini
Ancona
Pisa
Florence
Perugia
Rome
Salerno
Capua
Pozzuoli
Benevento
Foggia
ADRIATIC SEA
CORSICA
SARDINIA
SICILY
Palermo
Lilybaeum
Catania
Syracuse
Reggio
MELITA
MEDITERRANEAN
Northern Limit of Mohammedanism
Caesarea
Hippo Regius
Thabraca
Utica
Carthage
Tunis
Zama
Cirta
Milev
Tigisis
NUMIDIA
Badiae
MAURETANIA
Leptis Magna
From the Seventh Century
Extent of Christianity about 600 (pontificate of Gregory I, the Great, 590 - 604)
Area Christianized 600 - 800
" " 800 - 1100
" " 1100 - 1300
Damascus Churches of the apostolic period (33 - 100)
Nicaea Principal churches of the post apostolic period (100-311)
Alexandria Antioch Mission centres in both periods
Journeys of the Apostle Paul
Peoples converted from Arianism to Catholicism
Figures indicate approximate dates of conversion to Christianity
Scale 1 : 20 000 000
Miles
Long.

Christianity introduced by Swedes 1155
Esthonians
Livonians
Novgorod
Riga
Lithuanians
Moscow
Russians
Christianity introduced under Vladimir (988-1015)
Kiev
Dnieper R.
Dniester R.
Khazars
Patzinaks
Christianized 11th Century
Sea of Azov
Goths
Converted to Arian Christianity by Ulfilas (341-381)
Subsequent Migration to Italy and Spain
Bulgarians (865-900)
BLACK SEA
CASPIAN SEA
Balkan
Anchialus
Odessus
Durostorum
Tomi
THRACE
Constantinople
Chalcedon
Nicomedia
Heraclea
S. of Marmora
BITHYNIA
PONTUS
Amastris
Sinope
Trapezus
Amasia
Neocaesarea
Claudiopolis
Sebastea
GALATIA
CAPPADOCIA
Ancyra
Caesarea
Melitene
Amida
Nisibis
Edessa
Resaina
Carrhae
MESOPOTAMIA
Tigris R.
Euphrates R.
Circesium
Palmyra
Emesa
Beroea
Chalcis
Antioch
Seleucia
CYPRUS
Salamis
Paphos
SYRIA
Tripoli
Beirut
Sidon
Tyre
Damascus
Caesarea Philippi
Bostra
Caesarea
Joppa
Gaza
Jerusalem
Pella
Rhinocolura
Pelusium
Alexandria
Memphis
EGYPT
Nile R.
Ptolemais
Aelana
RED SEA
Iconium
Lystra
Derbe
Tarsus
Tyana
Mopsuestia
Dorylaeum
Nicaea
Pergamum
Thyatira
Sardis
Philadelphia
Magnesia
Smyrna
Ephesus
Tralles
Laodicea
Colossae
Hierapolis
Tabae
Miletus
LYCIA
PAMPHYLIA
Patara
Myra
Rhodes
RHODES
Cnossus
Gortyna
CRETE
MACEDONIA
Philippi
Abdera
Thessalonica
Apollonia
Larissa
Thebes
Athens
Corinth
Argos
Apollonia
Cyrene
Pityus
Greenwich

The Roman and Hunnic Empires about 450.

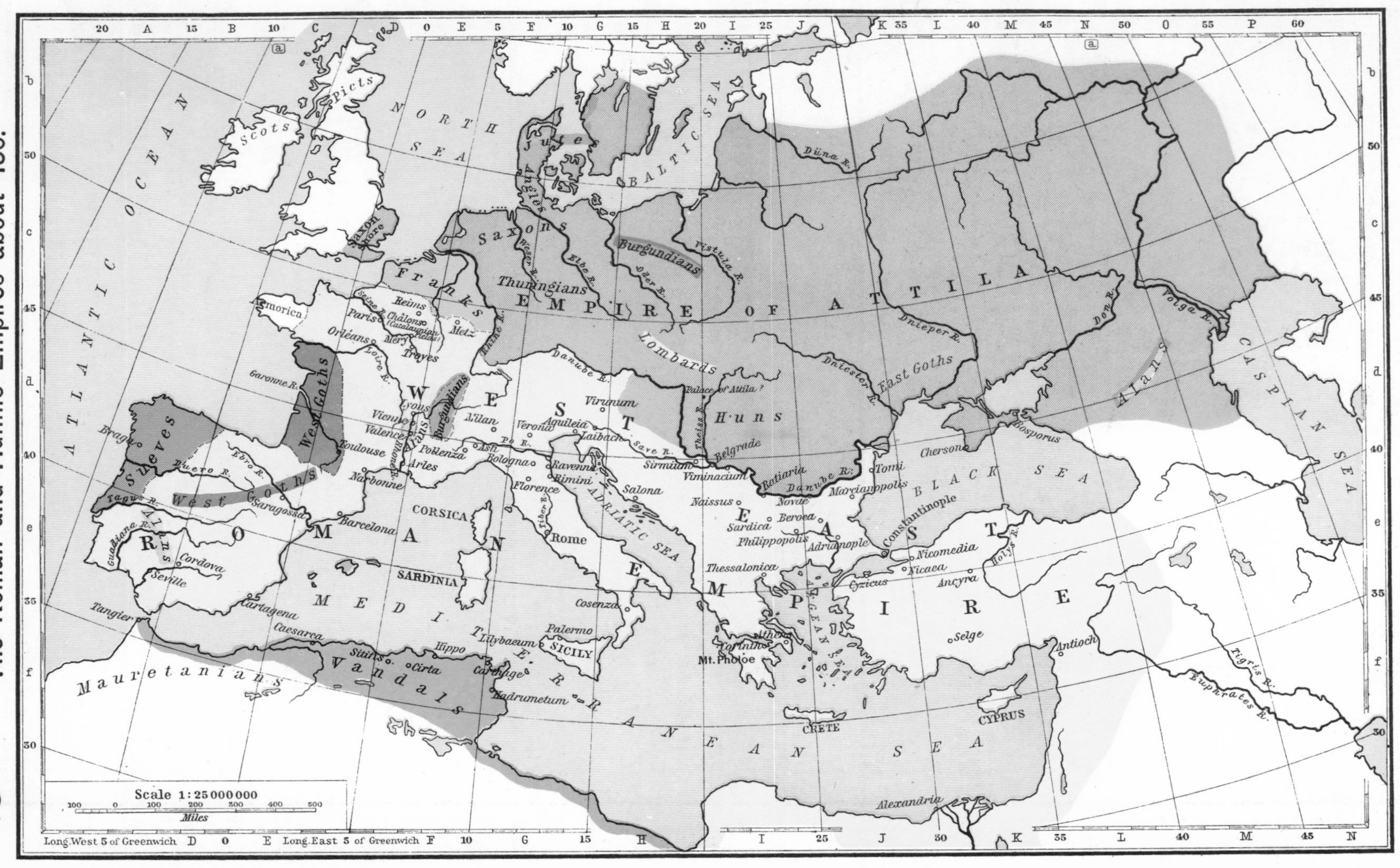

Physical Map of the British Isles.

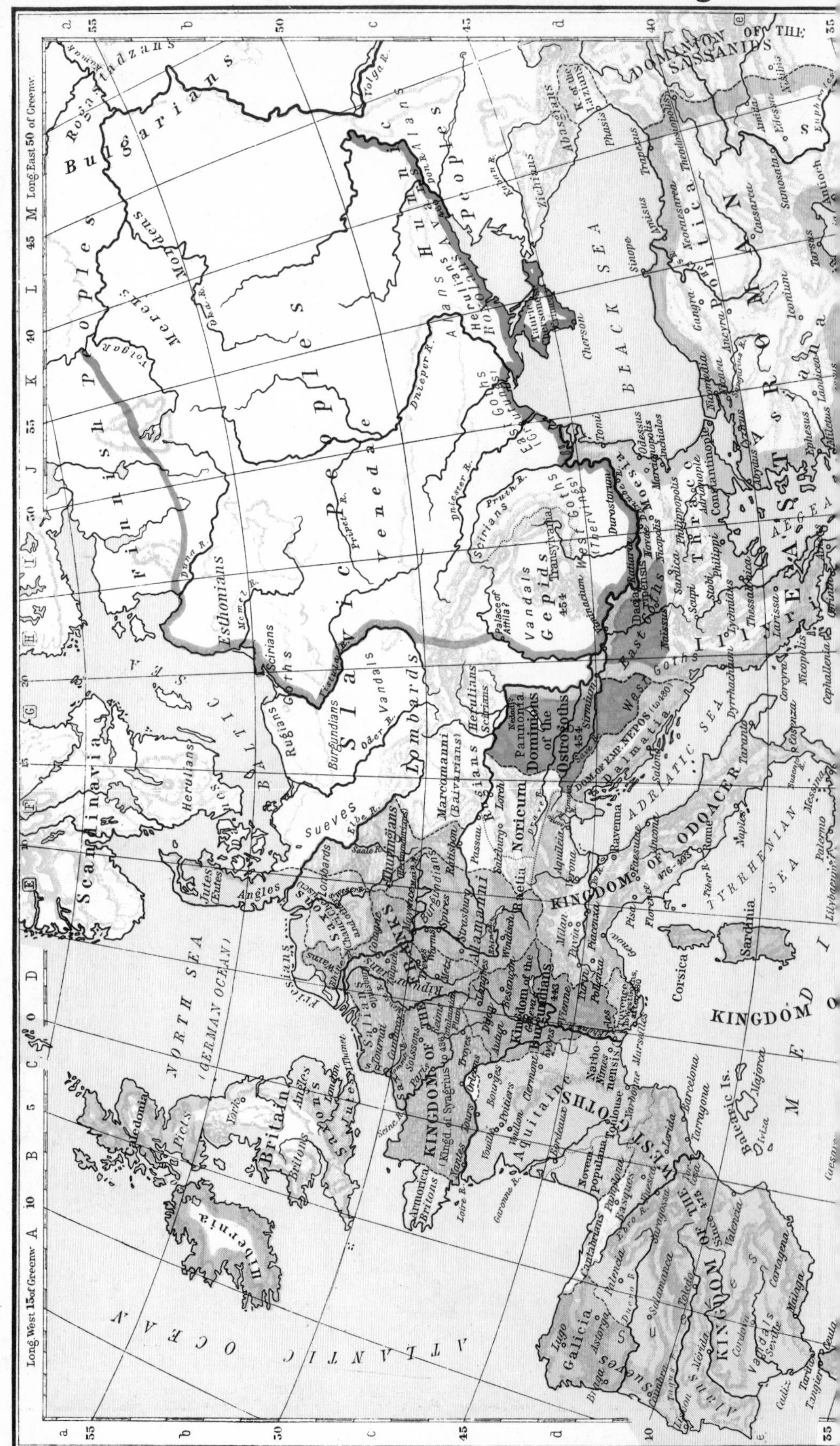
NORTH SEA
(GERMAN OCEAN)
ATLANTIC OCEAN
BLACK SEA
ADRIATIC SEA
TYRRHENIAN SEA
Scandinavia
Britain
Hibernia
Caledonia
Picts
Bulgarians
Esthonians
Lombards
Noricum
Pannonia
Dominions of the Ostrogoths
KINGDOM OF ODOACER
KINGDOM OF THE WEST GOTHS
KINGDOM OF THE BURGUNDIANS
KINGDOM OF SYAGRIUS
Aquitaine
Galicia
Corsica
Sardinia
Balearic Is.
Ravenna
Rome
Constantinople
Long. West 15 of Greenw.
Long. East 50 of Greenw.

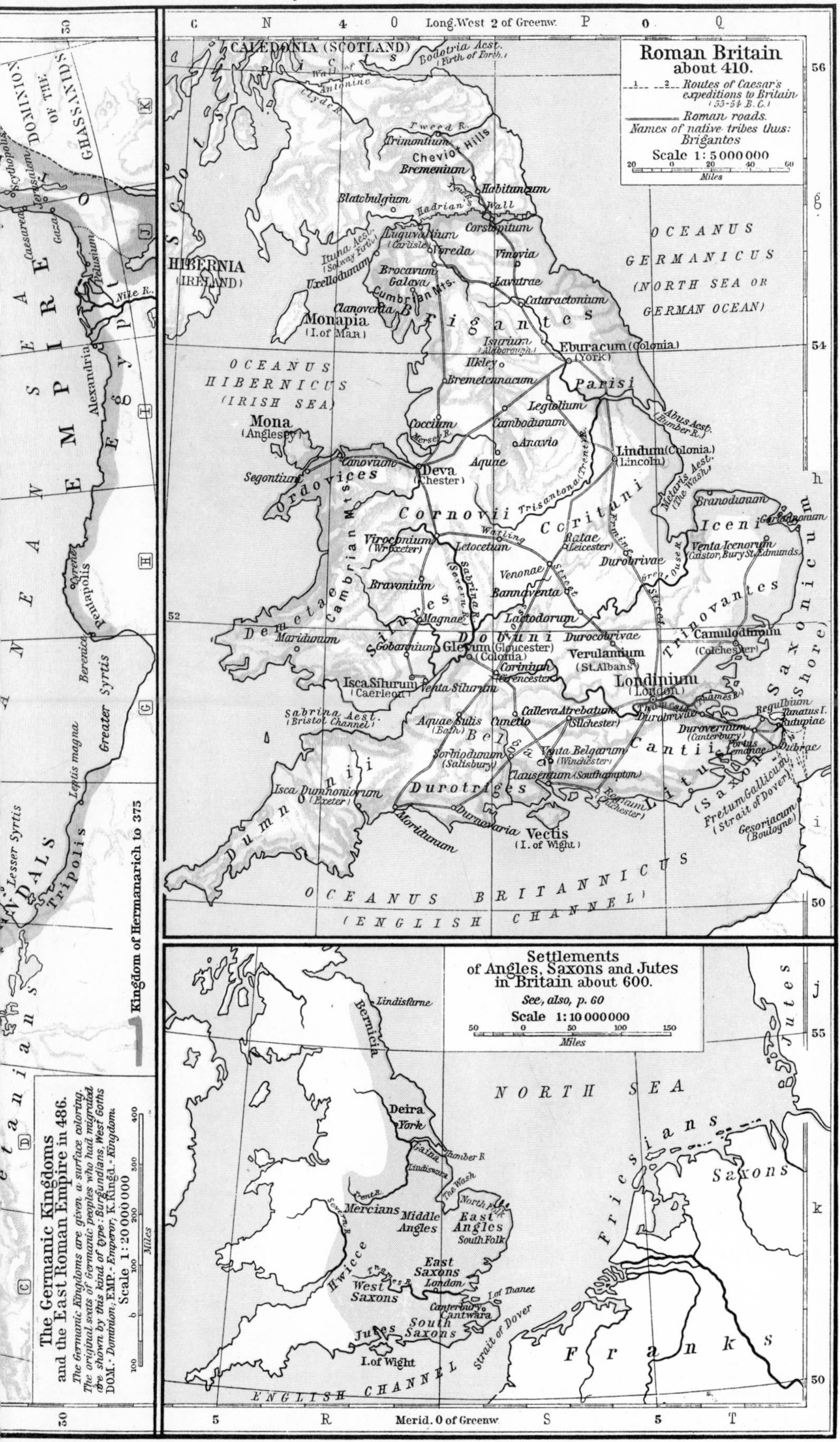
Roman Britain
about 410.
Routes of Caesar's expeditions to Britain (55-54 B.C.)
Roman roads.
Names of native tribes thus: Brigantes
Scale 1: 5 000 000
Miles
Settlements
of Angles, Saxons and Jutes
in Britain about 600.
See, also, p. 60
Scale 1:10 000 000
Miles
The Germanic Kingdoms
and the East Roman Empire in 486.
The Germanic Kingdoms are given a surface coloring. The original seats of Germanic peoples who had migrated are shown by this kind of type: Burgundians, West Goths
DOM. = Dominion; EMP. = Emperor; K. Kingd. = Kingdom.
Scale 1:20 000 000
Miles
Kingdom of Hermanarich to 375
Long. West 2 of Greenw.
Merid. 0 of Greenw.
CALEDONIA (SCOTLAND)
HIBERNIA (IRELAND)
OCEANUS GERMANICUS (NORTH SEA OR GERMAN OCEAN)
OCEANUS HIBERNICUS (IRISH SEA)
OCEANUS BRITANNICUS (ENGLISH CHANNEL)
Eburacum (Colonia) (York)
Lindum (Colonia) (Lincoln)
Deva (Chester)
Londinium (London)
Camulodunum (Colchester)
Verulamium (St. Albans)
Glevum (Gloucester) (Colonia)
Isca Silurum (Caerleon)
Isca Dumnoniorum (Exeter)
Aquae Sulis (Bath)
Venta Belgarum (Winchester)
Calleva Atrebatum (Silchester)
Durovernum (Canterbury)
Vectis (I. of Wight)
Mona (Anglesey)
Monapia (I. of Man)
Brigantes
Parisi
Iceni
Trinovantes
Cantii
Belgae
Durotriges
Dumnonii
Silures
Dobuni
Cornovii
Coritani
Demetae
Ordovices
Litus Saxonicum (Saxon Shore)
Fretum Gallicum (Strait of Dover)
Gesoriacum (Boulogne)
NORTH SEA
ENGLISH CHANNEL
Bernicia
Deira
Mercians
Middle Angles
East Angles
East Saxons
West Saxons
South Saxons
Jutes
Hwicce
Frisians
Saxons
Franks
Jutes
I. of Wight
EASTERN EMPIRE
DOMINION OF THE GHASSANIDS
Alexandria
Egypt
Nile R.
Cyrenaica
Pentapolis
Berenice
Greater Syrtis
Leptis magna
Tripolis
Lesser Syrtis
VANDALS

The Germanic Kingdoms and the East Roman Empire, 526—600.

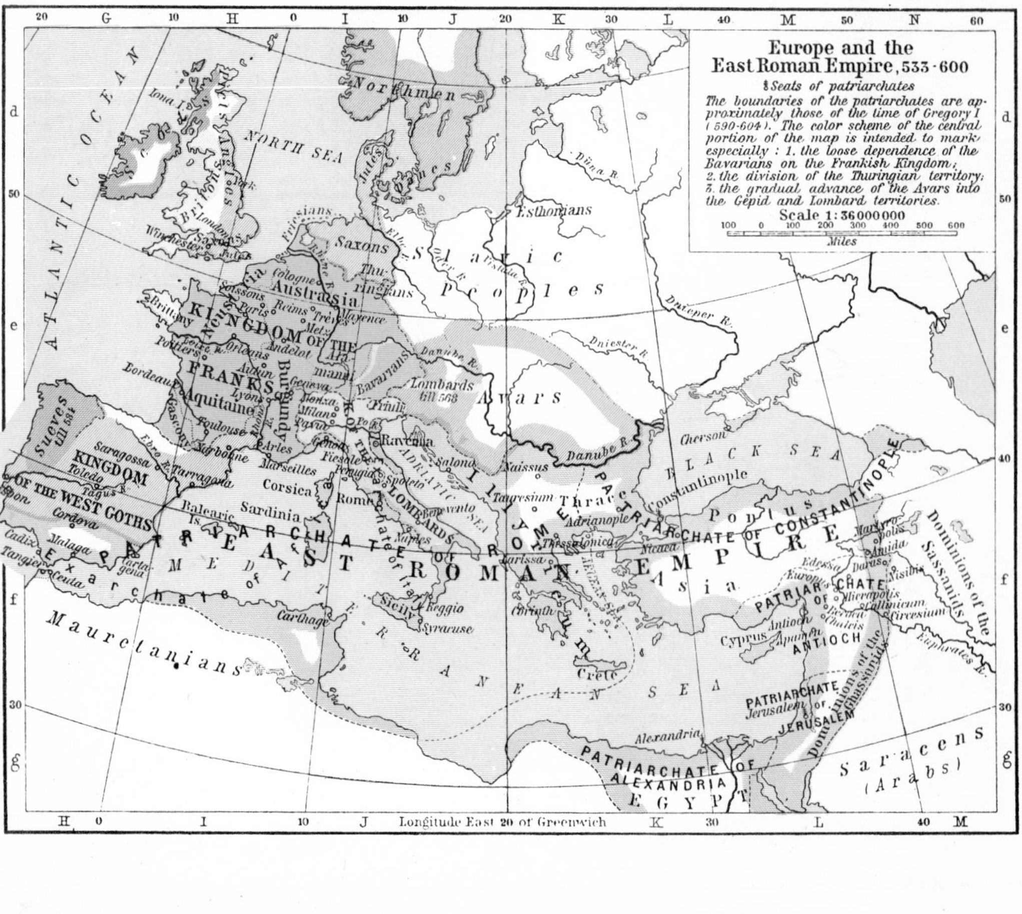

The Germanic Kingdoms and the East Roman Empire in 526

The headship of Theodoric and the East Goths over the West Goths is indicated by underlining the name of the latter in white. The colorings of the district occupied by the Alamanni are intended to show how checkered their career was. Of this district the area bordered in green corresponds roughly to that of the later duchy of Franconia.

Scale 1:30000000

100 0 100 200 300 400 500 600 Miles

Longitude East 10 of Greenwich

Europe and the East Roman Empire, 533-600

‡ *Seats of patriarchates*

The boundaries of the patriarchates are approximately those of the time of Gregory I (590-604). The color scheme of the central portion of the map is intended to mark especially: 1. the loose dependence of the Bavarians on the Frankish Kingdom; 2. the division of the Thuringian territory; 3. the gradual advance of the Avars into the Gepid and Lombard territories.

Scale 1:36000000

100 0 100 200 300 400 500 600 Miles

Longitude East 20 of Greenwich

The Califate in 750. Growth of Frankish Power, 481—814.

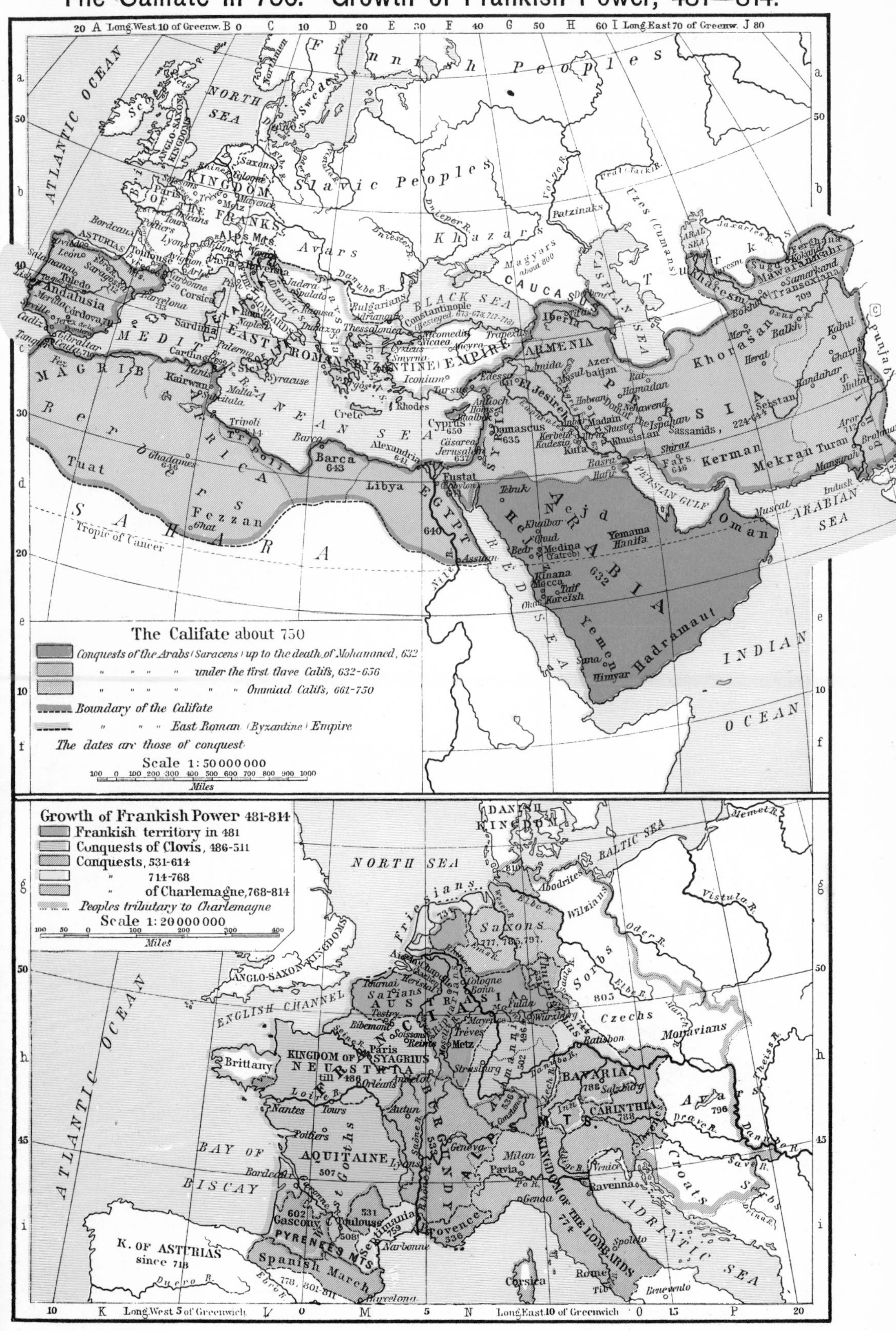

The Carolingian Empire
Slavic peoples tributary to Charlemagne
Slavs
Celts
The Byzantine Empire
The Califate
Boundary of the Patrimony of St. Peter, as determined in 774
Frontier station for trade with Slavs and Avars thus: Schesel
Site of important event thus: Poitiers
Seat of an archbishopric
" " a bishopric
In the East Frankish dominions about the end of the ninth century
Monastery
Castle or stronghold
Scale 1: 20 000 000
Miles
ATLANTIC OCEAN
NORTH SEA
Shetland Is.
Orkney Is.
The Hebrides
Iona
SCOTS
ANGLO SAXON KINGDOMS
Canterbury
London
Winchester
York
DANISH KINGDOM
Boulogne
Flanders
AUSTRASIA
NEUSTRIA
BRITTANY
March of Brittany
AQUITAINE
GASCONY
SEPTIMANIA
Spanish March
ALAMANNIA
BAVARIA
CARINTHIA
BOHEMIA
SAXONS
Magdeburg
Schesel
Cologne
Paris
Orleans
Tours
Poitiers
Bordeaux
Toulouse
Barcelona
Lombardy
Provence
Rome
Spoleto
DUCHY OF BENEVENTO
Ravenna
Venice
KINGDOM OF ASTURIAS
Oviedo
Santiago de Compostela
Oporto
Lisbon
Toledo
OMMIAD EMIRATE OF CORDOVA
Cordova
Seville
Granada
Cadiz
Strait of Gibraltar
Tangier
Balearic Is.
Majorca
Minorca
Corsica
SARDINIA
SICILY
Palermo
Messina
Syracuse
Malta
TYRRHENIAN SEA
ADRIATIC SEA
MEDITERRANEAN SEA
DOMINION OF THE IDRISIDS (since 788)
DOMINION OF THE AGHLABIDS (since 800)
Kairwan
Tripoli
CALIFATE
BYZANTINE
Long. West 5 of Greenwich

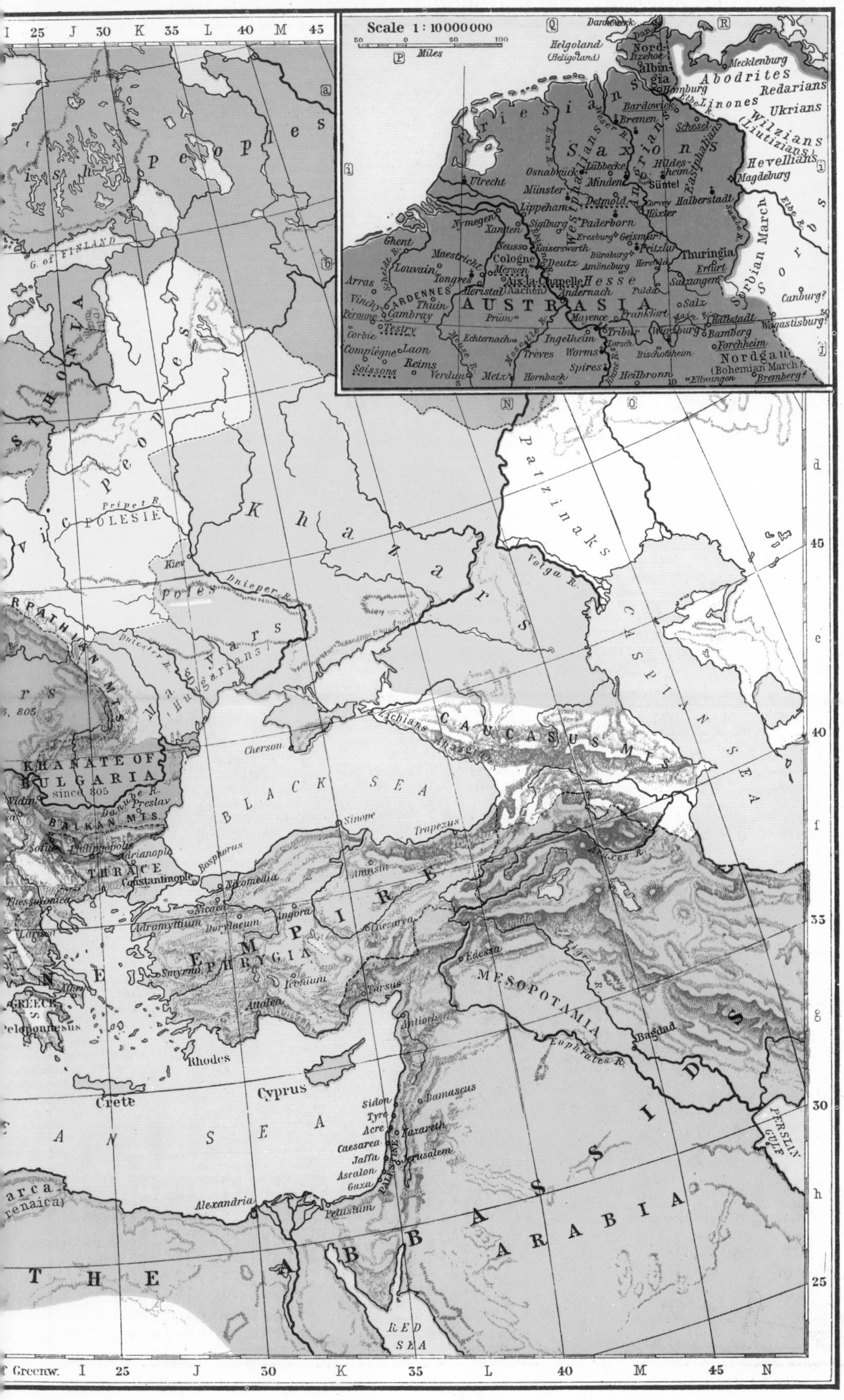
Scale 1 : 10000000
Miles
Helgoland (Heligoland)
Nord-albingia
Abodrites
Redarians
Ukrians
Wilzians (Liutizians)
Hevellians
Magdeburg
Mecklenburg
Hamburg
Bardowiek
Linones
Bremen
Frisians
Saxons
Westphalians
Angrians
Eastphalians
Utrecht
Osnabrück
Lübbecke
Minden
Hildesheim
Süntel
Münster
Detmold
Halberstadt
Lippeham
Paderborn
Nymegen
Xanten
Ghent
Maestricht
Louvain
Tongres
Neuss
Cologne
Kaiserswerth
Deutz
Thuringia
Erfurt
Aix-la-Chapelle (Aachen)
Hesse
Herstal
Andernach
Fritzlar
Salzungen
Arras
ARDENNES
Thuin
AUSTRASIA
Cambray
Péronne
Frankfort
Mayence
Salz
Hallstadt
Bamberg
Forchheim
Wogastisburg
Sorbian March
Canburg?
Testry
Prüm
Echternach
Ingelheim
Tribur
Würzburg
Compiègne
Laon
Reims
Treves
Worms
Spires
Soissons
Verdun
Metz
Hornbach
Heilbronn
Ellwangen
Nordgau
(Bohemian March)
Bremberg?
Peoples
G. of FINLAND
Pripet R.
POLESIE
Kiev
Poles
Dnieper R.
Khazars
Magyars (Hungarians)
Patzinaks
Volga R.
CASPIAN SEA
CARPATHIAN MTS
KHANATE OF BULGARIA since 805
Vidin
Danube R.
Preslav
BALKAN MTS.
Sofia
Philippopolis
Adrianople
THRACE
Constantinople
Bosphorus
Cherson
BLACK SEA
Sinope
Trapezus
CAUCASUS MTS
Araxes R.
Amastris
Nicomedia
Nicaea
Adramyttium
Dorylaeum
Angora
Caesarea
EMPIRE
PHRYGIA
Smyrna
Iconium
Attalea
Tarsus
Edessa
Tigris R.
MESOPOTAMIA
Antioch
Bagdad
Euphrates R.
Rhodes
Cyprus
Crete
Sidon
Damascus
Tyre
Acre
Nazareth
Caesarea
Jaffa
Jerusalem
Ascalon
Gaza
PALESTINE
Alexandria
Pelusium
THE ABBASSIDS
ARABIA
PERSIAN GULF
RED SEA
GREECE
Peloponnesus
Cyrenaica
Greenw.

Disruption of the Carolingian Empire, 843—888.

The Peoples of Europe about 900.

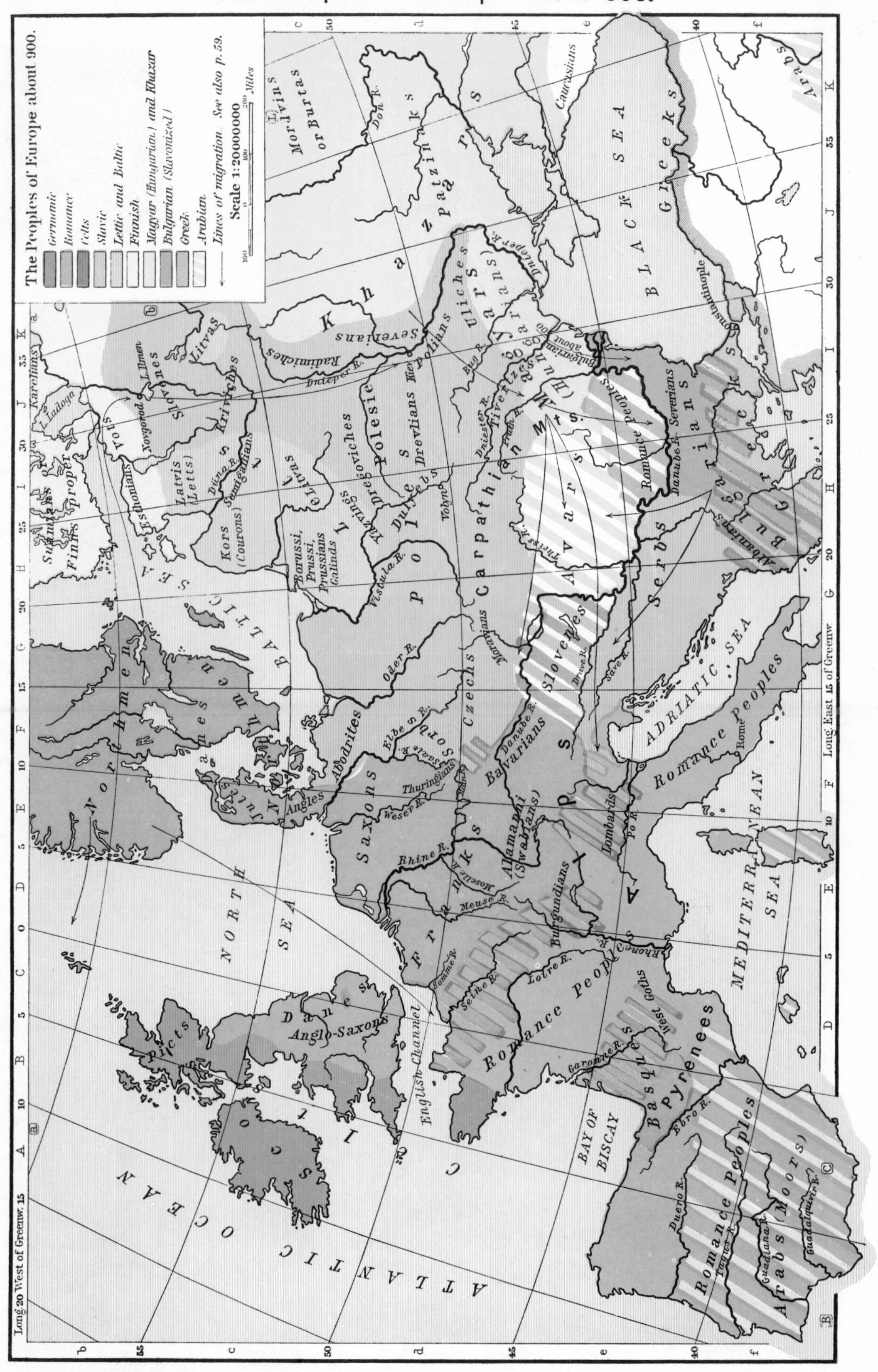

Route of the Varangians.
Scale 1:15000000
100 50 0 100 200 300
Miles.
C. County; D. Duchy; D.M. Danish March; K. Kingdom; M. March; Sax.M. Saxon March; Th. Theme.
ATLANTIC OCEAN
NORTH SEA
ENGLISH CHANNEL
KINGDOM OF NORWAY
KINGDOM OF DENMARK
IRELAND
Dublin
Cork
SCOTS
Edinburgh
Durham
York
Chester
WALES
Cardiff
ENGLAND
Norwich
Oxford
London
Thames R.
Canterbury
Boulogne
Ribe
Roeskilde
Slesvik
Nordalbingia
Hamburg
Bremen
FRIESLAND
Osnabrück
D. OF SAXONY
Minden
Verden
Magdeburg
Utrecht
Münster
Paderborn
Cologne
D. OF LOWER LORRAINE
Aix-la-Chapelle
D. OF FLANDERS
Tongres
Tournai
Liège
Arras
Cambray
D. OF WEST FRANCONIA
Frankfort
Fulda
Erfurt
Meissen
Mainz
Würzburg
Worms
Trèves
Verdun
Metz
Reims
Laon
C. OF CHAMPAGNE
Toul
Strasburg
UPPER LORRAINE
VOSGES MTS.
ALSACE
Bamberg
NORDGAU
Eichstädt
Ratisbon
Passau
Augsburg
Ulm
D. OF ALAMANNIA (SWABIA)
Constance
Basel (Bâle)
D. OF BAVARIA
Brixen
Villach
CARINTHIA
Trent
March of Verona
Aquileia
Venice
Rouen
Seine R.
D. OF NORMANDY
Paris
C. OF BRITTANY
D. OF Orléans
FRANCIA
Troyes
Nantes
Loire R.
Tours
Poitiers
Bourges
Langres
D. OF BURGUNDY
Besançon
Autun
FRANCE
Limoges
D. OF AQUITAINE
Bordeaux
Lyons
Geneva
KINGDOM OF BURGUNDY
Vienne
Rhône R.
Avignon
Arles
Nimes
C. OF TOULOUSE
Toulouse
Narbonne
Marseilles
Nice
Bayonne
D. OF GASCONY
Garonne R.
PYRENEES MTS.
ALPS
Ivrea
Milan
Bergamo
Susa
Pavia
LOMBARDY
Mantua
Parma
Canossa
Modena
Bologna
Genoa
Ravenna
Florence
Pisa
TUSCIA
Siena
Spoleto
STATES OF THE CHURCH
Rome
Gaeta
Naples
HOLY ROMAN EMPIRE
Oviedo
Asturias
Leon
KINGDOM OF LEON
Zamora
Burgos
CASTILE
K. OF NAVARRE
Pamplona
Aragon
Duero R.
Salamanca
Ebro R.
Saragossa
Lerida
C. OF BARCELONA
Barcelona
Tagus R.
Toledo
Lisbon
Cuenca
CALIFATE OF CORDOVA
SARACENIC POSSESSIONS
Guadiana R.
Cordova
Guadalquivir R.
Seville
Valencia
Murcia
Cartagena
Malaga
Strait of Gibraltar
Tangier
Balearic Isles
CORSICA
End of ninth century
SARDINIA
MEDITERRANEAN
Palermo 831
SICILY
Mazara 827
Algiers
Biserta
Tunis
Kairwan
Mehdiya
DOMINION OF THE FATIMIDES
Dates are those of Saracenic conquest or possession.
Long. West 5 of Greenwich
Long. East 5 of Greenwich

RUSSIA
Patzinaks
Bulgars
Merians
Muromans
Mordvins or Burtas
Veps
Esthonians
Livonians
Lithuanians
Prussians
Novgorod
L. Ilmen
Smolensk
Minsk
Pinsk
Chernigov
Kiev
Dnieper
Route of the Varangians
Donetz R.
Don R.
Kuban R.
Volga R.
Oka R.
Düna R.
Niemen R.
Pripet R.
Dniester R.
Bug R.
Pruth R.
Danube R.
CARPATHIAN MTS.
KINGDOM OF HUNGARY
Territory in dispute between Transylvania Hungary and the Patzinaks
DUCHY OF POLAND
CHROBATIA
Cracow
Danzig
Belz
Halicz
CAUCASUS MTS.
BLACK SEA
Cherson
THEME OF CHERSON (conquered by the Varangians 988)
Constantinople
Sinope
Trapezus
Amastris
Heraclea
THEME OF CHALDIA
ARMENIAC THEME
TH. OF PAPHLAGONIA
BUCELLARIAN TH.
TH. OF COLONEA
TH. OF SEBASTEA
TH. OF MESOPOTAMIA
THEME CHARSIANON
TH. OF LYCANDOS
CAPPADOCIA
THEME OF CILICIA
THEME OF ANTIOCH
ANATOLIC THEME
OPSICIAN THEME
THRACESIAN THEME
TH. OF THE CIBYRRHAEOTS
TH. OF SELEUCIA
TH. OF CYPRUS
TH. OF CRETE
THEME OF THE AEGEAN ISLANDS
THEME OF THRACE
THEME OF MACEDONIA
STRYMON
TH. OF THESSALONICA
THEME OF HELLAS
THEME OF NICOPOLIS
THEME OF PELOPONNESUS
CEPHALENIA
THEME OF DYRRHACHIUM
SERVIA
BALKAN MTS.
BYZANTINE EMPIRE
DOMINION OF THE HAMDANIDS
SYRIA
Aleppo
Antioch
Edessa
Homs
Tripoli
Damascus
Acre
Jerusalem
Belgrade
Varna
Nicopolis
Adrianople
Nicaea
Nicomedia
Ancyra
Caesarea
Iconium
Sardis
Smyrna
Ephesus
Attalea
Seleucia
Constantia
Paphos
Chandax
Larissa
Athens
Corinth
Argos
Ragusa
Diocleа
Bari
Brindisi
MEDITERRANEAN SEA

England in the Eighth and Ninth Centuries.

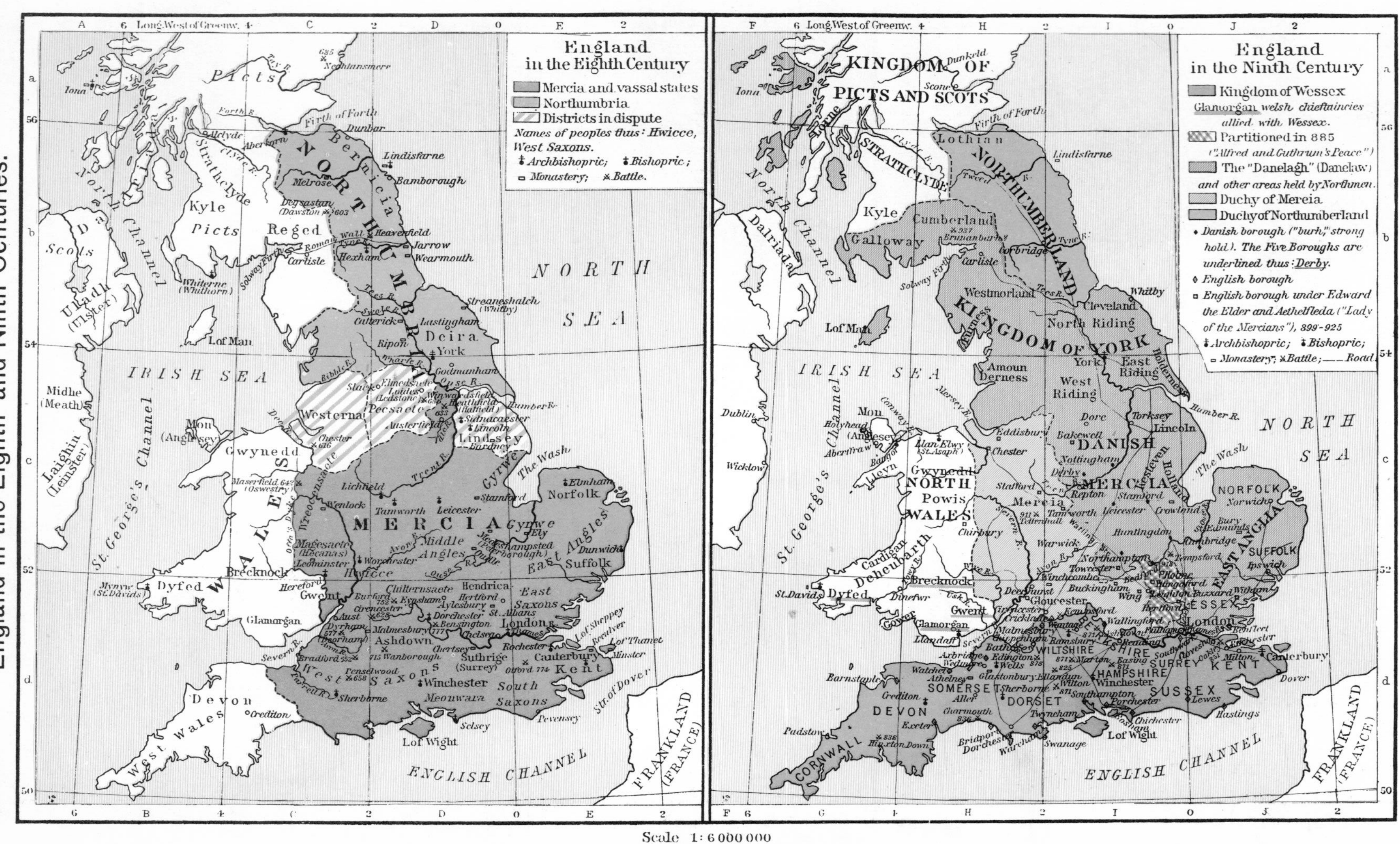

France about 1035.

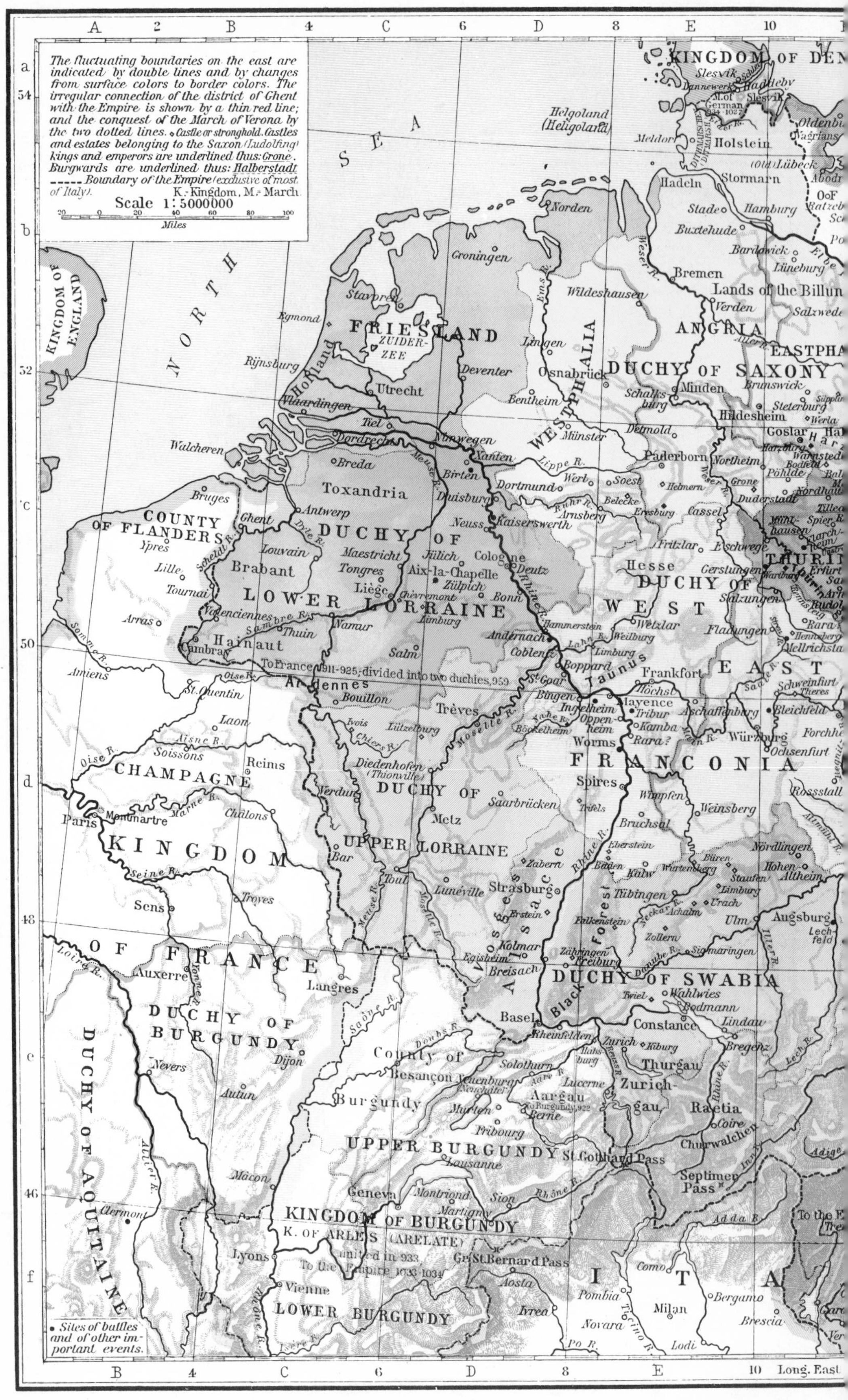

The fluctuating boundaries on the east are indicated by double lines and by changes from surface colors to border colors. The irregular connection of the district of Ghent with the Empire is shown by a thin red line; and the conquest of the March of Verona by the two dotted lines. Castle or stronghold. Castles and estates belonging to the Saxon (Ludolfing) kings and emperors are underlined thus: Grone. Burgwards are underlined thus: Halberstadt
Boundary of the Empire (exclusive of most of Italy).
K.= Kingdom, M.= March.
Scale 1: 5000000
Miles
Sites of battles and of other important events.
NORTH SEA
KINGDOM OF ENGLAND
KINGDOM OF DEN
Slesvik
Helgoland (Heligoland)
Holstein
Stormarn
Hadeln
Hamburg
Stade
Buxtehude
Bremen
Lands of the Billun
Verden
Lüneburg
Bardowick
Norden
Groningen
Wildeshausen
FRIESLAND
ZUIDER-ZEE
Stavoren
Egmond
Rijnsburg
Holland
Deventer
Utrecht
Vlaardingen
Tiel
Dordrecht
Nimwegen
Walcheren
Xanten
Birten
Breda
Toxandria
Bruges
Ghent
Antwerp
COUNTY OF FLANDERS
Ypres
Lille
Tournai
Arras
Louvain
Brabant
DUCHY OF LOWER LORRAINE
Maestricht
Tongres
Liège
Jülich
Aix-la-Chapelle
Zülpich
Cologne
Deutz
Bonn
Duisburg
Neuss
Kaiserswerth
Namur
Valenciennes
Hainaut
Cambrai
Thuin
Limburg
Salm
To France 911-925; divided into two duchies, 959
Ardennes
Bouillon
Amiens
St. Quentin
Laon
Soissons
Reims
CHAMPAGNE
Paris
Montmartre
Châlons
KINGDOM OF FRANCE
Sens
Troyes
Auxerre
Langres
DUCHY OF BURGUNDY
Dijon
Nevers
Autun
Mâcon
Clermont
DUCHY OF AQUITAINE
Trèves
Lützelburg
Diedenhofen (Thionville)
Verdun
DUCHY OF UPPER LORRAINE
Metz
Bar
Toul
Lunéville
Saarbrücken
Strasburg
Alsace
Vosges
Kolmar
Breisach
Basel
Lingen
Osnabrück
Bentheim
Münster
WESTPHALIA
Dortmund
Werl
Soest
Arnsberg
Paderborn
Detmold
DUCHY OF SAXONY
ANGRIA
EASTPHA
Minden
Hildesheim
Goslar
Northeim
Grone
Duderstadt
Cassel
Eschwege
Fritzlar
Hesse
DUCHY OF WEST FRANCONIA
Salzungen
Wetzlar
Fulda
Frankfort
Höchst
Mayence
Ingelheim
Oppenheim
Worms
Spires
Bingen
Boppard
Coblenz
Andernach
Taunus
Aschaffenburg
Würzburg
Ochsenfurt
FRANCONIA
Wimpfen
Weinsberg
Bruchsal
Baden
Tübingen
Ulm
Augsburg
Nördlingen
Zollern
Sigmaringen
Black Forest
DUCHY OF SWABIA
Zähringen
Freiburg
Constance
Lindau
Bregenz
Zurich
Thurgau
Zurichgau
Aargau
Berne
Solothurn
Lucerne
Raetia
Coire
Churwalchen
Septimer Pass
St. Gotthard Pass
Besançon
County of Burgundy
UPPER BURGUNDY
Lausanne
Geneva
Sion
KINGDOM OF BURGUNDY
K. OF ARLES (ARELATE)
united in 933
To the Empire 1033-1034
Lyons
Vienne
LOWER BURGUNDY
Gr. St. Bernard Pass
Aosta
Ivrea
Novara
Milan
Como
Bergamo
Brescia
Lodi
Pombia
ITA
Long. East

BALTIC SEA
Arkona
Rügen
Julin (Jomsburg)
Kolberg
Danzig
Vistula R.
Prussians
MARCH
Wolgast
Belgard
Demmin
Peene R.
Usedom
Wollin
POMERANIA
LLUNGS
Redarians
Stettin
Rhetra ?
Garz
Nakel
Ukrians
Netze R.
Pyritz
Wilzians
(Liutizians)
Prizlawa
Havelberg
Hevellians
Havel R.
Oder R.
Warthe R.
Gnesen
NORTH MARCH
(NORDMARK)
Lebus
Posen
Brandenburg
Spree R.
Vistula R.
Krossen
EAST MARCH
(OSTMARK)
Zerbst
Jüterbog
Lebusa
Pilica R.
Lusatians
March of Lusatia
Dobrilugk
Niemitsch
Sagan
Bober R.
Glogau
POLAND
Kingdom, 1025
Elbe R.
Mulde R.
Elster R.
Polish, 1002-1018, 1031
Halle
Belgern
Wurzen
Strehla
Milzienians
March of Meissen
Görlitz
Neisse R.
Liegnitz
Oder R.
Breslau
Warthe R.
M. of Merseburg
Leipzig
Merseburg
MARCH OF THURINGIA
Bautzen
Zeitz
Meissen
Dalaminzians
Dohna
Schweidnitz
Nimptsch
M. of Zeitz
Miriquidi
Leitmeritz
Warthe
Neisse R.
Under Poland since 999
CHROBATIA
Glatz
Melnik
Brüx (Gnevin)
Cracow
Eger R.
Saaz
Nimburg
Elbe R.
Vistula R.
Bunzlau
Prague
Wyschehrad
Leitomischl
Pilsen
DUCHY OF BOHEMIA
Oder R.
Leuchtenberg
Olmütz
GRAVATE
Nabburg
Böhmerwald
Under Poland, 1003-1004
MORAVIA
Under Poland, 1003-1029
RDGAU
Cham
Klattau
Moldau R.
Hohenburg
Regen R.
Brünn
Waag R.
Ratisbon
Netolitz
Trencsin
Znaym
Gran R.
Thaya R.
Mailberg
March R.
BAVARIAN EAST MARCH
(OSTMARK)
(MARGRAVATE OF AUSTRIA)
Isar R.
Passau
Freising
Mühldorf
Inn R.
Linz
Krems
Melk
Tulln
Hainburg
Presburg
Pöchlarn
St. Pölten
Vienna
Wels
Hungarian, 907-955
Duchy, 1156
Ebersberg
Steier
Leitha R.
Danube R.
DUCHY OF BAVARIA
Traun R.
Pitten
Ödenburg
(Sopron)
Buda
(Ofen)
Salzburg
Enns R.
HUNGARY
Eppenstein
MARCH OF
Established 970 ?
Hengistburg
Salzach R.
Raab R.
Mur R.
Detached from Carinthia 1035
Theiss R.
Brixen
Drave R.
Friesach
CARINTHIA
DUCHY OF CARINTHIA
Drave R.
Mur R.
Villach
Detached from Bavaria 976
From 1055
M. OF STYRIA
1180, Duchy
Souna
Belluno
Friuli
Save R.
Drave R.
OF VERONA
Laibach
MARCH OF CARNIOLA
Feltre
Bavaria, 952; to Carinthia, 976
Aquileia
Trieste
Detached from Carinthia
1040
Treviso
Grado
MARCH OF
ISTRIA
CROATIA
Danube R.
Duchy of
Venice
Save R.
12
G
14
H
16
I
J
K
22
18
20
a
b
c
d
e
f
54
52
50
48
46

ITALY about 1050.

- States of the Church
- Domains of the Countess Matilda
- Possessions of the Byzantine Empire
- Lombard principalities
- Norman conquests
- Saracenic territory

The figures indicate the date of acquisition by the Normans.
The territory bordered with purple was claimed by the Pope. C.: County; D.: Duchy; M.: March; Mqu.: Marquisate; P.: Principality.

Scale 1:9000000

Miles

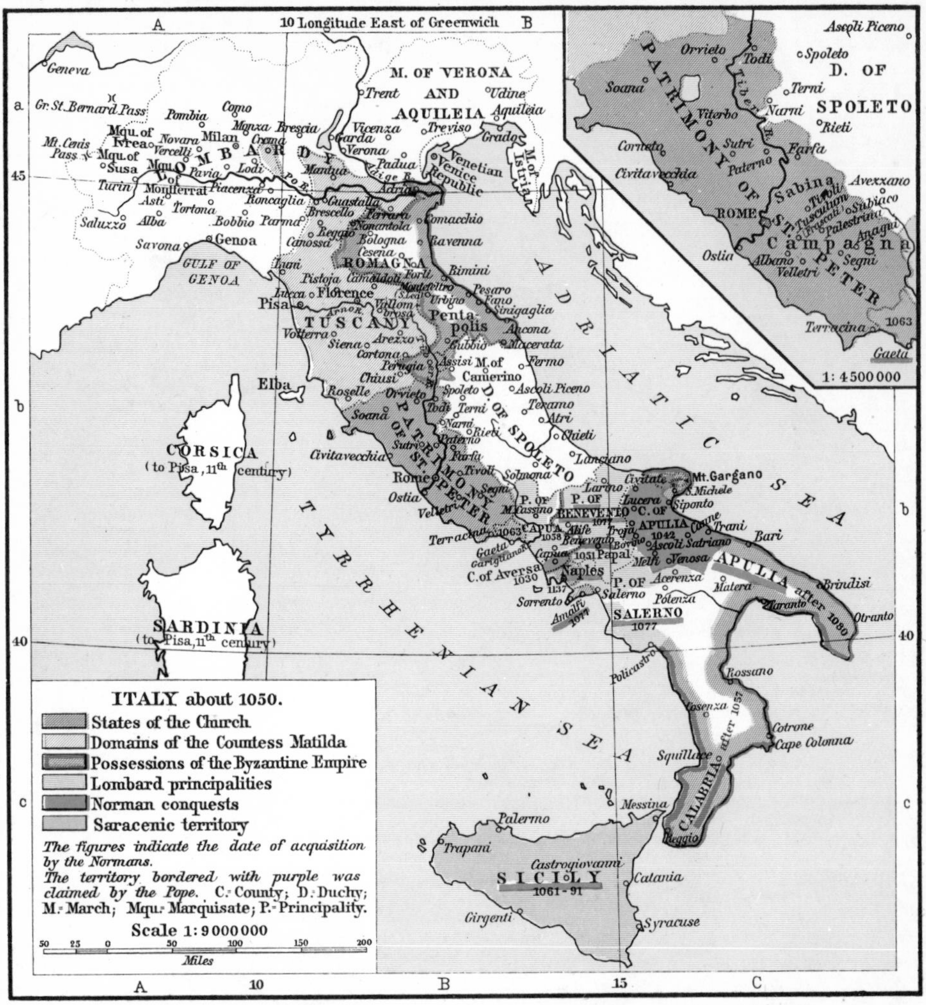

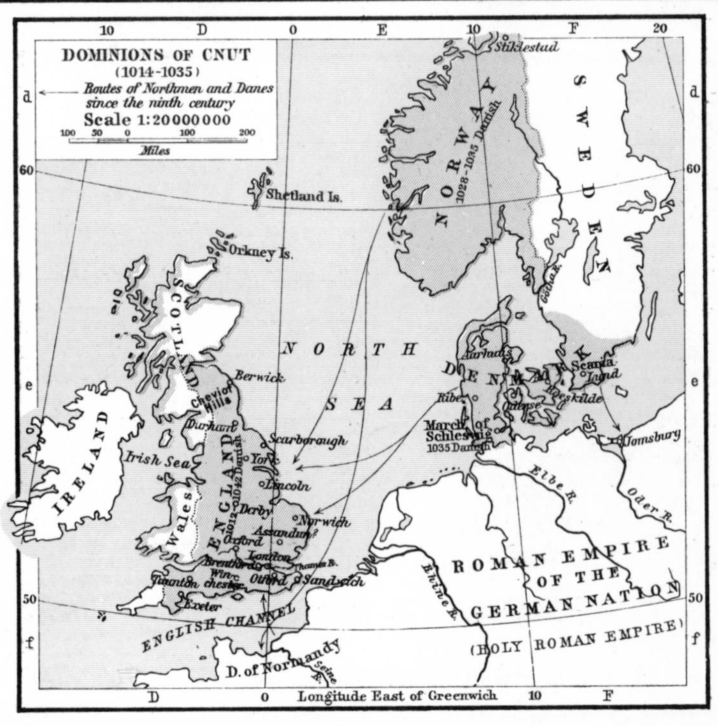

England, 1087—1154.

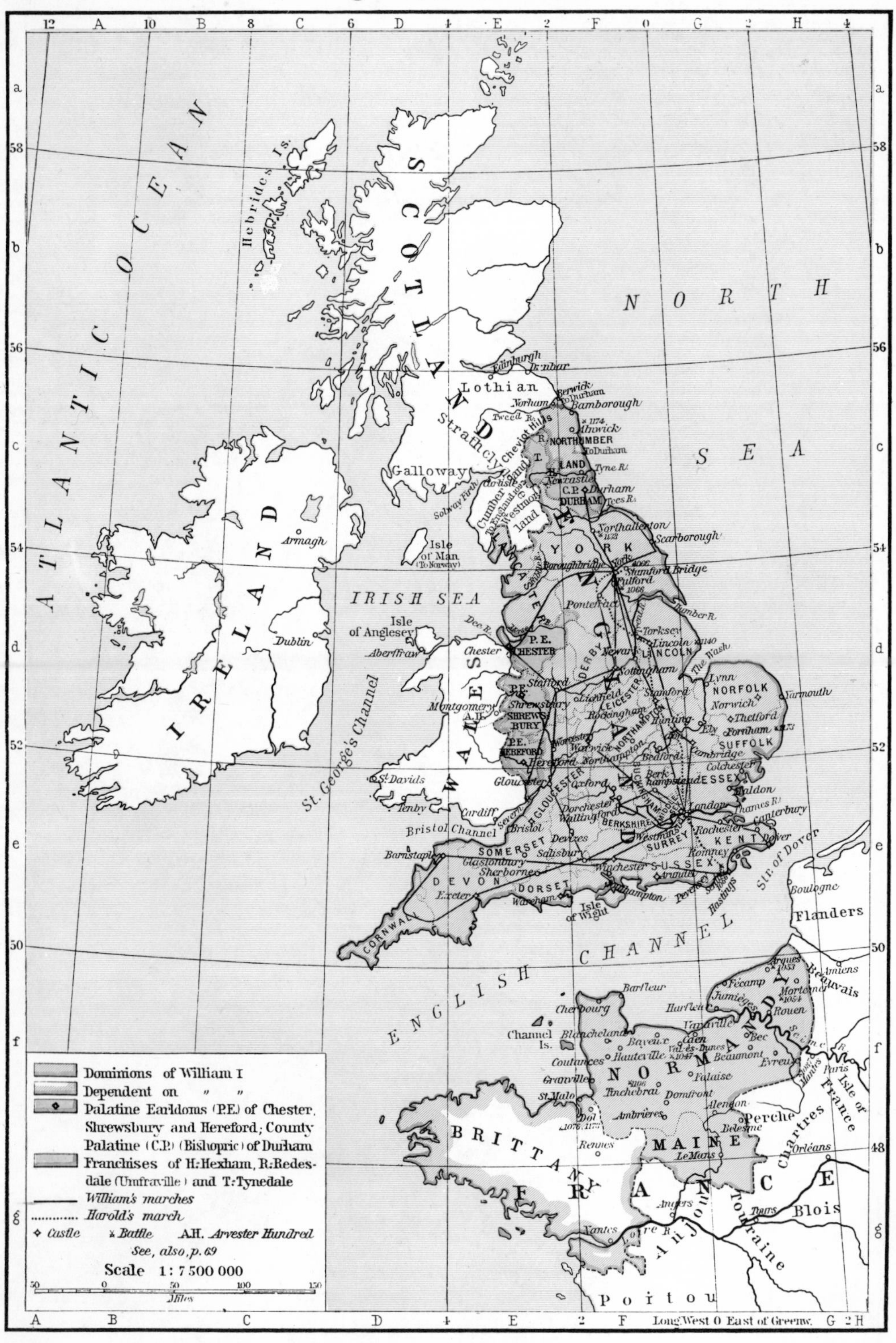

Routes of the leaders of the first Crusade
(1096-1099)
Godfrey of Bouillon
Adhemar of Puy and Raymond of Toulouse
Bohemond and Tancred
Robert of Flanders and Hugh of Vermandois
Route of the combined forces. C.-County; D.-Duchy; P.-Principality.
Scale 1:20 000 000
Miles
ATLANTIC OCEAN
NORTH SEA
IRELAND
Dublin
KINGDOM OF SCOTLAND
Edinburgh
KINGDOM OF ENGLAND
Chester
WALES
London
Canterbury
KINGDOM OF NORWAY
Tönsberg
KINGDOM OF SWEDEN
Upsala
GOTHLAND
KINGDOM OF DENMARK
Lund
Rügen
DUCHY OF POMERANIA
Posen
Hamburg
Bremen
Utrecht
Brunswick
Cologne
Calais
Flanders
Vermandois
Bouillon
Mayence
ROMAN EMPIRE OF THE GERMAN NATION
(HOLY ROMAN EMPIRE)
Nuremberg
Ratisbon
Prague (Praha)
Vienna
Danube R.
Normandy
Maine
Paris
St.Denis
Blois
Vezelay
KINGDOM OF FRANCE
Clermont
Le Puy
Toulouse
Montpellier
KINGDOM OF BURGUNDY
Geneva
Turin
Milan
Genoa
Piacenza
Avignon
Marseilles
Aquileia
Venice
Ravenna
Ancona
Pisa
Rome
KINGDOM OF CROATIA
Spalato
DALMATIA
ADRIATIC SEA
KINGDOM OF LEON
Leon
Santiago de Compostela
Porto
Burgos
Zamora
COUNTY OF PORTUGAL
Coimbra
KINGDOM OF CASTILE
KINGDOM OF NAVARRE
KINGDOM OF ARAGON
COUNTY OF BARCELONA OR CATALONIA
Saragossa
Barcelona
Tarragona
New Castile
Toledo
Lisbon
Tagus R.
DOMINION
Zalaca
Badajoz
Córdova
Seville
Silves
Guadiana R.
Valencia
Murcia
Granada
Jeréz
Algeciras
Almeria
Strait of Gibraltar
Tangier
Ceuta
Balearic Is.
Corsica (to Pisa)
SARDINIA (to Pisa)
TYRRHENIAN SEA
Capua
Naples
Amalfi
Salerno
Benevento
Bari
Taranto
Palermo
Messina
Reggio
Syracuse
C. OF SICILY
NORMAN PRINCIPALITIES
Malta 1090 to Sicily
MEDITERRANEAN
OF THE MAGRIB ALMORAVIDS
1060 - 1147
Tlemsen
Oran
Tenes
Bujaia (Bougie)
DOMINION OF THE HAMMADITES
Bona
Tunis
Zeirids
Kairwan
Gulf of Gabes
Tripoli
CALIFATE OF
Gulf of Sidra
Scale 1:90,000,000
The Growth of Islamic Power, 632-1097
Under Mohammed, up to 632
632 - 700
701 - 800
801 - 900
To 1097
Spain
Cordova
France
Italy
Rome
Sardinia
Sicily
Tunis
Kairwan
Tripoli
Magrib
667-99
Ifrikiya
Byzantine Empire
Constantinople besieged 672-78, 717-18
Bulgars
Crete
Cyprus
Tarsus
Armenia
Syria
Kerbela
Kufa
Bagdad
Basra
Persia
Ispahan
Kerman
Meshed
Herat
Balkh
Bokhara
Samarkand
Oxus R.
Multan
Mansurah
Egypt
Cairo
Arabia
Medina
Mecca
Long.

Scale 1: 40 000 000
Miles
Meridian of 0 Greenwich
Europe and the Mediterranean Lands by Religions about 1097.
Christians:
Belonging to the Roman Church
" " " Greek "
Mohammedans:
Under the Calif of Bagdad (Abbasid)
" " " " Cairo (Fatimite)
Dates are those of conversion to Christianity
ATLANTIC OCEAN
NORTH SEA
BALTIC SEA
NORWAY about 1000
SWEDEN about 1000
DENMARK
SCOTLAND
IRELAND
ENGLAND
Canterbury
Finns
Esthonians
Letts
Lithuanians
Prussians
Pomeranians 12 cent
Novgorod
Polock
Vitebsk
Smolensk
Chernigov
Kiev
Russ about 1000
Volga R.
Kama R.
Don R.
Dnieper R.
Dniester R.
Cumans
Poles End 10 cent.
Cracow
Gnesen
Czechs about 900
GERMANY
Mayence
Reims
FRANCE
BURGUNDY
Salzburg
Gran (Esztergom)
Hungarians about 1000
LEON
CASTILE
SPAIN
DOM. OF THE
Cordova
ALMORAVIDS
DOM. OF THE HAMMADITES
ITALY
Rome
NORMAN PRINCIPALITIES
MEDITERRANEAN SEA
BLACK SEA
BYZANTINE EMPIRE
Constantinople
Armenians
Nestorians
CALIFATE OF BAGDAD (ABBASID)
Bagdad
Antioch
Jerusalem
Alexandria
Cairo
CALIFATE OF CAIRO (FATIMITE)
Esthonians
Pskov
LITHUANIA
Minsk
Pinsk
Halicz
RUSSIA
Sea of Asov
Bosporus
Kuban R.
Khazars
Ossetes (Alans?)
CASPIAN SEA
Cumans about 1050
Patzinaks
Gothia
Cherson
Georgia
Tiflis
Shirvan
Kura R.
Aras R.
Kars
Ani
Trebizond
Sinope
EMPIRE
BULGARIA
Philippopolis
Adrianople
Constantinople
Chalcedon
MACEDONIA
Gallipolis
Thessalonica
Nicomedia
Nicaea
Amasia
Neocaesarea
Theodosiopolis (Erzerum)
Malazkert
DOMINION OF THE SELJUK TURKS
Danishmend
Angora
SULTANATE OF ROUM
Dorylaeum
Adramyttium
Pergamum
Sardis
Philadelphia
Smyrna
Ephesus
Laodicea
Philomelium
Iconium
Heraclea
Caesarea
Melitene
Petty Armenian States
Marash
Tarsus
Attalia
Myra
Rhodes
Armenia
Kurdistan
Azerbaijan
Tabriz
Shahr Zor
Hamadan
Amida
Edessa
Mardin
Harran
DOMINION OF MOSUL
Mosul (Seljuk 1055)
El Jesireh
Tigris R.
Euphrates R.
Bagdad (Seljuk 1055)
Iraq
Aleppo
Antioch
Seleucia
Nicosia
Cyprus
Limasol
Candia
Crete
Tripoli
Homs (Emesa)
Beirut
Sidon
Tyre
Acre
SYRIA
Damascus (Seljuk 1076)
PALESTINE
Jaffa
Ascalon
Gaza
Jerusalem Fatimite 969, Seljuk 1071, Fatimite 1098.
Dead Sea
Damietta
El Arish
Alexandria
EGYPT
Cairo
Nile R.
(FATIMITE)
RED SEA
ARABIA
AEGEAN SEA
GREECE
Athens
Thebes
K 25 L 30 M 35 N 40 O 45 P

Asia Minor and the States of the Crusaders in Syria, about 1140.

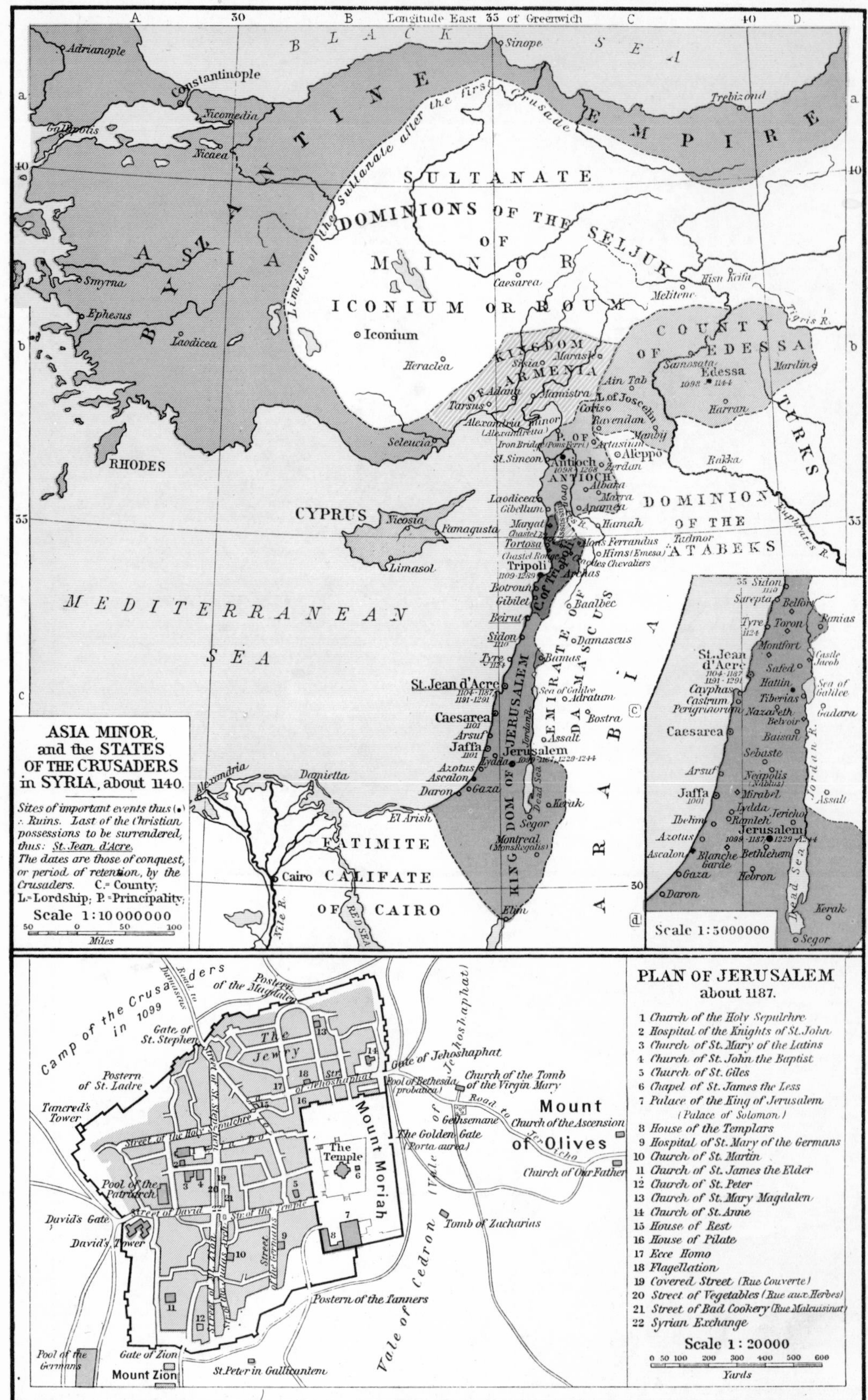

France, 1154—1184.

Royal Domain
Other fiefs
English possessions
English dominions held of the French Crown
B.- BISHOPRIC; C.- COUNTY; D.- DUCHY;
K.- KINGDOM; M.- MARQUISATE;
S.- SEIGNIORY; V.- VISCOUNTY.
ARM.- COUNTY OF ARMAGNAC
FEZ.- " " FEZENSAC
G.- " " GAURE
GA.- VISCOUNTY OF GABARDAN
LOM.- " " LOMAGNE
P.- COUNTY OF PARDIAC
F.-To Flanders; L.R.- COUNTY OF LA ROCHE.
Archbishopric, Bishopric, Monastery, Castle
Scale 1 : 7 500 000
Miles
See also, p. 70
KINGDOM OF ENGLAND
ENGLISH CHANNEL
BAY OF BISCAY
MEDITERRANEAN SEA
D. OF NORMANDY
C. OF BRITTANY
C. OF MAINE
C. OF ANJOU
POITOU
DUCHY OF AQUITAINE (GUIENNE)
D. OF GASCONY
C. OF TOULOUSE
D. OF BURGUNDY
KINGDOM OF GERMANY
HOLY ROMAN EMPIRE
KINGDOM OF ARLES
KINGDOMS OF LEON AND CASTILE
K. OF NAVARRE
K. OF ARAGON
Domain, Fiefs and Suzerains of the Count of Champagne in the Twelfth Century.
Held of the Emperor as suzerain
King of France " "
Duke of Burgundy " "
Archbishop of Reims " "
" " Sens " "
Bishop of Autun " "
" " Auxerre " "
" " Langres " "
Abbot " St. Denis " "
B.- BISHOPRIC; C.- COUNTY;
S.- SEIGNIORY; V.- VISCOUNTY.
Comp.- Compiègne; Prém.- Prémontré;
Montm.- Montmorency.
Scale 1 : 5000000
Miles

ATLANTIC OCEAN
NORTH SEA
KINGDOM OF NORWAY
KINGDOM OF DENMARK
KINGDOM OF SCOTLAND
IRELAND
KINGDOM OF ENGLAND
ENGLISH CHANNEL
KINGDOM OF FRANCE
HOLY ROMAN EMPIRE
KINGDOM OF GERMANY
KINGDOM OF ITALY
KINGDOM OF CASTILE
KINGDOM OF LEON
K. OF PORTUGAL
K. OF NAVARRE
KINGDOM OF ARAGON
DOMINIONS OF THE ALMOHADS
NORMAN KINGDOM OF THE TWO SICILIES
ADRIATIC SEA
MEDITERRA
Richard's Fleet
Philip Augustus
Balearic Is.
Corsica
Sardinia
Malta
Aberdeen
Perth
Edinburgh
Berwick
Carlisle
Durham
York
Chester
Dublin
Limerick
Wexford
Waterford
Milford
W.M.E.
Leicester
Northampton
Oxford
London
Winchester
Gloucester
Exeter
Southampton
Canterbury
Bruges
Ghent
Boulogne
Rouen
Paris
Reims
Orléans
Tours
Clairvaux
Vezelay
Poitiers
Bourges
Clermont
Limoges
Bordeaux
Toulouse
Narbonne
Arles
Marseilles
Lyons
Geneva
Bremen
Hamburg
Utrecht
Brunswick
Cologne
Trèves
Mayence
Metz
Spires
Strasburg
Basel
Constance
Augsburg
Salzburg
Nuremberg
Ratisbon
Prague
Vienna
Stettin
Rügen
Lund
Calmar
Tönsberg
Posen
Milan
Pavia
Turin
Alessandria
Genoa
Verona
Trent
Aquileia
Venice
Ravenna
Florence
Pisa
Ancona
Rome
Naples
Salerno
Bari
Brindisi
Taranto
Messina
Reggio
Palermo
Syracuse
Croatia
Slavonia
Zara
Spalato
Santiago de Compostela
Oviedo
León
Burgos
Valladolid
Oporto
Coimbra
Salamanca
Talavera
Santarem
Lisbon
Tagus R.
Alcantara
Mérida
Badajoz
Toledo
Calatrava
Cuenca
Valencia
Játiva
Murcia
Cordova
Seville
Silves
Guadiana
Guadalquivir
Jaen
Granada
Almeria
Malaga
Cadiz
Algeciras
Gibraltar
Tangier
Ceuta
Tetuan
Tudela
Saragossa
Lerida
Barcelona
Tarragona
Melilla
Oran
Tlemsen
Fez
Morocco
Tenes
Algiers
Bujaia
(Bougie)
Setif
Constantine
Bona
Tunis
Kairwan
Mahedia
Gabes
Tripoli
Sirt
De Cl.=De Clare; De Co.=De Courcy; De L.=De Lacy (Anglo-Norman Earldoms in Ireland); DOM.=Dominion; K.=Kingdom; PRINC.=Principality; W.M.E.=Welsh Marcher Earldoms; W.P.=Welsh Principalities.
Crusade of Louis VII and Conrad III (1147-1149)
Crusade of Richard I, Philip II (Augustus) and Frederick I (Barbarossa) (1189-1191)
Scale 1:20000000
100 50 0 100 200 300 400 500
Miles
E Long. West 5 of Greenwich F 0 G Long. East 5 of Greenwich H 10 I 15 J

Guelf, Hohenstaufen and Ascanian domains in Germany about 1176
Guelf
Hohenstaufen
Ascanian
Scale 1:15 000 000
The dark coloring indicates hereditary or imperial domains; light coloring, feudal territories, and border coloring, suzerainty.
Long. East 10 of Greenwich
DUCHY OF SAXONY
MARGRAVATE OF BRANDENBURG
DUCHY OF FRANCONIA
DUCHY OF SWABIA
DUCHY OF BAVARIA
(DUCHY OF AUSTRIA, 1156)
ALSACE
Lübeck
Lüneburg
Brunswick
Brandenburg
Magdeburg
Münster
Northeim
Anhalt
Elbe R.
Oder R.
Cologne
Aix-la-Chapelle
Vogtland
Prague
Frankfort
Mayence
Nuremberg
Waiblingen
Staufen
Ulm
Strasburg
Augsburg
Munich
Danube R.
Vienna
Altdorf
Lindau
Uri
Brixen
Gratz
Chiavenna
TERRITORY OF NOVGOROD
FINLAND
VIATKA
Lake Neva
Ladoga
Novgorod
Chuds
ESTHONIA
Dorpat
Pskov
Russo
Livonia
Courland
LITHUANIA
Polotsk (Polock)
Vitebsk
Toropetz
Yaroslavl
Rostov
Pereiaslavl
Suzdal
Kostroma
Volga R.
Kokshérev
Bulgarians
Dmietrov
Moscow
Murom
Mordvins
Riazan
Pronsk
Smolensk
Krasny
Minsk
Grodno
Yatvegs
Starodub
Dorogobuzh
Pinsk
Kursk
Chernigov
Vladimir
Lublin
Belz
Kiev
RUSSIA
Kiev
Sarub
Dnieper R.
Halicz
Svenigrod
Dniester R.
Polovzi
Khazars
Rostov
Don R.
Kherson
Cumans
Alans
Kassogs
CASPIAN SEA
BLACK SEA
GEORGIA
Tiflis
Kars
Trebizond
Sinope
Amasia
Erzerum
SHAH ARMEN
Lake Van
Tabriz
Azerbaijan
Atabeks
Kurdistan
Seljuks of Roum
Angora
Caesarea
Melitene
Tyana
Philomelium
Iconium (Konia)
Laranda
Tarsus
ARMENIA
Edessa
Harran
Mardin
Zengid Atabeks
Mosul
Irbil
Atabeks of Irbil
El Jesireh
Rakka
Aleppo
Principality of Antioch
Antioch
Bagdad
Califate
Iraq
Euphrates R.
Tigris R.
Basra
(Transylvania)
Orsova
Danube R.
Bulgarians
Philippopolis
Adrianople
Constantinople
Chalcedon
Nicomedia
Nicaea
Dorylaeum
Sardica
Thessalonica
Gallipoli
Adramyttium
Larissa
Thebes
Corinth
Athens
Pergamum
Thyatira
Sardis
Philadelphia
Smyrna
Ephesus
Laodicea
Attalia
Selinus
Rhodes
Myra
KINGDOM OF CYPRUS
Nicosia
Limasol
Famagusta
Candia
CRETE
Tortosa
County of Tripoli
Homs (Emesa)
Beirut
Baalbec
Damascus
Tyre
St. Jean d'Acre
Jaffa
Ramleh
Jerusalem
Ascalon
Damietta
Alexandria
Cairo
EGYPT
Nile R.
RED SEA
ARABIA
Saladin
Philip Augustus
Conrad III
Frederick I
Louis VII
The Fleet
BYZANTINE EMPIRE

72 The Holy Roman Empire under the Hohenstaufen, 1138—1254.

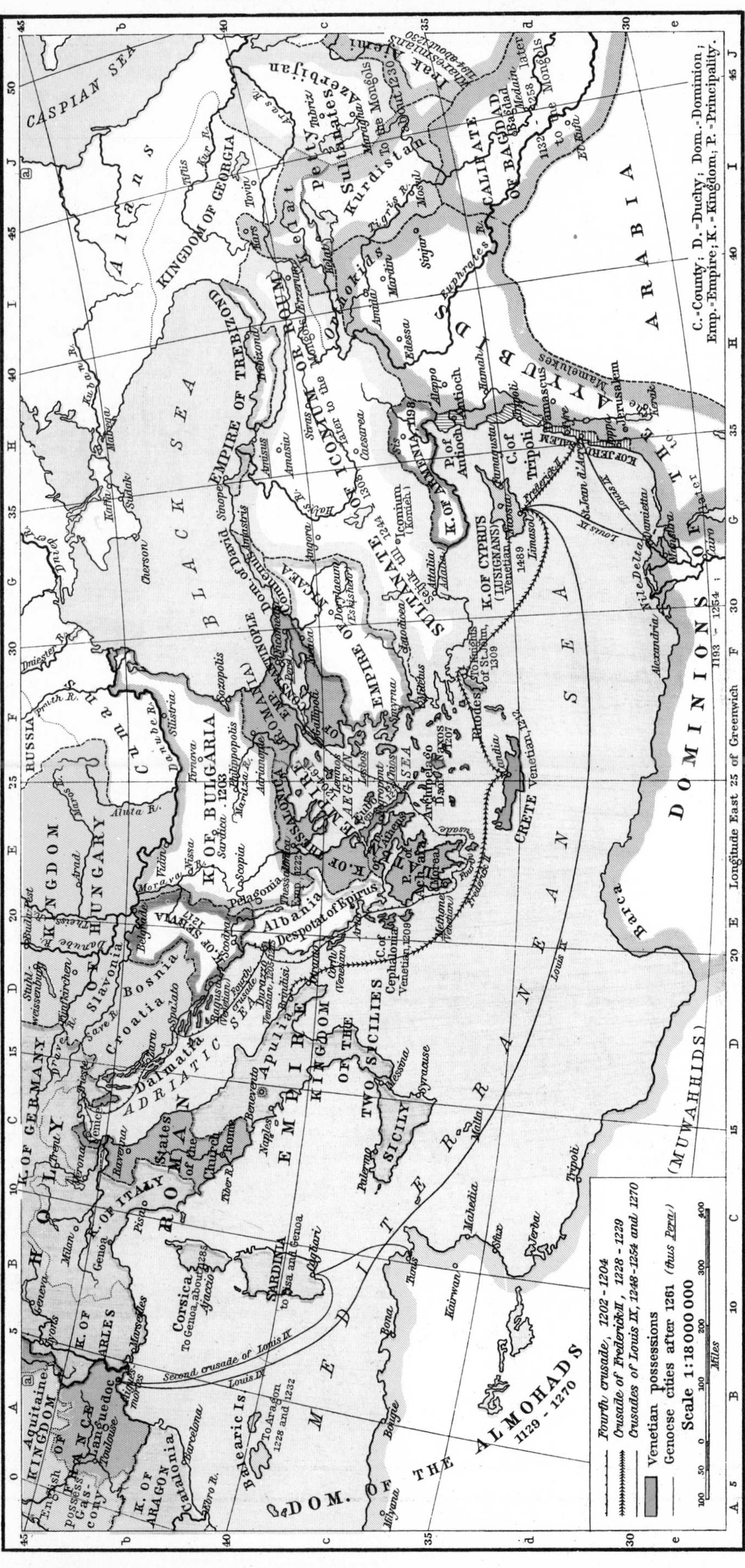

CASPIAN SEA
BLACK SEA
MEDITERRANEAN SEA
ADRIATIC SEA
AEGEAN SEA
KINGDOM OF GEORGIA
Alans
Azerbaijan
Irak Ajemi
Khwarezmians 1194-about 1230
Petty Sultanates
Kurdistan
Ortokids
CALIPHATE OF BAGDAD
Mongols 1258
ARABIA
EMPIRE OF TREBIZOND
SULTANATE OF ICONIUM OR ROUM
EMPIRE OF NICAEA
K. OF ARMENIA
P. of Antioch
C. of Tripoli
K. OF JERUSALEM
AYYUBIDS
Mamelukes
K. OF CYPRUS (LUSIGNANS)
Venetian 1489
Rhodes
To Knights of St. John 1309
CRETE Venetian 1212
EMPIRE OF ROMANIA (LATIN)
K. OF BULGARIA 1203
K. OF THESSALONICA
P. of Achaia
K. OF SERVIA 1217
Despotat of Epirus
Albania
Cumans
RUSSIA
KINGDOM OF HUNGARY
Slavonia
Croatia
Bosnia
Dalmatia
KINGDOM OF THE TWO SICILIES
SICILY
States of the Church
Rome
HOLY ROMAN EMPIRE
K. OF GERMANY
K. OF ITALY
K. OF ARLES
KINGDOM OF FRANCE
English possessions
Gascony
Languedoc
Aquitaine
K. OF ARAGON
Catalonia
Balearic Is.
To Aragon 1228 and 1232
Corsica
To Genoa, about 1283
SARDINIA
to Pisa and Genoa
DOM. OF THE ALMOHADS 1129-1270
DOMINIONS OF THE (MUWAHHIDS)
DOMINIONS OF THE AYYUBIDS 1193-1254
Barca
Nile Delta
Alexandria
Cairo
Damietta
Tunis
Tripoli
Malta
Second crusade of Louis IX
Louis IX
Frederick II
Fourth crusade
C.-County; D.-Duchy; Dom.-Dominion;
Emp.-Empire; K.-Kingdom; P.-Principality.
Fourth crusade, 1202-1204
Crusade of Frederick II, 1228-1239
Crusades of Louis IX, 1248-1254 and 1270
Venetian possessions
Genoese cities after 1261 (thus Pera)
Scale 1:18000000
Miles
Longitude East 25 of Greenwich

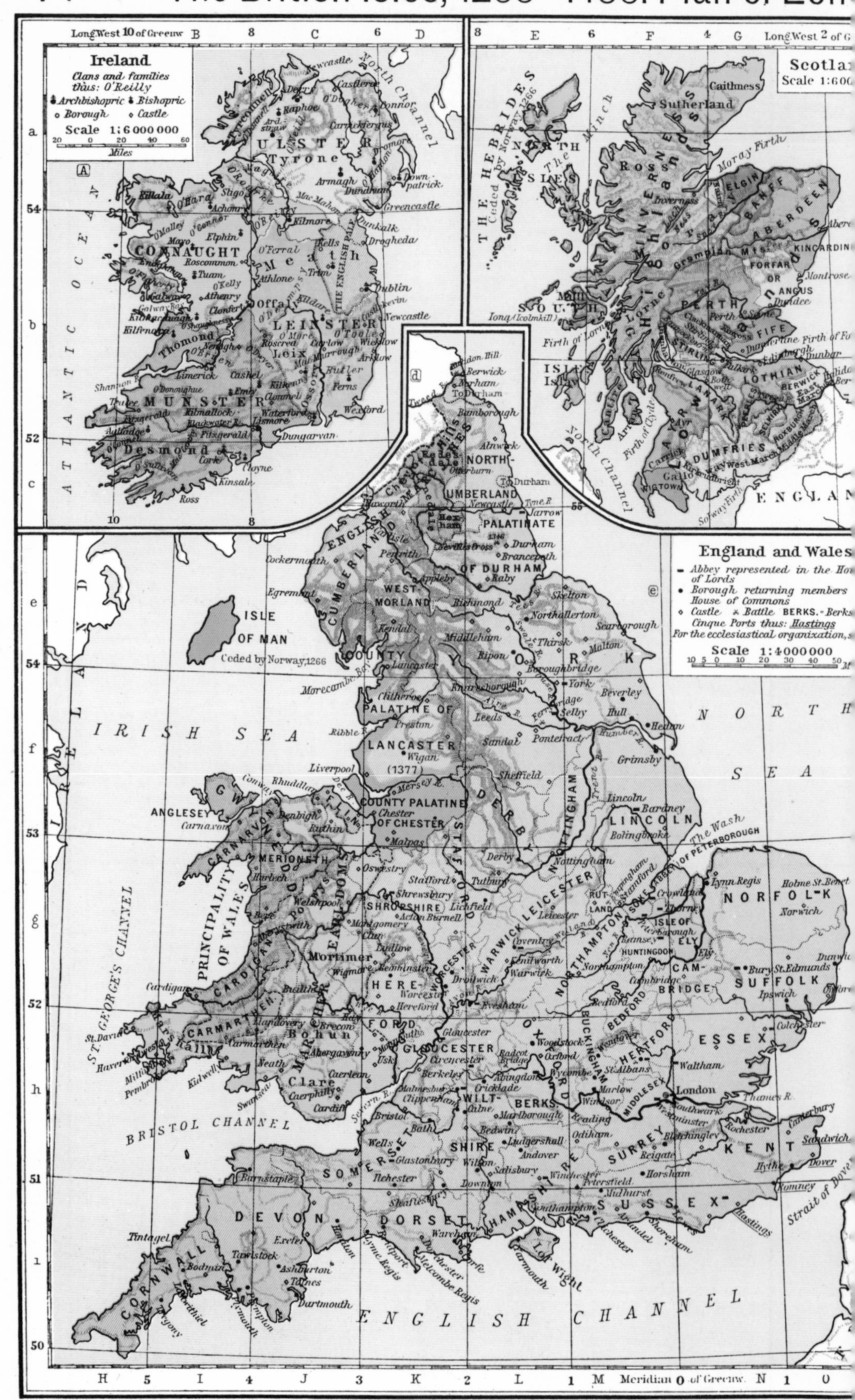
Ireland
Clans and families thus: O'Reilly
Archbishopric Bishopric
Borough Castle
Scale 1:6 000 000
Miles
ULSTER
Tyrone
CONNAUGHT
Meath
LEINSTER
Leix
Offaly
Thomond
MUNSTER
Desmond
ATLANTIC OCEAN
North Channel
Dublin
Armagh
Limerick
Cork
Waterford
Wexford
Kilkenny
Scotland
Scale 1:600
Caithness
Sutherland
Ross
ELGIN
BANFF
ABERDEEN
KINCARDINE
FORFAR OR ANGUS
PERTH
FIFE
STIRLING
LOTHIAN
BERWICK
LANARK
DUMFRIES
Galloway
THE HEBRIDES Ceded by Norway 1266
NORTH ISLES
SOUTH ISLES
Iona (Icolmkill)
Firth of Lorne
Firth of Forth
Firth of Clyde
Moray Firth
Inverness
Dunbar
Edinburgh
Glasgow
Dundee
Montrose
ENGLAND
England and Wales
Abbey represented in the House of Lords
Borough returning members House of Commons
Castle Battle BERKS. = Berks
Cinque Ports thus: Hastings
For the ecclesiastical organization,
Scale 1:4 000 000
ISLE OF MAN
Ceded by Norway, 1266
IRISH SEA
NORTH SEA
ST. GEORGE'S CHANNEL
BRISTOL CHANNEL
ENGLISH CHANNEL
Strait of Dover
IRELAND
NORTHUMBERLAND
PALATINATE OF DURHAM
CUMBERLAND
WESTMORLAND
YORK
COUNTY PALATINE OF LANCASTER (1377)
COUNTY PALATINE OF CHESTER
DERBY
NOTTINGHAM
LINCOLN
STAFFORD
LEICESTER
RUTLAND
NORTHAMPTON
HUNTINGDON
ISLE OF ELY
NORFOLK
SUFFOLK
CAMBRIDGE
ESSEX
HERTFORD
BEDFORD
BUCKINGHAM
OXFORD
MIDDLESEX
London
BERKS
WILTSHIRE
GLOUCESTER
HEREFORD
SHROPSHIRE
WORCESTER
WARWICK
SOMERSET
DORSET
DEVON
CORNWALL
HAMPSHIRE
SURREY
SUSSEX
KENT
PRINCIPALITY OF WALES
ANGLESEY
CARNARVON
MERIONETH
CARDIGAN
CARMARTHEN
Mortimer
Bohun
Clare
Isle of Wight
The Wash
Meridian 0 of Greenw.

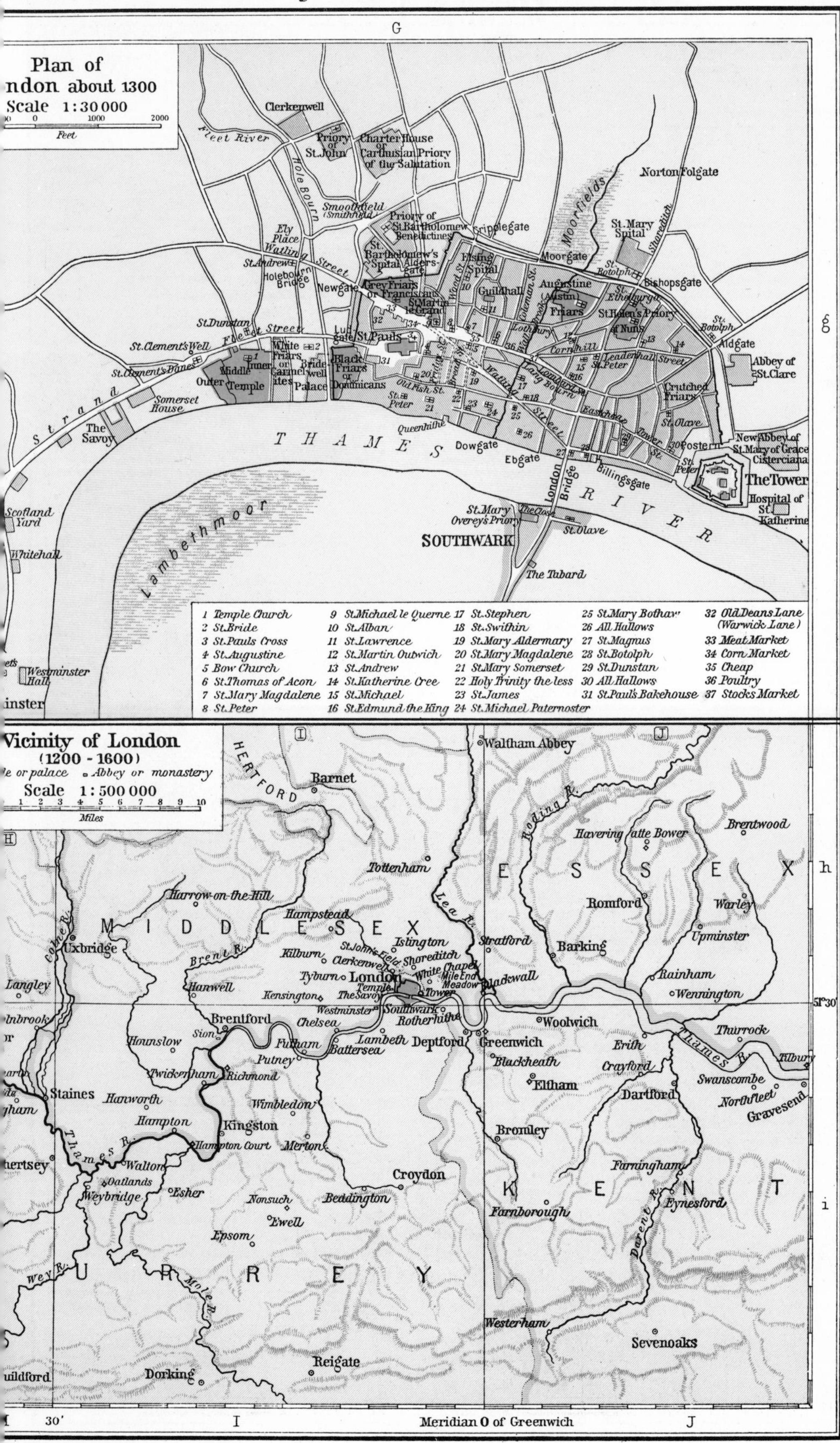
Plan of
ndon about 1300
Scale 1:30 000
Feet
THAMES
RIVER
SOUTHWARK
The Tower
1 Temple Church
2 St. Bride
3 St. Pauls Cross
4 St. Augustine
5 Bow Church
6 St. Thomas of Acon
7 St. Mary Magdalene
8 St. Peter
9 St. Michael le Querne
10 St. Alban
11 St. Lawrence
12 St. Martin Outwich
13 St. Andrew
14 St. Katherine Cree
15 St. Michael
16 St. Edmund the King
17 St. Stephen
18 St. Swithin
19 St. Mary Aldermary
20 St. Mary Magdalene
21 St. Mary Somerset
22 Holy Trinity the less
23 St. James
24 St. Michael Paternoster
25 St. Mary Bothaw
26 All Hallows
27 St. Magnus
28 St. Botolph
29 St. Dunstan
30 All Hallows
31 St. Paul's Bakehouse
32 Old Deans Lane (Warwick Lane)
33 Meat Market
34 Corn Market
35 Cheap
36 Poultry
37 Stocks Market
Vicinity of London
(1200 - 1600)
e or palace
Abbey or monastery
Scale 1:500 000
Miles
MIDDLESEX
ESSEX
KENT
URREY
London
Meridian 0 of Greenwich

France in 1328.

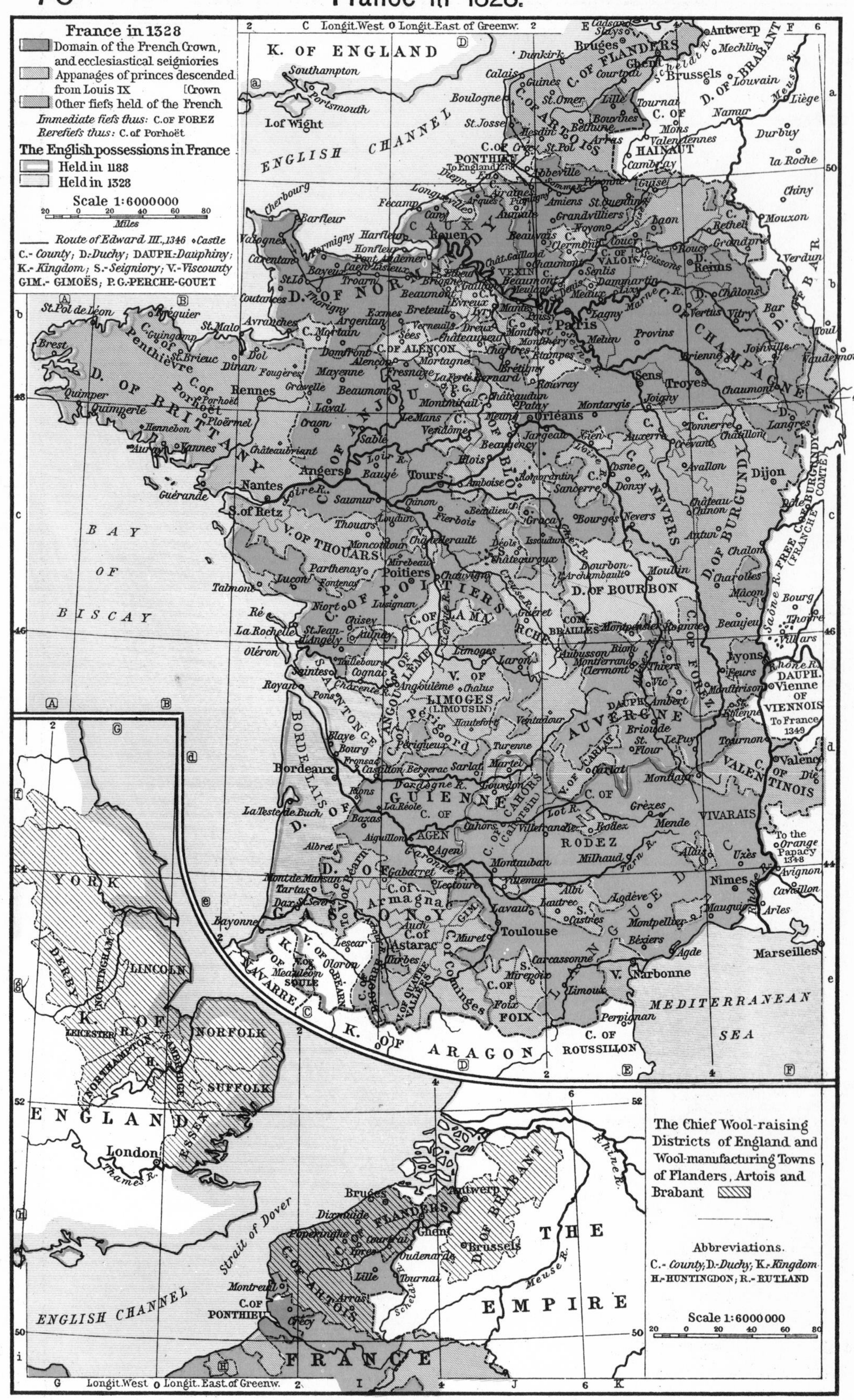

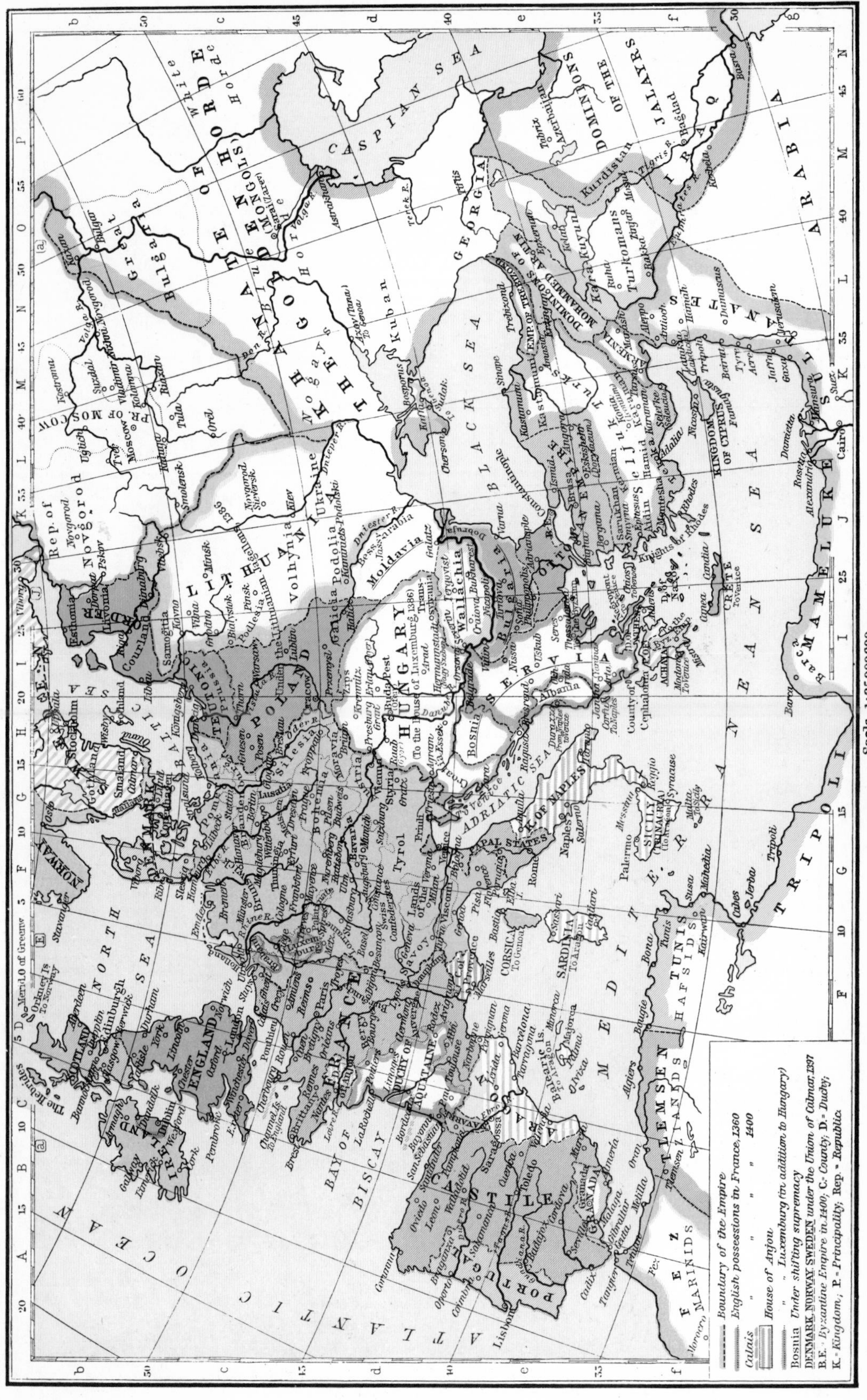
Boundary of the Empire
English possessions in France, 1360
Calais " " " 1400
House of Anjou
" " Luxemburg (in addition to Hungary)
Bosnia Under shifting supremacy
DENMARK, NORWAY, SWEDEN under the Union of Calmar, 1397
B.E. Byzantine Empire in 1400; C.= County; D.= Duchy;
K.= Kingdom; P.= Principality; Rep.= Republic.
Scale 1:25000000
Miles
ATLANTIC OCEAN
NORTH SEA
BALTIC SEA
BAY OF BISCAY
MEDITERRANEAN SEA
ADRIATIC SEA
BLACK SEA
CASPIAN SEA
ENGLAND
IRELAND
SCOTLAND
FRANCE
CASTILE
PORTUGAL
ARAGON
GRANADA
NORWAY
DENMARK
SWEDEN
POLAND
LITHUANIA
HUNGARY
BOHEMIA
SERVIA
Moldavia
Wallachia
Bulgaria
Bosnia
KINGDOM OF CYPRUS
MAMELUKES
TRIPOLI
ARABIA
IRAQ
GEORGIA
THE GOLDEN HORDE
PR. OF MOSCOW
Rep. of Novgorod
TLEMSEN
FEZ
HAFSIDS
SICILY
SARDINIA
CORSICA
CRETE

Central E

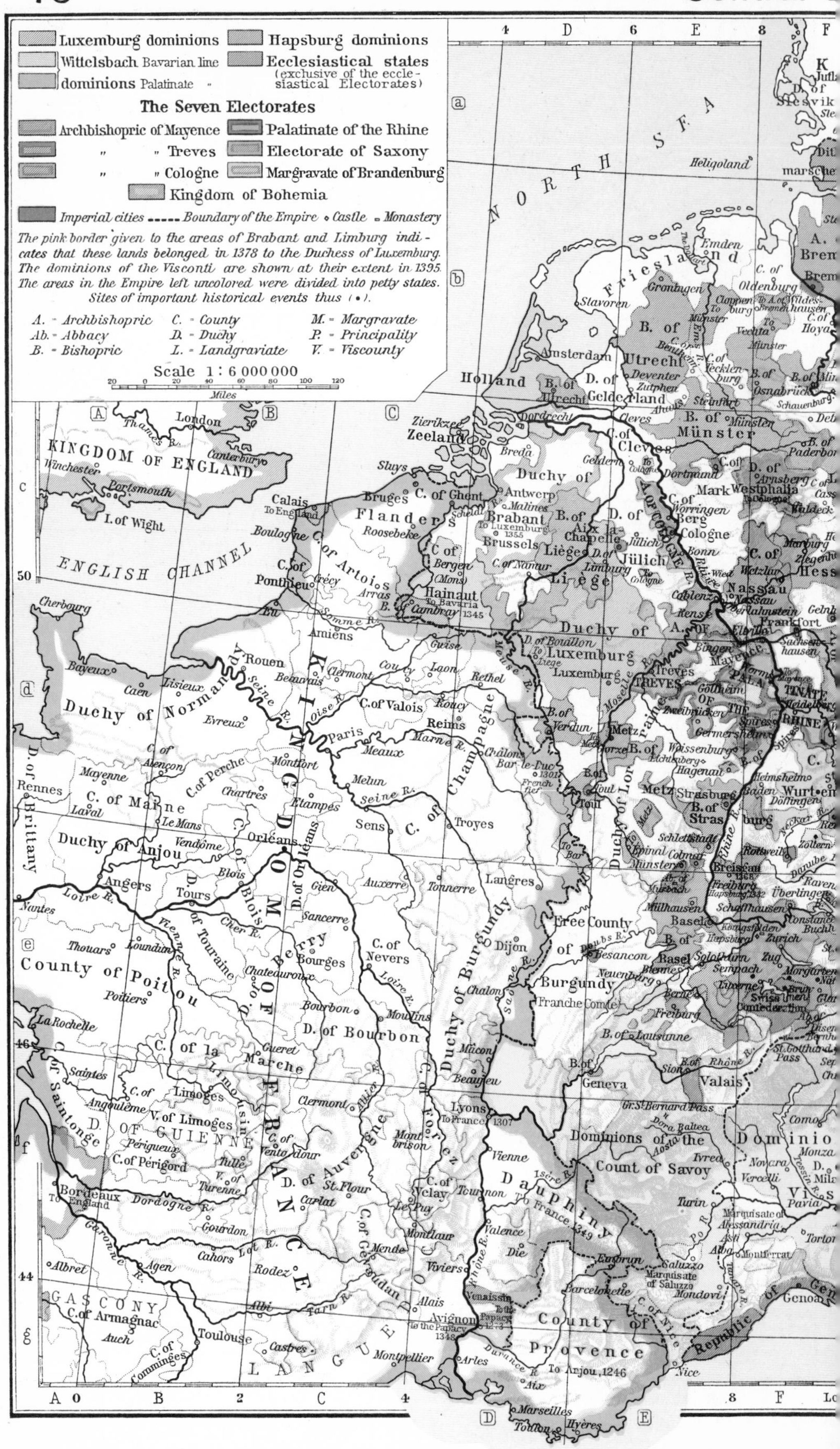

Luxemburg dominions
Wittelsbach dominions Bavarian line
Palatinate
Hapsburg dominions
Ecclesiastical states (exclusive of the ecclesiastical Electorates)
The Seven Electorates
Archbishopric of Mayence
" " Treves
" " Cologne
Palatinate of the Rhine
Electorate of Saxony
Margravate of Brandenburg
Kingdom of Bohemia
Imperial cities
Boundary of the Empire
Castle
Monastery
The pink border given to the areas of Brabant and Limburg indicates that these lands belonged in 1378 to the Duchess of Luxemburg.
The dominions of the Visconti are shown at their extent in 1395.
The areas in the Empire left uncolored were divided into petty states.
Sites of important historical events thus (•).
A. = Archbishopric
Ab. = Abbacy
B. = Bishopric
C. = County
D. = Duchy
L. = Landgraviate
M. = Margravate
P. = Principality
V. = Viscounty
Scale 1 : 6 000 000
Miles
NORTH SEA
Heligoland
Friesland
Emden
Groningen
Stavoren
Amsterdam
Holland
Utrecht
B. of Utrecht
D. of Gelderland
B. of Münster
KINGDOM OF ENGLAND
London
Thames R.
Canterbury
Winchester
Portsmouth
I. of Wight
ENGLISH CHANNEL
Zeeland
Sluys
Bruges
C. of Ghent
Flanders
Roosebeke
Calais
Boulogne
C. of Artois
Arras
Crécy
Duchy of Brabant
Antwerp
Malines
Brussels
Aix la Chapelle
Liège
Jülich
Cologne
Bonn
Coblenz
Duchy of Luxemburg
Luxemburg
Treves
Mayence
Frankfort
Nassau
Metz
Toul
Verdun
Strasburg
Basel
Zurich
Lucerne
Swiss Confederation
Amiens
Somme R.
Rouen
Beauvais
Cherbourg
Bayeux
Caen
Lisieux
Duchy of Normandy
Evreux
Paris
Meaux
Reims
Laon
Rethel
Châlons
C. of Champagne
Troyes
Sens
Melun
KINGDOM OF FRANCE
Orléans
D. of Orléans
Chartres
Étampes
Le Mans
C. of Maine
Duchy of Anjou
Angers
Tours
Blois
Loire R.
Nantes
D. of Brittany
Rennes
County of Poitou
Poitiers
La Rochelle
Berry
Bourges
C. of Nevers
D. of Bourbon
Duchy of Burgundy
Dijon
Free County of Burgundy
Besancon
Langres
Auxerre
Lyons
Vienne
Dauphiny
Valence
Grenoble
Avignon
County of Provence
Arles
Aix
Marseilles
Toulon
Hyères
Nice
Dominions of the Count of Savoy
Geneva
Turin
Limoges
C. of Périgord
Périgueux
D. of Guienne
Bordeaux
Dordogne R.
Garonne R.
Cahors
Agen
Rodez
Albi
Toulouse
Castres
Montpellier
Languedoc
Gascony
C. of Armagnac
Auch
C. of Comminges
D. of Auvergne
Clermont
Le Puy
Mende
Viviers
Alais
Carlat
St. Flour
Rhône R.
Isère R.
Saône R.
Seine R.
Marne R.
Oise R.
Meuse R.
Moselle R.
Rhine R.
Lake Constance
Republic of Genoa
Genoa
Milan
Pavia
Novara
Vercelli
Marquisate of Alessandria
Marquisate of Saluzzo
Como

BALTIC SEA
Bornholm
Möen
Falster
Fehmern
P. of Rügen
To Pomerania, 1325
Königsberg
Braunsberg
Ermeland
Elbing
Marienburg
Danzig
Dirschau
Lauenburg
Stolp
Pomerelia
To Teutonic Order, 1310
Domain of the Teutonic Order
Marienwerder
Kulm
Thorn
Vistula R.
Kolberg
Kammin
B. of Kammin
Wolgast
Neustettin
Stralsund
Greifswald
D. of Pomerania
Rostock
Wismar
Mecklenburg
Stettin
Stargard
Schivelbein
Neumark
Prenzlau
Ukermark
Prignitz
Ruppin
Chorin
MARGRAVIATE OF BRANDENBURG
Bavarian, 1324-1373
Altmark
Stendal
Tangermünde
Havelberg
Berlin
Küstrin
Frankfort
Magdeburg
Brandenburg
Lebus
Fürstenwalde
Margravate of Lusatia
To Luxemburg (Bohemian) 1368
Kottbus
Sorau
Sagan
Krossen
Oder R.
Schwiebus
Schwerin
Posen
Gnesen
Bromberg
Flatow
Netze R.
Inowrazlaw
Kujavia
Radziejow
Brest
Warthe R.
KINGDOM OF POLAND
Wlodawek
Masovia
Dobrzyn
Plock
Warsaw
Poland and Lithuania under the same ruling house, 1386
Peisern
Macijowice
Kalisz
Petrikau
Radom
Vielun
Czenstochova
Siewierz
Vistula R.
Cracow
Tarnow
Zator
Dessau
Wittenberg
ELECTORATE OF SAXONY
Anhalt
Halle
Leipzig
Merseburg
Naumburg
M. of Meissen
Osterland
Meissen
Dresden
Lucka
Walden
Pleissnerland
Freiberg
Plauen
Vogtland
Graslitz
Kaaden
Carlsbad
Eger
Bautzen
Görlitz
Zittau
Jauer
Liegnitz
Glogau
Duchy of
P. of Öls
P. of Breslau
To Luxemburg, 1335
Schweidnitz
Brieg
Münsterberg
P. of Oppeln
Silesia
Under Luxemburg (Bohemian) suzerainty since beginning of the 14th century
Ratibor
Auschwitz
Jägerndorf
P. of Troppau
P. of Teschen
Glatz
Königgrätz
Aussig
Leitmeritz
Melnik
Kolin
Pardubitz
Prague
Kuttenberg
Leitomischl
KINGDOM OF BOHEMIA
To Luxemburg, 1310
Olmütz
Iglau
Margravate of Moravia
To Luxemburg, 1310
Brünn
Znaim
Budweis
Rosenberg
Pisek
Moldau R.
March R.
Bamberg
Nuremberg
UPPER PALATINATE
Regensburg
Ratisbon
Straubing
Bavaria-Straubing
Passau
Ingolstadt
Landshut
D. of Bavaria
Munich
Bavaria-Munich
Salzburg
A. of Salzburg
Innsbruck
Tyrol
Linz
Enns
Vienna
Danube R.
Austria
Hapsburg, 1282
Baden
Duchy of Styria
Hapsburg, 1282
Gratz
Leoben
Judenburg
Friesach
Klagenfurt
D. of Carinthia
Hapsburg, 1335
Villach
Cilli
Laibach
D. of Carniola
Hapsburg 1282, 1335
Trieste
Agram
Croatia
Patriarchate of Aquileia
Udine
Aquileia
Trent
Belluno
Treviso
Venetian Republic
Venice
Padua
Verona
Vicenza
Carrara
Chioggia
Mantua
Ferrara
Este
Modena
Bologna
Ravenna
Cesena
Rimini
Pesaro
Ancona
Florence
PAPAL STATES
Pola
Zara
Dalmatia
To the Venetian Republic
KINGDOM OF BOSNIA
Save R.
Drave R.
Mur R.
Pressburg
Tyrnau
Neutra
Trentschin
Waag R.
Kremnitz
Altsohl (Zvolen)
Schemnitz
Liptau
Leutschau
Käsmark
Kaschau
Gran (Esztergom)
Erlau
Raab
Ödenburg
Güns
Güssing
Buda (Ofen)
Pest
KINGDOM OF HUNGARY
Luxemburg, 1386
Vesprem
Theiss R.
Szegedin
Dominions of Ottocar of Bohemia
Bohemia and Moravia
Acquisitions of Ottocar
Scale 1:12 000 000
Egerland 1266
Bohemia
Moravia
Austria 1251
Styria 1254
Carinthia 1269
Carniola 1269

Spread of German Settlements to the Eastward, 800—1400.

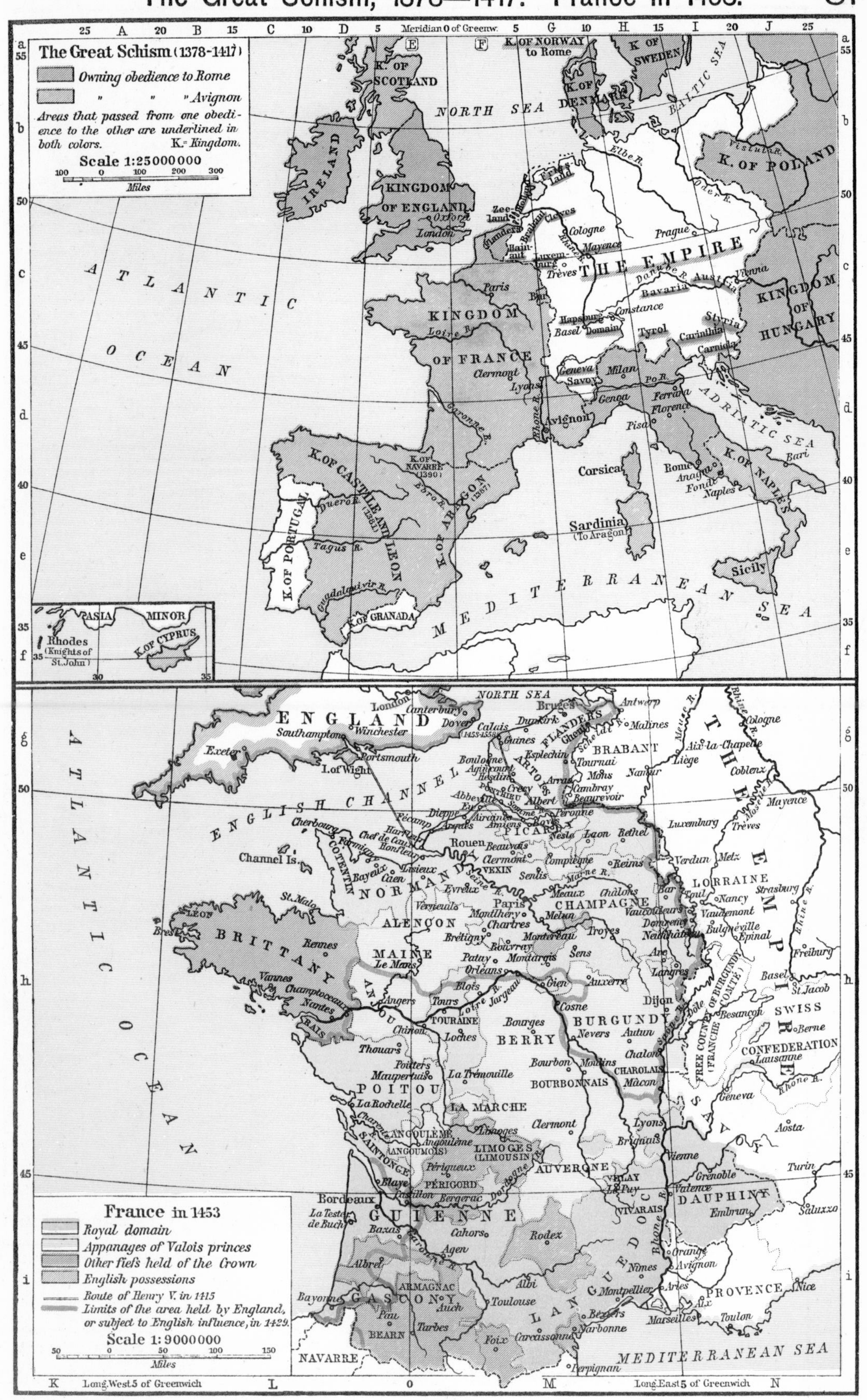
The Great Schism (1378-1417)
Owning obedience to Rome
" " " Avignon
Areas that passed from one obedience to the other are underlined in both colors. K.= Kingdom.
Scale 1:25000000
Miles
ATLANTIC OCEAN
NORTH SEA
BALTIC SEA
K. OF SCOTLAND
IRELAND
KINGDOM OF ENGLAND
Oxford
London
K. OF NORWAY to Rome
K. OF DENMARK
K. OF SWEDEN
K. OF POLAND
THE EMPIRE
Cologne
Mayence
Prague
Vienna
Treves
Bavaria
Austria
Constance
Basel
Tyrol
Styria
Carinthia
Carniola
KINGDOM OF HUNGARY
KINGDOM OF FRANCE
Paris
Clermont
Lyons
Avignon
Geneva
Savoy
Milan
Genoa
Ferrara
Florence
Pisa
ADRIATIC SEA
Rome
Anagni
Fondi
Naples
K. OF NAPLES
Bari
Corsica
Sardinia (To Aragon)
Sicily
K. OF NAVARRE (1390)
K. OF CASTILE AND LEON
K. OF ARAGON
K. OF PORTUGAL
K. OF GRANADA
MEDITERRANEAN SEA
ASIA MINOR
Rhodes (Knights of St. John)
K. OF CYPRUS
France in 1453
Royal domain
Appanages of Valois princes
Other fiefs held of the Crown
English possessions
Route of Henry V. in 1415
Limits of the area held by England, or subject to English influence, in 1429.
Scale 1:9000000
Miles
ENGLAND
London
Canterbury
Dover
Southampton
Winchester
Portsmouth
Exeter
I. of Wight
NORTH SEA
ENGLISH CHANNEL
Calais (1453-1558)
Bruges
Antwerp
Malines
FLANDERS
BRABANT
Tournai
Mons
Namur
Liège
Aix-la-Chapelle
Cologne
Coblenz
Mayence
Treves
Luxemburg
THE EMPIRE
ARTOIS
PICARDY
Rouen
Channel Is.
Cherbourg
COTENTIN
Bayeux
Caen
Lisieux
NORMANDY
Evreux
Paris
Chartres
CHAMPAGNE
Reims
Troyes
LORRAINE
Metz
Verdun
Nancy
Strasburg
Épinal
Freiburg
Basel
BRITTANY
Brest
Rennes
Vannes
Nantes
ALENÇON
MAINE
Le Mans
ANJOU
Angers
Tours
TOURAINE
Orléans
Blois
Bourges
BERRY
BURGUNDY
Dijon
Autun
Nevers
FREE COUNTY OF BURGUNDY (FRANCHE COMTÉ)
Besançon
SWISS CONFEDERATION
Berne
Lausanne
Geneva
SAVOY
POITOU
Poitiers
La Rochelle
LA MARCHE
BOURBONNAIS
Clermont
Lyons
ANGOULÊME
LIMOGES (LIMOUSIN)
AUVERGNE
PÉRIGORD
Bordeaux
GUIENNE
DAUPHINY
Grenoble
Turin
Aosta
Saluzzo
Cahors
Rodez
LANGUEDOC
Nîmes
Montpellier
Avignon
Arles
PROVENCE
Marseilles
Toulon
Nice
GASCONY
Bayonne
Toulouse
Narbonne
Carcassonne
Foix
BEARN
NAVARRE
Perpignan
MEDITERRANEAN SEA
Long. West 5 of Greenwich
Long. East 5 of Greenwich

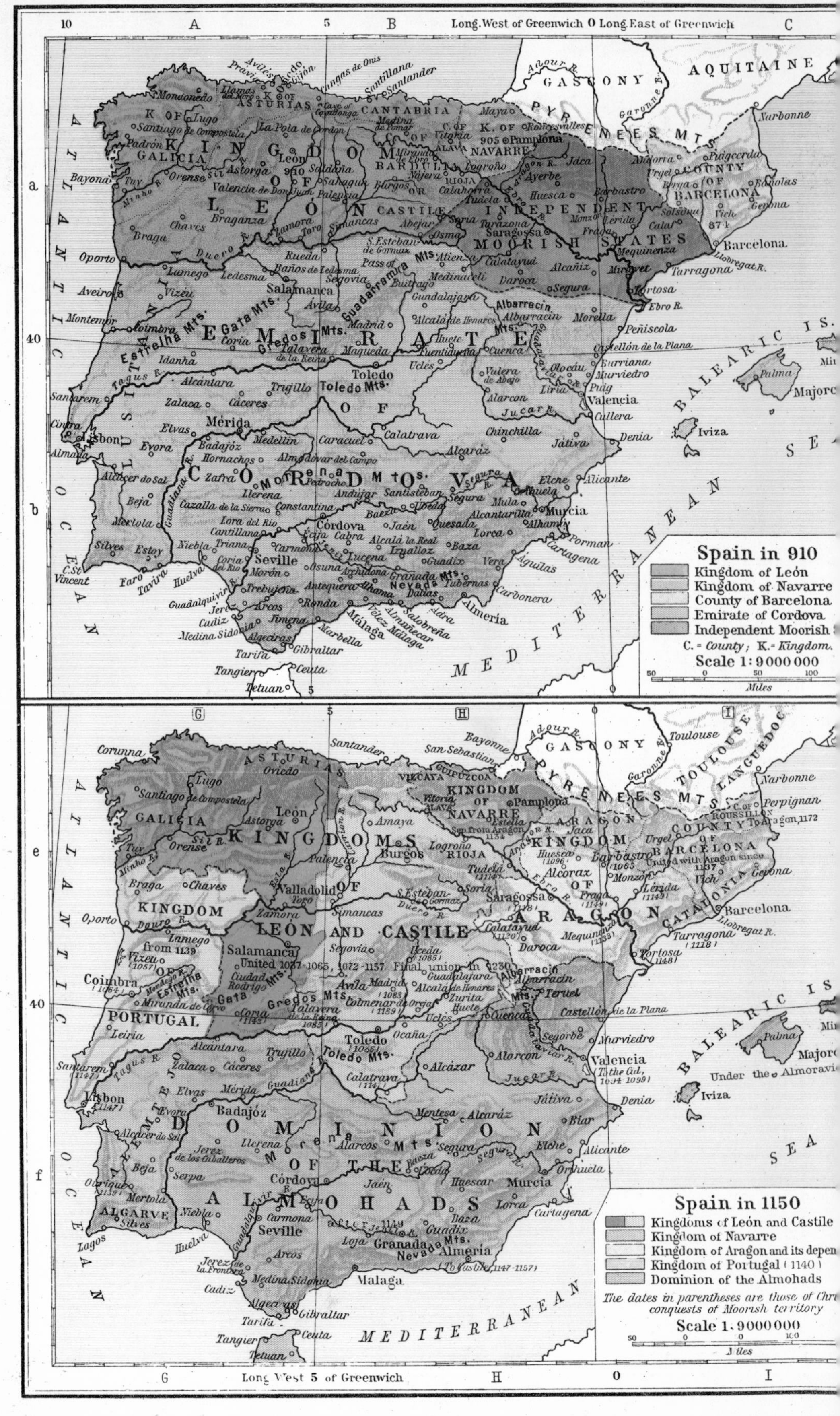
Long. West of Greenwich 0 Long. East of Greenwich
Spain in 910
Kingdom of León
Kingdom of Navarre
County of Barcelona
Emirate of Cordova
Independent Moorish
C. = County; K. = Kingdom.
Scale 1: 9000000
Miles
KINGDOM OF LEÓN
EMIRATE OF CORDOVA
INDEPENDENT MOORISH STATES
ATLANTIC OCEAN
MEDITERRANEAN SEA
BALEARIC IS.
Spain in 1150
Kingdoms of León and Castile
Kingdom of Navarre
Kingdom of Aragon and its depen
Kingdom of Portugal (1140)
Dominion of the Almohads
The dates in parentheses are those of Chr
conquests of Moorish territory
Scale 1: 9000000
Miles
KINGDOMS OF LEÓN AND CASTILE
United 1037-1065, 1072-1157. Final union in 1230
KINGDOM OF NAVARRE
KINGDOM OF ARAGON
KINGDOM OF PORTUGAL
DOMINION OF THE ALMOHADS
Long. West 5 of Greenwich

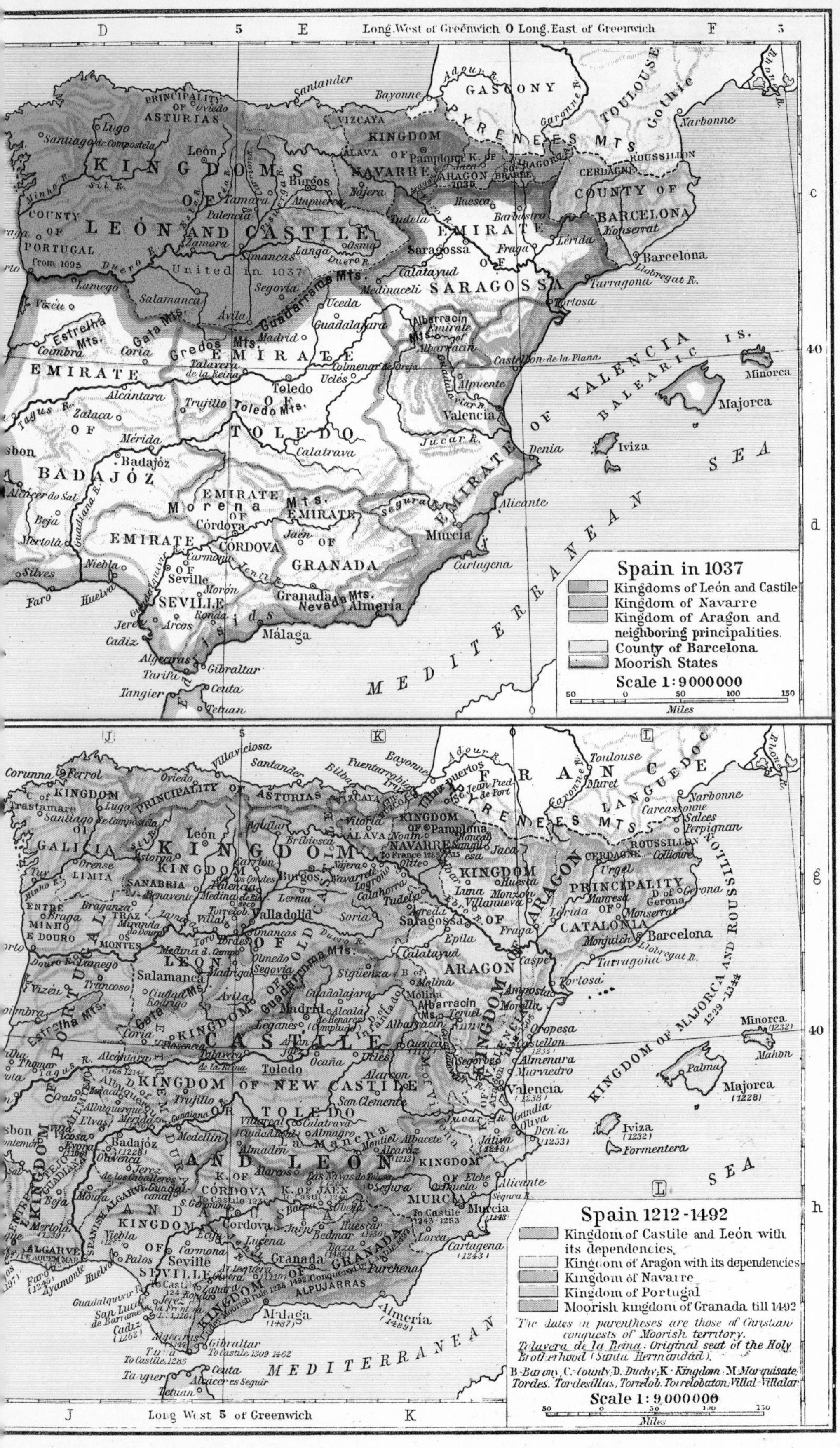
Long. West of Greenwich 0 Long. East of Greenwich
PRINCIPALITY OF ASTURIAS
KINGDOMS OF LEÓN AND CASTILE
United in 1037
COUNTY OF PORTUGAL
KINGDOM OF NAVARRE
K. OF ARAGON 1035
COUNTY OF BARCELONA
EMIRATE OF SARAGOSSA
EMIRATE OF TOLEDO
EMIRATE OF BADAJÓZ
EMIRATE OF VALENCIA
EMIRATE OF CÓRDOVA
EMIRATE OF GRANADA
EMIRATE OF SEVILLE
GASCONY
TOULOUSE
PYRENEES MTS.
BALEARIC IS.
MEDITERRANEAN SEA
Spain in 1037
Kingdoms of León and Castile
Kingdom of Navarre
Kingdom of Aragon and neighboring principalities
County of Barcelona
Moorish States
Scale 1: 9000000
Miles
FRANCE
LANGUEDOC
KINGDOM OF NAVARRE
KINGDOM OF ARAGON
PRINCIPALITY OF CATALONIA
KINGDOM OF CASTILE
KINGDOM OF NEW CASTILE
KINGDOM OF PORTUGAL
KINGDOM OF GRANADA
KINGDOM OF VALENCIA
KINGDOM OF MAJORCA AND ROUSSILLON 1229-1344
MEDITERRANEAN SEA
Spain 1212-1492
Kingdom of Castile and León with its dependencies
Kingdom of Aragon with its dependencies
Kingdom of Navarre
Kingdom of Portugal
Moorish kingdom of Granada till 1492
The dates in parentheses are those of Christian conquests of Moorish territory.
Talavera de la Reina: Original seat of the Holy Brotherhood (Santa Hermandad).
B. Barony, C. County, D. Duchy, K. Kingdom, M. Marquisate, Tordes. Tordesillas, Torrelob. Torrelobaton, Villal. Villalar.
Scale 1: 9000000
Miles
Long. West 5 of Greenwich

England and France, 1455—1494.

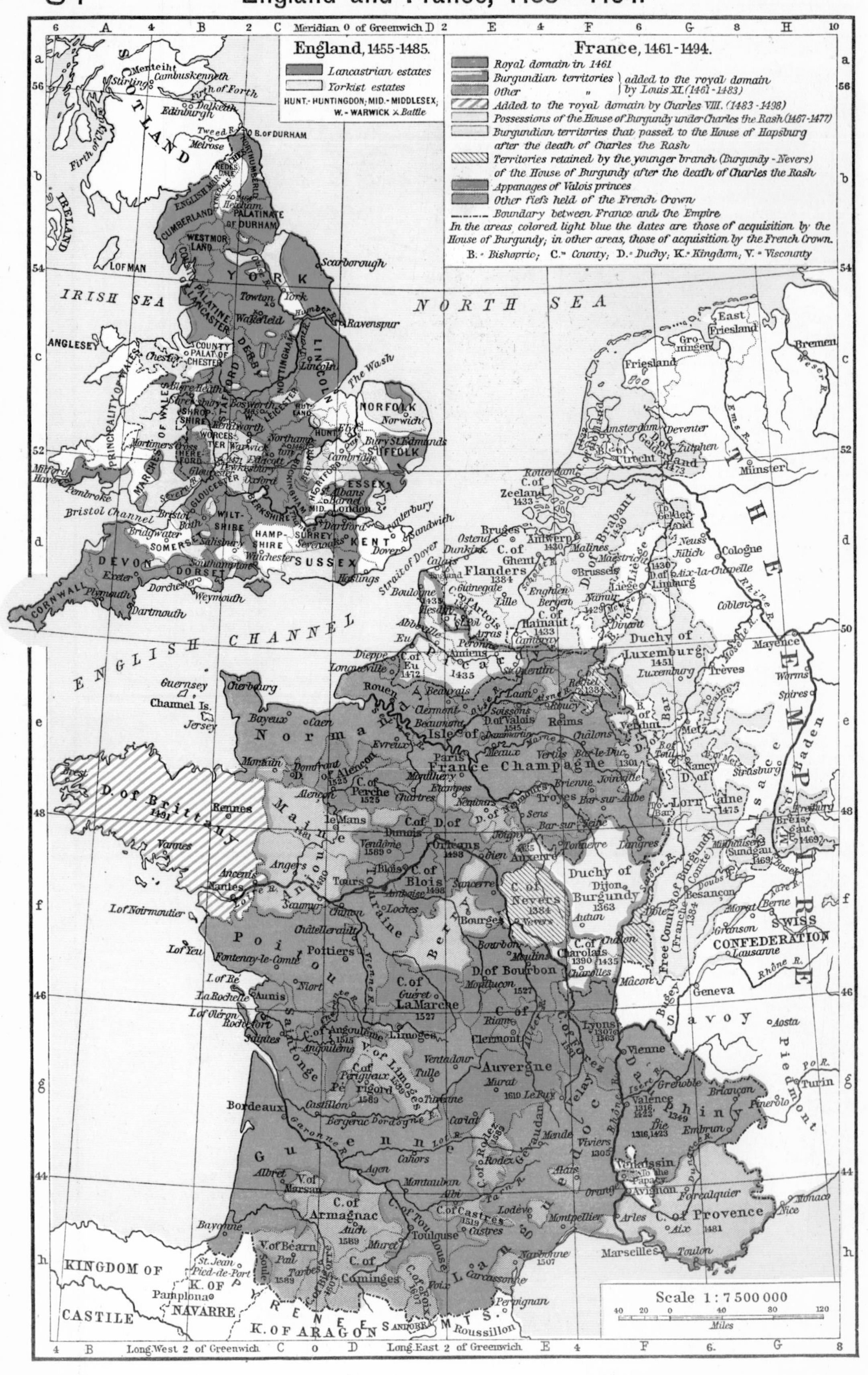

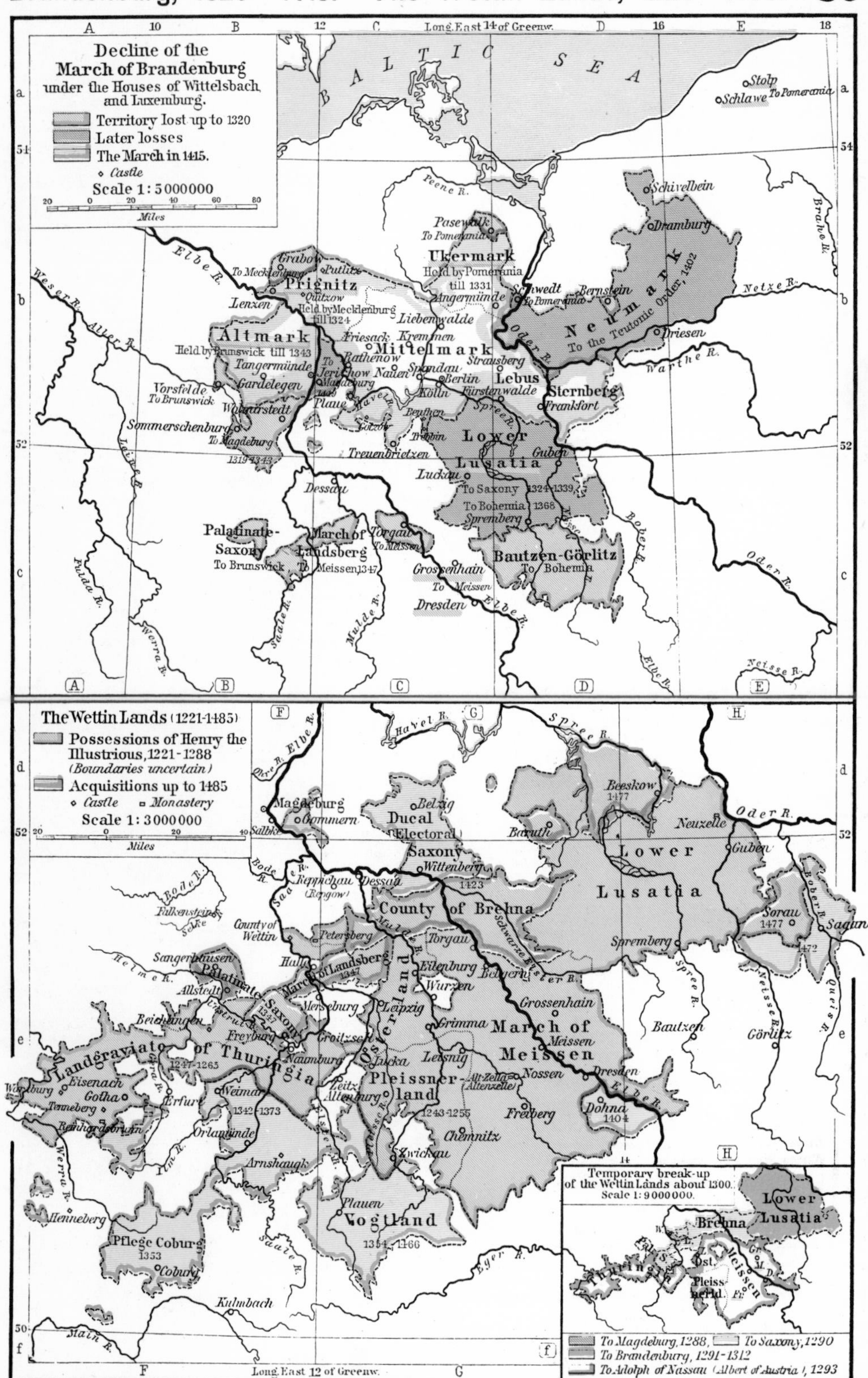
Decline of the March of Brandenburg under the Houses of Wittelsbach and Luxemburg.
Territory lost up to 1320
Later losses
The March in 1415.
Castle
Scale 1: 5000000
Miles
BALTIC SEA
Stolp
Schlawe
To Pomerania
Schivelbein
Dramburg
Neumark
To the Teutonic Order, 1402
Netze R.
Driesen
Warthe R.
Peene R.
Pasewalk
To Pomerania
Ukermark
Held by Pomerania till 1331
Angermünde
Schwedt
To Pomerania
Bernstein
Oder R.
Elbe R.
Grabow
To Mecklenburg
Putlitz
Prignitz
Quitzow
Held by Mecklenburg till 1324
Lenzen
Liebenwalde
Altmark
Held by Brunswick till 1343
Friesack
Kremmen
Mittelmark
Rathenow
Tangermünde
Gardelegen
Vorsfelde
To Brunswick
Wolmirstedt
Sommerschenburg
To Magdeburg
Jerichow
Nauen
Spandau
Strausberg
Berlin
Lebus
Köln
Fürstenwalde
Sternberg
Frankfort
Plaue
Havel R.
Spree R.
Beuthen
Zossen
Trebbin
Treuenbrietzen
Lower Lusatia
Guben
Luckau
To Saxony 1324-1339
To Bohemia 1368
Spremberg
Dessau
Palatinate-Saxony
To Brunswick
March of Landsberg
To Meissen 1347
Torgau
To Meissen
Bautzen-Görlitz
To Bohemia
Grossenhain
To Meissen
Dresden
Bober R.
Oder R.
Saale R.
Mulde R.
Werra R.
Fulda R.
Leine R.
Weser R.
Aller R.
Neisse R.
The Wettin Lands (1221-1485)
Possessions of Henry the Illustrious, 1221-1288 (Boundaries uncertain)
Acquisitions up to 1485
Castle
Monastery
Scale 1: 3000000
Miles
Havel R.
Spree R.
Elbe R.
Ohre R.
Magdeburg
Gommern
Salbke
Belzig
Ducal (Electoral) Saxony
Baruth
Beeskow 1477
Neuzelle
Oder R.
Guben
Lower Lusatia
Bode R.
Reppichau (Repgow)
Dessau
Wittenberg 1423
County of Brehna
Falkenstein
Selke R.
County of Wettin
Petersberg
Torgau
Schwarze Elster R.
Spremberg
Sorau 1477
Sagan
Bober R.
Queis R.
Neisse R.
Sangerhausen
Helme R.
Halle
March of Landsberg 1347
Eilenburg
Belgern
Wurzen
Palatinate Saxony 1347
Allstedt
Unstrut R.
Merseburg
Leipzig
Grossenhain
Bautzen
Görlitz
Beichlingen
Freyburg
Osterland
Grimma
March of Meissen
Croitzsch
Landgraviate of Thuringia 1247-1265
Naumburg
Leisnig
Nossen
Dresden
Eisenach
Gotha
Wartburg
Tenneberg
Reinhardsbrunn
Erfurt
Weimar 1342-1373
Zeitz
Altenburg
Pleissnerland 1243-1255
Altzella (Altenzelle)
Freiberg
Dohna 1404
Chemnitz
Orlamünde
Ilm R.
Zwickau
Arnshaugk
Werra R.
Plauen
Vogtland 1354-1466
Henneberg
Pflege Coburg 1353
Coburg
Saale R.
Eger R.
Kulmbach
Main R.
Long. East 12 of Greenw.
Long. East 14 of Greenw.
Temporary break-up of the Wettin Lands about 1300.
Scale 1: 9000000.
Lower Lusatia
Brehna
Thuringia
Ost.
Meissen
Pleissnerland
To Magdeburg, 1288
To Saxony, 1290
To Brandenburg, 1291-1312
To Adolph of Nassau (Albert of Austria), 1293

Meridian 0 of Greenw.
NORTH SEA
ENGLISH CHANNEL
KINGDOM OF ENGLAND
YORK
NORFOLK
SUFFOLK
ESSEX
KENT
SURREY
SUSSEX
I. of Wight
Friesland
East Friesland
B. of Utrecht
B. of Münster
D. of Geldepland
C. of Holland
C. of Zeeland
C. of Flanders
D. of Brabant
B. of Liège
C. of Hainaut
C. of Artois
Picardy
Ardennes
Duchy of Luxemburg
Normandy
Maine
Anjou
Poitou
Touraine
Isle of France
Champagne
KINGDOM OF FRANCE
D. of Valois
D. of Bar
Lorraine
B. of Metz
B. of Strasburg
PAL. OF THE RHINE
A. of Treves
A. of Cologne
C. of Nassau
Hess
C. of Nevers
DUCHY OF BURGUNDY
FREE COUNTY (FRANCHE COMTÉ)
Vaud
SWISS CONFEDERATI
Valais
Savoy
DUCHY OF SAVOY
Piedmont
Dauphiny
County of Provence
Republic of Genoa
Paris
London
Calais
Dijon
Lyons
Marseilles
Avignon
To France, 1481
Dominions of the House of Hapsburg
Dominions of the House of Burgundy
Possessions of Charles the Rash
" " the Burgundy-Nevers line
The possessions of Charles the Rash held of the French Crown are given a wide border; those of the Burgundy-Nevers line, similarly, a narrow border.
Ecclesiastical States
Imperial Cities
Boundary of the Empire
The two colorings given to the Bohemian region are intended to show that in 1477 a Polish Jagellon was reigning in Bohemia; and that Moravia and Silesia were subject to Hungary, but were reunited with Bohemia in 1490. The areas in the Empire left uncolored were divided into petty states.
Abbreviations
A: Archbishopric; Ab: Abbacy; B: Bishopric; C: County; D: Duchy; Lg: Landgraviate; M: Margravate; Marq: Marquisate; P: Principality; Pal.: Palatinate; Rep.: Republic; Castle; Monastery.
Scale 1:6 000 000
Miles

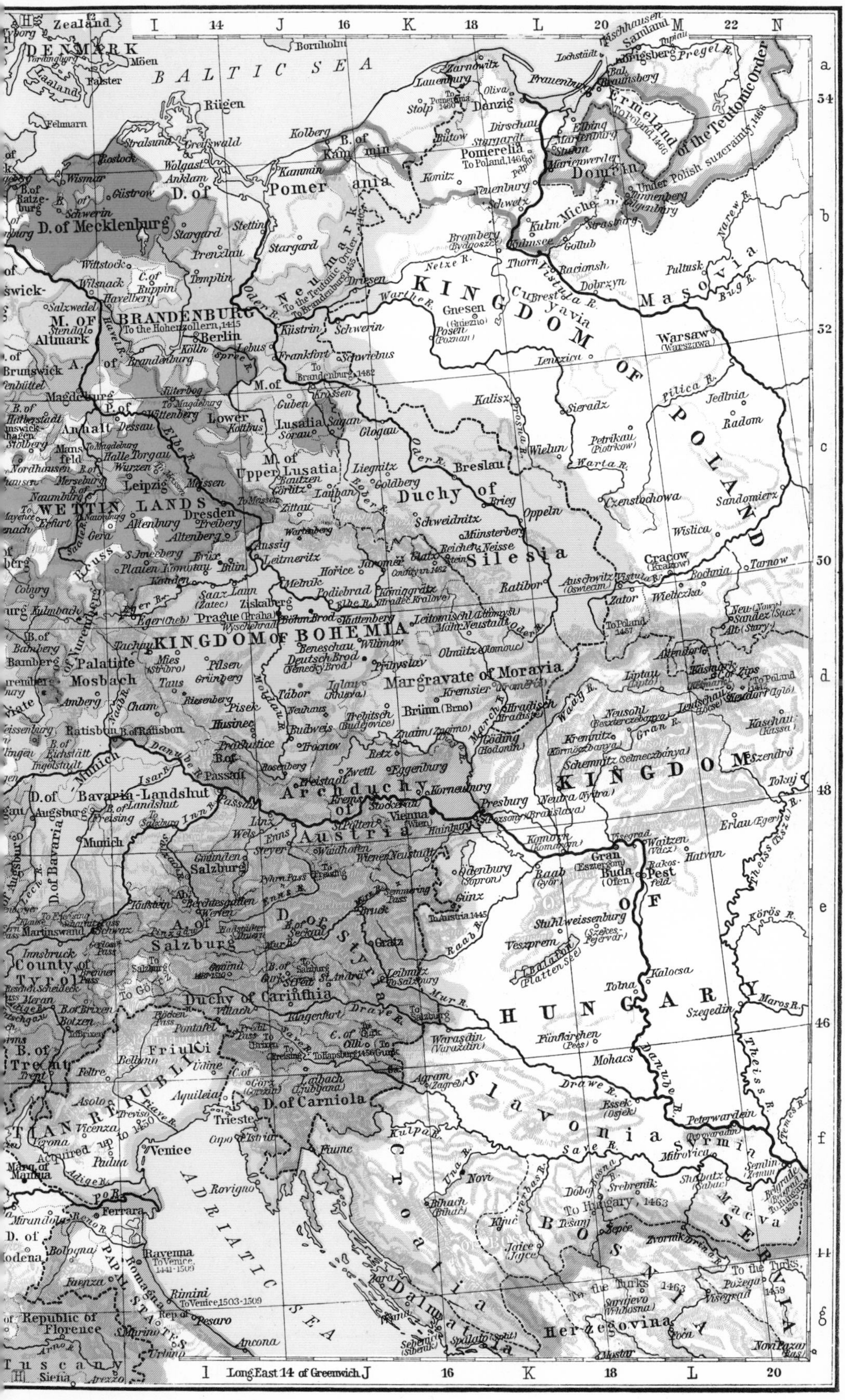
BALTIC SEA
DENMARK
Zealand
Bornholm
Rügen
D. of Mecklenburg
M. OF BRANDENBURG
To the Hohenzollern, 1415
Berlin
Pomerania
Neumark
Danzig
Pomerelia
To Poland, 1466
Ermeland
Domain of the Teutonic Order
Under Polish suzerainty, 1466
KINGDOM OF POLAND
Masovia
Warsaw
Cujavia
Gnesen
Posen
Kalisz
Cracow
Silesia
Duchy of
Breslau
Lusatia
WETTIN LANDS
Dresden
Leipzig
Magdeburg
KINGDOM OF BOHEMIA
Prague (Praha)
Margravate of Moravia
Brünn (Brno)
Olmütz
Palatinate
Bavaria-Landshut
Munich
Ratisbon
Archduchy of Austria
Vienna (Wien)
Salzburg
D. of Styria
Duchy of Carinthia
D. of Carniola
County of Tyrol
Friuli
Trieste
Venice
ADRIATIC SEA
KINGDOM OF HUNGARY
Presburg
Buda (Ofen)
Pest
Gran
Szegedin
Mohacs
Slavonia
Croatia
Dalmatia
Bosnia
Servia
Herzegovina
Belgrade
Ferrara
Ravenna
Republic of Florence
Tuscany
Papal States
Long. East 14 of Greenwich

Decline of German Power in the Baltic Region
(i.e of the Hanseatic League and the Teutonic Order)
I Rise of Scandinavia
Under the Union of Calmar, 1397-1523
Holstein (united with the Danish fief Schleswig in 1386) annexed to Denmark, 1460
II Rise of Poland
Poland and Lithuania (united in 1386) up to 1410
Acquired from the Teutonic Order up to 1466
III Further partitions of the domain of the Teutonic Order
Domain of the Order in 1466
Duchy of Prussia 1525
Territory still belonging to the Order in 1560
Scale 1 : 7 500 000
Miles
A. Archbishopric; B. Bishopric; D. Duchy.
M.a. = Seat of the merchant adventurers
Steelyard in London, closed, 1598
NORTH SEA
SKAGER RAK
KATTEGAT
BALTIC SEA
GULF OF FINLAND
KINGDOM OF NORWAY
KINGDOM OF SWEDEN
KINGDOM OF DENMARK
KINGDOM OF POLAND
GRAND PRINCIPALITY OF LITHUANIA
RUSSIA
DUCHY OF PRUSSIA
Livonia
Esthonia
Courland
Samogitia
Pomerelia
Finland
Dalecarlia
Gotland
Öland
Bornholm
Rügen
Neumark
Long. East of Greenw.

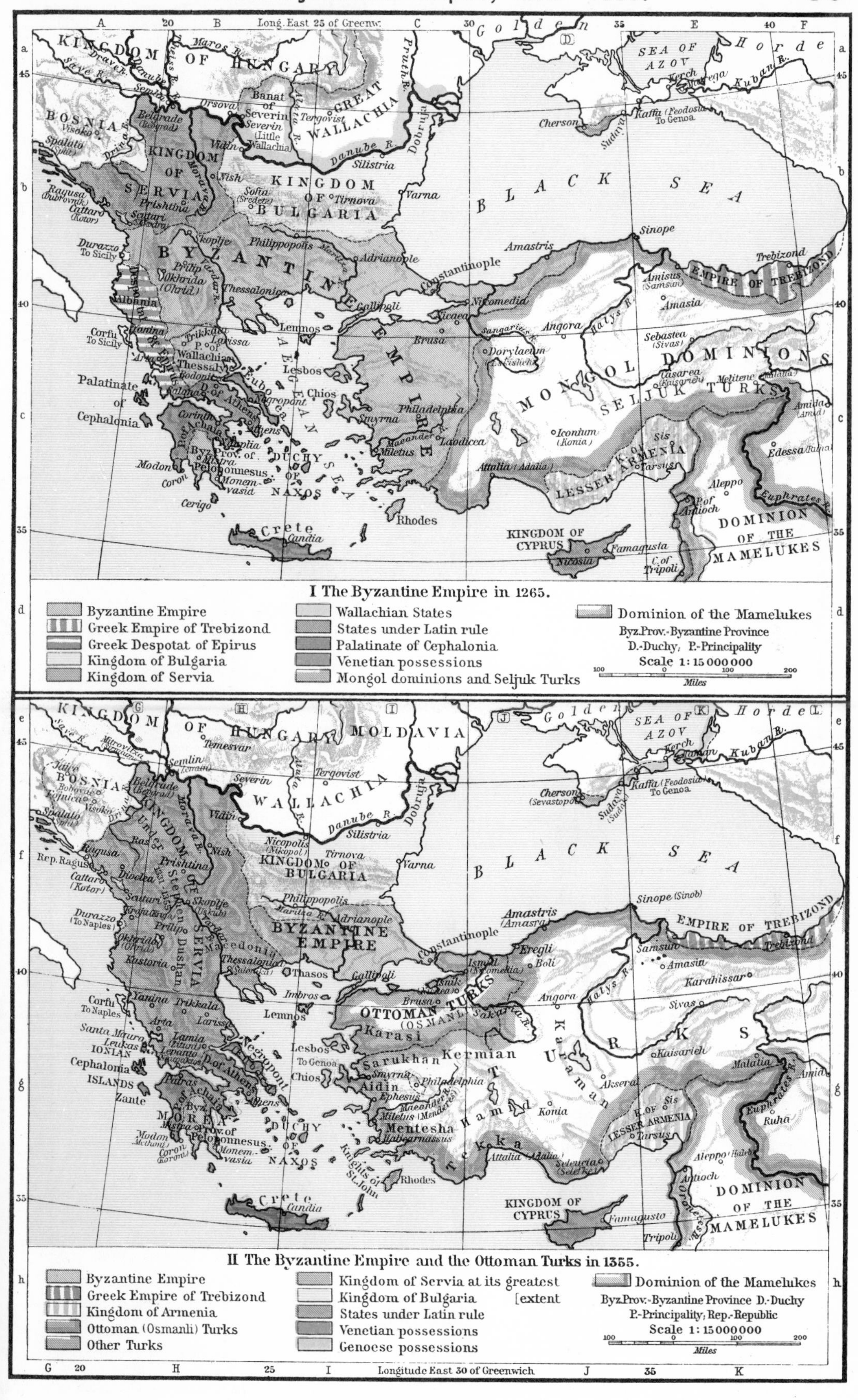
I The Byzantine Empire in 1265.
Byzantine Empire
Greek Empire of Trebizond
Greek Despotat of Epirus
Kingdom of Bulgaria
Kingdom of Servia
Wallachian States
States under Latin rule
Palatinate of Cephalonia
Venetian possessions
Mongol dominions and Seljuk Turks
Dominion of the Mamelukes
Byz.Prov.-Byzantine Province
D.-Duchy; P.-Principality
Scale 1: 15 000 000
Miles
KINGDOM OF HUNGARY
KINGDOM OF SERVIA
KINGDOM OF BULGARIA
GREAT WALLACHIA
BYZANTINE EMPIRE
BLACK SEA
SEA OF AZOV
Golden Horde
EMPIRE OF TREBIZOND
MONGOL DOMINIONS
SELJUK TURKS
LESSER ARMENIA
KINGDOM OF CYPRUS
DOMINION OF THE MAMELUKES
DUCHY OF NAXOS
AEGEAN SEA
Palatinate of Cephalonia
Constantinople
II The Byzantine Empire and the Ottoman Turks in 1355.
Byzantine Empire
Greek Empire of Trebizond
Kingdom of Armenia
Ottoman (Osmanli) Turks
Other Turks
Kingdom of Servia at its greatest [extent
Kingdom of Bulgaria
States under Latin rule
Venetian possessions
Genoese possessions
Dominion of the Mamelukes
Byz.Prov.-Byzantine Province D.-Duchy
P.-Principality; Rep.-Republic
Scale 1: 15 000 000
Miles
KINGDOM OF HUNGARY
MOLDAVIA
WALLACHIA
KINGDOM OF BULGARIA
KINGDOM OF SERVIA
BYZANTINE EMPIRE
OTTOMAN TURKS (OSMANLI)
EMPIRE OF TREBIZOND
BLACK SEA
SEA OF AZOV
Golden Horde
TURKS
Karaman
LESSER ARMENIA
KINGDOM OF CYPRUS
DOMINION OF THE MAMELUKES
DUCHY OF NAXOS
IONIAN ISLANDS
MOREA
Constantinople
Longitude East 30 of Greenwich

Long. East 12 of Greenw.
SWITZERLAND
Tyrol
Carinthia
RAETIAN ALPS
LEPONTINE ALPS
PENNINE ALPS
CARNIC ALPS
B. of Trent
Carniola
Istria
Croatia
HUN
KIN
DUCHY OF SAVOY
M. OF SALUZZO
DUCHY OF MILAN
M. OF MANTUA
D. OF FERRARA (Este)
D. OF MODENA (Este)
REP. OF GENOA
LIGURIAN ALPS
VENETIAN REPUBLIC
REP. OF FLORENCE
REP. OF SAN MARINO
REP. OF SIENA
FLORENCE
Corsica (To Genoa)
Elba
Emilia
Romagna
Umbria
The Marches
Sabina
Patrimony of St. Peter
Abruzzi
Molise
Capitanata
Campania
Principati
Basilicata
Apulia
KINGDOM OF THE TWO SICILIES
Lipari or Aeolian Is.
Sicily
Malta
ADRIATIC
Dalmatia
Rome
Naples
Venice
Milan
Genoa
Florence
Pisa
Siena
Bologna
Palermo
Messina
Ravenna
To Venice till 1509
The Milanese under the Visconti, 1339-1402.
Dominions of Azzo Visconti (1329-1339)
Acquired by Luchino and Giovanni Visconti (1339-54)
" " Bernabò and Galeazzo Visconti (1354-85)
" " Gian Galeazzo Visconti (1385-1402)
Areas given a border coloring are those which became dowries for Visconti heiresses, or were otherwise lost, before 1402.
Scale 1:5000000
Miles
The Republic of Florence, 1300-1494.
Boundaries of the Tuscan States in 1300
The Republic of Florence:
In 1300
Acquired, 1300-1377
" , 1377-1433
" , 1433-1494
Protected States
Scale 1:5000000
Miles
In the States of the Church the areas given a surface coloring of violet were under effective control.
ITA
B. = Bi
M. = Ma
For sites Milan du sixteenth

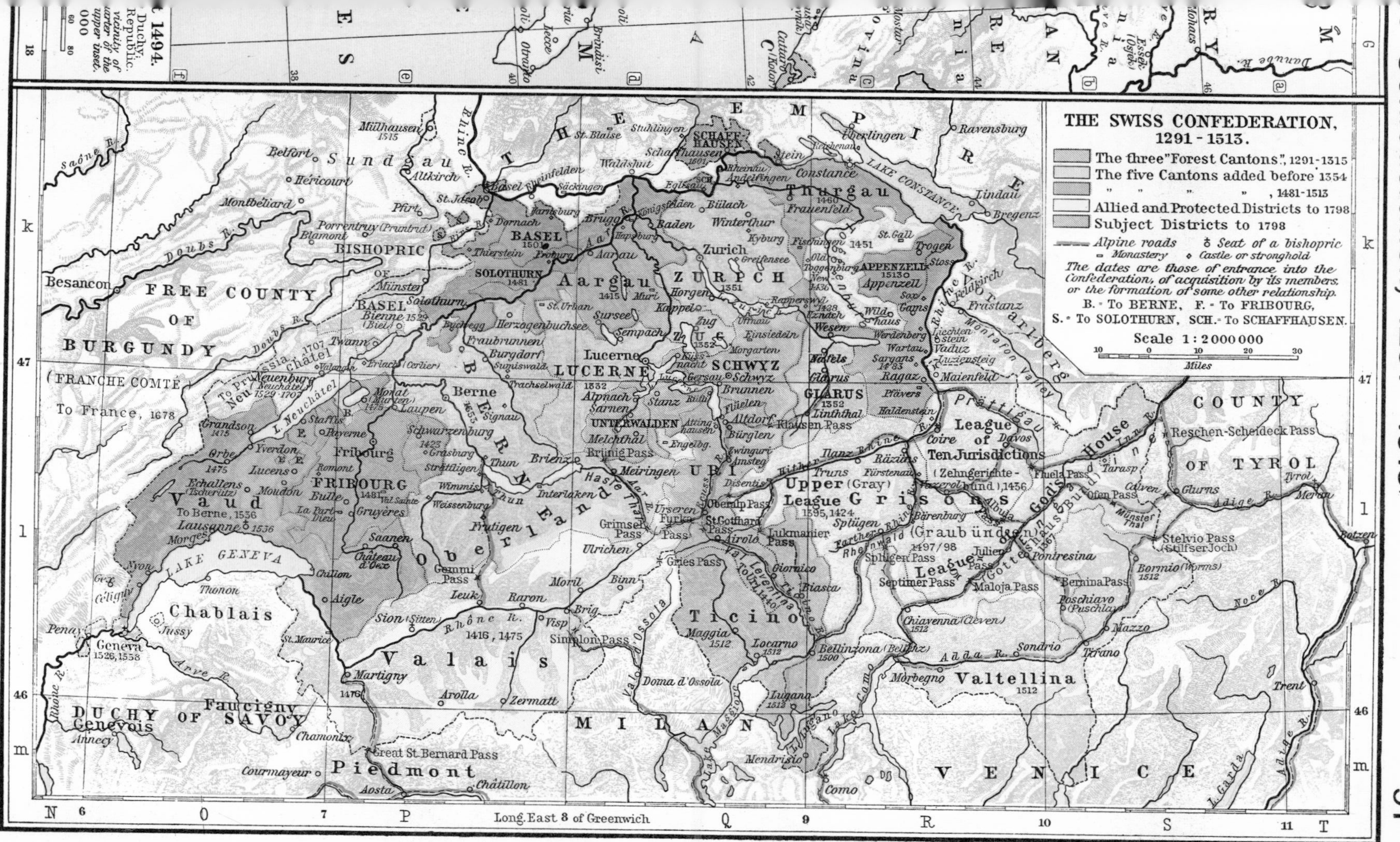
THE SWISS CONFEDERATION, 1291 - 1513.
The three "Forest Cantons", 1291-1315
The five Cantons added before 1354
" " " " , 1481-1513
Allied and Protected Districts to 1798
Subject Districts to 1798
Alpine roads
Seat of a bishopric
Monastery
Castle or stronghold
The dates are those of entrance into the Confederation, of acquisition by its members, or the formation of some other relationship.
B. - To BERNE, F. - To FRIBOURG,
S. - To SOLOTHURN, SCH. - To SCHAFFHAUSEN.
Scale 1:2000000
Miles
Long. East 8 of Greenwich

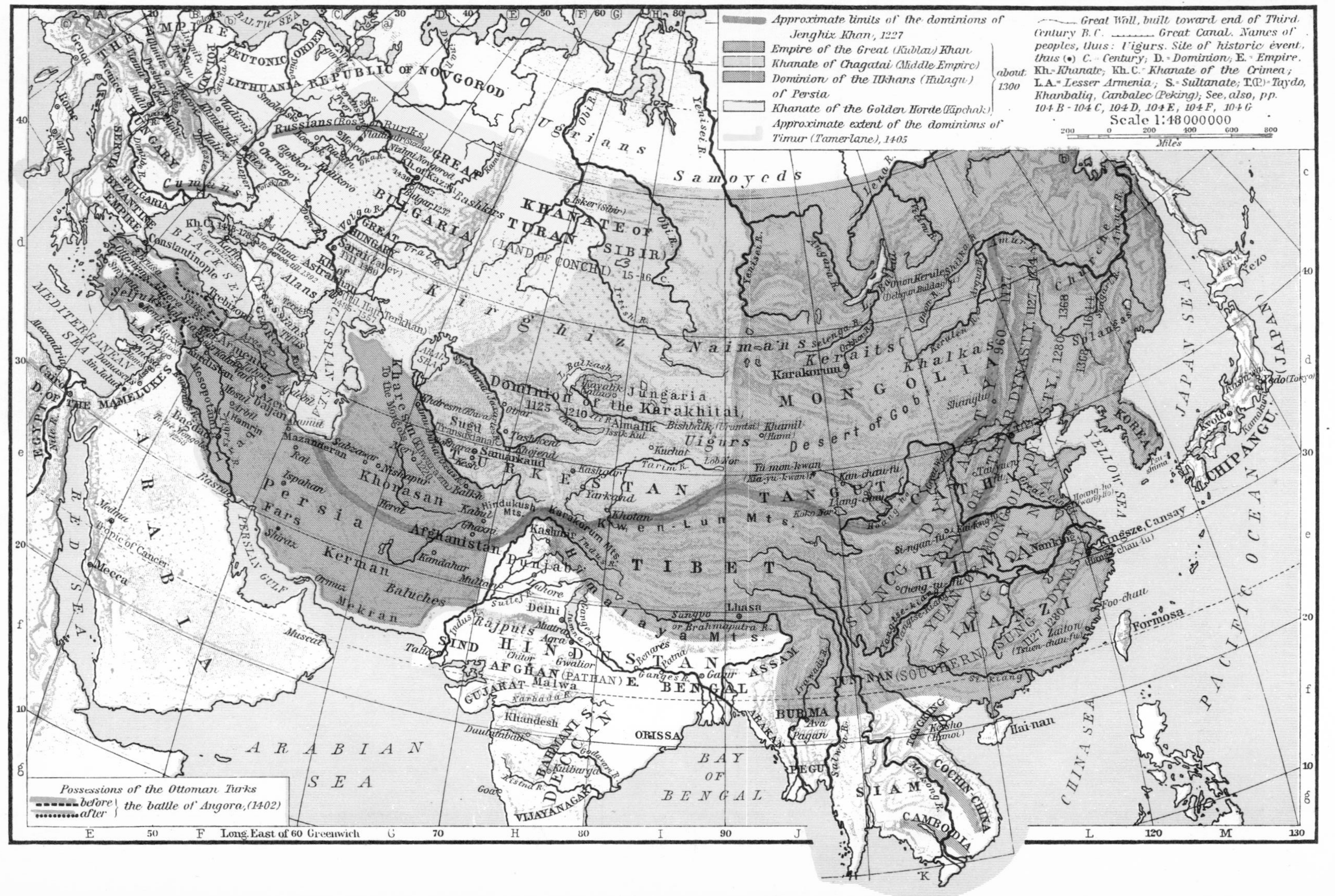
Approximate limits of the dominions of Jenghiz Khan, 1227
Empire of the Great (Kublai) Khan
Khanate of Chagatai (Middle Empire)
Dominion of the Ilkhans (Hulagu) of Persia
Khanate of the Golden Horde (Kipchak)
about 1300
Approximate extent of the dominions of Timur (Tamerlane), 1405
Great Wall, built toward end of Third Century B.C.
Great Canal. Names of peoples, thus: Uigurs. Site of historic event, thus (•) C.= Century; D.= Dominion; E.= Empire. Kh.= Khanate; Kh.C.= Khanate of the Crimea; L.A.= Lesser Armenia; S.= Sultanate; T.(P.)= Taydo, Khanbaliq, Canbalec (Peking); See, also, pp. 104 B - 104 C, 104 D, 104 E, 104 F, 104 G
Scale 1:48 000 000
Miles
Possessions of the Ottoman Turks before / after the battle of Angora (1402)
Long. East of 60 Greenwich
REPUBLIC OF NOVGOROD
LITHUANIA
TEUTONIC ORDER
POLAND
HUNGARY
SERVIA
BULGARIA
BYZANTINE EMPIRE
Cumans
Russians
GREAT BULGARIA
KHANATE OF SIBIR
TURAN (LAND OF CONCHI)
Ugrians
Samoyeds
Kirghiz
Naimans
Keraits
Karakorum
Khalkas
MONGOLIA
Desert of Gobi
Dominion of the Karakhitai 1125 1210
Jungaria
Uigurs
TURKESTAN
TANGUT
TIBET
Kwen-Lun Mts.
Himalaya Mts.
Persia
Khorasan
Afghanistan
Kerman
Fars
Baluches
Mekran
ARABIA
Mecca
Muscat
D. OF THE MAMELUKES
EGYPT
MEDITERRANEAN SEA
BLACK SEA
CASPIAN SEA
PERSIAN GULF
RED SEA
ARABIAN SEA
BAY OF BENGAL
CHINA SEA
YELLOW SEA
JAPAN SEA
PACIFIC OCEAN
SIND
HINDUSTAN
AFGHAN (PATHAN) E.
GUJARAT
Malwa
BENGAL
ASSAM
ORISSA
BAHMANI S.
DECCAN
VIJAYANAGAR
Delhi
Lhasa
BURMA
PEGU
SIAM
CAMBODIA
COCHIN-CHINA
TONGKING
YUN NAN
MANZI
SUNG (SOUTHERN) DYNASTY
KOREA
CHIPANGU (JAPAN)
Yedo (Tokyo)
Yezo
Formosa
Hai-nan
Kingsze, Cansay

The Ottoman Empire 1451 - 1481

KINGDOM OF HUNGARY
MOLDAVIA
KHANATE OF CRIMEA
SEA OF AZOV
Tartars
WALLACHIA
BOSNIA 1463
Herzego-vina 1463/83
Montenegro
Rep. of Ragusa
SERVIA 1459
Bulgaria
Dobruja
BLACK SEA
OTTOMAN EMPIRE
Rumelia
Macedonia 1389
Thessaly 1393
BYZANTINE EMPIRE Constantinople 1453
EMPIRE OF TREBIZOND 1462
KARAMAN 1466
DUCHY OF NAXOS
Knights of St. John
Rhodes
KINGDOM OF CYPRUS
DOMINION OF THE CIRCASSIAN MAMELUKES
Diarbekr
Crete
DESP. OF ROMANIA (EPIRUS)
Cephalonia Under the Tocci 1479

Remnant of the Byzantine Empire and its dependencies in the Morea (Peloponnesus) (in 1451)	Albania under George Castriota (Scanderbeg) [1443-1468	Dominions of the Ottoman Turks acquired between 1451 and 1481
Greek Empire of Trebizond (in 1451)	States under Latin rule (in 1451)	D.-Duchy; Desp.-Despotat; Rep.-Republic
Servia (in 1451)	Venetian possessions (in 1451)	*The dates are those of acquisition by the Turks* × *Battle*
Bosnia, Herzegovina, Montenegro (in 1451)	Genoese possessions (in 1451)	
	Dominion of the Circassian Mamelukes (in 1451)	
	Dominions of the Ottoman Turks (in 1451)	

Scale 1:15000000 — 100 0 100 200 Miles

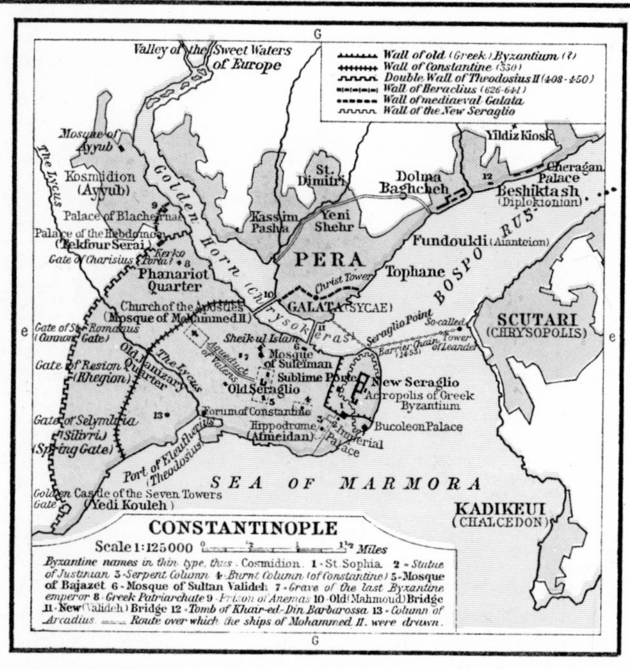

Ecclesiastical Map of Wes

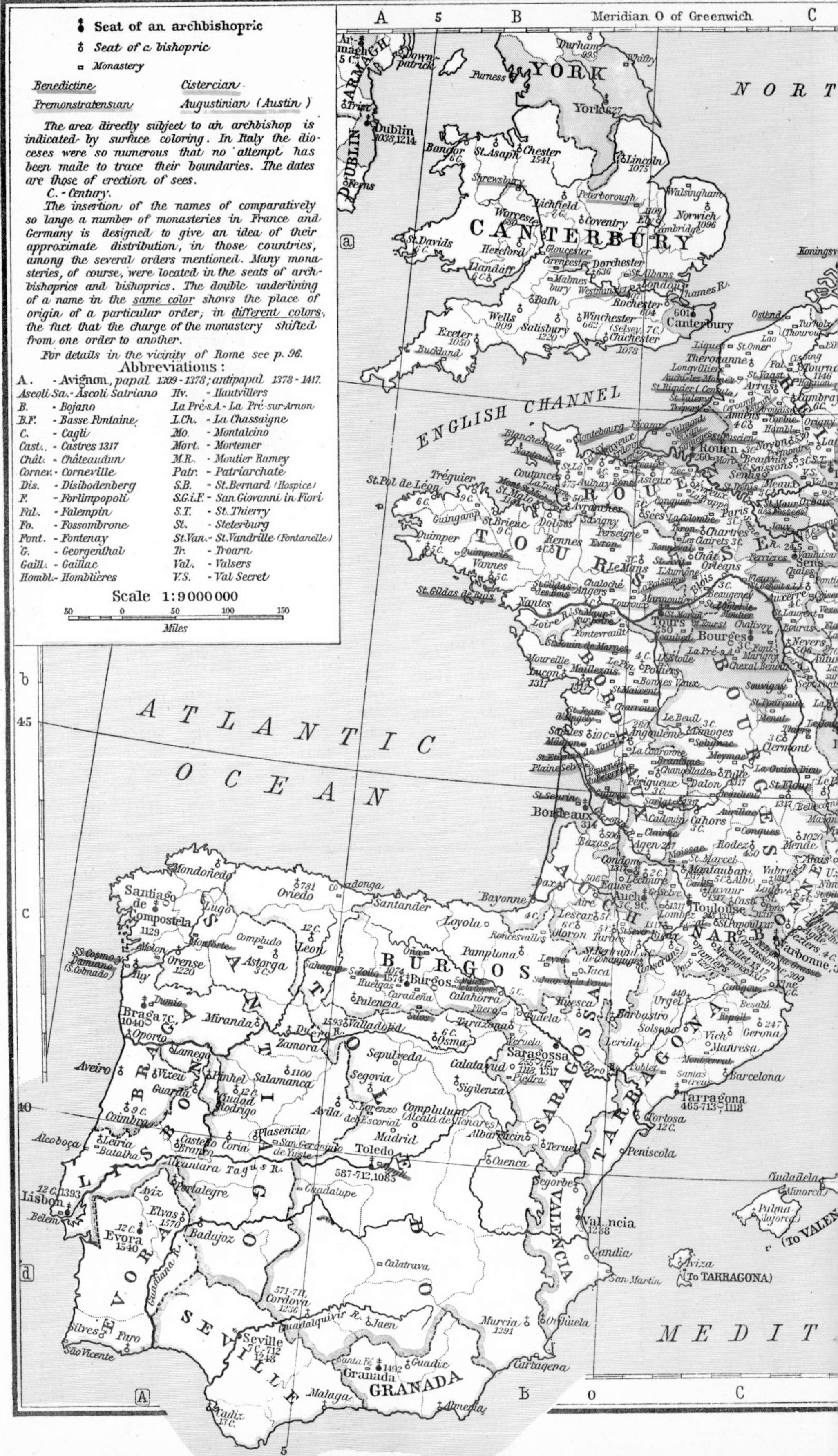

BALTIC SEA

LUND

BREMEN

MAGDEBURG

Bishopric of the Pomeranians

GNESEN

RIGA

TO GNESEN about 1200

COLOGNE

MAYENCE

TO MAYENCE

PRAGUE, after 1344

SALZBURG

GRAN

KALOCSA

BESANÇON

TARENTAISE

AQUILEIA

MILAN

RAVENNA

GENOA

EMBRUN

SPALATO

ZARA

ADRIATIC SEA

RAGUSA

ROME

TO GENOA

TO PISA

TORRES

ORISTANO

CAGLIARI

SIPONTO 1034

NAZARETH

TRANI

BARI

BRINDISI

OTRANTO

TARANTO

CATTARO

ANTIVARI (BAR)

DURAZZO (DURES)

CAPUA

BENEVENTO

CONZA

NAPLES

SORRENTO

AMALFI

SALERNO

ACERENZA

ROSSANO

COSENZA

S. SEVERINA

REGGIO

MESSINA

PALERMO

MONREALE

MEDITERRANEAN SEA

Plan of Rome in the Middle Ages. The Roman Suburbicarian Bishoprics.

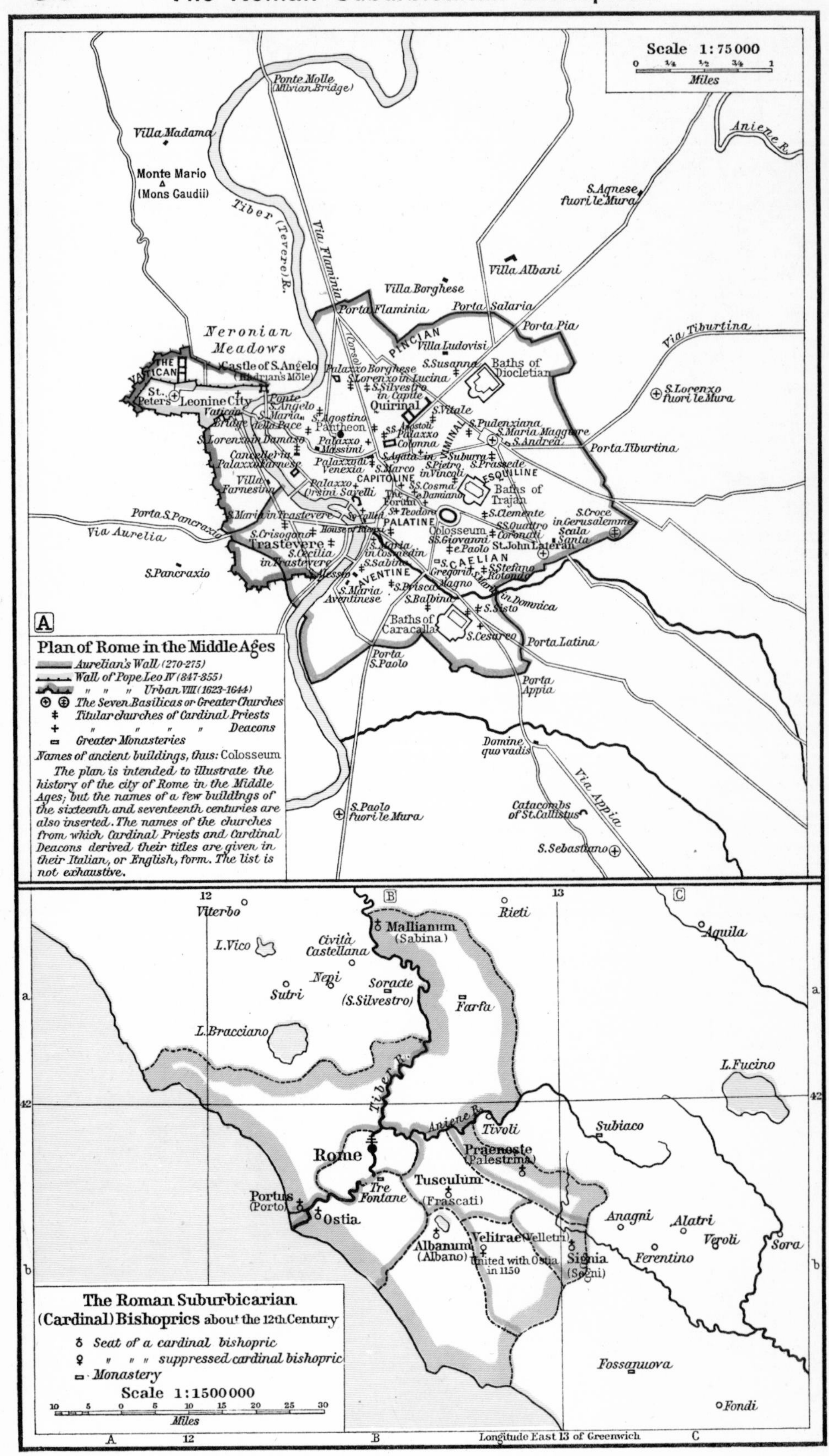

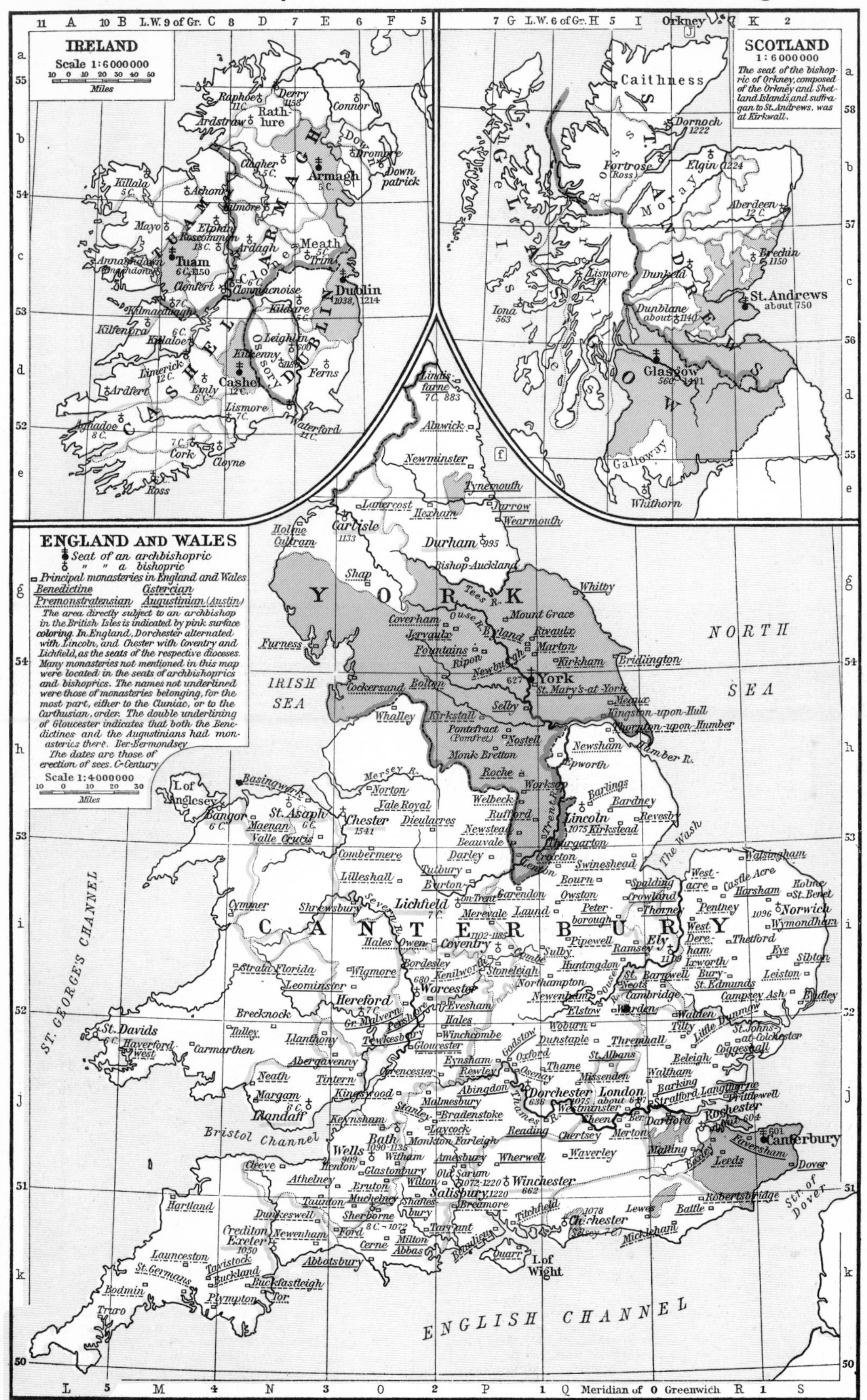
IRELAND
Scale 1:6000000
Miles
SCOTLAND
1:6000000
The seat of the bishopric of Orkney, composed of the Orkney and Shetland Islands and suffragan to St. Andrews, was at Kirkwall.
ENGLAND AND WALES
Seat of an archbishopric
" " a bishopric
Principal monasteries in England and Wales
Benedictine
Cistercian
Premonstratensian
Augustinian (Austin)
The area directly subject to an archbishop in the British Isles is indicated by pink surface coloring. In England, Dorchester alternated with Lincoln, and Chester with Coventry and Lichfield, as the seats of the respective dioceses. Many monasteries not mentioned in this map were located in the seats of archbishoprics and bishoprics. The names not underlined were those of monasteries belonging, for the most part, either to the Cluniac, or to the Carthusian, order. The double underlining of Gloucester indicates that both the Benedictines and the Augustinians had monasteries there. Ber.=Bermondsey
The dates are those of erection of sees. C=Century
Scale 1:4000000
Miles
Armagh
Dublin
Tuam
Cashel
York
Canterbury
St. Andrews
Glasgow
NORTH SEA
IRISH SEA
ST. GEORGE'S CHANNEL
Bristol Channel
ENGLISH CHANNEL
Str. of Dover
L.W. 9 of Gr.
L.W. 6 of Gr.
Meridian of 0 Greenwich

1: 10 000 000
IRISH SEA
GERMAN OCEAN
SEA OF ENGLAND OR WEST SEA (NORTH SEA)
ENGLISH CHANNEL
ATLANTIC OCEAN
SEA OF ROCHELLE (BAY OF BISCAY)
MITERETANE
IRELAND
SCOTLAND
ENGLAND
NORWAY
FRANCE
THE EMPIRE
SPAIN
PORTUGAL
ALPS
ITALY
APENNINES
PYRENEES MTS.
ATLAS MTS.
MAGRIB
AFRICA
CORSICA
SARDINIA
SICILY
Balearic Is.
Areas of relatively dense population
" " moderate sized "
Land routes (by navigable rivers, also)
Mongol Baltic trade route
Sea routes
" " of the Hanseatic League (Hansa)
" " " " Venetians
" " " " Genoese
In possession, also, of most of the commerce in the Black Sea.
Lübeck Centres of the Hanseatic League
Bergen Foreign offices of the " "
Soest Cities belonging to " " "
Dieppe Foreign cities in which the Hanseatic League, or any of its members, possessed trading privileges
Principal markets and fairs
Alpine passes
Roman missionary archbishopric
" " bishopric
Nestorian metropolitanate
in the fourteenth century
Fland.-Flanders
Thour.-Thourout
Mediaeval names in hair-line, thus: MITERETANE, Bambilonia. Names of peoples, thus: Bashkirs
See, also, pp. 102-103, 104 B-104 C and 104 G
Scale 1 : 20 000 000
Miles

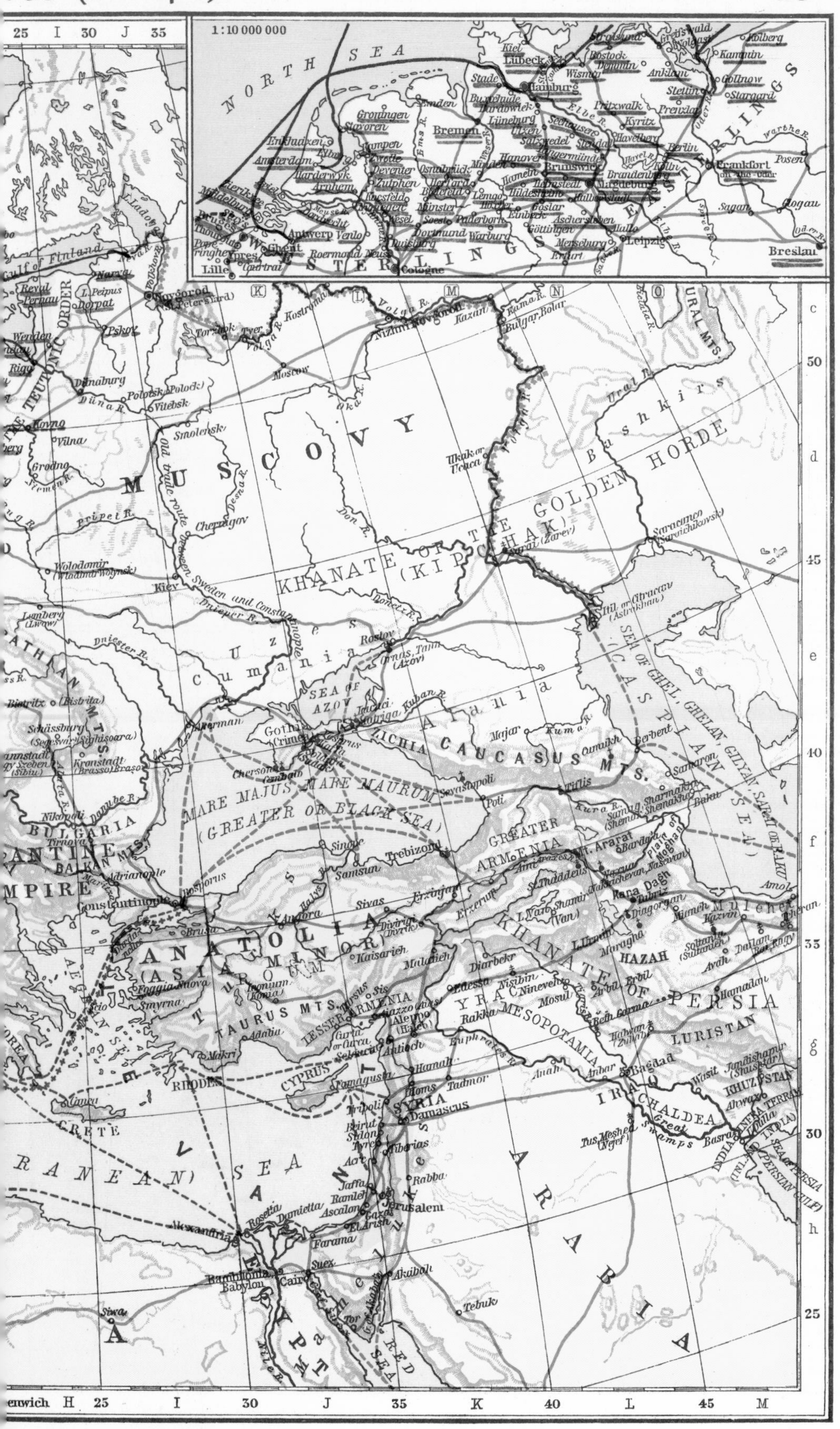
1:10 000 000
NORTH SEA
STERLINGS
EASTERLINGS
Kiel
Lübeck
Stralsund
Greifswald
Wolgast
Kolberg
Rostock
Demmin
Wismar
Anklam
Kammin
Stade
Hamburg
Gollnow
Stettin
Stargard
Buxtehude
Bardowiek
Pritzwalk
Prenzlau
Groningen
Stavoren
Emden
Bremen
Lüneburg
Uelzen
Seehausen
Kyritz
Enkhuizen
Kampen
Salzwedel
Stendal
Havelberg
Berlin
Amsterdam
Elburg
Zwolle
Deventer
Osnabrück
Minden
Hanover
Tangermünde
Brunswick
Kölln
Frankfort on the Oder
Posen
Harderwyk
Arnheim
Zutphen
Herford
Hameln
Hildesheim
Brandenburg
Magdeburg
Lemgo
Goslar
Halberstadt
Coesfeld
Bielefeld
Münster
Einbeck
Aschersleben
Sagan
Glogau
Wesel
Soest
Paderborn
Göttingen
Halle
Antwerp
Venlo
Dortmund
Warburg
Merseburg
Leipzig
Bruges
Ypres
Ghent
Roermond
Neuss
Duisburg
Erfurt
Breslau
Lille
Courtrai
Cologne
Gulf of Finland
Narva
Reval
Pernau
L. Peipus
Dorpat
Novgorod
(St. Petersburg)
Pskov
Torzhok
Tver
Volga R.
Nizhni Novgorod
Kazan
Kama R.
Bulgar, Bolar
URAL MTS.
Wenden
Riga
TEUTONIC ORDER
Dünaburg
Düna R.
Polotsk
Vitebsk
Moscow
Oka R.
Kovno
Vilna
Smolensk
Grodno
Niemen R.
MUSCOVY
Old trade route
Desna R.
Chernigov
Don R.
Ural R.
Bashkirs
KHANATE OF THE GOLDEN HORDE
KHANATE OF THE GOLDEN HORDE (KIPCHAK)
Ukak or Uvica
Saraicinco (Saraichikovsk)
Sarai (Zarev)
Pripet R.
Wolodomir (Wladimir Wolynsk)
Kiev
Between Sweden and Constantinople
Dnieper R.
Lemberg (Lwow)
Itil or Citracan (Astrakhan)
Dniester R.
Donetz R.
Rostov
Cumania
Uzes
Tana (Azov)
SEA OF GHEL, GHELAN, GILYAN, SARAI OR BAKU (CASPIAN SEA)
SEA OF AZOV
Alania
Bistritz (Bistrita)
Schässburg (Segesvar) (Sighisoara)
Kronstadt (Brasso) Brasov
Akkerman
Gothia (Crimea)
Kuban R.
ZICHIA
Majar
Kuma R.
Derbent
CAUCASUS MTS.
Chersonese
Sevastopoli
Tiflis
Samaron
Nikopoli
Danube R.
BULGARIA
Tirnova
MARE MAJUS, MARE MAURUM (GREATER OR BLACK SEA)
Poti
Kura R.
Shamakha
BALKAN MTS.
Adrianople
Sinope
Samsun
Trebizond
GREATER ARMENIA
Mt. Ararat
Bardah
Amol
Bosporus
Constantinople
Sivas
Erzinjan
Erzerum
Rana Dagh
Tabriz
Teheran
Angora
Brusa
ANATOLIA (ASIA MINOR)
RUM
Kaisarieh
Divrigi
L. Van
Dingorgan
Kazvin
Mulehet
KHANATE OF PERSIA
Maragha
HAZAH
Sultanieh
Dailam
Malatieh
Diarbekr
Foggia Nuova
Iconium (Konia)
Edessa
Nisibin
Nineveh
Mosul
Arbil, Erbil
Hamadan
Smyrna
TAURUS MTS.
LESSER ARMENIA
YRAC
Rakka
MESOPOTAMIA
Aleppo (Haleb)
LURISTAN
Adalia
Antioch
Euphrates R.
Beth Garma
Hulwan
Makri
RHODES
CYPRUS
Famagusta
Hamah
Anah
Anbar
Bagdad
Wasit
Jundishapur (Shushtar)
KHUZISTAN
Tadmor
Homs
IRAQ
CRETE
Tripoli
SYRIA
Damascus
CHALDEA
Ahwaz
Beirut
Sidon
Tyre
Tiberias
Tus, Meshed (Nejef)
Great Swamps
Basra
Acre
Jaffa
Ramleh
Rabba
Ascalon
Gaza
Jerusalem
El Arish
ARABIA
Alexandria
Rosetta
Damietta
Farama
Suez
Akabah
Cairo
Babylon
EGYPT
Tebuk
Tor
RED SEA
Siwa
Nile R.
Greenwich H 25 I 30 J 35 K 40 L 45 M
c d e f g h
50 45 40 35 30 25

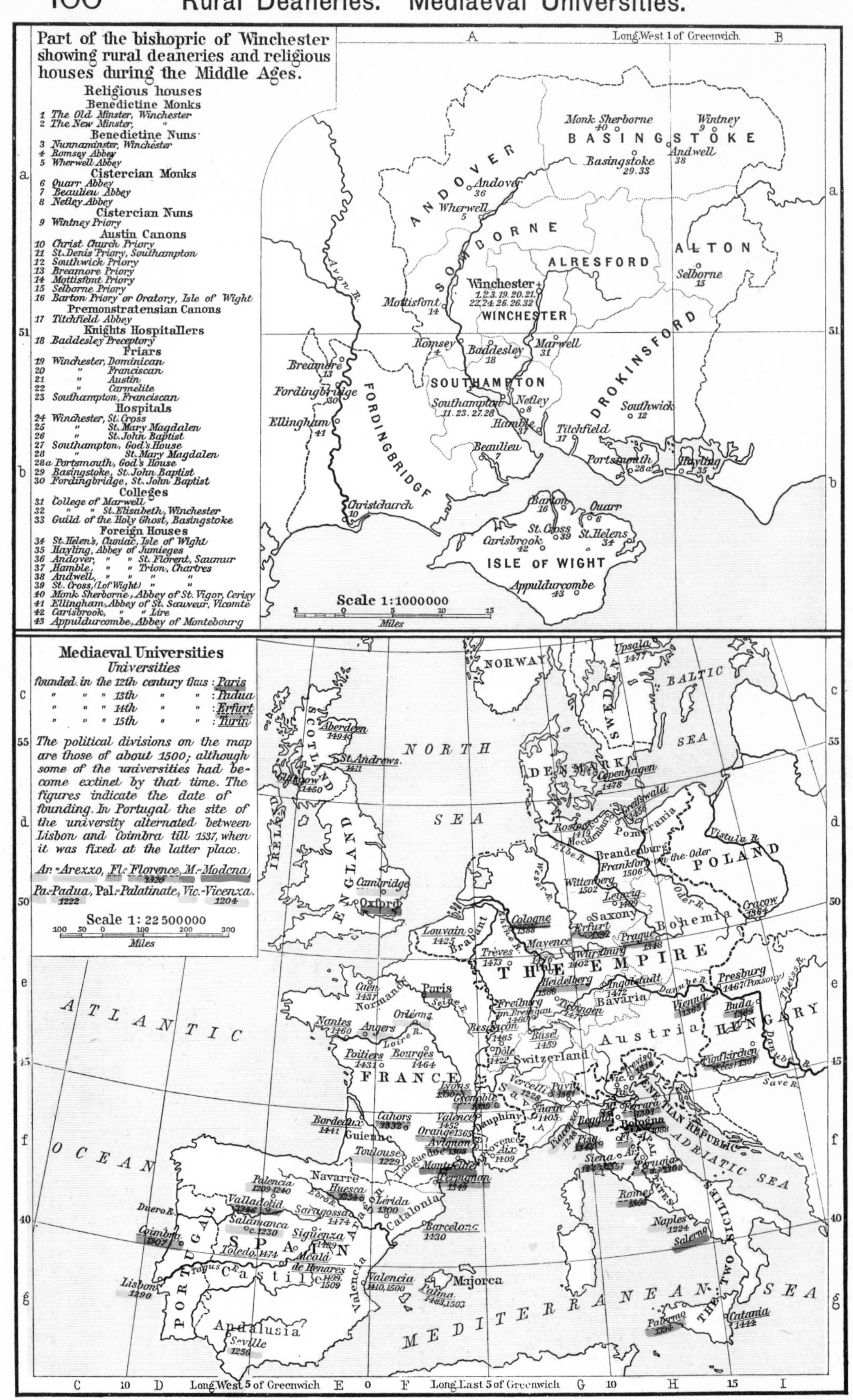
Part of the bishopric of Winchester showing rural deaneries and religious houses during the Middle Ages.
Religious houses
Benedictine Monks
1 The Old Minster, Winchester
2 The New Minster, "
Benedictine Nuns
3 Nunnaminster, Winchester
4 Romsey Abbey
5 Wherwell Abbey
Cistercian Monks
6 Quarr Abbey
7 Beaulieu Abbey
8 Netley Abbey
Cistercian Nuns
9 Wintney Priory
Austin Canons
10 Christ Church Priory
11 St. Denis Priory, Southampton
12 Southwick Priory
13 Breamore Priory
14 Mottisfont Priory
15 Selborne Priory
16 Barton Priory or Oratory, Isle of Wight
Premonstratensian Canons
17 Titchfield Abbey
Knights Hospitallers
18 Baddesley Preceptory
Friars
19 Winchester, Dominican
20 " Franciscan
21 " Austin
22 " Carmelite
23 Southampton, Franciscan
Hospitals
24 Winchester, St. Cross
25 " St. Mary Magdalen
26 " St. John Baptist
27 Southampton, God's House
28 " St. Mary Magdalen
28a Portsmouth, God's House
29 Basingstoke, St. John Baptist
30 Fordingbridge, St. John Baptist
Colleges
31 College of Marwell
32 " " St. Elisabeth, Winchester
33 Guild of the Holy Ghost, Basingstoke
Foreign Houses
34 St. Helen's, Cluniac, Isle of Wight
35 Hayling, Abbey of Jumieges
36 Andover, " " St. Florent, Saumur
37 Hamble, " " Trion, Chartres
38 Andwell, " " "
39 St. Cross, (I. of Wight) " " "
40 Monk Sherborne, Abbey of St. Vigor, Cerisy
41 Ellingham, Abbey of St. Sauveur, Vicomte
42 Carisbrook, " " Lire
43 Appuldurcombe, Abbey of Montebourg
Long. West 1 of Greenwich
BASINGSTOKE
ANDOVER
SOMBORNE
ALRESFORD
ALTON
WINCHESTER
DROKINSFORD
SOUTHAMPTON
FORDINGBRIDGE
ISLE OF WIGHT
Scale 1:1000000
Miles
Mediaeval Universities
Universities
founded in the 12th century thus: Paris
" " " 13th " " : Padua
" " " 14th " " : Erfurt
" " " 15th " " : Turin
The political divisions on the map are those of about 1500; although some of the universities had become extinct by that time. The figures indicate the date of founding. In Portugal the site of the university alternated between Lisbon and Coimbra till 1537, when it was fixed at the latter place.
Ar.=Arezzo, Fl.=Florence, M.=Modena, Pa.=Padua, Pal.=Palatinate, Vic.=Vicenza.
Scale 1: 22 500000
Miles
NORTH SEA
ATLANTIC OCEAN
MEDITERRANEAN SEA
BALTIC SEA
ADRIATIC SEA
SCOTLAND
ENGLAND
IRELAND
NORWAY
SWEDEN
DENMARK
POLAND
HUNGARY
FRANCE
SPAIN
PORTUGAL
THE EMPIRE
Long. West 5 of Greenwich
Long. East 5 of Greenwich

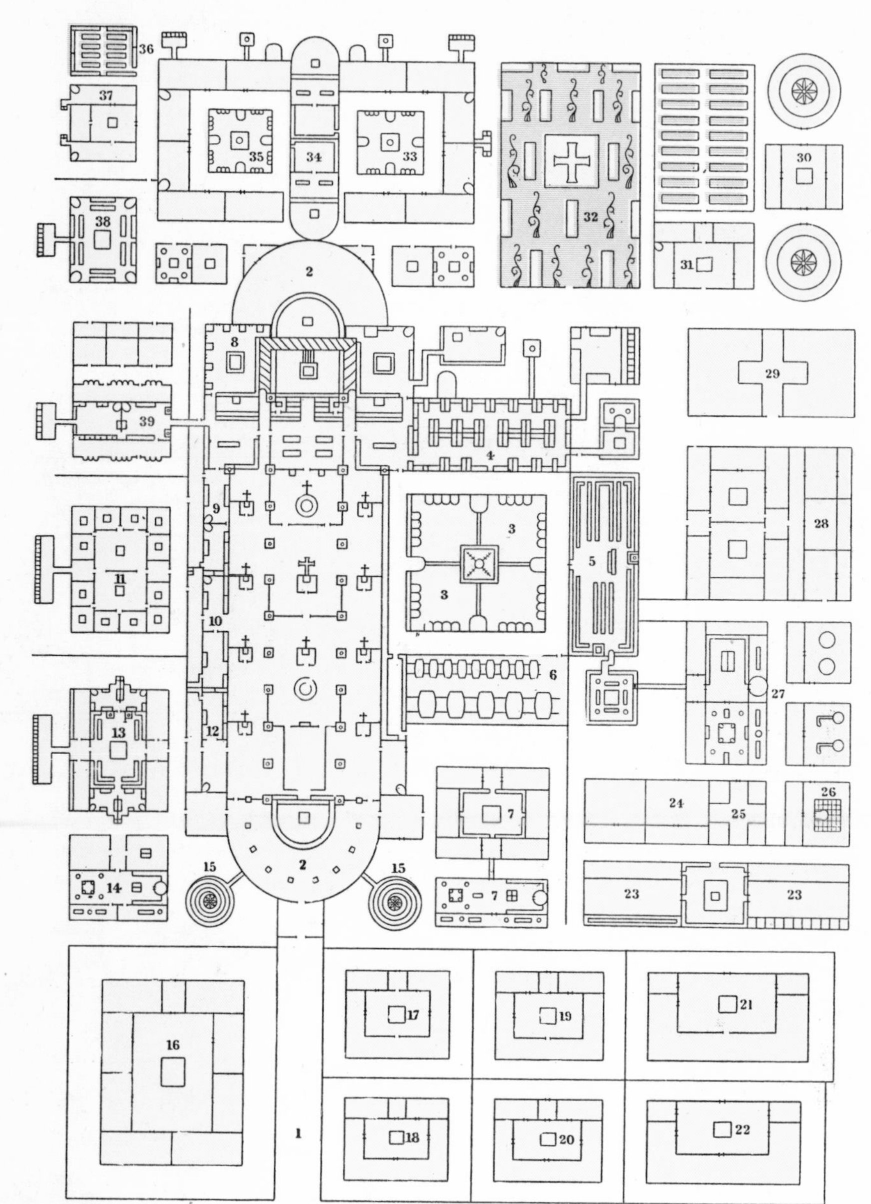

Explanation

This ground-plan is a reduced copy from the ninth century original preserved in the present monastery library. It represents an ideal Benedictine house, and was probably not carried out in complete detail. The enclosure, surrounded by a wall, was about four hundred feet long by about three hundred wide. - 1. *Entrance to the church from outside the walls.* 2. *Church with two apses and numerous altars.* 3. *Main cloister, showing arches.* 4. *Dormitory above; room with heating apparatus below.* 5. *Refectory below; wardrobe above.* 6. *Cellar with storehouses above.* 7. *House for pilgrims and poor travellers, with brewery and bakery adjoining.* 8. *Writing-room below; library above.* 9. *Living-room and dormitory for visiting monks.* 10. *Schoolmaster's lodging.* 11. *School-room for ordinary pupils with lodgings for the teachers.* 12. *Porter's lodge.* 13. *Quarters for guests of quality.* 14. *Brewery and bakery belonging to* 13. 15. *Towers with spiral staircases, overlooking the whole place.* 16. *Large building of unknown use.* 17. *Sheep-stall.* 18. *Servants' quarters.* 19. *Goat-stall with goatherds' quarters.* 20. *Swine-stall with swineherds' quarters.* 21. *Cattle-shed with cowherds' quarters.* 22. *Horse-barn with grooms' quarters.* 23. *Stable for mares and oxen with hay-lofts above and quarters for servants in the middle.* 24. *Workshops of coopers and turners.* 25. *Storehouse for brewery-grain.* 26. *Fruit-drying house.* 27. *Brewery and bakery for the resident monks, showing mortars and hand-mills.* 28. *Workshops of shoemakers, saddlers, sword and shield-makers, carvers, tanners, goldsmiths, blacksmiths, fullers.* 29. *Granary and threshing-floor.* 30. *House of poultry-keeper; hen-house and goose-pen adjoining.* 31. *House of the gardener; kitchen-garden adjoining. The original gives names of vegetables on the several beds.* 32. *Burying-ground.* 33. *Cloister and living-rooms of the "oblati" and their teacher, and of convalescents.* 34. *Church for the novices and the ill.* 35. *Cloister and living-rooms, especially for the seriously ill.* 36. *Hospital-garden.* 37. *Physician's quarters, apothecary-shop and rooms for patients.* 38. *Additional building for surgical purposes.* 39. *Abbot's house, showing entrance to church and to main cloister.*

Mediaeval Indus

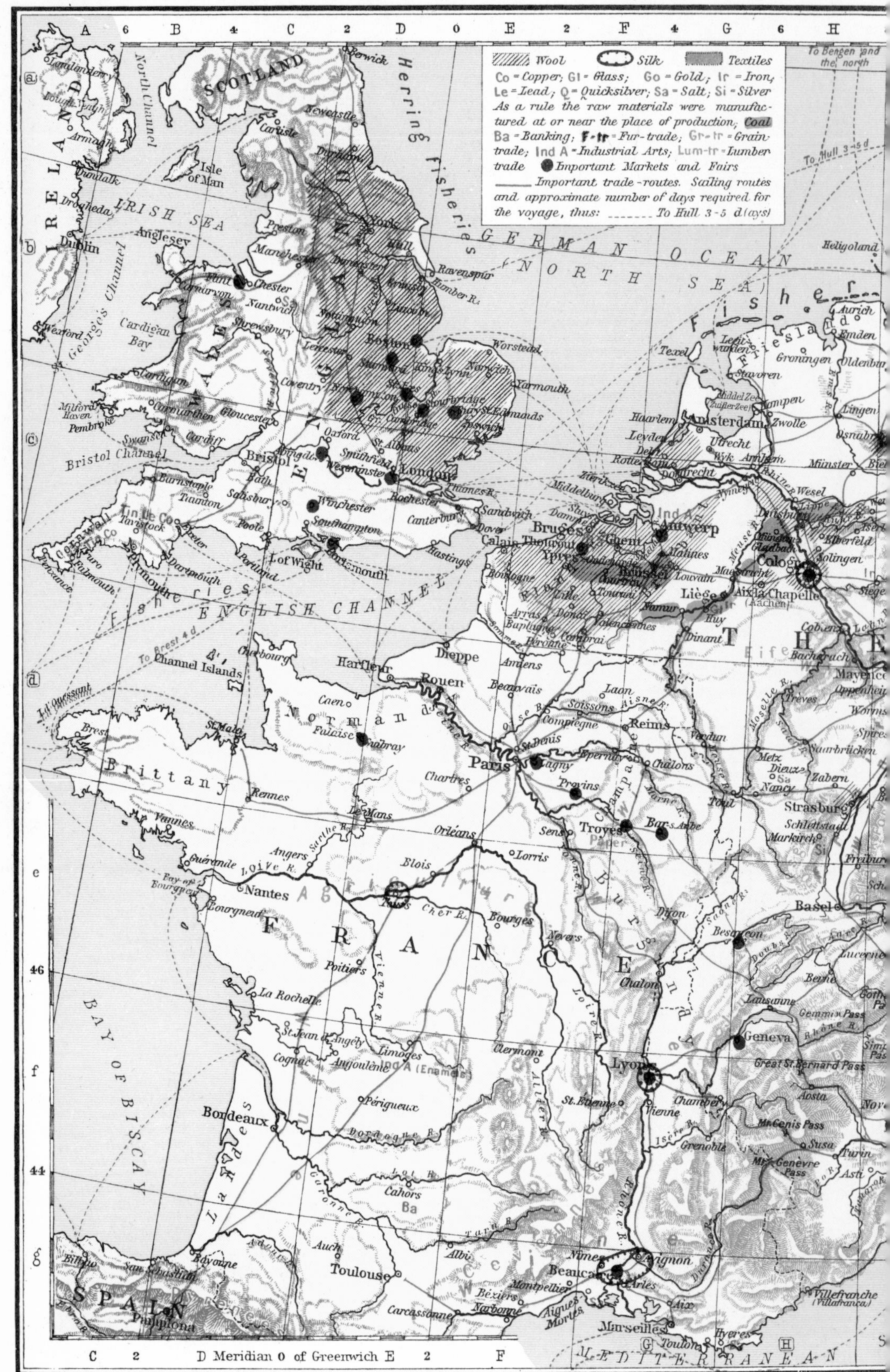

Scale 1: 7000000

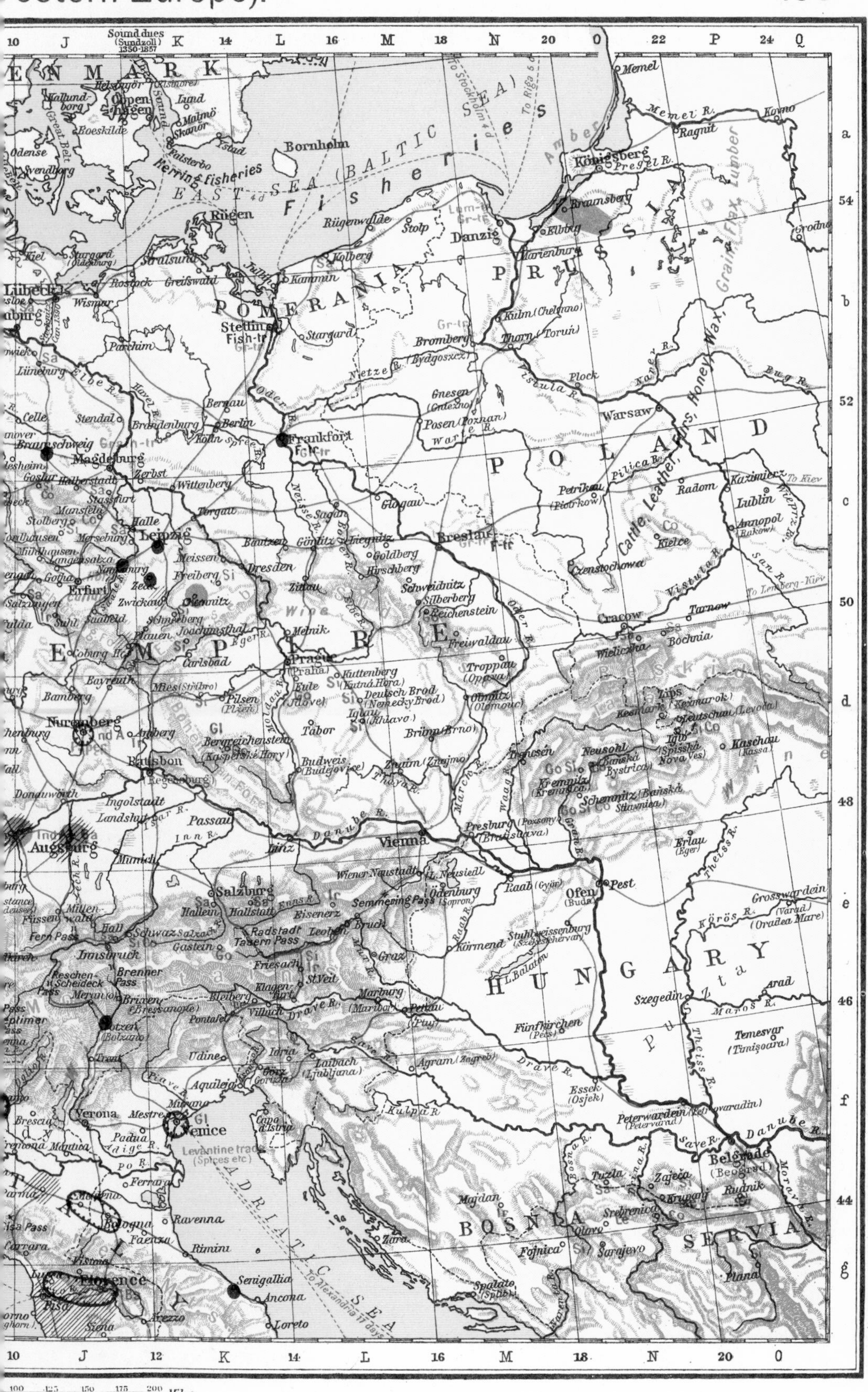

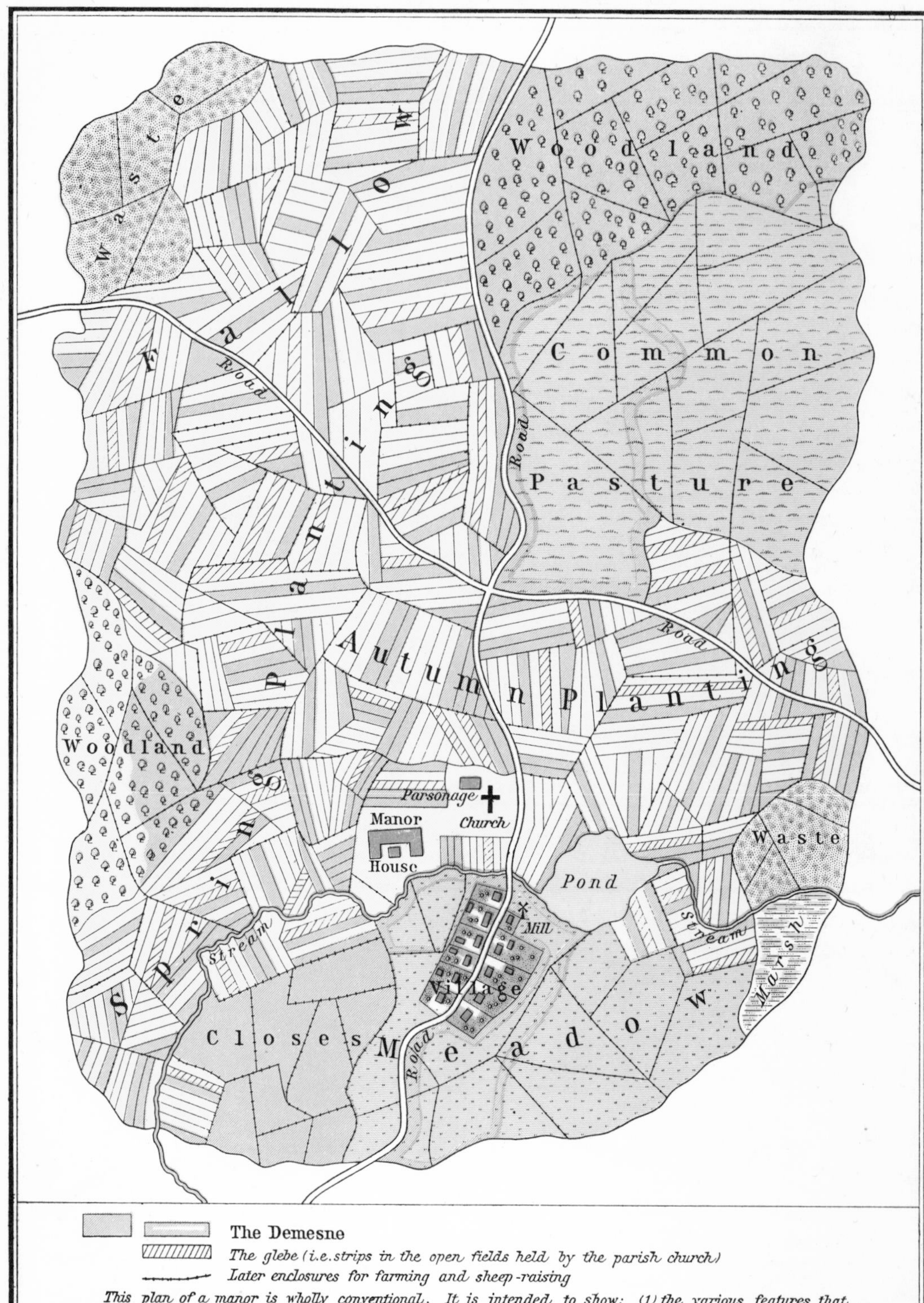

The Demesne

The glebe (i.e. strips in the open fields held by the parish church)

Later enclosures for farming and sheep-raising

This plan of a manor is wholly conventional. It is intended to show: (1) the various features that might be found in English manors (or vills) of the mediaeval period; (2) the more important changes in the agricultural system which occurred in England from the fourteenth century onward. Many of these manorial features, of course, appeared in similar domains on the continent.

Enfranchisement of Mediaeval Towns: Expansion of the Charter of Beaumont-en-Argonne, 1182—1300.

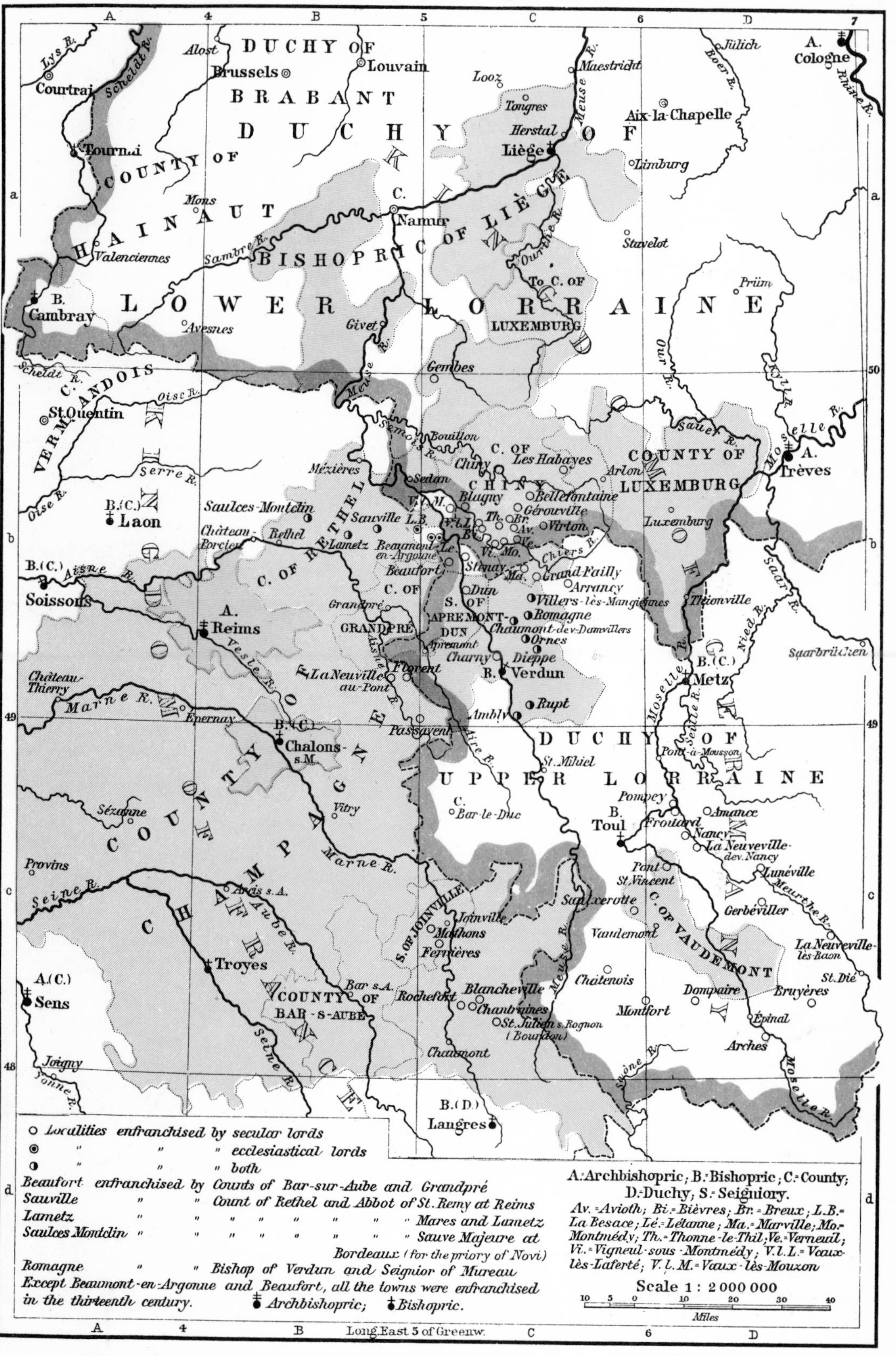

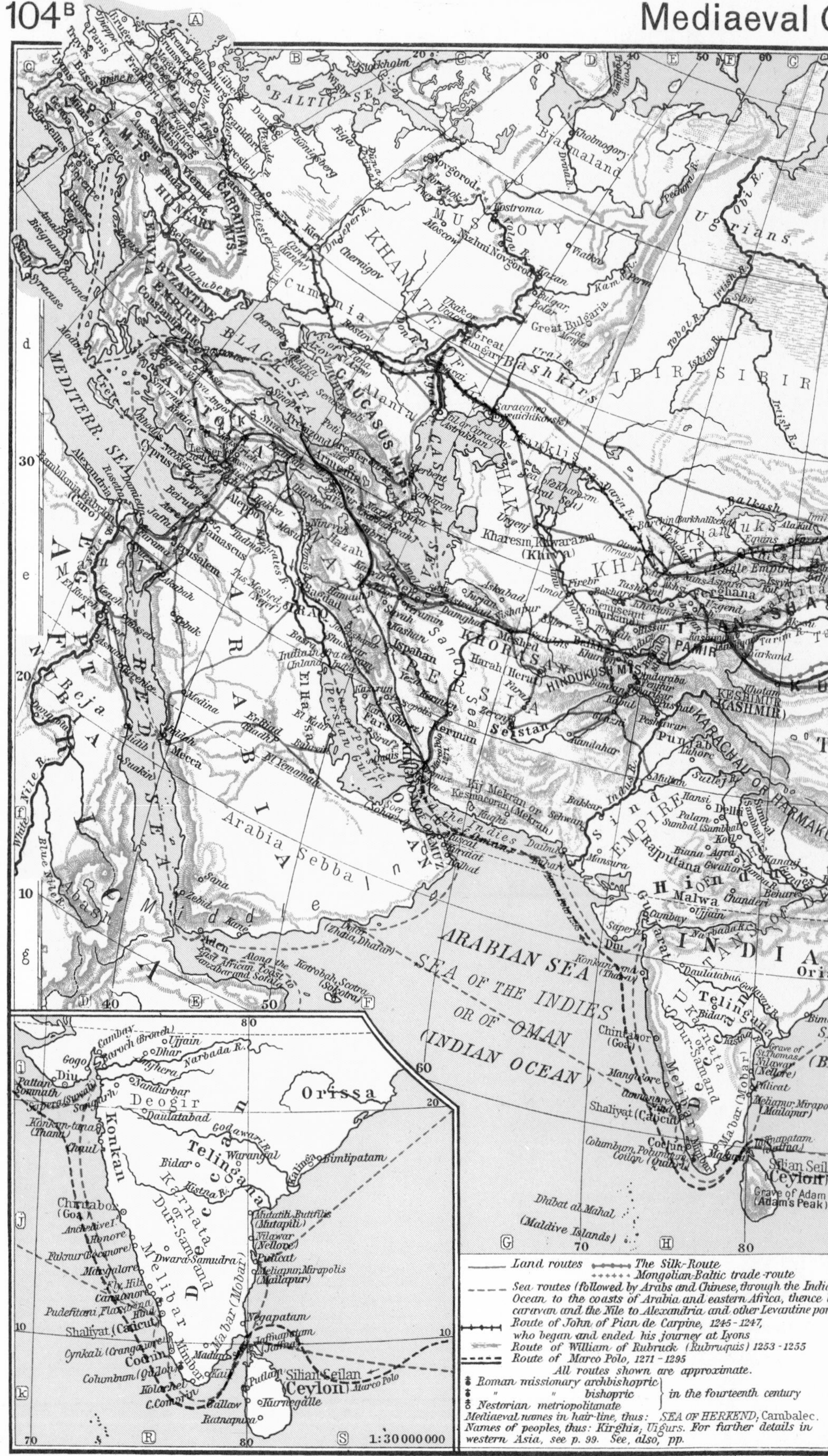

Scale 1:40 000 000

JAPAN SEA
ZIPANGU OR CHIPANGU
JAPAN (NIPPON)
YELLOW SEA
PACIFIC OCEAN
SEA OF CHIN
SEA OF SANDJY (CHINA SEA)
SEA OF THE INDIAN ISLANDS
SURROUNDING SEA
MANCHURIA
KHINGAN MTS.
Great Desert
Desert of Gobi
SIAM
CAMBODIA OR KHMER
CHAMPE
Borneo
Java
Yezo
Hondo
Kyushu
Shikoku
Hai-nan
Palawan
Spice Islands (Moluccas)
Celebes
Sumatra
Flores
Greenwich
Miles

Europe in 1490.

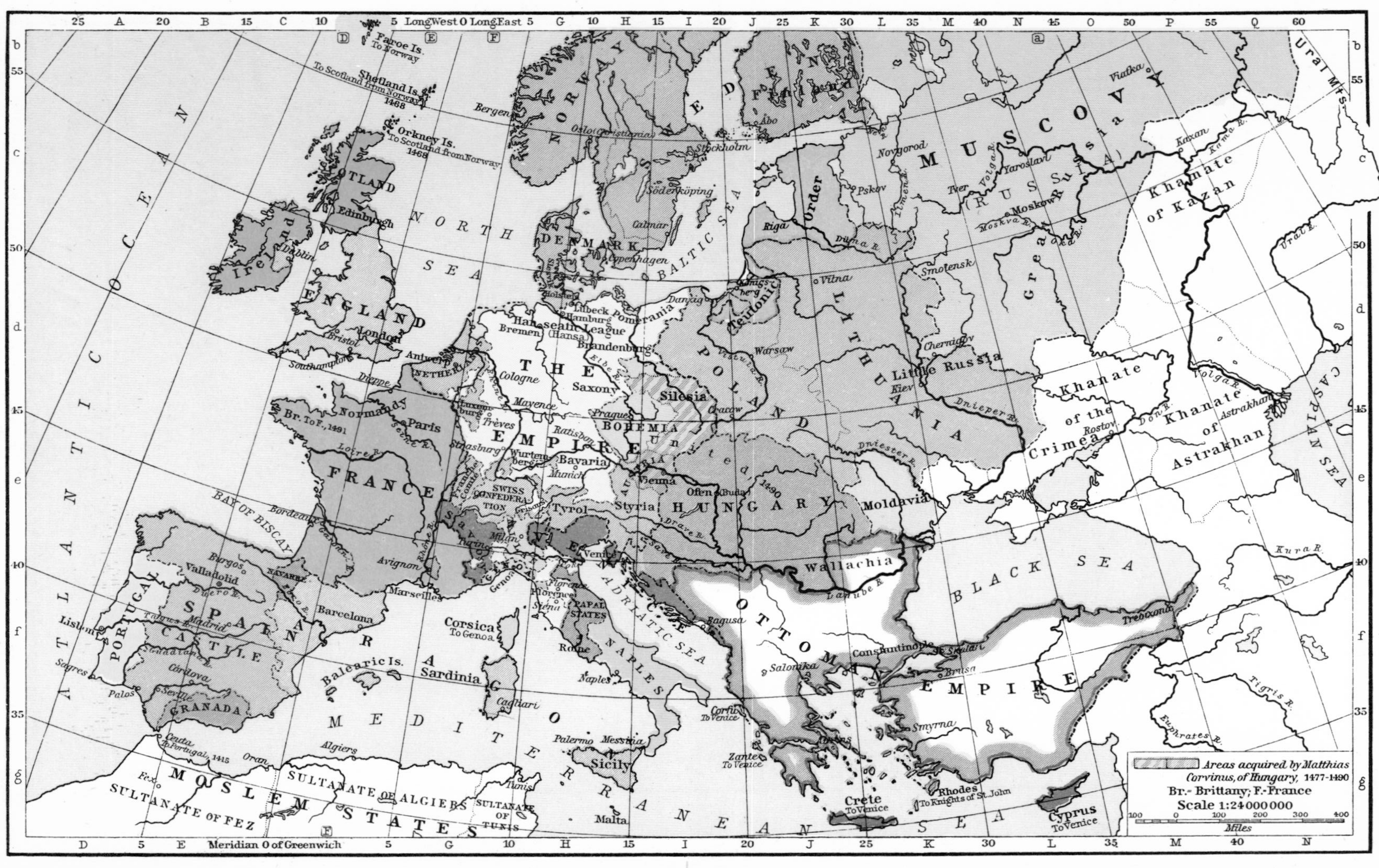

The Portuguese Colonial Dominions in India and the Malay Archipelago, 1498—1580.

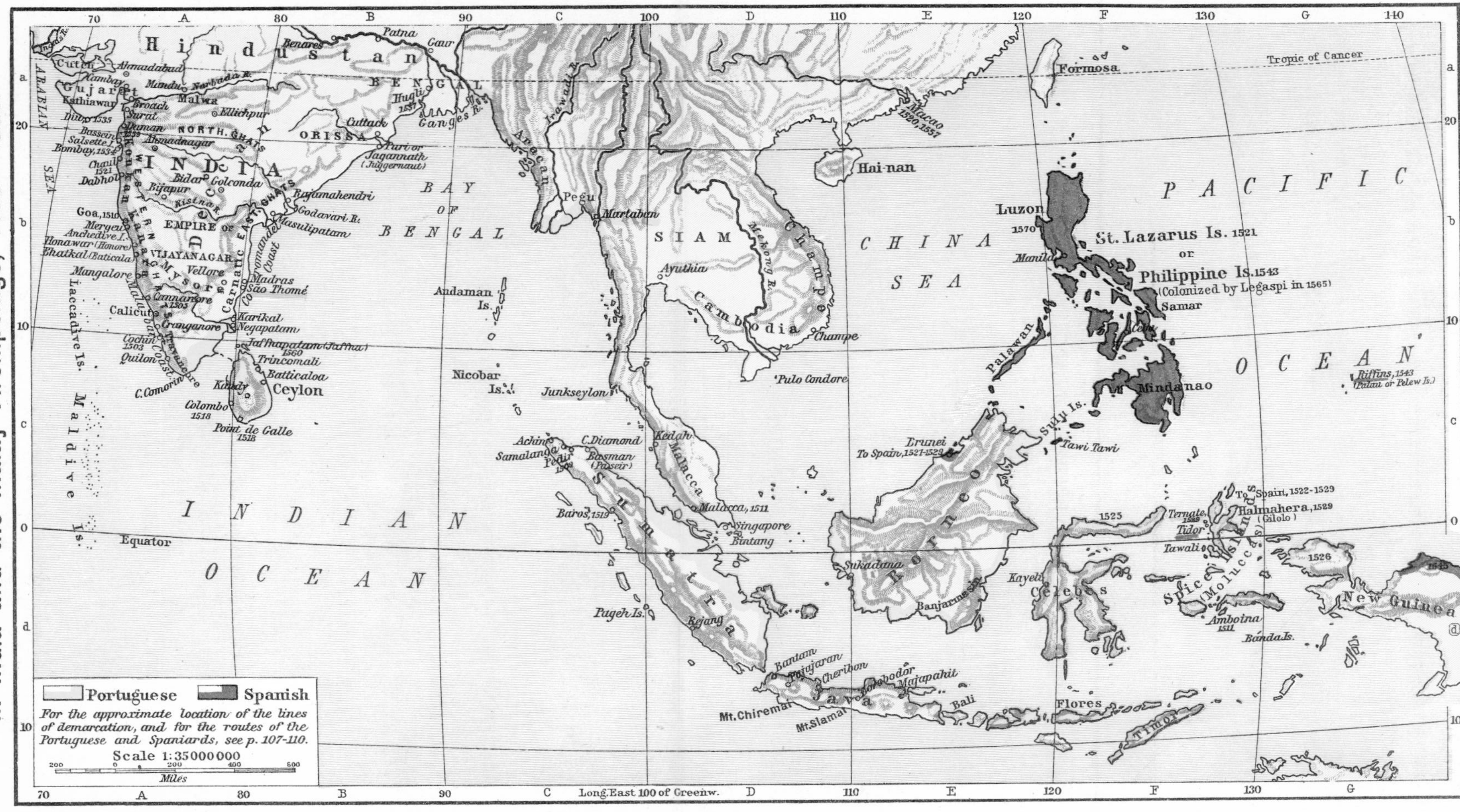

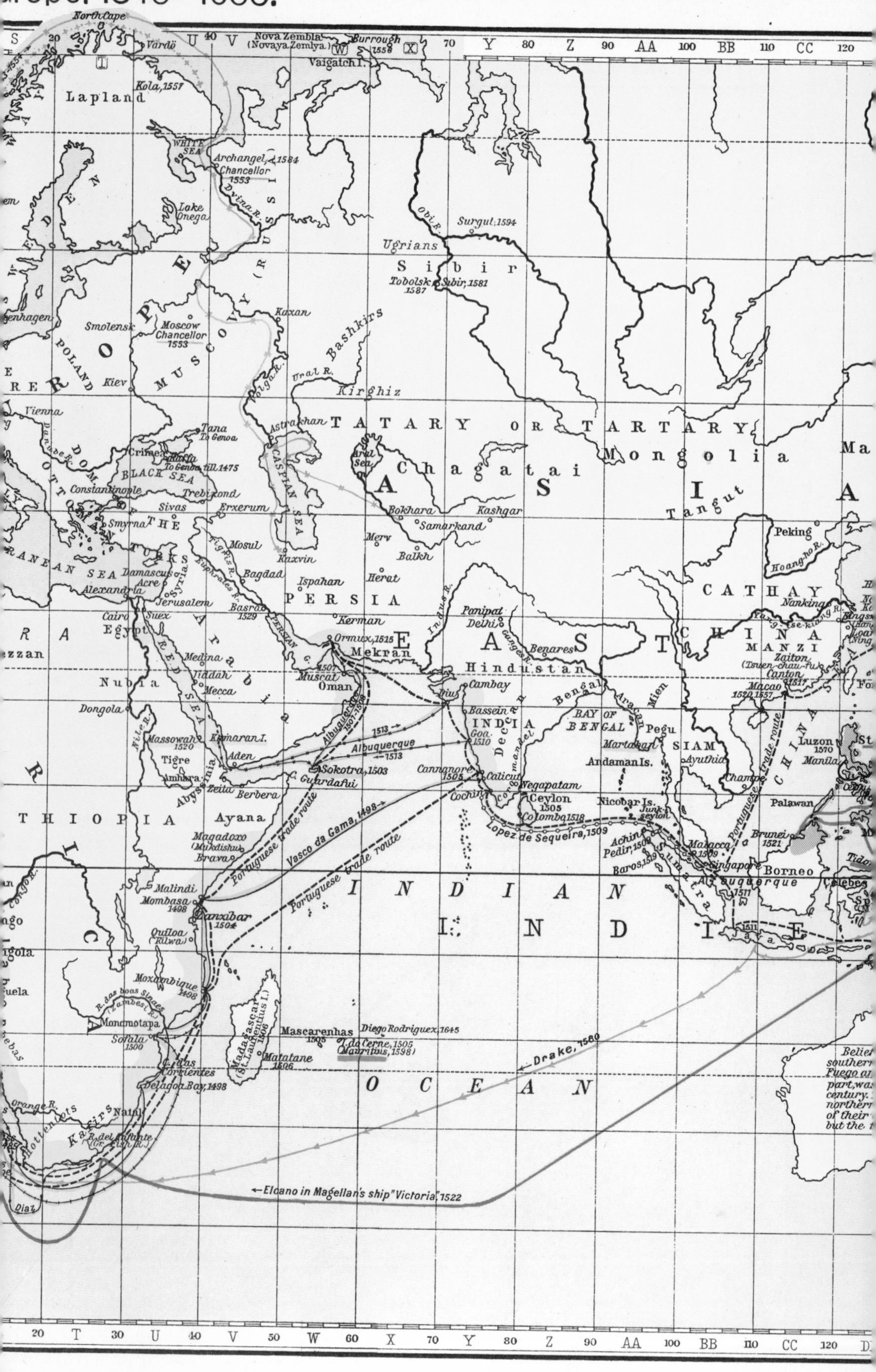

North Cape
Vardö
Nova Zembla (Novaya Zemlya)
Burrough 1558
Vaigatch I.
Kola, 1557
Lapland
WHITE SEA
Archangel, 1584
Chancellor 1553
Dvina R.
Lake Onega
S W E D E N
Copenhagen
Smolensk
Moscow Chancellor 1553
POLAND
Kiev
M U S C O V Y (R U S S I A)
E U R O P E
Kazan
Bashkirs
Ural R.
Kirghiz
Volga R.
Vienna
Danube R.
Tana To Genoa
Crimea
Kaffa To Genoa till 1475
BLACK SEA
Trebizond
Constantinople
Sivas
Erzerum
Smyrna
THE OTTOMAN TURKS
MEDITERRANEAN SEA
Damascus
Acre
Syria
Alexandria
Jerusalem
Cairo
Suez
Egypt
Astrakhan
CASPIAN SEA
Aral Sea
Mosul
Tigris R.
Euphrates R.
Bagdad
Kazvin
Basra 1529
PERSIAN G.
Ispahan
PERSIA
Kerman
Ormuz, 1515
Mekran
Muscat 1507
Oman
Arabia
Medina
Jiddah
Mecca
RED SEA
Nile R.
Nubia
Dongola
Massowah 1520
Kamaran I.
Tigre
Amhara
Abyssinia
Aden
Zeila
Berbera
Sokotra, 1503
C. Guardafui
Ayana
Magadoxo (Mukdishu)
Brava
Malindi
Mombasa 1498
Zanzibar 1504
Quiloa (Kilwa)
Mozambique 1498
R. das boas Sinaes (Zambesi R.)
Monomotapa
Sofala 1500
C. das Corrientes
Delagoa Bay, 1498
Natal
Kafirs
Hottentots
Orange R.
R. del Infante (Gr. Fish R.)
Diaz
Congo R.
Angola
Benguela
Madagascar (St. Laurentius I.) 1506
Matatane 1506
Mascarenhas 1505
Diego Rodriguez, 1645
I. do Cerne, 1505 (Mauritius, 1598)
AFRICA
ETHIOPIA
Tobolsk 1587
Sibir, 1581
Sibir
Ugrians
Obi R.
Surgut, 1594
TATARY OR TARTARY
Mongolia
Chagatai
ASIA
Bokhara
Samarkand
Kashgar
Merv
Balkh
Herat
Tangut
Peking
Hoang-ho R.
CATHAY
Nanking
Yang-tse-kiang R.
CHINA
MANZI
Zaiton (Tsuen-chau-fu)
Canton 1517
Macao 1520, 1557
Indus R.
Panipat
Delhi
Ganges R.
Benares
EAST
Hindustan
Diu
Cambay
Bassein
INDIA
Goa 1510
Deccan
Bengal
BAY OF BENGAL
Aracan
Mien
Pegu
Martaban
SIAM
Ayuthia
Champa
Andaman Is.
Nicobar Is.
Junk-seylon
Cannanore 1505
Calicut
Cochin
Coromandel
Negapatam
Ceylon 1505
Colombo 1518
Lopez de Sequeira, 1509
Achin
Pedir, 1509
Baros, 1519
Sumatra
Malacca 1509
Singapore
Albuquerque 1511
Brunei 1521
Borneo
Palawan
Luzon 1570
Manila
Celebes
Java
1511
Albuquerque 1507–1508
1513
Albuquerque 1513
Portuguese trade route
Vasco da Gama, 1498
Portuguese trade route
Portuguese trade route
INDIAN
INDIES
OCEAN
Drake, 1580
←Elcano in Magellan's ship "Victoria", 1522
SOUTH CHINA SEA

Arctic Circle
Approximate location of the demarcation line according to the treaty of Tordesillas, June 7, 1494.
Approximate location of the demarcation line according to the papal bull of May 4, 1493
Spanish
Portuguese
CHIPANGU OR CIPANGO (JAPAN)
Nippon
Kyūshū
Tanegashima I. 1542
Jesuit mission founded by St. Francis Xavier, 1549
PACIFIC OCEAN
Tropic of Cancer
Ladrones or Thieves Is. (Marianne Is.) March, 1521
Guam
Alvaro de Saavedra, 1527-1528
Spanish trade route to the Philippines
Coral Is. 1543
Riffins, 1543 (Palau or Pelew Is.)
Caroline Is.
Saavedra, 1528
Drake, 1579
Magellan, 1521
Equator
Ortiz de Retes 1545
New Guinea
Solomon Is.
Sta. Isabel de la Estrella (Mendaña, 1568)
S. Christóbal
Sta. Cruz Is. (Mendaña, 1595)
Tropic of Capricorn

The Conquest of Peru, 1531—1533.

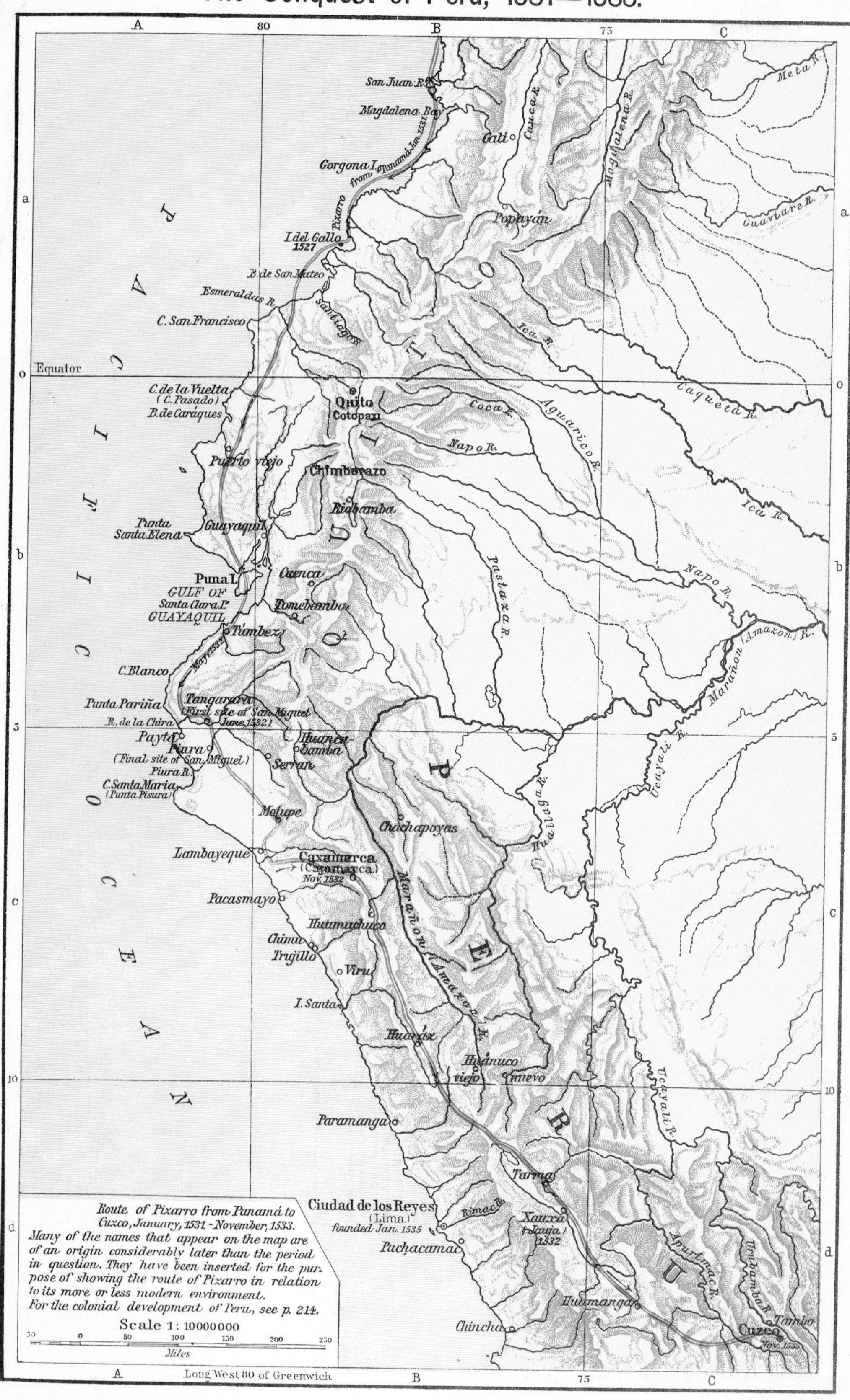

The Imperial Circles about 1512.

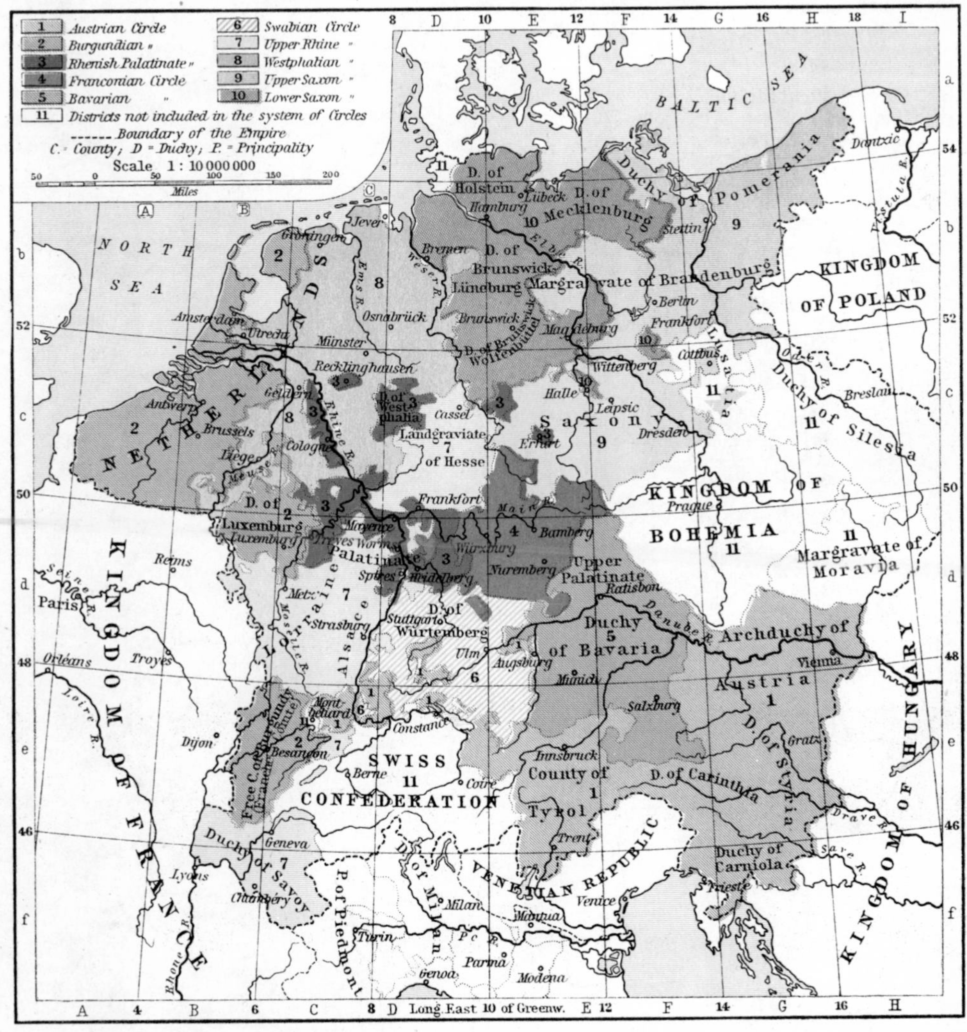

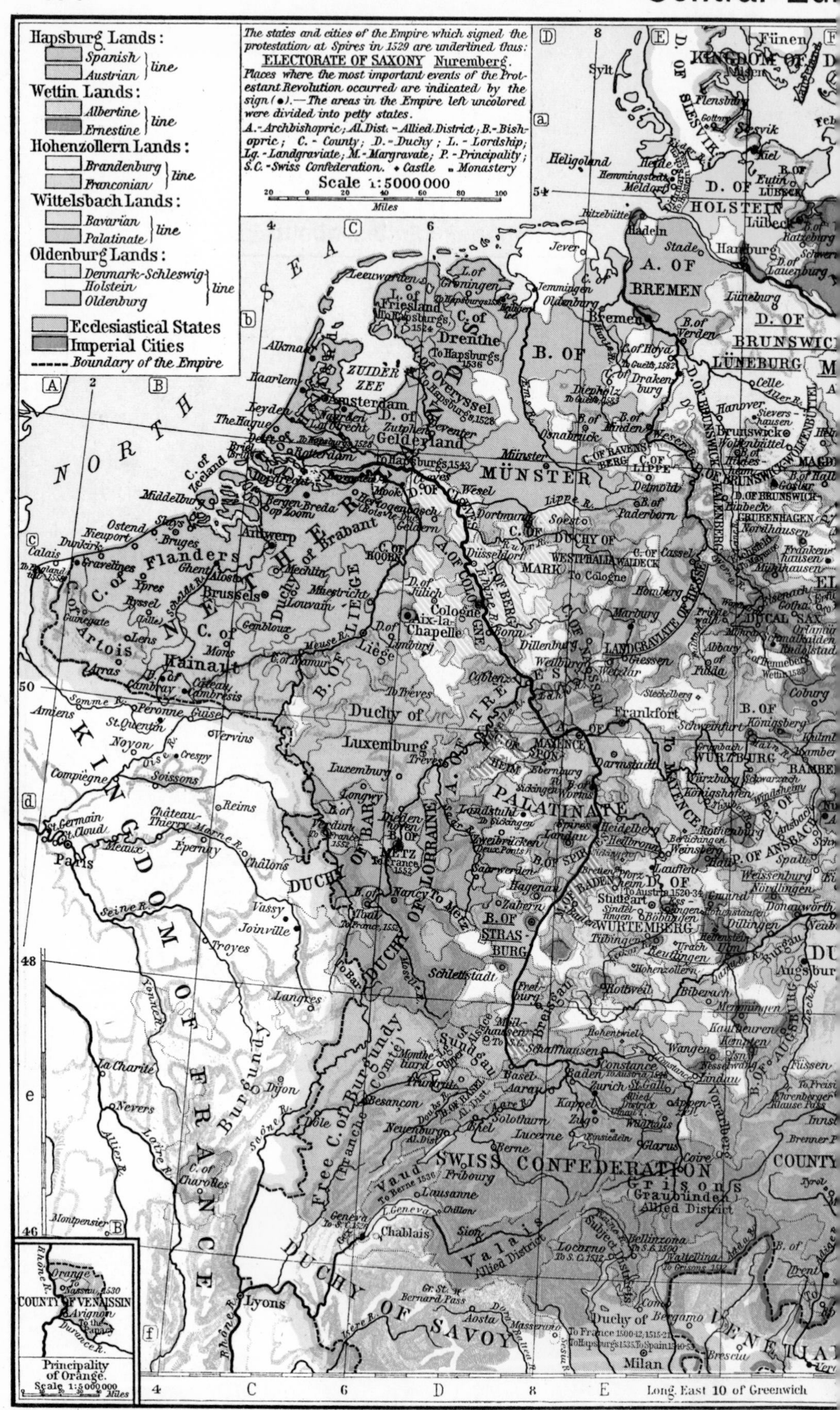
Hapsburg Lands:
Spanish
Austrian
line
Wettin Lands:
Albertine
Ernestine
line
Hohenzollern Lands:
Brandenburg
Franconian
line
Wittelsbach Lands:
Bavarian
Palatinate
line
Oldenburg Lands:
Denmark-Schleswig-Holstein
Oldenburg
line
Ecclesiastical States
Imperial Cities
Boundary of the Empire
The states and cities of the Empire which signed the protestation at Spires in 1529 are underlined thus: ELECTORATE OF SAXONY Nuremberg.
Places where the most important events of the Protestant Revolution occurred are indicated by the sign (●).—The areas in the Empire left uncolored were divided into petty states.
A.-Archbishopric; Al. Dist.-Allied District; B.-Bishopric; C.-County; D.-Duchy; L.-Lordship; Lg.-Landgraviate; M.-Margravate; P.-Principality; S.C.-Swiss Confederation. ◆ Castle ▪ Monastery
Scale 1:5000000
Miles
NORTH SEA
NETHERLANDS
KINGDOM OF FRANCE
SWISS CONFEDERATION
DUCHY OF SAVOY
PALATINATE
MÜNSTER
A. OF BREMEN
D. OF HOLSTEIN
Principality of Orange.
Scale 1:5000000
Long. East 10 of Greenwich

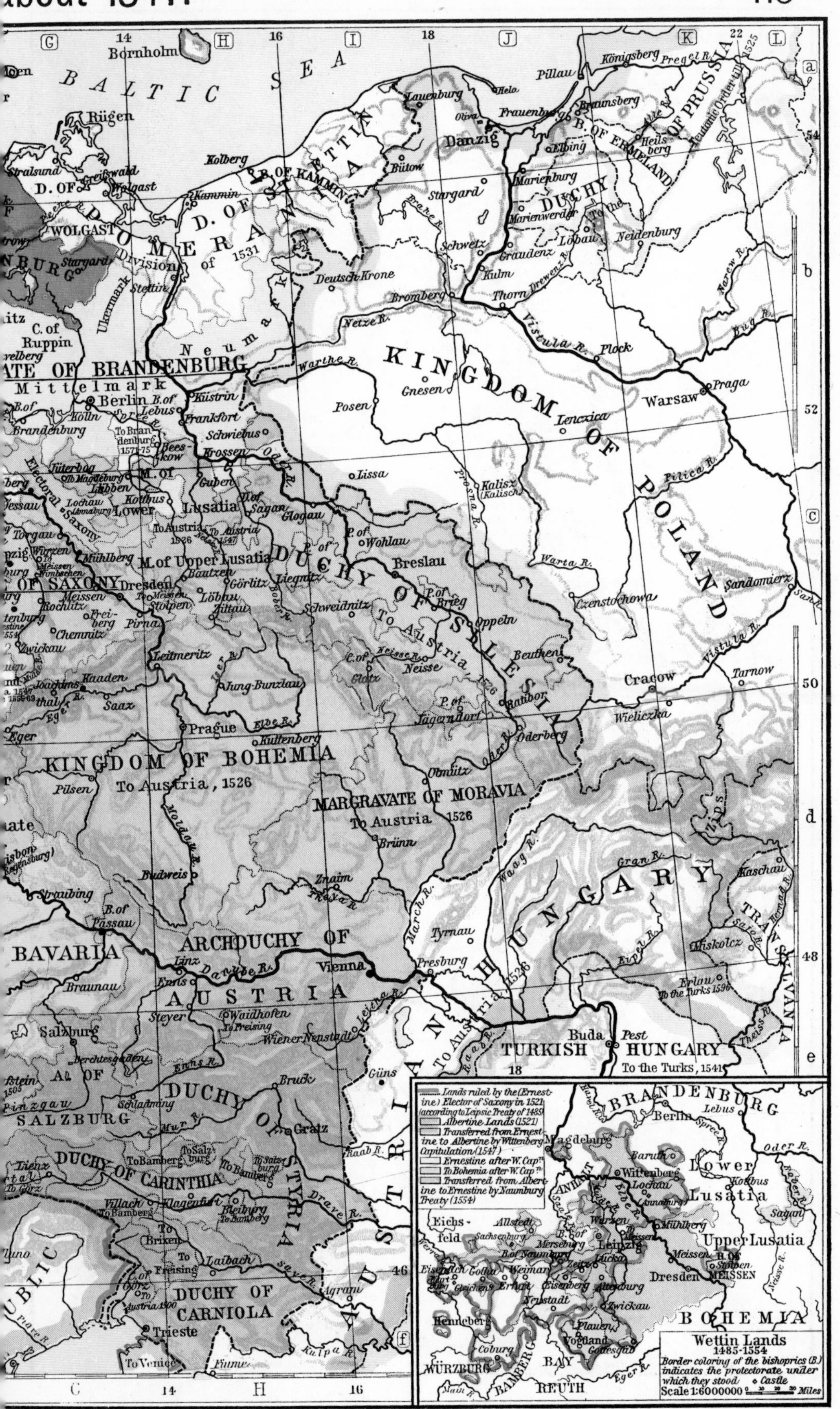
BALTIC SEA
Bornholm
Rügen
Stralsund
Greifswald
Wolgast
D. OF WOLGAST
POMERANIA
D. OF STETTIN
Division of 1531
Kolberg
B. OF KAMMIN
Kammin
Stettin
Stargard
Uckermark
Lauenburg
Danzig
Oliva
Hela
Pillau
Königsberg
Pregel R.
Frauenburg
Braunsberg
B. OF ERMELAND
DUCHY OF PRUSSIA
Teutonic Order till 1525
Heilsberg
Elbing
Marienburg
Marienwerder
Bütow
Stargard
Schwetz
Graudenz
Kulm
Thorn
Löbau
Neidenburg
Deutsch Krone
Bromberg
Netze R.
Narew R.
Bug R.
Vistula R.
Plock
Neumark
C. of Ruppin
ELECTORATE OF BRANDENBURG
Mittelmark
Berlin
Köln
B. of Lebus
Küstrin
Frankfort
Brandenburg
To Brandenburg 1571-75
Schwiebus
Beeskow
Krossen
Oder R.
Warthe R.
Posen
Gnesen
KINGDOM OF POLAND
Lenczica
Warsaw
Praga
Lissa
Kalisz (Kalisch)
Prosna R.
Pilica R.
Jüterbog
Electoral Saxony
Lübben
Lochau
M. of Lower Lusatia
Kottbus
Guben
D. of Sagan
Glogau
To Austria 1526
To Austria 1547
P. of Wohlau
Breslau
Torgau
Wurzen
Mühlberg
M. of Upper Lusatia
Bautzen
Görlitz
Liegnitz
DUCHY OF SILESIA
DUCHY OF SAXONY
Dresden
Meissen
Stolpen
Löbau
Zittau
Schweidnitz
P. of Brieg
To Austria 1526
Oppeln
Warta R.
Czenstochowa
Sandomierz
Rochlitz
Freiberg
Pirna
Chemnitz
Zwickau
C. of Glatz
Neisse
Beuthen
Leitmeritz
Jung-Bunzlau
Kaaden
Joachimsthal
Eger R.
Saaz
Ratibor
P. of Jägerndorf
Cracow
Tarnow
Wieliczka
Vistula R.
Eger
Prague
Elbe R.
Kuttenberg
Oderberg
KINGDOM OF BOHEMIA
To Austria, 1526
Pilsen
Olmütz
MARGRAVATE OF MORAVIA
To Austria 1526
Brünn
Zips
Moldau R.
Budweis
Znaim
Thaya R.
Waag R.
Gran R.
Kaschau
HUNGARY
Straubing
B. of Passau
March R.
Tyrnau
TRANSYLVANIA
Miskolcz
BAVARIA
ARCHDUCHY OF AUSTRIA
Linz
Danube R.
Vienna
Presburg
Eipel R.
Erlau
To the Turks 1596
Enns
Braunau
Steyer
Waidhofen
To Freising
Wiener Neustadt
Leitha R.
To Austria 1526
Salzburg
Berchtesgaden
AB. OF SALZBURG
Pinzgau
Enns R.
Bruck
DUCHY OF STYRIA
Schladming
Mur R.
Gratz
Güns
Buda
Pest
TURKISH HUNGARY
To the Turks, 1541
Theiss R.
Raab R.
DUCHY OF CARINTHIA
To Bamberg
To Salzburg
Tienz
Villach
Klagenfurt
Bleiburg
Drave R.
Brixen
Freising
Laibach
Save R.
Agram
C. of Görz
To Austria 1500
DUCHY OF CARNIOLA
Trieste
Kulpa R.
Fiume
To Venice
Piave R.
REPUBLIC
Wettin Lands 1485-1554
Lands ruled by the (Ernestine) Elector of Saxony in 1521 (according to Leipsic Treaty of 1485)
Albertine Lands (1521)
Transferred from Ernestine to Albertine by Wittenberg Capitulation (1547)
Ernestine after W. Capᵗⁿ
To Bohemia after W. Capᵗⁿ
Transferred from Albertine to Ernestine by Naumburg Treaty (1554)
Border coloring of the bishoprics (B.) indicates the protectorate under which they stood
Castle
Scale 1:6000000
Miles
BRANDENBURG
Berlin
Lebus
Spree R.
Oder R.
Havel R.
Magdeburg
Baruth
Wittenberg
ANHALT
Lower Lusatia
Lochau
Kottbus
Sagan
Mühlberg
Upper Lusatia
Eichsfeld
Allstedt
Sachsenburg
Leipzig
Merseburg
B. of Naumburg
Meissen
B. of Meissen
Stolpen
Dresden
Eisenach
Gotha
Weimar
Erfurt
Eisenberg
Altenburg
Zwickau
Neisse R.
Henneberg
Neustadt
Plauen
Vogtland
BOHEMIA
Coburg
WÜRZBURG
BAMBERG
BAYREUTH
Main R.
Eger R.
C
14
H
16
18
22
G
I
J
K
L
a
b
c
d
e
f
54
52
50
48
46

The Religious Situation in Europe about 1560.

The Religious Situation in Central Europe about 1560.
Lutherans
Calvinists and Zwinglians
Waldensians and Moravians
Anabaptists, Socinians, Antitrinitarians etc.
Roman Catholics
Abbreviations.
A.=Archbishopric; Ab.=Abbacy; B.=Bishopric; Brunsw.=Brunswick; C.=County; D.=Duchy; Elect.=Electorate; F.C.=Free County (Franche Comté); Hildeshm.=Hildesheim; K.=Kingdom; Kalenbg.=Kalenberg; L.=Lordship; M.=Margravate; P.=Principality; Pal.=Palatine.
Scale 1:9000000
Miles
The Religious Situation in Europe about 1560.
Lutherans
Anglicans
Calvinists and Zwinglians
Waldensians, Moravians
Anabaptists, Socinians Antitrinitarians etc.
Approximate extent of the revolt from the Roman Church
Roman Catholics
Greek Orthodox
Mohammedans
Scale 1:30000000
Miles.
Long. East 10 of Greenwich
Long. West 10 of Greenw.
Long. East 10 of Greenw.
BALTIC SEA
K. OF DENMARK
KINGDOM OF POLAND
K. OF BOHEMIA
M. of Moravia
HUNGARY
TURKISH HUNGARY
SWISS CONFEDERATION
VENETIAN REPUBLIC
NORTH SEA
ATLANTIC OCEAN
MEDITERRANEAN SEA
FRANCE
SPAIN
PORTUGAL
ITALY
OTTOMAN EMPIRE
RUSSIA
SCOTLAND
ENGLAND
IRELAND
NORWAY
SWEDEN
DENMARK
POLAND
BOHEMIA
AUSTRIA
NETHERLANDS

The Netherlands, 1559—1609.

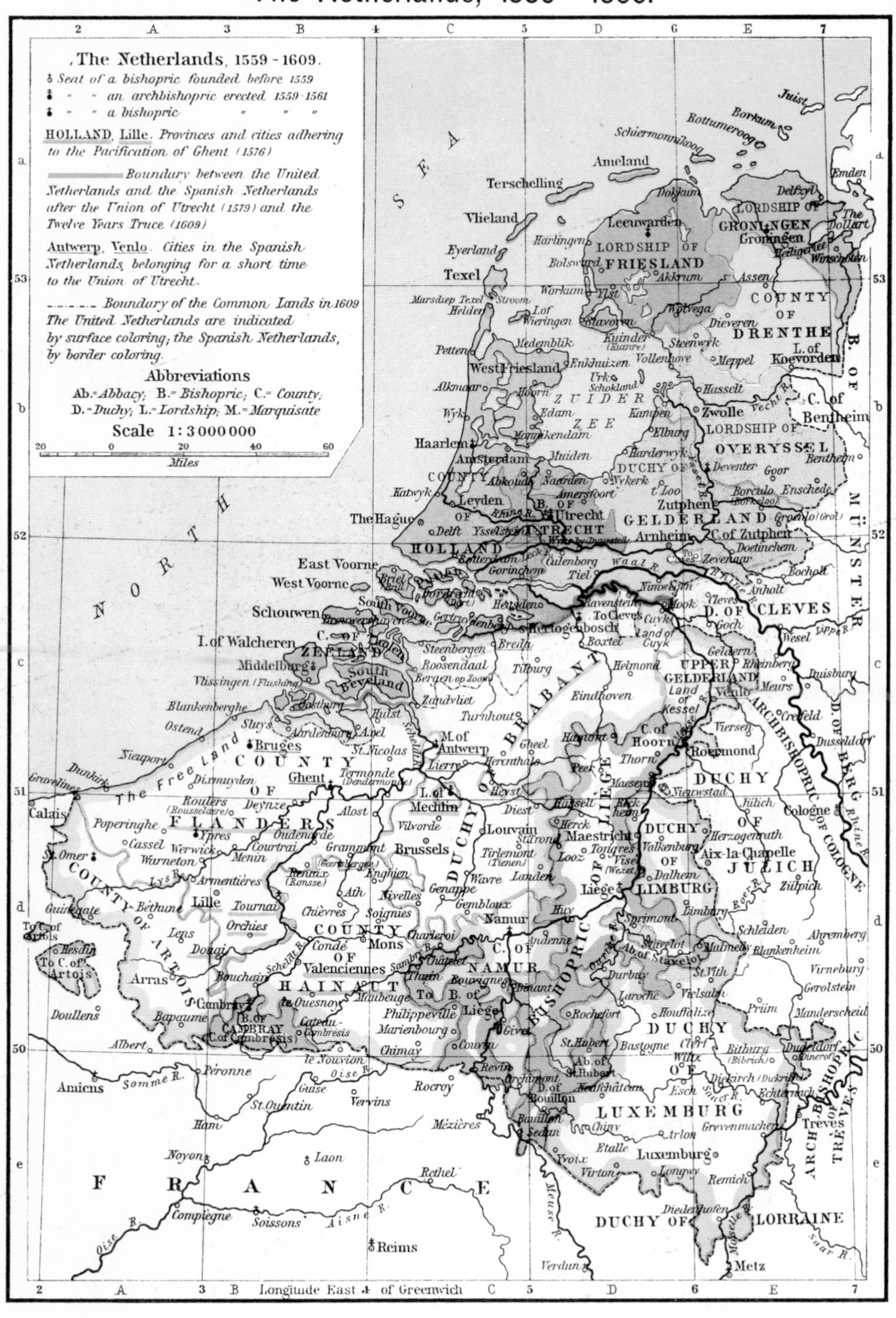

Meridian 0 of Greenwich
Shetland Is.
Orkneys
The Hebrides
KINGDOM OF SCOTLAND
KINGDOM OF NORWAY
Bergen
Stavanger
Kongsberg
Bohus
Inverness
Aberdeen
Perth
Stirling
St. Andrews
Firth of Forth
Dunbar
Edinburgh
Berwick
Flodden
Northumberland
Donegal Bay
Ulster
Armagh
Connaught
IRELAND
Galway
Leinster
Dublin
Limerick
Munster
Cork
Waterford
Dingle Bay
ATLANTIC OCEAN
NORTH SEA
KINGDOM OF ENGLAND
Isle of Man
Westmorland
Carlisle
Solway Moor
York
Shrewsbury
Tutbury
Leicester
Peterborough
Coventry
Norfolk
Norwich
Wales
Gloucester
Fotheringhay
Cambridge
Severn
Oxford
London
Canterbury
Portsmouth
Dover
Plymouth
Lizard Head
ENGLISH CHANNEL
Calais
Guernsey
Jersey
Cherbourg
Amsterdam
Utrecht
The Hague
NETHERLANDS
Bruges
Ghent
Flanders
Artois
Cambray
Brussels
Liège
Aix-la-Chapelle
Cologne
Marburg
Schmalkalden
Hamburg
Bremen
Oldenburg
Lübeck
Schwerin
Holstein
Schleswig
Jutland
K. OF DENMARK
Münster
Brunswick
Magdeburg
Eisleben
Cassel
Erfurt
Leipzig
SAXONY
THE EMPIRE
Frankfort
Mayence
Luxemburg
Metz
Lorraine
Nuremberg
Spires
Stuttgart
Ratisbon
Strasburg
Augsburg
BAVARIA
Munich
Freiburg
Basel
Zurich
Innsbruck
Tyrol
Franche Comté
Besançon
Berne
SWISS CONFEDERATION
Geneva
D. OF SAVOY
Turin
Milan
Pavia
Verona
Padua
Mantua
Venice
Parma
Modena
Ferrara
Bologna
Genoa
Lucca
Florence
Pisa
Siena
PAPAL STATES
Rome
Naples
Rouen
Noyon
Soissons
Brittany
Brest
Rennes
Paris
Meaux
Chalons
Nantes
Blois
Orléans
Amboise
Tours
Bourges
KINGDOM OF FRANCE
La Rochelle
Poitiers
Limoges
Clermont
Lyons
Grenoble
Dauphiny
Bordeaux
BAY OF BISCAY
Bayonne
Toulouse
Languedoc
Avignon
Provence
Marseilles
Toulon
Narbonne
Perpignan
Roussillon
Corunna
Santiago
Leon
Bilbao
Burgos
K. of Navarre
Zamora
Valladolid
Salamanca
Segovia
Saragossa
Lérida
Aragon
Barcelona
Tarragona
Madrid
KINGDOM OF SPAIN
Toledo
Castile
Valencia
Oporto
Braganza
K. OF PORTUGAL
Lisbon
Badajoz
Seville
Cordova
Granada
Malaga
Almeria
Cartagena
Murcia
Cadiz
Gibraltar
Ceuta
Tangier
Balearic Is.
Minorca
Majorca
Iviza
Corsica
To Genoa
K. OF SARDINIA
Cagliari
MEDIT
Oran
Melilla
Algiers
Bona
Bizerta
Tunis
FEZ AND MOROCCO
Tlemsen
ALGERIA
BARBARY STATES
TUNIS
Long. West 0 Long. East

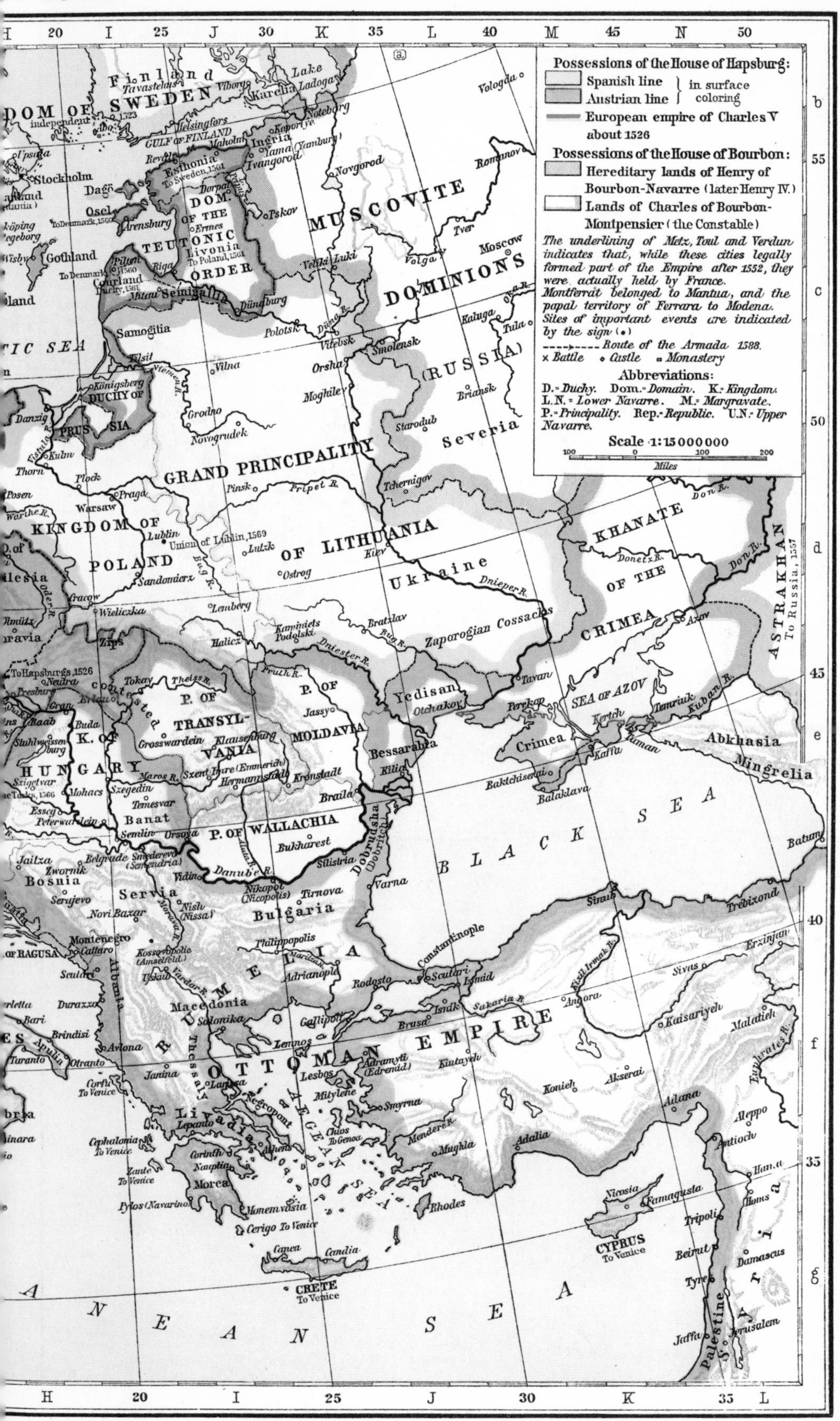
Possessions of the House of Hapsburg:
Spanish line
Austrian line
in surface coloring
European empire of Charles V about 1526
Possessions of the House of Bourbon:
Hereditary lands of Henry of Bourbon-Navarre (later Henry IV.)
Lands of Charles of Bourbon-Montpensier (the Constable)
The underlining of Metz, Toul and Verdun indicates that, while these cities legally formed part of the Empire after 1552, they were actually held by France.
Montferrat belonged to Mantua, and the papal territory of Ferrara to Modena.
Sites of important events are indicated by the sign (•)
Route of the Armada 1588.
× Battle
◆ Castle
▪ Monastery
Abbreviations:
D.= Duchy. Dom.= Domain. K.= Kingdom.
L.N.= Lower Navarre. M.= Margravate.
P.= Principality. Rep.= Republic. U.N.= Upper Navarre.
Scale 1:15000000
Miles
Finland
SWEDEN
Lake Ladoga
MUSCOVITE DOMINIONS (RUSSIA)
DOM. OF THE TEUTONIC ORDER
Livonia To Poland, 1561
Esthonia To Sweden, 1561
Courland
Samogitia
DUCHY OF PRUSSIA
GRAND PRINCIPALITY OF LITHUANIA
KINGDOM OF POLAND
Union of Lublin, 1569
Ukraine
Zaporogian Cossacks
Severia
KHANATE OF THE CRIMEA
ASTRAKHAN To Russia, 1557
SEA OF AZOV
Crimea
Abkhasia
Mingrelia
BLACK SEA
P. OF TRANSYLVANIA
P. OF MOLDAVIA
P. OF WALLACHIA
K. OF HUNGARY
Bessarabia
Yedisan
Dobrudsha (Dobritch)
Bosnia
Servia
Bulgaria
RUMELIA
Macedonia
Thessaly
Albania
Livadia
Morea
OTTOMAN EMPIRE
AEGEAN SEA
CYPRUS To Venice
CRETE To Venice
Syria
Palestine
Moscow
Novgorod
Smolensk
Kiev
Warsaw
Cracow
Stockholm
Riga
Danzig
Constantinople
Adrianople
Belgrade
Bukharest
Varna
Trebizond
Angora
Aleppo
Damascus
Jerusalem
Rhodes

The Religious Situation in Central Europe about 1618. Sweden about 1658.

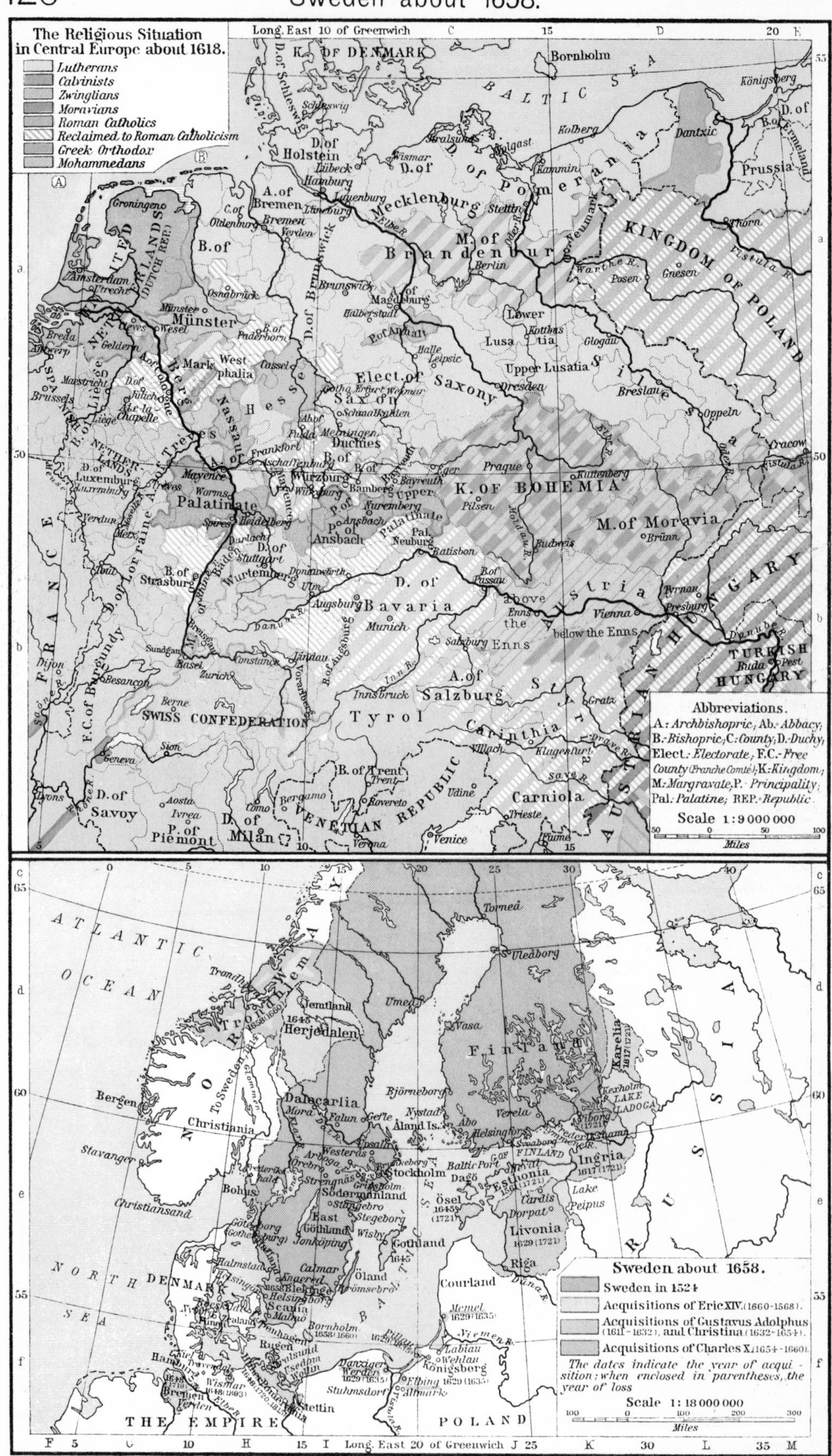

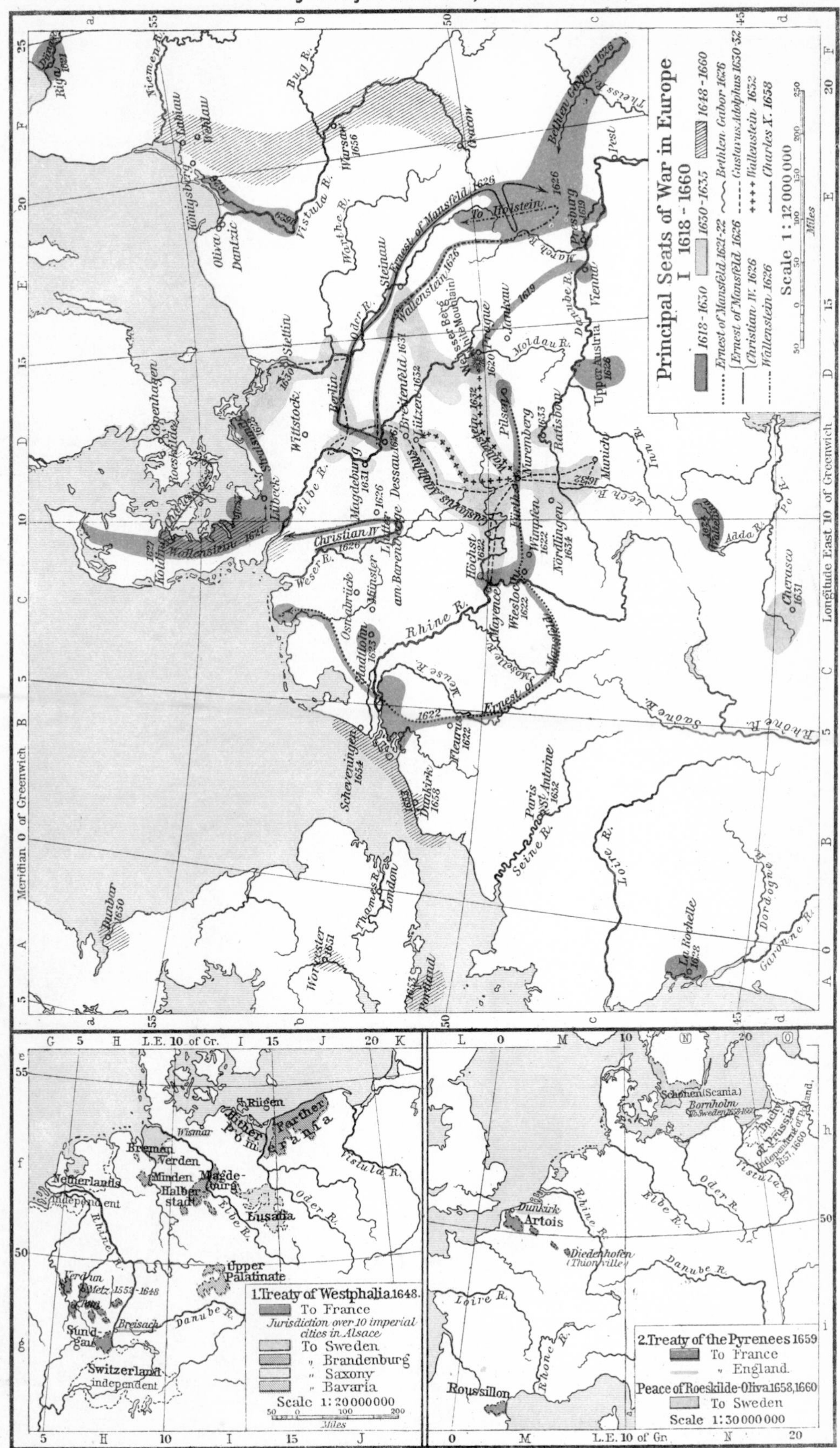
Principal Seats of War in Europe
I 1618-1660
1618-1630
1630-1635
1648-1660
Ernest of Mansfeld 1621-22
Bethlen Gabor 1626
Ernest of Mansfeld 1626
Gustavus Adolphus 1630-32
Christian IV. 1626
Wallenstein 1632
Wallenstein 1626
Charles X. 1658
Scale 1 : 12 000 000
Miles
1. Treaty of Westphalia 1648.
To France
Jurisdiction over 10 imperial cities in Alsace
To Sweden
Brandenburg
Saxony
Bavaria
Scale 1: 20 000 000
Miles
2. Treaty of the Pyrenees 1659
To France
England
Peace of Roeskilde-Oliva 1658, 1660
To Sweden
Scale 1: 30 000 000

NORTH SEA
UNITED NETHERLANDS
Independent of the Empire 1648
SPANISH NETHERLANDS
KINGDOM OF FRANCE
SWITZERLAND
Independent of the Empire, 1648
DUCHY OF SAVOY
PRINCIPALITY OF PIEDMONT
DUCHY OF BREMEN
DUCHY OF LÜNEBURG
HOLSTEIN
MÜNSTER
DUCHY OF WESTPHALIA
LANDGRAVIATE OF HESSE-CASSEL
WÜRZBURG
D. OF WURTEMBERG
Franche Comté
Flanders
Artois
Heligoland
To Holstein-Gottorp
To France, 1601
Duchy of Milan
Grisons
Amsterdam
Rotterdam
Antwerp
Brussels
Paris
Amiens
Lyons
Geneva
Strasburg
Frankfort
Cologne
Bremen
Hanover
Brunswick
Hamburg
Lübeck
Metz
Nancy
Dijon
Langres
Troyes
Reims
Soissons
Compiègne
Bourges
Nevers
Montluçon
Clermont
St. Etienne
Fontainebleau
Lausanne
Berne
Zurich
Lucerne
Basel
Constance
Mayence
Mannheim
Heidelberg
Stuttgart
Tübingen
Ulm
Trèves
Coblenz
Liège
Aix-la-Chapelle
Sedan
Verdun
Calais
Dunkirk
Ostend
Bruges
Ghent
Norwich
Groningen
Texel
Zuider Zee
Utrecht
Osnabrück
Paderborn
Cassel
Marburg
Giessen
Darmstadt
Besançon
Chalon
Lindau
Kempten
Memmingen
Locarno
Bergamo
Brescia
Como
Annecy
Aosta
Chambéry
Sion
Fribourg
Neuchâtel
Pontarlier
Vesoul
Montbéliard
Mülhausen
Breisach
Colmar
Speyer
Worms
Landau
Saarbrücken
Luxemburg
Rocroy
Mézières
St. Quentin
Noyon
Laon
Châlons
Bar-le-Duc
Toul
Cambray
Arras
Mons
Namur
Charleroi
10 Long. East

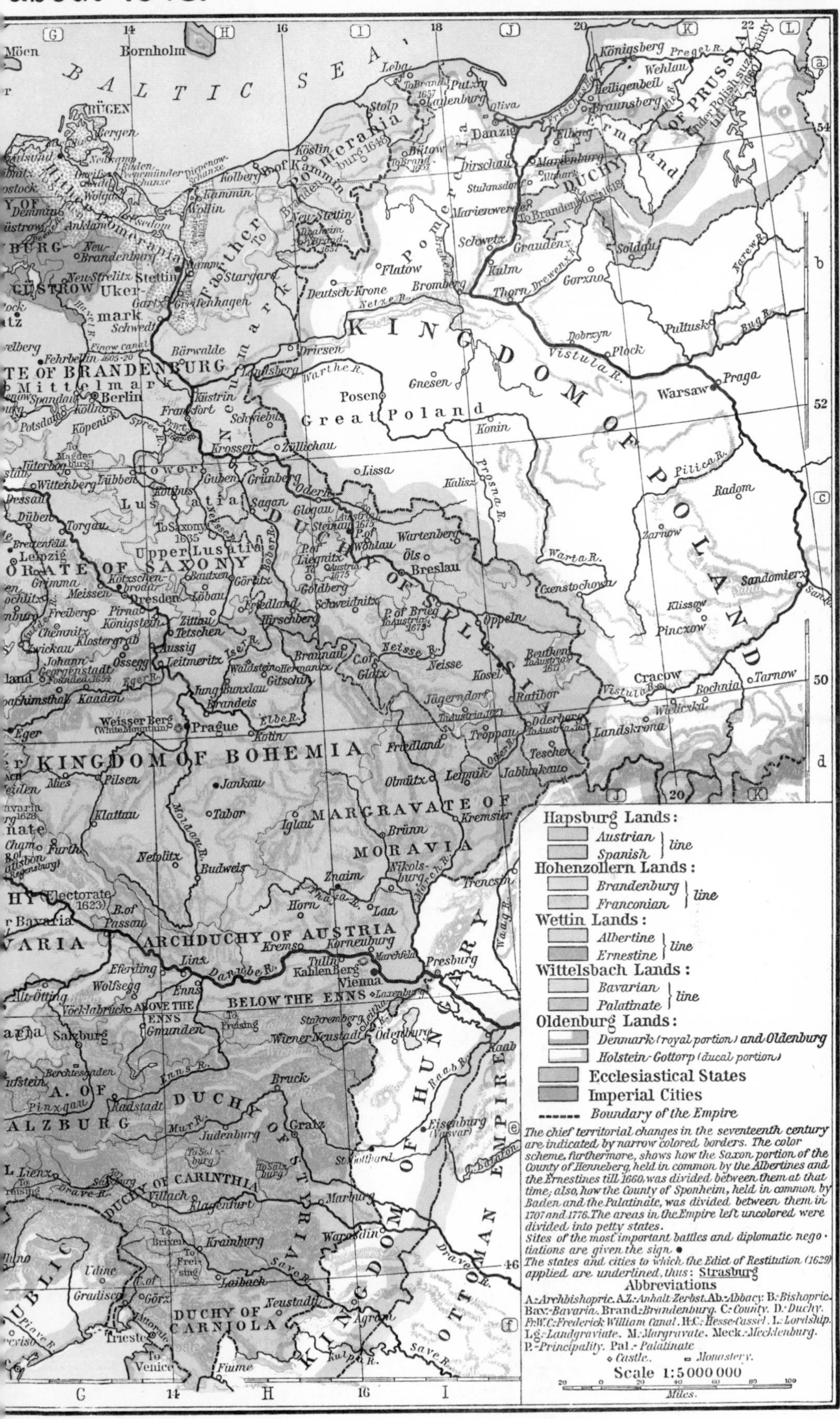
BALTIC SEA
KINGDOM OF POLAND
Great Poland
DUCHY OF PRUSSIA
Ermeland
Pomerania
Farther Pomerania
Hither Pomerania
Neumark
Uker-mark
Mittelmark
ELECTORATE OF BRANDENBURG
ELECTORATE OF SAXONY
Lower Lusatia
Upper Lusatia
DUCHY OF SILESIA
KINGDOM OF BOHEMIA
MARGRAVATE OF MORAVIA
ARCHDUCHY OF AUSTRIA
ABOVE THE ENNS
BELOW THE ENNS
DUCHY OF STYRIA
DUCHY OF CARINTHIA
DUCHY OF CARNIOLA
A. OF SALZBURG
KINGDOM OF HUNGARY
OTTOMAN EMPIRE
Königsberg
Danzig
Stettin
Berlin
Frankfort
Posen
Warsaw
Cracow
Breslau
Dresden
Leipzig
Prague
Brünn
Vienna
Presburg
Linz
Salzburg
Gratz
Laibach
Trieste
Venice
Fiume
Hapsburg Lands:
Austrian line
Spanish line
Hohenzollern Lands:
Brandenburg line
Franconian line
Wettin Lands:
Albertine line
Ernestine line
Wittelsbach Lands:
Bavarian line
Palatinate line
Oldenburg Lands:
Denmark (royal portion) and Oldenburg
Holstein-Gottorp (ducal portion)
Ecclesiastical States
Imperial Cities
Boundary of the Empire
The chief territorial changes in the seventeenth century are indicated by narrow colored borders. The color scheme, furthermore, shows how the Saxon portion of the County of Henneberg, held in common by the Albertines and the Ernestines till 1660, was divided between them at that time; also, how the County of Sponheim, held in common by Baden and the Palatinate, was divided between them in 1707 and 1776. The areas in the Empire left uncolored were divided into petty states.
Sites of the most important battles and diplomatic negotiations are given the sign ●
The states and cities to which the Edict of Restitution (1629) applied are underlined, thus: Strasburg
Abbreviations
A.=Archbishopric. A.Z.=Anhalt-Zerbst. Ab.=Abbacy. B.=Bishopric. Bav.=Bavaria. Brand.=Brandenburg. C.=County. D.=Duchy. Fr.W.C.=Frederick William Canal. H.C.=Hesse-Cassel. L.=Lordship. Lg.=Landgraviate. M.=Margravate. Meck.=Mecklenburg. P.=Principality. Pal.=Palatinate
◇ Castle. ▭ Monastery.
Scale 1:5 000 000
Miles.

Europe in 1648.

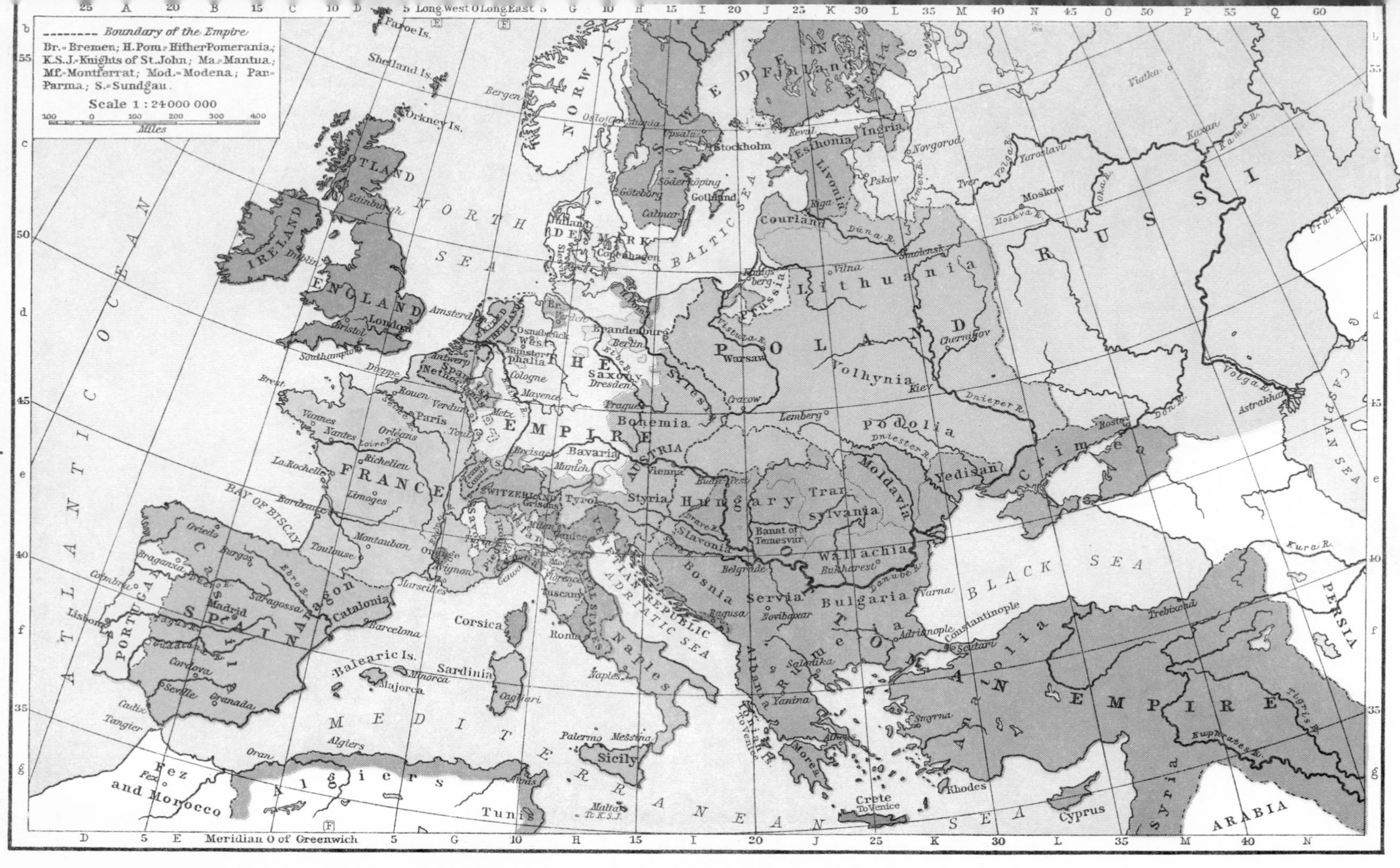

Principal Seats of War in Europe, 1672—1699.
Treaty Adjustments, 1688—1699.

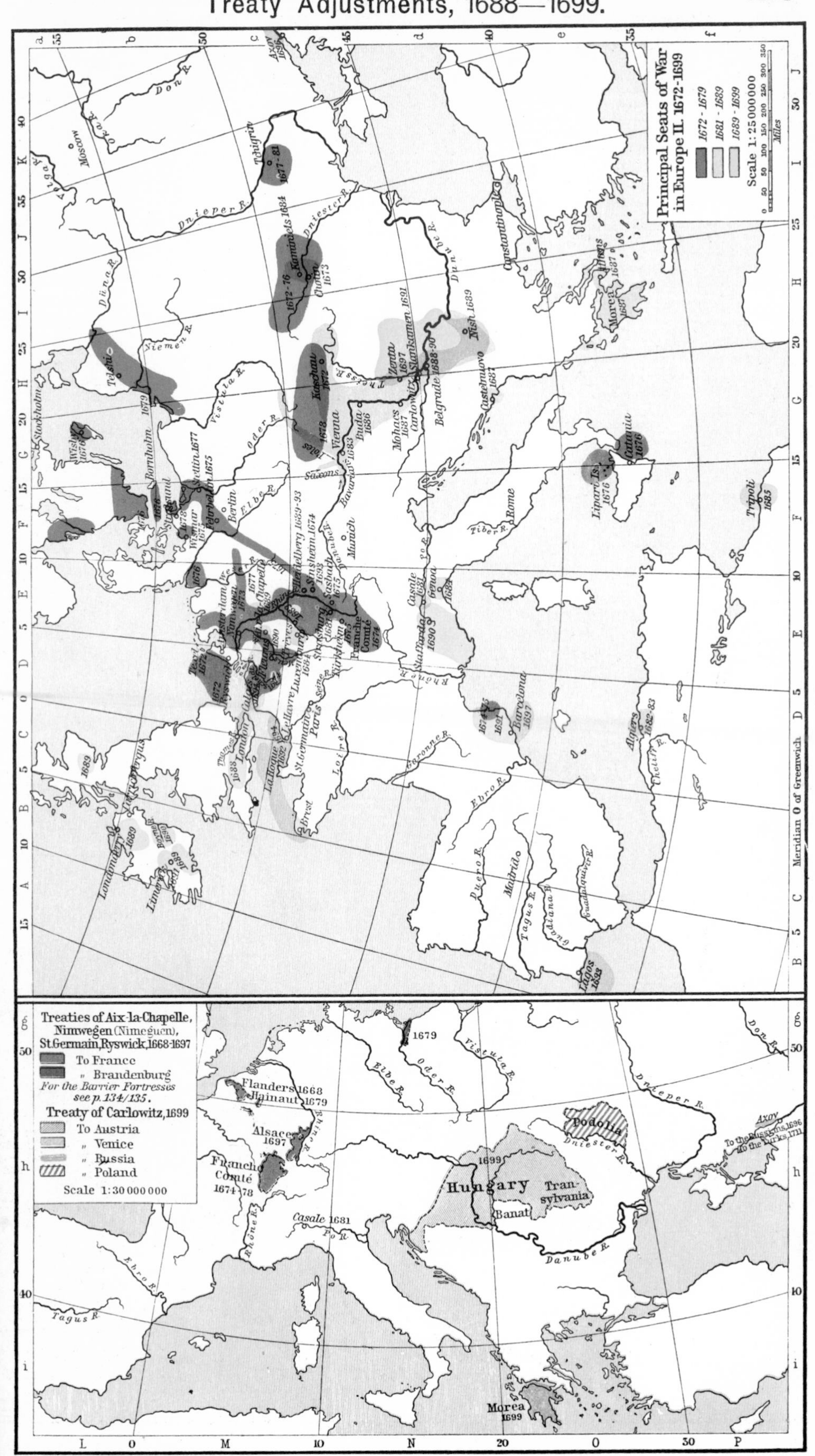

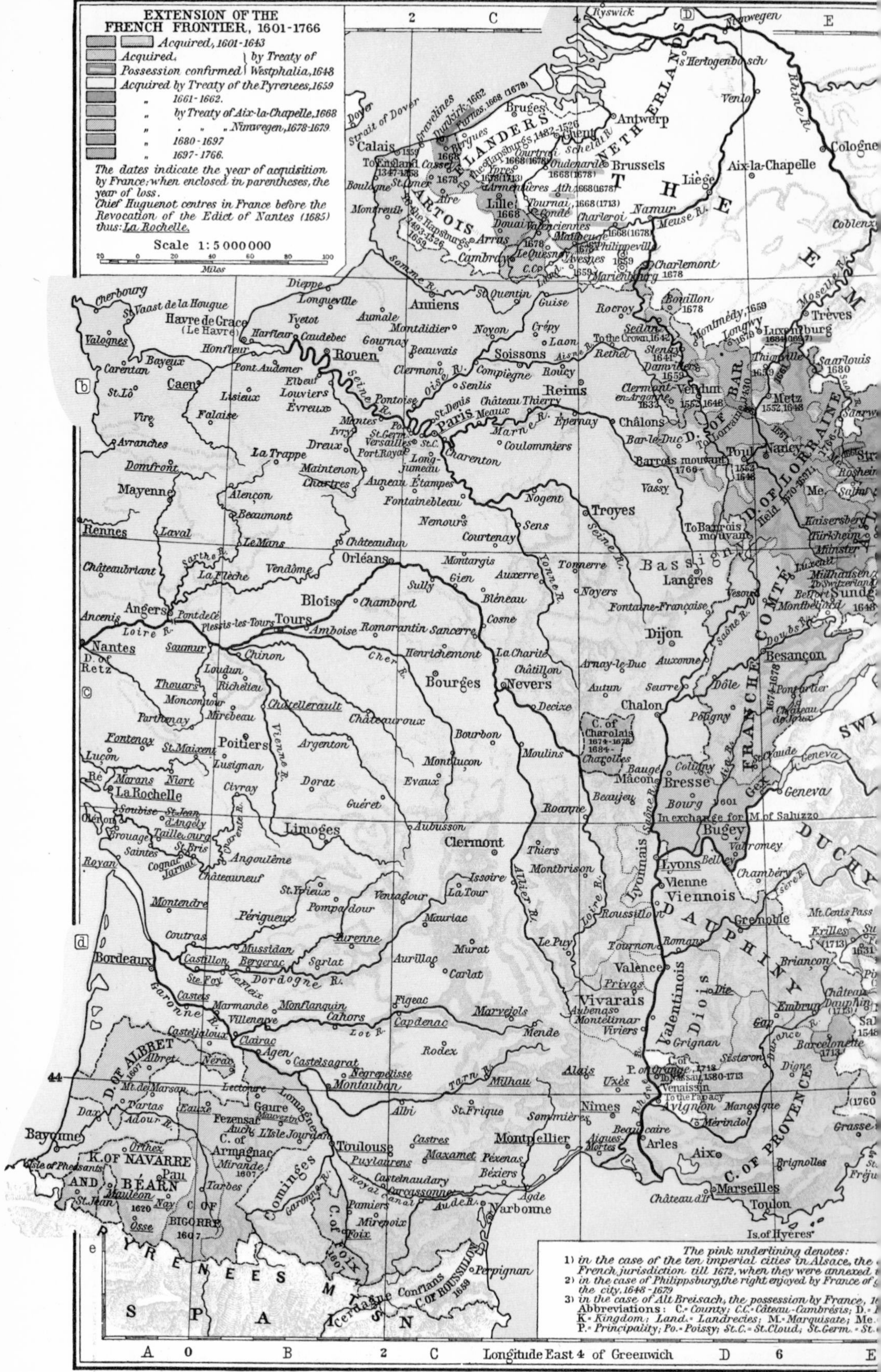
EXTENSION OF THE FRENCH FRONTIER, 1601-1766
Acquired, 1601-1643
Acquired. } by Treaty of
Possession confirmed } Westphalia, 1648
Acquired by Treaty of the Pyrenees, 1659
" 1661-1662.
" by Treaty of Aix-la-Chapelle, 1668
" " Nimwegen, 1678-1679.
" 1680-1697
" 1697-1766.
The dates indicate the year of acquisition by France; when enclosed in parentheses, the year of loss.
Chief Huguenot centres in France before the Revocation of the Edict of Nantes (1685) thus: La Rochelle.
Scale 1:5 000 000
Miles
The pink underlining denotes:
1) in the case of the ten imperial cities in Alsace, the
French jurisdiction till 1672, when they were annexed
2) in the case of Philippsburg, the right enjoyed by France of
the city, 1648-1679
3) in the case of Alt Breisach, the possession by France,
Abbreviations: C.= County; C.C.= Cateau-Cambresis; D.=
K.= Kingdom; Land.= Landrecies; M.= Marquisate; Me.
P.= Principality; Po.= Poissy; St.C.= St.Cloud; St.Germ.= St.
Longitude East 4 of Greenwich
FLANDERS
ARTOIS
NETHERLANDS
THE EM
D. OF BAR
D. OF LORRAINE
FRANCHE COMTÉ
Bassigny
Bresse
Bugey
In exchange for M. of Saluzzo
DUCHY
DAUPHINY
Valentinois
Diois
Vivarais
Lyonnais
C. of PROVENCE
C. of Charolais
D. OF ALBRET
K. OF NAVARRE AND BÉARN
C. OF BIGORRE
Cominges
C. of Foix
C. OF ROUSSILLON
Cerdagne
Lomagne
Armagnac
PYRENEES MTS
SPAIN
Paris
Rouen
Amiens
Reims
Orléans
Tours
Nantes
Bourges
Lyons
Bordeaux
Toulouse
Marseilles
Dijon
Besançon
Metz
Verdun
Toul
Nancy
Brussels
Antwerp
Liège
Aix-la-Chapelle
Cologne
Luxemburg
Strait of Dover
Calais
Dunkirk 1662
Lille 1668
Arras
Cambrai
La Rochelle
Limoges
Clermont
Montpellier
Avignon
Grenoble
Geneva
Narbonne
Perpignan 1659
Bayonne
Pau
Nîmes
Toulon
Is. of Hyères
Havre de Grace (Le Havre)
Cherbourg
Rennes
Angers
Blois
Poitiers
Troyes
Sedan
Loire R.
Seine R.
Rhône R.
Garonne R.
Dordogne R.
Meuse R.
Rhine R.
Moselle R.

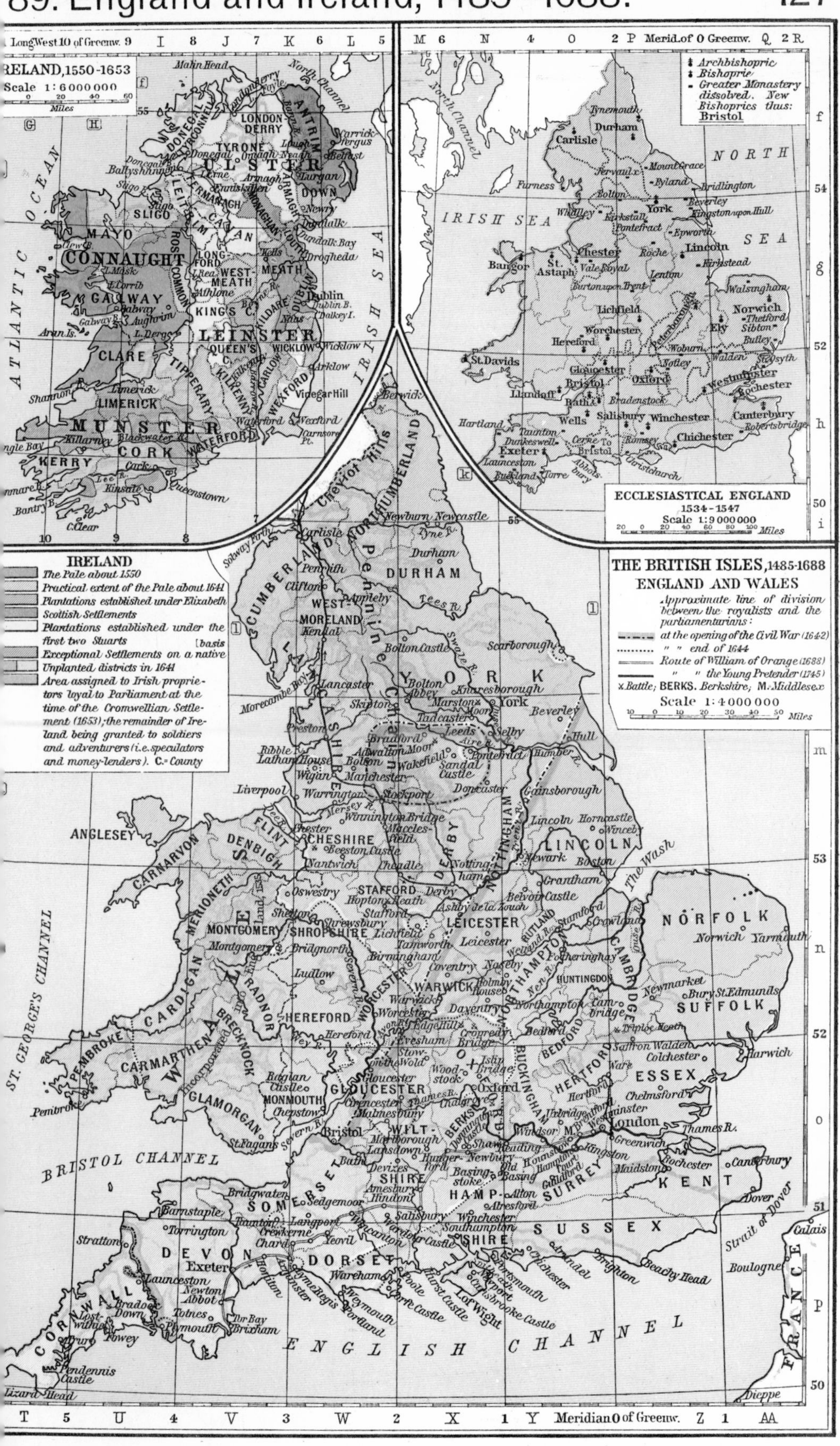
IRELAND, 1550-1653
Scale 1:6 000 000
Miles
ATLANTIC OCEAN
IRISH SEA
IRELAND
The Pale about 1550
Practical extent of the Pale about 1641
Plantations established under Elizabeth
Scottish Settlements
Plantations established under the first two Stuarts
Exceptional Settlements on a native basis
Unplanted districts in 1641
Area assigned to Irish proprietors loyal to Parliament at the time of the Cromwellian Settlement (1653); the remainder of Ireland being granted to soldiers and adventurers (i.e. speculators and money-lenders). C. = County
Archbishopric
Bishopric
Greater Monastery dissolved. New Bishoprics thus: Bristol
ECCLESIASTICAL ENGLAND 1534-1547
Scale 1:9 000 000
Miles
THE BRITISH ISLES, 1485-1688
ENGLAND AND WALES
Approximate line of division between the royalists and the parliamentarians:
at the opening of the Civil War (1642)
" " end of 1644
Route of William of Orange (1688)
" " the Young Pretender (1745)
× Battle; BERKS. Berkshire; M. Middlesex
Scale 1:4 000 000
Miles
NORTH SEA
ST. GEORGE'S CHANNEL
BRISTOL CHANNEL
ENGLISH CHANNEL
FRANCE
Meridian 0 of Greenw.

Scotland, 1488—1688.

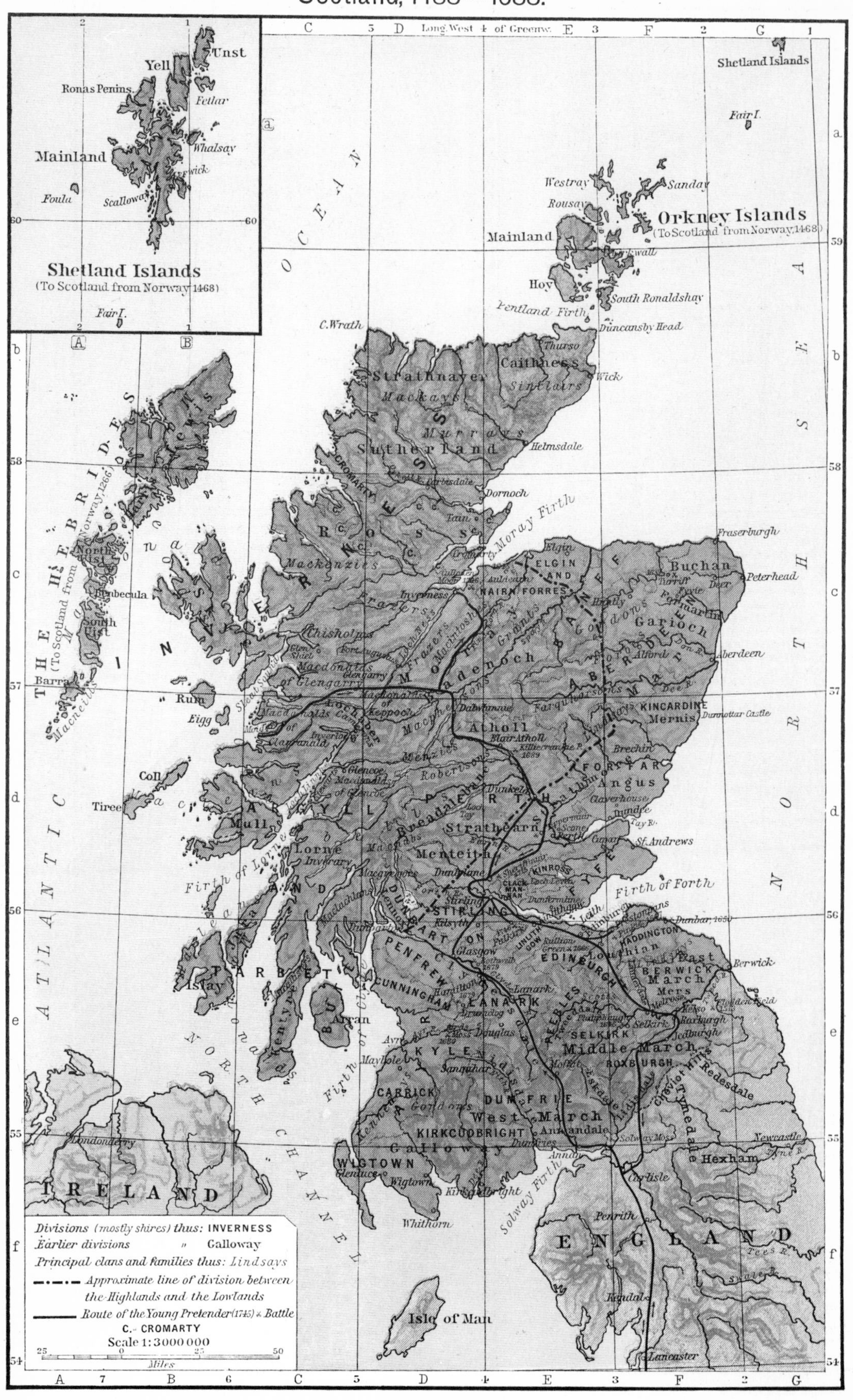

The Ottoman Empire, 1481—1683.

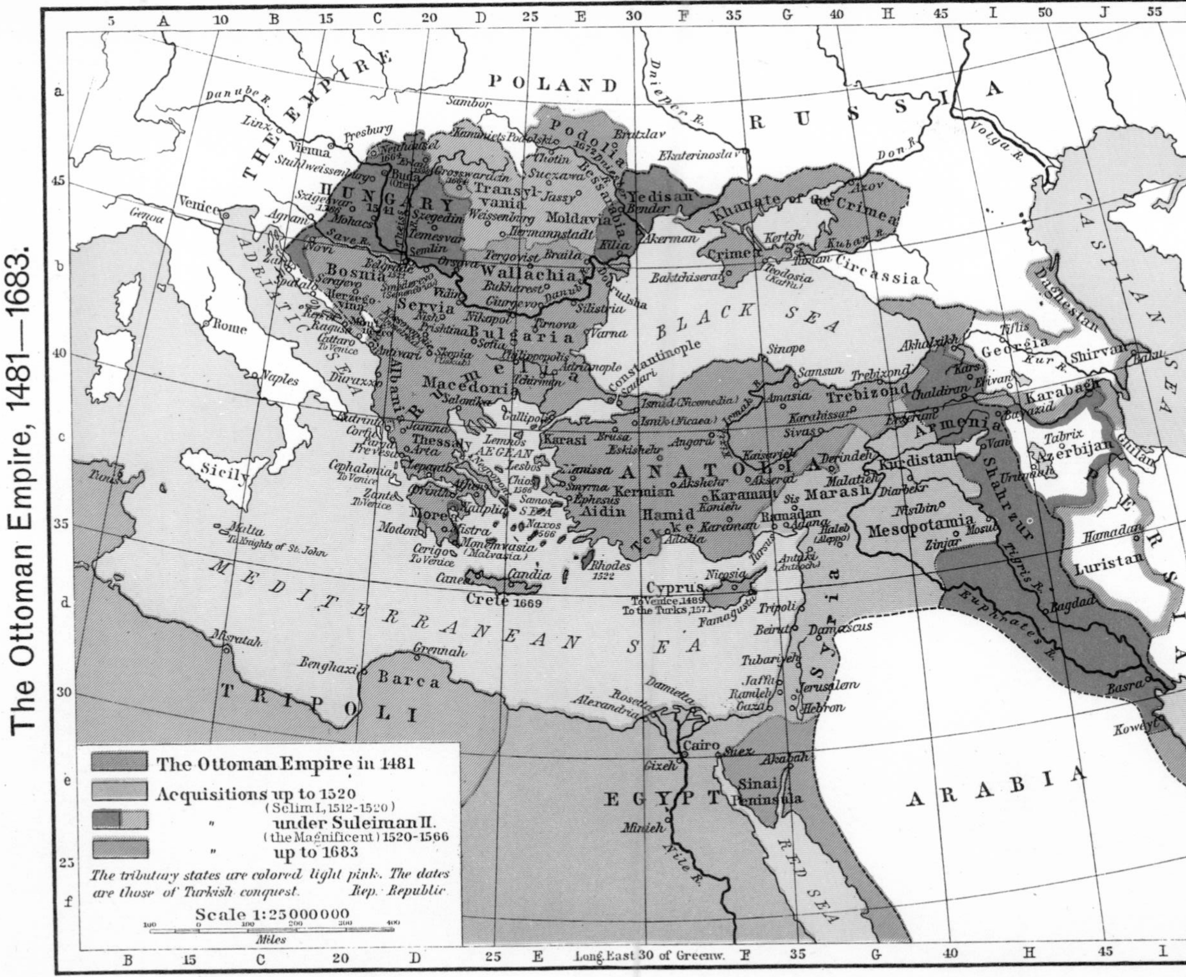

Greenland
To Denmark, 1605, 1721
Hudson, 1607
Iceland
To Denmark
Arctic Circle
Hudson Bay
Rupert's Land
Hudson, 1610-1611
(Hudson Bay Company)
1670
Ft. Albany, 1674
Ft. Rupert 1668
N O R T H
France
Quebec
Montreal
Newfoundland, 1623
Settled also by the French
A M E R I C A
New England
N.N.
Ft. Amsterdam, 1626
Jamestown 1607
New Sweden, 1638-1655
1655 D.
Louisiana
Virginia
Bermudas, 1609, 1612
Azores Is.
Portugal
Spain
Tangier 1661-1684
Madeira
Canary Is.
Santa Barbara Is. 1602
New Spain (Mexico)
Pensacola 1696
Florida
Gulf of Mexico
Tropic of Cancer
Cuba
St. Domingue
Hispaniola
Porto Rico
Belize 1638
Jamaica
Cape Verd Is.
Gambia
Gorce
Ft. James
Sierra Leone
P A C I F I C
New Andalusia
Guiana
New Granada
Equator
O C E A N
St. Louis, 1612-1615
1654, 1661
Olinda
Mauritsstad, Recife or Pernambuco
S O U T H
A M E R I C A
Brazil
Peru
New Castile
Bahia 1624-1626
Colonia do Sacramento, 1680
St. Helena
Sagittaria (Tahiti) 1606
Quiros
Tropic of Capricorn
Guaranis
La Plata
Chile
New Estremadura
C. Horn
Le Maire and Schouten, 1615
Long. West 70 of Greenw.
Tropic of Cancer
Bahama Is.
Cuba
Tortuga F. 1640, 1697 (Headquarters of the Buccaneers)
Hispaniola
Porto Rico
Leeward Is.
Jamaica 1655
Port Royal (Kingston)
St. Domingue F. 1640, 1697
Virgin Is., 1672
St. Croix (Santa Cruz) 1650 F.
St. Eustatius
St. Christopher Joint possession
Nevis
Montserrat
St. Bartholomew, 1648
Barbuda, 1628
Antigua, 1628
Guadeloupe, 1635
Dominica
Martinique, 1635
St. Lucia, E. 1639; F. 1667
Barbados, 1625
Honduras
C. Gracias á Dios
Caribbean Sea
Providence Is. 1630
Mosquito Coast
Curaçao, 1634
St. Vincent
Grenada 1650
Windward Is.
Tobago D. 1632; neutral, 1680
Trinidad
Porto Bello
Cartagena
Caledonia
Darien
Panama
Spanish Main
(Tierra Firme)
Valencia
Caracas
Cumana
Orinoco
Essequibo, 1625
Berbice, 1627
Surinam
E. 1640-1667
D. 1667
Cayenne 1626
Equator
Partition of Guiana and the West Indies (1600-1700)
English
Dutch
French
Spanish
Haunts of the Buccaneers.
Scale along the Equator 1:40000000
Delhi
L.E. 80 of Gr.
Jats
Rajputs
Agra
Ajmer
Ahmadabad
Tropic of Cancer
Cambay
Surat
Burhanpur
Diu
Daman
Bassein
Salsette
Bombay
Chaul
Goa
Mahrattas
D E C C A N
Godaveri R.
Kistna R.
Malabar
Coromandel
Cannanore, 1663
Calicut, 1656
Cranganore, 1662
Cochin, 1663
Quilon, 1661
Negumbo
Colombo, 1656
Pointe de Galle
Pulicat
Pondicherry
Negapatam
Trincomali
Ceylon

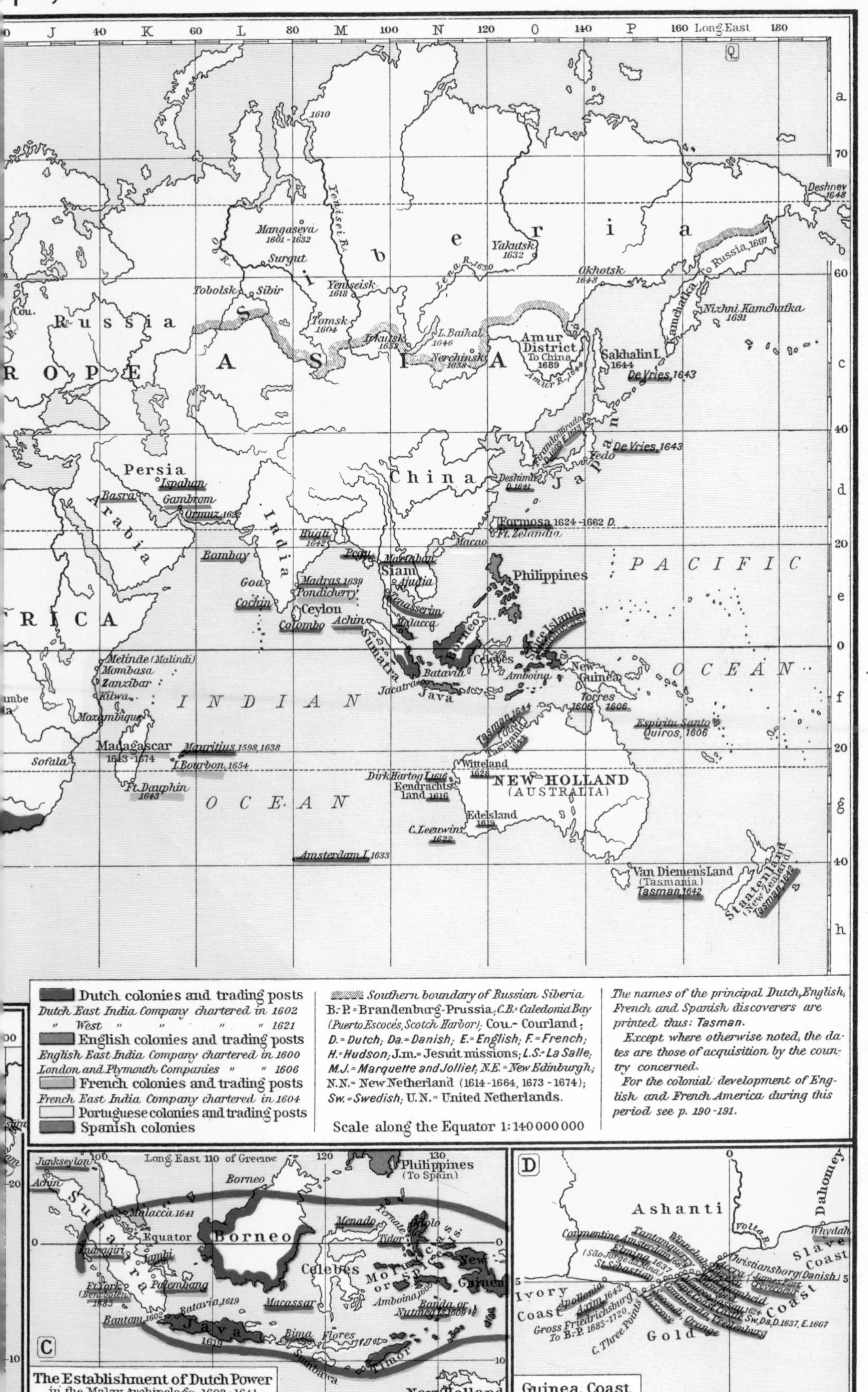
Long. East
Siberia
Russia
ASIA
EUROPE
AFRICA
Mangaseya 1601-1632
Surgut
Tobolsk
Sibir
Yeniseisk 1618
Tomsk 1604
Irkutsk 1652
L. Baikal 1646
Nerchinsk 1658
Yakutsk 1632
Lena R. 1630
Okhotsk 1648
Amur District To China 1689
Amur R. 1644
Kamchatka
to Russia 1697
Nizhni Kamchatka 1691
Deshnev 1648
Sakhalin I. 1644
De Vries 1643
Japan
Hirado
Yedo
Deshima
China
Formosa 1624-1662 D.
Ft. Zelandia
Macao
Philippines
PACIFIC OCEAN
Persia
Ispahan
Gambrom
Ormuz 1622
Basra
Arabia
India
Hugli 1642
Bombay
Goa
Madras 1639
Pondicherry
Cochin
Ceylon
Colombo
Achin
Pegu
Martaban
Siam
Ajudia
Tenasserim
Malacca
Sumatra
Borneo
Celebes
Spice Islands
Amboina
Batavia
Jacatra
Java
New Guinea
Torres 1606
Espiritu Santo Quiros 1606
Melinde (Malindi)
Mombasa
Zanzibar
Kilwa
Mozambique
Madagascar 1643-1674
Mauritius 1598, 1638
I. Bourbon 1654
Ft. Dauphin 1643
Sofala
INDIAN OCEAN
Tasman 1644
Dirk Hartog I. 1616
Eendrachts land 1616
Witteland 1628
NEW HOLLAND (AUSTRALIA)
Edelsland 1619
C. Leeuwin 1622
Amsterdam I. 1633
Van Diemen's Land (Tasmania) Tasman 1642
Staaten Land (New Zealand) Tasman 1642
Dutch colonies and trading posts
Dutch East India Company chartered in 1602
" West " " " 1621
English colonies and trading posts
English East India Company chartered in 1600
London and Plymouth Companies " " 1606
French colonies and trading posts
French East India Company chartered in 1604
Portuguese colonies and trading posts
Spanish colonies
Southern boundary of Russian Siberia
B.-P. = Brandenburg-Prussia; C.B. = Caledonia Bay (Puerto Escocés, Scotch Harbor); Cou. = Courland; D. = Dutch; Da. = Danish; E. = English; F. = French; H. = Hudson; J.m. = Jesuit missions; L.S. = La Salle; M.J. = Marquette and Jolliet; N.E. = New Edinburgh; N.N. = New Netherland (1614-1664, 1673-1674); Sw. = Swedish; U.N. = United Netherlands.
Scale along the Equator 1:140 000 000
The names of the principal Dutch, English, French and Spanish discoverers are printed thus: Tasman.
Except where otherwise noted, the dates are those of acquisition by the country concerned.
For the colonial development of English and French America during this period see p. 190-191.
C
The Establishment of Dutch Power in the Malay Archipelago, 1602-1641
Scale along the Equator 1:60000000
Long. East 110 of Greenw.
Junkseylon
Achin
Malacca 1641
Sumatra
Equator
Indragiri
Jambi
Palembang
Ft. York (Bencoolen) 1685
Bantam 1602
Batavia 1619
Java
Borneo
Celebes
Macassar
Menado
Ternate
Tidor
Gilolo
Moluccas or Spice Islands
Amboina 1605
Banda or Nutmeg Is. 1609
New Guinea
Bima
Flores
Sumbawa
Timor
Philippines (To Spain)
New Holland (Australia)
D
Guinea Coast
Scale 1:15000000
Meridian 0 of Greenw.
Ashanti
Dahomey
Volta R.
Whydah
Slave Coast
Ivory Coast
Gold Coast
Apollonia
Axim 1642
Gross Friedrichsburg 1683-1720 To B.-P.
C. Three Points
Commenda
Elmina 1637
St. Sebastian
Christiansborg (Danish)
Accra
Sw. D.8, D.1637, E.1667

Principal Seats of War in Europe, 1700—1721.

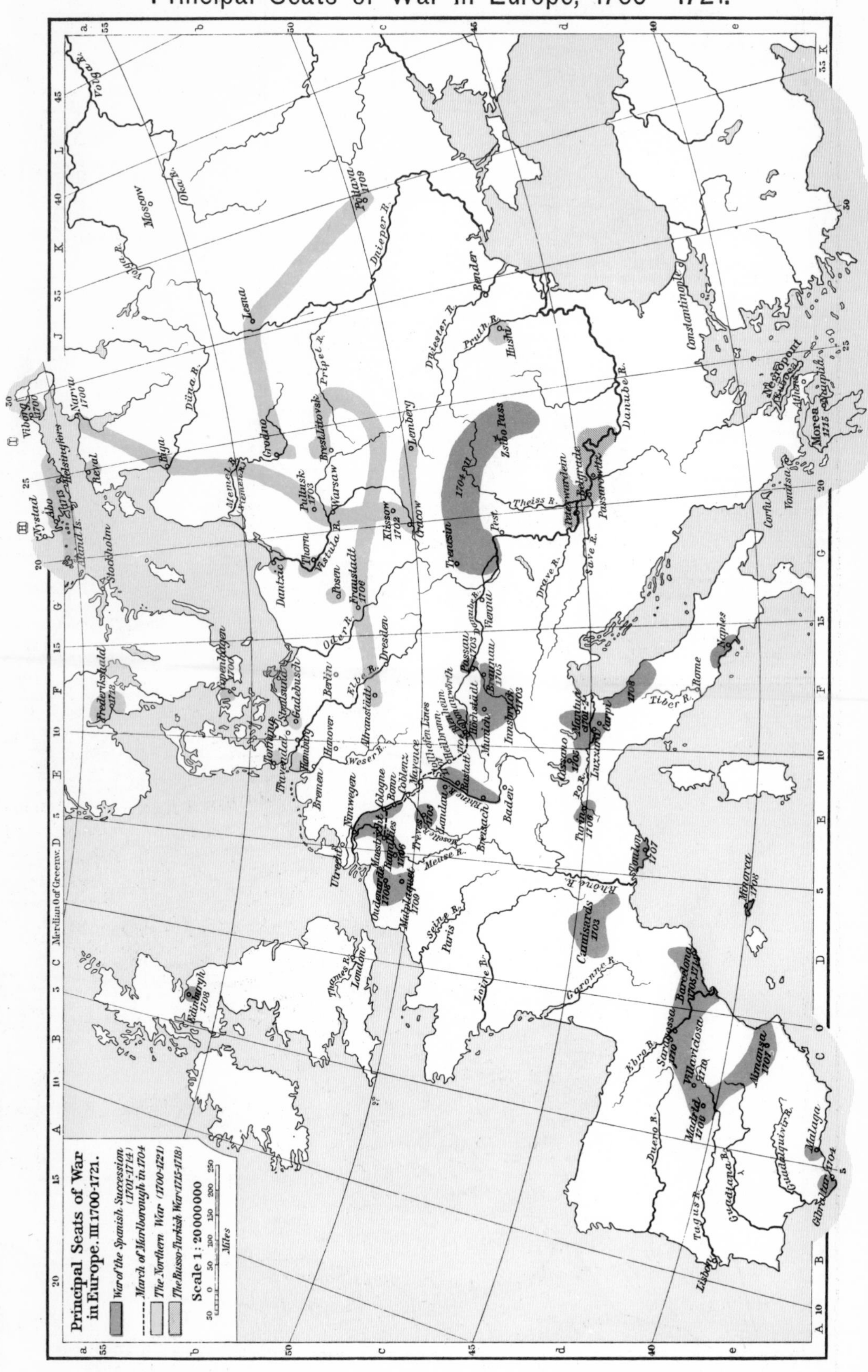

The Growth of Savoy, 1418-1748
The County of Savoy about 1280
Domain of the Duchy of Savoy in 1418
Territory acquired up to 1435
" " " " 1531
" lost " " 1536
" acquired " " 1601
" lost " " 1601
" acquired " " 1631
" " " " 1714
" " " " 1738
" " " " 1748
For other acquisitions of Savoy between 1714 and 1721, see the main map.
Co. - Cocconato Cr. - Crescentino
Scale 1:4 000 000
Miles
Free County of Burgundy
SAVOY
PIEDMONT
FRANCE
Valais
Chablais
Geneva
Lausanne
Fribourg
Berne
Chambéry
Grenoble
Lyons
Aosta
Turin
Ivrea
Vercelli
Novara
Milan
Casale
Asti
Alessandria
Pavia
Genoa
Nice
G. of Genoa
Little St. Bernard Pass
Great St. Bernard Pass
Simplon Pass
Mt. Cenis Pass
Mt. Genèvre Pass
NORTH SEA
ATLANTIC OCEAN
BAY OF BISCAY
ENGLISH CHANNEL
ENGLAND
KINGDOM OF FRANCE
KINGDOM OF SPAIN
K. OF PORTUGAL
Catalonia
Roussillon
Balearic Is.
Minorca To Great Britain 1708-1783
Majorca
Ivixa
Formentera
UNITED NETHERLANDS
Austrian Netherlands
SWITZERLAND
REPUBLIC OF GENOA
Corsica
K. OF SARDINIA
FEZ AND MOROCCO
ALGERIA
Gibraltar To England 1704
Ceuta To Spain
Melilla To Spain
Paris
London
Madrid
Lisbon
Seville
Barcelona
Bordeaux
Marseilles
Long. West 5 of Greenwich
Long. East 5 of Greenwich

KINGDOM OF SWEDEN
Finland
RUSSIAN EMPIRE
Govt. of Novgorod
Govt. of Moscow
Govt. of Smolensk
Govt. of Voronezh
Govt. of Biel-gorod
Govt. of Kiev
Esthonia
Livonia
Ingria
D. OF COURLAND
BALTIC SEA
K. OF PRUSSIA
KINGDOM OF POLAND
Lithuania
Great Poland
Little Poland
Volhynia
Podolia
Ukraine
Zaporogian Cossacks
Cossacks of the Don
Yedisan
Crimea
SEA OF AZOV
Moldavia
Bessarabia
Wallachia
Transylvania
KINGDOM OF HUNGARY
Bulgaria
Servia
Bosnia
Rumelia
Albania
Anatolia
OTTOMAN EMPIRE
BLACK SEA
KINGDOM OF THE TWO SICILIES
Sicily
Crete
Silesia
Bohemia
Moravia
AUSTRIA
Styria
Carinthia
Carniola
VENETIAN REPUBLIC
House of Bourbon
House of Hapsburg-Lorraine
Kingdom of Prussia and its dependencies
House of Savoy
Boundary of the Empire
Castle or Fortress
Monastery
Abbreviations.
A. = Austria. D. = Duchy. Govt. = Government.
GR.D. = Grand Duchy. Gr.P. = Grand Principality. H. = Holstein-Gottorp. K. = Kingdom.
P. = Principality. REP. = Republic.
Sites of battles, diplomatic negotiations and other events of historical importance are indicated by the sign (•).
Scale 1:15000000
Miles

Principal Seats of War, 1740—1763.

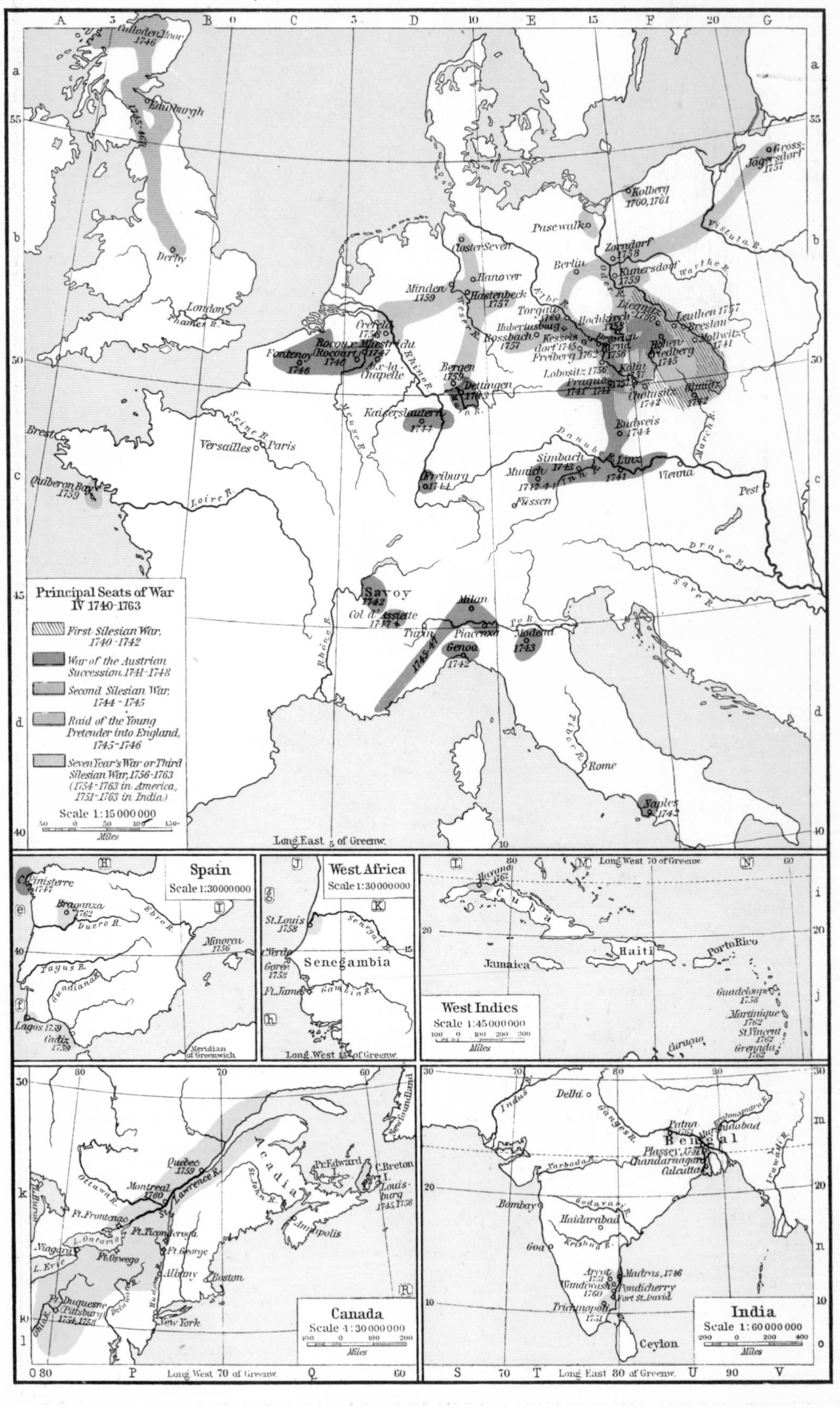

Treaty Adjustments, 1713—1763.

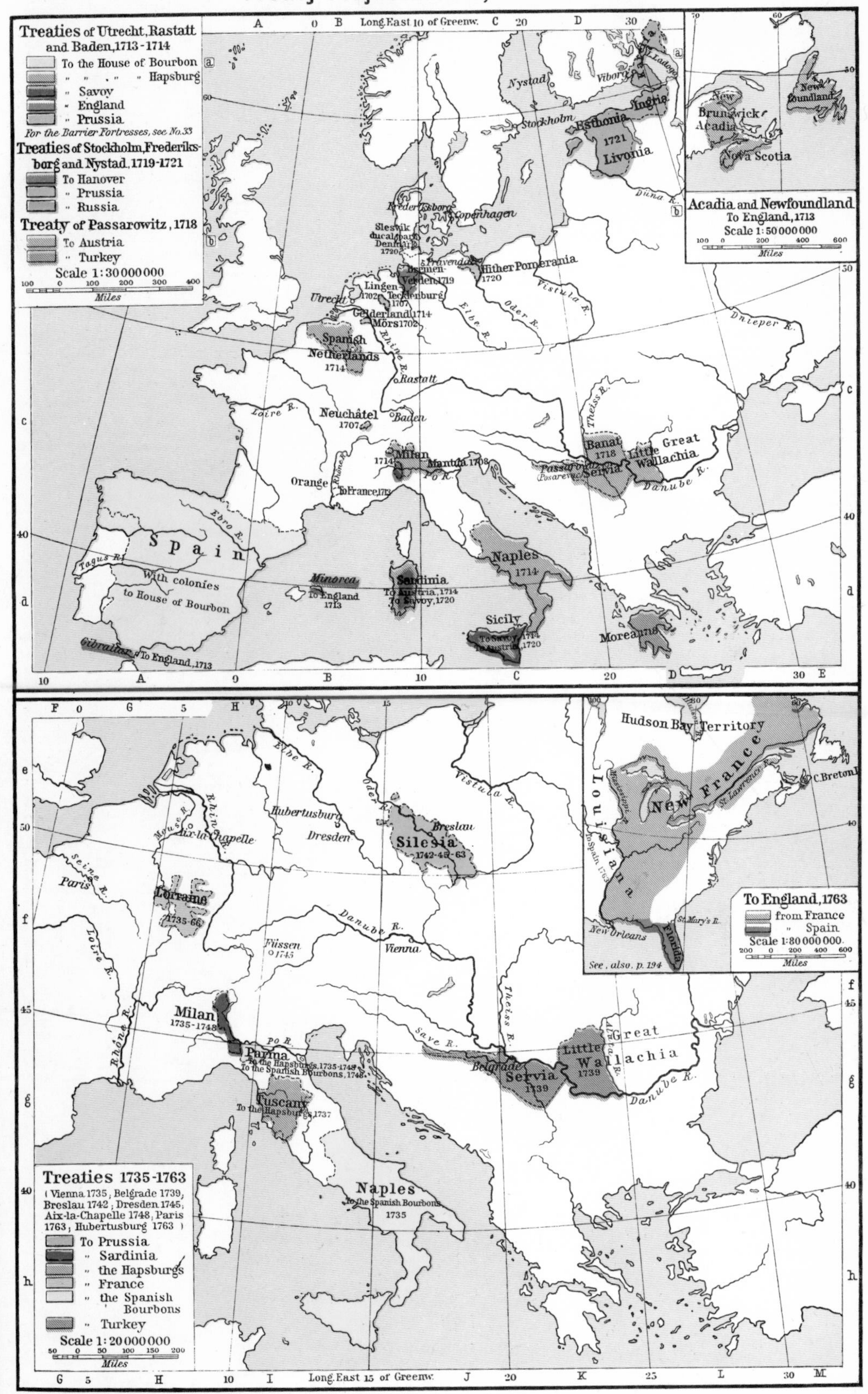
Treaties of Utrecht, Rastatt and Baden, 1713-1714
To the House of Bourbon
" " " Hapsburg
" Savoy
" England
" Prussia
For the Barrier Fortresses, see No.33
Treaties of Stockholm, Frederiksborg and Nystad, 1719-1721
To Hanover
" Prussia
" Russia
Treaty of Passarowitz, 1718
To Austria
" Turkey
Scale 1:30 000 000
Miles
Acadia and Newfoundland
To England, 1713
Scale 1:50 000 000
Miles
Treaties 1735-1763
(Vienna 1735; Belgrade 1739; Breslau 1742; Dresden 1745; Aix-la-Chapelle 1748; Paris 1763; Hubertusburg 1763)
To Prussia
" Sardinia
" the Hapsburgs
" France
" the Spanish Bourbons
" Turkey
Scale 1:20 000 000
Miles
To England, 1763
from France
" Spain
Scale 1:80 000 000
Miles
See, also, p. 194

BALTIC SEA
Bornholm
Rügen
Königsberg
Danzig
Elbing
East Prussia
Ermeland
KINGDOM OF PRUSSIA
West Prussia
Netze District
Farther Pomerania
Hither Pomerania
Neumark
Ukermark
Mittelmark
Berlin
New East Prussia
Warsaw
KINGDOM OF POLAND
South Prussia
Posen
Breslau
Silesia
Austrian Silesia
Upper Lusatia
Lower Lusatia
Dresden
Prague
KINGDOM OF BOHEMIA
M. of Moravia
Archduchy of Austria
Vienna
Below the Enns
Above the Enns
A. OF SALZBURG
D. of Styria
D. of Carinthia
D. of Carniola
Trieste
Istria
Croatia
Slavonia
KINGDOM OF HUNGARY
West Galicia
K. of Galicia
To Austria, 1772
New Silesia
Cracow
Zips
L. Balaton
Hapsburg Lands
Hohenzollern Lands:
Prussia
Franconian line
Wettin Lands:
Albertine
Ernestine
Wittelsbach Lands:
Bavaria (Palatinate-Sulzbach)
Palatinate-Zweibrücken (Deux-Ponts)
Oldenburg Lands:
Denmark (royal portion)
Holstein-Gottorp (ducal portion) and Oldenburg
Ecclesiastical States
Imperial Cities
Boundary of the Empire.
Barrier Fortresses are underlined thus: Ypres.
Stollhofen and Weissenburg lines.
The chief territorial changes in the eighteenth century are indicated by narrow colored borders.
Sites of the most important battles and diplomatic negotiations are given the sign (•).
The areas in the Empire left uncolored were divided into petty states.
Abbreviations:
A. = Archbishopric; A. Z. = Anhalt-Zerbst; B. = Bishopric; Br. C. = Bromberg Canal; C. = County; D. = Duchy; Fr. W. C. = Frederick William Canal; H. C. = Hesse-Cassel; K. = Kingdom; Lg. = Landgraviate; M. = Margravate; Meckl. = Mecklenburg; N. = Nassau; P. = Principality.
Castle or fortress
Monastery
Scale 1 : 5 000 000
Miles

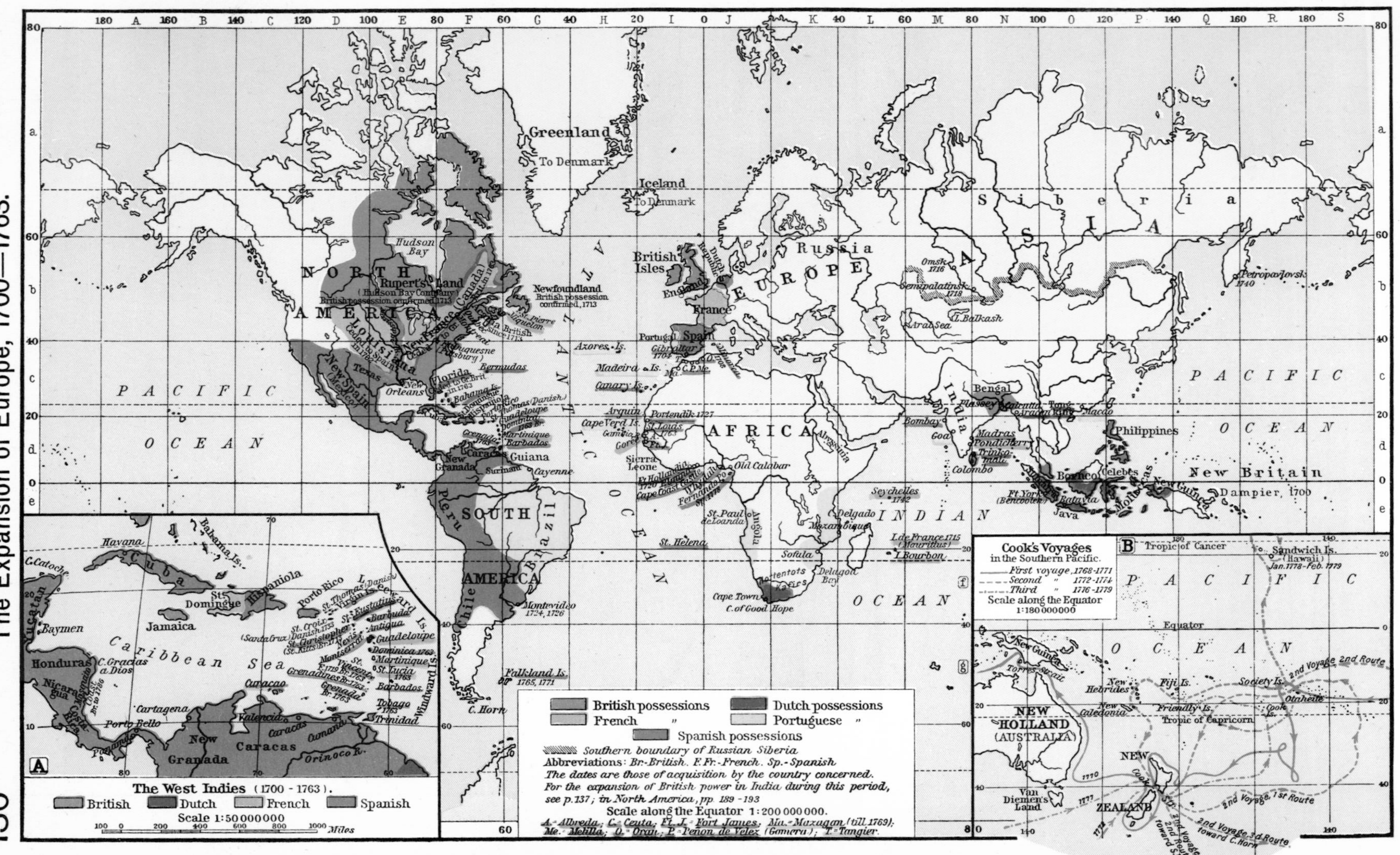

NORTH AMERICA
SOUTH AMERICA
AFRICA
EUROPE
ASIA
Siberia
Russia
India
PACIFIC OCEAN
ATLANTIC OCEAN
INDIAN OCEAN
Greenland
To Denmark
Iceland
To Denmark
British Isles
England
France
Spain
Portugal
Hudson Bay
Rupert's Land
(Hudson Bay Company)
British possession confirmed, 1713
Newfoundland
British possession confirmed, 1713
Louisiana
New France (Canada)
New Spain
(Mexico)
Texas
Florida
New Orleans
Bermudas
Azores Is.
Madeira Is.
Canary Is.
Cape Verd Is.
Sierra Leone
Old Calabar
St. Helena
Angola
Mozambique
Sofala
Delagoa Bay
Cape Town
C. of Good Hope
Seychelles
I. de France 1715
(Mauritius)
I. Bourbon
Bombay
Goa
Madras
Pondicherry
Colombo
Bengal
Macao
Philippines
Borneo
Celebes
Java
Moluccas
New Guinea
New Britain
Dampier, 1700
Omsk 1716
Semipalatinsk 1718
Aral Sea
L. Balkash
Petropavlovsk 1740
Guiana
Surinam
Cayenne
New Granada
Peru
Chile
Brazil
Montevideo 1724, 1726
Falkland Is. 1765, 1771
C. Horn
A
Havana
Cuba
Bahama Is.
Yucatan
Baymen
Honduras
C. Gracias a Dios
Nicaragua
Costa Rica
Jamaica
St. Domingue
Hispaniola
Porto Rico
Caribbean Sea
Leeward Is.
Windward Is.
Guadeloupe
Dominica 1763
Martinique
St. Lucia 1763
Barbados
Tobago 1763
Trinidad
Grenada Br. 1763
Curaçao
Cartagena
Porto Bello
New Granada
Caracas
Orinoco R.
The West Indies (1700 - 1763).
British
Dutch
French
Spanish
Scale 1:50000000
Miles
British possessions
French "
Spanish possessions
Dutch possessions
Portuguese "
Southern boundary of Russian Siberia
Abbreviations: Br.-British. F.Fr.-French. Sp.-Spanish
The dates are those of acquisition by the country concerned.
For the expansion of British power in India during this period, see p.137; in North America, pp. 189 - 193
Scale along the Equator 1:200000000.
A.-Albreda; C.-Ceuta; Ft. J.-Fort James; Ma.-Mazagan (till 1769); Me.-Melilla; O.-Oran; P.-Peñon de Velez (Gomera); T.-Tangier.
B
Cook's Voyages
in the Southern Pacific.
First voyage 1768-1771
Second " 1772-1774
Third " 1776-1779
Scale along the Equator
1:180000000
Tropic of Cancer
Sandwich Is. (Hawaii)
Jan. 1778 - Feb. 1779
Equator
Tropic of Capricorn
New Guinea
Torres Strait
NEW HOLLAND (AUSTRALIA)
Van Diemen's Land
New Hebrides
New Caledonia
Fiji Is.
Friendly Is.
Society Is.
Otaheite
Cook Is.
NEW ZEALAND
2nd Voyage 2nd Route
2nd Voyage 1st Route
2nd Voyage 3rd Route toward C. Horn

India, 1700—1792.

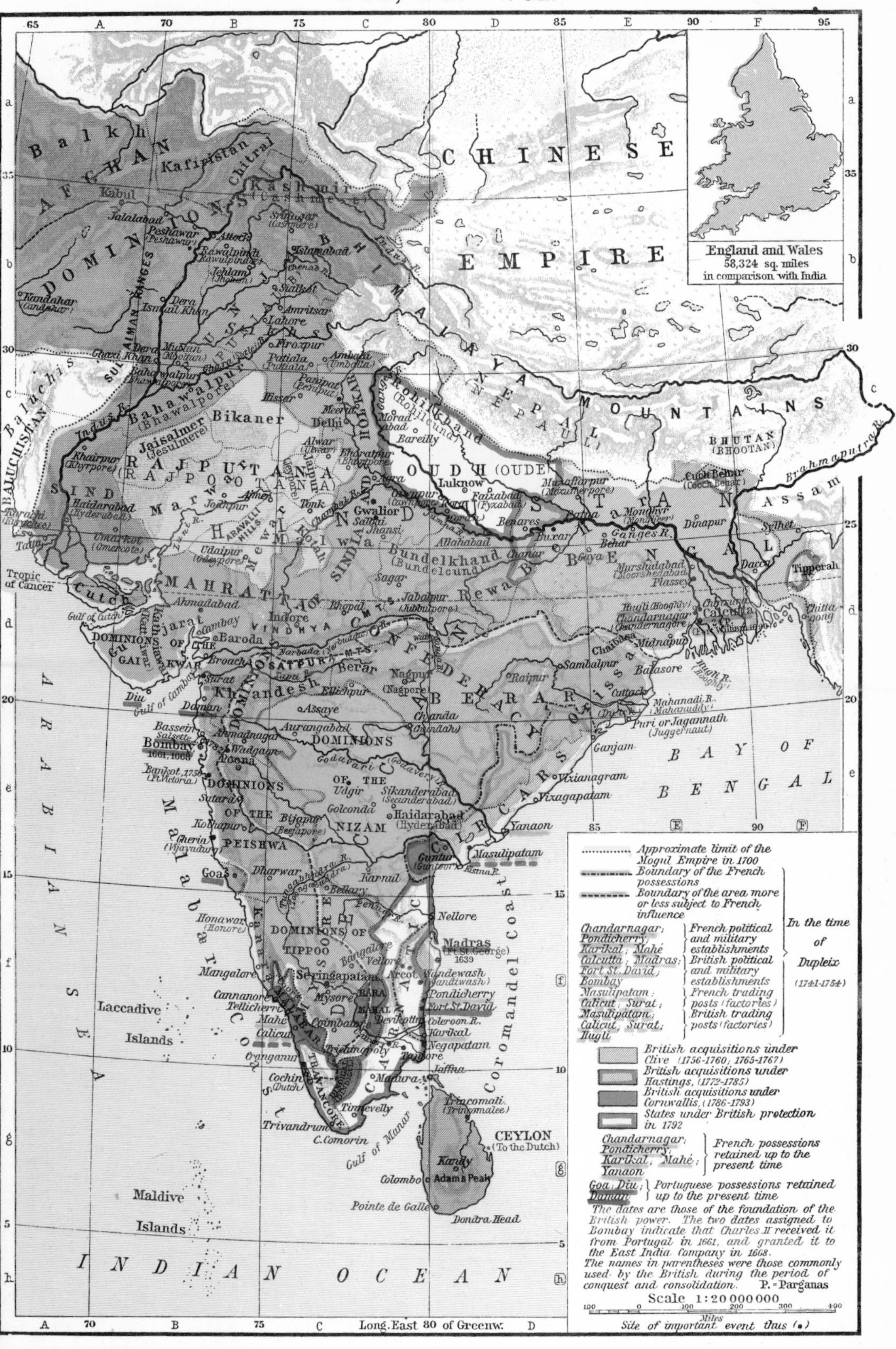

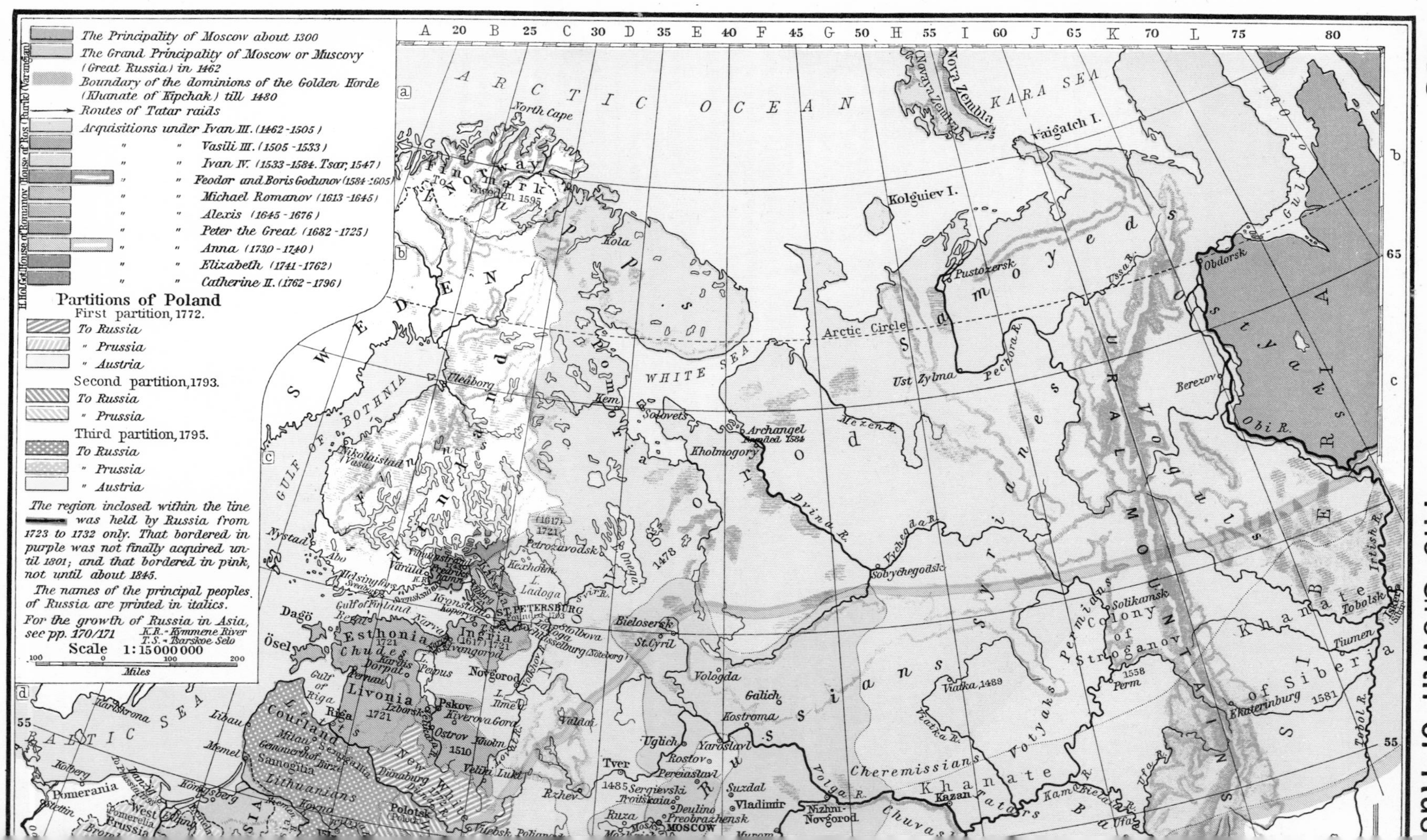

The Principality of Moscow about 1300
The Grand Principality of Moscow or Muscovy (Great Russia) in 1462
Boundary of the dominions of the Golden Horde (Khanate of Kipchak) till 1480
Routes of Tatar raids
Acquisitions under Ivan III. (1462-1505)
" " Vasili III. (1505-1533)
" " Ivan IV. (1533-1584. Tsar, 1547)
" " Feodor and Boris Godunov (1584-1605)
" " Michael Romanov (1613-1645)
" " Alexis (1645-1676)
" " Peter the Great (1682-1725)
" " Anna (1730-1740)
" " Elizabeth (1741-1762)
" " Catherine II. (1762-1796)
Partitions of Poland
First partition, 1772.
To Russia
" Prussia
" Austria
Second partition, 1793.
To Russia
" Prussia
Third partition, 1795.
To Russia
" Prussia
" Austria
The region inclosed within the line was held by Russia from 1723 to 1732 only. That bordered in purple was not finally acquired until 1801; and that bordered in pink, not until about 1845.
The names of the principal peoples of Russia are printed in italics.
For the growth of Russia in Asia, see pp. 170/171
K.R. = Kymmene River
T.S. = Tsarskoe Selo
Scale 1:15000000
Miles
ARCTIC OCEAN
KARA SEA
WHITE SEA
BALTIC SEA
GULF OF BOTHNIA
URAL MOUNTAINS
SWEDEN

BLACK SEA
SEA OF AZOV
CASPIAN SEA
ARAL SEA
AEGEAN SEA
MEDITERRANEAN SEA
OTTOMAN EMPIRE
PERSIA
HUNGARY
AUSTRIA
Little Poland
Galicia
Lodomeria
Volhynia
Podolia
Little Russia
Ukraine
Severia
Crimea
Zaporogian Cossacks
Khanate of the Crimea
Yedisan
Bessarabia
Moldavia
Wallachia
Transylvania
CARPATHIAN MTS.
Servia
Bulgaria
BALKAN MTS.
Rumelia
Greece
Cossacks of the Don
Kalmucks
Khanate of Astrakhan
Nogaians
German Settlements from 1763
Uralian Cossacks
Kirgiz
Ust-Urt
Transcaspian District
KHIVA
Turcomans
Kuban
Circassians
CAUCASUS MTS.
Kabardia
Cossacks of the Terek
Daghestan
Mingrelia
Imeritia
Georgia
Shirvan
Armenia
Azerbaijan
Ghilan
Mazanderan
Astrabad
Astrakhan
Constantinople
Tiflis
Teheran
Crete
Cyprus
Rhodes
Lesbos
Euphrates R.
Tigris R.
Danube R.
Don R.
Volga R.
Ural R.
Long. East 40 of Greenwich

Typical German States befo

I. Baden.

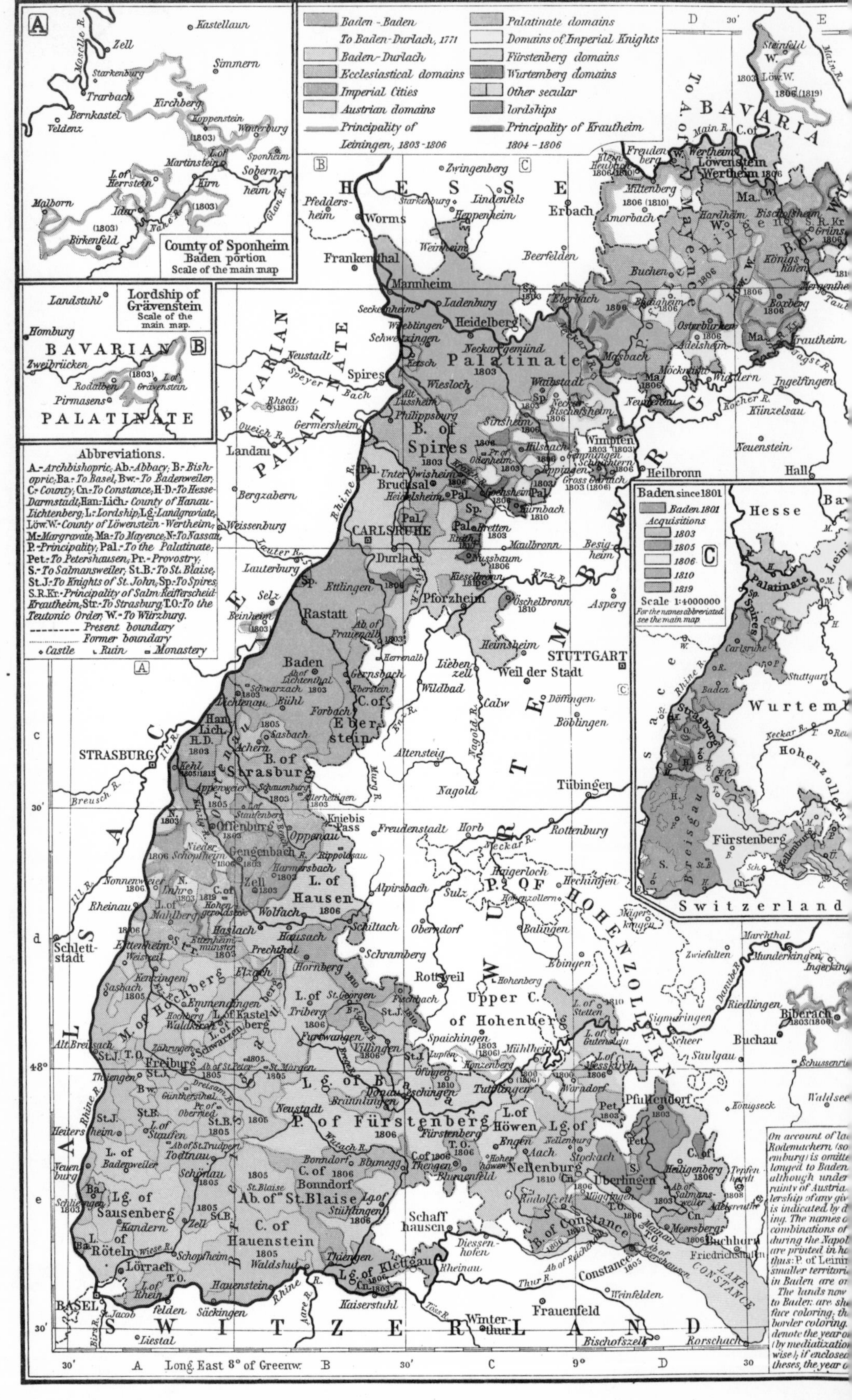

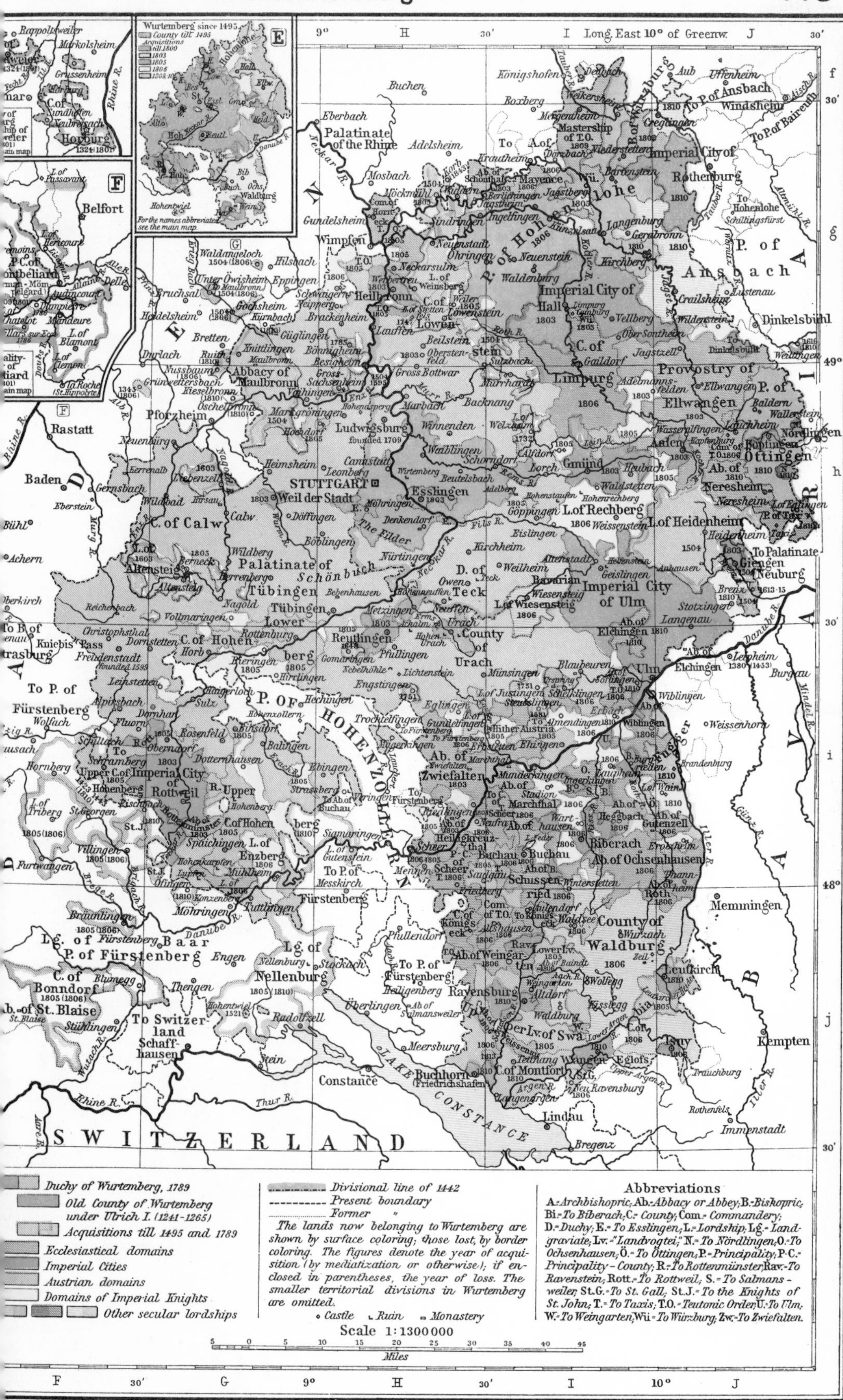
Duchy of Wurtemberg, 1789
Old County of Wurtemberg under Ulrich I. (1241-1265)
Acquisitions till 1495 and 1789
Ecclesiastical domains
Imperial Cities
Austrian domains
Domains of Imperial Knights
Other secular lordships
Divisional line of 1442
Present boundary
Former "
The lands now belonging to Wurtemberg are shown by surface coloring; those lost, by border coloring. The figures denote the year of acquisition (by mediatization or otherwise); if enclosed in parentheses, the year of loss. The smaller territorial divisions in Wurtemberg are omitted.
Castle
Ruin
Monastery
Scale 1:1300000
Miles
Abbreviations
A.-Archbishopric; Ab.-Abbacy or Abbey; B.-Bishopric; Bi.-To Biberach; C.-County; Com.-Commandery; D.-Duchy; E.-To Esslingen; L.-Lordship; Lg.-Landgraviate; Lv.-"Landvogtei;" N.-To Nördlingen; O.-To Ochsenhausen; Ö.-To Öttingen; P.-Principality; P-C.-Principality-County; R.-To Rottenmünster; Rav.-To Ravenstein; Rott.-To Rottweil; S.-To Salmansweiler; St.G.-To St. Gall; St.J.-To the Knights of St. John; T.-To Taxis; T.O.-Teutonic Order; U.-To Ulm; W.-To Weingarten; Wü.-To Würzburg; Zw.-To Zwiefalten.
Wurtemberg since 1495
STUTTGART
Palatinate of the Rhine
P. of Hohenlohe
P. of Ansbach
Imperial City of Rothenburg
Imperial City of Hall
Provostry of Ellwangen
P. of Öttingen
Imperial City of Ulm
County of Urach
P. of Hohenzollern
Imperial City of Rottweil
County of Waldburg
P. of Fürstenberg
Lg. of Nellenburg
Lake Constance
SWITZERLAND
Bavaria
Baden

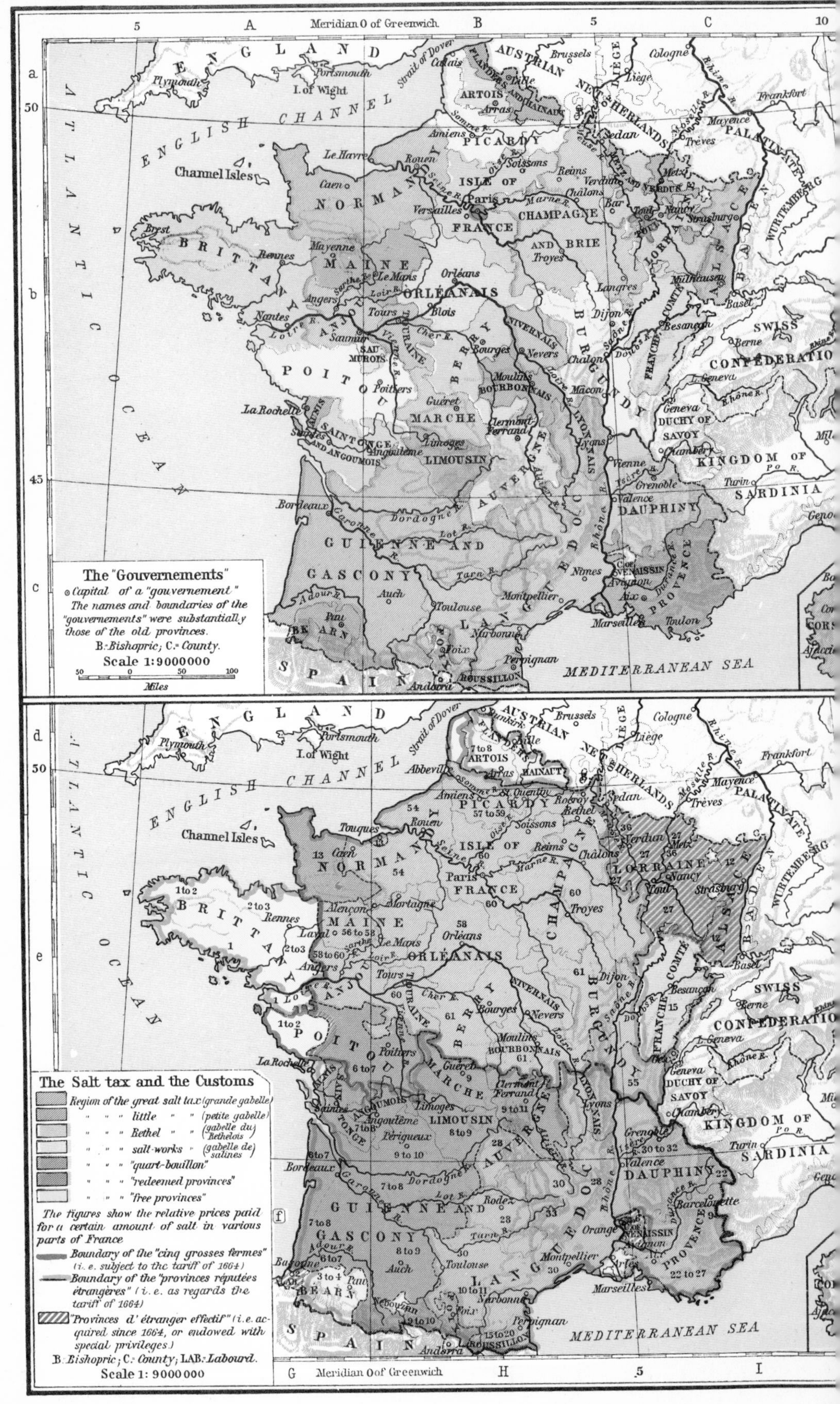

The "Gouvernements"
Capital of a "gouvernement"
The names and boundaries of the "gouvernements" were substantially those of the old provinces.
B.: Bishopric; C.: County.
Scale 1:9000000
Miles
ENGLAND
ENGLISH CHANNEL
ATLANTIC OCEAN
MEDITERRANEAN SEA
AUSTRIAN NETHERLANDS
SWISS CONFEDERATION
KINGDOM OF SARDINIA
SPAIN
BRITTANY
NORMANDY
PICARDY
ISLE OF FRANCE
CHAMPAGNE AND BRIE
MAINE
ORLÉANAIS
POITOU
MARCHE
LIMOUSIN
AUVERGNE
BURGUNDY
DAUPHINY
PROVENCE
GUIENNE AND GASCONY
LANGUEDOC
The Salt tax and the Customs
Region of the great salt tax (grande gabelle)
" " " little " " (petite gabelle)
" " " Rethel " " (gabelle du Rethelois)
" " " salt-works " (gabelle de salines)
" " " "quart-bouillon"
" " " "redeemed provinces"
" " " "free provinces"
The figures show the relative prices paid for a certain amount of salt in various parts of France
Boundary of the "cinq grosses fermes" (i. e. subject to the tariff of 1664)
Boundary of the "provinces réputées étrangères" (i. e. as regards the tariff of 1664)
"Provinces d' étranger effectif" (i. e. acquired since 1664, or endowed with special privileges.)
B.: Bishopric; C.: County; LAB.: Labourd.
Scale 1: 9000000
Meridian 0 of Greenwich

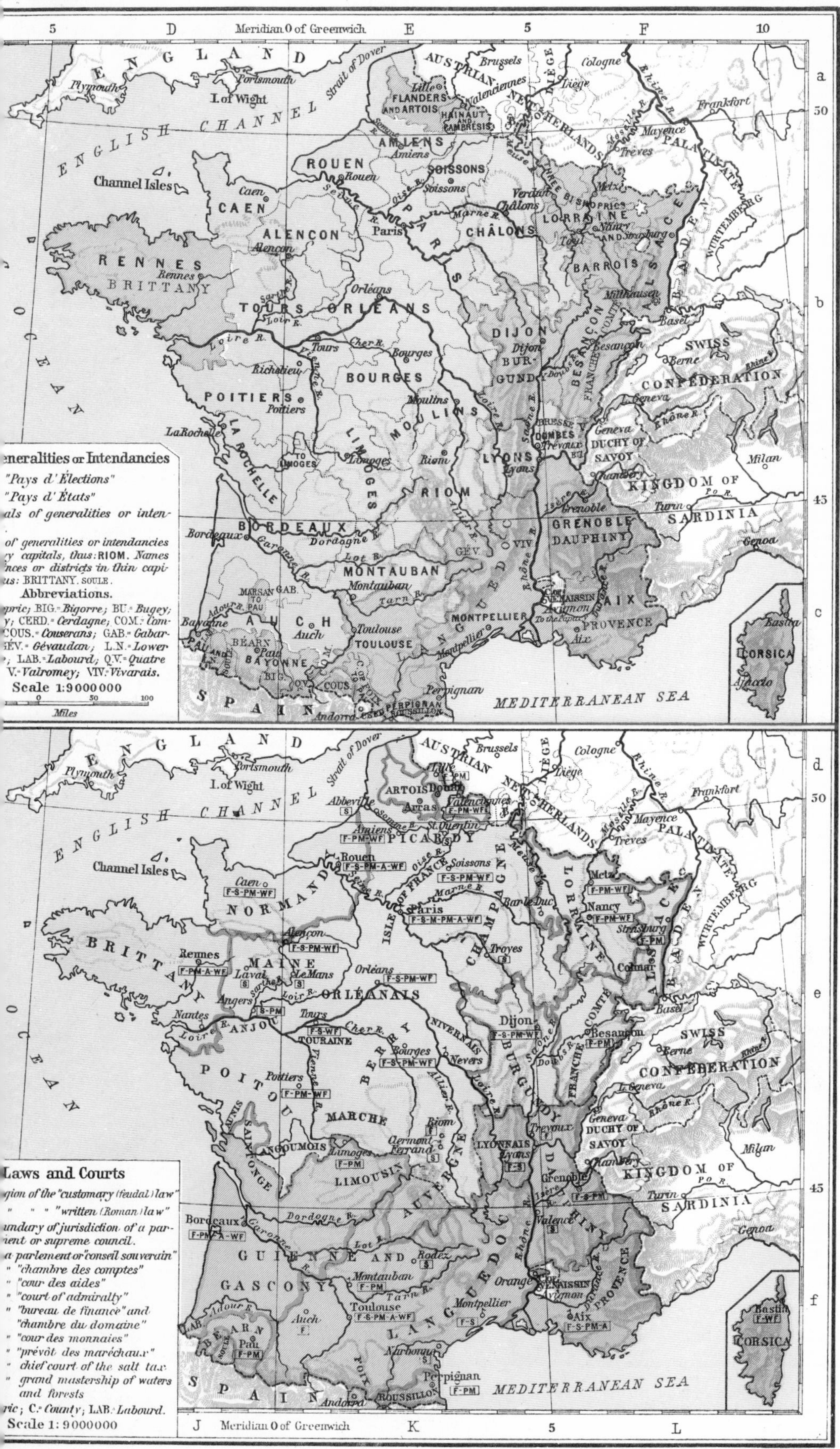
Generalities or Intendancies
"Pays d'Élections"
"Pays d'États"
Abbreviations.
Scale 1:9000000
Miles
Laws and Courts
Scale 1: 9000000
Meridian 0 of Greenwich
ENGLISH CHANNEL
MEDITERRANEAN SEA
AUSTRIAN NETHERLANDS
SWISS CONFEDERATION
KINGDOM OF SARDINIA
DUCHY OF SAVOY
SPAIN
CORSICA
OCEAN

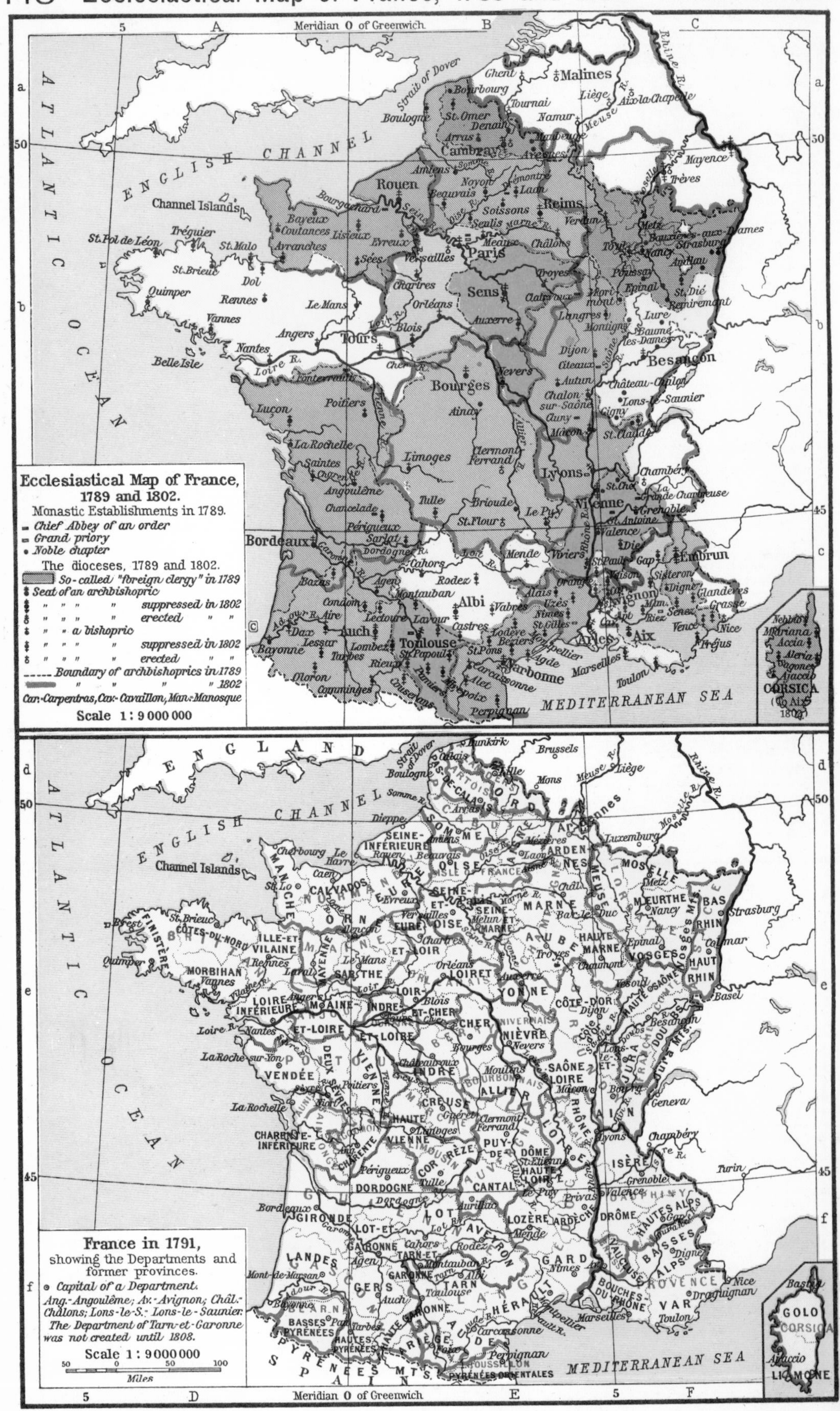
Ecclesiastical Map of France, 1789 and 1802.
Monastic Establishments in 1789.
Chief Abbey of an order
Grand priory
Noble chapter
The dioceses, 1789 and 1802.
So-called "foreign clergy" in 1789
Seat of an archbishopric
" " " suppressed in 1802
" " " erected " "
" " a bishopric
" " " suppressed in 1802
" " " erected " "
Boundary of archbishoprics in 1789
" " " 1802
Car.-Carpentras, Cav.-Cavaillon, Man.-Manosque
Scale 1 : 9 000 000
ATLANTIC OCEAN
ENGLISH CHANNEL
MEDITERRANEAN SEA
Strait of Dover
Channel Islands
CORSICA
France in 1791,
showing the Departments and former provinces.
Capital of a Department.
Ang.-Angoulême; Av.-Avignon; Châl.-Châlons; Lons-le-S.-Lons-le-Saunier.
The Department of Tarn-et-Garonne was not created until 1808.
Scale 1 : 9 000 000
Miles
ENGLAND
SPAIN
PYRENEES MTS.
Meridian 0 of Greenwich

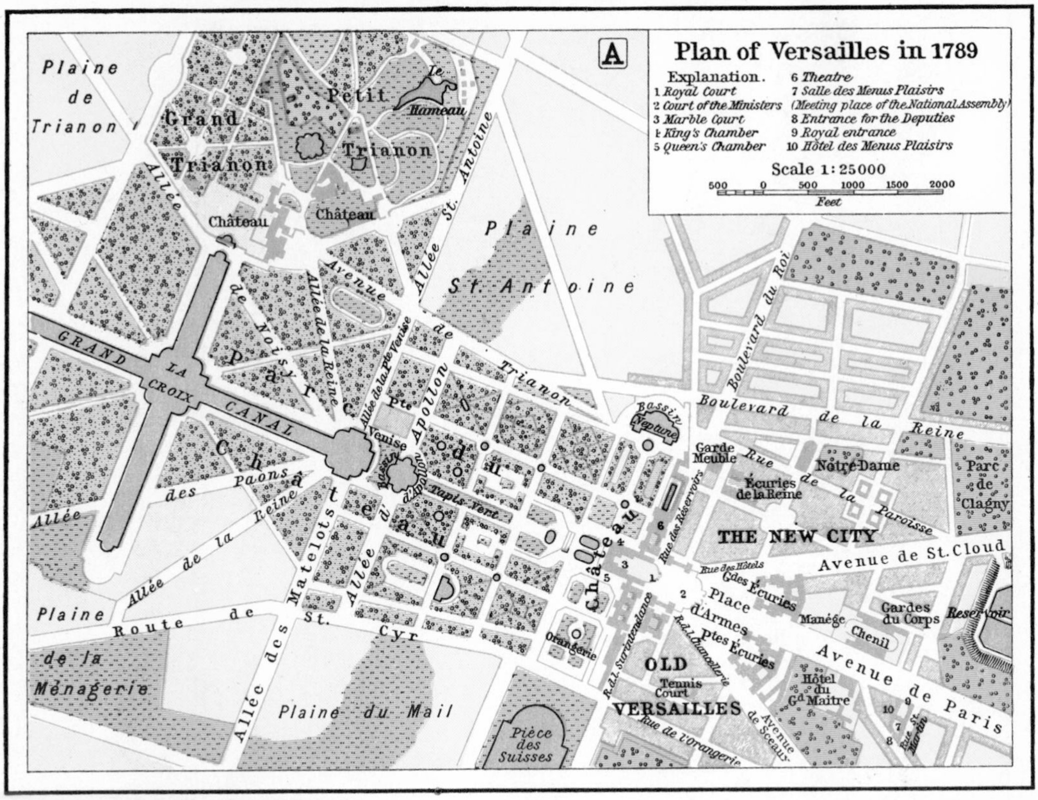
A
Plan of Versailles in 1789
Explanation.
1 Royal Court
2 Court of the Ministers
3 Marble Court
4 King's Chamber
5 Queen's Chamber
6 Theatre
7 Salle des Menus Plaisirs (Meeting place of the National Assembly)
8 Entrance for the Deputies
9 Royal entrance
10 Hôtel des Menus Plaisirs
Scale 1:25000
500 0 500 1000 1500 2000
Feet
Plaine de Trianon
Grand Trianon
Petit Trianon
le Hameau
Château
Château
Allée St. Antoine
Plaine St. Antoine
Avenue de Trianon
Allée de Noisy
Allée de la Reine
GRAND CANAL
LA CROIX
Parc du Château
Allée des Paons
Allée de la Reine
Pts Venise
Bassin d'Apollon
Allée d'Apollon
Tapis Vert
Allée des Matelots
Allée d'Apollon
Plaine de la Ménagerie
Route de St. Cyr
Allée des Matelots
Plaine du Mail
Pièce des Suisses
Orangerie
Château
Bassin Neptune
Garde Meuble
Boulevard du Roi
Boulevard de la Reine
Rue de la Paroisse
Notre Dame
Écuries de la Reine
Parc de Clagny
THE NEW CITY
Rue des Réservoirs
Rue des Hôtels
Avenue de St. Cloud
Gdes Écuries
Place d'Armes
Ptes Écuries
Manège
Chenil
Gardes du Corps
Reservoir
R.d.l. Surintendance
R.d.l. Chancellerie
OLD VERSAILLES
Tennis Court
Rue de l'Orangerie
Avenue de Sceaux
Hôtel du Gd Maitre
Avenue de Paris
Rue St. Martin

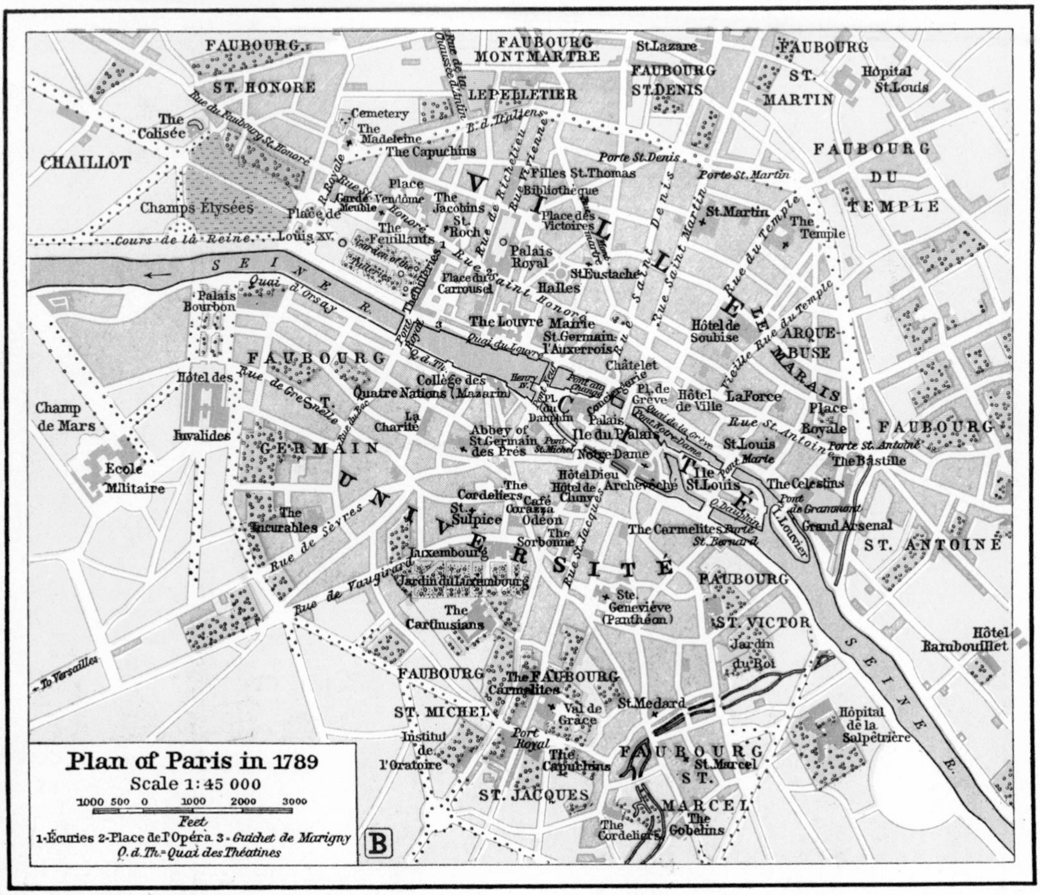
FAUBOURG ST. HONORE
FAUBOURG MONTMARTRE
St. Lazare
FAUBOURG ST. DENIS
FAUBOURG ST. MARTIN
Hôpital St. Louis
Chaussée d'Antin
LEPELLETIER
Cemetery
The Madeleine
The Capuchins
B.d. Italiens
The Colisée
CHAILLOT
Rue du Faubourg St. Honoré
Porte St. Denis
Porte St. Martin
FAUBOURG DU TEMPLE
Filles St. Thomas
Bibliothèque
R. Royale
Garde Meuble
Place Vendôme
The Jacobins
St. Roch
Champs Elysées
Place de Louis XV.
Cours de la Reine
The Feuillants
Jardin of the Tuileries
Place des Victoires
Rue de Richelieu
Rue Vivienne
Rue St. Honoré
Palais Royal
St. Eustache
Halles
Rue Saint Denis
Rue Saint Martin
St. Martin
The Temple
Rue du Temple
VILLE
SEINE R.
Quai d'Orsay
Palais Bourbon
Place du Carrousel
The Louvre
Marie
St. Germain l'Auxerrois
Quai du Louvre
Hôtel de Soubise
Vieille Rue du Temple
ARQUEBUSE
LE MARAIS
Châtelet
Pont Royal
FAUBOURG ST. GERMAIN
Hôtel des Invalides
Rue de Grenelle
Rue du Bac
Collège des Quatre Nations (Mazarin)
Henry IV
Pont Neuf
Pont au Change
Pl. de Grève
Hôtel de Ville
LaForce
Place Royale
Rue St. Antoine
FAUBOURG
Champ de Mars
La Charité
Pl. Dauphin
Palais
Ile du Palais
CITÉ
Abbey of St. Germain des Prés
Pont St. Michel
Notre Dame
St. Louis
Pont Marie
Porte St. Antoine
The Bastille
Ecole Militaire
Hôtel Dieu
Archevêché
Ile St. Louis
The Celestins
Hôtel de Cluny
The Cordeliers
Café Corazza
Odéon
St. Sulpice
The Incurables
Rue de Sèvres
The Sorbonne
UNIVERSITÉ
Rue St. Jacques
The Carmelites
Porte St. Bernard
Pont de Grammont
I. Louvier
Grand Arsenal
ST. ANTOINE
Luxembourg
Jardin du Luxembourg
Rue de Vaugirard
Ste. Geneviève (Panthéon)
FAUBOURG ST. VICTOR
Jardin du Roi
The Carthusians
Hôtel Rambouillet
To Versailles
FAUBOURG ST. MICHEL
The FAUBOURG Carmelites
Val de Grâce
St. Medard
Hôpital de la Salpêtrière
Institut de l'Oratoire
Port Royal
The Capuchins
FAUBOURG St. Marcel ST. MARCEL
ST. JACQUES
The Cordeliers
The Gobelins
Plan of Paris in 1789
Scale 1:45 000
1000 500 0 1000 2000 3000
Feet
1-Écuries 2-Place de l'Opéra 3-Guichet de Marigny
Q.d.Th.=Quai des Théatines
B

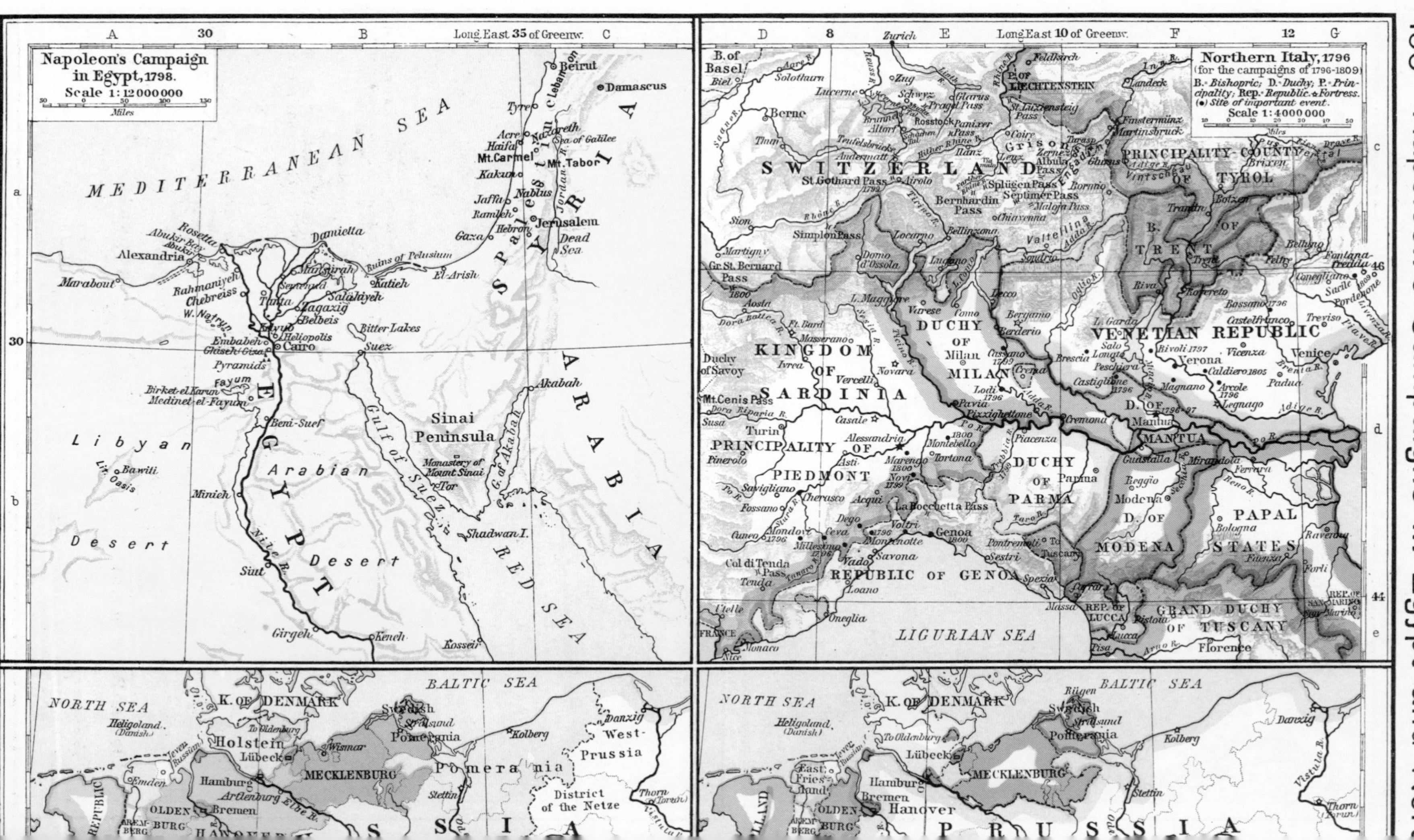
Napoleon's Campaign in Egypt, 1798.
Scale 1:12 000 000
Miles
MEDITERRANEAN SEA
EGYPT
Libyan Desert
Arabian Desert
Sinai Peninsula
ARABIA
SYRIA
RED SEA
Gulf of Suez
Alexandria
Rosetta
Damietta
Cairo
Pyramids
Suez
Gaza
Jaffa
Acre
Jerusalem
Damascus
Beirut
Northern Italy, 1796
(for the campaigns of 1796-1809)
B. Bishopric; D. Duchy; P. Principality; Rep. Republic. ⊕ Fortress.
(●) Site of important event.
Scale 1:4 000 000
SWITZERLAND
KINGDOM OF SARDINIA
PRINCIPALITY OF PIEDMONT
DUCHY OF MILAN
VENETIAN REPUBLIC
DUCHY OF PARMA
D. OF MODENA
PAPAL STATES
GRAND DUCHY OF TUSCANY
REPUBLIC OF GENOA
LIGURIAN SEA
PRINCIPALITY-COUNTY OF TYROL
MANTUA
NORTH SEA
BALTIC SEA
K. OF DENMARK
MECKLENBURG
PRUSSIA

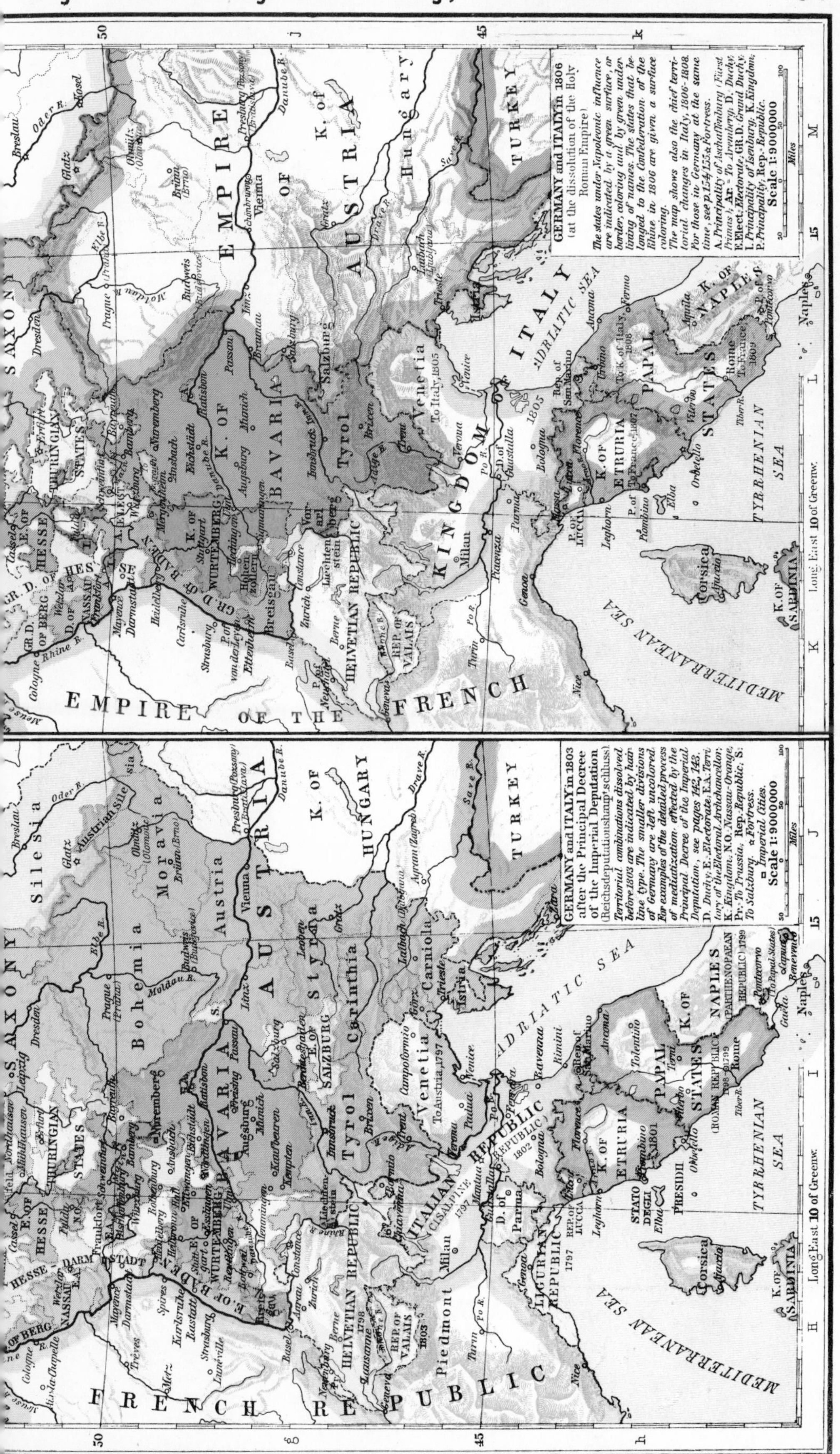
GERMANY and ITALY in 1806 (at the dissolution of the Holy Roman Empire)
Scale 1:9000000
GERMANY and ITALY in 1803 after the Principal Decree of the Imperial Deputation (Reichsdeputationshauptschluss)
Scale 1:9000000
MEDITERRANEAN SEA
TYRRHENIAN SEA
ADRIATIC SEA

Treaty Adjustments, 1801—1812.

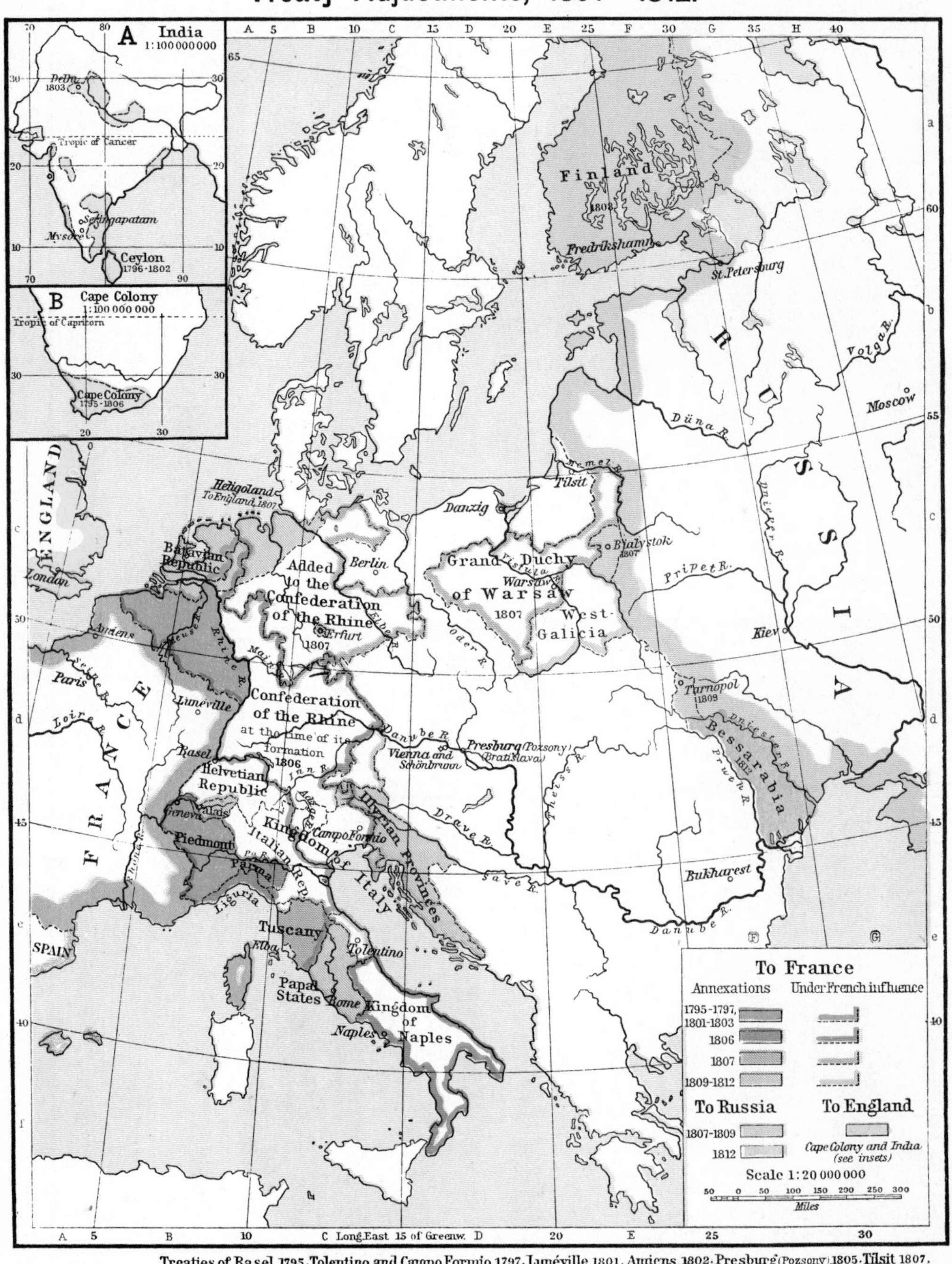

Treaties of Basel, 1795; Tolentino and Campo Formio, 1797; Lunéville, 1801; Amiens, 1802; Presburg (Pozsony), 1805; Tilsit 1807; Fredrikshamn and Vienna (Schönbrunn), 1809; Bukharest, 1812.

Principal Seats of War, 1788—1815.

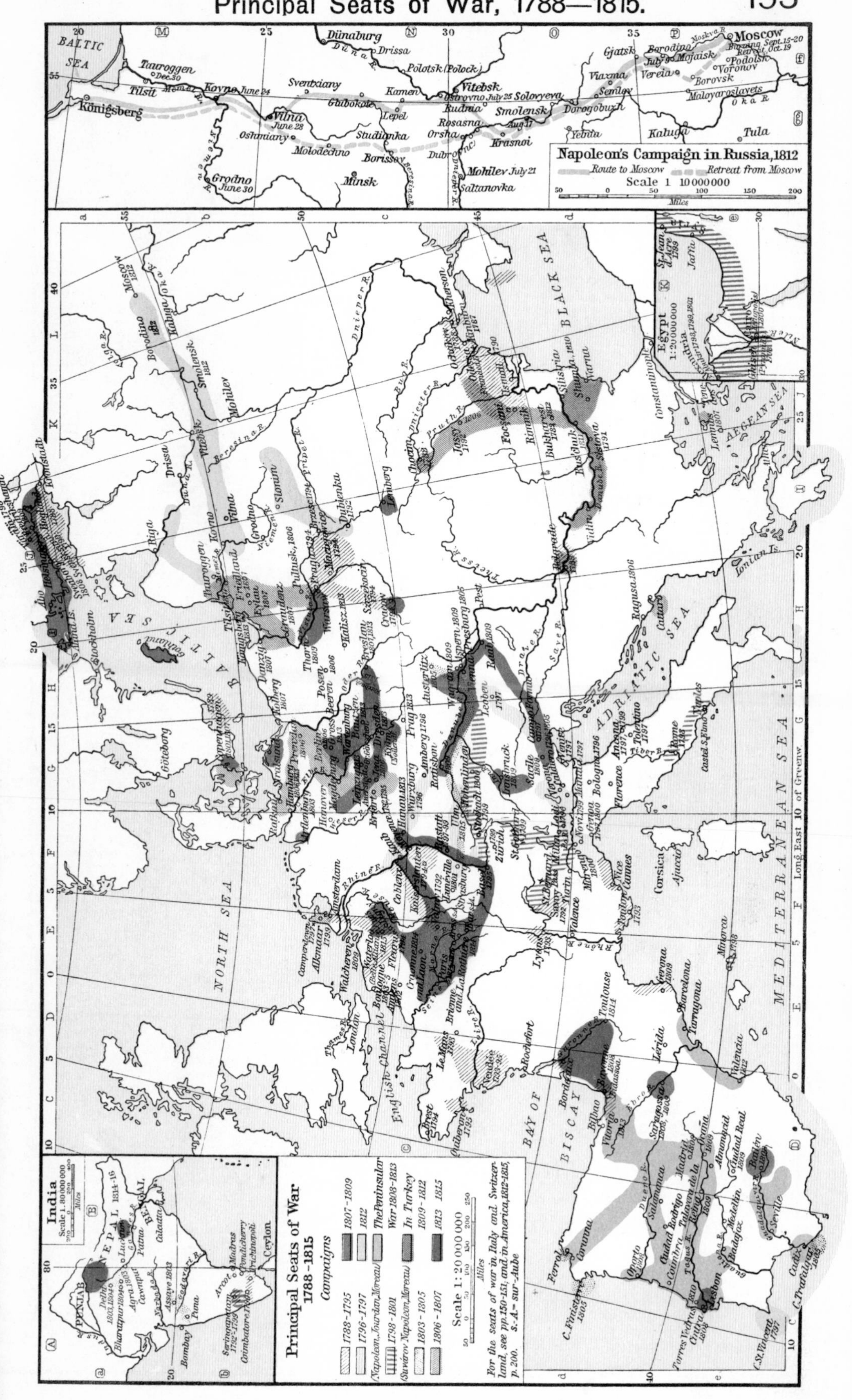
Napoleon's Campaign in Russia, 1812
Route to Moscow
Retreat from Moscow
Scale 1:10000000
Miles
Principal Seats of War
1788-1815
Campaigns
1788-1795
1796-1797
(Napoleon, Jourdan, Moreau)
1798-1801
(Suwarov, Napoleon, Moreau)
1803-1805
1806-1807
1807-1809
1812
The Peninsular War 1808-1813
In Turkey 1809-1812
1813
1815
Scale 1:20000000
Miles
For the seats of war in Italy and Switzerland, see pp. 150-151; and in America, 1812-1815, p. 200.
S.-A.= sur-Aube
India
Scale 1:80000000
Egypt
1:20000000
BALTIC SEA
NORTH SEA
BLACK SEA
BAY OF BISCAY
MEDITERRANEAN SEA
ADRIATIC SEA
AEGEAN SEA
Moscow
Borodino
Smolensk
Vitebsk
Vilna
Kovno
Tilsit
Königsberg
Grodno
Minsk
Borissov
Kaluga
Tula
Dünaburg
Polotsk
Drissa
Mohilev

NORTH SEA
Heligoland (British)
UNITED KINGDOM
Norwich
Ipswich
Deal
Dover
Calais
Dunkirk
Ostend
Bruges
Ghent
Antwerp
Brussels
Louvain
Maestricht
Waterloo
Belle Alliance
Quatre Bras
Ligny
Mons
Charleroi
Namur
Liège
Aix-la-Chapelle
Cologne
Bonn
Helder
Haarlem
Amsterdam
The Hague
Rotterdam
Leyden
Utrecht
Zuider Zee
Zwolle
Leeuwarden
Groningen
Emden
Jever
Oldenburg
To France, 1810
Bremen
Verden
Cuxhaven
Glückstadt
Stade
Harburg
Hamburg
Lübeck
Holstein
Kiel
K. of DENMARK
Zealand
Fühnen
Odense
Kolding
Slesvik
Flensburg
Fehmern
D. OF MECKLENBURG
Schwerin
Wismar
Rostock
Lauenburg
Lüneburg
Salzwedel
Celle
Hanover
Brunswick
Hildesheim
Magdeburg
Stendal
KINGDOM OF WESTPHALIA
Münster
Osnabrück
Minden
Bielefeld
Paderborn
Cassel
Göttingen
Nordhausen
Halberstadt
Quedlinburg
GR.D. OF BERG
Elberfeld
Düsseldorf
Dortmund
Arnsberg
Wesel
Cleves
Nymegen
Venlo
Breda
Hertogenbosch (Bois-le-Duc)
Flushing
I. of Walcheren
Middelburg
Marburg
Hersfeld
Giessen
Fulda
Wetzlar
D. OF NASSAU
Ehrenbreitstein
Coblenz
Wiesbaden
Mayence
Frankfort
Hanau
Darmstadt
Worms
Mannheim
Heidelberg
Erfurt
Weimar
Gotha
Eisenach
DUCHIES
Rudolstadt
Saalfeld
Schleiz
Coburg
Meiningen
GR.D. OF WURZBURG
Würzburg
Schweinfurt
Bamberg
Bayreuth
Nuremberg
Amberg
Ansbach
Neumarkt
Ratisbon
Eichstädt
Ingolstadt
Abensberg
Landshut
K. OF BAVARIA
Augsburg
Munich
Memmingen
Kaufbeuren
Kempten
Rosenheim
Donauwörth
Nördlingen
Bopfingen
Heilbronn
Mergentheim
Carlsruhe
Pforzheim
Rastatt
Stuttgart
K. OF WURTEMBERG
Ulm
Günzburg
Elchingen
Sigmaringen
GR.D. OF BADEN
Freiburg
Kehl
Strasburg
Colmar
Neu Breisach
Mülhausen
Belfort
Schaffhausen
Constance
Basel
Zurich
St. Gall
Lucerne
Berne
SWITZERLAND
Glarus
Coire
Fribourg
Lausanne
Lake Geneva
Geneva
Valais
Sion
To France, 1810
P. OF NEUCHATEL
Lindau
Bregenz
Vorarlberg
Feldkirch
Liechtenstein
Innsbruck
Tyrol
Brixen
Botzen
Meran
Trent
Rovereto
Bellinzona
Como
Bergamo
Milan
Brescia
Verona
Padua
Mantua
Cremona
Pavia
Piacenza
Parma
Reggio
Ferrara
Bologna
Genoa
KINGDOM OF ITALY
Vercelli
Ivrea
Aosta
Fort Bard
Turin
Susa
Alessandria
Annecy
Grenoble
Valence
Gap
Lyons
St. Étienne
Roanne
Clermont
Nevers
Bourges
Cosne
Auxerre
Châtillon
Langres
Dijon
Besançon
Chalon-sur-Saône
Chaumont
Troyes
Brienne
La Rothière
Bar-sur-Aube
Bar-sur-Seine
Sens
Nogent
Montereau
Fontainebleau
Melun
Nangis
Orleans
EMPIRE OF THE FRENCH
Paris
Versailles
Montmartre
Meaux
Château-Thierry
Montmirail
Champaubert
Vauchamps
Fère-Champenoise
Épernay
Châlons
Vitry
St. Dizier
Bar-le-Duc
Toul
Nancy
Lunéville
Épinal
Metz
Verdun
Thionville
Luxemburg
Sedan
Givet
Rheims
Soissons
Laon
Craonne
Rethel
Compiègne
Péronne
Ham
Cambrai
Arras
Abbeville
Montreuil
Boulogne
St. Omer
Ypres
Courtrai
Lille
Tournai
Valenciennes
Trèves
St. Wendel
Saarlouis
Kaiserslautern
Landau
Zweibrücken
Bitsch
Weissenburg
North Sea
Long. East 10 of Greenwich

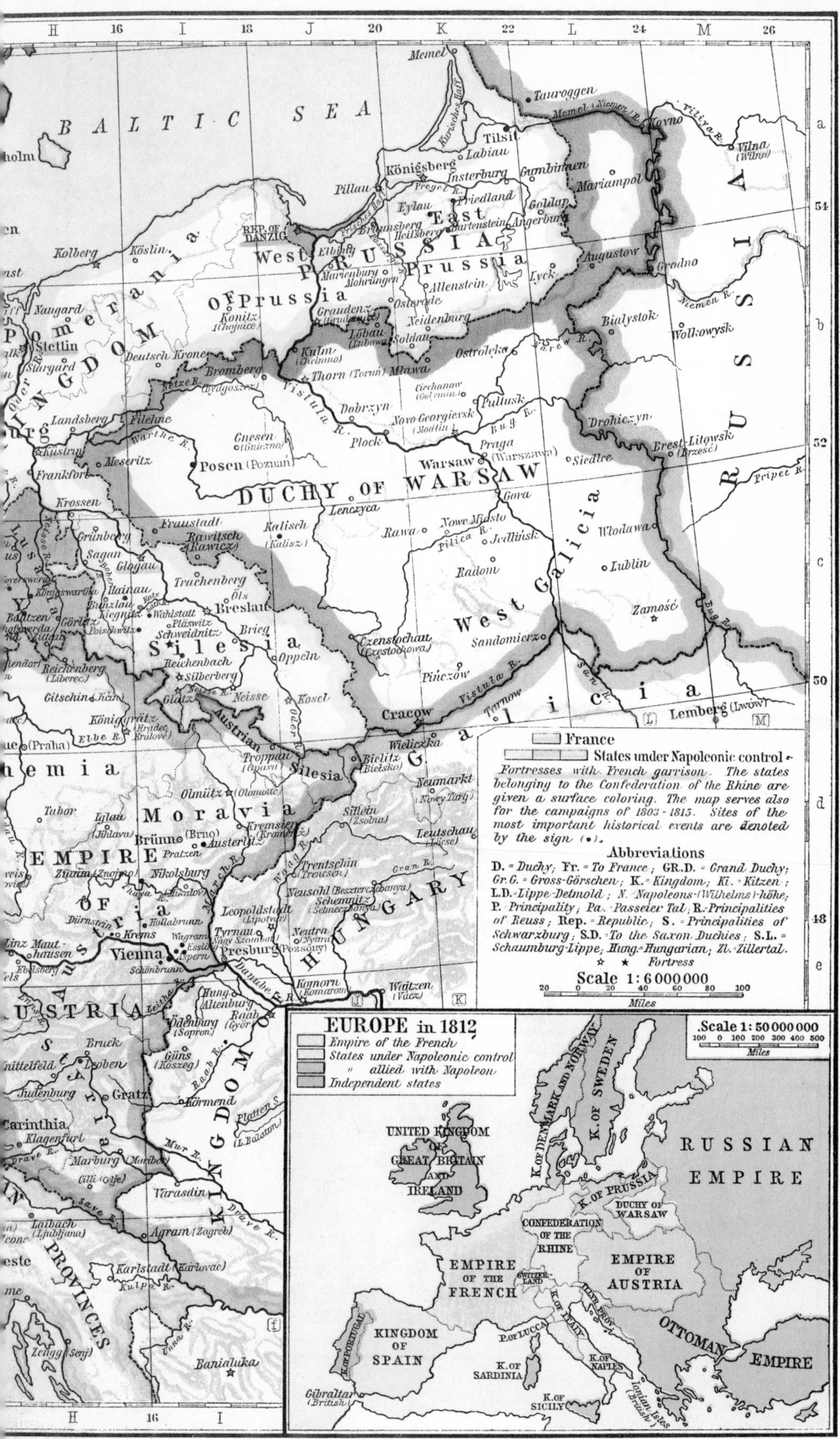
BALTIC SEA
REP. OF DANZIG
West Prussia
East Prussia
KINGDOM OF Prussia
Pomerania
DUCHY OF WARSAW
West Galicia
RUSSIA
Silesia
Moravia
Austrian Silesia
EMPIRE OF Austria
HUNGARY
KINGDOM OF HUNGARY
Galicia
Memel
Tauroggen
Tilsit
Königsberg
Pillau
Insterburg
Gumbinnen
Mariampol
Kovno
Vilna (Wilno)
Eylau
Friedland
Goldap
Braunsberg
Heilsberg
Bartenstein
Angerburg
Elbing
Marienburg
Mohrungen
Allenstein
Lyck
Augustow
Grodno
Köslin
Kolberg
Konitz (Chojnice)
Graudenz
Osterode
Neidenburg
Soldau
Löbau
Bialystok
Wolkowysk
Naugard
Stettin
Stargard
Deutsch Krone
Bromberg (Bydgoszcz)
Kulm (Chelmno)
Thorn (Toruń)
Mlawa
Ostrolenka
Ciechanow
Pultusk
Dobrzyn
Novo Georgievsk (Modlin)
Landsberg
Filehne
Gnesen (Gniezno)
Plock
Praga (Warszawa)
Drohiczyn
Brest-Litowsk (Brześć)
Küstrin
Meseritz
Posen (Poznań)
Warsaw
Siedlce
Frankfort
Lenczyca
Gora
Krossen
Fraustadt
Rawitsch (Rawicz)
Kalisch (Kalisz)
Rawa
Nowe Miasto
Jedlinsk
Wlodawa
Grünberg
Sagan
Glogau
Radom
Lublin
Trachenberg
Hainau
Bunzlau
Liegnitz
Katzbach
Wahlstatt
Pläswitz
Schweidnitz
Öls
Breslau
Brieg
Bautzen
Görlitz
Zamość
Czenstochau (Częstochowa)
Sandomierz
Oppeln
Reichenbach
Silberberg
Reichenberg (Liberec)
Pińczów
Glatz
Neisse
Kosel
Gitschin
Königgrätz (Hradec Králové)
Tarnow
Cracow
Lemberg (Lwów)
Wieliczka
Troppau (Opava)
Bielitz (Bielsko)
Neumarkt (Nowy Targ)
Olmütz (Olomouc)
Tabor
Iglau (Jihlava)
Brünn (Brno)
Austerlitz
Pratzen
Kremsier (Kroměříž)
Sillein (Žilina)
Leutschau (Lőcse)
Trentschin (Trencsén)
Znaim (Znojmo)
Nikolsburg
Neusohl (Besztercebánya)
Schemnitz (Selmeczbánya)
Dürnstein
Krems
Hollabrunn
Wagram
Essling
Aspern
Leopoldstadt (Lipótvár)
Tyrnau (Nagy Szombat)
Neutra (Nyitra)
Linz
Mauthausen
Vienna
Schönbrunn
Presburg (Pozsony)
Komorn (Komárom)
Waitzen (Vácz)
Hung. Altenburg
Raab (Győr)
Ödenburg (Sopron)
Bruck
Leoben
Güns (Kőszeg)
Judenburg
Gratz
Körmend
Carinthia
Klagenfurt
Marburg (Maribor)
Cilli (Celje)
Varasdin
Laibach (Ljubljana)
Agram (Zagreb)
Karlstadt (Karlovac)
PROVINCES
Zengg (Senj)
Banialuka
Vistula R.
Danube R.
Oder R.
Bug R.
Narew R.
Niemen R.
Pripet R.
Pilica R.
San R.
Warthe R.
Netze R.
Memel (Niemen) R.
Viliya R.
Drave R.
Save R.
Mur R.
Raab R.
Platten S. (L. Balaton)
Kulpa R.
Gran R.
March R.
Waag R.
Thaya R.
Leitha R.
Elbe R.
Una R.
France
States under Napoleonic control
Fortresses with French garrison. The states belonging to the Confederation of the Rhine are given a surface coloring. The map serves also for the campaigns of 1805-1815. Sites of the most important historical events are denoted by the sign (•).
Abbreviations
D. = Duchy; Fr. = To France; GR.D. = Grand Duchy; Gr.G. = Gross-Görschen; K. = Kingdom; Ki. = Kitzen; L.D. = Lippe-Detmold; N. Napoleons-(Wilhelms)-höhe; P. Principality; Pa. Passeier Tal; R. Principalities of Reuss; Rep. = Republic; S. = Principalities of Schwarzburg; S.D. = To the Saxon Duchies; S.L. = Schaumburg-Lippe; Hung. = Hungarian; Zl. = Zillertal.
Fortress
Scale 1: 6 000 000
20 0 20 40 60 80 100
Miles
EUROPE in 1812
Empire of the French
States under Napoleonic control
" allied with Napoleon
Independent states
Scale 1: 50 000 000
100 0 100 200 300 400 500
Miles
UNITED KINGDOM OF GREAT BRITAIN AND IRELAND
K. OF DENMARK AND NORWAY
K. OF SWEDEN
RUSSIAN EMPIRE
K. OF PRUSSIA
DUCHY OF WARSAW
CONFEDERATION OF THE RHINE
EMPIRE OF THE FRENCH
SWITZERLAND
EMPIRE OF AUSTRIA
K. OF ITALY
ILLYR. PROV.
OTTOMAN EMPIRE
K. OF PORTUGAL
KINGDOM OF SPAIN
P. OF LUCCA
K. OF SARDINIA
K. OF NAPLES
K. OF SICILY
Gibraltar (British)
Ionian Isles (British)

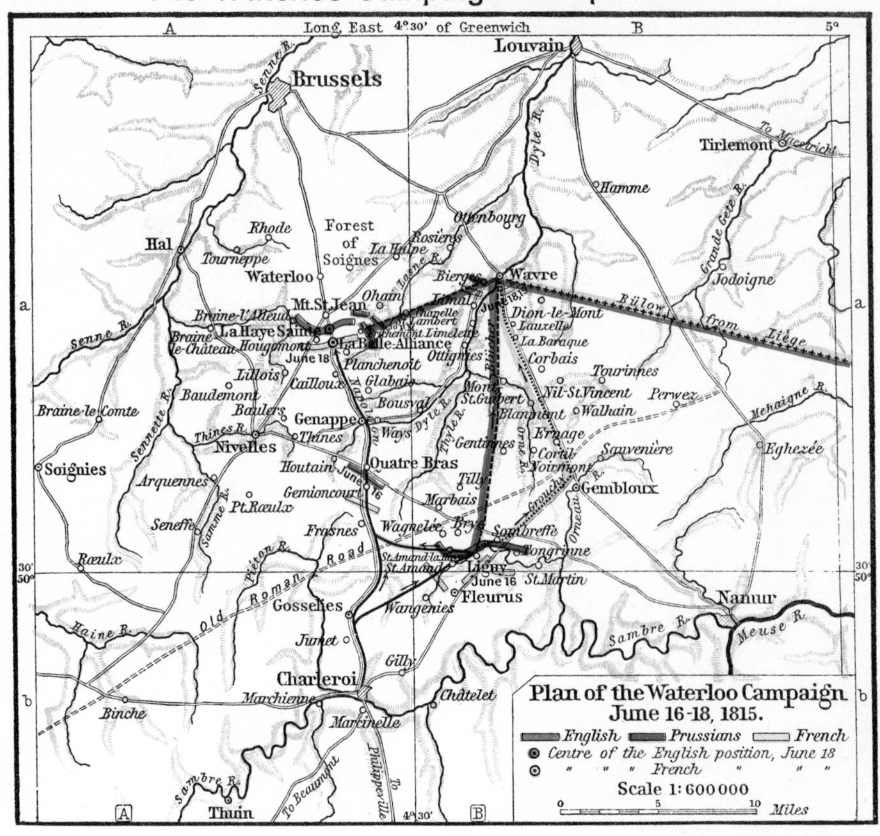
Plan of the Waterloo Campaign
June 16-18, 1815.
English
Prussians
French
Centre of the English position, June 18
" " " French " "
Scale 1: 600 000
Miles
Brussels
Louvain
Tirlemont
Waterloo
Wavre
Gembloux
Namur
Charleroi
Quatre Bras
Nivelles
Genappe
Fleurus
Ligny
Hal
Soignies
Binche
Thuin

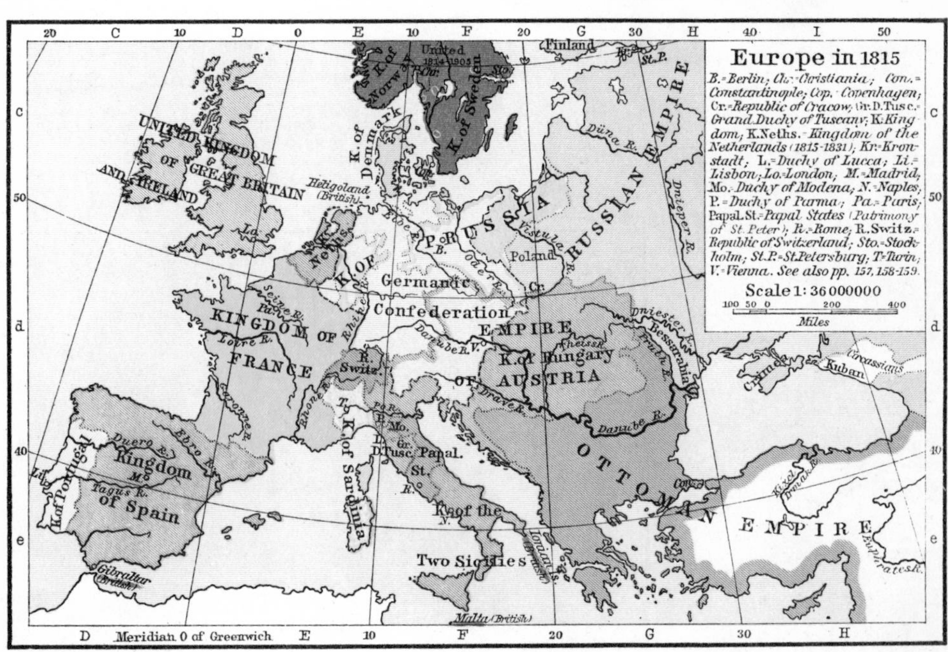
Europe in 1815
B.=Berlin; Ch.=Christiania; Con.=Constantinople; Cop.=Copenhagen; Cr.=Republic of Cracow; Gr.D.Tusc.=Grand Duchy of Tuscany; K.=Kingdom; K.Neths.=Kingdom of the Netherlands (1815-1831); Kr.=Kronstadt; L.=Duchy of Lucca; Li.=Lisbon; Lo.=London; M.=Madrid; Mo.=Duchy of Modena; N.=Naples; P.=Duchy of Parma; Pa.=Paris; Papal St.=Papal States (Patrimony of St. Peter); R.=Rome; R.Switz.=Republic of Switzerland; Sto.=Stockholm; St.P.=St.Petersburg; T.=Turin; V.=Vienna. See also pp. 157, 158-159.
Scale 1: 36 000 000
Miles
Meridian 0 of Greenwich
UNITED KINGDOM OF GREAT BRITAIN AND IRELAND
KINGDOM OF FRANCE
Kingdom of Spain
K. of Portugal
PRUSSIA
RUSSIAN EMPIRE
EMPIRE OF AUSTRIA
OTTOMAN EMPIRE
Germanic Confederation
K. of Sardinia
Two Sicilies
K. of Sweden
K. of Denmark
Poland
Heligoland (British)
Gibraltar (British)
Malta (British)

To Austria
To Prussia
" Bavaria
" Hanover
" Baden
" Wurtemberg
" Denmark
" Russia
" Sardinia
" Switzerland
Malta To Great Britain
The Austrian Netherlands united with the former Dutch Republic as the Kingdom of the Netherlands. - The Grand Duchy of Luxemburg, under the personal rule of the King of the Netherlands, was a member of the Germanic Confederation.
United with Sweden as the Kingdom of Sweden and Norway.
The states belonging to the Germanic Confederation are given a surface coloring. See also pp. 158-159
Scale 1: 12 000 000
Miles
KINGDOM OF SWEDEN AND NORWAY, 1814-1905
BALTIC SEA
NORTH SEA
Jutland
DENMARK
Slesvik
Holstein
Heligoland British 1814-1890
Mecklenburg
Swedish Pomerania
Rügen
Bornholm
Gothland
Öland
Ösel
Riga
Memel
Königsberg
Danzig
Stettin
Berlin
Hanover
Westphalia
GERMANIC CONFEDERATION
Posen
Warsaw
KINGDOM OF POLAND
RUSSIA
Silesia
Lusatia
Saxony
Thuringian States
Bohemia
Moravia
Galicia
AUSTRIA
EMPIRE OF AUSTRIA
HUNGARY
Vienna
Buda (Ofen)
Pest
Prague
Munich
Bavaria
Wurtemberg
Tyrol
Salzburg
Carinthia
Carniola
Croatia
Slavonia
Bosnia
Servia
OTTOMAN EMPIRE
Albania
Epirus
Greece
Ionian Is.
Montenegro
Herzegovina
Dalmatia
ADRIATIC SEA
Venetia
Lombardy
Piedmont
K. OF SARDINIA
SWITZERLAND
Savoy
Parma
Modena
Tuscany
Papal States
Rome
Naples
KINGDOM OF THE TWO SICILIES
Corsica (To France)
Sardinia To K. of Sardinia (Piedmont)
Balearic Is.
MEDITERRANEAN SEA
Malta (British)
FRANCE
Paris
NETHERLANDS
Amsterdam
The Hague
Austrian Netherlands
Brussels
Rhine Province
LUXEMBURG
Strasburg
Lyons
Marseilles
Tulin
Genoa
Nice
Monaco
(Austrian) Netherlands 1815
Rhine Prov. To Prussia 1815
Palatinate To Bavaria 1815
LUXEMBURG
FRANCE
Scale 1: 6 000 000 Miles
★ French frontier fortress held by the Allies, 1815
Eastern boundary of France in 1792
" " " " " 1814
" " " " " 1815
★ French frontier fortress held by the Allies, 1815
☆ Fortress of the Germanic Confederation
The four Free Cities thus: Hamburg
K.-Kingdom; Lux.-Luxemburg; Prov.-Province; R.-Republic; Ras.-Rastatt
L. East 15 of Greenwich

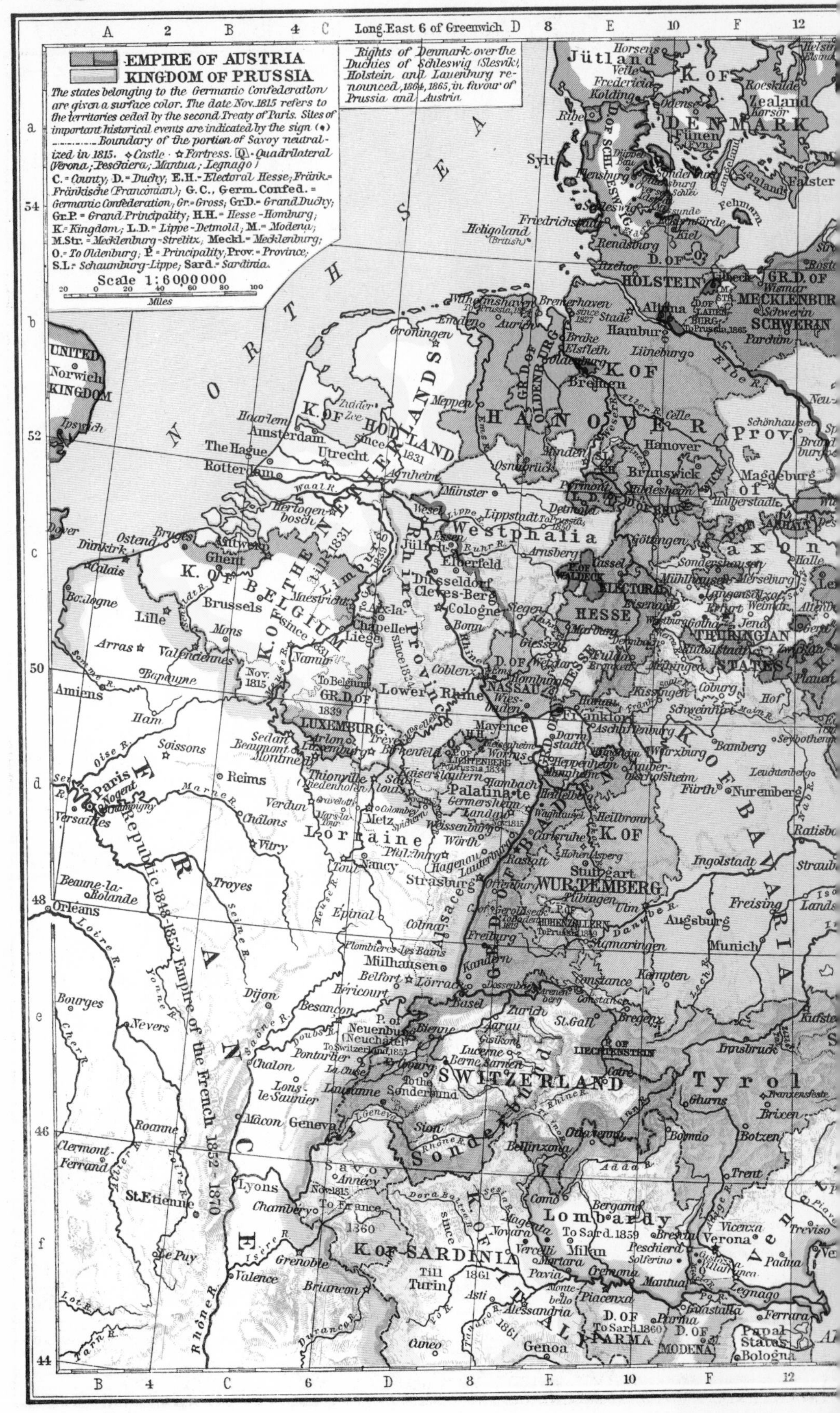
Long. East 6 of Greenwich
EMPIRE OF AUSTRIA
KINGDOM OF PRUSSIA
The states belonging to the Germanic Confederation are given a surface color. The date Nov. 1815 refers to the territories ceded by the second Treaty of Paris. Sites of important historical events are indicated by the sign (•)
Boundary of the portion of Savoy neutralized in 1815. ◇ Castle ☆ Fortress. Q - Quadrilateral (Verona; Peschiera; Mantua; Legnago)
C. = County; D. = Duchy; E.H. - Electoral Hesse; Fränk. = Fränkische (Franconian); G. C., Germ. Confed. = Germanic Confederation; Gr. = Gross; Gr.D. = Grand Duchy; Gr.P. = Grand Principality; H.H. = Hesse-Homburg; K. = Kingdom; L.D. = Lippe-Detmold; M. = Modena; M.Str. = Mecklenburg-Strelitz; Meckl. = Mecklenburg; O. = To Oldenburg; P. = Principality; Prov. = Province; S.L. = Schaumburg-Lippe; Sard. = Sardinia.
Scale 1:6000000
20 0 20 40 60 80 100
Miles
Rights of Denmark over the Duchies of Schleswig (Slesvik), Holstein and Lauenburg renounced, 1864, 1865, in favour of Prussia and Austria
NORTH SEA
K. OF DENMARK
Jütland
Zealand
UNITED KINGDOM
K. OF HOLLAND
K. OF BELGIUM
K. OF HANOVER
Westphalia
Rhine Province
Lower Rhine
GR. D. OF LUXEMBURG
ELECTORAL HESSE
THURINGIAN STATES
K. OF BAVARIA
K. OF WURTEMBERG
GR. D. OF BADEN
Lorraine
Alsace
FRANCE
Republic 1848-1852
Empire of the French 1852-1870
SWITZERLAND
Tyrol
Lombardy
Venetia
K. OF SARDINIA
K. OF ITALY
D. OF PARMA
D. OF MODENA
Papal States

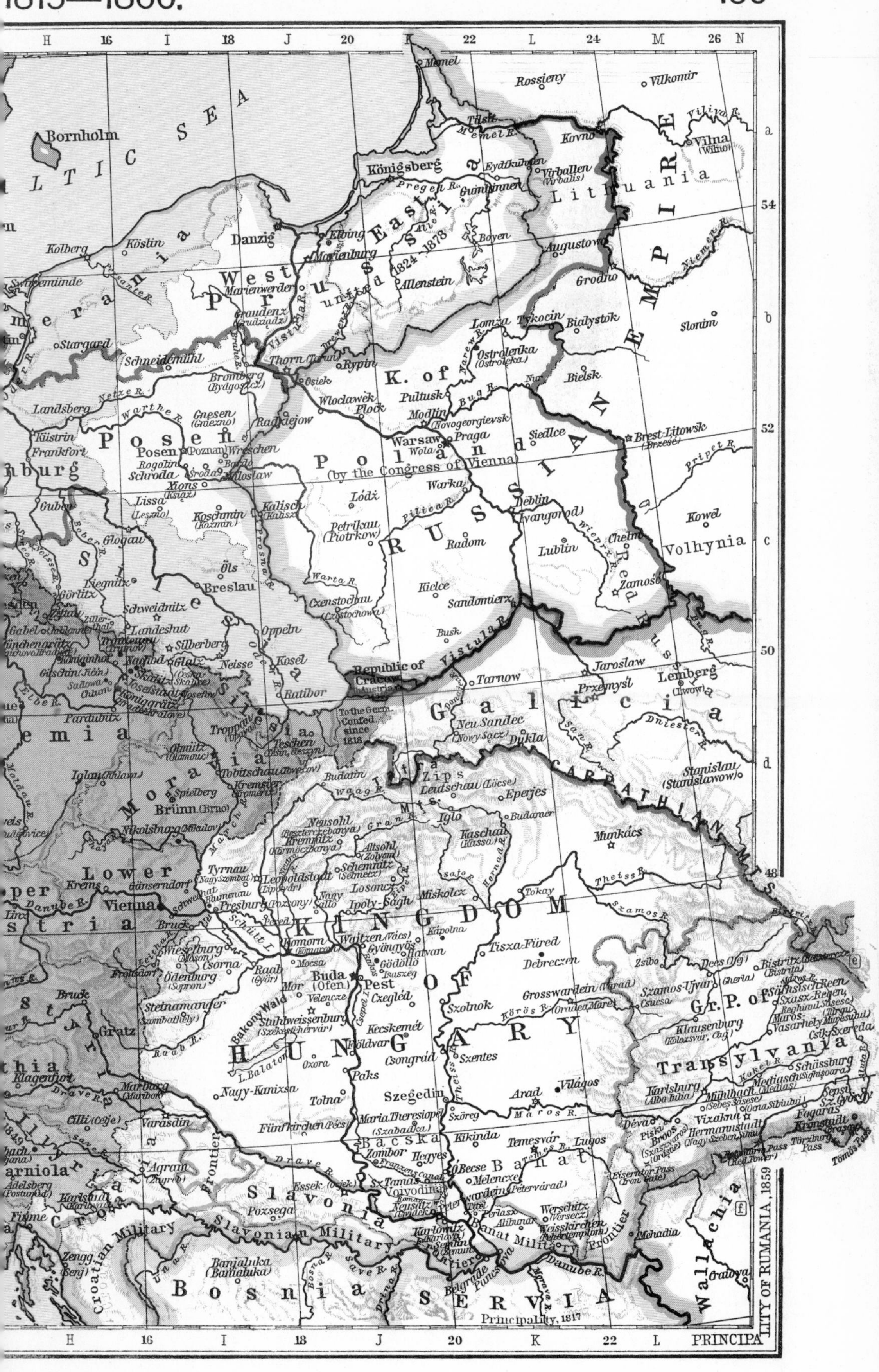
BALTIC SEA
Bornholm
Königsberg
Danzig
East Prussia
West Prussia
united 1824-1878
Memel
Tilsit
Kovno
Vilna
Lithuania
Grodno
Augustowo
Bialystok
Slonim
RUSSIAN EMPIRE
Pomerania
Stettin
Kolberg
Köslin
Stargard
Posen
Bromberg
Thorn
Gnesen
K. of Poland
(by the Congress of Vienna)
Warsaw
Praga
Modlin
Pultusk
Plock
Wloclawek
Siedlce
Brest-Litowsk
Lublin
Radom
Kielce
Lódź
Kalisch
Czenstochau
Sandomierz
Zamość
Volhynia
Kowel
Red Russia
Silesia
Breslau
Glogau
Liegnitz
Oppeln
Ratibor
Republic of Cracow
To the Germ. Confed. since 1818
Galicia
Tarnow
Jaroslaw
Przemysl
Lemberg
Stanislau
Bohemia
Moravia
Brünn
Olmütz
Troppau
Teschen
CARPATHIAN MTS.
Lower Austria
Vienna
Presburg
KINGDOM OF HUNGARY
Buda (Ofen)
Pest
Debreczen
Szegedin
Tokay
Kaschau
Eperjes
Munkács
Grosswardein
Arad
Világos
Temesvár
Transylvania
Gr. P. of
Klausenburg
Hermannstadt
Kronstadt
Banat
Slavonia
Croatia
Carniola
Illyria
Styria
Gratz
Agram
Fiume
Croatian Military
Slavonian Military
Banat Military Frontier
Bosnia
SERVIA
Principality, 1817
Belgrade
Wallachia
Mehadia
Craiova
PRINCIPALITY OF RUMANIA, 1859
Danube R.
Vistula R.

The German Zollverein (Customs-Union), 1828—1872.

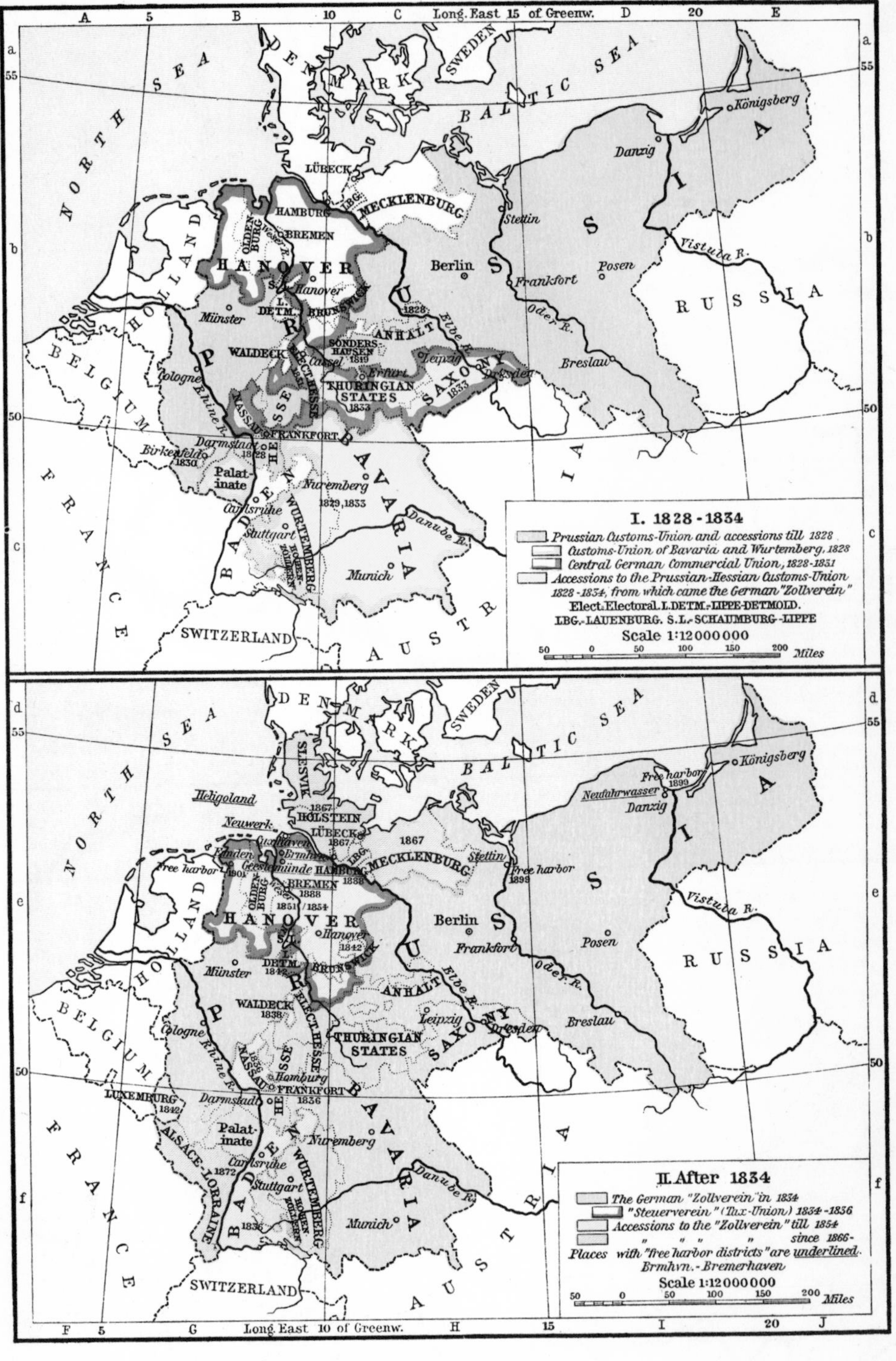

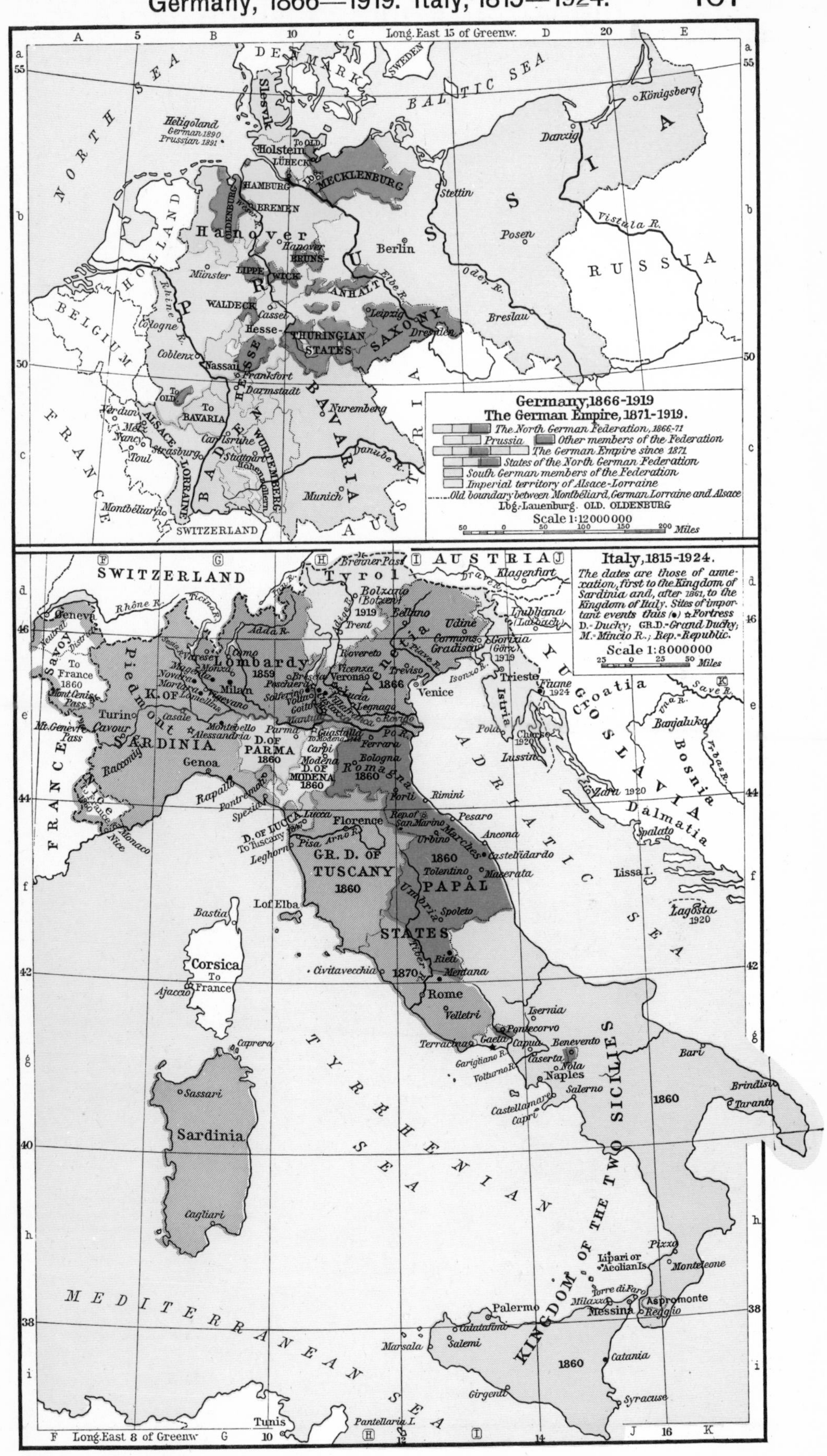
Germany, 1866-1919
The German Empire, 1871-1919.
The North German Federation, 1866-71
Prussia
Other members of the Federation
The German Empire since 1871
States of the North German Federation
South German members of the Federation
Imperial territory of Alsace-Lorraine
Old boundary between Montbéliard, German Lorraine and Alsace
Lbg.-Lauenburg. OLD. OLDENBURG
Scale 1:12000000
Miles
NORTH SEA
BALTIC SEA
DENMARK
SWEDEN
Heligoland German 1890 Prussian 1891
Slesvik
Holstein
LÜBECK
HAMBURG
BREMEN
MECKLENBURG
Königsberg
Danzig
Stettin
Posen
Berlin
Hanover
RUSSIA
Vistula R.
Oder R.
Elbe R.
Breslau
HOLLAND
BELGIUM
FRANCE
Münster
LIPPE
WALDECK
Cassel
ANHALT
Leipzig
SAXONY
Dresden
THURINGIAN STATES
Cologne
Coblenz
Nassau
Frankfort
Darmstadt
Nuremberg
BAVARIA
Verdun
Metz
Nancy
Toul
Strasburg
Carlsruhe
Stuttgart
ALSACE
LORRAINE
BADEN
WURTEMBERG
Danube R.
Munich
Montbéliard
SWITZERLAND
AUSTRIA
Italy, 1815-1924.
The dates are those of annexation, first to the Kingdom of Sardinia and, after 1861, to the Kingdom of Italy. Sites of important events thus (•) ☆ Fortress
D. = Duchy; GR.D. = Grand Duchy; M. = Mincio R.; Rep. = Republic.
Scale 1:8000000
Miles
SWITZERLAND
Tyrol
Brenner Pass
Bolzano (Botzen) 1919
Trent
Klagenfurt
Ljubljana (Laibach)
Udine
Gorizia
Trieste
Fiume 1924
Croatia
YUGOSLAVIA
Banjaluka
Bosnia
Save R.
Geneva
Rhône R.
Savoy
To France 1860
Mont Cenis Pass
Mt. Genèvre Pass
Piedmont
K. OF SARDINIA
Turin
Alessandria
Genoa
Lombardy 1859
Milan
Como
Novara
Magenta
Solferino
Brescia
Verona
Vicenza
Venetia 1866
Venice
Treviso
Mantua
D. OF PARMA 1860
Parma
Modena
D. OF MODENA 1860
Ferrara
Bologna
Romagna 1860
Nice
Monaco
Spezia
Lucca
Florence
Leghorn
GR. D. OF TUSCANY 1860
Rep. of San Marino
Rimini
Pesaro
Ancona
Castelfidardo
Urbino
Marches 1860
PAPAL STATES
Umbria
Spoleto
Istria
Pola
Zara 1920
Lussin
Dalmatia
Spalato
Lissa I.
Lagosta 1920
ADRIATIC SEA
Bastia
Corsica To France
Ajaccio
I. of Elba
Civitavecchia
Rome 1870
Mentana
Velletri
Gaeta
Capua
Caserta
Naples
Salerno
Benevento
Bari
Brindisi
Taranto
KINGDOM OF THE TWO SICILIES 1860
Caprera
Sassari
Sardinia
Cagliari
TYRRHENIAN SEA
MEDITERRANEAN SEA
Lipari or Aeolian Is.
Pizzo
Monteleone
Aspromonte
Messina
Reggio
Palermo
Calatafimi
Salemi
Marsala
Catania
Syracuse
Girgenti
Pantellaria I.
Tunis

Meridian 0 of Greenw.
Long. West 2 of Greenw.
SCOTLAND
NORTHUMBERLAND
Newcastle
Gateshead
South Shields
Sunderland
Ships
Coalfields
Durham
DURHAM
West Hartlepool
Stockton
Darlington
Middlesbrough
Iron
Pottery
Lead
Carlisle
CUMBERLAND
Solway Firth
Whitehaven
WESTMORLAND
Kendal
NORTH RIDING
Barrow in Furness
Ships
I. OF MAN
Lancaster
YORK
WEST RIDING
York
EAST RIDING
Blackpool
Preston
Leeds
Bradford
Burnley
Blackburn
Halifax
Huddersfield
Wakefield
Bolton
Wigan
Oldham
Salford
Manchester
Liverpool
Birkenhead
Southport
Goole
Hull
Ships
Iron
Grimsby
Humber R.
Barnsley
Rotherham
Sheffield
Cutlery
Machinery
Coalfield
IRISH SEA
NORTH SEA
ANGLESEY
Slate
Wrexham
Llangollen
Slate
WALES
Cardigan Bay
CHESTER
Chester
Northwich
Salt
Crewe
Stoke
Pottery
Derby
NOTTINGHAM
Nottingham
Lace
Cotton
Lincoln
Iron
LINCOLN
Boston
The Wash
Kings Lynn
NORFOLK
Norwich
Ellesmere
STAFFORD
Silk
SALOP
Shrewsbury
Newtown
Wolverhampton
West Bromwich
Walsall
Birmingham
Aston Manor
Coventry
Hardware
Stourport
LEICESTER
Leicester
Woolens
RUTLAND
Peterborough
NORTHAMPTON
Northampton
Linen
HUNTINGDON
CAMBRIDGE
Cambridge
Bedford
BEDFORD
SUFFOLK
Ipswich
WORCESTER
Worcester
WARWICK
HEREFORD
Hops
Fruit
Smelting
Merthyr Tydfil
Swansea
Pembroke
Ships
Great South Wales Coalfield
Cardiff
Newport
MONMOUTH
GLOUCESTER
Gloucester
Woolens
Oxford
OXFORD
BUCKINGHAM
HERTFORD
Colchester
ESSEX
LONDON
MIDDLESEX
Thames R.
Ships
Bristol Channel
Bristol
Bath
Iron
Coalfield
Devizes
BERKS
Reading
SURREY
Wheat
Maidstone
Chatham
Hops
KENT
Fruit
Barnstaple
SOMERSET
Bridgwater
Taunton
WILTS
Salisbury
HANTS
Winchester
Southampton
SUSSEX
Brighton
Hastings
Eastbourne
Strait of
DEVON
Exeter
DORSET
Sherborne
Dorchester
Bournemouth
Portsmouth
I. OF WIGHT
Lyme Regis
Portland
CORNWALL
Tin
Granite
Plymouth
Dartmouth
Copper
Falmouth
ENGLISH CHANNEL
Centres of population
Chief manufacturing centres
Districts in which manufacturing was carried on jointly with agriculture
Coalfields about 1800
Canals " "
Ro.=Ro
Centres of population
Important manufacturing centres
Principal districts in which manufacturing is carried on
at
pres
tim
The names of the more important products and
factures of England at the present time are printed th
Scale 1: 3700000
20 10 0 20 40 60
Miles
The violet coloring indicates that the areas concerned
centres of population both in 1750 and at the present

Meridian 0 of Greenw.
Ab. = Abingdon
Am. = Amersham
And. = Andover
Ayl. = Aylesbury
B.A. = Bere Alston
Blet. = Bletchingley
Chelt. = Cheltenham
Chipp = Chippenham
Ch.Wyc. = Chipping Wycombe
Chr. = Christchurch
Cirenc. = Cirencester
Crick. = Cricklade
E. = East
E.S. = East Surrey
Finsb. = Finsbury
Gat. = Gatton
Greenw. = Greenwich
Gr.M. = Great Marlow
Guildf. = Guildford
Heyt. = Heytesbury
Hind. = Hindon
Hudd. = Huddersfield
Kidderm. = Kidderminster
Lamb. = Lambeth
Lisk. = Liskeard
Malm. = Malmesbury
Marlb. = Marlborough
Maryleb. = Marylebone
MIDD. = Middlesex
Milb. = Milborne Port
N. = North
New Wood. = New Woodstock
NOTT. = Nottingham
Old S. = Old Sarum
Petersf. = Petersfield
Read. = Reading
S. = South
Salf. = Salford
Salisb. = Salisbury
Sherb. = Sherborne
Southw. = Southwark
Tewkesb. = Tewkesbury
W. = West
Wall. = Wallingford
Warr. = Warrington
W.B. = Wootton Bassett
We. = Wendover
Westm. = Westminster
Winch. = Winchester
Wolv. = Wolverhampton
Worc. = Worcester
NORTH NORTHUMBERLAND
SOUTH NORTHUMBERLAND
EAST CUMBERLAND
WEST CUMBERLAND
NORTH DURHAM
SOUTH DURHAM
WESTMORLAND
NORTH RIDING
EAST RIDING
WEST RIDING
NORTH LANCASTER
SOUTH LANCASTER
LINDSEY
NORTH CHESHIRE
SOUTH CHESHIRE
NORTH DERBY
SOUTH DERBY
NORTH NOTTINGHAM
S. NOTT
KESTEVEN AND HOLLAND
ANGLESEY
FLINT
DENBIGH
CARNARVON
MERIONETH
MONTGOMERY
NORTH SALOP
SOUTH SALOP
NORTH STAFFORD
SOUTH STAFFORD
N. LEICESTER
S. LEICESTER
RUTLAND
NORTHAMPTON
NORTH NORTHAMPTON
SOUTH NORTHAMPTON
HUNTINGDON
CAMBRIDGE
WEST NORFOLK
EAST NORFOLK
WEST SUFFOLK
EAST SUFFOLK
NORTH WARWICK
SOUTH WARWICK
EAST WORCESTER
WEST WORCESTER
RADNOR
CARDIGAN
HEREFORD
BRECKNOCK
PEMBROKE
CARMARTHEN
GLAMORGAN
MONMOUTH
E. GLOUCESTER
WEST GLOUCESTER
OXFORD
BUCKS
BEDFORD
HERTFORD
NORTH ESSEX
SOUTH ESSEX
MIDD.
LONDON
BERKS
N. WILTS
S. WILTS
EAST SOMERSET
WEST SOMERSET
N. HANTS
S. HANTS
W. SURREY
E.S.
WEST KENT
EAST KENT
W. SUSSEX
EAST SUSSEX
NORTH DEVON
SOUTH DEVON
DORSET
EAST CORNWALL
WEST CORNWALL
ISLE OF WIGHT
ENGLAND AND WALES
showing the system of representation in the House of Commons before and after the Reform Act of 1832
Haslemere — Borough returning two members before 1832 } disfranchised in 1832
Higham Ferrers — " one member " "
St. Ives — " that had its representation reduced in 1832
Birmingham — " enfranchised in 1832, and returning two members
Tynemouth — " " " " " " one member
Nottingham — " returning two members before and after 1832
Abingdon — " " one member " " " "
OXFORD — County " three members after 1832
BEDFORD — " " two " " "
SOUTH DEVON — Division of county returning two members after 1832.
Before 1832 each county in England returned two members, and each county in Wales one member; after 1832 nine counties in Wales, only, returned one member.
Scale 1:3 700 000
20 10 0 20 40 60 Miles

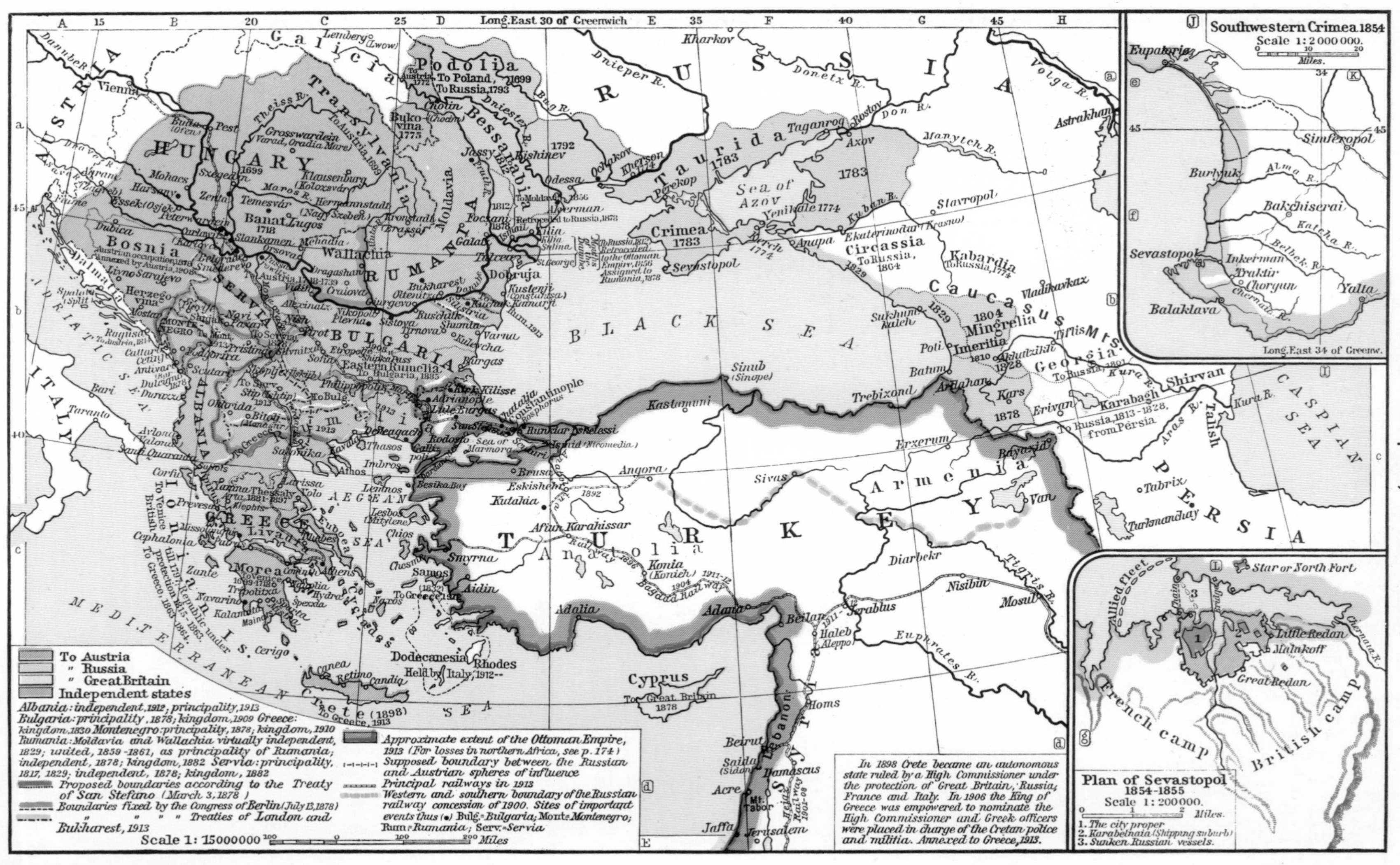
To Austria
" Russia
" Great Britain
Independent states
Albania: independent, 1912; principality, 1913
Bulgaria: principality, 1878; kingdom, 1909 Greece: kingdom, 1830 Montenegro: principality, 1878; kingdom, 1910
Rumania: Moldavia and Wallachia virtually independent, 1829; united, 1859-1861, as principality of Rumania; independent, 1878; kingdom, 1882 Servia: principality, 1817, 1829; independent, 1878; kingdom, 1882
Proposed boundaries according to the Treaty of San Stefano (March 3, 1878)
Boundaries fixed by the Congress of Berlin (July 13, 1878)
" " " " Treaties of London and Bukharest, 1913
Approximate extent of the Ottoman Empire, 1913 (For losses in northern Africa, see p. 174)
Supposed boundary between the Russian and Austrian spheres of influence
Principal railways in 1913
Western and southern boundary of the Russian railway concession of 1900. Sites of important events thus (•) Bulg.=Bulgaria; Mont.=Montenegro; Rum.=Rumania; Serv.=Servia
Scale 1: 15000000
Miles
In 1898 Crete became an autonomous state ruled by a High Commissioner under the protection of Great Britain, Russia, France and Italy. In 1906 the King of Greece was empowered to nominate the High Commissioner and Greek officers were placed in charge of the Cretan police and militia. Annexed to Greece, 1913.
Southwestern Crimea 1854
Scale 1: 2 000 000.
Miles.
Long. East 34 of Greenw.
Plan of Sevastopol
1854-1855
Scale 1: 200000.
Miles.
1. The city proper
2. Karabelnaia (Shipping suburb)
3. Sunken Russian vessels.
Long. East 30 of Greenwich
BLACK SEA
CASPIAN SEA
MEDITERRANEAN SEA
AEGEAN SEA
ADRIATIC SEA
RUSSIA
TURKEY
PERSIA
HUNGARY
BULGARIA
GREECE
RUMANIA
SERVIA
ALBANIA
ITALY
AUSTRIA

Peoples of Southeastern Europe and Asia Minor in 1913.

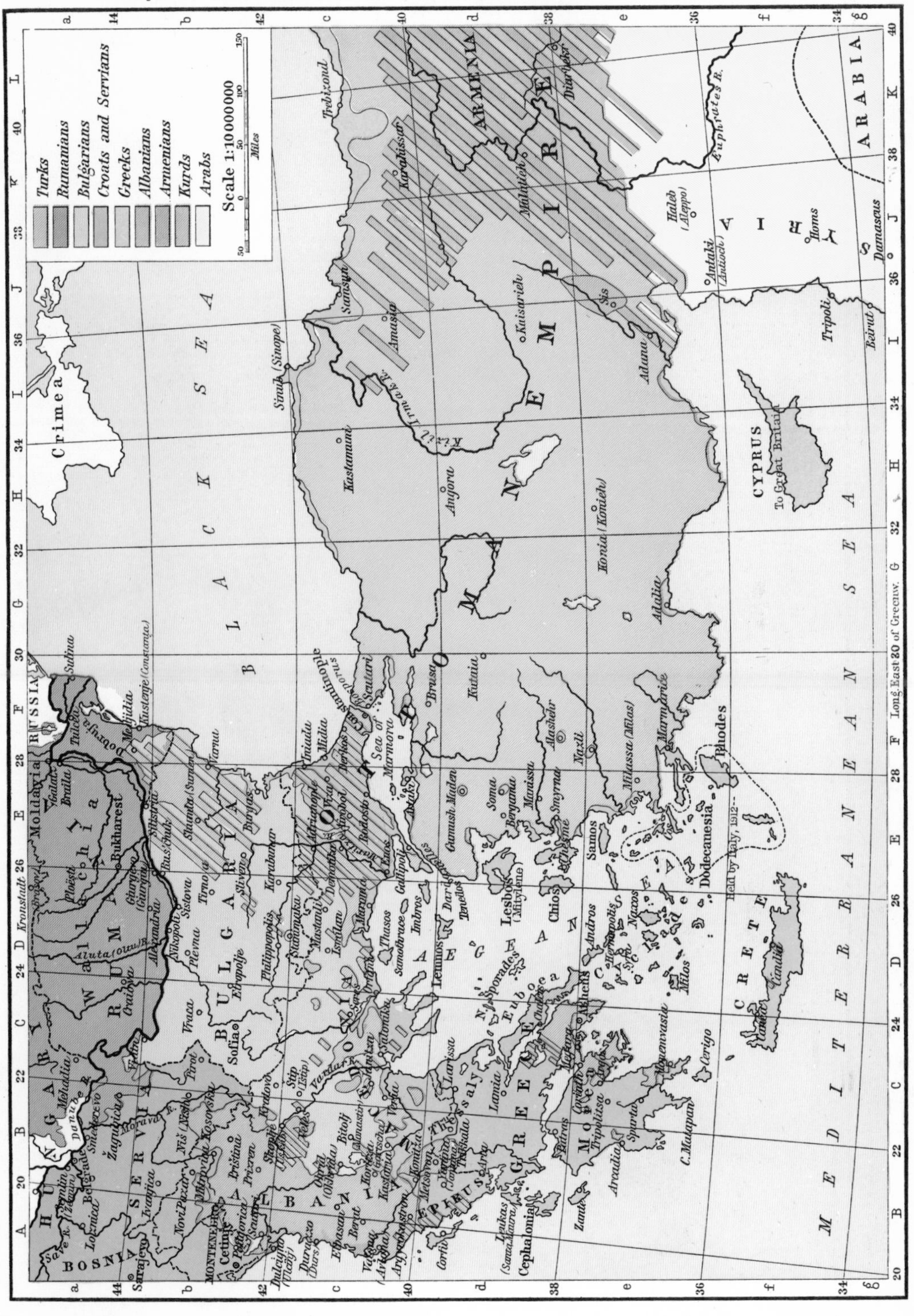

Illinois, 56,650 sq. miles in comparison with Europe
Iceland (To Denmark)
Jan Mayen
Arctic Circle
Faröe Is. (To Denmark)
Orkney Is.
Shetland Is.
The Hebrides
ATLANTIC OCEAN
IRELAND
GREAT BRITAIN
NORTH SEA
ENGLISH CHANNEL
London
Paris
FRANCE
SPAIN
PORTUGAL
Madrid
Lisbon
Pyrenees
Balearic Is.
MEDITERRANEAN
ITALY
Rome
Sardinia
Corsica
Sicily
SWITZERLAND
AUSTRIA
GERMANY
Berlin
DENMARK
Copenhagen
NORWAY
SWEDEN
SKAGER RAK
Heligoland (To Germany, 1890)
MOROCCO
French Protectorate 1912
ALGERIA
To France 1830
TUNIS
Fr. Prot. 1881
Malta (Brit.)
Gibraltar (Brit.)
Ceuta (Sp.)
Melilla (Sp.)
ADRIATIC SEA
TYRRHENIAN SEA
Meridian 0 of Greenwich

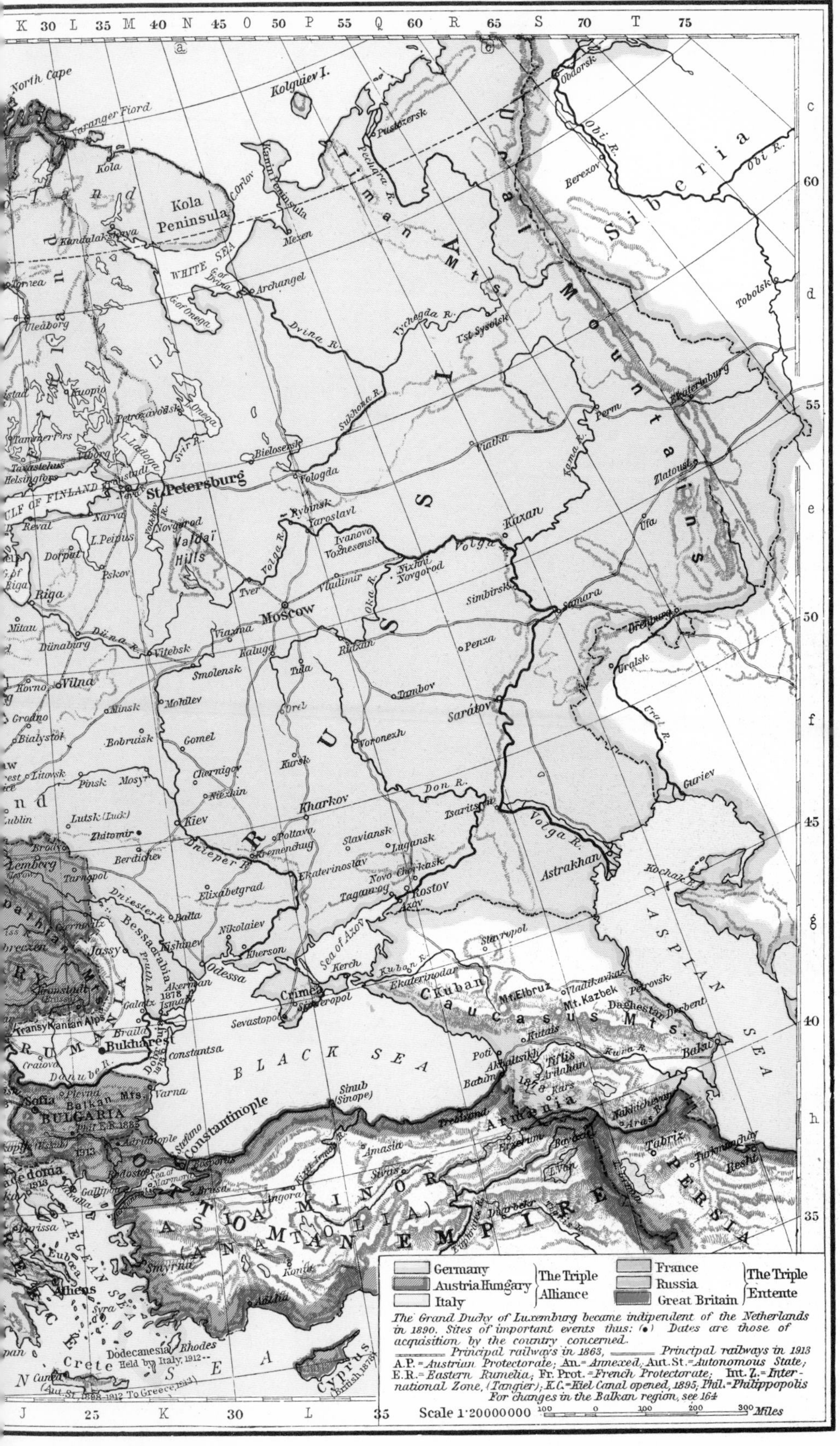

Germany
Austria Hungary
Italy
The Triple Alliance
France
Russia
Great Britain
The Triple Entente
The Grand Duchy of Luxemburg became indipendent of the Netherlands in 1890. Sites of important events thus: (•) Dates are those of acquisition by the country concerned.
Principal railways in 1863, Principal railways in 1913
A.P.=Austrian Protectorate; An.=Annexed; Aut.St.=Autonomous State; E.R.=Eastern Rumelia; Fr. Prot.=French Protectorate; Int. Z.=International Zone, (Tangier); K.C.=Kiel Canal opened, 1895; Phil.=Philippopolis
For changes in the Balkan region, see 164
Scale 1:20000000
Miles
North Cape
Kola Peninsula
WHITE SEA
Archangel
Kolguiev I.
Siberia
Ural Mountains
Obi R.
Tobolsk
Ekaterinburg
Perm
Vologda
St. Petersburg
GULF OF FINLAND
Helsingfors
Reval
Riga
Valdai Hills
Moscow
Vitebsk
Smolensk
Kaluga
Tula
Vilna
Minsk
Kiev
Kharkov
Kazan
Samara
Saratov
Simbirsk
Penza
Tambov
Voronezh
Kursk
Nizhni Novgorod
Volga R.
Don R.
Dnieper R.
Tsaritsyn
Astrakhan
Orenburg
Uralsk
Ural R.
Guriev
Odessa
Kherson
Nikolaiev
Kishinev
Jassy
Bessarabia
Crimea
Sevastopol
Sea of Azov
Rostov
Ekaterinodar
Stavropol
Kuban
Mt. Elbruz
Mt. Kazbek
Caucasus Mts.
Tiflis
Baku
Kars
Batum
CASPIAN SEA
BLACK SEA
Bukharest
Constantsa
Varna
Sofia
BULGARIA
Constantinople
Smyrna
Athens
AEGEAN SEA
Crete
Dodecanesia Held by Italy, 1912
Rhodes
Cyprus (British 1878)
Sinub (Sinope)
Trebizond
Erzerum
Armenia
Tabriz
Resht
PERSIA
ASIA MINOR
OTTOMAN EMPIRE
ANATOLIA
Angora
Konieh
Diarbekr
Euphrates R.
Tigris R.
Sivas
L. Van

Peoples of Austria-Hungary in 1914.

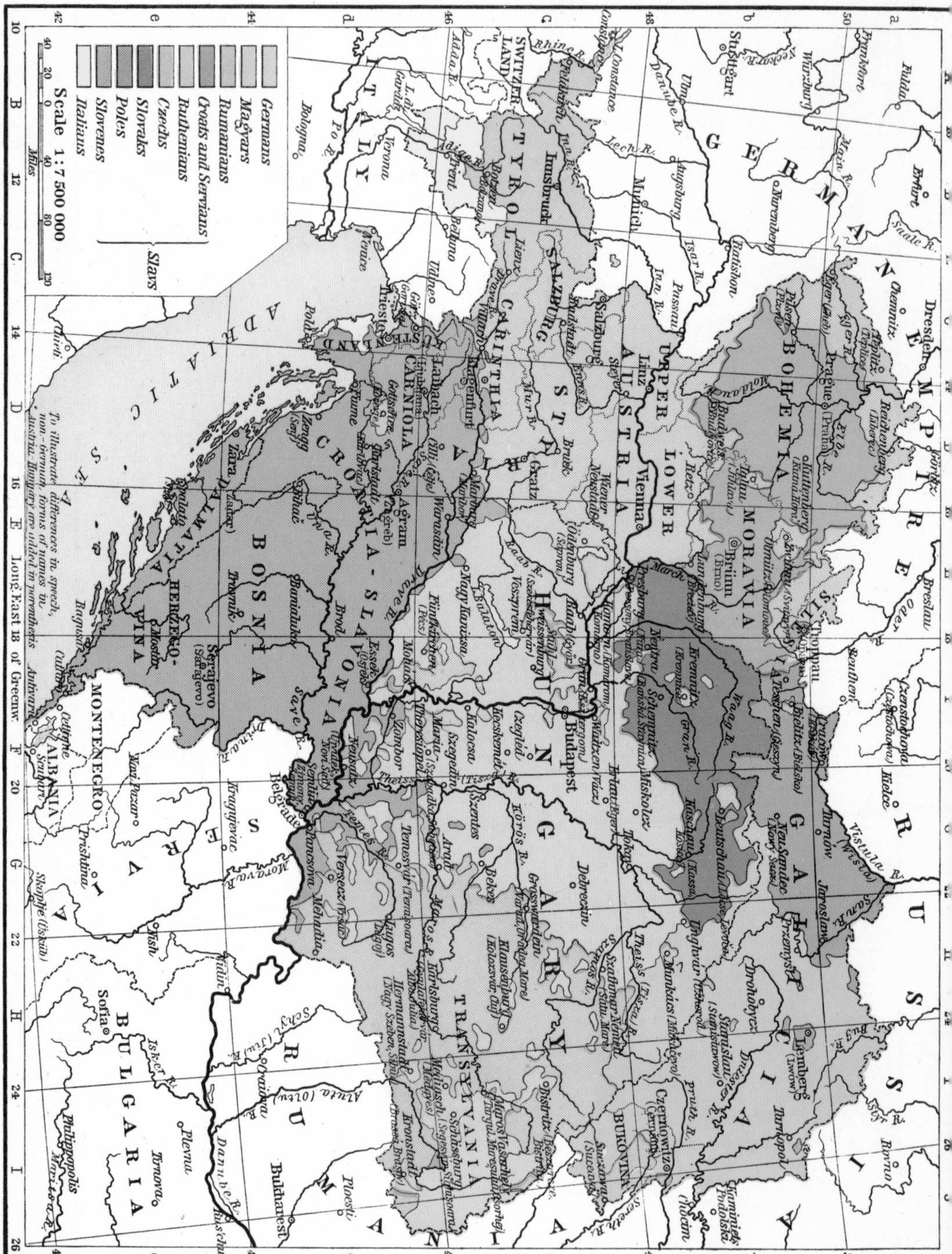

Germans
Magyars
Rumanians
Croats and Servians
Ruthenians
Czechs
Slovaks
Poles
Slovenes
Italians
Slavs

Scale 1 : 7 500 000
Miles

To illustrate differences in speech, non-German forms of names in Austria-Hungary are added in parenthesis

The World at War, 1914—1918.

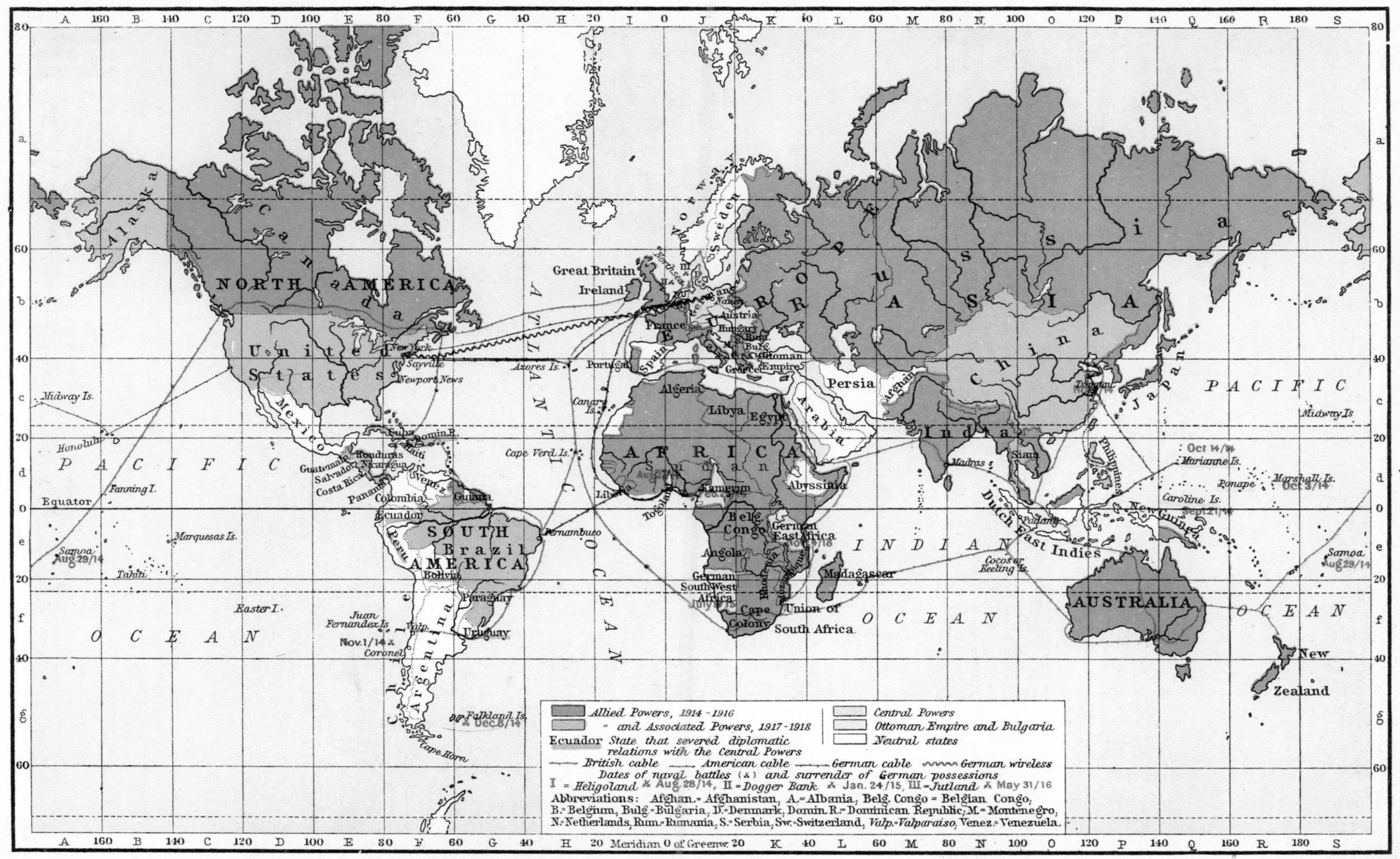

Principal Seats of War, 1914—1918.

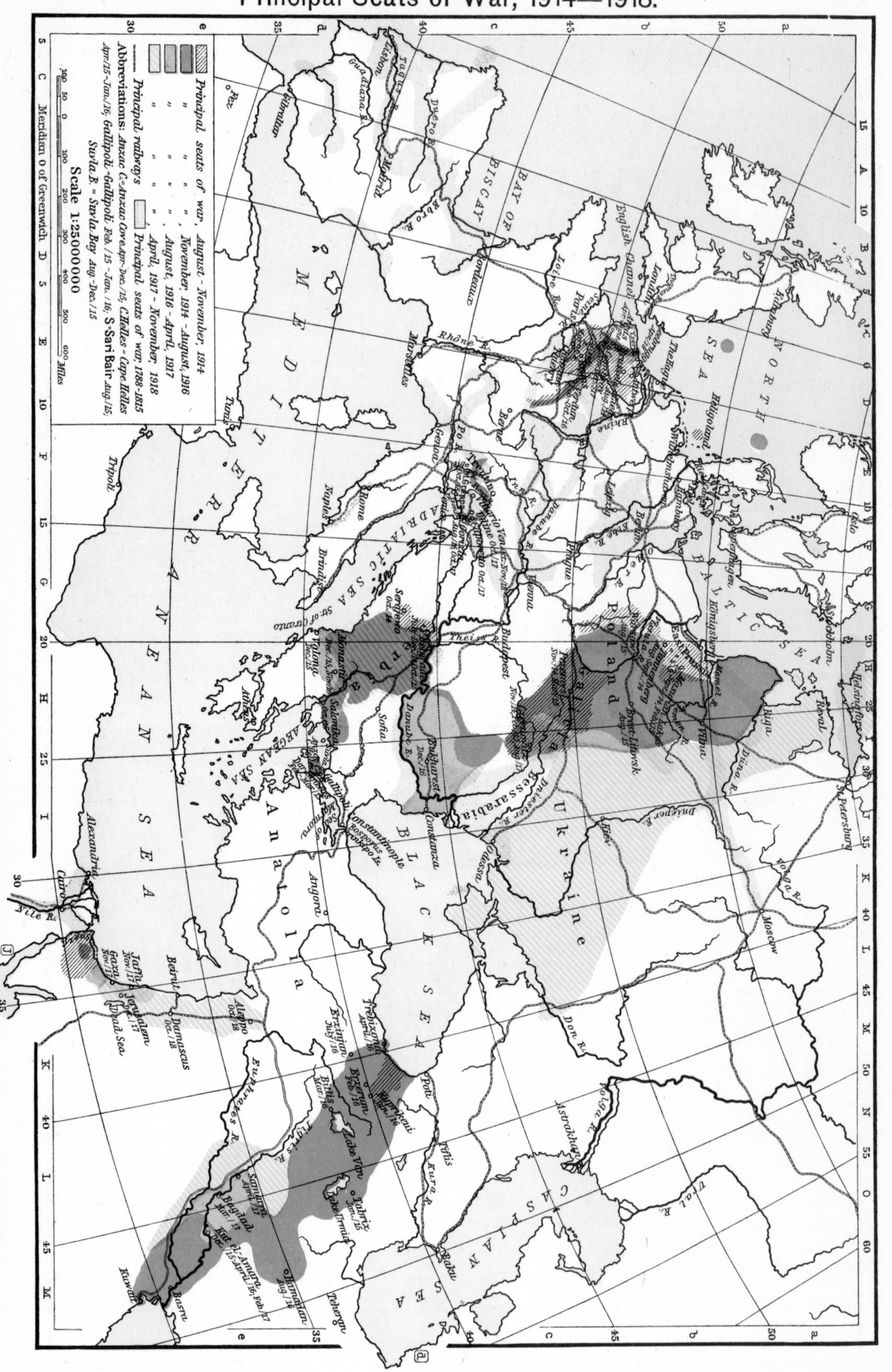

Principal seats of war, August - November, 1914
" " " " November, 1914 - August, 1916
" " " " August, 1916 - April, 1917
" " " " April, 1917 - November, 1918
Principal railways
Principal seats of war, 1788-1815
Abbreviations: Anzac C.=Anzac Cove, Apr.-Dec./15, C.Helles - Cape Helles Apr./15-Jan./16, Gallipoli - Gallipoli Feb./15-Jan./16, S-Sari Bair Aug./15, Suvla B. = Suvla Bay Aug.-Dec./15
Scale 1:25000000
Miles
Meridian 0 of Greenwich

The Western European Front, 1914—1918.

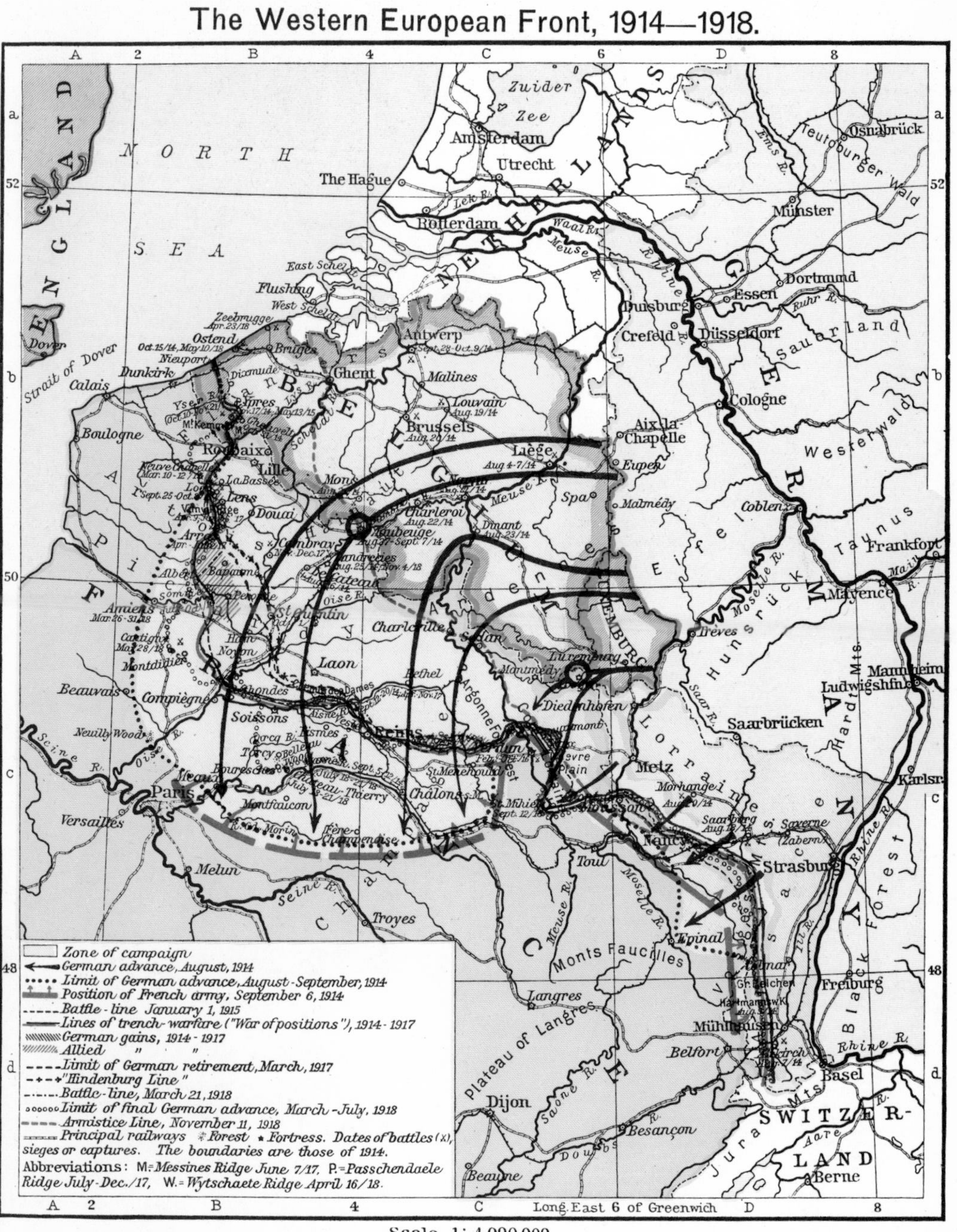

Scale 1: 4 000 000

25 0 25 50 75

Miles

Treaty Adjustments, 1919—1926.

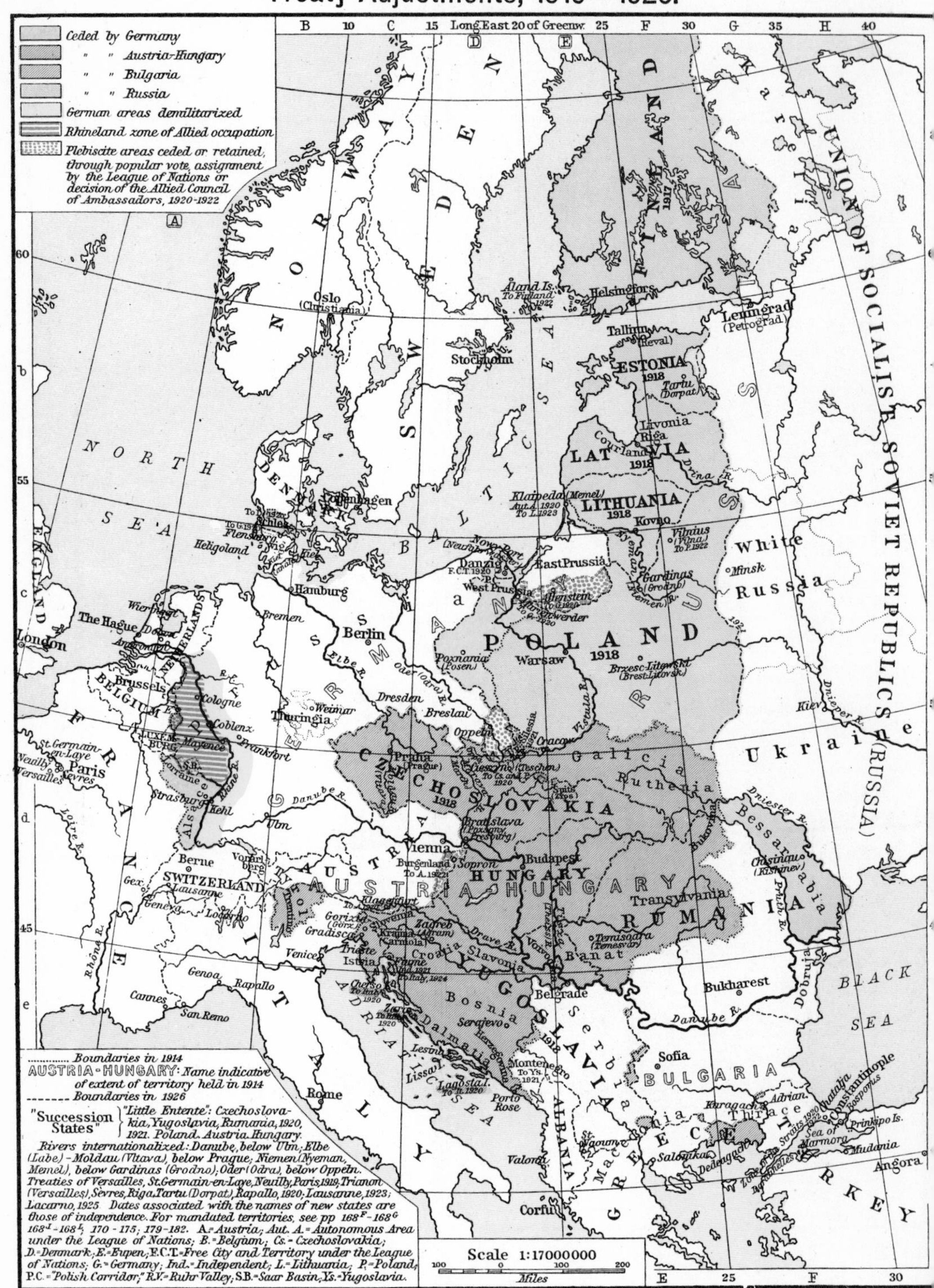

For the Rhineland see p 168E

Treaty Adjustments, 1919—1926. The Rhineland.

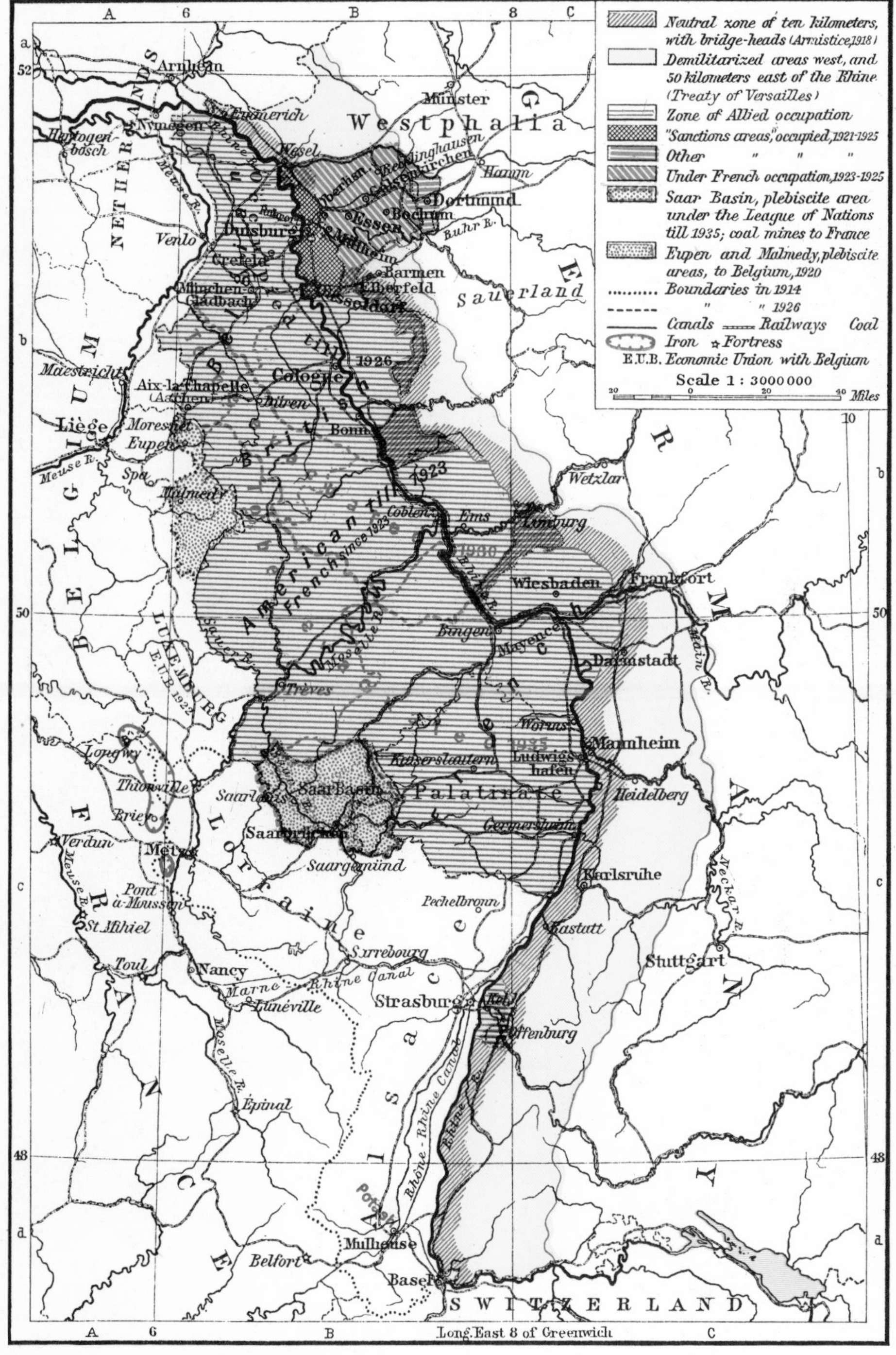

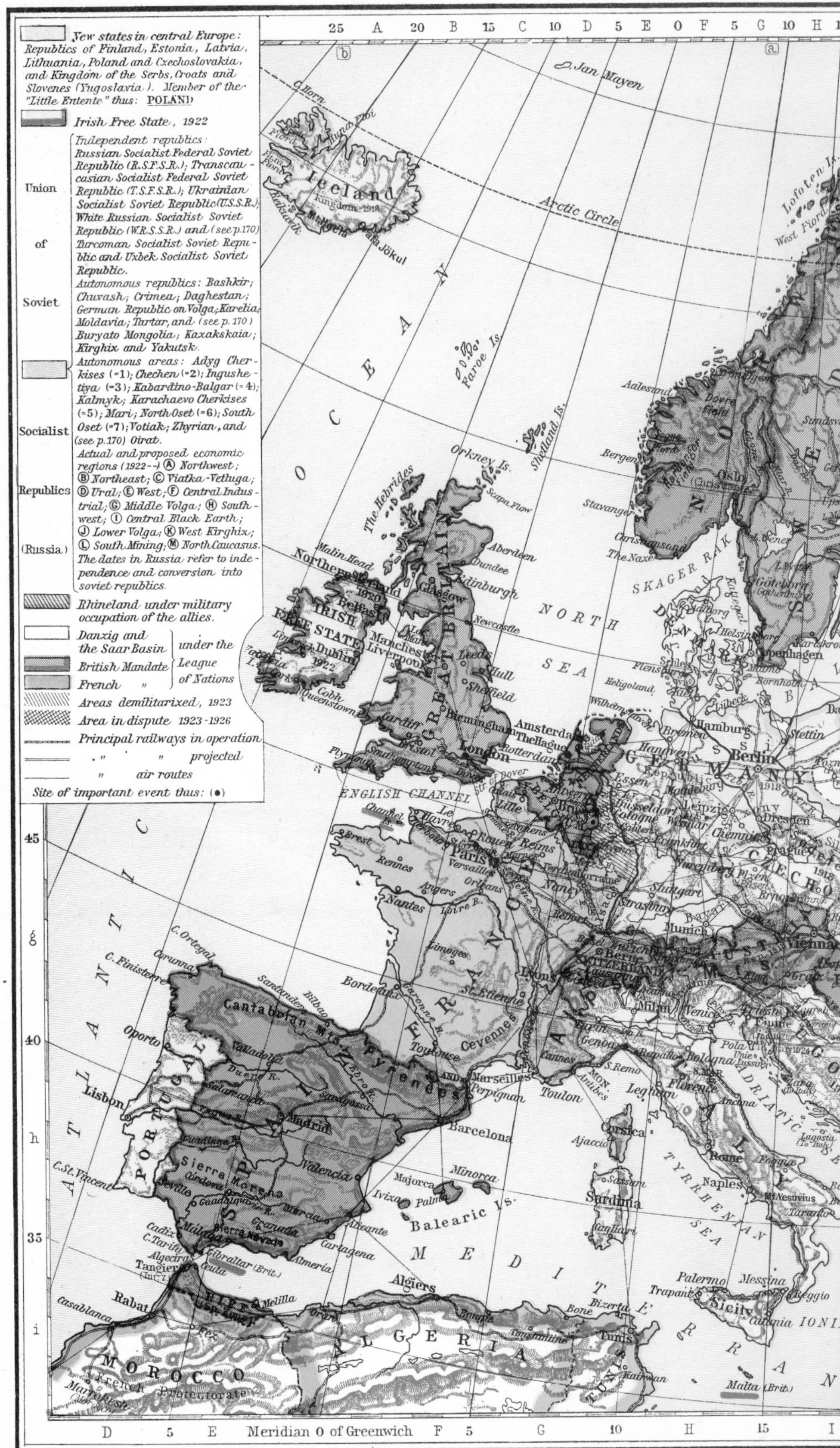
New states in central Europe: Republics of Finland, Estonia, Latvia, Lithuania, Poland and Czechoslovakia, and Kingdom of the Serbs, Croats and Slovenes (Yugoslavia). Member of the "Little Entente" thus: POLAND
Irish Free State, 1922
Union of Soviet Socialist Republics (Russia)
Independent republics: Russian Socialist Federal Soviet Republic (R.S.F.S.R.); Transcaucasian Socialist Federal Soviet Republic (T.S.F.S.R.); Ukrainian Socialist Soviet Republic (U.S.S.R.); White Russian Socialist Soviet Republic (W.R.S.S.R.) and (see p.170) Turcoman Socialist Soviet Republic and Uxbek Socialist Soviet Republic.
Autonomous republics: Bashkir; Chuvash; Crimea; Daghestan; German Republic on Volga; Karelia; Moldavia; Tartar, and (see p. 170) Buryato Mongolia; Kazakskaia; Kirghix and Yakutsk.
Autonomous areas: Adyg Cherkises (=1); Chechen (=2); Ingushetiya (=3); Kabardino-Balgar (=4); Kalmyk; Karachaevo Cherkises (=5); Mari; North Oset (=6); South Oset (=7); Votiak; Zhyrian, and (see p.170) Oirat.
Actual and proposed economic regions (1922--) Ⓐ Northwest; Ⓑ Northeast; Ⓒ Viatka-Vetluga; Ⓓ Ural; Ⓔ West; Ⓕ Central Industrial; Ⓖ Middle Volga; Ⓗ Southwest; Ⓘ Central Black Earth; Ⓙ Lower Volga; Ⓚ West Kirghix; Ⓛ South Mining; Ⓜ North Caucasus.
The dates in Russia refer to independence and conversion into soviet republics.
Rhineland under military occupation of the allies.
Danzig and the Saar Basin
British Mandate
French "
under the League of Nations
Areas demilitarized, 1923
Area in dispute 1923-1926
Principal railways in operation
" " projected
" air routes
Site of important event thus: (•)
Jan Mayen
Iceland
Arctic Circle
Lofoten Is.
West Fiord
Faroe Is.
Shetland Is.
Orkney Is.
The Hebrides
Aalesund
Bergen
Stavanger
Oslo
Christiansand
The Naze
SKAGER RAK
NORTH SEA
Aberdeen
Dundee
Edinburgh
Glasgow
Newcastle
GREAT BRITAIN
Malin Head
Northern Ireland
Belfast
IRISH FREE STATE
Dublin 1922
Cobh Queenstown
Manchester
Liverpool
Leeds
Hull
Sheffield
Birmingham
Cardiff
Bristol
Southampton
Plymouth
London
ENGLISH CHANNEL
Str. of Dover
Amsterdam
The Hague
Rotterdam
Heligoland
Flensburg
Copenhagen
Bornholm
Hamburg
Bremen
Hanover
Berlin
Stettin
Essen
Düsseldorf
Cologne
Leipzig
Dresden
Frankfurt
Prague
Munich
Vienna
Stuttgart
Strasbourg
Nancy
Lille
Calais
Havre
Rouen
Reims
Paris
Versailles
Orleans
Brest
Rennes
Nantes
Angers
Loire R.
Limoges
Bordeaux
Lyon
St. Etienne
Cevennes
Toulouse
Marseilles
Toulon
Perpignan
FRANCE
C. Ortegal
Corunna
C. Finisterre
Santander
Bilbao
Cantabrian Mts.
Pyrenees
Oporto
Valladolid
Salamanca
Madrid
Saragossa
Barcelona
Lisbon
PORTUGAL
SPAIN
Valencia
Sierra Morena
Seville
Granada
Murcia
Cartagena
Alicante
Almeria
Malaga
Sierra Nevada
Cadiz
C. Tarifa
Algeciras
Gibraltar (Brit.)
Ceuta
Tangier
C. St. Vincent
Majorca
Minorca
Ivixa
Palma
Balearic Is.
MEDITERRANEAN
Milan
Venice
Genoa
Florence
Leghorn
Bologna
Trieste
Fiume
Ancona
Rome
Naples
Corsica
Ajaccio
Sardinia
Cagliari
TYRRHENIAN SEA
Palermo
Messina
Trapani
Sicily
Catania
Reggio
Malta (Brit.)
Tunis
Bizerta
Bone
Algiers
ALGERIA
Melilla
Rabat
Casablanca
Fez
MOROCCO
French Protectorate
ATLANTIC OCEAN
Meridian 0 of Greenwich

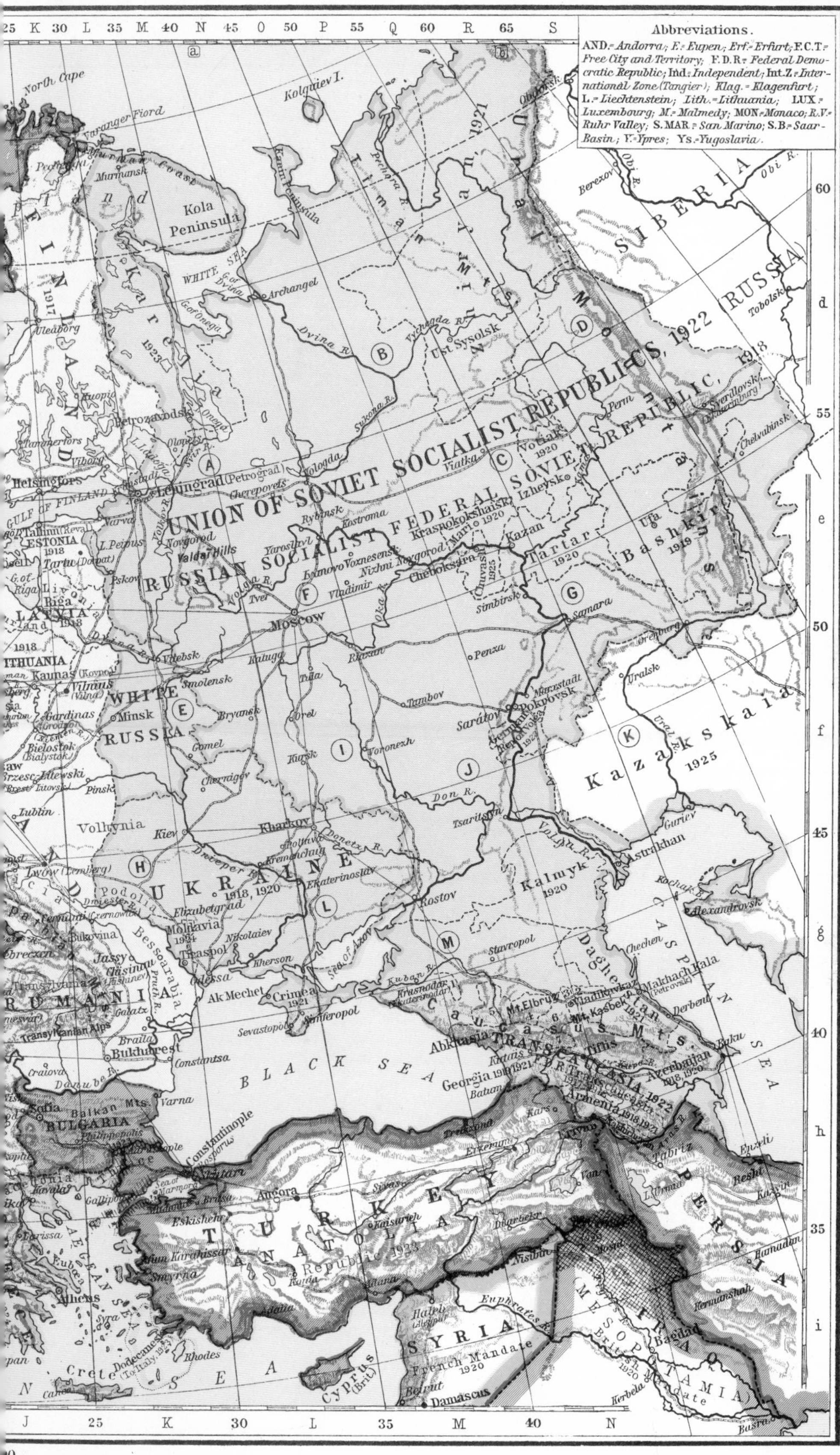
Abbreviations.
AND.= Andorra; E.= Eupen; Erf.= Erfurt; F.C.T.= Free City and Territory; F.D.R.= Federal Democratic Republic; Ind.= Independent; Int.Z.= International Zone (Tangier); Klag.= Klagenfurt; L.= Liechtenstein; Lith.= Lithuania; LUX.= Luxembourg; M.= Malmedy; MON.= Monaco; R.V.= Ruhr Valley; S.MAR.= San Marino; S.B.= Saar-Basin; Y.= Ypres; Ys.= Yugoslavia.
UNION OF SOVIET SOCIALIST REPUBLICS, 1922
RUSSIAN SOCIALIST FEDERAL SOVIET REPUBLIC, 1918
SIBERIA (RUSSIA)
Kola Peninsula
WHITE SEA
BLACK SEA
CASPIAN SEA
AEGEAN SEA
UKRAINE
WHITE RUSSIA
TRANSCAUCASIA, 1922
TURKEY
ANATOLIA
PERSIA
SYRIA
French Mandate 1920
MESOPOTAMIA
British Mandate 1920
BULGARIA
RUMANIA
ESTONIA
LATVIA
LITHUANIA
FINLAND
Karelia 1923
Kazakskaia 1925
Kalmyk 1920
Tartar 1920
Bashkir 1919
Chuvash 1925
Votiak 1920
Mari 1920
Daghestan
Caucasus Mts.
Ural Mts.
Timan Mts.
Moscow
Leningrad (Petrograd)
Kiev
Kharkov
Odessa
Crimea 1921
Archangel
Kazan
Samara
Astrakhan
Baku
Tiflis
Angora
Constantinople
Smyrna
Damascus
Bagdad
Helsingfors
Bukharest
Sofia
Athens
Cyprus (Brit.)
Crete
Dodecanese (To Italy, 1923)
Georgia 1921
Armenia 1918, 1921
Azerbaijan 1918, 1920
Abkhasia
Bessarabia
Volhynia
Podolia
Moldavia 1924
German Volga Republic 1923
Kolguiev I.
Kanin Peninsula
Dvina R.
Volga R.
Don R.
Dnieper R.
Ural R.
Obi R.
Euphrates R.

168H Peoples of Central Europe in 1929.

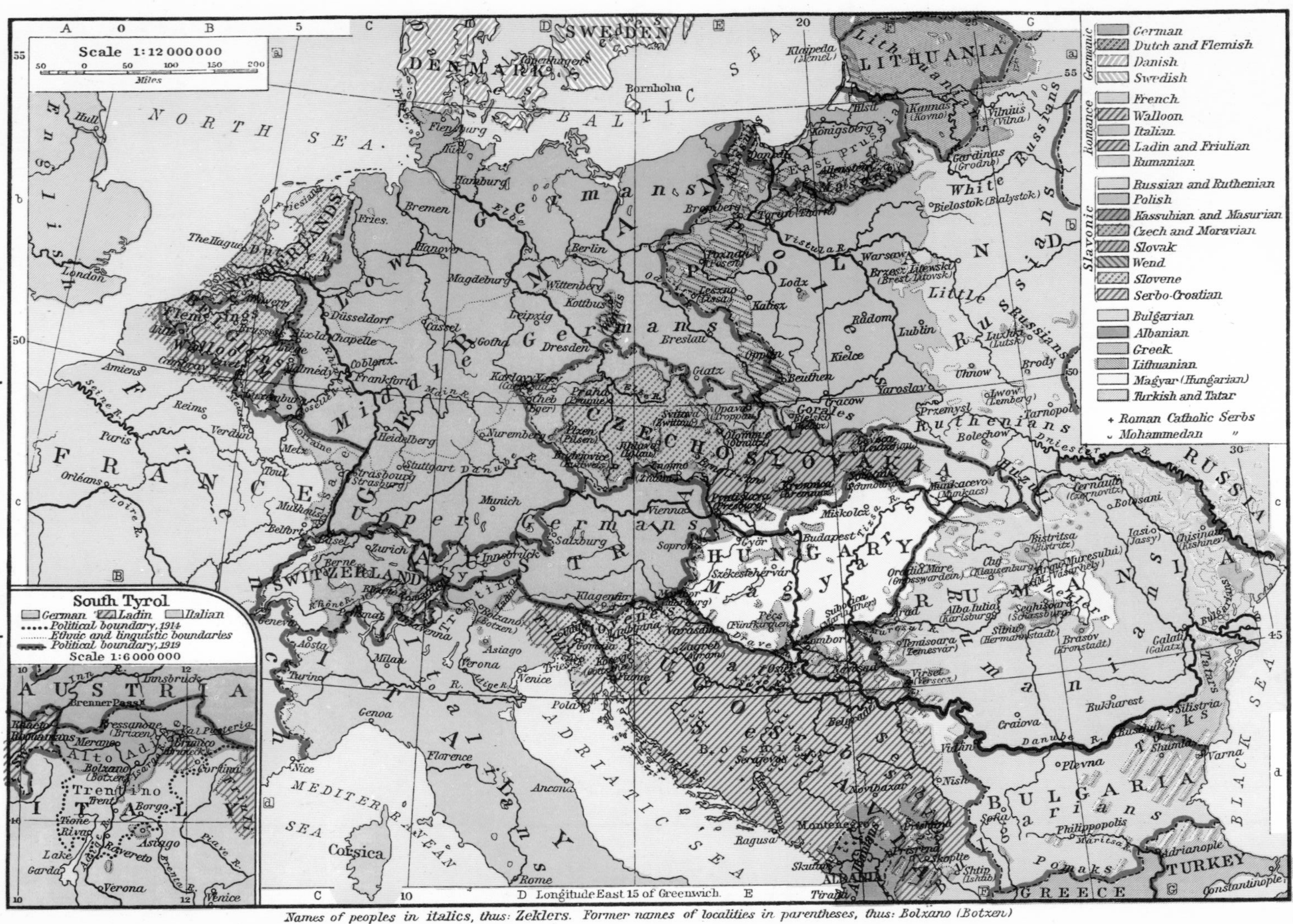

Names of peoples in italics, thus: Zeklers. Former names of localities in parentheses, thus: Bolzano (Botzen)

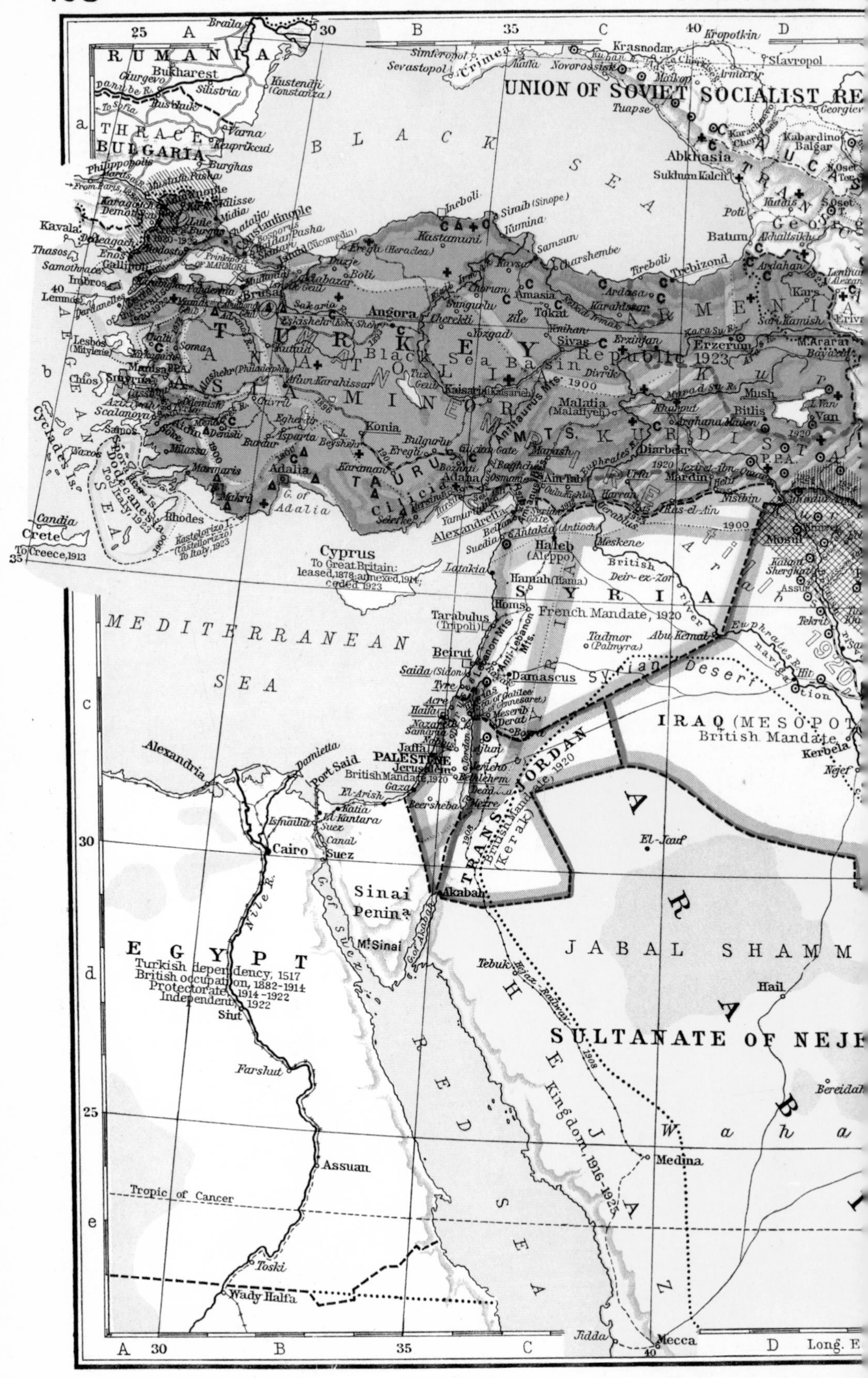
RUMANIA
Bukharest
BULGARIA
BLACK SEA
UNION OF SOVIET SOCIALIST RE
TURKEY
Republic 1923
ANATOLIA
ASIA MINOR
ARMENIA
KURDISTAN
Constantinople
Angora
Konia
Adana
Trebizond
Erzerum
Cyprus
To Great Britain: leased, 1878; annexed, 1914; ceded 1923
Crete
To Greece, 1913
Dodecanese Is.
To Italy, 1923
Rhodes
MEDITERRANEAN SEA
SYRIA
French Mandate, 1920
Haleb (Aleppo)
Beirut
Damascus
Syrian Desert
PALESTINE
British Mandate, 1920
Jerusalem
TRANS-JORDAN
British Mandate, 1920
IRAQ (MESOPOT
British Mandate
Mosul
Alexandria
Cairo
Suez
Sinai Penin.
EGYPT
Turkish dependency, 1517
British occupation, 1882-1914
Protectorate, 1914-1922
Independent, 1922
Siut
Assuan
Tropic of Cancer
Wady Halfa
RED SEA
HEJAZ
Kingdom, 1916-1925
Hejaz Railway
Medina
Mecca
Jidda
ARABIA
JABAL SHAMM
SULTANATE OF NEJ
Hail
Long. E

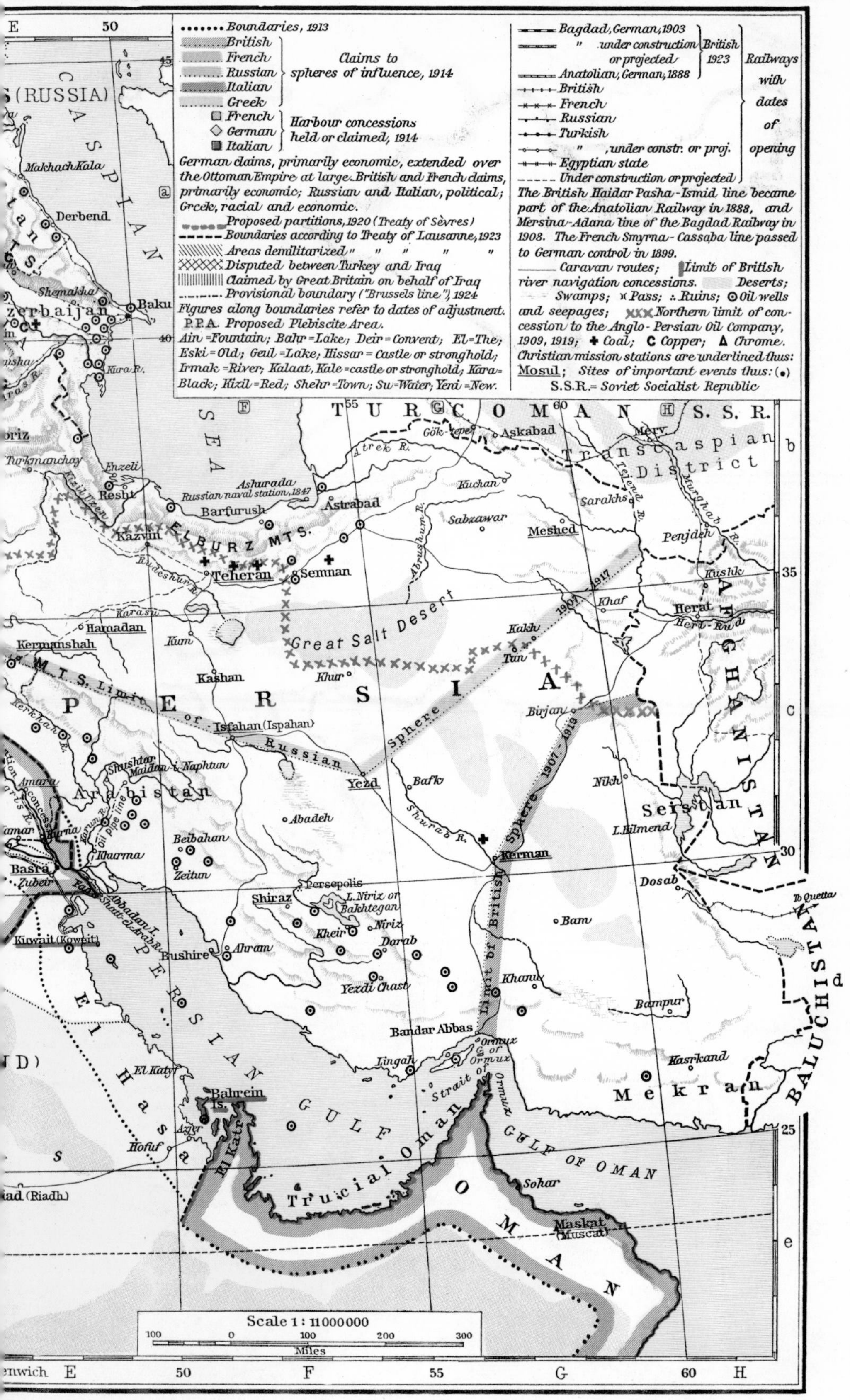
Boundaries, 1913
British
French
Russian
Italian
Greek
Claims to spheres of influence, 1914
French
German
Italian
Harbour concessions held or claimed, 1914
German claims, primarily economic, extended over the Ottoman Empire at large. British and French claims, primarily economic; Russian and Italian, political; Greek, racial and economic.
Proposed partitions, 1920 (Treaty of Sèvres)
Boundaries according to Treaty of Lausanne, 1923
Areas demilitarized " " " " "
Disputed between Turkey and Iraq
Claimed by Great Britain on behalf of Iraq
Provisional boundary ("Brussels line"), 1924
Figures along boundaries refer to dates of adjustment.
P.P.A. Proposed Plebiscite Area.
Ain = Fountain; Bahr = Lake; Deir = Convent; El = The; Eski = Old; Geul = Lake; Hissar = Castle or stronghold; Irmak = River; Kalaat, Kale = castle or stronghold; Kara = Black; Kizil = Red; Shehr = Town; Su = Water; Yeni = New.
Bagdad, German, 1903
" under construction or projected
British 1923
Anatolian, German, 1888
British
French
Russian
Turkish
" , under constr. or proj.
Egyptian state
Under construction or projected
Railways with dates of opening
The British Haidar Pasha-Ismid line became part of the Anatolian Railway in 1888, and Mersina-Adana line of the Bagdad Railway in 1908. The French Smyrna-Cassaba line passed to German control in 1899.
Caravan routes; Limit of British river navigation concessions. Deserts; Swamps; Pass; Ruins; Oil wells and seepages; Northern limit of concession to the Anglo-Persian Oil Company, 1909, 1919; Coal; Copper; Chrome.
Christian mission stations are underlined thus: Mosul; Sites of important events thus: (•)
S.S.R. = Soviet Socialist Republic
CASPIAN SEA
(RUSSIA)
Makhach Kala
Derbend
Shemakha
Azerbaijan
Baku
Kura R.
Araş R.
Tabriz
Turkmanchay
Enzeli
Resht
Ashurada
Russian naval station, 1847
Barfurush
Astrabad
Kazvin
ELBURZ MTS.
Teheran
Semnan
Rudeshur R.
Karasu
Hamadan
Kum
Kermanshah
Kashan
TURCOMAN S.S.R.
Gök-tepe
Askabad
Merv
Transcaspian District
Atrek R.
Kuchan
Sarakhs
Tejend R.
Murghab R.
Sabzawar
Meshed
Abrushum R.
Penjdeh
Kushk
AFGHANISTAN
Herat
Heri-Rud
Khaf
Great Salt Desert
Kakh
Tun
Khur
PERSIA
Limit of Russian Sphere
Limit of British Sphere
1907
1917
1907-1919
Birjan
Isfahan (Ispahan)
Kerkhah R.
Yezd
Bafk
Shurab R.
Shushtar
Maidan-i-Naphtun
Arabistan
Amara
Karun R.
Oil pipe line
Kurna
Abadeh
Nikh
Seistan
L. Hilmend
Beibahan
Kharma
Basra
Zubeir
Zeitun
Abbadan I.
Shat-el-Arab R.
Kerman
Persepolis
Shiraz
L. Niriz or Bakhtegan
Niriz
Kheir
Darab
Dosab
To Quetta
Bam
Kuwait (Koweit)
Bushire
Ahram
Yezdi Chast
Khanu
Bampur
BALUCHISTAN
PERSIAN GULF
El Hasa
Bandar Abbas
Ormuz or Ormuz
Lingah
Strait of Ormuz
Kasrkand
Mekran
El Katif
Bahrein Is.
Azier
Hofuf
El Katr
Trucial Oman
GULF OF OMAN
Sohar
Maskat (Muscat)
OMAN
Riad (Riadh)
Scale 1: 11 000 000
100 0 100 200 300
Miles
Greenwich E 50 F 55 G 60 H
45 40 35 30 25
b c d e

The Near East II.

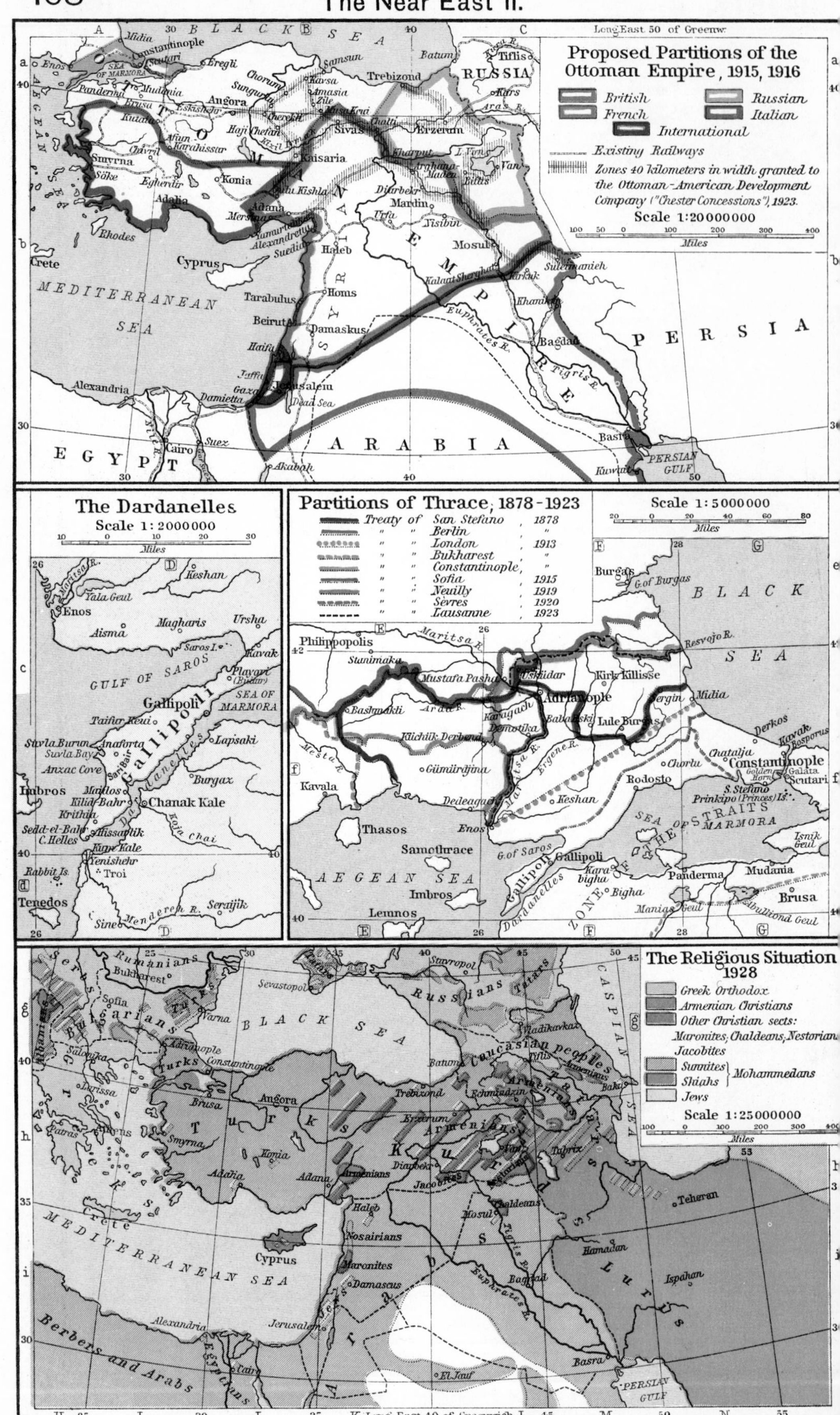

Proposed Partitions of the Ottoman Empire, 1915, 1916
British
Russian
French
Italian
International
Existing Railways
Zones 40 kilometers in width granted to the Ottoman-American Development Company ("Chester Concessions"), 1923.
Scale 1:20000000
Miles
The Dardanelles
Scale 1:2000000
Miles
Partitions of Thrace, 1878-1923
Treaty of San Stefano, 1878
" " Berlin, "
" " London, 1913
" " Bukharest, "
" " Constantinople, "
" " Sofia, 1915
" " Neuilly, 1919
" " Sèvres, 1920
" " Lausanne, 1923
Scale 1:5000000
Miles
The Religious Situation 1928
Greek Orthodox
Armenian Christians
Other Christian sects: Maronites, Chaldeans, Nestorians, Jacobites
Sunnites
Shiahs
Mohammedans
Jews
Scale 1:25000000
Miles

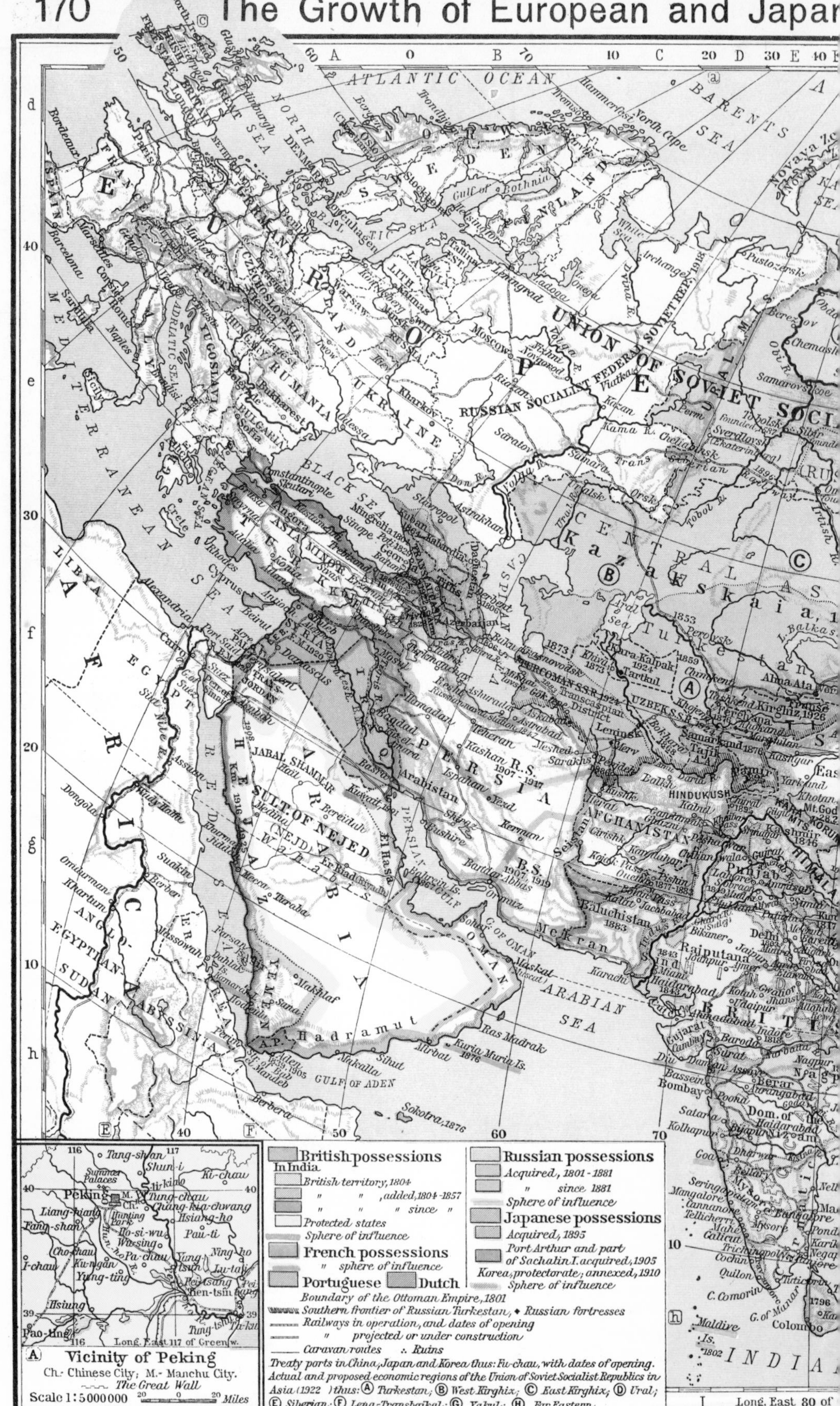

Abbreviations: A.A.= *Autonomous (Socialist Soviet) Area*; A.P.= *Aden Protectorate*; A.R.= *Autonomous (Socialist Soviet) Republic*; ALB.= *Alban*
EST.= *Estonia*; E.M.S= *Federated Malay States*; F.M.= *French Mandate*; J.= *Japan*; LEB.= *Lebanon*; LITH.= *Lithuania*; PAL.= *Palestine*; R.= *Russ*

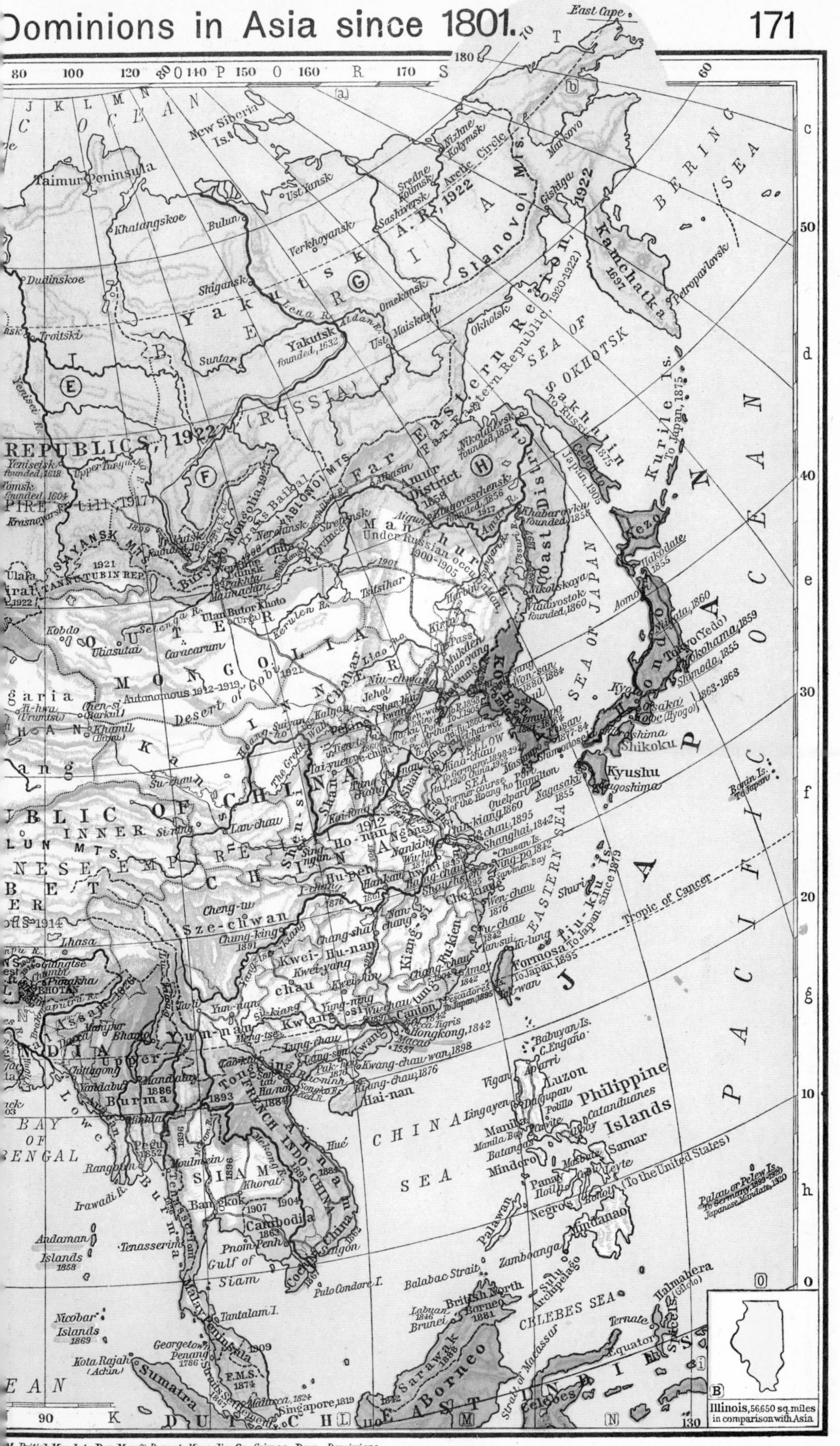

M.=British Mandate; Bur. Mong.=Buryato Mongolia; Cr.=Crimea; Dom.=Dominions; ...ere; REP.=Republic; S.S.R.=Socialist Soviet Republic; SULT.=Sultanate.

Scale 1:40 000 000 200 0 200 400 600 Miles

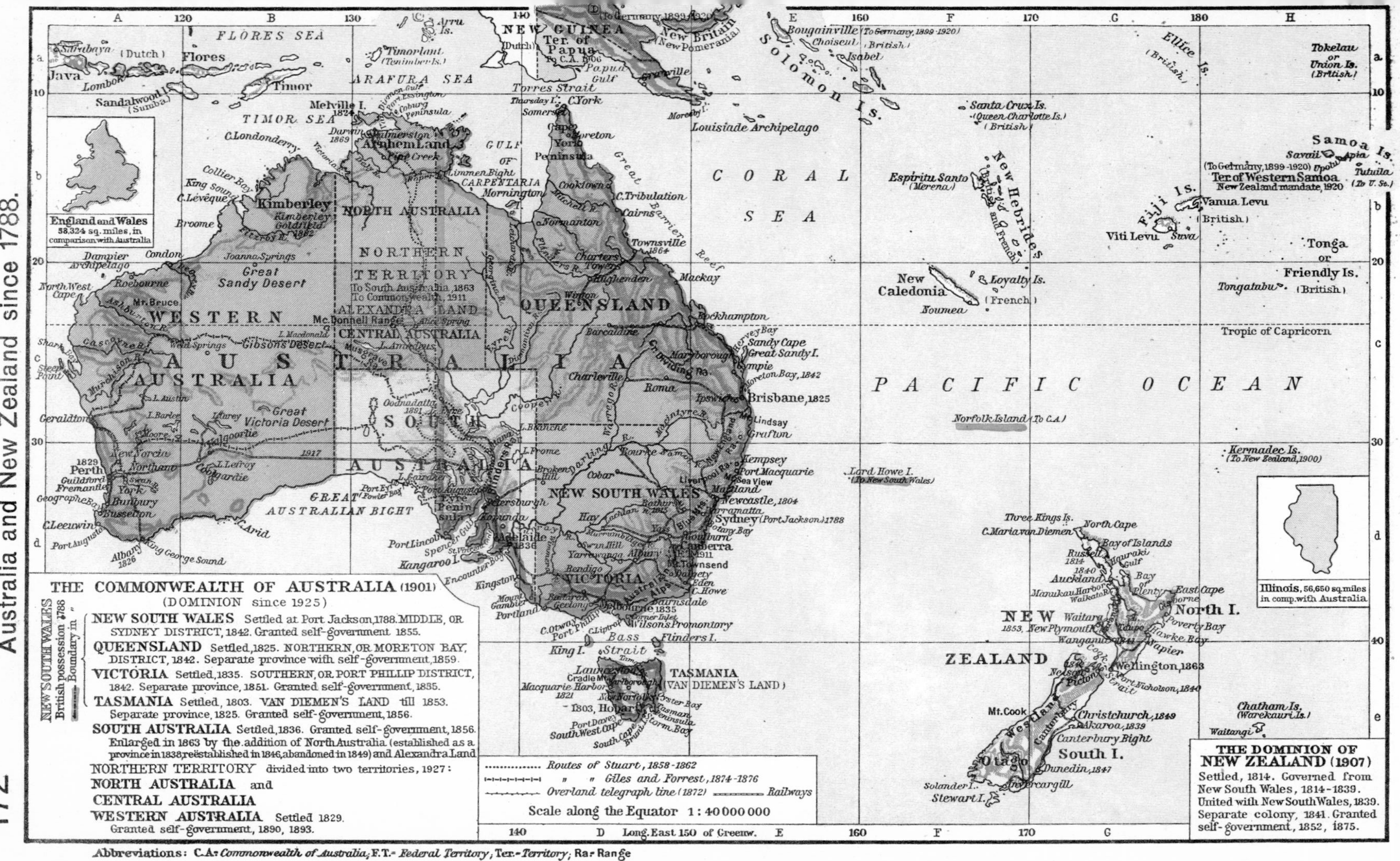
THE COMMONWEALTH OF AUSTRALIA (1901)
(DOMINION since 1925)
NEW SOUTH WALES
British possession 1788
Boundary in "
NEW SOUTH WALES Settled at Port Jackson, 1788. MIDDLE, OR SYDNEY DISTRICT, 1842. Granted self-government 1855.
QUEENSLAND Settled, 1825. NORTHERN, OR MORETON BAY, DISTRICT, 1842. Separate province with self-government, 1859.
VICTORIA Settled, 1835. SOUTHERN, OR PORT PHILLIP DISTRICT, 1842. Separate province, 1851. Granted self-government, 1855.
TASMANIA Settled, 1803. VAN DIEMEN'S LAND till 1853. Separate province, 1825. Granted self-government, 1856.
SOUTH AUSTRALIA Settled, 1836. Granted self-government, 1856. Enlarged in 1863 by the addition of North Australia (established as a province in 1838, reëstablished in 1846, abandoned in 1849) and Alexandra Land
NORTHERN TERRITORY divided into two territories, 1927:
NORTH AUSTRALIA and
CENTRAL AUSTRALIA
WESTERN AUSTRALIA Settled 1829. Granted self-government, 1890, 1893.
Abbreviations: C.A.: Commonwealth of Australia, F.T.: Federal Territory, Ter.: Territory, Ra.: Range
England and Wales 58,324 sq. miles, in comparison with Australia
Routes of Stuart, 1858-1862
" " Giles and Forrest, 1874-1876
Overland telegraph line (1872)
Railways
Scale along the Equator 1:40000000
Long. East 150 of Greenw.
Illinois, 56,650 sq. miles in comp. with Australia
THE DOMINION OF NEW ZEALAND (1907)
Settled, 1814. Governed from New South Wales, 1814-1839. United with New South Wales, 1839. Separate colony, 1841. Granted self-government, 1852, 1875.
AUSTRALIA
WESTERN AUSTRALIA
SOUTH AUSTRALIA
NORTHERN TERRITORY
To South Australia, 1863
To Commonwealth, 1911
ALEXANDRA LAND
NORTH AUSTRALIA
CENTRAL AUSTRALIA
QUEENSLAND
NEW SOUTH WALES
VICTORIA
TASMANIA (VAN DIEMEN'S LAND)
NEW ZEALAND
North I.
South I.
CORAL SEA
PACIFIC OCEAN
TIMOR SEA
ARAFURA SEA
FLORES SEA
GREAT AUSTRALIAN BIGHT
NEW GUINEA
Ter. of Papua
Great Sandy Desert
Great Victoria Desert
Gibsons Desert
Tropic of Capricorn
New Caledonia
Loyalty Is. (French)
Fiji Is. (British)
Samoa Is.
Ter. of Western Samoa
New Zealand mandate, 1920
Tonga or Friendly Is. (British)
Solomon Is.
New Hebrides
Norfolk Island (To C.A.)
Lord Howe I. (To New South Wales)
Kermadec Is. (To New Zealand, 1900)
Chatham Is. (Warekauri Is.)
Perth
Adelaide
Melbourne
Sydney (Port Jackson), 1788
Brisbane, 1825
Canberra
Wellington, 1863
Auckland
Christchurch, 1849
Dunedin, 1847

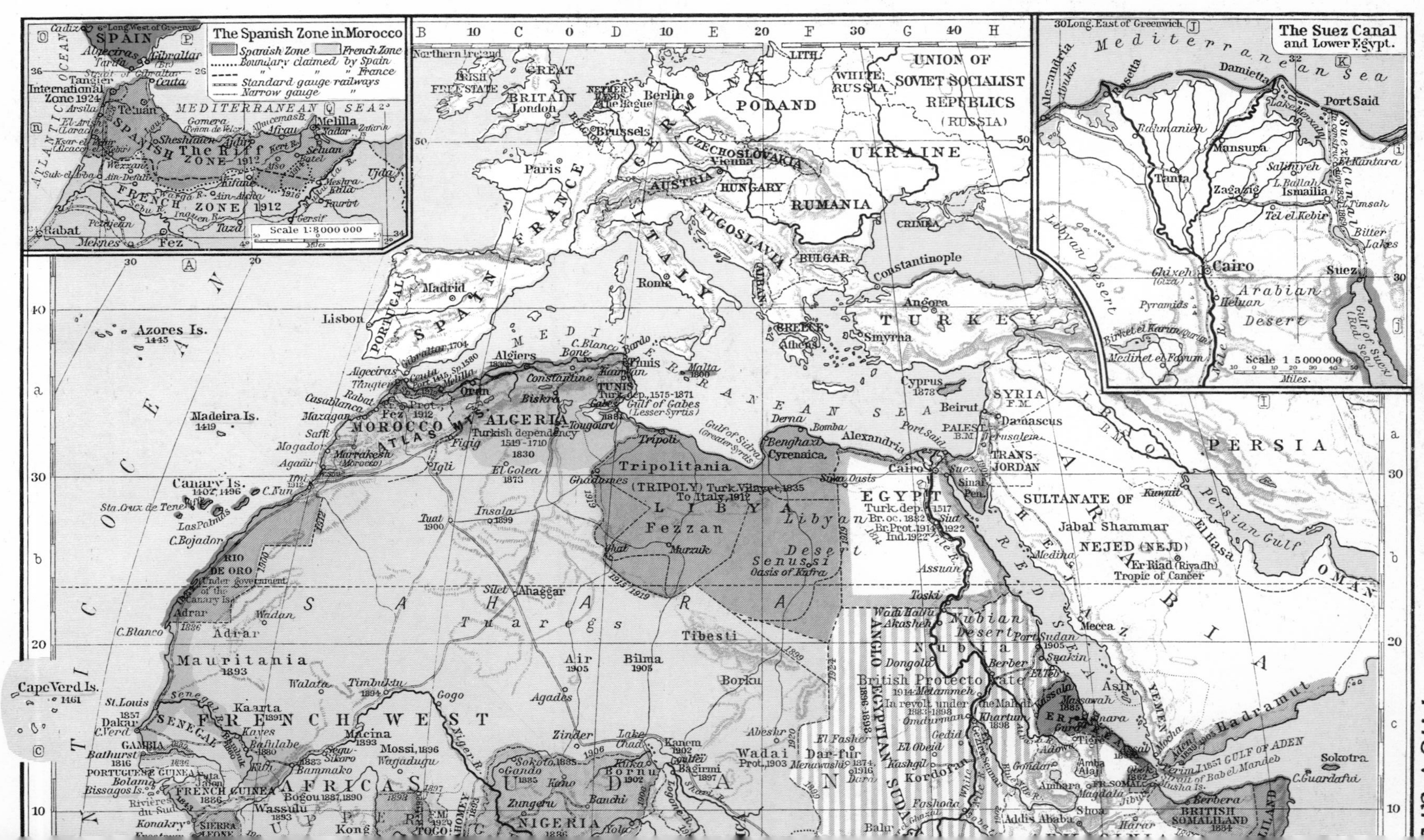
The Spanish Zone in Morocco
Spanish Zone
French Zone
Boundary claimed by Spain
" " " France
Standard gauge railways
Narrow gauge "
Scale 1:8 000 000
The Suez Canal and Lower Egypt.
Scale 1 5 000 000
UNION OF SOVIET SOCIALIST REPUBLICS (RUSSIA)
UKRAINE
POLAND
GERMANY
CZECHOSLOVAKIA
AUSTRIA
HUNGARY
RUMANIA
YUGOSLAVIA
ITALY
FRANCE
SPAIN
PORTUGAL
GREAT BRITAIN
TURKEY
PERSIA
ARABIA
SULTANATE OF Jabal Shammar
NEJED (NEJD)
EGYPT
LIBYA
ALGERIA
MOROCCO
Tripolitania
Fezzan
SAHARA
Mauritania
ANGLO EGYPTIAN SUDAN
FRENCH WEST AFRICA
NIGERIA
MEDITERRANEAN SEA
Azores Is.
Madeira Is.
Canary Is.
Cape Verd Is.

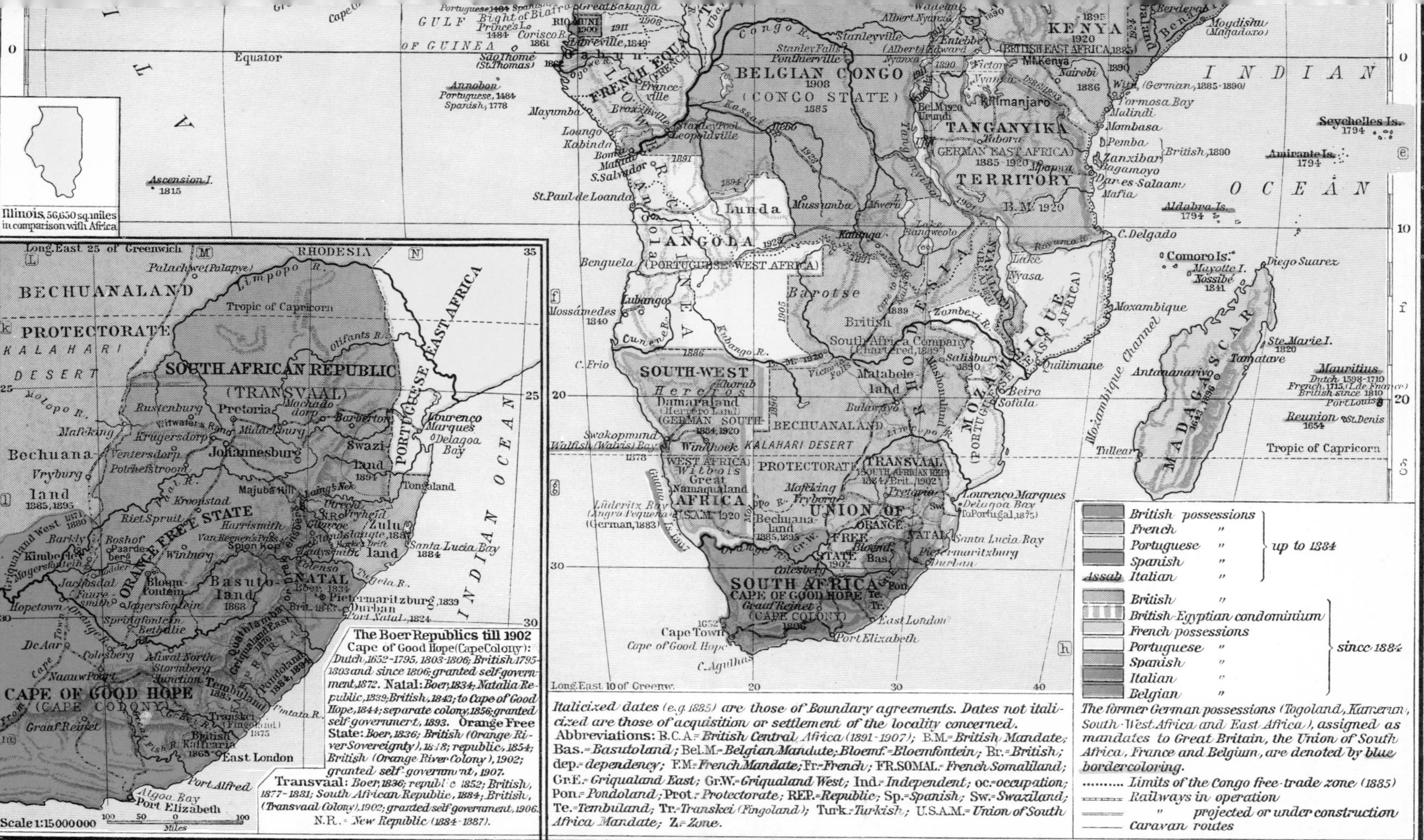
British possessions "
French "
Portuguese "
Spanish "
Assab Italian "
up to 1884
British "
British-Egyptian condominium
French possessions
Portuguese "
Spanish "
Italian "
Belgian "
since 1884
The former German possessions (Togoland, Kamerun, South-West Africa and East Africa), assigned as mandates to Great Britain, the Union of South Africa, France and Belgium, are denoted by blue bordercoloring.
.... Limits of the Congo free-trade zone (1885)
Railways in operation
" projected or under construction
Caravan routes
Italicized dates (e.g. 1885) are those of Boundary agreements. Dates not italicized are those of acquisition or settlement of the locality concerned.
Abbreviations: B.C.A.= British Central Africa (1891-1907); B.M.= British Mandate; Bas.= Basutoland; Bel.M.= Belgian Mandate; Bloemf.= Bloemfontein; Br.= British; dep.= dependency; F.M.= French Mandate; Fr.= French; FR.SOMAL.= French Somaliland; Gr.E.= Griqualand East; Gr.W.= Griqualand West; Ind.= Independent; oc.= occupation; Pon.= Pondoland; Prot.= Protectorate; REP.= Republic; Sp.= Spanish; Sw.= Swaziland; Te.= Tembuland; Tr.= Transkei (Fingoland); Turk.= Turkish; U.S.A.M.= Union of South Africa Mandate; Z.= Zone.
Scale 1:40 000 000
Miles
Illinois, 56,650 sq. miles in comparison with Africa
The Boer Republics till 1902
Cape of Good Hope (Cape Colony): Dutch, 1652-1795, 1803-1806; British 1795-1803 and since 1806; granted self-government, 1872. Natal: Boer, 1834; Natalia Republic, 1839; British, 1843; to Cape of Good Hope, 1844; separate colony, 1856; granted self-government, 1893. Orange Free State: Boer, 1836; British (Orange River Sovereignty), 1848; republic, 1854; British (Orange River Colony), 1902; granted self-government, 1907.
Transvaal: Boer, 1836; republic 1852; British, 1877-1881; South African Republic, 1884; British, (Transvaal Colony), 1902; granted self government, 1906.
N.R.= New Republic (1884-1887).
Scale 1:15 000 000
BELGIAN CONGO
(CONGO STATE)
TANGANYIKA
TERRITORY
KENYA
ANGOLA
(PORTUGUESE WEST AFRICA)
SOUTH-WEST AFRICA
SOUTH AFRICA
UNION OF
MADAGASCAR
INDIAN OCEAN
BECHUANALAND PROTECTORATE
SOUTH AFRICAN REPUBLIC
(TRANSVAAL)
ORANGE FREE STATE
NATAL
CAPE OF GOOD HOPE
(CAPE COLONY)
PORTUGUESE EAST AFRICA

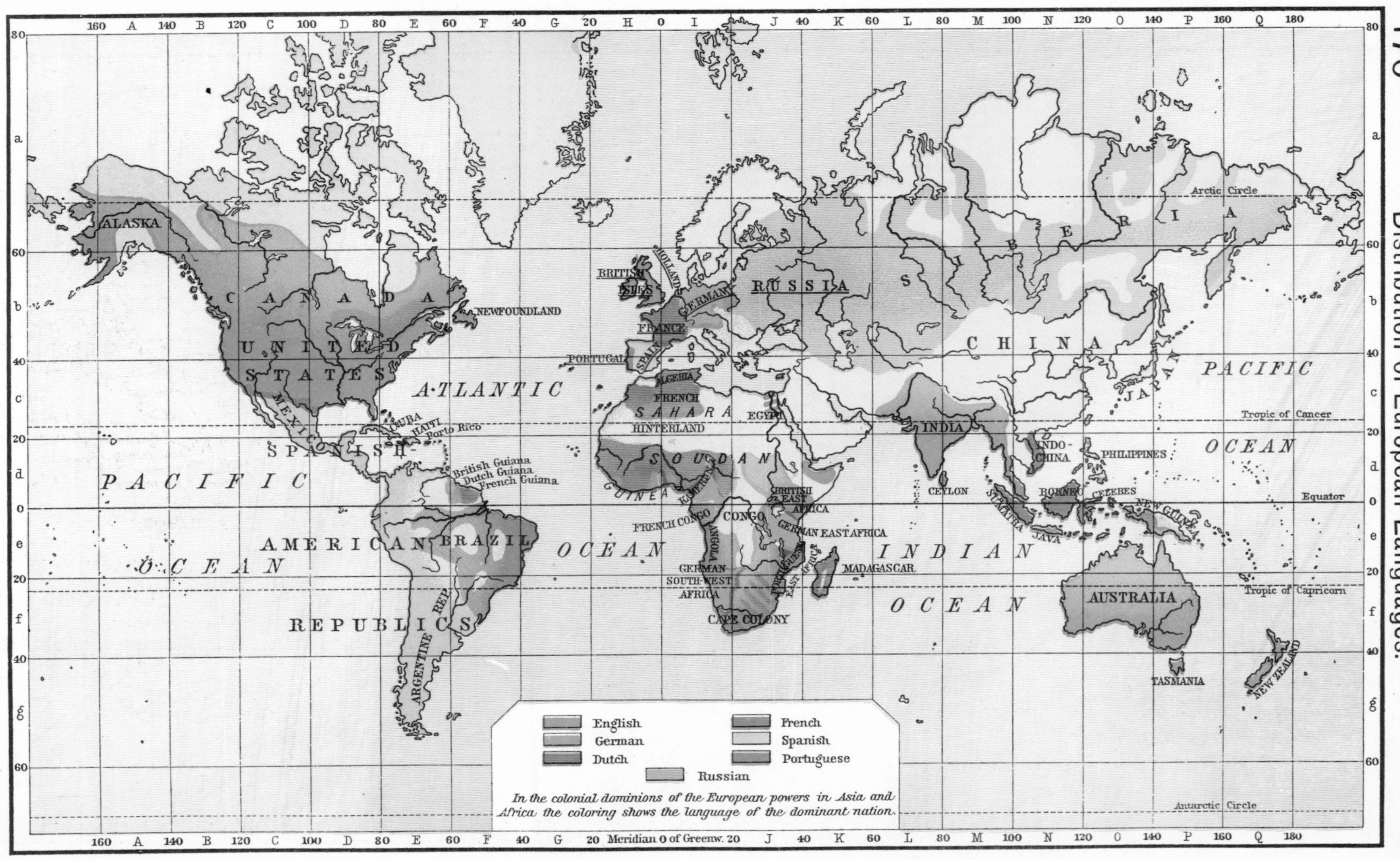
English
German
Dutch
French
Spanish
Portuguese
Russian
In the colonial dominions of the European powers in Asia and Africa the coloring shows the language of the dominant nation.
Meridian 0 of Greenw.
Arctic Circle
Tropic of Cancer
Equator
Tropic of Capricorn
Antarctic Circle
PACIFIC OCEAN
ATLANTIC OCEAN
INDIAN OCEAN
ALASKA
CANADA
UNITED STATES
MEXICO
NEWFOUNDLAND
CUBA
HAITI
Porto Rico
British Guiana
Dutch Guiana
French Guiana
SPANISH AMERICAN REPUBLICS
BRAZIL
ARGENTINE REP.
BRITISH ISLES
HOLLAND
GERMANY
FRANCE
SPAIN
PORTUGAL
RUSSIA
SIBERIA
CHINA
JAPAN
INDIA
CEYLON
INDO-CHINA
PHILIPPINES
BORNEO
CELEBES
SUMATRA
JAVA
NEW GUINEA
AUSTRALIA
TASMANIA
NEW ZEALAND
ALGERIA
FRENCH SAHARA
HINTERLAND
EGYPT
SOUDAN
GUINEA
FRENCH CONGO
CONGO
ANGOLA
GERMAN SOUTH-WEST AFRICA
CAPE COLONY
BRITISH EAST AFRICA
GERMAN EAST AFRICA
MADAGASCAR

European, African and Asiatic Migration.

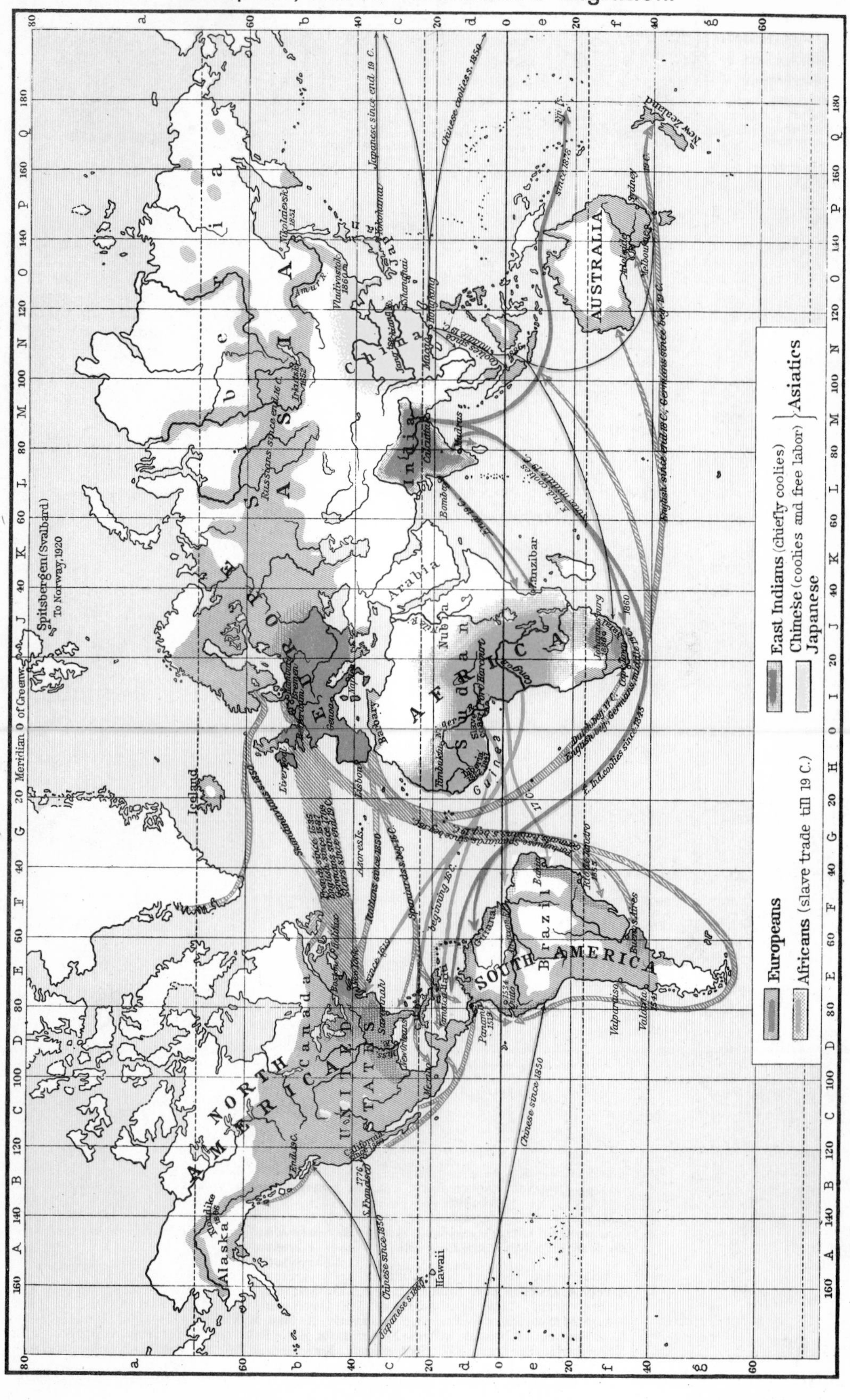

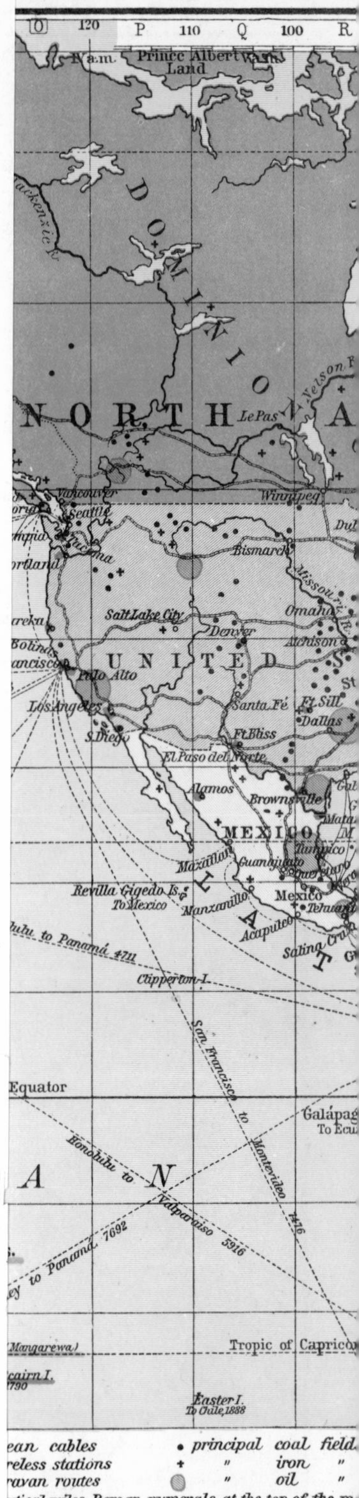

ean cables • principal coal field
reless stations + " iron "
ravan routes " oil "
utical miles; Roman numerals at the top of the m
ich.
ons
ago, **Arm.**= **Armenia**; Aus.= Australia, **AUST.**= **Austri**
Bel. M.= Belgian Mandate; *Bloemf.*= *Bloemfontei*
Republic, **EST.**= **Estonia**; F.M.= French Mandate; **EM**
HUNG.= **Hungary**; **LITH.**= **Lithuania**; **M.**= **Monteneg**
lestine; **Pr.**= **Prince**; **SS.**= **Straits Setflements**
ry; **W.** = **Western**; **U.S.**= **United States**; U.S.A.M
a.

BAFFIN LAND
Davis Strait
Godhavn
Godthaab
Lichtenfels
Hudson Str.
RICA
ANADA
NEWFOU
Anticosti
Quebec
Montreal
Drummondville
Ottawa
Pr. Edward I.
Louisburg
St. Pierre
Miquelon
C. Breton I.
C. Canso
Halifax
Boston
Springfield
Bar Harbor
Cape Cod
New York
Philadelphia
Baltimore
Washington
Norfolk
New Orleans to Southampton
Charleston
Savannah
Bermudas
Kingston to Southampton
Colón to Liverpool
Nassau
Bahama Is.
WEST INDIES
Santiago
Kingston
Jamaica
Porto Rico
To U.S. 1898
Virgin Is. from Denmark to U.S.
Leeward Is.
Guadeloupe
Martinique
Windward Is.
Barbados
Tobago, 1794
Trinidad, 1797
CARIBBEAN SEA
St. Martin
Colón
Cartagena
Caracas
VENEZUELA
Demerara
Georgetown
Paramaribo
1796
GUIANA
COLOMBIA
Bogotá
Boa Vista do Rio Branco
ECUADOR
Amazon R.
Benjamin Constant
Manáos
Iquitos
SOUTH
Bocca do Acre
Humaytá
PERU
BRA
Porto Velho
Callao
Lima
Riberalta
BOLIVIA
La Paz
Mollendo
Arica
AMERI
Iquique
Paraguay R.
PARAGUAY
Antofagasta
Caldera
Jujuy
Tucumán
Paraná R.
Paraná
Córdoba
Valparaiso
Mendoza
URUGUAY
Santiago
Buenos Aires
Montevideo
Talcahuano
Concepción
ARGENTINE REPUBLIC (ARGENTINA)
Puerto Belgrano
Puerto Montt
Punta Arenas to Montevideo 1807
Wellington I.
Falkland Is.
1833
Port Stanley
Straits of Magellan
Punta Arenas
Tierra del Fuego
Año Nuevo
Cape Horn

Localities in Western Europe, connected with American History

Scale 1 : 15 000 000

100 50 0 100 200 300 Miles

Localities in England, connected with American History.

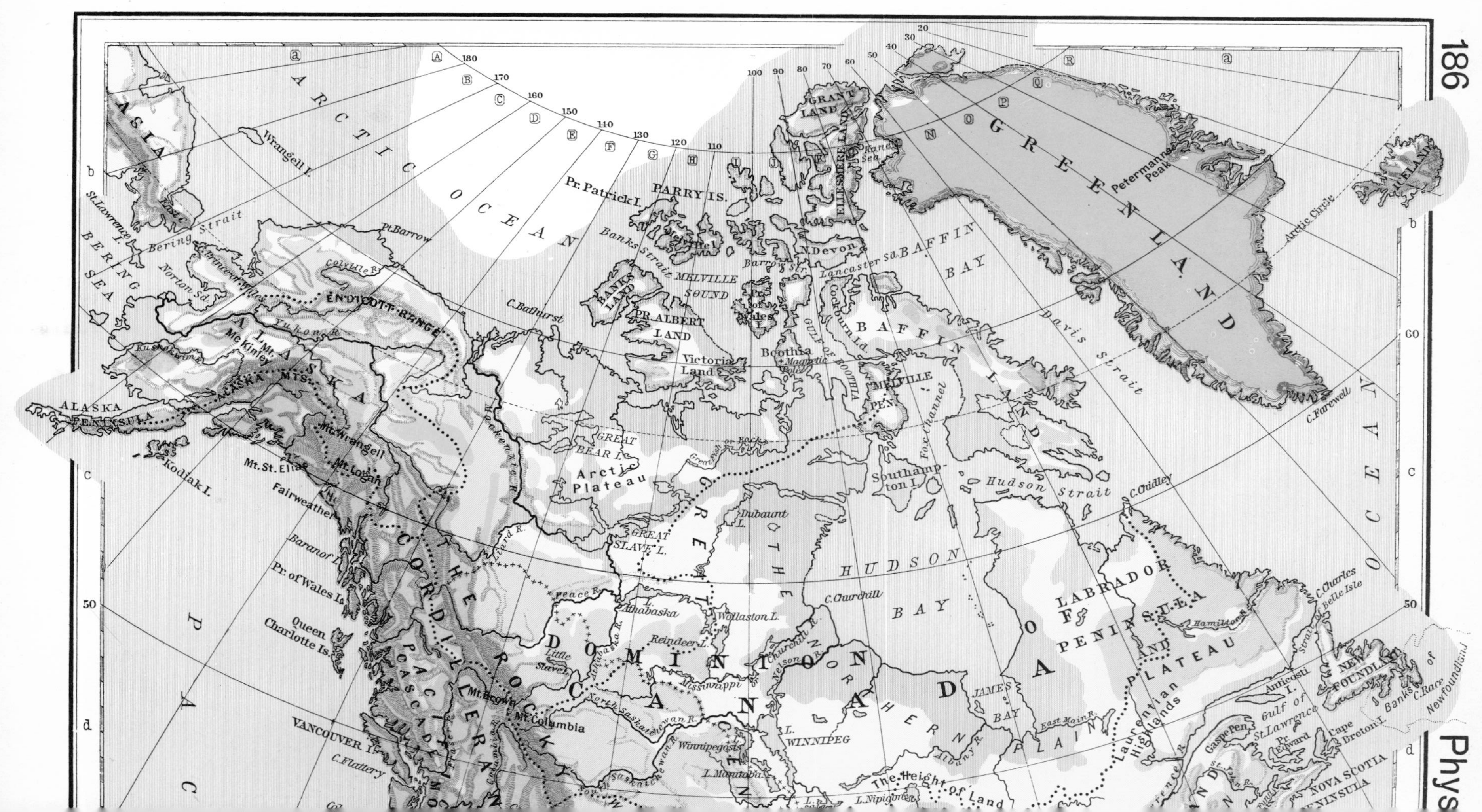
ARCTIC OCEAN
OCEAN
GREENLAND
Petermann Peak
Arctic Circle
C. Farewell
ICELAND
Davis Strait
BAFFIN BAY
BAFFIN LAND
Lancaster Sd.
Cockburn Ld.
GULF OF BOOTHIA
Boothia
MELVILLE PEN.
Fox Channel
Southampton I.
Hudson Strait
C. Chidley
HUDSON BAY
THE BAY
C. Churchill
JAMES BAY
LABRADOR
LABRADOR PENINSULA
PLATEAU
Laurentian Highlands
Gulf of St. Lawrence
Anticosti I.
Strait of Belle Isle
NEWFOUNDLAND
Banks of Newfoundland
Cape Breton I.
NOVA SCOTIA
Gaspé Pen.
ELLESMERE LAND
N. Devon
PARRY IS.
Pr. Patrick I.
Melville I.
MELVILLE SOUND
Banks Strait
BANKS LAND
PR. ALBERT LAND
Victoria Land
Arctic Plateau
GREAT BEAR L.
GREAT SLAVE L.
L. Athabaska
Reindeer L.
Wollaston L.
Dubawnt L.
L. WINNIPEG
L. Winnipegosis
L. Manitoba
L. Nipigon
The Height of Land
NORTHERN PLAIN
GREAT PLAIN
DOMINION OF CANADA
Nelson R.
Churchill R.
Peace R.
Mackenzie R.
C. Bathurst
Pt. Barrow
ENDICOTT RANGE
Yukon R.
ALASKA
ALASKA MTS.
Mt. McKinley
Mt. Wrangell
Mt. Logan
Mt. St. Elias
Fairweather
Baranof I.
Pr. of Wales Is.
Queen Charlotte Is.
VANCOUVER I.
C. Flattery
THE ROCKY MTS.
CORDILLERA
PACIFIC
CASCADE
Mt. Brown
Mt. Columbia
Kodiak I.
ALASKA PENINSULA
Norton Sd.
Bering Strait
BERING SEA
St. Lawrence I.
Wrangell I.
ASIA
P A C

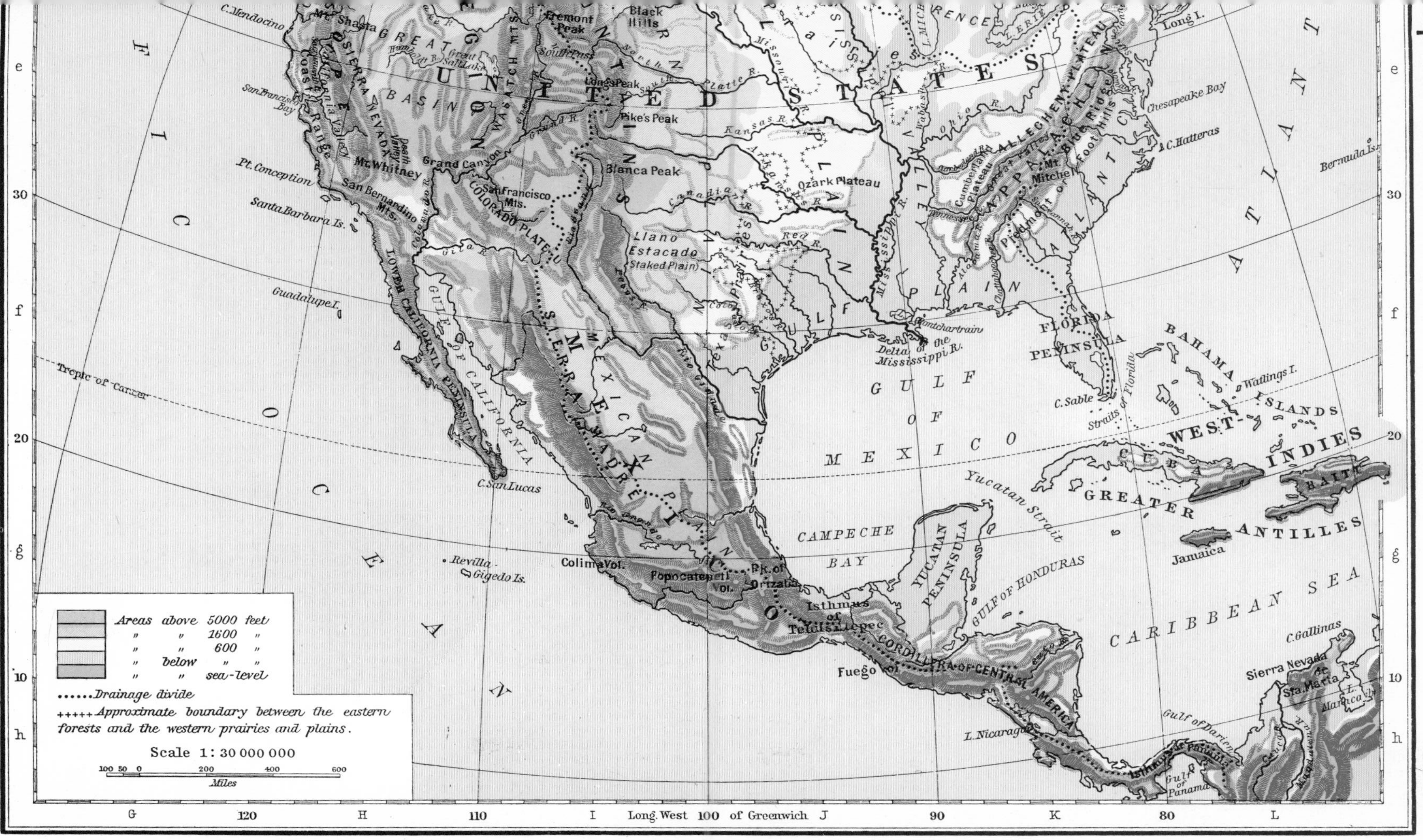
UNITED STATES
GULF OF MEXICO
CARIBBEAN SEA
WEST INDIES
GREATER ANTILLES
BAHAMA ISLANDS
CUBA
HAITI
Jamaica
YUCATAN PENINSULA
CAMPECHE BAY
GULF OF HONDURAS
Yucatan Strait
FLORIDA PENINSULA
C. Sable
C. Hatteras
Chesapeake Bay
Bermuda Is.
Ozark Plateau
Llano Estacado (Staked Plain)
Pike's Peak
Blanca Peak
Longs Peak
Black Hills
Fremont Peak
Grand Canyon
COLORADO PLATEAU
San Francisco Mts.
SIERRA NEVADA
GREAT BASIN
WASATCH MTS
Mt. Whitney
Death Valley
San Bernardino Mts.
Coast Range
California Valley
Mt. Shasta
C. Mendocino
San Francisco Bay
Pt. Conception
Santa Barbara Is.
Guadalupe I.
GULF OF CALIFORNIA
LOWER CALIFORNIA PENINSULA
C. San Lucas
Tropic of Cancer
SIERRA MADRE
MEXICAN PLATEAU
Colima Vol.
Popocatepetl Vol.
Pk. of Orizaba
Isthmus of Tehuantepec
Fuego
CORDILLERA OF CENTRAL AMERICA
L. Nicaragua
Gulf of Darien
Gulf of Panama
Sierra Nevada de Sta. Marta
C. Gallinas
Revilla Gigedo Is.
Delta of the Mississippi R.
Pontchartrain
Areas above 5000 feet
" " 1600 "
" " 600 "
" below " "
" " sea-level
Drainage divide
Approximate boundary between the eastern forests and the western prairies and plains.
Scale 1 : 30 000 000
Miles
Long. West 100 of Greenwich

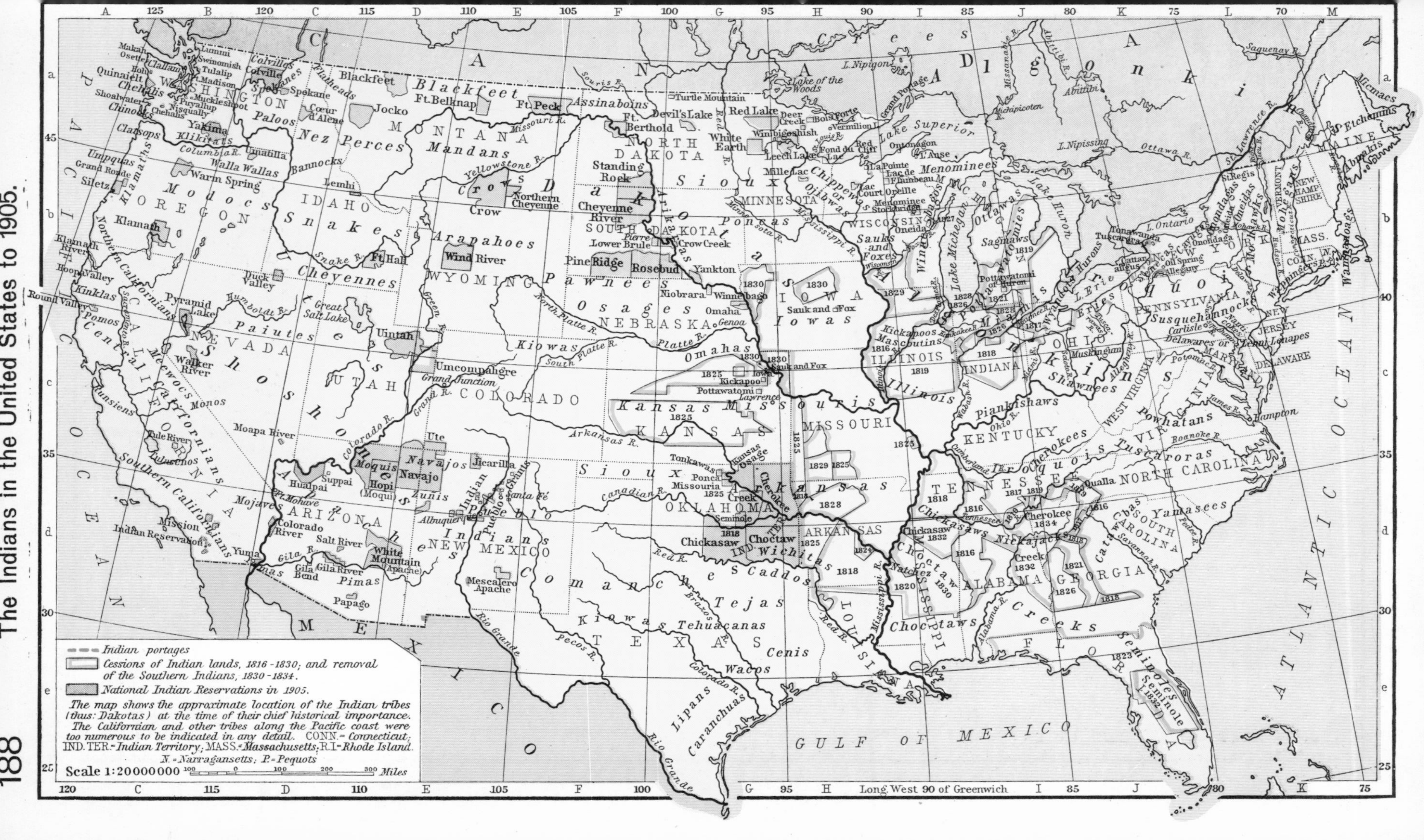
Indian portages
Cessions of Indian lands, 1816-1830; and removal of the Southern Indians, 1830-1834.
National Indian Reservations in 1905.
The map shows the approximate location of the Indian tribes (thus: Dakotas) at the time of their chief historical importance. The Californian and other tribes along the Pacific coast were too numerous to be indicated in any detail. CONN.=Connecticut; IND.TER.=Indian Territory; MASS.=Massachusetts; R.I.=Rhode Island.
N.=Narragansetts; P.=Pequots
Scale 1:20000000
Miles
GULF OF MEXICO
ATLANTIC OCEAN
Long. West 90 of Greenwich

Reference Map of the New England Colonies, 1607—1760.

English possessions about 1750
Approximate area of settlement in 1660
" " " " " 1750
" frontier of the "New England Confederation", 1643-1684
Dutch possessions, 1613-1664, 1673-1674
French possessions about 1750

MASSACHUSETTS BAY

Corporate colony under patent from the Council for New England, 1628, and under royal charter, 1629; charter annulled, 1684; royal Province under new charter, 1691; charter practically abrogated by Parliament, 1774.

New Plymouth

Corporate colony under patent from the London Company, 1620, and from the Council for New England, 1621, 1630; added to Massachusetts Bay, 1691.

MAINE: *(between the Merrimac and Kennebec Rivers)-*
Proprietary colony under patent from the Council for New England, 1622

": *(between the Piscataqua and Kennebec Rivers)-*
Proprietary colony under royal charter, 1637; held by Massachusetts Bay, 1651-1665, 1667-1679; nominally a royal province, but actually held by Massachusetts Bay, 1679-1686, 1689-1696

": *(between the Kennebec and St. Croix Rivers)-*
Proprietary colony under royal charter, 1664-1691.

": *(between the Piscataqua and St. Croix Rivers)-*
Added to Massachusetts Bay, 1691.

NEW HAMPSHIRE

Proprietary colony (part of MAINE*) under patent from the Council for New England, 1622; proprietary colony of* **New Hampshire** *(between the Merrimac and Piscataqua Rivers) under patent from the Council for New England, 1629; held by Massachusetts Bay, 1641-1679, 1690-1692; royal province, 1679-1690, 1692-1698; under same governor as Massachusetts Bay, 1698-1741; separate province, 1741-*

CONNECTICUT

Corporate colony under royal charter, 1662.

New Haven

United with Connecticut, 1664.

RHODE ISLAND

Corporate colony under charter from Parliament, 1644, and under royal charter, 1663.

Massachusetts Bay and the area in Maine subject to its control	1686-1689	under the rule of a royal governor-general
New Plymouth	"	
New Hampshire	"	
Rhode Island	"	
Connecticut	1687-1689	
New York	1688-1689	
East and West New Jersey	"	

The map is designed to serve as an index to localities in the New England Colonies which for lack of space could not be inserted in the map of European Exploration and Settlement in the United States, 1513-1776 (pages 190-191). The list of names given is not exhaustive. For names of Indian tribes, see page 188.

Dates associated with the names of localities having the sign (⊙○) are those of settlement, or of change of name, e.g.: Agawam, 1633; Ipswich, 1634. In the case of Corlaer or Schenectady, Agamenticus, Casco or Ft. Loyal, Pemaquid, and Penobscot or Ft. Pentagöet, the dates of settlement are underlined.

✦ *Fort, with date of construction.* × *Site of event in colonial warfare (1689-1760), with date of occurence. Other localities and dates of importance during the period of warfare in question are: Quebec, 1690, 1759; Port Royal (Acadia), 1690, 1707, 1710; Grand Pré, 1704; Canso, 1744; Louisburg, 1745, 1758; and St. Johns (Newfoundland), 1696, 1705, 1709. See p. 194.*

To the extent shown in the map, the artificial boundaries (..........) are those of the present States of Massachusetts, New Hampshire, Connecticut and Rhode Island. Boundary disputes are not indicated. For the extent of the various grants by royal charter, see pp. 190-191 (inset).

Abbreviations: *C.=To Connecticut till 1664; Dart.=Dartmouth; Ki.=Kittery, 1624; M.B.=To Massachusetts Bay; Mid.=Middleborough; N.Hv.=To New Haven till 1664; Nor=Norwich; Rich.=Richmond I.; Salisb.=Salisbury; S.B.=South Berwick; Sudb.=Sudbury; Th.R.=Thames R.*

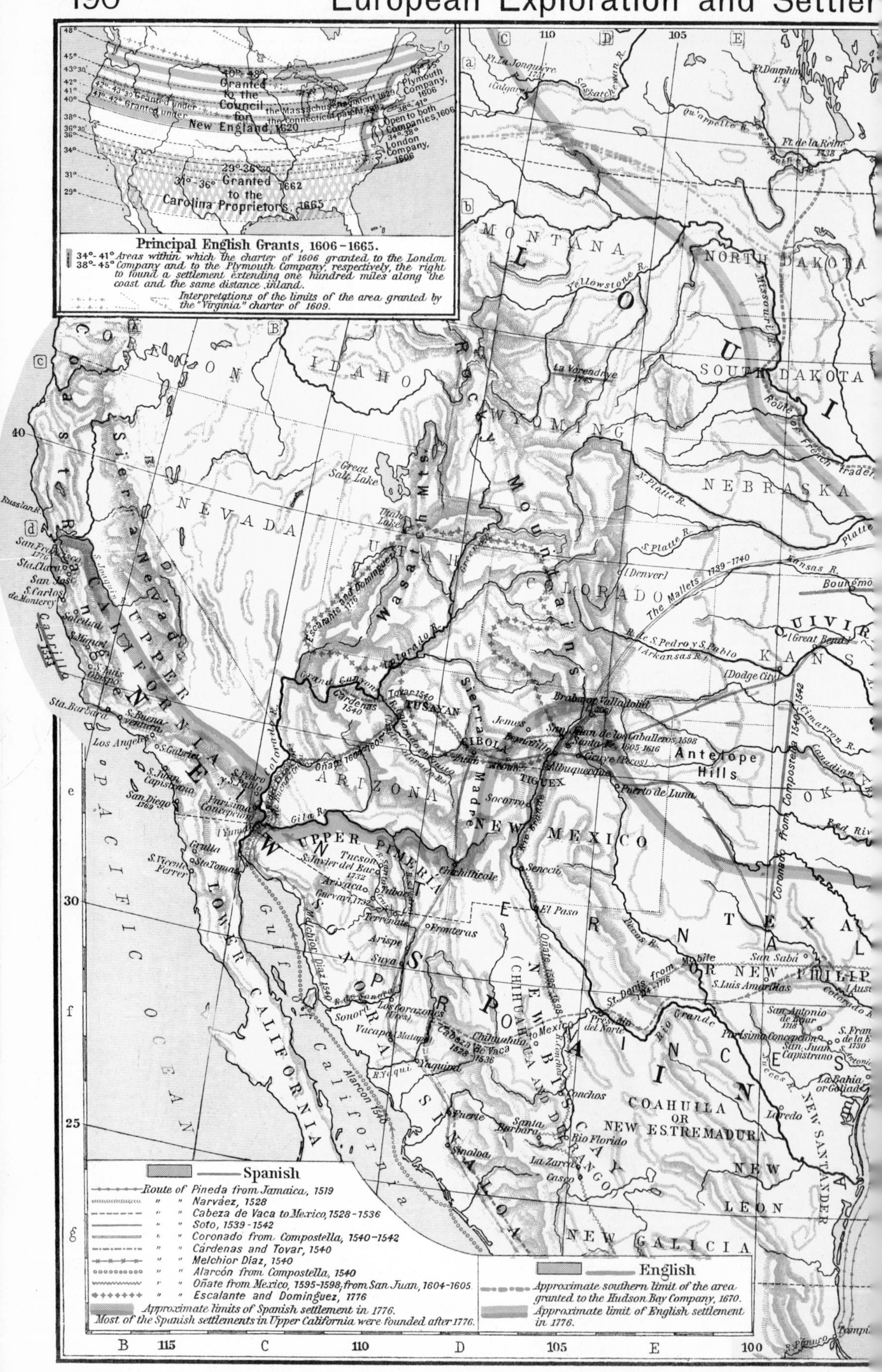
Principal English Grants, 1606-1665.
34°-41° 38°-45° Areas within which the charter of 1606 granted to the London Company and to the Plymouth Company, respectively, the right to found a settlement extending one hundred miles along the coast and the same distance inland.
Interpretations of the limits of the area granted by the "Virginia" charter of 1609.
40°-48° Granted to the Council for New England, 1620
29°-36° 31°-36° Granted to the Carolina Proprietors, 1662 1665
41°-45° Plymouth Company, 1606
38°-41° Open to both Companies, 1606
34°-38° London Company, 1606
Spanish
Route of Pineda from Jamaica, 1519
" " Narváez, 1528
" " Cabeza de Vaca to Mexico, 1528-1536
" " Soto, 1539-1542
" " Coronado from Compostella, 1540-1542
" " Cárdenas and Tovar, 1540
" " Melchior Díaz, 1540
" " Alarcón from Compostella, 1540
" " Oñate from Mexico, 1595-1598, from San Juan, 1604-1605
" " Escalante and Domínguez, 1776
Approximate limits of Spanish settlement in 1776.
Most of the Spanish settlements in Upper California were founded after 1776.
English
Approximate southern limit of the area granted to the Hudson Bay Company, 1670.
Approximate limit of English settlement in 1776.
MONTANA
NORTH DAKOTA
SOUTH DAKOTA
WYOMING
NEBRASKA
IDAHO
OREGON
NEVADA
UTAH
COLORADO
ARIZONA
NEW MEXICO
UPPER CALIFORNIA
LOWER CALIFORNIA
PACIFIC OCEAN
Gulf of California
NEW SPAIN
TEXAS OR NEW PHILIPPINES
COAHUILA OR NEW ESTREMADURA
NEW LEON
NEW SANTANDER
NEW GALICIA
NEW BISCAY (CHIHUAHUA AND DURANGO)
SONORA
SINALOA
UPPER PIMERIA
Rocky Mountains
Wasatch Mts.
Sierra Nevada
Sierra Madre
Great Salt Lake
Antelope Hills
CIBOLA
TIGUEX
TUSAYAN
QUIVIRA
Santa Fe
El Paso
San Diego 1769
San Francisco 1776
Los Angeles
B 115 C 110 D 105 E 100

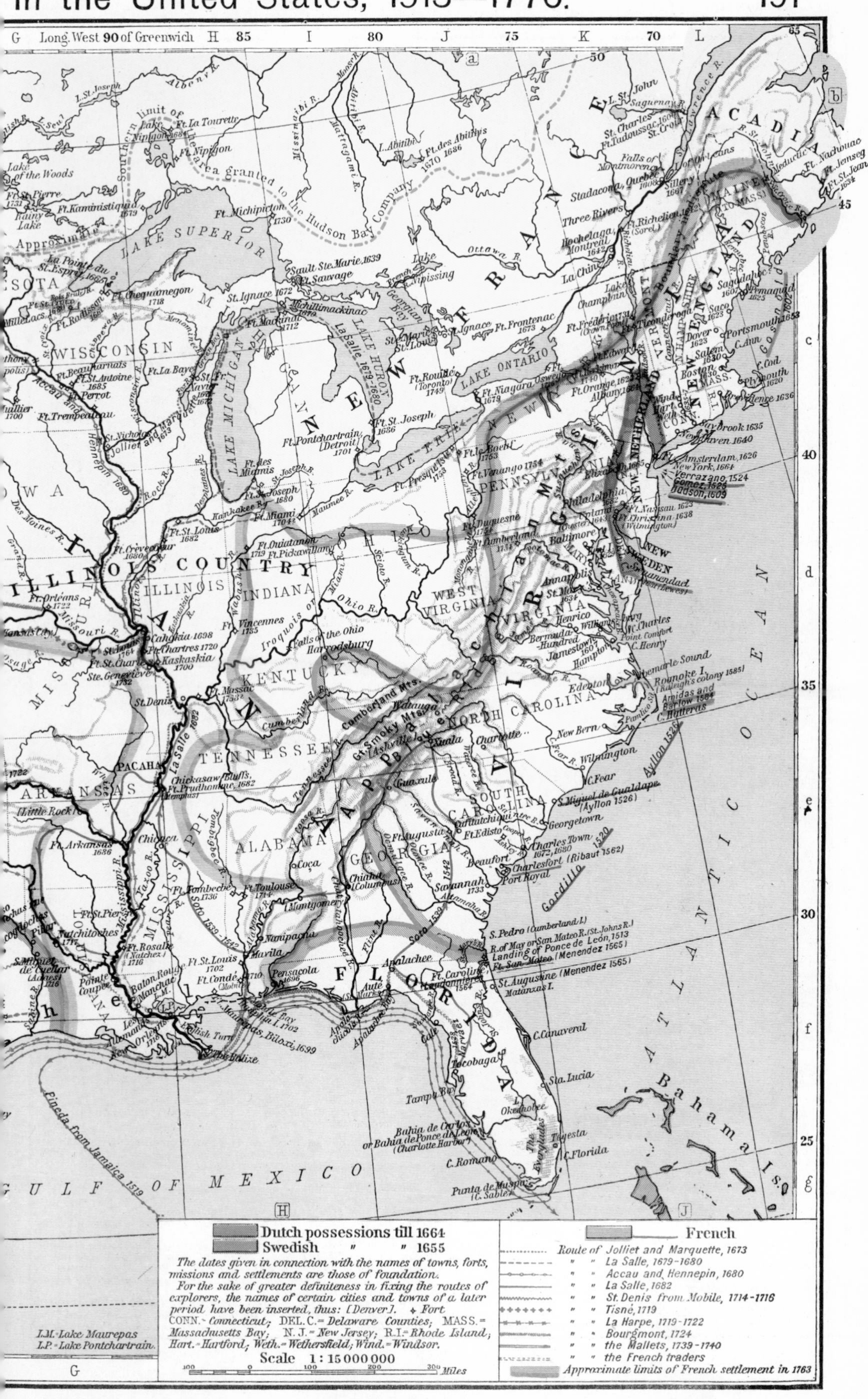

Long. West 90 of Greenwich
LAKE SUPERIOR
LAKE MICHIGAN
LAKE HURON
LAKE ONTARIO
LAKE ERIE
NEW FRANCE
ACADIA
NEW ENGLAND
NEW NETHERLAND
NEW SWEDEN
ILLINOIS COUNTRY
WISCONSIN
ILLINOIS
INDIANA
OHIO
KENTUCKY
TENNESSEE
WEST VIRGINIA
VIRGINIA
NORTH CAROLINA
SOUTH CAROLINA
GEORGIA
ALABAMA
MISSISSIPPI
ARKANSAS
PENNSYLVANIA
FLORIDA
GULF OF MEXICO
ATLANTIC OCEAN
Bahama Is.
Southern limit of the area granted to the Hudson Bay Company
Dutch possessions till 1664
Swedish " " 1655
The dates given in connection with the names of towns, forts, missions and settlements are those of foundation.
For the sake of greater definiteness in fixing the routes of explorers, the names of certain cities and towns of a later period have been inserted, thus: [Denver]. ✣ Fort
CONN.= Connecticut; DEL.C.= Delaware Counties; MASS.= Massachusetts Bay; N.J.= New Jersey; R.I.= Rhode Island; Hart.= Hartford; Weth.= Wethersfield; Wind.= Windsor.
Scale 1: 15 000 000
Miles
L.M.= Lake Maurepas
L.P.= Lake Pontchartrain.
French
Route of Jolliet and Marquette, 1673
" " La Salle, 1679-1680
" " Accau and Hennepin, 1680
" " La Salle, 1682
" " St. Denis from Mobile, 1714-1716
" " Tisné, 1719
" " La Harpe, 1719-1722
" " Bourgmont, 1724
" " the Mallets, 1739-1740
" " the French traders
Approximate limits of French settlement in 1763

Reference Map of the Middle Colonies, 1607—1760.

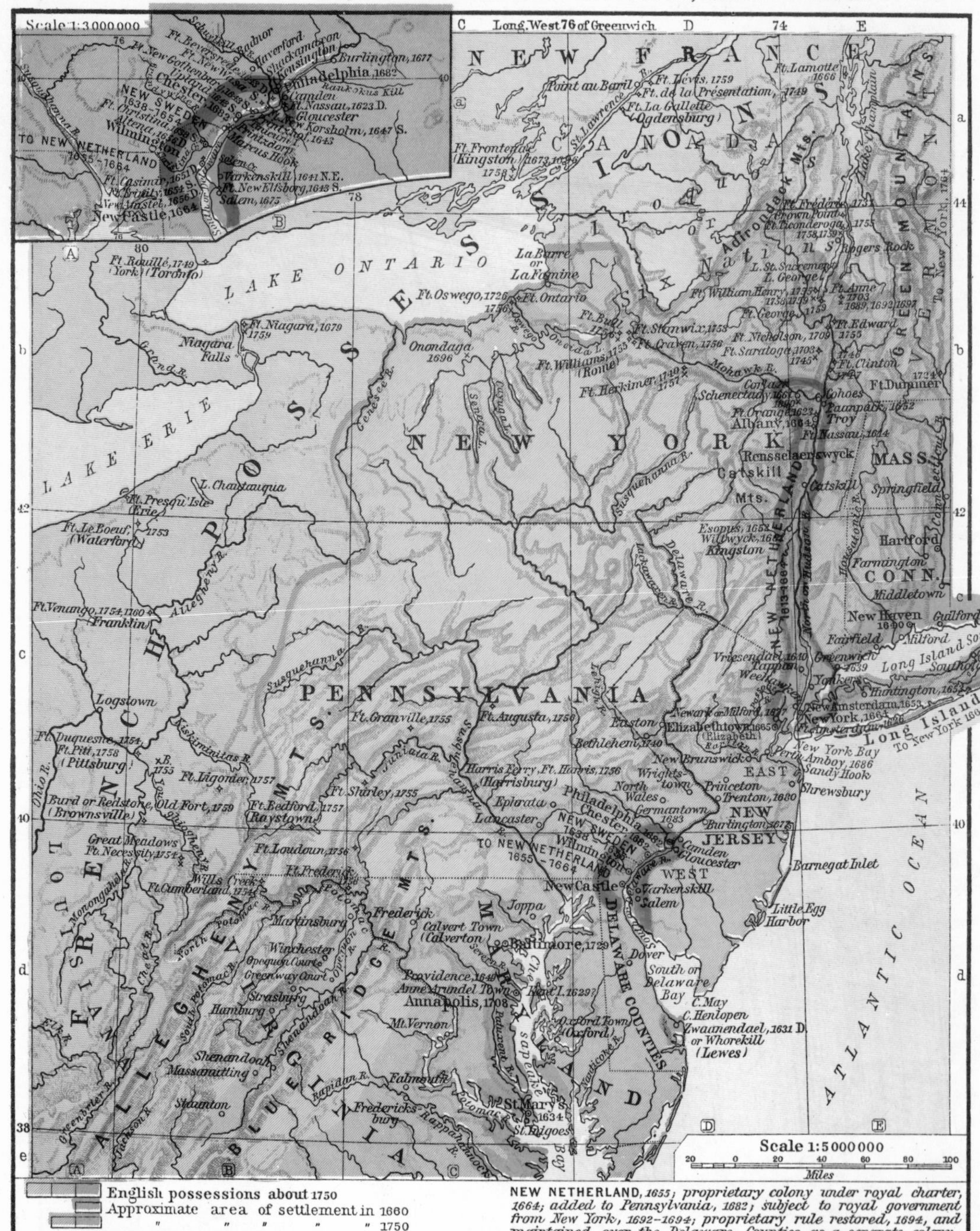

English possessions about 1750

Approximate area of settlement in 1660

" " " " " 1750

Line of the "Walking Purchase," 1737

Dutch possessions 1613-1664, 1655-1664, 1673-1674

Swedish possessions 1638-1655

French possessions about 1750

NEW YORK *As* NEW NETHERLAND, *under Dutch rule, 1623-1664, 1673-1674; proprietary colony under royal charter, 1664-1685; royal province, 1685-1688; united with the New England colonies under royal governor-general, 1688-1689; separate province, 1689-*

NEW JERSEY *Proprietary colony under royal charter, 1664, and under patent from the Duke of York, 1664-1674; divided into East New Jersey and West New Jersey, 1676; united with the New England colonies under royal governor-general, 1688-1689; proprietary colonies of East New Jersey and West New Jersey, 1689-1702; royal province of New Jersey, 1702; under same governor as New York, 1702-1738; separate province, 1738-*

PENNSYLVANIA *Proprietary colony under royal charter, 1681; subject to royal government from New York, 1692-1694; proprietary rule restored, 1694, and maintained till 1776*

DELAWARE COUNTIES (The Three Lower Counties on the Delaware) *As* NEW SWEDEN, *under Swedish rule, 1638-1655; annexed to* NEW NETHERLAND, *1655; proprietary colony under royal charter, 1664; added to Pennsylvania, 1682; subject to royal government from New York, 1692-1694; proprietary rule restored, 1694, and maintained over the Delaware Counties as a separate colony, 1704-1776.*

MARYLAND *Proprietary colony under royal charter, 1632; subject to royal government, 1692-1715; proprietary rule restored, 1715, and maintained till 1776.*

The map is designed to serve as an index to localities in the Middle Colonies which for lack of space could not be inserted in the map of European Exploration and Settlement in the United States, 1513-1776 (pages 190/191). The list of names given is not exhaustive. For names of Indian tribes, see p. 188.

Dates associated with the names of localities having the sign (◎ ○) are those of settlement, or of change of name.

✧Fort, with date of construction. × Site of event in colonial warfare (1689-1760), with date of occurrence.

To the extent shown in the map, the artificial boundaries (..........) are those of the present States of New York, New Jersey, Pennsylvania, Delaware and Maryland. Boundary disputes are not indicated. For the extent of the various grants by royal charter, see p. 190 (inset).

Abbreviations: *B.=Site of Braddock's defeat;* CONN.= CONNECTICUT, D.=*Founded or renamed by the Dutch;* MASS.= MASSACHUSETTS; N.E.=*Settled from New England;* S.=*Founded or renamed by the Swedes.*

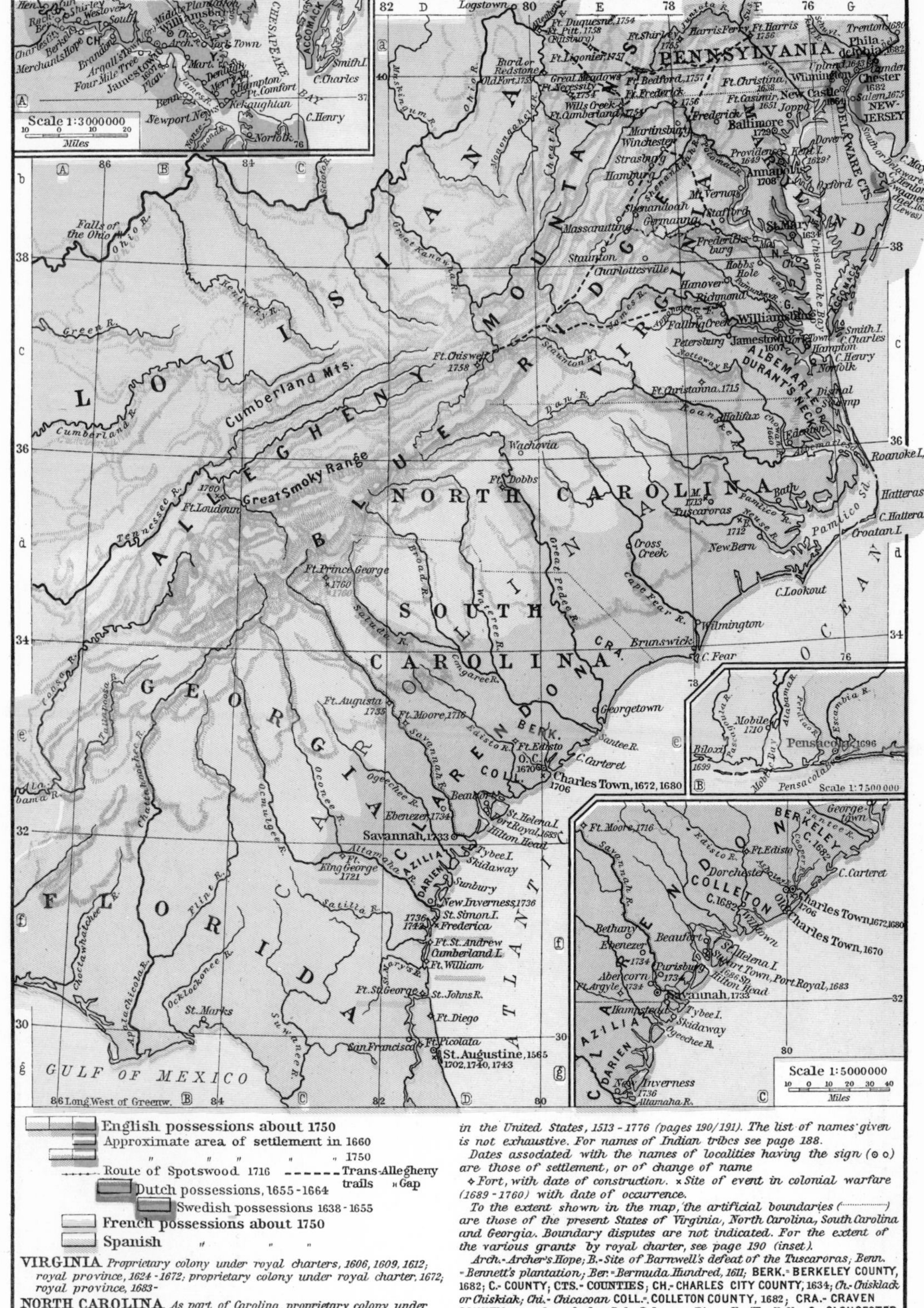

English possessions about 1750
Approximate area of settlement in 1660
" " " " " 1750
Route of Spotswood 1716
Trans-Allegheny trails " Gap
Dutch possessions, 1655-1664
Swedish possessions 1638-1655
French possessions about 1750
Spanish " " "

VIRGINIA *Proprietary colony under royal charters, 1606, 1609, 1612; royal province, 1624-1672; proprietary colony under royal charter, 1672; royal province, 1683-*

NORTH CAROLINA *As part of Carolina, proprietary colony under royal charters, 1663, 1665; separate colony, 1713; proprietary rights surrendered to the Crown, 1729; royal province, 1731-*

SOUTH CAROLINA *As part of Carolina, proprietary colony under royal charters, 1663, 1665; separate colony, 1713; royal province, 1719-; proprietary rights surrendered to the Crown, 1729.*

GEORGIA *Proprietary colony under royal charter, 1732; royal province, 1752, 1754-*

The map is designed to serve as an index to localities in the Southern Colonies which for lack of space could not be inserted in the map of European Exploration and Settlement in the United States, 1513-1776 (pages 190/191). The list of names given is not exhaustive. For names of Indian tribes see page 188.

Dates associated with the names of localities having the sign (⊙ ○) are those of settlement, or of change of name

✧ Fort, with date of construction. × Site of event in colonial warfare (1689-1760) with date of occurrence.

To the extent shown in the map, the artificial boundaries (..........) are those of the present States of Virginia, North Carolina, South Carolina and Georgia. Boundary disputes are not indicated. For the extent of the various grants by royal charter, see page 190 (inset).

Arch.-Archer's Hope; B.-Site of Barnwell's defeat of the Tuscaroras; Benn.-Bennett's plantation; Ber.-Bermuda Hundred, 1611; BERK.-BERKELEY COUNTY, 1682; C.-COUNTY; CTS.-COUNTIES; CH.-CHARLES CITY COUNTY, 1634; *Ch.-Chisklack or Chiskiak; Chi.-Chicacoan* COLL.-COLLETON COUNTY, 1682; CRA.-CRAVEN COUNTY, 1682; *Cur.-Curles; Del.-Delaware River; F.-The Falls;* G.-GLOUCESTER COUNTY, 1651; *Gr.-Greenspring; Hen.-Henrico, 1611; M.-Site of Moore's defeat of the Tuscaroras; Ma.-Mattox; Mart.-Martin's Hundred;* N.-NORTHUMBERLAND COUNTY, 1648; O.C.-*Site of* Old Charles Town; *Plan.-Plantations across the water; Rap.-Rappahannock River; Roch.-Rochdale Hundred; South.-Southampton Hundred; Sus.-Susquehanna River;* Sp.-*Attacked by the Spaniards;* Y.-YORK COUNTY, 1634; *Y.-York River*

Scale 1: 7500000
20 0 20 40 60 80 100 120 140 160 180
Miles

The British Colonies in North America, 1763—1775.

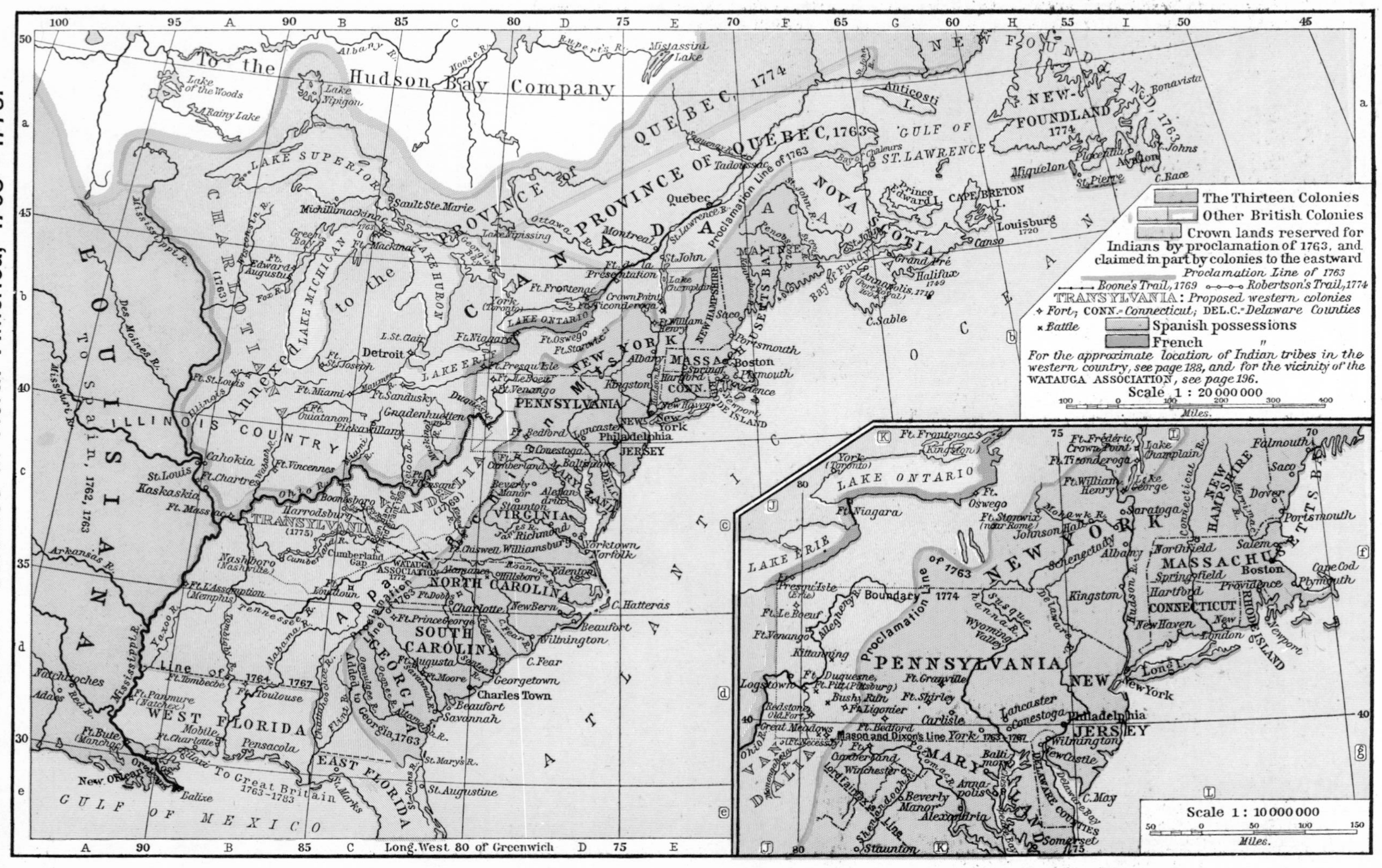

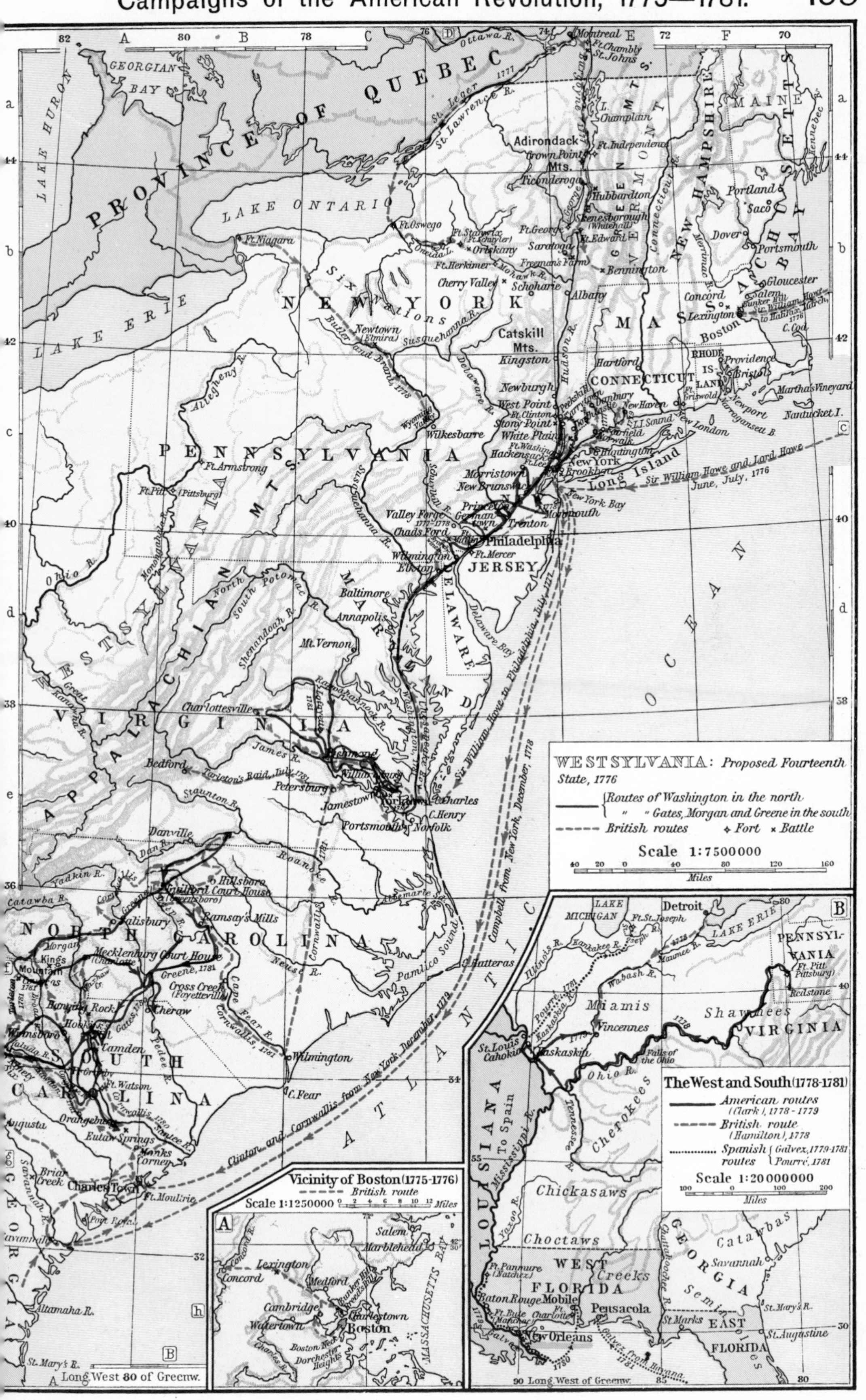
WESTSYLVANIA: Proposed Fourteenth State, 1776
Routes of Washington in the north
" " Gates, Morgan and Greene in the south
British routes
Fort
Battle
Scale 1:7500000
Miles
The West and South (1778-1781)
American routes (Clark), 1778-1779
British route (Hamilton), 1778
Spanish routes { Galvez, 1779-1781 Pourré, 1781
Scale 1:20000000
Miles
Vicinity of Boston (1775-1776)
British route
Scale 1:1250000
Miles
PROVINCE OF QUEBEC
LAKE HURON
GEORGIAN BAY
LAKE ONTARIO
LAKE ERIE
NEW YORK
PENNSYLVANIA
NEW JERSEY
DELAWARE
MARYLAND
VIRGINIA
NORTH CAROLINA
SOUTH CAROLINA
GEORGIA
VERMONT
NEW HAMPSHIRE
MASSACHUSETTS BAY
MAINE
CONNECTICUT
RHODE IS-LAND
APPALACHIAN MTS.
WESTSYLVANIA
ATLANTIC OCEAN
Montreal
Ft. Chambly
St. Johns
Adirondack Mts.
Crown Point
Ticonderoga
Ft. Independence
Hubbardton
Skenesborough (Whitehall)
Ft. Edward
Saratoga
Freeman's Farm
Bennington
Albany
Ft. Oswego
Ft. Stanwix (Ft. Schuyler)
Oriskany
Ft. Herkimer
Cherry Valley
Schoharie
Ft. Niagara
Six Nations
Newtown (Elmira)
Catskill Mts.
Kingston
Newburgh
West Point
Stony Point
White Plains
Ft. Washington
Hackensack
New York
Brooklyn
Long Island
Sir William Howe and Lord Howe June, July, 1776
Morristown
New Brunswick
Princeton
Monmouth
Trenton
Valley Forge 1777-1778
Chads Ford
Germantown
Philadelphia
Ft. Mercer
Wilmington
Elkton
Baltimore
Annapolis
Mt. Vernon
Wyoming Valley
Wilkesbarre
Ft. Armstrong
Ft. Pitt (Pittsburg)
Charlottesville
Richmond
Williamsburg
Yorktown
Jamestown
Petersburg
Bedford
Tarleton's Raid, July, 1781
Portsmouth
Norfolk
C. Charles
C. Henry
Sir William Howe to Philadelphia, July, 1777
Campbell from New York, December, 1778
Danville
Hillsboro
Guilford Court House (Greensboro)
Ramsay's Mills
Salisbury
Kings Mountain
Mecklenburg Court House (Charlotte)
Greene, 1781
Cross Creek (Fayetteville)
Cheraw
Hatteras
Pamlico Sound
Wilmington
C. Fear
Camden
Winnsboro
Ft. Watson
Orangeburg
Eutaw Springs
Monks Corner
Charles Town
Ft. Moultrie
Augusta
Briar Creek
Clinton and Cornwallis from New York, December, 1779
Portland
Saco
Dover
Portsmouth
Gloucester
Salem
Concord
Lexington
Boston
C. Cod
Providence
Bristol
Newport
Martha's Vineyard
Nantucket I.
Hartford
Danbury
New Haven
New London
Ft. Griswold
Fairfield
Norwalk
Huntington
Concord
Lexington
Medford
Salem
Marblehead
Cambridge
Charlestown
Watertown
Boston
Bunker Hill
Breeds Hill
Boston Neck
Dorchester Heights
MASSACHUSETTS BAY
LAKE MICHIGAN
Detroit
Ft. St. Joseph
LAKE ERIE
PENNSYLVANIA
Ft. Pitt (Pittsburg)
Redstone
Miamis
Vincennes
Shawnees
VIRGINIA
St. Louis
Cahokia
Kaskaskia
Falls of the Ohio
Cherokees
LOUISIANA To Spain
Chickasaws
Choctaws
Creeks
WEST FLORIDA
Ft. Panmure (Natchez)
Baton Rouge
Mobile
Pensacola
New Orleans
Galvez from Havana, 1781
St. Marks
EAST FLORIDA
St. Augustine
Catawbas
Savannah
Seminoles
Long. West 80 of Greenw.
90 Long. West of Greenw.

The United States, 1783—1803.

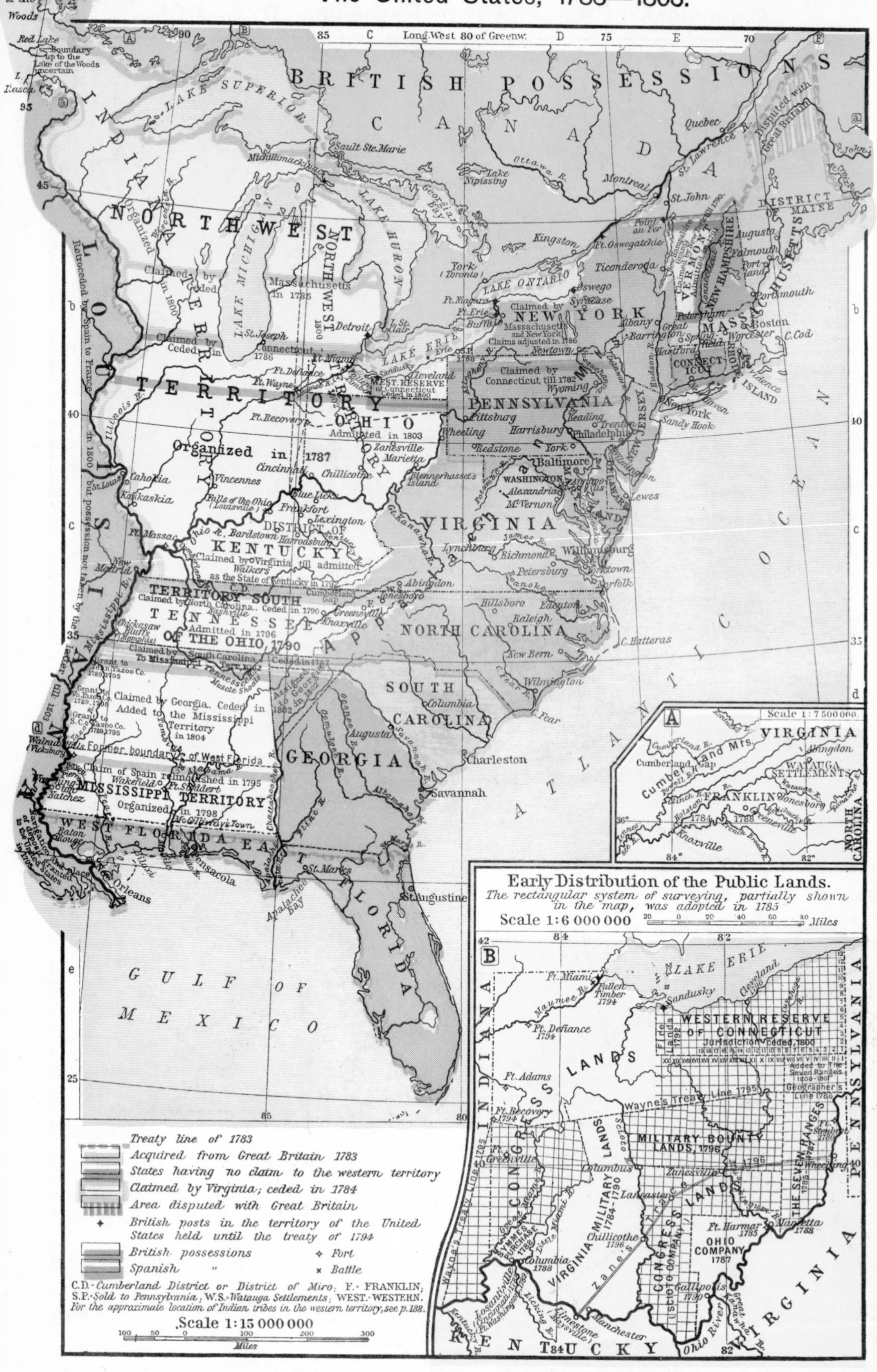

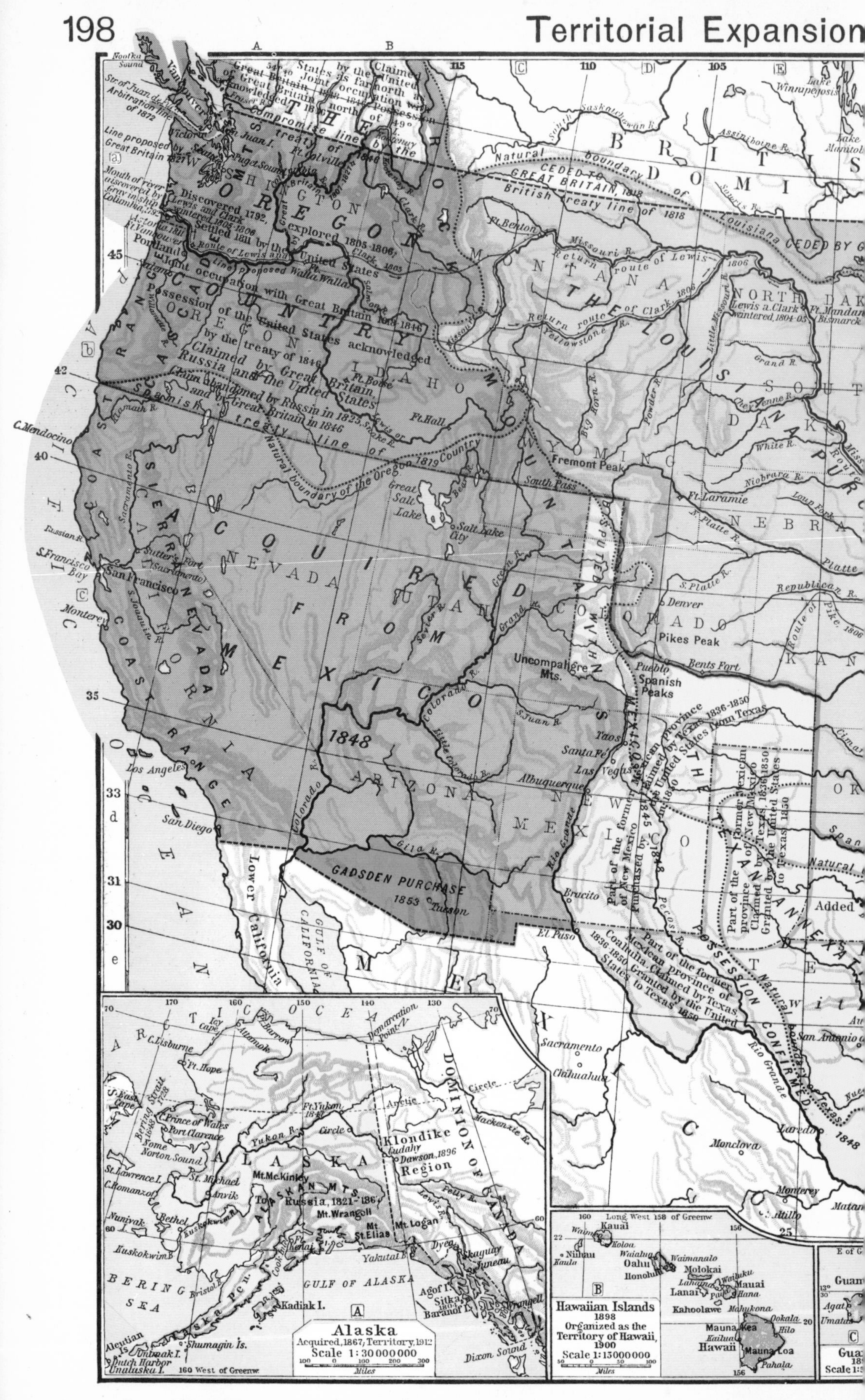
Alaska
Acquired, 1867; Territory, 1912
Scale 1:30 000 000
Hawaiian Islands
1898
Organized as the Territory of Hawaii, 1900
Scale 1:15 000 000
GADSDEN PURCHASE
1853
1848
Klondike Region
Great Salt Lake
Salt Lake City
San Francisco
Los Angeles
San Diego
Denver
Pikes Peak
Santa Fe
El Paso
Tucson

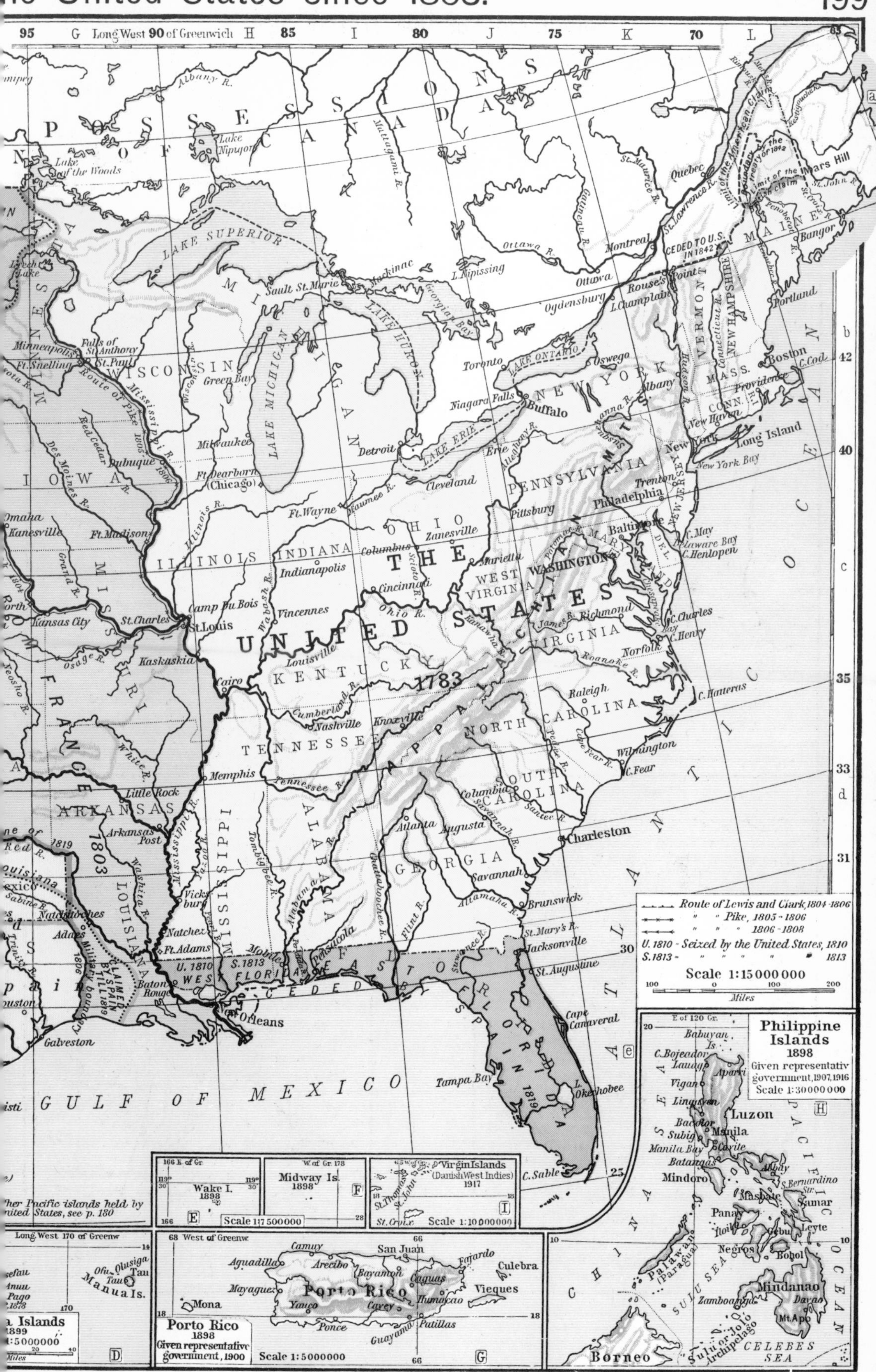

Long West 90 of Greenwich
POSSESSIONS OF CANADA
Lake of the Woods
Lake Nipigon
Albany R.
Mattagami R.
St. Maurice R.
Gatineau R.
Ottawa R.
Quebec
St. Lawrence R.
Montreal
Ottawa
Ogdensburg
L. Nipissing
Georgian Bay
Mackinac
Sault St. Marie
LAKE SUPERIOR
LAKE HURON
LAKE MICHIGAN
LAKE ONTARIO
LAKE ERIE
Toronto
Niagara Falls
Buffalo
Oswego
Detroit
Erie
Cleveland
MICHIGAN
WISCONSIN
Green Bay
Milwaukee
Ft. Dearborn (Chicago)
Falls of St. Anthony
Minneapolis
St. Paul
Ft. Snelling
Route of Pike
Mississippi R.
Dubuque
Red Cedar
Des Moines R.
IOWA
Omaha
Kanesville
Ft. Madison
Grand R.
MISSOURI
Kansas City
St. Charles
St. Louis
Camp Du Bois
Osage R.
Kaskaskia
Cairo
White R.
Little Rock
ARKANSAS
Arkansas Post
Red R.
Louisiana
Sabine R.
Natchitoches
Adaes
Military Road
Washita R.
LOUISIANA
CLAIMED BY SPAIN TILL 1819
Spain
Houston
Galveston
FRANCE
1803
ILLINOIS
Illinois R.
INDIANA
Indianapolis
Vincennes
Wabash R.
Ft. Wayne
Maumee R.
OHIO
Columbus
Zanesville
Scioto R.
Cincinnati
Marietta
THE UNITED STATES 1783
KENTUCKY
Louisville
Ohio R.
Cumberland R.
Nashville
Knoxville
TENNESSEE
Tennessee R.
Memphis
MISSISSIPPI
Yazoo R.
Vicksburg
Natchez
Ft. Adams
Pearl R.
Tombigbee R.
ALABAMA
Alabama R.
Mobile
Pensacola
Chattahoochee R.
Flint R.
GEORGIA
Atlanta
Augusta
Savannah
Savannah R.
Altamaha R.
Brunswick
St. Mary's R.
Jacksonville
St. Augustine
Suwannee R.
U. 1810 WEST FLORIDA
S. 1813
EAST FLORIDA
CEDED BY SPAIN 1819
Baton Rouge
New Orleans
Cape Canaveral
Tampa Bay
L. Okeechobee
C. Sable
GULF OF MEXICO
APPALACHIAN
WEST VIRGINIA
VIRGINIA
Kanawha R.
James R.
Richmond
Roanoke R.
Norfolk
C. Charles
C. Henry
WASHINGTON
Potomac R.
MARYLAND
Baltimore
DEL.
C. May
Delaware Bay
C. Henlopen
NORTH CAROLINA
Raleigh
Cape Fear R.
Pedee R.
Wilmington
C. Fear
C. Hatteras
SOUTH CAROLINA
Columbia
Santee R.
Charleston
PENNSYLVANIA
Pittsburg
Allegheny R.
Susquehanna R.
Philadelphia
Trenton
NEW JERSEY
NEW YORK
Albany
Hudson R.
New York
New York Bay
Long Island
New Haven
CONN.
R.I.
Providence
MASS.
Boston
C. Cod
VERMONT
NEW HAMPSHIRE
Connecticut R.
L. Champlain
Rouse's Point
CEDED TO U.S. IN 1842
MAINE
Portland
Bangor
Penobscot R.
Kennebec R.
St. Croix R.
St. John R.
Mars Hill
Limit of the American Claim
Boundary by the Treaty of 1842
Limit of the British claim
Restigouche R.
ATLANTIC OCEAN
Route of Lewis and Clark, 1804-1806
" " Pike, 1805-1806
" " " 1806-1808
U. 1810 - Seized by the United States, 1810
S. 1813 - " " " " 1813
Scale 1:15 000 000
Miles
Philippine Islands 1898
Given representativ government, 1907, 1916
Scale 1:30 000 000
E of 120 Gr.
Babuyan Is.
C. Bojeador
Laoag
Aparri
Vigan
Lingayen
Bacolor
Subig
Manila
Manila Bay
Cavite
Luzon
Batangas
Albay
Mindoro
S. Bernardino Str.
Masbate
Samar
Panay
Iloilo
Cebu
Leyte
Negros
Bohol
Palawan (Paragua)
SULU SEA
Mindanao
Zamboanga
Davao
Mt. Apo
Sulu or Jolo Archipelago
CELEBES SEA
Borneo
CHINA SEA
PACIFIC OCEAN
166 E. of Gr.
Wake I. 1898
Scale 1:7 500 000
W. of Gr. 178
Midway Is. 1898
Virgin Islands (Danish West Indies) 1917
St. Thomas
St. John
St. Croix
Scale 1:10 000 000
Other Pacific islands held by United States, see p. 180
Long. West 170 of Greenw.
Ofu
Olosiga
Tau
Manua Is.
Pago Pago
68 West of Greenw.
Aguadilla
Camuy
Arecibo
San Juan
Bayamon
Fajardo
Culebra
Caguas
Mayaguez
Porto Rico
Vieques
Humacao
Mona
Yauco
Cayey
Ponce
Patillas
Guayama
Porto Rico 1898
Given representative government, 1900
Scale 1:5 000 000

Campaigns of the War of 1812.

Campaigns of the War of 1812
Hull's route, 1812
Harrison's " 1813
Dearborn's " 1812-1813
Wilkinson's " 1813
Scale 1: 7 500 000
Miles

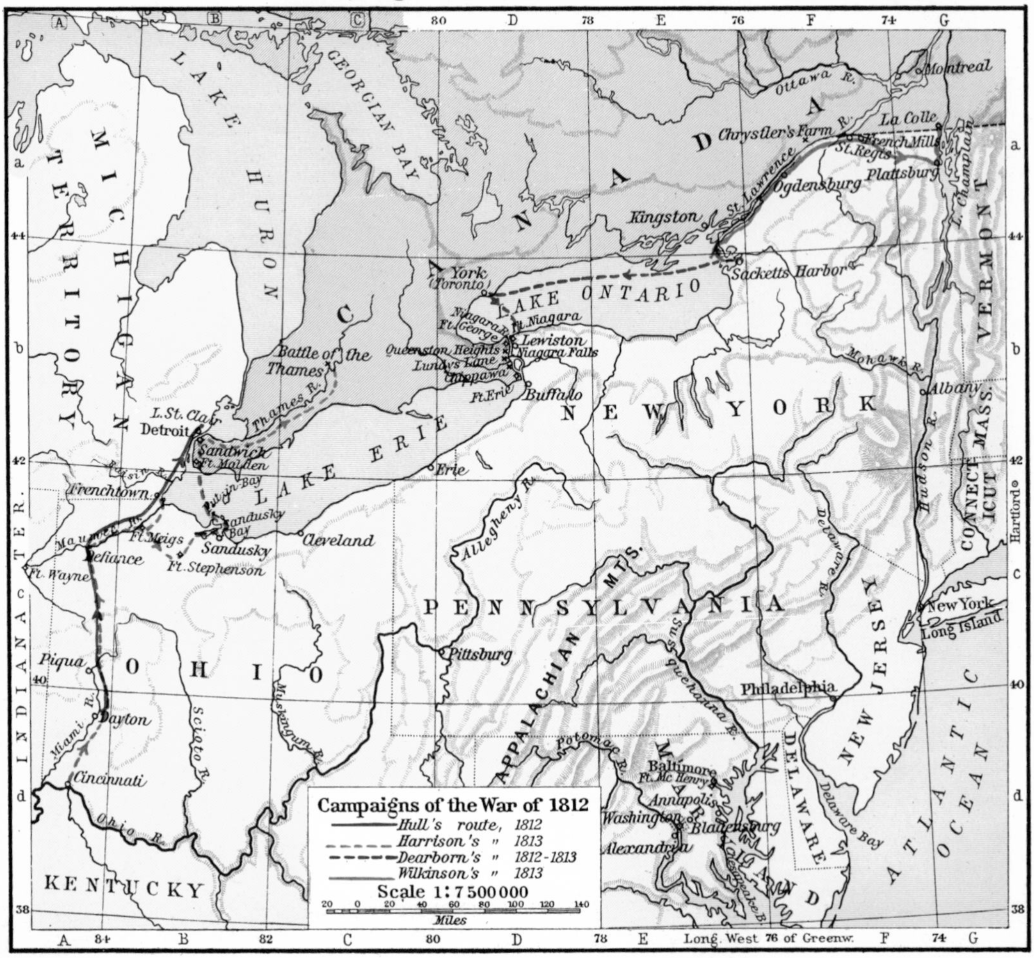

MASS.= MASSACHUSETTS; TER.= TERRITORY. ⋄ Fort × Battle

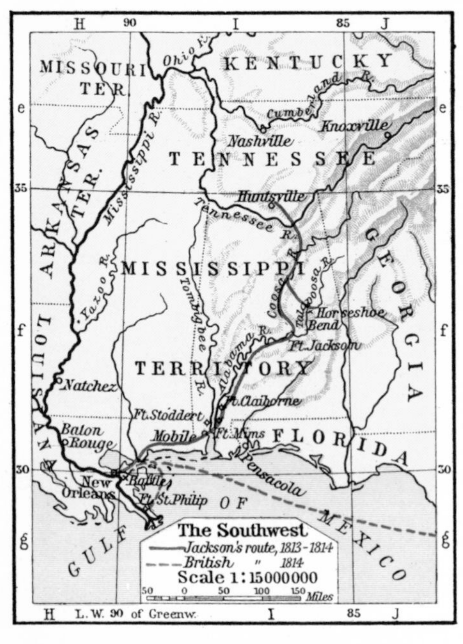

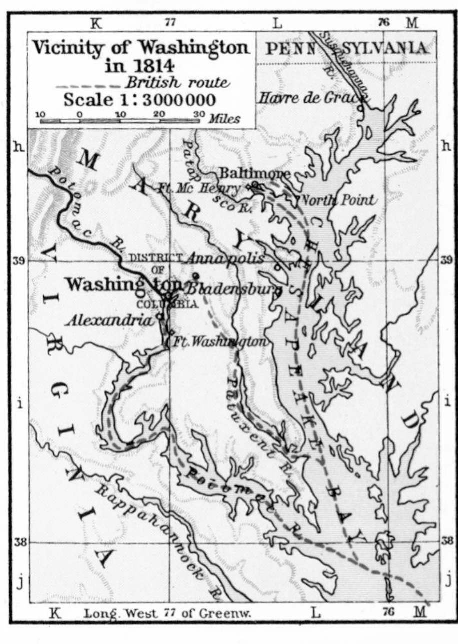

Campaigns of the Mexican War, 1846—1847.

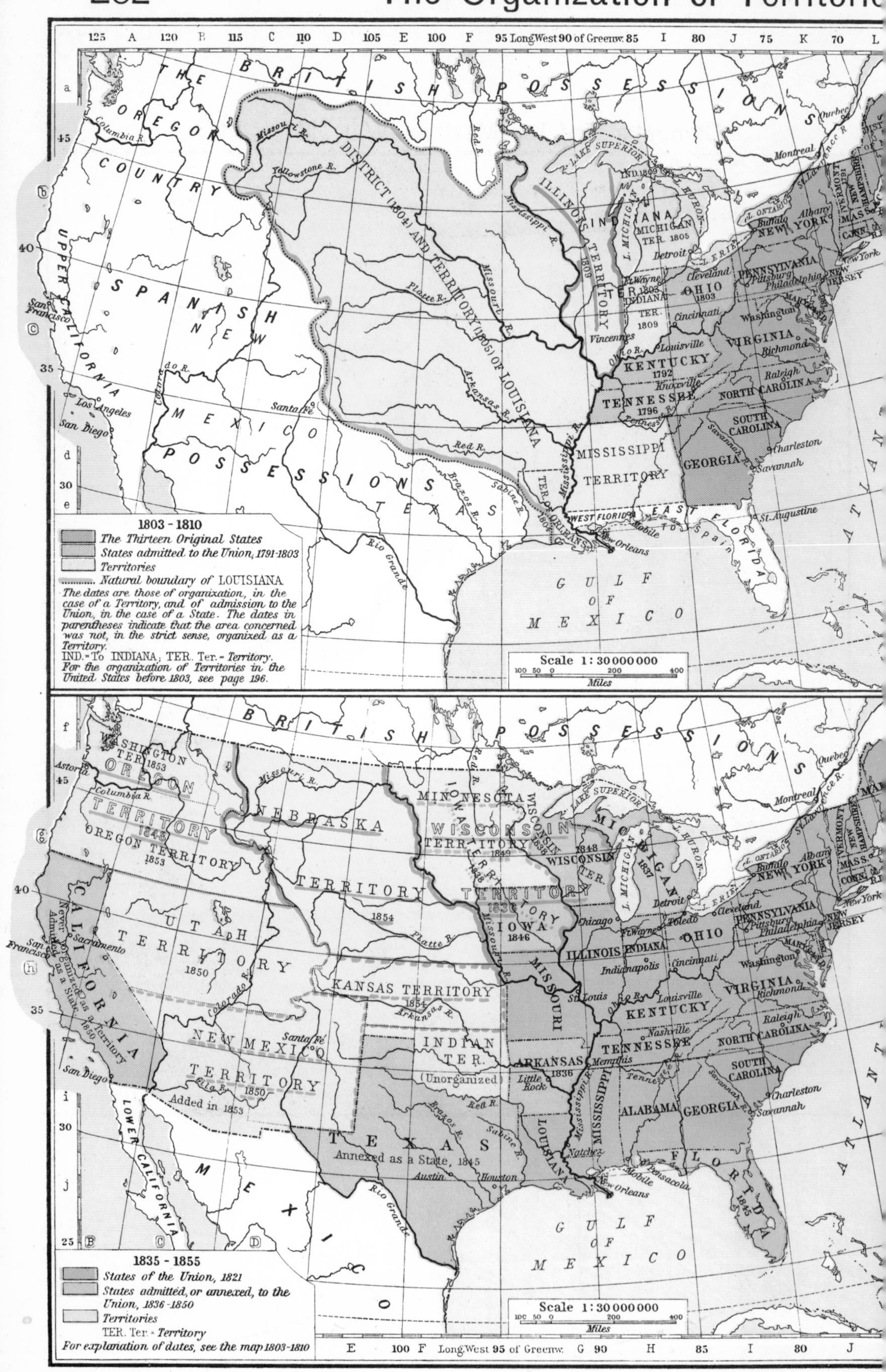
1803 - 1810
The Thirteen Original States
States admitted to the Union, 1791-1803
Territories
Natural boundary of LOUISIANA
The dates are those of organization, in the case of a Territory, and of admission to the Union, in the case of a State. The dates in parentheses indicate that the area concerned was not, in the strict sense, organized as a Territory.
IND.= To INDIANA; TER. Ter.= Territory.
For the organization of Territories in the United States before 1803, see page 196.
Scale 1: 30 000 000
Miles
THE BRITISH POSSESSIONS
OREGON COUNTRY
UPPER CALIFORNIA
SPANISH NEW MEXICO
MEXICO POSSESSIONS
TEXAS
DISTRICT (1804) AND TERRITORY (1805) OF LOUISIANA
ILLINOIS TERRITORY 1809
INDIANA TER. 1809
MICHIGAN TER. 1805
OHIO 1803
KENTUCKY 1792
TENNESSEE 1796
MISSISSIPPI TERRITORY
TER. OF ORLEANS 1804
WEST FLORIDA
EAST FLORIDA
To Spain
GULF OF MEXICO
1835 - 1855
States of the Union, 1821
States admitted, or annexed, to the Union, 1836-1850
Territories
TER. Ter.= Territory
For explanation of dates, see the map 1803-1810
Scale 1: 30 000 000
Miles
WASHINGTON TER. 1853
OREGON TERRITORY 1848
OREGON TERRITORY 1853
NEBRASKA TERRITORY 1854
MINNESOTA TERRITORY 1849
WISCONSIN TERRITORY 1836
IOWA TERRITORY 1838
IOWA 1846
WISCONSIN 1848
MICHIGAN 1837
CALIFORNIA
Never organized as a Territory
Admitted as a State, 1850
UTAH TERRITORY 1850
KANSAS TERRITORY 1854
NEW MEXICO TERRITORY 1850
Added in 1853
INDIAN TER. (Unorganized)
ARKANSAS 1836
TEXAS
Annexed as a State, 1845
FLORIDA 1845
LOWER CALIFORNIA
MEXICO
Long. West 95 of Greenw.

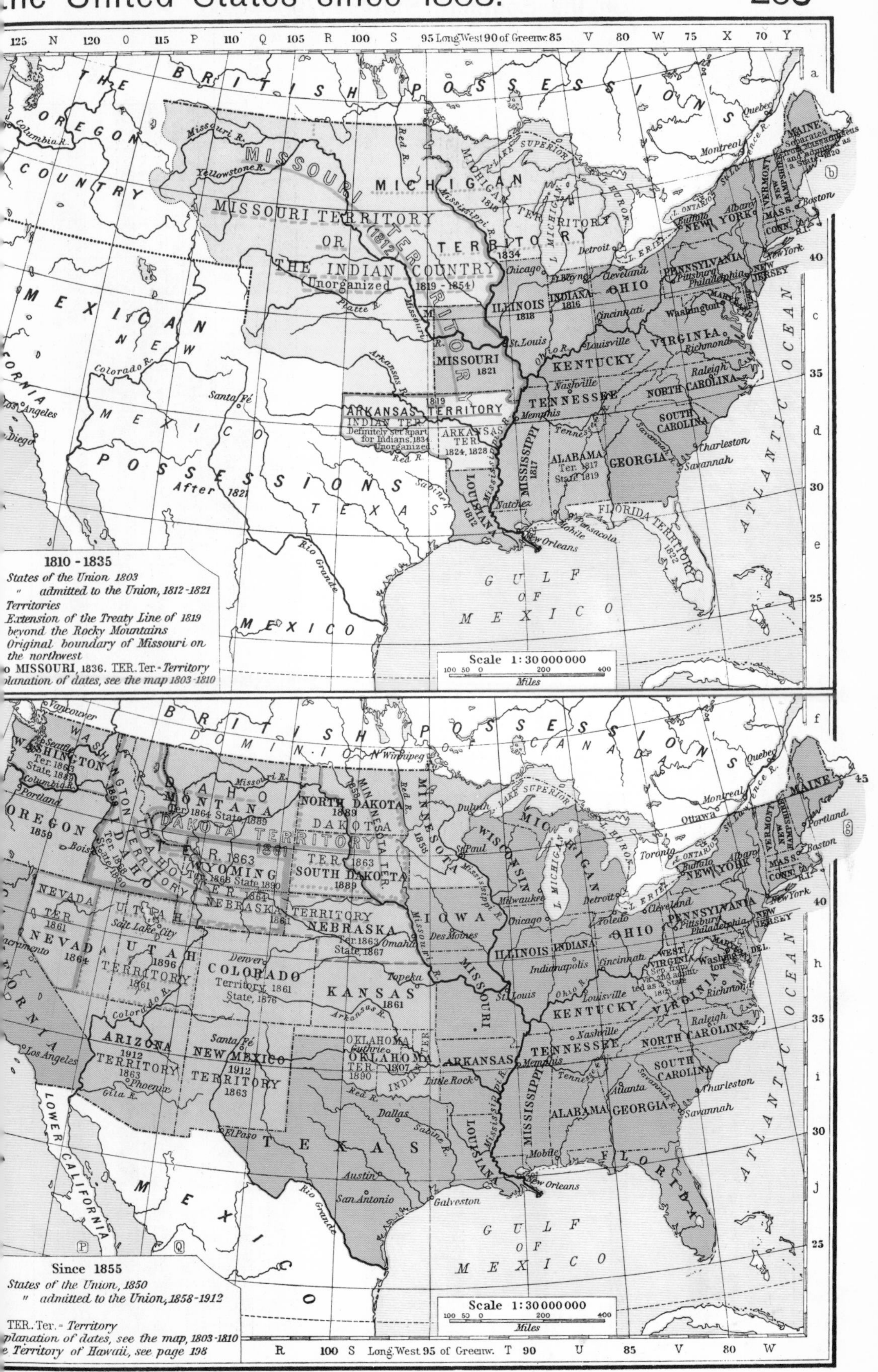
1810 - 1835
States of the Union 1803
" admitted to the Union, 1812-1821
Territories
Extension of the Treaty Line of 1819 beyond the Rocky Mountains
Original boundary of Missouri on the northwest
o MISSOURI, 1836. TER. Ter. = Territory
planation of dates, see the map 1803-1810
BRITISH POSSESSIONS
THE OREGON COUNTRY
MISSOURI TERRITORY
MISSOURI TERRITORY OR THE INDIAN COUNTRY (Unorganized 1819-1854)
MICHIGAN TERRITORY 1818 1834
MEXICAN NEW MEXICO POSSESSIONS After 1821
TEXAS
ARKANSAS TERRITORY 1819
INDIAN TER. Definitely set apart for Indians, 1834. Unorganized
ARKANSAS TER. 1824, 1828
MISSOURI 1821
ILLINOIS 1818
INDIANA 1816
OHIO
KENTUCKY
TENNESSEE
VIRGINIA
NORTH CAROLINA
SOUTH CAROLINA
GEORGIA
ALABAMA Ter. 1817 State 1819
MISSISSIPPI 1817
LOUISIANA 1812
FLORIDA TERRITORY 1822
PENNSYLVANIA
NEW YORK
NEW JERSEY
MARYLAND
MAINE Separated from Massachusetts and admitted as a State 1820
VERMONT
MASS.
CONN.
R.I.
GULF OF MEXICO
MEXICO
ATLANTIC OCEAN
Scale 1:30 000 000
Miles
Since 1855
States of the Union, 1850
" admitted to the Union, 1858-1912
TER. Ter. = Territory
planation of dates, see the map, 1803-1810
e Territory of Hawaii, see page 198
BRITISH POSSESSIONS
DOMINION OF CANADA
WASHINGTON Ter. 1863 State 1889
OREGON 1859
IDAHO TERRITORY Ter. 1863 State 1890
MONTANA Ter. 1864 State 1889
DAKOTA TERRITORY 1861
NORTH DAKOTA 1889
SOUTH DAKOTA 1889
WYOMING Ter. 1868 State 1890
NEBRASKA TERRITORY 1854
NEBRASKA Ter. 1863 State 1867
NEVADA TER. 1861
NEVADA 1864
UTAH TERRITORY 1861
UTAH 1896
COLORADO Territory 1861 State 1876
KANSAS 1861
MINNESOTA 1858
IOWA
MISSOURI
WISCONSIN
MICHIGAN
ILLINOIS
INDIANA
OHIO
KENTUCKY
WEST VIRGINIA Sep. from and admitted as a State 1863
VIRGINIA
NORTH CAROLINA
SOUTH CAROLINA
TENNESSEE
GEORGIA
ALABAMA
MISSISSIPPI
LOUISIANA
ARKANSAS
FLORIDA
TEXAS
OKLAHOMA TER. 1890
OKLAHOMA 1907
INDIAN TER.
ARIZONA TERRITORY 1863 1912
NEW MEXICO TERRITORY 1863 1912
CALIFORNIA
LOWER CALIFORNIA
MEXICO
PENNSYLVANIA
NEW YORK
NEW JERSEY
DEL.
MAINE
VERMONT
MASS.
CONN.
R.I.
GULF OF MEXICO
ATLANTIC OCEAN
Scale 1:30 000 000
Miles
Long. West 95 of Greenw.

Slavery and the Staple Agricultural Products in the Southern States, 1790—1860.

	ALABAMA	ARKANSAS	FLORIDA	GEORGIA	KENTUCKY	LOUISIANA	MARYLAND	MISSISSIPPI	MISSOURI	N.CAROLINA	S.CAROLINA	TENNESSEE	TEXAS	VIRGINIA	Totals
1860	395,982,000	146,957,200	26,061,200	280,736,000		311,095,200		481,002,800	16,475,200	58,205,600	141,364,800	118,585,600	172,585,200	5,090,800	2,154,141,600
	232,914	989,980	828,815	919,318	108,126,840	39,940	38,410,965	159,141	25,086,196	32,853,250	104,412	43,448,097	97,914	123,968,312	375,266,094
	493,465	16,831	223,704	52,507,652		6,331,257		809,082	9,767	7,593,796	119,100,528	40,372	26,031	8,325	187,160,710
	175,000		1,669,000	1,167,000		221,726,000		506,000	402,000	38,000	198,000	2,000	5,099,000		230,982,000
	435,080	111,115	61,745	462,198	225,483	331,726	87,189	436,631	114,931	331,059	402,406	275,719	182,566	490,865	3,948,713
1850	225,775,600	26,137,600	18,052,400	199,636,400	303,200	71,494,800		193,716,800		29,538,000	120,360,400	77,812,800	23,228,800	1,578,800	987,635,600
	164,990	218,936	998,614	423,924	55,601,196	26,878	21,407,497	49,960	17,113,784	11,984,786	74,285	20,148,932	66,897	56,803,227	185,083,906
	2,312,252	63,179	1,075,090	38,950,691	5,688	4,425,349		2,719,856	700	5,465,868	159,930,613	258,854	88,203	17,154	215,313,397
	8,242,000		2,750,000	1,642,000	284,000	226,001,000		388,000			671,000	248,000	7,351,000		247,583,000
	342,844	47,100	39,310	381,682	210,981	244,809	90,368	309,878	87,422	288,548	384,984	239,459	58,161	472,528	3,198,074
1840	117,138,823	6,028,042	12,110,533	163,392,396	691,456	152,555,368	5,673	193,401,577	121,121	51,926,190	61,710,274	27,701,277		3,494,483	790,277,213
	273,302	148,439	75,274	162,894	53,436,909	119,824	24,816,012	83,471	9,067,913	16,772,359	51,519	29,550,432		75,347,106	209,905,454
	149,019	5,454	481,420	12,384,732	16,736	3,604,534		777,195	50	2,820,388	60,590,861	7,977		2,956	80,841,322
	10,143	1,542	275,317	329,744	1,377,835	119,947,720	36,266	77	274,853	17,163	30,000	258,073		1,541,833	124,100,566
	253,532	19,935	25,717	280,944	182,258	168,452	89,737	195,211	58,240	245,817	327,038	183,059		449,087	2,479,027
1830	117,549	4,576	15,501	217,531	165,213	109,588	102,994	65,659	25,091	245,601	315,401	141,603		469,757	1,996,065
1820	47,439	1,617		149,656	126,732	69,064	107,398	32,814	10,222	205,017	258,475	80,107		425,153	1,513,694
1810				105,218	80,561	34,660	111,502	17,088	3,011	168,824	196,365	44,535		392,518	1,154,282
1800				59,404	40,343		105,635	3,489		133,296	146,151	13,584		345,796	847,698
1790				29,264	11,830		103,036			100,572	107,094	3,417		293,427	648,640

Slavery and the Staple Agricultural Products in the Southern States, 1790-1860

Slaves
Cotton — Rice
Tobacco — Sugar-cane

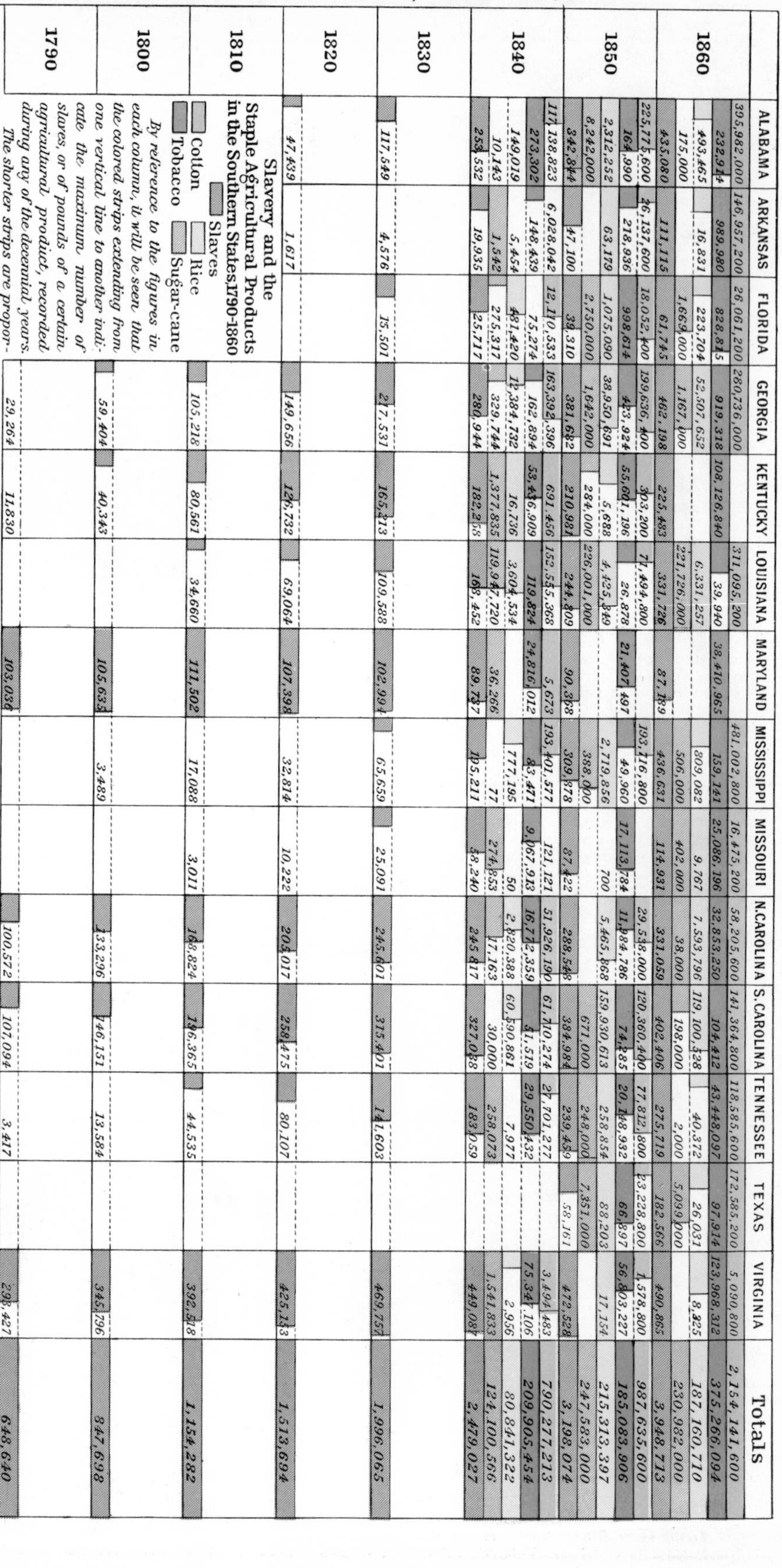

By reference to the figures in each column, it will be seen that the colored strips extending from one vertical line to another indicate the maximum number of slaves, or of pounds of a certain agricultural product, recorded during any of the decennial years.

The shorter strips are proportioned in size to this representation of the maximum number. In the absence of any strip, the figures alone mean that the number of slaves, or of pounds of a certain agricultural product, was less than one tenth of the maximum.

The purpose of this chart is to suggest a possible relation between the sectionalization of slavery and the growth of the staple agricultural products in the Southern States. Unfortunately the Reports of the Census Bureau of the United States, from which the figures are taken, do not supply agricultural statistics before 1840. – Although a slave-holding State, Delaware is not included in the list, because the amount of any of the staple agricultural products raised there was too small for the purpose of comparison.

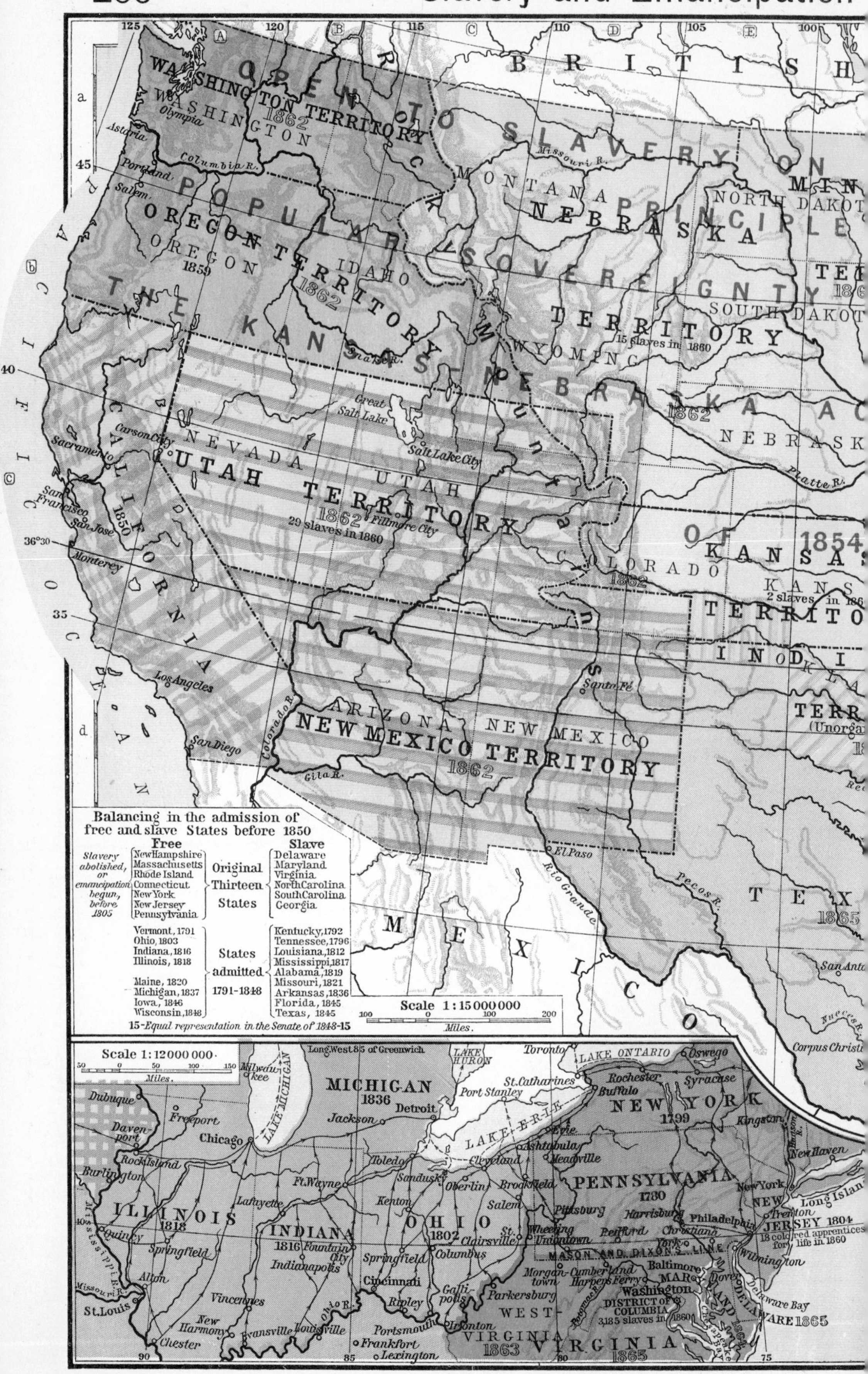
BRITISH
OPEN TO SLAVERY ON PRINCIPLE OF POPULAR SOVEREIGNTY
THE KANSAS-NEBRASKA ACT OF 1854
WASHINGTON TERRITORY
WASHINGTON
1862
Olympia
Astoria
Portland
Salem
Columbia R.
OREGON TERRITORY
OREGON
1859
IDAHO
1862
MONTANA
NEBRASKA
Missouri R.
NORTH DAKOTA
SOUTH DAKOTA
NEBRASKA TERRITORY
15 slaves in 1860
WYOMING
Snake R.
Great Salt Lake
Salt Lake City
NEBRASKA
Platte R.
NEVADA
UTAH
UTAH TERRITORY
1862
29 slaves in 1860
Fillmore City
Carson City
Sacramento
San Francisco
San Jose
CALIFORNIA
1850
Monterey
Los Angeles
San Diego
PACIFIC OCEAN
ROCKY MOUNTAINS
COLORADO
1862
KANSAS
KANSAS TERRITORY
2 slaves in 1860
INDIAN TERRITORY
(Unorganized)
Santa Fé
ARIZONA
NEW MEXICO
NEW MEXICO TERRITORY
1862
Colorado R.
Gila R.
El Paso
Rio Grande
Pecos R.
TEXAS
1865
San Antonio
Nueces R.
Corpus Christi
MEXICO
Balancing in the admission of free and slave States before 1850
Free
Slave
Slavery abolished, or emancipation begun, before 1805
New Hampshire
Massachusetts
Rhode Island
Connecticut
New York
New Jersey
Pennsylvania
Original Thirteen States
Delaware
Maryland
Virginia
North Carolina
South Carolina
Georgia
Vermont, 1791
Ohio, 1803
Indiana, 1816
Illinois, 1818
Maine, 1820
Michigan, 1837
Iowa, 1846
Wisconsin, 1848
States admitted 1791-1848
Kentucky, 1792
Tennessee, 1796
Louisiana, 1812
Mississippi, 1817
Alabama, 1819
Missouri, 1821
Arkansas, 1836
Florida, 1845
Texas, 1845
15-Equal representation in the Senate of 1848-15
Scale 1:15000000
Miles
Scale 1:12000000
Miles
Long. West 85 of Greenwich
LAKE HURON
LAKE MICHIGAN
Milwaukee
MICHIGAN
1836
Detroit
Jackson
Dubuque
Freeport
Davenport
Chicago
Rock Island
Burlington
ILLINOIS
1818
Quincy
Springfield
Alton
Mississippi R.
Missouri R.
St. Louis
Chester
Lafayette
Ft. Wayne
Toledo
Sandusky
INDIANA
1816
Fountain City
Indianapolis
Vincennes
New Harmony
Evansville
Louisville
Ohio R.
Kenton
OHIO
1802
Oberlin
Cleveland
Springfield
Columbus
Cincinnati
Ripley
Gallipolis
Portsmouth
Ironton
Frankfort
Lexington
Toronto
LAKE ONTARIO
Oswego
St. Catharines
Port Stanley
Buffalo
Rochester
Syracuse
LAKE ERIE
NEW YORK
1799
Erie
Ashtabula
Meadville
Brookfield
Salem
St. Clairsville
Wheeling
Uniontown
Pittsburg
PENNSYLVANIA
1780
Harrisburg
Bedford
Christiana
York
Philadelphia
Kingston
Hudson R.
New Haven
New York
Long Island
NEW JERSEY 1804
Trenton
18 colored apprentices for life in 1860
Wilmington
Delaware Bay
DELAWARE 1865
Dover
MARYLAND
1864
Baltimore
MASON AND DIXON'S LINE
Cumberland
Morgantown
Harpers Ferry
Washington
DISTRICT OF COLUMBIA
3,185 slaves in 1860
Parkersburg
WEST VIRGINIA
1863
VIRGINIA
1865
Chesapeake Bay

Long. West 85 of Greenwich
POSSESSIONS
LAKE SUPERIOR
LAKE MICHIGAN
LAKE HURON
LAKE ONTARIO
LAKE ERIE
Quebec
Montreal
Ottawa R.
St. Lawrence R.
Kingston
Toronto
Collingwood
St. Catharines
NEW BRUNSWICK
MAINE 1780
Augusta
Bangor
Portland
To St. John, New Brunswick
To England
VERMONT 1777
NEW HAMPSHIRE 1783
MASS. 1780
Boston
CONN. 1784
RHODE ISLAND, 1784
NEW YORK 1799
Buffalo
Oswego
Utica
Albany
Troy
Springfield
Hartford
New London
New Haven
New York
Long I.
PENNSYLVANIA 1780
Pittsburg
Philadelphia
Erie
NEW JERSEY 1804
Trenton
MASON AND DIXON'S LINE
Baltimore
MARYLAND 1864
Washington D.C.
Harpers Ferry
Alexandria
DELAWARE 1865
Delaware Bay
Dover
WEST VIRGINIA 1863
VIRGINIA 1865
Richmond
Petersburg
Norfolk
Dismal Swamp
Portsmouth
Lexington
NORTH CAROLINA 1865
Raleigh
Newbern
Wilmington
Salisbury
SOUTH CAROLINA 1865
Columbia
Charleston
GEORGIA 1865
Atlanta
Milledgeville
Savannah
Amelia Island
FLORIDA 1865
Tallahassee
St. Augustine
Pensacola
L. Okechobee
The Everglades
Key West
ALABAMA 1865
Montgomery
Tuskegee
Tuscaloosa
Mobile
MISSISSIPPI 1865
Vicksburg
Jackson
Natchez
LOUISIANA 1865
Baton Rouge
New Orleans
Barataria Bay
Galveston
TENNESSEE 1865
Nashville
Knoxville
Chattanooga
Memphis
KENTUCKY 1865
Frankfort
Lexington
Louisville
OHIO 1802
Columbus
Cincinnati
Cleveland
Salem
Toledo
Wheeling
INDIANA 1816
Indianapolis
Evansville
Vincennes
Ft. Wayne
ILLINOIS 1818
Springfield
Chicago
Alton
Quincy
Cairo
Chester
Rock Island
MICHIGAN 1836
Detroit
Lansing
Jackson
WISCONSIN 1848
Madison
Milwaukee
Green Bay
St. Paul
IOWA 1846
Dubuque
Davenport
Iowa City
Burlington
Des Moines
Grinnell
MISSOURI 1864
St. Louis
St. Joseph
Jefferson City
Kansas City
Independence
Carthage
ARKANSAS 1865
Little Rock
Arkansas R.
Mississippi R.
Ohio R.
Tennessee R.
Cumberland R.
Sabine R.
APPALACHIAN MTS.
ATLANTIC OCEAN
GULF OF MEXICO
Bahama Is.
Nassau
Area of the Original Thirteen States
Slave
Free
…ing part of the Union before
…t admitted as States until later
Free before 1850
Free territory by the Ordinance of 1787 (held by the courts not to free pre-existent slaves), supplemented by territorial Acts of Congress and by State constitutions
…ve States …Arkansas) …d, 1792-1845
…ve State …tion, 1845
Free territory by Act of Congress annexing Texas
Free territory by the Missouri Compromise, 1820
Free State admitted from the area subject to the Missouri Compromise
Free by the Missouri Compromise; slave by addition to Missouri in 1836
Slave State admitted from the area subject to the Missouri Compromise
Open to slavery by the Missouri Compromise
Free by the Missouri Compromise; but opened to slavery by the Compromise of 1850
Territory acquired from Mexico in 1848; free by Mexican law, but opened to slavery by the Compromise of 1850
Free State admitted from the territory acquired from Mexico
Free territory by act of organization, 1848
The areas opened to slavery under the principle of the Kansas-Nebraska Act of 1854 are indicated by the red lettering. The territorial organization shown in the map is that of 1854.
…e dates of immediate abolition or of the beginnings of gradual emancipation by State action before 1861 are printed thus: 1780;
…se of immediate abolition by State or national action between 1861 and 1865 are printed thus: 1863.
…reference is made to the "Dred Scott dicta" of 1857, or to the Emancipation Proclamation of 1863; because, legally, the one did not authorize
…duction of slavery into the Territories any more than the other effected the abolition of slavery in the Southern States.
Land } routes of the
Sea } slave trade
"Underground" routes } land
of fugitive slaves } water
The area east of the present State of Oregon formed part of Washington Territory in 1862. The names printed in thin capitals are those of States admitted subsequent to 1854

Seat of the Civil War, 1861—1865.

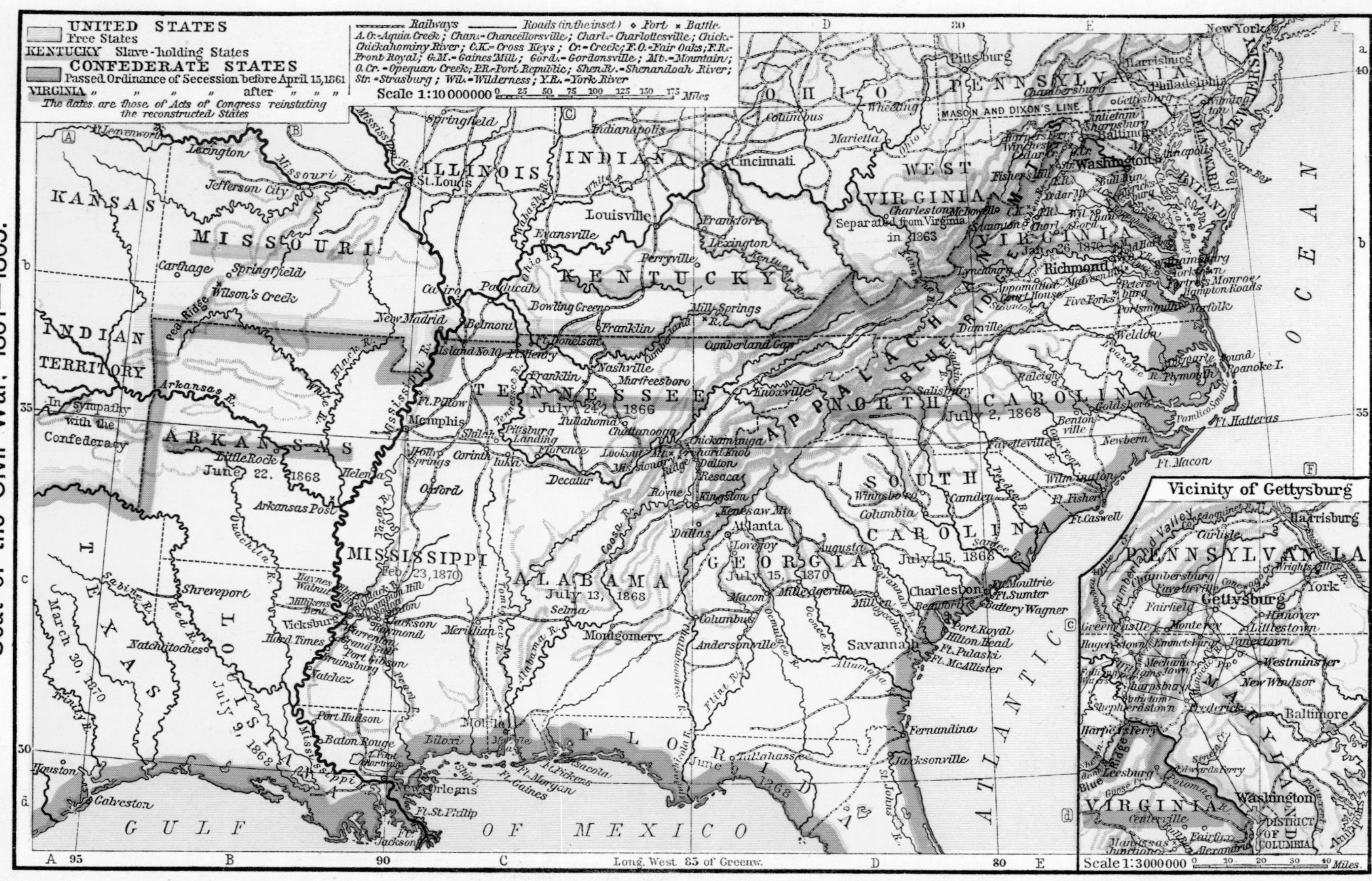

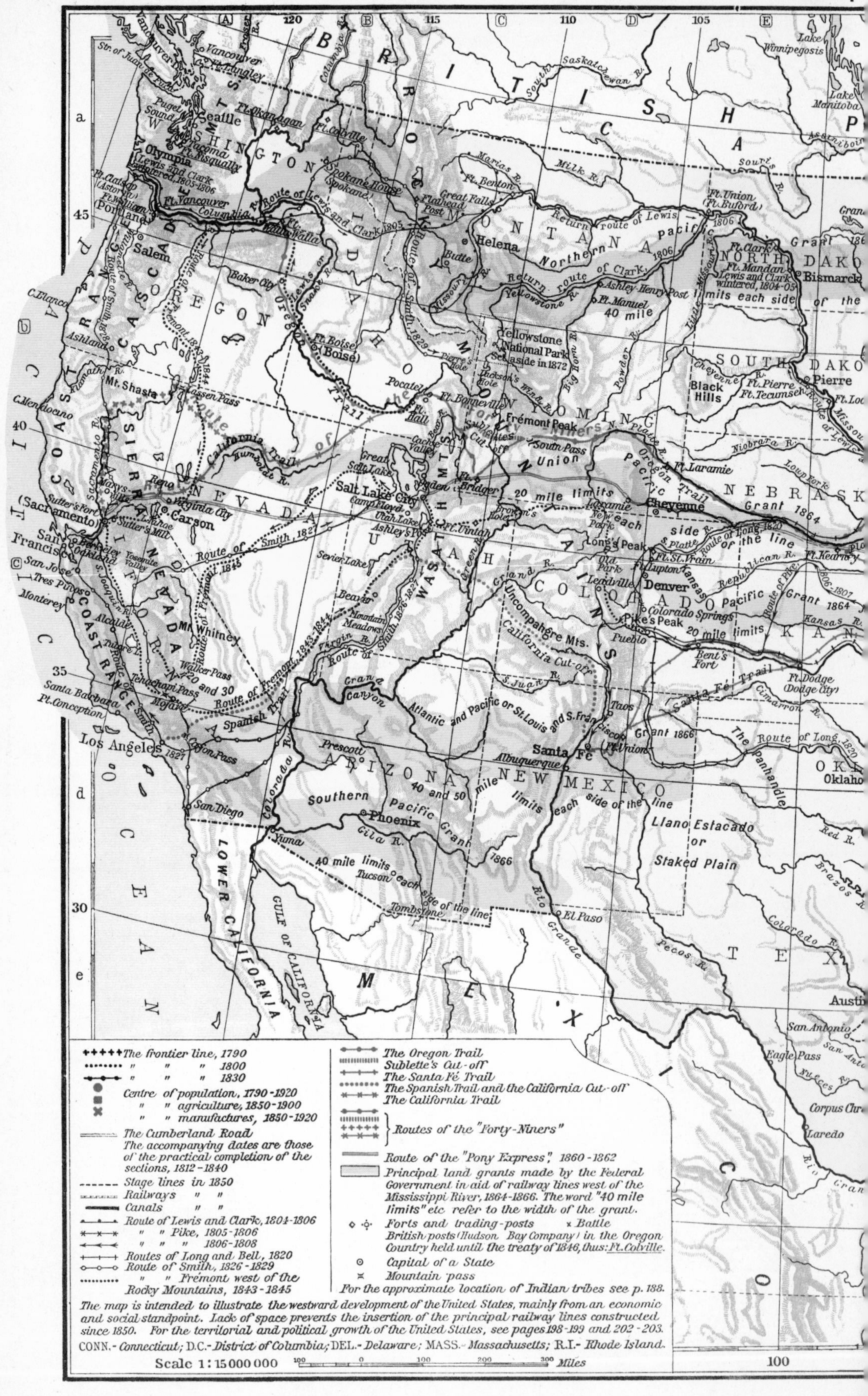
The frontier line, 1790
" " " 1800
" " " 1830
Centre of population, 1790-1920
" " agriculture, 1850-1900
" " manufactures, 1850-1920
The Cumberland Road
The accompanying dates are those of the practical completion of the sections, 1812-1840
Stage lines in 1850
Railways " "
Canals " "
Route of Lewis and Clark, 1804-1806
" " Pike, 1805-1806
" " " 1806-1808
Routes of Long and Bell, 1820
Route of Smith, 1826-1829
" " Frémont west of the Rocky Mountains, 1843-1845
The Oregon Trail
Sublette's Cut-off
The Santa Fé Trail
The Spanish Trail and the California Cut-off
The California Trail
Routes of the "Forty-Niners"
Route of the "Pony Express", 1860-1862
Principal land grants made by the Federal Government in aid of railway lines west of the Mississippi River, 1864-1866. The word "40 mile limits" etc refer to the width of the grant.
Forts and trading-posts
Battle
British posts (Hudson Bay Company) in the Oregon Country held until the treaty of 1846, thus: Ft. Colville.
Capital of a State
Mountain pass
For the approximate location of Indian tribes see p. 188.
The map is intended to illustrate the westward development of the United States, mainly from an economic and social standpoint. Lack of space prevents the insertion of the principal railway lines constructed since 1850. For the territorial and political growth of the United States, see pages 198-199 and 202-203.
CONN.-Connecticut; D.C.-District of Columbia; DEL.-Delaware; MASS.-Massachusetts; R.I.-Rhode Island.
Scale 1:15 000 000
Miles

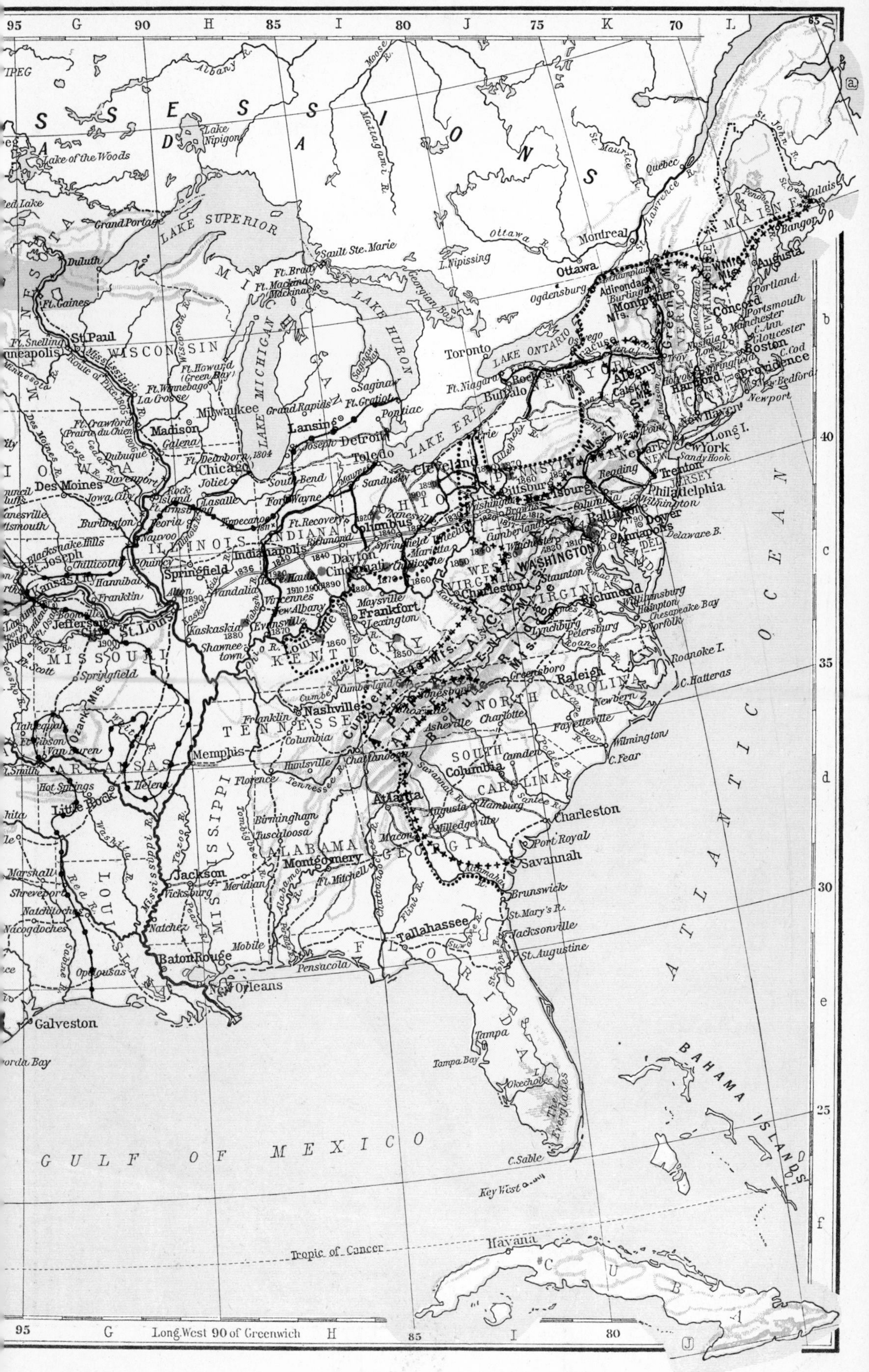
BRITISH POSSESSIONS
LAKE SUPERIOR
LAKE MICHIGAN
LAKE HURON
LAKE ERIE
LAKE ONTARIO
Lake Nipigon
Lake of the Woods
Georgian Bay
L. Nipissing
Ottawa R.
Sault Ste. Marie
Quebec
Montreal
Ottawa
Toronto
Duluth
St Paul
Grand Portage
WISCONSIN
Madison
Milwaukee
Chicago
Detroit
Lansing
Toledo
Cleveland
Buffalo
NEW YORK
Albany
Boston
Providence
Portland
Augusta
Bangor
Calais
MAINE
VERMONT
Montpelier
Concord
Hartford
New Haven
New York
Newark
Trenton
Philadelphia
Harrisburg
Pittsburg
Baltimore
Dover
Annapolis
WASHINGTON
Richmond
Norfolk
Chesapeake Bay
OHIO
Columbus
Cincinnati
Dayton
INDIANA
Indianapolis
ILLINOIS
Springfield
St. Louis
MISSOURI
Jefferson City
Kansas City
IOWA
Des Moines
KENTUCKY
Frankfort
Lexington
Louisville
TENNESSEE
Nashville
Memphis
Chattanooga
NORTH CAROLINA
Raleigh
Greensboro
SOUTH CAROLINA
Columbia
Charleston
GEORGIA
Atlanta
Savannah
Augusta
ALABAMA
Montgomery
Birmingham
MISSISSIPPI
Jackson
Vicksburg
Natchez
LOUISIANA
Baton Rouge
New Orleans
ARKANSAS
Little Rock
Hot Springs
Galveston
FLORIDA
Tallahassee
Jacksonville
St. Augustine
Pensacola
Tampa
Tampa Bay
Okechobee
The Everglades
C. Sable
Key West
GULF OF MEXICO
ATLANTIC OCEAN
BAHAMA ISLANDS
Havana
CUBA
Tropic of Cancer
C. Hatteras
C. Fear
Wilmington
C. Cod
APPALACHIAN Mts.
Long. West 90 of Greenwich

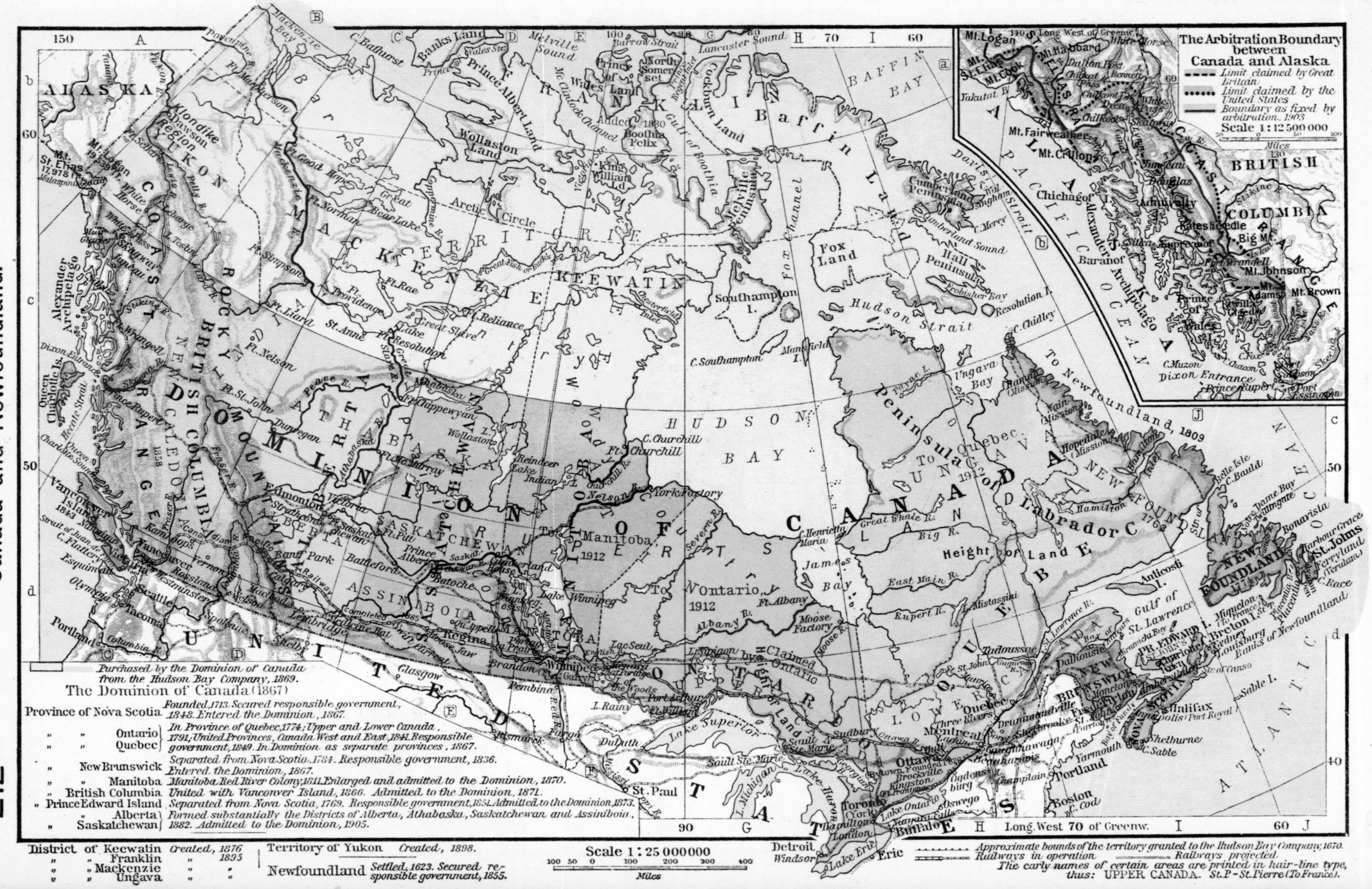
The Arbitration Boundary between Canada and Alaska
Limit claimed by Great Britain
Limit claimed by the United States
Boundary as fixed by arbitration, 1903
Scale 1: 12 500 000
Purchased by the Dominion of Canada from the Hudson Bay Company, 1869.
The Dominion of Canada (1867)
Province of Nova Scotia Founded, 1713. Secured responsible government, 1848. Entered the Dominion, 1867.
" " Ontario / Quebec In Province of Quebec, 1774; Upper and Lower Canada, 1791; United Provinces, Canada West and East, 1841. Responsible government, 1849. In Dominion as separate provinces, 1867.
" New Brunswick Separated from Nova Scotia, 1784. Responsible government, 1836. Entered the Dominion, 1867.
" " Manitoba Manitoba Red River Colony, 1811. Enlarged and admitted to the Dominion, 1870.
" British Columbia United with Vancouver Island, 1866. Admitted to the Dominion, 1871.
" Prince Edward Island Separated from Nova Scotia, 1769. Responsible government, 1851. Admitted to the Dominion, 1873.
" Alberta / Saskatchewan Formed substantially the Districts of Alberta, Athabaska, Saskatchewan and Assiniboia, 1882. Admitted to the Dominion, 1905.
District of Keewatin Created, 1876
" " Franklin " 1895
" " Mackenzie " "
" " Ungava " "
Territory of Yukon Created, 1898.
Newfoundland Settled, 1623. Secured responsible government, 1855.
Scale 1: 25 000 000
Miles
Approximate bounds of the territory granted to the Hudson Bay Company, 1670.
Railways in operation
Railways projected.
The early names of certain areas are printed in hair-line type, thus: UPPER CANADA. St. P.—St. Pierre (To France).
Long. West 70 of Greenw.

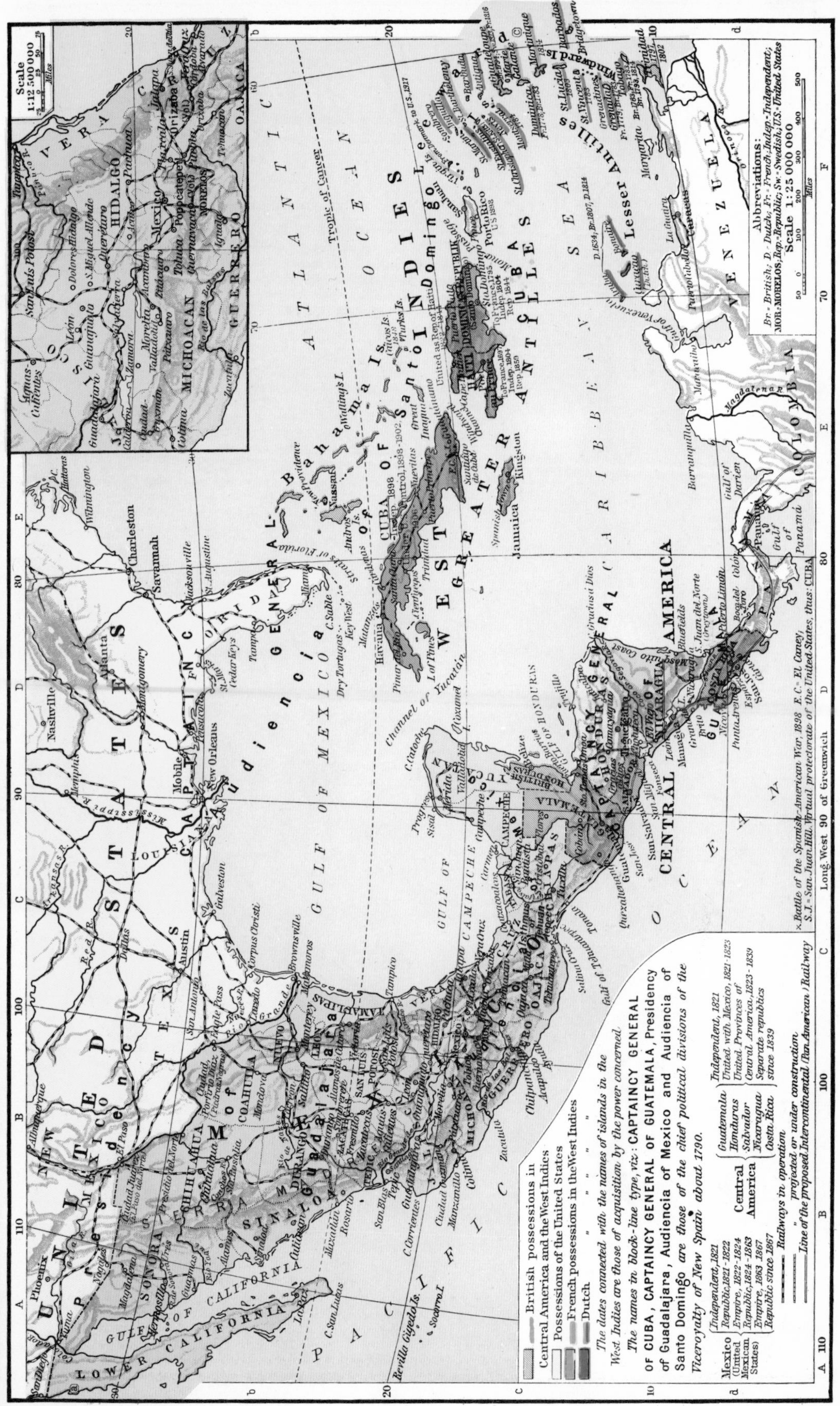
British possessions in Central America and the West Indies
Possessions of the United States
French possessions in the West Indies
Dutch
The dates connected with the names of islands in the West Indies are those of acquisition by the power concerned.
The names in block-line type, viz: CAPTAINCY GENERAL OF CUBA, CAPTAINCY GENERAL OF GUATEMALA, Presidency of Guadalajara, Audiencia of Mexico and Audiencia of Santo Domingo are those of the chief political divisions of the Viceroyalty of New Spain about 1790.
Railways in operation
projected or under construction
Line of the proposed Intercontinental (Pan-American) Railway
Abbreviations:
Br.=British; D.=Dutch; Fr.=French; Indep.=Independent; MOR.=MORELOS; Rep.=Republic; Sw.=Swedish; U.S.=United States
Scale 1:25 000 000
× Battle of the Spanish-American War, 1898. E.C.=El Caney.
S.J.=San Juan Hill. Virtual protectorate of the United States, thus: CUBA
Long. West 90 of Greenwich

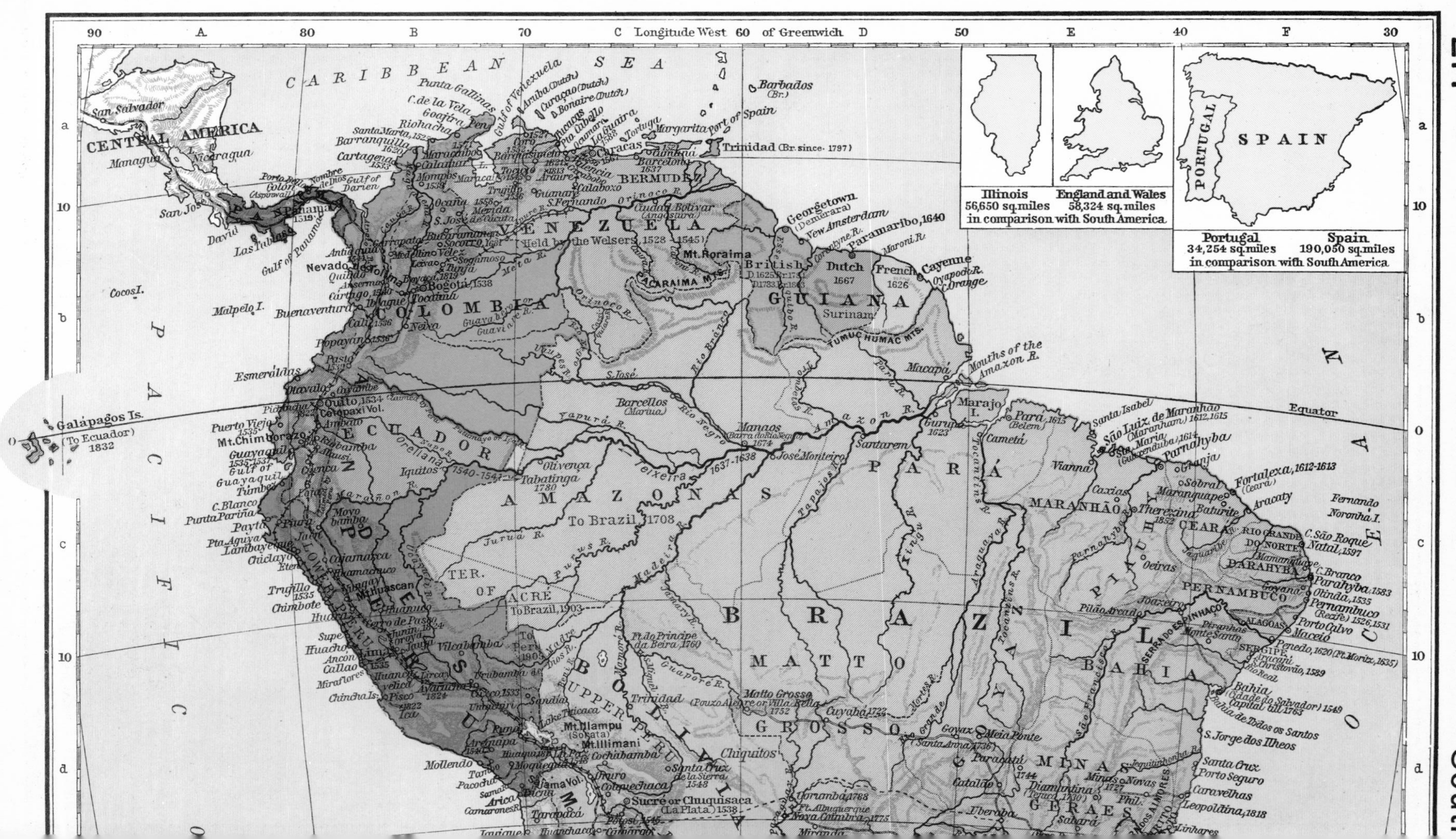
90 A 80 B 70 C Longitude West 60 of Greenwich D 50 E 40 F 30
CARIBBEAN SEA
CENTRAL AMERICA
Illinois
56,650 sq.miles
England and Wales
58,324 sq.miles
in comparison with South America.
SPAIN
PORTUGAL
Portugal
34,254 sq.miles
Spain
190,050 sq.miles
in comparison with South America.
Barbados
(Br.)
Trinidad (Br. since 1797)
VENEZUELA
Held by the Welsers, 1528-1545
COLOMBIA
GUIANA
British
Dutch
1667
French
1626
Surinam
Georgetown
(Demerara)
New Amsterdam
Paramaribo, 1640
Cayenne
Mouths of the Amazon R.
Equator
Galapagos Is.
(To Ecuador)
1832
ECUADOR
AMAZONAS
To Brazil 1708
TER. OF ACRE
To Brazil, 1903
PERU
LOWER PERU
UPPER PERU
BOLIVIA
BRAZIL
PARÁ
MARANHÃO
PIAUHY
CEARÁ
PERNAMBUCO
BAHIA
MATTO GROSSO
MINAS GERAES
PACIFIC

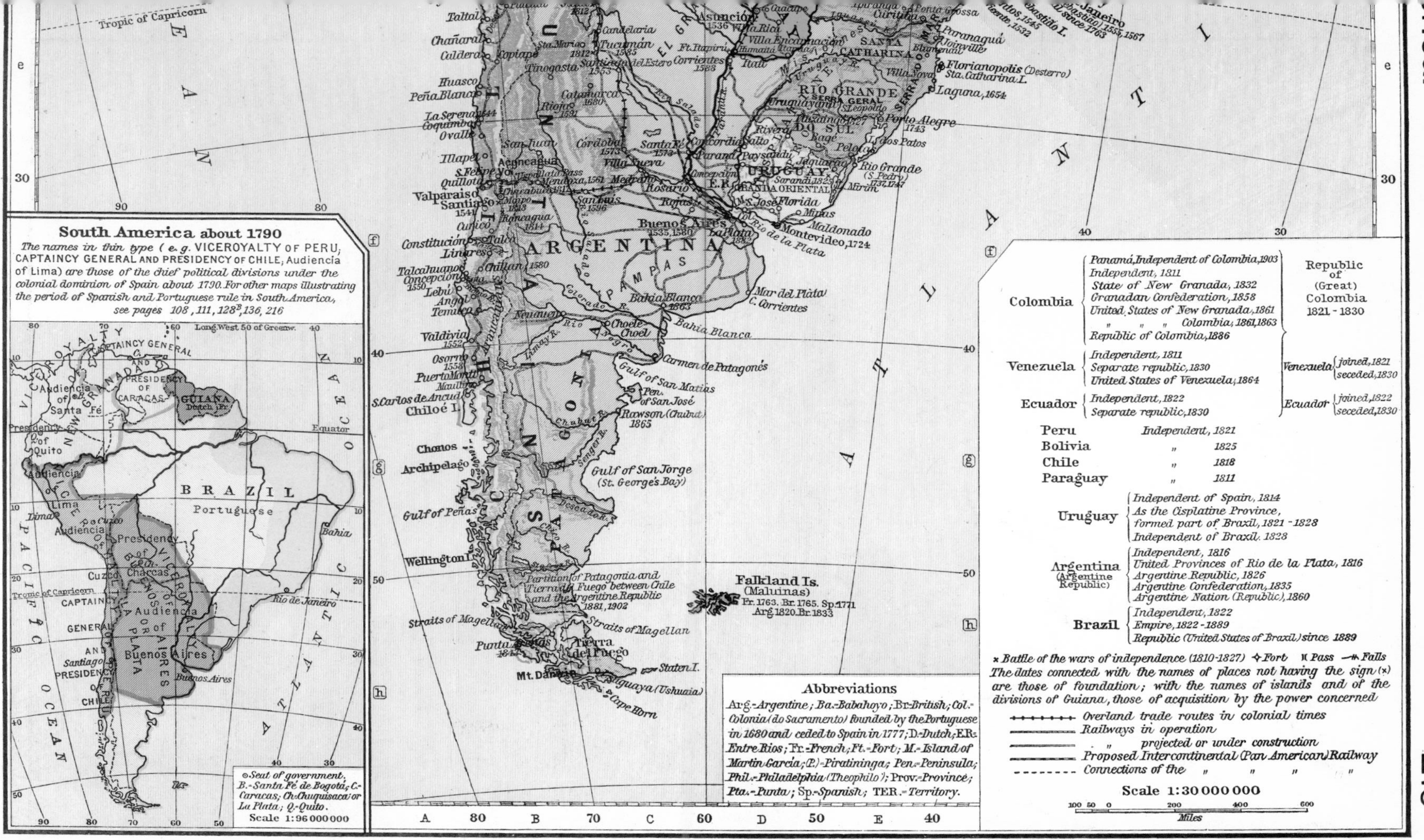
South America about 1790
The names in thin type (e.g. VICEROYALTY OF PERU; CAPTAINCY GENERAL AND PRESIDENCY OF CHILE; Audiencia of Lima) are those of the chief political divisions under the colonial dominion of Spain about 1790. For other maps illustrating the period of Spanish and Portuguese rule in South America, see pages 108, 111, 128B, 136, 216
Long. West 50 of Greenw.
VICEROYALTY OF NEW GRANADA
CAPTAINCY GENERAL AND PRESIDENCY OF CARACAS
Audiencia of Santa Fé
Presidency of Quito
GUIANA Dutch, Fr.
Equator
BRAZIL
Portuguese
Bahia
Lima
Cuzco
Presidency of Charcas
Audiencia of Buenos Aires
VICEROYALTY OF BUENOS AIRES OR LA PLATA
Tropic of Capricorn
Rio de Janeiro
CAPTAINCY GENERAL AND PRESIDENCY OF CHILE
Santiago
Buenos Aires
PACIFIC OCEAN
ATLANTIC OCEAN
⊙Seat of government. B.-Santa Fé de Bogotá; C.-Caracas; Ch.-Chuquisaca or La Plata; Q.-Quito.
Scale 1:96 000 000
Tropic of Capricorn
ARGENTINA
PAMPAS
PATAGONIA
URUGUAY
BANDA ORIENTAL
RIO GRANDE DO SUL
SANTA CATHARINA
Asunción 1536
Buenos Aires 1535, 1580
Montevideo, 1724
Rio de la Plata
Valparaiso
Santiago 1541
Valdivia 1552
Chiloé I.
Chonos Archipelago
Gulf of Peñas
Wellington I.
Gulf of San Jorge (St. George's Bay)
Gulf of San Matias
Bahia Blanca
Carmen de Patagones
Rawson (Chubut) 1865
Partition of Patagonia and Tierra del Fuego between Chile and the Argentine Republic 1881, 1902
Straits of Magellan
Tierra del Fuego
Staten I.
Ushuaya (Ushuaia)
Cape Horn
Falkland Is. (Maluinas) Fr. 1763. Br. 1765. Sp. 1771 Arg. 1820. Br. 1833
Florianopolis (Desterro)
Porto Alegre 1743
Laguna, 1654
Colombia { Panamá, Independent of Colombia, 1903; Independent, 1811; State of New Granada, 1832; Granadan Confederation, 1858; United States of New Granada, 1861; " " " Colombia, 1861, 1863; Republic of Colombia, 1886 } Republic of (Great) Colombia 1821 - 1830
Venezuela { Independent, 1811; Separate republic, 1830; United States of Venezuela, 1864 } Venezuela { joined, 1821; seceded, 1830 }
Ecuador { Independent, 1822; Separate republic, 1830 } Ecuador { joined, 1822; seceded, 1830 }
Peru Independent, 1821
Bolivia " 1825
Chile " 1818
Paraguay " 1811
Uruguay { Independent of Spain, 1814; As the Cisplatine Province, formed part of Brazil, 1821 - 1828; Independent of Brazil, 1828 }
Argentina (Argentine Republic) { Independent, 1816; United Provinces of Rio de la Plata, 1816; Argentine Republic, 1826; Argentine Confederation, 1835; Argentine Nation (Republic), 1860 }
Brazil { Independent, 1822; Empire, 1822 - 1889; Republic (United States of Brazil) since 1889 }
× Battle of the wars of independence (1810-1827) ✧ Fort)(Pass ⇥ Falls
The dates connected with the names of places not having the sign (×) are those of foundation; with the names of islands and of the divisions of Guiana, those of acquisition by the power concerned
Overland trade routes in colonial times
Railways in operation
" projected or under construction
Proposed Intercontinental (Pan American) Railway
Connections of the " " "
Scale 1:30 000 000
Miles
Abbreviations
Arg.-Argentine; Ba.-Babahoyo; Br.-British; Col.-Colonia (do Sacramento) founded by the Portuguese in 1680 and ceded to Spain in 1777; D.-Dutch; E.R.-Entre Rios; Fr.-French; Ft.-Fort; M.-Island of Martin Garcia; (P.)-Piratininga; Pen.-Peninsula; Phil.-Philadelphia (Theophilo); Prov.-Province; Pta.-Punta; Sp.-Spanish; TER.-Territory.

Hispanic America, 1828—1929.

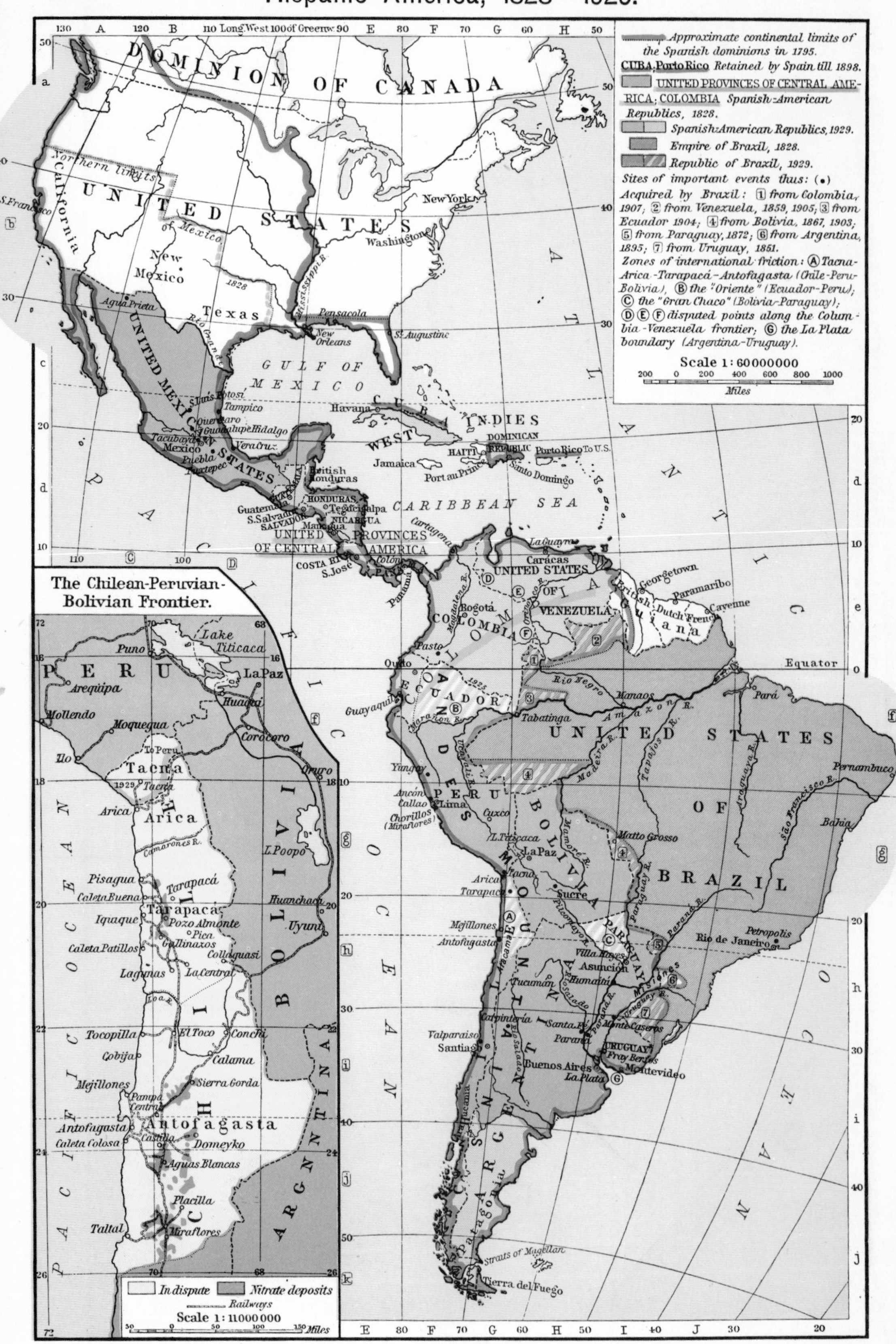

MAPS SINCE 1929

PREPARED BY C. S. HAMMOND & COMPANY

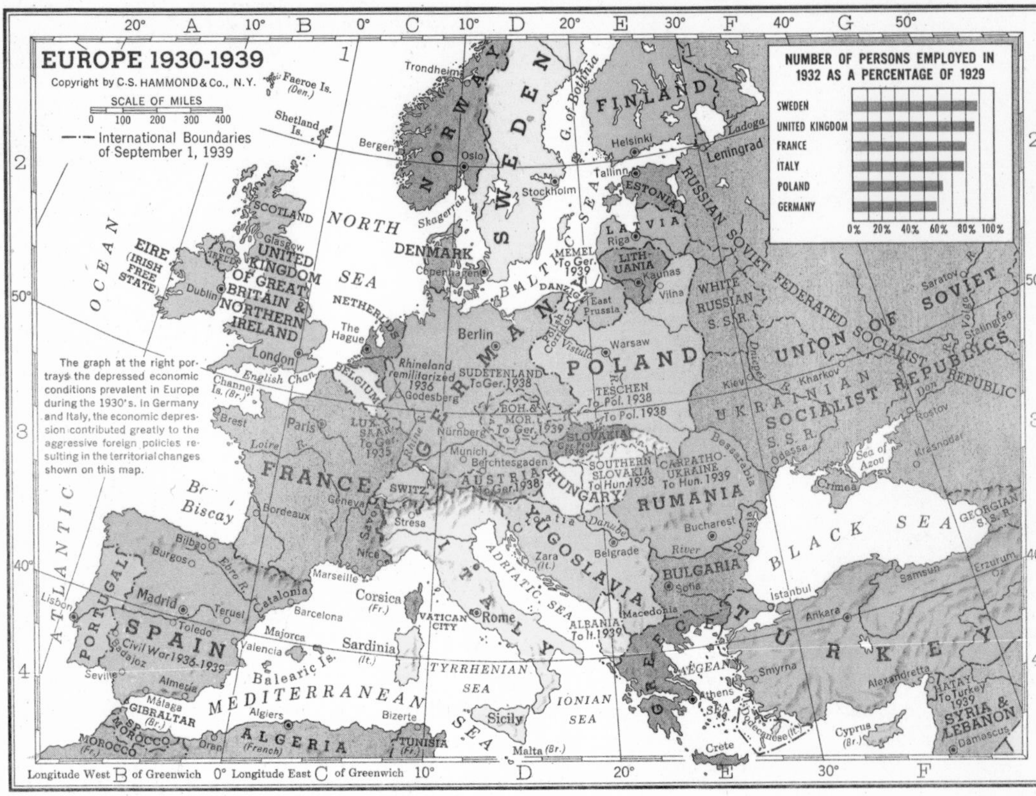

EUROPE 1930-1939

SCALE OF MILES
0 100 200 300 400

—·— International Boundaries of September 1, 1939

NUMBER OF PERSONS EMPLOYED IN 1932 AS A PERCENTAGE OF 1929

SWEDEN
UNITED KINGDOM
FRANCE
ITALY
POLAND
GERMANY

0% 20% 40% 60% 80% 100%

The graph at the right portrays the depressed economic conditions prevalent in Europe during the 1930's. In Germany and Italy, the economic depression contributed greatly to the aggressive foreign policies resulting in the territorial changes shown on this map.

Longitude West B of Greenwich 0° Longitude East C of Greenwich 10° D 20° E 30° F

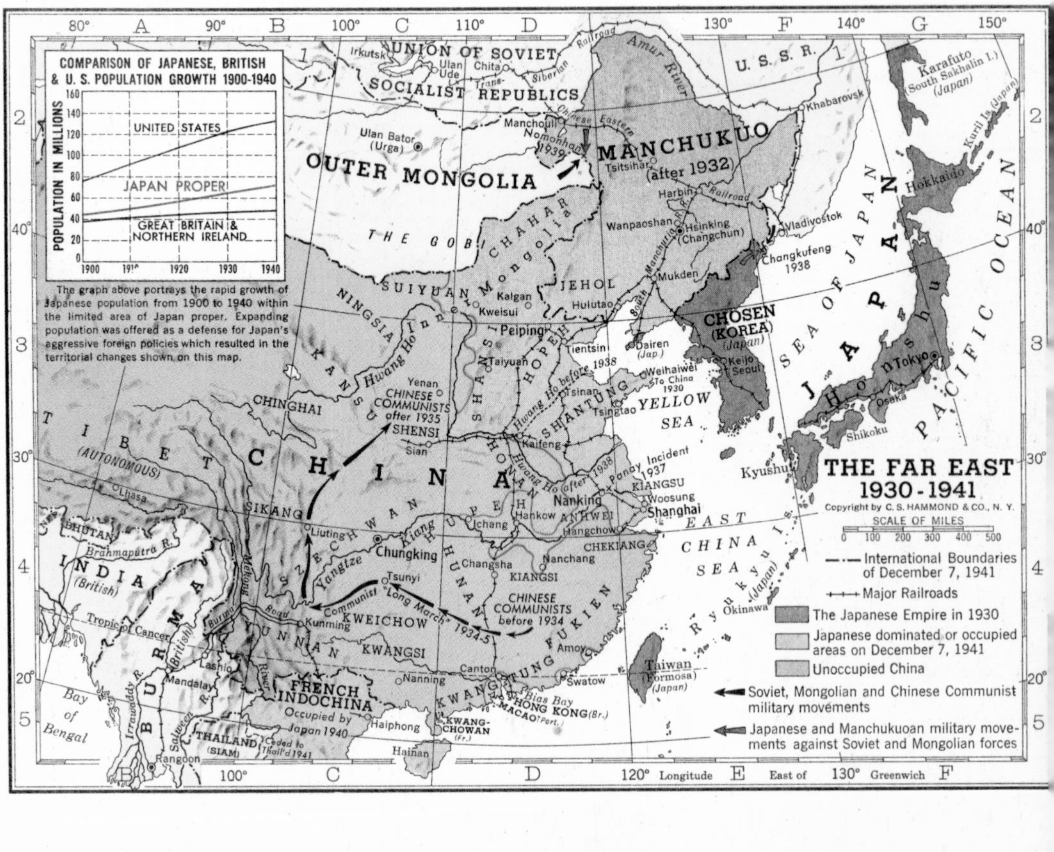

THE FAR EAST 1930-1941

SCALE OF MILES
0 100 200 300 400 500

COMPARISON OF JAPANESE, BRITISH & U. S. POPULATION GROWTH 1900-1940

POPULATION IN MILLIONS
160 140 120 100 80 60 40 20 0

UNITED STATES
JAPAN PROPER
GREAT BRITAIN & NORTHERN IRELAND

1900 1910 1920 1930 1940

The graph above portrays the rapid growth of Japanese population from 1900 to 1940 within the limited area of Japan proper. Expanding population was offered as a defense for Japan's aggressive foreign policies which resulted in the territorial changes shown on this map.

—·— International Boundaries of December 7, 1941
Major Railroads
The Japanese Empire in 1930
Japanese dominated or occupied areas on December 7, 1941
Unoccupied China
Soviet, Mongolian and Chinese Communist military movements
Japanese and Manchukuoan military movements against Soviet and Mongolian forces

120° Longitude E East of 130° Greenwich F

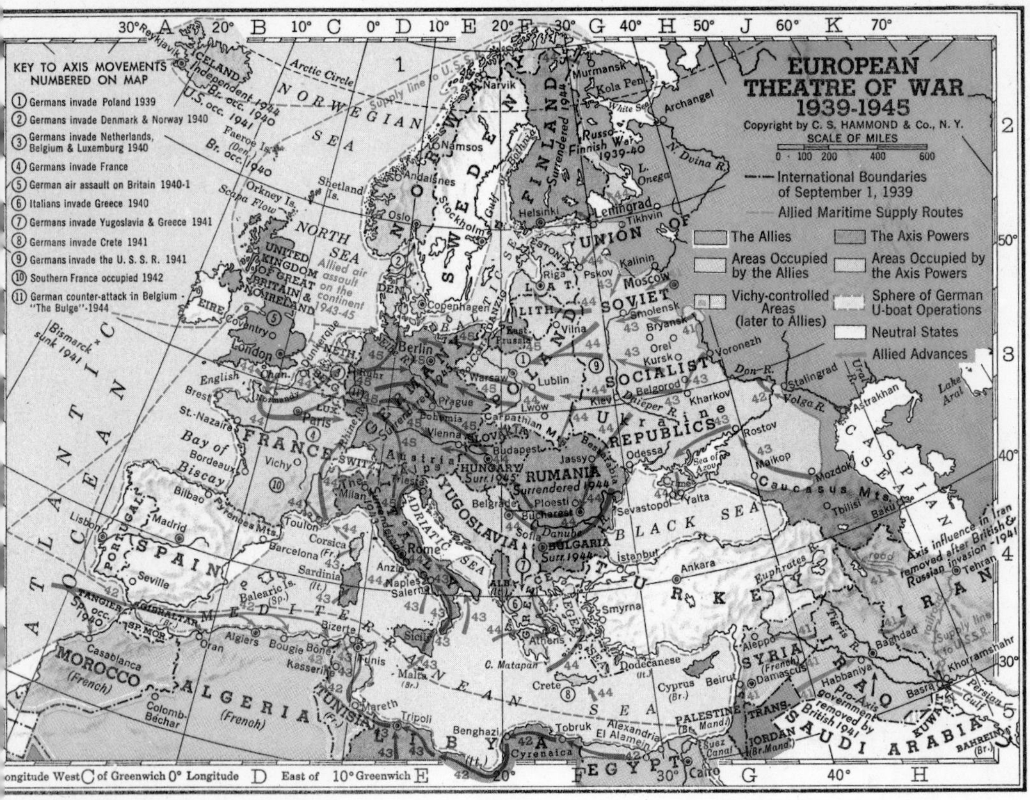
EUROPEAN THEATRE OF WAR 1939-1945
Copyright by C. S. HAMMOND & Co., N. Y.
SCALE OF MILES
0 100 200 400 600
International Boundaries of September 1, 1939
Allied Maritime Supply Routes
The Allies
The Axis Powers
Areas Occupied by the Allies
Areas Occupied by the Axis Powers
Vichy-controlled Areas (later to Allies)
Sphere of German U-boat Operations
Neutral States
Allied Advances
KEY TO AXIS MOVEMENTS NUMBERED ON MAP
1 Germans invade Poland 1939
2 Germans invade Denmark & Norway 1940
3 Germans invade Netherlands, Belgium & Luxemburg 1940
4 Germans invade France
5 German air assault on Britain 1940-1
6 Italians invade Greece 1940
7 Germans invade Yugoslavia & Greece 1941
8 Germans invade Crete 1941
9 Germans invade the U. S. S. R. 1941
10 Southern France occupied 1942
11 German counter-attack in Belgium "The Bulge"-1944
Arctic Circle
NORWEGIAN SEA
NORTH SEA
Allied air assault on the continent 1943-45
UNITED KINGDOM OF GREAT BRITAIN & N. IRELAND
EIRE
ICELAND Independent 1944 Br. occ. 1940 U.S. occ. 1941
Faeroe Is. (Den.) Br. occ. 1940
Bismarck sunk 1941
ATLANTIC OCEAN
FRANCE
Bay of Biscay
SPAIN
PORTUGAL
MOROCCO (French)
ALGERIA (French)
TUNISIA
MEDITERRANEAN SEA
ITALY
YUGOSLAVIA
RUMANIA Surrendered 1944
HUNGARY Surr. 1945
BULGARIA Surr. 1944
BLACK SEA
TURKEY
SYRIA (French)
IRAQ
IRAN
SAUDI ARABIA
EGYPT
LIBYA
PALESTINE (Br. Mand.)
TRANS-JORDAN (Br. Mand.)
CASPIAN SEA
UNION OF SOVIET SOCIALIST REPUBLICS
FINLAND Surrendered 1944
Russo-Finnish War 1939-40
SWEDEN
NORWAY
POLAND
GERMANY
Axis influence in Iran removed after British & Russian invasion-1941
Pro-Axis government removed by British 1941
Supply line to U.S.S.R.
Longitude West of Greenwich 0° Longitude East of 10° Greenwich

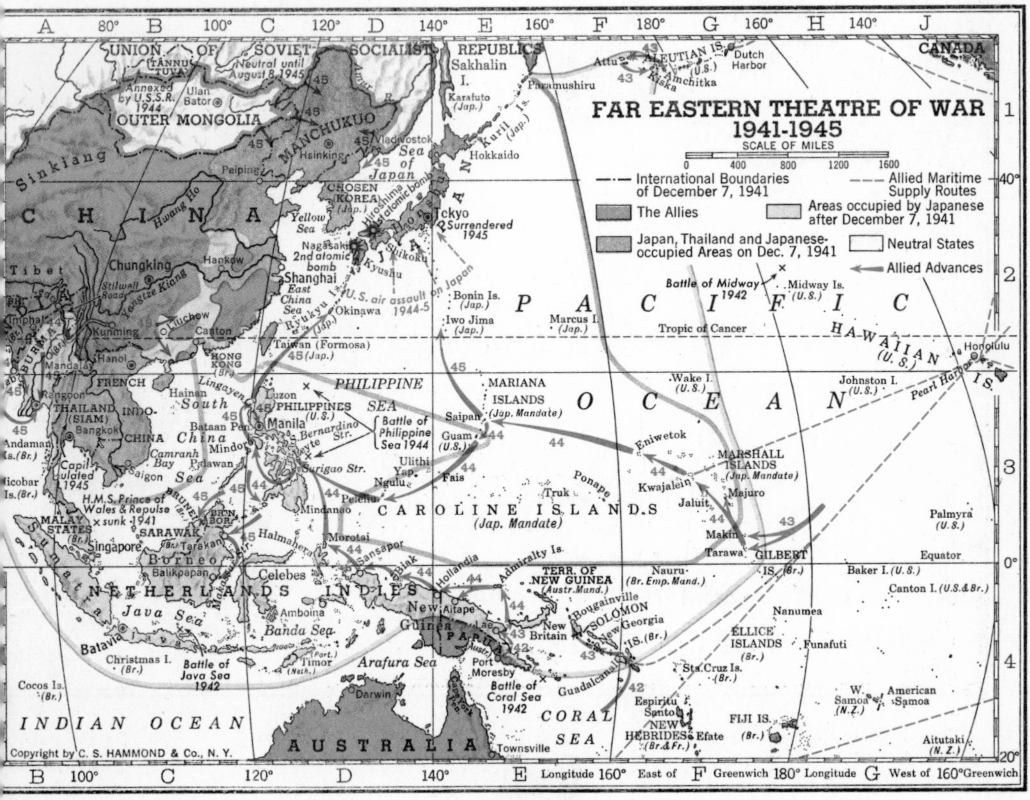
FAR EASTERN THEATRE OF WAR 1941-1945
SCALE OF MILES
0 400 800 1200 1600
International Boundaries of December 7, 1941
Allied Maritime Supply Routes
The Allies
Areas occupied by Japanese after December 7, 1941
Japan, Thailand and Japanese-occupied Areas on Dec. 7, 1941
Neutral States
Allied Advances
UNION OF SOVIET SOCIALIST REPUBLICS
OUTER MONGOLIA
MANCHUKUO
CHINA
CHOSEN (KOREA) (Jap.)
Tokyo Surrendered 1945
Hiroshima 1st atomic bomb
Nagasaki 2nd atomic bomb
U.S. air assault on Japan 1944-5
Battle of Midway 1942
PACIFIC OCEAN
PHILIPPINE SEA
Battle of Philippine Sea 1944
CAROLINE ISLANDS (Jap. Mandate)
MARIANA ISLANDS (Jap. Mandate)
MARSHALL ISLANDS (Jap. Mandate)
NETHERLANDS INDIES
H.M.S. Prince of Wales & Repulse sunk 1941
Battle of Java Sea 1942
Battle of Coral Sea 1942
CORAL SEA
AUSTRALIA
INDIAN OCEAN
HAWAIIAN IS. (U.S.)
Pearl Harbor
Tropic of Cancer
CANADA
Copyright by C. S. HAMMOND & Co., N. Y.
Longitude 160° East of Greenwich 180° Longitude West of 160° Greenwich

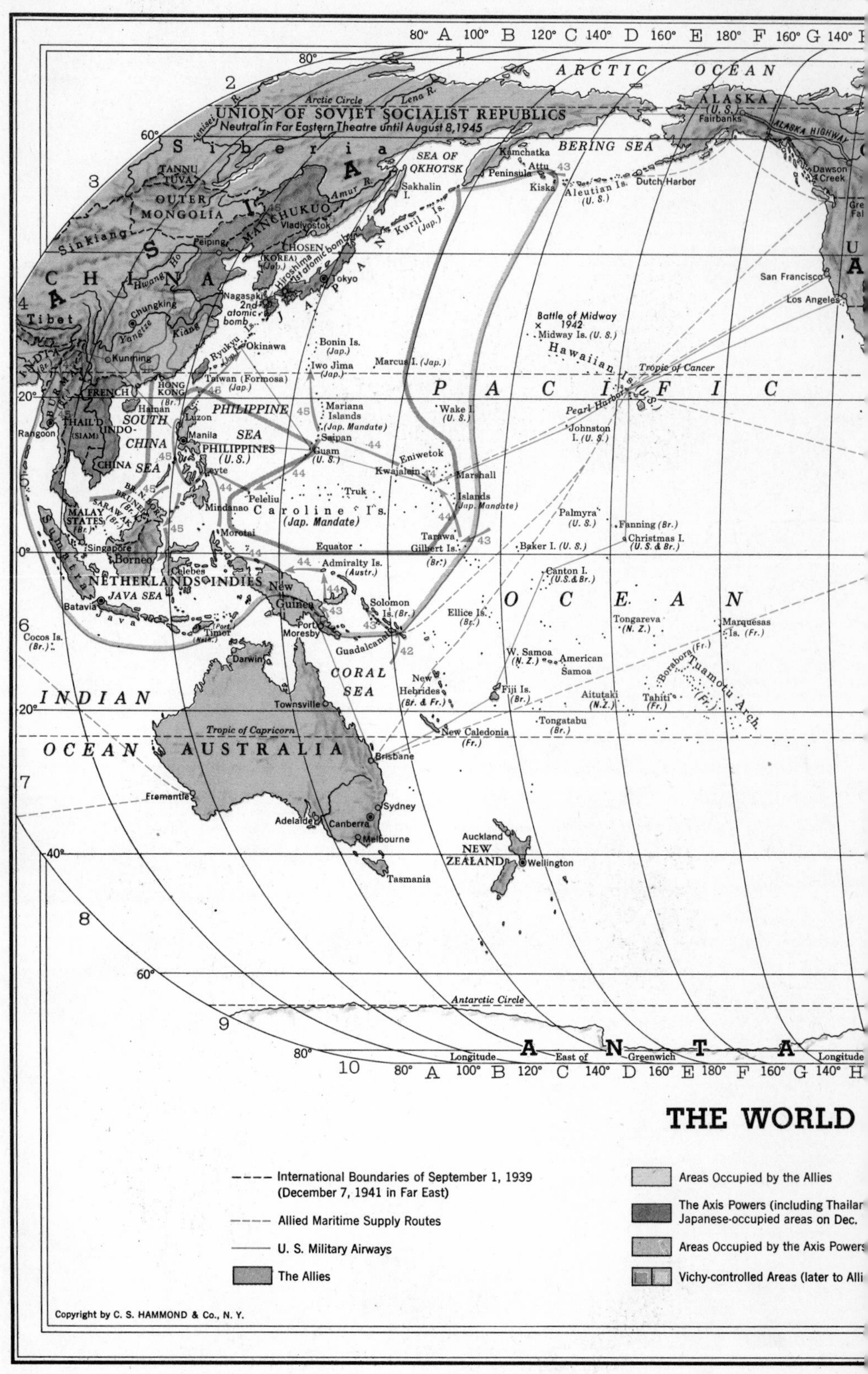
ARCTIC OCEAN
UNION OF SOVIET SOCIALIST REPUBLICS
Neutral in Far Eastern Theatre until August 8, 1945
Arctic Circle
Lena R.
Siberia
ASIA
SEA OF OKHOTSK
BERING SEA
ALASKA (U. S.)
Fairbanks
ALASKA HIGHWAY
Dawson Creek
Kamchatka Peninsula
Attu
Kiska
Aleutian Is. (U. S.)
Dutch Harbor
TANNU TUVA
OUTER MONGOLIA
MANCHUKUO
Amur R.
Vladivostok
Sakhalin I.
Kuril Is. (Jap.)
Sinkiang
CHINA
Peiping
CHOSEN (KOREA) (Jap.)
Hiroshima 1st atomic bomb
JAPAN
Tokyo
Nagasaki 2nd atomic bomb
Tibet
Chungking
Yangtze
Kunming
INDIA
Okinawa
Ryukyu Is.
Bonin Is. (Jap.)
Iwo Jima (Jap.)
Marcus I. (Jap.)
Battle of Midway 1942
Midway Is. (U. S.)
Hawaiian Is. (U. S.)
Tropic of Cancer
San Francisco
Los Angeles
Taiwan (Formosa) (Jap.)
HONG KONG (Br.)
FRENCH INDO-CHINA
BURMA
Rangoon
THAIL'D (SIAM)
Hainan
SOUTH CHINA SEA
Luzon
Manila
PHILIPPINE SEA
PHILIPPINES (U. S.)
Leyte
Mindanao
Mariana Islands (Jap. Mandate)
Saipan
Guam (U. S.)
PACIFIC
Wake I. (U. S.)
Pearl Harbor
Johnston I. (U. S.)
Eniwetok
Kwajalein
Marshall Islands (Jap. Mandate)
Truk
Peleliu
Caroline Is. (Jap. Mandate)
BR. N. BORNEO
BRUNEI (Br.)
SARAWAK (Br.)
MALAY STATES (Br.)
Singapore
Borneo
Sumatra
Morotai
Equator
Tarawa
Gilbert Is. (Br.)
Palmyra (U. S.)
Fanning (Br.)
Christmas I. (U. S. & Br.)
Baker I. (U. S.)
Celebes
NETHERLANDS INDIES
JAVA SEA
Batavia
Java
Timor (Port.) (Neth.)
Admiralty Is. (Austr.)
New Guinea
Port Moresby
Solomon Is. (Br.)
Guadalcanal
Canton I. (U.S.& Br.)
OCEAN
Ellice Is. (Br.)
Tongareva (N. Z.)
Marquesas Is. (Fr.)
Cocos Is. (Br.)
Darwin
CORAL SEA
New Hebrides (Br. & Fr.)
W. Samoa (N. Z.)
American Samoa
Fiji Is. (Br.)
Aitutaki (N.Z.)
Tahiti (Fr.)
Borabora (Fr.)
Tuamotu Arch. (Fr.)
INDIAN OCEAN
Townsville
Tropic of Capricorn
AUSTRALIA
New Caledonia (Fr.)
Tongatabu (Br.)
Brisbane
Fremantle
Sydney
Adelaide
Canberra
Melbourne
Tasmania
Auckland
NEW ZEALAND
Wellington
Antarctic Circle
ANTARCTICA
Longitude East of Greenwich
80° A 100° B 120° C 140° D 160° E 180° F 160° G 140°
THE WORLD
International Boundaries of September 1, 1939 (December 7, 1941 in Far East)
Allied Maritime Supply Routes
U. S. Military Airways
The Allies
Areas Occupied by the Allies
The Axis Powers (including Thailar
Japanese-occupied areas on Dec.
Areas Occupied by the Axis Powers
Vichy-controlled Areas (later to Alli
Copyright by C. S. HAMMOND & Co., N. Y.

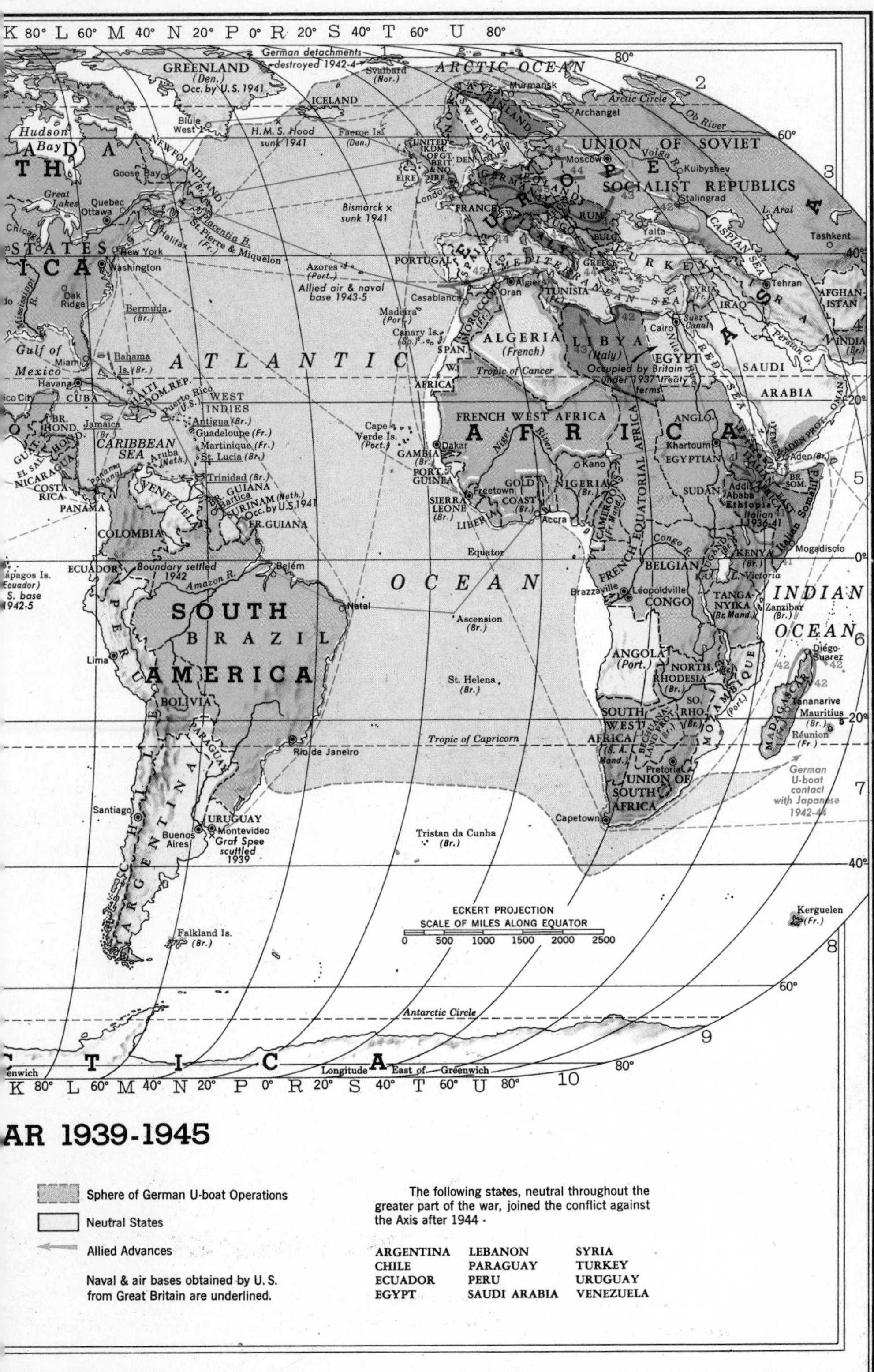

AR 1939-1945

Sphere of German U-boat Operations

Neutral States

Allied Advances

Naval & air bases obtained by U. S. from Great Britain are underlined.

The following states, neutral throughout the greater part of the war, joined the conflict against the Axis after 1944 -

ARGENTINA
CHILE
ECUADOR
EGYPT
LEBANON
PARAGUAY
PERU
SAUDI ARABIA
SYRIA
TURKEY
URUGUAY
VENEZUELA

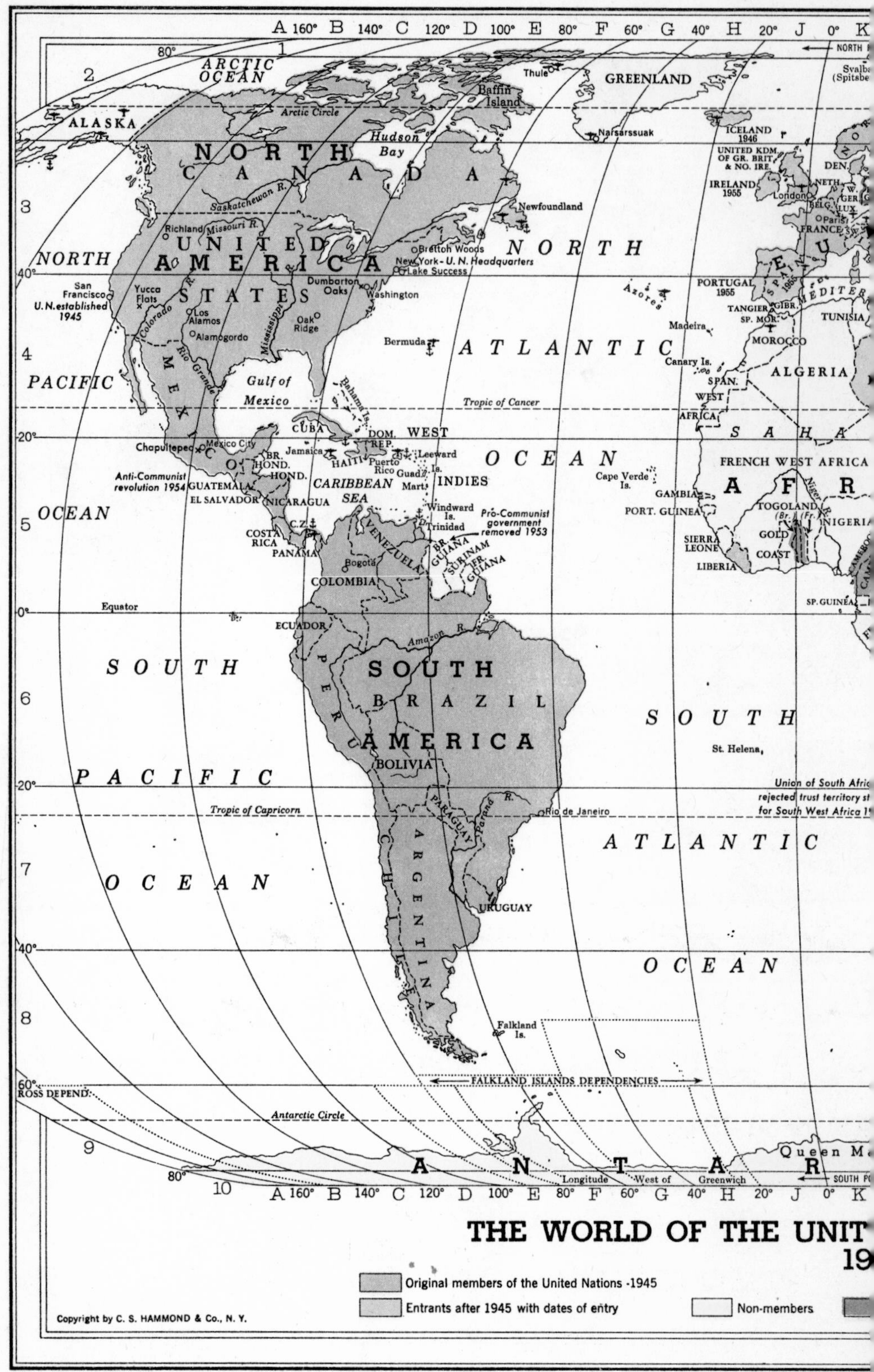
ARCTIC OCEAN
ALASKA
GREENLAND
Thule
Baffin Island
Arctic Circle
Hudson Bay
NORTH
CANADA
Narsarssuak
ICELAND 1946
UNITED KDM. OF GR. BRIT. & NO. IRE.
IRELAND 1955
London
Paris
FRANCE
Saskatchewan R.
Newfoundland
Richland
Missouri R.
UNITED STATES
AMERICA
Bretton Woods
New York - U. N. Headquarters
Lake Success
NORTH
NORTH
San Francisco
U.N. established 1945
Yucca Flats
Los Alamos
Alamogordo
Dumbarton Oaks
Washington
Oak Ridge
Azores
PORTUGAL 1955
SPAIN
TANGIER
GIBR.
SP. MOR.
Madeira
MOROCCO
TUNISIA
ALGERIA
Bermuda
ATLANTIC
Canary Is.
SPAN. WEST AFRICA
PACIFIC
Gulf of Mexico
MEXICO
Rio Grande
Tropic of Cancer
CUBA
DOM. REP.
WEST INDIES
HAITI
Jamaica
Puerto Rico
Leeward Is.
Guad.
Mart.
Chapultepec
Mexico City
BR. HOND.
HOND.
Anti-Communist revolution 1954
GUATEMALA
EL SALVADOR
NICARAGUA
CARIBBEAN SEA
OCEAN
Cape Verde Is.
GAMBIA
PORT. GUINEA
FRENCH WEST AFRICA
AFRICA
SAHARA
Windward Is.
Trinidad
Pro-Communist government removed 1953
OCEAN
C.Z.
COSTA RICA
PANAMA
VENEZUELA
BR. GUIANA
SURINAM
FR. GUIANA
Bogotá
COLOMBIA
SIERRA LEONE
LIBERIA
TOGOLAND (Br.) (Fr.)
GOLD COAST
NIGERIA
SP. GUINEA
Equator
ECUADOR
Amazon R.
SOUTH
SOUTH
AMERICA
BRAZIL
PERU
BOLIVIA
SOUTH
St. Helena
PACIFIC
Tropic of Capricorn
PARAGUAY
Paraná R.
Rio de Janeiro
Union of South Afric
rejected trust territory st
for South West Africa 1
ATLANTIC
OCEAN
ARGENTINA
CHILE
URUGUAY
OCEAN
Falkland Is.
FALKLAND ISLANDS DEPENDENCIES
ROSS DEPEND.
Antarctic Circle
Queen M
ANTAR
Longitude West of Greenwich
NORTH
SOUTH P
THE WORLD OF THE UNIT
19
Original members of the United Nations -1945
Entrants after 1945 with dates of entry
Non-members
Copyright by C. S. HAMMOND & Co., N. Y.

TIONS AND THE COLD WAR
55

es

The Soviet Union and Soviet dominated states

Overseas air bases of the United States

Overseas naval bases of the United States

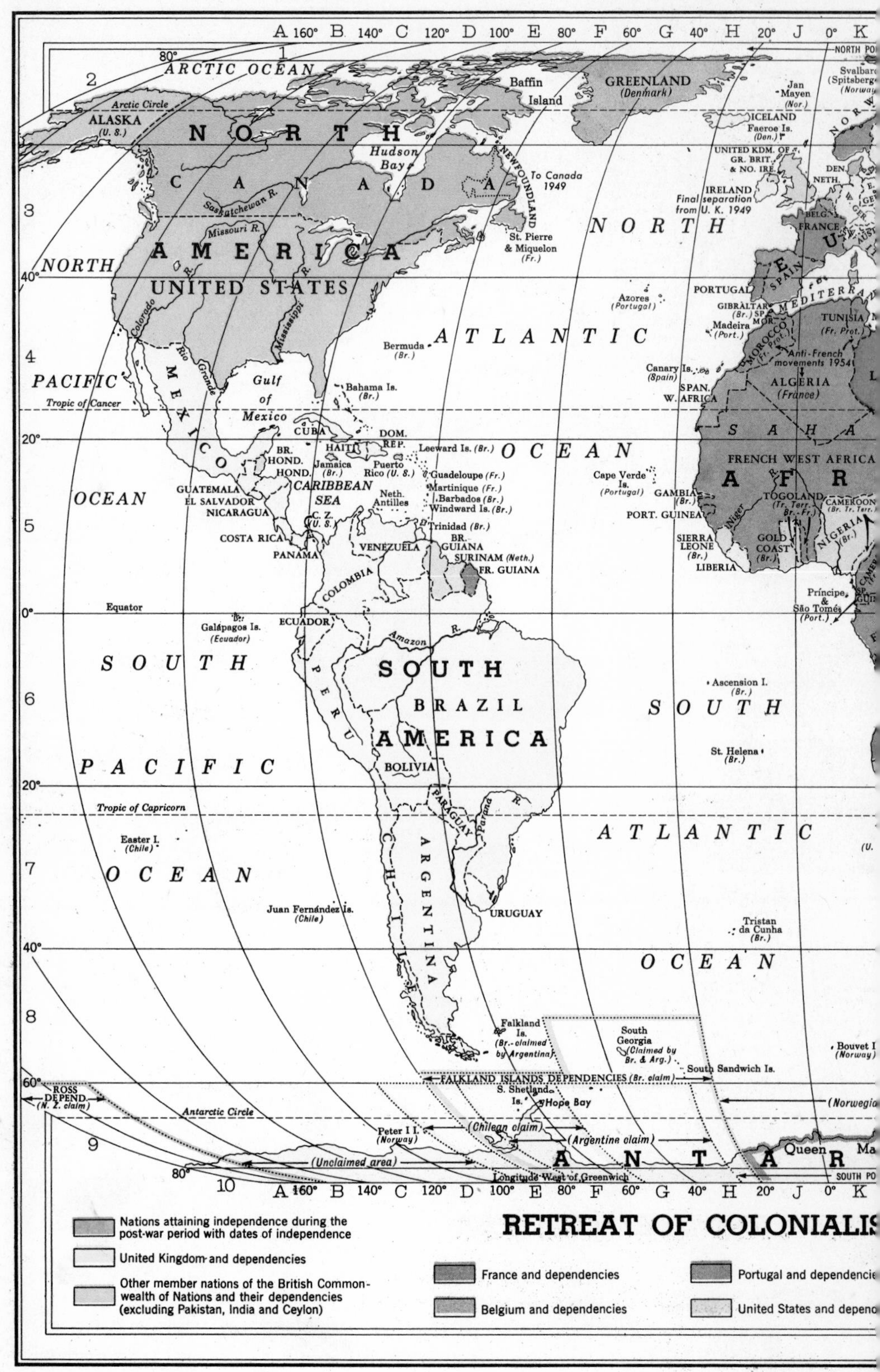

RETREAT OF COLONIALIS

- Nations attaining independence during the post-war period with dates of independence
- United Kingdom and dependencies
- Other member nations of the British Commonwealth of Nations and their dependencies (excluding Pakistan, India and Ceylon)
- France and dependencies
- Belgium and dependencies
- Portugal and dependencie
- United States and depend

THE POST-WAR PERIOD

- Netherlands and dependencies
- Spain and dependencies
- Italy and dependency
- Denmark and dependency
- Norway and dependencies
- Other countries
- Areas of the Soviet Union in which Great Russians constitute a majority of the population. Names of other peoples are underlined.

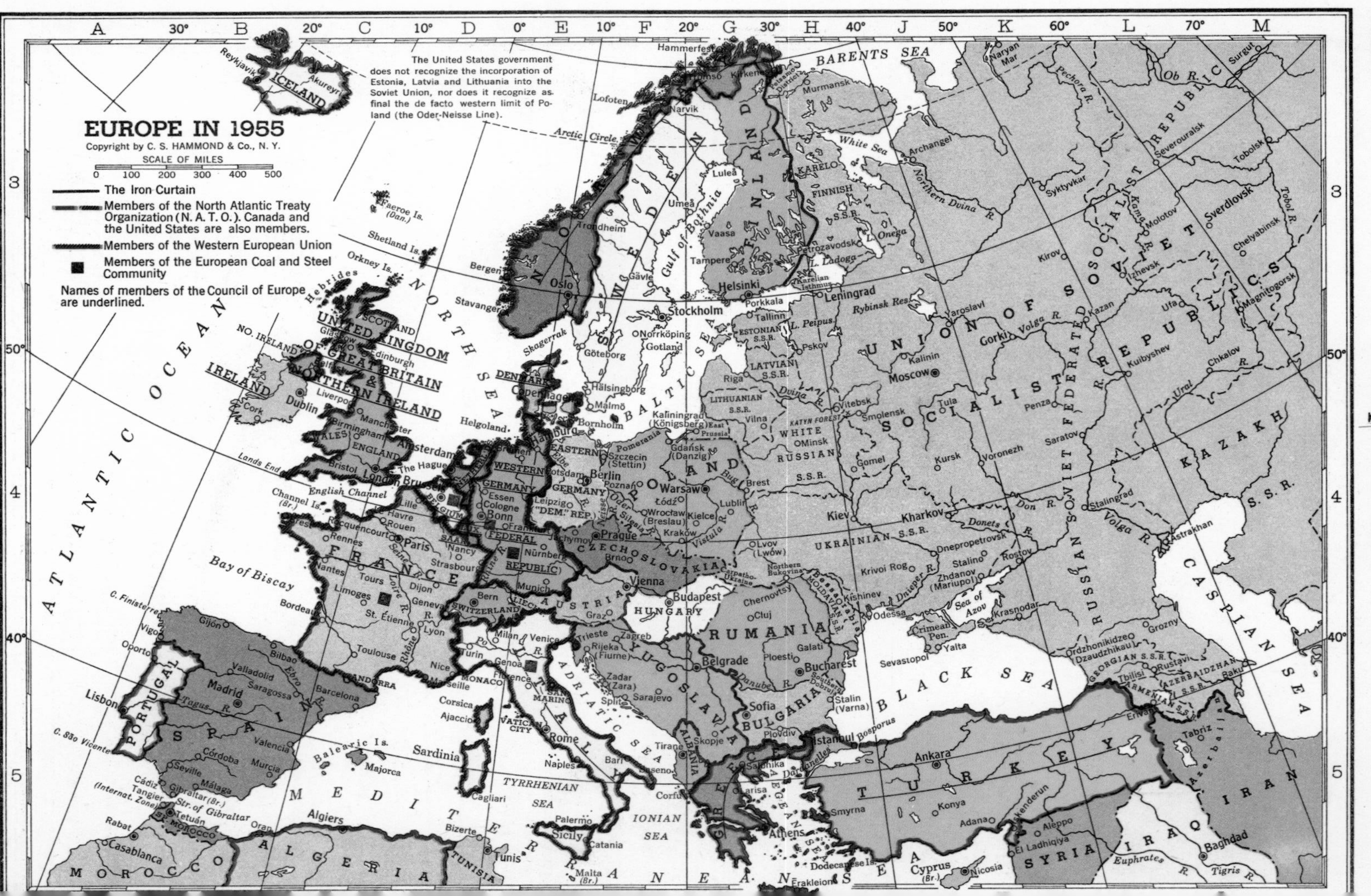
EUROPE IN 1955
Copyright by C. S. HAMMOND & Co., N. Y.
SCALE OF MILES
0 100 200 300 400 500
The Iron Curtain
Members of the North Atlantic Treaty Organization (N. A. T. O.). Canada and the United States are also members.
Members of the Western European Union
Members of the European Coal and Steel Community
Names of members of the Council of Europe are underlined.
The United States government does not recognize the incorporation of Estonia, Latvia and Lithuania into the Soviet Union, nor does it recognize as final the de facto western limit of Poland (the Oder-Neisse Line).
ATLANTIC OCEAN
NORTH SEA
BARENTS SEA
BALTIC SEA
BLACK SEA
CASPIAN SEA
MEDITERRANEAN SEA
ADRIATIC SEA
TYRRHENIAN SEA
IONIAN SEA
AEGEAN SEA
Bay of Biscay
English Channel
Gulf of Bothnia
White Sea
UNION OF SOVIET SOCIALIST REPUBLICS
RUSSIAN SOVIET FEDERATED SOCIALIST REPUBLIC
UKRAINIAN S.S.R.
WHITE RUSSIAN S.S.R.
KAZAKH S.S.R.
FINLAND
SWEDEN
NORWAY
DENMARK
POLAND
CZECHOSLOVAKIA
HUNGARY
RUMANIA
BULGARIA
YUGOSLAVIA
ALBANIA
GREECE
TURKEY
SYRIA
IRAQ
IRAN
ITALY
AUSTRIA
SWITZERLAND
FRANCE
SPAIN
PORTUGAL
IRELAND
UNITED KINGDOM OF GREAT BRITAIN & NORTHERN IRELAND
ICELAND
ALGERIA
MOROCCO
TUNISIA

INDEX

Unless otherwise indicated, the names given are those of towns. The Index does not furnish a complete set of references to the more important countries at successive periods of time. The maps needful for this purpose may be found by consulting the Table of Contents.

Modern names of ancient localities and different spellings of the same name are sometimes inclosed in parentheses, sometimes noted by cross-references. Though not appearing on the maps themselves, a considerable number of classical and medieval Latin names, and of different spellings of the same name, have been inserted in the Index with the proper cross-reference to the modern or customary form of such names.

If not accompanied by the letters B. C., the dates cited are A. D.

The number following a name refers to the page on which the name appears. The capital letter or letters following this number usually refer to a strip on that page inclosed by lines of longitude, and the small letter or letters, to a strip inclosed by lines of latitude. The name itself lies within the block formed by the intersection of the two strips. Thus the name *Madrid* 83 K g will be found on page 83, within the block formed by the intersection of the strip lettered K and the strip lettered g. In some cases, however, the letter or letters refer to a particular plan or inset on the page concerned.

Names which appear in the original Index without indication of the block in which they lie, are repeated with full information in the Index-Supplement. Names contained in the maps for the period 1911-1929 also appear in the Index-Supplement, as well as a number of names for the old maps which were omitted in the original Index.

ABBREVIATIONS

ab. = abbacy
abp. = archbishopric
Arg. Rep. = Argentine Republic
Aug. Reg. = Augustan Region
auton. = autonomous
bldg. = building
bp. = bishopric
Cal. = California
calif. = califate
cap. = captaincy
cent. = century
ch. = church
col. = colony
Conn. = Connecticut
cty. = county
cy. = city
dept. = department
desp. = despotat
dioc. = diocese
dist. = district
dom. = dominion(s)
E. = East
elect. = electorate
emir. = emirate
emp. = empire
exarch. = exarchate
fam. = family or clan
for. off. = foreign office
Frank. = Frankish
gen. = general or generality
gouv. = gouvernement
gov. = government
gr. = grand
Hanse. = Hanseatic
imp. = imperial
Ind. Res. = Indian Reservation
ins. = inset
isl. = island(s)
khan. = khanate
km. = kingdom
landgr. = landgraviate
leg. = legend
loc. = locality
margr. = margravate
marq. = marquisate
Mass. = Massachusetts
Miss. = Mississippi
mon. = monastery
mt., mts. = mountain(s)
N. = North
Ore. = Oregon
Pa. = Pennsylvania
palat. = palatinate
parl. bor. = parliamentary borough
patr. = patriarchate
pen. = peninsula
poss. = possessions
pref. = prefecture
pres. = presidency
princ. = principality
proc. = proconsultate
prom. = promontory
prot. = protectorate
prov. = province
R. = River
reg. = region
rep. = republic
Rom. = Roman
S. = South
satr. = satrapy
S. C. = South Carolina
seign. = seigniory
sen. = senatorial
set. = settlement
str. = strait
ter. = territory
univ. = university
U. S. = United States
Va. = Virginia
viscty. = viscounty
vol. = volcano
W. = West or Western

I

Aach 142 C e
Aachen (Aix-la-Chapelle) 55 Q i
Aalborg 88 C c
Aalen 143 J h
Aalesund 166 G c
Aarau 91 Q k
Aardenburg 117 B c
Aar or Aare River 91 Q k
Aargau, distr. 91 Q k
Aargau, region 62 D e
Abacaenum 30 E d
Abæ 11 D d
Aballo, see Avallon
Abalus (Helgoland), isl. 38 D b
Abana River 6 E a
Abarim, Mountains of 7 D f
Abaris, promontory 9 B c
Abasgi, people 35 M e
Abasgians, people 50 L d
Abbassids, Calif. of the 55 K h
Abbeville 76 D a
Abbotsbury, mon. 97 O k
Abdera, in Spain 12 C c
Abdera, in Thrace 12 H b
Abejar 82 B a
Abel 6 D b
Abel-Keramin 7 D e
Abella 30 D b
Abellinum 30 D b
Abensberg 154 F d
Abercorn, in Georgia 193 ins. C
Abercorn, in Scotland 185 C b
Aberdeen
Aberdeen, bp. 97 K b
Aberdeen, cty.
Aberdeen, univ. 100 E c
Aberffraw
Abergavenny
Abergavenny, mon. 97 O j
Aberystwith, parl. bor.
Abeshr 174 F c
Abia 14 C c
Abila, in Gilead 6 D c
Abila, in Mauretania 38 A e
Abila, in Syria 6 E a
Abingdon, in England 98 ins. A
Abingdon, mon. 97 P j
Abingdon, parl. bor. 163 M f (Ab.)
Abingdon, in Virginia 196 ins. A
Abittibi, lake 188 J a
Abittibi, river 188 J a
Abkhasia, reg. 119 L e
Abkoude 117 C b
Abnakis, people 188 M b
Abnoba Mountains 38 D c
Åbo 120 J d
Abodrites, people 55 R i
Abomey 174 D d
Abrincas or Abrincates, see Avranche
Abruzzi, dist. 90 D c
Abruzzo, bp. 95 E c
Absalom, Tomb of 6 ins. A
Abukir 174 J i
Abukir Bay 150 A a
Abus, mt. 20 I c
Abus Fluvius (Humber River).
Abu Simbel 4 F d
Abusina 38 E c
Abydos, in Egypt 4 F d
Abydos, on the Hellespont
Abyssinia, reg. 109 U g
Abyssinia, cty. 174 G d
Acadia, reg. 194 F a
Acalán, reg. 105 B c
Acalander River 31 F b
Acamas, prom. 20 E e
Acambaro 213 ins.
Acampsis River 20 I b
Acanthian Gulf 11 E b
Acanthus 11 E b
Acapulco 107, 108 H f
Acarnania, reg. 10 B d
Accau, route of 191 G c
Acci 38 B e
Accia 148 C c
Accomack, cty. 193 ins. A
Accra 175 C d
Aceldama, loc. near Jerusalem 6 ins. A
Acelum 26 F b
Acerenza 64 C b
Acerenza, abp. 95 F c
Acerra, bp. 95 ins.
Acerræ, in Campania 30 D b
Acerræ, in Venetia 26 D b
Aceruntia 30 E b
Acervo 27 I b
Acesines River, in India 19 L d
Acesines River, in Sicily 30 E e
Achaia, dioc. 43 G f
Achaia, princ. 89 B c
Achaia, prov. 35 I f
Achaia, reg. 14 B a
Achaia (Phtiotis), reg. 11 D c
Achaia, state 13 B b
Achaian, League 19 ins. A
Achaian Mountains 10 D d
Achalm, castle 62 E d
Achalm, ruin 143 H h
Acharnae 15 D a
Acharnian Gate 23 D
Achelous River 10 C d
Achern 142 B c
Acheron River 10 B c
Acherusia, lake in Campania 31 ins. A
Acherusia, lake in Epirus 10 B c
Achilles, Burial mound of
Achilleum
Achillis Island 18 D a
Achin 112 C c
Achonry, bp. 97 C b
Achradina, quarter in Syracuse 31 ins. B
Achrida 59 I e
Achshaph 6 C b
Achzib 6 C b
Acilii, Gardens of the 22 A
Aciris (Agri) River 31 F b
Acium 30 E e
Acla 105 E e
Acoma 190 D e
Aconcagua, mt. 215 C f
Acqui 90 I h
Acqui, bp. 95 D c
Acræ 30 D e
Acraephia 11 E d
Acragas (Girgenti) 30 C e
Acre, see Saint Jean d'Acre 73 G d
Acre, ter. 214 B c
Acriæ 15 C c
Acritas, mt. 14 B c
Acritas, prom. 14 B c
Acroceraunia, prom 31 I b
Acroceraunia, reg. 17 A a
Acroceraunian Mountains 10 A b
Acrocorinthus 15 C b
Acropolis of Athens, plan of the 23 C
Acroria, reg. 14 B b
Acrothoi 11 F b
Acte, reg. in Argolis 15 D b
Acte, reg. in Attica 16 D c
Acte, reg. in Chalcidice 11 F b
Actium 10 B d
Aculco 213 ins.
Adadah 7 C f
Adaes 191 G e
Adalia 77 K e
Adams, Fort, in Mississippi 199 G d
Adams, Fort, in Ohio 196 ins. B
Adams, mt. 212 ins.
Adamawa, Adamaua, reg. 174 E d
Adana 20 F d
Ad Aquilam 27 F d
Ad Castores 26 E b
Adda River 90 I h
Addis Abeba
Addua (Adda) River 26 D a
Adelaide 172 C d
Adelberg, mon. 143 I h
Adelmannsfelden 143 I h
Adelsberg 159 H f
Adelsheim 142 D b
Adelsreuthe 142 E e
Aden
Aden, Gulf of 170 F g
Aden Protectorate 170 F g (A.P.)
Ad Fines
Adiabene, reg. 20 J e
Adige River 90 J h
Adirondack Mountains 192 D b
Adis Ababa
Admiralty Island 212 ins.
Admont, mon. 80 D h
Ad Novas, on Lake Sabatinus 35 ins. B
Ad Novas, near L. Trasimenus 27 F d
Adoraim 7 C e
Adour River 76 C e
Adowa 174 G c
Ad Padum 27 G c
Adra 82 B b
Adraha 6 E c
Adramyttium
Adramyttium, Gulf of
Adrana River 39 J h
Adrar, reg. 174 B b
Adratum 68 C c
Adria 64 B a
Adria, bp. 95 E b
Adrianople 43 H e
Adrianopolis 35 J e
Adrianus River 27 F b
Adriatic Sea 2 E d
Ad Sabatum 31 F c
Adsalluta River 27 I a
Ad Sextum 27 F d
Ad Statuas 35 ins. B
Adua see Adowa
Aduatuca 39 H h
Aduatuci, people 39 H h
Adula, mt. 26 C a
Adullam 7 B e
Adwalton Moor 127 X m
Æane 10 C b
Æas River 10 A b
Æcæ 30 E a
Æclanum 30 D a
Ædepsus 11 E d
Ædro, Portus 27 G b
Ædui, see Autun
Ædui, people 38 C c
Æfula 35 ins. B
Ægæ, in Achaia 14 C a
Ægæ, in Euboea 11 E d
Ægæ or Agææ, in Macedonia 10 D b
Ægaleos, mountain in Attica 16 B b
Ægaleus, mountain in Messenia 14 B b
Ægates, isl. 30 B d
Æge 11 E c
Ægeae 20 F d
Ægean Islands, Theme of the 59 I f
Ægean Sea 2 G e
Ægiæ 14 C c
Ægialea, reg. 14 B a
Ægilia, in Attica 16 B b
Ægilia, island near Crete 15 D d
Ægilia, island near Euboea 15 E a
Ægilips, isl. 10 B d
Ægilos, isl. 26 D d
Ægina 15 D b
Ægina, isl. 15 D b
Æginium 10 C c
Ægira 14 C a
Ægitium 10 D d
Ægium 14 C a
Ægospotami River
Ægosthena 15 D a
Ægusa, isl. 30 B e
Ægyptus, Rom. prov., see Egypt 35 J h
Ægys 14 C b
Ælana 35 K h
Ælia Capitolina (Jerusalem) 35 L g
Ælian Bridge 22 A
Ælmere, bay, see Zuider Zee

Æmilia, reg. 26 E c
Æmilia, Rom. prov. 42 E e (2)
Æmilia, Basilica, bldg. 24 B
Æmilian Bridge 24 A
Æmilian Portico 22 A
Æmilian Way, road 26 C c
Æmilian Way of Scaurus, road 26 D c
Ænaria, (Ischia), isl. 30 C b
Ænea 11 D b
Æneum, prom. 11 D b
Ænianìa, reg. 10 D d
Ænis, reg. 8 N h
Ænona 27 J c
Ænus
Ænus, mt. 10 B d
Ænus (Inn) River 38 E c
Ænyra 11 F b
Æoli, (Stromboli), isl. 30 E d
Æoliæ, (Lipari), isl. 30 D d
Æolian Islands 90 E e
Æolians, people 8 O h
Æolis, reg. 8 Q h
Æpea 14 B c
Æqui, people 27 H e
Æquians, people
Æquimelium 24 A
Æquum Tuticum 30 E a
Ærarium, bldg. in Rome
Aëre 6 E b
Æsar River 31 G c
Æsculapius, Temple of, in Carthage 34 ins. A (5)
Æsculapius, Temple of, in Rome 22 A
Æsepus River
Æsernia 30 D a
Æsis 27 H d
Æsis (Esino) River 27 H d
Æsium, see Jesi
Æson River 11 D b
Æstui, people 38 G a
Æthalia, (Elba), isl. 26 E e
Æthices, people 10 C c
Ætna 30 D e
Ætna, mt., see Etna
Ætolia, reg. 10 C d
Ætolian League 19 ins. A
Æxone 16 B b
Afghanistan, cty. 170 H e
Afghans, people
Africa, continent 174, 175
Africa, dioc. 42
Africa, exarch. 52 I f
Africa, Proconsular, Rom. prov. 34 F f
Africa, prov. 38 D e
Agade 4 G c
Agades 174 D c
Agalassa 19 L d
Agamenticus 189 C c
Agaña 198 ins. C
Agaraci, people 35 L g
Agat 198 ins. C
Agatha, Agathe (Agde) 12 D b
Agathyrnum 30 D b
Agawam (Ipswich, Mass.) 189 C c
Agawam (Springfield, Mass.) 189 B c
Agde 61 E e
Agedincum (Sens) 38 C c
Agen 46 G e
Agen, bp. 94 C c
Agen, cty. 69 D d
Agenais, cty. 61 D d
Agennum, see Agde
Agenorium 18 ins. B
Ager Gallicus, dist. 27 G d
Ager Romanus, dist. 35 ins. B
Ager Solonius, dist. 35 ins. B
Ager Vaticanus, dist. 22 A
Aggershuus (Christiania)
Aghadoe, bp. 97 B d
Aghlabids, Dom. of the 54 G g
Agida 27 H b
Agincourt 81 M g
Aginnum (Agen) 38 C d
Agnadello 90 I h
Agnus 16 B b
Agogna River 90 I h
Agora (Lysimachia)
Agordo 90 J g
Agostinho, Cape 108 R i
Agra 137 C c
Agræ 16 B b
Agræ, reg. 23 D
Agræi, people 10 C d
Agræna 6 E c
Agram 72 D b
Agram, bp. 95 F b
Agrianes, people 18 B b
Agri Decumates (Tithe Lands), distr. 39 J i
Agrigentum (Girgenti) 30 C e
Agrinium 10 C d
Agrippa, Baths of 22 A
Agrippa, Field of 22 A
Agrippa, Monument of
Agrippa's Bridge 22 A
Agrippina, Gardens of 22 A
Agryle 16 B b
Aguadilla 199 ins. G
Aguantum 27 G a
Aguarico River 111 B b
Agua Salud River
Aguas Blancas 215 B e
Aguas Calientes 213 ins.
Aguilar 83 K g
Aguilas 82 B b
Aguinum 30 C a
Agulhas, Cape 175 E h
Aguya, Punta 214 A c
Agyrium 30 D e
Ahausen 122 F d
Ahmadabad 137 B d
Ahmadnagar 137 B e
Ahorca Lagarto
Ahremberg 117 E d
Ahwaz 99 M g
Ai 7 C e
Aianteion, quarter 93 G e
Aianteum
Aibar 83 K g
Aidin 164 D c
Aidin, reg. 77 J e
Aigle 91 P l
Aigues-mortes 73 A b
Aiguillon 76 D d
Aigun 171 N c
Aimores, Serra dos 214 E d
Ain, dept. 148 F e
Ain River 126 D c
Ainay, mon. 148 B b
Aini 99 L e
Ainos 12 I b
Ain-Tab 68 C b
Aiquebelle, mon. 95 D c
Air, reg. 174 D c
Airaines 76 D b
Aird's Moss
Aire 126 C a
Aire, bp. 94 B c
Aire River 127 X m
Airebolu 165 E c
Airolo 91 Q l
Aisne, dept. 148 E e
Aisne River 126 C b
Aix 61 F e
Aix, (Aix-les-Bains) 130 N i
Aix, abp. 95 D c
Aix, gen. 147 F c
Aix, univ. 100 G f
Aix-la-Chapelle (Aachen) 55 Q i
Aix-la-Chapelle, imp. cy. 78 D c
Ajaccio 72 B c
Ajaccio, bp. 95 D c
Ajalon 7 C e
Ajana, reg.
Ajax, Burial mound of
Ajmere 137 B c
Akabah 99 K h
Akabah, Gulf of 99 J h
Akaroa 172 G e
Akasheh 174 F b
Ake 6 C c
Akerman 99 J d
Akhalzikh 164 G b
Akhsi
Akkad, reg. 4 G c
Akko 6 C c
Akkrum 117 D a
Akra 6 ins. A
Akrabbi 7 C d
Akrabbim, mts. 7 B g
Akserai 89 J g
Akshehr 93 D c
Akshi-Kioi
Aksu
Akureyri 166 B b
Alabama River 187 K e
Alabama, state 203 U d
Alabama, ter. 203 U d
Alabanda 20 C d
Alagoas, state 214 F c
Alagonia 14 C c
Alais 76 E d
Alalcomenæ 10 B d
Alalia 12 E b
Alamance, battle 194 D c
Alamanni, people in 486 50 E c
Alamanni, people about 900 57 E d
Alamannia, duchy about 1000 58 F d
Alamannia, Frank. prov. 53 N h
Alamannia, reg. 54 F d
Álamo, battle 201 F d
Álamos 213 B b
Álamos de Catorce 213 B b
Alamut 92 F d
Alancione, see Alençon
Åland Islands 120 I d
Alans, people in Russia
Alans, people in France 48 F d
Alans, people in Spain 45 C e
Alara River 39 J g
Alarcon 82 B b
Alarcon, route of 190 C f
Alashehr 93 C c
Alaska, Gulf of 198 ins. A
Alaska, dist. 186 D b
Alaska Mountains 186 D b
Alaska Peninsula 186 D c
Alatri, bp. 95 E c
Alausi 214 B c
Álava, cty. 82 B a
Álava, reg. 83 K g
Alazones, people 35 K d
Alba River, see Aube River
Alba 90 I h
Alba, bp. 95 D c
Albacete 83 K h
Alba Fucens 27 H e
Alba Longa 35 ins. B
Alba Mountains 38 D c
Albana 35 N e
Albania, princ. 93 A b
Albania, reg. in Caucasia 19 G b
Albania, reg. in Epirus 73 E b
Albanian Principalities 77 I d
Albanians, people 165 leg.
Albano 64 ins.
Albano, bp. 96 B b
Albanum, bp. 96 B b
Albanus, lake 35 ins. B
Albanus, mt. 30 B a
Albany, in W. Australia 172 A d
Albany, in New York 192 D b
Albany, Fort 212 G c
Albany, New 211 H c
Albany River 186 K c
Alba Pompeia 26 C c
Albara 68 C b
Albarracin 82 B a
Albarracin, emir. 83 E c
Albasin 171 N c
Albay 199 ins. H
Albemarle 184 D c

Albemarle, reg. 193 F c
Albemarle Sound 193 F c
Albenga 90 B b
Albenga, bp. 95 D c
Albert 81 M g
Alberta, prov. 212 D c
Albert Edward Nyanza lake, see Edward Nyanza
Albert Nyanza, lake 175 F d
Albi 61 E e
Albi, abp. 148 B c
Albi, bp. 94 C c
Albi, viscty. 61 E e
Albici, people 38 D d
Albiga (Albi) 38 C d
Albigeois, cty. 69 E e
Albingaunum 26 C c
Albinia River 27 F e
Albintimilium 26 B d
Albion, name applied at first to Britain, later to England
Albis (Elbe) River 38 E b
Albon, cty. 69 F d
Albret, castle 76 C d
Albret, duchy 126 A d
Albret, seign. 69 C d
Albuera 130 B f
Albula Pass 91 R l
Albuquerque, in New Mexico 188 E d
Albuquerque, in Spain 83 J h
Albuquerque, duchy 83 J h
Albuquerque, Fort 214 D d
Albuquerque, route of 109 X h, 110 BB h
Alburnus, mt. 30 E b
Albury 172 D d
Alcácer do Sal 82 A b
Alcácer es Seguir 83 J h
Alcalá de Henares 82 B a
Alcalá de Henares, univ. 100 E f
Alcalá la Real 82 B b
Alcalde 210 A c
Alcañiz 82 B a
Alcántara 82 A b
Alcantarilla 82 B b
Alcaráz 82 B b
Alcázar 82 H f
Alcluyd
Alcmona River, see Altmühl R.
Alcobaça, mon. 94 A d
Alcoraz 66 F e
Alcyonian Gulf 15 D a
Aldabra Islands 175 H e
Aldan River
Aldborough, parl. bor. 163 M c
Aldeburgh, parl. bor. 163 P e
Alderney, isl. 69 B b
Aldersbach, mon. 95 E b
Aldersgate, in London 75 G g
Aldgate, in London 75 G g
Aldobrandeschi, fam. 90 L j
Alea 14 C b
Alemtejo, reg. 82 G f
Alençon 76 D b
Alençon, cty. 76 D b
Alençon, duchy 84 D e
Alençon, gen. 147 D b
Alençon, reg. 81 L h
Alençon, seign. 69 H f
Aleppo 68 C b
Alerheim 122 F d
Aleria 26 D e
Aleria, bp. 148 C c
Aleshki 131 J d
Alesia 38 C c
Alesium 14 B b
Alessandria 78 F f
Alessandria, bp. 95 D c
Alet 61 C b
Alet, bp. 94 C c
Aletium 31 H b
Aletrium 30 C a
Aletum, see Alet
Aleutian Islands 179 I b
Alexander Archipelago 212 ins.
Alexander's Mole 18 ins. B
Alexandra Land, reg. 172 C c
Alexandretta 68 C b
Alexandria, in Babylonia 19 G d
Alexandria, in Egypt 4 ins.
Alexandria, in India Superior 19 L d
Alexandria, near Parapanisus Mts. 19 K c
Alexandria, in Rumania 165 D b
Alexandria, in Syria (Iscanderum) 20 G d
Alexandria, in Virginia 194 K g
Alexandria, plan of 34 ins. C
Alexandria, patr. 52 K f
Alexandria Arachosiorum 19 K d
Alexandria Ariorum 19 J d
Alexandria eschata 19 K b
Alexandria Margiana 19 J c
Alexandria minor (Alexandretta) 68 C b
Alexandria Opiana 19 L e
Alexandria Oxiana
Alexandria Sogdiana 19 K e
Alexandria Troas
Alexandrine Aqueduct 35 ins. B
Alexinatz 164 C b
Alfdorf 143 I h
Alford
Algarve, dist. 82 G f
Algarve, Spanish, dist. 83 J h
Algarve de Aquem Mar, dist. 83 J h
Algeciras 82 A b
Algeria, col. 174 D a
Algeria, reg.
Algeria, state 118 E g
Algerian Plateaus 2 E e
Algerian Sahara 2 E e
Algidus, mt. 35 ins. B
Algiers 58 E f
Algoa Bay 175 M m
Algonkins, tribes 188 I b
Alhama, near Granada 82 B b
Alhama, near Murcia 82 B b
Alibunar 159 K f
Alicante 82 B b
Alice Spring Station 172 C c
Alife 64 B b
Alife, bp. 95 ins.
Aligarh 170 I f
Aliphera 14 B b
Aliso 39 I h and J h
Aliwal 170 I e
Aliwal North 175 M m
Aljubarrota 83 J h
Alkmaar 117 C b
Allahabad 137 D c
Allaine River 143 ins. F
Allegany, Ind. Res. 188 K b
Allegheny Mountains 193 B d-E a
Allegheny Plateau 187 K e
Allegheny River 192 B c
Allenstein 155 K b
Allerheiligen, mon. 142 B c
Alle River (Allaine R.) 143 ins. F
Alle River (Prussia) 115 K a
Aller River 78 F b
All Hallows, church in London 75 G g (26.30)
Allier, dept. 148 E e
Allier River 76 E d
Allifae 30 D a
Allobroges, people 26 A b
Allstedt 63 F c
Almada 82 A b
Almagro 83 K h
Almagro, route of 108 K i
Almalik 92 I c
Almansa 130 C f
Alma River 164 J f
Almazan 184 C d
Almeida 214 F d
Almendingen 143 I i
Almería 82 B b
Almería, bp. 94 B d
Almirante, Bahia del, bay 105 D e
Almissa, bp. 95 F c
Almodóvar del Campo 82 B b
Almohads, Dom. of the 70 H g
Almopia 10 D b
Almopia, reg. 10 D b
Almoravids, Dom. of the
Almuñecar 82 B b
Alnwick
Alnwick, mon. 97 P f
Alonæ 12 C c
Alope, in Locris 11 D d
Alope, in Phthiotis 11 D d
Alopece 16 B b
Alorus 11 D b
Alost 117 B d
Alpeni 16 F e
Alpheus River 14 B b
Alpirsbach 143 F i
Alpirsbach, mon. 95 D b
Alpis Graia, pass 26 A b
Alpis Poenina, pass 26 B b
Alpnach 91 Q l
Alps, The, mts. 2 E d
Alpuente 83 E d
Alpujarras, mts. 83 K h
Alresford 127 X o
Alresford, parl. bor.
Alsace, gen. 147 F b
Alsace, gouv. 146 C b
Alsace, prov. 148 F e
Alsace-Lorraine, imp. ter. 161 B c
Alsek River 212 ins.
Alsen, isl. 114 F a
Alsietinus, lake 35 ins. B
Alsietine Aqueduct 35 ins. B
Alsium
Altai Mountains 102 I c
Altamaha River 193 C f
Altamura 90 F d
Alta Ripa 39 J i
Alta Semita, loc. in Rome 22 A
Alt-Breisach 142 A d
Altdorf, near Nuremberg 114 F d
Altdorf, in Swabia 143 I j
Altdorf, in Switzerland 91 Q l
Altefähr 123 G a
Alteia 39 I i
Altena (Wilmington) 192 ins.
Altenburg, in Hungary 72 D b
Altenburg, in Thuringia 72 C a
Altenburg, mon. in Austria 95 F b
Altenkirchen 134 D c
Altenstadt 143 I h
Altensteig 143 G h
Altensteig, lordship 143 G h
Altenzaun 154 F b
Altenzella, mon., near Würzburg 95 D b
Altenzelle, mon., near Meissen 85 G e
Alternus River 27 H e
Altheim, Hohen- 62 F d
Altinum 27 G b
Altis, loc. in Olympia
Alt-Lussheim 142 C b
Altmark, reg. 79 G b
Altmühl River 62 F d
Altomünster, mon. 95 E b
Alton, in England 127 Y o
Alton, in Illinois 211 G c
Alton, parl. bor.
Altona 122 E b
Altorf (Altdorf), in Switzerland 150 E c
Alt-Ötting 123 G d
Altötting, mon. 95 E b
Altranstädt 135 G c
Altshausen 143 I j
Altsohl 159 J d
Aluta River 73 E a
Alutus River (Aluta R.) 39 M l
Alvarado 213 ins.
Alvarado, route of 105 B c
Alvaro de Saavedra, route of 110 I f
Alvona 27 I b
Alwar 137 C c

Alyzia 10 B d
Amadeus, lake 172 C c
Amalekites, people 7 ins. C
Amalfi 64 B b
Amalfi, abp. 95 E c
Amalphis, see Amalfi
Amanus Mountains 20 G d
Amapuemecan
Amardi, people 19 H c
Amardians, people 8 D b
Amasea 35 L e
Amaserah 93 D b
Amasia 20 F b
Amastra 59 K e
Amastris 47 M e
Amatha 6 D c
Amathus, in Cyprus 20 E e
Amathus, in Peræa 7 D d
Amaya 82 H e
Amazonas, state 214 C c
Amazon River 214 D c
Amba Alaji, mt. 174 G c
Ambacia, see Amboise
Ambala 137 C b
Ambarri, people 38 C c
Ambato 214 B c
Amberg 122 F d
Ambérieu 130 N i
Ambert 76 E d
Ambiani or Ambianis, see Amiens
Amboise 69 H g
Amboyna, isl. 112 F d
Ambracia (Arta) 10 C c
Ambracia, state 13 B b
Ambracian Gulf (Gulf of Arta) 10 B d
Ambracus 10 B c
Ambras, castle 122 F e
Ambrières 65 F f
Ambrysus 11 D d
Ameland, isl. 117 D a
Amelia Island 207 I d
Ameria 27 G e
America, name on Waldseemüller map 108 K j
America, Central, reg. 213 D c
America, North, continent 186, 187
America, South, continent 214, 215
Amersfœrt 189 ins. C
Amersfoort 117 D b
Amersham, parl. bor. 163 N f (Am.)
Amesbury 127 X o
Amesbury, mon. 97 P j
Amestratus 30 D e
Amhara, reg. 174 G c
Amherstburg 212 I d
Amichel, reg. 191 F f
Amid or Amida (Diarbekr) 4 G c
Amida, abp. 43 K f
Amidas, route of 191 J d
Amiens 46 G d
Amiens, bp. 94 C b
Amiens, cty. 69 I f
Amiens, gen. 147 E b
Amirante Islands 175 I e
Amisia (Ems) River 38 D b
Amisus 20 G b
Amiternum 27 H e
Amjhera
Ammon, reg. 4 F c
Ammonites, people 7 ins. D
Ammonium 18 C e
Amnias River 20 F b
Amol, in Persia
Amol, in Turkestan
Amöneburg 134 E c
Amöneburg, mon. 95 D a
Amorbach 142 D a
Amorbach, mon. 95 D b
Amorgos, isl. 4 C b
Amorgus 13 D c
Amorium 20 D c
Amoy 171 M f
Ampelus, prom. in Chalcidice 11 E c
Ampelus, prom. in Crete 14 ins.
Ampfing 79 H d
Amphaxitis, reg. in Mygdonia 11 D b
Amphaxitis, reg. in Pæonia
Amphia 14 C b
Amphiale, prom. 16 B b
Amphiaræum 16 B a
Amphicæa 11 D d
Amphictionium 16 F e
Amphilochia, reg. 10 C c
Amphipagus, prom. 10 A c
Amphipolis 11 E b
Amphissa 11 D d
Amphitrope 16 C b
Amposta 83 L g
Ampsivarii, people 38 D b
Amritsar 137 B b
Amselfeld, battle 93 B b
Amsteg 91 Q l
Amsterdam 117 C b
Amsterdam, Hanse. cy. 99 ins. B
Amsterdam, Fort (New York) 189 ins. C
Amsterdam, New, in Dutch Guiana 214 D b
Amsterdam, New (New York) 189 ins. C
Amu-Daria River
Amur District 171 N c
Amur River
Amyclæ 14 C b
Amygdolon, Pool of 6 ins. A (6)
Amyrus 11 D c
Amyrus River 11 D c
Anab 7 B f
Anacæa 16 B a
Anactorium 10 B d
Anæa 17 E c
Anagni 90 D d
Anagni, bp. 95 E c
Anagnia (Anagni) 30 C a
Anagyrus 16 B b
Anah 99 L g
Anahuac, Plateau of 106 C a
Anam
Anamari, people 26 D c
Anamis River 19 I e
Anaphe, isl. 13 D c
Anaphlystus 15 D b
Anapus River, in Acarnania 10 C d
Anapus River, in Sicily 30 E e
Anas (Guadiana) River 38 A e
Anathoth 7 C e
Anatolia, reg. 99 I f
Anatolic Theme 59 K f
Anaua 20 C d
Anauni, people 26 E a
Anaunium 26 E a
Anazarbus 43 J f
Anbar 99 L g
Ancenis 84 C f
Anchedive Island
Anchesmus, mt. 16 B a
Anchialus 43 H e
Ancón 214 B d
Ancona 27 H d
Ancona, bp. 95 E c
Ancona, march 72 C c
Ancúd, San Carlos de 215 B g
Ancyra, in Galatia 20 E c
Ancyra, in Mysia 20 C c
Andaca 19 L d
Andagoya, route of 108 J g
Andahan
Andalos, reg. 53 B b
Andalusia, reg. 83 J h
Andaman Islands 103 J f
Andania 14 C b
Andaraba
Andecavi, see Angers
Andecavi, people 38 B c
Andechs, castle 72 C b
Andechs, mon. 95 E b
Andegavis, see Angers
Andelfingen, castle 91 Q k
Andelaus, see Andelot
Andelot 53 N h
Andelys 69 H f
Andematunnum 39 H j
Andenne 117 D d
Anderida or Anderidæ (Pevensey) 51 Q i
Anderitum, see Javols
Andermatt 150 E c
Andernach 62 D c
Andersonville 208 D c
Andes 26 E b
Andes Mountains 214 B bg
Andijan
Andlau, mon. 148 C b
Andorra 82 C a
Andover, in Mass. 189 C c
Andover, deanery, in England 100 A a
Andover, mon. 100 A a
Andover, parl. bor. 163 M f (And.)
Andoverpis, see Antwerp
Andros 15 E b
Andros, isl., Cyclades 15 E b
Andros Islands, Bahama Is. 213 E b
Androscoggin River 189 C b
Andrussov 138 D e
Andújar 82 B d
Andwell, mon. 100 B a
Anemas, Prison of 93 G e (9)
Anemo River 27 F c
Anemoria 11 D d
Anemurium, prom. 20 E d
Angara River
Angele 16 B b
Angerburg 155 K a
Angeriacus, see Saint Jean-d'Angély
Angermünde 85 D b
Angers 61 C c
Angers, bp. 94 B b
Angers, univ. 100 E e
Anghiari 90 M j
Angites River 11 E b
Angles, people, in Britain 51 R k
Angles, people, in Holstein 38 D b
Angles, people, about 900 57 E c
Anglesey, isl. 49 D e
Anglesey, cty. 127 U m
Anglesey, parl. dist. 163 J d
Anglo-Egyptian Sudan, reg. 174 F c
Anglo-Saxon kingdom, about 1000
Anglo-Saxon kingdoms, about 814 54 D c
Angol 215 B f
Angola, dist. 175 E e
Angora 55 K f
Angostura 214 C b
Angoulême 61 D d
Angoulême, bp. 94 C b
Angoulême, cty. 69 D d
Angoumois, cty. 61 C d
Angoumois, prov. 148 D e
Angra das Voltas 108 S j
Angra Pequena, bay 175 E g
Angria, reg. 62 E b
Angrians, people 55 Q i
Angrivarii, people 39 J g
Anguilla, isl. 213 F c
Angus, cty.
Angus, reg.
Anhalt, castle 71 S j
Anhalt, princ. 79 G c
Anhausen, mon. 143 J h
Anholt 117 E c
Ani 67 O e
Aniane, mon. 94 C c
Anicium, see Le Puy
Aniene River 96 B b
Anio River 27 G f
Anio novus, aqueduct 35 ins. B
Anisus River, see Enns River
Anjou, cty. 61 C c
Anjou, duchy 78 B e
Anjou, gouv. 146 A b
Anjou, prov. 148 D e
Anklam 87 I b
Anklam, Hanse. cy. 99 ins. B

Ann, Cape 189 C c
Annaburg, castle 115 ins. B
Annandale, reg.
Annapolis, in Maryland 192 C d
Annapolis, in Nova Scotia 212 I d
Anne, Fort 192 E b
Anne Arundel Town 192 C d
Annecy 130 O i
Anneianum, in Etruria 27 F d
Anneianum, in Venetia 27 F b
Annobon, isl. 175 D e
Anopæa Mountains 16 F e
Ansbach 114 F d
Ansbach, princ. 114 F d
Anserma 214 B b
Antaki
Antananarivo 175 H f
Antandrus
Antaradus 20 F e
Antelope Hills 190 E d
Antemnæ 35 ins. B
Antequera 82 B b
Anthedon, in Bœotia 11 E d
Anthedon, in Philistæa 7 A e
Anthela 16 F e
Anthemus 11 E b
Anthemus, reg. 11 E b
Anthemusias 35 L f
Anthena 15 C b
Antian Way, road 35 ins. B
Antibes 126 E e
Anticosti, isl. 186 M d
Anticyra, in Locris Ozolis 10 D d
Anticyra, in Malis 11 D d
Anticyra, in Phocis 11 D d
Antietam, battle 208 ins.
Antietam River 208 ins.
Antigonia, in Arcadia 14 C b
Antigonia, in Chalcidice 11 E b
Antigonia, in Epirus 10 A b
Antigua, isl. 105 H c
Antigua, Rio de la, river 106 D a
Anti-Lebanon Mountains 6 E a
Antinoë 43 I h
Antinum 27 H f
Antioch, in Phrygia 20 D c
Antioch, in Syria 20 G d
Antioch, patr. 52 L f
Antioch, princ. about 1140 68 C b
Antioch, princ. about 1190 71 N f
Antioch, theme 59 L f
Antiochia, in Asia Minor 43 I f
Antiochia, in Margiana 19 J c
Antioquia 214 B b
Antipatria 10 A b
Antipatris 7 B d
Antipodes Islands 179 I l
Antipolis 26 B d
Antirrhium, prom. 10 C d
Antirrhodus, isl. 34 ins. C (2)
Antissa 13 D b
Antitaurus Mountains 20 I c
Antium 30 B a
Antivari 164 B b
Antivari, abp. 95 F c
Antofagasta 215 B e
Antonine, Wall of 51 O g
Antoninus Pius, Column of 22 A
Antonius, Temple of 24 B (19)
Antrim, cty. 127 K f
Antron 11 E d
Antunnacum 39 I h
Antwerp 117 C c
Antwerp, Hanse. for. cy. 99 ins. B
Antwerp, marg. 117 C c
Anuu, isl. 199 ins. D
Anvik 198 ins. A
Anxa 31 G b
Anxanum 27 I e
Anxia 30 E b
Anxur (Terracina) 30 C a
Anydrus, mt. 16 B b
Anzican, reg. 109 S h
Aomori 171 P d
Aornus, in Bactria 19 K c
Aornus, in India 19 L d
Aorsi, people 35 N d
Aosta 90 A b
Aosta bp. 95 D b
Aous mt. 20 E e
Aous River 10 A b
Apache, Ind. Res. 188 E d
Apaches, tribe 188 D c
Apalachee 191 I e
Apalachee Bay 191 I f
Apalachicola River 193 B f
Apamea, in Osrhoëne 20 G d
Apamea, in Syria 20 G e
Apamea Cibotus 20 D c
Aparri 199 ins. H
Apenestae 31 F a
Apennines, mts. 2 F d
Aperanti, people 10 C d
Aperantia 10 C d
Aperopia (Doko), isl. 15 D b
Aphek
Aphetæ 11 E c
Aphidnæ 16 B a
Aphnitis Lake
Aphrodisias 43 H f
Aphrodisium 16 D c (4)
Aphytis 11 E b
Apia 172 H b
Apidanus River 10 D c
Apo, mt. 199 ins. H
Apodoti, people 10 C d
Apollo, Cave of 23 C
Apollo, Temple of 24 A
Apollon, Allée d' 149 A
Apollonia, in Illyricum 31 I b
Apollonia, in Mysia
Apollonia, in Palestine 7 B d
Apollonia, in Pieria 11 F b
Apollonia, in Sicily 30 D d
Apollonia, in Thrace 12 I b
Apollonia Chalcidice 11 E b
Apollonia Mygdonia 11 E b
Aponus 26 F b
Apostles, Church of the 93 G e
Appalachian Highland 187 K e
Appenweier 142 A c
Appenzell 91 R k
Appenzell, canton 91 R k
Appian Aqueduct 35 ins. B (3)
Appian Gate 22 A
Appian Way, road 30 B a
Appian Way, Old, road 35 ins. B
Appleby 127 W l
Appleby, dist. 84 B b
Appomattox Court House 208 E b
Appomattox River 193 E c
Appuldurcombe, mon. 100 A b
Apsinthii, people
Apsorus 27 I c
Apsorus, isl. 27 I c
Apsus 31 I b
Apsus River 10 A b
Apt, bp. 95 D c
Apta or Apta Iulia, see Apt
Apuani, people 26 D c
Apulia, cty. 64 C b
Apulia, duchy 70 I e
Apulia, reg. 30 E a
Apulia and Calabria, Aug. Reg. 38 F d (2)
Apulia and Calabria, prov. 42 F e (5)
Apulum 35 I d
Apure River 214 C b
Apurimac River 111 C d
Aquæ, see Aquæ Sextiæ
Aquæ, see Dax
Aquæ 39 J j
Aquæ Albulæ 35 ins. B
Aquæ Apollinares 35 ins. B
Aquæ Aureliæ 39 J i
Aquæ Bormiæ 26 E a
Aquæ Cutiliæ 27 G e
Aquæ Grani or Aquæ Granni, see Aix-la-Chapelle
Aquæ Mattiacæ 39 J h
Aquæ Pisanæ 26 E d
Aquæ Populoniæ 26 E d
Aquæ Sextiæ (Aix) 38 D d
Aquæ Solis or Aquæ Sulis (Bath) 51 O i
Aquæ Statiellæ 26 C c
Aquæ Volaterranæ 26 E d
Aquia Creek 208 E b (A. Cr.)
Aquidaban River 215 D e
Aquidneck Island 189 ins. A
Aquila 90 D c
Aquileia, in Germany 39 J i
Aquileia, in Venetia 27 H b
Aquileia, abp. 95 E b
Aquileia, march 64 B a
Aquileia, patr. 79 H e
Aquilonia, in E. Samnium
Aquilonia, in W. Samnium
Aquilo River 30 E a
Aquincum (Budapest) 38 F c
Aquino, bp. 95 E c
Aquis, see Aquæ Sextiæ (Aix)
Aquis, see Dax
Aquis Granum, see Aix-la-Chapelle
Aquitaine, duchy, 11 cent. 61 C c d
Aquitaine, duchy, 14 cent. 77 D d
Aquitaine, reg., about 814 54 E d
Aquitaine (Aquitania), Rom. prov. 38 C c (5)
Aquitaine I, Rom. prov. 42 C d (10)
Aquitaine II, Rom. prov. 42 B d (11)
Aquitania (Aquitaine), Rom. prov. 38 C c (5)
Aquitania Propria, reg. 38 B d
Arabah Valley 7 D e
Arabia, Rom. prov. 43 Y g (15)
Arabia, pen. 170 F f
Arabia, Rom. prov. 35 K g
Arabia, reg. 53 G d
Arabia, table land 3 I f
Arabia Deserta, reg. 20 H f
Arabian Desert, in Egypt 150 B b
Arabian Sea
Arabii, people 19 K e
Arabius River 19 K e
Arab raids, 9 cent. 45 G d
Arabs, people, in Arabia 4 G d
Arabs, people, in North Africa 45 D I-f
Arabs, people, in Sicily 45 G e
Arabs, people, in S. France 45 EF d
Arabs, people, in Spain, 711 45 D e
Arabs, people, in Spain, about 900 57 B f
Aracajú 214 F d
Aracan 136 N c
Aracan, reg. 112 C a
Aracaty 214 F c
Arachnæus, mt. 15 C b
Arachosia, prov. 19 K d
Arachosia, satr. 18 R h
Arachotus 8 E b
Arachotus River 19 K d
Arachthus River 10 C c
Aracynthus, mt. 10 C d
Arad, in Hungary 77 I c
Arad, in Palestine 7 C f
Arad, reg. 53 G b
Araden 14 ins.
Aradus 12 K d
Aræ Flaviæ 39 J i
Aræthyrea 14 C b
Arafura Sea 172 C a
Aragon, km., 12 cent. 82 H e
Aragon, km., 13—15 cent. 83 L g
Aragon, distr. 82 H e
Araguaya River 214 E c
Arakan, reg. 92 J e
Aral Sea 3 J d
Aramæans, people 7 ins. D
Ara Maxima 24 A
Aran Islands 127 H h
Arantia 14 C b
Arapahoes, tribe 188 E b
Araphen 15 E a

Ararat, mt. 3 I e
Arar River 38 C c
Araris River, see Aar or Aare River
Aras River 73 J c
Araucanians, people 215 B f
Araure 214 C b
Arausio or Arausione (Orange) 38 D d
Aravalli Hills 137 B c
Araxes River, in Armenia 5 D b
Araxes River, in Mesopotamia 20 I e
Araxes River, in Persis 19 H d
Araxus prom. 14 B a
Arba, isl. 27 I c
Arbe, bp. 95 E c
Arbela 4 G c
Arbela, abp. 43 K f
Arboga 88 F b
Arbor Felix 39 J j
Arc 81 N h
Arcadia, Rom. prov. 43 I h (5)
Arcadia, reg. 14 C b
Arcadia, state 13 B c
Arcadius, Column of 93 G e (13)
Archangel 138 F c
Archas 68 C c
Archelaïs (Akserai), in Cappadocia 20 F c
Archelaïs, in Palestine 7 C d
Archers Hope 103 ins. A (Arch.)
Archidona 82 B b
Arcis-sur-Aube 154 C d
Arcole 150 F d
Arcos 82 A b
Arcot 137 C f
Arctic Ocean 2 E a
Arctic Plateau 186 H b
Ardabil 92 E d
Ardagh, bp. 97 D c
Ardea 30 B a
Ardea Gate 22 A
Ardèche, dept. 148 E f
Arden, forest 49 F e
Ardenne, mon. 94 B b
Ardennes, dept. 148 E e
Ardennes, mts. 62 C d
Ardettus, mt. 23 D
Ardfert, bp. 97 B d
Ardmore 210 F d
Ardstraw, bp. 97 D b
Arduenna Forest 39 H i
Arebrigium 26 B b
Arecibo 199 ins. G
Arelate 38 C d
Arelate (Arles), km. 62 D f
Aremberg, dist. 151 H f
Aremorica, reg. 38 B c
Arenacum 39 H f
Arenas, Punta, in Chile 215 B l
Arenas, Punta, in Costa Rica 213 D d
Arendal 130 E b
Arenenberg, castle 158 E e
Arensburg 119 I b
Areopagus (Mars Hill)
Areopolis 7 D f
Arequipa 214 B d
Arethon River 10 C c
Arethusa 11 E b
Arevaci, people 38 B d
Arezzo 90 L j
Arezzo, bp. 95 E c
Arezzo, univ. 100 H f (Ar.)
Argæus, mt. 20 F c
Argall's Town 193 ins. A
Argen River 143 I j
Argen River, Lower 143 I j
Argen River, Upper 143 I j
Argentan 76 C b
Argentarius, mt. 27 F e
Argenteus River 26 A d
Argentina, see Argentoratum (Strasburg)
Argentina, or the Argentine Republic, cty. 215 C e f
Argenton 126 B c
Argentoratum (Strasburg) 39 I i
Argiletum, street 22 A
Argilus 11 E b
Arginussæ Islands 17 E b
Argithea 10 C c
Argob, reg.
Argolic Gulf 4 B b
Argolis, reg. 15 C b
Argonauts, Portico of the 22 A
Argonnes, mts. 134 C d
Argos 14 C b
Argos Amphilochicum 10 C d
Argos Oresticum 10 C b
Argous Portus 26 E e
Arguin, isl.
Argun Islands 108 P e
Argun River 92 L b
Argura 11 D c
Argyle, bp. in Scotland
Argyle, cty.
Argyle, dist.
Argyle, Fort 193 ins. C
Argyrus (Argyrokastron) 10 B b
Aria, prov. 19 J d
Aria, reg. 8 E b
Aria, satr. 18 R h
Arialbinnum, see Basel
Ariana, reg. 19 H d
Ariano, bp. 95 F c
Arica 214 B d
Aricia 30 B a
Arid, Cape 172 A d
Ariège, dept. 148 E f
Arikaras, tribe 188 G b
Arilica 26 E b
Arimathea 7 C d
Ariminum 27 G c
Ariminus River 27 G c
Ariola 39 H i
Ariolica, in Gaul 39 I j
Ariolica, in Italy 26 B b
Arisbe
Arispe 190 C e
Aristonautæ 14 C a
Arius, lake 19 J d
Arius River 19 J d
Arivaca 190 C e
Arizona, ter. 203 P h
Arkansas, Fort 191 G e
Arkansas, tribe 188 G c
Arkansas, state 202 G h
Arkansas, ter. 1819 203 S c
Arkansas, ter. 1824 203 T d
Arkansas Post 199 G d
Arkansas Post, battle 208 B c
Arkansas River 190 E d
Arklow
Arkona 63 G a
Arles 61 F e
Arles, abp. 94 C c
Arles, km., about 1035 61 F d
Arles, km., 13 cent. 72 B b
Arlon 117 D e
Armagh
Armagh, abp. 97 D c
Armagh, cty. 127 K g
Armagnac, cty. 12 cent. 69 C e (Arm.)
Armagnac, cty. 14 cent. 76 D e
Armagnac, cty. 17 cent. 126 B e
Armagnac, dist. 81 M i
Armavir, Armavira 20 J b
Armenia, km., about 1140 68 C b
Armenia, km., 13 cent.
Armenia, km., 14 cent.
Armenia, reg., about 600 B. C. 8 C b
Armenia, reg., about 750 53 G c
Armenia, reg., about 1097 67 O f
Armenia, satr. 8 I e
Armenia I, Rom. prov. 43 J f (10)
Armenia II, Rom. prov. 43 J f (11)
Armenia, Great, reg. 99 L e
Armenia, Lesser, reg. in Cilicia 99 J f
Armenia, Lesser, reg. in Pontus 35 L f
Armenia minor, reg. 20 H c
Armeniac Theme 59 L e
Armenian Highlands 3 I d
Armenians, people
Armenta River 27 F e
Armentières 117 A d
Armstrong, Fort, in Illinois 211 G b
Armstrong, Fort, in Pa. 195 B c
Arnay-le-Duc 126 D c
Arne 10 D c
Arneburg 63 F b
Arnheim 117 D b
Arnhem, Hanse. cy. 99 ins. B
Arnhem Land, reg. 172 C b
Arnissa, in Illyricum 31 I b
Arnissa, in Macedonia 10 C b
Arno River 90 L j
Arnon River 7 D f
Arnsberg 62 D c
Arnshaugk 85 F e
Arnstadt 62 F c
Arnus (Arno) River 26 E d
Aro River 27 G f
Aroania, mt. 14 C b
Aroanius River 14 C b
Arœ 14 B a
Arœr, in Idumæa 7 C f
Arœr, in Peræa 7 D f
Arogas River 31 F c
Arolla 91 P l
Arolsen 154 E c
Arona 90 I h
Arouaise, mon. 94 C a
Arpad (Tel-Erfâd)
Arpi 30 E a
Arpinum (Arpino) 30 C a
Arquebuse 149 B
Arquennes 156 A a
Arques, castle 76 D b
Arrabo River, see Raab River
Arrabona 38 F c
Arran, isl.
Arras 117 A d
Arras, bp. 94 C a
Arraticum, see Arras
Arretium (Arezzo) 27 F d
Arru Islands 172 C a
Arsacids, Kingdom of the, about 200 B. C. 19 X k
Arsacids, Kingdom of the, about 90 B. C. 33 N f
Arsamosata 20 H c
Arsanias River 20 I c
Arsia (Arsa) River 27 I b
Arsian Forest 35 ins. B
Arsinoë, in Cyrenaica 34 H g
Arsinoë, on L. Mœris 4 ins.
Arsinoë, on the Red Sea 35 K g
Arsissa Lake 20 J c
Arsuf 68 ins. A
Arta 73 E c
Artabri, people 38 A d
Artacana 19 H d
Artace
Artacoana 19 J d
Artaki 165 E c
Artasium 68 C b
Artaxata 20 K c
Artemis, Temple of 31 ins. B (3)
Artemis Agrotera, temple 23 D
Artemis Brauronia, temple 23 C (3)
Artemisium, prom. 11 E c
Artemisius, mt. 14 C b
Artemita 35 M g
Artemita, isl. 10 C d
Artena 35 ins. B
Artlenburg 122 F b
Artois, cty. 14 cent. 76 E a
Artois, cty. 16 cent. 117 A d
Artois, gouv. 146 B a
Artois, prov. 148 E d
Artynia Lake
Aruba, isl. 214 C a
Arundel 127 Y p

Arundel, castle . . . . 65 F e
Arundel, mon. . . . . 74 E f
Arundel, parl. bor. . . . . 163 N g
Arupium . . . . 27 J c
Arurius (Aar or Aare) River . 39 I j
Arvad . . . . 4 F c
Arverni, see Clermont-Ferrand
Arverni, people . . . . 38 C c
Arx (citadel) on Capitoline Mt. 24 A
Arx (citadel) on the Janiculum 22 A
Arx Regia, in Tyre . . . . 18 ins. B
Asabara . . . . 7 D e
Asalmanus Mountains . . . . . . 6 F c
Asamon Mountains . . . . 6 C c
Asbach, mon. . . . . 95 E b
Ascalon . . . .
Ascania Lake . . . .
Ascanian Domains . . . . 71 ins.
Ascension Island . . . . 108 P h
Aschaffenburg . . . . 86 G d
Aschaffenburg, princ. . . . . . . 151 K j (A)
Aschersleben, Hanse. cy. . . . . 99 ins. B
Asciburgium . . . . 39 I h
Asciburgius Mountains . . . . . 38 F b
Asclepieum . . . . 23 C
Ascoli Piceno . . . . 64 B b
Ascoli Piceno, bp. . . . . 95 E c
Ascoli Satriano . . . . 64 C b
Ascoli Satriano, bp. . . . . 95 F c
Ascordus River . . . . 11 D b
Ascra . . . . 11 E d
Asculum (Ascoli Piceno) . . . . 27 H e
Ascuris . . . . 11 D c
Asea . . . . 14 C b
Ashanti, reg. . . . . 174 C d
Ashburton, parl. bor . . . . 163 K g
Ashburton River . . . . 172 A c
Ashby de la Zouch . . . . 127 X n
Ashdod . . . . 7 B e
Ashdown . . . .
Asher . . . . 7 C d
Asher, tribe . . . . 7 ins. D
Asheville . . . . 211 I c
Ashland . . . . 210 A b
Ashley River . . . . 193 ins. C
Ashley-Henry Post . . . . 210 D a
Ashley's Post . . . . 210 C c
Ashtabula . . . . 206 ins.
Ashtaroth-Karnaim . . . . 6 E c
Ashton, parl. bor . . . . 163 L d
Ashurada . . . . 170 G e
Asia, continent 170, 171
Asia, Rom. dioc. . . . . 43 I f
Asia, East Rom. prov. . . . . . . 43 H f
Asia, Rom. prov. . . . . 35 J f
Asia Minor, reg. 20
Asia Minor, table-land . . . . . 3 H e
Asiana, reg. . . . . 50 I e
Asinarian Gate . . . . 22 A
Asine, in Argolis . . . . 15 C b
Asine, in Messenia . . . . 14 B c
Asines River . . . . 30 E e
Asir, reg. . . . . 170 F g
Asisium . . . . 27 G d
Askabad . . . .
Asmak River . . . .
Asmara . . . . 174 G c
Asmonæan Palace . . . . 6 ins. A
Asola . . . . 90 J h
Asopus . . . . 15 C c
Asopus River, in Bœotia . . . . 11 E d
Asopus River, in Corinth . . . 14 C b
Asopus River, in Malis . . . . . 14 D d
Aspadana (Ispahan) . . . . 19 H d
Aspara . . . .
Aspern . . . . 155 I d
Aspinwall . . . .
Aspisii, people . . . . 19 J a
Aspledon . . . . 11 D d
Aspona . . . .
Aspromonte, mt. . . . . 161 K h
Assa . . . . 11 E b
Assab . . . . 174 H c
Assaba . . . . 174 D d
Assaceni, people . . . . 19 L d
Assalt . . . . 68 ins. A
Assam, prov. . . . . 171 K f
Assam, reg. . . . . 92 J e
Assandun . . . . 64 E e
Assassins, sect, in Persia . . . . 92 F d
Assassins, sect, in Syria . . . . 68 C b
Assaye . . . . 137 C d
Assen . . . . 117 E a
Assenisipia, proposed state in U. S. . . . . 196 B b
Assens . . . . 88 D d
Assera . . . . 11 E b
Asseria . . . . 27 J c
Asseritis, reg. . . . . 11 E b
Assinaboins, tribe . . . . 188 F a
Assinarus River . . . . 30 E e
Assiniboia, prov. . . . . 212 E c
Assiniboine River . . . .
Assisi . . . . 90 D c
Assisi, bp. . . . . 95 E c
Assisium, see Assisi
Assorus . . . . 30 D e
Assuan . . . . 174 G b
Assur . . . . 4 G c
Assus . . . .
Assyria, prov. . . . . 18 F c
Assyria, reg. . . . . 8 C b
Assyria, satr. . . . . 8 I e
Assyrian Empire 5
Asta, see Asti
Astacus, in Acarnania . . . . . . 10 C d
Astacus, in Bithynia . . . . . . 9 E c
Astacus, bay of . . . . 9 E c
Astæ, people . . . . 9 D b
Astapa . . . . 38 B e
Astarac, cty. . . . . 76 D e
Astauene, reg. . . . . 19 I c
Asteris, isl. . . . . 10 B d
Asthala, isl. . . . . 19 J d
Asti . . . . 90 I h
Asti, bp. . . . . 95 D b
Aston Manor . . . . 162 E e
Astorga . . . . 82 A a
Astorga, abp. . . . . 42 A e
Astorga, bp. . . . . 94 A c
Astoria . . . . 198 A a
Astrabad . . . .
Astrabad, reg. . . . . 139 H h
Astrakhan . . . . 139 G f
Astrakhan, Khanate of . . . . . . 139 F f
Astroni, crater . . . . 31 ins. A
Astura . . . . 30 B a
Astures, people . . . . 38 A d
Asturias, cty. . . . . 82 A a
Asturias, Kingdom of . . . . . . 54 C e
Asturias, princ. . . . . 83 D c
Asturias, reg. . . . . 58 C e
Austurica Augusta (Astorga) . . 38 A d
Astypalæa, isl. . . . . 13 E c
Astypalæa, prom. . . . . 16 B b
Astyra . . . .
Asunción . . . . 215 D e
Asylum . . . . 24 A
Atabeks, Dom. of the . . . . . . 68 C c
Atabeks, Ildijiz, dom. . . . . . . 71 P f
Atabeks, Zengid, dom. . . . . . . 71 O f
Atabeks of Irbil, dom. . . . . . . 71 O f
Atacama, Desert of . . . . 215 C e
Atacama, reg. . . . . 108 K j
Atalante . . . . 11 D a
Atalante, isl. near Locris Opuntia 11 E d
Atalante, isl. near Salamis . . . 16 B b
Atalia . . . . 26 D e
Atapuerca . . . . 83 E c
Atarneus . . . .
Ataroth . . . . 7 D e
Atbara River . . . . 174 G c
Atchison . . . . 210 F c
Atella, in Basilicata . . . . 90 E d
Atella, in Campania . . . . 30 D b
Aternum (Pescara) . . . . 27 I e
Aternus (Pescara) River . . . . 27 H e
Ateste (Este) . . . . 26 F b
Ath . . . . 117 B d
Athabaska, lake . . . . 186 H c
Athabaska, prov. . . . . 212 D c
Athabaska River . . . . 186 H c
Athamania, reg. . . . . 10 C c
Athelney
Athelney, mon. . . . . 97 O j
Athena . . . . 20 I b
Athena, Temple of, in Athens . 23 C (1)
Athenæ . . . . 16 B b
Athenæ Diades . . . . 11 E d
Athenæum, in Arcadia . . . . . 14 C b
Athenæum, in Epirus . . . . . . 10 C c
Athene, Temple of, in Syracuse 31 ins. B (2)
Athene Promachos, monument . 23 C (5)
Athenian Empire 13
Athenopolis . . . . 26 A d
Athens, in Attica . . . . 15 D b
Athens, bp. . . . . 43 G f
Athens, duchy, 13 cent. . . . . . 73 E c
Athens, duchy, 15 cent. . . . . . 93 B c
Athens, plan of ancient . . . . . 23 D
Athens, plan of modern . . . . . 23 D
Athesis (Adige) River . . . . . . 26 E a
Athlone . . . .
Athmonum . . . . 16 B a
Athol, reg. . . . .
Athos, mt. . . . . 11 F b
Athyras River . . . .
Atienza . . . . 82 B a
Atina, in Latium . . . . 30 C a
Atina, in Lucania . . . . 30 E b
Atintania, reg. . . . . 10 B b
Atkinson, Fort . . . . 210 F b
Atlanta . . . . 211 I d
Atlantic and Pacific Railroad Grant . . . . 210 C c
Atlantic Ocean . . . . 108 Nc-Pk
Atlantic Plain . . . . 187 K e
Atlas Mountains . . . . 2 D e
Atmeidan . . . . 93 G e
Atoyac River . . . .
Atrans . . . . 27 I a
Atrato River . . . . 105 E e
Atrax . . . . 11 D c
Atrebates or Atrebatis, see Arras
Atrebates, people, in Britain . . 51 P i
Atrebates, people, in Gaul . . . 38 C b
Atrectian Alps, mts. . . . . 26 B b
Atri . . . . 90 D c
Atri, bp. . . . . 95 E c
Atria . . . . 26 F b
Atropatene, Media, reg. . . . . . 35 N f
Atropatene, Media, satr. . . . . . 18 P h
Attalea . . . . 59 K f
Attalia . . . . 20 D d
Attalids, Kingdom of the . . . . 33 legend
Attalus, Stoa of . . . . 23 D
Attamok . . . . 198 ins. A
Attica, reg. 16
Attidium . . . . 27 G d
Attila, Empire of . . . . 48 F L b
Attilla, Palace of . . . . 48 I c
Attinghausen . . . . 91 Q l
Attium, prom. . . . . 26 C e
Attock . . . . 137 B b
Atur or Aturius (Adour) River . 38 B d
Atwood Cay . . . . 105 F b
Aube, dept. . . . . 148 E e
Aube River . . . . 69 I f
Aubenas . . . . 126 D d
Aubeterre, mon. . . . . 94 B b
Aubusson . . . . 76 E d
Auch . . . . 61 D e
Auch, abp. . . . . 94 B c
Auch, gen. . . . . 147 D c
Auchi-les-Moines, mon . . . . . 94 C a
Auckland . . . . 172 G d
Aude, dept. . . . . 148 E f
Aude River . . . . 126 C e
Audincourt . . . . 143 ins. F
Auerstädt . . . . 154 F c
Aufidena, in Apulia . . . . 31 F a
Aufidena, in Samnium . . . . . . 31 D a

Aufidus, Bridge of . . . . 30 E a
Aufidus (Ofanto) River . . . . . 31 F a
Aufinum. . . . . 27 H e
Aughrim . . . . 127 I h
Augila . . . . 18 B e
Augsburg . . . . 62 F d
Augsburg, bp. . . . . 79 G e
Augsburg, imp. city . . . . 79 G d
Augusta, in Cilicia . . . . 20 F d
Augusta, in Maine . . . . 211 L b
Augusta, in Sicily . . . . 131 G f
Augusta, in S. C. . . . . 196 C d
Augusta, Asturica (Astorga) . . 38 A d
Augusta, Bracara (Braga) . . . . 38 A d
Augusta, Emerita (Mérida) . . . 38 A e
Augusta, Fort, in Georgia . . . 193 D e
Augusta, Fort, in Pa. . . . . . . 192 C c
Augusta Bagiennorum (Bene) . 26 B c
Augusta Prætoria (Aosta). . . . 26 B b
Augusta Rauricorum (Augst). . 39 I j
Augusta Suessionum, see Soissons
Augusta Taurinorum (Turin) . 26 B b
Augusta Treverorum (Trèves) . 39 I i
Augusta Vindelicorum (Augsburg) 38 E c
Augustamnica, Rom. prov. . . . 43 I g (6)
Augustan Canal . . . . 27 G c
Augustanus, Vicus . . . . 35 ins. B
Augusti, Lucus (Luc-en-Die) . 38 D d
Augusti, Lucus (Lugo) . . . . . 38 A d
Augusti, Portus . . . . 27 G f
Augustine Friars, mon. of . . . 75 G g
Augustobona (Troyes) . . . . . . 38 C c
Augustobriga (Talavera la Vieja) 38 B e
Augustodunum (Autun) . . . . . 38 C c
Augustodurum (Bayeux) . . . . 38 B c
Augustonemetum (Clermont-Ferrand) . . . . 38 C c
Augustoritum (Limoges). . . . . 38 C c
Augustowo . . . . 155 L b
Augustus, Arch of . . . .
Augustus, Forum of . . . . 24 B
Augustus, Mausoleum of . . . . 22 A
Augustus,, Naumachia of. . . . 22 A
Augustus, Palace of . . . . 24 B
Augustus, Port of . . . . 35 ins. B
Augustus, Temple of . . . . .
Aujila . . . . 99 H h
Auldearn . . . . 127 Q g
Aulendorf . . . . 143 I j
Aulerci Cenomani, people . . . 38 B c
Aulis. . . . . 11 E d
Aulnay . . . . 76 C c
Aulnay, mon. . . . . 94 B b
Aulon . . . . 31 I b
Aulon, valley in Laconia . . . . 14 C c
Aulon, valley in Macedonia . . 11 E b
Aulon, valley in Palestine . . . 7 D d
Aumale . . . . 76 D b
Aumône, L', mon. . . . . 94 C b
Auneau . . . . 126 B b
Aunis, gouv. . . . . 146 A b
Aunis, prov. . . . . 148 D e
Aurangabad . . . . 137 C e
Auranitis, reg. . . . . 7 E d
Auray . . . . 76 B c
Aureus, Mt. . . . . 26 C e
Aurelian Bridge. . . . . 22 A
Aurelian Gate . . . . 22 A
Aurelian Gate, New . . . . 22 A
Aurelian Wall . . . . 22 A
Aurelian Way, road . . . . 26 E d
Aureliani or Aurelianis (Orléans) 38 C c
Aurelii, Forum . . . . 27 F e
Aureoli, Pons . . . . 26 D b
Aurich . . . . 158 D b
Aurillac . . . . 69 E d
Aurillac, mon. . . . . 94 C c
Aurunci, people. . . . . 30 C a
Ausava . . . . 39 I h
Auscii or Ausciis, see Auch
Ausculum . . . . 30 E a
Ausetani, people . . . . 38 C d
Auser River . . . . 26 E c
Ausonians, people . . . . 29 C d
Aussig . . . . 87 J c
Austerfield . . . . 185 E d
Austerlitz . . . . 155 I d
Austin . . . . 210 F d
Austin, Lake . . . . 172 A c
Austral Islands . . . . 180 M j
Australia, continent 172
Australia, North, reg . . . . . . 172 C b
Australian Alps . . . . 172 D d
Australian Bight, Great . . . . . 172 B d
Austrasia, reg.. . . . . 54 F c
Austria, archduchy . . . . 87 J d
Austria, duchy, 12 cent. . . . . 72 D b
Austria, duchy, 13 cent. . . . . 79 I d
Austria, empire, 1806 . . . . . . 151 M j
Austria, empire, 1812 . . . . . . 155 ins.
Austria, empire, 1815 158–159
Austria, march . . . . 59 H d
Austria, margr. . . . . 63 I d
Austria, Lower, dist. . . . . . . 159 H d
Austria, Upper, dist . . . . 159 H d
Austrian Netherlands, prov. . . 134 B c
Austrian Silesia, dist. . . . . . 135 I c
Ausugum . . . . 27 F a
Autariatæ, people . . . . 39 L l
Auté . . . . 191 I e
Autessiodurum or Autissiodurum, see Auxerre
Autricum (Chartres) . . . . 38 C c
Autrigones, people . . . . 38 B d
Autun . . . . 61 F c
Autun, bp. . . . . 94 C b
Auvergne, cty.. . . . . 61 E d
Auvergne, duchy . . . . 78 C f
Auvergne, gouv. . . . . 146 B b
Auvergne, prov. . . . . 148 E e
Auxerre . . . . 69 E c
Auxerre, bp. . . . . 69 I g
Auxerre, cty.. . . . . 76 E c
Auxerre, dist. . . . . 84 E f
Auximum (Osimo) . . . . 27 H d
Auxonne . . . . 126 D c
Ava . . . . 103 J e
Ava, reg. . . . . 103 J e
Avah . . . . 99 M f
Avallon, Avallone . . . . 76 F c
Avalon Peninsula.. . . . . 212 J d
Avaricum (Bourges) . . . . 38 C c
Avars, people . . . . 54 H d
Avasgians, people . . . . 55 M e
Aveia . . . . 27 H e
Aveiro . . . . 82 A a
Avellino. . . . . 90 E d
Avellino, bp.. . . . . 95 ins.
Avendo . . . . 27 J c
Avenio or Avenione, see Avignon
Avens River . . . . 27 H e
Aventicum (Avenches). . . . . . 39 I j
Aventine, quarter . . . . 96 A
Aventine, Augustan, Region of Rome . . . . 22 A
Aventine Mount. . . . . 22 A
Avenue de Paris, Versailles . . 149 A
Avenue de Saint Cloud, Versailles . . . . 149 A
Avenue de Trianon, Versailles 149 A
Averni, see Clermont, in Auvergne
Avernus Lake . . . . 31 ins. A
Aversa . . . . 90 E d
Aversa, bp. . . . . 95 ins.
Aversa, cty. . . . . 64 B b
Avesica . . . . 27 H b
Avesnes . . . . 69 F a
Avesnes, mon. . . . . 148 B a
Aveyron, dept. . . . . 148 E f
Avezzano . . . . 64 ins.
Avignon . . . . 61 F d
Avignon, bp. . . . . 94 C c
Avignon, papal dom. . . . . . . 78 D f
Avignon, univ. . . . . 100 F f
Avila. . . . . 82 B a
Avila, bp. . . . . 94 B c
Avilés . . . . 82 A a
Aviones, people . . . . 38 D a
Aviz . . . . 94 A d
Avlona . . . . 164 B b
Avola . . . . 90 E f
Avona River . . . . 38 B b
Avon River . . . . 127 W n
Avranches . . . . 61 C b
Avranches, bp. . . . . 94 B b
Avranches, cty. . . . . 69 C b
Axbridge, parl. bor. . . . .
Axel . . . . 117 B c
Axima . . . . 26 A b
Axiupolis . . . . 43 H e
Axius (Vardar) River . . . . . . 11 D b
Axminster. . . . . 127 V p
Axona River, see Aisne River
Axtopolis . . . . 47 L e
Axuenna . . . . 39 H i
Axuenna River, see Aisne River
Ayacucho, battle . . . . 214 B d
Ayamonte . . . . 83 J h
Ayas . . . . 99 K f
Ayerbe . . . . 82 B a
Aylesbury, parl. bor. . . . . 163 N f (Ayl.)
Aylesbury, parl. dist . . . . 163 N f (Ayl.)
Ayllon, route of . . . . 191 J e
Ayotta . . . . 201 H g
Ayr . . . .
Ayr, cty. . . . . 127 P i
Ayr, reg. . . . .
Ayuthia . . . .
Ayutla . . . . 213 C c
Ayyubids, Dominion of the . . 73 H d
Azania, reg. . . . . 14 B b
Azenia. . . . . 16 B b
Azerbijan, reg.. . . . .
Azetium. . . . . 31 F b
Azilia, dist.. . . . . 193 ins. C
Aziris . . . . 18 B d
Azores Islands. . . . . 175 A a
Azorus . . . . 10 D c
Azotus . . . . 7 B e
Azov . . . . 139 E f
Azov, Sea of. . . . . 3 H d
Aztecs, Dominion of the . . . . 107 G e
Azzo Visconti, Dominion of . . 90 I h

Baalbec . . . . 6 E a
Baal Gad . . . . 6 D b
Baar, landgr. . . . . 142 B e
Babadagh . . . . 131 I e
Babahoyo . . . . 214 B c (Ba)
Baba Mahal, reg. . . . .
Bab el Mandeb, strait . . . . . . 170 F g
Babenberg, see Bamberg . . . . 62 F d
Babuyan Islands . . . . 171 N g
Babylon . . . . 4 G c
Babylonia, prov.. . . . . 18 G d
Babylonia, reg. . . . . 8 C b
Babylonia, satr. . . . . 8 I e
Bacallaos, Tierra de los. . . . . 108 L c
Bacanore . . . .
Bacca . . . . 77 L e
Bacenis Forest. . . . . 39 J h
Backnang . . . . 143 H h
Back's River . . . . 212 E b
Bac-ninh . . . . 171 L f
Bacolor . . . . 199 ins. H
Bacs, reg. . . . .
Baotra . . . . 8 E b
Bactria, prov. . . . . 19 K c
Bactria, reg. . . . . 8 E b
Bactria, satr. . . . . 8 K e
Bactrians, Kingdom of the . . . 19 Y k
Badajóz . . . . 83 D d
Badajóz, bp. . . . . 94 A d
Badajóz, emir. . . . . 83 D d
Badakshan, reg. . . . .
Baddesley, preceptory . . . . . . 100 A b
Baden, in Baden . . . . 142 B c
Baden, in Switzerland . . . . . . 91 Q k
Baden, near Vienna . . . . 79 J c
Baden, castle. . . . . 62 E d
Baden, elect. . . . . 151 H g

Baden, gr. duchy . . . 151 K j
Baden, margr. . . . 86 G d
Badenoch, reg. . . .
Badenweiler . . . 142 A e
Badenweiler, lordship . . . 142 A e
Badiæ . . . 46 H g
Bæbiani . . . 30 D a
Bæcula . . . 38 B e
Bæterræ, see Béziers
Bætica, West Rom. prov. . . . 42 A f (1)
Bætica, Farther, senat. prov. . . . 34 C f
Bætica (Farther Spain) Augustan prov. . . . 38 A e (3)
Bætica, Hither, senat. prov. . . . 34 D f
Bætis River (Guadalquivir) . . . 38 A e
Bæto . . . 38 A e
Bæza . . . 82 B b
Baffin Bay . . . 186 L a
Baffin Land . . . 186 L a
Bafulabe . . . 174 B c
Bagæ . . . 42 D f
Bagamoyo . . . 175 G e
Bagdad . . . 53 G c
Bagdad, calif. . . . 73 I d
Bagé, in Brazil . . . 215 D f
Bagé, in France . . . 130 M h
Bagienni, people . . . 26 B c
Bagirmi, reg. . . . 174 E c
Bagistana (Behistun) . . .
Bagno di Romagna . . . 90 M j
Bagnolo . . . 90 J h
Bagnorea, bp. . . . 95 E c
Bagradas River . . . 38 D e
Bahama Islands . . . 105 E b
Bahawalpur . . . 137 B c
Bahawalpur, reg. . . . 137 B c
Bahia . . . 214 F d
Bahia, cap. . . . 108 M i
Bahia, state . . . 214 E d
Bahia Blanca . . . 215 C f
Bahia Blanca, bay . . . 215 C f
Bahia del Almirante, bay . . . 105 D e
Bahia de Todos os Santos, bay 214 F d
Bahmanid Sultanate . . . 92 H f
Bahrein, isl. . . .
Bahr el Ghazal, reg. . . . 174 F d
Bahr el Ghazal, R. . . . 174 F d
Baiæ . . . 31 ins. A
Baikal, lake . . .
Baila Monos River . . .
Bailén . . . 130 C f
Baindt, ab. . . . 143 I j
Baisan . . . 68 ins. A
Bajazet, Mosque of . . . 93 G e (5)
Bajocas or Bajocasses, see Bayeux
Baker City . . . 210 B b
Baker Island . . . 180 J h
Bakkar . . .
Bakony Wald, mts. . . . 159 I e
Baktchiserai . . . 93 D b
Baku . . . 139 G g
Balabac Strait . . . 171 M h
Balabo, mt. . . . 30 E b
Balaklava . . . 164 J f
Balasor . . .
Balaton, lake . . .
Balboa, route of . . . 105 E e
Balbus, Crypta of . . . 22 A
Balbus, Theatre of . . . 22 A
Baldern . . . 143 J h
Bâle, see Basel
Balearic Islands . . . 2 E e
Balearic Isles, Rom. prov. . . . 42 C f (7)
Balearic Sea . . . 38 C e
Balesium . . . 31 H b
Bali, isl. . . . 112 E d
Balingen . . . 143 G i
Balize . . . 191 H f
Balkan Mountains . . . 2 G d
Balkan Peninsula . . . 2 G d
Balkash, lake . . .
Balkh
Balkh, reg. . . . 137 A a
Balla . . . 11 D b
Ballaarat . . . 172 D d
Ballah, lake . . . 174 K i
Ballenstedt . . . 62 F c
Ballinasloe . . . 98 B c
Ballyshannon . . . 127 I g
Balsas, Rio de las, R. . . . 213 ins.
Balta . . . 139 C f
Baltic Port . . . 120 J e
Baltic Sea . . . 2 F c
Baltimore, in Ireland . . . 184 B b
Baltimore, in Maryland . . . 192 C d
Baltischport (Baltic Port) . . . 120 J e
Baluches, people . . . 92 G e
Baluchistan, state . . . 170 H f
Balyra River . . . 14 B b
Bamberg . . . 62 F d
Bamberg, bp. . . . 79 G d
Bamborough . . .
Bamborough, parl. bor. . . .
Bambuk, reg. . . . 174 B c
Bamian . . . 102 G d
Bammako . . . 174 C c
Banat, reg. . . . 159 K f
Banbury, parl. bor. . . . 163 M e
Banda, isl. . . .
Banda Oriental, prov. . . . 215 D f
Bandar Abbas . . . 170 G f
Bandusia, Fount of . . . 30 E b
Banff, cty. . . .
Banff Park, town . . . 212 D c
Bangalore . . . 137 C f
Bangkok . . . 171 K g
Bangor, in Maine . . . 199 L b
Bangor, in Wales . . .
Bangor, bp. . . . 97 M h
Bangweolo, lake . . . 175 F f
Banialuka . . . 159 I f
Banias . . . 68 ins. A
Banjermassin, reg. . . . 112 E d
Banks Land, isl. . . . 186 G a
Banks Strait . . . 186 G a
Bann River . . . 49 C d
Bannocks, people . . . 188 C a
Bañolas . . . 82 C a
Baños de Ledesma . . . 82 C a
Bantam . . . 112 D d
Bantia . . . 31 F b
Bantry Bay . . . 127 G j
Banz, mon. . . . 95 E a
Bauli . . . 31 ins. A
Bapaume . . . 117 A d
Baphyras River . . . 11 D b
Bar (Antivari) . . . 164 B b
Bar, in Podolia . . . 131 I d
Bar-le-Duc . . . 84 F e
Bar-sur-Aube . . . 61 F b
Bar-sur-Aube, cty. . . . 69 J f
Bar-sur-Seine . . . 69 J f
Bar, duchy, 14 cent. . . . 76 F b
Bar, duchy, 15 cent. . . . 84 F e
Bar, duchy, 17 and 18 cent. . . . 126 D b
Bar, dist., 18 cent. . . . 134 C d
Baranof Island . . . 212 ins.
Baraque, La . . . 156 B a
Barathrum, mt. . . . 23 D
Barataria Bay . . . 207 G e
Barbados, isl. . . . 213 F c
Barbary, reg. . . . 108 Q d
Barbary States . . . 118 D g
Barbastro . . . 82 C a
Barberton . . . 175 N l
Barbuda, isl. . . . 213 F c
Barca . . . 8 G e
Barca, reg. . . . 66 K g
Barcaldine . . . 172 D c
Barcellos . . . 214 C c
Barcelona, in Spain . . . 82 C a
Barcelona, in Venezuela . . . 214 C b
Barcelona, bp. . . . 94 C c
Barcelona, cty. . . . 82 C a
Barcelona, univ. . . . 100 F f
Barcelonette . . . 126 E d
Barchin
Barchinona or Barcino (Barcelona) 38 C d
Bard, Fort . . . 150 D d
Bardenwick, see Bardowiek
Bardney, mon. . . . 97 Q h
Bardo . . .
Bardowiek . . . 62 F b
Bardstown . . . 196 B c
Barduli . . . 31 F a
Bardulia, cty. . . . 82 B a
Barea . . . 38 B e
Bareilly . . . 137 C c
Bärenburg, castle . . . 91 R l
Barfleur . . . 65 F f
Barga . . . 90 L i
Bargu, reg. . . .
Bargylia . . . 17 E c
Bari . . . 64 C b
Bari, abp. . . . 95 F c
Baris . . . 31 H c
Barium . . . 31 F a
Barka Plateau . . . 2 G e
Barkhalikend . . .
Barking . . . 75 J h
Barking, mon. . . . 97 R j
Barkly . . . 175 L l
Barkul . . .
Barlee, lake . . . 172 A c
Barletta . . . 90 F d
Barlings, mon. . . . 97 Q h
Barlow, route of . . . 191 J d
Barnegat Inlet . . . 192 D d
Barnet . . . 75 I h
Barnim, reg. . . . 80 ins.
Barnsley . . . 162 E d
Barnstable . . . 189 C d
Barnstaple . . . 65 D e
Barnstaple, parl. bor. . . . 163 J f
Barnus, mt. . . . 10 C b
Barnwell, mon. . . . 97 R i
Barroch . . .
Baroda . . . 137 B d
Baros . . . 112 C c
Barotse, people . . . 175 F f
Barquisimeto . . . 105 G d
Barra do Rio Negro . . . 214 D c
Barra Island . . .
Barranquilla . . . 214 B a
Barre, La . . . 192 C b
Barren Country, reg. . . . 212 C b
Barrios, Puerto . . . 213 D c
Barrois mouvant, dist. . . . 126 D b
Barrow, Point . . . 186 D a
Barrow River . . . 49 C e
Barrow Strait . . . 186 J a
Barrum, see Bar-le-Duc and Bar-sur-Aube
Bartenstein, in Prussia . . . 155 K a
Bartenstein, in Wurtemberg . . . 143 I g
Bartfeld . . . 131 H d
Barton, priory . . . 100 A b
Barton-on-Humber, parl. bor. .
Baruth . . . 85 G d
Bärwalde . . . 123 H b
Basel . . . 91 P k
Basel, bp. . . . 78 E e
Basel, canton . . . 91 P k
Basel, imp. cy. . . . 78 E e
Basel, univ. . . . 100 G e
Basentus (Busento) River . . . 31 F c
Bashan, reg. . . . 6 E c
Bashkirs, people . . . 139 H e
Basilica Æmilia, bldg. . . . 24 B
Basilica Julia, bldg. . . . 24 B
Basilica Porcia, bldg. . . .
Basilica Sempronia, bldg. . . . 24 A
Basilica Ulpia, bldg. . . . 24 B
Basilicata, dist. . . . 90 E d
Basilia, see Basel
Basingstoke . . . 127 X o
Basingstoke, college . . . 100 A a (33)
Basingstoke, deanery . . . 100 A a
Basingstoke, hospital . . . 100 A a (29)
Basingstoke, parl. bor. . . .
Basingwerk, mon. . . . 97 N h
Basle, see Basel
Basman . . . 112 C c

Basques, people . . . . . 57 C e
Basra . . . . 53 G c
Bas-Rhin, dept. . . . . . . 148 F e
Bassam, Grand . . . . . . 175 C d
Bassania . . . . 31 I a
Bassano . . . . 72 C b
Basse-Fontaine, mon. . . . 94 C b (B. F.)
Bassein . . . . 112 A b
Basses-Alps, dept. . . . . 148 F f
Basses-Pyrénées, dept. . . 148 D f
Bassignano . . . . 130 Q j
Bassigny, dist. . . . . . . 126 D c
Bass Strait . . . . 172 D d
Bastarnæ, people . . . . . 35 I c
Bastetani, people . . . . . 38 B e
Basti . . . . 38 B e
Bastia . . . . 77 F d
Bastidas, route of . . . . 105 E d
Bastille, bldg. . . . . . . 149 B
Basutoland, col. . . . . . 175 M l
Bastogne . . . . 117 D d
Batalha . . . . 83 J h
Batalha, mon. . . . . 94 A d
Batanæa, reg. . . . . 6 E c
Batanga, Gross . . . . . .
Batangas . . . . 171 N g
Batava, Castra (Passau) . . 38 E c
Batavian Republic . . . . . 151 H f
Batavians, people . . . . . 38 C b
Batavodurum . . . . 39 H g
Bate . . . . 16 B a
Bateia . . . .
Bath, in England . . . . .
Bath, in N. Carolina . . . 193 F d
Bath, bp. . . . . 97 O j
Bath, parl. bor. . . . . . 163 L f
Bathurst, in Gambia . . . . 174 B c
Bathurst, in N. S. Wales . . 172 D d
Bathurst, Cape . . . . . . 212 C a
Baticala . . . . 112 A b
Batinus River . . . . 27 I e
Batnæ . . . . 20 H d
Batoche . . . . 212 E c
Baton Rouge . . . . 191 G e
Battas, people . . . . . .
Battersea . . . . 75 I i
Battery Wagner, fort . . . . 208 E c
Battikalva . . . . 112 B c
Battle, mon. . . . . 97 R k
Battleford . . . . 212 E c
Baturin . . . . 131 J c
Baturite . . . . 214 F c
Bau . . . . 158 E a
Bauconia . . . . 39 J i
Baudemont . . . . 156 A a
Baugé, in Anjou . . . . . 70 C c
Baugé, in Bresse . . . . . 126 D c
Bauld, Cape . . . . 212 J c
Baume-les-Dames, mon. . . 95 D b
Baumgartenberg, mon. . . . 95 E b
Bautzen . . . . 63 H c
Bautzen-Görlitz, dist. . . . 85 D c
Bauzanum . . . . 27 F a
Bavaria, duchy, 10 cent. . . 63 G e
Bavaria, duchy, 13 cent. . . 72 C b
Bavaria, duchy, 16 cent. . . 115 G d
Bavaria, elect. . . . . . . 123 G d
Bavaria, Frank. prov., 8 cent. . 53 O h
Bavaria, Frank. prov., 9 cent. . 54 G d
Bavaria, km., 1806 . . . . 151 L j
Bavaria, km., 1812 . . . . 154 F d
Bavaria, km., 1815—1866 . . 158 F d
Bavaria, km., since 1866 . . 161 C c
Bavaria-Landshut, duchy . . 79 H d
Bavaria-Munich, duchy . . . 79 G e
Bavaria-Straubing, duchy . . 79 H d
Bavarian East March (Ostmark) 63 H d
Bavarians, people . . . . . 46 I d
Bawiti . . . . 150 A b
Bawtry . . . . 185 E d
Bayamon . . . . 199 ins. G
Bayeux . . . . 61 C b
Bayeux, bp. . . . . 94 B b
Baymen, people . . . . . . 136 ins. A
Bay of Chaleurs . . . . . . 212 I d
Bayona . . . . 82 A a
Bayonne . . . . 58 D e
Bayonne, bp. . . . . 94 B c
Bayou Pierre, R. . . . . . 196 A d
Bayreuth . . . . 114 F d
Bayreuth, princ. . . . . . 114 F d
Baza . . . . 82 B b
Bazadais, dist. . . . . . . 69 C d
Bazas . . . . 61 C d
Bazas, bp. . . . . 94 B c
Beachy Head . . . . 127 Z p
Bear River . . . . 198 C b
Béarn, gouv. . . . . 146 A c
Béarn, prov. . . . . 148 D f
Béarn, viscty. . . . . . . 76 C e
Bearroc Wood . . . . 49 F f
Beata, isl. . . . . 105 F c
Beaucaire . . . . 126 D e
Beauce, dist. . . . . 69 H f
Beau-Chêne . . . . 156 C c
Beaufort . . . . 193 ins. C
Beaugency . . . . 69 H g
Beaugency, mon. . . . . .
Beauharnais, Fort . . . . . 191 G c
Beauharnois . . . . 212 H d
Beaujeu . . . . 76 F c
Beaujeu, seign. . . . . . . 69 F c
Beaulieu, ab. . . . . 100 A b
Beaulieu, castle . . . . . 76 D c
Beaulieu, mon., near Tours . 94 C b
Beaulieu, mon., near Tulle . 94 C b
Beaumaris, parl. bor. . . . 163 J d
Beaumont, in Anjou . . . . 76 C b
Beaumont, in Hainaut . . . 157 ins.
Beaumont, in Normandy . . . 65 G f
Beaumont, on the Oise . . . 76 E b
Beaumont, cty., in Normandy . 76 D b
Beauvais . . . . 61 E b
Beauvais, bp. . . . . 94 C b
Beauvais, cty. . . . . . . 61 E b
Beauvale, mon. . . . . . . 97 P h
Beaver . . . . 210 C c
Bebenhausen, mon . . . . . 143 H h
Bec . . . . 65 G f
Bec, mon. . . . . 94 C b
Bechuanaland, dist. . . . . 175 F g
Bechuanaland, prot., col. . . 175 F g
Beda . . . . 39 I i
Beddington . . . . 75 I i
Bedesis (Ronco) River . . . 27 E d
Bedford, in England . . . .
Bedford, in Virginia . . . . 195 B e
Bedford, cty. . . . . 127 Y n
Bedford, Fort . . . . 192 B c
Bedford, New . . . . 211 K b
Bedford, parl. bor. . . . . 163 N e
Bedlington . . . .
Bedwyn, parl. bor. . . . .
Beejapore . . . . 137 C e
Beerfelden . . . . 142 C a
Beer Alston, parl. bor. . . .
Beersheba . . . . 7 B f
Beeskow . . . . 85 H d
Beeston Castle . . . . . . 127 W m
Behar . . . . 137 E c
Behar, reg. . . . . 137 D d
Beichlingen . . . . 85 F e
Beilan . . . . 164 F c
Beilstein . . . . 143 H g
Beinheim . . . . 142 B c
Beira . . . . 175 G f
Beira, Fort do Principe da . . 214 C d
Beirut . . . . 68 C c
Beja . . . . 82 A b
Beka, The, reg. . . . . . . 6 D a
Bekes . . . . 168 G c
Belbek River . . . . 164 J f
Belbina, isl. . . . . 15 D b
Belbuck, mon. . . . . 80 D d
Belecke, castle . . . . . . 62 E c
Beleigh, mon. . . . . 97 R j
Belem, in Brazil . . . . . . 214 E c
Belem, in Portugal . . . . . 83 J h
Belem, mon. . . . . 94 A d
Belemina . . . . 14 C b
Belen . . . . 105 D e
Belesme . . . . 65 G f
Belfast . . . . 127 L g
Belfort, in the Sundgau . . . 122 D e
Belfort, in Syria, castle . . . 68 ins. A
Belgæ, people . . . . 51 O i
Belgard . . . . 63 H b
Belgern . . . . 63 G c
Belgian Congo, col. . . . . 175 F e
Belgica . . . . 39 I h
Belgica, Rom. prov. . . . . 38 D c (3)
Belgica I, Rom. prov. . . . 42 D d (5)
Belgica II, Rom. prov. . . . 42 C c (6)
Belgium, km. . . . . 158 C c
Belgrade . . . . 43 G e
Belgrade, bp. . . . . 95 G c
Belize . . . . 213 D c
Belkesheim, dist. . . . . . 63 F b
Belknap, Fort, Ind. Res. . . 188 D a
Bell, route of . . . . 210 F c
Bellac . . . . 69 D c
Bellagio see Bellaggio . . . 90 I h
Bellary . . . . 137 C e
Belle-Alliance, La, farm . . 156 C c
Bellecombe, mon. . . . . . 94 C c
Belle Ile, isl. . . . . 69 B c
Belle Isle . . . . 148 A b
Belle Isle, Strait of . . . . 186 N c
Bellême, seign. . . . . . . 69 H f
Belleville, mon. . . . . . . 94 C b
Belley . . . . 69 F d
Belley, bp. . . . . 95 D b
Belli, people . . . . 38 B d
Bellinzona . . . . 91 R l
Bellona, Temple of . . . . . 24 A
Bellovaci or Bellovacis, see Beauvais
Bellovaci, people . . . . . 38 C c
Belluno . . . . 63 G e
Belluno, bp. . . . . 95 E b
Bellunum . . . . 27 G a
Belmont . . . . 208 C b
Belrain . . . . 69 J f
Belt, Great, str. . . . . . . 88 D d
Belt, Little, str. . . . . . . 88 C d
Beltana . . . . 172 C d
Belts . . . . 59 I c
Belus River . . . . 6 C c
Belvoir, in Syria, castle . . 68 ins. A
Belvoir Castle, in England . . 127 Y n
Belzig . . . . 85 G d
Benacus (Garda), lake . . . 26 E b
Benadir, reg. . . . . 175 H d
Benafrum, see Venafrum (Venafro)
Benares . . . . 137 D c
Benavente . . . . 83 J g
Bencoolen . . . .
Bender . . . .
Bendigo . . . . 172 D d
Benediktbeuren, mon. . . . 95 E b
Beneschau . . . . 135 H d
Benevento . . . . 46 I e
Benevento, abp. . . . . . . 95 E c
Benevento, duchy . . . . . 54 G e
Benevento, princ. . . . . . 64 B b
Beneventum (Benevento) . . . 30 D a
Bengal, dist. . . . .
Bengal, prov. . . . . 137 E d
Bengal, Bay of . . . . . . 112 B b
Benghazi . . . . 174 F a
Benguela . . . . 175 E f
Benguela, reg. . . . . . . 109 S i
Beni River . . . . 214 C d
Benin . . . . 174 D d
Benin, Bight of . . . . . . 174 D d
Benin, reg. . . . . 108 R g
Bénisson-Dieu, La, mon. . . 94 C b
Beni-Suef . . . . 150 B b
Benjamin, tribe . . . . . . 7 ins. D
Bennet, lake . . . . 212 ins.
Bennett's Plantation . . 193 ins. A (Benn.)
Ben Nevis, mt. . . . . 49 D c

Bennington . . . 195 E b
Bentheim . . . 62 D b
Bentheim, cty. . . . 134 D b
Benton, Fort . . . 198 C a
Bentonville . . . 208 E b
Bent's Fort . . . 198 E c
Benue River . . . 174 D d
Berar, dist. . . . 137 C d
Berar, prov. . . . 170 I f
Berar, Rajah of, princ. . . .
Berat . . . 165 A c
Berber . . . 174 G c
Berbera . . . 174 H c
Berbers, people . . . 53 B-D c-d
Berchtesgaden . . . 79 H e
Berchtesgaden, ab. . . . 79 H e
Berchtesgaden, mon. . . . 72 C b
Berdera . . . 175 H d
Berditchev . . . 131 I d
Berea . . . 7 C e
Bereïdah . . . 170 F f
Berenice . . . 34 H g
Beresina River . . . 153 N g
Berezov . . . 170 H b
Berg, cty. . . . 78 E c
Berg, duchy . . . 86 F c
Berg, gr. duchy . . . 154 D c
Bergalei, people . . . 26 D a
Berga . . . 82 C a
Bergama . . . 77 J e
Bergamo . . . 90 I h
Bergamo, bp. . . . 95 D b
Berge, in Macedonia . . . 11 E b
Berge, mon. near Magdeburg . . . 95 E a
Bergen, near Frankfort . . . 134 E c
Bergen, in Netherlands . . . 134 C b
Bergen, in New Jersey . . . 189 ins. C
Bergen, in Norway . . . 166 F c
Bergen, on Rugen Island . . . 123 G a
Bergen, Hanse. for. off. . . . 98 D a
Bergen, mon., on Rugen I. . . . 80 C d
Bergen op Zoom . . . 117 C c
Bergerac . . . 69 D d
Bergerac, castle . . . 76 D d
Bergomum (Bergamo) . . . 26 D b
Bergues . . . 126 C a
Bergula . . .
Bergzabern . . . 142 B b
Berhampur . . . 171 J f
Bering Sea . . . 179 I b
Bering Strait . . . 186 C b
Beritini, people . . . 26 A d
Berkeley, in California . . . 210 A c
Berkeley, in England . . . 185 D f
Berkeley, in Virginia . . . 193 ins. A
Berkeley, castle . . .
Berkeley County . . . 193 ins. C
Berkhampstead . . . 65 F e
Berkhampstead, parl. bor. 163
Berks, parl. dist. . . . 163 M f
Berkshire, cty. . . . 60 M i
Berlichingen . . . 143 I g
Berlichingen, castle . . . 114 E d
Berlin . . . 85 C b
Berlin, Hanse. cy. . . . 99 ins. B
Bermejo River . . . 215 C e
Bermius, mt. . . . 10 C b
Bermondsey, mon. . . . 97 Q j
Bermuda, isl. . . . 108 K d
Bermuda Hundred . . . 191 J d
Bermudez, state . . . 214 C b
Bermudez, route of . . . 108 K d
Bernalillo . . . 190 D d
Bernardino River . . .
Bernburg . . . 154 F c
Berne . . . 91 P l
Berne, canton . . . 91 P l
Berne, New (Newbern) . . . 193 F d
Berneck, castle . . . 143 G h
Bernhardin Pass . . . 150 E c
Bernicia, dist. . . .
Bernicians, people . . .
Bernina Pass . . . 91 S l
Bernkastel . . . 142 ins. A
Bernstein . . . 85 D b
Berœa, in Macedonia . . . 10 D b
Berœa, in Syria . . . 20 G d
Berœa, in Thrace . . . 39 N l
Berones, people . . . 38 B d
Berothai . . . 6 D a
Berrhœa . . . 10 D b
Berry, duchy . . . 78 C e
Berry, gouv. . . . 146 B b
Berry, prov. . . . 148 E e
Berthold, Fort, Ind. Res. . . . 188 F a
Bertinoro, bp. . . . 95 E c
Bertiscus, mt. . . . 11 E b
Berwick, in England . . .
Berwick, in New Hampshire . . . 189 C c
Berwick, cty. . . .
Berwick on Tweed, parl. bor. . . . 163 M b
Berwick, South . . . 189 C c (S. B.)
Berytus (Beirut) . . . 6 D a
Besa . . . 16 C b
Besalú, mon. . . . 94 C c
Besançon . . . 62 D e
Besançon, abp. . . . 95 D b
Besançon, gen. . . . 147 F b
Besançon, imp. cy. . . . 78 E e
Besançon, univ. . . . 100 G e
Beshicktash, quarter . . .
Besigheim . . . 143 H g
Besika Bay . . .
Besor River . . . 7 B f
Bessapara . . . 39 M l
Bessarabia, dist. in the Ottoman Empire . . .
Bessarabia, dist. in Russia . . . 139 C f
Bessi, people . . . 39 M l
Bethany, in Georgia . . . 193 ins. C
Bethany, in Palestine . . . 7 C e
Bethar . . . 7 B d
Betharbel . . .
Beth-Aven . . . 7 C e
Bethel, in Alaska . . . 198 ins. A
Bethel, in Palestine . . . 7 C e
Bethelea . . . 7 A e
Bethencourt, route of . . . 108 O e
Bethesda, Pool of . . . 6 ins. A
Beth-Haran . . . 7 D e
Beth-Horon . . . 7 C e
Beth-Jeshimoth . . . 7 D e
Bethlehem, in Palestine . . . 7 C e
Bethlehem, in Pennsylv. . . . 192 D c
Bethlen Gabor, route of . . . 121 F c
Beth-Markaboth . . . 7 C f
Beth-Meon . . .
Beth-Nimrah . . . 7 D e
Beth-Peor . . . 7 D e
Bethsaida . . . 6 D c
Bethshean . . . 7 C d
Beth-Shemesh . . . 7 B e
Bethso . . . 6 ins. A
Bethulie . . . 175 M m
Béthune . . . 117 A d
Bethzur . . . 7 C e
Betifulus . . .
Betogabra . . . 7 B e
Betonim . . . 7 D e
Betriacum . . . 26 E b
Beuil, Le, mon. . . . 94 C b
Beutelsbach . . . 143 H h
Beuthen . . . 115 J c
Beveland, South, isl. . . . 117 B c
Beverley . . . 127 Y m
Beverley, parl. bor. . . . 163 N d
Beverly Manor . . . 194 K g
Bevern . . . 134 E c
Beversrede, Fort . . . 192 ins.
Beverswyck . . . 189 A c
Bewdley, parl. bor. . . . 163 L e
Bezabde . . . 20 J d
Bézenas . . . 126 C e
Bezetha . . . 6 ins. A
Bezetha, Hill of . . . 6 ins. A
Béziers . . . 76 E e
Béziers, bp. . . . 94 C c
Bhamo . . . 171 K f
Bhartpur . . .
Bhatkal . . . 112 A b
Bhawalpore . . . 137 B c
Bhawalpore, dist. . . . 137 B c
Bhootan, Bhutan, princ. . . . 137 E c
Bhopal . . . 137 C d
Bhotan, Bhutan, princ. . . . 171 K f
Bhurtpore . . .
Biafra, reg. . . . 109 I g
Biafra, bight . . . 175 D d
Bialystok . . . 138 B e
Biana . . .
Biandrate . . . 72 B b
Biar . . . 82 H f
Bias River . . .
Biasca . . . 91 Q l
Biberach . . . 142 E d
Biberach, imp. cy. . . . 143 I i
Bibracte . . . 38 C c
Bibrax . . . 38 C c
Bibrich . . . 117 E e
Bibroci, people . . .
Biocca . . . 90 I h
Bidar . . .
Bidassoa River . . . 130 C e
Biel . . .
Bielefeld . . . 154 E b
Bielefeld, Hanse. cy. . . . 99 ins. B
Bielgorod . . . 139 E e
Bielgorod, gov. . . . 131 K e
Bielitz . . . 135 J d
Biella . . . 90 I h
Bielosersk . . . 138 E c
Bielsk . . . 159 L b
Bienne . . . 91 P k
Bierges . . . 156 B a
Bieringen . . . 143 G i
Big Mountain . . . 212 ins.
Big River . . . 212 H c
Big Black River . . . 208 B c
Big Black River, battle . . . 208 B c
Bigha . . . 77 J d
Big Horn River . . . 198 D b
Bigorre, cty. . . . 76 C e
Bigorre, dist. . . . 147 D c (Big.)
Bigorritis, lake . . . 10 C b
Big Sioux River . . . 198 F b
Bihacs . . . 119 H e
Bijapur . . . 137 C e
Bikaner . . . 170 I f
Bikaner, dist. . . . 137 B c
Bilbao . . . 83 K g
Bilbilis . . . 38 B d
Bilitio . . . 26 C a
Billæus River . . . 20 E b
Billingsgate, loc. in London . . . 75 G g
Billungs, Lands of the . . . 62 F b
Billungs, March of the . . . 63 F b
Biloxi . . . 191 H f
Bima . . .
Bimlipatam . . .
Binche . . . 156 A b
Binchester . . .
Bingen . . . 62 D d
Bingerville . . . 174 C d
Bingium (Bingen) . . . 39 I i
Binn . . . 91 Q l
Binsdorf . . . 143 G i
Bintang, isl. . . .
Biobio River . . . 215 B f
Birkenfeld . . . 142 ins. A
Birkel-el-Kerun, lake . . .
Birket Israel . . . 6 ins. A
Birmingham, in Alabama . . . 211 H d
Birmingham, in England . . . 127 X n
Birmingham, parl. bor. . . . 163 M e
Birs River . . . 91 P k
Birten . . . 62 D c
Bisaltia . . . 11 E b
Bisaltia, reg. . . . 11 E b
Bisanthe . . .
Biscay, Bay of . . . 2 D d
Bisceglie . . . 90 F d
Bischoflack . . . 135 H e

Bischofsheim . . . . 142 E a
Bischofsheim, mon. . . . . 95 D b
Bischofswerda . . . . 155 H c
Bischofszell . . . . 142 D e
Biserta . . . . 58 F f
Bishbalk (Urumtsi) . . . .
Bishop-Auckland, mon. . . . . . . 97 P g
Bishop's Castle, parl. bor. . . .
Bishopsgate, loc. in London . . 75 G g
Bishops Stortford, parl. bor. 163 O f (Bish. St.)
Bisignano . . . . 98 G f
Biskra . . . . 174 D a
Bismarck . . . . 210 E a
Bismarck Archipelago . . . . . . 179 F h
Bissagos Islands . . . . 174 B c
Bistritz . . . .
Bitburg . . . . 117 E d
Biterræ, see Béziers
Bitervium, see Viterbo
Bithynia, dist. . . . . 20 D b
Bithynia, East Rom. prov. . . . 43 He (1.)
Bithynia, reg. . . . . 8 B a
Bithynia, Rom. prov. . . . . 35 K e
Bithynium . . . . 20 D b
Bitolia . . . . 164 C b
Bitonto . . . . 90 F d
Bitsch, fortress . . . . 154 D d
Bitter Lakes . . . . 174 K i
Bitterne . . . . 51 P i
Biturgia . . . . 27 F d
Bituriges or Biturigis, see Bourges
Bituriges, people . . . . 38 C c
Bivium . . . . 35 ins. B
Bizerta . . . .
Bizye . . . . 39 N l
Björneborg . . . . 120 J d
Blachernæ, palace . . . . 93 G e
Blackburn, parl. bor. . . . . . . 163 L d
Blackfeet, Ind. Res. . . . . 188 D a
Blackfeet, tribe . . . . 188 D a
Black Forest, mts. . . . . 62 D e
Black Friars, mon. in London . 75 G g
Blackheath . . . . 75 J i
Black Hills . . . . 210 E b
Black River . . . . 208 B b
Black Russia, reg. . . . . 139 C e
Black Sea . . . . 3 H d
Blacksnake Hills, fort . . . . . . 211 G b
Blackwall . . . . 75 J h
Blackwater River . . . .
Bladensburg . . . . 200 L i
Blagovestchensk . . . .
Blakeney, parl. bor. . . . .
Blamont . . . . 143 ins. F
Blamont, lordship . . . . 143 ins. F
Blanca Peak . . . . 187 I e
Blanche, lake . . . . 172 D c
Blanche Garde, castle . . . . . . 68 ins. A
Blanchelande . . . . 65 F f
Blanchelande, mon. . . . . 94 B b
Blanco, Cape, in Guinea . . . . 174 B b
Blanco, Cape, in Oregon . . . . 210 A b
Blanco, Cape, in Peru . . . . . . 111 A b
Blanco, Cape, in Tunis . . . . . 174 D a
Blanda, in Italy . . . . 30 E c
Blanda, in Spain . . . . 38 C d
Blandford, parl. bor. . . . .
Blankenberghe . . . . 117 B c
Blankenheim . . . . 117 E d
Blanmont . . . . 156 B a
Blariacum . . . . 39 H h
Blaubeuren . . . . 143 I i
Blaubeuren, mon. . . . . 95 D b
Blaye . . . . 76 C d
Bleiburg . . . . 115 H e
Bleichfeld . . . . 62 F d
Blekinge, dist. . . . . 88 F c
Bléneau . . . . 126 C c
Blenheim . . . . 129 F c
Blennerhasset's Island . . . . . . 196 C c
Blera, in Apulia . . . . 31 F b
Blera, in Etruria . . . . 27 G e
Blesum, see Blois
Bletchingley, parl. bor. . . . 163 N f (Blet.)
Blindheim . . . . 134 F d
Block Island . . . . 189 C d
Bloemfontein . . . . 175 M l
Blois . . . . 61 D c
Blois, cty. . . . . 61 D c
Blore Heath . . . . 84 B c
Bluefields . . . . 213 D c
Blue Horde, people . . . .
Blue Licks . . . . 196 C c
Blue Mountains . . . . 172 D d
Blue Nile River . . . . 174 G c
Blue Ridge, mts. . . . . . . 193 C d — E b
Blumegg . . . . 142 B e
Blumenau, in Brazil . . . . 215 E e
Blumenau, in Hungary . . . . . 159 I d
Blumenfeld . . . . 142 C e
Boactes River . . . . 26 D c
Bobbio . . . . 90 I h
Bobbio, bp. . . . . 95 D c
Bober River . . . . 63 H c
Bobium Castrum (Bobbio) . . . 26 D c
Böblingen . . . . 143 H h
Bobruisk . . . . 167 K e
Boca del Dragón, str. . . . . . . 105 H d
Boca del Sierpe, str. . . . . . . 105 H d
Boca del Toro, bay . . . . 213 D d
Bocca Tigris . . . . 171 M f
Bocchetta Pass, La . . . . 150 E d
Bochnia . . . . 123 K c
Bocholt . . . . 117 E c
Böckelheim, castle . . . . 62 D d
Bode River . . . . 85 F e
Boderiæ Æstuarium (Firth of Forth) 38 B a
Bodetia . . . . 26 D c
Bodfeld, castle . . . . 62 F c
Bödigheim . . . . 142 D b
Bodmann . . . . 62 E e
Bodmin, mon. . . . . 97 M k
Bodmin, parl. bor. . . . . 163 J g
Bodonitza . . . . 89 B c
Bodotria Æstuarium (Firth of Forth) 51 O g
Bœæ . . . . 15 D c
Bœæ, Bay of . . . . 15 D c
Bœbe . . . . 11 D c
Bœbeis, lake . . . . 11 D c
Bœotia, reg. . . . . 11 E d
Bœum . . . . 11 D d
Bogesund . . . . 88 E c
Bogotá . . . . 214 B b
Bohemia, duchy . . . . 63 H d
Bohemia, km. . . . . 72 C b
Bohemia, plain of . . . . 2 F d
Bohemia, reg. . . . . 54 G d
Bohemian March . . . . 55 R j
Bohemians, people . . . .
Bohio . . . .
Böhmer Wald, mts. . . . . 63 G d
Böhmisch-Brod . . . . 87 J c
Bohol, isl. . . . . 199 ins. H
Bohus, dist. . . . . 88 D b
Boii, people, in Italy . . . . . . 26 E c
Boii, people, in Pannonia . . . 38 F c
Bois Brulé River . . . . 191 G b
Boisé . . . . 210 B b
Boisé, Fort . . . . 198 B a
Bois Forte, Ind. Res. . . . . . . 188 H a
Bois-le-Duc . . . . 114 C c
Boissière, La, mon. . . . . 94 C b
Boïus, mt. . . . . 10 B b
Bojador, Cape . . . . 174 B b
Bojano, bp. . . . . 95 ins.
Bojeador, Cape . . . . 199 ins. H
Bojohæmum (Bohemia), reg . . 38 E c
Bokhara . . . .
Bokhara, emir. . . . .
Bola . . . . 35 ins. B
Bolama . . . . 174 B c
Bolan Pass . . . . 170 H f
Bolar . . . . 99 N c
Bolbe, lake . . . . 11 E b
Bolghars, people . . . .
Boli . . . . 89 J f
Bolkhov . . . . 139 E e
Bolivia, country . . . . 214 C d
Bologna . . . . 90 C b
Bologna, bp. . . . . 95 E c
Bologna, univ. . . . . 100 H f
Bolsena, lake . . . . 90 L j
Bolsward . . . . 117 D a
Bolton, in England . . . . 127 W m
Bolton, in Mississippi . . . . . . 208 B c
Bolton, mon. . . . . 97 P h
Bolton, parl. bor. . . . . 163 L d
Bolton Abbey . . . . 127 X l
Bolton Castle . . . . 127 X l
Boma . . . . 175 E e
Bomarsund . . . . 131 H a
Bombay . . . . 137 B e
Bona . . . . 66 H f
Bona Dea, Temple of . . . . . . 22 A
Bonaire, isl. . . . . 214 C a
Bonavista . . . . 212 J d
Bonavista, Cape . . . . 194 I a
Bone . . . . 174 D a
Bonifacio . . . . 72 B c
Bonn . . . . 62 D c
Bonna (Bonn) . . . . 39 I h
Bonndorf . . . . 142 B e
Bonndorf, cty. . . . . 142 B e
Bonneval, mon. . . . . 94 C b
Bonnes Vaux, mon. . . . . 94 C b
Bonnevaux, mon. . . . . 95 D b
Bonneville, Fort . . . . 210 C b
Bönnigheim . . . . 143 H g
Bononia (Bologna) . . . . 27 F c
Bononia (Boulogne) . . . . 38 C b
Bontobrica . . . . 39 I h
Boonesboro . . . . 194 C c
Boone's Trail . . . . 194 C c
Boonville . . . . 211 G c
Boothia, Gulf of . . . . 186 K b
Boothia, isl. . . . . 186 J a
Boothia Felix, pen. . . . . 212 F a
Bopfingen, imp. cy. . . . . 143 J h
Boppard . . . . 62 D c
Bora, mt. . . . . 10 C a
Borbetomagus (Worms) . . . . . 39 J i
Borborus, lake . . . . 11 D b
Borculo . . . . 117 E b
Bordeaux . . . . 61 C d
Bordeaux, abp. . . . . 94 B b
Bordeaux, gen. . . . . 147 D c
Bordeaux, univ. . . . . 100 E f
Bordelais, dist. . . . . 76 C d
Bordesley, mon. . . . . 97 P i
Borgo San Donnino . . . . 90 J h
Borgo San Lorenzo . . . . 90 L j
Borgo San Sepolcro . . . . 90 M j
Borgo Sesia . . . . 130 Q i
Boriquen, isl. . . . . 105 G c
Borisov . . . .
Borkeloo . . . . 117 E b
Borku, reg. . . . . 174 E c
Borkum, isl. . . . . 117 E a
Bormio . . . . 90 J g
Borneo, isl. . . . .
Bornholm, isl. . . . . 88 F d
Bornhöved . . . . 72 C a
Bornu, reg. . . . . 174 E c
Borobodor . . . .
Borodino . . . . 131 K b
Boroughbridge . . . . 65 F c
Boroughbridge, parl. bor. . . . 163 M c
Borovsk . . . . 153 P f
Borsippa . . . . 4 G c
Borysthenes (Dnieper) River . . 35 K d
Boscaudun, mon. . . . . 95 D c
Boshof . . . . 175 M l
Bosna River . . . . 159 J f
Bosnia, reg. . . . .
Bosnia, km. . . . . 93 A b
Bosnia, prov. in the Ottoman Empire . . . . 124 C b
Bosnia, prov. in Austria . . . . 164 B b
Bosporus, Bosphorus, strait . . 2 G d
Bosporus, Kingdom of the Cimmerian . . . . 35 K e
Bosrah . . . . 6 F c

Bossiney, parl. bor. 163 J g
Boston, in England 127 Y m
Boston, Hanse. for. cy. 98 ins. A
Boston, parl. bor. 163 O d
Boston, in Mass. 189 ins. B
Boston Neck, pen. 195 ins. A
Bostra 6 F c
Bostrenus River 6 C a
Bosworth 84 C c
Botany Bay 172 E d
Bothnia, Gulf of 2 G b
Bothwell
Botroun 68 C c
Bottiæis, reg. 11 D b
Bottice, reg. 11 E b
Bottwar, Gross 143 H h
Botzen 62 F e
Bouchain 117 B d
Bouches-du-Rhône, dept. 148 E f
Bouet, Port 175 C d
Bougainville, isl. 172 E a
Bougie 66 G f
Bouillon 117 D e
Bouillon, duchy 117 D e
Boulers 156 A a
Boulevard de la Reine, in Versailles 149 A
Boulevard du Roi, in Versailles 149 A
Boulogne 61 D a
Bounty Islands 179 I l
Bouras, mon. 94 C b
Bourbon 61 E c
Bourbon, cty 61 E c
Bourbon, duchy 76 E c
Bourbon, isl.
Bourbon, Palais, bldg. in Paris 149 B
Bourbon, seign. 69 E c
Bourbon-Lancy 69 I g
Bourbon-l'Archambault 76 E c
Bourbonnais, gouv. 146 B b
Bourbonnais, prov. 148 E e
Bourbonnais, seign. 69 E c
Bourbourg, mon. 148 B a
Bourg, in Bresse 126 D c
Bourg, in Saintonge 76 C d
Bourgachard, mon. 148 B b
Bourges 61 E c
Bourges, abp. 94 C b
Bourges, gen. 147 E b
Bourges, univ. 100 F e
Bourges, viscty. 69 D c
Bourgmont, route of 190 F d
Bourke 172 D d
Bourn, mon. 97 Q i
Bournet, mon. 94 B b
Boussac 69 D c
Bousval 156 A a
Bouvignes 117 C d
Bouvines 69 E a
Bouxières-aux-Dames, mon. 148 C b
Boves 81 M h
Bovianum Undecumanorum 30 D a
Bovianum vetus
Bovillæ 35 ins. B
Bovino 64 C b
Bovino, bp. 95 F c
Bow Church, in London 75 G g (5)
Bowling Green 208 C b
Boxberg 142 E b
Boxley, mon. 97 R j
Boxtel 117 D c
Boyacá, battle 214 B b
Boyen, fortress 159 K a
Boyne River 127 J h
Brà 90 H h
Braba 190 D d
Brabant, dist. 62 B c
Brabant, duchy, 12 cent. 72 A a
Brabant, duchy, 14 cent. 78 D c
Brabant, duchy, 16 cent. 117 C c
Bracara Augusta (Braga) 38 A d
Bracciano, lake 96 B a
Bracito 198 D d
Brackenheim 143 H g
Brackley, parl. bor. 163 M e
Bradanus (Bradano) River 31 F b
Braden Forest 49 E f
Bradenstoke, mon. 97 P j
Bradford, in Wiltshire
Bradford, in Yorkshire 127 X m
Bradninch, parl. bor.
Bradock Down 127 U p
Brady, Fort 211 H a
Braga 82 A a
Braga, abp. 94 A c
Braganza 82 A a
Brahe River 115 I b
Braila 93 C a
Braine-l'Alleud
Braine-le-Château 156 A a
Braine-le-Comte 156 A a
Braintree 189 C c
Brake 158 E b
Bramber and Steyning, parl. bor. 163 N g
Branco, Cape 214 F c
Brandeis 123 H c
Brandenburg 63 G b
Brandenburg, bp. 79 H b
Brandenburg, castle 143 J i
Brandenburg, Hanse. cy. 99 ins. B
Brandenburg, march 85
Brandenburg, margr. 71 S j
Brandenburg, prov. 158 G b
Brandenburg, Neu 123 G b
Brandon, in Manitoba 212 F d
Brandon, in Virginia 193 ins. A
Brandywine River 192 ins.
Branford 189 B d
Brannkirka 88 G b
Branodunum (Brancaster) 51 Q h
Brant, route of 195 C c
Brantôme, mon. 94 C b
Braschimov
Bratzlav 139 C f
Braunau, in Austria 135 G d
Braunau, in Bavaria 115 G d
Braunau, in Bohemia 123 I c
Bräunlingen 142 B e
Braunsberg 79 L a
Braunsberg, Hanse. cy. 99 H c
Brauron 15 D b
Brava 109 V g
Bray 69 I f
Brazen Gate 6 ins. A
Brazil, col. 108 M i
Brazil, country 214 D d
Brazos River 191 F f
Brazos Santiago 201 F d
Brazza, isl. 90 F c
Brazzaville 175 E e
Breadalbane, dist.
Bread Street, in London 75 G g
Breamore, priory 100 A b
Brechin, bp. 97 K c
Brecknock, cty. 127 V n
Brecknock, mon. 97 N i
Brecknock, parl. dist. 163 K e
Brecon, parl. bor. 163 K f
Breda 117 C c
Brede Fiord 166 A b
Breed's Hill 195 ins. A
Brege River 142 B d
Bregenz 134 E e
Brehna, cty. 85 G e
Breisach 62 D e
Breisach, Alt (Old) 142 A d
Breisach, New 134 D e
Breisgau, dist. 142 B e
Breitenfeld 123 G c
Breitenwang 72 C b
Brema, see Bremen
Bremberg 55 R j
Breme, mon. 95 D b
Bremen 62 E b
Bremen, abp. 95 D a
Bremen, duchy 134 E b
Bremen, Hanse. cy. 99 ins. B
Bremen, imp. cy. 78 F b
Bremerhaven 158 E b
Bremetennacum, see Ribchester
Brenner, pass 63 F e
Brenneville 69 H f
Brennus, mt. 26 E b
Brent River 75 I h
Brenta River 63 F f
Brentford 75 I i
Brentwood 75 J h
Brenz 143 J h
Brenz River 143 J h
Brescello 64 B b
Brescia 90 J h
Brescia, bp. 95 E b
Breslau 72 D a
Breslau, bp. 95 F a
Breslau, Hanse. cy. 99 ins. B
Bresse, dist. 126 D c
Brest, in France 69 A b
Brest, in Poland
Brest Litovsk
Breteuil, near Amiens 69 I f
Breteuil, in Normandy 76 D b
Brétigny 76 D b
Breton, Cape 108 K c
Bretones, Tierra de los 108 L c
Bretones, people
Bretten 142 C b
Breuckelen (Brooklyn) 189 ins. C
Briançon 84 G g
Briansk 139 D e
Briantica, reg.
Briar Creek 195 A g
Bridewell Palace, in London 75 G g
Bridgenorth 65 E d
Bridgeport 189 B d
Bridges, Fort 210 C b
Bridgetown 213 F c
Bridgnorth 127 W n
Bridgnorth, parl. bor. 163 L e
Bridgwater 84 B d
Bridgwater, parl. bor. 163 K f
Bridlington, mon. 97 Q g
Bridport, parl. bor. 163 L g
Brie, dist. 69 I f
Brieg 79 J c
Brieg, princ. 79 J c
Briel 117 C c
Briel, Hanse. cy. 99 ins. B
Brienne 76 F b
Brienz 91 P l
Brienz, lake 91 P l
Brig 91 Q l
Brigach River 142 B d
Brigæcium 38 A d
Brigantes, people, in England
Brigantes, people, in Ireland 38 A b
Brigantinus, lake 39 J j
Brigantio 26 A c
Brigantium (Bregenz), in Rætia 39 J j
Brigantium (Corunna), in Spain 38 A d
Brigetio 38 F c
Brighton 127 Y p
Brighton, parl. bor. 163 N g
Brignais 81 M h
Brignolles 126 E e
Brilessus, mt. 15 D a
Brill 117 C c
Brindisi 90 G d
Brindisi, abp. 95 F c
Brinta River 27 F b
Brionne 76 D b
Brioude 76 E d
Brioude, mon. 148 B b
Brisbane 172 E c
Bristol, in England
Bristol, in Rhode Island 189 ins. A
Bristol, castle
Bristol, parl. bor. 163 L f
Bristol Bay 198 ins. A
Bristol Channel 49 D f
Bristol Coalfield 162 D f
Britain, West Rom. dioc. 42 B c
Britain, Rom. prov. 34 D c

Britain I, West Rom. prov. . . . . 42 B c (3)
Britain II, West Rom. prov. . . . 42 B c (4)
Britain, about 410 and 600 . . . 51
Britain, Lower, Rom. prov. . . . 38 B b (2)
Britain, Upper, Rom. prov. . . . 38 B b (1)
Britannia, Rom. prov., see Britain 34 D c
Britannia I, II, Rom. prov. . . . 38 B b
British Central Africa, see Nyasaland . . . . 175 G f
British Columbia, prov. . . . . 212 C c
British East Africa, col. . . . . 175 G d
British Guiana, col. . . . . . . 214 D b
British Honduras, col. . . . . . 213 D c
British India, emp. . . . . 170 I f
British Isles . . . . 2 C c
British Kaffraria, dist. . . . . . 175 M m
British New Guinea, col. . . . . 172 D a
British Somaliland, col. . . . . 174 H d
British South Africa Company 175 F f
Brito . . . . 213 D c
Britons, people . . . .
Brittany, cty. . . . . 61 B b
Brittany, duchy . . . . 76 B c
Brittany, gouv. . . . . 146 A b
Brittany, march . . . . 54 D d
Brittany, prov. . . . . 148 E d
Brittany, reg. . . . . 52 B b
Brivas, see Brioude
Brixellum . . . .
Brixen . . . . 63 F e
Brixen, bp. . . . . 79 G e
Brixham . . . . 127 V p
Brixia (Brescia) . . . . 26 E b
Broach . . . . 137 B d
Broad River . . . . 193 D d
Broad Way, street in Rome . . 22 A
Brocavium (Brougham) . . . . .
Brockville . . . . 212 H d
Brod, Böhmisch . . . . 87 I c
Brod, Deutsch . . . . 87 I d
Brode, mon. . . . . 80 C e
Brody . . . . 139 C e
Brogne, mon. . . . . 94 C a
Broken Hill . . . . 172 D d
Bromberg . . . . 79 J b
Bromberg Canal . . . . . 135 I b (Br. C.)
Bromiscus . . . . 11 E b
Bromley . . . . 75 J i
Brömsebro . . . . 120 I e
Bromsgrove, parl. bor. . . . . .
Bromyard, parl. bor. . . . . . .
Bronzell . . . . 158 E c
Brookfield, in Mass. . . . . . . 189 B c
Brookfield, in Ohio . . . . . . 206 ins.
Brooklyn . . . . 189 ins. C
Broome . . . . 172 B b
Broos . . . . 159 L f
Brou . . . . 69 H f
Brouage . . . . 126 A d
Brouwershaven . . . . 117 B c
Brown, mt., in Coast Range . . 212 ins.
Brown, mt., in Rocky Mts. . . . 186 H c
Brown, Fort . . . . 201 F d
Brown's Hole, dist. . . . . . . 210 D b
Brownsville, Pa. . . . . 192 B c
Brownsville, Texas . . . . 201 F d
Bruanium . . . . 10 C a
Bruce, mt. . . . . 172 A c
Bruchium, quarter in Alexandria 34 ins. C
Bruchsal . . . . 142 C b
Bruck, on the Leitha R. . . . . 159 I d
Bruck, on the Mur R. . . . . . . 87 J e
Bructeri, people . . . . 39 I h
Bruges . . . . 117 B c
Bruges, Hanse. for. off. . . . . 99 ins. B
Brugg . . . . 91 Q k
Brügge (Bruges) . . . . 117 B c
Brugnato, bp. . . . . 95 D c
Bruinsburg . . . . 208 B c
Bruja Point . . . .
Brundisium or Brundusium (Brindisi) . . . . 31 G b
Brundulum . . . . 27 G b
Brunei . . . .
Bruni Island . . . . 172 D e
Brünig Pass . . . . 91 Q l
Brunkeberg, mt. . . . . 88 H b
Brünn . . . . 63 I d
Brunnen . . . . 91 Q l
Brunswick, in Germany . . . . . 62 F b
Brunswick, in Georgia . . . . . 199 I d
Brunswick, in Maine . . . . . . 189 C b
Brunswick, duchy, 14 cent. . . . 79 G b
Brunswick, duchy, 18 cent. . . . 134 F c
Brunswick, duchy, 19 cent. . . . 158 F c
Brunswick, Hanse. cy. . . . . . 99 ins. B
Brunswick-Grubenhagen, duchy 79 G c
Brunswick-Kalenberg, duchy . 86 G b
Brunswick-Lüneburg, duchy . . 79 G b
Brunswick-Wolfenbüttel, duchy 114 F b
Brusa . . . . 77 J d
Brussels . . . . 117 C d
Bruton, mon. . . . . 97 O j
Bruttia and Lucania, West Rom. prov. . . . . 42 F f (6)
Bruttium, reg. . . . . 31 F d
Brüx . . . . 63 G c
Brye . . . . 156 B a
Bryges, people . . . . 17 B a
Bryseæ . . . . 14 C c
Bubastis or Bubastus (Tel Basta) 4 ins.
Buca . . . . 27 I e
Bucaramanga . . . . 214 B b
Buccaneers, head quarters of the
Bucellarian Theme . . . . 59 K e
Bucephala . . . . 19 L d
Bucephala, prom. . . . . 15 D b
Buch, captalat . . . . 69 C d
Buch, mon. . . . . 95 E a
Buchan, dist. . . . .
Buchau, ab. . . . . 143 I i
Buchau, imp. cy. . . . . 143 I i
Buchau, mon. . . . . 95 D b
Buchegg, castle . . . . 91 P k
Buchen . . . . 142 D a
Buchenberg . . . . 122 E d
Buchetium . . . . 10 B c
Buchhorn, imp. cy. . . . . 143 I j
Buckfastleigh, mon. . . . . . . 97 N k
Buckingham . . . .
Buckingham, cty. . . . . 127 Y o
Buckingham, parl. bor. . . . . . 163 N f
Buckland, mon. . . . . 97 M k
Bucks, cty. . . . . 163 N f
Bucoleon Palace . . . . 93 G e
Buda (Ofen) . . . . 66 J d
Buda, univ. . . . . 100 I e
Budamer . . . . 159 K d
Budapest . . . . 166 I f
Budatin . . . . 159 J d
Budini, people . . . . 35 K c
Budorus River . . . . 11 E d
Budshaja (Bougie) . . . . 66 G f
Budua, bp. . . . . 95 F c
Budweis . . . . 79 I d
Budziak . . . . 131 I d
Buea . . . . 175 D d
Buena Guia, Rio de, R. . . . . . 190 C e
Buenaventura . . . . 214 B b
Buena Vista, battle . . . . 201 E e
Buenos Ayres . . . . 215 D f
Buenos Ayres, audiencia . . . . 215 ins.
Buenos Ayres, viceroyalty . . . 215 ins.
Buffalo . . . . 196 D b
Buford, Fort . . . . 210 E a
Bug River, in Podolia . . . . . . 139 D f
Bug River, in Poland . . . . . . 99 H c
Bugey, dist. . . . . 126 D d
Bühl . . . . 142 B c
Buitrago, pass . . . . 82 B a
Bukharest . . . . 93 C b
Bukowina, dist. . . . . 139 C f
Bülach . . . . 91 Q k
Bulawayo . . . . 175 F g
Buleuterium . . . .
Bulgar . . . . 77 N b
Bulgaria, princ., about 1000 . . 59 I e
Bulgaria, km., 1203 . . . . 73 E b
Bulgaria, km., 1265 . . . . 89 B b
Bulgaria, km., 14 cent. . . . . . 89 H f
Bulgaria, km., 1909 . . . . 164 C b
Bulgaria, prov., 15 cent. . . . . 93 B b
Bulgaria, reg., 11 cent. . . . . . 67 K e
Bulgarians, people, about 900 . 57 H e
Bulgarians, people, about 1190 71 K e
Bulgarians, people, 19 cent. . .
Bulgarians, Kama-, people . . . 71 P b
Bulis . . . . 11 D d
Bull, Fort . . . . 192 D b
Bulla . . . . 38 D e
Bulle . . . . 91 P l
Bull Run, battle . . . . 208 ins.
Bulotus River . . . . 31 F d
Bulun . . . . 171 N a
Bumodus River . . . . 20 J d
Bunarbashi . . . .
Bunarbashi Brook, canal . . . .
Bunbury . . . . 172 A d
Bundelcund, reg. . . . . 137 C d
Bundelkhand, reg. . . . . 137 C d
Bunker Hill, battle . . . . 195 ins. A
Bunzelwitz . . . . 135 I c
Bunzlau, in Bohemia . . . . . . 63 H c
Bunzlau, in Silesia . . . . 155 H c
Buonconvento . . . . 72 C c
Buporthmus, prom. . . . . 15 D b
Buprasion . . . . 14 B a
Bura . . . . 14 C a
Büraburg . . . . 55 Q i
Buraicus River . . . . 14 C a
Burchana . . . . 38 D b
Burd . . . . 192 B c
Burdegala, Burdigala (Bordeaux) 38 B d
Büren, castle . . . . 62 E d
Burford . . . . 60 F e
Burford, parl. bor. . . . .
Burgau . . . . 143 J i
Burgau, margr. . . . . 79 G d
Burghas . . . .
Bürglen . . . . 91 Q l
Burgos . . . . 83 E a
Burgos, abp. . . . . 94 B c
Burgoyne, route of . . . . 195 E a
Burgrieden . . . . 143 I i
Burgsdorf . . . . 91 P k
Burgundarholm (Bornholm), isl. 38 E a
Burgundians, Kingdom of the . 50 D c
Burgundians, people . . . . . . 45 H b, E c
Burgundy, cty. . . . . 61 F c
Burgundy, duchy . . . . 58 E d
Burgundy, gouv. . . . . 146 B b
Burgundy, km. . . . . 58 F de
Burgundy, prov. . . . . 148 E e
Burgundy, Cisjurane (Arles) . . 56 CD cd
Burgundy, Free County of, 14 cent. 78 D e
Burgundy, Free County of, 17 cent. 126 D e
Burgundy, Lower, dist. . . . . . 62 C f
Burgundy, Transjurane or Upper, km. . . . . 56 D c
Burgundy, Upper, dist. . . . . . 62 D e
Buri, people . . . . 34 H d
Burkersdorf . . . . 135 I c
Burlington, in Iowa . . . . 211 G b
Burlington, in New Jersey . . . 192 D c
Burlington, in Vermont . . . . . 211 K b
Burlyuk . . . . 164 J f
Burma, reg. . . . .
Burma, Lower, prov. . . . . . . 171 K g
Burma, Upper, prov. . . . . . . 171 K f
Burnum . . . . 38 F c
Burriana . . . . 82 B b
Burrough, route of . . . . 109 W a
Bursfelde, mon. . . . . 95 D a
Burshena see Purchena . . . . . 83 K h
Burton-on-Trent, mon. . . . . . 97 P i
Bury, parl. bor. . . . . 163 L d
Bury Saint Edmunds . . . .
Bury Saint Edmunds, mon. . . .
Bury St. Edmunds, parl. bor. . 163 O e
Burzenland, dist. . . . . 80 I i
Busaco . . . . 130 B e
Busento River . . . . 50 G e

Bushire . . . . . . 170 G f
Bushwick . . . . . . 189 ins. C (Bush.)
Bushy Run, battle . . . . . . 194 K f
Busiris. . . . . . 4 ins.
Busk . . . . . . 159 K c
Busselton . . . . . . 172 A d
Bussière, La, mon. . . . . . . 94 C b
Busuluk . . . . . . 139 H e
Bute, cty. . . . . . .
Bute, Fort . . . . . . 195 ins. B
Buthrotum (Butrinto) . . . . . . 10 B c
Butler, route of . . . . . . 195 C b
Butlers, The, fam. . . . . . .
Butley, mon. . . . . . . 97 S i
Buto . . . . . . 4 ins.
Butonti . . . . . .
Bütow . . . . . . 115 I a
Butrinto . . . . . . 93 A c
Butte . . . . . . 210 C a
Buxar . . . . . . 137 D c
Buxentum . . . . . . 30 E b
Buxentum, prom. . . . . . . 30 E c
Buxentus River . . . . . . 30 E c
Buxtehude . . . . . . 62 E b
Buxtehude, Hanse. cy. . . . . . . 99 ins. B
Buzzards Bay . . . . . . 189 C d
Byblus . . . . . . 4 F c
Byland, mon. . . . . . . 97 P g
Byllis . . . . . . 31 I b
Byrsa, citadel . . . . . . 34 ins. A (4)
Bytown (Ottawa) . . . . . . 212 H d
Byzacium, reg. . . . . . . 38 D e
Byzacium, West Rom. prov. . . 42 D g (1)
Byzantine Empire, about 814 54-55 F f
Byzantine Empire, about 1000 . 59 H-L f
Byzantine Empire, 12 cent. . . . 71 K e
Byzantine Empire, in 1265 . . . 89
Byzantine Empire, in 1355 . . . 89
Byzantine Empire, in 1451 . . . 93 C b
Byzantium (Constantinople) . .

Caacupe . . . . . . 215 D e
Cabalia, reg. . . . . . . 20 C d
Cabasa . . . . . . 43 I g
Cabellio or Cabellione, see Cavaillon
Cabes . . . . . .
Cabeza de Vaca, route of . . . 190 D f
Cabillonum or Cabilonum (Chalon) . . . . . . 39 H j
Cabira . . . . . . 20 G b
Cabo das Corrientes, cape . . . 109 U j
Cabot, John, route of . . . 108 O b, M c
Cabot, Sebastian, route of . . . 108 L k
Cabra . . . . . . 82 B b
Cabral, route of . . . . . . 108 O h, Q j
Cabrillo, route of . . . . . . 107 E d
Cabul (Kabul), in Afghanistan 53 I c
Cabul, in Palestine . . . . . . 6 C c
Cabura (Kabul in Afghanistan) 19 K d
Caburrum . . . . . . 26 B c
Cáceres . . . . . . 82 A b
Cache Valley, dist. . . . . . . 210 C b
Cacyparis River . . . . . . 30 E e
Caddos, tribe . . . . . . 188 G d
Cadiz . . . . . . 82 A b
Cadiz, bp. . . . . . . 94 A d
Cadore . . . . . . 90 D a
Cadouin, mon. . . . . . . 94 C c
Cadurci or Cadurcis, see Cahors
Cadurci, people . . . . . . 38 C d
Cadusii (Cadusians), people . . 19 G c
Cæcina River . . . . . . 26 E d
Cæcinus River . . . . . . 30 E e
Cæcuban Territory . . . . . . 30 C a
Cælemontane Gate . . . . . . 23 B
Cælia, in Apulia . . . . . . 31 F a
Cælia, in Calabria . . . . . . 31 G b
Cælian Mount . . . . . . 22 A
Cælian, quarter . . . . . . 96 A
Cælimontium, Aug. Reg. of Rome . . . . . . 22 A
Caen . . . . . . 69 C b
Caen, gen. . . . . . . 147 D b
Caen, mon. . . . . . . 94 B b
Caen, univ. . . . . . . 100 E e
Cænæ . . . . . . 20 J e
Cænepolis . . . . . . 14 C c
Cænia, mt. . . . . . . 26 A c
Cænys, prom. . . . . . . 31 E d
Cære . . . . . . 27 G e
Cærleon-upon-Usk . . . . . . 42 B c
Cærwent . . . . . .
Cæsar, Statue of . . . . . . 24 B (12)
Cæsar, Gardens of . . . . . . 22 A
Cæsaraugusta (Saragossa) . . . . 38 B d
Cæsarea, in Cappadocia (Kaisarieh) . . . . . . 20 F c
Cæsarea, in Mauretania . . . . 38 C e
Cæsarea, in Samaria . . . . . . 6 B c
Cæsarea Philippi . . . . . . 6 D b
Cæsarea, isl. (Jersey) . . . . . . 38 B c
Cæsarobriga (Talavera de la Reina) . . . . . . 38 B d
Cæsarodunum (Tours) . . . . . . 38 C c
Cæsaromagus, see Beauvais
Cæsar's Forum . . . . . . 24 B
Cæsena . . . . . . 27 G c
Cagli, bp. . . . . . . 95 E c (C.)
Cagliari . . . . . . 42 D f
Cagliari, abp. . . . . . . 95 D d
Caguas . . . . . . 199 ins. G
Cahokia . . . . . . 191 H d
Cahors . . . . . . 91 D d
Cahors, bp. . . . . . . 94 C c
Cahors, univ. . . . . . . 100 F f
Cahorsin, cty. . . . . . . 76 D d
Caiatia . . . . . . 30 D a
Caicos Islands . . . . . . 213 E b
Caicus River . . . . . .
Caieta (Gaëta) . . . . . . 30 C a
Caieta, bay . . . . . . 30 C a
Cailac . . . . . .
Cailloux, farm . . . . . .
Caimitillo River . . . . . .
Caino or Cainone, see Chinon
Cairns . . . . . . 172 D b
Cairo, in Egypt . . . . . . 67 M h
Cairo, in Illinois . . . . . . 199 H c
Cairo, in Italy . . . . . . 130 Q j
Cairo, calif. . . . . . .
Caithness, bp. . . . . . . 97 I a
Caithness, cty. . . . . . .
Caithness, dist. . . . . . .
Caius Cestius, Tomb of . . . . 22 A
Cajamarca . . . . . . 111 B c
Cajon Pass . . . . . . 210 B d
Calabar . . . . . . 175 D d
Calabozo . . . . . . 214 C b
Calabria, dist., in Rom. times . 31 G b
Calabria, dist., 15 cent. . . . . . 90 F e
Calabria, duchy, 11 cent. . . . . 66 J f
Calabria, theme, 10 cent. . . . . 59 H f
Caladunum, see Châlons
Calaf . . . . . . 82 C a
Calagurris (Calahorra) . . . . . . 38 B d
Calahorra . . . . . . 82 B a
Calahorra, bp. . . . . . . 94 B c
Calais, in France . . . . . . 76 D a
Calais, in Maine . . . . . . 211 L a
Calama, in Algeria . . . . . . 42 D f
Calama, in Chile . . . . . . 215 C e
Calamar . . . . . . 214 B a
Calamine, dist. . . . . . . 10 B c
Calanicum . . . . . . 26 C c
Calatafimi . . . . . . 161 I i
Calatayud . . . . . . 82 B a
Calatha . . . . . . 38 D e
Calatia . . . . . . 30 D a
Calatrava . . . . . . 82 B b
Calatrava, mon. . . . . . . 94 B d
Calauria, isl. . . . . . . 15 D b
Calaurus, mt. . . . . . . 11 E b
Calcaria, see Tadcaster
Calchedon . . . . . .
Calchu . . . . . . 5 D b
Calcutta . . . . . . 137 E d
Caldera . . . . . . 215 B e
Calderon . . . . . . 213 ins.
Caldiero . . . . . . 150 F d
Cale . . . . . . 191 I f
Cale, Portus (Oporto) . . . . . . 38 A d
Caleacte . . . . . . 30 D e
Cale acte, Cape . . . . . . 15 E a
Caledonia (Scotland) . . . . . . 38 B a
Caledonia, New, isl. . . . . . . 172 F c
Caledonii, people . . . . . . 38 B a
Cales (Calvi), in Campania . . . 30 D a
Cales, in Umbria . . . . . . 27 G d
Caletes, people . . . . . .
Calgary . . . . . . 212 D c
Calhoun, Fort . . . . . . 210 F b
Cali . . . . . . 111 B a
Calicut . . . . . . 137 C f
Califate, emp. . . . . . .
Califate, reg. . . . . . . 71 O g
California, Gulf of . . . . . . 187 H f
California, state . . . . . . 202 A h
California, Lower, pen. . . . . . 187 H e-f
California, Lower, prov. . 107—108 F d e
California, Upper, prov. . . . . 190 A B d e
California Cut-off, route . . . . 210 D c
California Trail . . . . . . 210 B b
California Valley . . . . . . 187 G e
Caligula, Palace of . . . . . . 24 B
Calindœa . . . . . .
Call, parl. bor. . . . . . . 163 J g
Callao . . . . . . 214 B d
Callas River . . . . . . 11 E c
Callatis . . . . . . 39 N l
Calleva (Silchester) . . . . . .
Callidromus, mt. . . . . . . 11 D e
Callipolis, in Calabria . . . . . . 31 G b
Callipolis, in Thrace . . . . . . 39 N l
Callirrhoe . . . . . . 23 D
Callium . . . . . . 10 D d
Calliupolis . . . . . .
Callone . . . . . . 18 G d
Calmar . . . . . . 88 G c
Calmar, Hanse. for. cy. . . . . . 98 G b
Calne, parl. bor. . . . . . . 163 L f
Calor River . . . . . . 30 D a
Calpe, in Bithynia . . . . . . 20 D b
Calpe, in Spain . . . . . . 12 B c
Calpulalpan . . . . . .
Caltanisetta . . . . . . 90 D f
Caluso . . . . . . 130 P i
Calvados, dept. . . . . . . 148 D e
Calverton . . . . . . 192 C d
Calvert Town . . . . . . 192 C d
Calvi, bp. . . . . . . 95 ins.
Calw . . . . . . 143 G h
Calw, cty. . . . . . . 143 G h
Calycadnus River . . . . . . 20 E d
Calydon . . . . . . 10 C d
Calydon, Gulf of . . . . . . 14 B a
Calymna, isl. . . . . . . 17 E c
Calynda . . . . . . 20 C d
Cam, Diogo, route of . . . . . . 108 R h
Camaldoli . . . . . . 90 L j
Camaldoli, mon. . . . . . . 95 E c
Camaracus, see Cambray
Camargo, in Bolivia . . . . . . 214 C e
Camargo, in Mexico . . . . . . 201 F d
Camarina . . . . . . 30 D e
Camarones River . . . . . . 214 B d
Cambalec (Peking) . . . . . .
Cambay . . . . . . 137 B d
Cambay, Gulf of . . . . . . 137 B d
Cambete . . . . . . 39 I j
Cambodia, reg. . . . . . .
Cambodunum, in Britain . . . . 51 P h
Cambodunum, in Rætia . . . . . 39 K j
Camboricum (Cambridge) . . . .
Cambray . . . . . .
Cambray, bp. . . . . . . 117 B d
Cambrésis, cty. . . . . . . 117 B d
Cambrian Mountains . . . . . . 49 E e
Cambridge, in England . . . .
Cambridge, in Mass. . . . . . . 189 ins. B
Cambridge, castle . . . . . . 65 G d

Cambridge, cty. 127 Z n
Cambridge, mon. 97 R i
Cambridge, parl. bor. 163 O e
Cambridge, parl. dist. 163 O e
Cambridge, shire
Cambridge, univ. 100 F d
Cambridge, univ., parl. bor. 163 O e
Cambunian Mountains 10 C c
Cambuskenneth 84 B a
Camden, in N. S. Wales
Camden, in New Jersey 192 D d
Camden, in S. Carolina 195 A f
Camelford, parl. bor. 163 J g
Cameria 35 ins. B
Camerino 90 D c
Camerino, bp. 95 E c
Camerino, march 64 B b
Camerinum 27 H d
Camerons, fam. 97 H c
Cameroons, see Kamerun
Cameta 214 E c
Camexa
Camillomagus 26 D b
Camirus 13 E c
Camisards, people 129 D d
Campagna, dist. 64 ins.
Campanha 214 E e
Campania, dist. 30 D b
Campania, Rom. prov. 42 E e (1)
Campbell, route of 195 D f
Campbells, fam. 97 H c
Camp du Bois 199 H c
Campeche 213 C c
Campeche, state 213 C c
Campeche Bay 187 J f
Camperdown 153 E b
Camp Floyd 210 C b
Campidona, see Kempten
Campi Raudii or Raudian Plain, dist. 26 C b
Campobasso 90 E d
Campos 214 E e
Campo Vitale 62 F f
Campsey Ash, mon. 97 S i
Campus Martius, loc. in Rome 22 A
Campus Sceleratus, loc. in Rome 23 B
Campylus River 10 C c
Camulodunum (Colchester)
Camunni, people 26 E b
Camuy 199 ins. G
Cana 6 C c
Cana River 7 B d
Canaan 207 L b
Canaan, reg. 4 F c
Canaanites, people 7 ins. D
Canada, col. 194 Cb, Ea
Canada, Dominion of 212 H c
Canadian Pacific Railway 212 D c
Canadian River 190 F d
Canal du Midi 130 D e
Canal Zone, dist.
Cananea, bay of 108 M j
Caña Quebrada, R.
Canary Islands 174 B b
Canastræum, prom. 11 E c
Canatha 6 F c
Canaveral, Cape 191 I f
Canbury 55 R i
Cancellaria 96 A
Candahar 137 A b
Candavia 10 B a
Candavian Mountains 10 B a
Candelaria 215 C e
Canea 77 I e
Cangas de Onis 82 A a
Canigou, mon. 94 C c
Cannæ 31 F a
Cannanore 137 C f
Canne 64 C b
Canninefates, people 39 H g
Cannock Chase 49 E e
Cannon Gate 93 G e
Cannstadt 143 H h
Canonicut Island 189 C d
Canopic Gate 34 ins. C
Canopus 4 ins.
Canossa 64 B b
Canso 194 G a
Canso, strait of 212 J d
Cantabri, people 38 B d
Cantabria, reg. 82 B a
Cantabrian Mountains 2 D d
Cantal, dept. 148 E e
Canterbury, in Conn. 207 L b
Canterbury, in England
Canterbury, abp. 97 N i
Canterbury, dist. in N. Zealand 172 G e
Canterbury, Hanse. for. cy. 98 ins. A
Canterbury, parl. bor. 163 P f
Canterbury Bight 172 G e
Cantharus Port 16 D c
Cantii, people 51 Q i
Cantillana 82 A b
Canton 171 M f
Cantuaria, see Canterbury
Canusium 31 F a
Cany 76 D b
Caononabo, chieftain 105 F c
Caorle, bp. 95 E b
Capara 38 A d
Capdenac 126 C d
Cape Ann 189 C c
Cape Coast Castle 175 C d
Cape Cod Bay 189 C d
Cape Colony, col. 175 F h
Cape Fear River 193 E d
Cape Haitien 213 E c
Capena 27 G e
Capena Gate, in Rome 23 B
Capena Gate, Aug. Reg., Rome 22 A
Cape of Good Hope, cape 175 E h
Cape of Good Hope, col. 175 F h
Cape of Storms 109 S k
Cape Porpoise 189 C c
Capernaum 6 D c
Cape Town 175 E h
Cape Verd 174 B c
Cape Verd Islands 174 A c
Cape York Peninsula 172 D b
Caphereus, prom. 15 E a
Caphyæ 14 C b
Capitanata, dist. 90 E d
Capitolias 6 D c
Capitoline, quarter 96 A
Capitoline Mount 24 A
Capo d'Istria
Capo d'Istria, bp. 95 E b
Cappadocia, dist. 20 F c
Cappadocia, imp. prov. 35 L f
Cappadocia, prov. 18 D c
Cappadocia, reg. 8 B b
Cappadocia, satr. 8 H d
Cappadocia, theme 59 K f
Cappadocia I, East Rom. prov. 43 I f (6)
Cappadocia II, East Rom. prov. 43 I f (7)
Capraria, isl., near Corsica 26 D e
Capraria, isl., Balearic Is. 38 C e
Caprasia 31 F c
Capreæ (Capri), isl. 30 D b
Caprera, isl. 161 G g
Capri, bp. 95 ins.
Capri, isl. 90 E d
Caprus 11 E b
Capsa 34 F g
Capua (ancient) 30 D a
Capua (modern) 90 E d
Capua, abp. 95 E c
Capua, princ. 64 B b
Capucines, The, ch.
Caput Africæ 22 A
Caputvada 52 D c
Caqueta River 111 C b
Carabaros 105 D e
Carabobo, battle 214 C b
Caracalla, Baths of 22 A
Caracarum or Karakorum
Caracas 214 C a
Caracas, cap. gen. and pres. 215 ins.
Caraceni, people 27 I f
Caracuel 82 B b
Caradeña, mon. 94 B e
Caralis (Cagliari) 12 B c
Caramagna, mon. 95 D e
Caramoran River
Carana 20 I c
Caranchuas, tribe 188 G e
Caraques, Bahia de, bay 111 A b
Caravaggio 90 B b
Caravelhas 214 F d
Carbonera 82 B b
Carcaso, Carcasona or Carcasso (Carcassonne) 38 C d
Carcassonne 76 E e
Carcassonne, bp. 94 C c
Carchemish 4 F c
Carcinus River 31 F e
Cardamyle 14 C c
Cárdenas 213 D b
Cárdenas, route of 190 C d
Cardenas River
Cardia
Cardiff 65 E e
Cardiff, parl. bor. 163 K f
Cardigan, castle 74 C e
Cardigan, cty. 127 U n
Cardigan, parl. bor. 163 J e
Cardigan, parl. dist. 163 J e
Cardigan Bay
Cardona 130 D e
Careiæ 35 ins. B
Carentan 76 C b
Carentonus River, see Charente River
Careta 105 E e
Carey, lake 172 B c
Caria, dist. 20 C d
Caria, East Rom. prov. 43 H f (3)
Caria, reg. 5 B b
Caria, satr. 18 N h
Cariæ 14 C b
Cariari 105 D d
Caribbean Sea 187 L g
Carical
Carinæ 22 A
Carinthia, duchy, about 1000 63 H e
Carinthia, duchy, 14 cent. 79 I e
Carinthia, march 63 H e
Carinthia, reg. 54 G d
Carioli 35 ins. B
Carisbrooke
Carisbrooke, mon. 100 A b
Carisbrooke Castle 127 X p
Carisiacus, see Kiersy
Carlat 76 E d
Carlat, viscty. 76 E d
Carlingford
Carlisle, in England
Carlisle, in Pa. 188 K b
Carlisle, bp. 97 O g
Carlisle, parl. bor. 163 L c
Carlos, Bahia de, bay 191 I f
Carlow
Carlow, cty. 127 K i
Carlowitz 159 J f
Carlsbad 79 H c
Carlskrona 131 G b
Carlsruhe 142 B b
Carlstein, castle 79 H c
Carmagnola 130 P j
Carmalas River 20 F d
Carmana (Kirman) 19 I d
Carmania (Kirman), prov. 19 I e
Carmania, satr. 18 Q i
Carmanians, people 8 J e
Carmarthen, castle
Carmarthen, cty. 127 U o
Carmarthen, mon. 97 M j
Carmarthen, parl. bor. 163 J f
Carmarthen, parl. dist. 163 J f
Carmel 7 C f
Carmel, mt. 6 C e
Carmelites, mon. in London 75 G g
Carmelites, The, mon. in Paris 149 B

Carmen 213 C c
Carmen de Patagonés 215 C g
Carmenta Gate 24 A
Carmona 82 A b
Carnarvon, castle
Carnarvon, cty. 127 U n
Carnarvon, parl. bor. 163 J d
Carnarvon, parl. dist. 163 J e
Carnatic, reg. 112 A b
Carni, people 27 H a
Carnic Alps, mts. 27 G a
Carnicum Julium 27 G a
Carniola, duchy 79 I f
Carniola, march 63 H f
Carniola, reg. 56 E c
Carnsore Point 127 K i
Carnuntum 38 F c
Carnus, isl. 10 B d
Carnotes or Carnutes, see Chartres
Carnutes, people 38 C c
Carolina, col. 193 C f-E e
Carolina, North, col. 193 E d
Carolina, North, state 196 C c
Carolina, South, col. 193 D d
Carolina, South, state 196 C d
Carolina Proprietors, Grants to the 190 ins.
Caroline, Fort 191 I e
Caroline Island 180 M h
Caroline Islands 179 F g
Caroline River 214 C b
Carolingian Empire 54
Carpathian Mountains 2 G d
Carpathian Sea 17 E d
Carpathos, isl. 4 C b
Carpentaria, Gulf of 172 C b
Carpentoracte, see Carpentras
Carpentras, bp. 95 D c
Carpetani, people 38 B d
Carpi 131 F e
Carpi, people 38 F i
Carpis 46 I f
Carrara, near Pisa 90 L i
Carrara, near Venice 90 J h
Carrara, dist. 79 G f
Carrea Potentia 26 B c
Carrhæ 20 H d
Carrick, dist.
Carrickfergus
Carrión de los Condes 83 K g
Carsioli 27 H e
Carson 210 B c
Carson City 206 A c
Carsulæ 27 G e
Cartagena, in Colombia 214 B a
Cartagena, in Spain 82 B b
Cártago, in Colombia 214 B b
Cártago, in Costa Rica 213 D d
Carteia 38 A e
Cartenna 38 C e
Carteret, Cape 193 ins. C
Carthæa 15 E b
Carthage (ancient) 38 E e
Carthage, in Missouri 207 G c
Carthage, New (Cartagena) 38 B e
Carthage, plan of 34 ins. A
Carthaginiensis, West Rom. prov. 42 B f(5)
Carthago 12 E c
Carthusian Priory of the Salutation 75 G g
Carthusians, The, mon. in Paris 149 B
Cartier, routes of 108 M b, O c
Caruanca, mt. 27 I a
Carus River, see Cher River
Carystus, in Eubœa 15 E a
Carystus, in Laconia 14 C b
Casablanca 174 C a
Casale 90 I h
Cascadas, Las
Cascade Mountains 186 G c
Casco, in Maine 189 C c
Casco, in Mexico 190 E f
Casco Bay 189 C c
Caserta 90 E d
Caserta, bp. 95 ins.
Cashel
Cashel, abp. 97 C d
Cashmere or Kashmir, reg.
Casilinum 30 D a
Casimir, Fort 192 ins.
Casinum 30 C a
Casmenæ 30 D e
Caspe 83 L g
Caspian Depression, plain 3 I d
Caspian Gates, pass 19 H c
Caspian Sea 3 I d
Caspians, people 8 I d
Cassander, Kingdom of 18
Cassandrea 11 E b
Cassano 134 E f
Cassano, bp. 95 F d
Cassel, in Flanders 117 A d
Cassel, in Hesse 62 E c
Cassian Way, road 27 F e
Cassii, Forum 27 G e
Cassim Pasha, quarter
Cassinelle 130 Q j
Cassiope 10 A c
Cassiquiare River 214 C b
Cassiterides Islands 34 C c
Cassope 10 B c
Cassopia, reg. 10 B c
Casteldelfino 130 O j
Castelfidardo 161 I f
Casteljaloux 126 B d
Castell 122 F d
Castellammare 161 J g
Castellaneta 90 F d
Castello Branco 94 A d
Castellón de la Plana 83 E a
Castellum (Kastel) 39 J h
Castellum Felicitatis, see Città di Castello
Castellum Firmanum 27 H d
Castellum Flevum 39 H g
Castelnaudary 69 D e
Castelnuovo 125 G d
Castelsagrat 126 B d
Castets 126 A d
Casthanæa 11 D c
Castiglione, in Calabria 90 F e
Castiglione, near Florence 90 L j
Castiglione, near Mantua 150 F d
Castiglione dalla Pescaja 90 L j
Castile, cty. 82 B a
Castile, km., 11 cent. 83 E c
Castile, km., 12 cent. 82 H e
Castile, km., 15 cent. 83 K g
Castilla del Oro, reg. 105 D e
Castillon 76 C d
Castine 189 D b
Castle Acre, mon. 97 R i
Castle Jacob 68 ins. A
Castle of the Seven Towers 93 G e
Castle Rising, parl. bor. 163 O e
Castor, near Norwich 51 Q h
Castor, Temple of
Castor and Pollux, Temple of
Castores, Ad 26 E b
Castoria 59 I e
Castra Batava (Passau) 38 E c
Castra Hannibalis 31 F d
Castra Sarræ 39 H i
Castra Vetera 39 I h
Castres 76 E e
Castres, bp. 94 C c (Cast.)
Castres, cty. 84 E h
Castres, seign. 76 E e
Castrimœnium 35 ins. B
Castriota, Dominion of 93 A b
Castro, bp. 95 E c
Castrogiovanni 64 B c
Castrovillari 90 F e
Castrum Bobium (Bobbio) 26 D c
Castrum Gordonis, see Sancerre
Castrum Minervæ 31 H b
Castrum Nantonis, see Château-Landon
Castrum novum, in Etruria 27 F e
Castrum novum, in Picenum 27 I e
Castrum Peregrinorum 68 ins. A
Castrum Truentinum 27 H e
Castulo 38 B e
Castulo, bp. 42 B f
Castulonensis, Saltus, mts. 38 B e
Casuentus (Basento) River 31 F b
Casus, isl. 17 E d
Caswell, Fort 208 E c
Catacombs of Saint Callistus 96 A
Catalão 214 E d
Catalauni or Catalaunis, see Châlons
Catalaunian Fields 48 E c
Catalonia, princ. 83 L g
Catalonia, reg. 82 I e
Catamarca 215 C e
Catana 30 E e
Catania 90 E f
Catania, bp. 95 F d
Catania, univ. 100 I g
Catanzaro 90 F e
Catanzaro, bp. 95 F d
Cataractonium (Catterick) 51 P g
Catawba River 195 A f
Catawbas, tribe 188 J d
Cateau-Cambrésis 117 B d
Cathay (China), cty. 92 K d
Catholic Hennersdorf 135 H c
Catillus, mt. 35 ins. B
Cat Island 105 E b
Catoche, Cape 105 C b
Catskill 192 E b
Catskill Mountains 192 D b
Cattaraugus, Ind. Res. 188 K b
Cattaro 90 G c
Cattaro, abp. 95 F c
Caturiges 39 H i
Caturiges, people 26 A c
Catuvellauni, people
Caub 154 D c
Cauca 38 B d
Cauca River 214 B b
Caucasians, people 57 K e
Caucasus Mountains 3 I d
Cauci, people 38 A b
Caudebec 126 B b
Caudine Forks, passes, near Caudium
Caudini, people 30 D a
Caudium 30 D a
Caughnawaga 212 H d
Caulonia 31 F d
Caunus 20 C d
Caura River 214 C b
Causannæ 51 P h
Caux, dist. 69 H f
Caux, Chef de, cape 81 L h
Cava, La, mon. 95 ins.
Cavaillon 76 F e
Cavaillon, bp. 95 D c
Cavan, cty. 127 J g
Cavite 199 ins. H
Cavore, mon. 95 D c
Cavour 130 P j
Cawnpur, Cawnpore 137 D c
Caxamarca 111 B c
Caxias 214 E c
Cayambe 214 B b
Cayenne 214 D b
Cayay 199 ins. G
Cayos, Los, isl. 105 E b
Cayphas 68 ins. A
Cayster River 13 E b
Caystrupedium
Cayuga Lake 192 C b
Cayugas, tribe 188 K b
Cazalla de la Sierra 82 A b
Cazlona 46 F f
Cé, Pont de 130 C d
Ceará 214 F c
Ceará, state 214 F c
Ceba 26 C c

Cebenna Mountains 38 C d
Cebrene
Cebu 112 F b
Cebu, isl. 110 D D f
Cecryphalæ, isl.
Cedar Creek, battle 208 E b
Cedar Keys 213 D b
Cedar Mountain, battle 208 E b
Cedar River 211 G b
Cedron, Vale of 6 ins. A
Cefalù 90 E e
Cefalù, bp. 95 E d
Ceiriadæ, deme 23 D
Celadussæ, isl. 27 J d
Celebes, isl.
Celebes Sea 171 N h
Celeia 27 J a
Celenderis 15 D b
Celetrum 10 C b
Céligny 91 O l
Cellæ 10 C b
Celle 79 G b
Celtiberians, people 32 A c
Celtic Gaul 38 ins.
Celtici, people 38 A e
Celts, people 5 A a
Cemenelum 26 B d
Cempoalla 106 D a
Cenabum (Orléans) 38 C c
Cenæum, prom. 11 D d
Cenchreæ, near Argos 14 C b
Cenchreæ, near Corinth 15 D b
Ceneda, bp. 95 E b
Ceneda 27 G b
Cenis, Mont, pass 26 A b
Cenis, people 188 G d
Cenomani or Cenomanis see Le Mans
Cenomani, people 26 E b
Centerville 208 ins.
Central Africa, British, see Nyasaland 175 G f
Central America, reg. 213 D c
Central America, Cordillera of 187 K g
Central Asia, reg. 170 G I d
Central Californians, tribes 188 B c
Central German Commercial Union 160 D c
Centripæ 30 D e
Centula or Centulum (Saint Riquier), mon. 94 C a
Centumcellæ (Civitavecchia) 27 F e
Centum Gradus 24 A
Centurinum 26 D e
Ceos (Cea), isl. 15 E b
Cephale 16 B b
Cephalenia, theme 59 H f
Cephallenia (Cephalonia), isl. 10 B d
Cephalonia, cty. 73 D c
Cephalonia, isl. 89 H g
Cephalonia, palat. 89 A c
Cephalœdium 30 D d
Cephisia 16 B a
Cephisus River, in Attica 16 B a
Cephisus River, in Bœotia 11 D d
Ceprano 72 C c
Ceramic Gulf 17 E c
Ceramicus, Inner, quarter 23 D
Ceramicus, Outer, quarter 23 D
Ceramon-agora 20 C c
Cerasus 20 H b
Ceraunii Mountains
Cerbalus River 30 E a
Cercamp, mon. 94 C a
Certetius, mt. 10 C c
Cercina, isl. 38 E f
Cercinitis, lake 11 E b
Cerdagne, reg. 83 F c
Cerdylium 11 E b
Cereatæ 30 C a
Ceredigion, reg.
Ceres, Temple of 24 B
Ceresius (Lugano) lake 26 C a
Ceretani, people 38 C d
Cereus River 11 E d
Cerignola 90 E d
Cerigo, isl. 89 B c
Cerillæ 30 E c
Cerinthus 11 E d
Cérisy, mon. 94 B b
Cerlier, castle 91 P k
Cermalus, quarter
Cerne, Ilha do, isl. 109 W j
Cerne, mon. 97 O k
Cerro Columbia, hill
Cerro Comboy, hill
Cerro Culebra, hill
Cerro de Cabras, hill
Cerro de los Harmigueros, hill
Cerro de Pasco 214 B d
Cerro de San Juan, hill
Cerro Gordo, battle 201 H g
Cerro Mitra, hill
Certosa, mon. 95 D b
Ceruglio 90 L j
Cervia 90 M i
Cervia, bp. 95 E c
Cerynia 14 C a
Cesena 90 D b
Cesena, bp. 95 E c
Cessetani, people 38 C d
Cestian Bridge 22 A
Cestrine, reg. 10 B c
Cestrus River 20 D d
Cettigne 166 I g
Ceuta
Ceutrones, people 26 A b
Ceva 90 I h
Ceylon, isl. 137 D g
Chablais, dist. 91 O l
Chaboras River 20 I e
Chacabuco, battle 215 B f
Chachapoyas 111 B c
Chacon, Cape 212 ins.
Chad, lake 174 E c
Chads Ford, battle 195 C c
Chæronea 11 D d
Chagatai, khan.
Chagos Islands 182 II h
Chagres
Chagres River
Chaibasa, reg. 137 E d
Chaillot 149 B
Chaise-Dieu, La, mon. 94 C b
Chalæum 11 D d
Chalastra 11 D b
Chalcedon
Chalcidice, reg. 11 E b
Chalcis, in Ætolia 10 C d
Chalcis, in Epirus 10 C c
Chalcis, in Eubœa 11 E d
Chalcis, in Syria 6 D a
Chalco 106 B a
Chalco, lake 106 B a
Chaldæi, people 18 G d
Chaldea, reg. 4 G c
Chaldean Empire 8
Chaldeans, people
Chaldia, theme 59 L e
Chaldiran
Chales, mon. 94 C b
Chaleurs, Bay of 194 G a
Chalgrove 127 X o
Chalia 11 E d
Chalish (Karashar)
Chalivoy, mon. 94 C b
Chaloché, mon. 94 B b
Chalon 61 F c
Chalon, cty. 69 J f
Chalon, sur-Saône, bp. 94 C b
Châlons 61 F b
Châlons, cty. 61 F b
Châlons, duchy 76 F b
Châlons, gen. 147 E b
Châlons-sur-Marne, bp. 94 C b
Chalus, castle 69 D d
Cham 63 G d
Chamavi, people 39 I g
Chambal River 137 C c
Chambersburg 208 ins.
Chambéry 130 N i
Chambly, Fort 189 B b
Chambord 126 B c
Champa
Champa, reg.
Champagne, cty. 11 cent. 61 E b
Champagne, cty. 12 cent. 69
Champagne, cty. 14 cent. 76 F b
Champagne, prov. 148 E e
Champagne and Brie, gouv. 146 B b
Champ de Mars, loc. in Paris 149 B
Champaubert 154 B d
Champion Hill 208 B c
Champlain, lake 189 B b
Champs Elysées, loc. in Paris 149 B
Champtoceaux 81 L h
Chanar 187 D c
Chañaral 215 B e
Chancellade, mon. 94 C b
Chancellerie, Rue de la, street in Versailles 149 A
Chancellor, route of 109 Ub, Va
Chancellorsville 208 E b (Chan.)
Chanda 137 C d
Chandarnagar 137 E d
Chandax 59 J f
Chanderi
Chandernagore 137 E d
Changanor
Chang-chau 171 M f
Chang-chau-fu
Chang-kia-chwang 170 ins. A
Chang-sha 171 M f
Channel Islands 49 E g
Chaoni, people
Chaonia, dist. 10 A b
Chapelle-Saint-Lambert
Chapultepec, castle 201 H g
Charadra 10 B c
Charadrus 11 F b
Charadrus River 14 C b
Charcas, pres. 215 ins.
Chard 127 V p
Chard, parl. bor.
Chardjui
Charente, dept. 148 E e
Charente River 76 C d
Charente-Inférieure, dept. 148 D e
Charenton 126 C b
Charidemi, prom. 38 B e
Charikar
Charing Cross, loc. in London 75 G g
Charisius, gate 93 G e
Charité, La, near Nevers 126 C c
Charité, La, in Paris 149 B
Charkov
Charlemont 126 D a
Charleroi 117 C d
Charles, Cape, in Labrador 186 N c
Charles, Cape, in Virginia 193 ins. A
Charles X., route of 121 D a
Charles City 193 ins. A
Charles City County 193 ins. A (Ch.)
Charlesfort 191 I e
Charles River 189 ins. B
Charleston, in S. C. 211 J d
Charleston, in W. Va. 211 I c
Charlestown, near Boston 189 ins. B
Charles Town, in S. Carolina 193 ins. C
Charleville 172 D c
Charlotiana, proposed col. in U.S. 194 A a
Charlotte 191 I d
Charlotte, Fort 195 ins. B
Charlotte Harbor 191 I f
Charlottenburg 135 G b
Charlottesville 193 E c
Charlottetown 212 I d
Charolais, cty. 126 D c
Charolais, dist. 81 M h
Charolles 76 F c
Charolles, cty. 114 C e
Charroux, mon. 94 C b
Charsianon, theme 59 K f

Charter House, bldg. in London 75 G g
Charters Towers 172 D b
Chartres 61 D b
Chartres, bp. 94 C b
Chartres, Fort 191 G d
Chartreuse, mon. 69 F d
Charudes, people 38 D a
Chassaigne, La, mon. 95 D b (L. Ch.)
Chastel Blanc, castle 68 C bc
Chastel Rouge, castle 68 C c
Châteaubriant, castle 76 C c
Château-Chalon, mon. 148 C b
Château Chinon 76 F c
Château Dauphin 126 E d
Château de Joux 126 E c
Château d'If 126 D e
Château d'Œx 91 P l
Châteaudun 61 D b
Châteaudun, bp. 94 C b (Chât.)
Château Gaillard, castle 76 D b
Château-Landon 61 E b
Châteauneuf, in Angoumois 126 B d
Châteauneuf, in Perche 76 D b
Château-Porcien 69 F b
Château-Renard 69 I g
Châteauroux 76 D c
Châteauroux, seign. 69 H g
Château-Thierry 69 I f
Châtelet, near Charleroi 117 C d
Châtelet, loc. in Paris 149 B
Châtellerault 76 D c
Châtellerault, viscty. 76 D c
Chatelot 143 ins. F
Chatelot, lordship 143 ins. F
Chatham, parl. bor. 163 O f
Chatham Islands 172 H e
Châtillon, on the Marne R. 69 I f
Châtillon, near Nevers 126 C c
Châtillon, in Savoy 91 P m
Châtillon, on the Seine R. 76 F c
Chattahoochee River 193 B e
Chattanooga 208 C b
Chatti, people 39 J h
Chauci, people 38 D b
Chaudière River 188 L a
Chaul
Chaumont, in Champagne 76 F b
Chaumont, in Vexin 76 E b
Chauon 18 F c
Chaussée, la 154 C d
Chautauqua, lake 192 B b
Chauvigny 76 D c
Chaves 82 A a
Cheadle 127 X n
Cheap, loc. in London 75 G g (35)
Cheat River 192 B d
Chef de Caux, Cape 81 L h
Chehalis, Ind. Res. 188 B a
Chehalis, tribe 188 B a
Che-kiang, prov. 171 M f
Cheliabinsk 170 H c
Chelidoniæ Islands 20 D d
Cheliff, or Sheliff, River 118 E f
Chelmsford 127 Z o
Chelmsford, parl. bor.
Chelonatas Gulf 14 B b
Chelonatas, prom. 14 B b
Chelsea 75 I i
Cheltenham, parl. bor. 163 L f (Chelt.)
Chemashevskoe 170 H b
Cheminon, mon. 94 C b
Chemmis 18 D e
Chemnitz 85 G e
Chemulpo 171 N e
Chenab River 137 C b
Cheng-tu-fu
Chen-si
Chepstow 127 W o
Chequamegon, Fort
Cher, dept. 148 E e
Cher River 69 H g
Cherasco 90 H h
Cheraw 195 B f
Cherbourg 76 C b
Cheremissians, people 138 G d
Cheribon
Chernaia River 164 J f
Cherokee, Ind. Res. 188 G c
Cherokee, Ind. Res. 1834 188 I d
Cherokees, tribe 188 J c
Cherronesus, proposed state in U. S.
Cherry Valley 195 D b
Cherson, in the Crimea 43 I e
Cherson, on the Dnieper
Cherson, theme 59 K e
Chersonese, Thracian, pen. 13 E a
Chersonese, Tauric, pen. 35 K d
Chersonesus, prom. 11 F d
Chertsey 75 H i
Chertsey mon.
Cherusci, people 38 J h
Chesapeake Bay 193 F c
Cheshire, cty. 127 W m
Chester, in England
Chester, in Illinois 207 H c
Chester, in Pa. 192 D d
Chester, bp. 97 O h
Chester, castle
Chester, cty. 162 D d
Chester, cty. palat.
Chester, parl. bor. 163 L d
Chesterfield Inlet 212 F b
Cheval-de-Bois
Cheviot Hills 49 E d
Chèvremont, castle 62 C c
Cheyenne 210 E b
Cheyenne River 198 E b
Cheyenne River, Ind. Res. 188 F a
Cheyennes, tribe 188 D b
Chezal-Benoît, mon. 94 C b
Chiaha 191 I e
Chiapa 105 B c
Chiapas, state 213 C c
Chiari 130 E d
Chiavari 90 I h
Chiavenna 91 R l
Chicaça 191 G e
Chicacoan 193 F c (Chi.)
Chicago 211 H b
Chichagof Island 212 ins.
Chichester
Chichester, bp. 97 Q k
Chichester, parl. bor. 163 N g
Chichilticale 190 D e
Chiclayo 214 A c
Chickamauga 208 D b
Chickasaw, Ind. Res. 188 G d
Chickasaw, Ind. Res. 1832 188 I d
Chickasaw Bluffs 191 H d
Chickasaws, tribe 188 I d
Chico River 215 B g
Chidley, Cape 186 M b
Chiemsee, bp. 95 E b
Chienti, bp. 95 F c
Chieri 130 P i
Chiers River 62 C d
Chieti 90 E c
Chieti, bp. 95 E c
Chièvres 117 B d
Chi-fu 171 N e
Chihuahua 213 B b
Chihuahua, prov. 190 D f
Chihuahua, state 213 B b
Chilau
Chile, capt. gen. and pres. 215 ins.
Chile, cty. 215 B g e
Chilenfu
Chilianwala 170 I e
Chilkat Pass 212 ins.
Chilcoot 212 ins.
Chilcoot Pass 212 ins.
Chillan 215 B f
Chillicothe, in Missouri 211 G c
Chillicothe, in Ohio 196 ins. B
Chillon, castle 91 O l
Chiloé Island 215 B g
Chilpancingo 213 B c
Chiltern Hills 49 F i
Chimalhuacan
Chimay 117 B d
Chimborazo, mt. 214 A c
Chimbote 214 B c
Chimerium 10 B c
Chimkent
Chimu 111 B c
China, country 171 L e
China Sea 112 E b
Chinalaph River, see Cheliff River
Chincha 111 B d
Chincha Islands 214 B d
Chinchilla 82 B b
Chinese City, loc. in Peking 170 ins. A
Chinese Empire 171 J M e
Chinilla River
Chin-kiang 171 M e
Chinon 69 H g
Chinon, castle 76 D c
Chinooks, tribe 188 B a
Chinsura 137 E d
Chintabor
Chiny
Chioggia 72 C b
Chioggia, bp. 95 E b
Chios, isl. 13 D b
Chipangu, empire (Japan)
Chippawa, battle 200 D b
Chippenham
Chippenham, parl. bor. 163 L f (Chipp.)
Chippewa River 191 G c
Chippewas, tribe 188 H a
Chippewyan, Fort 212 D c
Chipping Norton, parl. bor.
Chipping Wycombe, parl. bor. 163 N f (Ch. Wyc.)
Chiquitos, tribe 214 C d
Chira, Rio de la, river 111 A b
Chiremai, mt. 112 D d
Chiriqui Lagoon 105 D e
Chisey 76 C c
Chiskiak or Chisklack 193 ins. A (Ch.)
Chiswell, Fort 193 D c
Chita 171 M c
Chitral 170 I e
Chitral, reg. 137 B a
Chittagong 137 F d
Chiusi 90 L j
Chiusi, bp. 95 E c
Chivasso 130 P i
Chlum 159 H c
Chmielnik 92 C b
Choarene, reg. 19 H c
Choaspes River 19 L c
Choaspis River 19 G d
Cho-chau 170 ins. A
Choctaw, Ind. Res. 188 G d
Choctaw, Ind. Res. 1830 188 I d
Choctawhatchee River 193 B f
Choctaws, tribe 188 H d
Chœle-Chœl 215 C f
Chœrades Islands, in Eleusinian Gulf 16 B a
Chœrades Islands, in Gulf of Tarentum 31 G b
Choiseul, isl. 172 E a
Cholet 130 C d
Cholm 159 L c
Cholula 106 B a
Choluteca 213 D c
Chonos Archipelago 215 B g
Chorasmii, people 19 I b
Chorazin 6 D c
Chorin, mon. 79 H b
Chorsia(e) 11 D d
Chotin 131 I d
Chouteau's Landing 210 F c
Chotusitz 135 H d
Chowan River 193 F c
Christanna, Fort 193 F c
Christchurch, in New Zealand 172 G e
Christchurch, parl. bor. 163 M g
Christchurch, priory 100 A b

Christian IV., route of 121 C b
Christiana 206 ins.
Christiania (Aggershuus)
Christiansand 166 G c
Christiansborg
Christina, Fort 192 ins.
Christmas I., Indian Ocean 179 B i
Christmas I., Pacific Ocean 180 L g
Christophsthal 143 F i
Chrobatia, reg. 59 I c
Chrysas River 30 D e
Chrysea, isl. 14 ins.
Chrysokeras (Golden Horn) str. 93 G e
Chrysopolis
Chrysorrhoas River 6 E a
Chrystler's Farm, battle 200 F a
Chubut 215 C g
Chubut River 215 C g
Chudes, people 138 B d
Chumbi 171 J f
Chundah 137 C e
Chung-kiang 171 L f
Chuquisaca 214 C d
Chur, see Coire
Church, States of the, 9 cent. 56 E d
Church, States of the, 13 cent. 73 C b
Church, States of the, see also Papal States and Patrimony of Saint Peter
Churchill, Cape 186 J c
Churchill, Fort 212 F c
Churchill River 212 F c
Churubusco, battle 201 H g
Churwalchen 62 E e
Chusan, Islands 171 N e
Chuvashes, people 138 G d
Chylemath River 38 C e
Ciabrus River 39 M l
Ciando
Cibalis
Cibao, reg. 105 F c
Cibola, reg. 190 D d
Cibotus, Harbor of 34 ins. C (4)
Cibyra 20 C d
Cibyrrhæots, Theme of the 59 K f
Cicero, House of 24 A
Cichyrus 10 B c
Cicuye 190 D d
Cicynethus, isl. 11 E c
Cidade do Salvador (Bahia) 214 F d
Ciechanow 155 K b
Cienfuegos 213 D b
Cierium 10 D c
Cilicia, imp. prov. 35 K f
Cilicia, Macedonian prov. 18 D c
Cilicia, reg. 4 F c
Cilicia, Rom. prov.
Cilicia, satr. 18 O h
Cilicia, Strait of 20 E e
Cilicia, theme 59 L f
Cilicia I, E. Rom. prov. 43 I f (4)
Cilicia II, E. Rom. prov. 43 I f (13)
Cilli 72 D b
Cimarron River 190 F d
Cimbebas, people 109 S i
Cimbric Chersonese (Denmark) 38 D a
Ciminius, lake 27 G e
Cimmerian Bosporus, km. 33 L d
Cimolus (Kimolo), isl. 15 E c
Cincinnati 211 I c
Cinga River 38 C d
Cingulum 27 H d
Cintra 82 A b
Cipango, emp. (Japan)
Circæum, prom. 30 B a
Circars, reg. 137 D e
Circassia, reg.
Circassian Mamelukes, Dom. of the 93 E c
Circassians, people 139 E g
Circei or Circeii (San Felice) 30 C a
Circesium 20 I e
Circidius River 26 C e
Circle 198 ins. A
Circus Maximus, loc. in Rome 24 B
Circus Maximus, Aug. Reg., Rome 22 A
Cirencester 51 P i
Cirencester, mon. 97 O j
Cirencester, parl. bor. 163 M f (Cirenc.)
Cirphis, mt. 11 D d
Cirrha 11 D d
Cirta 38 D e
Cisa, La, pass 26 D c
Cisalpine Gaul, reg. 38 ins.
Cisalpine Republic 151 H g
Cisjurane Burgundy, km. 56 C d
Cisoing, mon. 94 C a
Cispadane Gaul, reg. 26 E c
Cispadane Gaul, Aug. Reg. 38 E d (8)
Cispius, mt. 22 A
Cisplatine Province 215 D f
Cissia, prov. 19 G d
Cissus 11 E b
Cissus, mt. 11 E b
Cité, Paris 149 B
Citeaux, mon. 95 D b
Cithæron Mountains 11 E d
Citium, in Cyprus 4 F c
Citium, in Macedonia 10 D b
Citlaltepec 106 A a
Citlaltepetl, mt. 106 C a
Citracan (Astrakhan) 99 M d
Città di Castello 90 D c
Città di Castello, bp. 95 E c
Cittanuova, bp. 95 E b
Cittavecchia, bp. 95 F c
City of Salt 7 C f
Ciudad Bolivar 214 C b
Ciudad de los Reyes 111 B d
Ciudadela, bp. 94 C d
Ciudad Guzman 213 ins.
Ciudad Juarez (El Paso del Norte) 213 B a
Ciudad Porfirio Diáz 213 B b
Ciudad Real 130 C f
Ciudad Rodrigo 82 G e
Ciudad Rodrigo, bp. 94 A c
Cius
Cius, Bay of
Cividale 90 D a
Civitá Castellana 96 B a
Civitate 64 C b
Civitavecchia 64 ins.
Civitella 90 D c
Civray 126 B c
Clackmannan, cty.
Cladeus River 14 B b
Clagny, Parc de, loc. in Versailles 149 A
Claiborne, Fort 200 I f
Clairac 126 B d
Clairac, mon. 94 C c
Clairets, Les, mon. 94 C b
Clairlieu, mon. 95 D b
Clairvaux 69 J f
Clairvaux, mon. 94 C b
Clallams, people 188 B a
Clampetia 31 F c
Clanis (Chiana) River 27 G e
Clanius River 30 C b
Clare, cty. 127 H i
Clarendon 69 B a
Clarendon, castle
Clarendon, dist. 193 ins. C
Clark, Fort 210 E a
Clark, route of 210 B a and D a
Clarke River 186 H d
Clarksville 210 F d
Clarus Mons, see Clermont-Ferrand
Clasis River 27 G d
Classes 27 G c
Clastidium 26 D c
Claterna 27 F c
Clatsop, Fort 210 A a
Clatsops, tribe 188 B a
Claudian Aqueduct 35 ins. B
Claudian Augustan Way, road 27 G b
Claudian Valerian Way, road 27 H e
Claudiopolis 20 D b
Claudius, Arch of 22 A
Clausentum (Bitterne) 51 P i
Clavenna (Chiavenna) 26 D a
Claverack 189 B c
Clazomenæ 13 E b
Clear, Cape 49 B f
Cleeve, mon. 97 N j
Clemont 143 ins. F
Clemont, lordship 143 ins. F
Cleonæ, on Acte Pen. 11 F b
Cleonæ, in Argolis 15 C b
Clepsydra, Spring of 23 C (4)
Clerf 117 E d
Clerkenwell, loc. in London 75 G g
Clermont, in Auvergne 61 E d
Clermont-en-Beauvoisis 76 E b
Clermont, bp. 94 C b
Clermont, cty. 76 E b
Clermont-en-Argonne 126 D b
Clermont-Ferrand 134 B f
Clesis River 26 E b
Cleveland 196 ins. B
Cleves 78 E c
Cleves, cty. 78 E c
Cleves, duchy 114 D c
Clew Bay 127 H h
Clifton 127 W l
Clinch River 196 ins. A
Clinton 208 B c
Clinton, Fort, near Saratoga 192 E b
Clinton, Fort, near West Point 195 D c
Clinton, route of 195 B g
Clipperton Island 180 P f
Clisius River 26 B c
Clitæ, people 20 E d
Cliternia 30 E a
Clitor 14 C b
Clitumnus River 27 G e
Clivus Argentarius, loc. in Rome 24 A
Clivus Capitolinus, loc. in Rome 24 A
Clivus Scauri, loc. in Rome 22 A
Clivus Victoriæ, loc. in Rome 24 A
Cloaca Maxima, loc. in Rome 24 A
Clodiana 31 I a
Clodian Way, road 27 F e
Clodius, Port of 35 ins. B
Clodii, Forum, near L. Sabatinus 35 ins. B
Clodii, Forum, near Luca 26 E d
Clogher, bp. 97 D b
Clomnacnoise, bp.
Clone, bp.
Clonfert, bp. 97 C c
Clonmel
Closter-Seven
Clota Æstuarium (Firth of Clyde) 38 A a
Cloyne, bp. 97 C e
Cluentus River 27 H d
Clugia, see Chioggia
Clunia, in Rætia 39 J j
Clunia, in Spain 38 B d
Cluny, mon. 94 C b
Clusium (Chiusi) 27 F d
Cluviæ 27 I f
Clyde, Firth of 49 D d
Clyde River 49 D e
Clydesdale, dist.
Cnemides 11 D d
Cnemis, mt. 11 D d
Cnidus 12 I c
Cnossus 14 ins.
Coahuila, prov. 190 E f
Coahuila, state 213 B b
Coast District 171 O d
Coast Range, mts., California 187 G d
Coast Range, mts., Canada 212 B b
Coatepec 106 B a
Coatzacoalco River 105 B c
Coatzacoalcos 213 C c
Coban 213 C c
Cobar 172 D d
Cobija 214 B e
Coblenz 62 D c
Coburg 85 F e
Coburg, Pflege, dist. 85 F e
Coburg Peninsula 172 C b

Coca . . . . . 191 H e
Coca River . . . . . 111 B b
Cocala . . . . . 19 K e
Coccium (Ribchester) . . . . .
Cocconato . . . . . 130 Q i (Co.)
Cochaba . . . . . 6 E b
Cochabamba . . . . . 214 C d
Cocheco . . . . . 189 B c
Cochin . . . . . 137 C g
Cochin-China, country . . . . . 171 L g
Cockburn Land . . . . . 186 K a
Cockermouth, parl. bor. . . . . . 163 K c
Cockersand, mon. . . . . . 97 O h
Coco River . . . . . 213 D c
Cocos I., Pacific Ocean . . . . . 214 A b
Cocos Is., Indian Ocean . . . . . 179 A i
Cocynthum, prom. . . . . . 31 F d
Cocytus River . . . . . 10 B c
Cod, Cape . . . . . 186 M d
Codfish Land . . . . . 108 L c
Cœle, Deme of . . . . .
Cœle, reg. . . . . . 14 B b
Cœel Syria, reg. . . . . .
Cœletæ, people . . . . . 39 N l
Cœnyra . . . . . 11 F b
Cœur d'Alene, Ind. Res. . . . . . 188 C a
Coggeshall, mon. . . . . . 97 R j
Cognac . . . . . 76 C d
Cogolla, San Millan de la, mon. 94 B c
Cohœs . . . . . 192 E b
Coiba, isl. . . . . . 105 D e
Coimbatore . . . . . 137 C f
Coimbra . . . . . 82 G e
Coimbra, bp. . . . . . 94 A c
Coimbra, univ. . . . . . 100 D f
Coire . . . . . 91 R l
Coire, bp. . . . . . 78 F e
Colapis River . . . . . 27 J b
Colatio . . . . . 27 J a
Colberg . . . . .
Colchester . . . . .
Colchester, parl. bor. . . . . . 163 O f
Colchis, reg. . . . . . 20 J a
Colchis, satr. . . . . . 8 I d
Cold Harbor, battle . . . . . 208 E b
Col di Tenda Pass . . . . . 130 P j
Coleman Street, in London . . . 75 G g
Colendonck . . . . . 89 ins. C
Colenso . . . . . 175 M l
Colesberg . . . . . 175 M m
Colias, prom. . . . . . 16 B b
Coligny . . . . . 126 D c
Colima . . . . . 213 ins.
Colima, vol. . . . . . 187 I g
Collatia . . . . . 35 ins. B
Colle . . . . . 90 L j
Colle, La . . . . . 200 G a
Colleton County . . . . . 193 ins. C
Collier Bay . . . . . 172 B b
Colline Gate . . . . . 22 A
Collingwood . . . . . 207 I b
Colmar . . . . . 143 ins. D
Colmar, imp. city . . . . . 78 E d
Colmenar de Oreja . . . . . 82 H e
Cöln, see Cologne
Colnbrook . . . . . 75 H i
Colne River . . . . . 75 H h
Cologne (Cöln) . . . . . 62 D c
Cologne, abp. . . . . . 78 E c
Cologne, Hanse. cy. . . . . . 99 ins. B
Cologne, imp. city . . . . . 78 E c
Cologne, univ. . . . . . 100 G d
Colombe, La, mon. . . . . . 94 C b
Colombia, cty. . . . . . 214 B b
Colombo . . . . . 137 C g
Colón . . . . . 214 A b
Colonea . . . . . 59 L e
Colonea, theme . . . . . 59 L f
Colonia Agrippina (Cologne) . 39 I h
Colonia Copia . . . . . 31 F c (Col. Copia)
Colonia do Sacramento . . .
Colonia Neptunia 31 G b (Col. Neptunia)
Colonia Traiana . . . . . 39 I h
Colonides . . . . . 14 B c
Colonna, Cape . . . . . 64 C c
Colonna, Piazza . . . . . 22 A
Colonus . . . . . 16 B b
Colonus, Deme of . . . . .
Colorado, ter. . . . . . 203 Q h
Colorado, state . . . . . 203 Q h
Colorado Chiquito, R. . . . . . 190 C d
Colorado Plateau . . . . . 187 H e
Colorado River, flowing into G. of Mexico . . . . . 187 J e
Colorado River, flowing into G. of California . . . . . 187 H e
Colorado River, in Arg. Rep. . 215 C f
Colorado River, Little . . . . . 190 C d
Colorado River, Ind. Res. . . . 188 D d
Colorado Springs . . . . . 210 E c
Colossæ . . . . . 20 C d
Colosseum, bldg. in Rome . . . 24 B
Colquechaca . . . . . 214 C d
Columbia, in Ohio . . . . . 196 ins. B
Columbia, in Pa. . . . . . 211 J c
Columbia, in S. Carolina . . . . 211 I d
Columbia, in Tennessee . . . . 211 H c
Columbia, District of . . . . . 208 ins.
Columbia, mt. . . . . . 186 H c
Columbia Plateau . . . . . 187 H d
Columbia River . . . . . 186 G d
Columbus, in Georgia . . . . . 191 I e
Columbus, in Ohio . . . . . 199 I c
Columbus, voyages of . . 105, 108 M N e f
Columna Rhegium . . . . . 30 E d
Colville, Fort . . . . . 198 B a
Colville, Ind. Res. . . . . . 188 C a
Colville River . . . . . 186 D b
Colvilles, tribe . . . . . 188 C a
Comacchio . . . . . 90 K h
Comacchio, bp. . . . . . 95 E c
Comacenus, lake . . . . . 26 D a
Comaclum, see Comacchio
Comana, in Çappadocia . . . . . 20 G c
Comana, in Pontus . . . . . 20 G b
Comanches, tribe . . . . . 188 F d
Comayagua . . . . . 213 D c
Combe, mon. . . . . . 97 P i
Combermere, mon. . . . . . 97 O i
Combrailles, cty. . . . . . 76 E c
Comburg, castle . . . . . 143 I g
Comfort, Point . . . . . 193 ins. A
Cominges, cty. . . . . . 76 D e
Comitium, loc. in Rome . . . . 24 A
Commagene, reg. . . . . . 20 G d
Commendah . . . . .
Comminges, bp. . . . . . 94 C c
Common Lands, dist. . . . . .
Communipaw . . . . . 189 ins. C
Como . . . . . 90 I h
Como, bp. . . . . . 95 D b
Como, lake . . . . . 90 I h
Comorin, Cape . . . . . 137 C g
Comoro Islands . . . . . 175 H f
Compendium, see Compiègne
Compiègne . . . . . 126 C b
Compludo, mon. . . . . . 94 A c
Complutum . . . . . 38 B d
Compostella, Santiago de . . . .
Compostella, Santiago de, abp.
Compsa . . . . . 30 E b
Compton, Little . . . . . 189 ins. A
Comum (Como) . . . . . 26 D b
Concepción, in Arg. Rep. . . . 215 D f
Concepción, in Chile . . . . . 215 B f
Concepción, in Paraguay . . . . 215 D e
Conception, Point . . . . . 187 G e
Conception Island . . . . . 108 P h
Conchos . . . . . 190 D f
Conchos River . . . . . 191 D f
Conciergerie, bldg. in Paris . . 149 B
Concord, Massachusetts . . . . . 189 ins. B
Concord, New Hampshire . . . 211 K b
Concord, Temple of . . . . .
Concord River . . . . . 195 ins. A
Concordia, in Arg. Rep. . . . . 215 D f
Concordia, in Upper Germany 39 I i
Concordia, in Venetia . . . . . 27 G b
Concordia, bp. . . . . . 95 E b
Condé . . . . . 126 C a
Condevincum or Condivincum (Nantes) . . . . . 38 B c
Condom, bp. . . . . . 94 C c
Condrusi, people . . . . . 39 H h
Conedoquinet River . . . . . 208 ins.
Conegliano . . . . . 150 G d
Conembriga . . . . . 38 A d
Conestoga . . . . . 194 K f
Conewago Creek . . . . .
Confederation of the Rhine . . 155 leg.
Conflans, cty. . . . . . 69 E e
Conflans, dist. . . . . . 126 C e
Confluens, see Münster
Confluentes or Confluentia (Coblenz) . . . . . 39 I h
Congaree River . . . . . 193 D e
Congo, reg. . . . . . 109 S h
Congo, Belgian, col. . . . . . 175 F e
Congo, French, col. . . . . . 175 E d
Congo River . . . . . 175 F d
Congo State . . . . . 175 F e
Congress Lands . . . . . 196 ins. B
Conii, people . . . . . 38 A e
Connaught, prov. . . . . .
Connecticut, col. . . . . . 189 B d
Connecticut, state . . . . 211 K b (Conn.)
Connecticut River . . . . . 189 B c
Connor, bp. . . . . . 97 E b
Conococheague Creek . . . . . 208 ins.
Conope . . . . . 10 C d
Conovium (Conway) . . . . . 51 O h
Conques, mon., near Evreux . . 94 C b
Conques, mon., near Rodez . . 94 C c
Conrad III., crusade of . . . . . 70 I d
Consentia (Cosenza) . . . . . 31 F c
Conserans, bp. . . . . . 94 C c
Constance . . . . . 62 E e
Constance, bp. . . . . . 142 D e
Constance, imp. cy. . . . . . 78 F e
Constantia (Constance) . . . . . 39 J j
Constantia, see Coutances
Constantia, in Cyprus . . . . . 43 I f
Constantina . . . . . 82 A b
Constantine . . . . . 70 H f
Constantine, Arch of . . . . . 24 B
Constantine, Basilica of . . . . 24 B
Constantine, Baths of . . . . . 22 A
Constantine, Burnt Column of 93 G e (4)
Constantine, Church of . . . . . 23 D
Constantine, Statue of . . . . .
Constantine, Forum of . . . . . 93 G e
Constantine, Wall of . . . . . 93 G e
Constantinople . . . . . 43 H e
Constantinople, patr. . . . . . 52 L f
Constantinople, plan of . . . . . 93 G e
Constantinople, Emp. of . . . . 73 F b
Constanz (Constance), bp. . . . 95 D b
Constanza . . . . . 164 D b
Constitución . . . . . 215 B f
Contestani, people . . . . . 38 B e
Contrebia . . . . . 38 B d
Contreras, battle . . . . . 201 H g
Conway . . . . .
Conway, parl. bor. . . . . .
Conz, bridge of . . . . . 122 D d
Conza, abp. . . . . . 95 F c
Cooch Behar, reg. . . . . . 137 E c
Cook, mt., in Alaska . . . . . 212 ins.
Cook, mt., in New Zealand . . 172 F e
Cook Inlet . . . . . 198 ins. A
Cook Islands . . . . . 180 L i
Cook Strait . . . . . 172 G e
Cooktown . . . . . 172 D b
Coolgardie . . . . . 172 B d
Cooper River, in Australia . . . 172 D c
Cooper River, in S. Carolina . 193 ins. C
Coorg, reg. . . . . . 137 C f
Coosa River . . . . . 208 C c
Copæ . . . . . 11 E d
Copais, lake . . . . . 11 E d
Copan . . . . . 105 C d
Copenhagen . . . . . 77 G a

Copenhagen, Hanse. for. cy. 98 F b
Copenhagen, univ. 100 H c
Cophen River 19 L d
Cophos Port 16 D c
Copia, col. 31 F c
Copiapó 215 B e
Coppermine River 212 D b
Coquimbo 215 B f
Cora 35 ins. B
Coracesium 20 E d
Corah 137 D c
Coral Islands 110 FF g
Coral Sea 172 E b
Corax, mt. 11 D d
Corbais 156 B a
Corbeia, see Corbie
Corbeil 61 E b
Corbie, mon. 55 P k
Corbridge
Corbridge, parl. bor.
Corcora River, in Noricum 27 I a
Corcora River, in Pannonia 27 J b
Corcyra (Corfu), isl. 10 A c
Corcyra Nigra 38 F d
Cordilleran Region 186 G c
Córdoba, in Arg. Rep 215 C f
Córdoba, in Mexico 213 ins.
Cordova, in Spain 82 B b
Cordova, by. 94 B d
Cordova, calif. 58 C f
Cordova, emir. 54 D f
Cordova, km. 83 J h
Corduba (Cordova) 38 A e
Corduēne, reg. 20 J c
Corentine River 214 D b
Coressus 15 E b
Corfe Castle 127 W p
Corfinium 27 H e
Corfu, isl. 77 H e
Coria 82 A a
Coria, bp. 94 A d
Coria del Rio 82 A b
Corinium (Cirencester) 51 P i
Corinth, in Greece 15 C b
Corinth, in Mississippi 208 C c
Corinth, Gulf of 14 C a
Corinth, Isthmus of 2 G e
Corinthian Gate 6 ins. A
Coriovallum 39 H h
Coris 68 C b
Corisco Bay 175 D d
Coritani, people 51 P h
Cork
Cork, bp. 97 C e
Cork, cty. 127 I i
Corlær 192 D b
Cormons 161 I e
Cornavii, people
Cornelimünster, mon. 95 D a
Corner Gate 6 ins. A
Corner Inlet 172 D d
Corneto 64 ins.
Corneto, bp. 95 E c
Corneville, mon. 94 E b (Cornev.)
Cornhill, in London 75 G g
Corniculum 35 ins. B
Corn Market, in London 75 G g (34)
Cornouailles, cty. 69 B b
Cornwall, cty. 127 T p
Cornwall, reg.
Cornwallis, route of 195 A g, B f, C f
Coro 105 G d
Corobilium, see Corbeil
Coromandel Coast 137 D f
Coron
Coronado, route of 190 F e
Corone 14 B c
Corone, Cape 16 C b
Coronea, in Bœotia 11 D d
Coronea, in Thessaly 11 D c
Coronea, lake 11 E b
Corope 11 E c
Corozal
Corpus Christi 201 F d
Correggio 90 J h
Corrèze, dept. 148 E e
Corrientes 215 D e
Corrientes, Cabo das, cape in Africa 109 U j
Corrientes, cape, in Arg. Rep. 215 D f
Corrientes, Cape, in Mexico 213 B b
Corsica, isl. 2 E d
Corsica, gen. 147 F c
Corsica, gouv. 146 C c
Corsica, French prov. 148 F f
Corsica, W. Rom. prov. 42 D e (9)
Corsote 20 I e
Corso Umberto I, street in Rome 22 A
Corstopitum (Corbridge) 51 O g
Corte 146 C c
Cortemiglia 130 Q j
Cortenuova 72 B b
Cortereal, route of 108 L b
Cortez, routes of 105, 106
Cortil-Noirmont 156 B a
Cortona 27 G d
Cortona, bp. 95 E c
Cortoriacus or Corturiacus, see Courtrai
Corumbá 214 D d
Corunna 82 G e
Corvey 151 H f
Corvey, mon. 95 D a
Corycium, prom. 20 B c
Corydalus 16 B b
Corydalus, mt. 16 B b
Coryphasium, prom. 14 B c
Cos 13 E c
Cos, isl. 13 E c
Cosa 27 F e
Cosa, route of 108 M g
Cosedia, see Coutances
Cosenza 90 F e
Cosenza, abp. 95 F d
Cosmidion, quarter
Cosmin
Cosmo y Damiano, Saints, mon. 94 A c
Cossium, see Bazas
Cosne 76 E c
Cossacks of the Don, people 139 F f
Cossacks of the Terek, people 139 G g
Cossacks, Uralian, people 139 H e
Cossack, Zaporogian, people 139 D f
Cossæi, people 19 G d
Cosseans, people 8 C b
Cossonay 130 O h
Cossyra, isl. 38 E e
Costa Rica, reg. 105 C d
Costa Rica, country 213 D c
Costnitz, (Constance), bp. 95 D b
Cotaxtla, river 106 D b
Côte-d'Or, dept. 148 E e
Côte-d'Or, mts. 148 E e
Cotentin, dist. 81 L h
Côtes-du-Nord, dept. 148 D e
Cotini, people 38 F c
Cotopaxi, mt. 111 B b
Cotrone 90 F e
Cotrone, bp. 95 F d
Cotswold Hills 49 E f
Cottbus 155 H c
Cottian Alps, mts. 26 B c
Cottian Alps, W. Rom. prov. 42 D e (5)
Cottius, Kingdom of 26 A c
Cotyaēum 20 C c
Cotyora 20 G b
Coucou, le 156 C c
Coucy 76 E b
Coucy, seign. 69 I f
Coulommiers 126 C b
Council Bluffs 211 F b
Council House, bldg. in Jerusalem 6 ins. A
Courland, duchy 88 J c
Courland, reg. 138 B d
Courmayeur 91 O m
Couronne, La, mon. 94 C b
Courtenay 69 I f
Courtrai 117 B d
Couserans, cty. 69 D e
Couserans, dist. 147 E c (Cous.)
Coutances 61 C b
Coutances, bp. 94 B b
Coutances, cty. 69 C b
Coutras 126 A d
Couvin 117 C d
Covadonga, cave 82 A a
Covadonga, mon. 94 A c
Coventry
Coventry, bp. 97 P i
Coventry, parl. bor. 163 M e
Coverham, mon. 97 P g
Cowpens, battle 195 A f
Coyohuacan
Cozumel, isl. 105 C b
Crac des Chevaliers, castle 68 C c
Cracow 70 J c
Cracow, bp. 95 F a
Cracow, Hanse. cy. 98 G c
Cracow, rep. 159 J c
Cracow, univ. 100 I d
Cradle Mount 172 D e
Crailsheim 143 J g
Craiova 164 C b
Cranæa 10 B c
Cranganore
Crania, mt. 10 B c
Cranii 10 B d
Crannon 11 D c
Craon 76 C c
Craon, castle 69 C c
Craonne 154 B d
Craterus, route of 19 I d
Crathis, mt. 14 C a
Crathis River, in Achaia 14 C a
Crathis (Crati) River, in Bruttium 31 F c
Crato 83 J h
Craven County 193 E e (Cra.)
Craven, Fort 192 D b
Crawford, Fort 211 G b
Crayford 75 J i
Crécy 76 D a
Crediton
Crediton, parl. bor.
Creek, Ind. Res. 188 G c
Creek, Ind. Res. 1832 188 I d
Creeks, tribe 188 I d
Crefeld 117 E c
Creglingen 143 J g
Crema 90 I h
Cremera River 35 ins. B
Cremisa, see Krems
Cremona 26 E b
Cremona, bp. 95 E b
Crenæ 10 C d
Crenides 11 F a
Crépy, near Laon 126 C b
Crépy, in Valois 69 I f
Crescentino 130 Q i (Cr.)
Crespy 114 B d
Crestonia, reg. 11 E b
Cretan Sea 15 D c
Crete, isl. 14 ins.
Crete, East Rom. prov. 43 H f (2)
Crete, Rom. prov. 35 I g
Crete, theme 59 J g
Creuse, dept. 148 E e
Creuse River 76 D c
Creusis 11 E d
Creussen, castle 63 F d
Crevacuore 130 Q i
Crévant 76 E c
Crèvecœur, Fort 191 H c
Crewe 162 D d
Crewkerne 127 W p
Crexa 27 I c
Crexi, isl. 27 I c
Cricklade, parl. bor. 163 M f (Crick.)
Crillon, mt. 212 ins.
Crimea, Khan of the
Crimea, pen. 3 H d
Crimisa 31 G c
Crimisa, prom. 31 G c

Crimisius River 30 C e
Cripplegate, in London 75 G g
Crisa or Crissa 11 D d
Crisa or Crissa (Salona), Gulf of 11 D d
Crisenon, mon. 94 C b
Crithote, prom. 10 B d
Criumetopon, prom. 14 ins.
Crius River 14 C a
Crixia 26 C c
Croatan Island 193 G d
Croatia, dist. 159 H f
Croatia, km. 59 H e
Croatia, reg. 54 H e
Croatian Military Frontier 159 H f
Croats, people 53 P i
Croceæ 14 C c
Crocian Field 11 D c
Crocylia, isl. 10 B d
Cromarty, cty.
Crommyon 15 D b
Cronos Hill
Crooked Island 105 F b
Cropredy Bridge 127 X n
Cross, Cape 109 S k
Crossæa, reg. 11 E b
Cross Creek 195 B f
Cross Keys 208 E b (C. K.)
Crotalus River 31 F c
Croton 31 G c
Crow, Ind. Res. 188 E b
Crow Creek, Ind. Res. 188 G b
Crowland
Crown Point 192 E h
Crows, tribe 188 E a
Croxton, mon. 97 Q i
Croydon 75 I i
Croyland, mon.
Crozet Island 182 GG l
Crusade, fourth 73
Crusade of Conrad III. 70
Crusade of Frederick Barbarossa 70
Crusade of Frederick II. 73
Crusade of Louis VII. 70
Crusade of Louis IX. 73
Crusade of Philip II. (Augustus) 70
Crusade of Richard I. 70
Crusis, reg. 11 E b
Crustumerium 35 ins. B
Crustumium River 27 G d
Crutched Friars, mon. in London 75 G g
Cruzblanca 201 H g
Cruz del Marqués 106 A a
Csanad, bp. 95 G b
Csepel Island 159 J e
Csik-Sereda 159 M e
Csongrád 159 J e
Csorna 159 I e
Csucsa 159 L e
Ctesiphon 20 K f
Ctimene 10 D c
Cuarius River 11 D c
Cuba, Capt. Gen. of 213 C/F a/c
Cuba, isl. 105 E b
Cubagua, isl. 105 H d
Cuch Behar, reg. 137 E c
Cuco River 187 K g
Cudahy 198 ins. A
Cuddalore
Cuenca, in Ecuador 111 B b
Cuenca, in Spain 82 B a
Cuernavaca 106 A b
Cufitatchiqui 191 I e
Cugerni, people 39 H h
Cuitlahuac 106 B a
Cujavia, reg. 138 A e
Cularo (Grenoble) 38 D c
Culebra
Culebra, isl. 199 ins. G
Culenborg 117 D c
Culhuacan
Culiacan 213 B b
Cullera 82 B b
Culloden Moor
Cumæ 31 ins. A
Cumaná 105 H d
Cumaná, reg. 105 H e
Cumania, reg.
Cumans, people 71 L d
Cumberland 211 J c
Cumberland, cty.
Cumberland, Fort 192 B d
Cumberland District 196 B c (C. D.)
Cumberland Gap, pass 194 C c
Cumberland House 212 E c
Cumberland Island 193 D f
Cumberland Mountains 193 C c
Cumberland Peninsula 212 I b
Cumberland Plateau 187 K e
Cumberland River 191 H d
Cumberland Road, see legend 210
Cumberland Sound 212 I b
Cumberland Valley 208 ins.
Cumbria, reg.
Cumbrian Mountains 49 E d
Cume 12 F b
Cumeoberg, mt. 54 H d
Cunaxa 20 J f
Cunene River 175 E f
Cuneo 90 H h
Cunerum, prom. 27 H d
Cuneus aureus
Cupra Maritima 27 H d
Curaçao, isl. 214 C a
Curalius River 10 C c
Curca 99 J f
Curetes, people 10 B d
Curia (Coire) 39 J j
Curia Hostilia 24 A
Curico 215 B f
Curicum 27 I b
Curitiba 215 E e
Curium 20 E e
Curles 193 ins. A (Cur.)
Curictæ, isl. 27 I b
Curta 99 J f
Curus 27 G e
Curzola, bp. 95 F c
Curzola, isl. 90 F c
Cusentia, see Consentia (Cosenza)
Cush, reg. 4 F e
Customs-Union of Bavaria and Wurtemberg 160 D c
Custoza 158 F f
Cutch, Gulf of 137 A d
Cutch, reg. 137 A d
Cutiliæ, Aquæ 27 G e
Cuttack 137 E d
Cuttiæ 26 C b
Cuttyhunk Island 189 C d
Cuxhaven 134 E b
Cuyabá 214 D d
Cuyahoga River 196 ins. B
Cuyk 117 D c
Cuyk, Land of 117 D c
Cuzco 111 C d
Cuzco, audiencia 215 ins.
Cyamosorus River 30 D e
Cyana, Shrine of 31 ins. B
Cyane River 31 ins. B
Cyathus River 10 C d
Cyclades, isl. 4 B b
Cycloborus River 23 D
Cydathenæum, deme 23 D
Cydnus (Tersus) River 20 F d
Cydonia 14 ins.
Cyllene 14 B b
Cyllene, gulf 14 B a
Cyllene, mt. 14 C b
Cyme, in Eubœa 11 F d
Cyme, in Italy 5 A a
Cymmer, mon. 97 N i
Cynætha 14 C a
Cynetes, people 38 A e
Cynkalan (Canton)
Cynkali
Cynosarges, loc. near Athens 23 D
Cynoscephalæ, mts. 11 D c
Cynosura, prom. in Diacria 16 C a
Cynosura, prom. in Salamis 16 B b
Cyntia, lake 10 C d
Cynuria, dist. in Arcadia 14 B b
Cynuria, dist. in Argolis 14 C b
Cynus 11 E d
Cypariseis River 14 B b
Cyparissia 15 C c
Cyparissiæ 14 B b
Cyparissian Gulf (Gulf of Arcadia) 14 B b
Cyparissium, prom. 14 B b
Cyphanta 15 D c
Cyprus, isl. 20 E e
Cyprus, km. 71 M g
Cyprus, East Rom. prov. 43 I g (5)
Cyprus, Rom. prov. 35 K g
Cyprus, theme 59 K g
Cypsela 9 B c
Cyrene 12 H d
Cyrenaica, reg. 12 H d
Cyrenaica, Rom. prov. 35 I g
Cyreschata 19 K c
Cyretiæ 10 D c
Cyropolis 8 K e
Cyrrhus, in Macedonia 11 D b
Cyrrhus, in Syria 20 G d
Cyrus River (Kur R.) 18 G b
Cythera 15 D c
Cythera (Cerigo), isl. 15 C c
Cythnus 15 E b
Cythnus (Termia), isl. 15 E b
Cytinium 11 D d
Cyzicus
Czaslau 135 H d
Czechs, people 56 E c
Czegléd 159 J e
Czenstochowa 79 K c
Czenstochowa, mon. 95 F a
Czernowitz 131 I d

Dabayba, reg. 105 E e
Dacca 137 F d
Dacia, Rom. prov. 35 I d
Dacia, East Rom. dioc. 43 G e
Dacia Apulensis, Rom. prov. 39 M k
Dacia Maluensis, Rom. prov. 39 M l
Dacia mediterranea, East Rom. prov. 43 G e (1)
Dacia ripensis, East Rom. prov. 50 H d
Daghestan, reg. 139 G g
Dagö, isl. 88 I b
Dagupan 171 N g
Dahæ, people 19 I c
Dahbul 112 A b
Dahlak Islands 170 F g
Dahomey, col. 174 D d
Daibul
Dakar 174 B c
Dakota, ter. 1861 203 P f
Dakota, ter. 1863 203 R f
Dakota, North, state 203 R f
Dakota, South, state 203 R g
Dakota River 198 F b
Dakotas, tribe 188 F a
Dalaminzians, people 63 G c
Dalecarlia, reg. 88 F a
Dalgety 172 D d
Dalhem 117 D d
Dalhousie 212 I d
Dalias 82 B b
Dalkeith 84 B b
Dalkey Island 127 K h
Dallas, in Georgia 208 D c
Dallas, in Texas 210 F d
Dalmatia, imp. prov. 34 H e
Dalmatia, reg. 56 F d
Dalmatia, theme 59 H e
Dalmatia, West Rom. prov. 43 F e (11)
Dalny 171 N e
Dalon, mon. 94 C b
Dalriada, km.
Dal River 88 F a
Dalton 208 D c
Daly River 172 C b

Daman 137 B d
Damaraland, reg. 175 E g
Damariscotta 189 D b
Damascene, reg. 6 E b
Damascus 5 C b
Damascus, emir. 68 C c
Damgarten 154 G a
Damghan
Damietta 150 B a
Damm 123 H b
Dammartin 76 E b
Dammeshek (Damascus) 6 E a
Damnii, people 38 B a
Dampier Archipelago 172 A b
Dampierre 143 ins. F
Damvillers 126 D b
Dan 6 D b
Dan River 193 E c
Dan, tribe 7 ins. D
Danbury 195 E c
Danelaw, The, reg.
Danes, people 46 H b
Danes, people, in England 57 C c
Danewerk, wall 63 E a
Danish Kingdom 54 F b
Danish March 58 F c (D.M.)
Danish Mercia, reg.
Danish Northumbria, reg.
Dankov 139 E e
Dannenberg 79 G b
Dantzic 63 J a
Dantzic, Hanse. cy. 98 G c
Dantzic, rep. 155 J a
Danube River 2 F d
Danuvius (Danube) River 34 G d
Danville 195 B e
Daphne 4 ins.
Daphnus 11 D d
Daphnus River 10 C d
Dara, in Dar-fur 174 F c
Dara, in Mesopotamia 20 I d
Darantasia 26 A b
Daras 52 M f
Dardanelles, str. 2 G e
Dardani, people 39 M l
Dardania, reg.
Dardania, East Rom. prov. 43 G e (4)
Dardanus
Dar-es-Salaam 175 G e
Darent River 75 J i
Dar-fur, reg. 174 F c
Dargun, mon. 80 C e
Darien, Gulf of 105 E e
Darien, reg., in Colombia, see Urabá 105 E e
Darien, dist., in Georgia 193 ins. C
Darini, people 38 A b
Dariorigum, see Vannes
Darley, mon. 97 P i
Darling River 172 D d
Darlington 162 E c
Darmstadt 114 E d
Darnis 43 G g
Daroca 82 B a
Daron 68 ins. A
Dartford 75 J i
Dartfort, mon. 97 R j
Dartmoor 49 D f
Dartmouth, in England 84 B d
Dartmouth, parl. bor. 163 K g
Dartmouth, in Mass. 189 C d (Dart.)
Darwin, mt. 215 B h
Dascon 31 ins. B
Dascylium
Dassaretæ, people 10 B b
Dassel 72 B a
Datis' fleet, route of 13 D c
Datum 11 F b
Daulatabad
Daulis 11 D d
Daunii, people 30 E a
Daunus River 30 E a
Dauphin, Fort
Dauphin, isl. 191 H e
Dauphin, Place du, Paris 149 B
Dauphiny, gouv. 146 C c
Dauphiny, prov. 148 F f
Davao 199 ins. H
Davenport 211 G b
Daventry 127 X n
Davey, Port 172 D e
David 214 A b
David, Street of 68 ins. B
David, Tomb(s) of 6 ins. A
David and Solomon, Wall of 6 ins. A
David Comnenus, Dom. of 73 G b
David's Gate 68 ins. B
Davids house, Jerusalem 6 ins. A (3)
Davids Tower 68 ins. B
Davis Islands 108 L l
Davis, routes of 108 P b
Davis Strait 186 N b
Davos 91 R l
Dawson 212 B b
Dax 69 C e
Dax, bp. 94 B c
Dayton 200 A d
De Aar 175 L m
Dead Sea 7 C f
Dean, Forest of 49 E f
Dearborn, Fort (Chicago) 199 H b
Dearborn, route of 200 C d
Death Valley 187 H e
Debeltum 43 H e
Debreczin
Decastadium 30 E e
Decatur 208 C c
Deccan, reg. 137 C f
Decelea 15 D a
Decempagi 39 I i
Deciates, people 26 A d
Decise 126 C c
Decius, Baths of
Decuman Gate 22 A
Deddington, parl. bor.
Dedham 189 ins. B
Deer Creek, Ind. Res. 188 H a
Deerfield, battle 189 B c
Deep River 195 B f
Dee River, in England
Dee River, in Scotland
Dees 159 L e
Defiance 200 A c
Defiance, Fort 196 ins. B
Dego 150 E d
De Grey River 172 B c
Deheubarth, reg.
Dehkergan
Dei Consentes, Portico of the
Deiotarus, Kingdom of 35 K e
Deira, reg.
Deirades 16 C b
Deirans, people
Dekapolis, dist. 7 D d
Delagoa Bay 175 G g
Delaware, state 199 J c (Del.)
Delaware Bay 192 D d
Delaware Counties, col. 192 D d
Delaware River 192 D c
Delawares, tribe 188 K c
Deleus
Delft 117 C b
Delftshaven 184 D b
Delfzyl 117 E a
Delgado, Cape 175 H f
Delhi 137 C c
Delhi, Empire of the Sultans of
Delian Amphictyony 8 P i
Delium 11 E d
Della Scala Dominions 79 G f
Dello 143 ins. F
Delminium 38 F d
Delos 15 F b
Delos, isl. 8 P i
Delphi (Kastri) 11 D d
Delphic Amphictyony 8 O h legend
Delphini, Portus 26 D c
Demarcation Point, cape 198 ins. A
Demerara 214 D b
Demetæ, people 51 N i
Demeter, Temple of 31 ins. B (12)
Demetrias 11 E c
Demmin 63 G b
Demmin, Hanse. cy. 99 ins. B
Demonesi Islands
Demotika 131 I e
Denain 134 B c
Denain, mon. 148 B a
Denbigh, in Virginia 193 ins. A
Denbigh, cty. in Wales 127 V m
Denbigh, parl. bor. 163 K d
Denbigh, parl. dist. 163 K d
Dendera 4 F d
Dendermonde 117 C c
Denia 82 C b
Denkendorf 143 H h
Denmark, kingdom, about 1000 58 G b
Denmark, kingdom, 19 cent. 158 F a
Denmark and Norway, km. in 1812 155 ins.
Dennewitz 154 G c
Dennis, East 207 M b
Dentheletæ, people 39 M l
Dentheliatis, dist. 14 C c
Denver 210 E c
Deogir, reg.
Déols 61 D c
Déols, castle 76 D c
Déols, seign. 61 D c
Deorham
Deptford 75 I i
Dera Ghazi Khan 137 B b
Dera Ismail Khan 137 B b
Derbe 20 E d
Derbend
Derbiccans, people 8 J e
Derby
Derby, cty.
Derby, parl. bor. 163 M e
Derby, shire
Derg, Lough, lake 127 I h
Derindeh 124 G c
Derkos 165 F c
Dermbach 158 E c
Derrhis, prom. 11 E c
Derry, bp. 97 D b
Dertona 26 C c
Dertosa (Tortosa) 38 C d
Desastre, Rio del, river 105 D d
Deseado, Cape 108 J l
Deseado River 215 C g
Deseret, see Utah 211 C b c
Des Moines 211 G b
Des Moines River 191 G c
Desna River 139 D e
Desplaines River 191 H c
Dessau 79 H c
Desterro 215 E e
Detmold 62 E c
Detroit, fort 191 I c
Detroit 199 I b
Dettingen 134 E c
Deulino 138 E d
Deuriopes, people 10 C a
Deutsch-Brod 87 J d
Deutsch-Krone 115 I b
Deuts 55 Q i
Deux Ponts (Zweibrücken) 86 F d
Deux Ponts, princ. 134 D d
Deux-Sèvres, dept. 148 D e
Deva (Chester) 51 O h
Deva, in Transylvania 159 L f
Deventer 117 E b
Deventer, Hanse. cy. 99 ins. B
Deventer, mon. 95 D a
Devil's Lake, Ind. Res. 188 G a
Devizes 65 F e
Devizes, castle
Devizes, parl. bor. 163 M f
Devol 67 K e
Devon, cty.
Devon, shire
Devonport, parl. bor. 163 J g

De Vries, route of
Deynze 117 B d
Dhar
Dharwar 137 C e
Dia, isl. 14 ins.
Diacira 20 J f
Diacria, dist. 16 B a
Diadochi, Kingdoms of the, about 200 B. C. 19
Diadochi, Kingdoms of the, 301 B. C. 18
Diagon River 14 B b
Dialas River 18 G c
Diamantina 214 E d
Diamantine River 172 C c
Diamond, Cape 112 C c
Diana, Grove of 35 ins. B
Diana, Temple of 22 A
Dianium 38 C e
Dianium, isl. 26 F e
Diarbekir, reg.
Diarbekr 99 L f
Diaz, Bartholomew, route of. 108 Q g
Diaz, Melchior, route of 190 C f
Dibio, see Dijon
Dibon 7 D f
Dicæa 13 J d
Dicæarchia 31 ins. A
Dickrich 117 E e
Dicte 4 C b
Dicte, mt. 14 ins.
Didyma, mt. 15 D b
Didyme, isl. 30 D d
Die 61 F d
Die, bp. 95 D c
Diedenhofen (Thionville) 62 C d
Diego, Fort 193 D f
Diego Garcia, isl 182 II h
Diego Rodriguez, isl. 109 X i
Diego Suarez 175 H f
Diekirch 117 E e
Diepenow-Schanze, fort 123 H a
Diepholz 86 G b
Diepholz, cty. 86 G b
Dieppe 76 D a
Dieppe, Hanse. for. cy. 98 D d
Diessenhofen 142 C e
Diest 117 C d
Dieulacres, mon. 97 O h
Dieveren 117 E b
Digentia River 35 ins. B
Digne 69 G d
Digne, bp. 95 D c
Dijon 61 F c
Dijon, gen. 147 E b
Dillenburg 114 D c
Dillingen 114 F d
Dinan 76 B b
Dinant 117 C d
Dinant, Hanse. cy. 98 D d
Dinapur 137 E c
Dinaretium, prom. 20 F e
Dindigal, Dindigul, dist. 137 C g
Dindymus, mt. near Cyzicus
Dindymus, mt. near Sardis 20 C c
Dine, isl. 15 C b
Dinerof 117 E e
Dingle Bay 127 G i
Dinia, see Digne
Diocæsarea 6 C c
Diochares Gate 23 D
Dioclea 59 H e
Diocletian, Baths of 22 A
Diogenium 23 D
Diois, dist. 126 D d
Diomean Gate 23 D
Dion-le-Mont 156 B a
Dionysiades, isl. 14 ins.
Dionysius, Citadel of 31 ins. B (4)
Dionysopolis 39 N l
Dionysus, Temple of
Dionysus, Theatre of 23 C
Dioryctus 10 B d
Dioscurias 12 L b
Dioscurias, prom. 31 G d
Diospolis, in Bithynia 20 D b
Diospolis, in Egypt 4 F d
Diospolis, in Palestine 7 B e
Dipæa 14 C b
Diplokionion, quarter 93 G e
Dipylum 23 D
Diribitorium, loc. in Rome 24 B
Dirphys, mt. 11 E d
Dirschau 123 J a
Disentis, ab. 78 F e
Disentis, mon. 91 Q l
Disibodenberg, mon. 95 D b (Dis.)
Dismal Swamp 193 F c
District of Columbia 211 J c (D. C.)
Dithmarschen (Ditmarsh) reg. 62 E a
Dittani, people 38 B d
Diu 137 B d
Dium, in Chalcidice 11 F b
Dium, in Eubœa 11 D d
Dium, in Macedonia 11 D b
Dium, in Syria 6 D c
Divini, Portus 38 B e
Divione, see Dijon
Divirigi 99 K f
Divitia 39 I h
Divodurum (Metz) 39 I i
Divona, see Cahors
Divus Augustus, Temple of 24 B
Divus Claudius, Portico of 22 A
Divus Claudius, Temple of 22 A
Divus Julius, Temple of
Divus Romulus, Temple of
Divus Trajanus, Temple of 24 B
Dixcove
Dixmuide
Dixmuyden 117 A c
Dixon Entrance 212 ins.
Dixon Sound 198 ins. A
Dmietrov 71 N b
Dnieper River
Dniester River 139 C f
Dobbs, Fort 193 D d
Doberan, mon. 80 B d
Doberus 17 E a
Dobrilugk 63 G c
Dobritch, Dobrudja, Dobrudsha, dist. 119 J e
Dobrzyn 79 K b
Dobuni, people 51 O i
Doclea 39 L l
Dodendorf 154 F b
Dodge, Fort 210 E c
Dodge City 210 E c
Dodona 10 B c
Dœtinchem 117 E c
Doffingen 143 G h
Dohna 85 G e
Dohna, castle 63 G c
Dokkum 117 D a
Dol 61 C b
Dol, bp. 94 B b
Dolceacqua 130 P k
Dôle 114 C e
Dôle, univ. 100 G e
Doliche 10 D b
Doliche, isl. 10 C d
Dollart, The, bay 78 E b
Dolma Baghtcheh
Dolopes, people, in Scyrus 11 F d
Dolopes, people, in Thessaly 8 N h
Dolopia, reg. 10 C c
Dolores Hidalgo 213 ins.
Dolyani, bp. 95 F c
Domana 20 H b
Dombes, gen. 147 F b
Domfront 69 C b
Domine quo vadis, loc. near Rome 96 A
Dominguez, route of 190 C d
Dominica, isl., Antilles 105 H c
Dominica, isl., Marquesas 107 D h
Dominican Republic, country 213 E c
Dominion of Canada 212 C c
Domitian, Gardens of 22 A
Domitian, Palace of 24 B
Domitian, Stadium of 22 A
Dömitz 122 F b
Domo d'Ossola 90 I g
Domremy 81 N h
Domstadtl 135 I d
Don, Cossacks of the, people 139 F f
Donajec River 159 K d
Donaueschingen 142 B e
Donauwörth, imp. cy. 79 G d
Doncaster
Doncaster, parl. bor.
Donegal 127 J g
Donegal, cty. 127 J g
Donegal Bay 49 B d
Donelson, Fort 208 C b
Donetz River 139 F f
Dongola 174 F c
Donnington Castle 127 X o
Donnybrook, fair in Dublin 98 ins. A
Don River 139 F f
Donzy 76 E c
Dor, Dora 6 B c
Dora Baltea River 130 P i
Dora Ripaira River 130 O i
Dorat 126 B c
Dorchester, in Dorsetshire
Dorchester, in Oxfordshire
Dorchester, in Conn. 189 B d
Dorchester, in Mass. 189 ins. B
Dorchester, bp. 97 P j
Dorchester, parl. bor. 163 L g
Dorchester Heights 195 ins. A
Dordogne, dept. 148 E e
Dordogne River 76 D d
Dordrecht 117 C c
Dordrecht, Hanse. cy. 99 ins. B
Dorians, people
Doris, region, in Asia Minor 8 Q i
Doris, state, in Greece 13 C b
Doriscus
Dorium 14 B b
Dorking 75 I i
Dormition, loc. in Jerusalem 6 ins. A
Dornach, castle 91 P k
Dornhan 143 G i
Dornonia, see Dordogne
Dornstetten 143 G i
Dorocas, see Dreux
Dorogobusch
Dorogobuzh 153 O g
Dorostorium 43 H e
Dorpat 71 L b
Dorpat, Hanse. cy. 99 I b
Dorsætas, people
Dorset, cty.
Dorset, parl. dist. 163 L g
Dorset, shire
Dort 117 C c
Dortmund 62 D c
Dortmund, Hanse. cy. 99 ins. B
Dortmund, imp. city 78 E c
Dorylæum 20 D c
Dörzbach 143 I g
Dossenbach 158 E e
Dothan 7 C d
Dotian Field 11 D c
Dotternhausen 143 G i
Douai 117 B d
Doubs River 62 D e
Doubs, dept. 148 F e
Douglas 212 ins.
Douglas, castle 118 D b
Douglas, fam.
Doullens 117 A d
Dour 157 ins.
Douro (Duero) River 82 G e
Dover, in England
Dover, castle 65 G e
Dover, mon. 97 S j
Dover, parl. bor. 163 P f
Dover, in Delaware 192 D d
Dover, in New Hampshire 189 C c

Dovre Field 166 G c
Downgate, in London 75 G g
Down, bp. 97 E b
Down, cty. 127 K g
Downpatrick, bp. 97 F b
Downs, North, dist. 49 G f
Downs, South, dist. 49 F f
Downton, parl. bor. 163 M g
Drabescus 11 F a
Dragashan 164 C b
Dragon's Mouth, str. 105 H d
Dragovitches, people 71 K c
Draguignan 148 F f
Draheim 123 I b
Drake, route of 107 C e
108 M k
109 I j
110 H f
Drake's Bay 107 E d
Drakenburg 114 E b
Drakensberg, mts. 175 M l
Dramburg 85 D b
Drangiana, prov. 19 J d
Drangiana, satr. 8 K e
Drapsaca 19 K c
Drave River 63 I f
Dravus (Drave) River 38 E c
Dred Scott „dicta", see legend 207
Dreisam River 142 A e
Drenthe, cty. 117 E b
Drepanum, in Asia Minor
Drepanum, in Sicily 30 B e
Drepanum, prom. 14 B a
Dresden 85 G e
Dreux 61 D b
Driesen 85 D b
Drilon River 17 B a
Drina River 89 G f
Drinus River 39 L l
Drissa 153 N f
Drišti, bp. 95 F c
Drobetæ 39 M l
Drogheda
Drohiczin 155 L b
Droitwich, parl. bor. 163 L e
Drokinsford, deanery 100 A b
Drôme, dept. 148 F f
Drömling, dist. 62 F b
Dromore, bp. 97 E b
Dromos, in Alexandria 34 ins. C
Drübeck 122 F c
Druentia (Durance) River 26 A c
Drummondville 212 H d
Drusi, Pons, bridge 27 F a
Drusus, Arch of 22 A
Drusus, Canal of 39 I h
Drymæa 11 D d
Dryopes, people 15 E a
Dry Tortugas, isl. 213 D b
Dubaunt Lake 186 I b
Düben 123 G c
Dubienka 139 B e
Dubis (Doubs) River 39 I j
Dubitza 131 G d
Dublin
Dublin, abp. 97 E d
Dublin, cty. 127 K h
Dublin Bay 127 K h
Dubra, see Dubræ
Dubræ (Dover) 51 Q i
Dubrovna 153 O g
Dubuque 199 G b
Ducal Saxony 85 G d
Duck Valley, Ind. Res. 188 C b
Dudeldorf 117 E d
Duderstadt 62 F c
Dudinskœ 171 J b
Dudley, parl. bor. 163 L e
Duero (Douro) River 82 A a
Dufile 175 G d
Duisburg, in Belgium 50 D b
Duisburg, in Germany 62 D c
Duisburg, Hanse. cy. 99 ins. B
Dukla 159 K d
Dulcigno, bp. 95 F c
Dulcis Portus, bay 10 B c
Duluth 211 G a
Dumah 7 B f
Dumbarton
Dumbarton, cty.
Dumbarton, dist.
Dumbrek, R.
Dumfries
Dumfries, cty.
Dumfries, reg.
Dumio, mon. 94 A c
Dummer, Fort 189 B c
Dumnonii, people 51 N i
Dünaburg 88 L c
Düna River 138 C d
Dunbar
Dunblaine, bp.
Duncansby Head
Dundalk
Dundalk Bay 127 K h
Dundee
Dundra Head, cape
Dunedin 172 G e
Dunfermline
Dung Gate, loc. in Jerusalem 6 ins. A
Dunkeld
Dunkeld, bp. 97 J c
Dunkeswell, mon. 97 N k
Dunkirk 117 A c
Dunmow, Little, mon. 97 R j
Dunnottar Castle
Dunois, cty. 84 D e
Dunstable, castle
Dunstable, mon. 97 Q j
Dunstable, parl. bor.
Dunster, parl. bor.
Dunum, see Châteaudun
Dunwich
Dunwich, parl. bor. 163 P e
Düppel 158 E a
Duquesne, Fort 192 A c
Dura in Assyria 20 J e
Dura in Mesopotamia 20 I e
Durance River 69 F e
Durango 213 B b
Durango, prov. 190 D f
Durango, state 213 B b
Duranius (Dordogne) River 38 C d
Durant's Neck, dist. 193 F c
Durazzo 42 F e
Durazzo, abp. 95 F c
Durban 175 N l
Durbuy 117 D d
Durham
Durham, battle 189 C c
Durham, bp. 97 P g
Durham, castle 65 F c
Durham, cty. 127 X l
Durham, palat.
Durham, shire
Duria Major (Dora Baltea) River 26 B b
Duria Minor River 26 B b
Dur-Ilu 5 D b
Durius (Douro) River 38 A d
Dur Kurigalzu 4 G c
Durlach 142 B c
Durnkrut 79 J d
Durnomagus 39 I h
Durnovaria (Dorchester) 51 O i
Durobrivæ (Castor) 51 P h
Durobrivae (Rochester) 51 Q i
Durocasses, see Dreux
Durocatalaunum, see Châlons
Durocornovium, see Corinium (Cirencester)
Durocortorum (Reims) 38 C c
Durolipons
Durostorum (Silistria) 39 N l
Durotriges, people 51 O i
Durovernum (Canterbury) 51 Q i
Dürrenstein, castle 72 D b
Dur-Samand, reg.
Dur-Sharukin (Khorsabad) 5 D b
Düsseldorf 86 F c
Dutch Guiana 214 D b
Dutch Harbor 198 ins. A
Duxbury, in England 185 D d
Duxbury, in Mass. 189 C c
Dwara-Samudra
Dwina, Gulf
Dwina River
Dyea 212 ins.
Dyle River 62 C c
Dyme 14 B a
Dynevwor
Dyras River 16 E e
Dyrrhachium (Durazzo) 31 I a
Dyrrhachium, theme 59 H e
Dyrta 19 L c
Dyscus 11 F d
Dysoron, mt. 11 E a

Eagle Pass 210 E e
East, Dioc. of the 43 J g
East, Pref. of the 43 I h
East Africa, British, col.
East Africa, German, col.
East Africa, Portuquese, col.
East Africa Company, German
East Africa Company, Imperial British
East Angles, people 51 S k
East Anglia, km.
East Anglia Heights 49 G e
East Cape, in Asia 171 T b
East Cape, in New Zealand 172 G d
Eastcheap, in London 75 G g
East Cornwall, parl. dist. 163 J g
East Cumberland, parl. dist. 163 L c
East Dennis 207 M b
Easter Island 180 Q j
Eastern Euphrates River 20 H c
Eastern Ghats, mts. 112 B b
Eastern Rumelia, prov. 164 C b
Eastern Sea 171 N f
East Florida, col. 194 C de
East Franconia, duchy 62 E d
East Frankish Kingdom 56 C b
East Friesland, cty. 122 D b
East Friesland, dist. 86 F b
East Friesland, princ. 134 D b
East Gloucester, parl. dist. 163 L f
East Göthland, reg.
East Goths, Kingdom of the 52 D b
East Goths, people, in Asia Minor, in 382
East Goths, people, on the Dnieper, in 200 45 K c
East Goths, people, in Italy, in 493 45 G d
East Goths, people, in Pannonia, in 454 45 H c
East Greenwich 189 ins. A
East Grinstead, parl. bor. 163 O f
Eastham 189 D d
Easthampton 189 B d
East Indies, reg. 109, 110 X-D D, e-h
East Kent, parl. dist. 163 O f
East London 175 M m
East Looe, parl. bor. 163 J g
East Main River 186 L c
East March, Bavarian 63 H d
East March, in Scotland
East Marches, in Northumberland
East New Jersey, col. 192 D c
East Norfolk, parl. dist. 163 P e
Easton 192 D c
Eastphalia, dist. 62 F b
Eastphalians, people 55 R i
East Prussia, prov. 159 K a
East Prussia, reg. 135 K a
East Retfort, parl. dist. 163 N d
East Riding, dist. 162 F d
East Riding, parl. dist. 163 N d
East Roman Empire about 395 43
East Roman Empire in 486 50—51
East Roman Empire, 6 cent. 52

East Roman Empire, in 750 . . 53
East Saxons, people 51 R k
East Somerset, parl. dist. 163 L f
East Suffolk, parl. dist. 163 P e
East Surrey, parl. dist. 163 N f (E. S.)
East Sussex, parl. dist. 163 O g
East Turkestan, reg. 170 I e
East Voorne, isl. 117 B c
East Worcester, parl. dist. 163 L e
Eause (Eauze) 94 C c
Ebal, mt. 7 C d
Ebelsberg 155 H d
Ebenezer, in Georgia 193 ins. C
Ebenezer, in Judæa 7 B e
Eberbach 142 C b
Eberbach, mon. 95 D a
Ebernburg, castle 114 D d
Ebersberg, castle 63 F d
Eberstein, castle 142 B c
Eberstein, cty. 142 B c
Ebgate, in London 75 G g
Ebingen 143 H i
Eblana 34 C c
Eboracum or Eburacum (York in England) 51 P h
Ebrach, mon. 95 E b
Ebrodunum, see Embrun
Ebroicas, see Evreux
Ebro River 82 B a
Ebron 6 C c
Ebudae Islands (The Hebrides) 34 C b
Eburacum or Eboracum (York in England) 38 B b
Eburodunum (Embrum) 26 A c
Eburodunum (Yverdon) 39 I j
Eburones, people 39 H h
Eburovices, see Evreux
Eburovices, people 38 C c
Eburum 30 E b
Ebusus, isl. 38 C e
Ecbatana (Hamadan) 5 D b
Ecdippa 6 C b
Ecetra 30 C a
Echallens 91 O l
Echedamia 11 D d
Echedorus River 11 D b
Echinades, isl. 10 B d
Echinus 11 D d
Echternach 117 E e
Echternach, mon. 95 D b
Écija 82 A b
Eckernförde 158 F a
Ecnomus, mt. 30 C e
Ecolesima, see Angoulême
Ecuador, country 214 B c
Écuries, Grandes, in Versailles 149 A
Écuries, Petites, in Versailles 149 A
Écuries de la Reine, in Versailles 149 A
Edam 117 D b
Edenton 193 F c
Edessa, in Macedonia 10 D b
Edessa, in Mesopotamia 20 H d
Edessa, cty. 68 C b
Edgartown 189 C d
Edgecote 84 C c
Edge Hill 49 F e
Edge Hill, village 127 X n
Edinburgh
Edinburgh, cty.
Edisto, Fort 193 ins. C
Edisto River 193 D e
Edmonton 212 D c
Edom, reg. 5 C b
Edomites, people 7 ins. D
Edones, people 11 E b
Edrei 6 E c
Edrisids, Dom. of the 83 E d
Edrum 26 E b
Edward, Fort 192 E b
Edward Augustus, Fort 194 B b
Edward Nyanza, lake 175 G d
Edwards Ferry 208 ins.
Eetionea 16 D c
Eferding 123 G d
Eger 72 C a
Egerland, dist. 79 ins.
Eger River 63 G c
Egersund 166 G d
Egg Harbor, Little 192 D d
Eggmühl 154 G d
Egham 75 H i
Eghezée 156 B a
Egisheim 62 D d
Eglaim 7 D f
Eglingen 143 H i
Eglingen, lordship 143 J h
Eglisau, castle 91 Q k
Eglofs, cty. 143 I j
Eglon 7 B e
Egmond, castle 62 C b
Egmond, mon. 94 C a
Egnatia 31 G b
Egnatian Way
Egremont, parl. bor.
Egrigaia
Egypt, emp. 4 F d
Egypt, Rom. prov. 35 J h
Egypt, East Rom. dioc. 43 H h
Egypt, East Rom. prov. 43 I g (4)
Egypt, prov. 12 cent. 71 M h
Egypt, state 174 F b
Egypt, Port of 18 ins. B
Ehingen 143 I i
Ehnheim, Ober- 122 D d
Ehrenberger Klause Pass 114 F e
Ehrenbreitstein 122 D c
Eichsfeld, dist. 114 F c
Eichstädt
Eichstädt, bp.
Eider River 62 E a
Eiham, mon. 94 C a
Eilenburg 85 G e
Einbeck 114 F c
Einbeck, Hanse. cy. 99 ins. B
Eindhoven 117 D c
Einsiedeln, mon. 91 Q k
Eïon 11 E b
Eipel River 115 J d
Eisack River 62 F e
Eisenach 85 F e
Eisenberg 115 ins. B
Eisenburg 123 I e
Eiserntor Pass 159 L f
Eisleben 114 F c
Eislingen 143 I h
Ekaterinburg 138 J d
Ekaterinodar 167 M g
Ekaterinoslav 139 D f
Ekron (Akir) 7 B e
Elæa 10 B c
Elæatis, reg. 10 B c
Elæum, mt. 14 B b
Elæus, in Ætolia 10 C d
Elæus, in Argolis 14 C b
Elæus, in Epirus 10 B b
Elæus, in Thrace
Elæussa Island 16 B b
Elam, reg. 4 G c
Elandslaagte 175 N l
El Araish 118 C f
El Arish
Elatea, in Bœotia 11 D d
Elath 5 C c
Elatia 11 D c
Elatria 10 B c
Elatus, mt. 14 A b
Elaver (Allier) River 38 C c
Elba, isl. 90 L j
Elbassan
Elbe River 62 F b
Elberfeld 158 D c
Elbeuf 76 D b
Elbing 72 D a
Elbing, Hanse. cy. 98 G c
Elbruz, mt. 3 I d
Elburg 117 D b
Elburg, Hanse. cy. 99 ins. B
Elburz Mountains 3 J e
Elcano, route of 109 W k
Elche 82 B b
Elchingen, ab. 143 J i
Elchingen, mon. 143 J i
Eldena, mon. 80 C e
Elea 30 E b
Elealah 7 D e
Electoral Archchancellor, Ter. of the 151 H f (E. A.)
Electoral Hesse, state 158 E c
Electoral Saxony, state 85 G d
Electorates, The Seven 78 leg.
Elen 214 B c
Eleon 11 E d
Elephantine Island (Gezeret-Assuan) 4 F d
Eleusinian Gulf 16 B a
Eleusis (Levsina) 15 D a
Eleutheræ 15 D a
Eleuthernæ 14 ins.
Eleutheropolis 7 B e
Eleutherus River 30 C e
El Fasher 174 F c
Elgin
Elgin, bp. 97 J b
Elgin, cty.
El Golea 174 D a
El Gran Chaco, region 215 C e
El Hasa, reg.
El Hejas, Hedjaz, reg. 170 E f
Elim 68 C d
Elimea 10 C b
Elimea, reg. 10 C b
Elis 14 B b
Elis, reg. 14 B b
Elis, state 13 B c
Elizabetgrad 167 L f
Elizabeth 192 D c
Elizabeth, Cape 189 C c
Elizabethtown 192 D c
El Jesireh, reg. 67 O f
El Kantara 174 K i
El Katif
Elk River 192 A d
Elkton 195 C d
El Kufa 73 I d
Ellesmere 162 D e
Ellesmere Land 186 K a
Ellice Islands 172 G a
Ellichpur 137 C d
Ellingham, mon. 100 A b
Ellomenen 10 B d
Ellwangen 143 J h
Ellwangen, mon. 95 E b
Ellwangen, provostry 143 J h
El-Mahdiya 73 C c
Elmet, Forest of 49 F e
Elmet, dist.
Elmham
Elmina
Elmira 195 C b
Elne, bp. 94 C c
El Obeid 174 F c
Elosa or Elusa, see Eause (Eauze)
El Pardo, castle 130 C e
El Paso 190 D e
El Paso del Norte 213 B a
Elphin, bp. 97 C c
Elsfleth 122 E b
Elsing Spital, bldg. in London 75 G g
Elster, Schwarze, river 85 G e
Elster, Weisse, river 85 G e
Elstow, mon. 97 Q i
El Teb 174 G c
Eltham 75 J i
Eltville 78 F c
Elusa, in France, see Eause (Eauze)
Elusa, in Palestine 7 B f
Elvas 82 A b
El Viejo 213 D c
Elvira 42 B f
Ely, in England
Ely, in India
Ely, bp. 97 R i

Ely, Isle of, dist.
Ely, parl. bor.
El Yemamah
Elymæi, people 19 G d
Elymi, people 30 B e
Elymia 14 C b
Elymians, people
Ely Place, loc. in London 75 G g
Elz River 142 A d
Elzach 142 B d
Emathia, reg. 11 D b
Embrun 69 G d
Embrun, abp. 95 D c
Emden 78 E b
Emerita Augusta (Mérida) 38 A e
Emesa 35 L g
Emilia, dist. 90 C b
Emly, bp. 97 C d
Emmaus 7 B e
Emmendingen 142 A d
Emmerich, in Germany 122 D c
Emmerich, in Transylvania 119 I d
Emmetsburg 208 ins.
Emona (Laibach) 27 I a
Emperador
Empire, The 81 H c
Empire of the French 155 ins.
Empire of the Sultans of Delhi
Emporiæ 38 C d
Emporium, loc. in Rome 22 A
Emporium, in Spain 12 D b
Empulum 35 ins. B
Ems 134 D c
Ems River 62 D b
Enaghdune, bp.
Enchelei, people 31 I a
Encounter Bay 172 C d
Endicott Range 186 D b
Endidæ 27 F a
Endor 6 C c
En-Eglaim 7 C e
Engadine, valley 91 S l
Enganna 7 D d
Engannim 7 C d
Engaño, Cape 171 N g
Engaño, Punta del, cape 107 F e
Engeddi 7 C f
Engelberg, mon. 91 Q l
Engen 142 C e
Enghien 117 C d
England, km. 66 F c
English, people
English Channel 2 D d
English Grants in North America 190 ins.
English Kingdom, 9 cent. 56 B b
English Marches, dist.
English Mercia, reg.
English Northumbria, km.
English Pale, The, dist.
English River 212 F c
English Turn, loc. on Miss. R. 191 H f
Engstingen 143 H i
Engyum 30 D e
Enipeus River, in Elis 14 B b
Enipeus River, in Macedonia 11 D b
Enipeus River, in Thessaly 11 D c
Enkhuizen 117 D b
Enkhuizen, Hanse. cy. 99 ins. B
Enna 72 C d
En-Nasirah 150 C a
Enniskillen 127 J g
Enns 115 H d
Enns River 63 H e
Enos 165 E c
Enschede 117 E b
Ensisheim 86 F e
Entella 30 C e
Entre Minho e Douro, reg. 83 J g
Entre Rios, prov., in Argentina 215 D f (E. R.)
Entre Tejo e Guadiana, reg. 83 J h
Enzberg, lordship 143 G i
Enzheim 122 D d
Enz River 143 H h
Eordæa, reg. 10 C b
Eordaïcus River 10 B b
Eordi, people
Epamantodurum
Eperies 159 K d
Épernay 69 I f
Épernay, mon. 94 C b
Ephesus 17 E c
Ephraim, Gate of 6 ins. A
Ephraim, mt. 7 C d
Ephraim, tribe 7 ins. D
Ephrata 192 C c
Ephyra, in Elis 14 B b
Ephyra, in Epirus 10 B c
Ephyra, isl., near Melos 15 E c
Ephyra, isl., near Argolis 15 C b
Epidamnus (Durazzo) 12 G b
Epidaurum 38 F d
Epidaurus, in Argolis 15 D b
Epidaurus Limera 15 D c
Epidelium, prom. 15 D c
Epila 83 K g
Épinal 78 E d
Épinal, mon. 95 D b
Épineuil 69 I g
Epiphania 20 G e
Epipolæ, quarter in Syracuse 31 ins. B
Epirus, country 10 B b
Epirus, desp., 13 cent. 73 E c
Epirus, desp., 15 cent. 93 B c
Epirus, Rom. prov. 35 I f
Epirus, state 13 B b
Epirus nova, East Rom. prov. 43 G e(5)
Epirus vetus, East Rom. prov. 43 G f(4)
Epitalium 14 B b
Epium 14 B b
Epizephyrii, Locri 31 F d
Epoissum 39 H i
Epopeus, mt. 30 C b
Eporedia (Ivrea) 26 B b
Eppenstein, castle 63 H e
Eppingen 142 C b
Epping Forest 49 F f
Epsom 75 I i
Epternacus, see Echternach
Epworth, mon. 97 Q h
Equatorial Provinces under Emin Pascha 1878—1889 174 F d
Equius
Erasinus River, in Arcadia 14 C b
Erasinus River, in Attica 16 C b
Eratyra 10 C b
Erbach, in Hesse 142 C a
Erbach, in Wurtemberg 143 I i
Erbstetten 143 I i
Ercavica
Erchia 16 B b
Ercte, mt. 30 C d
Erechtheum
Eresburg, stronghold 55 Q i
Eretria, in Eubœa 11 E d
Eretria, in Thessaly 11 D c
Eretum 27 G e
Erfurt 62 F c
Erfurt, mon. 95 E a
Erfurt, univ. 100 H d
Ergines River
Erginul, Erginur
Ergitium 30 E a
Ericinium 10 D c
Ericussa, isl. 30 D d
Eridanus River, see Po River
Eridu (Abu Shahrein) 4 G c
Erie 199 I b
Erie, Fort 200 D b
Erie, lake 187 K d
Erie Canal 211 J b
Eries, tribe 188 J b
Erigon River 10 C b
Erineus, in Achaia 14 B a
Erineus, in Doris 11 D d
Erith 75 J i
Eritium 10 D c
Eritrea, Italian col. 174 G c
Erivan
Erivan, reg.
Erlach, castle 91 P k
Erlangen 122 F d
Erlau 77 I c
Erlau, bp. 95 G b
Ermeland, reg. 87 M a
Ermeland, bp. 115 K a
Ermes 88 K c
Ermine Street, road 51 P g
Erms River 143 H h
Ernage 156 B a
Erolzheim 143 J i
Erpisfurt, see Erfurt
Er Riad
Er Rimmon 7 B f
Erstein, castle 62 D d
Eryces River 30 D e
Erymanthus mt. 14 B b
Erymanthus River 14 B b
Erythræ, in Ionia 13 E b
Erythræ, in Locris 10 D d
Eryx 30 B d
Erzerum 71 O f
Erzgebirge, mts., in Germany 2 F c
Erz Gebirge, mts., in Hungary 159 J d
Erzinjan 77 L e
Escalante, route of 190 C d
Escambia River 193 ins. B
Escaut River, see Scheldt River
Esch 117 D e
Eschwege 62 E c
Escondido, Rio 105 D d
Escorial, San Lorenzo del, mon. 94 B c
Escurial, see Escorial
Esdrælon
Eshcol, vale 7 C e
Esher 75 I i
Eskishehr 164 E c
Esmeraldas 214 B b
Esmeraldas River 111 A a
Esmûn, Temple of 34 ins. A (5)
Esopus 192 D c
Española, isl. 105 F c
Esparza 213 D d
Espinhaço, Serra do, mts. 214 E d
Espinosa 130 C e
Espinosa, route of 105 D e
Espirito Santo 214 E e
Espirito Santo, state 214 E d
Espiritu Santo, isl. 172 F b
Espiritu Santo, Rio del (Mobile R.) 107 I d
Esplechin 81 M g
Esquiliæ, Aug. Reg. of Rome 22 A
Esquiline, quarter 96 A
Esquiline Gate 22 A
Esquiline Mount 22 A
Esquimalt 212 C d
Es-Salihiyeh 150 B a
Esseg
Essen 158 D c
Essen, mon. 95 D a
Essequibo River 214 D b
Essex, cty.
Essex, km.
Essex, shire
Essington, Port 212 ins.
Essling 155 I d
Esslingen, imp. city 143 H h
Este 90 J h
Este, duchy 90 C b
Estella 82 H e
Esthonia, reg., 9 cent. 55 I c
Esthonia, reg., 14 cent. 88 K b
Esthonians, people 59 I b
Estoy 82 A b
Estremadura, reg. 83 J h
Estrun, mon. 94 C a
Etalle 117 D e
Etam 7 C e
Étampes 76 E b
Etawah 170 I f
Etchemins, tribe 188 M a

Eteocretes, people 14 ins.
Ether
Ethiopia, reg., Egyptian emp. 4 F d
Ethiopia, reg., Sudan 109 S U g
Etna, mt. 36 E e
Étoges 154 C d
Étoile, L', mon. 94 C b
Eton 75 H i
Etropol 164 C b
Etruria, Aug. Reg. 38 E d (7)
Etruria, reg. 27 F d
Etruscans, people
Ettenheim 142 A d
Ettenheimmünster, mon. 142 A d
Ettlingen 142 B c
Etymander River 19 J d
Eu 61 D a
Eu, cty. 76 D a
Eubœa (Negropont), isl. 4 B b
Eubœa, state 13 C b
Euboic Gulf 11 E d
Eudemia, isl. 11 F c
Euenus River 10 C d
Eufratensis, E. Rom. prov. 43 J f (9)
Euganei, people 26 E b
Eugubium, see Gubbio
Euhydrium 11 D c
Eumenes, Stoa of 23 C
Eumenia 20 C c
Eunostus, Portus 34 ins. C
Euonymus, isl. 30 E d
Eupalium 10 C d
Eupatoria, in Crimea 139 D f
Eupatoria, in Pontus 33 U h
Euphrates River 18 F d
Eupilis, lake 26 D b
Euporia 11 E b
Eure, dept. 148 E e
Eure-et-Loir, dept 148 E e
Euripus, strait 11 E d
Eurœa 10 B c
Europe, continent 2—3, 166—167
Europe, E. Rom. prov. 43 H e (1)
Europus, in Almopia 10 D b
Europus, in Emathia 11 D a
Europus, in Syria 52 L f
Europus River 10 D c
Eurotas (Iri) River 14 C b
Euryalus 31 ins. B
Eurychorus 18 ins. B
Eurymedon River 20 D d
Eurymenæ 11 D c
Eurytanes, people 10 C d
Eutæa 14 C b
Eutaw Springs, battle 195 A g
Eutin 114 F a
Eutresia, reg. 14 C b
Evangelista, isl. 105 D b
Evansville 208 C b
Evaux 126 C c
Everest, mt. 171 J f
Everglades, The, swamp 191 I f
Evesham 127 X n
Evesham, mon. 97 P i
Evesham, parl. bor. 163 M e
Evora 82 A b
Evora, abp. 94 A d
Évreux 61 D b
Évreux, bp. 94 C b
Évreux, cty. 76 D b
Evron, mon. 94 B b
Ewell 75 I i
Exarchate of Italy 53 D b
Exeter, in England 127 V p
Exeter, bp. 97 N k
Exeter, castle 65 E e
Exeter, parl. bor. 163 K g
Exeter, in New Hampshire 189 C c
Exeter, in Rhode Island 189 ins. A
Exilles 126 E d
Exmes 76 D b
Exmoor 49 E f
Eyach River 143 G i
Eydtkuhnen 159 L a
Eye, mon. 97 S i
Eye, parl. bor. 163 P e
Eyerland, isl. 117 C a
Eylau 155 K a
Eynesford 75 J i
Eynsham, mon. 97 P j
Eyoub, mosque
Eyoub, quarter
Eyre, lake 172 C c
Eyre Peninsula 172 C d
Eyre River 172 C c
Ezion-Geber 5 C c

Fabrateria nova 30 C a
Fabrician Bridge 22 A
Faenza 90 J h
Faenza, bp. 95 E c
Fæsulæ (Fiesole) 27 F d
Fagifulæ 30 D a
Fagundes, route of 108 L c
Fagutal 22 A
Fairfax 208 ins.
Fairfield, in Conn. 192 E c
Fairfield, in Pa. 208 ins.
Fair Oaks, battle 208 E b (F. O.)
Fairweather, mt. 212 ins.
Faizabad 137 D c
Fajardo 199 ins. G
Faknur
Falaise 65 F f
Falempin, mon. 94 C a (Fal.)
Falerii 27 G e
Falerio 27 H d
Falernian District 30 D a
Falesia 26 E e
Falkenstein, castle 62 E d
Falkirk
Falkland Islands 215 D h
Fallen Timber, battle 196 ins. B
Falling Creek 193 F c
Falling Waters, falls 208 ins.
Falls of the Ohio 193 B b
Falmouth, in Maine 189 C c
Falmouth, in Virginia 192 C d
Falmouth, parl. bor. 163 J g
Falster, isl. 114 F a
Falsterbo, Hanse. for. cy. 98 F b
Falun 88 F a
Famagusta 68 B b
Famine, La 192 C b
Fanestris, Julia 27 H d
Fang-shan 170 ins. A
Fanning Island 180 L g
Fano 90 M j
Fano, bp. 95 E c
Fansur
Fanum or Fanum Fortunæ (Fano) 27 H d
Farah
Farama 99 J g
Farentia 27 F c
Farewell, Cape 186 O c
Farfa 64 ins.
Farfa, mon. 96 B a
Fargo 210 F a
Farmington 192 E c
Farnborough 75 J i
Farnham, parl. bor.
Farningham 75 J i
Farnsburg, castle 91 P k
Faro 82 A b
Farœ Islands 2 D b
Farquhar Island 182 G G i
Fars, reg.
Farsan Islands 170 F g
Farther India, reg.
Farther Pomerania, dist. 123 H b
Farther Rhine River 91 R l
Farther Spain, prov. 38 A e (3)
Fasher, El- 174 F c
Fashoda 174 G c
Fatimite, dynasty, about 1097 67 M g
Fatimites, Dom. of the, about 1000 58 D F f
Faubourg du Temple, quarter in Paris 149 B
Faubourg Montmartre, quarter in Paris 149 B
Faubourg Saint Antoine, quarter in Paris 149 B
Faubourg Saint Denis, quarter in Paris 149 B
Faubourg Saint Germain, quarter in Paris 149 B
Faubourg Saint Honoré, quarter in Paris 149 B
Faubourg Saint Honoré, Rue du, street in Paris 149 B
Faubourg Saint Jacques, quarter in Paris 149 B
Faubourg Saint Marcel, quarter in Paris 149 B
Faubourg Saint Martin, quarter in Paris 149 B
Faubourg Saint Michel, quarter in Paris 149 B
Faubourg Saint Victor, quarter in Paris 149 B
Faucigny 130 O h
Fauresmith 175 L l
Faustina, Temple of
Faventia, see Faenza
Faverney, mon. 95 D b
Faversham, mon. 97 R j
Faversham, parl. bor.
Favianæ 50 G c
Faxa Fiord 166 A c
Fayetteville, in N. Carolina 193 E d
Fayetteville, in Pa. 208 ins.
Fayum, reg. 4 ins.
Fear, Cape 191 J e
Fécamp 65 G f
Fécamp mon. 94 C b
Fecht River 143 ins. D
Feder, lake 143 I i
Fehmern, isl. 114 F a
Fehrbellin 123 G b
Feldkirch 78 F e
Felicitas Julia 38 A e
Felsina 27 F c
Feltre 63 F e f
Feltre, bp. 95 E b
Feltria (Feltre) 27 F a
Fenestrelle 126 E d
Fenni, people 35 I a
Fens, The, dist. 49 F e
Feodosia 89 E b
Ferdi, see Verden
Fère-Champenoise 154 B d
Ferentinian Grove 35 ins. B (4)
Ferentino 72 C c
Ferentinum, in Etruria 27 G e
Ferentinum, in Latium 30 C a
Ferghana, reg.
Ferlech
Fermanagh, cty. 127 J g
Fermo 90 D c
Fermo, bp. 95 E c
Fernandina 208 D c
Fernandina, isl. 105 F b
Fernando Noronha Island 214 F c
Fernando Po, isl. 175 D d
Ferns, bp. 97 E d
Feronia 27 G e
Ferrara 90 J h
Ferrara, bp. 95 E c
Ferrara, duchy, 15 cent. 90 C b
Ferrara, univ. 100 H f
Ferraria, see Ferrara
Ferrières, mon. 94 C b
Ferro, Bay of 118 C e
Ferryland 212 J d
Ferté-sur-Grône, La, mon. 94 C b
Fertur River 30 D a
Feuillants, The, mon. in Paris 149 B
Feurs 76 F d
Fez 70 E g
Fez, state 118 C g
Fezensac, dist. 126 B e
Fezenzac, cty. 69 D e (Fez)

Fezzan, Oases of 2 F f
Fezzan, reg. 174 E b
Ficulea 35 ins. B
Fidenæ 27 G f
Fidentia 26 E c
Field of Blood, loc. near Jerusalem 6 ins. A
Fierbois 76 D c
Fiesole 52 J e
Fiesole, bp. 95 E c
Fife, cty.
Figeac 126 C d
Figig 174 C a
Fiji Islands 172 G b
Filehne 155 I b
Filles Saint Thomas, mon. in Paris 149 B
Fillmore City 206 C c
Fils River 143 I h
Fines, near Divodurum 39 H i
Fines, Ad-, near Florentia 27 F d
Fingoland, reg. 175 M m
Finisterre, Cape 83 J g
Finistère, dept. 148 D e
Finland, Gulf of 138 C d
Finland, prov. 167 K c
Finland, reg. 138 C c
Finns, people 138 B c
Finow Canal 123 G b
Finsbury, parl. bor. 163 N f (Finsb.)
Finstermünz 134 F e
Fiorentino, castle 72 D c
Firebr
Fire Lands, dist. 196 ins. B
Firenzuola 90 L i
Firmanum, Castellum 27 H d
Firmum (Fermo) 27 H d
Firozabad 170 I f
Fiscannum, see Fécamp
Fischa River 63 I d e
Fischbach 142 B d
Fischhausen 80 F d
Fischingen, mon. 91 Q k
Fiscellus, mt. 27 H e
Fisher, Fort 208 E c
Fisher's Hill, battle 208 E b
Fish Gate 6 ins. A
Fish River, Great 175 M m
Fitchburg 207 L b
Fitero, mon. 94 B c
Fitzgeralds, The, fam.
Fitzroy River 172 B b
Fiume 135 H f
Five Forks, battle 208 E b
Fivizzano 90 C b
Fixtuinum, see Meaux, in France
Fladungen 62 E c
Flamborough
Flamenco Island
Fläming, mts. 80 ins.
Flaminia and Picenum Annonarium, West. Rom. prov. 42 E e (4)
Flaminian Circus 24 A
Flaminian Circus, Aug. Reg. of Rome 22 A
Flaminian Gate 22 A
Flaminian Way, road 27 G e
Flaminian Way, Old, road 27 G e
Flanders, cty. 61 E a
Flanders, duchy, about 1000 58 E c
Flanders, prov. 148 E d
Flanders and Artois, gen. 147 E a
Flanders and Hainaut, gouv. 146 B a
Flandrina
Flanola, Gulf of 27 I c
Flanona 27 I b
Flarchheim 62 F c
Flatbush 189 ins. C
Flathead Post 210 C a
Flatheads, tribe 188 C a
Flatlands 189 ins. C
Flattery, Cape 186 G d
Flatow 79 J b
Flavia Cæsariensis, West. Rom. prov. 42 B c (5)
Flaviæ, Aræ 39 J i
Flavian Amphitheatre 24 B
Flavian Canal 27 G c
Flavian Way, road 27 H b
Flavigny, mon. 94 C b
Flaviobriga 38 B d
Fleet River, in London 75 G g
Fleet Street, in London 75 G g
Flensborg, Hanse. for. cy.
Flensburg 86 G a
Fleurus 156 B b
Fleury, mon. 94 C b
Flevo, lake (Zuider Zee) 39 H g
Flinders Range 172 C d
Flinders River 172 D b
Flinders Island 172 D d
Flint, cty. 127 V m
Flint, parl. bor. 163 K d
Flint, parl. dist. 163 K d
Flint River 193 B f
Flochberg, castle 72 C b
Flodden 118 D b
Flora, Temple of 23 B
Florence, in Alabama 211 H d
Florence, in Italy 64 B b
Florence, abp. 95 E c
Florence, rep. 90 M j
Florence, univ. 100 H f (Fl.)
Florentia (Florence, in Italy) 27 F d
Florentiola 26 D c
Flores 213 C c
Flores, isl. 112 F d
Flores Sea 172 B a
Floriacus, see Fleury
Florianopolis 215 E e
Florida 215 D f
Florida, Cape 191 I f
Florida, pen. 187 K f
Florida, col. 191 I e f
Florida, state 211 I e
Florida, Straits of 187 L f
Florida, ter. 203 V d
Florida, East, col. 194 C d e
Florida, West, col. 194 B d
Floyd, Camp 210 C b
Fluela Pass 91 R l
Flüelen 91 Q l
Fluorn 123 F i
Flushing, in Holland 117 B c
Flushing, in New York 189 ins. C
Flusor River 27 H d
Fobbing 98 ins. A
Fogaras 159 M f
Foggia 90 E d
Foggia Nuova 99 I f
Foligno, bp. 95 E c
Foix 61 D e
Foix, cty. 76 D e
Foix, gouv. 146 B c
Foix, prov. 148 E f
Fokchani 131 I d
Fo-kien, prov. 171 M f
Földvar 159 J e
Foligno 90 D c
Fond du Lac, Ind. Res. 188 H a
Fondi 90 D d
Fondi, bp. 95 E c
Fontainebleau 126 C b
Fontaine de Bèze, La, mon. 95 D b
Fontaine Française 126 D c
Fontanelle, mon. 94 C b (St. Van.)
Fontenay, in Auxerrois 56 C c
Fontenay, in Poitou 69 C c
Fontenay, castle 76 C c
Fontenay, mon. 94 B b (Font.)
Fontenay-le-Comte 84 C f
Fontenay, seign. 69 C c
Fontenoy, near Tournay 134 B a
Fontevrault 69 H g
Fontevrault, mon. 94 B b
Font-Marigny, mon. 94 C b
Fontus, Gate of
Foo-chau 92 M e
Foot Hills 187 L e
Forbach 142 B c
Forcalquier 69 F e
Forcalquier, cty. 69 F d
Forchheim 55 R j
Forchheim, mon. 95 E b
Ford, mon. 97 O k
Fordingbridge, deanery 100 A b
Fordingbridge, hospital 100 A b
Forentum 30 E b
Forest Cantons, Three 91 S k
Forez, cty. 61 F d
Forfar, cty.
Forli, in Romagna 90 C b
Forli, bp., in Romagna 95 E c
Forli, bp., in Venetia 95 E b
Forlimpopoli, bp. 95 E c (F.)
Formentera, isl. 83 L h
Formiæ 30 C a
Formigny 76 C b
Formio River 27 H b
Formosa, isl. 171 N f
Formosa Bay 175 H e
Fornix Fabianus 24 A
Fornovo 90 B b
Forest, routes of 172 leg.
Fors Fortuna, Temple of 22 A
Fort Adams, in Miss. 199 G d
Fort Adams, in Ohio 196 ins. B
Fort Albany 212 G c
Fort Albuquerque 214 D d
Fortaleza 214 F c
Fort Amsterdam (New York) 189 ins. C
Fort Anne 192 E b
Fort Argyle 193 ins. C
Fort Arkansas 191 G e
Fort Armstrong, in Illinois 211 G b
Fort Armstrong, in Pa. 195 B c
Fort Atkinson 210 F b
Fort Augusta, in Georgia 193 C e
Fort Augusta, in Pa. 192 C c
Fort Bard 150 D d
Fort Beauharnais 191 G c
Fort Bedford 192 B c
Fort Belknap, Ind. Res. 188 D a
Fort Benton 198 C a
Fort Berthold, Ind. Res. 188 F a
Fort Beversrede 192 ins.
Fort Boisé 198 B a
Fort Bonneville 210 C b
Fort Brady 211 H a
Fort Bridger 210 C b
Fort Brown 201 F d
Fort Buford 210 E a
Fort Bull 192 D b
Fort Bute 195 ins. B
Fort Calhoun 210 F b
Fort Caroline 191 I e
Fort Casimir 192 ins.
Fort Caswell 208 E c
Fort Chambly 189 B b
Fort Charlotte 195 ins. B
Fort Chartres 191 G d
Fort Chequamegon
Fort Chippewyan 212 D c
Fort Chiswell 193 D c
Fort Christanna 193 F c
Fort Christina 192 ins.
Fort Churchill 212 F c
Fort Claiborne 200 I f
Fort Clark 210 E a
Fort Clatsop 210 A a
Fort Clinton, near Saratoga 192 E b
Fort Clinton, near West Point 195 D c
Fort Colville 198 B a
Fort Craven 192 D b
Fort Crawford 211 G b
Fort Crèvecœur 191 H c
Fort Cumberland 192 B d
Fort Dauphin
Fort Dearborn 199 H b
Fort de la Présentation 192 D a
Fort Defiance 196 ins. B
Fort d'Huillier 191 G c
Fort Diego 193 D f

Fort Dobbs . . . 193 D d
Fort Dodge . . . 210 E c
Fort Donelson . . . 208 C b
Fort do Principe da Beira . . . 214 C d
Fort Dummer . . . 189 B c
Fort Duquesne . . . 192 A c
Fort Edisto . . . 193 ins. C
Fort Edward . . . 192 C b
Fort Edward Augustus . . . 194 B b
Fort Erie . . . 196 D b
Fort Fisher . . . 208 E c
Fort Frédéric . . . 192 E a
Fort Frederick . . . 192 C d
Fort Frontenac . . . 192 C a
Fort Gaines, in Alabama . . . 208 C c
Fort Gaines, in Minnesota . . . 211 G a
Fort George, in Canada . . . 200 D b
Fort George, in Maine . . . 189 D c
Fort George, in New York . . . 192 E b
Fort Good Hope . . . 212 C b
Fort Gibson . . . 211 G c
Fort Granby . . . 195 A g
Fort Granville . . . 192 C c
Fort Gratiot . . . 211 I b
Fort Greenville . . . 196 ins. B
Fort Griswold . . . 195 F c
Forth, Firth of . . . 49 E c
Fort Hall . . . 198 C b
Fort Hall, Ind. Res. . . . 188 D b
Fort Halifax . . . 189 D b
Fort Harmar . . . 196 ins. B
Fort Hatteras . . . 208 E b
Fort Henry . . . 208 C b
Fort Herkimer . . . 192 D b
Fort Howard . . . 211 H b
Fort Independence . . . 195 E a
Fort Jackson, in Louisiana . . . 208 C d
Fort Jackson, in Mississippi . . . 200 I f
Fort James . . .
Fort Kaministiquia . . . 191 G b
Fort Kearney . . . 210 F b
Fort Kenai . . . 198 ins. A
Fort King George . . . 193 C f
Fort La Baye . . . 191 H c
Fort Lac Pepin . . .
Fort La Gallette . . . 192 D a
Fort La Jonquière . . . 190 C a
Fort Lamotte . . . 189 B b
Fort Langley . . . 210 A a
Fort Laramie . . . 198 E b
Fort La Reine . . . 190 F b
Fort L'Assomption . . . 194 B c
Fort Leavenworth . . . 198 F c
Fort Le Bœuf . . . 192 A c
Fort Lee . . . 195 D c
Fort Lévis . . . 192 D a
Fort Liard . . . 212 C b
Fort Ligonier . . . 192 B c
Fort Lisa . . . 210 F b
Fort Loudoun, in Pa. . . . 192 B d
Fort Loudoun, in Tennessee . . . 193 B d
Fort Louis . . . 154 D d
Fort Lupton . . . 210 E c
Fort Loyal . . . 189 D c
Fort Mac Allister . . . 208 D c
Fort Mac Henry . . . 200 L h
Fort Mackinac . . . 194 C a
Fort Mac Murray . . . 212 D c
Fort Macon . . . 208 E c
Fort Macpherson . . . 212 B b
Fort Madison . . . 199 G b
Fort Madison, Ind. Res. . . . 188 B a
Fort Malden . . . 200 B b
Fort Mandan . . . 210 E a
Fort Manuel . . . 210 D a
Fort Massac . . . 194 B c
Fort Maurepas, in Mississippi . 191 H e
Fort Maurepas, on L. Winnipeg 191 F a
Fort Meigs . . . 200 B c
Fort Mercer . . . 195 D d
Fort Miami . . . 196 ins. B
Fort Mifflin . . . 195 D d
Fort Mims . . . 200 I f
Fort Mitchell . . . 211 H d
Fort Mohave . . . 188 D c
Fort Moore . . . 193 ins. C
Fort Morgan . . . 208 C c
Fort Moritz . . . 214 F d
Fort Moultrie . . . 195 B g
Fort Nassau, in New Jersey . . 191 K d
Fort Nassau, in New York . . . 192 E b
Fort Necessity . . . 192 B d
Fort Nelson . . . 212 C b
Fort New Elfsborg . . . 192 ins.
Fort New Gothenburg . . . 192 ins.
Fort New Korsholm . . . 192 ins.
Fort New Wasa . . . 192 ins.
Fort Niagara . . . 192 B b
Fort Nicholson . . . 192 E b
Fort Nipigon . . . 191 H b
Fort Nisqually . . . 210 A a
Fort Norman . . . 212 C b
Fort Okanagan . . . 210 B a
Fort Ontario . . . 192 C b
Fort Orange . . . 192 D b
Fort Orleans . . . 191 G d
Fortore River, see Frento River
Fort Osage . . . 211 G c
Fort Oswegatchie . . . 196 D b
Fort Oswego . . . 192 C b
Fort Ouiatanon . . . 191 H c
Fort Panmure . . . 194 A d
Fort Peck, Ind. Res. . . . 188 E a
Fort Pejepscort . . . 189 C b
Fort Pentagöet . . . 189 D b
Fort Pickens . . . 208 C c
Fort Picolata . . . 193 D g
Fort Pierre . . . 210 E b
Fort Pillow . . . 208 C b
Fort Pitt . . . 212 E c
Fort Pontchartrain . . . 191 I c
Fort Presqu'Isle . . . 192 B b
Fort Prince George . . . 193 C d
Fort Providence . . . 212 D b
Fort Prudhomme . . . 191 H d
Fort Pulaski . . . 208 D c
Fort Rae . . . 212 D b
Fort Recovery . . . 196 ins. B
Fort Reliance . . . 212 E b
Fort Resolution . . . 212 D b
Fortress Monroe . . . 208 E b
Fort Richelieu . . . 189 B a
Fort Rosalie . . . 191 G e
Fort Rouge . . .
Fort Rouillé . . . 192 B b
Fort Saint Andrew . . . 193 D f
Fort Saint Charles, or Kaskaskia 191 G d
Fort Saint Charles, near Lake of the Woods . . . 191 F b
Fort Saint David (Cuddalore) . 137 C f
Fort Saint Thérèse . . . 189 B b
Fort Saint George, in Florida . 193 D f
Fort Saint George (Madras) . . 137 D f
Fort Saint John, in Brit. Columbia . . . 212 C b
Fort Saint John, on Richelieu R. 189 B b
Fort Saint Joseph . . . 191 H c
Fort Saint Louis, in Illinois Country . . . 191 H c
Fort Saint Louis, in Texas . . 190 F f
Fort Saint Philip . . . 200 I g
Fort Saint Pierre . . . 191 G b
Fort Saint Vrein . . . 210 E b
Fort Sandusky . . . 194 C b
Fort San Mateo . . . 191 I e
Fort Saratoga . . . 192 E b
Fort Saskatchewan . . . 212 D c
Fort Schuyler, near Montreal . 189 B b
Fort Schuyler (Oriskany) . . . 195 D b
Fort Scott . . . 211 G c
Fort Selkirk . . . 212 B b
Fort Shirley . . . 192 C c
Fort Simpson . . . 212 C b
Fort Smith . . . 211 G c
Fort Snelling . . . 199 G b
Fort Stanwix . . . 192 D b
Fort Stephenson . . . 200 B c
Fort Steuben . . . 196 ins. B
Fort Stoddert . . . 196 B d
Fort Sumter . . . 208 E c
Fort Tecumseh . . . 210 E b
Fort Ticonderoga . . . 192 E b
Fort Tombecbé . . . 191 H e
Fort Toulouse . . . 191 H e
Fort Trinity . . . 192 ins.
Fortuna, Temple of . . . 22 A
Fortuna, Fanum . . . 27 H d
Fortunæ, Tres . . . 23 B
Fort Union, in New Mexico . . 210 D c
Fort Union, in North Dakota . 210 E a
Fort Uintah . . . 210 C b
Fort Vancouver . . . 210 A a
Fort Venango . . . 192 A c
Fort Vincennes . . . 194 B c
Fort Walla Walla . . . 198 B a
Fort Washington (Cincinnati) . 196 ins. B
Fort Washington, in Maryland . 200 L i
Fort Washington, near New York 195 D c
Fort Washita . . . 210 F d
Fort Watson . . . 195 A g
Fort Wayne . . . 196 B b
Fort Western . . . 189 D b
Fort William (Calcutta) . . . 137 E d
Fort William, in Florida . . . 193 D f
Fort William, in Ontario . . . 212 F d
Fort William (Portland, Ore.) . 210 A a
Fort William Henry . . . 192 D b
Fort Williams . . . 192 D b
Fort Winnebago . . . 211 H b
Fort Wrangell . . . 212 ins.
Forty-Niners, route of . . . 210 legend
Fort York . . .
Fort Yukon . . . 198 ins. A
Foruli . . . 27 H e
Forum, loc. in Carthage . . 34 ins. A (3)
Forum, loc. in Rome . . . 24 A and B
Forum Aurelii . . . 27 F e
Forum Boarium, loc. in Rome 24 A
Forum Cassii . . . 27 G e
Forum Clodii, near L. Sabatinus 35 ins. B
Forum Clodii, near Luca . . . 26 E d
Forum Cornelii . . . 27 F c
Forum Fulvii . . .
Forum Gallorum . . . 27 F c
Forum Germanorum . . . 26 B c
Forum Holitorium, loc. in Rome 24 A
Forum Julii (Fréjus), in Gaul . 26 A d
Forum Julii (Cividale), in Venetia 27 H a
Forum Livii (Forli) . . . 27 F c
Forum novum . . . 26 E c
Forum Popilii (Forlimpopoli), in Cispadane Gaul . . . 27 G c
Forum Popilii, in Lucania . . . 30 E b
Forum Sempronii . . . 27 G d
Forum Vibii . . . 26 B c
Forum Vulcani (Solfatara), vol. 31 ins. A
Fossæ Papirianæ . . . 26 E d
Fossalta . . . 72 C c
Fossano . . . 150 D d
Fossanuova, mon. . . . 96 C b
Fosse Way, road . . . 51 P h
Fossombrone, bp. . . . 95 E c (Fo.)
Fotheringhay . . . 127 Y n
Fougères . . . 69 C b
Fougères, castle . . . 76 C b
Fountain City . . . 206 ins.
Fountains, mon. . . . 97 P g
Four Mile Tree . . . 193 ins. A
Fowey . . . 127 U p
Fowey, parl. bor. . . . 163 J g
Fowler Bay . . . 172 C d
Fox, Cape . . . 212 ins.
Fox, Sauk and, Ind. Res. . . . 188 H b
Fox Land . . . 212 H b
Fox Channel . . . 186 K b
Fox River . . . 188 I b
Foxes, tribe . . . 188 H b
Foyle, lake . . . 127 J f
Fraga . . . 82 C a
Francavilla . . . 131 F f
France, km., 11 cent. . . . 58 E d
France, km., 12 cent. . . . 70 G d

France, km., 18 cent. 130 D d
France, rep. 166 F f
France, Plain of 2 E d
Franceville 175 E e
Franche Comté, gouv. 146 C b
Franche Comté, prov. 148 F e
Franche Comté, see also Free County of Burgundy
Francia, duchy, about 1000 58 E d
Francia, reg. 53 M h
Franconia, Frankish prov., 9 cent. 56 D b
Franconia, duchy, 12 cent. 71 R k
Franconia, E., duchy 62 E c d
Franconia, W., duchy 62 E c d
Franconofurt, see Frankfort-on-the-Main and Frankfurt-on-the-Oder
Frankenhausen 114 F c
Frankenthal 122 E d
Frankfort, in Kentucky 196 C c
Frankfort-on-the-Main 55 Q i
Frankfort-on-the-Oder 79 I b
Frankfort-on-the-Oder, Hanse. cy. 99 ins. B
Frankfort-on-the-Oder, univ. 100 H d
Frankfort, gr. duchy 154 E c
Frankfort, imp. cy. 78 F c
Fränkische Saale, river 158 E c
Franklin, in Kentucky 208 C b
Franklin, in Pa. 192 A c
Franklin, in Tennessee 208 C b
Franklin, dist. in Canada 212 E a
Franklin, proposed state in U. S. 196 ins. A
Franks, Kingdom of the, 486 50 D c
Franks, Kingdom of the, 526—600 52 C b
Franks, Kingdom of the, 6 cent. 52 I e
Franks, people in France, 486-496 45 E c
Franks, people in Italy, 774 45 G d
Franks, people, about 900 57 D E c
Franzensfeste 158 F e
Franzens Canal 159 J f
Frascati, see Tusculum 64 ins.
Frascati, bp. 96 B b
Fraser River 212 C c
Frasnes 156 A a
Frastanz 91 R k
Fraubrunnen 91 P k
Frauenalb, ab. 142 B c
Frauenburg 115 J a
Frauenburg, bp. 95 F a
Frauenfeld 91 Q k
Fraustadt 135 I c
Fraxinet or Fraxinetum (Garde-Frainet) 56 D d
Frazers, fam. 97 I b
Frédéric, Fort 192 E a
Frederica 193 D f
Fredericia 158 E a
Frederick 192 C d
Frederick, Fort 192 B d
Frederick Barbarossa, crusade of 70 I d
Fredericksburg 193 F b
Frederick William Canal 135 H b (Fr. W. C.)
Fredericton 212 I d
Frederikshamn
Frederiksholm, castle 120 H e
Free County of Burgundy, 14 cent. 78 D e
Free County of Burgundy, 17 cent. 126 D c
Freeman's Farm, battle 195 E b
Freeport 207 H b
Freetown 174 B d
Fregellæ 30 C a
Fregenæ 27 G f
Freiberg 85 G e
Freiburg, in Breisgau 78 E e
Freiburg, in Breisgau, univ. 100 G e
Freiburg, in Switzerland, see Fribourg 91 P l
Freiburg, canton, see Fribourg 91 P l
Freising 63 F d
Freising, bp. 79 G d
Freyburg, on the Unstrut R. 85 F e
Fréjus 69 G e
Fréjus, bp. 95 D c
Fremantle 172 A d
Fremington, parl. bor.
Fremont 210 F b
Frémont, routes of 210 leg.
Fremont Peak 187 I d
French, empire of the, 1806 151 K j
French, people, about 900
French Bay 105 ins.
French Broad River 196 ins. A
French Congo, col. 175 E e
French Frigate Island 180 J e
French Guiana, col. 214 D b
French Guinea, col. 174 B c
French Indo-China, col. 171 L g
French Mills 200 F a
French Republic 151 H g
French Somaliland, col. 174 H c (Fr. Somal.)
Frenchtown 200 B c
French West Africa, col. 174 C c
Frentani, people 27 I e
Frentanians, people
Frento (Fortore) River 30 E a
Fresnaye 76 D b
Fresnillo 213 B b
Fréteval 69 H g
Fretum Gallicum (Strait of Dover) 51 Q i
Freudenberg 142 D a
Freudenstadt 143 F i
Fribourg 91 P l
Fribourg, canton 91 P l
Frichemont
Friday Street, in London 75 G g
Friedberg, in Swabia 143 H j
Friedberg, on the Taunus 122 E c
Friedewald 114 E c
Friedland, in Bohemia 123 H c
Friedland, in Moravia 123 I d
Friedland, in Prussia 155 K a
Friedrichshafen, imp. city 143 I j
Friedrichstadt 158 E a
Friedrich Wilhelm Canal 123 H b
Friendly Islands 172 H c
Friesach 63 H e
Friesack 85 C b
Friesack, castle 72 C a
Friesians, people 38 D b
Friesland, reg., 9 cent. 56 C b
Friesland, reg., 13 cent. 72 B a
Friesland, reg., 14 cent. 78 E b
Friesland lordship, 16 cent. 117 D a
Friesland, East, reg. 86 F b
Friesland, West, dist. 117 C b
Frigidus River 27 H b
Frijoles
Friniates, people 26 E c
Frio, Cape, in Brazil 215 E e
Frio, Cape, in Africa 175 E f
Frisches Haff, bay 123 J a
Frisians, people, see Friesians
Frisinga, see Freising
Fritzlar 55 Q i
Fritzlar, mon. 95 D a
Friuli, March of 54 G d
Friuli, people 52 J e
Friuli, dist. 63 G e
Frobisher, route of 108 L b
Frobisher Bay 212 I b
Froburg, castle 91 P k
Frohse 63 F b
Frohsdorf 159 I e
Frome, lake 172 D d
Frome, parl. bor. 163 L f
Fronsac, castle 76 C d
Frontenac, Fort 192 C a
Fronteras 190 D e
Frontiacus, see Fronsac
Front Royal 208 E b (F. R.)
Frutigen, castle 91 P l
Fruttuaria, mon. 95 D b
Fucens, Alba 27 H e
Fu-chau
Fucino, lake 96 C a
Fucinus (Fucino) lake 27 H f
Fuego, Tierra del, isl. 215 C h
Fuego, volcano 187 J g
Fuenterrabia 83 K g
Fuentes de Oñoro 130 B e
Fuentidueña 82 B a
Fuerte 190 D f
Fugger, lordship 143 J i
Fugui
Fulda 72 B a
Fulda, ab. 78 F c
Fulda, bp. 122 E c
Fulda, mon. 55 Q i
Fulginium (Foligno)
Fulham
Fulvii, Forum 26 C c
Fundi 30 C a
Fundoukli, quarter 93 G e
Fundy, Bay of 186 M d
Fünfkirchen 72 D b
Fünfkirchen, bp. 95 F b
Fünfkirchen, univ. 100 I e
Fünen, isl.
Furculæ Caudinæ, passes, see Caudine Forks
Furka Pass 91 Q l
Furlo Pass 27 G d
Furnes 69 E a
Furness, mon. 97 N g
Furth, in Bavaria 123 G d
Fürth, in Ansbach 122 F d
Fürstenau, castle 91 R l
Fürstenberg 142 C e
Fürstenberg, cty. 122 E e
Fürstenberg, princ. 142 B e
Fürstenfeld, mon. 95 E b
Fürstenwalde 79 I b
Fürstenwalde, bp. 95 E a
Furtwangen 142 B d
Fusan 171 N e
Füssen 134 F e
Futa, la-, Pass 27 F c
Futa Jalon, reg. 174 B c
Fuzo
Fyriswall 59 H b
Fyzabad 137 D c

Gabales or Gabalis, see Javols
Gabara 6 C c
Gabardan, dist. 147 E c (Gab.)
Gabarret 76 D d
Gabel 159 H c
Gabes 174 D a
Gabes, Gulf of 174 E a
Gabii 27 G f
Gabun, reg. 175 D e
Gad, tribe 7 ins. D
Gadara
Gadda 7 E d
Gadebusch 134 F b
Gades (Cadiz) 38 A e
Gadsden Purchase, reg. 1853 198 C d
Gaëta 90 D d
Gaëta, bp. 95 E c
Gaëtulia, reg. 34 F g
Gaikwar, Dom. of the 137 B d
Gaildorf 143 I g
Gaillac, mon. 94 C c (Gaill.)
Gaillard, castle 76 D b
Gaillon 76 D b
Gainas, people 51 F
Gaines, Fort, in Alabama 208 C c
Gaines, Fort, in Minnesota 211 G a
Gaines' Mill, battle 208 E b (G. M.)
Gainsborough 127 Y m
Gairdner, lake 172 C d
Galaaditis, reg. 7 D d
Galapagos Islands 214 A b
Galata, dist. in Constantinople 93 G e
Galatia, E. Rom. prov. 43 I f (2)
Galatia, Rom. prov.
Galatia Salutaris, E. Rom. prov. 43 I e (5)
Galatz 131 I d
Galeazzo Visconti, Dom. of 90
Galena 211 G b

Galepsus, in Pieria 11 F b
Galepsus, in Sithonia 11 E b
Galera 118 D f
Galicia, cty. in Spain 82 A a
Galicia, dist. in Austria-Hungary 159 K d
Galicia, dist. in Poland 139 B f
Galicia, km. in Spain 83 J g
Galicia, W. Rom. prov. 42 A e (3)
Galilee, dist. 6 C c
Galilee, Sea of 6 D c
Galitch
Gallæci, people 38 A d
Gallæcia, reg. 34 C e
Gallette, La, Fort 192 D a
Gallia, see Gaul 34 E d
Gallia Belgica, see Belgica 38 D c (3)
Gallia Cisalpina, see Cispadane and Transpadane Gaul 26
Gallia Cispadana, see Cispadane Gaul 26 E c
Gallia Lugdunensis, see Lugdunensis 38 C c (4)
Gallia Narbonensis, see Narbonensis 38 D d (6)
Gallia Transalpina, see Gaul 34 E d
Gallia Transpadana, see Transpadane Gaul 26 C b
Gallienus, Arch of 22 A
Gallinas, Cape 187 L g
Gallinas, Punta, cape 214 B a
Gallipoli, in Italy 90 F d
Gallipoli, in Thrace 71 L e
Gallipolis, in Ohio 196 ins. B
Gallo, Isla del, isl. 111 B a
Galloway, bp. 97 I e
Galloway, dist.
Galtelli 72 B c
Galveston 199 G e
Galvez, route of 195 ins. B
Galway
Galway, cty. 127 H h
Galway Bay 49 B e
Gamala 6 D c
Gambia, col. 174 B c
Gambia River 108 P f
Gambier Islands 180 N j
Gambrium
Gams 91 R k
Gandamak 170 H e
Gandavum, see Ghent
Gander River 212 J d
Gandersheim, mon. 95 D a
Gandia
Gando 174 D c
Gangani, people 38 A b
Ganges River 137 E c
Gangra 20 E b
Ganjam 137 E e
Gänserndorf 159 I d
Gap 126 E d
Gap, bp. 95 D c
Gard, dept. 148 E f
Garda 90 J h
Garda, lake 90 J h
Garde-Frainet, see Fraxinet or Fraxinetum
Gardelegen 85 B b
Gardiner's Island 189 C d
Gard Meuble, loc. in Versailles 149 A
Garendon, mon. 97 P i
Garessio 130 Q j
Gargano, mt. 64 C b
Garganum. prom. 31 F a
Garganus (Gargano), mt. 30 E a
Gargara
Gargettus 16 B a
Garigliano River 90 D d
Garmantes, people 35 G h
Garonne, Haute, dept. 148 E f
Garonne River 61 D d
Garrapata 214 B b
Garsaura 20 F c
Gartach, Gross 142 D b
Garts 123 H b
Garumna (Garonne) River 38 B d
Garz 63 H b
Gascony, dist. 50 C d
Gascony, duchy 61 C e
Gascony, prov. 148 D f
Gascoyne River 172 A c
Gaspé Peninsula 186 M d
Gastein 158 G e
Gates, route of 195 A f
Gateshead, parl. bor. 163 M c
Gath 7 B e
Gath Rimmon 7 B e
Gatheæ 14 C b
Gâtinais, dist. 69 I f
Gatineau River 199 J a
Gattinara 118 F d
Gatton, parl. bor. 163 N f (Gat.)
Gatun
Gatun River
Gaudus, isl. 14 ins.
Gaugamela 20 J d
Gaul, reg. 12 D a
Gaul, W. Rom. dioc. 42 C d
Gaul, W. Rom. pref. 42
Gaul, Cisalpine, reg. 38 ins.
Gaul, Cispadane, reg. 27 E c
Gaul, Transalpine, reg. 34 E d (Gaul)
Gaul, Transpadane reg. 26 C b
Gaur 92 I e
Gaure, dist. 126 B e
Gaurium 15 E b
Gaurus, mt. 31 ins. A
Gaya 137 E d
Gaza
Gazaca 35 N f
Gazaria, reg.
Gaziura 20 G b
Geba 7 C d
Gebal 6 D a
Gebal, reg.
Gebu, isl. 199 ins. H
Gederoth 7 B e
Gedid 174 G c
Gedrosia, prov. 19 J e
Gedrosia, satr. 8 K f
Geelong 172 G d
Geertsbergen 117 B d
Gefle 88 G a
Geislingen 143 I h
Geismar 55 Q i
Gela 30 D e
Gelas River 30 D e
Geldern 78 E e
Gelderland, Upper, dist. 117 E c
Gelderland, duchy 117 D b
Gelduba 39 I h
Gelnhausen 72 B a
Gelnhausen, imp. cy. 78 F c
Gembloux 156 B a
Gembloux, mon. 94 C a
Gemelli Hills 30 C e
Gemeticum, see Jumièges
Geminiacum (Gembloux) 39 H h
Gemioncourt 156 A a
Gemmingen 142 D b
Gemmi Pass 91 P l
Genappe 156 A a
Genava (Geneva) 26 A a
Generality Lands, see Common Lands
Genesee River 192 C b
Geneva 91 O l
Geneva, bp. 95 D b
Geneva, cty. 69 G d
Geneva, dist. 91 O l
Geneva, lake 39 I j
Genèvre, Mont, pass 26 A c
Genf, see Geneva 91 O l
Genfer See, see L. Geneva 91 O l
Gengenbach 142 B d
Gennath Gate 6 ins. A
Gennesaret, Lake of 6 D c
Gennesaret, Plain of 6 D c
Genoa, in Italy 90 I h
Genoa, abp. 95 D c
Genoa, Gulf of 26 C d
Genoa, rep. 90 B b
Genoa, in Nebraska 188 G b
Gentinnes 156 B a
Genua (Genoa) 26 C c
Genusia 31 F b
Genusus River 10 B a
Geographe Bay 172 A d
Geographer's Line 196 ins. B
George, Fort, in Canada 200 D b
George, Fort, in Maine 189 D c
George, Fort, in New York 192 E b
George, lake 192 E b
Georgeana 189 D c
Georgenthal, mon. 95 E a (G.)
Georgetown, in Brit. Guiana 214 D b
Georgetown, in Pulo Penang 171 K h
Georgetown, in S. Carolina 193 E e
Georgia, col. 193 C e
Georgia, km. 73 I b
Georgia, prov. 139 F g
Georgia, reg. 67 O e
Georgia, state 199 I d
Georgian Bay 191 I b
Georgina River 172 C c
Gepidæ, people 35 I d
Gepids, people 50 H c
Gera 87 I c
Gera River 85 F e
Gerabronn 143 I g
Gerace 90 F e
Gerace, bp. 95 F d
Geræstus, prom. 15 E b
Geraldton 172 A c
Gerania, mt. 15 D a
Gerasa 7 D d
Gerata, mt.
Gerberoy, castle 69 H f
Gerenia
Gergesa 6 D c
Gergithes 9 C c
Gergovia 38 C c
Geringswalde, mon. 80 ins.
Gerizim, mt. 7 C d
Germalus, mt. 23 B
German Confederation 157 C b
German East Africa, col.
German East Africa Company
German Empire
German South-West Africa, col.
Germania reg., see Germany
Germania I, West Rom. prov. 42 D d (3)
Germania II, West Rom. prov. 42 D c (4)
Germania Inferior, Rom. prov., see Lower Germany
Germania Superior, Rom. prov., see Upper Germany
Germanic Peoples, about 900 57
Germanicopolis 20 E b
Germanna 193 F b
German Ocean
Germanorum, Forum 26 B c
Germantown 192 D c
Germany, country, see German Empire
Germany, reg. 34 G c
Germany, Greater, reg.
Germany, km. 70 I d
Germany, Lower, Rom. prov.
Germany, Upper, Rom. prov.
German Zollverein, customs-union 160 D c
Germersheim 78 F d
Gernsbach 142 B c
Gerstungen
Geroldseck, castle 154 D d
Geroldseck, cty. 158 E d
Gerolstein 117 E d
Gerona 82 C a
Gerona, bp. 94 C c
Gerona, duchy 83 L g
Gerónimo de Yuste, San, mon. 94 A c
Geronthræ 14 C c

Gerontia, isl. 11 F c
Gerresheim, mon. 95 D a
Gerrha 19 H e
Gerrhæi, people 19 G e
Gers, dept. 148 E f
Gersau 91 Q k
Gersoriacum, see Boulogne
Gertruydenberg 117 C c
Gerunium 30 E a
Geshur, reg. 6 D c
Gesoriacum 38 C b
Getæ, people 18 B b
Gethsemane, loc. near Jerusalem 6 ins. A
Gettysburg 208 ins.
Gévaudan, cty. 61 E d
Gévaudan, dist. 84 E g
Gex, dist. 130 N h
Gezer 7 B e
Ghadames 174 D b
Ghara River 137 B b
Ghassanids, Dom. of the 52 L f
Ghazal, Bahr el, reg. 174 F d
Ghazal, Bahr el, R. 174 F d
Ghazni 170 H e
Gheel 117 D c
Ghent 117 B c
Ghent, Hanse. for. cy. 99 ins. B
Gherardesca 90 L j
Ghilan, reg. 139 G h
Gian Galeazzo Visconti, Dom. of 90
Giangtse 171 K f
Giants, Stoa of the
Gibeah
Gibellum 68 C b
Gibeon 7 C e
Gibilet 68 C c
Gibraltar 82 A b
Gibraltar, strait of 2 D e
Gibson, Fort 211 G c
Gibson's Desert 172 B c
Giebichenstein, castle 63 F c
Gien 76 E c
Giengen, imp. cy. 79 G d
Giessen 114 E c
Giglio Island 90 L j
Gigny, mon. 148 C b
Gigonus 11 E b
Gijón 82 A a
Gila Bend, Ind. Res. 188 D d
Gila River 187 H e
Gila River, Ind. Res. 188 D d
Gilbert Islands 179 I g
Gilboa 7 C d
Gilboa, mt. 6 C c
Gilead, mts. 7 D d
Gilead, dist.
Giles, routes of 172 leg.
Gilgal, near Jericho
Gilgal, near Ramathaim
Gilgal, in Samaria 7 B d
Gilgit 170 I e
Gilly 156 A b
Gilolo, isl. 112 F c
Gimoës, cty. 76 D e (Gim.)
Ginœa
Giornico 91 Q l
Giovanni Visconti, Dom. of 90 I h
Giovi, pass 26 D c
Giovinazzo 90 F d
Girgeh 150 B b
Girgenti 90 D f
Girgenti, bp. 95 E d
Girishk 170 H e
Gironde, dept. 148 D f
Gisborne 172 G d
Giseh 150 B a
Gishiga 171 R b
Gislikon
Gisors 69 H f
Gitana 10 B c
Gitschin 159 H c
Gitta 7 C d
Giurgevo 93 C b
Givet 117 C d
Gizeh
Glabais 156 A a
Glacier Bay 212 ins.
Glamorgan, cty. 127 V o
Glamorgan, parl. dist. 163 K f
Glandève, bp. 95 D c
Glaphyræ 11 D c
Glarus 91 R k
Glarus, canton 91 R l
Glasgow
Glasgow, abp. 97 G b
Glasgow, univ. 100 E c
Glastonbury 60 E e
Glastonbury, mon. 97 O j
Glastonbury, parl. bor. 163 L f
Glatz 63 I c
Glatz, cty. 87 K c
Glaucus River, in Achaia 14 B a
Glaucus River, in Armenia 20 I b
Gleichen, castle 115 ins. B
Glen Coe, in Scotland
Glencoe, in Natal 175 N l
Glengarry
Glen Shiel
Glevum (Gloucester) 51 O i
Glisas 11 E d
Globukoie
Glogau 63 I c
Glogau, princ. 79 I c
Glom River 166 H c
Glommen River 120 H d
Gloucester, in England
Gloucester, castle
Gloucester, cty.
Gloucester, mon.
Gloucester, parl. bor. 163 L f
Gloucester, shire
Gloucester, in Mass. 189 D c
Gloucester, in New Jersey 192 D d
Gloucester, cty. in Virginia 193 F c (G.)
Glücksburg 158 E a
Glückstadt 122 E b
Glurns
Glykys Limen, bay 10 B c
Glympeis 15 C b
Gmünd, imp. cy. 143 I h
Gmunden 123 G e
Gnadenhuetten 194 C b
Gnatia 31 G b
Gnesen
Gnesen, abp.
Gnevin 63 G c
Goa 137 B e
Goajíra Peninsula 214 B a
Gobæum, prom. 38 A c
Gobannium (Abergavenny) 51 O i
Gobi, desert 92 K c
Goch 117 E c
Gochsheim 142 C b
Godavari River 137 C e
Godmundingham
Gödöllö 159 J e
Gods, Portico of the 24 B
God's House, League of, dist. 91 R l
Godstow, mon. 97 P j
Godwin Austen, mt. 170 I e
Gogana 19 H e
Gogo, in Africa 174 D c
Gogo, in India
Gogo, reg. 108 R f
Göhrde 154 F b
Goito 161 H e
Gök-tepe 170 G e
Golan 6 D c
Golan, reg. 6 D c
Golconda 137 C e
Goldberg 123 H c
Gold Coast, col. 174 C d
Golden Castile, reg. 105 D e
Golden Gate, in Constantinople 93 G e
Golden Gate, The, in Jerusalem 68 ins. B
Golden Horde, khan. of the 77 M c
Golden Horn, bay 93 G e
Goldenkron, mon. 80 D g
Golden Mile-stone, in Rome
Goldsboro 208 E b
Golea, El 174 D a
Golfo Dulce 105 C c
Golgatha, loc. near Jerusalem 6 ins. A
Goliad 198 F e
Göllheim 78 E d
Gollnow 135 H b
Gollnow, Hanse. cy. 99 ins. B
Golo, dept. 148 F f
Golowczyn 131 I c
Golymin 155 K b
Gomaringen 143 H i
Gomel 139 D e
Gomera, isl. 108 P e
Gomez, route of 108 J c
Gommern 85 F d
Gomphi 10 C c
Gondar 174 G c
Gonnus 11 D c
Gonzaga, fam. 79 G f
Gonzales de Avila, route of 105 C d
Good Hope, Cape of 109 S k
Good Hope, Fort 212 C b
Goole 162 F d
Goor 117 E b
Goose Creek 208 ins.
Gophna 7 C e
Göppingen 143 I h
Gora 155 K c
Gordieum 20 D c
Gordillo, route of 191 J e
Gordons, fam.
Gordonsville 208 E b (Gord.)
Gorée
Gorgiana 189 D c
Gorgon, isl. 26 D d
Gorgona
Gorgona Island 111 B a
Gorinchem 117 C c
Goritza 165 B c
Görlitz 63 H c
Gortyna
Gortys 14 C b
Görz 72 C b
Görz, cty. 79 H f
Gorze, mon. 95 D b
Gorzno 123 J b
Goshen, reg. 4 ins.
Goslar 62 F c
Goslar, Hanse. cy. 99 ins. B
Goslar, imp. cy. 79 G c
Gosnold, route of 191 L c
Göss, mon. 80 D h
Gosselies 156 A b
Göteborg
Gotha 85 F e
Götha River
Götheborg
Gothenburg
Gothia, dist. 46 I b
Gothia, marq. 61 E e
Gothland, dist. 66 I b
Gothland, isl.
Göthland, E., dist.
Göthland, W., dist.
Goths, people, in Dacia 47 K d
Goths, people, in Scandia 38 E a
Gotland, see Gothland and Göthland
Gottenburg 184 F a
Gottesgab 115 ins. B
Gotteshausbund, dist. 91 R l
Gotthard, Sankt 131 G d
Göttingen 78 F c
Göttingen, Hanse. cy. 99 ins. B
Gottlieben, castle 86 G e
Gottorp, castle 114 E a
Gottschee 80 D h
Göttweig, mon. 80 D g
Gough Island 181 A A l
Goulas 4 B b
Goulburn 172 E d
Gourdon 76 D d

Gournay . . . . 126 B b
Govola River . . . . 26 D e
Goyana . . . . 214 F c
Goyaz . . . . 214 D d
Goyaz, state . . . . 214 E d
Gozo, isl. . . . . 131 F f
Graaf Reinet . . . . 175 L m
Grabow . . . . 85 B b
Graçay . . . . 76 D c
Gracias á Dios, Cape . . . . 105 D c
Grado . . . . 63 G f
Gradus Monetæ . . . . 24 A
Græcia, Magna, reg. . . . . 29 E e
Græcostasis, in Rome . . . .
Grafton . . . . 172 E c
Graham Harbor . . . . 105 ins.
Graia, Alpis, pass . . . . 26 A b
Graian Alps, mts. . . . . 26 B b
Graïce, dist. . . . . 16 B a
Grain Coast, reg. . . . . 174 B d
Graioceli, people . . . . 26 A b
Grammont . . . . 117 B d
Grampian Mountains . . . . 49 D c
Grampound, parl. bor. . . . .
Gramzow, mon. . . . . 80 ins.
Gran . . . . 59 H d
Gran, abp. . . . . 95 F b
Gran River . . . . 63 J d
Granada, in Nicaragua . . . . 105 C d
Granada, in Spain . . . . 83 E d
Granada, abp. . . . . 94 B d
Granada, emir. . . . . 83 E d
Granada, km. . . . . 83 K h
Granby, Fort . . . . 195 A g
Gran Chaco, El, reg. . . . . 215 C e
Grand Bassam . . . . 175 C d
Grand Canyon . . . . 187 H e
Grande Chartreuse, La, mon. . . 95 D b
Grande Gete River . . . . 156 B a
Grande Ronde, Ind. Res. . . . . 188 B b
Grandes Écuries, in Versailles 149 A
Grand Forks . . . . 210 F a
Grand Gulf . . . . 208 B c
Grand Junction . . . . 188 E c
Grand Portage . . . . 211 G a
Grand Portage, Ind. Res. . . . . 188 I a
Grandpré, in France . . . .
Grand Pré, in Nova Scotia . . . 194 G b
Grand Rapids . . . . 211 H b
Grand River, in Missouri . . . . 199 G b
Grand River, in Utah . . . . 198 D c
Grand River, in S. Dakota . . . 198 E a
Grand Selve, mon. . . . . 94 C c
Grandson . . . . 91 O l
Grand Trianon, in Versailles . 149 A
Grandvilliers . . . . 76 E b
Granges . . . . 143 ins. F
Granges, lordship . . . . 143 ins. F
Granicus River . . . .
Granja . . . . 214 E c
Granja, La, castle . . . . 130 C e
Granson . . . . 130 O h
Grantham . . . . 127 Y n
Grantham, parl. bor. . . . . 163 N e
Grant Land . . . . 186 L a
Granville . . . . 172 D a
Granville, Fort . . . . 192 C c
Grasburg, castle . . . . 91 P l
Grasse . . . . 126 E e
Grasse, bp. . . . . 95 D c
Gratianopolis, see Grenoble
Gratiot, Fort . . . . 211 I b
Gratz . . . . 72 D b
Graubünden (Grisons), dist. . . 91 R l
Graudenz . . . . 115 J b
Gravelines . . . . 126 C a
Gravelle . . . . 76 C b
Grävenstein, castle . . . . 142 ins. B
Grävenstein, lordship . . . . 142 ins. B
Gravesend, in Kent . . . . 75 J i
Gravesend, in Long Island . . . 189 ins. C
Graviscæ . . . . 27 F e
Great Armenia, reg. . . . . 99 L e
Great Australian Bight . . . . 172 B d
Great Barrier Reef . . . . 172 D b
Great Barrington . . . . 196 E b
Great Basin . . . . 187 H d
Great Bear Lake . . . . 186 H b
Great Belt, str. . . . . 88 D d
Great Bend . . . . 190 F d
Great Bulgaria, reg. . . . . 77 N b
Great Canal . . . .
Great Cayman, isl. . . . . 105 D c
Great Central Plain . . . . 186 I b
Great Desert . . . .
Greater Antilles, isl. . . . . 187 L g
Greater Armenia, reg. . . . . 33 N e
Greater Germany, reg. . . . .
Greater Phrygia, satr. . . . . 18 O h
Greater Syrtis, gulf . . . . 51 G f
Great Exuma, isl. . . . . 105 E b
Great Falls . . . . 210 C a
Great Fish River, in Canada . 186 I b
Great Fish River, in Cape Col. 175 M m
Great Grimsby, parl. bor. . . . . 163 N d
Great Harbor . . . . 189 C d
Great Inagua, isl. . . . . 213 E b
Great Kanawha River . . . . 193 D b
Great Kei River . . . . 175 M m
Great Khan, Empire of the . . .
Great Lakes, The . . . . 186 K d
Great Lowland Plain . . . . 2 E c
Great Malvern, mon. . . . . 97 O i
Great Marlow, parl. bor. . 163 N f (Gr. M.)
Great Meadows, battle . . . . 192 B d
Great Miami River . . . . 196 ins. B
Great Namaqualand, reg. . . . . 175 E g
Great Northern Coalfields, England . . . . 162 E b
Great Oasis . . . . 4 E d
Great Ouse River . . . . 49 F e
Great Pedee River . . . . 193 E d
Great Poland, reg. . . . . 131 G c
Great Redan, Fort . . . . 164 L g
Great Russia, see Muscovy
Great Russians, people . . . . 139 E e
Great Saint Bernard Pass . . . 91 P m
Great Salt Lake . . . . 190 C c
Great Sandy Desert . . . . 172 B c
Great Sandy Island . . . . 172 E c
Great Siberian Plain . . . . 3 K c
Great Slave Lake . . . . 186 H b
Great Slave River . . . . 212 D b
Great Smoky Range . . . . 193 C d
Great South Wales Coalfield . 162 C f
Great Valley . . . . 187 K e
Great Victoria Desert . . . . 172 B b
Great Wall . . . .
Great Wallachia, reg. . . . . 89 C b
Great Wahle River . . . . 212 H c
Great Yarmouth, parl. bor. . . . 163 P e
Grecian Peninsula . . . . 2 G e
Greece, km. . . . . 164 C c
Greece, reg. . . . . 4 B b
Greek Patriarchate . . . . 93 G e (8)
Greeks, people . . . . 165 leg.
Green Bay . . . . 191 H c
Green Bay, cy. . . . . 199 H b
Greenbrier River . . . . 192 A d
Greencastle . . . .
Greene, route of . . . . 195 B f
Greenland, isl. . . . . 186 O a
Green Mountains . . . . 192 E b
Green River, in Kentucky . . . 193 A c
Green River, in Utah . . . . 190 D d
Greensboro . . . . 211 J c
Greenspring . . . . 193 ins. A (Gr.)
Greenville . . . . 196 ins. A
Greenville, Fort . . . . 196 ins. B
Greenway Court . . . . 192 B d
Greenwich, in Conn. . . . . 192 E c
Greenwich, in England . . . . 75 I i
Greenwich, parl. bor. . . . . 163 O f
Greenwich, E. . . . . 189 ins. A
Greetsiel . . . . 122 D b
Greifenhagen . . . . 123 H b
Greifensee, castle . . . . 91 Q k
Greifswald . . . . 80 C d
Greifswald, Hanse. cy. . . . . 99 ins. B
Greifswald, univ. . . . . 100 H d
Greiz . . . . 135 G c
Grenade, isl. . . . . 213 F c
Grenadines, isl. . . . . 213 F c
Grenoble . . . . 61 F d
Grenoble, bp. . . . . 95 D b
Grenoble, gen. . . . . 147 F c
Grenoble, univ. . . . . 100 G e
Greutungs, people . . . . 50 I c
Grève, Place de, Paris . . . . 149 B
Grève, Quai de la, Paris . . . . 149 B
Grevenmacher . . . . 117 E e
Grey Friars, mon. in London . 75 G g
Greytown . . . . 213 D c
Grèzes . . . . 76 E d
Gries Pass . . . . 91 Q l
Grignan . . . . 126 D d
Grijalva River . . . . 213 C c
Grijalva, route of . . . . 105 B c
Grimma . . . . 85 G e
Grimsby, Hanse. for. cy. . . . 98 ins. A
Grinsel Pass . . . .
Grinnell . . . . 207 G b
Gripsholm, castle . . . . 120 I e
Griqualand East, dist. . . . . 175 M m
Griqualand, West, dist. . . . . 175 L l
Grisons, dist. . . . . 91 R l
Griswold, Fort . . . . 195 F c
Grobe, mon. . . . . 80 D d
Grodno . . . . 138 B e
Groenlo . . . . 117 E b
Groitzsch . . . . 63 G c
Grol . . . . 117 E b
Grone, castle . . . . 62 E c
Groningen . . . . 117 E a
Groningen, Hanse. cy. . . . . 99 ins. B
Groningen, lordship . . . . 117 E a
Gross Batanga . . . .
Gross Beeren . . . . 154 G b
Gross Bottwar . . . . 143 H h
Grossenhain . . . . 85 G e
Grosseto . . . . 90 L j
Grosseto, bp. . . . . 95 E c
Gross Friedrichsburg . . . .
Gross Gartach . . . . 142 D b
Gross Görschen . . . . 154 G c (Gr. G.)
Gross Jägersdorf . . . . 135 K a
Gross Mariazell, mon. . . . . 95 F b
Gross Sachsenheim . . . . 143 H h
Gross Scheuern . . . . 159 M f
Groton, in Conn. . . . . 189 C d
Groton, in England . . . . 185 G e
Groton, in Mass. . . . . 189 C c
Grotzko . . . .
Grubenhagen, castle . . . . 122 F c
Grulla . . . . 190 B e
Grumbach, castle . . . . 114 E d
Grumentum . . . . 30 E b
Grumum . . . . 31 F b
Grünberg . . . . 123 H c
Grünhain, mon. . . . . 80 ins.
Grünsfeld . . . . 142 E a
Grünwettersbach . . . . 143 G h
Grussenheim . . . . 143 ins. D
Gruyères . . . . 91 P l
Gryneum . . . . 17 E b
Guadalajara, in Spain . . . . 82 B e
Guadalajara, in Mexico . . . . 213 ins.
Guadalajara, pres. . . . . 213 B b
Guadalquivir River . . . . 82 A b
Guadalupe . . . . 214 C e
Guadalupe, isl., Antilles . . . . 105 H c
Guadalupe, isl. off Lower Cal. . 187 H f
Guadalupe, mon. . . . . 94 A d
Guadalupe Hidalgo . . . . 201 F f
Guadeloupe, isl. . . . . 105 H c
Guadiana River . . . . 82 A b
Guadix . . . . 82 B b
Guadix, bp. . . . . 94 B d
Guaira . . . . 108 L j
Guaira, La, see Guayra, La
Gualtieri . . . . 90 J h
Guam, isl. . . . . 179 F f

Guanahani, isl. . . . . 105 F b
Guanajuato . . . . 213 ins.
Guanare . . . . 214 C b
Guangja, isl. . . . . 105 D c
Guano Islands . . . . 175 E g
Guantánamo . . . . 213 E b
Guapore River . . . . 214 C d
Guarda, bp. . . . . 94 A c
Guardafui, Cape . . . . 174 I c
Guardia, bp. . . . . 95 F c
Guarionex, chieftain . . . . 105 F c
Guastalla . . . . 90 C b
Guastalla, duchy . . . . 151 L k
Guatemala . . . . 105 B d
Guatemala, capt. gen. and pres. 213 D c
Guatemala, country . . . . 213 C c
Guatemala, reg. . . . . 105 B d
Guaviare River . . . . 214 B b
Guaxenduba . . . . 214 E c
Guaxule . . . . 191 I e
Guayabero River . . . . 214 B b
Guayama . . . . 199 ins. G
Guayaquil . . . . 111 B b
Guayaquil, Gulf of . . . . 111 A b
Guaymas . . . . 213 A b
Guayra, La . . . . 214 C a
Gubbio . . . . 90 D c
Gubbio, bp. . . . . 95 E c
Guben . . . . 85 H e
Guelf Domains . . . . 71 ins.
Guerande . . . . 76 B c
Guéret . . . . 69 E c
Guernsey, isl. . . . . 69 B b
Guerrero, state . . . . 213 ins.
Guevara, route of . . . . 108 J j
Guevari . . . . 190 C e
Güglingen . . . . 143 G g
Guiana, British, col. . . . . . . 214 D b
Guiana, Dutch, col. . . . . 214 D b
Guiana, French, col. . . . . 214 D b
Guiana, reg. . . . .
Guidi, fam. . . . . 90 L j
Guienne, dist. . . . . 84 C g
Guienne, duchy, 11 cent. . . . . 61 D d
Guienne, duchy, 14 cent. . . . . 76 D d
Guienne, prov. . . . . 148 D f
Guienne and Gascony, gouv. . . 146 A c
Guildford, in England . . . . . . 75 H i
Guildford, parl. bor. . . . 163 N f (Guildf.)
Guildford, in W. Australia . . . 172 A d
Guildhall, bldg. in London . . . 75 G g
Guild of the Holy Ghost, college 100 A a (33)
Guilfort, in Conn. . . . . 192 E c
Guilford Court House . . . . . . 195 B e
Guinea, Gulf of . . . . 175 D d
Guinea, reg. . . . . 108 Q g
Guinea, French, col. . . . . 174 B c
Guinea, Lower, reg. . . . . 175 E e
Guinea, Portuguese, col. . . . . 174 B c
Guinea, Upper, reg. . . . . 174 C d
Guinegate . . . . 114 B c
Guines . . . . 69 D a
Guines, cty. . . . . 69 D a
Guingamp, castle . . . . 76 B b
Guingamp, mon. . . . . 94 B b
Guipúzcoa, dist. . . . . 83 K g
Guise . . . . 76 E b
Guîtres, mon. . . . . 94 B b
Gujarat, reg. . . . . 137 B d
Gujrat . . . . 170 I e
Gulf Plain . . . . 187 J f
Gumbinnen . . . . 159 L a
Gum Coast . . . . 108 P e
Gumush Maden . . . . 165 E d
Gundelfingen . . . . 143 H i
Gundelfingen, lordship . . . . . 143 H i
Gundelsheim . . . . 143 H g
Güns . . . . 115 I e
Günsburg . . . . 154 F d
Günthersthal, mon. . . . . 142 A e
Guntia . . . . 39 K i
Guntoor, Guntur . . . . 137 D e
Günz River . . . . 143 J i
Gura . . . . 174 G c
Gurgures Mountains . . . . 27 G e
Guriev . . . . 139 H f
Gurk . . . . 80 D h
Gurk, bp. . . . . 95 E b
Gurupa . . . . 214 D c
Gustavus Adolphus, route of . 121 D b
Güstrow . . . . 79 H b
Güstrow, princ. . . . . 79 H b
Gutenberg, castle . . . .
Gutenstein . . . . 142 D d
Gutenstein, lordship . . . . . . 142 D d
Gutensell, ab. . . . . 143 J i
Guthrie . . . . 210 F c
Guthrum's Kingdom . . . .
Gutones, people . . . . 38 F b
Guzerat, reg., see Gujarat
Guzman, route of . . . . 107 G e
Gwalior . . . . 137 C c
Gwent, dist. . . . .
Gwynedd, dist. . . . .
Gyarus, isl. . . . . 15 E b
Gympie . . . . 172 E c
Gyöngyös . . . . 159 J e
Gyrton . . . . 11 D c
Gythium . . . . 14 C c
Gzhatsk . . . . 153 O f

Haarlem . . . . 117 C b
Habbard, mt. . . . . 212 ins.
Habitancium (Risingham) . . . .
Habsburg, see Hapsburg
Habsburg (Hapsburg), castle . . 62 E e
Hackensack . . . . 189 ins. C
Hacsány . . . . 131 G d
Hadad-Rimmon . . . . 6 C c
Haddeby . . . . 62 E a
Haddington, cty. . . . . . . 127 R i (HA.)
Hadeln, Land, dist. . . . . 86 G b
Hadley . . . . 189 B c
Hadramut, Hadramaut, reg. . . . 53 G e
Hadranus River . . . . 30 D e
Hadranum . . . . 30 D e
Hadria . . . . 27 I e
Hadrian, Mausoleum of . . . . . 22 A
Hadrian, Wall of, in Athens . . 23 D
Hadrian, Wall of, in Britain . . 42 B c
Hadrian, Stoa of . . . . 23 D
Hadrianopolis, in Epirus . . . . 10 B c
Hadrianopolis, in Thrace . . . . 39 N l
Hadrian's Circus . . . . 22 A
Hadrian's Gate . . . . 23 D
Hadrian's Mole . . . . 96 A
Hadrian's Villa . . . . 35 ins. B (7)
Hadrian's Wall . . . . 51 O g
Hadrumetum . . . . 38 E e
Haegsted, see Eichstädt
Hæmimont, theme . . . . 59 J e
Hæmimontium, E. Rom. prov. . . 43 H e (3)
Hæmus Mons (Mountains) . . . 39 M l
Haff, Kurisches, bay . . . . . . 155 K a
Haff, Stettiner, bay . . . . 155 H b
Hafsids, dynasty . . . . 77 F e
Hagelberg . . . . 154 G b
Hagenau . . . . 72 B b
Hagerstown . . . . 208 ins.
Hague, de la, Cape, battle off .
Hague, The . . . . 117 C b
Haidarabad, in Deccan . . . . . 137 C e
Haidarabad, in Sind . . . . 137 A c
Haigerloch . . . . 143 G i
Haïl . . . . 170 F f
Hain River . . . .
Hai-nan, isl. . . . .
Hainau . . . . 155 H c
Hainault Forest . . . . 49 G f
Hainaut, cty. . . . . 117 B d
Hainaut, dist. . . . . 62 B c
Hainaut and Cambrésis, gen. . . 147 E a
Hainburg . . . . 63 I d
Haine River . . . . 156 A b
Haiti, isl. . . . . 187 L g
Haiti, rep. . . . . 213 E c
Hakodate . . . . 171 P d
Hal . . . . 156 A a
Halæ . . . . 11 E d
Halæ Araphenides . . . . 16 C b
Halæ Æxonides . . . . 16 B b
Halæsa . . . . 30 D d
Halberstadt . . . . 62 F c
Halberstadt, bp. . . . . 95 E a
Halberstadt, Hanse. cy. . . . . 99 ins. B
Halberstadt, princ. . . . . 122 F c
Haldensleben . . . . 72 C a
Haldenstein, castle . . . . 91 R l
Hales, mon. . . . . 97 P i
Hales Owen, mon. . . . . 97 O i
Hales River . . . . 30 E b
Halex River . . . . 30 E e
Haliacmon River . . . . 10 D b
Haliartus . . . . 11 E d
Halica . . . . 15 D b
Halicarnassus . . . . 13 E c
Halicyæ . . . . 30 B e
Halicz . . . . 59 I d
Halicz, princ. . . . . 71 K d
Halidon Hill . . . .
Halieis . . . . 15 D b
Halifax, in England . . . . 162 E d
Halifax, parl. bor. . . . . 163 M d
Halifax, in Nova Scotia . . . . . 212 I d
Halifax, Fort . . . . 189 D b
Halil-Eli . . . .
Halimus . . . . 16 B b
Halipedon, dist. . . . . 16 D c
Haliussa Island . . . . 15 D b
Hall, in Tyrol . . . . 154 F e
Hall, imp. cy., in Wurtemberg . 143 I g
Hall, Fort . . . . 198 C b
Hall, Fort, Ind. Res. . . . . . . 188 D b
Hall Peninsula . . . . 212 I b
Halland, dist. . . . . 88 E c
Halle . . . . 63 G c
Halle, Hanse. cy. . . . . 99 ins. B
Halles, loc. in Paris . . . . . . 149 B
Hallstadt . . . .
Halmahera, isl. . . . . 112 F c
Halmstad . . . . 120 H e
Halonnesus, isl. . . . . 11 F c
Haluntium . . . . 30 D d
Haluc . . . . 11 D c
Halycus River . . . . 30 C e
Halys River . . . . 20 F b
Ham . . . . 117 B e
Hamadan . . . .
Hamah . . . . 68 C b
Hamar . . . . 131 F a
Hamath, on Lake of Gennesaret 6 D c
Hamath, on the Orontes R. . . 4 F c
Hamaxitos, road . . . . 23 D
Hambach . . . . 158 E d
Hamble, mon. . . . . 100 A b
Hamburg, in Germany . . . . . . 62 F b
Hamburg, Hanse. cy. . . . . . . 99 ins. B
Hamburg, imp. cy. . . . . 78 F b
Hamburg, in S. Carolina . . . . 211 I d
Hamburg, in Virginia . . . . . . 193 E b
Hamdanids, Dom. of the . . . . 59 L f
Hameln . . . . 122 E b
Hameln, Hanse. cy. . . . . 99 ins. B
Hami . . . .
Hamid, reg. . . . . 89 J g
Hamilton, in Canada . . . . 212 G d
Hamilton, in Scotland . . . . . .
Hamilton Inlet . . . . 212 J c
Hamilton River . . . . 212 I c
Hamiltons, fam. . . . . 97 I d
Hamme . . . . 156 B a
Hammerfest . . . . 167 J a
Hammerstein, castle . . . . 62 D c
Hammon . . . . 6 C b
Hamont . . . . 117 D c
Hampshire, cty. . . . .
Hampstead, in England . . . . . 75 I h
Hampstead, in Georgia . . . . . 193 ins. C
Hampton, in England . . . . . . 75 I i
Hampton, in N. Hampshire . . . 189 C c
Hampton, in Virginia . . . . . . 193 ins. A
Hampton Court, castle . . . . . 75 I i

Hampton Roads, harbor 208 E b
Hana 198 ins. B
Hanau 122 E c
Hang-chau-fu
Hanging Rock, battle 195 A f
Hangö, isl. 131 H b
Hannibal 211 G c
Hannibalis, Castra 31 F d
Ha-noi 171 L f
Hanolelet
Hanover, in Germany 86 G b
Hanover, Hanse. cy. 99 ins. B
Hanover, elect. 134 E b
Hanover, km. 158 E b
Hanover, in Pa. 208 ins.
Hanover, in Virginia 193 F c
Hansi
Hanwell 75 I h
Hanworth 75 I i
Haparanda 167 J b
Happiness, Temple of 24 A
Hapsburg, castle 91 Q k
Haran 5 C b
Harar 174 H d
Harbin 171 N d
Harbour Grace 212 J d
Harburg 134 E b
Hardanger Field 166 G c
Harderwyk 117 D b
Harderwyk, Hanse. cy. 99 ins. B
Hardheim 142 D a
Hard Times 208 B c
Harfleur 76 D b
Harfleur, Hanse. for. cy. 98 D d
Harlech, castle
Harlingen 117 D a
Harmakut, mts.
Harmar, Fort 196 ins. B
Harmene 20 F a
Harmersbach 142 B d
Harmony, New 206 ins.
Harmozia 8 D c
Harmozica 20 K b
Harpers Ferry 208 ins.
Harplea
Harran 67 N f
Harris, dist. 127 N g
Harris, Fort 192 C c
Harrisburg 196 D b
Harris Ferry 192 C c
Harrismith 175 M l
Harrison, route of 200 C d
Harrodsburg 191 I d
Harrow-on-the-Hill 75 I h
Harsany 164 B a
Hartford, in Conn. 189 B d
Hartford, in England 185 D d
Hartland, mon. 97 M k
Harvard 189 C c
Harwich 127 A A o
Harwich, parl. bor. 163 P f
Harz, mts. 62 F c
Harzburg, castle 62 F c
Hasa, El, reg.
Haslach 142 B d
Haslemere, parl. bor. 163 N f
Hasle Thal, valley 91 Q l
Hasnon, mon. 94 C a
Hasselt, in Liège 117 D d
Hasselt, in Overyssel 117 E b
Hasta, in Liguria 26 C c
Hasta, in Spain 38 A e
Hastenbeck 134 E b
Hastings
Hastings, parl. bor. 163 O g
Hatera 11 D b
Hatfield, in England
Hatfield, in Mass. 189 B c
Hatita 7 E d
Hatra 20 J e
Hatria, see Atria 27 G b
Hatria, see Hadria 27 I e
Hatteras, Cape 193 G d
Hatteras, Fort 208 E b
Hatteras Island 193 G d
Hattin 68 ins. A
Hatvan 159 J e
Hauara 18 E e
Hauenstein 142 B e
Hauenstein, cty. 142 B e
Hauran, reg. 6 E c
Hauraki Gulf 172 G d
Hausach 142 B d
Hausbergen 72 B b
Hausen, lordship 142 B d
Haute-Crête, mon. 95 D b
Hauteford, castle 76 D d
Haute-Garonne, dept. 148 E f
Haute-Loire, dept. 148 E e
Haute-Marne, dept. 148 E e
Hauterive, mon. 95 D b
Hautes-Alps, dept. 148 F f
Haute-Saône, dept. 148 F e
Hautes-Pyrénées, dept. 148 D f
Haute-Vienne, dept. 148 E e
Hauteville 65 F f
Haut-Rhin, dept. 148 F e
Hautvillers, mon. 94 C b (Hv.)
Havana 105 D b
Havel River 63 G b
Havelberg 63 G b
Havelberg, bp. 95 E a
Havelberg, Hanse. cy. 99 ins. B
Haverford 192 ins.
Haverfordwest, mon. 97 M j
Haverfordwest, parl. bor. 163 I f
Haverhill 189 C c
Havering-atte-Bower 75 J h
Havre 69 H f
Havre de Grace, in France 126 B b
Havre de Grace, in Maryland 200 L h
Hawaii, isl. 198 ins. B
Hawaii, ter. 198 ins. B
Hawaiian Islands 198 ins. B
Hawke Bay 172 G d
Haye, la, farm
Haye Sainte, la, farm
Hayling, mon. 100 B b
Haynes Bluff 208 B c
Hazah, reg. 99 M f
Hazor, near Asamon Mts. 6 C c
Hazor, near Ashdod 7 B e
Hazor, near waters of Merom 6 D b
Heathfield
Hebdomon, palace 93 G e
Hebrides, The, isl. 49 C c
Hebrides, New, isl. 172 F b
Hebron 7 C e
Hebrus River 39 N l
Hebulae Islands (The Hebrides) 38 A a
Hecate Strait 212 B c
Hecatompylus 19 I c
Hechingen 143 G i
Hecla, mt. 166 B c
Hedjaz, El Hejas, reg.
Hedon, parl. bor. 163 N d
Heemstede 189 B d
Heggbach, ab. 143 I i
Hegyes 159 J f
Heide 114 E a
Heidelberg 142 C b
Heidelberg, univ. 100 G e
Heidelsheim 142 C b
Heidenheim 143 J h
Heidenheim, lordship 143 J h
Heidenheim, mon. 95 E b
Height of Land, The 186 K c
Heilbronn 72 B b
Heilbronn, imp. cy. 143 H g
Heiligenbeil 123 K a
Heiligenberg 142 D e
Heiligenberg, cty. 142 D e
Heiligenhafen 122 F a
Heiligenkreuz, mon. 80 E h
Heiligerlee 117 E a
Heiligkreuzthal, ab. 143 H i
Heilsberg 80 G d
Heimsheim 143 G h
Heinrichau, mon. 95 F a
Heisterbach, mon. 95 D b
Heitersheim 142 A e
Hejas, El, Hedjaz, reg.
Hela 115 J a
Hela, pen. 88 H d
Helbon 6 E a
Helder 117 C b
Heldua 6 C a
Helena, Baths of 22 A
Helena, in Arkansas 208 B c
Helena, in France, see Elne
Helena, in Montana 210 C a
Helena, isl. 15 E b
Helenopontus, East Rom. prov. 43 J e (8)
Helfenstein, castle 114 E d
Helfenstein, ruin 143 I h
Helgoland, isl. 62 D a
Helice 14 C a
Helicon, mt. 11 D d
Helicon River 11 D b
Helicranum 10 B c
Heliopolis, in Egypt 4 F c
Heliopolis, in Syria 6 E a
Heliopolis, ruins of 150 B a
Helisson River 14 C b
Hellas, seg. 8 A b
Hellas, theme 59 I f
Helleporus River 31 F d
Hellespont (Dardanelles), strait
Hellespontine Phrygia, satr.
Hellespontus, dioc. 43 H f
Hellopia, dist. 10 B c
Helme River 85 F e
Helmern, castle 62 E c
Helmond 117 D c
Helmstedt 114 F b
Helmstedt, Hanse. cy. 99 ins. B
Helorine Way 31 ins. B
Helorus 30 E e
Helorus River 30 D e
Helos 15 C c
Helsingborg 120 H e
Helsingborg, Hanse. for. cy. 98 F b
Helsingfors 119 J a
Helsingör 120 H e
Helsingör, Hanse. for. cy. 98 F b
Helston, parl. bor. 163 I g
Heluan 174 J j
Helvetian Republic 151 H g
Helvetii, people 38 D c
Helvii, people 38 C d
Helvillum 27 G d
Helvinus River 27 I e
Hemeroscopium 12 C c
Hemesa 20 G e
Hemmingstedt 86 G a
Hempstead 189 B d
Hengstburg 63 H e
Heniochi, people 35 L e
Henlopen, Cape 192 D d
Henna 30 D e
Henneberg, castle 85 F e
Henneberg, cty. 114 F c
Hennebont, castle 76 B c
Hennegau, see Hainaut
Hennepin, route of 191 G c
Hennersdorf, Catholic 135 H c
Henrichemont 126 C c
Henrico 193 ins. A (Hen.)
Henrico County 207 K c
Henrietta Maria, Cape 212 G c
Henry, Cape 193 ins. A
Henry, Fort 208 C b
Henry the Illustrious, Poss. of 85
Henton, mon. 97 O j
Hepha 6 B c
Heppenheim 142 C a
Heptastadium, loc. in Alexandria 34 ins. C
Heraclea, in Acarnania 10 C d
Heraclea, in Cappadocia 67 M f
Heraclea, in Elis 14 B b
Heraclea, in Epirus 10 C c
Heraclea, in Lucania 31 F b

Heraclea, in Macedonia 10 C a
Heraclea (Perinthus)
Heraclea Chersonesus 12 J b
Heraclea Minoa 30 C e
Heraclea Pontica 20 D b
Heraclea Trachinia 11 D d
Heracleopolis 4 ins.
Heracleum, in Athens 23 D
Heracleum, in Syracuse 31 ins. B (10)
Heracleum, cy. in Macedonia 11 D b
Heraclius, Wall of 93 G e
Heræa 14 B b
Heræan Mountains 30 D e
Heræum, cy. in Thrace
Heræum, temple, in Olympia
Heræum, prom. 15 C a
Herat
Hérault, dept. 148 E f
Herault River 148 E f
Herbertshöhe 172 E a
Herbita 30 D e
Herbrechtigen 122 F d
Herck 117 D d
Herculaneum 30 D b
Hercules, isl. 18 ins. B
Hercules, Pillars of, (Calpe, or Gibraltar, and Abila), promontories 38 B e
Hercules, prom. 31 F e
Hercules, Temple of 24 A
Hercules Custor, Temple of
Herculian Way 30 E a
Herculis Monœci, Portus (Monaco) 26 B d
Hercynian Forest, mts. 38 E b
Herdoniæ 30 E a
Hereford
Hereford, bp. 97 O i
Hereford, castle 65 E d
Hereford, cty.
Hereford, parl. bor. 163 L e
Hereford, parl. dist. 163 L e
Hereford, shire
Herenthals 117 C c
Herford 122 E b
Herford, Hanse. cy. 99 ins. B
Herford, mon. 95 D a
Héricourt 143 ins. F
Héricourt, lordship 143 ins. F
Heristal 53 N g
Herjedalen, dist. 120 H d
Herkimer, Fort 192 D b
Hermanitz 123 H c
Hermannstadt 80 I i
Herminius, mt. 38 A d
Herminones, people 38 E b
Hermione 15 D b
Hermon, mts. 6 D b
Hermopolis (Eshmun) 18 D e
Hermosillo 213 A b
Hermunduri, people 38 E b
Hermus 16 B a
Hermus River 20 C c
Hernad River 115 K d
Hernandez de Cordova, route of 105 C b
Hernici, people 27 H f
Hernösand 166 I c
Herod, Tomb of 6 ins. A
Herod Agrippa, Wall of 6 ins. A
Herodes Atticus, Exedra of
Herodes Atticus, Odeum of 23 C
Herodium 7 C e
Herod's Palace, in Jerusalem 6 ins. A
Heroopolis 4 ins.
Herrenalb, mon. 95 D b
Herrenberg 143 G h
Herrenbreitungen, mon. 95 E a
Herrenhausen, castle 134 E b
Herrero Land, reg. 175 E g
Herrstein 142 ins. A
Herrstein, lordship 142 ins. A
Hersfeld 56 D b
Hersfeld, ab. 78 F c
Hersfeld, mon. 95 D a
Hersfeld, princ. 122 E c
Hertford
Hertford, cty.
Hertford, parl. bor. 163 O f
Hertford, parl. dist. 163 N f
Hertford, shire
Herulians, people, in Denmark 38 E a
Herulians, people, in Hungary 50 G c
Hervey Bay 172 E c
Hervey Islands 180 K i
Herzogenbuchsee 91 P k
Herzogenrath 117 E d
Herzegovina, dist., 15 cent. 93 A b
Herzegovina, dist., 20 cent. 164 B b
Hesdin 117 A d
Heshbon 7 D e
Hesperis 12 G d
Hesse, dist. 62 E c
Hesse, gr. duchy, 1812 154 E c
Hesse, gr. duchy, 1866 158 E c
Hesse, landgr. 78 F c
Hesse, people 55 Q i
Hesse, Electoral, state 158 E c
Hesse-Cassel, landgr. 122 E c
Hesse-Darmstadt, landgr. 122 E c
Hestia, Temple of 16 D c (2)
Histiæotis, dist.
Heubach 143 I h
Heubach, Klein 142 D a
Heusden 117 C c
Hevellians, people 63 G b
Hexamilion
Hexapylum, loc. in Syracuse 31 ins. B (11)
Hexham
Hexham, mon.
Hexham, dist.
Heyst 117 C c
Heystesbury, parl. bor. 163 L f (Heyt.)
Hezekiah, Pool of 6 ins. A (6)
Hezekiah, Wall of 6 ins. A
Hibernia (Ireland) 34 C c
Hibernii, people 38 A b
Hiberus River, see Ebro River
Hildalgo, state 213 ins.
Hiera, isl., Ægates Island 30 B e
Hiera, isl., Liparææ Island 30 E d
Hierapolis, in Asia Minor
Hierapolis, in Syria 20 G d
Hierapytna 14 ins.
Hieromyces River 6 D c
Hieron Æsculapii 15 D b
Hierosolyma (Jerusalem) 35 L g
Higham Ferrers, parl. bor. 163 N e
Highlanders, people 184 C a
Highlands, reg. 49 D c
Highworth, parl. bor.
Higuey, reg. 105 G c
Hilara River 39 J i
Hildburghausen 134 F c
Hildesheim 62 E b
Hildesheim, bp. 95 D a
Hildesheim, Hanse. cy. 99 ins. B
Hilerda, see Lérida
Hili
Hill of Evil Counsel 6 ins. A
Hill of the Muses 23 D
Hill of the Nymphs 23 D
Hillsboro 195 B e
Hilo 198 ins. B
Hilsbach 142 C b
Hilton Head, cape 193 ins. C
Hilton Head, cy. 208 D c
Himalaya Mountains 170 I e
Himella River 27 H e
Himera 30 C e
Himera River, N. 30 C e
Himera River, S. 30 D e
Himmelpforte, mon. 80 ins.
Himmelpforten 122 E b
Hims, see Homs 59 L g
Hindon 127 W o
Hindon, parl. bor. 163 L f (Hind.)
Hindukush, mts.
Hindustan, reg. 137 B-E c
Hingham 189 ins. B
Hinnom, valley 6 ins. A
Hinter-Rhein, see Farther Rhine River 91 R l
Hinterpommern, see Farther Pomerania 123 H b
Hiogo
Hippicus Tower 6 ins. A
Hippodamea 16 D c
Hippodrome, loc. in Rome 24 B
Hippola 14 C c
Hipponiates, gulf 31 F d
Hipponium (Vibo) 31 F d
Hippo Regius 38 D e
Hippo Zarytus 38 D e
Hippus 6 D c
Hiram's Grave 6 C b
Hirato, isl.
Hiroshima 171 O e
Hirpini, people 30 D b
Hirrlingen 143 G i
Hirsau, mon. 95 D b
Hirschberg 123 H c
Hisn Keifa, on the Euphrates 68 C b
Hisn Keifa, on the Tigris 71 O f
Hispalis (Seville) 38 A e
Hispania, see Spain
Hispania Bætica, prov. 38 A e (3)
Hispania Lusitania, prov. 38 A d (2)
Hispania Tarraconensis, prov. 38 B d (1)
Hispaniola, isl. 105 F c
Hispellum 27 G c
Hissar, in India 137 C c
Hissar, in Turkestan
Hissarlik
Histiæa 11 E d
Histiæotis, dist. 11 E d
Histonium 27 I e
Histria, reg., see Istria 27 H b
Hither Pomerania, dist. 123 G a
Hither Rhine River 91 R l
Hither Spain, prov. 38 B d (1)
Hittites, people 4 F c
Hlidbeki, see Lübeck
Hoang-ho, R.
Hobart 172 D e
Hobkirks Hill, battle 195 A f
Hoboken 189 ins. C
Hochberg, castle 142 A d
Hochberg, margr. 142 A d
Hochdorf 143 G h
Hochelaga 191 K b
Hochkirch 135 H c
Höchst, S. of Frankfort 122 E c
Höchst, W. of Frankfort 62 E c
Höchstädt 134 F d
Hodeida 170 F g
Hof 154 F c
Hogland, isl. 131 I a
Hogue or Hougue, la, see Saint Vaast-de-la-Hougue
Hoh, Ind. Res. 188 B a
Hohen-Altheim 62 F d
Hohenasperg 143 H h
Hohenberg, ruin 143 G i
Hohenberg, Lower, cty. 143 G i
Hohenberg, Upper, cty. 143 G i
Hohenburg, in Alsace 72 B b
Hohenburg, in Bavaria 63 F d
Hohenems 72 B b
Hohenfriedeberg 135 I c
Hohengeroldseck, cty. 142 A d
Hohengeroldseck, mon. 142 A d
Hohenhöwen, castle 142 C e
Hohenkarpfen, ruin 143 G i
Hohenlinden 135 G d
Hohenlohe, princ. 143 I g
Hohen-Mölsen 63 G c
Hohenneuffen, ruin 143 H h
Hohenrechberg, ruin 143 I h
Hohenstaufen, castle 114 E d
Hohenstaufen, ruin 143 I h
Hohenstaufen Domains 71
Hohentwiel, castle 114 E c

Hohen Urach, ruin 143 H i
Hohenzollern, castle 154 G b
Hohenzollern, princ. 143 H i
Hohnstein 122 F c
Hojeda, route of 105 G d, 108 M g
Hole Bourn, loc. near London 75 G g
Holebourn Bridge 75 G g
Holkar, Dom. of 137 C c
Hollabrunn 155 I d
Holland, cty. 117 C c
Holland, dist.
Holland, km., 1806 151 K i
Holland, km., 1831 158 C b
Höllental, valley 134 E e
Holly Springs 208 C c
Holmby House 127 X n
Holme Cultram, mon. 97 N g
Holmiæ, prom. 15 C a
Holstein, cty. 72 B a
Holstein, dist. 62 E a
Holstein, duchy, 15 cent. 86 G b
Holstein, duchy, 19 cent. 151 H f
Holston River 196 ins. A
Holwan
Holyoke 211 K b
Holy Rock, loc. in Jerusalem 6 ins. A (1)
Holy Roman Empire about 1000 58, 59
Holy Roman Empire, 1138—1254 72
Holy Sepulchre, Church of the 6 ins. A
Holy Sepulchre, street of the 68 ins. B
Holy Trinity the less, ch. in London 75 G g (22)
Homberg 114 E c
Homblières, mon. 94 C b (Hombl.)
Homburg, in Bavarian Palatinate 142 ins. B
Homburg, in Hesse 158 E c
Homolium 11 D c
Homs 68 C c
Ho-nan, prov. 171 M e
Honawar 137 B f
Hondo, isl. 171 O e
Honduras, Cape 105 C c
Honduras, country 213 D c
Honduras, reg. 105 C d
Honduras, Gulf of 105 C c
Hondschoote 134 B c
Honfleur 76 D b
Hongkong 171 M f
Honiton 127 V p
Honiton, parl. bor. 163 K g
Honolulu 198 ins. B
Honor, Temple of 22 A
Honore 137 B f
Honorias, E. Rom. prov. 43 I e (4)
Hood, mt. 187 G d
Hoogly
Hoogly River
Hoogstraeten 72 B a
Hoogwoud 72 A a
Hoopa Valley, Ind. Res. 188 B b
Hoorn 117 D b
Hoorn, cty. 117 D c
Hope, Temple of
Hopedale 212 I c
Hopetown 175 L l
Hopi, Ind. Res. 188 D c
Hopton Heath 127 W n
Horace, Villa of 35 ins. B
Horb 143 G i
Horburg 143 ins. D
Horburg, cty. 143 ins. D
Horgen 91 Q k
Horma
Horn 123 H d
Horn, Cape, in Iceland 166 A b
Horn, Cape, in S. America 215 C h
Hornachos 82 A b
Hornbach, mon. 95 D b
Hornberg 142 B d
Horncastle 98 ins. A
Horneck 143 H g
Hornisgrinde, pass 134 E d
Horologium, in Athens 23 D
Horrea 26 A d
Horrea, loc. in Rome 23 A
Horse Gate 6 ins. A
Horseham, parl. bor.
Horsens 158 E a
Horseshoe Bend, battle 200 I f
Horsham, mon. 97 S i
Horta 27 G e
Ho-si-wu 170 ins. A
Hostilia 26 F b
Hôtel des Invalides, in Paris 149 B
Hôtel de Ville, in Paris 149 B
Hôtel Dieu 149 B
Hôtel du Grand Maître in Versailles 149 A
Hôtels, Rue des, street in Versailles 149 A
Hot Springs 211 G d
Hottentots, people 109 S k
Houffalize 117 D d
Hougomont, castle
Hougue, La 130 C d
Hounslow 75 I i
Housatonic River 189 B c
House of Hope 189 B d
House of the Mighty Men, in Jerusalem 6 ins. A (4)
Houston 198 F d
Houtain 156 A a
Howard, Fort 211 H b
Howe, Cape 172 E d
Howe, route of Lord 195 F c
Howe, route of Sir William 105 F c, D e
Höwen, lordship 142 C e
Howland Island 180 J g
Höxter 55 Q i
Höxter, mon. 95 D a
Höxter, Hanse. cy. 99 ins. B
Hoya 78 F b
Hoya, cty. 78 F b
Hoyerswerda 155 H c
Hradisch, mon. 80 E g
Hsiang-ho 170 ins. A
Hsiang-yang
Hsiung 170 ins. A
Huacho 214 B d
Huallaga River 111 B c
Hualpai, Ind. Res. 188 B c
Huamachuco 111 B c
Huamanga 111 C d
Huancabamba 111 B c
Huancavelica 214 B d
Huanchaca 214 C e
Huanuco nuevo 111 B c
Huanuco viejo 111 B c
Huaqui 214 C d
Huaraz 111 B c
Huascan (Huascaran), mt. 214 B c
Huasco 215 B e
Hubbardton 195 E b
Hubermont, Farm
Hubermont, Woods of
Hubert, Saint 117 D d
Hubertusburg 135 G c
Huddersfield, parl. bor. 163 M d (Hudd.)
Hude, mon. 95 D a
Hudson, route of
Hudson Bay 186 K b
Hudson River 189 B d
Hudson Strait 186 L b
Hudson's Bay Company
Hué 171 L g
Huejotlipan
Huejotzingo
Huelgas, mon. 94 B c
Huelva 82 A b
Huesca 82 B a
Huesca, bp. 94 B c
Huesca, univ. 100 E f
Huescar 82 H f
Huete 82 B a
Hughenden 172 D c
Hugli 137 E d
Hugli River 137 E d
Hühnerwasser 159 H c
Huillier, Fort d' 191 G c
Hull, in Canada 212 H d
Hull, in England 127 Y m
Hull, Hanse. for. cy. 98 ins. A
Hull, parl. bor. 163 N d
Hull, in Massachus 189 ins. B
Hull, route of 200 C d
Hulst 117 C c
Hulwan 99 M g
Humacao 199 ins. G
Humaitá 215 D e
Humber River 49 G e
Humboldt River 187 H d
Huna Floi 166 A b
Hu-nan, prov. 171 M f
Hundheim 158 E d
Hungarian Plain 2 F d
Hungarians, people, on the Dniester 55 J d
Hungarians, people, on the Theiss 168 G c
Hungary, km., about 1000 59 H-I d
Hungary, km., about 1190 70 K d
Hungary, km., part of the Ottoman Empire 119 H d
Hungary, km., about 1740 131 H d
Hungary, km., 19 cent. 159 J e
Hungerford 127 X o
Hun-ho, R. 170 ins. A
Hüningen 122 D e
Hunkiar Skelessi 164 D b
Hunnic (Attila's) Empire 48 F-L b
Huns, people, on the Volga R.
Huns, people, in Hungary
Hunte River 114 E b
Huntingdon 127 Y n
Huntingdon, castle 65 F d
Huntingdon, cty.
Huntingdon, mon. 97 Q i
Huntingdon, parl. bor. 163 N e
Huntingdon, parl. dist. 163 N e
Huntingdon, shire
Huntington 192 E c
Huntsville 211 H d
Hu-pei, prov. 171 M e
Huriel 69 I g
Huron, lake 187 K d
Hurons, tribe 188 J b
Hurst Castle 127 X p
Hushi 131 I d
Hussinetz 79 H d
Huy 117 D d
Hwang-chau
Hwiccas, people
Hyampolis 11 D d
Hybla Heræa 30 D e
Hybla Maior 30 D e
Hyblæus River 30 D e
Hyccara 30 C d
Hydaspes River 19 L d
Hyderabad, in Deccan 137 C e
Hyderabad, in Sind 137 A c
Hydraotes River 19 L d
Hydrea (Hydra), isl. 15 D b
Hydruntum (Otranto) 31 H b
Hydrusa, isl. 16 B b
Hyeres, isl. 126 E e
Hilæthus River 11 D d
Hyle 11 E d
Hylias River 31 F c
Hylice, lake 11 E d
Hymettus, mt. 15 D b
Hypæpa 20 B c
Hypanis River (Bug R.) 18 D a
Hypanis River (Kuban R.) 18 E a
Hypata 10 D d
Hypatus, mt. 11 E d
Hyphasis River 19 D d
Hyphormus, Port of 16 B b
Hypsas River 30 B e
Hyrcania, reg. 19 H c
Hyrcania, satr. 8 J e
Hyria, lake 10 C d
Hyrmine 14 B a
Hyrminus River 30 D e

Hyrtacina 14 ins.
Hysiæ 14 C b
Hythe
Hythe, parl. bor. 163 P f

Iaccetani, people 38 C d
Iader 27 J c
Ialysus 4 C b
Iamo 38 C e
Iamnia 7 B e
Iamnia maritima 7 B e
Iamzai
Ianiculum, mt. 22 A
Iapis River 16 A a
Iapydes, people 27 I b
Iapygians, people 29 E d
Iapygium, prom. 31 H c
Iardanus River, in Crete 14 ins.
Iardanus River, in Elis 14 B b
Iassus 13 E c
Iazyges Metanastæ, people 38 F c
Ibagué 214 B b
Ibebin
Iberia, reg. (Caucasia) 18 F b
Iberia, reg. (Spain) 12 B c
Iberian Peninsula 2 D d
Iberian Sea 38 B e
Iberus River, see Ebro River
Ibir-Sibir, reg. 102 G b
Iburg, mon. 95 D a
Ica, battle 214 B d
Iça River
Icaria 16 B a
Icaria, isl. 13 E c
Icaros, see Icaria 17 E c
Icauna or Icaunus River, see Yonne River
Ice Cape 170 I a
Iceland, isl. 166 B c
Iceni, people 51 Q h
I-chang 171 M e
I-chau 170 ins. A
Ichnæ 11 D b
Ichtershausen, mon. 95 E a
Ichthyophagi, people 19 J e
Ichthys, prom. 14 B b
Iciodurum, see Issoire
Icknield Way, road 51 P i
Icolmkill, isl.
Iconium (Konieh) 20 E d
Iconium, sultanate, 12 cent. 68 B b
Iconium, sultanate, 13 cent. 73 H c
Icorigium 39 I h
Icosium 12 D c
Iculisna, see Angoulême
Icus 11 E c
Icus (Khiliodromia), isl. 11 E c
Icy Cape 198 ins. A
Ida, mt., in Crete 14 ins.
Idaho, state 210 B a
Idaho, ter. 1863 203 P f
Idaho, ter. 1864 203 P g
Idaho, ter. 1868 203 O g
Ida Mountains, in Troas
Idanha 82 A b
Idar 142 ins. A
Idex River 27 F c
Idistaviso 39 J g
Idomene
Idrisids, dom. of the 54 E f
Idstedt 158 E a
Idubeda Mountains 38 B d
Idumæa, reg. 7 B f
Ieracia, isl.
Ierne (Ireland), isl. 38 A b
Igilgilis 38 D e
Igilium, isl. 26 E e
Iglau 79 I d
Igli 174 C a
Iglo 159 K d
Iguala 213 ins.
Iguassú, river and falls 215 D e
Iguvium 27 G d
Ilanz 91 R l
Ilchester, parl. bor. 163 L g
Ildijis Atabeks, people 71 P f
Ile du Palais, loc. in Paris 149 B
Ilei 15 D b
Ilerda (Lérida) 38 C d
Ilergetes, people 38 B d
Ilfeld, mon. 95 E a
Ilheos, cap. 108 M i
Ili River 92 H c
Ilici 38 B e
Ilipula Mountains 38 B e
Ilissus River 16 B b
Ilium (Troy)
Ilium, in Epirus 10 B c
Il-Khans of Persia, Dom. of the
Illampu, Mount 214 C d
Illapel 215 B f
Ille-et-Vilaine, dept. 148 D e
Iller River 62 F d
Illiberi or Illiberis (Elvira) in Spain 38 B e
Illiberis, in France, see Elne
Illimani, Mount 214 C d
Illinoia, proposed state in U. S.
Illinois, tribe 188 H c
Illinois Country, reg. 191 G H c
Illinois, ter. 1809 202 G a
Illinois, state 203 T b
Illinois River 191 G d
Illiturgi 38 B e
Illkirch 122 D d
Illurgavonenses, people 38 C d
Illyria, reg. 12 G b
Illyria, km. 159 H e
Illyrian Provinces 155 G e
Illyrians, people 5 A a
Illyricum, reg., 1st cent. 34 H e
Illyricum, reg., 5 cent. 50 H d
Illyricum, E. Rom. pref. 43 G f
Illyrii, people 17 B a
Illyris, dist. 10 B b
Ilm River 85 F e
Ilmen, lake 59 K b
Iloilo 199 ins. H
Iluro, see Oloron
Ilus, Burial mound of
Ilva (Elba), isl. 26 E e
Imbros, isl.
Imil
Immenstadt 143 J j
Imola 90 J h
Imola, bp. 95 E c
Imperial Canal 171 M e
Inachus River, in Æniania 10 D d
Inachus River, in Argolis 14 C b
Inachus River, in Epirus 10 C c
Inagua, isl. 105 F b
Incas, Dom. of the 108 J h K j
In Castello 27 F c
Incia River 26 E c
Inda, mon. 95 D a
Independence, in Missouri 211 G c
Independence, in Texas 210 F d
Independence, Fort, in Vermont 195 E a
India, emp. 137
India, reg. 112 A b
India Inferior, prov. 19 K e
India infra terram, reg. 99 M g
Indiana, ter. 1803 202 H b
Indiana, ter. 1809 202 H b
Indiana, state 203 U b
Indianapolis 199 H c
Indian Country, reg. 1819 203 R b
Indian Lake 212 F c
Indian Ocean 109 W-A A h
Indian Pueblo Grants 188 E c
India Superior, prov. 19 L d
Indian Territories, in Canada 212 C c
Indian Territory, in the U. S. 203 S c
Indians in the United States 188
Indigetes, people 38 C d
Indies, E., reg. 109, 110 X-D D e-h
Indies, The, reg. 107, 108, leg.
Indien, W., reg. 107, 108 E-O, a-l
Indo-China, French col. 171 L g
Indore 137 C d
Indragiri
Indre, dept. 148 E e
Indre-et-Loire, dept. 148 E e
Indus River, in Caria 20 C d
Indus River, in India 137 A c
Industria 26 C b
Inessa 30 D e
Infantado, duchy 83 K g
Infante, Rio del, R. 109 T k
Ingævones, people 38 D b
Ingauni, people 26 C c
Ingelfingen 143 I g
Ingelheim 62 D d
Ingerkingen 143 I i
Ingermanland, reg. 138 C d
Ingolstadt 79 G d
Ingolstadt, univ. 100 H e
Ingria, reg. 138 C d
Iniada 165 F c
Inkerman 164 J f
Inland India, reg. 99 M g
Inn River 63 G d
Innichen 54 G d
Innichen, mon. 80 C h
Inn Quarter, dist. 135 G d
Innsbruck 72 C b
Innviertel, dist. 157 C c
Inowraclaw (Hohensalza) 135 J b
In Portu 26 E d
Insala 174 D b
Insterburg 155 K a
Insubres, people 26 C b
Interamna or Interamne (Terni), in Umbria 27 G e
Interamna Lirenas (Termini), in Latium 30 C a
Interamnia, in Picenum 27 H e
Interamnium 31 F c
Interlaken 91 P l
Internal Provinces, New Spain 190 B F e f
Interocrium 27 H e
Interpromium 27 H e
Intimilii, people 26 B d
Inverary
Invercargill 172 F e
Inverloch
Inverness
Inverness, cty.
Inycum 30 C e
Iol 38 C e
Iolcus 11 D c
Ion River 10 C c
Iona, bp. 97 G c
Iona, isl. 49 C c
Ionia, reg. 8 Q h
Ionia, satr. 8 G e
Ionian Islands 164 B c
Ionians, people
Ionian Sea 5 A b
Ios 13 D c
Iovavum (Salzburg), see Iuvavum
Ioventio, pass 26 D c
Iowa City 211 G b
Iowa, Ind. Res. 188 G c
Iowa, ter. 1838 202 F f
Iowa, state 202 G g
Iowa River 211 G b
Iowa, tribe 188 H b
Ipni Promontorium 11 E c
Ipoly-Ságh 159 J d
Ipsus 20 D c
Ipswich, in England
Ipswich, Hanse. for. cy. 98 ins. A
Ipswich, parl. bor. 163 P e
Ipswich, in Mass. 189 D c
Ipswich, in Queensland 172 E c
Iquique 214 B e
Iquitos 214 B c
Ira 14 B b
Ira River 26 D c
Irak, reg.
Irak Ajemi, reg.
Irak Arabi, reg.

Iran, Plateau of 3 J f
Irawadi River
Irbil 71 O f
Ireland, isl.
Iria 26 C b
Irish, people, about 900
Irish Sea 49 D e
Iris River 20 G b
Irkutsk 171 L c
Iron 6 C b
Iron Bridge, over the Orontes R. 68 C b
Ironton 206 ins.
Iroquois, tribes 192 D a
Iroquois River 191 H
Irrhesia, isl. 11 F c
Irtish River
Is (Hit) 18 F d
Isabel, isl. 172 E a
Isabella 105 F c
Isabella, isl. 105 F b
Isar River 63 G d
Isara, see Pontoise
Isara River (Isère R.) 38 D c
Isara River (Oise R.) 38 C c
Isarci, people 27 F a
Isarcus River 27 F a
Isaszeg 159 J e
Isatis (Yezd) 19 H d
Isaura 20 E d
Isauria, reg.
Isauria, E. Rom. prov. 43 I f (14)
Isauria, Rom. prov.
Isca Dumnoniorum (Exeter) 51 O i
Isca Silurum (Caerleon-upon-Usk) 51 O i
Ischia, bp. 95 ins.
Ischia, isl. 90 D d
Ischl 158 G e
Isel-Berg, mt. 154 F e
Isenburg, princ. 154 E c
Iser River 115 H c
Isère, dept. 148 F e
Isère River 84 F g
Isernia 161 J g
Isernia, bp. 95 E c
Iseum 22 A
Ishim River
Ishmaelites, people 7 ins. C
Isis, Temple of 22 A
Isis and Serapis, Aug. Reg. of Rome 22 A
Isker 138 K d
Isker River 168 H e
Iskut River 212 ins.
Isla del Gallo, isl. 111 B a
Isla de Pinos, isl. 105 C c
Isla de Sacrificios, isl. 106 D a
Isla de Términos, isl. 105 B c
Islamabad 137 C b
Island No. 10, fort 208 C b
Islands, Bay of 172 G d
Isla Santa, isl., off coast of Perú 111 B c
Isla Santa, i. e. South America 105 F e
Islay, isl. 49 C d
Isle de France, isl. 175 I f
Isle of France, gouv. 146 B b
Isle of France, prov. 148 E e
Isle of Wight 100 A b
Isle of Wight, parl. dist. 163 M g
Isles, The, bp. 97 G c
Islington 75 I h
Islip Bridge 127 X o
Ismail 131 I d
Ismailia 174 K i
Ismenus River 11 E d
Ismid 77 K d
Ismilan 165 D c
Isnik 89 I f
Isny 114 F e
Isny, imp. city 143 J j
Isocum 38 C e
Isontus River, see Salzach River
Isonzo River 50 F c
Ispahan 53 H c
Israel, Kingdom of 6 ins. B
Issachar, tribe 7 ins. D
Issoire 126 C d
Issoudun 61 E c
Issoudun, castle 76 E c
Issoudun, seign. 61 D c
Issus 20 G d
Issus, Gulf of 20 F d
Issyk-kul, lake
Istævones, people 38 D b
Ister (Danube) River 35 I e
Istib
Istone, mt. 10 A c
Istria, reg. 27 H b
Istria, march 63 G f
Istropolis 39 N l
Istrus 12 I b
Istvæones, see Istævones
Isurium (Aldborough) 51 P g
Italia, dist. in Bruttium 30 E d
Italia, see Italy
Italians, people
Italian Peninsula 2 F d
Italian Republic 151 H g
Italian Somaliland, col. 174 H d
Italica 38 A e
Italy, reg. 12 F b
Italy, West. Rom. dioc. 42 E d
Italy, exarch. of 52 J e
Italy, km., 9 cent. 56 E d
Italy, km., 12 cent. 70 I e
Italy, km., 19 cent. 154 F f
Itanus 14 ins.
Itapirú, Fort 215 D e
Itapua 215 D e
Itasca, lake 186 J d
Itati 215 D e
Ithaca 10 B d
Ithaca, isl. 10 B d
Ithaca (Leucas), isl. 10 B d
Ithome 10 C c
Ithome, mt. 14 B b
Ithoria 10 C d
Itil (Astrakhan) 99 M d
Itius, Portus, bay 38 C b
Itonus 11 D c
Ituna Æstuarium (Solway Firth) 51 O g
Iturea, dist. 6 D a
Ituzaingó, battle 215 D f
Ityke 12 F c
Itzehoe 55 Q i
Iuenna 27 I a
Iuka 208 C c
Iuliabriga 38 B d
Iuliacum (Jülich) 39 I h
Iulia Fanestris 27 H d
Iuliobona 38 B c
Iuliomagus (Angers) 38 B c
Iulis 15 E b
Iulius, Vicus 39 J i
Iulium Carnicum 27 G a
Iunonia Falisca 27 G e
Iuvanum 27 I f
Iuvavum (Salzburg) 38 E c
Ivangorod, in Ingria 138 C d
Ivangorod, in Poland 159 L c
Ivanitza 165 B b
Ivanovo Vosnessensk
Iviza, bp. 94 C d
Iviza, isl. 82 C b
Ivois, castle 62 C d
Ivory Coast, French col. 174 C d
Ivrea 90 A b
Ivrea, bp. 95 D b
Ivrea, marq. 64 A a
Ivry 76 D b
Ixtacamaxtitlan
Ixworth, mon. 97 R i
Izium 139 E f
Iznalloz 82 B b
Iztaban 105 B c
Iztaccihuatl, volcano of 106 B a
Iztapalapan
Iztaplatzinco
Jabalpur, Jubbulpore 137 C d
Jabbok River 7 D d
Jabesh-Gilead
Jablunkau 123 J d
Jabneel, in Galilee 6 D c
Jabneel, in Philistæa 7 B e
Jaca 82 B a
Jackson, in Michigan 207 I b
Jackson, in Mississippi 211 G d
Jackson, Fort, in Alabama 200 I f
Jackson, Fort, in Louisiana 208 C d
Jackson, route of 200 I g
Jackson's Hole, dist. 210 C b
Jacksonville 199 I d
Jacob, castle 68 ins. A
Jacobins, The, bldg. in Paris 149 B
Jacobsdal 175 L l
Jadera 54 H e
Jaén, in Peru 214 B c
Jaén, in Spain 82 B b
Jaén, bp. 94 B d
Jaén, km. 83 K h
Jaffa 68 ins. A
Jafna 112 B c
Jafnapatam 112 B c
Jagannath 137 E e
Jägerndorf 115 I c
Jägerndorf, princ. 115 I c
Jagersfontein 175 M l
Jagst River 143 J g
Jagstberg 143 I g
Jagstheim 143 H g
Jagstzell 143 J g
Jaguarão 215 D f
Jaguaribe River 214 F c
Jahna, castle 63 G c
Jaipur, in Madras 170 J g
Jaipur, in Rajputana 170 I f
Jaipur, Jaypore, dist. 137 C c
Jaisalmer, dist. 137 B c
Jaitza
Jalalabad 137 B b
Jalapa 106 D a
Jalayrs, Dom. of the 77 N f
Jaligny 69 E c
Jalisco, state 213 ins.
Jamaica 189 ins. C
Jamaica, isl. 105 E c
Jamapa, R. 106 D a
Jamary River 214 C d
Jambi
James, Fort 132 J h
James Bay 186 K c
James River 188 K c
Jamestown 193 ins. A
Janiculan citadel 23 B
Janina
Janitza 165 C c
Janizary Quarter, Old, in Constantinople 93 G e
Jankau 123 H d
Jan Mayen, isl. 166 D a
Janus, Temple of, in Rome
Janus quadrifrons, in Rome 24 B
Japan, emp.
Japan Sea
Jargeau 76 E c
Jarmuth Ramoth 7 C d
Jarnac 126 A d
Jaroslaw 159 L c
Jarrow
Jarrow, mon. 97 P g
Jassy 139 C f
Játiva 82 B b
Jauer 79 I c
Jauja 111 B d
Java, isl.
Javols, about forty miles northeast of Rodez
Jaxartes River (Syr-Daria) 19 J a
Jazer 7 D e
Jean-Loo
Jeba 6 B c
Jeblaam 7 C d

Jedburgh
Jefferson City 211 G c
Jehlam 137 B b
Jehol 171 M d
Jehoshaphat, gate, in Jerusalem 68 ins. B
Jehoshaphat, street 68 ins. B
Jehoshaphat, Tomb of 6 ins. A
Jehoshaphat, Valley of 6 ins. A
Jelairs, people
Jemappas 134 B c
Jemes 190 D d
Jemmingen 114 D b
Jemtland, dist. 120 E d
Jena 114 F c
Jeni-Kivi
Jeni-Shehr
Jenkinson, route of 108 R a
Jequitinhonha River 214 E d
Jerba, isl. 73 C d
Jerez de la Frontera 82 G f
Jerez de los Caballeros 82 G f
Jericho 7 C e
Jerichow 85 C b
Jerichow, mon. 80 ins.
Jersey, isl. 69 B b
Jersey City 189 ins. C
Jerusalem 7 C e
Jerusalem, plan of ancient 6 ins. A
Jerusalem, plan of mediaeval 68 ins. B
Jerusalem, km., 12 cent. 68 C c
Jerusalem, km., 13 cent. 73 G d
Jerusalem, patr. 52 L f
Jervaulx, mon. 97 P g
Jeshua 7 B f
Jesi 90 D c
Jesi, bp. 95 E c
Jesireh, El, see El Jesireh
Jesulmere, reg. 137 B c
Jever 114 D b
Jever, lordship 122 D b
Jeypore, Jaipur, dist. 137 C c
Jezreel 6 C c
Jezreel, Plain of 6 C c
Jhansi 137 C c
Jheelum
Jibuti 174 H c
Jicarilla, Ind. Res. 188 E c
Jiddah
Jimena 82 A b
Jiphtha 6 C c
Jitomir 139 C e
Joachimsthal 115 G c
Joanna Springs 172 B b
Joazeiro 214 E c
Jocko, Ind. Res. 188 D a
Jodhpur 137 B c
Jodoigne 156 B a
Johann Georgenstadt 123 G c
Johannesburg 175 M l
John Cabot, route of 108 O b M c
John of Pian de Carpine, route of
Johnson, mt. 212 ins.
Johnson Hall 194 L f
Johnstones, fam. 97 J d
Johnston Islands 180 K f
Joigny 61 E c
Joinville, in Brazil 215 E e
Joinville, in France 76 F b
Joinville, seign. 69 J f
Jokneam 6 C c
Joli-Bois
Joliet 211 H b
Jolliet, route of 191 G c
Joló Archipelago 199 ins. H
Jomsburg 63 H b
Jonesboro 196 ins. A
Jönköping 120 H e
Joppa, in Maryland 192 C d
Joppa, in Palestine 7 B d
Joppe 7 B d
Jordan River 7 D d
Josefstadt 159 I c
José Monteiro 214 D c
Joug-Dieu, Le, mon. 94 C b
Jouy, mon. 94 C b
Juana (Cuba), isl. 105 D b
Juan de Fuca, Strait of 198 A a
Juan Fernandez Island 107 I k
Juba River 175 H d
Jubbulpore, Jabalpur 137 C d
Judæa, reg. 7 B e
Judah, Kingdom of 6 ins. B
Judah, tribe 7 ins. D
Judah, Mountains of 7 C e
Judah, Wilderness of 7 C e
Judenburg 123 H a
Judith, Point, cape 189 ins. A
Juggernaut 137 E e
Juist, isl. 117 E a
Jujuy 215 C e
Julian Alps, mts. 27 H a
Julian Aqueduct 22 A
Julian Augustan Way, road 26 B d
Julias 6 D c
Julica, Basilia, bldg. in Rome 24 B
Jülich 62 D c
Jülich, duchy 78 E c
Jülich-Cleves-Berg, prov. 158 D c
Julier, pass 26 D a
Jumet 156 A b
Jumièges 65 G f
Jumièges, mon. 94 C b
Jumna River
Junction City 210 F c
Juneau 212 ins.
Jungaria, reg. 92 I c
Jung-Bunzlau 115 H c
Juniata River 192 C c
Junin, battle 214 B d
Junkseylon 112 C c
Juno Lucina, Temple of 22 A
Juno Moneta, Temple of 24 A
Juno Regina, Temple of 22 A
Jupiter Capitolinus, Temple of 24 A
Jupiter Dolichenus, Temple of 22 A
Jupiter Latiaris, Temple of 35 ins. B (5)
Jupiter Stator, Temple of 24 A
Jupiter Victor, Temple of 24 A
Jura, dept. 148 F e
Jura Mountains 38 D c
Jurjan 102 F d
Juruá River 214 B c
Jussy 91 O l
Justingen 143 I i
Justingen, lordship 143 I i
Justinian, Statue of 93 G e (2)
Jüterbog 63 G c
Jutes, people, 5 cent.
Jutes, people, about 900
Jutigalpa 213 D c
Jutland, reg. 70 H b
Juttah 7 C f
Juturna, Lake of

Kaaden 79 H c
Kabarda, reg.
Kabinda 175 E e
Kabul 137 A b
Kadesh 4 F c
Kadesh Barnea 7 ins. C
Kadesh Naphtali 6 ins. B
Kadesia 53 G d
Kadiak, isl. 198 ins. A
Kadikeui 93 G e
Kafche-kué, reg.
Kaffa 73 H a
Kaffraria, reg. 175 M m
Kaffraria, British, dist. 175 M m
Kafiristan, reg. 137 B a
Kafr Embabeh
Kagoshima 171 O e
Kahlen Berg, mt. 123 I d
Kahoolawe, isl. 198 ins. B
Kai-fong-fu
Kail
Kailua 198 ins. B
Kaindu
Kairwan 53 C c
Kais, isl.
Kaisarieh
Kaisersberg 126 E b
Kaiserslautern 122 D d
Kaiserstuhl 142 B e
Kaiserswerth 62 D c
Kaiserswerth, mon. 55 Q i
Kaiser Wilhelms Land, col. 179 F h
Kaisheim, mon. 95 E b
Kalahari Desert 175 F g
Kalamata 164 C c
Kalenberg, Brunswick-, duchy 86 G b
Kalgan 171 M d
Kalhat
Kalifati
Kalinga, reg.
Kalisz, Kalisch 79 K c
Kallundborg, Hanse. for. cy. 98 F b
Kalmucks, people 139 F f
Kalocsa 168 F c
Kalocsa, abp. 95 F c
Kalpi 170 I f
Kaluga 139 E e
Kalw 62 E d
Kama-Bulgarians, people 71 P b
Kama River 138 H d
Kamakura
Kamaran Island 170 F g
Kamba 62 E d
Kamburg 63 F c
Kamen 153 N f
Kamens 80 ins.
Kamerun, Cameroons, German col. 174 E d
Kaminiets Podolski 119 J d
Kaministiquia, Fort 191 G b
Kamloops 212 C c
Kammin 72 D a
Kammin, bp. 79 J a
Kammin, Hanse. cy. 99 ins. B
Kamp, mon. 95 D a
Kampen 117 D b
Kampen, Hanse. cy. 99 ins. B
Kamrup, reg.
Kamtchatka, pen.
Kanah 6 C b
Kanara, reg. 137 B f
Kanata 6 E c
Kanauj
Kanawha River, Great 193 D b
Kan-chau-fu
Kandahar
Kandalakskaya 167 L b
Kandern 142 A e
Kandy 137 D g
Kané
Kane Sea 186 L a
Kanem, reg. 174 E c
Kanesville 199 F c
Kangaroo Island 172 C d
Kanin Peninsula 167 N b
Kankakee River 191 H c
Kanklis, reg.
Kano 174 D c
Kansan
Kansas, tribe 188 F c
Kansas, state 203 S h
Kansas, ter. 1854 202 E h
Kansas City 211 G c
Kansas Osage, Ind. Res. 188 G c
Kansas Pacific Grant 210 E c
Kansas River 198 F c
Kan-su, prov. 171 L e
Kantara, El 174 K i
Kaoli, reg. (Korea)
Kao-tai
Kapfenburg, castle 143 J h
Kaphar Saba 7 B d
Kapolna 159 K e
Kappel 91 Q k
Kappenberg, mon. 95 D a
Kapunda 172 C d
Karabunar 165 D b

Karachal, mts.
Karachi 137 A c
Kara Dagh, mts. 99 M f
Karahissar 89 K f
Karajang
Karajang, reg.
Karakhitai, reg. 92 H c
Karakodja
Karakoram (Karakorum) Mountains
Karakorum, Caracarum 92 K c
Kara-Kuyunli, people 77 L e
Karaman 93 D c
Karaman, princ. 93 D c
Karaman, reg. 89 J g
Kara Sea 170 H a
Karashar
Karasi, reg. 89 I g
Karatova 165 C b
Karchedon (Carthage) 5 A b
Kardis
Karelia, reg. 138 C c
Karikal 137 D f
Karlsburg, near Bremen 122 E b
Karlsburg, in Transylvania 159 L e
Karlstadt 155 H f
Karnak 4 F d
Karnata, reg.
Karnul 137 C e
Kars 67 O e
Kartha 6 B c
Kasbek, mt. 167 O g
Kaschau
Kashan
Kashgar
Kashgil 174 F c
Kashmir, Cashmere, reg.
Kaskaskia 191 H d
Kaskaskia River 191 H d
Kasr el Kebir 118 C g
Kassai River 175 E e
Kassites, people 5 D b
Kassogs, people 71 O e
Kastamuni 77 K d
Kastamuni, dist. 77 K d
Kastelberg, lordship 142 B d
Kastellaun 142 ins. A
Kastoria 71 K e
Katcha River 164 J f
Kates Needle, mt. 212 ins.
Kathiawar, Kattiwar, dist. 137 B d
Katieh 150 B a
Katif, El
Kattegat, str. 88 D c
Katwyk 117 C b
Katzbach River 155 I c
Kauai, isl. 198 ins. B
Kaufbeuren, imp. city 79 G e
Kaula, isl. 198 ins. B
Kavala 131 H e
Kaveri River
Kawar, oasis 2 F g
Kay 135 H b
Kayalik
Kayoli
Kayes 174 B c
Kayna 72 C a
Kaysersberg 143 ins. D
Kazan 138 G d
Kazan, khan. 139 G e
Kazerun
Kazvin
Kearney, Fort 210 F b
Kearney, route of 201 legend
Kecskemét 159 J e
Kedah
Kedesh Naphtali 6 D b
Keeling Islands 179 A i
Keewatin, dist. 212 F b
Kehl 142 A c
Keilah 7 B e
Kei River, Great 175 M m
Kekaughtan 193 ins. A
Kelat 67 O f
Kelat, reg. 73 I c
Kehlheim 122 F d
Kells 127 K h
Kelso
Kem 138 D c
Kemkemjuts, people
Kempsey 172 E d
Kempten, ab. 79 G e
Kempten, mon. 95 E b
Kenai, Fort 198 ins. A
Kenath 6 F c
Kendal 127 W l
Kendal, parl. bor. 163 L c
Kendal, reg. 84 B b
Keneh 150 B b
Kenesaw Mount, battle 208 D c
Kenia, mt. 175 G e
Kenilworth
Kenilworth, castle
Kenilworth, mon. 97 P i
Kenites, people 7 ins. D
Kenmare Bay 127 G j
Kennebec River 189 D b
Kennedys, fam.
Kensington, in Pa. 192 ins.
Kensington, castle, in England 75 I h
Kent, cty.
Kent, kingdom
Kentishmen, people
Kent Island 192 C d
Kenton 206 ins.
Kentucky, dist. 196 B c
Kentucky, state 211 H c
Kentucky River 193 B c
Kenzingen 142 A d
Keraits, people
Kerak 68 ins. A
Kerbela 77 M f
Kerguelen Islands 182 H H l
Kerith River 7 C c
Kerko Porta 93 G e
Kermadec Islands 172 H d
Kermian, reg. 89 I g
Kerry, cty. 127 H j
Kertch
Kerulen River
Kerun, Birket el, lake
Kesho
Kesmacoran, reg.
Kessel, dist. 117 D c
Kesselsdorf 135 G c
Kessin 63 F a
Kesteven and Holland, parl. dist. 163 N d
Ketsch 142 C b
Kexholm 138 D c
Keynsham, mon. 97 O j
Key West 211 I f
Khabarovka 171 O d
Khaibar Pass 170 I e
Khair-ed-Din Barbarossa, Tomb of 93 G e (12)
Khairpur 137 A c
Khalkas, people
Khalman (Aleppo) 5 C b
Khamil
Khanate of the Golden Horde
Khanbalig (Peking)
Khandesh, reg. 137 B d
Kharesm
Kharesm, Khuwarizm, reg.
Kharesmians, people 8 K d
Kharezmians, dynasty 73 I d
Kharkov 139 E e
Kharluks, people
Khartum 174 G c
Khatanga River
Khatangskoe 171 L a
Khatmandu 171 J f
Khazars, people 55 K c
Khelat
Kherson 139 D f
Khingan Mountains
Khitans, people
Khiva 170 G d
Khiva, khan.
Khojent
Khokand
Kholm 131 J b
Kholmogory 138 F c
Khorasan, reg. 53 H c
Khorat 171 L g
Khoritza 139 D f
Khorsabad 5 D b
Khotan
Khuram
Khuwarizm, Kharesm, reg.
Khuzistan, reg.
Khyrpore 137 A c
Kiakhta
Kiang-si, prov. 171 M f
Kiang-su, prov. 171 M e
Kiao-chau 171 N e
Kia-yu-kwan
Kiburg, castle 62 E e
Ki-chau 170 ins. A
Kickapoo, Ind. Res. 188 G c
Kickapoos, tribe 188 H b
Kichinev 139 C f
Kidderminster, parl. bor. 163 L e (Kidderm.)
Kiel 79 G a
Kiel, Hanse. cy. 99 ins. B
Kielce 159 K c
Kien-chang-fu
Kiersy 56 C c
Kieselbronn 142 C c
Kiev 71 M c
Kiev, prov. 131 J c
Kiev, dist. 71 L c
Kievits Hoeck 189 B d
Kiffhausen, castle 72 C a
Kij Mekran, reg.
Kikinda 159 K f
Kilburn 75 I h
Kildare, bp. 97 E c
Kildare, cty. 127 K h
Kilfenora, bp. 97 B d
Kilia 164 D a
Kilia, mouth of the Danube R. 164 D a
Kilimandjaro, mt. 175 G e
Kilkenny
Kilkenny, bp. 97 D d
Kilkenny, cty. 127 J i
Killala, bp. 97 B b
Killaloe, bp. 97 C d
Killarney 127 H i
Killiecrankie
Kilmacduagh, bp. 97 C c
Kilmore, bp. 97 D c
Kilsyth
Ki-lung 171 N f
Kilwa 109 U h
Kimberley, in Africa 175 L l
Kimberley, dist. in Australia 172 B b
Kimberley Goldfield 172 B b
Kinburn 139 D f
Kincardine, cty.
Kincardine, dist.
Kinchat
Kingdom of the Two Sicilies, 15 cent. 90 E e
King George, Fort 193 C f
King George Sound 172 A d
King Island 172 D e
King of Jerusalem, Palace of the 68 ins. B (7)
King's County 127 J h
King's Garden, isl. 105 E b
Kings Lynn, parl. bor. 163 O e
Kings Mountain, battle 195 A f
King Sound 172 B b
Kingston, in Canada 200 E a
Kingston, in Georgia 208 D c
Kingston, in Jamaica 213 E c
Kingston, in New York 192 D c
Kingston, in S. Australia 172 C d
Kingston, South, Rhode Island 189 ins. A
Kingston-upon-Hull, mon. 97 Q h

Kingston-upon-Thames . . . . . 75 I i
Kingswood, mon. . . . . 97 O j
King William Land . . . . . . 212 F b
Kinklas, tribe . . . . 188 B b
Kinross, cty. . . . .
Kinross, dist. . . . .
Kinsai (Hang-chau-fu) . . . . .
Kinsale . . . .
Kinzig Pass . . . . 134 E e
Kinzig River . . . . 142 A d
Kiovia, dist. . . . . 139 C e
Kiowas, tribe, in Colorado . . 188 E b
Kiowas, tribe, in Texas . . . . 188 F d
Kipchak, khan. . . . .
Kirchberg, on the Hunsrück Mts. . . . . 142 ins. A
Kirchberg, on the Jagst R. . . 143 I g
Kirchheim . . . . 143 H h
Kirghiz, people, in Turkestan . 92 G c
Kirghiz, people, on the Yenisei R.
Kirghiz Steppe . . . . 3 J d
Kiriathaim . . . . 7 D e
Kirin . . . . 171 N d
Kirjath-Jearim . . . . 7 C e
Kirkcudbright . . . .
Kirkcudbright, cty. . . . .
Kirkcudbright, dist. . . . .
Kirkham, mon. . . . . 97 Q g
Kirkstall, mon. . . . . 97 P h
Kirkstead, mon. . . . . 97 Q h
Kirkwall, seat of bishopric . . 97 Ka leg.
Kirman . . . .
Kirman, reg. . . . . 53 H d
Kirn . . . . 142 ins. A
Kir of Moab . . . . 7 D f
Kish . . . .
Kishm, isl. . . . .
Kishon River . . . . 6 C c
Kiskiminitas River . . . . . . 192 B c
Kissingen . . . . 158 F c
Kisslegg . . . . 143 I j
Kistna River . . . . 112 A b
Kittanning . . . . 194 K f
Kittery . . . . 189 C c (Ki.)
Kitzen . . . . 154 G c (Ki.)
Kitzingen . . . . 72 C b
Kitzingen, mon. . . . . 95 E b
Kiung-chau . . . . 171 M g
Kiushiu, isl. . . . .
Kiutayeh . . . . 164 D c
Kiverova Gora . . . . 138 C d
Kizil Irmak River . . . . . . 93 D b
Kladrau . . . . 79 H d
Kladrau, mon. . . . . 95 E b
Klagenfurt . . . . 79 I e
Klamath, Ind. Res. . . . . . . 188 B b
Klamath River . . . . 198 A b
Klamath River, Ind. Res. . . . 188 B b
Klamaths, tribe . . . . 188 B b
Klar River . . . . 88 E a
Klause Pass . . . . 72 C b
Klausen Pass . . . . 91 Q l
Klausenburg . . . . 80 H h
Klein-Heubach . . . . 142 D a
Klein-Mariazell, mon. . . . . . 95 F b
Klein-Schnellendorf . . . . . . 135 I c
Klephts, people . . . . 164 C c
Klettgau, landgr. . . . . 142 B e
Klissow . . . .
Klikitats, tribe . . . . 188 B a
Klondike Region . . . . 212 B b
Klostergrab . . . . 123 G c
Klosterneuburg, mon. . . . . . 80 E g
Knaered . . . . 120 H e
Knaresborough . . . . 127 X l
Knaresborough, parl. bor. . . . 163 M d
Kniebis Pass . . . . 142 B d
Knights of Saint John, Dom. of the . . . . 89 I g
Knights of Saint John, Hospital of the . . . . 68 ins. B (2)
Knin . . . . 131 G e
Knin, bp. . . . . 95 F c
Knittelfeld . . . . 155 H e
Knittlingen . . . . 143 G g
Knocke . . . . 134 B c
Knoxville . . . . 196 ins. A
Kobdo . . . . 171 K d
Kobdo, Plateau of . . . . 3 N d
Kobe . . . . 171 O e
Kocher River . . . . 143 J g
Kodiak, isl. . . . . 186 D c
Koesfeld, Hanse. cy. . . . . . . 99 ins. B
Koevorden . . . . 117 E b
Koevorden, lordship . . . . . . 117 E b
Koil . . . .
Kojak Pass . . . . 170 H e
Kokel River . . . . 159 M e
Koko-nor, lake . . . .
Koksherev . . . . 71 P b
Kola . . . . 138 D b
Kola Peninsula . . . . 3 H b
Kolachel . . . .
Kolapore . . . .
Kolbatz, mon. . . . . 80 ins.
Kolberg . . . . 63 H a
Kolberg, Hanse. cy. . . . . . . 99 ins. B
Kolberger Heide, dist. . . . . . 122 F a
Kolding . . . . 154 E a
Kolditz . . . . 154 G c
Kolguiev, isl. . . . . 138 H b
Kolhapur . . . . 137 B e
Kolimsk, Nijne . . . .
Kolimsk, Sredne . . . . 171 Q b
Kolin . . . . 79 I c
Kölln, on the Spree . . . . . . 85 C b
Kölln, Hanse. cy. . . . . 99 ins. B
Kolmar . . . . 62 D d
Köln, see Cologne
Koloa . . . . 198 ins. B
Kolomna . . . . 138 E d
Kolonos . . . . 16 E e
Komorn . . . . 159 J e
Konakry . . . . 174 B d
Kongsberg . . . . 88 C b
Konieh . . . .
Königgrätz . . . . 135 H c
Königinhof . . . . 159 H c
Königsberg, in Prussia . . . . . 79 L a
Königsberg, Hanse. cy. . . . . 99 H c
Königsberg, imp. cy. in Franconia . . . . 114 F c
Königsbronn . . . . 122 F d
Königseck, castle . . . . 143 H j
Königseck, cty. . . . . 143 H j
Königsfelden, mon. . . . . . . 91 Q k
Königshofen . . . . 142 E a
Königslutter, mon. . . . . . . 95 E a
Königstein . . . . 123 H c
Königswartha . . . . 155 H c
Königs-Wusterhausen . . . . . . 135 G b
Konin . . . . 123 J b
Koningsveld, mon. . . . . 94 C a
Konitz . . . . 135 I b
Konkan, reg. . . . .
Konkan-tana . . . .
Konstanz, see Constance
Konzenberg . . . . 142 C d
Kootenay, lake . . . . 198 B a
Kootenay River . . . . 198 B a
Köpenick . . . . 123 G b
Koporiye . . . .
Koppenstein, castle . . . . . . 142 ins. A
Korb . . . . 143 H g
Kordofan, reg. . . . . 174 F c
Korea, Jap. prot. . . . . 171 N e
Korea, reg. . . . .
Körmend . . . . 155 I e
Körmöczbanya . . . .
Korneuburg . . . . 123 I d
Körös River . . . . 159 K e
Korsör . . . . 158 F a
Kortrijk . . . . 122 B c
Koschmin . . . . 159 I c
Kosel . . . . 123 J c
Köslin . . . . 123 I a
Koslov . . . . 139 F e
Kosseir . . . . 150 B b
Kossovopolje, valley . . . . . . 93 B b
Kostnitz, see Constance
Kostroma . . . . 138 F d
Kotah . . . . 170 I f
Kotah, reg. . . . . 137 C c
Kota Rajah . . . . 171 K h
Kotchak Bay . . . . 167 P f
Kottbus . . . . 72 C a
Köthen . . . . 154 F c
Kötzschenbroda . . . . 123 G c
Kovel . . . . 159 M c
Kovno . . . . 77 I a
Kovno, Hanse. for. cy. . . . . . 99 H b
Koweyt . . . .
Kraich River . . . . 142 C b
Krainburg . . . . 123 H e
Krajova . . . .
Krasnoi . . . . 153 O g
Krasnoi-Yar . . . . 139 G f
Krasnovodsk . . . . 170 G d
Krasnoyarsk . . . . 171 K c
Krasny . . . . 71 M c
Krautheim . . . . 142 E b
Krementchug . . . .
Kremmen . . . . 85 C b
Kremnitz . . . . 80 F g
Krems . . . . 63 H d
Kremsier . . . .
Kremsmünster, mon. . . . . . . 80 D h
Kreuzberg, pass . . . . 27 G a
Kreuznach . . . . 122 D d
Kriechingen . . . . 134 D d
Kroia . . . .
Kroia, bp. . . . . 95 F c
Kroissenbrunn . . . . 72 D b
Kronstadt, in Russia . . . . . . 138 C c
Kronstadt, in Transylvania . . .
Kroonstad . . . . 175 M l
Krossen . . . . 63 H b
Krugersdorp . . . . 175 M l
Krumau . . . . 135 H d
Kuban, dist. . . . . 170 E d
Kuban, reg. . . . . 77 L c
Kuban River . . . . 73 H a
Kubango River . . . . 175 E f
Kuchar . . . .
Kuen-lun Mountains . . . . . .
Kufstein . . . . 115 G e
Kufra, oases . . . . 2 G f
Kughi . . . .
Kuinder . . . . 117 D b
Kuinre . . . . 117 D b
Kuka, Kukawa . . . . 174 E c
Kulbarga . . . . 92 H f
Kuldja . . . .
Kulevdcha . . . .
Kulikovo . . . . 92 D b
Kulm, in Bohemia . . . . 72 C a
Kulm, in Prussia . . . . 72 D a
Kulm, bp. . . . . 95 F a
Kulm, Hanse. cy. . . . . 98 G c
Kulmbach . . . . 87 H c
Kulmerland, dist. . . . . 72 D a
Kulmsee, seat of bishopric . . . 95 F a
Kuma River . . . . 99 M e
Kumaon, reg. . . . . 170 I e
Kumassi . . . . 174 C d
Kum-Kale . . . .
Kum-Kioi . . . .
Kunde . . . . 174 E d
Kunduz . . . .
Kunersdorf . . . . 135 H b
Ku-ngan . . . . 170 ins. A
Künzelsau . . . . 143 I g
Kuopio . . . . 167 K c
Kupiansk . . . . 139 E f
Kupreanof Island . . . . 212 ins.
Kur River . . . .
Kura River . . . .
Kurachee . . . . 137 A c
Kuraiyat . . . .
Kurdistan, reg. . . . . 67 O f
Kurdistan Highlands . . . . . . 3 I e
Kurds, people . . . .

Kuria Muria Islands 170 G g
Kurile Islands 171 P d
Kurisches Haff, bay 155 K a
Kürnbach 142 C b
Kurnegalle
Kursk 139 E e
Kushk 170 H e
Kuskokwim River 186 C b
Küssnacht 91 Q k
Kustendji
Küstrin 79 I b
Kutais 167 N g
Kutchuk Kainardji
Kutha (Tel Ibrahim) 4 G c
Kuttenberg 79 I d
Kwang-chau-wan 171 M f
Kwang-si, prov. 171 L f
Kwang-tung, prov. 171 M f
Kwei-chau, prov. 171 L f
Kwei-lin-fu
Kwei-yang 171 L f
Kyburg, castle 91 Q k
Kyle, dist.
Kymmene River 120 K d
Kyoto 171 O e
Kyritz, Hanse. cy. 99 ins. B

Láa 123 I d
Laach, mon. 95 D a
Laaland, isl. 114 F a
La Bahia 190 F f
La Baraque 156 B a
La Barre 192 C b
La Baye, Fort 191 H c
Labdalum 31 ins. B
Labeates Lake 39 L l
La Belle-Alliance, farm
La Bénisson-Dieu, mon. 94 C b
Labiau 131 H c
Labican Way, road 35 ins. B
Labicum 35 ins. B
La Boca
La Bocchetta Pass 150 E d
La Boissière, mon. 94 C b
Labourd, dist. 147 D c (Lab.)
Labrador Peninsula 186 L c
Labrador Plateau 186 L c
Labranda 13 E c
Labuan 171 M h
La Bussière, mon. 94 C b
La Cava, mon. 95 ins.
Laccadive Islands 137 B f
Lac Court Oreille, Ind. Res. 188 H a
Lac de Flambeau, Ind. Res. 188 I a
Lacedæmon 14 C b
Lacedæmonia, state 14 C b
Laceria 11 D c
La Chaise-Dieu, mon. 94 C b
La Charité, on the Loire R. 126 C c
La Charité, in Paris 149 B
La Chassaigne, mon. 95 D b (L. Ch.)
La Chaussée 154 C d
La Chine, Lachine 191 K b
Lachine Rapids 189 A b
Lachish 7 B e
Lachlan River 172 D d
Laciadæ, deme 23 D
Lacinium, prom. 31 G c
La Cisa, Pass 26 D c
Lackawaxen River 192 D c
Lacmus, mt. 10 C c
La Colle 200 G a
La Colombe, mon. 94 C b
Laconia, reg. 14 C c
Laconia, gulf of 14 C c
La Couronne, mon. 94 C b
Lac Pepin, Fort G c
La Crosse 211 G b
Lac Seul, lake 212 F c
Lactarius, mt. 52 D b
Lactora, see Lectoure
Lacus Asphaltites (Dead Sea) 7 C f
Lade, isl. 13 E c
Ladenburg 142 C b
Lado 174 G d
Ladoga 138 D c
Ladoga, lake 138 D c
Ladon River, in Arcadia 14 B b
Ladon River, in Elis 14 B b
Ladrones, isl. 110 FF f
Ladysmith 175 M l
Laebactes 27 G a
Laevi, people 26 D b
La Famine 192 C b
Lafayette 206 ins.
La Ferté-Bernard 76 D b
La Ferté-sur-Grône, mon. 94 C b
La Flèche 126 A c
La Fontaine de Bèze, mon. 95 D b
La Force, bldg. in Paris 149 B
La Gallette, Fort 192 D a
Lagash 4 G c
Lagina River 39 J g
Lagny 76 E b
Lago Maggiore, lake 90 I h
Lagos, in Nigeria 174 D d
Lagos, in Portugal 82 J h
Lagos, dist. 174 D d
La Grande Chartreuse, mon. 95 D b
La Granja, castle 130 C e
La Guayra, La Guaira 214 C a
Laguna 215 E e
Laguna das Patos, lake 215 D f
Lagussa, isl. 15 F c
La Hague, Cape de, battle off 125 C c
Lahaina 198 ins. B
Lahari
La Harpe, route of 191 F e
La Haye, farm 156 C c
La Haye Sainte, farm
Lahn River 62 D c
La Hogue or La Hougue, see Saint Vaast-de-la-Hougue
Lahore 137 B b
La Hougue 130 C d
Lahr 142 A d
La Huerta, isl. 105 D d
La Hulpe 156 A a
Laibach 63 H f
Laietani, people 38 C d
Laino 90 E e
Laish 6 D b
Lajazzo 99 K f
La Jonquière, Fort 190 C a
Lake Country 49 E d
Lake of the Woods 191 G b
Lake Region 2 G b
Laknaoti
La Levette, farm
La Lusern, mon. 94 B b
La Maison-du-Roi 156 C c
La Mancha, dist. 83 K h
La Marche or Marche, cty. 61 D c
La Marche or Marche, gouv. 146 B b
La Marche or Marche, prov. 148 E e
Lambach, mon. 80 C g
Lambaesis 38 D e
Lambayeque 111 B c
Lambeth 75 I i
Lambeth, parl. bor. 163 N f (Lamb.)
Lambethmoor, dist. 75 G g
Lambrus River 26 D b
Lamego 82 A a
Lamego, bp. 94 A c
Lametus River 31 F d
Lamia 11 D d
Laminium 38 B e
Lamotte, Fort 189 B b
Lampsacus 5 B a
Lamptræ inferior 16 B b
Lamptræ superior 16 B b
Lanai, isl. 198 ins. B
Lanark 127
Lanark, cty. 127
Lanark, dist.
Lancashire, cty.
Lancaster, in England
Lancaster, cty. palat.
Lancaster, parl. bor. 163 L c
Lancaster, in Mass. 189 C c
Lancaster, in Ohio 196 ins. B
Lancaster, in Pa. 192 C c
Lancaster Sound 186 K a
Lancastrian Estates 84
Lan-chau-fu
Lancia 38 A d
Lanciano 64 B b
Landau 114 E d
Landeck 79 G e
Landen 117 D d
Landes, dept. 148 D f
Landeshut, in Silesia 135 H c
Landrecies 126 C a (Land.)
Landsberg, in Styria 135 H e
Landsberg, on the Warthe 80 ins.
Landsberg, march 85 G e
Land's End, cape 49 C f
Landshut, in Bavaria 115 G d
Landskrona 123 J d
Landstuhl 114 D d
Lanercost, mon.
Lang Bourn, in London 75 G g
Langenargen 143 I j
Langenau 143 J h
Langenburg 143 I g
Langensalza 158 F c
Langley 75 H h
Langley, Fort 210 A a
Langport 127 W o
Langport, parl. bor.
Langres 61 F c
Langres, bp. 95 D b
Langres, cty. 61 F c
Langres, duchy 76 F c
Langside 118 D b
Langs Nek
Lang-soi
Languedoc, dist. 69 E e
Languedoc, gouv. 146 B c
Languedoc, prov. 148 E f
Lankavi Island
Lansdown 127 X o
L'Anse, Ind. Res. 188 I a
Lansing 211 H b
Lanuvium 35 ins. B
Laodicea, in Coele-Syria 20 G e
Laodicea, in Lycaonia 20 E c
Laodicea, in Phrygia 20 C d
Laodicea, in Syria 20 F e
Lao-kai 171 L f
Laon 61 E b
Laon, bp. 94 C b
Laon, cty. 61 E b
La Part-Dieu, mon. 91 O l
Lapathus 11 D c
La Paz, in Bolivia 214 C d
La Paz, in Lower Cal. 213 A b
Lapis Niger, in Rome
Lapithas, mt. 14 B b
Lapland, reg. 167 J b
La Plata, in the Arg. Rep. 215 D f
La Plata, in Bolivia 214 C d
La Plata, viceroyalty 215 ins.
La Pointe, Ind. Res. 188 H a
La Pointe du Saint Esprit 191 G b
La Pola de Gordon 82 A a
Lappa 14 ins.
Lapps, people 138 B b
La Prairie 189 B b
La Pré-sur-Arnon, mon. 94 C b
Lapurdum, see Bayonne
La Rábida 184 B e
Laramie 210 D b
Laramie, Fort 198 E b
Laranda 71 M f
Laredo, in Spain
Laredo, in Texas 198 F e
La Reine, Fort 190 F b
La Réole, castle 76 D d
Larga 39 I j
Larino 64 B b
Larino, bp. 95 E c

Larinum 30 D a
Larisa, see Larissa
Larissa, in Assyria 20 J d
Larissa, in Thessaly 11 D c
Larissa Cremaste 11 D d
Larisus River 14 B a
Larius (Como), lake 26 D a
Larix 27 H a
La Roche, in Burgundy 143 ins. F
Laroche, in Luxemburg 117 D d
La Roche, cty. 69 F a (L. R.)
La Rochelle 130 C d
La Rochelle, gen. 147 D b
Laron 76 D d
La Rothière 154 C d
Larsa or Larsam (Senkereh) 4 G c
Larymna 11 E d
Las 14 C c
Lasalle, in France 184 D d
Lasalle, in Illinois 211 H b
La Salle, routes of 191 H d, I c, F d
Las Cascadas
Las Cruces
La Serena 215 B e
Lasion 14 B b
Las Navas de Tolosa 83 K h
Lasne
Lasne River 156 A a
Las Palmas 174 B b
Las Salinas 108 J i
Lassen Pass 214 B b
L'Assomption, Fort 194 B c
Las Tabbas 214 A b
Las Vegas 198 D c
Las Vigas 201 H g
Lateran, Palace 22 A
Laterani, Palace of the 22 A
La Teste de Buch 76 C d
Latham House 127 W m
Latin Empire 73 E c
Latin Gate 22 A
Latini or Latins, people 30 B a
Latin Way, road 30 B a
Latis River 26 B c
Latium, reg. 30 B a
Latium and Campania, Aug. Reg. of Rome 38 E d (1)
Latomiæ, loc. in Syracuse 31 ins. B (7)
La Tour 69 E d
Latovici, people 27 I b
Latovicorum Prætorium 27 I b
La Trappe 126 B b
La Trappe, mon. 94 C b
La Tremouille 81 M h
Lauag 199 ins. H
Lauban 80 ins.
Lauchert River 143 H i
Lauchheim 143 J h
Laudonnière, set. of 191 I e
Lauenburg, on the Elbe 72 C a
Lauenburg, in Pomerania 123 I a
Lauenburg, duchy 87 H b
Lauffen 143 H g
Laumellum 26 C b
L'Aumône, mon. 94 C b
Launceston, in England 127 U p
Launceston, mon. 97 M k
Launceston, parl. bor. 163 J g
Launceston, in Tasmania 172 D e
Laund, mon. 97 Q i
Laupen 91 P l
Lanpheim 143 I i
Laurentian Highlands 186 L d
Laurentum 35 ins. B
Lauresham, see Lorch, mon.
Lauriacum, (Lorch, in Austria) 38 E c
Laurium, mt. 16 C b
Laurvik 166 G d
Laus 30 E c
Laus, Pompeia 26 D b
Laus, bay 30 E c
Laus (Lao) River 30 E c
Lausanne 91 O l
Lausanne, bp. 95 D b
Lausitz, march 58 G c
Lausitz, margr. see Lusatia 79 I c
Lausitz, Nieder. margr. see Lusatia, Lower 87 I c
Lausitz, Ober, margr. see Lusatia, Upper 87 I c
Lausonna, see Lausanne
Lautern 72 B b
Lautrec 76 E e
Lautulæ 30 C a
Lautumiæ 24 A
Lauzelle 156 B a
Laval 76 C b
Lavant 80 D h
Lavant, bp. 95 E b
Lavant River 63 H e
Lavatræ
Lavaur 76 D e
Lavaur, bp. 94 C c
La Vérendrye, route of 190 D c
Laverna, Gate of 23 B
Lavinium 30 B a
Lawrence 206 F c
Laxenburg, castle
Laybach, see Laibach
Laycock, mon. 97 O j
La Zarca 190 E f
Lea River 75 I h
Leadenhall Street, in London 75 G g
Leadville 210 D c
League of God's House, dist. 91 R l
League of Ten Jurisdictions, dist. 91 R l
Leander, Tower of 93 G e
Leavenworth, Fort 198 F c
Leba 123 I a
Lebadea 11 D d
Lebanon, House of 6 ins. A
Lebanon Mountains 6 D a
Lebarge, lake 212 B b
Lebedos 13 E b
Le Beuil, mon. 94 C b
Lebinthus, isl. 17 E c
Le Boeuf, Fort 192 A c
Lebonah 7 C d
Lebú 215 B f
Lebus 63 H b
Lebus, bp. 79 I b
Lebus, dist. 85 D b
Lebusa, castle 63 G c
Lecce 90 G d
Lecco 150 E d
Lech River 62 F e
Lechæum 15 C b
Lechfeld, dist. 62 F d
Leck River 117 D c
Lecompton 206 F c
Le Coucou
Lectoure 76 D e
Lectoure, bp. 94 C c
Lectum, prom. 17 D b
Ledbury, parl. bor.
Ledesma 82 A a
Lee, Fort 195 D c
Lee River 127 H j
Leech Lake 199 G a
Leech Lake, Ind. Res. 188 H a
Leeds, in Yorkshire 127 X m
Leeds, mon. in Kent 97 R j
Leeds, parl. bor. 163 M d
Leesburg 208 ins.
Leeuwarden 117 D a
Leeuwin, Cape 172 A d
Leeward Islands 213 F c
Le Fleix 126 B d
Lefroy, lake 172 B d
Legæ, people 35 N e
Legedia, see Avranches
Leghorn 90 L j
Legnago 150 F d
Legnano 72 B b
Le Havre 126 B b
Lehigh River 192 D c
Lehnin, mon. 72 C a
Leicester
Leicester, cty.
Leicester, parl. bor. 163 M e
Leicester, shire
Leichardt River 172 C b
Leighlin, bp. 97 D d
Lein River 143 I h
Leine River 158 E b
Leiningen, princ. 142 D a
Leinster, prov.
Leinstetten 143 G i
Leipheim 143 J i
Leipnik 123 I d
Leipsic, Leipzig
Leipsic, Leipzig, univ.
Leiria 82 G f
Leisnig 85 G e
Leiston, mon. 97 S i
Leith
Leitha River 63 I e
Leitmeritz 63 H c
Leitomischl 63 H d
Leitrim, cty. 127 I g
Leitzkau 63 F b
Leitzkau, mon. 80 ins.
Leiva 214 B b
Le Jafs, farm
Le Joug-Dieu, mon. 94 C b
Lelantian Fields 11 E d
Lelantus River 11 E d
Le Maire, route of
Le Mans 61 C b
Le Mans, bp. 94 C b
Lemanus (Geneva), lake 26 A a
Lemanus Portus (Lymne) 38 C b
Lemberg 139 B f
Le Mesnil
Lemgo, Hanse. cy. 99 ins. B
Lemhi, Ind. Res. 188 D a
Lemnos, isl. 13 D b
Lemovices or Lemovicis, see Limoges
Lemovices, people 38 C c
Lemovii, people 38 F b
Lena River 171 N b
Lenczyca 135 J b
Lenni-Lenapes, tribe 188 K c
Lennox, dist.
Lens 117 A d
Lenton, mon. 97 P i
Lenzen 63 F b
Lenzin
Leo IV, Wall of Pope 96 A
Leoben 135 H e
Leodicum, see Liège
Leominster, mon. 97 O i
Leominster, parl. bor. 163 L e
Léon, in France 61 B b
León, in Mexico 213 ins.
León, in Nicaragua 105 C d
León, in Spain 82 A a
León, bp. 94 A c
Léon, dist. 81 L h
Léon, km. 82 A a, G e
Léon, viscty. 69 A b
Leonberg 143 H h
Leone 199 ins. D
Leonidæum
Leonine City, in Rome 96 A
Leontine Way 31 ins. B
Leontini 30 D e
Leontium 14 B a
Leontopolis 43 I g
Leopoldina 214 F d
Leopoldstadt 155 I d
Leopoldville 175 E e
Lepanto 89 H g
Le Paraclet, mon. 94 C b
Lepel 153 N g
Lepelletier 149 B
Lepidum, Regium 26 E c
Le Pin, mon. 94 C b
Lepontii, people 26 C a
Lepontine Alps, mts. 90 B a

Lepreum . . . 14 B b
Lepsydrium . . . 16 B a
Leptis maior or magna . . . 34 G g
Leptis minor . . . 38 E e
Le Puiset . . . 69 H f
Le Puy . . . 61 E d
Le Puy, bp. . . . 94 C b
Le Quesnoy . . . 117 B d
Lérida . . . 82 C a
Lérida, bp. . . . 94 C c
Lérida, univ. . . . 100 F f
Lérins, mon. . . . 95 D c
Lerma, lake . . . 106 A a
Lerna . . . 14 C b
Leros, isl. . . . 16 B b
Le Roussart . . .
Lerus . . . 13 E c
Lerus, isl., Sporades . . . 13 E c
Les Allemands . . . 191 G f
Lesbos, isl. . . . 13 D b
Lescar . . . 61 C e
Lescar, bp. . . . 94 B c
Les Clairets, mon. . . . 94 C b
Lesina, bp. . . . 95 F c
Lesina, isl. . . . 90 F c
Lesje . . . 130 E a
Lesna . . . 131 J c
Lessa . . . 15 D b
Lesser Antilles, isl. . . . 213 F c
Lesser Armenia, reg. in Pontus . . . 33 M e
Lesser Armenia, reg. in Syria . . . 99 J f
Lesser Scythia, reg. . . . 39 N l
Lesser Syrtis, gulf . . . 51 F f
Lete . . . 11 D d
Lethæus River, in Crete . . . 14 ins.
Lethæus River, in Thessaly . . 10 C c
Lethbridge . . . 212 D d
Letoa, isl. . . . 14 ins.
Letocetum . . . 51 P h
L'Etoile, mon. . . . 94 C b
Letrini . . . 14 B b
Letts, people . . . 57 H c
Leubus, mon. . . . 80 E f
Leuca . . . 31 H c
Leuca, mt. . . . 14 ins.
Leucadia, isl. . . . 89 H g
Leucæ Islands . . . 14 ins.
Leucas . . .
Leucas (Santa Maura), isl. . . .
Leucate, prom. . . .
Leuce, isl. . . . 18 D a
Leuce acte . . . 15 E b
Leuceræ . . . 26 D b
Leuchtenberg . . . 63 G d
Leuci, see Toul
Leuci, people . . . 38 D c
Leucimma, prom. . . . 10 B c
Leucopetra, prom. . . . 30 E d
Leuctra . . . 11 E d
Leuctrum . . . 14 C c
Leuk . . . 91 P l
Leuthen . . . 135 I c
Leutkirch, imp. cy. . . . 143 J j
Leutkircher Heide, dist. . . . 143 J j
Leutschau . . .
Levadia, reg. . . . 131 H f
Leventina, valley . . . 91 Q l
Lévêque, cape . . . 172 B b
Levette, la, farm . . . 156 C c
Lévis, Fort . . . 192 D a
Lewes, in England . . .
Lewes, castle . . .
Lewes, mon. . . . 97 Q k
Lewes, parl. bor. . . . 163 O g
Lewes, in Delaware . . . 192 D d
Lewis, dist. . . . 127 N f
Lewis River, in Canada . . . 198 ins. A
Lewis River, in Idaho . . . 198 C b
Lewis and Clark, routes of . . 198, 199
Lewiston . . . 200 D b
Lexington, in Kentucky . . . 208 D b
Lexington, in Mass. . . . 195 ins. A
Lexington, in Missouri . . . 208 B b
Lexington, in Virginia . . . 207 K c
Lexovii or Lexoviis, see Lisieux
Leyden . . . 117 C b
Leyre, mon. . . . 94 B c
Leyte, isl. . . . 199 ins. H
Lezat, mon. . . . 94 C c
Lhasa . . . 92 J d
Liamone, dept. . . . 148 F f
Liang-hiang . . . 170 ins. A
Liao-yang . . . 171 N d
Liard, Fort . . . 212 C b
Liard River . . . 212 C c
Liau-ho, R. . . .
Liau-tung, pen. . . .
Libarna . . . 26 C c
Libau . . . 77 I a
Libau, Hanse. cy. . . . 99 H b
Liberia, country . . . 174 C d
Libici, people . . . 26 C b
Libisonis, Turris . . . 38 D d
Libreville . . . 175 D d
Liburnia, reg. . . . 27 I b
Libya, reg. . . . 18 C d
Libyan Desert . . . 2 G f
Lichades Islands . . . 11 D d
Lichfield . . . 65 F d
Lichfield, bp. . . . 97 P i
Lichfield, parl. bor. . . . 163 M e
Lichtenau . . . 142 A c
Lichtenberg, princ. . . . 158 D d
Lichtenstein, castle . . . 143 H i
Lichtenthal, ab. . . . 142 B c
Licking River . . . 196 ins. B
Licus (Gail) River . . . 27 H a
Licus (Lech) River . . . 39 K j
Lidford, parl. bor. . . .
Liebenwalde . . . 85 C b
Liebenzell . . . 143 G h
Liechtenstein . . . 154 E e
Liechtenstein, princ. . . . 150 E c
Liège . . . 117 D d
Liège, bp. . . . 117 D d
Liegnitz . . . 63 I c
Liegnitz, princ. . . . 79 J c
Lienz . . . 115 G e
Lierre . . . 117 C c
Lies, Field of . . . 56 D c
Liestal . . . 142 A e
Liger (Loire) River . . . 38 C c
Ligny . . . 156 B a
Ligonier, Fort . . . 192 B c
Ligures Baebiani . . . 30 D a
Liguria, Aug. Reg. . . . 39 D d (9)
Liguria, reg. . . . 26 B c
Liguria, French prov. . . . 152 B e
Liguria, West Rom. prov. . 42 D d (3)
Ligurian Alps, mts. . . . 90 B b
Ligurian Republic . . . 151 H h
Ligurian Sea . . . 150 E e
Ligurians, people . . . 12 E b
Lilæa . . . 11 D d
Lilienfeld, mon. . . . 95 F b
Lille . . . 117 B d
Lilleshall, mon. . . . 97 O i
Lillois . . . 156 A a
Lilybæum . . . 30 B e
Lima . . . 214 B d
Lima, audiencia . . . 215 ins.
Limal . . . 156 B a
Limasol . . . 68 B c
Limay River . . . 215 C f
Limburg . . . 117 E d
Limburg, castle in Lower Lorraine . . . 62 D c
Limburg, castle in Swabia . 62 E d
Limburg, castle in W. Franconia . . . 62 E c
Limburg, duchy . . . 117 D d
Limburg, prov. . . . 158 C c
Limburg-on-the-Hardt, mon. . 95 D b
Limburg-on-the-Lahn, mon. . . 95 D a
Limelette . . . 156 B a
Limerick . . . 74 A e
Limerick, bp. . . . 97 C d
Limerick, cty. . . . 127 H i
Limes (Roman Wall) . . . 38 D c
Limestone . . . 196 ins. B
Limia, dist. . . . 83 J g
Limmen Bight . . . 172 C b
Limnæ, in Athens . . . 23 D
Limnæ, in Messenia . . . 14 C b
Limonum, see Poitiers
Limousin, prov. . . . 148 E e
Limpurg, castle . . . 143 I g
Limpurg, cty. . . . 143 I h
Linares . . . 215 B f
Lin-ching . . .
Lincoln, in England . . .
Lincoln, bp. . . . 97 Q h
Lincoln, castle . . . 65 F d
Lincoln, cty. . . .
Lincoln, parl. bor. . . . 163 N d
Lincoln, shire . . .
Lincoln, in Nebraska . . . 210 F b
Lincoln Heights . . . 49 F e
Lincoln Wolds . . . 49 F e
Lindau . . . 62 E e
Lindau, imp. cy. . . . 78 F e
Lindau, mon. . . . 95 D b
Lindenfels . . . 142 C a
Lindisfarne, mon. . . . 97 P f
Lindisfarne Island . . .
Lindiswaras, people . . .
Lindsay, mt. . . . 172 E c
Lindsey, parl. dist. . . . 163 N d
Lindum (Lincoln) . . . 51 P h
Lindus . . . 13 F c
Lingayen . . . 199 ins. H
Lingen . . . 62 D b
Lingones, see Langres
Lingones, people, in Gaul . . . 38 D c
Lingones, people, in Italy . . . 27 F c
Linhares . . . 214 F d
Linköping . . . 46 J b
Linlithgow . . .
Linlithgow, cty. . . .
Linones, people . . . 55 R i
Lindsays, fam. . . . 97 K d
Linth River . . . 150 E c
Linththal . . . 91 R l
Lin-tsing-chau . . .
Linz . . . 63 H d
Lion Hill, village . . .
Lipans, people . . . 188 G e
Lipara . . . 30 E d
Liparææ (Æolin or Lipari) Islands . . . 30 D d
Lipari Islands . . . 90 E e
Lippe, cty. . . . 114 C e
Lippe, princ. . . . 134 E c
Lippe, reg. . . . 86 G c
Lippe River . . . 62 D c
Lippe-Detmold, princ. . . 154 E b (L.D.)
Lippeham . . . 55 Q i
Lippstadt . . . 158 E c
Liptrap, Cape . . . 172 D d
Liquentia River . . . 27 G b
Liques, mon. . . . 94 C a
Lircay . . . 214 B d
Liria . . . 82 B b
Liris (Garigliano) River . . . 30 C a
Lisa, Fort . . . 210 F b
Lisaine River . . . 143 ins. F
Lisbon . . . 82 A b
Lisbon, abp. . . . 94 A d
Lisbon, univ. . . . 100 D g
Lisburne, Cape . . . 198 ins. A
Lisieux . . . 69 D b
Lisieux, bp. . . . 94 C b
Liskeard, parl. bor. . . . 163 J g (Lisk.)
L'Isle . . . 143 ins. F
L'Isle Jourdan . . . 126 B e
Lismore, bp. in Ireland . . . 97 D d
Lismore, bp. in Scotland . . . 97 H c
Lissa . . . 115 I c
Lissa, island, off Spalato . . . 90 F c
Lissa, island, off Zara . . . 27 J c

Lissa Island 161 J f
Lissabon, see Lisbon
Lissus 31 I a
Lissus, prom. 14 ins.
Lita River
Litani River
Liternum 30 C b
Lithuania, gr. princ. 119 J c
Lithuania, reg., about 1190 71 K b
Lithuania, reg., about 1360 77 J b
Lithuanians, people 59 I b
Littanum 27 G a
Little Belt, strait 88 C d
Little Burgundy, duchy 69 G c
Little Cayman, isl. 105 D c
Little Colorado River 198 C c
Little Compton 189 ins. A
Little Dunmow, mon. 97 R j
Little Egg Harbor 192 D d
Little Harbour 189 C c
Little Miami River 196 ins. B
Little Missouri River 198 E a
Little Oasis 4 E d
Little Poland, reg. 131 H c
Little Redan, fort 164 L g
Little Rock 211 G d
Little Russia, reg. 139 C e
Little Russians, people 139 C e
Little Saint Bernard Pass 130 O i
Little Slave Lake 186 H c
Littlestown 208 ins.
Little Tatary, reg. 139 D f
Little Wallachia, reg. 131 H d
Little Yarmouth, parl. bor.
Littorale, reg. 123 G f
Litus Saxonicum (Saxon Shore) 51 Q i
Liu-kiu Islands 171 N f
Liutizians, people 63 G b
Liverpool 127 V m
Liverpool, parl. bor. 163 K d
Liverpool Range 172 E d
Livia, Palace of 24 B
Livia, Portico of 22 A
Livno 164 B b
Livny 139 E e
Livonia, reg., 9—14 cent. 80 I c
Livonia, reg., 14—16 cent. 88 K c
Livonia, reg., 17—18 cent. 138 C d
Livonia, Polish, reg. 131 I b
Livonians, people 59 I b
Livorno, see Leghorn 90 L j
Livraimont, farm
Lixus 38 A e
Lizard Head 127 T p
Llamas del Moro 82 A a
Llandaff
Llandaff, bp. 97 N j
Llangollen 162 C e
Llano Estacado, plain 210 E d
Llanthony, mon. 97 N j
Llerena 82 A b
Loa River 214 B e
Loampo 110 D D e
Loanda, Saint Paul de 175 E e
Loana 130 Q j
Loango 175 E e
Löbau, in Lusatia 115 H c
Löbau, in Prussia 115 J b
Löbau, dist. 72 D a
Lobbes, mon. 94 C a
Lobetani, people 38 B e
Lobos, isl. 201 F e
Lobositz 135 G c
Locarno 91 Q l
Locca, see Loches
Loccum, mon. 95 D a
Locedia, mon. 95 D b
Lochaber, dist.
Lochau 115 ins. B
Loches 61 D c
Lochias 34 ins. C
Lochleven 118 D b
Locoritum 39 J h
Locras River 26 C f
Locris Epicnemidia, dist. 11 D d
Locris Epizephyrii, dist. 31 F d
Locris Opuntia, dist. 11 E d
Locris Ozolis, dist. 10 D d
Lod 7 B e
Lodève 76 E e
Lodève, bp. 94 C c
Lodi 90 I h
Lodi, bp. 95 D b
Lodz 159 J c
Lofoten Islands 2 E b
Logan, mt. 186 F b
Logroño 82 B a
Logstown 192 A c
Loidis
Loir River 76 C c
Loire, dept. 148 E e
Loire River 61 C c
Loire-Inférieure, dept. 148 D e
Loiret, dept. 148 E e
Loir-et-Cher, dept. 148 E e
Loja, in Ecuador 214 B c
Loja, in Spain 82 H f
Lomagne, dist. 126 B e
Lomas de Ahorca Lagarto, hills
Lomas de Palenquillo, hills
Lombards, Kingdom of the 53 O i
Lombards, people 45 F b, G d
Lombard Street, in London 75 G g
Lombardy, Plain of 2 F d
Lombardy, prov. 158 E f
Lombardy, reg. 58 F d
Lombardy, theme 59 H e
Lombez, bp. 94 C c
Lombok, isl. 172 A a
Lome 174 D d
Lomellina, dist. 161 G e
Lomello 90 I h
Lomond, loch, lake 49 D c
Lomzha
Lonato 150 F d
Londinium (London) 51 P i
London, in Canada 212 G d
London, in England
London, plan, about 1300 75 G g
London, bp. 97 Q j
London, Hanse. for. off. 98 ins. A
London, parl. bor. 163 O f
London, New. 189 B d
London Bridge 75 G g
London Compagny, Grants to the 190 ins.
Londonderry, in Ireland 127 J f
Londonderry, in N. Hampshire 189 C c
Londonderry, cty. 127 J g
Londonderry, Cape 172 B b
Long, route of 210 E b
Longaticum 27 I b
Longford, cty. 127 J h
Long Island, in the Bahamas 105 F b
Long Island, off New York 189 B d
Long Island Sound 189 B d
Longjumeau 126 C b
Long's Peak 210 D b
Longueville 76 D b
Longula 30 B a
Longvilliers, mon. 94 C a
Longwy 114 C d
Lonicum 27 H a
Lons-le-Saunier 69 J f
Lons-le-Saunier, mon. 148 C b
Loo, mon. 94 C a
Lookout, Cape 193 F d
Lookout, Fort 210 F b
Lookout Mountain, battle 203 C c
Looz 117 D d
Lop
Lopadusa 34 G f
Lopez de Sequeira, route of 109 Y g
Lop-nor, lake 92 I c
Lopodunum 39 J i
Lora del Rio 82 A b
Lorca 82 B b
Lorch, in Austria 42 E d
Lorch, in Wurtemberg 143 I h
Lorch, mon. 95 D b
Lord Fairfax's Line 194 K g
Lord Howe, route of 195 F c
Lord Howe Island 172 F d
Lorenzo Marques
L'Orient 130 C d
Lorne, dist.
Lorne, Firth of 49 C c
Lörrach 142 A e
Lorraine, duchy 126 E b
Lorraine, gouv. 146 C b
Lorraine, prov. 148 F e
Lorraine, Lower, duchy 62 C c
Lorraine, Upper, duchy 62 D d
Lorraine and Barrois, gen. 147 F b
Lorris 98 D d
Lorsch, mon. 95 D b
Los Angeles 190 B e
Losantiville (Cincinnati) 196 ins. B
Los Cayos, isl. 105 E b
Los Corazones 190 C f
Losoncz 159 J d
Lostwithiel 127 U p
Lostwithiel, parl. bor. 163 J g
Lot, dept. 148 E f
Lot River 76 E d
Lota 215 B f
Lot-et-Garonne, dept. 148 E f
Lotharingia, duchy 56 D b
Lothbury 75 G g
Lothian, dist.
Lothian
Loudoun, Fort, in Pa. 192 B d
Loudoun, Fort, in Tennessee 193 B d
Loudun, in France 61 D c
Lough Corrib, lake 127 H h
Lough Derg, lake 127 I h
Lough Erne, lake 127 J g
Lough Mask, lake 127 H h
Lough Neagh, lake 127 K g
Lough Ree, lake
Louis VII., crusade of 70 H d
Louis, Fort 191 H e
Louisbourg 212 J d
Louisiade Archipelago 172 E b
Louisiana, dist. 202 G c
Louisiana, reg. 190 D b — H e
Louisiana, state 203 T d
Louisiana, ter. 202 G c
Louisville 199 H c
Loup Fork, R. 198 E b
Louroux, mon. 94 C b
Lousonna (Lausanne) 26 A a
Louth, cty. in Ireland 127 K h
Louth, parl. bor. in England
Louvain 117 C d
Louvain, univ. 100 F d
Louvier, Ile 149 B
Louviers 126 B b
Louvre, The, palace, in Paris 149 B
Louvre, Quai du, in Paris 149 B
Lovat River 88 N c
Lovejoy 208 D c
Low Archipelago 180 N i
Lowell 211 K b
Löwen, see Louvain
Löwenstein 143 H g
Löwenstein, cty. 143 H g
Löwenstein-Wertheim, cty. 142 D a
Lower Argen River 143 I j
Lower Bavaria, dist. 123 G d
Lower Britain, prov. 38 B b (2)
Lower Brule, Ind. Res. 188 F b
Lower Burgundy, dist. 62 C f
Lower Burma, reg. 171 K g
Lower California, pen. 187 H e
Lower California, reg. 190 C f
Lower California, ter. 213 A b
Lower Canade, reg. 212 H d
Lower Dacia, prov. 39 N k (1 b)
Lower Egypt, reg.
Lower Germany, prov.
Lower Gihon, well 6 ins. A
Lower Guinea, reg. 175 E c

Lower Libya, East Rom. prov. 43 H g (2)
Lower Lorraine, duchy 62 C c
Lower Lusatia, dist. 85 H e
Lower Lusatia, margr. 87 J c
Lower Moesia, prov. 35 J e
Lower Pannonia, prov. 34 H d
Lower Peru, reg. 214 B c
Lower Rhenish Province 158 D c
Lower Silesia, dist. 72 D a
Lower Tunguska River
Lowlands, reg. 49 D d
Loyalty Islands 172 F c
Lo-yang
Loyola 94 B c
Lozère, dept. 148 E f
Loznitza 165 A a
Lübbecke 55 Q i
Lübben 115 G c
Lübeck 62 F b
Lübeck, bp. 95 E a
Lübeck, Hanse. cy. 99 ins. B
Lübeck, imp. cy. 79 G b
Lublin 139 B e
Luca (Lucca) 26 E d
Lucania, reg. 30 E b
Lucania and Bruttium, Aug. Reg. 38 F e (3)
Lucca 90 L j
Lucca, bp. 95 E c
Lucca, duchy 161 G f
Lucca, princ. 151 K j
Lucca, rep. 150 F e
Lucena 82 B b
Lucens 91 O l
Lucentum 38 B e
Lucera 64 C b
Luceria 30 E a
Luceria, bp. 95 F c
Lucerne 91 Q k
Lucerne, canton 91 Q k
Lucerne, Lake of 91 Q l
Lucignano 118 G e
Lucka 79 H c
Luckau 85 C c
Lucknow, see Luknow
Luçon 76 C c
Luçon, bp. 94 B b
Lucretilis, mt. 35 ins. B
Lucrinus Lake 31 ins. A
Lucullus, Gardens of 23 B
Lucus. Augusti (Luc-en-Die) 38 D d
Lucus Augusti (Lugo) 38 A d
Lüderitz Bay 175 E g
Lüderitzbucht, see Lüderitz Bay
Ludgate, loc. in London 75 G g
Ludgershall, parl. bor.
Ludias River 11 D b
Ludlow 127 W n
Ludlow, parl. bor. 163 L e
Ludomeria, dist.
Ludwigsburg 143 H h
Lueg, pass 154 G e
Lugano 91 Q l
Lugano, lake 91 Q m
Lugansk 167 M f
Lugdunensis, Rom. prov. 38 C c (4)
Lugdunensis, West Rom. prov. 42 C d (2)
Lugdunum (Bagnères de Luchon) 38 C d
Lugdunum, see Laon
Lügenfeld (Field of Lies) 56 D c
Lugeus, lake 27 I b
Lugii, people 38 F c
Lugo 82 A a
Lugo, bp. 94 A c
Lugos 131 H d
Lugudunensis, prov. 34 D d
Lugudunum (Lyons) 38 C c
Lugudunum Batavorum (Leyden) 38 C b
Luguvallium (Carlisle) 51 O g
Luith
Lu-kiang, R. 171 K f
Lukmanier Pass 91 Q l
Luknow, Lucknow 137 D c
Lule River 166 I b
Luleå 167 J b
Lummi, Ind. Res. 188 B a
Luna 26 E c
Lunæ Portus (Gulf of Spezia) 26 D d
Lund 46 I b
Lund, abp. 95 D a
Lundenburg 168 E b
Lundy's Lane, battle 200 D b
Lüneburg 62 F b
Lüneburg, duchy 122 E b
Lüneburg, Hanse. cy. 99 ins. B
Lunéville 62 D d
Lung-chau 171 L f
Luni 64 B b
Luni River 137 B c
Lupercal, grotto 24 A
Lupfen, ruin 143 G i
Lupia (Lippe) River 39 I h
Lupiæ 31 H b
Lupton, Fort 210 E c
Lure, mon. 148 C b
Lurgan 127 K g
Luristan, reg. 99 M g
Lusatia, march 62 H c
Lusatia, margr. 76 C a
Lusatia, Lower, margr. 87 J c
Lusatia, Upper, margr. 87 J c
Lusatians, people 63 G c
Lusern, La, mon. 94 B b
Lusignan 126 B c
Lusignan, castle 76 D c
Lusignan, seign. 69 D c
Lusignans, dynasty 73 G c
Lusitani, people 38 A e
Lusitania, prov. 38 A d (2)
Lusitania, reg. 82 A b
Lusitania, West Rom. prov. 42 A e (2)
Lusones 38 B d
Lussheim, Alt 142 C b
Lustenau 143 J g
Lu-tai 170 ins. A
Lutetia (Paris) 38 C c
Luteva, see Lodève
Lutter am Barenberge 122 F c
Lutterberg 134 E c
Lutterworth, about thirtheen miles north-east of Coventry 97 P i
Lüttich, see Liège
Lützelburg 62 C d
Lützen 123 G c
Lutzk 139 C e
Luxembourg, palace 149 B
Luxemburg 117 D e
Luxemburg, duchy 78 D d
Luxemburg, gr. duchy 158 C d
Luxeuil, mon. 95 D b
Luxor 4 F d
Luxovium (Luxeuil) 39 I j
Luzern, see Lucerne
Luzon, isl. 199 ins. H
Luzy 69 I g
Lycabettus, mt. 23 D
Lycæus, mt. 14 B b
Lycaonia, East Rom. prov. 43 I f (5)
Lycaonia, Macedonian prov. 18 D c
Lycaonia, Rom. prov.
Lycandos, theme 59 L f
Lyceum, quarter 23 D
Lychnidus 10 B a
Lychnites, lake, in Epirus 10 B a
Lychnitis, lake, in Armenia 20 K b
Lycia, East Rom. prov. 43 H f (4)
Lycia, Macedonian prov. 18 C c
Lycia, reg. 8 A b
Lycia, Rom. prov. 20 C d
Lycia, satr. 18 N h
Lyck 155 L b
Lycosura 14 C b
Lycus River, in Phœnicia 6 D a
Lycus River, in Pontus 20 H b
Lycus, The, river, in Constantinople 93 G e
Lydda 7 B e
Lydia, East Rom. prov. 43 H f (2)
Lydia, Macedon. prov. 18 C c
Lydia, reg. 8 A b
Lydia, Rom. prov. 20 C c
Lydia, satr. 18 N h
Lydian Kingdom 5 B b
Lyme Regis 127 W p
Lyme Regis, parl. bor. 163 L g
Lymington, parl. bor. 163 M g
Lyncestis, dist. 10 C a
Lynchburg 208 E b
Lyncus, mt. 10 C c
Lynn, in England 65 G d
Lynn, Hanse. for. cy. 98 ins. A
Lynn, in Mass. 189 ins. B
Lynn Canal 212 ins.
Lyonnais, cty. 69 F d
Lyonnais, gouv. 146 B b
Lyonnais, prov. 148 E e
Lyons 70 G d
Lyons, abp. 94 C b
Lyons, gen. 147 E b
Lyons, Gulf of 38 C d
Lyrcea 14 C b
Lys River 117 A d
Lysikrates, Monument of
Lysimachia, in Ætolia 10 C d
Lysimachia, on the Propontis
Lysimachus, Kingdom of 18
Lysimelian Marsh 31 ins. B
Lystra 20 E d
Lyttus 14 ins.

Maacha, reg. 6 D b
Ma'bar, reg. 102 H f
McAllister, Fort 208 D c
Macao 110 CC e
Macapá 214 D b
Macara 30 C e
Macaria, dist. 14 C b
Macassar
Macassar, Strait of 171 M h
Macclesfield 127 W m
Macclesfield, parl. bor. 163 L d
McClintock Channel 212 E a
Macdonald, lake 172 B c
MacDonalds, fam.
McDonnell Range 172 C c
McDowell 208 E b
Macedonia, East Rom. dioc. 43 G e
Macedonia, East Rom. prov. 43 Ge (1.)
Macedonia, reg. 10 C b
Macedonia, Rom. imp. prov. 39 M l (4.)
Macedonia, Rom. sen. prov. 35 I e
Macedonia, state 18 B b
Macedonia, theme 59 J e
Macedonia Salutaris, East Rom. prov. 43 Ge (6.)
Macedonian Empire, The 18, 19
Maceió 214 F c
Macellum Liviae, in Rome 22 A
Macellum magnum, in Rome 22 A
Macerata 90 D c
Macerata, bp. 95 E c
Macestus River
Maceta, Cape 19 I e
McGillivray's Town 196 B d
Machadodorp 175 N e
Machærus 7 D e
McHenry, Fort 200 L h
Machias 189 E b
Macijowice
MacIntoshes, fam.
Macintyre River 172 D c
Macistus 14 B b
Macistus, mt. 11 E d
Mackay 172 D c
MacKays, fam.
Mackenzie, dist. 212 C b
MacKenzies, fam.
Mackenzie Bay 212 B b
Mackenzie River 186 G b
Mackinac 211 H a
Mackinac, Fort 194 C a
McKinley, mt. 186 D b

MacLeans, fam.
Macleod 212 D d
MacLeods, fam.
McMurray, Fort 212 D c
Macomades 46 H f
Mâcon, in France 61 F c
Mâcon, bp. 94 C b
Macon, in Georgia 208 D c
Macon, Fort, in N. Carolina 208 E c
MacPhersons, fam.
Macpherson, Fort 212 B b
Macquarie Harbor 172 D e
Macra River 26 D c
Mactan, isl. 110 D D g
Macynia 10 C d
Madagascar, isl. 175 H g
Madaura 38 D e
Madeira Islands 174 B a
Madeira River 214 C c
Madeket 189 C d
Madeleine, The, church, in Paris 149 B
Mâdion, mon. 94 B b
Madison 211 H b
Madison, Fort 199 G b
Madison, Fort, Ind. Res. 188 B a
Madrak, Ras 170 G g
Madras 137 D f
Madre de Dios River 214 C d
Madrid 83 K g
Madura 137 C g
Madytus
Mæander (Mendere) River 20 C d
Mæcenas, Gardens of 22 A
Mædi, people 39 M l
Mæetae, people 35 L d
Mænalus 14 C b
Mænalus, mt. 14 C b
Mænan, mon. 97 N h
Mæotis, lake (Sea of Azov) 12 K a
Maeseyck 117 D c
Maestricht 117 D d
Mafeking 175 F g
Mafia, isl. 175 H e
Magadaburg, see Magdeburg
Magadoxo 175 H d
Magalhães (Magellan) Strait 108 K l
Magalhães, route of, see Magellan 107—110 leg.
Magalia, quarter in Carthage 34 ins. A
Magdala, in Abyssinia 174 G c
Magdala, in Palestine 6 D c
Magdalen, Postern of the 68 ins. B
Magdalena 213 A a
Magdalena, isl. 107 D i
Magdalena Bay 111 B a
Magdalena River 214 B b
Magdeburg 63 F b
Magdeburg, abp. 95 E a
Magdeburg, duchy 122 F b
Magdeburg, Hanse. cy. 99 ins. B
Magdiel 6 B c
Magdolum 4 ins.
Magellan, route of 107 Ah, 108 Ng, 110 DDg
Magellan, Straits of 215 B h
Magenta 158 E f
Mägerkingen 143 H i
Magersfontein 175 L l
Magetobriga 39 H j
Maggia 91 Q l
Maggiore, Lake 91 Q m
Magia 39 J j
Magna Charta Island 75 H i
Magna Græcia, reg. 29 E e
Magna Mater, Temple of 24 A
Magnano 150 F d
Magnesia (Manissa) 93 C c
Magnesia, reg. 11 D c
Magnetic Pole, Northern 186 J a
Mago 38 C e
Magoras River 6 D a
Magrib, reg. 98 C g
Maguelonne, bp. 94 C c
Magyars, people, 800
Magyars, people, about 900
Mahanadi River 137 E d
Mahanaim 7 D d
Mahanuddy River 137 E d
Mahé 137 C f
Mahedia 70 I f
Mahlberg 142 A d
Mahlberg, lordship 142 A d
Mahmoud Bridge 93 Ge (10.)
Maholm 88 L b
Mahon 83 L h
Mahra, reg. 53 H e
Mahratta Confederacy 137 B d
Mahukona 198 ins. B
Maidstone, in England 127 Z o
Maidstone, parl. bor. 163 O f
Maidstone (Easthampton), in New York 189 C d
Maienfeld 91 R k
Mail, Plaine du, Versailles 149 A
Mailand, see Milan
Mailapur
Mailberg 63 H d
Maillezais, bp. 94 B b
Mailly 69 I g
Maimatchin 171 L d
Mainau, isl. 142 D e
Maine, cty., in France 61 D b
Maine, gouv., in France 146 A b
Maine. prov., in France 148 D e
Maine, col., in U. S. 189 C c
Maine. dist., in U. S. 196 F b
Maine, state, in U. S. 203 Y a
Maine-et-Loire, dept. 148 D e
Mainots, people 164 C c
Main River 62 F c
Main River, East 186 L c
Maintenon 126 B b
Maintenon, castle 130 D d
Mainz, see Mayence
Maior (Majorca), isl. 38 C e
Maipo, battle 215 B f
Maison-du-Roi, la 156 C c
Maitland 172 E d
Majapahit 112 E d
Majar 99 L e
Majella, Mount, mon. 95 E c
Majorca, bp. 94 C d
Majorca, isl. 82 C b
Majorca and Roussillon, km. 83 L g
Majuba Hill, mt. 175 M l
Majumas 7 A e
Makah, Ind. Res. 188 A a
Makalla 170 F g
Makarska, bp. 95 F c
Makhlaf 170 F g
Makri 99 I f
Makua River 175 F d
Malabar, reg. 137 C f
Malabar Coast 137 B e
Malaca (Málaga) 38 B e
Malacca 112 D c
Malacca, pen. 112 D c
Málaga 82 B b
Málaga, bp. 94 B d
Malakoff, Fort 164 L g
Mälar, lake 119 H b
Malaspina, fam. 90 L i
Malaspina Glacier 212 A c
Malatia 99 K f
Malatieh
Malay Peninsula 171 L h
Malborn 142 ins. A
Malden 189 ins. B
Malden, Fort 200 B b
Malden Island 180 L h
Maldive Islands 112 A c
Maldon 65 G e
Maldon, parl. bor. 163 O f
Maldonado 215 D f
Malea, prom. in Laconia 15 D c
Malea, prom. in Lesbos
Malécites, mission 189 E a
Malian Gulf 11 D d
Malian Plain 16 E e
Malindi 175 H e
Malines, abp. 148 B a
Malin Head 127 J f
Malis, dist. 11 D d
Mallets, route of the 190 E d
Malli, people 19 L d
Mallianum, bp. 96 B a
Malling, mon. 97 R j
Malmedy 117 E d
Malmedy, mon. 95 D a
Malmesbury
Malmesbury, mon
Malmesbury, parl. bor. 163 L f (Malm.)
Malmö 88 E d
Malmö, Hanse. for. cy. 98 F b
Mallœa 10 D c
Maloja Pass 91 R l
Maloyaroslavets 153 P g
Malpelo Island 214 A b
Malplaquet 134 B c
Malta, isl. 50 F e
Malton, parl. bor. 163 N c
Maluentum 30 D a
Maluinas (Falkland), isl. 215 D h
Malvasia 124 D c
Malvern, Great, mon. 97 O i
Malvern Hill, in Virginia 208 E b
Malvern Hills, in England 49 E e
Malwa, reg. 137 C c
Mamanguape 214 F c
Mamei
Mamelukes, Dom. of the 73 H d
Mameluke Sultanates 77 I e
Mamertium 31 F d
Mamistra 68 C b
Mamoré River 214 C d
Man, Isle of 49 D d
Manado
Managua 213 D c
Manahiki Islands 180 L i
Manaos 214 D c
Manar, Gulf of 137 C g
Manassas Junction 208 ins.
Manasseh, tribe 7 ins. D
Manbij 68 C b
Mancha, La, dist. 83 K h
Manchac 191 G e
Manche, dept. 148 D e
Manchester, in England 127 W m
Manchester, parl. bor. 163 L d
Manchester, in New Hampshire 211 K b
Manchester, in Ohio 196 ins. B
Manchu City, in Peking 170 ins. A
Manchuria, reg. 171 N c d
Manchus, people
Mancunium (Manchester)
Mandalay 171 K f
Mandans, tribe 188 D a
Mandan, Fort 210 E a
Manderscheid 117 E d
Mandeure 143 ins. F
Mandingo River
Mandræ
Mandu 112 A a
Mandubii, people 38 C c
Manduessedum
Manduria 31 G b
Manfredonia (Siponto) 90 F d
Mangalore 137 B f
Mangarewa Island 180 O j
Mangaseya
Manhardsberg, mt. 54 H d
Manhattan 189 ins. C
Manhattan Island 189 ins. C
Manila 171 N g
Manila Bay 171 N g
Manipur 171 K f
Manissa (Magnesia) 93 C c
Manitoba, lake 186 I c
Manitoba, prov. 212 F c
Mannheim 142 B a
Manosque 126 D c

Manosque, mon. 148 C c (Man.)
Manresa
Mans, Le 61 C b
Mans, Le, bp. 94 C b
Mansfeld 62 F c
Mansfeld, cty. 114 F c
Mansfeld, Ernest of, route 121 C c
Mansfield Island 212 G b
Mansura, in Egypt 174 J i
Mansurah, in India 53 I d
Mantes 69 H f
Manthyrea 14 C b
Mantinea nova 14 C b
Mantinea vetus 14 C b
Mantinum 26 D e
Mantua 26 E b
Mantua, bp. 95 E b
Mantua, duchy 150 F d
Mantua, marq. 90 C b
Manua Islands 199 ins. D
Manuel, Fort 210 D a
Manukau Harbor 172 G d
Manytch River 164 G a
Manzanillo 213 B c
Manzanillo, Bay of
Manzi, reg. 92 L e
Manzikert 67 O f
Maon 7 C f
Maqueda 82 B a
Mar, dist.
Maracaibo 214 B a
Maracaibo Lake 105 F e
Maracanda 19 K c
Maragha 73 J c
Marajo Island 214 E c
Marakesh (Morocco) 174 C a
Maranguape 214 F c
Maranham 214 E c
Maranhão, state 214 E c
Marañon River 214 B c
Marans 126 A c
Maransart
Marash 68 C b
Marash, reg. 124 G c
Marathon 15 D a
Marathon, Plain of 16 B a
Marbach 143 H h
Marbais 156 B a
Marbella 82 B b
Marblehead 189 ins. B
Marburg 123 H e
Marcellus, Theatre of 22 A
March River 63 I d
Marche, or La Marche, cty. 61 D c
Marche, or La Marche, gouv. 146 B b
Marche, or La Marche, prov. 148 E e
Marches, The, dist. 90 D c
Marchfeld, dist. 79 J d
Marchienne 156 A b
Marchthal, ab. 143 I i
Marchthal, mon. 143 I i
Marcian Aqueduct 35 ins. B
Marcianopolis 39 N l
Marcinelle 156 A b
Marcodurum 39 I h
Marcomagus 39 I h
Marcomanni, people 38 E c
Marco Polo, route of
Marcus Aurelius, Arch of 22 A
Marcus Aurelius, Column of 22 A
Marcus Aurelius, Temple of 22 A
Marcus Hook 192 ins.
Mar del Norte (Caribbean Sea) 108 J f
Mar del Plata 215 D f
Mar del Sur (South Sea or Pacific Ocean) 107 F H g
Mardin 68 D b
Mardocho 6 F c
Mardonius' Fleet, route of 13 D b
Mardyck 122 B c
Marengo 150 E d
Mareotis, lake 4 ins.
Margalæ 14 B b
Margam, mon. 97 N j
Margarita, isl. 105 H d
Margat 68 C b
Marghilan 170 I e
Margiana, prov. 19 J c
Margus River (Morava R.) 39 M l
Margus River (Murgab R.) 19 J c
Maria Galante, isl. 105 H c
Mariamne 6 ins. A
Mariampol 155 L a
Mariana 26 D e
Marianne Islands 110 F F f
Marias River 210 C a
Maria Theresiopel 159 J e
Maria van Diemen, Cape 172 G d
Mariazell, Gross, mon. 95 F b
Mariazell, Klein, mon. 95 F b
Marici, people 26 D b
Maridunum (Carmarthen) 51 N i
Marie Galante, isl. 213 F c
Marienbourg 117 C d
Marienburg 79 K b
Marienburg, Hanse. cy. 98 G c
Marienstern, mon. 95 E a
Marienthal, mon. 95 E a
Marienwalde, mon. 80 ins.
Marienwerder 72 D a
Marienwerder, bp. 95 F a
Marietta 196 ins. B
Marignano 90 I h
Mariguana, isl. 105 F b
Marinids, dynasty 77 C f
Mario, Monte 96 A
Mariposa 201 B b
Maritima, isl. 30 A e
Maritime Alps, mts. 26 B c
MaritimeAlps, West Rom. prov. 42 D e (7)
Maritza River 89 C b
Mariua 214 C c
Mariupol 139 E f
Mark, cty. 78 E c
Mark, see Brandenburg
Market Harborough 98 ins. A
Markgröningen 143 H h
Markovo 171 S b
Marlborough, in England 127 X o
Marlborough, parl. bor. 163 M f (Marlb.)
Marlborough, route of 129 leg.
Marlborough, in Tasmania 172 D e
Marle 69 I f
Marmande 126 B d
Marmarica, dist. 35 I g
Marmarium 15 E a
Marmora, Sea of 3 H d
Marmoutier, mon. 94 C b
Marne, dept. 148 E e
Marne River 69 I f
Maroneus, mt. 30 D e
Maronia 13 D a
Maroni River 214 D b
Maros River 73 E a
Maros-Vasarhely 159 M e
Marpessa, mt. 15 F b
Marquesas de Mendoza, isl. 107 D h
Marquesas Islands 180 M h
Marquette, route of 191 H c
Marra 68 C b
Marrucini, people 27 I e
Marruvium 27 H f
Mars, Temple of 22 A
Mars the Avenger, Temple of 24 B
Marsala 90 D f
Marsalquivir 130 C f
Marsan, dist. 147 D c
Marsan, viscty. 84 C g
Marsdiep, strait 117 C b
Marseilles 61 F e
Marseilles, bp. 95 D c
Marshall 211 G d
Marshall Islands 179 I f
Mars' Hill, (Areopagus) in Athens
Mars Hill, mt. in Maine 199 L a
Marsi, people, in Germany 39 I h
Marsi, Marsians, people, in Italy
Marsico, bp. 95 F c
Marston Moor 127 X m
Martaban
Marta River 27 F e
Martel 76 D d
Martha's Vineyard, isl. 189 C d
Martigny 91 P l
Martin Garcia, Island of 215 D f (M.)
Martinino (Martinique), isl. 105 H d
Martinique, isl. 213 F c
Martinsbruck 150 F c
Martinsburg 193 F b
Martin's Hundred 193 ins. A (Mart.)
Martinstein 142 ins. A
Martinstein, lordship 142 ins. A
Martinswand 87 H e
Martirano 72 D d
Marton, mon. 97 Q g
Martyropolis 52 M f
Marusium 31 I b
Marus River (March R.) 38 F c
Marvejols 126 C d
Marwar, dist. 137 B c
Marwell, college 100 A b
Maryborough 172 E c
Maryland, col. 192 C d
Maryland, state 211 J c
Mary-le-bone, parl. bor.
Marysville 210 A c
Masada 7 C f
Masampo, Masampho 171 N e
Masbate, isl. 199 ins. H
Mascara 130 D f
Mascarenhas, isl. 109 W i
Mascoutins, tribe 188 H b
Masefau 199 ins. D
Maserfield (Oswestry)
Mases 15 D b
Mashonaland, dist. 175 G f
Masis, mt. 18 F c
Masius Mountains 20 I d
Maskat 170 G f
Mason and Dixon's Line 194 K g
Mason and Gorges' Claim 189 C c
Masovia, dist. 138 B e
Massa 90 L j
Massa, bp. 95 E c
Massa Marittima 90 L j
Massa Veternensis 26 E d
Massac, Fort 194 B c
Massaca 19 L d
Massachusetts, state, till 1820 202 K b
Massachusetts, state, since 1820 203 X b
Massachusetts Bay 189 C c
Massachusetts Bay, col. 189 C c
Massagetæ, Massagetans, people 19 J b
Massanutting 193 E b
Massaua or Massawa, see Massowah
Masserano 130 Q i
Massicus, mt. 30 C a
Massilia (Marseilles) 38 D d
Massowah 174 G c
Massylii, people 38 D e
Mastanli 165 D c
Masulipatam 137 D e
Matabeleland, reg. 175 F f
Matachin
Matagorda Bay 190 F f
Matamoros 201 F d
Matanzas 213 D b
Matanzas Island 191 I f
Matapan, Cape 167 J h
Matape 190 D f
Matatane 109 V j
Matelots, Allée des, Versailles 149 A
Matera 64 C b
Matera, abp. 95 F c
Maternum 27 F e
Mathia, mt. 14 B c
Mathis River 31 I a
Mathraval
Matianus, lake 18 G c

Matifu, Cape 118 E f
Matilica 27 H d
Matinum 31 F a
Matisco or Matiscone (Mâcon, in France) 39 H j
Matrega, Matriga 73 H b
Matrinum 27 I e
Matrona, Mount (Mt. Genèvre), pass 26 A c
Matrona (Marne) River 38 C c
Mattagami River 211 I a
Mattium 39 J h
Matto Grosso (Villa Bella) 214 D d
Matto Grosso, state 214 D d
Mattox 193 F b (Ma.)
Mauai, isl. 198 ins. B
Maubeuge 117 B d
Maubeuge, mon. 148 B a
Maugio 76 F e
Maulbronn, ab. 143 G h
Maulbronn, mon. 143 G g
Maule River 215 B f
Mauléon 126 A e
Maullin 215 B g
Maultasch, castle 79 G e
Maumee River 200 A c
Mauna Kea, mt. 198 ins. B
Mauna Loa, mt. 198 ins. B
Maupertuis 81 M h
Maurepas, lake 191 G e (L. M.)
Maurepas, Fort (Biloxi) 191 H e
Maurepas, Fort (on Winnipeg L.) 191 F a
Mauretania, reg. 46 F g
Mauretania Cæsariensis, prov. 34 D g
Mauretania Cæsariensis, West Rom. prov. 42 C f (5.)
Mauretania Sitifensis, West Rom. prov. 42 C f (4.)
Mauretania Tingitana, imp. prov. 34 C g
Mauretania Tingitana, West Rom. prov. 42 B g (6.)
Mauretanians, people 51 C f
Mauriac 126 C d
Maurici, Portus 26 C d
Maurienne, bp. 95 D b
Mauritius, isl. 175 I f
Mauritsstad
Maursmünster, mon. 95 D b
Mauvezin 126 B e
Mauze, castle 69 C c
Mavila 191 H e
Maxen 135 G c
Maxima Cæsariensis, West Rom. prov. 42 B c (1.)
Maxima Sequanorum, West Rom. prov. 42 D d (9.)
Maximianopolis 6 C c
May, Cape 192 D d
May, River of 191 I e
Maya 82 B a
Mayaguana, isl. 105 F b
Mayaguez 199 ins. G
Mayas, people 105 C c
Mayence 62 E d
Mayence, abp. 95 D b
Mayence, univ. 100 G d
Mayenne 76 C b
Mayenne, dept. 148 D e
Mayo, bp. 97 B c
Mayo, cty. 127 H h
Mayotte Island 175 H f
Maysi, Cape 105 F c
Maysville 211 I c
Mayumba 175 D e
Mazaca (Kaisarieh) 20 F c
Mazagan 108 P d
Mazamet 126 C e
Mazan, mon. 94 C c
Mazanderan, reg. 139 H h
Mazara 30 B e
Mazatlan 213 B b
Mazovia, reg. 59 I c
Mazzara 90 D f
Mazzara, bp. 95 E d
Mazzo 91 S l
McCarthys, The, fam.
McGuires, The, fam.
McMahons, The, fam.
McMurroughs, The, fam.
Meadville 206 ins.
Meara 6 D a
Mearns, dist.
Meath, bp. 97 E c
Meath, cty. 127 K h
Meath, dist.
Meat Market, in London 75 G g (33.)
Meauléon 76 C e
Meaux, in France 61 E b
Meaux, bp. 94 C b
Meaux, mon., in England 97 Q h
Mecca
Mechanicstown 208 ins.
Mechlin 76 F b
Mechlin, abp. 148 B a
Mechlin, lordship 117 C d
Mecklenburg 55 R i
Mecklenburg, castle 63 F b
Mecklenburg, dist. 79 G b
Mecklenburg, duchy 87 H b
Mecklenburg Court House 195 A f
Mecklenburg-Güstrow, duchy 123 G b
Mecklenburg-Schwerin, duchy 122 F b
Mecklenburg-Schwerin, gr. duchy 158 F b
Mecklenburg-Strelitz, duchy 135 G b
Mecklenburg-Strelitz, gr. duchy 158 G b
Mecyberna 11 E b
Medama 12 G c
Medeba
Medellin, in Columbia 214 B b
Medellin, in Mexico 106 D a
Medellin, in Spain 82 A b
Medemblik 117 D b
Medeon 10 C d
Medes, people 5 D b
Medeshamstead
Medford 189 ins. B
Medgyes 159 M e
Media, prov. 19 G c
Media, reg. 8 C b
Media, satr. 8 I e
Media Atropatene, reg. 35 N f
Media Atropatene, satr. 18 P h
Media Magna, satr. 18 P h
Median Empire 8
Median Wall 18 F d
Mediasch 159 M e
Medicine Hat 212 D d
Medina
Medinaceli 82 B a
Medina del Campo 83 K g
Medina de Pomar 82 B a
Medina de Rioseco
Medina Sidonia 82 A b
Medinet el Fayum 174 J j
Mediolanium, Mediolanum (Milan) 26 D b
Mediolanum, see Evreux
Mediolanum, see Saintes
Mediomatrici, see Metz
Mediomatrici, people 38 D c
Mediterranean Sea 2 E e
Medjidie 165 F a
Medma 30 E d
Medma River 31 F d
Medrano 215 C f
Meduacus (Brenta) River 27 F b
Medulli, people 26 A b
Medullia 35 ins. B
Meenen
Meersberg 142 D e
Meerut 137 C c
Meewocs, tribe 188 B c
Megalopolis 14 C b
Megara, in Greece 15 D a
Megara, quarter in Carthage 34 ins. A
Megara Hyblæa 30 E e
Megaris, dist. 15 D a
Megaris, isl. 31 ins. A
Megiddo 6 C c
Mehadia 159 L f
Mehaigne River 156 B a
Meia Ponte 214 E d
Meigs, Fort 200 B c
Meiningen 154 F c
Meiringen 91 Q l
Meisenheim 158 D d
Meissen 63 G c
Meissen, bp. 95 E a
Meissen, march 85 G e
Me-Jarkon 7 B d
Mejillones 215 B e
Mekong River
Mekran, reg. 170 H f
Melænæ 16 B a
Melæneæ 14 B b
Melas, gulf
Melas River 16 E e
Melbourne 172 D d
Melcart, Island of 18 ins. B
Melchior Diaz, route of 190 C f
Melchthal 91 Q l
Melcombe Regis, parl. bor. 163 L g
Meldæ or Meldis, see Meaux
Meldorf 62 E a
Meleda, isl. 90 F c
Melodunum, see Melodunum
Melencze 159 K f
Melfi 90 E d
Melfi, bp. 95 F c
Melgueil, cty. 69 E e
Melibocus Mountains 39 K h
Melibœa 11 D c
Melilla 118 D f
Melinde
Melita (Malta), isl. 34 G f
Melita (Meleda), isl. 38 F d
Melitæa 11 D c
Melite, deme of 23 D
Melite, lake 10 C d
Melitean Gate 23 D
Melitene (Malatieh) 20 H c
Melk 63 H d
Melk, mon. 95 F b
Mella River 26 E b
Melli 108 Q f
Mellrichstadt 62 F c
Melnik 63 H c
Melno, lake 88 H e
Melodunum (Melun) 38 C c
Melon, mon. 94 A c
Meloria, isl. 72 C c
Melos 15 E c
Melos (Milo), isl. 15 E c
Melpes River 30 E c
Melrose
Melton Mowbray, parl. bor.
Melun 76 E b
Mellville Island, off Australian coast 172 B b
Melville Island, Parry Is. 186 H a
Melville Peninsula 212 G b
Melville Sound 186 H a
Memel 80 G d
Memleben 63 F c
Memleben, mon. 95 E a
Memmingen 79 G d
Memphis, in Egypt 4 ins.
Memphis, in Tennessee 199 H c
Menæum 30 D e
Menam River 171 K g
Menapii, people 39 H h
Menat, mon. 94 C b
Menawaski 174 F c
Mendana, route of 110 HH h
Mende, in Chalcidice 11 E c
Mende, in France 61 E d
Mande, bp. 94 C c
Mendere River (Scamander R.)
Mendere River (Mæander R.)
Mendes 4 ins.
Mendip Hills 49 E f
Mendocino, Cape 187 G d
Mendon 189 C c

Mendoza . . . . 215 C f
Mendoza, route of . . . . 107 G f
Mendrisio . . . . 91 Q m
Menendez, set. of . . . . 191 J e
Mengen . . . . 143 H i
Meng-tsze . . . .
Menin . . . . 117 B d
Meninx . . . . 34 G d
Men-nofer (Memphis) . . . . . . 4 F d
Menominee, Ind. Res. . . . . . 188 I a
Menominee River . . . . 191 H b
Menominees, tribe . . . . 188 I a
Mentana . . . . 161 I f
Menteith, dist. . . . .
Mentesa . . . . 82 H f
Mentesha, reg. . . . . 89 I g
Mentone . . . . 130 P k
Mentorides, isl. . . . . 27 I c
Mentz, see Mayence
Menzaleh, lake . . . .
Meonwara, people . . . .
Meppel . . . . 117 E b
Meppen . . . . 122 D b
Meppen, mon. . . . . 95 D a
Mequinenza . . . . 82 C a
Meran . . . . 114 F e
Meran, mon. . . . . 95 E b
Merash . . . .
Merbe Braine . . . .
Mercer, Fort . . . . 195 D d
Merchant's Hope . . . . 193 ins. A
Mercia, Kingdom . . . .
Mercia, Danish, reg. . . . . . .
Mercia, English, reg. . . . . . .
Mercians, people . . . . 51 R k
Mercoeur, castle . . . . 69 E d
Mercurii, prom. . . . . 38 E e
Mercury, Temple of . . . . . . 22 A
Mercy, Cape . . . . 212 I b
Mere, parl. bor. . . . .
Merena, isl. . . . . 172 F b
Merevale, mon. . . . . 97 P i
Mergens, Pitinum . . . . 27 G d
Mergentheim . . . . 143 I g
Mergen . . . . 112 A b
Mérida, in Spain . . . . 82 A b
Mérida in Venezuela . . . . . . 214 B b
Mérida, in Yucatan . . . . 213 D b
Meridian . . . . 208 C c
Mérindol . . . . 126 D e
Mering . . . . 62 F d
Merinum . . . . 31 F a
Merioneth, cty. . . . . 74 D e
Merioneth, parl. dist. . . . . . . 163 K e
Merkits, people . . . .
Merom . . . . 6 C c
Merom, Waters of . . . . 6 D b
Merrimac River . . . . 189 C c
Merry Mount, in Mass. . . . . . 189 C c
Merry Mount, in Virginia . . . 193 ins. A
Merse, dist. . . . .
Merseburg . . . . 63 G c
Merseburg, bp. . . . . 95 E a
Merseburg, Hanse. cy. . . . . . 99 ins. B
Merseburg, march . . . . 63 G c
Mersen . . . . 55 Q i
Mersey River . . . . 127 W m
Merthyr Tydfil, parl. bor. . . . 163 K f
Merry Mount, village . . . . . . 189 C c
Mertola . . . . 82 A b
Merton . . . . 75 I i
Merton, mon. . . . . 97 Q j
Merv . . . . 53 I c
Méry . . . . 45 E c
Mesambria, on the Ægean Sea 17 D a
Mesambria, Mesembria, on the Black Sea . . . . 12 I b
Mescalero Apache, Ind. Res. . 188 E d
Meseritz . . . . 155 H b
Meseritz, mon. . . . . 95 F a
Meshed . . . .
Meshed-Ali . . . . 99 L g
Mesogæa, dist. . . . . 15 D b
Mesopotamia, Rom. prov. . . . 35 M f
Mesopotamia, East Rom. prov 43 J f (12.)
Mesopotamia, reg. . . . . 4 G c
Mesopotamia, satr. . . . . 18 P h
Mesopotamia, theme . . . . . . 59 L f
Mesopotamia Plains . . . . . . 3 I e
Messa . . . . 14 C c
Messana (Messina) . . . . 30 E d
Messapii, Messapians, people . 31 G b
Messene . . . . 14 B b
Messenia, Gulf of . . . . 14 C c
Messenia,, state . . . . 14 B b
Messina . . . . 90 E e
Messina, abp. . . . . 95 E d
Messina, Strait of . . . . 30 E d
Messkirch . . . . 142 D d
Messkirch, lordship . . . . . . 142 D d
Meta River . . . . 214 B b
Metammeh . . . . 174 G c
Metanastæ, Jazyges, people . . 38 F c
Metapontum, Metapontium . . . 31 F a
Metaris Æstuarium (The Wash) 51 Q h
Meta sudans, in Rome . . . . . 24 B
Metauro River . . . . 90 M j
Metaurus River, in Bruttium . . 30 E d
Metaurus River, in Umbria . . 27 G d
Methana . . . . 15 D b
Methone, in Macedonia . . . . . 11 D b
Methone, in Magnesia . . . . . 11 E c
Methone (Modoni), in Messenia 14 B c
Methydrium . . . . 14 E b
Methymna . . . .
Metis River . . . . 199 L a
Metropolis, in Acarnania . . . 10 C d
Metropolis, in Epirus . . . . . . 10 C d
Metropolis, in Pelasgiotis . . . . 11 D c
Metropolis, in Thessaliotis . . . 10 C c
Metropotamia, proposed state in U. S. . . . .
Metroum . . . .
Metrovian Gate . . . . 22 A
Metsovo . . . .
Mettis (Metz) . . . . 39 I i
Metulum . . . . 27 J b
Metz . . . . 62 D d
Metz, bp. . . . . 78 E d
Metz, imp. cy. . . . . 78 E d
Metz and Verdun, gouv. . . . . 146 C b
Metzingen . . . . 143 H h
Meulant, castle . . . . 76 D b
Meung . . . . 76 D c
Meurs . . . . 117 E c
Meurthe, dept. . . . . 148 F e
Meuse, dept. . . . . 148 F e
Meuse River . . . . 62 C c
Mevania . . . . 27 G e
Mevaniola . . . . 27 F c
Mewar, dist. . . . . 137 B d
Mexicaltzinco . . . .
Mexican Plain . . . . 187 I f
Mexico . . . . 106 A a
Mexico, audiencia . . . . 213 C c
Mexico, viceroyalty, see New Spain
Mexico, country . . . . A — D a — c
Mexico, Gulf of . . . . 187 J f
Mexico, New, ter. . . . . 203 Q h
Meymac, mon. . . . . 94 C b
Mezen . . . . 167 N b
Mézières . . . . 69 J f
Miami . . . . 213 D b
Miami, Fort . . . .
Miami River . . . . 191 I d
Miamis, tribe . . . . 188 I b
Miana . . . .
Miani . . . . 170 H f
Miantonomo . . . . 189 ins. A
Michael, parl. bor. . . . .
Michaelovsk . . . .
Michigan, lake . . . . 187 K d
Michigan, state . . . . 202 H f
Michigan, ter. 1805 . . . . 202 H b
Michigan, ter. 1818 . . . . 203 T a
Michigan, ter. 1834 . . . . 203 S a
Michigania, proposed state in U. S. . . . .
Michilimackinac, or Michillimackinac . . . . 191 I b
Michipicoten . . . .
Michipicoten River . . . . 188 J a
Michmash . . . . 7 C e
Michoacan, state . . . . 213 ins.
Mickleham, mon. . . . . 97 R k
Micmacs, tribe . . . . 188 M a
Middelburg, in Holland . . . . . 117 B c
Middelburg, Hanse. cv. . . . . . 99 ins. B
Middelburg, in Transvaal . . . . 175 M l
Middelfart . . . . 88 C d
Middle Angles, people . . . . . 51 R k
Middleborough . . . . . . 189 C d (Mid.)
Middle District, New South Wales . . . . 172 leg.
Middle Empire, see Chagatai .
Middle March, dist. . . . .
Middle Plantation . . . . 193 ins. A
Middle Saxons, people . . . . .
Middlesbrough . . . . 162 E c
Middlesex, cty. . . . .
Middlesex, dist. . . . .
Mindlesex, parl. dist. . . .
Middletown . . . . 189 B d
Midea . . . . 15 C b
Midhurst, parl. bor. . . . . . . 163 N f
Midi, Canal du . . . . 130 D e
Midia . . . . 165 F c
Midian, dist. . . . . 4 F d
Midianites, people . . . . 7 ins. C
Midnapur . . . . 137 E d
Midway Islands . . . . 180 J e
Midwout . . . . 189 ins. C
Mien . . . .
Mien, reg. . . . . 109 A A e
Mies . . . . 87 I d
Mifflin, Fort . . . . 195 D d
Migdol . . . . 4 ins.
Milan . . . . 90 B b
Milan, abp. . . . . 95 D b
Milan, duchy, 1395 . . . . 78 F f
Milan, duchy, 1494 . . . . 90 B b
Milan, duchy, 1796. . . . . 150 E d
Milanese, The, dist., 1339–1402 90 H-K g-h
Milassa (Miletus) . . . .
Milazzo . . . . 161 J h
Milborne Post, parl. bor.
Mile End Meadow . . . . 75 I h
Miletopolis . . . .
Miletus . . . . 20 B d
Mileve . . . . 42 D f
Milford, in Conn. . . . . 192 E c
Milford, in New Jersey . . . . . 192 D c
Milford, in Wales . . . . 70 E c
Milford Haven . . . . 84 A d
Milhaud . . . . 76 E d
Milhaud, viscty. . . . . 69 E d
Milid (Maladieh) . . . . 5 C b
Military boundary, 1806 . . . . . 199 G e
Military Bounty Lands . . . . . 196 ins. B
Military Frontier, Croatian, Slavonian and Banat . . . . . . 159 H-L f
Milk River . . . . 210 D a
Milledgeville . . . . 208 D c
Mille Lac, Ind. Res. . . . . . . 188 H a
Millen . . . . 208 D c
Millesimo . . . . 130 Q j
Millikens Bend, point on Miss. R. 208 B c
Mill Springs, battle . . . . 208 D b
Miloslaw . . . . 159 I b
Miltenberg . . . . 142 D a
Milton Abbas, mon. . . . . 97 O k
Milvian Bridge . . . . 96 A
Milwaukee . . . . 199 H b
Milyana . . . . 73 A c
Milyas, dist. . . . . 20 D d
Milzienians, people . . . . 63 H c
Mimate, see Mende
Mimigerniford, see Münster
Mims, Fort . . . . 200 I f
Minagara . . . . 18 R i
Minas . . . . 215 D f

Minas Geraes, state . . . . . . 214 E d
Minas Novas . . . . 214 E d
Minch, The, strait . . . . 49 C c
Mincio River . . . . 150 F d
Mincius (Mincio) River . . . . . 26 E b
Minda, see Minden
Mindanao, isl. . . . . 199 ins. H
Mindel River . . . . 143 J i
Minden . . . . 62 E b
Minden, bp. . . . . 95 D a
Minden, Hanse, cy. . . . . 99 ins. B
Minden, princ. . . . . 122 E b
Mindi . . . .
Mindoro, isl. . . . . 199 ins. H
Minehead, parl. bor. . . . . . 163 K f
Minerva, Temple of, on the Aventine Mt. . . . . 22 A
Minerva, Temple of, in the Forum . . . . 24 B
Minerva, Temple of, on Sunium Promontory . . . . 16 C b
Minerva, prom. . . . . 30 D b
Minerva Archegetis . . . . 23 D
Minervæ, Castrum . . . . 31 H b
Minervia, see Scolacium (Squillace)
Mingio . . . . 103 M e
Mingrelia, reg. . . . . 164 G b
Minhla . . . . 171 K g
Minho River . . . . 82 A a
Minibar, reg. . . . .
Minieh . . . . 150 B b
Minio River . . . . 27 F e
Minius (Minho) River . . . . . 38 A d
Minneapolis . . . . 199 G a
Minnesota, state . . . . 203 S f
Minnesota, ter. . . . . 202 F f
Minnesota River . . . . 198 F b
Minnith . . . . 7 D e
Minnodunum . . . . 39 I j
Minoa, in Laconia . . . . 15 D c
Minoa, on Siphnus I. . . . . . .
Minoa, isl. . . . .
Minor (Minorca), isl. . . . . . . 38 C d
Minorca, bp. . . . . 94 C d
Minorca, isl. . . . . 82 C b
Minsk . . . . 138 C e
Minthe, mt. . . . . 14 B b
Minturnæ . . . . 30 C a
Minucian Portico . . . . 22 A
Minyæ, people . . . . 11 D d
Miquelon, isl. . . . . 212 J d
Mirabel, in France . . . . . . 69 D d
Mirabel, castle in Palestine . . 68 ins. A
Miraflores, in Panamá . . . . .
Miraflores, in Perú . . . . 214 B d
Miramichi Bay . . . . 212 I d
Miranda . . . . 214 D e
Miranda de Corvo . . . . 82 G e
Miranda do Douro . . . . 83 J g
Miranda de Ebro . . . . 82 B a
Mirande, in France . . . . 126 B e
Mirandola . . . . 90 J h
Miravet . . . . 82 C a
Mirbat . . . . 170 G g
Mirebeau . . . . 69 H g
Mirebeau, castle . . . . 76 D c
Mirepoix . . . . 76 D e
Mirepoix, bp. . . . . 94 C c
Mirepoix, seign. . . . . 76 D e
Mirim, lake . . . . 215 D f
Miriquidi, mts. . . . . 63 G c
Miró, District of . . . . . 196 B c (C. D.)
Miscus River . . . .
Misenum, harbor of . . . . 31 ins. A
Misenum, prom. . . . . 30 C b
Mishawum . . . . 189 ins. B
Misiones, dist. . . . . 215 D e
Miskolcz . . . . 159 K d
Miso River . . . . 27 H d
Misquamicut . . . . 189 ins. A
Missanabie River . . . .
Missema . . . . 6 E b
Missenden, mon. . . . . 97 Q j
Missinnippi River . . . . 186 I c
Mission Indian Reservation . . . 188 C d
Missionary Ridge, battle . . . . 208 C c
Mississippi, state . . . . 203 U d
Mississippi, ter. . . . . 202 H d
Mississippi River . . . . 191 G e
Mississippi River, Delta of the 187 J f
Mississippi Valley . . . . 187 J d
Missolonghi . . . . 164 C c
Missouri, state . . . . 203 F c
Missouri, ter. 1812 . . . . . . 203 Q a
Missouri, ter. 1819 . . . . . . 203 Q b
Missouri Plateau . . . . 186 I d
Missouri River . . . . 187 J d
Missouri River, Little . . . . . 198 E a
Missouria, Ind. Res. . . . . . . 188 G c
Missouris, tribe . . . . 188 G c
Missunde . . . . 158 E a
Mistassini, lake . . . . 212 H c
Mistra . . . . 89 B c
Mistra, desp. . . . . 93 B c
Mitau . . . . 88 J c
Mitchell, Fort . . . . 211 H d
Mitchell, mt. . . . . 187 K e
Mitchell, parl. bor. . . . . . . 163 I g
Mitchell River . . . . 172 D b
Mithradates VI., Kingdom of . 33 leg.
Mitla . . . . 213 C c
Mitrovitza, in Slavonia . . . . .
Mitrovitza, in Turkey . . . . . .
Mittelmark, dist. . . . . 85 C b
Mitys River . . . . 11 D b
Mizpah, N. of Jerusalem . . . . 7 C e
Mizpah, W. of Jerusalem . . . . 7 B e
Mizpah, mt. . . . .
Mizpah, Valley of . . . . 6 D a
Mizquiz . . . .
Mława . . . . 155 K b
Moab, dist. . . . . 7 D f
Moabites, people . . . . 7 ins. D
Moapa River, Ind. Res. . . . . 188 C c
Mobar, reg. . . . .
Mobile . . . . 191 H e
Mobile Bay . . . . 191 H e
Mocha . . . . 174 H c
Möckern, near Leipsic . . . . . 154 G c
Möckern, near Magdeburg . . . 154 G b
Möckmühl . . . . 143 H g
Mocsa . . . . 159 J e
Modbury, parl. bor. . . . . . .
Modder River . . . . 175 M l
Modena . . . . 90 J h
Modena, bp. . . . . 95 E c
Modena, duchy . . . . 90 C b
Modicia . . . . 26 D b
Modigliana . . . . 90 L i
Modin . . . . 7 C e
Modlin . . . . 155 K b
Modocs, tribe . . . . 188 B b
Modon . . . .
Modrush, bp. . . . .
Möen, isl. . . . . 115 G a
Mœnus (Main) River . . . . . . 38 D b
Mœris, lake . . . . 4 ins.
Mœsia, reg. . . . . 47 K e
Mœsia, Lower, imp. prov. . . 35 J e
Mœsia, Upper, imp. prov. . . 35 I e
Mœsia I, East Roman prov. 43 F e (2.)
Mœsia II, East Roman prov. 43 H e (5.)
Mogadisho . . . . 175 H d
Mogador . . . . 174 B a
Mogaung . . . .
Möggingen . . . . 142 D e
Moghan, plain . . . . 99 M f
Moghilev . . . .
Mogul Empire in 1700 . . . . 137 leg.
Mogontia or Mogontiacum (Mayence) . . . . 39 J i
Mohammed Artin, Dom. of . . 77 L e
Mohammed II., mosque . . . . 93 G e
Mohammedans . . . . 67 ins., leg.
Mohave, Mojave . . . . 210 B d
Mohave, Fort . . . . 188 D c
Mohaves, Mojaves, tribe . . . . 188 C d
Mohawk River . . . . 192 D b
Mohawks, tribe . . . . 188 L b
Mohegans, tribe . . . . 188 L b
Mohi . . . . 92 C c
Möhra . . . . 114 F c
Möhringen . . . . 143 H h
Mohrungen . . . . 155 J b
Moidart . . . .
Moissac, mon. . . . . 94 C c
Mola . . . . 90 F d
Moldau River . . . . 63 H d
Moldavia, dist. 19 cent. . . . . 164 D a
Moldavia, princ. 16 cent. . . . 119 J d
Moldavia, reg., 14 cent. . . . . 77 J c
Moldavia, reg., 18 cent. . . . . 131 I d
Mole River . . . . 75 I i
Molesme, mon. . . . . 94 C b
Molina . . . . 83 K g
Molina, barony . . . . 83 K g
Molino del Rey, battle . . . . . 201 H g
Molinos, R. . . . . 106 B b
Molise, dist. . . . . 90 E d
Mollendo . . . . 214 B d
Mollwitz . . . . 135 I c
Molodechno . . . . 153 N g
Molokai, isl. . . . . 198 ins. B
Molopo River . . . . 175 E g
Molossi, people . . . .
Molossis, dist. . . . . 10 B c
Moluccas, isl. . . . . 112 F d
Molycria . . . . 10 C d
Mombasa . . . . 175 H e
Momemphis . . . . 8 B b
Mömpelgard . . . . 143 ins. F
Mömpelgard, cty., see Montbéliard . . . . 86 F e
Mömpelgard, princ. cty. . . . . 143 ins. F
Mompos . . . . 214 B b
Mona (Anglesey), isl. . . . . . 51 N h
Mona, isl., West Indies . . . . 105 G c
Monaco . . . . 90 A c
Monaco, princ. . . . . 161 F f
Mona Passage, str. . . . . 213 F c
Monaghan, cty. . . . . 127 K g
Monapia (Isle of Man) . . . . . 51 N g
Monastir . . . . 164 C b
Moncalieri . . . . 130 P j
Monchique . . . . 83 J h
Monclova . . . . 213 B b
Moncontour . . . . 76 D c
Moncton . . . . 212 I d
Mondego River . . . . 82 G e
Mondoñedo . . . . 82 A a
Mondoñedo, bp. . . . . 94 A c
Mondovi . . . . 90 H h
Mandovi, bp. . . . . 95 D c
Mondsee, mon. . . . . 95 E b
Monemvasia . . . . 89 B c
Monflanquin . . . . 126 B d
Monforte, mon. . . . . 94 A c
Monghyr, Mongheer . . . . . . 137 E c
Mongolia, reg. . . . . 92 K c
Mongols, Khanate of the . . .
Mongols, people . . . .
Monhegan Island . . . . 189 D c
Monilia . . . . 26 D c
Monk-Bretton, mon. . . . . . . 97 P h
Monkey Hill, village 216
Monk Sherborne, mon. . . . . 100 A a
Monks Corner . . . . 195 B g
Monkton Farleigh, mon. . . . . 97 O j
Monmouth, in England . . . . .
Monmouth, cty. . . . . 127 W o
Monmouth, parl. bor. . . . . . 163 L f
Monmouth, parl. dist. . . . . . 163 K f
Monmouth, in New Jersey . . . 195 D c
Monnikendam . . . . 117 D b
Monocacy River . . . . 208 ins.
Monœcus (Monaco) . . . . 26 B d
Monongahela River . . . . . . 192 A d
Monopoli . . . . 90 F d
Monos, tribe . . . . 188 C c
Mon Plaisir, farm . . . .
Monreale, abp. . . . . 95 E d

Monroe, Fortress . . . . 208 E b
Monrovia . . . . 174 B d
Mons, in Hainaut . . . . 117 C d
Mons Brisiacus (Breisach) . . . 39 I i
Mons Casinus, see Monte Cassino
Monserrate, isl. . . . . 105 H c
Mons Ferrandus, castle . . . . 68 C c
Mons Gaudii, mt. . . . . 96 A
Mons Regalis, see Montreal, in Syria . . . . 68 C c
Montacute, parl. bor. . . . . .
Montafon Valley . . . . 91 R k
Montaigu . . . . 69 C c
Montaigu, seign. . . . . 69 C c
Montalcino, bp. . . . . . . 95 E c (Mo.)
Montana, ter. 1864 . . . . 203 P f
Montana, state . . . . 203 P f
Montaperto . . . . 90 L j
Montargis . . . . 69 I f
Montauban . . . . 76 D d
Montauban bp. . . . . 94 C c
Montauban, gen. . . . . 147 E c
Montbard . . . . 69 J f
Montbéliard . . . . 143 ins. F
Montbéliard, cty. . . . . 86 F e
Montbéliard, princ.-cty. . . . . 143 ins. F
Mont Blanc, mt. . . . . 2 E d
Montbrison . . . . 69 E d
Mont Cenis Pass . . . . 130 O i
Montcontour . . . . 118 D d
Mont-de-Marsan . . . . 148 D f
Montdidier . . . . 126 C b
Montebello . . . . 150 E d
Montebourg, mon. . . . . 94 B b
Montecarlo, near Pisa . . . . . 90 L j
Monte Cassino . . . . 64 B b
Monte Cassino, bp. . . . . 95 E c
Monte Cassino, mon. . . . . . . 95 E c
Montechiaro, near Asti . . . . . 130 Q j
Montechiaro, near Brescia . . . 90 J h
Montefeltro . . . . 64 B b
Monteleone . . . . 161 K h
Montélimart . . . . 126 D d
Monte Mario . . . . 96 A
Montemór, near Coimbra . . . . 82 A a
Montemór, near Evora . . . . . 83 J h
Montendre . . . . 126 A d
Montenegro, princ. . . . . 164 B b
Montenegro, reg. . . . . 93 A b
Montenotte . . . . 150 E d
Monte Nuovo, mt. . . . . 31 ins. A
Montepulciano . . . . 90 L j
Montereau . . . . 154 B d
Monterey, in California . . . . 198 A c
Monterey, in Mexico . . . . . . 201 E d
Monterey, in Pa. . . . . 208 ins.
Monte Rosa, mt. . . . . 2 E d
Monte Santo, town . . . . 214 F d
Montesha, reg. . . . . 77 J e
Montes Serrorum (Transylvanian Alps) . . . . 39 M k
Monte Testaccio . . . . 22 A
Montevideo . . . . 215 D f
Montfaucon, mon. . . . . 95 D b
Montferrat, marq. . . . . 90 B b
Montfort, in France . . . . . .
Montfort, in Syria . . . . 68 ins. A
Montfort, castle, in France . . . 69 H f
Montfort, castle, in Vorarlberg 78 F e
Montfort, cty., in France . . . . 76 D b
Montfort, cty., in Swabia . . . . 143 I j
Mont Genèvre Pass . . . . 130 O j
Montgomery, in Alabama . . . 211 H d
Montgomery, in Wales . . . . . 127 V n
Montgomery, castle . . . .
Montgomery, cty. . . . . 127 V n
Montgomery, parl. bor. . . . . . 163 K e
Montgomery, parl. dist. . . . . 163 K e
Montiel . . . . 83 K h
Montigny, mon. . . . . 148 C b
Montlaur . . . . 76 E d
Montlhéry . . . . 76 E b
Montlucon . . . . 69 I g
Montluel . . . . 130 N i
Montmartre, Faubourg, quarter in Paris . . . . 149 B
Montmartre, mt. . . . . 62 B d
Montmédy . . . . 126 D b
Montmirail, in Champagne . . . 154 B d
Montmirail, in Perche . . . . . 76 D b
Montmorency . . . . 69 I f (Montm.)
Montmorency, Falls of . . . . . 191 K b
Montpelier . . . . 211 K b
Montpellier . . . . 76 E e
Montpellier, gen. . . . . 147 E c
Montpellier, univ. . . . . 100 F f
Montpensier . . . . 76 E c
Montreal, in Canada . . . . . . 189 B b
Montreal, in Syria . . . . 68 C c
Montreuil . . . . 61 D a
Montreuillon . . . . 69 I g
Montriond . . . . 62 D e
Montrose . . . .
Mont-Saint-Guibert . . . . 156 B a
Mont-Saint-Jean, farm . . . . .
Mont-Saint-Jean, village . . . .
Mont-Saint-Michel, mon. . . . . 94 B b
Montserrat, isl. . . . . 213 F c
Montserrat, mon. . . . . 94 C c
Monza . . . . 90 I h
Mook . . . . 117 D c
Mooltan . . . . 137 B b
Moon, Gate of the, in Alexandria . . . . 34 ins. C
Moon, Temple of the, in Rome 24 B
Moore, Fort . . . . 193 ins. C
Moore, lake . . . . 172 A c
Moorfields, in London . . . 75 G g
Moorgate, in London . . . 75 G g
Moorish States, in Spain . . . 82 B a
Moors, people, in Spain . . . 57 C f
Moorshedabad . . . . 137 E d
Moose Factory . . . . 212 G c
Moose Jaw, post . . . . 212 E c
Moose River . . . . 212 G c
Mopsium . . . . 11 D c
Mopsuestia, Mopsuhestia . . . . 20 F d
Moquegua . . . . 214 B d
Moqui, Ind. Res. . . . . 188 D c
Moquis, tribe . . . . 188 D c
Mor . . . . 159 J e
Mora . . . . 88 F a
Moradabad . . . . 137 C c
Morat . . . . 91 P l
Morava River . . . . 119 I e
Moravia, march, about 1000 . . 59 H d
Moravia, march, 12 cent. . . . . 72 D b
Moravian Kingdom, 9 cent. . . 56 F c
Moravians, people, about 900 . 57 G d
Moray, bp. . . . . 97 I b
Moray, dist. . . . .
Moray Firth . . . . 49 E c
Morbegno . . . . 91 R l
Morbihan, dept. . . . . 148 D e
Mordvins, people . . . . 139 G e
Morea Peninsula . . . . 2 G e
Morecambe Bay . . . . 127 V m
Morelia . . . . 213 ins.
Morella . . . . 82 B a
Morelos, state . . . . 213 ins.
Moresby Island . . . . 172 E b
Moreton . . . . 172 D b
Moreton Bay . . . . 172 E c
Moreton Bay District . . . . . 172 leg.
Morgan, Fort . . . . 208 C c
Morgan, route of . . . . 195 A f
Morgantina . . . . 30 D e
Morgantown . . . . 206 ins.
Morgarten . . . . 91 Q k
Moriah, mt. . . . . 68 ins. B
Moril . . . . 91 Q l
Morimont, mon. . . . . 148 C b
Morini, see Thérouanne
Morini, people . . . . 38 C b
Moritz, Fort . . . . 214 F d
Mornington Island . . . . 172 C b
Morocco . . . . 174 C a
Morocco, reg., 14 cent. . . . . 77 C f
Morocco, state, 16 cent. . . . . 118 C g
Morocco, state, 20 cent. . . . . 174 C a
Morón . . . . 82 A b
Morontobara . . . . 19 K f
Morpeth, parl. bor. . . . . . . 163 M b
Morristown . . . . 195 D c
Mortagne . . . . 61 D b
Mortain . . . . 69 C b
Mortain, cty. . . . . 69 C b
Mortara . . . . 130 Q i
Mortemer . . . . 65 G f
Mortemer, mon. . . . . . . 94 C b (Mort.)
Mortes River . . . . 214 D d
Mortimers Cross . . . . 84 B c
Mosa (Meuse) River . . . . . . 38 D b
Mosbach . . . . 142 D b
Mosbach, Palatine, princ. . . . 87 H d
Moschi, people . . . . 35 M e
Moscow . . . . 138 E d
Moscow, princ. . . . . 77 L a
Moscow, gov. . . . . 131 K b
Mosella (Moselle) River . . . . 38 D c
Moselle, dept. . . . . 148 F e
Moselle River . . . . 62 D d
Moskva River . . . . 153 P f
Mosomagus . . . . 39 H i
Mosquito Coast . . . . 213 D c
Moss . . . . 131 F b
Mossámedes . . . . 175 E f
Mostar . . . . 93 A b
Mosul . . . . 67 O f
Mosul, Dominion of . . . . . . 67 O f
Mosyr . . . . 167 K e
Motola . . . . 90 F d
Motrone . . . . 90 L j
Mottisfont, priory . . . . 100 A a
Motupe . . . . 111 B c
Motyca . . . . 30 D e
Motye . . . . 30 B e
Moulins . . . . 76 E c
Moulins, gen. . . . . 147 E b
Moulmein . . . . 171 K g
Moultrie, Fort . . . . 195 B g
Mount Desert Island . . . . . . 189 D b
Mount Gambier, town . . . . . 172 C d
Mount Grace, mon. . . . . . . 97 P g
Mount Hope, town . . . . . . 189 ins. A
Mount Majella, mon. . . . . . . 95 E c
Mount of Offense . . . . 6 ins. A
Mount of Olives . . . . 6 ins. A
Mount Sinai, mon. of . . . . . . 150 B b
Mount Vernon, town . . . . . . 193 F b
Mount Wollaston, village . . . . 189 C c
Mount Zion, Street of . . . . . 68 ins. B
Moura . . . . 83 J h
Moureille, mon. . . . . 94 B b
Mouse River, see Souris River
Moutier-Ramey, mon. . . . 94 C b (M. R.)
Moutiers . . . . 130 O i
Mouzon . . . . 76 F b
Mouzon, mon. . . . . 95 D b
Moyobamba . . . . 214 B c
Moys . . . . 135 H c
Mozambique . . . . 175 H f
Mozambique, see Portuguese East Africa
Mozambique Channel . . . . . . 175 H g
Mozhaisk . . . . 138 E d
Mozufferpore . . . . 137 D c
Mpapwa . . . . 175 G e
Muchelney, mon. . . . . 97 O k
Much Wenloch, parl. bor. . . . 163 L e
Muckleshoot, Ind. Res. . . . . . 188 B a
Mudki . . . . 170 I e
Mugonian Gate . . . . 24 A
Mühlberg . . . . 115 G c
Mühldorf . . . . 79 H d
Mühlenbach . . . . 159 L f
Mühlhausen, in Thuringia . . . . 62 F c
Mühlhausen, in Thuringia, imp. cy. . . . . 79 G c
Mühlheim, on the Danube R. . . 143 G i
Muiden . . . . 117 D b
Muir Glacier . . . . 212 B c

Mukden . . . . 171 N d
Mukdishu . . . . 175 H d
Mula . . . . 82 B b
Mulde River . . . . 85 G e
Mülhausen, in Alsace, imp. cy. 78 E f
Mul-Java (Malacca), pen. . . . .
Mull, isl. . . . .
Multan . . . . 137 B b
Mulucha River . . . . 38 B e
Müncheberg . . . . 80 ins.
München, see Munich
Münchengrätz . . . . 159 H c
Müdnen . . . . 134 E c
Munderkingen . . . . 143 I i
Munich . . . . 72 C b
Munkacs . . . . 131 H d
Münsingen . . . . 143 I i
Munster, in Ireland, prov. . . .
Münster, in Alsace . . . . 126 E b
Münster, in Bp. of Basel . . . . 91 P k
Münster, in Westphalia . . . . . 62 D c
Münster, bp. . . . . 78 E c
Münster, Hanse. cy. . . . . . . 99 ins. B
Münsterberg . . . . 79 J c
Münsterberg, princ. . . . . . . 79 J c
Münster Thal, valley . . . . . 91 S l
Munychia, dist. . . . . 16 D c
Munychia Port . . . . 16 D c
Muota Tal, valley . . . . 150 E c
Mur River . . . . 63 I e
Muranum . . . . 31 F c
Murat, viscty. . . . . 69 E d
Murbach, ab. . . . . 78 E e
Murbach, mon. . . . . 95 D b
Murbogi, people . . . . 38 B d
Murchison River . . . . 172 A c
Murcia . . . . 82 B b
Murcia, bp. . . . . 94 B d
Murcia, Km. . . . . 83 K h
Muret . . . . 76 D e
Murfreesboro . . . . 208 C b
Murg River . . . . 142 B c
Murshidabad . . . . 137 E d
Muri, mon. . . . . 91 Q k
Murom . . . . 138 F d
Murr River . . . . 143 H d
Murray River . . . . 172 D d
Murrays, fam. . . . . 97 I c
Murrhardt . . . . 143 I h
Murrumbidgee River . . . . . . 172 D d
Mursa . . . . 42 F d
Murten . . . . 91 P l
Murus (Mur) River . . . . 38 E c
Murviedro . . . . 82 B b
Musarna . . . . 19 J d
Muscat . . . .
Musciacus, see Moissac
Muscle Shoals . . . . 196 B d
Muscovite Dominions, 16 cent. 119 K b
Muscovy, reg. . . . . 109 U b
Musgrave Range . . . . 172 C c
Musha Islands . . . . 174 H c
Mushki, people . . . . 5 C b
Muskingum River . . . . 196 ins. B
Muskingum, tribe . . . . 188 J c
Muspa, Punta de, cape . . . . . 191 I f
Mussidan . . . . 126 B d
Mussumba . . . . 175 F e
Musulami, people . . . . 38 D e
Mutapili . . . .
Muthul River . . . . 38 D e
Mutilum . . . . 27 G c
Mutina (Modena) . . . . 26 E c
Muttra . . . . 170 I f
Muwahhids, Dom of the . . . . 73 C d
Muzaffarpur . . . . 137 D c
Muzon, Cape . . . . 212 ins.
Mweru, lake . . . . 175 F e
Mycale, mt. . . . . 13 E c
Mycalessus . . . . 11 E d
Mycenæ . . . . 15 C b
Mycenean Greece . . . . 4 B b
Mygdonia, dist., in Macedonia 11 D b
Mygdonia, dist., in Mesopotamia 20 I d
Mykonos . . . . 13 D c
Mylæ, in Sicily . . . . 30 E d
Mylæ, in Thessaly . . . . 10 D c
Mylasa . . . . 17 E c
Myndus . . . . 17 E c
Mynyw (Saint Davids) . . . . . 60 D e
Myonia . . . . 11 D d
Myonnesus . . . . 20 B c
Myra . . . . 20 D d
Myrcinus . . . . 11 E b
Myriandrus . . . . 18 E c
Myrina . . . . 17 E b
Myrmex . . . . 34 ins. C
Myrrhinus . . . . 16 B b
Myrtea . . . . 9 D c
Myrto, isl. . . . . 15 E b
Myrtoum Sea . . . . 15 D b
Myrtuntium . . . . 14 B b
Myrtuntium, lake . . . . 10 B d
Mysia, Macedonian prov. . . . . 18 C c
Mysia, Rom. prov. . . . . 20 B c
Mysia, reg. . . . . 8 G e
Mysore . . . . 137 C f
Mysore, reg. . . . . 137 C f
Mystic . . . . 189 C d
Mystic River . . . . 189 ins. B
Mytilene . . . .
Mytilene, isl. . . . .
Myus . . . . 13 E c

Naarath . . . . 7 C e
Naarden . . . . 117 D b
Naas . . . . 127 K h
Naauw Poort . . . . 175 L m
Nab River . . . . 63 G d
Nabatæi, people . . . . 35 L h
Nabburg . . . . 63 G d
Nablus, see Neapolis . . . . . . 68 ins. A
Nachod . . . . 159 C c
Nacogdoches . . . . 191 G e
Naqjivan . . . . 99 M f
Nævian Gate . . . . 23 B
Näfels . . . . 91 R k
Nagasaki . . . . 171 N e
Nagold . . . . 143 G h
Nagold River . . . . 143 G h
Nagpur, Nagpore . . . . 137 C d
Nagpur, state . . . . 170 I f
Nagy-Kanizsa . . . . 159 I e
Nagy Sallo . . . . 159 J d
Nahe River . . . . 62 D d
Naimans, people . . . .
Nain, in Galilee . . . . 6 C c
Nain, in Labrador . . . . 212 I c
Nairi, people . . . .
Nairn, cty. . . . .
Naissus . . . . 39 M l
Nájera . . . . 82 B a
Nakel . . . . 63 I b
Namaqualand, Great, dist. . . . 175 E g
Namnetes, see Nantes
Namnetes, people . . . . 38 B c
Namnetum, isl. . . . . 38 B c
Namnetum, Portus (Nantes) . . 38 B c
Namoi River . . . . 172 D d
Namugum, see Namur
Namur . . . . 117 C d
Namur, cty. . . . . 117 C d
Nan-chan-fu . . . .
Nancy . . . . 84 G e
Nandurbar . . . .
Nangis . . . . 154 B d
Nanipacna . . . . 191 H e
Nanking . . . .
Nanrantsouck Mission . . . . . 189 D b
Nansemond River . . . . 193 ins. A
Nantasket . . . . 189 ins. B
Nantes . . . . 61 C c
Nantes, bp. . . . . 94 B b
Nantes, cty. . . . . 69 C c
Nantes, univ. . . . . 100 E e
Nanteuil, mon. . . . . 94 B b
Nanticoke River . . . . 192 D d
Nanticokes, tribe . . . . 188 K b
Nantuates, people . . . . 26 A a
Nantucket, isl. . . . . 189 D d
Nantwich . . . . 127 W m
Napata (Jebel Barkal) . . . . . 4 F e
Naphtali, Mountains of . . . . . 6 C c
Naphtali, tribe . . . . 7 ins. D
Napier . . . . 172 G e
Naples . . . . 90 E d
Naples, abp. . . . . 95 E c
Naples, Bay of . . . . 30 D b
Naples, km., 14 cent. . . . . . 81 I d
Naples, km., 16 cent. . . . . . 119 H e
Naples, km., 1812 . . . . 152 D e
Naples, theme . . . . 58 G e
Naples, univ. . . . . 100 H f
Napo River . . . . 111 B b
Napoca . . . . 35 I d
Napoleonshöhe, castle . . 154 E c (N.)
Nar River . . . . 27 H e
Naragarra . . . . 38 D e
Narbada River . . . . 137 C d
Narbata . . . . 6 B c
Narbo Martius (Narbonne) . . . 38 C d
Narbonensis, Rom. prov. . . 38 D d (6)
Narbonne . . . . 61 E e
Narbonne, abp. . . . . 94 C c
Narbonne, viscty. . . . . 76 E e
Narbonnensis I, West Rom. prov. . . . . 42 C e (13)
Narbonnensis II, West Rom. prov. . . . . 42 D e (14)
Narew River . . . . 87 M b
Narni . . . . 90 D c
Narnia . . . . 27 G e
Narona . . . . 38 F d
Narova River . . . . 88 L b
Narragansett Bay . . . . 189 ins. A
Narragansetts, tribe . . . . . . 189 ins. A
Narthacius, mt. . . . . 11 D c
Narva . . . . 88 M b
Narva, Hanse. cy. . . . . 99 I b
Narvaez, route of . . . . 191 I f
Naseby . . . . 127 Y n
Nashboro . . . . 194 B c
Nashua . . . . 211 K b
Nashville . . . . 199 H c
Nasium . . . . 39 H i
Nasos, quarter in Syracuse . . 31 ins. B
Nass River . . . . 212 ins.
Nassau, Bahama Is. . . . . . . 213 E b
Nassau, in Germany . . . . . . 72 B a
Nassau, cty. . . . . 78 F c
Nassau, duchy . . . . 154 E c
Nassau, princ. . . . . 122 E c
Nassau, Fort, in New York . . 192 E b
Nassau, Fort in Pa. . . . . . . 192 ins.
Natal . . . . 214 F c
Natal, col. . . . . 175 N l
Natchez . . . . 208 B c
Natchez, tribe . . . . 188 H d
Natchitoches . . . . 191 G e
Natick . . . . 189 C d
Natiso River . . . . 27 H b
Natuna, isl. . . . .
Naucratis . . . . 4 ins.
Nauen . . . . 85 C b
Naugard . . . . 155 H b
Naulinco . . . . 106 C a
Naulochus . . . . 30 E d
Naumachia of Augustus . . . . 22 A
Naumburg . . . . 63 F c
Naumburg, bp. . . . . 95 E a
Naumkeag . . . . 189 ins. B
Naupactus . . . . 10 C d
Nauplia . . . . 15 C b
Nauportus . . . . 27 I b
Nautaca . . . . 19 K c
Nauvoo . . . . 211 G b
Nava River . . . . 39 I i
Navajo, Ind. Res. . . . . 188 E c
Navajos, tribe . . . . 188 E c
Navalia (shipyards in Rome) . 22 A
Navalia River . . . . 39 I g
Navari, people . . . . 35 J d

Navarre, dist. . . . . 56 B d
Navarre, km. . . . . 82 H e
Navarre and Béarn, km. . . . . 126 A e
Navarrete . . . . 83 K g
Navas de Tolosa, Las . . . . . 83 K h
Navidad . . . . 105 F c
Navigator Islands . . . . 180 K i
Nawsett . . . . 189 D d
Naxos . . . . 13 D c
Naxos, duchy . . . . 89 C c
Naxos, isl. . . . . 13 D c
Naxua . . . . 99 M f
Naxus . . . .
Nay . . . . 126 A e
Nazareth, in Palestine . . . . . 6 C c
Nazareth, abp. in Italy . . . . . 95 F c
Nazas, Rio de, R. . . . . 213 B b
Nazianzus . . . . 20 F c
Nazli . . . . 165 F d
Neæ, isl. . . . .
Neæthus (Neto) River . . . . . 31 F c
Neagh, lough, lake . . . . 49 C d
Neapel, see Naples
Neapolis, in Africa . . . . 38 E e
Neapolis, in Apulia . . . . 31 G a
Neapolis, in Campania (Naples) 30 D b
Neapolis, in Chalcidice . . . . . 11 E b
Neapolis, in Istria . . . . 27 H b
Neapolis, in Macedonia . . . . 11 F b
Neapolis, in Palestine . . . . . 7 C d
Neapolis, in Sardinia . . . . . 38 D e
Neapolis, quarter in Syracuse . 31 ins. B
Nearchus, route of . . . . 19 H e
Neath, mon. . . . . 97 N j
Nebbio . . . . 148 C c
Nebelhöhle . . . . 143 H i
Nebo, mt. . . . . 7 D e
Nebouzan, reg. . . . . 146 B f
Nebraska City . . . . 206 F b
Nebraska, state . . . . 203 R g
Nebraska, ter. 1854 . . . . . . 202 C f
Nebraska, ter. 1861 . . . . . . 203 Q g
Nebraska, ter. 1863 . . . . . . 203 R g
Nebrodes Mountains . . . . . . 30 D e
Necessity, Fort . . . . 192 B d
Neckar River . . . . 62 E d
Neckar-Bischofsheim . . . . . . 142 C b
Neckargemünd . . . . 142 C b
Neckarsulm . . . . 143 H g
Necropolis, dist. . . . . 16 D c
Nectansmere . . . .
Neda River . . . . 14 B b
Nedad River . . . . 50 G c
Nedjed, reg. . . . .
Nedjef . . . .
Nedon River . . . . 14 C b
Neerwinden . . . . 122 C c
Neetum . . . . 30 E e
Negapatam . . . . 137 D f
Nègrepelisse . . . . 126 B d
Negro, Cabo, cape . . . . 108 R i
Negropont, isl. . . . . 89 H g
Negros, isl. . . . . 199 ins. H
Neidenburg . . . . 115 K b
Neïus, mt. . . . . 10 B d
Neipperg . . . . 143 H g
Neisse . . . . 115 I c
Neisse River, Glatzer . . . . . 63 I c
Neisse River, Görlitzer . . . . . 63 H c
Neiva . . . . 214 B b
Nelea . . . . 11 E c
Neleus River . . . . 11 E d
Nellenburg, castle . . . . 142 C e
Nellenburg, landgr. . . . . . . 142 C e
Nellore . . . . 137 D f
Nelson, in Alberta . . . . 212 D d
Nelson, in New Zealand . . . . 172 G e
Nelson, Fort . . . . 212 C c
Nelson River . . . . 186 J c
Nemara . . . . 6 F c
Nemausus (Nîmes) . . . . 38 C d
Nemea . . . . 15 C b
Nemetacus, see Arras
Nemetes, see Spires
Nemetes, people . . . . 39 I i
Nemorensis, lake . . . . 35 ins. B
Nemossus . . . . 38 C c
Nemours . . . . 69 I f
Nemours, duchy . . . . 84 E e
Nen River . . . . 127 Y n
Neocæsarea . . . . 20 G b
Neosho River . . . . 198 F c
Nepal, Nepaul, state . . . . . . 171 J f
Nepete . . . . 27 G e
Nepi, bp. . . . . 95 E c
Nepomuk, mon. . . . . 95 E b
Neponset River . . . . 189 ins. B
Nepos, Dom. of emperor . . . . 50 G d
Neptune, Basilica of . . . . . . 22 A
Neptune, Mts. of . . . . 30 E d
Neptune, Temple of . . . . . . 34 ins. C (8)
Neptunia, Colonia (Taranto) . . 31 G b
Nequinum . . . . 27 G e
Nérac . . . . 126 B d
Nerbudda River . . . . 137 C d
Neresheim . . . . 143 J h
Neresheim, ab. . . . . 143 J h
Neretum . . . . 31 G b
Neris . . . . 14 C b
Nēritus, mt. . . . . 10 B d
Nerium, prom. . . . . 38 A d
Nero, Aqueduct of . . . . 22 A
Nero, Baths of . . . . 22 A
Nero, Circus of . . . . 22 A
Nero, Colossus of . . . . 24 B
Nero, Villa of . . . . 22 A
Neronian Meadows . . . . 96 A
Nerós house, in Olympia . . . .
Nertchinsk . . . .
Nertobriga . . . . 38 B d
Nerulum . . . . 31 F c
Nerva, Forum of . . . . 24 B
Nervii, people . . . . 38 C b
Nesactium . . . . 27 H c
Nesis, isl. . . . . 31 ins. A
Nesle . . . . 69 I f
Ness, loch, lake . . . . 49 D c
Nesselwang . . . . 114 F e
Nessonis, lake . . . . 11 D c
Nestorians, sect . . . . 67 X m
Nestus River . . . . 11 F b
Netherlands, Austrian, prov. . . 134 B c
Netherlands, Kingdom of the . 158 C c
Netherlands, Spanish, prov. . . 122 B c
Netherlands, The, reg. 117
Netherlands, United, country . 122 C b
Netley, ab. . . . . 100 A b
Netolitz . . . . 63 G d
Netze District . . . . 135 I b
Netze River . . . . 63 I b
Neu-Brandenburg . . . . 123 G b
Neubreisach . . . . 154 D e
Neuburg . . . . 62 F d
Neuburg, palat. . . . . 122 F d
Neuburg, princ. . . . . 134 F d
Neuchâtel . . . . 91 O l
Neuchâtel, dist. . . . . 91 O l
Neuchâtel, lake . . . . 91 O l
Neuchâtel, princ. . . . . 151 K j
Neudenau . . . . 142 D b
Neuenburg, in Baden . . . . . . 142 A e
Neuenburg, in Switzerland . . . 91 O l
Neuenburg, (Neuchâtel) princ. . 134 D e
Neuenstadt . . . . 143 H g
Neuenstein . . . . 143 I g
Neufchâteau . . . . 117 D e
Neuffen . . . . 143 H h
Neufra . . . . 143 H i
Neuhaldensleben . . . . 122 F b
Neuhaus . . . . 154 F b
Neuhäusel . . . . 131 G d
Neukamp . . . . 123 G a
Neumark, dist. . . . . 85 D b
Neumarkt, in Bavaria . . . . . . 154 F d
Neumarkt, in Galicia . . . . . . 135 K d
Neumarkt, in Styria . . . . . . 135 H e
Neumünster . . . . 72 B a
Neuquen . . . . 215 C f
Neu-Ravensburg . . . . 143 I j
Neu-Ruppin . . . . 158 G b
Neu-Sandec . . . . 159 K d
Neusatz . . . . 159 J f
Neuse River . . . . 193 F d
Neusohl . . . . 159 J d
Neuss . . . . 62 D c
Neuss, Hanse. cy. . . . . 99 ins. B
Neustadt, in the Black Forest . 142 B e
Neustadt, on the Hardt . . . . 142 B b
Neustadt, in Moravia . . . . . . 135 I d
Neustadt, on the Orla . . . . . 114 F c
Neustadtl . . . . 123 H f
Neu-Stettin . . . . 123 I b
Neu-Strelitz . . . . 123 G b
Neustria, reg. . . . . 54 E d
Neutra . . . . 72 D b
Neutra, bp. . . . . 95 F b
Neutra River . . . . 159 J d
Neuzelle, mon. . . . . 80 ins.
Neva, lake . . . . 71 M a
Nevada, state . . . . 203 O h
Nevada, ter. . . . . 203 O g
Nevada, Sierra, mts. . . . . . . 187 H e
Nevado de Tolima, mt. . . . . . 214 B b
Neve . . . . 6 E c
Nevers . . . . 61 E c
Nevers, bp. . . . . 94 C b
Nevers, cty. . . . . 61 E c
Nevilles Cross . . . .
Nevirnum, see Nevers
Nevis, isl. . . . . 213 F c
New Albany . . . . 211 H c
New Abbey of Saint Mary of Grace Cisterciana . . . . . . 75 G g
New Amstel . . . . 192 ins.
New Amsterdam, in Dutch Guiana . . . . 214 D b
New Amsterdam (New York) . 189 ins. C
New Amsterdam Island . . . . . 182 II k
New Andalusia, reg. . . . . . . 105 E e
Newark, in England . . . . . . 74 E e
Newark, parl. bor. . . . . 163 N d
Newark, in New Jersey . . . . 192 D c
New Athens . . . . 23 D
New Aurelian Gate . . . . 22 A
New Bedford . . . . 211 K b
New Berne, Newbern . . . . .
New Biscay, prov. . . . . 190 D f
Newborough, parl. bor. . . . .
New Breisach . . . . 134 D e
New Brunswick, in New Jersey 192 D c
New Brunswick, col. . . . . . . 212 I d
Newburgh, in New York . . . . 195 D c
Newburgh, mon. in England . . 97 P g
Newburn . . . . 127 X k
Newbury, in England . . . . . 127 X o
Newbury, parl. bor. . . .
Newbury, in Mass. . . . . 189 C c
New Caledonia, isl. . . . . . . 172 F c
New Caledonia, reg. . . . . . . 212 C c
New Carthage (Cartagena) . . . 38 B e
New Castle, (Newcastle), in Delaware . . . . 192 D d
Newcastle, New South Wales . 172 E d
Newcastle-on-Tyne . . . . 65 F c
Newcastle, parl. bor. . . . . . 163 M b
Newcastle-under-Lyme, parl. bor. . . . . 163 L d
New Castile, km., in Spain . . 83 K h
New Castile (Peru), reg. . . .
New Claudian Way . . . . 27 H e
New East Prussia, dist. . . . . 138 B e
New Elfsborg, Fort . . . . 192 ins.
New England Colonies, The . . 189
New England Confederation, see . . . . 189 leg.
New England Range . . . . . . 172 E d
Newenham, mon. in Bedford . 97 Q i
Newenham, mon. in Devon . . 97 N k
New Estremadura (Chile), reg. 108 J k
New Estremadura, prov. in Mexico . . . . 190 E f
New Forest, The . . . . 49 F f

Newfoundland, col. . . . . 212 I c
New France, reg. . . . . . 191 I c K b
New Galicia, prov. . . . .
Newgate, loc. in London . . . . 75 G g
New Gothenburg, Fort . . . . . 192 ins.
New Granada, reg. . . . . 108 J g
New Granada, viceroyalty . . 215 ins.
New Guinea, isl. . . . . 110 F F h
New Hampshire, col. . . . . . 189 C c
New Hampshire, state . . . . . 199 K b
New Harmony . . . . 206 ins.
New Haven, in Conn. . . . . . 189 B d
Newhaven, in England . . . . . 185 G g
New Haven, col. . . . . 189 B d
New Hebrides, isl. . . . . 172 F b
New Inverness . . . . 193 ins. C
New Jersey, col. . . . . 192 D c
New Jersey, East, col. . . . . 192 D c
New Jersey, West, col. . . . . 192 D d
New Jersey, state . . . . 199 K c
New Korsholm, Fort . . . . . . 192 ins.
New León, prov. . . . . 190 E f
New London . . . . 189 B d
New Madrid . . . . 208 C b
Newmarket . . . . 127 Z n
New Mecklenburg, isl. . . . . 179 G h
New Mexico, prov. . . . . 190 D e
New Mexico, ter. 1850 . . . . . 202 C h
New Mexico, ter. 1863 . . . . . 203 Q h
Newminster, mon. . . . . 97 P f
New Netherland, col. . . . . . 192 D c
New Norcia . . . . 172 A d
New Norfolk . . . . 172 D e
New Orleans . . . . 191 G f
New Park, dist. . . . . 210 D b
New Philippines, prov. . . . . . 190 F e
New Plymouth, col. . . . . . . 189 C d
New Plymouth, in New Zealand 172 G d
New Pomerania, isl. . . . . . . 172 E a
Newport, parl. bor. in Cornwall 163 J g
Newport, in I. of Wight . . . 127 X p
Newport, parl. bor., I. of Wight 163 M g
Newport, in Rhode Island . . . 189 ins. A
Newport News . . . . 193 ins. A
New Providence . . . . 213 E b
New Romney, parl. bor. . . . . 163 P g
Newry . . . . 127 K g
New Santander, prov. . . . . . 190 F f
New Seraglio, loc. in Constantinople . . . . 93 G e
New Seraglio, Wall of the . . 93 G e
Newsham, mon. . . . . 97 Q h
New Shops, loc. in Rome . . .
New Shoreham, parl. bor. . . . 163 N g
New Shoreham, parl. dist. . . 163 N g
New Silesia, dist. . . . . 135 J c
New Siberia Islands . . . . . . 171 O a
New Spain, viceroyalty . . . . . 213 leg.
New South Wales, col. . . . . 172 leg.
New South Wales, state . . . 172 D d
Newstead, mon. . . . . 97 P h
New Sweden, col. . . . . 192 ins.
New Toggenburg, castle . . . . 91 R k
Newton, parl. bor. . . . . 163 L d
Newton Abbot . . . . 127 V p
Newtown, in Conn. . . . . 189 B d
Newtown, in Mass. . . . . 189 ins. B
Newtown, in New York . . . . 195 C b
Newtown, in Wales . . . . . . 162 C e
Newtown, parl. bor., I. of Wight 163 M g
New Utrecht . . . . 189 ins. C
New Wasa, Fort . . . . 192 ins.
New White Russia, reg. . . . . 138 C d
New Windsor, in Maryland . . 208 ins.
New Windsor, parl. bor. in England . . . . 163 N f
New Woodstock, parl. bor. . . 163 M f (New. Wood.)
New York . . . . 189 ins. C
New York, col. . . . . 192 D b
New York, state . . . . 199 J b
New York Bay . . . . 189 ins. C
New Zealand, col. . . . .
Nez Percés, tribe . . . . 188 C a
Ngan-hwei, prov. . . . . 171 M e
Nganking . . . .
Niagara, Fort . . . . 192 B b
Niagara Falls . . . . 192 B b
Niagara River . . . . 200 D b
Nicæa, in Bithynia . . . . 20 C b
Nicæa, in India . . . . 19 L d
Nicæa (Nice), in Liguria . . . 26 B d
Nicæa, in Locris . . . . 16 F e
Nicæa, Empire of . . . . 73 G c
Nicaragua, lake . . . . 105 C d
Nicaragua, country . . . . 213 D c
Nicaragua, reg. . . . . 105 C d
Nice . . . . 61 G e
Nice, bp. . . . . 95 D c
Nicephorium . . . . 20 H e
Nicer (Neckar) River . . . . . . 39 J i
Nicholson, Fort . . . . 192 E b
Nickajacks, tribe . . . . 188 I d
Nicobar Islands . . . .
Nicomedia . . . . 20 C b
Nicopolis, in Epirus . . . . . . 10 B c
Nicopolis, in Mœsia . . . . . . 39 N l
Nicopolis, in Palestine . . . . . 7 B e
Nicopolis, in Pontus . . . . . . 20 H b
Nicopolis, on the Danube . . .
Nicopolis, theme . . . . 59 I f
Nicosia . . . . 68 B b
Nicotera . . . . 30 E d
Nicoya . . . . 213 D c
Nicoya, Gulf of . . . . 105 D e
Nictheroy . . . . 215 E e
Nida . . . . 39 J h
Nidum (Neath) . . . .
Niebla . . . . 82 A b
Nieder Schopfheim . . . . 142 A d
Niederstetten . . . . 143 I g
Niemîtsch . . . . 63 H c
Niemen River . . . . 138 B e
Nienburg, on the Saale . . . . 63 F c
Nienburg, on the Weser . . . . 134 E b
Nienburg, mon. . . . . 95 E a
Nieuport . . . . 117 A c
Nieuwstad . . . . 117 D c
Nièvre, dept. . . . . 148 E e
Niezhin . . . . 167 L e
Niger River . . . . 174 D c
Nigeria, col. . . . . 174 D d
Nigritia, reg. . . . . 108 Q f
Niigata . . . . 171 O e
Niihau, isl. . . . . 198 ins. B
Nijne Kolimsk
Nijni Novgorod . . . . 138 F d
Nike, Temple of . . . . 23 C (7)
Niklashausen . . . . 86 G d
Nikolaiev . . . . 139 D f
Nikolaievsk . . . . 171 O c
Nikolaistad . . . . 138 B c
Nikolsburg . . . . 159 I d
Nikolskaya . . . . 171 O d
Nikopol . . . .
Nile, Delta of the . . . . 4 ins.
Nile River . . . . 174 G b
Nile River, Blue . . . . 174 G c
Nile River, White . . . . 174 G c
Nil-Saint-Vincent . . . . 156 B a
Nimbschen, mon. . . . . 80 ins.
Nimburg . . . . 63 H c
Nimeguen, see Nimwegen
Nimes . . . . 76 F e
Nimes, bp. . . . . 94 C c
Nimptsch . . . . 63 I c
Nimwegen . . . . 117 D c
Nimwegen, Hanse. cy. . . . . . 99 ins. B
Ninety Six . . . . 195 A f
Nineveh . . . . 4 G c
Ning-hia . . . .
Ning-ho . . . . 170 ins. A
Ning-po . . . . 171 N f
Ningus River . . . . 27 H b
Ninus . . . . 20 J d
Niobrara, Ind. Res. . . . . . . 188 G b
Niobrara River . . . . 198 E b
Niort . . . . 69 C c
Nipigon, Fort . . . . 191 H b
Nipigon, lake . . . . 191 H a
Nipissing, lake . . . . 191 I b
Nippon (Japan), empire . . . . .
Nippur (Niffer) . . . . 4 G c
Nisæa . . . . 15 D b
Nisæa, dist. . . . . 18 R h
Nisæan Plain . . . . 19 G c
Nish . . . . 93 B b
Nishapur . . . .
Nisibin . . . .
Nisibis . . . . 5 D b
Nisqually, Fort . . . . 210 A a
Nisqually, Ind. Res. . . . . . . 188 B a
Nissa (Nish) . . . . 59 I e
Nisyrus, isl. . . . . 17 E c
Nithsdale, dist. . . . .
Nitiobroges, people . . . . 38 C d
Niuche, people . . . . 103 M c
Niu-chwang . . . . 171 N d
Niumaga, see Nimwegen
Nivelles . . . . 117 C d
Nivelles, mon. . . . . 94 C a
Nivernais, gouv. . . . . 146 B b
Nivernais, prov. . . . . 148 E e
Nivernis, see Nevers
Nizam, Dom. of the . . . . . . 137 C e
Nizib . . . . 164 F c
Nizza, see Nice
Nizza della Paglia . . . . 130 Q j
Noas Island 216
Noce River . . . . 91 S l
Nocera . . . . 90 E d
Nocera, bp. in Campania . . . 95 ins.
Nocera, bp. in Umbria . . . . . 95 E c
Nogaians, people . . . . 139 E f
Nogales . . . . 213 A a
Nogays, people . . . . 77 L c
Nogent . . . . 69 I f
Nogent-le-Rotrou . . . . 69 H f
Noirmoutier, isl. . . . . 69 B c
Noisy, Allée de, in Versailles . 149 A
Nola . . . . 30 D b
Nola, bp. . . . . 95 ins.
Noli, bp. . . . . 95 D c
Nollendorf . . . . 155 H c
Nombre de Dios . . . . 105 E e
Nome . . . . 198 ins. A
Nomentan Gate . . . . 22 A
Nomentan Way, road . . . . . . 35 ins. B
Nomentum . . . . 27 G e
Nomia, mt. . . . . 14 B b
Nona, bp. . . . . 95 F c
Nonacris . . . . 14 C a
Nonantola . . . . 64 B b
Nonantola, mon. . . . . 95 E c
Nonnenweier . . . . 142 A d
Nonsuch, castle . . . . 75 I i
Nora, in Cappadocia . . . . . . 18 O h
Nora, in Sardinia . . . . 38 D e
Norba . . . . 35 ins. B
Norba Cæsarea . . . . 38 A e
Norbona, see Narbo Martius (Narbonne)
Narcia, New . . . . 172 A d
Nord, dept . . . . 148 E d
Nordalbingia, dist. . . . . 55 Q i
Norddeutscher Bund, see North German Federation
Norden . . . . 62 D b
Nordgau, dist. . . . . 55 R j
Nordgau, margr. . . . . 63 F d
Nordhausen . . . . 62 F c
Nordhausen, imp. cy. . . . . . . 79 G c
Nordheim, mon. . . . . 95 E a
Nördlingen . . . . 62 F d
Nördlingen, imp. cy. . . . . . . 79 G d
Nordmark, march . . . . 63 G b
Noreia . . . . 38 E c
Norfolk, in Virginia . . . . . . 193 ins. A
Norfolk, cty. in England . . . .
Norfolk, shire . . . .
Norfolk Island . . . . 172 F c
Norfolk, New . . . . 172 D e

Norham
Noricum, Rom. prov. 38 E c
Noricum mediterraneum, West Rom. prov. 42 E d (12)
Noricum ripense, West Rom. prov. 42 E d (13)
Norman, Fort 212 C b
Norman Principalities 66 I f
Normandy, duchy 61 D b
Normandy, gouv. 146 A b
Normandy, prox. 148 D e
Normanton 172 D b
Normans, people, in England 45 D b
Normans, people, in France 45 D c
Normans, people, in Italy 45 H e
Norridgewock 189 C b
Norrköping 131 G b
Northallerton 65 F c
North Allerton, parl. bor.
Northam, in N. Hampshire 189 C c
Northam, in W. Australia 172 A d
North America, continent, 186 187
Northampton, in England
Northampton, cty.
Northampton, mon. 97 Q i
Northampton, parl. bor. 163 N e
Nordhamptan, shire
Northampton, in Mass. 189 B c
North Australia, reg.
North Borneo, col. 171 M h
North Cape, in Europe 2 G a
North Cape, in New Zealand 172 G d
North Channel. 49 C d
North Carolina, col. 193 E d
North Carolina, state 199 I c
North Castle 195 E c
North Chester, parl. dist. 163 L d
North Dakota, state 203 R f
North Derby, parl. dist. 163 M d
North Devon, isl. 186 K a
North Devon, parl. dist. 163 J g
Nord Downs, dist. 49 G f
North Durham, parl. dist. 163 M c
Northeim 62 E c
Northern Californians, tribes 188 B b
Northern Cheyenne, Ind. Res. 188 E a
Northern District, Queensland 172 leg.
Northern Dwina River 3 I b
Northern Ghats, mts. 112 A a
Northern Pacific Grant 210 D a
Northern Plain, The 186 J c
Northern Territory, S. Australia 172 C b
North Essex, parl. dist. 163 O f
Northfield 189 B c
Northfleet 75 J i
North Folk (Angles), people 51 S k
North Fort, Sevastopol 164 L g
North Gate, in Olympia
North German Federation 161 D c
North Hants, parl. dist. 163 M f
North Humbrians, people
North Isles (Hebrides)
North Island, New Zealand 172 G d
North Lancaster, parl. dist. 163 L c
North Leicester, parl. dist. 163 M e
North March, dist. 58 G c
Northmen, people, in Scandinavia 45 F a
Northmen, people, in Russia 45 K b
North Northampton, parl. dist. 163 N e
North Northumberland, parl. dist. 163 L b
North Nottingham, parl. dist. 163 M d
North Platte River 190 E c
North Point, in Maryland 200 L h
North Potomac River 192 B d
North Riding, parl. dist. 163 M c
North (Hudson) River 189 B d
North Salop, parl. bor. 163 L e
North Saskatchewan River 186 H c
North Sea 2 E c
North Somerset, isl. 212 F a
North Sporades, isl.
North Stafford, parl. dist. 163 L e
Northumberland, cty., in England
Northumberland County, in Virginia 193 F b (N.)
Northumberland, shire
Northumbria, km.
Northumbria, Danish, reg.
Northumbria, English, km.
North Wales, town in Pa. 192 D c
North Wales, dist.
North Warwick, parl. dist. 163 M e
North West Cape, Australia 172 A c
North West Territories, Canada
Northwest Territory, in U. S., 1787 196 B b
Northwest Territory, in U. S., 1800—1802 196 C b
Northwich 162 D d
North Wilts, parl. dist. 163 L f
Norton, mon. 97 O h
Norton Folgate 75 G g
Norton Sound 186 C b
Norwalk 189 B d
Norway, km., about 1000 58 F a
Norway, km. 1910 166 G d—I b
Norwegians, people 46 H a
Norwich, in Conn. 189 B d (Nor.)
Norwich, in England 84 D c
Norwich, bp. 97 S i
Norwich, castle 65 G d
Norwich, Hanse. for. cy. 98 ins. A
Norwich, parl. bor. 163 P e
Nossen 85 G e
Nossi Bé, isl.
Nostell, mon. 97 P h
Noteborg 119 K b
Notium 17 E c
Notium, prom. 38 A b
Notre Dame, church, Paris 149 B
Notre Dame, bridge, Paris 149 B
Notre Dame, church, Versailles 149 A
Notre Dame Bay 212 J c
Notre-Dame-de-la-Grasse, mon. 94 C c
Nottingham
Nottingham, castle 65 F d
Nottingham, cty.
Nottingham, parl. bor. 163 M e
Nottingham, shire
Nottoway River 193 F c
Noumea 172 F c
Nouvion, le 117 B e
Nova Coimbra 214 D d
Novæ 39 N l
Novæsium 39 I h
Nova Friburgo 215 E e
Novantæ, people 38 B a
Novara 90 I h
Novara, bp. 95 D b
Novaria 26 C b
Novas, Ad, on the Clanis R. 27 F d
Novas, Ad, on L. Sabatinus 35 ins. B
Nova Scotia, prov. 212 I d
Nova Scotia Peninsula 186 M d
Novaya Zemlya (Nova Zembla) islands 170 G a
Novempopulana 42 B e (12)
Novgorod 57 J b
Novgorod, gov. 131 J b
Novgorod, Hanse. for. off. 99 J b
Novgorod, reg. 138 D d
Novgorod, rep. 92 D b
Novgorod, ter. 71 N a
Novgorod Seiversk 77 K b
Novi, in Bosnia
Novi, in Italy 90 I h
Novi Bazar 119 I e
Noviodunum, in Aquitania 38 C c
Noviodunum, in Lugdunensis 38 B c
Noviodunum, in Mœsia 39 N k
Noviodunum, in Pannonia
Noviomagus, see Lisieux
Noviomagus (Neufchâteau), on the Meuse 39 H i
Noviomagus (Neumagen), near the Moselle 39 I i
Noviomagus (Nimwegen), on the Waal 39 H h
Noviomagus, see Noyon
Noviomagus (Spires), on the Rhine 39 J i
Noviomum, see Noyon
Novo-Georgievsk 155 K b
Novogrudek 119 J c
Novo-Tscherkask
Novum Castrum 29 D c
Noyers 126 D c
Noyon 61 E b
Noyon, bp. 94 C b
Noyon, cty. 61 E b
Nubia, reg. 174 G c
Nubian Desert 3 H f
Nuceria Alfaterna 30 D b
Nuceria Camellaria 27 G d
Nudionnum, see Sées
Nueces River 190 F f
Nuevitas 213 E b
Nuevo León, state 213 B b
Numana 27 H d
Numantia 38 B d
Numicus River 35 ins. B
Numidia, reg. 38 D e
Numidia, Rom. prov. 34 F f
Numidia, West Rom. prov. 42 D f (2)
Numistro 30 E b
Nun, Cape 174 B b
Nunivak, isl. 198 ins. A
Nur 159 L b
Nure River 26 D c
Nuremberg 62 F d
Nuremberg, burgraviate 79 G d
Nuremberg, imp. cy. 79 G d
Nursia 27 H e
Nürtingen 143 H h
Nusco, bp. 95 F c
Nussbaum 142 C c
Nutmeg Islands
Nyasa, lake 175 G f
Nyasaland, col. 175 G f
Nykerk 117 D b
Nyköping 131 G b
Nymphæum, loc. in Rome 22 A
Nymphæum, prom. 11 F b
Nymphenburg, castle 134 F d
Nysa 17 F c
Nyssa 20 F c
Nystad 138 B c

Oahu, isl. 198 ins. B
Oajaca 213 C c
Oajaca, state 213 C c
Oakala 198 ins. B
Oak forest, near Mizpah 7 B e
Oakland 210 A c
Oaracta, isl. 19 I e
Oatlands, castle 75 I i
Oaxas
Oaxes River 14 ins.
Obdorsk 170 H b
O Becse 159 K f
Obeid, El 174 F c
Oberalp Pass 91 Q l
Ober-Ehnheim 122 D d
Oberlahnstein 78 E c
Oberlin 206 ins.
Oberndorf 143 G i
Oberried, mon. 142 A e
Oberried, provostry 142 A e
Ober-Sontheim 143 I g
Oberstenfeld 143 H g
Obi, Gulf of 138 L b
Obi River
Obilinnum 26 A b
Obispo
Obok 174 H c
O'Brennans, The, fam.
O'Briens, The, fam.
Observatory Inlet 212 ins.
Ocaña, in Colombia 214 B b
Ocaña, in Spain 82 H f

Oceanus Britannicus (English Channel) . . . 51 O i
Oceanus Germanicus (North Sea) . . . 51 Q g
Oceanus Hibernicus (Irish Sea) 51 N h
Ocelum . . . 26 B b
Ocha, mt. . . . 15 E a
Ochrida . . .
Ochsenfurt . . . 62 F d
Ochsenfurt, mon. . . . 95 E b
Ochsenhausen, ab. . . . 143 I i
Ochus River . . . 19 J c
Ockley . . .
Ocklockonee River . . . 193 B f
Ocmulgee River . . . 193 C e
Oconee River . . . 193 C e
O'Connels, The, fam. . . .
O'Connors, The, fam. . . .
Ocra, mt. . . . 27 I b
Ocriculum . . . 27 G e
Octavia, Portico of . . . 24 B
Octovius, Portico of . . . 22 A
Octodurus . . . 26 B a
Octagesa . . . 38 C d
Octogon, in Olympia . . .
Ocumare . . . 214 C a
O'Dempseys, The, fam. . . .
Ödenburg (Sopron) . . . 63 I e
Odenheim, mon. . . . 142 C b
Odenheim, princ. . . . 142 C b
Odense . . . 154 F a
Odéon, bldg. in Paris . . . 149 B
Oderberg . . . 115 J d
Oder River . . . 63 H b
Odessa . . . 139 D f
Odessus . . . 39 N l
Odeum vetustissimum, bldg. in Athens . . . 23 D
Odeypore . . . 137 B d
Odiham, parl. bor. . . .
Odoacer, Kingdom of . . . 50 F d
Odomanti, people . . . 11 E a
O'Donnells, The, fam. . . .
O'Donoghues, The, fam. . . .
O'Doughertys, The, fam. . . .
Odrysæ, people . . . 39 N l
O'Dwyers, The, fam. . . .
Oea . . . 34 G g
Oeanthea . . . 11 D d
Oechalia, in Ætolia . . . 10 C d
Oechalia, in Messenia . . . 14 B b
Oedenburg, see Ödenburg
Oee . . . 16 B a
Oeiras . . . 214 E c
Oeneon . . . 10 C d
Oeniadæ . . . 10 C d
Oenoë, in Argolis . . . 14 C b
Oenoë, near Cythæron Mts. . 16 A a
Oenoë, in Elis . . . 14 B b
Oenoë, on the Istmus of Corinth 15 D a
Oenoë, near Marathon . . . 16 B a
Oenophyta . . . 11 E d
Oenotrians, people . . . 29 D e
Oenus (Inn) River . . . 14 C b
Oenussæ Island . . . 14 B c
Oëroë River . . . 11 E d
Oescus . . . 39 M l
Oescus River (Isker R.) . . . 39 M l
Oesyme . . . 11 F b
Oeta, mt. . . . 11 D d
Oetæa, dist. . . . 10 D d
Oetylus . . . 14 C c
Oeum . . .
O'Farrells, The, fam. . . .
Ofen (Buda) . . . 63 J e
Ofen (Buda) univ. . . . 100 I e
Ofen Pass . . . 91 S l
Offa's Dike . . .
Offenburg . . . 142 A d
Öfingen . . . 142 C e
O'Flahertys, The, fam. . . .
Ofu, isl. . . . 199 ins. D
Ogden . . . 210 C b
Ogdensburg . . . 192 D a
Ogeechee River . . . 193 C e
Oglasa, isl. . . . 26 E e
Oglio River . . . 90 J h
Ogowe River . . . 175 E e
Ohain . . .
Ohain, Woods of . . .
Ohain River . . .
O'Hanlons, The, fam. . . .
O'Haras, The, fam. . . .
Ohiv Company . . . 196 ins. B
Ohio, Falls of the . . . 196 B c
Ohio, state . . . 202 I b
Ohio, ter. . . . 196 C b
Ohio River . . . 187 K e
Ohrdruf, mon. . . . 95 E a
Ohre River . . . 85 F d
Öhringen . . . 143 H g
Oil River, dist. . . . 174 D d
Oil Spring, Ind. Res. . . . 188 K b
Oise dept. . . . 148 E e
Oise River . . . 126 C b
Ojibwas, Chippewas, tribe . . . 188 H a
Okanagan, Fort . . . 210 B a
Oka River . . . 139 E e
Okechobee, lake . . . 191 I f
Okehampton, parl. bor. . . . 163 J g
O'Kellys, The, fam. . . .
Okhotsk . . . 171 P c
Okhotsk, Sea of . . . 171 P c
Oklahoma . . . 210 F c
Oklahoma, state . . . 203 S h
Oklahoma, ter. . . . 203 S h
Olana River . . . 27 F c
Öland, isl. . . . 77 H a
Olbia, in Gaul . . . 12 E b
Olbia, in Sardinia . . . 38 D d
Olbia, in Sarmatia . . . 35 K d
Old Appian Way, road . . . 35 ins. B
Old Basing . . . 127 X o
Old Castile, km. . . . 83 K g
Old Celtic Church, area under influence of the . . . 46 E c
Olp Charles Town . . . 193 ins. C
Old Dean's Lane, in London 75 G g (32)
Oldenburg, in Holstein . . . 62 F a
Oldenburg, in Oldenburg . . . 72 B a
Oldenburg, cty. . . . 78 F b
Oldenburg, duchy . . . 134 E b
Oldenburg, gr. duchy . . . 158 E b
Oldenesche . . . 72 B a
Oldesloe . . . 72 C a
Old Fish Street, in London . . 75 G g
Old Flaminian Way, road . . . 27 G e
Old Gate, in Jerusalem . . . 6 ins. A
Oldham, parl. bor. . . . 163 L d
Old Park, dist. . . . 210 D c
Old Sarum . . .
Old Sarum, parl. bor. 163 M f (Old S.)
Old Seraglio, loc. i. Constantinople 93 G e
Old Shops, loc. in Rome . . .
Old Toggenburg, castle . . . 91 R k
Old Tyre . . . 18 ins. B
Old Versailles . . . 149 A
Olenus . . . 14 B a
Oléron, isl. . . . 76 C d
Oliarus (Antiparos), isl. . . . 15 F b
Olid, route of . . . 105 D c
Olifants River . . . 175 N k
Oligyrtus, mt. . . . 14 C b
Olinda . . . 214 F c
Olisipo (Lisbon) . . . 38 A e
Olite . . . 83 K g
Oliva, mon. . . . 95 F a
Olivença, in Brazil . . . 214 C c
Olivenza, in Portugal . . . 83 J h
Olives, Mount of . . . 68 ins. B
Olizon . . . 11 E c
Ollius River . . . 26 E b
Olmedo . . . 83 K g
Olmütz . . . 63 I d
Olmütz, bp. . . . 95 F b
Olocáu . . . 82 B b
Oloosson . . . 10 D c
Olophyxus . . . 11 F b
Oloron . . . 76 C e
Oloron, bp. . . . 94 B c
Olorone, see Oloron
Olpæ . . . 10 C d
Öls . . . 79 J c
Öls, princ. . . . 79 J c
Oltenitza . . . 164 D b
Oltis (Lot) River . . . 38 C d
Olubria River . . . 26 C c
Olusiga, isl. . . . 199 ins. D
Olympia, in Elis . . . 14 B b
Olympia, Plan of . . . 9
Olympia, in Washington . . . 210 A a
Olympieum, in Athens . . . 23 D
Olympieum, in Syracuse . . . 31 ins. B
Olympus, mt., in Attica . . . 16 B b
Olympus, mt., in Cyprus . . . 20 E e
Olympus, mt., in Macedonia . . 11 D b
Olympus Mysius, mt. . . .
Olynthus . . . 11 E b
Omagh . . . 127 J g
Omaha . . . 198 F c
Omaha, Ind. Res. . . . 188 G b
Omahas, tribe . . . 188 G b
O'Malleys, The, fam. . . .
Oman, Gulf of . . .
Oman, reg. . . .
Oman, Sea of . . .
Ombrone River . . . 90 L j
Omdurman . . . 174 G c
Omekonsk . . . 171 P b
Omercote . . . 137 A c
Ommiad Emirate of Cordova . 54 C e
Omoa . . . 213 D c
Omont . . . 61 F b
O'Mores, The, fam. . . .
Omphalium . . . 10 B b
Omsk . . . 170 I c
On . . . 4 F d
Oñate, routes of . . . 190 C e, D e
Onchesmus . . . 10 B c
Onchestus River . . . 11 D c
Onea, mt. . . . 15 C b
Onega, Gulf of . . . 167 M c
Onega, lake . . . 138 E c
Oneglia . . . 130 Q k
Oneida Ind. Res. . . . 188 I b, K b
Oneida Lake . . . 192 D b
Oneidas, tribe . . . 188 L b
O'Neills, The, fam. . . .
Onis, Cangas de . . . 82 A a
Ono . . . 7 B d
Onochonus River . . . 10 D c
Onondaga, battle . . . 192 C b
Onondaga, Ind. Res. . . . 188 K b
Onondagas, tribe . . . 188 K b
Onon River . . .
Ontario, Fort . . . 192 C b
Ontario, lake . . . 187 L d
Ontario, prov. . . . 212 G d
Ontonagon, Ind. Res. . . . 188 I a
Onugnathos, prom. . . . 15 C c
Oodnadatta . . . 172 C c
Oostburg . . . 117 B c
Opelousas . . . 211 G d
Opequan Creek . . . 208 E b (O. Cr.)
Opequon Court . . . 192 B d
Opequon River . . . 192 B d
Ophel . . . 6 ins. A
Ophiones, people . . . 10 C d
Ophis River . . . 14 C b
Ophiussa, isl. . . . 38 C e
Ophrah . . . 7 C e
Ophrynium . . .
Opis . . . 20 K f
Opisthomarathus . . . 11 D d
Opitergium . . . 27 G b
Oporto . . . 82 A a
Oporto, bisp. . . . 94 A c
Oppeln . . . 79 K c
Oppeln, princ. . . . 79 K c
Oppenau . . . 142 B d
Oppenheim . . . 62 E d
Oppius, mt. . . . 22 A

Opsician Theme 59 J f
Opslo 88 D b
Optimaton, Theme of the 59 K e
Opus 11 E d
Opus, prom. 11 D d
Oraculum Fauni, loc. near Rome 35 ins. B
Oräfa Jökul, mt. 166 B c
Oran, in Algeria 174 C a
Orán, in Arg. Rep. 215 C e
Orange 61 F d
Orange, bp. 94 C c
Orange, Cape 214 D b
Orange, Fort 192 D b
Orange, princ. 114 ins. A
Orange, univ. 100 F f
Orangeburg 195 A g
Orange Free State, rep. 175 M l
Orangerie, Rue de l', street in Versailles 149 A
Orange River 175 E g
Orange River Colony 175 F g
Orbais, mon. 94 C b
Orbe 91 O l
Orbelus, mt. 11 F a
Orbetello 90 L j
Orcades Islands (Orkneys) 34 D b
Orchard Knob, battle 208 C b
Orchies 117 B d
Orchimont 117 C e
Orchoë 18 G d
Orchomenus, in Arcadia 14 C b
Orchomenus, in Bœotia 11 D d
Ordessus River 39 N l
Ordovices, people
Örebro 88 F b
Oregon Country, The 198 A a
Oregon, state 203 N g
Oregon, ter. 1848 202 A f
Oregon, ter. 1853 202 A g
Oregon Trail, route 210 B b
O'Reillys, The, fam.
Orel 139 E e
Orellana, route of 214 B c
Orenburg 139 I e
Orense 82 A a
Orense, bp. 94 A c
Oreshek
Oresticum 10 C b
Orestis, dist. 10 C b
Oretani, people 38 B e
Oretum 38 B e
Oreus 11 E d
Orfani 165 D c
Orford, parl. bor. 165 P e
Orgellis, see Urgel
Orgus River 26 B b
Oria 90 F d
Oricum 31 I b
Orient, L' 130 C d
Origny, mon. 94 C b
Orihuela 82 B b
Orinoco River 214 C b
Oriskany, battle 195 D b
Orissa, reg. 137 D d
Oristano, abp. 95 D d
Oritæ, people 19 K e
Orizaba 106 C b
Orizaba, vol. 106 C b
Orkhon River
Orkney, bp. 97 J a
Orkney Islands 49 E b
Orlamünde 85 F e
Orléanais, gouv. 146 B b
Orléanais, prov. 148 E e
Orléans 61 E c
Orléans, bp. 94 C b
Orléans, duchy 84 D f
Orléans, gen. 147 E b
Orléans, univ. 100 F e
Orleans, ter. 202 G d
Orleans, Fort 191 G d
Orleans, Island of, Mississippi R. 194 A e
Orleans, Island of, St. Lawrence R. 191 K b
Orlov, Cape 167 N b
Ormea 130 P j
Ormenium
Ormskirk 98 ins. A
Ormuz, isl.
Ormuz, km.
Ornas
Orne, dept. 148 D e
Orne River, in Belgium 156 B a
Orne River, in France 148 D e
Orneæ 14 C b
Orneau River 156 B a
Oro, Rio de, dist. 174 B b
Orobiæ 11 E d
Orolaunum 39 H i
Orontes River 68 C b
Oropus 15 D a
Oropus River 10 B c
O'Rorkes, The, fam.
Oroya 214 B d
Orsha 153 O g
Orsini, fam. 90 L j
Orsk 139 I e
Orsovo 71 K e
Orte, bp. 95 E c
Ortegal, Cape 166 D g
Ortenau, dist. 142 A c
Ortez de Retes, route of
Orthez 126 A e
Orthokids, people 75 I c
Orthospana (Kabul) 19 K d
Ortona 27 I e
Ortopla 27 I c
Ortospana, see Orthospana
Ortygia, quarter in Syracuse 31 ins. B
Orumbovii, people 26 D b
Oruro 214 C d
Orval 69 I g
Orval, mon. 95 D b
Orvieto 90 M j
Orvieto, bp. 95 E c
Oryxis, mt. 14 C b
Osage, Fort 211 G c
Osage River 191 G d
Osages, tribe 188 F b
Osaka 171 O e
Osawatomie 206 F c
Osca (Huesca) 38 B d
Oscela 26 C a
Öschelbronn 142 C c
Ösel, isl. 138 B d
Osenay, mon. 97 P j
Osette, Ind. Res. 188 A a
O'Shaugnessys, The, fam.
Oshmiany 153 N g
Osi, people 38 F c
Osimii, people 38 B c
Osimo 90 D c
Osma 82 B a
Osma, bp. 94 B c
Osmanli (Ottoman Turks), Dom. of the 89 I g
Osnabrück 62 D b
Osnabrück, bp. 78 F b
Osnabrück, Hanse. cy. 99 ins. B
Osoppo 158 G e
Osopus 27 H a
Osorno 215 B g
Osrhoëne, dist. 20 H d
Osrhoëne, prov. 43 J f (11)
Ossa, mt. 11 D c
Ossawatomie, see Osawatomie
Osse 126 A e
Osseg, in Bohemia 123 G c
Osseg, on the Vistula R.
Osseg, mon. 80 ins.
Ossero, bp. 95 E c
Ossola, val d', valley 91 Q l
Ossory, bp. 97 D d
Ostend 117 A c
Ostend, mon. 94 C a
Osteodes, isl. 30 C d
Osterburken 142 D b
Osterland, margr. 79 H c
Osterland, dist. 85 G e
Osterode 155 K b
Ostia 27 G f
Ostia, bp. 96 B b
Ostiaks, people
Ostian Gate 22 A
Ostian Way, road 35 ins. B
Ostmark (Austria), march 63 H d
Ostmark, march. in Brandenburg 63 G c
Ostrach 134 E e
Ostrog 119 J c
Ostrogoths, Dom. of the 50 G c
Ostrolenka 155 K b
Ostrov 138 C d
Ostrovno 153 N f
Ostrowo 135 I c
O'Sullivans, The, fam.
Osuna 82 A b
Oswegatchie, Fort 196 D b
Oswego 196 D b
Oswego, Fort 192 C b
Oswego River 192 C b
Oswestry 127 V n
Otago, prov. 172 F e
Otaheite, isl. 136 ins. B
Otalini, people 38 B a
Otavalo 214 B b
Otchakov 139 D f
Otford
Othrys, mt. 11 D c
Otochatz, bp.
O'Tooles, The, fam.
Otranto 90 G d
Otranto, abp. 95 F c
Otrar
Otryne 16 C a
Ottawa 212 H d
Ottawa River 199 J a
Ottawas, tribe 188 I b
Ottenbourg 156 B a
Ottensen 154 E b
Ottignies 156 B a
Ottilienberg, mon. 95 D b
Ötting, Alt 123 G d
Öttingen 122 F d
Öttingen, princ. 143 J h
Ottobeuren, mon. 95 E b
Ottocar of Bohemia, Dom. of 79 ins.
Ottoman (Turkish) Empire, 1451—1481 93
Ottoman (Turkish) Empire, 1481—1683 124
Ottoman (Turkish) Empire, since 1683 164
Ottoman Turks, Dom. of the, 14 cent. 89 I g
Ottoman Turks, Dom. of the, early 15 cent. 92 C d
Otumba 106 B a
Otway, Cape 172 D d
Oudenarde 117 B d
Oudh, Oude, reg. 137 D c
Ouiatanon, Fort 191 H c
Ourique 82 G f
Ouro Prereto 214 E e
Ourthe River 117 D d
Ouse River, R. 49 F d
Ouse River, Great 49 F e
Ovalle 215 B f
Oven Tower, loc. in Jerusalem 6 ins. A
Översee 158 E a
Overton, parl. bor.
Overyssel, Lordship of 117 E b
Oviedo 82 A a
Oviedo, bp. 94 A c
Ovilava 38 E c
Ovile (Sæpta) 23 B
Owen 143 H h
Öwisheim, Unter 142 C b
Owston, mon. 97 Q i
Oxford, in England 127 X o
Oxford, castle 94 E f
Oxford, cty. 127 X o
Oxford, mon. 97 P j

Oxford, parl. bor. . . . . 163 M f
Oxford, parl. dist. . . . . 163 M f
Oxford, univ. . . . . 100 E d
Oxford University, parl. bor. . . 163 M f
Oxford, in Maryland . . . . 192 C d
Oxford, in Mass. . . . . 189 C c
Oxford, in Miss. . . . . 208 C c
Oxford Town . . . . 192 C d
Oxus (Amu-Daria) River . . . . 92 G d
Oxybii, people . . . . 26 A d
Oxynia . . . . 10 C c
Oxyrhynchus . . . .
Oyapock River . . . . 214 D b
Oyster Bay, town in New York 189 B d
Oyster Bay . . . . 172 D e
Ozark Mountains . . . . 211 G c
Ozark Plateau . . . . 187 J e
Ozora . . . . 159 J e

Paanpack . . . . 192 E b
Paardeberg, mt. . . . . 175 M l
Pacaha, reg. . . . . 191 G d
Pacaraima Mountains . . . . . . 214 C b
Pacasmayo . . . . 111 B c
Pachacamac . . . . 111 B d
Pa-chau . . . . 170 ins. A
Pachuca . . . . 213 ins.
Pachynus, prom. . . . . 30 E e
Pacific Ocean . . . . 179—180
Pacific Slope . . . . 186 G c
Pacocha . . . . 214 B d
Pactolus River . . . . 20 B c
Pactyans, people . . . . 8 E b
Pactye . . . .
Paderborn . . . . 62 E c
Paderborn, bp. . . . . 95 D a
Paderborn, Hanse. cy. . . . . . . 99 ins. B
Padrabrunna, see Paderborn
Padrão, Rio do, river . . . . . . 108 R h
Padrón . . . . 82 A a
Padua . . . . 90 J h
Padua, bp. . . . . 95 E b
Padua, univ. . . . . 100 H e (Pa.)
Paducah . . . . 208 C b
Padum, Ad . . . . 27 G c
Padus River, see Po River
Padusa River . . . . 27 F c
Pæania . . . . 16 B b
Pædagogium, loc. in Rome . . . 24 B
Pæligni, people . . . . 27 H e
Pæmani, people . . . . 39 H h
Pæonia, dist. . . . . 17 B a
Pæonidæ . . . . 16 B a
Pæstum . . . . 30 D b
Pæstum, Bay of . . . . 30 D b
Pagæ . . . . 15 D a
Pagan . . . .
Pagasæ . . . . 11 D c
Pagasæan Gulf . . . . 11 D c
Pageh Islands . . . .
Pago Pago . . . . 199 ins. D
Pagus Ianiculensis, dist. in Rome 22 A
Pahala . . . . 198 ins. B
Paia . . . . 198 ins. B
Paiutes, Piutes, tribe . . . . 188 C b
Paja River . . . .
Pajajaran . . . . 112 D d
Pajeau . . . .
Pak-hoi . . . . 171 L f
Paks . . . . 159 J e
Palachwe . . . . 175 M k
Palæbyblus . . . . 6 D a
Palæo-Kastro . . . .
Palæopolis . . . . 31 ins. A
Polærus . . . . 10 B d
Palæstra . . . .
Palætyrus . . . . 6 C b
Palais Bourbon, bldg. in Paris . 149 B
Palais Royal, bldg. in Paris . . 149 B
Palam . . . .
Palatinate, see Rhenish Bavaria 158 D d
Palatinate, Bavarian, dist. . . . . 142 C b
Palatinate, Upper, dist. . . . . . 79 G d
Palatinate of the Rhine, elect. . 78 F d
Palatinate-Saxony . . . . 85 F e
Palatine, quarter in Rome . . . 96 A
Palatine, Aug. Reg. of Rome . 22 A
Palatine Library, bldg. in Rome 24 B
Palatine Mosbach, princ. . . . . 87 H d
Palatine Mount . . . . 24 A
Palatine Simmern, princ. . . . . 86 F d
Palatine Zweibrücken, princ. . . 86 F d
Palau Islands . . . . 179 E g
Palawan, isl. . . . . 112 E c
Palazzo Borghese, bldg. in Rome 96 A
Palazzo Colonna, bldg. in Rome 96 A
Palazzo di Venezia, bldg. in Rome . . . . 96 A
Palazzo Farnese, bldg. in Rome 96 A
Palazzo Massimi, bldg. in Rome 96 A
Palazzò Orsini Savelli, bldg. in Rome . . . . 96 A
Pale . . . . 10 B d
Pale, The English, dist. . . . . .
Palea . . . . 14 B a
Palembang . . . .
Palencia . . . . 82 B a
Palencia, bp. . . . . 94 B c
Palencia, univ. . . . . 100 E f
Palenque . . . . 105 B c
Palermo . . . . 90 D e
Palermo, abp. . . . . 95 E d
Palestine, reg. . . . . 6—7
Palestine I, East Rom. prov. . . 43 I g (1)
Palestine II, East Rom. prov. . 43 J g (6)
Palestine (Salutaris), East Rom. prov. . . . . 43 I h (7)
Palestrina . . . . 64 ins.
Palestrina, bp. . . . . 96 B b
Palice . . . . 30 D e
Pa-li-kioa . . . . 170 ins. A
Palinurus, prom. . . . . 30 E c
Pallacopas Canal . . . . 18 G d
Pallantia . . . . 38 B d
Pallantium . . . . 14 C b
Pallanum . . . . 27 I e
Pallanza . . . . 90 I h
Pallas, Gardens of . . . . 22 A
Pallene, in Attica . . . . 16 B a
Pallene, pen. . . . . 11 E b
Pallia River . . . . 27 F e
Palma . . . . 38 C e
Palma, bp. . . . . 94 C d
Palma, univ. . . . . 100 F g
Palmanova . . . . 158 G f
Palmaria, isl. . . . . 30 B b
Palmas, Cape . . . . 175 C d
Palmas, Las . . . . 174 B b
Palmerston . . . . 172 C b
Palmyra . . . . 20 H e
Palmyra Island . . . . 180 K g
Palo Alto, battle . . . .
Paloos, tribe . . . . 188 C a
Palos . . . . 83 J h
Pambotis, lake . . . . 10 B c
Pamiers . . . . 126 B e
Pamiers, bp. . . . . 94 C c
Pamier, plateau . . . . 3 L e
Pamir, reg. . . . . 170 I e
Pamisus River, in Messenia . . 14 B b
Pamisus River, in Thessaly . . 10 C c
Pamlico River . . . . 193 F d
Pamlico Sound . . . . 193 F d
Pamodus . . . . 27 I c
Pampeluna, see Pamplona
Pamphia . . . . 10 C d
Pamphylia, Macedonian prov. . 18 D c
Pamphylia, Rom. prov. . . . . . 35 K f
Pamphylia, East Rom. prov. . . 43 I f (1)
Pamphylia, reg. . . . . 20 D d
Pamphylia, satr. . . . . 8 H e
Pamphylians, people . . . . 5 C b
Pamplona . . . . 82 B a
Pamplona, bp. . . . . 94 B c
Pamunkey River . . . . 193 F c
Pan, Cave of . . . . 23 C
Panachaicus, mt. . . . . 14 B a
Panactum . . . . 16 B a
Panætolius, mt. . . . . 10 C d
Panamá . . . .
Panamá, Bay of . . . .
Panamá, Gulf of . . . . 213 E d
Panamá, country . . . . 214 A b
Panay, isl. . . . . 199 ins. H
Pancalieri . . . . 130 P j
Pancsova . . . . 159 K f
Pandarani . . . .
Pandateria, isl. . . . . 30 C b
Pandosia, in Epirus . . . . 10 B c
Pandosia, in Lucania . . . . . . 31 F b
Paneas . . . . 6 D b
Pangæus, mt. . . . . 11 E b
Panhandle, The, reg. . . . . . . 210 E c
Panionium . . . . 13 E c
Panipat, Paniput . . . . 137 C c
Panixer Pass . . . . 150 E c
Panjdeh . . . . 170 H e
Panmure, Fort . . . . 194 A d
Pannonia, reg. . . . . 38 F c
Pannonia I, West Rom. prov. . 42 F d (10)
Pannonia II, West Rom. prov. 42 F d (8)
Pannonia, Lower, Rom. prov. . 34 H d
Pannonia, Upper, Rom. prov. . 34 H d
Pannonian March . . . . 54 H d
Panopeus . . . . 11 D d
Panopolis (Chemmis) . . . . . . 18 D e
Panormus, in Peparethus . . . . 11 E c
Panormus (Palermo), in Sicily 30 C d
Panormus, port, in Epirus . . . 10 A b
Pantanus, lake . . . . 30 E a
Pantelleria Island . . . . 161 H i
Pantheon, bldg. in Rome . . . . 22 A
Panticapæum (Kertch) . . . . . . 12 K a
Pánuco River . . . . 201 F e
Paons, Allée des, Versailles . . 149 A
Pao-ting . . . . 170 ins. A
Papago, Ind. Res. . . . . 188 D d
Papal States . . . . 131 F e
Papelotte, farm . . . .
Paphlagonia, Macedonian prov. 18 D b
Paphlagonia, reg. . . . . 8 B a
Paphlagonia, Rom. prov. . . . . 20 E b
Paphlagonia, East Rom. prov. . 43 I e (3)
Paphlagonia, satr. . . . . 18 O g
Paphlagonia, theme . . . . 59 K e
Paphos . . . . 20 E e
Papia (Pavia) . . . . 26 D b
Papirianæ, Fossæ . . . . 26 E d
Pappua, mt. . . . . 52 C c
Papua, col., see British New Guinea
Papua Gulf . . . . 172 D a
Pará . . . . 214 E c
Pará, state . . . . 214 D c
Paracatú . . . . 214 E d
Paraclet, Le, mon. . . . . 94 C b
Paradies, mon. . . . . 95 F a
Paraetacene, reg. . . . . 19 K c
Parætaceni, people . . . . 19 H d
Parætonium . . . . 18 C d
Paragua, isl. . . . . 199 ins. H
Paraguay, country . . . . 215 D e
Paraguay River . . . . 21 D d
Parahyba . . . . 214 F c
Parahyba, state . . . . 214 F c
Parahyba River . . . . 214 E e
Paraiso 216
Paralia, dist. . . . . 15 D b
Paramanga . . . . 111 B d
Paramaribo . . . . 214 D b
Paraná . . . . 215 C f
Paraná, state . . . . 215 D e
Paraná River . . . . 214 D e
Paranaguá . . . . 215 E e
Paranapema River . . . . 215 D e
Parapanisadæ, people . . . . . . 19 K d
Parapanisus Mountains . . . . . 19 K c
Parapotamii . . . . 11 D d
Parauæa, dist. . . . . 10 B b
Parchim . . . . 158 F b
Pardiac, cty. . . . . 69 D e (P.)
Pardo, El, castle . . . . 130 C c

Pardubitz 159 H d
Parentium (Parenzo) 27 H b
Parenzo 90 D b
Parenzo, bp. 95 E b
Parga 93 B c
Paria, Gulf of 105 H d
Paria, reg. 105 H d
Paricanii, Paricanians, people 19 K e
Pariña, Punta, cape 111 A b
Paris 61 E b
Paris in 1789, plan of 149 B
Paris, bp. 94 C b
Paris, gen. 147 E b
Paris, univ. 100 F e
Parisii or Parisius, see Paris
Parisii, people 38 C c
Parita, reg. 105 D e
Parium
Parkersburg 206 ins.
Parma 26 E c
Parma, bp. 95 E c
Parma, duchy 150 E d
Parma River 26 E c
Parnahyba 214 E c
Parnahyba River 214 E c
Parnassus, mt. 11 D d
Parnes Mountains 15 D a
Parnon Mountains 14 C b
Paroisse, Rue de la, street in Versailles 149 A
Paros 15 F b
Paros, isl. 15 F b
Parramatta 172 E d
Parrhasia, reg. 14 B b
Parrtown 212 I d
Parry Islands 186 H a
Parsdorf 134 F d
Part-Dieu, La, mon. 91 O l
Partenkirchen 72 C b
Partenkirchen, mon. 95 E b
Parthanum 38 E c
Parthenay 69 C c
Parthenius, mt. 14 C b
Parthenius River 20 E b
Parthenon, bldg. in Athens 23 C
Parthenopæan Republic 151 I h
Parthenope (Naples) 5 A a
Parthia, prov. 19 I c
Parthia, reg. 8 D b
Parthia, satr. 18 Q h
Parthians, Empire of the 35 N g
Paru River 214 D b
Paryadres Mountains 20 H b
Pasado, Cape 111 A b
Pasargadæ 19 H d, H e
Pasargadæ, people 8 D c
Pas-de-Calais, dept. 148 E d
Paseir 112 C c
Pasewalk 85 C b
Pashat
Pasitigris River 19 G d
Passaic River 189 ins. C
Passarge River 155 J a
Passaro, Cape 131 G f
Passaron 10 B c
Passarowitz
Passau 63 G d
Passau, bp. 95 E b
Passavant, castle 143 ins. F
Passavant, lordship 143 ins. F
Passeier Tal, valley 154 F e (Pa.)
Pastaza River 111 B b
Pasto 214 B b
Patagonia, reg. 215 C g
Patani
Patapsco River 200 L h
Patara 20 C d
Patavia, see Passau
Patavium (Padua) 26 F b
Patay 76 D b
Paterno 64 ins.
Paternum 31 G c
Patiala 137 C b
Patillas 199 ins. G
Patmos, isl. 13 E c
Patna 137 D c
Patos, Laguna dos 215 D f
Patræ 14 B a
Patras 89 H g
Patras, desp. 93 B c
Patriarchates, 593—600 52
Patrimony of Saint Peter (States of the Church), 9 cent.
Patrimony of Saint Peter (States of the Church), 12 cent. 70 I e
Patrimony of Saint Peter (States of the Church), 15 cent. 90 C c
Patroclus, Burial mound of
Patroclus Island 15 D b
Pattala 19 K e
Pattan Somnath
Patti, bp. 95 E d
Patuca River 105 D c
Patuxent River 192 C d
Patzinaks or Petchenegs, people
Pátzcuaro 213 ins.
Pau 69 C e
Pau and Bayonne, gen. 147 D c
Paul, journeys of the Apostle 46, 47 leg.
Paulinzella, mon. 95 E a
Paulus Hoeck 189 ins. C
Paumotu, isl. 180 M i
Paus 14 B b
Pausilypum 31 ins. A
Pausulæ 27 H d
Pau-ti 170 ins. A
Pavia 90 I h
Pavia, bp. 95 D b
Pavia, univ. 100 G e
Pavonia 189 ins. C
Pawnees, tribe 188 F b
Pawtucket 189 ins. A
Pawtuxed 189 ins. A
Pax Iulia 38 A e
Paxo, isl. 157 D e
Paxus, isl. 10 B c
Payerne 91 O l
Payne Lake 212 H c
Paysandú 215 D f
Payta 111 A c
Paz, La 214 C d
Peace, Altar of 22 A
Peace, Temple of 24 B
Peace River 186 H c
Peakland, dist.
Pea Ridge, mts. 208 B b
Pearl Coast 105 G d
Pearl River 191 H e
Pe-chi-li, gulf. 171 M e
Pe-chi-li, prov. 171 M e
Pechora, River 3 J b
Peck, Fort, Ind. Res. 188 E a
Pecos 190 E d
Pecos River 190 E e
Pedasus (Methoni) 14 B c
Pedee River, Great 193 E d
Pediæus River 20 E e
Pedias, dist. 15 D a
Pedion, dist. 16 B b
Pedir 112 C c
Pedo 26 B c
Pedroche 82 B b
Pedro Miguel 216
Pedum 35 ins. B
Peebles, cty.
Peebles, dist.
Peekskill 195 E c
Peene River 63 G b
Peenemünder Schanze, fort 123 G a
Peer 117 D c
Pegau, mon. 80 ins.
Pegu
Pegu, reg.
Pei-ho, R. 170 ins. A
Peipus, lake 88 L b
Peishwa, Doms. of the 137 B e
Pei-tang 170 ins. A
Pei-tsang 170 ins. A
Pejepscot, Fort 189 C b
Peking
Pelagonia 10 C a
Pelagonia, dist. 17 B a
Pelasgiotis, dist. 11 D c
Pelendones, people 38 B d
Pelew Islands 179 E g
Pelican Point, cape 108 R j
Pelinnæum 10 C c
Pelion, mt. 11 E c
Pelisipia, proposed state in U.S.
Pelium 10 B b
Pella, in Gilead 7 D d
Pella, in Macedonia 11 D b
Pellana 14 C b
Pellene 14 C a
Pelly River 212 B b
Pelopium
Peloponnesus, Byzantine prov. 89 B c
Peloponnesus, pen. 13 C c
Peloponnesus, theme 59 I f
Pelorus, prom. 30 E d
Pelotas 215 D f
Pelplin, mon. 95 F a
Peltuinum 27 H e
Pelusium 4 ins.
Pelusium, ruins of 150 B a
Pemaquid 189 D c
Pemba, isl. 175 H e
Pembroke 84 A d
Pembroke, castle
Pembroke, cty. 127 U o
Pembroke, parl. bor. 163 J f
Pembroke, parl. dist. 163 J f
Peña Blanca 215 B e
Penas (Peñas) Gulf of 215 B g
Penay 91 N l
Pendennis Castle 127 T p
Penedo 214 F d
Peneus River, in Elis 14 B b
Peneus River, in Thessaly 11 D c
Peñiscola 82 C a
Penjhir
Pennar River
Penneloci 26 A a
Pennine Alps, mts. 26 B a
Pennine Chain, mts. 49 E d
Pennine Valley 26 B a
Pennine and Graian Alps, West Rom. prov. 42 D d (8)
Pennsylvania, col. 192 C c
Pennsylvania, state 199 J b
Penobscot 189 D b
Penobscot Bay 189 D b
Penobscot River 189 D b
Peñon de Velez 130 C f
Penrhyn Islands 180 L i
Penryn and Falmouth, parl. bor. 163 I g
Penrith 127 W l
Pensacola 191 H e
Pensacola Bay 193 ins. B
Pentagöet, Fort 189 D b
Pentapolis, dist., in Cyrenaica 43 G g
Pentapolis, dist., in Italy 64 B b
Pentapylum 31 ins. B (5)
Pentele 16 B a
Pentelicus, mt. 16 B a
Penthièvre, cty. 69 B b
Pentney, mon. 97 R i
Pentri, people 30 D a
Penuel 7 D d
Penza 139 G e
Peoria 212 G b
Peparethus, isl. 11 E c
Pephnos 14 C c
Pequots, tribe 189 C d
Pera 93 G c
Peræa, dist., in Palestine 7 D e
Peræa, dist., in Greece 15 C a
Perche, cty. 69 H f
Perche-Gouet, dist. 76 D b (P. G.)
Percote
Perdido River 193 ins. B
Pered 159 J d

Perekop 139 D f
Perekop, Isthmus of 3 H d
Pereslawl 138 E d
Pergamum
Pergamum, km. 33 C b
Pergamus 11 F b
Perge 43 I f
Périgord, cty. 61 D d
Périgueux 61 D d
Périgueux, bp. 94 C b
Perim Island 174 H c
Perinthus
Peristhlava 59 J e
Perlas, Isla de, isl. 105 E e
Perlasz 159 K f
Perleberg 154 G b
Perm 138 I d
Permians, people 138 H d
Pernambuco or Recife 214 F c
Pernambuco, state 214 F c
Pernau 88 K b
Pernau, Hanse. cy. 99 H b
Péronne 76 E b
Perosa 130 P j
Perote 106 C a
Perote, Cofre de, mt. 106 C a
Perovsk 170 H d
Perpignan 61 E e
Perpignan, gen. 147 E c
Perpignan, univ. 100 F f
Perrhæbi, people 10 C c
Perrhæbia, dist. 10 C c
Perryville 208 C b
Persante River 159 I b
Perseigne, mon. 94 C b
Persephone, Temple of 31 ins. B (12)
Persepolis 8 J f
Pershore, mon 97 O i
Pershore, parl. bor.
Persia, country 170 G e
Persia, khan.
Persia, reg.
Persian Empire, about 500 B. C. 8
Persian Gulf 3 I f
Persis, prov. 19 H e
Persis, reg. 8 D b
Persis, satr. 8 J f
Perth, in Australia 172 A d
Perth, in Scotland
Perth, cty.
Perth, dist.
Perth Amboy 192 D c
Peru, Conquest of 111
Peru, reg. 111 B c
Peru, rep. 214 B c
Peru, viceroyalty 215 ins.
Peru, Lower, reg. 214 B c
Peru, Upper, reg. 214 C d
Perugia 90 D c
Perugia, bp. 95 E c
Perugia, univ. 100 H f
Perusia (Perugia) 27 G d
Perwez 156 B a
Pesaro 90 D c
Pesaro, bp. 95 E c
Pescado River
Pescadores, isl. 171 M f
Pescara 90 E c
Peschiera 90 C b
Peshawar, Peshawur 137 B b
Pessinus 20 D c
Petaliæ Islands 15 E b
Petchenegs or Patzinaks, people
Petchora River
Petelia 31 G c
Peten, isl. 105 B c
Petenisca 39 I j
Peterborough
Peterborough, mon.
Peterborough, parl. bor. 163 N e
Peterborough, soke and abbey of
Peterhead
Peterhof 131 I b
Peterlingen, mon. 95 D b
Petermann's Peak 186 P a
Petersberg, mon. 85 G e
Petersburg, in Virginia 193 F c
Petersburg, Saint, in Russia 138 D c
Petersburgh, in S. Australia 172 C d
Petersfield, parl. bor. 163 M g (Petersf.)
Petersham 196 E b
Petershausen, ab. 142 D e
Peterwardein 159 K f
Petitarus River 10 C d
Petites Écuries, loc. in Versailles 149 A
Petite Venise, loc. in Versailles 149 A
Petite Venise, Allée de la, in Versailles 149 A
Petit Rœulx 156 A a
Petit Trianon, loc. in Versailles 149 A
Petra, in Arabia 18 E d
Petra, in Macedonia 11 D b
Petra, in Sicily 30 D e
Petracoris, see Périgueux
Petræantheatre 16 D c (3)
Petro-Alexandrovsk 170 H d
Petrocorii, see Périgueux
Petronell 54 H d
Petropavlovsk 171 Q c
Petropolis 215 E e
Petrovsk 167 O g
Petrozavodsk 138 D c
Pettau 54 H d
Petten 117 C b
Petty Armenian States 67 N f
Peuce Island 18 C a
Peucelaotis 19 L d
Peucetii, people 31 F b
Pevensey
Pfaffenhofen 134 F d
Pfalzburg 158 D d
Pfävers, mon. 91 R l
Pfeddersheim 142 B a
Pfinz River 142 C c
Pflege Coburg, dist. 85 F e
Pforta, mon. 95 E a
Pforzheim 142 C c
Pfullendorf 142 D e
Pfullingen 143 H i
Phacium 10 D c
Phæca 10 C c
Phæna 6 E b
Phæstus, in Crete 14 ins.
Phæstus, in Locris 11 D d
Phæstus, in Thessaly 10 D c
Phagres 11 E b
Phalacrum, prom. in Corcyra 10 A c
Phalacrum, prom. in Sicily 30 E d
Phalæsiæ 14 C b
Phalanna 11 D c
Phalara 11 D d
Phalasia, prom. 11 E d
Phalerum 15 D b
Phaliga 20 I e
Phaloria 10 C c
Phanagoria 12 K a
Phanariote Quarter, in Constantinople 93 G e
Phanote 10 A b
Phara 10 B d
Pharæ, in Achaia 14 B a
Pharæ, in Messenia 14 C b
Pharcadon 10 C c
Pharis 14 C b
Pharmacussa, isl. 16 B b
Pharnacia 20 H b
Pharpar River 6 E b
Pharos, isl. 12 G b
Pharos, lighthouse 34 ins. C
Pharsalus (Pharsala) 11 D c
Pharus, isl. 38 F d
Phaura, isl.
Phasael 6 ins. A
Phasaëlis 7 C d
Phaselis 20 D d
Phasis 12 L b
Phasis River 20 J a
Phea 14 B b
Pheasants, Isle of 126 A e
Pheneus 14 C b
Pheræ 11 D c
Phigæa 16 B b
Phigalia 14 B b
Phila 11 D c
Philadelphia, in Asia Minor 20 C c
Philadelphia, in Brazil 214 E d (Phil.)
Philadelphia, in Pa. 192 D c
Philadelphia, in Syria 7 D e
Philæ Island 4 F d
Philiphaugh
Philippeum, in Olympia
Philippeville 117 C d
Philippi 11 F a
Philippine Islands 199 ins. H
Philippopolis, in Syria 6 F c
Philippopolis, in Thrace 39 M l
Philippopolis, in Bulgaria 167 J g
Philippsburg 142 B b
Philippus, Portico of 22 A
Philistæa, dist. 7 A f
Philistines, people 7 ins. D
Philomelium 67 M f
Philopappus, Monument of 23 D
Phinopolis
Phintias 30 C e
Phlegra, pen. 11 E c
Phlegræan Fields 31 ins. A
Phlius 14 C b
Phlya 16 B a
Phlygonium 11 D d
Phocæa 12 I c
Phocian Wall 16 F e
Phocis, state 11 D d
Phœnice 10 B c
Phœnicia, country 6 C c
Phœnicia, East Rom. prov. 43 J g (2)
Phœnicia, reg. 4 F c
Phœnicia Libani, East Rom. prov. 43 J g (8)
Phœnicians, people 7 ins. D
Phœnicus, in Cythera 15 D c
Phœnicus Port, in Messenia 14 B c
Phœnicussa, isl. 30 D d
Phœnix 210 C d
Phœnix Islands 180 J h
Phœnix River, in Achaia 14 B a
Phœnix River, in Malis 16 F e
Pholegandrus, isl. 15 E c
Pholoë, mt. 14 B b
Phorbantia, isl. 30 B d
Phoron, Port of 16 B b
Photice 10 B c
Phra 19 J d
Phrixa 14 B b
Phrygia, reg. 20 D c
Phrygia, Macedonian prov. 18 D c
Phrygia Pacatiana, East Rom. prov. 43 H f (7)
Phrygia Salutaris, East Rom. prov. 43 I f (8)
Phrygians, people 5 C b
Phthiotis, reg. 11 D c
Phylacæ, in Macedonia 10 D b
Phylace, in Epirus 10 B c
Phylace, in Thessaly 11 D c
Phyle 15 D a
Phyllus 10 D c
Phytia 10 C d
Piacenza 90 I h
Piacenza, bp. 95 D c
Piacenza, univ. 100 G f
Pialia 10 C c
Pian de Carpine, John of, route of
Piankishaws, tribe 188 I c
Piauhy, state 214 E c
Piave River 90 D b
Picardy, gouv. 146 B b
Picardy, prov. 148 E d
Picentes, Picentians, people
Picentia 30 D b
Picentini, people 30 D b
Picenum, dist. 27 H d

Picenum Suburbicarium, West Rom. prov. 42 E e (3)
Pichincha, battle 214 B c
Pickawillany 194 C b
Pickens, Fort 208 C c
Pickering, parl. bor.
Picolata, Fort 193 D g
Pictavi, see Poitiers
Pictavi, people 38 B c
Pictland (Scotland), reg.
Picton 172 G e
Picts, people, 5 cent. 50 C a
Picts, people, 9 cent. 54 D b
Piedmont, dist. 90 A b
Piedmont, princ. 150 D d
Piedmont Hills 187 K e
Piedra, mon. 94 B c
Piedras Negras 213 B b
Pieria, dist., on the Strymonic Gulf 11 F b
Pieria, dist., on the Thermaic Gulf 11 D b
Pierre 210 F b
Pierre, Fort 210 E b
Pierre's Hole, dist. 210 C b
Pierus, mt. 10 D b
Pierus River 14 B a
Pietas Iulia, col. 27 H c
Pietermaritzburg 175 N e
Piéton River 156 A a
Pietramala 90 L i
Pietra Santa 90 C c
Pigeon Creek 105 ins.
Pike, route of 198 F c, 199 G b
Pike's Peak 198 E c
Pilar 191 G e
Pilate, House of 68 ins. B (16)
Pilcomayo River 214 C e
Pilica River 87 M c
Pillars of Hercules (Calpe, or Gibraltar, and Abila), prom. 12 B c
Pillau 115 J a
Pillnitz, castle 135 G c
Pillow, Fort 208 C b
Pilsen 63 G d
Pilten 88 I c
Pimas, tribe 188 D d
Pimería, Upper, dist. 190 C e
Pin, Le, mon. 94 C b
Pinacotheca, bldg. in Athens 23 C
Pinar del Rio 213 D b
Pinciacus, see Poissy
Pincian, qnarter in Rome 96 A
Pincian Gate 22 A
Pincian Mount 22 A
Pincian Way 22 A
Pinczow 123 K c
Pindus 11 D d
Pindus Mountains 10 C c
Pine Creek 172 C b
Pineda, route of 191 G f
Pine Ridge, Ind. Res. 188 F b
Pinerolo 90 A b
Pines, Isle of 105 D b
Ping-yang, in China
Ping-yang, in Corea 171 N e
Pinhel 94 A c
Pinkie 118 D b
Pinna 27 H e
Pinos Puente 184 C e
Pinsk 139 C e
Pinto, route of
Pinzgau, valley 115 G e
Pinzon, route of, 1499 108 N g
Pinzon, route of, 1508 105 D c
Piombino 90 L j
Piombino, princ. 151 L k
Piotrkow 159 J c
Pipe Creek, stream 208 ins.
Pipewell, mon. 97 Q i
Piqua 200 A c
Piquentum 27 H b
Piræus, The 16 B b
Piræus, harbor of the 16 D c
Piraic Gate 23 D
Piranhas 214 F c
Piranum 27 H b
Piratininga 215 E e (P.)
Piresiæ 10 D c
Pirmasens 134 D d
Pirna 115 G c
Pirot 164 C b
Pirus River 14 B a
Pisa, ruins, in Elis 14 B b
Pisa, in Italy 90 L j
Pisa, abp. 95 E c
Pisa, univ. 100 H f
Pisæ (Pisa, in Italy) 26 E d
Pisanus, Portus 26 E d
Pisatis, dist. 14 B b
Pisaurum (Pesaro) 27 G d
Pisaurus River 27 G d
Piscataqua 189 C c
Piscina Publica, in Rome 23 B
Piscina Publica, Aug. Reg. of Rome 22 A
Pisco 214 B d
Pisek 79 H d
Pisgah, mt. 7 D e
Pishin 170 H e
Pisidia, E. Rom. prov. 43 I f (6)
Pisidia, Macedonian prov. 18 D c
Pisidia, reg. 20 D d
Pisino, bp. 95 E b
Pisistratus, Aqueduct of 23 D
Piski 159 L f
Pistoja
Pistoriæ (Pistoja) 26 E d
Pistum 31 I a
Pistyrus 11 F b
Pisura, Punta, cape 111 A c
Pitcairn Island 180 O j
Pithecussæ, isl. 30 C b
Pithom 4 ins.
Pitinum Mergens 27 G d
Pitinum Pisaurense 27 G d
Pitt, Fort, in Canada 212 E c
Pitt, Fort, in Pa. 192 A c
Pittsburg 195 B c
Pittsburg Landing 208 C b
Pityus 12 L b
Pityusæ, isl. 38 C e
Pityussa, isl. 15 D b
Piura 111 A c
Piura River 111 A c
Pizarro, route of 111
Place d'Armes, in Versailles 149 A
Place de Grève, in Paris 149 B
Place de Louis XV., in Paris 149 B
Place des Victoires, in Paris 149 B
Place du Carrousel, in Paris 149 B
Place du Dauphin, in Paris 149 B
Place Vendôme, in Paris 149 B
Placentia (Piacenza), in Italy 26 D b
Placentia. in Newfoundland 212 J d
Placentia Bay 212 J d
Placilla 215 C e
Plaine de la Ménagerie, loc. in Versailles 149 A
Plaine de Trianon, loc. in Versailles 149 A
Plaine du Mail, loc. in Versailles 149 A
Plaine Saint Antoine, loc. in Versailles 149 A
Plaine-Selve, mon. 94 B b
Planasia, isl. 26 E e
Planchenoit
Plantations across the Water 193 ins. A (Plan.)
Plasencia 83 J g
Plasencia, bp. 94 A c
Plassey 137 E d
Plata, La, in the Arg. Rep. 215 D f
Plata, La, in Bolivia 214 C d
Plata, La, viceroyalty 215 ins.
Platææ 11 E d
Platamodes, prom. 14 B b
Platanistus, prom. 15 C c
Platte River 190 F c
Platte River, North 190 E c
Platte River, South 190 E c
Plattsburg 200 G a
Plattsmouth 210 F b
Plaue 85 C b
Plauen 85 G e
Plauer Canal 135 G b
Plavis (Piave) River 85 G e
Pleissnerland, dist. 85 G e
Plemmyrium, dist. 31 ins. B
Plemmyrium, prom. 30 E e
Plenty, Bay of 172 G d
Pleskau 88 M c
Pless 135 J d
Plessis-les-Tours 126 B c
Plestinus, lake 27 G d
Pleuron 10 C d
Plevlie 164 B d
Plevna 164 C b
Plistus River 11 D d
Plock 115 J b
Plock, bp. 95 F a
Ploërmel 76 B c
Ploesti 165 D a
Plökenpass 27 G a
Plombières-les-Bains 158 D e
Plothia 16 B a
Plymouth, in England
Plymouth, parl. bor. 163 J g
Plymouth, in Mass. 189 C d
Plymouth, in N. Carolina 208 E b
Plymouth, New, col. in Mass. 189 C d
Plymouth, New, New Zealand 172 G d
Plymouth Company, Grants to the 190 ins.
Plympton, mon. 97 M k
Plympton, parl. bor. 163 K g
Pnom-Penh 171 L g
Pnyx, loc. in Athens 23 D
Poblet, mon. 94 C c
Pocasset 189 ins. A
Pocatello 210 C b
Pöchlarn 63 H d
Podandus 59 K f
Podgoritza 164 B b
Podiebrad 87 J c
Podlesia, dist. 139 C e
Podolia, dist. 139 C f
Podolsk 153 P f
Pœcilus, mt. 16 B a
Pœdiculi, people 31 F a
Pœessa 15 E b
Poel, isl. 122 F a
Pœnina, Alpis, pass 26 B b
Pœtovio 42 F d
Pöhlde 62 F c
Point au Baril 192 D a
Point au Fer 196 E b
Point Comfort, cape 193 ins. A
Pointe Coupée 191 G e
Point de Galle, cape 112 B c
Point Pleasant, battle 194 C c
Poischwitz 155 H c
Poissy 76 E b
Poitiers 61 D c
Poitiers, bp. 94 C b
Poitiers, gen. 147 D b
Poitiers, univ. 100 F e
Poitou, cty. 61 C c
Poitou, gouv. 146 A b
Poitou, prov. 148 D e
Pojang Lake
Pola 27 H c
Pola, bp. 95 E c
Pola de Gordon, La 82 A a
Polabians, people 62 F b
Poland, duchy 59 H c
Poland, km., 11 cent. 63 I c
Poland, km., 12 cent. 70 J c
Poland, km., 16 cent. 119 I c
Poland, km., 18 cent. 131 I c
Poland, km., 19 cent. 159 J b
Poland, Great, dist. 139 A e
Poland, Little, dist. 139 B e
Polati, bp. 95 F c
Polaticum, prom. 27 H c

Polden Hills 49 E f
Poles, people 57 H c
Polesina, dist. 90 C b
Policastro 90 E e
Policastro, bp. 95 F c
Polichne, quarter in Syracuse. 31 ins. B
Poligny 126 D c
Polillo, isl. 171 N g
Polish Livonia, dist. 131 I b
Pollentia, Balearic Is. 38 C e
Pollentia, in Liguria 26 B c
Pollenza 50 E d
Polling 62 F e
Polling-places, loc. in Rome 24 B
Polo, Marco, route of
Polotsk 71 L b
Polotsk, princ. 71 L b
Polovzians, people 71 N d
Poltava 139 D f
Polyægus, isl. 15 E c
Polypotamia, proposed state in U. S.
Polyrrhenia 14 ins.
Polytimetus River 19 K b
Pombia 62 E f
Pomerania, dist. 59 H c
Pomerania, Farther, dist. 123 H b
Pomerania, Hither, dist. 123 G b
Pomerania, duchy, 12 cent. 72 D a
Pomerania, duchy, 15 cent. 87 J b
Pomerania, prov. 159 H b
Pomerania, Swedish, dist. 154 G a
Pomeranians, Bp. of the 95 E a
Pomeranians, people 46 J c
Pomerelia, dist. 72 D a
Pomoria, dist. 138 D b
Pomos, tribe 188 B c
Pompadour 126 B d
Pompælo (Pamplona) 38 B d
Pompeii 30 D b
Pompeiopolis, in Cilicia 20 F d
Pompeiopolis, in Paphlagonia 20 F b
Pompey, Gardens of 23 B
Pompey, Portico of 22 A
Pompey, Senate-house of 22 A
Pompey, Theatre of 22 A
Pompey's Pillar 34 ins. C (7)
Pomptine Marshes 30 B a
Ponca, Ind. Res. 188 G c
Poncas, tribe 188 G b
Ponce 199 ins. G
Ponce de León, Bahia de, bay 191 I f
Ponce de León, landing-place of 191 I e
Pondicherry 137 C f
Pondoland, dist. 175 M m
Pons, castle 76 C d
Pons Ælii (Newcastle)
Pons Aureoli 26 D b
Pons Drusi 27 F a
Pons Ferri (Iron Bridge) 68 C b
Pons Saravi 39 I i
Ponta Grossa
Pontafel Pass 135 G e
Pontarlier 122 D e
Pont au Change, loc. in Paris. 149 B
Pont Audemer 76 D b
Pontchartrain, Fort 191 I c
Pontchartrain, lake 208 B c
Pont de Cé 126 A c
Pont de l'Arche 76 D b
Ponteamas
Pontecorvo 90 D d
Pontecorvo, princ. 151 L k
Pontefract 65 F d
Pontefract, mon. 97 P h
Pontefract, parl. bor. 163 M d
Ponte Molle, loc. in Rome 96 A
Ponte Sant' Angelo, loc. in Rome 96 A
Ponthieu, cty. 76 D a
Pontiac 211 I b
Pontiæ, isl. 30 B b
Pontiæ Islands 30 C b
Pontica, reg. 50 J d
Ponticus, lake 19 J d
Pontifex Maximus, House of the 24 A
Pontigny 69 I g
Pontigny, mon. 94 C b
Pont Notre Dame, loc. in Paris 149 B
Pont Neuf, loc. in Paris 149 B
Pontoise 126 C b
Pontremoli 90 I h
Pontresina 91 R l
Pont Royal, loc. in Paris 149 B
Pont Saint Michel, loc. in Paris 149 B
Pontus, East Rom. dioc. 43 J f
Pontus, reg.
Pontus, Rom. prov.
Pontus Euxinus (Black Sea) 12 J b
Pontus Polemoniacus, East Rom. prov. 43 J e (9)
Pony Express, route of the 210 F b
Ponzone 130 Q j
Pool of the Aqueduct 6 ins. A (5)
Poole 127 X p
Poole, parl. bor. 163 L g
Poona 137 B e
Popayan 111 B a
Poperinghe 117 A d
Popilian Way, road 27 G c, 31 F d
Popocatepetl, vol. 106 B a
Popotlan
Poppi 90 L j
Populoniæ, Aquæ 26 E d
Populonium 26 E e
Po River 90 J h
Porchester
Porcien, cty. 69 J f
Porcobera River 26 C c
Porcupine River 212 A b
Porfirio Diaz, Ciudad 213 B b
Porhoët, castle 76 B b
Porhoët, cty. 76 B b
Porman 82 B b
Porphyrion 6 C a
Porpoise, Cape 189 C c
Porta Appia, loc. in Rome 96 A
Porta aurea, loc. in Jerusalem. 68 ins. B
Portæ Caspiæ, pass, see Caspian Gates 19 H c
Portæ Caucasiæ, pass, see Caucasian Gates 18 F b
Porta Flaminia, loc. in Rome 96 A
Portage la Prairie 212 F c
Porta Latina, loc. in Rome 96 A
Portalegre 94 A d
Porta Pia, loc. in Rome 96 A
Port Arthur, in Canada 212 F d
Port Arthur, in Asia 171 N e
Porta Salaria, loc. in Rome 96 A
Porta San Pancrazio, loc. in Rome 96 A
Porta San Paolo, loc. in Rome 96 A
Porta Tiburtina, loc. in Rome. 96 A
Port Augusta, S. Australia 172 C d
Port Augusta, W. Australia 172 A d
Port au Prince 213 E c
Port Bouet 175 C d
Port Clarence 198 ins. A
Port Darwin 172 B b
Port Davey 172 D e
Port Elizabeth 175 M m
Porte Saint Denis, loc. in Paris 149 B
Porte Saint Martin, loc. in Paris 149 B
Portese, Porta, loc. in Rome 22 A
Port Essington, in Australia 172 C b
Port Essington, in Canada 212 ins. A
Port Eyre 172 C d
Port Gibson 208 B c
Port Hamilton 171 N e
Porthmus 11 F d
Port Hope 198 ins. A
Port Hudson 208 B c
Portico of the Gods, loc. in Rome 24 B
Port Jackson 172 E d
Portland, in Australia 172 D d
Portland, in England 127 W p
Portland, in Maine 179 K b
Portland, in Oregon 198 A a
Portland Canal 212 ins.
Port Lincoln 172 C d
Port Louis 175 I g
Port Macquarie 172 E d
Port Natal 175 N l
Port Nicholson 172 G e
Porto, bp. 96 B b
Porto Alegre 215 D e
Porto Bello 105 E e
Porto Cabello, see Puerto Cabello
Porto Calvo 214 F c
Port of Spain 214 C a
Porto Maurizio 90 B c
Porto Novo 174 D d
Porto Rico, col.
Porto Rico, isl. 199 ins. G
Porto Santo 108 P d
Porto Seguro 214 F d
Porto Viejo
Port Phillip 172 G d
Port Phillip District 172 leg.
Port Republic 208 E b (P. R.)
Port Royal, in Jamaica
Port Royal, in Nova Scotia 212 I d
Port Royal, loc. in Paris 149 B
Port Royal, near Paris 126 B b
Port Royal, in S. C. 193 ins. C
Port Said 174 K i
Port Simpson 212 ins.
Portsmouth, in England 69 C a
Portsmouth, parl. bor.
Portsmouth, hospital 100 A b
Portsmouth, in N. Hampshire 189 C c
Portsmouth, in Ohio 206 ins.
Portsmouth, in Rhode Island 189 ins. A
Portsmouth, in Virginia 207 K c
Portsmouth Harbor 51 P i
Port Stanley 206 ins.
Port Sudan 174 G b
Portugal, cty. 83 D c
Portugal, km., 12 cent. 82 G e
Portugal, km., 15 cent. 83 J g
Portuguese, people
Portuguese East Africa, col. 175 G g
Portuguese Guinea, col. 174 B c
Portuguese West Africa, col. 175 E f
Portunata, isl. 27 I c
Portunus, Temple of 24 A
Portus, bp. 96 B b
Portus Ædro 27 G b
Portus Augusti 27 G f
Portus Cale (Oporto) 38 A d
Portus Delphini 26 D c
Portus Divini 38 B e
Portus Eunostus 34 ins. C
Portus Herculis Monœci (Monaco) 26 B d
Portus Itius 38 C b
Portus Lemanus (Lymne) 38 C b
Portus Magnus (Portsmouth Harbor)
Portus Maurici (Porto Maurizio) 26 C d
Portus Namnetum (Nantes) 38 B c
Portus Pisanus 26 E d
Portus Traianus 26 E e
Portus Veneris 26 D e
Port Way, road 35 ins. B
Poschiavo 91 S l
Posen 63 I b
Posen, bp. 95 F a
Posen, prov. 159 I b
Posidium, near Alexandria 34 ins. C
Posidium, near Corinth 15 D b
Posidium, prom., Acanthian Gulf 11 E b
Posidium, prom., Bay of Pæstum 30 D b
Posidium, prom., Phthiotis 11 E c
Posidium, prom., Propontis
Posidium, prom., Thermaic Gulf 11 E c
Posidonia 12 F b
Posilipo, mt. 31 ins. A
Pospol, farm
Postern, loc. in London 75 G g
Postumian Way, in Liguria, road 26 C c
Postumian Way, in Venetia, road 27 G b
Poswol 131 H b

Potaïssa . . . 35 I d
Potamii . . . 16 C b
Potchefstroom . . . 175 M l
Potentia, in Lucania . . . 30 E b
Potentia, in Picenum . . . 27 H d
Potenza . . . 90 E d
Poti . . . 99 L e
Potidæa . . . 11 E b
Potomac River . . . 187 L e
Potosí . . . 214 C d
Potsdam . . . 123 G b
Pottawatomi, Ind. Res. . . . 188 G c
Pottawatomi of Huron, Ind. Res. 188 I b
Pottawatomies, tribe . . . 188 I b
Poultry, loc. in London . . . 75 G g (36)
Pourré, route of . . . 195 ins. B
Poussay, mon. . . . 148 C b
Pouzo Alegre . . . 214 D d
Poverty Bay . . . 172 G d
Powder River . . . 198 D b
Powell River . . . 196 ins. A
Powhatans, tribes . . . 188 J c
Pozhega . . . 159 I f
Pozzuoli . . . 46 I e
Pozzuoli, bp. . . . 95 ins.
Præneste . . . 27 G f
Præneste, bp. . . . 96 B b
Prænestine Gate . . . 22 A
Prænestine Way, road . . . 35 ins. B
Prætorian Camp, loc. in Rome 22 A
Prætorian Gate . . . 22 A
Prætorium Latovicorum . . . 27 I b
Prætuttii, people . . . 27 H e
Prævalitana, prov. . . . 43 F e (3)
Praga . . . 115 K b
Pragel Pass . . . 150 E c
Prague . . . 63 H c
Prague, abp. . . . 95 E b
Prague, univ. . . . 100 H d
Prairie, La, battle . . . 189 B b
Prairie du Chien . . . 211 G b
Prasiæ, in Attica . . . 16 C b
Prasiæ, in Laconia . . . 15 C b
Prata Quinctia, loc. in Rome . 22 A
Prato, near Florence . . . 90 L j
Prattigau, valley . . . 91 R l
Pratzen . . . 155 I d
Právia . . . 82 A a
Pré-sur-Arnon, La, mon. . . . 94 C b
Préaux, mon. . . . 94 C b
Prechthal . . . 142 B d
Pregel River . . . 87 M a
Prela . . . 130 P k
Prémontré . . . 69 I f (Prém.)
Prémontré, mon. . . . 94 C b
Prenzlau . . . 79 H b
Prenzlau, Hanse. cy . . . 99 ins. B
Preobrazhensk . . . 138 E d
Prepesinthus, isl. . . . 15 E c
Presburg . . . 63 I d
Presburg, univ. . . . 100 I e
Prescott . . . 210 C d
Présentation, Fort de la . . . 194 D b
Presidio del Norte . . . 190 E f
Presidio, State of the . . . 151 I h
Presqu'Isle, Fort . . . 192 B b
Presteign, parl. bor. . . .
Preston . . . 127 V m
Preston, parl. bor. . . . 163 L d
Prestonpans . . .
Pretoria . . . 175 M l
Preussisch-Eylau . . . 153 I b
Prevesa . . . 93 B c
Priapus . . .
Pribilof Islands . . . 180 K b
Priene . . . 13 E c
Prignitz, dist. . . . 85 B b
Prilip . . . 89 B b
Prilius, lake . . . 26 E e
Prince Albert, town . . . 212 E c
Prince Albert Land . . . 186 H a
Prince Edward Island, Canada 186 M d
Prince Edward Island, Ind. Oc. 182 E E l
Prince George, Fort . . . 193 C d
Prince of Wales, Cape . . . 186 C b
Prince of Wales Island, Arctic Ocean . . . 186 J a
Prince of Wales Island, Pacific Ocean . . . 212 ins.
Prince of Wales Land . . . 212 F a
Prince of Wales Strait . . . 212 D a
Prince Patrick, isl. . . . 186 G a
Prince Regent Inlet . . . 212 F a
Prince Rupert, town . . . 212 ins.
Prince's Island . . . 175 D d
Princeton . . . 192 D c
Principati, dist. . . . 90 E d
Principe da Beira, Fort do . . . 214 C d
Printzdorp . . . 192 ins.
Printzhof . . . 192 ins.
Pripet, Marshes of the . . . 2 G c
Pripet River . . . 139 C e
Prishtina . . . 89 B b
Prison Gate, in Jerusalem . . . 6 ins. A
Prisrend . . . 77 I d
Prittlewell, mon. . . . 97 R j
Pritzwalk, Hanse. cy. . . . 99 ins. B
Privas . . . 126 D d
Privernum . . . 30 C a
Prizlawa . . . 63 G b
Probalinthus . . . 16 B a
Probus, Bridge of . . . 22 A
Prochyta, isl. . . . 30 C b
Procida, isl. . . . 90 D d
Proclamation Line of 1763 . 194 C d, E a
Proconnesus . . .
Proconnesus, isl. . . .
Proconsular Africa, Rom. prov. 34 F f
Proërna . . . 11 D c
Progreso . . . 213 D b
Prome . . .
Promontorium pulchrum, cape . 15 E a
Pronni . . . 10 B d
Pronsk . . . 71 N c
Propaxus, isl. . . . 10 B c
Prophthasia . . . 19 J d
Propylæa, bldg. in Athens . . . 23 C (6)
Propylæum, bldg. in Olympia .
Propontis (Sea of Marmora) . .
Proschium . . . 10 C d
Propopis . . . 4 ins.
Prospalta . . . 16 B b
Prote, isl. . . . 14 B b
Provence, cty., 11 cent. . . . 61 F e
Provence, cty., 12 cent. . . . 69 G e
Provence, cty., 15 cent. . . . 84 F h
Provence, gouv. . . . 146 C c
Provence, marq. . . . 69 F d
Provence, prov. . . . 148 F f
Providence, in Rhode Island . 189 ins. A
Providence, in Maryland . . . 192 C d
Providence, Fort . . . 212 D b
Providence Islands . . .
Provins . . . 76 E b
Prudhomme, Fort . . . 191 H d
Prüm . . . 117 E d
Prüm, mon. . . . 95 D a
Pruntrut . . .
Prusa . . .
Prussia, dist. . . . 77 I b
Prussia, duchy . . . 88 I d
Prussia, km., 1701 . . . 135 K a
Prussia, km., 1812 . . . 155 J a
Prussia, km., 1815—1866 . . . 158—159
Prussia, km., 1910 . . . 161 B-E b
Prussian Customs-Union . . . 160 D c
Prussian Hessian Customs-Union 160 D c
Prussians, people, about 1000 . 59 I c
Pruth River . . . 59 J d
Pruvinum, see Provins
Prytaneum, bldg. in Athens . . 23 D
Prytaneum, bldg. in Olympia .
Przemysl . . . 159 L d
Psacum, prom. . . . 15 D d
Psamathus Port . . . 14 C c
Psaphara . . . 11 E b
Psaphis . . . 15 D a
Psephinus Tower, in Jerusalem 6 ins. A
Pskov . . . 88 M c
Pskov, Hanse. for. cy. . . . 99 I b
Psophis . . . 14 B b
Psyra, isl. . . . 13 D b
Psyttalea, isl. . . . 16 B b
Pteleum . . . 11 D c
Ptolemaïs, in Cyrenaica . . . 35 I g
Ptolemaïs, in Egypt . . . 47 M k
Ptolemaïs (Acre), in Phœnicia . 6 C c
Ptolemies, Kingdom of the . . . 19 U l
Ptolemy, Kingdom of . . . 18 P i, leg.
Ptoon, mt. . . . 11 E d
Ptychia, isl. . . . 10 A c
Pucinum . . . 27 H b
Puebla de los Ángeles (Puebla) 106 B a
Pueblo . . . 198 E c
Pueblo Indians, tribe . . . 188 E c
Puerto Barrios . . . 213 D c
Puerto Bello, see Porto Bello . 214 B b
Puerto Cabello . . . 214 C a
Puerto de Bastimentos . . . 105 E e
Puerto de Caballos . . . 105 C c
Puerto de Luna . . . 190 E e
Puerto de Retrete . . . 105 E e
Puerto de Santa Gloria . . . 105 E c
Puerto Limon . . . 213 D c
Puerto Mexico, see Coatzacoalcos
Puerto Montt . . . 215 B g
Puerto Principe . . . 213 E b
Puerto Plata . . . 213 E c
Puerto viejo . . . 111 A b
Puget Sound . . . 198 A a
Puig . . . 82 B b
Puigcerda . . . 82 C a
Puiset, Le . . . 69 H f
Pukapuka, isl. . . . 107 D i
Pulaski, Fort . . . 208 D c
Pulicat . . .
Pullaria . . . 27 H c
Pulo Condore, isl. . . .
Pulo Penang, isl. . . . 171 K h
Pultusk . . . 87 M b
Puna, see Poona
Puna Island . . . 111 A b
Punakha . . . 171 K f
Punicum . . . 27 F e
Punitz . . . 135 I c
Punjab, Punjaub, reg. . . . 137 B b
Puno . . . 214 B d
Punta Arenas, in Chile . . . 215 B h
Punta Arenas, in Costa Rica . 213 D d
Punta Bernal . . . 106 D a
Puntarenas, see Punta Arenas, in Costa Rica
Pura . . . 19 J e
Purchena . . . 83 K h
Puri . . . 137 E e
Purísima Concepción, in California . . . 190 C e
Purísima Concepción, in Texas 190 F f
Purus River . . . 214 C c
Purysbourg . . . 193 ins. C
Pustertal, valley . . . 115 G e
Pustozersk . . . 138 H b
Puteoli . . . 31 ins. A
Put-in-Bay . . . 200 B c
Putlam . . .
Putlitz . . . 85 C b
Putney . . . 75 I i
Putten, isl. . . . 117 C c
Puttiala . . . 137 C b
Putzig . . . 123 J a
Puy, Le . . . 61 E d
Puy, Le, bp. . . . 94 C b
Puy-de-Dôme, dept. . . . 148 E e
Puyallup, Ind. Res. . . . 188 B a
Puylaurens . . . 126 C e
Pydna . . . 11 D b
Pydna vetus . . . 11 D b
Pylæ Caucasiæ, pass, see Caucasian Gates . . . 18 F b
Pylene . . . 10 C d
Pylos or Pylus, in Messenia . . 14 B c
Pylus, in Elis . . .

Pyramid Lake, Ind. Res. . . . . 188 C b
Pyramids, in Egypt. . . . . 174 J j
Pyramus River . . . . 20 F d
Pyrasus . . . . 11 D c
Pyrenæum, prom. . . . . 38 C d
Pyrenees Mountains . . . . . . 38 B d
Pyrénées, Hautes, dept. . . . . 148 D f
Pyrénées Orientales, dept. . . . 148 E f
Pyrgi, in Greece . . . .
Pyrgi, in Italy. . . . .
Pyritz . . . . 63 H b
Pyrmont. . . . . 158 E b
Pyrrha. . . . .
Pyrrha, prom. . . . . 11 D c
Pyrrhichus . . . . 14 C c
Pythium, in Athens. . . . . 23 D
Pythium, in Thessaly . . . . . . 11 D b
Pyxus . . . . 30 E b
Pyxus River . . . . 30 E c

Quadi, people . . . . 38 F c
Quadratæ. . . . . 26 C b
Quai de la Grève, loc. in Paris 149 B
Quai du Louvre, loc. in Paris. 149 B
Quakenbrück. . . . . 122 E b
Qualla, Ind. Res. . . . . 188 J c
Qu'Appelle. . . . . 212 E c
Quarr, ab. . . . . 100 A b
Quathlamba, mts. . . . . 175 M m
Quatres Bras. . . . . 156 A a
Quatre Vallées, dist. . . . 147 E c (Q. V.)
Quatre Vallées, viscty . . . . . . 76 D e
Quauhtitlan. . . . .
Quebec . . . . 191 K b
Quebec, prov. 1763. . . . . 194 E a
Quebec, prov. 1774. . . . . 194 E a
Quebec, prov. 1910. . . . . 212 H d
Quebrancha River . . . .
Quedlinburg . . . . 62 F c
Quedlinburg, mon. . . . . 95 E a
Queenborough, parl. bor. . . . . 163 O f
Queen Charlotte Islands, near British Columbia . . . . 186 F c
Queen Charlotte Islands (Santa Cruz Island) north east of Queensland . . . . 172 F b
Queen Charlotte Sound. . . . . 212 C c
Queenhithe, loc. in London . . 75 G g
Queen's County. . . . . 127 J i
Queen's Garden, isl. . . . . 105 E b
Queensland, state. . . . . 172 D c
Queenston Heights, battle . . . 200 D b
Queenstown . . . . 127 I j
Queis River . . . . 85 H e
Quelpart, isl. . . . . 171 N e
Quengian . . . .
Quercy, cty. . . . . 61 D d
Querétaro. . . . . 213 ins.
Querquetulan Gate. . . . . 23 B
Querquetulum . . . . 35 ins. B
Quesada. . . . . 82 B b
Quesnoy, le . . . . 117 B d
Quetta. . . . . 170 H e
Quezaltenango. . . . . 105 B d
Quiaca. . . . . 214 C e
Quibdo . . . . 214 B b
Quiberon . . . . 130 C d
Quiberon Bay . . . . 132 B c
Quierzy, see Kiersy
Quilimane . . . . 175 G f
Quillota . . . . 215 B f
Quiloa. . . . . 109 U h
Quilon. . . . .
Quimper . . . . 76 A b
Quimper, bp. . . . . 94 B b
Quimperlé . . . . 76 B c
Quimperlé, mon. . . . . 94 B b
Quinaielt, Ind. Res. . . . . 188 B a
Quincy . . . . 211 G c
Quinsai (Hang-chau-fu) . . . .
Quirinal, palace. . . . . 96 A
Quirinal Gate . . . . 23 B
Quirinal Hill. . . . . 22 A
Quirinus, Temple of. . . . . . . 22 A
Quiros, discoveries of . . . . . .
Quito . . . . 111 B b
Quito, pres. . . . . 215 ins.
Quito, reg. . . . . 111 C b
Quitzow . . . . 85 B b
Quivira, reg. . . . . 190 F d

Raab . . . .
Raab, bp. . . . . 95 F b
Raab River . . . . 159 I e
Raba River, see Raab River
Rabat . . . . 174 C a
Rabba . . . . 99 K g
Rabbath Ammon . . . . 7 D e
Rabbath Moab . . . . 7 D f
Rabida, La . . . . 184 B e
Racca . . . .
Radkersburg . . . . 135 I e
Radnor, in Pa.. . . . . 192 ins.
Radnor, in Wales. . . . . 163 K e
Radnor, cty. . . . . 127 V n
Radnor, parl. bor. . . . . 163 K e
Radnor, parl. dist. . . . . 163 K e
Radolfzell. . . . . 142 C e
Radom. . . . . 87 M c
Radstadt . . . . 123 G e
Radusculan Gate . . . . 23 B
Radziejewo . . . .
Radzin. . . . . 131 H c
Rae, Fort . . . . 212 D b
Raetia, dist. . . . . 62 E e
Rætia, prov. . . . . 38 D c
Rætia I, prov. . . . . 42 E d (6)
Rætia II, prov. . . . . 42 E d (7)
Rætian Alps, mts. . . . . 26 D a
Ragaba . . . . 7 D d
Ragaz . . . . 91 R k
Raglan Castle . . . . 127 W o
Ragusa, in Dalmatia . . . . . . 73 D b
Ragusa, abp. . . . . 95 F c
Ragusa, rep. . . . . 131 G e
Ragusa, in Sicily . . . . 90 E f
Ragy . . . .
Rahin River . . . . 143 ins. F
Rahmanieh or Rahmaniyeh . . . 174 J i
Rai . . . .
Rain . . . . 122 F d
Rainham . . . . 75 J h
Rainier, mt. . . . . 186 G d
Rainy Lake . . . . 191 G b
Raipur. . . . . 137 D d
Rais, dist. . . . . 81 L h
Rais, seign. . . . . 69 C c
Raisin River . . . . 200 B c
Rajamahendri . . . . 112 B b
Rajpootana or Rajputana, dist. . 137 B c
Rajputs, people . . . . 92 H e
Rakka . . . . 99 K f
Rakosfeld, dist. . . . . 159 J e
Raleigh . . . . 211 J c
Raleigh's col. . . . . 191 J d
Rama, dist. . . . . 72 D c
Ramadan, reg. . . . .
Ramah, in Galilee . . . . 6 C c
Ramah, in Judæa. . . . . 7 C e
Rahmah, in Labrador . . . . . . 212 I c
Ramah, in Phœnicia . . . . 6 C b
Ramathaim . . . . 7 C d
Rambacia . . . . 19 K e
Ramillies . . . . 134 C c
Ramleh . . . . 68 ins. A
Ramoth-Gilead . . . .
Ramsay's Mills . . . . 195 B f
Ramsey, mon. . . . . 97 Q i
Rancagua . . . . 215 B f
Rangoon . . . . 171 K g
Rankokus Kill, stream. . . . . . 192 ins.
Ransbecke . . . .
Rapallo . . . . 130 R j
Rapidan River. . . . . 192 B d
Raphia. . . . . 7 A f
Raphoe, bp. . . . . 97 D b
Rappahannock River. . . . 193 F c (Rap.)
Rapperswyl, castle . . . . 91 Q k
Rappoltsweiler. . . . . 143 ins. D
Rara . . . . 62 E d, F c
Raritan River . . . . 192 D c
Raron . . . . 91 P l
Rasa . . . .
Ras Madrak . . . . 170 G g
Rastatt. . . . . 142 B c
Ratæ (Leicester) . . . . 51 P h
Ratanpura. . . . .
Rathenow . . . . 85 C b
Rathlure, bp. . . . . 97 D b
Ratiaria . . . . 39 M l
Ratibor . . . . 79 K c
Ratibor, princ. . . . . 79 K c
Ratisbon. . . . . 63 G d
Ratisbon, bp. . . . . 79 H d
Ratisbon, imp. cy. . . . . 79 G d
Ratkau. . . . . 154 F a
Rat Portage . . . . 212 F d
Ratzeburg. . . . . 62 F b
Ratzeburg, bp. . . . . 79 G b
Raudii, or Raudian Plain, Campi, dist. . . . . 26 C b
Raurici, people . . . . 39 I j
Rauricorum, Augusta (Augst) . 39 I j
Ravendal . . . .
Ravenna. . . . . 27 G c
Ravenna, abp. . . . . 95 E c
Ravensburg . . . . 72 B b
Ravensburg, cty. . . . . 86 G b
Ravensburg, imp. cy. . . . . . . 143 I j
Ravensburg, Neu . . . . 143 I j
Ravenspur . . . . 84 D c
Ravenstein . . . . 117 D c
Rawa . . . . 135 K c
Rawalpindi . . . . 137 B b
Rawdon, route of. . . . . 195 A g
Rawicz . . . .
Rawka . . . . 135 J c
Rawson . . . . 215 C g
Rawulpindee, see Rawalpindi
Raymond . . . . 208 B c
Raystown . . . . 192 B c
Razlawice. . . . . 135 K c
Räzüns . . . . 91 R l
Ré, isl. . . . . 76 C c
Reading, in England . . . . .
Reading, mon. . . . . 97 Q j
Reading, parl. bor. . . . . 163 N f (Read.)
Reading, in Mass. . . . . 189 ins. B
Reading, in Pa. . . . . 196 D b
Reate . . . . 27 G e
Rechberg, Hohen, ruin . . . . . 143 I h
Rechberg, lordship . . . . 143 I h
Recife, or Pernambuco . . . . . 214 F c
Reckheim . . . . 117 D d
Recknitz River . . . . 63 G a
Recovery, Fort . . . . 196 ins. B
Reculver . . . .
Red Lake. . . . . 211 F a
Red Lake, Ind. Res. . . . . 188 G a
Red River, in southern U. S. . 211 G d
Red River, in Tongking . . . . 171 L g
Red River of the North, in U. S. and Canada . . . . 210 F a
Redan, Great and Little, forts 164 L g
Redarians, people . . . . 63 G b
Red Cedar River. . . . . 199 G b
Red Cliff, Ind. Res. . . . . . . 188 H a
Redesdale, dist. . . . .
Redones, people . . . . 38 B c
Redonis, see Rennes
Red Russia, reg. . . . . 139 B e
Red Sea . . . . 3 H f
Redstone, Old, Fort . . . . 195 ins. B
Reepsholt, mon. . . . . 95 D a
Reganesburg, see Ratisbon
Regen River . . . . 63 G d
Regensburg, see Ratisbon
Reggio, in Calabria . . . . 90 E e
Reggio, abp. . . . . 95 F d
Reggio, in Emilia . . . . 90 J h
Reggio, bp. . . . . 95 E c
Reggio, univ. . . . . 100 H f

Regia, in Rome
Regia, quarter in Alexandria . 34 ins. C
Regillus, lake 35 ins. B
Regina, in Saskatchewan 212 E c
Regina castra (Ratisbon) 38 E c
Regium (Reggio in Emilia) 26 E c
Regium, see Riez
Regni, people 51 P i
Regnitz River 62 F d
Regnum (Chichester) 51 P i
Regulbium (Reculver) 51 Q i
Rehoboth, in Mass. 189 ins. A
Rehoboth, in Palestine 7 B f
Reichenau, ab. 142 D e
Reichenau, mon. 95 D b
Reichenbach 135 I c
Reichenbach, mon. 143 F h
Reichenberg 135 H c
Reichenweier 143 ins. D
Reichenweier, lordship 143 ins. D
Reichersberg, mon. 95 E b
Reigate 75 I i
Reigate, parl. bor. 163 N f
Reims 61 F b
Reims, abp. 94 C b
Reims, cty. 61 F b
Reims, duchy 76 F b
Rein, mon. 95 F b
Reindeer Lake 212 E c
Reinhardsbrunn, mon 95 E a
Rejaf 175 G d
Rejang 112 D d
Reliance, Fort 212 E b
Remesiana 43 G e
Remi or Remis, see Reims
Remi, people 38 C c
Remich 117 E e
Remiremont, mon. 148 C b
Rems River 143 I h
Remuria, in Rome 23 B
Renaix 117 B d
Rench River 142 B d
Rendsburg 78 F a
Renfrew, cty.
Rennes 61 C c
Rennes, bp. 94 B b
Rennes, cty. 69 C b
Rennes, gen. 147 D b
Rennsteig, road 62 F c
Reno 210 B c
Reno River 150 F d
Rense 78 E c
Rensselærswyck, dist. 192 D b
Renus (Reno) River 27 F c
Rephaim, Valley of 6 ins. A
Republican River 198 E c
Resaca, battle 208 D c
Resaca de la Palma, battle 201 F d
Resaina 20 H d
Reschen-Scheideck Pass 91 S l
Resengo
Reseph 6 ins. C
Réservoirs, Rue des, street in Versailles 149 A
Resht 170 F e
Resolution, Fort 212 D b
Resolution Island 212 I b
Rest, House of, in Jerusalem 68 ins. B (15)
Restigouche River 199 L a
Retford, parl. bor. 163 N d
Rethel 69 J f
Rethel, cty. 76 F b
Retimo 164 C c
Retovium 26 D c
Retz, duchy 126 A c
Retz, seign. 76 C c
Reuben, tribe 7 ins. D
Reunion, isl. 175 I g
Reuss, cty. 114 F c
Reuss River 91 Q l
Reutlingen, imp. cy. 78 F d
Reval 88 K b
Reval, Hanse. cy. 99 H b
Revesby, mon. 97 R h
Revilla Gigedo Island, Alaska 212 ins.
Revilla Gigedo Islands, to Mexico 213 A c
Revin 117 C e
Rewa 170 J f
Rewa, dist. 137 D d
Rewley, mon. 97 P j
Reyes, Ciudad de los (Lima) . 111 B d
Reykjavik
Rha (Volga) River 35 N d
Rhætian Wall 39 K i
Rhagæ 8 D b
Rhakotis, quarter in Alexandria 34 ins. C
Rhamnus 15 E a
Rheba
Rhegium (Reggio in Calabria). 30 E d
Rhein River, see Rhine River
Rheinau 142 A d
Rheinau, mon. 91 Q k
Rheinberg 117 E c
Rheinbund, see Confederation of the Rhine
Rheinfelden 91 P k
Rheinfelden, lordship 142 A e
Rheinsberg 135 G b
Rheinwald, valley 91 R l
Rheitoi, lake 16 B a
Rheneia, isl. 15 F b
Rhenish Prussia, prov. 158 D c
Rhense, see Rense
Rhenus (Rhine) River 34 F c
Rhesus River
Rhetra 63 G b
Rhin, Bas, dept. 148 F e
Rhin, Haut, dept. 148 F e
Rhine River 2 E c
Rhinocolura 47 M g
Rhion 14 B c
Rhium, prom., in Corsica 26 C e
Rhium, prom., in Greece 14 B a
Rhizus, in Magnesia 11 D c
Rhizus, in Pontus 20 I b
Rhitymna 14 ins.
Rhoda or Rhodæ, in Spain 38 C d
Rhodanus River, see Rhône River
Rhode, in Belgium 156 A a
Rhode Island, col. 189 C d
Rhode Island, isl. 189 ins. A
Rhode Island, state 199 K b (K l)
Rhodes, state 33 C b
Rhodes, isl. 4 C b
Rhodes, Knights of 77 J e
Rhodesia, prot. 175 F f
Rhodius River
Rhodope, mt. 39 M l
Rhodope, Rom. prov. 43 H e (4)
Rhodt 142 B b
Rhodus 43 H f
Rhœdias River 10 D b
Rhœteum
Rhœteum, prom.
Rhône, dept. 148 E e
Rhône River 61 F d
Rhotanus River 26 D e
Rhyndacus River
Rhypes 14 C a
Riade 62 F c, 63 G c
Riadh
Riazan 139 E e
Ribagorza, dist. 83 F c
Ribaut, set. by 191 J e
Ribble River 127 V m
Ribchester
Ribe 158 E a
Ribemont 56 C c
Riblah 6 ins. C
Ribnitz 123 G a
Ricciacum 39 I i
Richelieu, in France 126 B c
Richelieu, Fort, in Canada 189 B a
Richelieu River 189 B b
Richelieu, Rue de, street in Paris 149 B
Richmond, in England
Richmond, parl. bor. 163 M c
Richmond, in Indiana 211 H b
Richmond, in Virginia 193 F c
Richmond, castle, near London 75 I i
Richmond Island 189 C c (Rich.)
Ricina 27 H d
Ricomagus, see Riom
Riddagshausen, mon. 95 E a
Riding Rocks, cape 105 ins.
Ried 135 G d
Riedlingen 143 H i
Rienzi, so-called House of 96 A
Riesa 135 G c
Riesa, mon. 95 E a
Riesenberg, castle 87 I d
Rieti 161 I f
Rieti, bp. 95 E c
Riet Spruit 175 M l
Rieux, bp. 94 C c
Riez, bp. 95 D c
Riffins, isl. 112 G c
Riga 138 B d
Riga, abp. 95 F a
Riga, Hanse. cy. 99 H b
Riga, Gulf of 80 H c
Rigomagus, on the Po R. 26 C b
Rigomagus (Remagen), on the Rhine R. 39 I h
Rigodulum 39 I i
Rijnsburg 62 B b
Rimac River 111 B d
Rimini 90 M i
Rimini, bp. 95 E c
Rimmon, in Galilee 6 C c
Rimmon, in Judæa 7 C e
Rimouski River 199 L a
Rinteln 122 E b
Riobamba 111 B b
Rio Blanco, in Mexico 106 D b
Rio Branco, in Brazil 214 C b
Rio Colorado Chiquito, R. 190 C d
Rio das Boas Sinaes, R. 108 U i
Rio de Janeiro 215 E e
Rio de Janeiro, state 215 E e
Rio de la Antigua, R. 106 D a
Rio de la Buena Guia, R. 190 C e
Rio de la Chira, R. 111 A b
Rio de la Plata, R. 215 D f
Rio de las Balsas, R. 213 ins.
Rio de Nazas, R. 213 B b
Rio de Oro, dist. 175 B b
Rio Dulce (delta of the Orinoco R.) 105 H e
Rio Florido 190 D f
Rio Grande, cty. in Brazil 215 D f
Rio Grande, river, in south central Brazil 214 D d
Rio Grande, river, in south-eastern Brazil 214 E e
Rio Grande, river, between Mexico and U. S. 187 I f
Rio Grande, river, in Panamá. 216
Rio Grande de Santiago, river, in Mexico 213 B b
Rio Grande do Norte, state 214 F c
Rio Grande do Sul, state 215 D e
Riohacha 214 B a
Rioja 215 C e
Rioja, dist. 82 B a
Riom 76 E d
Riom, gen. 147 E b
Riomum, see Riom
Rio Muni, dist. 175 D d
Rio Negro, river, in Arg. Rep. 215 C f
Rio Negro, river, in Brazil 214 C c
Rions, castle 76 C d
Rio Real, R. 214 F d
Rio Salado, river, northern Arg. Rep. 215 C e
Rio Salado, river, southern Arg. Rep. 215 C f
Ripa, Alta 39 J i
Ripaille, mon. 86 F e

Ripley . . . . 206 ins.
Ripoll, mon. . . . . 94 C c
Ripon . . . . 65 F c
Ripon, mon. . . . . 97 P g
Ripon, parl. bor. . . . . 163 M c
Rippoldsau, mon. . . . . 142 B d
Ripuarians, people . . . . 50 E c
Risano, bp. . . . . 95 F c
Risingham . . . .
Risinum . . . . 38 F d
Riss River . . . . 143 I i
Ritzebüttel . . . . 114 E b
Riu-kiu (Liu-kiu) Islands . . . 171 N f
Riva . . . . 134 F f
Rivaulx, mon. . . . . 97 Q g
Rivera . . . . 215 D f
River Gate . . . .
Rivières du Sud, dist. . . . . . . 174 B c
Rivoli, near Turin . . . . 130 P i
Rivoli, near Verona . . . . 150 F d
Roanne . . . . 76 E c
Roanoke Island . . . . 193 G d
Roanoke River . . . . 193 F c
Robertsbridge, mon. . . . . 97 R k
Robertsons, fam. . . . .
Robertson's Trail, route . . . . . 194 B c
Roberval . . . . 184 D c
Rocca San Casciano . . . . 90 L i
Roccasecca . . . . 90 D d
Rochdale, parl. bor. . . . . 163 L d
Roche, mon., in England . . . . 97 P h
Roche, la, in Belgium . . . . . . 76 F a
Roche, la, in France . . . . . . 143 ins. F
Roche, la, cty. . . . . 69 F a
Rochedale Hundred . . 193 ins. A (Roch.)
Rochefort, in Belgium . . . . . . 117 D d
Rochefort, in France . . . . 84 C g
Rochelle, La . . . . 76 C c
Rochelle, La, gen. . . . . 147 D b
Rochester, in England . . . . . . 127 Z o
Rochester, bp. . . . . 97 R j
Rochester, castle and mon. . . 74 F f
Rochester, Hanse. for. cy. . . . .
Rochester, parl. bor. . . . . 163 O f
Rochester, in New York . . . 211 J b
Rochlitz . . . . 115 G c
Rock Island . . . . 211 G b
Rock River . . . . 191 H c
Rockhampton . . . . 172 E c
Rockingham . . . . 65 F d
Rocky Mountains, The . . . . . 186 H c
Rocoux . . . . 134 C c
Rocroy . . . . 157 ins.
Rodalben . . . . 142 ins. B
Rodez . . . . 76 E d
Rodez, bp. . . . . 94 C c
Roding River . . . . 75 J h
Rodomum, see Rouen
Rodosto . . . . 93 C b
Rodriguez Island . . . . 182 HHi
Roebourne . . . . 172 A c
Roer River . . . . 117 E d
Roermond . . . . 117 E c
Roermond, Hanse. cy. . . . . . . 99 ins. B
Roeskilde . . . . 58 G b
Roeskilde, Hanse. for. cy. . . . . 98 F b
Rœulx . . . . 156 A a
Rogalin . . . . 159 I b
Rogel, Well of . . . . 6 ins. A
Rohan . . . . 69 B c
Rohilcund, Rohilkhand, dist. . . 137 C c
Roidomna, see Roanne
Rojas . . . . 215 C f
Roma, Temple of . . . .
Roma, in Queensland . . . . . . 172 D c
Roma, see Rome, in Italy
Roma quadrata, loc. in Rome, Italy . . . . 23 B
Romagna, dist. . . . . 90 D b
Roman Empire about 395 . . . . 42, 43
Roman Empire of the German Nation about 1000 . . . . 58, 59
Roman Empire of the German Nation, 1138—1254 72
Roman Empire, Holy, about 1000 58, 59
Roman Empire, Holy, 1138—1254 72
Roman Forum, The . . . . 24 B
Roman Forum, Aug. Reg. of Rome . . . . 22 A
Roman Gate, in Olympia . . . .
Romania, desp. . . . . 93 A c
Romania, emp. . . . . 73 F b
Romano, Cape . . . . 191 I f
Roman Republic, 1803 . . . . . . 151 I h
Romans . . . . 126 D d
Romanula Gate . . . . 24 A
Roman Wall, in England . . . .
Roman Wall, in Hungary . . . . 159 J f
Romanzof, Cape . . . . 198 ins. A
Rome, in Georgia . . . . 208 C c
Rome, in Italy . . . . 27 G f
Rome, abp. . . . . 95 E c
Rome, ancient imperial, plan of 22 A
Rome, ancient republican, plan of 23 B
Rome, medieval, plan of . . . . 96 A
Rome, modern, plan of . . . . . 22 A
Rome, patr. . . . . 52 J f
Rome, territorial expansion of 34, 35
Rome, univ. . . . . 100 H f
Rome, vicinity of ancient . . . . 35 ins. B
Rome, in New York . . . . 192 D b
Rome, Temple of . . . . 24 B
Rome, City of, Rom. dioc. . . . 42 E e
Romford . . . . 75 J h
Romney . . . .
Romont, castle . . . . 91 O l
Romorantin . . . . 126 B c
Romorantin, castle . . . . 76 D c
Romsey, ab. . . . . 100 A b
Romulus, Grave of . . . .
Romulus, Hut of . . . . 24 A
Roncaglia . . . . 72 B c
Roncesvalles . . . . 82 B a
Roncesvalles, mon. . . . . 94 B c
Ronda . . . . 82 A b
Ronnenberg . . . . 52 C a
Ronsse . . . . 117 B d
Roosbeke . . . .
Roosendaal . . . . 117 C c
Roper River . . . . 172 C b
Ropicum . . . . 26 C e
Roraima, mt. . . . . 214 C b
Rorkes Drift . . . . 175 N l
Rorschach . . . . 142 D e
Rosalie, Fort . . . . 191 G e
Rosario, in Arg. Rep. . . . . . . 215 C f
Rosario, in Mexico . . . . 213 B b
Rosasna . . . . 153 O g
Roscianum . . . . 31 F c
Roscommon, bp. . . . . 97 C c
Roscommon, cty. . . . . 127 I h
Rosebud, Ind. Res. . . . . 188 F b
Roselle . . . . 64 B b
Rosenfeld . . . . 143 G i
Rosemarkie, bp. . . . .
Rosetta . . . . 174 J i
Rosheim . . . . 126 E b
Rosières . . . . 156 B a
Ross, bp., in Ireland . . . . . . 97 B e
Ross, bp., in Scotland . . . . . . 97 H b
Ross, cty. . . . .
Ross, parl. bor. . . . .
Ross, dist. . . . .
Rossano . . . . 64 C c
Rossano, abp. . . . . 95 F d
Rossbach . . . . 134 F c
Rossbühl Pass . . . . 134 E d
Rossieny . . . . 159 L a
Rossland . . . . 212 D d
Rosslau . . . . 123 G c
Rossomme, farm . . . . 156 C c
Rossstall . . . . 62 F d
Rosstock, mt. . . . . 150 E c
Rostock, Hanse. cy. . . . . 99 ins. B
Rostock, univ. . . . . 100 H d
Rostov, on the Don R. . . . . . 71 N d
Rostov, north-east of Moscow 138 E d
Rostra, loc. in Rome . . . . 24 A (6)
Rostra Julia, loc. in Rome . . . 24 B (15)
Rostro Hermoso . . . . 108 N h
Röteln, lordship . . . . 142 A e
Rotenturm Pass . . . . 159 M f
Roth, ab. . . . . 143 J j
Roth River, flowing into Danube R. . . . . 143 I i
Roth River, flowing into Kocher River . . . . 143 J g
Rothenburg, imp. cy. on the Tauber . . . . 143 J g
Rothenfels, ruin . . . . 143 J j
Rotherham . . . . 162 E d
Rotherhithe . . . . 75 I i
Rothesay . . . .
Rothière, La . . . . 154 C d
Rotomagus (Rouen) . . . . 38 C c
Rottenburg . . . . 143 G i
Rottenmünster, ab. . . . . 143 G i
Rotterdam . . . . 117 C c
Rottumeroog, isl. . . . . 117 E a
Rottweil, imp. cy. . . . . 143 G i
Roucy . . . . 69 I f
Roucy, cty. . . . . 69 I f
Rouen . . . . 61 D b
Rouen, abp. . . . . 94 B b
Rouen, gen. . . . . 147 E b
Rouergue, cty. . . . . 61 E d
Rouge, Fort . . . .
Rouillé, Fort . . . . 192 B b
Roulers . . . . 117 B d
Roum, sultanate . . . . 67 M f
Round Valley . . . . 188 B c
Rouse's Point . . . . 199 K b
Roussart, Le . . . . 156 C c
Rousselaere . . . . 117 B d
Roussillon . . . . 126 D d
Roussillon, cty. . . . . 61 E e
Roussillon, gouv. . . . . 146 B c
Roussillon, prov. . . . . 148 E f
Roussy . . . . 69 J f
Rouvray . . . . 76 E b
Rovereto . . . . 114 F f
Rovigno . . . . 90 D b
Rovigo . . . . 90 J h
Rovuma River . . . . 175 G f
Roxburgh . . . .
Roxbury . . . . 189 ins. B
Roxolani or Roxolans, people . 35 L d
Royal Canal . . . . 126 B e
Royal Castle, in Athens . . . . . 23 D
Royal Niger Company . . . . . . 174 D c
Royan . . . . 76 C d
Rubi . . . . 31 F a
Rubicon River . . . . 27 G c
Rubruck or Rubruquis, William of, route of . . . .
Rudau . . . . 79 L a
Ruden, isl. . . . . 123 G a
Rudiæ . . . . 31 H b
Rudnia . . . . 153 O f
Rudolf, lake . . . . 175 G d
Rudolstadt . . . . 62 F c
Rueda . . . . 82 A a
Rue de la Chancellerie, street in Versailles . . . . 149 A
Rue de la Paroisse, street in Versailles . . . . 149 A
Rue de la Surintendance, street in Versailles . . . . 149 A
Rue de l'Orangerie, street in Versailles . . . . 149 A
Rue de Richelieu, street in Paris 149 B
Rue des Hôtels, street in Versailles . . . . 149 A
Rue des Réservoirs, street in Versailles . . . . 149 A
Rue de Faubourg Saint Honoré, street in Paris . . . . 149 B
Rue du Temple, street in Paris 149 B
Rue Saint Antoine, street in Paris 149 B
Rue Saint Denis, street in Paris 149 B
Rue Saint Honoré, street in Paris 149 B
Rue Saint Jacques, street in Paris 149 B

Rue Saint Martin, street in Paris 149 B
Rue Saint Martin, street in Versailles 149 A
Rue Vivienne, street in Paris 149 B
Rufford, mon. 97 P h
Rugeley 162 D e
Rügen, isl. 63 G a
Rügen, princ. 79 I a
Rügenwalde 135 I a
Rügenwalde, Hanse. cy. 98 G c
Rugia (Rugen), isl. 38 E b
Rugians or Rugii, people
Ruginium (Rovigno) 27 H b
Ruha 77 L e
Ruhr River 62 D c
Ruith 142 C b
Rûm, sultanate, see Roum
Rumania, km. 164 D b
Rumania, princ. 164 D b
Rumanians, people 165 leg.
Rum Cay, isl. 105 F b
Rumelia, dist. 93 B b
Rumelia, Eastern, prov. 164 C b
Rumigny 69 J f
Runnymede 75 H i
Runsiens, people 188 B c
Rupert River 212 H c
Rupert's Land
Ruppin 79 H b
Ruppin, cty. 87 I b
Rura (Ruhr) River 39 I h
Rusa 138 E d
Rusaddir 38 B e
Rusellæ 27 F e
Rusicade 38 D e
Ruspæ or Ruspe 12 F c
Ruspina 38 E e
Russell 172 G d
Russia, reg., about 1000 59 J L c
Russia, reg., about 1190 71 L c
Russian Empire, about 1740 131 J b
Russian Empire, 14—18 cent. 138/139
Russian Empire, 1910 170 F/O c
Russians, people 47 L c
Russian States, 14 cent. 77 K a
Russo 71 M b
Rustchuk
Rustdorp 189 ins. C
Rustenburg 175 M l
Ruteni or Rutenis, see Rodez
Ruteni, people 38 C d
Ruthenians, people 168 leg.
Rutland, cty. 127 Y n
Rutland, parl. dist. 163 N e
Rütli 91 Q l
Rutuba River 26 B d
Rutuli, people 35 ins. B
Rutupiæ (Richborough) 51 Q i
Ruvo 90 F d
Rybinsk 167 M d
Rye 189 D c
Rye, parl. bor. 163 O g
Rypin 159 J b
Ryswick 122 C b
Rzhev 138 D d

Saale River, flowing into Elbe R. 63 F c
Saale River, flowing into Main R. 62 E c
Saalfeld 63 F c
Saalkreis, dist. 122 F c
Saanen 91 P l
Saane River 150 D c
Saarbrücken 62 D d
Saarlouis 122 D d
Saar River 114 D d
Saarwerden 114 D d
Saavedra, route of ... 107 B f, 110 F F g
Saaz 63 G c
Sabará 214 E d
Sabaria 42 F d
Sabate 27 G e
Sabatia, Vada 26 C c
Sabatinus, lake 27 G e
Sabatus River, in Bruttium 31 F c
Sabatus River, in Samnium 30 D b
Sabatum, Ad 31 F c
Sabellians, people 39 C c
Sabina, bp. 96 B a
Sabina, dist. 90 D c
Sabine River 211 G d
Sabini, people, west of L. Benacus 26 E b
Sabines, or Sabini, north-east of Rome 27 G e
Sabino 189 D c
Sabis River 39 H h
Sablé 76 C c
Sable, Cape, in Florida 187 K f
Sable, Cape, in Nova Scotia 186 M d
Sable Island 212 J d
Sabrata 12 F d
Sabrina (Severn) River 38 B b
Sabrina Æstuarium (Bristol Channel) 51 O i
Sabutum
Sacæ, Sacans, people 18 S h
Sacaraucæ, people 19 H b
Sacasene, dist. 35 N e
Sacaseni, people 18 G b
Sacer River 26 D e
Sachion
Sachsenburg, in Carinthia 135 G e
Sachsenburg, castle in Thuringia 115 ins. B
Sachsenhausen 78 F c
Sachsenheim, Gross 143 H h
Sachsenklemme, pass 154 F e
Sacile 154 G f
Sacketts Harbor 200 E b
Säckingen 142 A e
Säckingen, mon. 95 D b
Saco 189 C c
Saco River 189 C b
Sacramento, in Cal. 210 A c
Sacramento, in Mexico 198 D e
Sacramento River 210 A c
Sacra Urbs, Temple of 24 B
Sacred Mount 35 ins. B
Sacred Gate 23 D
Sacred Way, street in Athen 23 C
Sacred Way, street in Rome 24 A, B
Sacrificios, Isla de, isl. 106 D a
Sacriportus 35 ins. B
Sacrum, prom., in Corsica 26 D d
Sacrum, prom., in Portugal 38 A e
Sadowa 159 H c
Sæpinum 30 D a
Sæpta Julia, loc. in Rome 24 B
Sætabis 38 B e
Sævo, mt. 34 F a
Safed 68 ins. A
Sagadahoc 191 L c
Sagadahoc River 189 D b
Sagan 85 H e
Sagan, duchy 115 H c
Sagar 137 C d
Sagartians, people 8 D b
Sagartii 19 I d
Sagii, see Sées
Saginaw 211 I b
Saginaw Bay 211 I b
Saginaws, tribe 188 I b
Sagis River 27 G c
Sagone 148 C c
Sagra River 31 F d
Sagres 82 A b
Sagrus (Sangro) River 27 I e
Saguenay River 212 H d
Saguntum 38 C e
Sahagun 82 B a
Sahagun, mon. 94 A c
Sahara, desert 175 C b
Saigon 171 L g
Saint, see also Sankt
Saint-Affrique see Saint-Frique 126 C e
Saint Alban, church in London 75 G g (10)
Saint Albans, in England
Saint Albans, mon.
Saint Albans, parl. bor. 163 N f
Saint Albans, in Vermont 207 L b
Saint-Amand 156 B a
Saint-Amand-la-Haye 156 B a
Saint Andrew, church in London, near Holebourn Bridge 75 G g
Saint Andrew, church in London, on Leadenhall Street 75 G g (13)
Saint Andrew, Fort, in Georgia 193 D f
Saint Andrews, in Scotland
Saint Andrews, abp. 97 I b
Saint Andrews, univ. 100 E c
Saint Anne, in Mackenzie Ter. 212 D b
Saint Anne, church in Jerusalem 68 ins. B (14)
Saint Anthony, Falls of 191 G a
Saint-Antoine, near Paris 122 B d
Saint-Antoine, Faubourg, quarter in Paris 149 B
Saint-Antoine, mon. 148 C b
Saint-Antoine, Plaine, loc. in Versailles 149 A
Saint-Antoine, Rue, street in Paris 149 B
Saint Asaph, bp. 97 N h
Saint Augustine, in Florida 193 D g
Saint Augustine, church in London 75 G g (4)
Saint-Avit, mon. 94 C b
Saint Barthélemy, isl., in West India 213 F c
Saint Bartholomew, priory in London 75 G g
Saint Bartholomew's Spital, in London 75 G g
Saint Benets-at-Hulme, mon.
Saint-Benoit-sur-Loire, mon. 94 C b
Saint-Bernard, mon. 95 D b (S. B.)
Saint Bernard, Great, pass 26 B b
Saint Bernard, Little, pass 26 A b
Saint Bernardino, pass 26 D a
Saint Blaise, ab. 142 B e
Saint Blaise, mon. 142 B e
Saint Botolph, church near Aldgate, in London 75 G g
Saint Botolph, church near Bishopsgate, in London 75 G g
Saint Botolph, church near London Bridge, in London 75 G g (28)
Saint Bride, church in London 75 G g (2)
Saint-Brieuc 61 B b
Saint-Brieuc, bp. 94 B b
Saint-Bris 126 A d
Saint Callistus, Catacombs of 96 A
Saint Catharines 207 I b
Saint Charles, in Missouri 199 G c
Saint Charles, Fort, in Illinois 191 G d
Saint Charles, Fort, in Manitoba 191 F b
Saint-Chef, mon. 148 C b
Saint Christopher (St. Kitts), isl. 213 F c
Saint Clair, lake 200 B b
Saint Clairsville 206 ins.
Saint Clare, abbey in London 75 G g
Saint-Claude 126 D c
Saint-Claude, mon. 148 C b
Saint Clement's Danes, church in London 75 G g
Saint Clement's Well, loc. in London 75 G g
Saint-Cloud 114 B d
Saint-Cloud, Avenue de, in Versailles 149 A
Saint Croix, isl. 105 H c
Saint Croix River, between Minnesota and Wisconsin 191 G b
Saint Croix River, eastern boundary of Maine 191 L b
Saint Cross, mon. 100 A b
Saint Cyril 138 E d
Saint David, Fort (Cuddalore) 137 C f
Saint Davids (Mynyw)
Saint Davids, bp. 97 L j
Saint Demetrius, loc. near ancient Troy
Saint Denis, in Illinois 191 H d
Saint-Denis, near Paris 76 E b
Saint-Denis, mon. 94 C b

Saint Denis, on Réunion I. 175 I g
Saint-Denis, Faubourg, quarter in Paris 149 B
Saint-Denis, Porte, loc. in Paris 149 B
Saint-Denis, route of 190 E e
Saint-Denis, Rue, street in Paris 149 B
Saint-Dié, mon. 95 D b
Saint Dimitri, quarter in Constantinople 93 G e
Saint-Dizier 134 C d
Saint Domingue, col.
Saint Dunstan, in the East, church in London 75 G g (29)
Saint Dunstan, in the West, church in London 75 G g
Saint Edmund the King, church in London 75 G g (16)
Sainte-Foy 126 B d
Sainte-Geneviève 191 G d
Sainte-Geneviève, church in Paris 149 B
Saint Elias, mt. 186 E b
Saint Elias Range 212 ins.
Sainte-Marguerite, isl. 126 E e
Sainte-Marie 191 I c
Sainte-Marie, isl. 175 I f
Sainte-Menehould 134 C d
Saintes 76 C d
Saintes, bp. 94 B b
Saint Ethelburga, church in London 75 G g
Sainte-Thérèse, Fort 189 B b
Saint-Étienne 76 F d
Saint-Étienne-de-Vaux, mon. 94 B b
Saint-Eustache, Saint Eustatius, isl. 213 F c
Saint Fagans 127 V o
Saint-Flour 76 E d
Saint-Flour, bp. 94 C b
Saint Francis River 189 B b
Saint-François-de-Sales 189 C a
Saint-Frique 126 C e
Saint-Fuscien, mon. 94 C b
Saint Gall 56 D c
Saint Gall, mon. 95 D b
Sainte-Geneviève, church in Paris 149 B
Saint George, Fort, in Florida 193 D f
Saint George, Fort (Madras) 137 D f
Saint George Mouth, Danube R. 164 D b
Saint Georges, in Maine 189 D c
Saint George's Bay 215 C g
Saint George's Channel 49 C f
Saint-Germain-en-Laye 126 C b
Saint-Germain, Faubourg, quarter in Paris 149 B
Saint-Germain-des-Prés, church in Paris 149 B
Saint Germans, mon. 97 M k
Saint Germans, parl. bor. 163 J g
Saint-Gildas-de-Ruis, mon. 94 B b
Saint-Gildas-de-Bois, mon. 94 B b
Saint Giles, church in Jerusalem 68 ins. B (5)
Saint-Gilles, mon. 94 C c
Saint Gotthard Pass 91 Q l
Saint Helena, isl., in the Atlantic Ocean 108 Q i
Saint Helena Island, off S. C. 193 ins. C
Saint Helens, mon. 100 A b
Saint Helen's Priory, in London 75 G g
Saint-Hippolyte 143 ins. F
Saint-Honorat, isl. 126 E e
Saint-Honoré, Faubourg, quarter in Paris 149 B
Saint-Honoré, Rue, street in Paris 149 B
Saint-Honoré, Rue du Faubourg, street in Paris 149 B
Saint-Hubert 117 D d
Saint-Hubert, ab. of 117 D e
Saint-Hubert, mon. 95 D a
Saint-Ignace, in Canada 191 J c
Saint-Ignace, in Michigan 191 H b
Saint Inigoes 192 C d
Saint Ives 98 ins. A
Saint Ives, parl. bor. 163 I g
Saint-Jaques, Faubourg, quarter in Paris 149 B
Saint-Jaques, Rue, street in Paris 149 B
Saint James, church, in London 75 G g (23)
Saint James the Elder, church, in Jerusalem 68 ins. B (11)
Saint James the Less, chapel, in Jerusalem 68 ins. B (6)
Saint-Jean-d'Acre 68 ins. A
Saint-Jean-d'Angély 76 C c
Saint-Jean-d'Angély, mon. 94 B b
Saint-Jean-de-Losne 69 J g
Saint-Jean-de-Maurienne 130 O i
Saint-Jean-Pied-de-Port 126 A e
Saint John, in Quebec 194 E a
Saint John, in New Brunswick 212 I d
Saint John, Fort, on Peace R. 212 C c
Saint John, Fort, on Richelieu R. 189 B b
Saint John, Knights of 73 F c
Saint John, lake 212 H d
Saint John, priory in London 75 G g
Saint John River 211 L a
Saint John Lateran, ch. 96 A
Saint John the Baptist, ch. 68 ins. B (4)
Saint Johns, in Newfoundland 212 J d
Saint Johns-at-Colchester, mon. 97 R j
Saint John's Field 75 I h
Saint John's Island (Prince Edward Island) 212 I d
Saint Johns River 211 I e
Saint Joseph, in Missouri 211 G c
Saint Joseph, in Michigan 211 H b
Saint Joseph, Fort
Saint Joseph River 191 H c
Saint-Josse 76 D a
Saint-Jouin-de-Marnes, mon. 94 B b
Saint Julian, Port 108 K l
Saint Katherine, hospital in London 75 G g
Saint Katherine Cree, bldg. in London 75 G g (14)
Saint Kitts (St. Christopher), isl. 213 F c
Saint Ladre, postern, gate in Jerusalem 68 ins. B
Saint-Laurent, mon. 94 C b
Saint Laurentius Island 109 V j
Saint Lawrence, church in London 75 G g (11)
Saint Lawrence, Gulf of 186 M d
Saint Lawrence Basin 187 K-L d
Saint Lawrence Island 180 J a
Saint Lawrence River 186 L d
Saint-Lazare, ch. 149 B
Saint Lazarus Islands 212 F b
Saint Leger, route of 195 D a
Saint-Lô 76 C b
Saint-Lô, mon. 94 B b
Saint-Lomer-le-Moutier, mon. 94 C b
Saint Louis, in Canada 191 I c
Saint Louis, in Missouri 191 G d
Saint Louis, in Senegal 174 B c
Saint Louis, Fort, in Illinois Country 191 H c
Saint Louis, Fort, in Texas 190 F f
Saint-Louis, Ile, isl. 149 B
Saint Louis River 188 H a
Saint Louis and San Francisco Grant 210 D c
Saint Lucia, isl. 213 F c
Saint Magnus, church in London 75 G g (27)
Saint-Maixent 126 A c
Saint-Maixent, mon. 94 B b
Saint-Malo 76 B b
Saint-Malo, bp. 94 B b
Saint-Marcel, Faubourg, quarter in Paris 149 B
Saint-Marcel, mon. 94 C c
Saint Margarets Church, London 75 G g
Saint Marks 193 B f
Saint-Martin, near Ligny 156 B b
Saint Martin, ch. 68 ins. B (10)
Saint-Martin, Faubourg, quarter in Paris 149 B
Saint Martin, isl. 213 F c
Saint-Martin, Porte, loc. in Paris 149 B
Saint-Martin, Rue, street in Paris 149 B
Saint-Martin, Rue, street in Versailles 149 A
Saint Martin le Grand, church in London 75 G g
Saint Martin of Tours, mon. 94 C b
Saint Martin Outwich, church in London 75 G g (12)
Saint Mary Aldermary, church in London 75 G g (19)
Saint Mary Bothaw, church in London 75 G g (25)
Saint Mary Magdalen, church in Jerusalem 68 ins. B (13)
Saint Mary Magdalene, church in London, east of St. Pauls 75 G g (7)
Saint Mary Magdalene, church in London, south of St. Pauls 75 G g (20)
Saint Mary of Grace, abbey in London 75 G g
Saint Mary of the Germans, hospital 68 ins. B (9)
Saint Mary of the Latins, ch. 68 ins. B (3)
Saint Mary Overey's Priory, in London 75 G g
Saint Mary Spital, bldg. in London 75 G g
Saint Mary's-at-York, mon. 97 Q h
Saint Mary's, in Maryland 192 C d
Saint Mary Somerset, church in London 75 G g (21)
Saint Mary's River 193 D f
Saint-Maur-des-Fossées, mon. 94 C b
Saint-Maur-sur-Loire, mon. 94 B b
Saint-Maurice, mon. 91 O l
Saint Maurice River 212 H d
Saint Mawes, parl. bor. 163 J g
Saint Maximin, mon. 95 D b
Saint Michael, in Alaska 198 ins. A
Saint Michael, church in London 75 G g (15)
Saint Michael le Querne, church in London 75 G g (9)
Saint Michael Paternoster, church in London 75 G g (24)
Saint-Michel, Faubourg, quarter in Paris 149 B
Saint-Michel, Pont, loc. in Paris 149 B
Saint-Mihiel 184 E c
Saint Neots, mon. 97 Q i
Saint Nicolas 117 C c
Saint Olave, church in London 75 G g
Saint-Omer 76 E a
Saint-Omer, mon. 94 C a
Saintonge, cty. 61 C d
Saintonge, prov. 148 D e
Saintonge and Angumois, gouv. 146 A b
Saint-Papoul 94 C c
Saint-Paul, near Nice 126 E e
Saint Paul, in Minnesota 199 G b
Saint-Paul, bp., near Orange 94 C c
Saint Paul Island 182 II k
Saint Paul de Loanda 175 E e
Saint Paul's, church in London 75 G g
Saint Paul's Bakehouse, in London 75 G g (31)
Saint Paul's Cross, in London 75 G g (3)
Saint Peter in Gallicantem, church in Jerusalem 68 ins. B
Saint Peter, church in Cheapside, London 75 G g (8)
Saint Peter, church in Cornhill, London 75 G g
Saint Peter, church in Jerusalem 68 ins. B (12)
Saint Peter, Patrimony of (States of the Church) 64 ins.
Saint Peter's, church in Rome 22 A, 96 A
Saint Petersburg 138 D c
Saint Peters' Yard, Hanse. for. off. 88 N b

Saint Philip, Fort 200 I g
Saint-Pierre, Fort 191 G b
Saint-Pierre, isl. 212 J d (St. P.)
Saint-Pol 76 E a
Saint-Pol-de-Leon 76 A b
Saint-Pol-de-Leon, bp. 94 B b
Saint-Pons, bp. 94 C c
Saint-Pourçain, mon. 94 C b
Saint-Quentin 61 E b
Saint-Rambert, mon. 95 D b
Saint Regis 200 F a
Saint Regis, Ind. Res. 188 L b
Saint-Riquier, mon. 94 C a
Saint-Roch, church in Paris 149 B
Saint Romanus, Late of
Saint-Sacrement, lake 192 E b
Saint-Sauveur 69 I g
Saint-Seine, mon. 95 C b
Saint-Seurin, mon. 94 B c
Saint-Sever, castle 76 C e
Saint-Sever, mon. 94 C c
Saint Simeon 68 C b
Saint Simon Island 193 D f
Saint Sophia, church in Constantinople 93 G e (1)
Saint Stephen, church in London 75 G e (17)
Saint Stephen, gate 68 ins. B
Saint Stephen, street 68 ins. B
Saint-Sulpice, mon. 95 D b
Saint Swithin, church in London 75 G g (18)
Saint-Thierry, mon. 94 C b (S.T.)
Saint Thomas, isl., Gulf of Guinea 175 D e
Saint Thomas, isl., West Indies 213 F c
Saint Thomas of Acon, church in London 75 G g (6)
Saint-Trond 117 C d
Saint-Trond, mon. 95 D a
Saint Trudpert, mon. 95 D b
Saint-Urbain, mon., in France 95 D b
Saint Urban, mon., in Switzerland 91 P k
Saint-Vaast, mon., near Arras 94 C a
Saint-Vaast-de-la-Hougue 126 A b
Saint-Valery, mon. 94 C a
Saint-Vandrille, mon. 94 C b (St. Van.)
Saint-Victor, Faubourg, quarter in Paris 149 B
Saint Vincent, cape 83 J h
Saint Vincent, isl. 213 F c
Saint Vincent Gulf 172 C d
Saint-Vrain, Fort 210 E b
Saint Xavier 191 H c
Saint-Wandrille, mon. see Saint-Vandrille
Saint-Yrieux 126 B d
Sairam
Sais 4 F c
Sajama, volcano 214 C d
Sajo River 115 K d
Sakaria River 93 C b
Sakhalin, isl. 171 P c
Sala (Saale) River 38 E b
Saladin, Dom. of 71 M g
Salamanca 82 A a
Salamanca, bp. 94 A c
Salamanca, univ. 100 D f
Salamis, in Attica 16 B b
Salamis, on Cyprus I. 47 M f
Salamis, isl. 15 D b
Salapia 31 F a
Salapia, lake 31 F a
Salarian Gate 22 A
Salarian Way, road 27 H e
Salassi, people 26 B b
Saldæ 38 C e
Saldaña 82 B a
Salem, in Mass. 189 ins. B
Salem, in New Jersey 192 D d
Salem, in Ohio 207 I b
Salem, in Oregon 198 A b
Salem, in Palestine 7 C d
Salem Creek 192 ins.
Salemi 161 I i
Saleph River 67 M f
Salerno 90 E d
Salerno, abp. 95 F e
Salerno, princ. 64 C b
Salerno, univ. 100 H f
Salernum (Salerno) 30 D b
Saletio 39 J i
Salford 162 D d
Salford, parl. bor. 163 L d (Salf.)
Salians, people 50 D b
Salihiyeh 174 J i
Salina Cruz 213 C c
Salinæ (Castellane) 26 A d
Salins 69 J f
Salinus (Saline) River 27 I e
Salisbury, in England
Salisbury, bp. 97 P j
Salisbury, parl. bor. 163 M f (Salisb.)
Salisbury, in Mass. 189 C c (Salisb.)
Salisbury, in N. Carolina 195 A f
Salisbury, in Rhodesia 175 G f
Salisbury Plain 49 F f
Salkhat 6 F c
Sallentini 31 G b
Sallentinum, prom. 31 H c
Sallust, Gardens of 22 A
Salm, in the Ardennes 62 C c
Salm, in the Vosges 126 E b
Salm, cty. in the Vosges 134 D d
Salm, cty., in Westphalia 151 H f
Salmansweiler, ab. 142 D e
Salmantica (Salamanca) 38 A d
Salmon Falls, town 189 C c
Salmon River 198 B a
Salmydessus 39 N l
Salò 150 F d
Salobreña 82 B b
Salodurum (Solothurn) 39 I j
Salofo, reg. 108 P f
Salona, in Dalmatia 42 F e
Salona, in Greece 89 B c
Salonæ (Salona, in Dalmatia) 38 F d
Salonica or Saloniki 59 I e
Salsette Island 137 B e (S.)
Salt River, Ind. Res. 188 D d
Salta 215 C e
Saltanovka 153 O g
Saltillo 201 E d
Salt Lake City 198 C b
Salto 215 D f
Saltus Castulonensis, mts. 38 B e
Saluda River 193 C d
Salurnis 27 F a
Salus, Gate of 23 B
Salus, Temple of 22 A
Saluzzo 90 H h
Saluzzo, marq. 126 E d
Salvador, country 213 D c
Salvatierra 213 ins.
Salwin River
Salz 55 R i
Salza 72 C a
Salzach River 63 G e
Salzburg 63 G e
Salzburg, abp. 95 E b
Salzburg, elect. 157 I g
Salzungen 62 E c
Salzungen, mon. 95 E a
Salzwedel 62 F b
Salzwedel, Hanse. cy. 99 ins. B
Sama River 214 B d
Samag 99 M e
Samalanga 112 C c
Samana, cape 105 G c
Samana, isl. 105 F b
Samar, isl. 199 ins. H
Samara 139 H e
Samara River, see Sambre River and Somme River
Samaria 7 C d
Samaria, dist. 7 C d
Samarcand or Samarkand 92 G d
Samarobriva (Amiens) 38 C c
Samaron 99 M e
Samarovskoe 170 H b
Sambalpur 137 D d
Sambhal
Sambhal, reg.
Sambor
Sambracitan Gulf 26 A d
Sambre River 62 C c
Sambreffe 156 B a
Same 10 B d
Samicum 14 B b
Samme River 156 A a
Samnites, people
Samnium, reg. 30 D a
Samnium, Rom. prov. 42 E e (7)
Samoa Islands 199 ins. D
Samogitia, reg. 88 J d
Samonium, prom. 14 ins.
Samos 13 E c
Samos, isl. 13 E c
Samos, theme 59 J f
Samosata 20 H d
Samothrace, isl.
Samsun 89 K f
Samoyedes, people
San River 159 L d
Sana
Sanabria, dist. 83 J g
San Agostinho, Cabo, cape
San Antonio 210 F e
San Antonio, Cape 105 D b
San Antonio River 190 F f
San Antonio de Béjar 190 F f
San Bernardino, pass, see Saint Bernardino
San Bernardino Mountains 187 H e
San Bernardino Strait 199 ins. H
San Bernardo, isl. 107 A h
San Blas 213 B b
San Buenaventura 190 B e
San Carlos de Ancud 215 B g
San Carlos de Monterey 190 A d
Sancerre 76 E c
Sancerre, cty. 76 E c
San Cesareo, ch. 96 A
San Clemente, ch. 96 A
San Crisogono, ch. 96 A
San Cristóbal 213 C c
San Cristóbal, isl. 110 HH i
Sanctus Ægidius, see Saint-Gilles
Sanctus Dionysius, see Saint-Denis
Sanctus Gallus, see Saint Gall
Sancus, Gate of 23 B
Sand 154 F e
Sandal Castle 127 X m
Sandalwood Island 172 A b
Sandau 154 G b
Sandía 214 C d
San Diego 190 B e
Sandomierz 87 M c
Sandrocotta, Kingdom of 18 S h
Sandu
Sandusky 200 B c
Sandusky, Fort 194 C b
Sandusky Bay 200 B c
Sandwich, in Canada 200 B b
Sandwich, in England
Sandwich, parl. bor. 163 P f
Sandwich, in Mass. 189 C d
Sandy Cape 172 E c
Sandy Desert, Great 172 B c
Sandy Hook, cape 192 E c
Sandy Island, Great 172 E c
Sandy Sea, desert
Sane, in Acte 11 E b
Sane, in Pallene 11 E b
San Estéban
Sanf, reg.
San Felipe 215 B f
San Fernando 214 C b
San Francisco, in California 190 A d
San Francisco, in Florida 193 D g
San Francisco, Cape 111 A a

San Francisco Bay 187 G e
San Francisco Mountains 187 H e
San Francisco de la Espada 190 F f
San Francisco de los Nechas 191 F e
San Francisco de los Tejas 191 F e
Sanga River 175 E d
San Gabriel 190 B e
Sangala 19 L d
Sangarius (Sakaria) River 20 D b
San Germano 72 C c
San Gerónimo de Yuste, mon. 94 A c
San Gimignano 90 L j
San Giovanni, Porta, gate 22 A
San Giovanni in Fiori, mon. 95 F d (S. G. i. F.)
San Giusto, mon. 95 D b
Sangpo River
San Gregorio Magno, mon. 96 A
San Ildefonso 184 C d
San Ildefonso, castle 130 C e
Sanitium, see Senez
San Javier del Bac 190 C e
San Joaquin River 198 A c
San Jorge, Gulf of 215 C g
San Jorge da Mina
San Jorge da Minha, see San Jorge da Mina
San José, in California 190 A d
San José, in Costa Rica 213 D d
San José, in Guatemala 213 C c
San José, in Uruguay 215 D f
San José, pen. 215 C g
San José de Cúcuta 214 B b
San Juan, in Arg. Rep. 215 C f
San Juan, in Porto Rico 199 ins. G
San Juan Island 198 A a
San Juan River, in Ecuador 111 B a
San Juan River, in New Mexico 198 D c
San Juan River, in Nicaragua 213 D c
San Juan Bautista, in Mexico 213 C c
San Juan Bautista (Porto Rico), isl. 105 G c
San Juan Capistrano, in California 190 B e
San Juan Capistrano, in Texas 190 F f
San Juan de la Peña, mon. 94 B c
San Juan del Norte 213 D c
San Juan de los Caballeros 190 D d
San Juan de Ulúa, Fort 106 D a
Sankt-Blasien, see Saint Blaise
Sankt-Florian, mon. 95 E b
Sankt-Gallen, see Saint Gall
Sankt-Georgen 142 B d
Sankt-Goar 62 D c
Sankt-Goar, mon. 95 D a
Sankt-Gotthard Pass 91 Q l
Sankt-Gotthard, in Hungary 123 I e
Sankt-Jacob 91 P k
Sankt-Lambrecht, mon. 80 D h
Sankt-Leonhardt 154 F e
Sankt-Luziensteig, pass 150 E c
Sankt-Märgen, mon. 142 B d
Sankt-Maximin, mon. 95 D b
Sankt-Peter, ab. 142 B d
Sankt-Pölten 63 H d
Sankt-Pölten, mon. 80 D g
Sankt-Trudpert, ab. 142 A e
Sankt-Trudpert, mon. 95 D b
Sankt-Urban, mon. 91 P k
Sankt-Vith 117 E d
Sankt-Wendel 154 D d
San Leo 64 B b
San Leo, bp. 95 E c
San Lorenzo del Escorial, mon. 94 B c
San Lorenzo in Damaso, ch. 96 A
San Lorenzo in Lucina, ch. 96 A
San Lorenzo fuori le Mura, ch. 96 A
San Lucar de Barrameda 83 J h
San Lucas, Cape 187 H f
San Luis, in Arg. Rep. 215 C f
San Luis Amarillas 190 F e
San Luis Obispo 190 A d
San Luis Potosí 201 E e
San Luis Potosí, state 213 B b
San Marco, in Calabria 90 F e
San Marco, bp. 95 F d
San Marco, church in Rome 96 A
San Marino, rep. 90 D c
San Martin, isl. 105 H c
San Martin, mon. 94 C d
San Mateo, Bahia de, bay 111 B a
San Mateo, Fort 191 I e
San Mateo River 191 I e
San Matias, Gulf of 215 C g
San Michele 64 C b
San Michele, mon. 95 F c
San Miguel, in California 190 A d
San Miguel (Piura) 111 A c
San Miguel, in Salvador 213 D c
San Miguel (Tangarara) 111 A b
San Miguel Allende 213 ins.
San Miguel de Cuellar 191 G e
San Miguel de Gualdape 191 J e
San Miguel, Cape 105 F c
San Miguel, Gulf of 105 E e
San Miguel River 214 C d
San Millan de la Cogolla, mon. 94 B c
San Miniato al Tedesco 90 L j
San-mun Bay
San Pablo 216
San Pablo, isl. 107 D i
San Pancrazio, ch. 96 A
San Pancrazio, Porta, gate 22 A
San Paola, Porta, gate 22 A
San Paolo fuori le Mura, ch. 96 A
San Pedro 191 I e
San Pedro, Rio, R. 190 C e
San Pedro y San Pablo, Rio de (Arkansas R.) 190 E d
San Pietro, Piazza di, loc. in Rome 22 A
San Pietro in Vincoli, ch. 96 A
San Remo 130 P k
San Roman, Cape 105 F d
San Roque, Cape
San Sabá 190 F e
San Salvador, in Angola 175 E e
San Salvador (Bahia)
San Salvador, in Salvador 105 C d
San Salvador, isl. 105 F b
San Sebastian, in Columbia 105 E e
San Sebastian, in Spain 82 H e
San Sebastiano, ch. 96 A
San Sebastiano, Porta, gate 22 A
San Sebastiano, Via di Porta, street 22 A
San Severino 90 E d
San Severo 90 E d
San Silvestro, mon. 95 E c
San Silvestro in Capite, ch. 96 A
San Sisto, ch. 96 A
San Stefano, near Constantinople 164 D b
San Stefano Rotondo, ch. 96 A
Santa Anna (Goyaz) 214 D d
Santa Balbina, ch. 96 A
Santa Bárbara, in California 190 B e
Santa Bárbara, in Mexico 190 D f
Santa Bárbara Islands 187 H e
Santa Catalina Island 108 M j
Santa Catharina, state 215 D e
Santa Catharina Island 215 E e
Santa Cecilia in Trastevere, ch. 96 A
Santa Clara, in California 190 A d
Santa Clara, in Cuba 213 D b
Santa Clara Island 111 A b
Santa Croce in Gerusalemme, ch. 96 A
Santa Cruz, in Brazil 214 F d
Santa Cruz de la Sierra 214 C d
Santa Cruz de Teneriffe 174 B b
Santa Cruz Quiché 105 B c
Santa Cruz, Cape 105 E c
Santa Cruz, Rio, R. 190 C e
Santa Cruz, Terra de (Brazil) 108 M i
Santa Cruz, isl., Atlantic Ocean 105 H c
Santa Cruz Islands, Pacific Ocean 172 F b
Santa Cruz River, in Patagonia 215 B g
Santa Elena, Punta, cape 111 A b
Santa Fé, in Arg. Rep. 215 C f
Santa Fé, in New Mexico 190 D d
Santa Fé, in Spain 184 C e
Santa Fé, audiencia 215 ins.
Santa Fé, mon. in Spain 94 B d
Santa Fé Trail, route 210 E c
Sant'Agata in Suburra, ch. 96 A
Sant'Agata, bp. 95 ins.
Santa Gloria, Puerto de 105 E c
Sant'Agnese fuori le Mura, ch. 96 A
Sant'Agostino, ch. 96 A
Santa Isabel 214 E c
Santa Isabel de la Estrella, isl. 110 G G h
Sant'Alessio 96 A
Santa Lucia, in Italy 161 H e
Santa Lucia, in Florida 191 I f
Santa Lucia Bay 175 N l
Santa Maria, in Arg. Rep. 215 C e
Santa Maria, in Brazil 214 E c
Santa Maria Aventinese, ch. 96 A
Santa Maria de la Concepción, isl. 105 F b
Santa Maria della Pace, ch. 96 A
Santa Maria in Cosmedin, ch. 96 A
Santa Maria in Domnica, ch. 96 A
Santa Maria in Trastevere, ch. 96 A
Santa Maria la Antigua del Darien 105 E e
Santa Maria Maggiore, ch. 96 A
Santa Maria Rotonda, ch. 22 A
Santa Marta 105 F d
Santander 82 B a
Santander, bp. 94 B c
Sant'Andrea, mon. 96 A
Sant'Angelo, castle 96 A
Sant'Apollinare in Classe, mon. 95 E c
Santa Prassede, ch. 96 A
Santa Prisca, ch. 96 A
Santa Pudenziana, ch. 96 A
Santarem, in Brazil 214 D c
Santarem, in Portugal 82 A b
Santa Rosalia 213 B b
Santa Sabina, ch. 96 A
Santas Creus, mon. 94 C c
Santa Severina, in Calabria 90 F e
Santa Severina, abp. 95 F d
Santa Susanna, ch. 96 A
Santee River 193 E e
San Teodore, ch. 96 A
Santhià 130 Q i
San Thomé 112 B b
San Thomé, Cape
Santiago, in Chile 215 B f
Santiago de Compostella
Santiago de Compostella, abp.
Santiago de Cuba 213 E c
Santiago del Estero 215 C e
Santiago, isl. (Jamaica) 105 E c
Santiago River 111 B a
Santi Apostoli, ch. 96 A
Santi Cosma e Damiano, ch. 96 A
Santi Giovanni e Paolo, ch. 96 A
Santillana 82 B a
Santi Quattro Coronati, ch. 96 A
Santistéban 82 B b
Santo Colmado, mon. 94 A c
Santo Domingo 105 G c
Santo Domingo, rep. 213 E c
Santo Domingo, Audiencia of. 213 E b
Santones, see Saintes
Santones, people 38 B c
Sant'Onofrio, ch. 22 A
Santos, city in Brazil 215 E e
Santos Cosmoy Damiano, mon. 94 A c
Santo Spirito, mon. 95 E c
Santo Stefano 164 D b
Santo Tomas, in Guatemala 213 D c
Santo Tomas, in Lower Cal. 190 B e
San Vicente Ferrer 190 B e
San Vitale, ch. 96 A
San Zoilo, mon. 94 B c
Sanzumata
São Christovão 214 F d
São Francisco River 214 E d
São João, in Minas Geraes 214 E e
São João da Barra 214 E e

São Jorge dos Ilheos . . . . . . 214 F d
São José, in Amazonas . . . . . 214 C b
São Leopoldo . . . . 215 D e
São Luiz de Maranhão . . . . . 214 E c
Saona, isl. . . . . 105 G c
Saône River . . . . 62 C e
Saône, Haute, dept. . . . . 148 F e
Saône-et-Loire, dept. . . . . . . 148 E e
São Paulo . . . . 215 E e
São Paulo, state . . . . 214 D e
São Pedro (Rio Grande) . . . . 215 D f
São Salvador . . . . 214 F e
São Sebastião . . . . 215 E e
São Sebastião Island . . . . 215 E e
São Thomé, cape, see San Thomé
São Thomé, isl. . . . . 108 R h
São Vicente, in Brazil . . . . . . 215 E e
São Vicente, mon., in Portugal . 94 A d
Sapera . . . .
Sapis River . . . . 27 F d
Sapphe . . . . 20 J d
Saracano . . . . 99 N d
Saracenic poss. . . . . 58 D F f
Saracens, people, see Arabs . . 45 leg.
Saragossa . . . . 82 B a
Saragossa, abp. . . . . 94 B c
Saragossa, emir. . . . . 83 E c
Saragossa, univ. . . . . 100 E f
Sarai . . . . 92 E c
Saraitchikovsk . . . .
Sarakhs . . . .
Sarandi . . . . 215 D f
Sarangians, people . . . . 8 E b
Saransk . . . . 139 G e
Saratoga . . . . 194 L f
Saratoga, proposed state in U.S.
Saratoga, Fort . . . . 192 E b
Saratov . . . . 139 G e
Saravus (Saar) River . . . . 39 I i
Sarawak, col. . . . . 171 M h
Sardica . . . . 39 M l
Sardinia, isl. . . . . 2 E d
Sardinia, km., 16 cent. . . . . . 118 F e
Sardinia, km., 18 cent. . . . . . 130 E e
Sardinia, km., 19 cent. . . . . . 161 F e
Sardinia, Rom. prov. . . . . . . 34 F e
Sardinia, W. Rom. prov. . . . . 42 D e (8)
Sardis . . . . 13 F b
Sared River . . . . 7 D f
Sarepta . . . . 6 C b
Sari . . . .
Sarius (Serio) River . . . . 26 D b
Sarlat . . . . 76 D d
Sarlat, mon. . . . . 94 C c
Sarmatæ, people . . . . 18 F a
Sarmatia, reg. . . . . 35 J c
Sarmizegetusa . . . . 39 M k
Sarnen . . . . 91 Q l
Sarni . . . . 26 F b
Sarnia, isl. . . . . 38 B c
Sarnius (Atrek) River . . . . . . 19 H c
Sarno, bp. . . . . 95 ins.
Sarnus (Sarno) River . . . . . . 30 D b
Saronic Gulf . . . . 15 D b
Sarpedon, prom. . . . . 33 D b
Sarsina . . . . 27 G d
Sarsina, bp. . . . . 95 E c
Sarta River, see Sarthe River
Sartaba, mt. . . . . 7 C d
Sarthe, dept. . . . . 148 D e
Sarthe River . . . . 69 C c
Sarukhan, reg. . . . . 89 I g
Sarum, Old . . . . 60 F e
Sarus River . . . . 20 F d
Sarzana . . . . 90 L i
Sarzana, bp. . . . . 95 D c
Sasbach, near Achern . . . . . . 142 B c
Sasbach, near Alt-Breisach . . 142 A d
Sashiversk . . . . 171 P b
Saskatchewan, Fort . . . . 212 D c
Saskatchewan, prov. . . . . 212 E c
Saskatchewan River . . . . 186 I c
Saskatchewan River, North . . . 186 I c
Saskatchewan River, South . . . 186 I c
Sason . . . . 31 I b
Saspirans, people . . . . 8 I d
Sassanids, Dom. of the . . . . . 43 K g
Sassari . . . . 77 F d
Sassula . . . . 35 ins. B
Saszvaros . . . . 159 L f
Satara . . . . 137 B e
Saternus (Santerno) River . . . 27 F c
Satganw . . . .
Saticula . . . . 30 D a
Satilla River . . . . 193 C f
Satpura Mountains . . . . 137 C d
Satricum . . . . 30 B a
Sattagydans, people . . . . 8 K e
Saturn, Temple of . . . .
Saturnia . . . . 27 F e
Saucourt . . . . 56 C b
Sauer River . . . . 117 E e
Saufeld . . . . 62 F c
Saugona River, see Saône River
Saugus River . . . . 189 ins. B
Sauk and Fox, Ind. Res. . . . . 188 H b
Sauks and Foxes, tribes . . . . 188 H b
Saulgau . . . . 143 H i
Sault Sainte Marie, in Michigan 191 I b
Sault Sainte Marie, in Ontario . 212 G d
Saumur . . . . 76 C c
Saumurois, gouv. . . . . 146 B b
Sausenberg, landgr. . . . . 142 A e
Sauvenière . . . . 156 B a
Savah . . . .
Savaii, isl. . . . . 172 H b
Savannah . . . . 193 ins. C
Savannah River . . . . 193 D e
Savaria . . . . 38 F c
Save River . . . . 87 J e
Savia, West Rom. prov. . . . . . 42 F d (9)
Savigliano, mon. . . . . 95 D c
Savigny, mon. . . . . 94 B b
Savo . . . . 26 C c
Savo River . . . . 30 C a
Savona . . . . 90 I h
Savona, bp. . . . . 95 D c
Savoy, cty. . . . . 69 G d
Savoy, duchy . . . . 86 F f
Savoy, growth of, 1418—1748 . 130 ins.
Savoy, neutral dist. . . . . 161 F e
Savoy, The, bldg. in London . 75 G g
Savus (Save) River . . . . 38 F c
Saxa Rubra . . . . 35 ins. B
Saxon March . . . . 58 G c (Sax. M.)
Saxons, people, before fifth cent. 38 D b
Saxons, people, in Britain . . . 51 R k
Saxons, people, in Germany . . 45 F b
Saxon Shore, dist. . . . . 51 Q i
Saxony, Frankish prov., 9 cent. 56 D b
Saxony, duchy, 10 cent. . . . . . 62 E b
Saxony, duchy, 13 cent. . . . . . 72 B a
Saxony, elect., 14 cent. . . . . . 79 H c
Saxony, elect., 16 cent. . . . . . 115 G c
Saxony, elect., 17—18 cent. . . 123 G c
Saxony, km., 1812 . . . . 154 G c
Saxony, km., 1815 . . . . 158 G c
Saxony, prov. of Prussia . . . . 158 F c
Saxony-Lauenburg, dist. . . . . 79 G b
Sayansk Mountains . . . . 171 K c
Saybrook . . . . 189 B d
Scalæ Caci, loc. in Rome . . . 24 A
Scalæ Gemoniæ, loc. in Rome .
Scala Santa, loc. in Rome . . . 96 A
Scaldis (Scheldt) River . . . . . 38 C b
Scallabis . . . . 38 A e
Scamander River . . . .
Scambonidæ, deme . . . . 23 D
Scampa . . . . 10 B a
Scandea . . . . 15 D c
Scandia (Scandinavia), reg. . . . 38 E a
Scandile, isl. . . . . 11 F c
Scandinavian Highlands . . . . . 2 E b
Scandinavian Peninsula . . . . . 2 F c
Scania, dist. . . . . 88 E c
Scapsa . . . . 11 D b
Scara . . . .
Scarbantia (Ödenburg) . . . . . . 38 F c
Scarborough . . . . 60 J g
Scarborough, parl. bor. . . . . . 163 N c
Scardona . . . . 38 F d
Scardona, bp. . . . . 95 F c
Scardus, mt. . . . . 39 M l
Scarphea . . . . 11 D d
Scarpona . . . . 39 H i
Scepsis . . . .
Schächen Tal, valley . . . . . . 150 E c
Schaffhausen . . . . 91 Q k
Schaffhausen, canton . . . . . . 91 Q k
Schaffhausen, imp. cy. . . . . . 78 F e
Schaftersheim . . . . 122 F d
Schalksburg . . . . 62 E b
Schärding . . . . 79 H d
Scharnitz, fort . . . . 154 F e
Scharnitz Pass . . . . 134 F e
Schässburg . . . . 159 M e
Schauenburg, castle . . . . 142 B b
Schaumburg, castle . . . . 72 B a
Schaumburg-Lippe, princ. 155 E b (S. L.)
Scheer . . . . 143 H i
Scheer, princ. cty. . . . . 143 H i
Scheidungen . . . . 63 F c
Scheldt River . . . . 117 B d
Schelklingen . . . . 143 I i
Schemnitz . . . . 155 J d
Schenectady . . . . 192 D b
Schenkenschanz . . . . 122 D c
Schesel . . . . 55 R i
Scheyern, castle . . . . 62 F d
Schiermonnikoog, isl. . . . . . . 117 D a
Schillingsfürst, castle . . . . . . 143 J g
Schiltach . . . . 142 B d
Schivelbein . . . . 85 D b
Schladming . . . . 115 G e
Schlawe . . . . 85 E a
Schlei, inlet . . . . 62 E a
Schleiden . . . . 117 E d
Schleiz . . . . 154 F c
Schleswig . . . . 62 E a
Schleswig, bp. . . . . 95 D a
Schleswig, duchy . . . . 158 E a
Schleswig, march . . . . 62 E a
Schleswig-Holstein, prov. . . . 161 B b
Schlettstadt . . . . 126 E b
Schlettstadt, imp. cy. . . . . . . 78 E d
Schliengen . . . . 142 A e
Schluchtern . . . . 142 D b
Schlüsselburg . . . . 138 D d
Schmalkalden . . . . 114 F c
Schneidemühl . . . . 159 I b
Schœnus . . . . 15 D b
Schoharie . . . . 195 D b
Schokland, isl. . . . . 117 D b
Schönau . . . . 142 A e
Schönbrunn, castle . . . . 135 I d
Schönbuch, dist. . . . . 143 H h
Schonen, dist., see Scania
Schönhausen . . . . 158 F b
Schönthal, ab. . . . . 143 H g
Schopfheim . . . . 142 A e
Schopfheim, Nieder . . . . 142 A d
Schorndorf . . . . 143 I h
Schouten, route of . . . .
Schouwen, isl. . . . . 117 B c
Schramberg . . . . 143 F i
Schroda . . . . 159 I b
Schussen River . . . . 143 I j
Schussenried, ab. . . . . 143 I i
Schütt Island . . . . 159 I e
Schuyler, Fort . . . . 189 B b
Schuylkill River . . . . 195 D c
Schwabach . . . . 114 F d
Schwaigern . . . . 143 H g
Schwarzach, in Bavaria . . . . . 114 F d
Schwarzach, mon. in Baden . . 142 B c
Schwarzburg, castle . . . . 79 G c
Schwarzburg, principalities . . . 154 F c (S.)
Schwarze Elster, R. . . . . 85 G e
Schwarzenburg, in Switzerland . 91 P l
Schwarzenberg, lordship in Baden . . . . 142 A d
Schwaz . . . . 154 F e

Schwechat . . . . 159 I d
Schwedt . . . . 85 D b
Schweidnitz . . . . 63 I c
Schweinfurt . . . . 62 F c
Schweinfurt, imp. cy. . . . . . . 79 G c
Schweinschädel . . . .
Schwerin, in Mecklenburg . . . 62 F b
Schwerin, on the Warthe R. . . 79 I b
Schwerin, bp. . . . . 95 E a
Schwerin, duchy . . . . 79 G b
Schwetz . . . . 87 L b
Schwetzingen . . . . 142 C b
Schwiebus . . . . 115 H b
Schwyz . . . . 91 Q k
Schwyz, canton . . . . 91 Q k
Schyl River . . . . 168 H d
Sciathus . . . . 11 E c
Sciathus, isl. . . . . 11 E c
Scidrus . . . . 30 E b
Scillus . . . . 14 B b
Scilly Islands . . . . 130 B d
Scingomagus . . . . 26 A b
Scione . . . . 11 E c
Scioto Company, grant . . . . . 196 ins. B
Scioto River . . . . 196 ins. B
Scipios, Tomb of the . . . . . . 22 A
Scipio's camp . . . . 34 ins. A
Scipio's mole . . . . 34 ins. A
Sciri, people . . . .
Sciritis, dist. . . . . 14 C b
Scituate . . . . 189 ins. B
Scodra (Scutari in Albania) . . 39 L l
Scolacium (Squillace) . . . . . . 31 F d
Scollis, mt. . . . . 14 B b
Scolus, in Bœotia . . . . 11 E d
Scolus, in Chalcidice . . . . . . 11 E b
Scomius, mt. . . . . 39 M l
Scone . . . .
Scopia (Uskub) . . . . 73 E b
Scordisci, people . . . . 39 L k
Scotch, people . . . .
Scotland, km. . . . . 58 D b
Scotland Yard, in London . . . 75 G g
Scots, people . . . . 54 C c
Scots, people in Ireland . . . .
Scott, Fort . . . . 211 G c
Scott, route of . . . . 201 leg.
Scott, fam. . . . .
Scotussa . . . . 11 D c
Scrooby . . . . 185 E d
Scultenna (Panaro) River . . . 27 F c
Scupi (Uskub) . . . . 39 M l
Scutari, in Albania . . . . 93 A b
Scutari, on the Bosporus . . . . 93 G e
Scutari, bp. . . . . 95 F c
Scylla . . . . 90 E e
Scylacium (Squillace) . . . . . . 31 F d
Scylacium, gulf . . . . 31 F d
Scyllæum . . . . 30 E d
Scyllæum, prom., in Greece . . 15 D b
Scyllæum, prom., in Italy . . . 30 E d
Scylletium (Squillace) . . . . . . 31 F d
Scyrians, people . . . . 50 F c
Scyrus . . . . 11 F d
Scyrus (Skyros), isl. . . . . . . 11 F d
Scythia, East Rom. prov. . . . . 43 H e (6)
Scythia, Lesser, reg. . . . . . . 39 N l
Scythians, people, in Asia . . . 8 J d, L e
Scythians, people, in Europe . 18 D a
Scythopolis . . . . 7 C d
Seaford, parl. bor. . . . . 163 O g
Sea of the Indies (Arabian Sea)
Seattle . . . . 210 A a
Sea View, mt. . . . . 172 E d
Sebago, lake . . . . 189 C c
Sebaste, in Palestine . . . . . . 7 C d
Sebaste, in Pontus . . . . 43 J f
Sebastea . . . . 59 L f
Sebastea, theme . . . . 59 L f
Sebastia . . . . 20 G c
Sebastian Cabot, route of . . . 108 L k
Sebastopolis (Phasis) . . . . . . 20 I a
Seben . . . . 62 F e
Sebenico . . . . 90 E c
Sebenico, bp. . . . . 95 F c
Sebennytos . . . . 4 ins.
Sebinus (Iseo), lake . . . . . . 26 E b
Sebzewar . . . . 92 F d
Secia (Secchia) River . . . . . . 26 E c
Seckau . . . . 80 D h
Seckau, bp. . . . . 95 E b
Seckenheim . . . . 142 C b
Secondee . . . .
Secunderabad . . . . 137 C e
Sedan . . . . 126 D b
Sedetani, people . . . . 38 B d
Sedge Moor, dist. . . . . 49 E f
Sedgemoor . . . . 127 W o
Seduni, people . . . . 26 B a
Sedunum (Sion) . . . . 26 B a
Seehausen, Hanse. cy. . . . . . 99 ins. B
Seekonk . . . . 189 ins. A
Sées . . . . 76 D b
Sées, bp. . . . . 94 C b
Segeberg . . . . 72 C a
Segeberg, mon. . . . . 95 D a
Segedunum . . . . 38 B a
Segesta, in Liguria . . . . 26 D c
Segesta, in Sicily . . . . 30 B e
Segni . . . . 64 ins.
Segni, bp. . . . . 96 C b
Segobodium . . . . 39 H j
Segobriga . . . .
Segodunum, see Rodez
Segontia (Sigüenza) . . . . 38 B e
Segontium (Carnarvon) . . . . . 51 N h
Segor . . . . 68 ins. A
Segorbe . . . . 82 H f
Segorbe, bp. . . . . 94 B d
Segovia . . . . 38 B d
Segovia, bp. . . . . 94 B c
Segovia River . . . . 213 D c
Segura, near Murcia . . . . 82 B b
Segura, near Saragossa . . . . . 82 B a
Segura de la Frontera . . . . . 106 C b
Seguro, captaincy . . . . 108 M i
Segusio (Susa) . . . . 26 A b
Segustero or Segusterone, see Sisteron
Sehwan . . . .
Seine-et-Marne, dept. . . . . . 148 E e
Seine-et-Oise, dept. . . . . . . 148 E e
Seine-Inférieure, dept. . . . . . 148 E e
Seine River . . . . 61 D b
Seistan, reg. . . . .
Selas River . . . . 14 B b
Selborne, priory . . . . 100 B a
Selby . . . . 127 X m
Selby, mon. . . . . 97 P h
Selefke . . . . 93 D c
Selenga River . . . .
Seleucia, in Babylonia . . . . . 18 P h
Seleucia, in Cilicia . . . . 20 E d
Seleucia, in Syria . . . . 20 F d
Seleucia, theme . . . . 59 K f
Seleucids, Kingdom of the . . . 19 W k
Seleucus, Kingdom of . . . . . . 18 P i
Selge . . . . 20 D d
Selgovæ, people . . . . 38 B a
Seligenstadt, mon. . . . . 95 D a
Selinus, in Cilicia . . . . 20 E d
Selinus, in Laconia . . . . 14 C b
Selinus, in Sicily . . . . 30 B e
Selinus River . . . . 14 C a
Seljuk Turks, Dom. of the . . . 67 O f
Seljuk Turks, people . . . . . . 77 K e
Selkirk . . . .
Selkirk, cty. . . . .
Selkirk, dist. . . . .
Selkirk, Fort . . . . 212 B b
Selkirk Forest . . . . 49 F d
Sella . . . . 98 G h
Sellasia . . . . 14 C b
Selleis River . . . . 14 B b
Selles . . . . 69 H g
Selma . . . . 208 C c
Selsey . . . .
Selwood . . . . 49 E f
Selymbria . . . .
Selz . . . . 142 B c
Selz, mon. . . . . 95 D b
Semana (Thuringian) Forest . . 39 K h
Semendria . . . . 93 B b
Semenud . . . . 150 B a
Semgallia, dist. . . . .
Seminara . . . . 90 E e
Seminole, Ind. Res. . . . . 118 G c
Seminoles, tribe . . . . 188 J e
Semipalatinsk . . . . 170 J c
Semlin . . . .
Semlov . . . . 153 O f
Semmering Pass . . . . 135 H e
Semnones, people . . . . 38 E b
Semo Sancus, Temple of . . . . 23 B
Sempronii, Forum . . . . 27 G d
Sempach . . . . 91 Q k
Sempronia Basilica, bldg. in Rome . . . . 24 A
Senaculum, bldg. in Rome . . .
Sena Gallica (Sinigaglia) . . . . 27 H d
Sena Iulia . . . . 27 F d
Sena (Cesano) River . . . . 27 H d
Senate House, in Rome . . . . . 24 B
Seneca Creek . . . . 208 ins.
Seneca Lake . . . . 192 C b
Senecas, tribe . . . . 188 K b
Senécu . . . . 190 D e
Seneffe . . . . 156 A a
Senegal, col. . . . . 174 B c
Senegal River . . . . 174 B c
Senez, bp. . . . . 95 D c
Senger River . . . . 215 C g
Senia . . . . 27 I c
Senigallia, see Sinigaglia . . . . 90 M j
Senlis . . . . 61 E b
Senlis, bp. . . . . 94 C b
Senlac . . . . 65 F G e
Sennabrin . . . .
Sennar, dist. . . . . 174 G c
Senne River . . . . 156 A a
Sennette River . . . . 156 A a
Senones (Sens) . . . . 38 C c
Senones, people, in Gaul . . . . 38 C c
Senones, people, in Italy . . . . 27 G d
Sens . . . . 61 E b
Sens, abp. . . . . 94 C b
Sens, cty. . . . . 69 I f
Sentinum . . . . 27 G d
Seoul . . . . 171 N e
Seph . . . . 6 C c
Sepharvaim, see Sippar
Sepias, prom. . . . . 11 E c
Sepphoris . . . . 6 C c
Sepsi-Szent-György . . . . 159 M e
Septem peda . . . . 27 H d
Septimania, reg. . . . . 53 M i
Septimer, Pass . . . . 26 D a
Septimian Gate . . . . 22 A
Septimius Severus, Arch of . .
Septimius Severus, Palace of . 24 B
Septizonium, loc. in Rome . . . 22 A
Septs-Fonts, mon. . . . . 94 C b
Sepulcretum, loc. in Rome . . . 24 A
Sepulveda . . . . 94 B c
Sequana (Seine) River . . . . . 38 C c
Sequani, people . . . . 38 D c
Seraglio, New and Old, in Constantinople . . . . 93 G e
Seraglio Point . . . . 93 G e
Serai . . . . 77 N c
Serajevo . . . . 119 H e
Serapeum, loc. in Alexandria 34 ins. C (7)
Serapeum, loc. in Rome . . . . 22 A
Serapis, Temple of . . . . 22 A
Serbs, people . . . . 57 G e
Serena, La . . . . 215 B e
Seres . . . . 93 B b
Sergievski . . . . 138 E d
Sergipe, state . . . . 214 F d
Seringapatam . . . . 137 C f
Seriphus (Serpho) . . . . 15 E b
Seriphus (Sériphos), isl. . . . . 15 E b

Sermyle 11 E b
Serpa 38 A e
Serpent Column, in Constantinople 93 G e (3)
Serpent Pool, in Jerusalem 6 ins. A
Serpent's Mouth, str. 105 H e
Serra do Espinhaço, mts. 214 E d
Serra do Mar, mts. 215 E e
Serra dos Aimores, mts. 214 E d
Serra Geral, mts. 215 D e
Serran 111 B c
Serra parda, Cabo, cape 108 R j
Serravalle 90 K h
Serrhæ 11 E a
Serrhium, prom.
Serrorum Montes (Transylvanian Alps), mts. 39 M k
Servia, reg. 54 H e
Servia, km., 13 cent. 89 B b
Servia, km., 14 cent. 89 H f
Servia, km., 15 cent. 93 B b
Servia, km., 19 cent. 164 C b
Servia, princ., 19 cent. 164 C b
Servia, prov. of Ottoman Empire
Servian Principalities, 14 cent. 77 I d
Servians, people
Servian Wall 23 B
Sesamus 20 E b
Sesia River 130 Q i
Sesites River 26 C b
Sessa 90 E d
Sessa, bp. 95 ins.
Sessorium 22 A
Sestinum 27 G d
Sestus
Setauket 189 B d
Setia 30 C a
Setif 70 H f
Setons, fam. 97 J d
Setu, isl.
Setúbal 83 J h
Seul, see Seoul 171 N e
Seurre 126 D c
Sevastopol, in the Crimea
Sevastopol, plan of 164 L g
Sevastopoli, in Abkhasia 99 L e
Seven Basilicas, churches 96 A
Seven Lakes 27 F c
Sevenoaks, battle 75 J i
Seven Ranges, The, dist. 196 ins. B
Seven Towers, Castle of the 93 G e
Severia, dist. 139 D e
Severians, people 71 M c
Severian Way, road 35 ins. B
Severin 77 I d
Severin, banat 89 B b
Severn River, in England 49 E e
Severn River, in Canada 212 G c
Severus, wall of 34 E b
Sevier, lake 210 C c
Sevier River 198 C c
Seville 82 A b
Seville, abp. 94 A d
Seville, emir. 83 D d
Seville, km. 83 J h
Seville, univ. 100 D g
Sevre River 148 D e
Sewan-hacky (Long Island) 189 B d
Sexi 38 B e
Sextum, Ad 27 F d
Seybothenreuth 158 F d
Seychelles Islands 175 I e
Sfax 73 C d
Sha-chau
Shackamaxon 192 ins.
Shaftesbury
Shaftesbury, mon.
Shaftesbury, parl. bor. 163 L g
Shahr Zor 67 P f
Shahrzur, reg.
Shah-Armen, Dom. of 71 O f
Shaliyat
Shanghai 171 N e
Shangtu
Shan-hai-kwan 171 M d
Shannon River 49 B e
Shan-si, prov. 171 M e
Shan-tung, prov. 171 M e
Shap, mon. 97 O g
Shari River 174 E c
Shark Bay 172 A c
Shark's Island 107 C i
Sharmakhi 99 M e
Sharon, Plain of 7 B d
Sharpness 162 D f
Sharpsburg 208 ins.
Shasta, mt. 210 A b
Shau-hsien 171 N f
Shavly 131 H b
Shaw 127 X o
Shawmut 189 ins. B
Shawnee Mission 206 F c
Shawnees, tribe 188 J c
Shawneetown 211 H c
Shawomet 189 ins. A
Shechem 7 C d
Sheen, mon. 97 Q j
Sheep Gate, in Jerusalem 6 ins. A
Sheffield 162 E d
Sheffield, parl. bor. 163 M d
Sheik-ul-Islam, loc. in Constantinople 93 G e
Shelburne 212 I d
Sheliff River 125 D e
Shelter Island 192 E c
Shelton 127 W n
Shenandoah 193 E b
Shenandoah River 193 E b
Shen-si, prov. 171 L e
Shephela, Plain of 7 B e
Shepherdstown 208 ins.
Sheppey, isl.
Sherborne 65 E e
Sherborne, mon. 97 O k
Sherborne, parl. bor. 163 L g (Sherb.)
Sherboro, Island 174 B d
Sherbrooke 212 H d
Sheriffmuir
s'Hertogenbosch 117 D c
Sherwood Forest 49 F e
Shetland Islands 49 F a
Shigansk 171 N b
Shikoku, isl. 171 O e
Shilka River
Shiloh, in Palestine 7 C d
Shiloh, in Tennessee 208 C b
Shimoda 171 O e
Shimonoseki 171 O e
Ship Island 208 C c
Shipka Pass 164 C b
Shipyards, loc. in Rome 22 A
Shiraz
Shirley 193 ins. A
Shirley, Fort 192 C c
Shirpurla 4 G c
Shirvan, reg.
Shoa, dist. 174 G d
Shoalwater, Ind. Res. 188 B a
Shoebury
Shomron 7 C d
Shoreditch 75 I h
Shoreditch, street in London 75 G g
Shoreham
Shoshones, tribe 188 C c
Shreveport 208 B c
Shrewsbury, in England
Shrewsbury, castle
Shrewsbury, mon. 97 O i
Shrewsbury, parl. bor. 163 L e
Shrewsbury, in New Jersey 192 E c
Shropshire, cty.
Shropshire, shire
Shtiplie 164 C b
Shubra Kheit
Shumagin Islands 198 ins. A
Shumla 131 I e
Shunem 6 C c
Shun-i 170 ins. A
Shuri, isl. 171 N f
Shuster
Sialkot 137 B b
Siam, km. 171 L g
Siam, Gulf of 171 L h
Siam, reg.
Siberia, khan. of 138 J d
Siberia, reg. 171 J-R b
Sibir
Sibir, khan. 92 H b
Sibir, reg. 109 X b
Sibota Islands 10 B c
Sibton, mon. 97 S i
Sicani or Sicanians, people 30 C e
Sicca 42 D f
Sicels, people
Sicilia, see Sicily
Sicilian Sea 34 H f
Sicilies, Kingdom of the Two 72 C d
Sicily, Rom. prov. 30 C d
Sicily, isl. 2 F e
Sicily, km. 77 G d
Sicily, West Rom. prov. 42 E f (4)
Sicinus (Sikinos), isl. 15 F c
Sickingen, castle 114 E d
Sicoris River 38 C d
Siculi, people 30 D e
Sicyon 14 C b
Side, in Laconia 15 D c
Side, in Pamphylia 18 D c
Sidicinum, Teanum 30 D a
Sidodone 19 H e
Sidon 6 C a
Sidon, Port of, in Tyre 18 ins. B
Sidra, Gulf of 174 E a
Sidus 15 D b
Siedlce 155 L b
Siegburg, mon. 95 D a
Siegen 158 E c
Siena 90 L j
Siena, abp. 95 E c
Siena, univ. 100 H f
Sierra de Piña, mts.
Sierra Leone, col. 174 B d
Sierra Madre, mts. in Mexico 187 I f
Sierra Madre, mts. in New Mexico 190 D d
Sierra Mindi, mts.
Sierra Morena, mts. 2 D e
Sierra Nevada, mts. in Spain 2 D e
Sierra Nevada, mts. in California 190 A d
Sierra Nevada de Santa Marta, mts. 187 L g
Sierra Quebrancha, mts.
Sievershausen 114 F b
Siga 38 B e
Sigeum
Sigeum, prom. 9 A a
Sigiburg 55 Q i
Sigmaringen 143 H i
Sigmaringen, castle 62 E d
Signau, castle 91 P l
Signia 35 ins. B
Signia, bp. 96 C b
Signy, mon. 94 C b
Sigtuna 46 J b
Sigüenza 83 K g
Sigüenza, bp. 94 B c
Sigüenza, univ. 100 E f
Sihuatan, Puerto 107 G f
Sihut 170 G g
Sikanderabad
Sikhim
Sikh States
Si-kiang, R.
Sila Mountains 31 F d
Silarus River, in Æmilia 27 F c
Silarus River, in Campania 30 D b
Silberberg, fortress 155 I c
Silesia, dist. 59 H c
Silesia, duchy 72 D a
Silesia, Austrian, dist. 159 I c
Silesia, Lower, dist. 72 D a

Silesia, Prussian, prov. 159 I c
Silesia, Upper, dist. 72 D a
Siletz, Ind. Res. 188 B b
Silingæ, people 38 F b
Silis River 19 K b
Silistria 73 F b
Siloam, Pool of 6 ins. A
Silures, people 51 O i
Silves 82 A b
Silves, bp. 94 A d
Silvium 31 F b
Simancas 82 B a
Simbach 135 G d
Simbirsk 139 G e
Simeon, tribe 7 ins. D
Simferopol 139 D g
Simla 170 I e
Simmern 86 F d
Simmern, princ. 86 F d
Simœis River (Dumbrek R.)
Simplon Pass 91 Q l
Simpson, Fort 212 C b
Simpson, Port 212 ins.
Sinaes, Rio das boas, R. 108 U i
Sinai, mt. 3 H f
Sinai Peninsula 150 B b
Sinaloa 190 D f
Sinaloa, prov. 190 D f
Sinaloa, state 213 B b
Sinclairs, fam.
Sind, reg. in 8 cent. 53 I c
Sind, reg. in 18 cent. 137 A c
Sindelfingen 114 E d
Sindi, people 35 L e
Sindia, Dom. of 137 C c
Sindomana 19 K e
Sindringen 143 H g
Sindus 11 D b
Si-ngan-fu
Singapore
Singara 20 I d
Singidunum (Belgrade) 50 H d
Singitic Gulf (Gulf of Monte Santo) 11 E b
Sing-ngan 171 L e
Singus 11 E b
Sinigaglia 90 M j
Sinigaglia, bp. 95 E c
Si-ning-fu
Sinjar
Sin-kiang, prov. 171 J d
Sinnius River 27 F c
Sinonia, isl. 30 C b
Sinope (Sinub) 20 F a
Sinsheim 142 C b
Sintleozesavia, see Reichenau
Sinuessa (Mondragone) 30 C a
Sion 91 P l
Sion, bp. 95 D b
Sion, mon. 75 I i
Sioux, tribe 188 F c, G a
Sioux City 210 F b
Sioux Falls, town 210 F b
Sioux River, Big 198 F b
Siphæ 11 E d
Siphnus 15 E c
Siphnus (Siphnos), isl. 15 E c
Siponto 64 C b
Siponto, abp. 95 F c
Sipontum (Manfredonia) 30 E a
Sippar (Abu Habba) 4 G c
Sippara 20 J f
Sipylus, mt. 20 B c
Siraca 19 J c
Siracæ, people 35 M e
Siraf
Sirgune River 72 D a
Siris, in Lucania 31 F b
Siris, in Macedonia 11 E a
Siris River 31 F b
Sirmio (Sermione) 26 E b
Sirmium (Mitrovitza) 38 F d
Sirt 98 G g
Sis 73 H c
Sisal 213 C b
Sisapon 38 A e
Siscia 38 F c
Sisia 68 C b
Sissek 54 H d
Sisteron 126 D d
Sisteron, bp. 95 D c
Sistova 93 C b
Sit River 92 D b
Sitacus River 19 H e
Sithiu, see Saint-Omer
Sithonia, pen. 11 E b
Sitifis 38 D e
Sitka 198 ins. A
Sitomagus
Sitones, people 34 G a
Sittace 20 K f
Sitten, see, Sion 91 P l
Siugui
Siut 174 G b
Sivas 89 E c
Siwah Oasis
Six Nations, tribes 192 D b
Sixt, mon. 95 D b
Skaga Fiord 166 B b
Skager Rak, str. 88 C c
Skagway 198 ins. A
Skalitz 159 I c
Skåne, dist. 88 E d
Skanör, Hanse. for. cy. 98 F b
Skeena River 212 C c
Skenesborough 195 E b
Skidaway 193 ins. C
Skipton 127 V m
Skopia (Uskub), see Scopia
Skye, isl. 49 C c
Slamat, mt.
Slankamen 131 H d
Slatoust 167 Q d
Slave Coast, reg. 174 D d
Slaviansk 167 M f
Slavic Peoples about 900 57 leg.
Slavinia, reg. 58 G c
Slavonia, reg. 70 J d
Slavonian Military Frontier 159 I f
Sligo 127 I g
Sligo, cty. 127 I g
Sligo Bay 49 B d
Sliven 165 E b
Slivnitza 164 C b
Sloboneva 153 O f
Slonim 139 C e
Slovaks, people 168 leg.
Slovenes, people, about 900
Slovenes, people, 1910
Sluys 117 B c
Sluys, Hanse. for. cy. 99 ins. B
Smaland, dist. 88 F c
Smederevo 93 B b
Smenus River 14 C c
Smith, Fort, town 211 G c
Smith, routes of 210 B c
Smithfield, loc. near London 75 G g
Smith Island 193 ins. A
Smohain
Smoky Range, Great 193 C d
Smolensk 153 O g
Smolensk, gov. 131 J b
Smoothfield (Smithfield), loc. near London 75 G g
Smyrna 20 B c
Smyrna vetus 20 B c
Snake River 198 C b
Snakes, tribe 188 C b
Snelling, Fort 199 G b
Snowdon, mt. 49 E e
Soana 64 ins.
Soana, bp. 95 E c
Sobat River 174 G d
Sobernheim 142 ins. A
Sobral 214 E c
Sobràon 170 I e
Sobrarbe, dist. 83 E c
Society Islands 180 L i
Socoh, in Idumæa 7 B f
Socoh, in Judæa 7 B e
Soconusco, reg. 105 B c
Socorro, in Colombia 214 B b
Socorro, in New Mexico 190 D e
Socorro Island 213 A c
Socotra, isl., see Sokotra
Socrates, Prison of, in Athens 23 D
Söderhamn 166 I c
Söderköping 88 G b
Soest 62 E c
Soest, Hanse. cy. 99 ins. B
Sofia 93 B b
Soflingen 143 I i
Soflingen, ab. 143 I i
Sogamoso 214 B b
Sogd, reg.
Sogdiana, prov. 19 K c
Sogdiana, satr. 18 R h
Sogne Fiord 166 G c
Sohar 170 G f
Soignes, Forest of 156 A a
Soignies 117 C d
Soissons 61 E b
Soissons, bp. 94 C b
Soissons, gen. 147 E b
Sokoto 174 D c
Sokotra, isl. 174 I c
Solander Island 172 F e
Soldaia (Sudak) 99 K e
Soldau 123 K b
Soledad 190 A d
Solent, str. 49 F f
Solfatara, vol. 31 ins. A
Solferino 158 F f
Solignac, mon. 94 C b
Solikamsk 138 I d
Solimariaca 39 H i
Solis, route of 105 D d
Solis River (Rio de la Plata) 108 L k
Solitaria, isl. 107 A i
Sollium 10 B d
Solmona 64 B b
Solomon, Palace of, in ancient Jerusalem 6 ins. A
Solomon, Palace of, in medieval Jerusalem 68 ins. B (7)
Solomon Islands 172 E a
Solomon's Pool, in ancient Jerusalem 6 ins. A (2)
Solona 27 F c
Solothurn 91 P k
Solothurn, canton 91 P k
Solovets 138 E c
Solsona 82 C a
Solsona, bp. 94 C c
Soluntum, or Solus 30 C d
Solway Firth
Solway Moor 118 D c
Solway Moss
Solygea 15 D b
Somah 165 E d
Somaliland, British, col. 174 H d
Somaliland, Italian, col. 174 H d
Somborne, deanery 100 A a
Somberete 213 B b
Sombrero, isl. 213 F c
Somena River, see Somme River
Somersætas, people
Somerset, in Maryland 194 K g
Somerset, in Queensland 172 D b
Somerset, cty. in England
Somerset, shire
Somerset House, in London 75 G g
Somme, dept. 148 E e
Somme River 76 E b
Sommerschenburg 85 B b
Sommerschenburg, castle 72 C a
Sommières 126 D e
Somnath, Pattan
Somosierra 130 C e
Sonderburg 88 C d
Sondershausen 134 F c
Sondrio 91 R l

Songhar
Song-ka River
Sonoma 201 A b
Sonora 190 C f
Sonora, prov. 190 C e
Sonora, Rio de, R. 190 C f
Sonora, state 213 A b
Son-tai 171 L f
Sontheim, Ober 143 I g
Sontius (Isonzo) River 27 H b
Soor 135 H c
Sophene, reg. 20 H c
Sophia
Sopianæ 38 F c
Sopron (Ödenburg) 63 I e
Sora 30 C a
Sora, bp. 95 E c
Soracte, mon. 95 E c
Soracte, mt. 27 G e
Sorata, mt. 214 C d
Sorau 79 I c
Sorbian March 55 R i
Sorbiodunum (Old Sarum)
Sorbiodurum (Straubing) 38 E c
Sorbonne, bldg. in Paris 149 B
Sorbs, people 53 O g
Sorek River 7 B e
Sorel 189 B b
Soria 82 H e
Sorocaba 215 E e
Soros 16 B a
Sorrento 90 E d
Sorrento, abp. 95 E c
Soto, route of 191 H e, I e
Soubise, near La Rochelle 126 A d
Soubise, loc. in Paris 149 B
Soule, dist. 147 D c
Soule, viscty. 76 C e
Souna, dist. 63 H e
Sound, The, strait 88 E d
Souris River 198 E a
South Africa Company, British 175 F f
South African Republic 175 M k
South America, continent 214, 115
Southampton, in England
Southampton, deanery 100 A b
Southampton, hospitals 100 A b
Southampton, mon. 100 A b
Southampton, parl. bor. 163 M g
Southampton, on Long Island 189 B d
Southampton, Cape, in Canada 212 G b
Southampton County, in Virginia 207 K c
Southampton Hundred 193 ins. A (South.)
Southampton Island 212 G b
South Angles, people
South Australia, state 172 C c
South (Delaware) Bay 192 D d
South Bend, tower 211 H b
South Berwick 189 C c (S. B.)
South Beveland, isl. 117 B c
South Cape, Tasmania 172 D e
South Carolina, col. 193 D e
South Carolina, state 199 I d
South Carolina Yazoo Company 196 A d
South Chester, parl. dist. 163 L d
South Dakota, state 210 E b
South Derby, parl. dist. 163 M d
South Devon, parl. dist. 163 K g
South Downs, dist. 49 F f
South Durham, parl. dist. 163 M c
Southern Californians, tribes 188 C d
Southern District, Victoria 172 leg.
Southern Pacific Grant 210 C d
Southern Uplands, Scotland 49 E d
South Essex, parl. dist. 163 O f
South Folk (Angles), people
South Hants, parl. dist. 163 M g
South Island, New Zealand 172 G e
South Isles, Scotland
South Kingston 189 ins. A
South Lancaster, parl. dist. 163 L d
South Leicester, parl. dist. 163 M e
South Molton, parl. bor. 163
South Northampton, parl. dist. 163 N e
South Northumberland, parl. dist. 163 L b
South Nottingham, parl. dist. 163 N d
Southold 189 B d
South Pass 210 D b
South Platte River 210 E b
South Potomac River 192 B d
South Prussia, dist. 135 I c
South (Delaware) River 192 D d
South Salop, parl. dist. 163 L e
South Saskatchewan River 186 H c
South Saxons, people 51 R k
South Sea (Pacific Ocean) 107 F h
South Shields, parl. bor. 163 M c
South Sporades, isl. 164 D c
South Stafford, parl. dist. 163 L e
South Stafford Coalfield 162 D e
South Voorne, isl. 117 C c
South Wales Coalfield, Great 162 C f
Southwark, suburb of London 75 G g
Southwark, parl. bor. 163 N f (Southw.)
South Warwick, parl. dist. 163 M e
South West Africa, German, col.
South West Cape, Tasmania 172 D e
Southwest Gate, in Olympia
Southwick, priory 100 A b
South Wilts, parl. dist. 163 L f
Söul, see Seoul 171 N e
Souvigny, mon. 94 C b
Sox, castle 91 R k
Sozopolis, in Asia Minor 71 M f
Sozopolis, in Bulgaria 73 F b
Spaichingen 143 G i
Spain, country, 910—1492 82, 83
Spain, km., about 1560 118 D e
Spain, km., about 1740 130 C f
Spain, reg., in Roman times 34 C e
Spain, Rom. dioc. 42 B e
Spalato 90 F c
Spalato, abp. 95 F c
Spalauthræ 11 E c
Spalding, mon. 97 Q i
Spalding, parl. bor.
Spalt 114 F d
Spandau 85 C b
Spanish Algarve, dist. 83 J h
Spanish March, 8 cent. 53 L i
Spanish March, 9 cent. 56 C d
Spanish Netherlands, prov. 122 B c
Spanish Peaks 198 D c
Spanish Plateau 2 D d
Spanish Town 213 E c
Spanish Trail, route 210 B d
Sparnacus, see Épernay
Sparta 14 C b
Spartel, Cape 2 D e
Spartolus 11 E b
Speen
Spencer Gulf 172 C d
Spercheus River 10 D d
Spes Vetus, Temple of 22 A
Speyer, see Spires
Spey River
Spezia 90 B b
Spezzia, isl. 164 C c
Sphacteria, isl. 14 B c
Sphagia, isl. 14 B c
Sphendale 16 B a
Sphettus 16 B b
Spice Islands 112 F d
Spielberg, castle 159 I d
Spier 62 F c
Spina 27 G c
Spinæ (Speen)
Spineticum Ostium, mouth of Po R. 27 G c
Spion Kop, mt. 175 M l
Spiræum, prom. 15 D b
Spira (Spires) 39 J i
Spires 62 E d
Spires, bp. 78 F d
Spires, imp. cy. 78 F d
Splügen 91 R l
Splügen Pass 91 R l
Spokane, or Spokane House 210 B a
Spokane, Ind. Res. 188 C a
Spokanes, tribe 188 C a
Spoletium (Spoleto) 27 G e
Spoleto 90 D c
Spoleto, bp. 95 E c
Spoleto, duchy 54 G e
Sponheim, castle 142 ins. A
Sponheim, cty. 114 D d
Sponheim, mon. 95 D b
Sporades, isl. 13 E c
Spree River 85 G d
Spremberg 85 H e
Sprimont 117 D d
Springfield, in Illinois 211 H c
Springfield, in Mass. 189 B c
Springfield, in Missouri 211 G c
Springfield, in Ohio 211 I c
Sprinfontein 175 M m
Squillace 90 F e
Squillace, bp. 95 F d
Sredne Kolimsk 171 Q b
Stabiæ 30 D b
Stabulaus, see Stavelot
Stadaconá (Quebec) 191 K b
Stade 62 E b
Stade, Hanse. cy. 99 ins. B
Stadion, castle and town 143 I i
Stadtlohn 122 D b
Staffarda 130 P j
Staffis 91 O l
Stafford, in England 127 W m
Stafford, in Virginia 193 F b
Stafford, cty. 127 W n
Stafford, parl. bor. 163 L l
Staggia 90 L j
Stagira, or Stagirus 11 E b
Stagno, bp. 95 F c
Stagnum Tuneticum (Bay of Tunis) 34 ins. A
Stahremberg, castle
Staines 75 H i
Stainforth 162 F d
Staked Plain 210 E d
Stalida, isl. 16 D c
Stamford, in Connecticut 189 B d
Stamford, in England 127 Y n
Stamford, castle 65 F d
Stamford, parl. bor. 163 N e
Stamford Bridge 65 F d
Stampæ, see Étampes
Standing Rock, Ind. Res. 188 F a
Standish 185 D d
Stanislau 168 I b
Stanislawow 159 M d
Stanley, mon. 97 O j
Stanley Falls 175 F d
Stanley Pool, lake 175 E e
Stanleyville 175 F d
Stanovoi Mountains 171 Q b
Stanwix, Fort 192 D b
Stanz 91 Q l
Starbuck Island 180 L h
Star Fort 164 L g
Stargard, in Mecklenburg 79 H b
Stargard, duchy 79 H b
Stargard, in Pomerania 79 I b
Stargard, Hanse cy. 99 ins. B
Starkenburg, castle, in Hesse 142 C a
Starkenburg, castle, on the Moselle R. 142 ins. A
Starodub 139 D e
Staten Island, South America 215 C h
Staten Island, U. S. 189 ins. C
States of the Church, 9 cent. 56 E d
States of the Church, 13 cent. 73 C b
States of the Church, see also Papal States and Patrimony of St. Peter
State Treasury, in Rome
Statilii, Tomb of the 22 A
Statonia 27 F e
Statuas, Ad 35 ins. B
Staufen, in Baden 142 A e

Staufen, lordship 142 A e
Staufen or Hohenstaufen, castle in Wurtemberg 62 E d
Staufenberg, castle 142 B d
Staufenberg, lordship 142 B d
Staunton 193 E b
Staunton River 193 E c
Stavanger 88 A b
Stavelot 117 D d
Stavelot, ab. 117 D d
Stavelot, mon. 95 D a
Stavoren 117 D b
Stavoren, Hanse. cy. 99 ins. B
Stavropol 139 F f
Steckelberg, castle 86 G c
Stecknitz Canal 79 G b
Stedingen, dist. 72 B a
Steelyard, The, loc. in London 98 ins. A
Steenbergen 117 C c
Steenkerque 122 C c
Steenwyk 117 E b
Steep Point, cape 172 A c
Stegeborg 119 H b
Steier, castle 63 H d
Stein 91 Q k
Steinamanger 135 I e
Steinau 123 I c
Steinfeld 142 E a
Steinfurt 122 D b
Steinhuder Lake 39 J g
Stelvio Pass 91 S l
Stenay 126 D b
Stendal 72 C a
Stendal, Hanse. cy. 99 ins. B
Stenimakhos 165 D c
Stenyclarus 14 B b
Stephenson, Fort 200 B c
Sternberg, dist. 85 D b
Sterzing 154 F e
Steterburg 62 F b
Steterburg, mon. 95 E a (St.)
Stetten 142 D d
Stetten, lordship 142 D d
Stettenfels, castle 143 H g
Stettenfels, lordship 143 H g
Stettin 63 H b
Stettin, duchy, 14 cent. 79 I b
Stettin, duchy, 16 cent. 115 I a
Stettin, Hanse. cy. 99 ins. B
Stettin, Neu 123 I b
Steuben, Fort 196 ins. B
Steuerverein (Tax-Union) 160 I f
Steusslingen 143 I i
Stewart Island 172 F e
Stewarts, fam.
Steyning, parl. bor. 163 N g
Steyr, in Austria 135 H e
Stikine River 212 ins.
Stiklestad 64 F d
Stilfser Joch, pass 26 E a
Stiria 16 C b
Stiris 11 D d
Stirling
Stirling, cty.
Stobi 39 M l
Stockach 142 D e
Stockbridge, Ind. Res. 188 I a
Stockelsdorf 88 D e
Stockholm 77 H a
Stockholm, Hanse. for. cy. 98 G b
Stockport 127 W m
Stockport, parl. bor. 163 L d
Stocks Market, in London 75 G g (37)
Stockton 162 E c
Stoddert, Fort 200 I f
Stœni, people 26 E b
Stoke-upon-Trent, parl. bor. 163 L d
Stoke-Courcy, parl. bor.
Stolbovo 138 D d
Stollhofen 134 D d
Stollhofen Lines, military dist. 129 E c
Stolp 123 I a
Stolp, Hanse. cy. 98 G c
Stolpen 115 H c
Stoneleigh, mon. 97 P i
Stonington 189 C d
Stony Point, on Hudson R. 195 D c
Stork Tower, in Jerusalem 6 ins. A
Storkyro 131 H a
Stormarn, dist. 62 E b
Storm Bay 172 D e
Stormberg Junction 175 M m
Storms, Cape of 109 S k
Stoss, Pass 91 R k
Stotzingen 143 J h
Stour River 49 G e
Stourbridge 98 ins. A
Stourport 162 D e
Stow-on-the-Wold 127 X o
Stradella 130 R i
Straits Settlements, col. 171 L h
Stralsund 79 H a
Stralsund, Hanse. cy. 99 ins. B
Strand, street in London 75 G g
Strasburg, in Alsace 62 D d
Strasburg, bp. 78 E d
Strasburg, imp. cy. 78 E d
Strasburg, in Virginia 193 E b
Strata Florida, mon. 97 N i
Stratford, near London 75 J h
Stratford, in Connecticut 189 B d
Stratford Langthorne, mon. 97 R j
Strathclyde, km.
Strathcona 212 D c
Strathearn, dist.
Strathnaver, dist.
Stratonicea 11 E b
Straton's Tower in Jerusalem 6 B d
Strättligen, castle 91 P l
Stratton 127 U p
Stratus 10 C d
Straubing 79 H d
Strausberg 85 D b
Strawberry Bank, village 189 D c
Strehla 63 G c
Strehlen 135 I c
Strengnäs 119 H b
Stresow 135 G a
Stretensk 171 M c
Streu River 62 F c
Stridon 42 F e
Striegau 135 I c
Strivali Islands 157 E e
Strogonov, Colony of
Strongyle, isl. 30 E d
Strood 98 ins. A
Strophades Islands 14 B b
Stroud, parl. bor. 163 L f
Stryme
Strymon River 11 E a
Strymonic Gulf 11 F b
Stuart, routes of 172 leg.
Stuart Town 193 ins. C
Studzianka 153 N g
Stühlingen 142 B e
Stühlingen, landgr. 142 B e
Stuhlweissenburg 159 J e
Stuhmsdorf 123 J b
Stura River (Stura di Demonte) 26 B c
Stura River (Stura di Lanzo) 26 B b
Sturni 31 G b
Stuttgart 143 H h
Styberra 10 C a
Stymphalus 14 C b
Styra 15 E a
Styria, duchy, 12 cent. 72 D b
Styria, duchy, 14 cent. 79 I e
Styria, march, 11 cent. 63 H e
Styx River 14 C b
Suakin 174 G c
Suana 27 F e
Suanetes, people 26 D a
Subiaco 64 ins.
Subiaco, mon. 96 C b
Subig 199 ins. H
Sublaqueum (Subiaco) 27 H f
Sublavio (Seben) 27 F a
Sublette's Cut-off, route 210 C b
Sublician Bridge, Rome 24 A
Sublime Porte, loc. in Constantinople 93 G e
Subura, quarter in Rome 22 A
Succoth 7 D d
Succur
Su-chau, in Kan-su 171 K e
Su-chau, in Kiang-su 171 N e
Suchester
Sucré 214 C d
Sucro River (Júcar R.) 38 B e
Suczawa 168 J c
Sudak 99 K e
Sudan, reg. 174 C c
Sudan, Anglo-Egyptian, reg. 174 F c
Sudbury, in England 163 O e
Sudbury, parl. bor. 163 O e
Sudbury, in Mass. 189 C c (Sudb.)
Sudbury, in Ontario 212 G d
Sudermania, dist. 119 H b
Sudetes, mts. 166 I e
Sudeti Mountains 38 E b
Sueones, people 38 E a
Suessa Aurunca or Suessa (Sessa) 30 C a
Suessa Pometia 30 B a
Suessiones or Suessionis, see Soissons
Suessiones, people 38 C c
Suessula (Torre di Sessola) 30 D a
Sueves, people, in Germany 45 G b
Sueves, people, in Spain 45 C d, 50 B d, 52 H e
Suez 174 K i
Suez, Gulf of 174 K j
Suez, Isthmus of 3 H e
Suez Canal 174 K i
Sufes 42 D f
Suffolk, cty. 127 Z n
Sugambri, people 39 I h
Suhar
Suhl 154 F c
Suhlingen 154 E b
Sui-chau-fu
Suindinum, see Le Mans
Suipacha 214 C e
Sukadana 112 E d
Sukhona River 167 N c
Sukhum Kaleh 164 G b
Sulby, mon. 97 Q i
Sulci 38 D e
Suleïman, mosque 93 G e
Sulina 165 F a
Sulina Mouth of Danube 164 D a
Suliots, people 164 C c
Sully 126 C c
Sulmo 27 H e
Sulmone 90 E c
Sultaniyeh 99 M f
Sultan's Pool 6 ins. A
Sultan Valideh, mosque 93 G e (6)
Sulu, isl.
Suluan, isl. 110 D D g
Sulu Archipelago 199 ins. H
Sulu Sea 199 ins. H
Sulz 143 G i
Sulzbach, in Bavaria 79 G d
Sulzbach, in Wurtemberg 143 I g
Sulzbach, palat. 123 G d
Sumatium
Sumatra, isl. 112 C c
Sumba, isl. 172 A b
Sumbal
Sumbal, reg.
Sumbawa, isl.
Sumelocenna 39 J i
Sumer, reg. 4 G c
Sumiswald, castle 91 P k
Summo lacu 26 D a
Summus Pœninus, see Great Saint Bernard
Sumter, Fort 208 E c
Sun, Gate of the, in Alexandria 34 ins. C
Sunarganw
Sunderland, parl. bor. 163 M c
Sundgau, dist. 114 D e

Sundhofen 143 ins. D
Sun Dial, in Rome 22 A
Sundswall 166 I c
Sungari River
Sumian Gate, in Athens
Suntar 171 M b
Süntel, mts. 55 Q i
Supe 214 B d
Superior, lake 186 K d
Suppai, Ind. Res. 188 D c
Süpplingenburg, castle 62 F b
Sura, Baths of
Surabaja 172 A a
Surat 137 B d
Surgut 170 I b
Surinam, col. 214 D b
Surintendance, Rue de la, street in Versailles 149 A
Surrentum (Sorrento) 30 D b
Surrey, cty. 127 Y o
Surreymen, people
Sursee 91 Q k
Surt
Susa, in Italy 90 A b
Susa, marq. 64 A a
Susa, in **Persia** 19 G d
Susia 19 I c
Susiana, prov. 19 G d
Susiana, reg. 8 C b
Susiana, satr. 18 P h
Susquehanna River 192 C c
Susquehannocks, tribe 188 K b
Sussex, cty. 127 Y p
Sussex, km.
Sutherland, cty.
Sutherland, dist.
Sutherlands, fam. 97 I a
Sutley River 137 B a
Sutri 64 ins.
Sutri, bp. 95 E c
Sutrium (Sutri) 27 G e
Sutter's Fort (Sacramento) 198 A c
Sutter's Mill 210 A c
Suva 172 G b
Suwali
Suwanee River 193 C f
Suya 190 C e
Suzdal 138 F d
Sveaborg, fortress 131 H a
Svendborg 88 D d
Svendborg, Hanse. for. cy. 98 E b
Svenigrod 71 L d
Sventziany 153 N f
Svir River 167 L c
Swaanendael see Zwaanendael 191 J d
Swabia, Frank. prov., 9 cent. 56 D c
Swabia, duchy, about 1000 58 F d
Swabia, duchy, 11 cent. 62 E e
Swabia, duchy, 12 cent. 72 B b
Swabia, Lower, "landvogtei" 143 I j
Swabia, Upper, "landvogtei" 143 I j
Swabians, people 57 E d
Swakopmund 175 E g
Swale River 127 X l
Swan Hill, town 172 D d
Swan River 172 A d
Swanscombe 75 J i
Swansea 189 ins. A
Swansea, parl. bor. 163 J f
Swaziland, reg. 175 N l
Sweet Waters, Valley of the, loc. in Constantinople 93 G e
Sweden, km., about 1000 59 H b
Sweden, km., about 1097 66 J b
Sweden, km., about 1190 70 J a
Sweden, km., about 1569 119 I a
Sweden, km., about 1658 120 leg.
Sweden, km., about 1740 131 H a
Sweden, km., about 1812 155 ins.
Sweden, km., 1910 166 H d
Swedes, people 46 I b
Swedish Pomerania, dist. 154 G a
Swift Current, town 212 E d
Swinemünde 135 H b
Swineshead, mon. 97 Q i
Swinomish, Ind. Res. 188 B a
Swiss Confederation, 14—18 cent. 91
Syagrius, km. of 33 M h
Sybaris 31 F c
Sybaris River 31 F c
Sycæ 93 G e
Sycaminon 6 B c
Sycurium 11 D c
Sydney, on Cape Breton I. 212 J d
Sydney, in New South Wales 172 E d
Sydney District 172 leg.
Syene (Assuan) 4 F d
Sylhet 137 F c
Sylt, isl. 114 E a
Sylvania, proposed state in U. S.
Symæthus River 30 D e
Syme, isl. 13 E c
Symmes Purchase, dist. 196 ins. B
Synnada 20 D c
Sypalettus 16 B a
Syracusæ, see Syracuse, in Sicily
Syracuse, in New York 196 D b
Syracuse, in Sicily 30 E e
Syracuse, bp. 95 F d
Syracuse, plan of 31 ins. B
Syra Orda
Syrastrene, reg. 19 L f
Syr Daria, River
Syria, km. 33 E b
Syria, Macedon. prov. 18 E d
Syria, reg. 67 N g
Syria, Rom. prov. 35 L g
Syria, satr. 18 O h
Syria I, E. Rom. prov. 43 J f (3)
Syrian Desert 3 H e
Syria Salutaris, Rom. prov. 43 J f (10)
Syrias, prom. 20 F a
Syros, isl. 15 E b
Syrtis, Greater, gulf 174 E a
Syrtis, Lesser, gulf 174 E a
Syrtis Maior (Greater Syrtis), gulf 34 H g
Syrtis Minor (Lesser Syrtis), gulf 34 G g
Sys River, in Achaia 14 C b
Sys River, in Macedonia 11 D c
Sythas River 14 C b
Szamos Rirer 159 L e
Szamos-Ujvar 159 M e
Szasz-Regen 159 M e
Szathmar
Sze-chwan, prov. 171 L e
Szentes 159 K e
Szent Imre 119 I d
Szent Tamas 159 J f
Szolnok 159 K e
Szöreg 159 K e

Taanach 6 C c
Tabæ, in Asia Minor 47 L f
Tabæ, in Palestine 6 D c
Tabæ, in Persia 19 I d
Tabard, The, inn, near London 75 G g
Tabasco 107 H f
Tabasco, reg. 105 B c
Tabasco River 105 B c
Tabasco, state 213 C c
Tabatinga 214 C c
Tabbas, Las 214 A b
Tabernæ (Zabern) 39 I i
Tabernæ (Rheinzabern) 39 J i
Taberna frigida 26 E d
Tabernas 82 B b
Tabernilla
Tabor, in Bohemia 87 J d
Tabor, in Iowa 206 F b
Tabor, mt. 6 C c
Tabora 175 G e
Tabriz 139 G H
Tabularium (Record Office) in Rome 24 A
Taburi, people 19 H c
Tacape 12 F d
Tacna 214 B d
Tacoma 210 A a
Tacubaya 106 A a
Tadcaster 127 X m
Tadmor 20 H e
Tadousac 212 H d
Tænarum 14 C c
Tænarum, prom. (Cape Matapan) 14 C c
Tænia 34 ins. A
Tæzalorum, prom. 38 B a
Taff River
Tafilet 98 C g
Taganrog 139 E f
Tagaste 42 D f
Tagernauseo, see Tegernsee
Taghaza 108 Q e
Taginæ 52 D b
Tagliacozzo 72 C c
Tagliamento River 135 G e
Tagong
Tagus River 82 A b
Tahiti, isl. 180 M i
Tahlequah 211 G c
Tahoe, lake 210 B c
Taido (Peking)
Taillebourg 69 C d
Taillebourg, castle 76 C d
Taimur Peninsula 171 K a
Tai-wan 171 N f
Tai-yuen-fu
Taiza 105 C c
Ta-ku 170 ins. A
Taku River 212 ins.
Talabriga 38 A d
Talamone 72 C c
Talas
Talavera de la Reina 82 A a
Talay River
Talca 215 B f
Talcahuano 212 B f
Ta-lien-wan 171 N e
Ta-li-fu
Tallahassee 211 I d
Tallapoosa River 193 B e
Talley, mon. 97 N j
Talmont 69 C c
Talmont, seign. 69 C c
Taltal 215 B e
Talva, see Tarbes
Taman 93 E a
Tamar 7 C f
Tamar River, in Cornwall
Tamar River, in Tasmania 172 D e
Tamara 83 E c
Tamarus River 30 D a
Tamatave 175 H f
Tamaulipas, state 213 C b
Tambo, near Cuzco 111 C d
Tambo, near Mollendo 214 B d
Tambov 139 F e
Tamesa (Thames) River 38 C b
Tampico 201 F e
Tammerfors 131 H a
Tampa 211 I e
Tampa Bay 211 I e
Tampico 107 H f
Tamworth 127 X n
Tamworth, parl. bor. 163 M e
Tamynæ 11 F d
Tamyras River 6 C a
Tana (Azov) 77 M c
Tanager River 30 E b
Tanagra 11 E d
Tanaïs 35 L d
Tanaïs (Don) River 35 M d
Tanana River 212 A b
Tanarus (Tanaro) River 26 C c
Tanatis Island 38 C b
Tancred's Tower, in Jerusalem 68 ins. B
Tanegashima Island 110 E E e
Taneytown 208 ins.
Tangarara 111 A b
Tanganyika, lake 175 F e
Tangermünde 85 B b
Tangermünde, Hanse. cy. 99 ins. B
Tangier 174 C a

Tang-shan . . . . . 170 ins. A
Tangut, reg. . . . .
Tanis . . . . . 4 ins.
Tanjore . . . . . 137 C f
Tannenberg . . . . . 87 L b
Tanners, Postern of the, loc. in Jerusalem . . . . . 68 ins. B
Tannetum . . . . . 26 E c
Tan-sui . . . . . 171 N f
Tanta . . . . . 150 B a
Tantalam Island . . . . . 171 L h
Tanus River . . . . . 14 C b
Taormina . . . . . 90 E f
Taos . . . . . 190 D d
Tapajos River . . . . . 214 D c
Tophiæ Islands . . . . . 10 B d
Taphus, isl. . . . . . 10 B d
Tappahannock . . . . . 193 F c
Tappan . . . . . 192 D c
Tapti River . . . . . 137 C d
Taranaki, prov. . . . . . 172 G d
Taranto . . . . . 90 F d
Taranto, abp. . . . . . 95 F c
Tarapacá . . . . . 214 C d
Taras (Taranto) . . . . . 31 G b
Tarascon, in Foix . . . . . 69 D e
Tarascon, in Provence . . . . . 72 A c
Tarasp . . . . . 122 F e
Tarazona . . . . . 82 B a
Tarazona, bp. . . . . . 94 B c
Tarbes . . . . . 61 C e
Tarbes, bp. . . . . . 94 C c
Tarentaise . . . . . 61 G d
Tarentaise, abp. . . . . . 95 D b
Tarentum (Taranto) . . . . . 31 G b
Tarentum, dist. in Rome . . . . . 23 B
Tarentum, Gulf of . . . . . 31 G c
Targovitza . . . . . 131 J d
Tarifa . . . . . 82 A b
Tarifa, Cape . . . . . 166 D h
Tarija . . . . . 214 C e
Tarim River . . . . .
Tarleton, raid of . . . . . 195 B e
Tarleton, route of . . . . . 195 A f
Tarma . . . . . 111 B d
Tarn, dept. . . . . . 148 E f
Tarn River . . . . . 76 E d
Tarn-et-Garonne, dept. . . . . . 148 E f
Tarnaiæ . . . . . 26 A a
Tarnis River, see Tarn River
Tarnopol . . . . . 139 C f
Tarnow . . . . . 87 M c
Taro River . . . . . 150 E d
Tarphe . . . . . 16 F e
Tarquinii . . . . . 27 F e
Tarracina (Terracina) . . . . . 30 C a
Tarraco (Tarragona) . . . . . 38 C d
Tarraconensis, Rom. prov. . . . . 38 B d (1)
Tarraconensis, West Rom. prov. 42 B e (4)
Tarragona . . . . . 82 C a
Tarragona, abp. . . . . . 94 C c
Tarrant, mon. . . . . . 97 O k
Tarrytown . . . . . 195 E c
Tarsatica . . . . . 27 I b
Tarshish, reg. . . . . . 12 B c
Tarsi, people . . . . .
Tarsius River . . . . .
Tarsus . . . . . 20 F d
Tartars or Tatars, people, north of Black Sea . . . . . 93 D a
Tartars or Tatars, people in eastern Asia . . . . .
Tartars or Tatars, people in eastern Russia . . . . . 138 H d
Tartarus River . . . . . 27 F b
Tartary or Tatary, reg. . . . . 109 W-BB c
Tartary or Tatary, Little, reg. . 139 D f
Tartas . . . . . 76 C e
Tarua . . . . . 8 D c
Taruana or Taruenna, see Thérouanne
Tarus (Taro) River . . . . . 26 E c
Tarvis . . . . . 135 G e
Tarvisium (Treviso) . . . . . 27 G b
Tashkent . . . . .
Tasman, route of . . . . .
Tasman Peninsula . . . . . 172 D e
Tasmania, state . . . . . 172 D e
Tatars, see Tartars
Tatary, reg., see Tartary
Tatra, mts. . . . . . 166 I f
Tatta . . . . . 137 A d
Tatta, lake . . . . . 20 E c
Tau . . . . . 199 ins. D
Tau, isl. . . . . . 199 ins. D
Tauber River . . . . . 114 E d
Tauberbischofsheim . . . . . 158 E d
Taulantii, people . . . . . 10 A b
Taungu . . . . .
Taungu, reg. . . . . .
Taunton, in England . . . . . 127 V p
Taunton, mon. . . . . . 97 N k
Taunton, parl. bor. . . . . . 163 K f
Taunton, in Mass. . . . . . 189 ins. A
Taunus Mountains . . . . . 39 J h
Taupo, lake . . . . . 172 G d
Taurasia (Turin) . . . . . 26 B b
Tauresium . . . . . 52 K e
Taurianum, prom. . . . . . 30 E d
Tauric Chersonese (Crimea) . . 35 K d
Taurida, reg. . . . . . 139 D f
Taurini, people . . . . . 26 B c
Taurinum, see Turin
Taurisci, people . . . . . 38 E c
Tauroggen . . . . . 131 H b
Tauromenium . . . . . 30 E e
Taurus Mountains . . . . . 3 H e
Taurus, prom. . . . . . 30 E e
Taus . . . . . 87 I d
Tavan . . . . . 119 K d
Tavastehus . . . . . 119 I a
Tavira . . . . . 82 A b
Tavoy . . . . .
Tavoy, reg. . . . . .
Tavistock, mon. . . . . . 97 M k
Tavistock, parl. bor. . . . . . 163 J g
Tavium . . . . . 20 F c
Tawali, isl. . . . . . 112 F d
Tawalisi, people . . . . .
Tawi-Tawi, isl. . . . . . 112 F c
Taxila . . . . . 19 L d
Taxis, castle . . . . . 143 J h
Taxis, princ. . . . . . 143 J h
Tay River . . . . . 49 D c
Taygetus Mountains . . . . . 14 C b
Taylor, route of . . . . . 201 leg.
Tcheragan Palace
Tcherkasy . . . . . 139 D f
Tchernigov . . . . . 139 D e
Tchernoi-Yar . . . . . 139 G f
Tchesme . . . . . 164 D c
Tchigrin . . . . . 139 D f
Tchirmen . . . . . 93 C b
Tchorgun . . . . . 164 J f
Tchuds, people . . . . . 71 K b
Tchuguiev . . . . . 139 E f
Teano, bp. . . . . . 95 ins.
Teanum Apulum . . . . . 30 E a
Teanum Sidicinum . . . . . 30 D a
Teate, Apulum . . . . . 30 E a
Teate, Marrucinum (Chieti) . . 27 I e
Teb, El . . . . . 174 G c
Tebuk . . . . . 99 K h
Teck, duchy . . . . . 143 H h
Teck, ruin . . . . . 143 H h
Tecklenburg . . . . . 78 E b
Tecklenburg, cty. . . . . . 78 E b
Tecmon . . . . . 10 B c
Tecumseh, Fort . . . . . 210 E b
Tees River . . . . . 49 F d
Tegea . . . . . 14 C b
Tegernsee, mon. . . . . . 95 E b
Tegesta . . . . . 191 I f
Tegianum . . . . . 30 E b
Tegucigalpa . . . . . 213 D c
Tehachapi Pass . . . . . 210 B c
Teheran . . . . . 170 G e
Tehuacan . . . . . 213 ins.
Tehuacanas, tribe . . . . . 188 G d
Tehuantepec . . . . . 105 A c
Tehuantepec, Gulf of . . . . . 213 C c
Tehuantepec, Isthmus of . . . . 213 C c
Teixeira, route of . . . . . 214 C c
Tejada . . . . . 46 F f
Tejas, tribe . . . . . 188 G d
Tejuco . . . . . 214 E d
Tekfour Serai, loc. in Constantinople . . . . . 93 G e
Tekka, reg. . . . . . 89 J g
Tekoa . . . . . 7 C e
Tela . . . . . 20 H d
Telamon . . . . . 27 F e
Telesia . . . . . 30 D a
Telethrius, mt. . . . . . 11 E d
Telium . . . . . 26 E a
Tell, The, reg. . . . . . 2 E e
Tellicherri . . . . . 137 C f
Tell el Kebir . . . . .
Tellena . . . . .
Tellus, Temple of, Rome . . . . 22 A
Telmessus, Telmissus . . . . . 20 C d
Telo Martius (Toulon) . . . . . 38 D d
Telshi . . . . . 125 H a
Telus . . . . . 13 E c
Tembuland, reg. . . . . . 175 M m
Temenites . . . . . 31 ins. B
Temenium . . . . . 15 C b
Temes River . . . . . 159 K f
Tempe, valley . . . . . 11 D c
Templars, House of the, Jerusalem . . . . . 68 ins. B (8)
Temple, Faubourg du, quarter in Paris . . . . . 149 B
Temple, Rue du, street in Paris 149 B
Temple, Inner, Middle and Outer, loc. in London . . . . 75 G g
Temple, The, in Jerusalem . . . 68 ins. B
Temple, Rue du, street in Paris 149 B
Temple, Street of the, Jerusalem 68 ins. B
Temple, The, bldg. in Paris . . 149 B
Temple, Vieille, Rue du, street in Paris . . . . . 149 B
Temple Church, in London . . 75 G g (1)
Temple of Peace, Aug. Reg. of Rome . . . . . 22 A
Tempsa . . . . . 31 F c
Temrink . . . . . 119 L d
Temuco . . . . . 215 B f
Tenancingo . . . . . 106 A a
Tenasserim . . . . .
Tenasserim, prov. . . . . . 171 K g
Tenby . . . . . 65 D e
Tencteri, people . . . . . 38 D b
Tenda . . . . . 130 P j
Tenda, Col di, pass . . . . . 150 D d
Tenduc, people . . . . .
Tenea . . . . . 15 C b
Tenebrium, prom. . . . . . 38 C e
Tenedos . . . . . 13 E b
Tenedos, isl. . . . . . 13 E b
Teneriffe, isl. . . . . . 108 P e
Teneriffe, Santa Cruz de . . . . 174 B b
Tenes . . . . . 66 G f
Tenimber Islands . . . . . 172 C a
Ten Jurisdictions, League of, dist. . . . . . 91 R l
Tenneberg . . . . . 85 F e
Tennessee, state . . . . . 202 H c
Tennessee River . . . . . 211 H d
Tennessee Yazoo Company . . 196 A d
Tennis Court, loc. in Versailles 149 A
Tenochtillan . . . . . 106 A a
Tenos . . . . . 15 F b
Tenos, isl. . . . . . 15 F b
Tentura or Tentyris (Dendera) 4 F d
Teodosia . . . . . 124 G b
Teos . . . . . 13 E b
Teotihuacan . . . . . 106 B a
Tepeaca . . . . . 106 C b
Tepexacac . . . . .
Tepfenhardt . . . . . 142 D e
Tepic . . . . . 213 B b

Tepic, ter. . . . . 213 B b
Tepl, mon. . . . . 95 E a
Teplitz . . . . . 154 G c
Tepotzotlan . . . . . 106 A a
Tepulaw Aqueduct . . . . . 22 A
Teramo . . . . . 90 D c
Teramo, bp. . . . . . 95 E c
Teredon . . . . . 19 G d
Terek River . . . . . 139 G g
Terek, Cossacks of the, people 139 G g
Tergeste (Trieste) . . . . . 27 H b
Tergeste, Gulf of . . . . . 27 H b
Tergovist . . . . . 77 J c
Terina . . . . . 31 F d
Terjan . . . . . 93 E c
Ter la Haye . . . . .
Termes . . . . . 38 B d
Termini . . . . . 90 D f
Termoli . . . . . 90 E c
Termoli, bp. . . . . . 95 E c
Termonde . . . . . 117 C c
Ternate, isl. . . . . . 112 F c
Terni . . . . . 90 D c
Terni, bp. . . . . . 95 E c
Ternodurum, see Tonnerre
Terracina . . . . . 90 D d
Terracina, bp. . . . . . 95 E c
Terranova, in Calabria . . . . . 90 F e
Terranova, in Sicily . . . . . 90 E f
Terre Haute . . . . . 211 H c
Terrenate . . . . . 190 C e
Terrington, parl. bor. . . . . .
Terschelling, isl. . . . . . 117 D a
Teruel . . . . . 82 H e
Terventum . . . . .
Teschen . . . . . 79 K d
Teschen, princ. . . . . . 79 K d
Teslin, lake . . . . . 212 B b
Tessin (Ticino) River . . . . . 78 F f
Tessin, dist., see Ticino . . . . . 91 Q l
Testaccio, Monte, Rome . . . . . 22 A
Teste de Buch, la . . . . . 76 C d
Testry . . . . . 55 P j
Tetrica, mt. . . . . . 27 H e
Tetschen . . . . . 123 H c
Tettnang . . . . . 143 I j
Tetuan . . . . . 70 E f
Teufelsbrücke, bridge . . . . . 150 E c
Teumessus . . . . . 11 E d
Teurnia . . . . . 27 H a
Teuthrania, dist. . . . . .
Teuthrone . . . . . 14 C c
Teutoburger Forest, Teutoburgiensis Saltus, mts. . . . . . 39 J g
Teutones, people . . . . . 34 F c
Teutonic Order, Dom. of the, 14 cent. . . . . . 77 H b
Teutonic Order, Dom. of the, 16 cent. . . . . . 119 J b
Teviotdale, dist. . . . . .
Tewkesbury . . . . . 84 B d
Tewkesbury, mon. . . . . . 97 O j
Tewkesbury, parl. bor. 163 L f (Tewkesb.)
Texas, prov. . . . . . 190 F e
Texas, state . . . . . 202 E i
Texas Prairies, reg. . . . . . 187 J f
Texel, isl. . . . . . 117 C a
Textricum, see Testry
Texuandri, people . . . . . 39 H h
Tezcuco . . . . .
Tezcuco, lake . . . . .
Thabraca . . . . . 46 H f
Thagines River . . . . . 31 F c
Thala . . . . . 38 D e
Thamatha . . . . . 7 D e
Thame, mon. . . . . . 97 Q j
Thames River, in Canada . . . 200 B b
Thames River, in Connecticut 189 B d (Th.R.)
Thames River, in England . . . 49 F f
Thames, Battle of the . . . . . 200 C b
Thamesis Æsturianum (Thames River) . . . . . 51 Q i
Thana . . . . .
Thanet, island of . . . . . 51 S k
Thann . . . . . 154 G d
Thannheim . . . . . 143 J i
Thantia . . . . . 7 E d
Thapsacus . . . . . 20 H e
Thapsus, in Algeria . . . . . 12 E c
Thapsus, in Sicily . . . . . 30 E e
Thapsus, in Tunis . . . . . 38 E e
Thara . . . . . 19 H c
Thasos . . . . . 11 F b
Thasos, isl. . . . . . 11 F b
Thaumaci . . . . . 11 D c
Thaya River . . . . . 63 I d
Theanum, see Teano
Thebæ Phthiotides . . . . . 11 D c
Thebais, Rom. prov. . . . . . 43 I h (3)
Thebes, in Bœotia . . . . . 11 E d
Thebes, in Egypt . . . . . 4 F d
Thebez, in Samaria . . . . . 7 C d
The Close, loc. in London . . . 75 G g
The Danelaw, reg. . . . . .
The Downs, roadstead . . . . . 185 H f
The Filder, dist. . . . . . 143 H h
The Free Land, reg. . . . . . 117 A c
Theganussa, isl. . . . . . 14 B c
The Hague . . . . . 117 C b
The Isles, bp. . . . . . 97 G c
Theiss River . . . . . 73 D a
Thelepte . . . . . 34 F g
Thelpusa . . . . . 14 B b
Themiscyra . . . . . 20 G b
Themistocles, Grave of . . . . . 16 D c
Themistocles, Wall of . . . . . 23 D
Thenæ . . . . . 34 G g
The Naze, cape . . . . . 166 G d
Thengen . . . . . 142 C e
Thengen, cty. . . . . . 142 C e
Theocoleum . . . . .
Theodonis Villa, see Thionville
Theodosia . . . . . 12 K a
Theodosiopolis (Erzerum) . . . 20 I c
Theodosius II., Wall of, Constantinople . . . . . 93 G e
Theophilo . . . . . 214 E d (Phil.)
Theotmelli, see Detmold
Thera . . . . . 13 D c
Thera, isl. . . . . . 13 D c
Therambus . . . . . 11 E c
Therapne . . . . . 14 C b
Theres, castle . . . . . 62 F c
Therezina . . . . . 214 E c
Therma (Salonika) . . . . . 11 D b
Thermæ Himerææ . . . . . 30 C e
Thermæ Selinuntiæ . . . . . 30 C e
Thermaic Gulf . . . . . 11 D b
Therme . . . . .
Thermessa, isl. . . . . . 30 E d
Thermodon River . . . . . 20 G b
Thermopylæ, pass . . . . . 11 D d
Thermopylæ, plan of 16
Thermum, in Ætolia . . . . . 10 C d
Thérouanne, bp. . . . . . 94 C a
Thervings, people . . . . . 50 I d
Theseum, loc. in Athens . . . . 23 D
Theseum, loc. in the Pyræus . 16 D c
Thespiæ . . . . . 11 E d
Thesprotia, dist. . . . . . 10 B c
Thesprotian Gulf . . . . . 10 B c
Thessaliotis, dist. . . . . . 10 D c
Thessalonica (Salonika) . . . . . 11 D b
Thessalonica, km. . . . . . 73 E b
Thessalonica, theme . . . . . 59 I e
Thessaly, Rom. prov. . . . . . 43 G f (3)
Thessaly, Turkish prov. . . . . . 164 C c
Thessaly, reg. . . . . . 10 C c
Thessaly, Wallachian, princ. . . 89 B c
Thestium . . . . . 10 C d
Thetford . . . . .
Thetford, castle . . . . . 65 G d
Thetford, mon. . . . . . 97 R i
Thetford, parl. bor. . . . . . 163 O e
Theudoria . . . . . 10 C c
Theveste . . . . . 38 D e
Thiengen, near Freiburg in Breisgau . . . . . 142 A e
Thiengen, near Waldshut in Baden . . . . . 142 B e
Thiers . . . . . 69 E d
Thiers, mon. . . . . . 94 C b
Thierstein, castle . . . . . 91 P k
Thieves Islands . . . . . 110 GG f
Thilabus . . . . . 20 J e
Thimnathah . . . . .
Thines . . . . . 156 A a
Thines River . . . . . 156 A a
Thionville, or Diedenhofen . . 62 C d
Thirsk, parl. bor. . . . . . 163 M c
This . . . . . 4 F d
Thisbæ . . . . .
Thisoa . . . . . 14 C b
Thoire . . . . . 76 F c
Tholen . . . . . 117 C c
Tholey . . . . . 157 ins.
Thoræ . . . . . 15 D b
Thoricus . . . . . 15 E b
Thorigny . . . . . 76 C b
Thorn, in the Netherlands . . . 117 D c
Thörn, in Prussia . . . . . 72 D a
Thorn, Hanse. cy. . . . . . 98 G c
Thorney, mon. . . . . . 97 R i
Thornton-upon-Humber, mon. 97 Q h
Thospitis, lake . . . . . 20 J c
Thouars . . . . . 61 C c
Thouars, viscty. . . . . . 76 C c
Thourout, mon. . . . . . 94 C a
Thrace, East Rom. prov. . . . . 43 G e (2)
Thrace, reg. . . . . . 8 A a
Thrace, Rom. dioc. . . . . . 43 H e
Thrace, Rom. prov. . . . . . 35 I e
Thrace, theme . . . . . 59 J e
Thracesian Theme . . . . . 59 J f
Thracian Bosporus, str. . . . . .
Thracian Chersonese, pen. . . . 17 E a
Thracian Sea . . . . . 17 C b
Three Bishoprics, gen. . . . . . 147 F b
Three Kings Islands . . . . . 172 G d
Three Points, cape . . . . .
Three Rivers, town . . . . . 191 K b
Thremhall, mon. . . . . . 97 R j
Thria . . . . . 16 B a
Thriasian Plain . . . . . 16 B a
Thronium . . . . . 11 D d
Thuin . . . . . 117 C d
Thun . . . . . 150 D c
Thun, lake of . . . . . 91 P l
Thun, stronghold . . . . . 91 P l
Thurgarton, mon. . . . . . 97 Q h
Thurgau, dist. . . . . . 62 E e
Thurii . . . . . 31 F c
Thüringer Wald (Thuringian Forest), mts. . . . . . 62 F c
Thuringia, dist. . . . . . 62 F c
Thuringia, landgr. . . . . . 85 F e
Thuringia, march . . . . . 63 G c
Thuringians, people . . . . . 45 F b
Thurrock . . . . . 75 J i
Thursday Island . . . . . 172 D b
Thyamis (Kalamas) River . . . . 10 B c
Thyamus, mt. . . . . . 10 C d
Thyatira . . . . . 20 C c
Thyle River . . . . . 156 B a
Thymbra . . . . .
Thymbrius River . . . . .
Thymœtadæ . . . . . 16 B b
Thynias, prom. . . . . . 20 C b
Thyreum . . . . . 10 C d
Thyrides, prom. . . . . . 14 C c
Thyssagetæ, people . . . . . 19 G a
Thyssus . . . . . 11 F b
Tian-shan Mountains . . . . .
Tiber River . . . . . 64 B b
Tiber Island . . . . . 22 A
Tiberias . . . . . 6 D c
Tiberine Way, road . . . . . 35 ins. B
Tiberinum . . . . . 27 G d
Tiberis River, see Tiber River
Tiberius, Arch of, on the Campus Martius . . . . . 22 A
Tiberius, Arch of, in the Forum

Tiberius, Palace of . . . 24 B
Tibesti, reg. . . . 174 E b
Tibet, reg. . . .
Tibiscus River . . . 39 M k
Tibur (Tivoli) . . . 27 G f
Tiburon, Cape . . . 105 F c
Tiburones, Isla de los, isl. . . . 107 C h
Tiburtian Way, road . . . 35 ins. B
Tiburtine Gate . . . 22 A
Ticino, dist. . . . 91 Q l
Ticino River . . . 130 Q i
Ticinum (Pavia) . . . 26 D b
Ticinus (Ticino) River . . . 26 C a
Tickhill, parl. bor. . . .
Ticonderoga . . . 196 E b
Ticonderoga, Fort . . . 192 E b
Tidore, isl. . . . 112 F c
Tiel . . . 117 D c
Tie-ling, see Tie Pass . . . 171 N d
Tienen . . . 117 C d
Tien-tsin . . . 170 ins. A
Tie Pass . . . 171 N d
Tierra del Fuego, isl. . . . 215 C h
Tierra de los Bacallaos, reg. . . . 108 L c
Tierra de los Bretones, reg. . . . 108 L c
Tierra Firme, reg. . . . 105 G e
Tieté River . . . 214 D e
Tifata, mt. . . . 30 D a
Tifernum . . . 27 G d
Tifernus, mt. . . . 30 D a
Tifernus (Biferno) River . . . 27 I f
Tiflis . . . 67 O e
Tiger Hill, village . . . 216
Tigisis, in Mauretania . . . 42 C f
Tigisis, in Numidia . . . 46 H f
Tigranocerta . . .
Tigre, dist. . . . 174 G c
Tigris River . . . 5 D b
Tiguex, reg. . . . 190 D e
Ti-hwa (Urumtsi) . . . 171 J d
Tilburg . . . 117 D c
Tilburg, castle . . . 75 J i
Tilingana . . .
Tiliventus (Tagliamento) River 27 G a
Tilleda . . . 62 F c
Tilly . . . 156 B a
Tilox, prom. . . . 26 D e
Tilsit . . . 88 I d
Tilty, mon. . . . 97 R j
Timan Mountains . . . 3 I b
Timavus (Timavo) River . . . 27 H b
Timbuktu . . . 174 C c
Timnah . . . 7 B e
Timonium . . . 34 ins. C (3)
Timor, isl. . . . 112 F d
Timor Sea . . . 172 B b
Timorlaut, isl. . . . 172 C e
Timsah, lake . . . 174 K i
Timur, Dom. of . . .
Tinchebrai . . . 65 F f
Tinetio . . . 26 D a
Tingis (Tangier) . . . 38 A e
Tinia River . . . 27 G d
Tinicum Island . . . 192 ins.
Tinna River . . . 27 H d
Tinnevelli . . .
Tinogasta . . . 215 C e
Tintern, mon. . . . 97 O j
Tiphsach . . . 6 ins. C
Tippecanoe, battle . . . 211 H b
Tipperah, dist. . . . 137 F d
Tipperary, cty. . . . 127 I i
Tippermuir . . .
Tippoo, Dominions of . . . 137 C f
Tirano . . . 91 S l
Tirhut, reg. . . .
Tirlemont . . . 117 C d
Tirmidh . . .
Tirnova . . . 59 J e
Tiron, mon. . . . 94 C b
Tiryns . . . 15 C b
Tirzah . . . 7 C d
Tisæus, mt. . . . 11 E c
Tisia (Theiss) River . . . 35 I d
Tisné, route of . . . 190 F d
Tisza, River, see Theiss River 43 G d.
Tisza-Füred . . . 159 K e
Titane . . . 14 C b
Titanus, mt. . . . 10 D c
Titaresius River . . . 10 D c
Titarius, mt. . . . 10 D b
Titchfield, ab. . . . 100 A b
Titel . . . 159 K f
Tithe Lands, dist. . . . 39 J i
Tithorea . . . 11 D d
Tithronium . . . 11 D d
Titicaca, lake . . . 214 C d
Titulcia . . . 38 B d
Titus, Arch of . . . 24 B
Titus, Baths of . . . 22 A
Tium . . . 20 E b
Tiumen . . . 138 K d
Tiveden, dist. . . . 88 F b
Tiverton . . . 189 C d
Tiverton, parl. bor. . . . 163 K g
Tivoli . . . 96 B b
Tivoli, bp. . . . 95 E c
Tizón, Rio del, R. . . . 190 C e
Tlacopan . . .
Tlalmanalco . . . 106 B a
Tlalpan . . . 201 H g
Tlascala, Tlaxcala . . . 106 B a
Tlemsen . . . 66 F g
Tlemsen, dist. . . . 118 D g
t'Loo . . . 117 D b
Tmolus, mt. . . . 20 C c
Toarcis, see Thouars
Tobago, isl. . . . 105 H d
Tobitschau . . . 159 I d
Tobol River . . .
Tobolsk . . . 170 H c
Tocaima . . . 214 B b
Tocantins River . . . 214 E c
Tocci, Dom. of the . . . 93 B c
Tocobaga . . . 191 I f
Tocopilla . . . 214 B e
Tocuyo . . . 214 C b
Todi . . . 64 ins.
Todi, bp. . . . 95 E c
Todos os Santos, Bahia de, bay 214 F d
Todtnau . . . 142 A e
Toggenburg, dist. . . . 91 R k
Toggenburg, New, castle . . . 91 R k
Toggenburg, Old, castle . . . 91 R k
Togoland, German col. . . .
Tokay . . . 159 K d
Tokelau Islands . . . 172 H a
Tokyo . . . 171 O e
Tolbiacum . . . 39 I h
Toledo, in Ohio . . . 211 I b
Toledo, in Spain . . . 82 B b
Toledo, abp. . . . 94 A c
Toledo, emir. . . . 83 E d
Tolentino . . . 151 I h
Tolenus (Turano) River . . . 27 G e
Toleria . . . 35 ins. B
Tolerus (Sacco) River . . . 30 C a
Toletum (Toledo) . . . 38 B e
Tolima, Nevada de, mt. . . . 214 B b
Tolna . . . 159 J e
Tolone, see Toulon
Tolophon . . . 10 D d
Tolosa (Toulouse) . . . 38 C d
Toluca . . . 106 A a
Tomarus, mt. in Epirus . . . 10 B c
Tomarus, mt. in Illyris . . . 10 B b
Tombecbé, Fort . . . 191 H e
Tombigbee River . . . 191 H e
Tombs of the kings, in Jerusalem 6 ins. A
Tombstone . . . 210 C d
Tomebamba . . . 111 B b
Tomi . . . 39 N l
Tomis . . . 35 J e
Tömös Pass . . . 159 M f
Tomsk . . . 171 J c
Tonala . . . 213 C c
Tonawanda, Ind. Res. . . . 188 K b
Tondern . . . 80 A d
Tonga Islands . . . 180 J i
Tongaland, dist. . . . 175 N l
Tongatabu, isl. . . . 172 H c
Tongking, reg. . . . 92 K e
Tongres . . . 117 D d
Tongrinne . . . 156 B a
Tonk . . . 137 C c
Tonkawas, Ind. Res. . . . 188 G c
Tonnerre . . . 61 E c
Tonnerre, cty. . . . 76 F c
Tönning . . . 134 E a
Toongabuddra River . . . 137 C e
Topeka . . . 198 F c
Tophane, quarter in Constantinople . . . 93 G e
Tor, mon. . . . 97 N k
Tor Bay . . . 127 V p
Torcello, bp. . . . 95 E b
Tordesillas . . .
Torgau . . . 115 G c
Torinna, see Turenne
Torksey, castle . . . 65 F d
Torne River . . . 167 J b
Torneå . . . 167 J b
Tornodorum, see Tonnerre
Toro . . . 82 A a
Toron . . . 68 ins. A
Toronaic Gulf . . . 11 E b
Torone . . . 11 E b
Toronto . . . 199 J b
Toropetz . . . 71 M b
Torre di Faro . . . 161 J h
Torrens, lake . . . 172 C d
Torreon . . . 213 B b
Torres, abp. . . . 95 D c
Torres Strait . . . 172 D a
Torres Vedras . . . 130 B f
Torrington . . . 127 U p
Torris . . . 72 B c
Tortona . . . 90 I h
Tortona, bp. . . . 95 D c
Tortosa, in Spain . . . 82 C a
Tortosa, bp. . . . 94 C c
Tortosa, in Syria . . . 68 C c
Tortuga, isl., near Haiti . . . 105 F b
Tortuga, isl., near Venezuela . 105 G d
Toryne . . . 10 B c
Törzburger Pass . . . 159 M f
Torzhok . . . 99 J b
Toskih . . .
Totnes . . . 127 V p
Tottenham . . . 75 I h
Toul . . . 62 C d
Toul, bp. . . . 95 D b
Toul, gouv. . . . 146 C b
Toul, imp. cy. . . . 78 D d
Toulon . . . 69 F e
Toulon, bp. . . . 95 D c
Toulouse, in France . . . 61 D e
Toulouse, abp. . . . 148 B c
Toulouse, cty. about 1000 . . . 58 E e
Toulouse, cty. 12 cent. . . . 69 E e
Toulouse, cty. 15 cent. . . . 84 D h
Toulouse, gen. . . . 147 E c
Toulouse, univ. . . . 100 F f
Toulouse, Fort, in Alabama . . 191 H e
Touques . . . 146 G e
Touraine, cty. . . . 69 H g
Touraine, duchy . . . 78 B e
Touraine, gouv. . . . 146 B b
Touraine, prov. . . . 148 E e
Tourcoing . . . 134 B c
Tourinnes . . . 156 B a
Tournai . . . 117 B d
Tournai, bp. . . . 94 C a
Tournai, cty. . . . 61 E a
Tourneppe . . . 156 A a
Tournon . . . 76 F d
Tours . . . 61 D c
Tours, abp. . . . 94 B b
Tours, cty. . . . 69 H g
Tours, gen. . . . 147 D b
Tovar, route of . . . 190 C d
Tovin . . . 73 I b

Tower, in London 75 G g
Tower of Leander, in Constantinople 93 G e
Tower of the Winds, in Athens 23 D
Tower Hamlets, parl. bor. 163 O f
Tower Street, in London 75 G g
Townsend, mt. 172 D d
Townsville 172 D b
Towton 84 C c
Toxandria, dist. 62 C c
Tozan, people
Trachea, dist. 33 L e
Trachenberg 154 I c
Trachinia 11 D d
Trachinian Cliffs 16 F e
Trachis 16 E e
Trachonitis, dist. 6 E c
Trachselwald, castle 91 P l
Trafalgar, Cape 130 B f
Tragia, isl. 20 B d
Traiana, Colonia 39 I h
Traianopolis, in Cilicia 20 E d
Traianopolis, in Thrace 39 N l
Traianus, Portus 26 E e
Traiectum (Utrecht, in the Netherlands) 39 H g
Traiectus, see Maestricht
Traietto 90 D d
Trais River 31 F c
Traisen River 63 H d e
Trajan, Caths of 22 A
Trajan, Port of 35 ins. B
Trajan, Statue of 24 B
Trajan's Aqueduct 35 ins. B (6)
Trajan's Column 22 A (14)
Trajan's Forum 24 B
Trajan's Way, road 30 E a
Traktir 164 J f
Tralles 17 E c
Tramin 150 F c
Trancoso 83 J g
Trani 90 F d
Trani, abp. 65 F c
Transalpine Gaul, reg. 34 E d (Gaul)
Trans Baikal Province 171 M c
Transcaspian District 170 G e
Transjurane Burgundy, km. 56 D c
Transkei, reg. 175 M m
Transpadane Gaul, reg. 26 B b
Trans Siberian Railway 170 G c
Trans Tiberim, Aug. Reg of Rome 22 A
Transvaal Colony
Transvaal, rep. 175 M l
Transylvania, gr. prim. in Hungary 131 H d
Transylvania, princ. 119 I d
Transylvania, reg. 59 I d
Transylvania, proposed col. in U. S. 194 B c
Transylvanian Alps, mts. 39 M l
Trapani 90 D f
Trapezus, in Arcadia 14 C b
Trapezus, in Pontus (Trebizond) 20 H b
Trappe, La, mon. 94 C b
Trarbach 134 D d
Trasimenus (Trasimeno), lake 27 G d
Trastamare, cty. 83 J g
Trastevere, quarter 96 A
Trasyllus, Monument of 23 C (9)
Traú, bp. 95 F c
Trauchburg, ruin 143 J j
Traungau, dist. 63 G e
Trausnitz, castle 79 H d
Trautenau 135 H c
Travancore, reg. 137 C g
Travendal, castle 134 F b
Travemünde 154 E a
Traz os Montes, dist. 83 J g
Trea 27 H d
Treba 27 H f
Trebia 27 G e
Trebia (Trebbia) River 26 D c
Trebizond 67 N e
Trebizond, empire, 13 cent. 73 H b
Trebizond, empire, 14 cent. 89 K I
Trebizond, empire, 15 cent. 93 E b
Trebnitz, mon. 80 E f
Trebujena 82 A b
Trebula, in Samnium 30 D a
Trebula Mutuesca 27 G e
Trecas, see Troyes
Tre Fontane, mon. 96 B b
Tregony, parl. bor. 163 J g
Tréguier 61 B b
Tréguier, bp. 94 B b
Trémoins 143 ins. F
Tremouille, La 81 M h
Trencsin
Trent 62 F e
Trent, bp. 79 G e
Trent River 49 F e
Trenton 192 D c
Tréport, mon. 94 C a
Trerus River, see Tolerus R. 30 C a
Tres Pinos 210 A c
Treuenbrietzen 85 C b
Treveri or Treveris, see Trèves
Treveri, people 38 D c
Trèves 62 D d
Trèves, abp. 95 D b
Trèves, univ. 100 G d
Treviso 90 K h
Treviso, bp. 95 E b
Treviso, univ 100 H e
Trévoux 147 F b
Triaditza 59 I e
Triana 82 A b
Trianon, Avenue de, in Versailles 149 A
Trianon, Grand, loc. in Versailles 149 A
Trianon, Petit, loc. in Versailles 149 A
Trianon, Plaine de, loc. in Versailles 149 A
Triballi, people 39 M l
Triberg 142 B d
Triberg, lordship 142 B d
Triboci, people 39 I i
Tribulation, Cape 172 D b
Tribur 62 E d
Tricameron 52 C c
Tricasses, see Troyes
Tricca (Trikala) 10 C c
Trichinopoly 137 C f
Trichonis, lake 10 C d
Trichonium 10 C d
Tricorythus 16 C a
Tricrana, isl. 15 D b
Tridentine Alps 27 F a
Tridentini, people 27 F a
Tridentum (Trent) 27 F a
Trient, see Trent
Trier, see Trèves
Trieste 63 G f
Trieste, bp. 95 E b
Trifanum 30 C a
Trifels, castle 62 D d
Trigemina Gate 23 B
Trikala 89 B c
Trileucum, prom. 38 A d
Trim, bp. 97 E c
Trimenia 16 B a
Trinacria, km. 77 G e
Trincomalee 137 D g
Trinidad, in Bolivia 214 C d
Trinidad, in Cuba 213 E b
Trinidad, isl. 105 H d
Trinidad River
Trinity, Fort 192 ins.
Trinity River 191 G e
Trinius River 27 I f
Trinkomali
Trino 130 Q i
Trinobantes, people
Triopium, prom. 20 B d
Triparadisus 18 O h
Triphylia, dist., in Elis 14 B b
Triphylia, dist., in Epirus 10 B c
Tripodiscus 15 D a
Tripoli, in Africa 53 D c
Tripoli, reg. 77 G f
Tripoli, vilayet 174 E a
Tripoli, in Syria 68 C c
Tripoli, cty. 68 C b
Tripolis, in Phœnicia 20 F e
Tripolis, in Pontus 20 H b
Tripolis, dist., in Thessaly 10 D b
Tripolis, reg., in Africa 34 G g
Tripolitana, W. Rom. prov. 42 E g (3)
Tripolitza 131 H f
Tristan da Cunha, isl. 108 P k
Tritæa, in Achaia
Tritæa, in Locris 11 D d
Triumphal Way, road 35 ins. B
Trivandrum 137 C g
Trivento, bp 95 E c
Troarn 76 C b
Troarn, mon. 94 B b (Tr.)
Troas, reg. 9 B d
Trochtelfingen 143 H i
Trœsmis 39 N l
Trœzen 15 D b
Trogen 91 R k
Trogilus Port 31 ins. B
Troglodytes, people 4 F d
Troian Plain
Trois Fontaines, mon. 94 C b
Troitsa 138 E d
Troitski 171 J b
Troitzkoi, mon. 131 K b
Troja, in Asia Minor, see Ilium
Troja, in Italy 90 E d
Troja, bp. 95 F c
Trombetas River 214 D c
Tromsoe 166 I b
Tropea, bp. 95 F d
Troppau 79 J d
Troppau, princ. 79 J d
Troy, in Asia Minor
Troy, in New York 192 E b
Troyes 61 E b
Troyes, bp. 94 C b
Troyes, cty. 61 E b
Troyland, reg.
Trubchevsk 131 J c
Truentus (Tronto) River 27 I e
Trujillo, in Honduras 213 D c
Trujillo, in Peru 111 B c
Trujillo, in Spain 82 A b
Trujillo, in Venezuela 214 B b
Trumplini, people 26 E b
Truro 127 T p
Truxillo (Trujillo, in Honduras) 105 C c
Tsanpu River 171 J f
Tshiblak
Tsi-nan 171 M e
Tsi-ning-chau
Tsitsihar 171 N d
Tsuen-chau-fu 103 L e
Tuam, abp. 97 C c
Tuamotu, isl. 180 N i
Tuat, oasis 2 D f
Tubac 190 C e
Tubantes, people 39 I g
Tubariyeh
Tübingen 143 H h
Tübingen, palat. 143 G h
Tübingen, univ. 100 G e
Tublinum 26 E a
Tubuai Islands 180 M j
Tucacas 214 C a
Tucci 42 B f
Tuchcov 131 I d
Tucson 190 C e
Tucumán 215 C e
Tuder 27 G e
Tugela River 175 N l
Tuileries, The, loc. in Paris 149 B
Tula 139 E e
Tulalip, Ind. Res. 188 B a
Tulare, lake 210 B c
Tularenos, tribe 188 C c
Tule River, Ind. Res. 188 C c
Tullahoma 208 C b

Tulle 84 D g
Tulle, bp. 94 C b
Tullear 175 H g
Tullianum 24 A (3)
Tulln 63 I d
Tullum (Toul) 39 H i
Tultcha 164 D a
Tumbez 111 A b
Tumuc Humac Mountains 214 D b
Tumut
Tunbridge, parl. bor.
Tunes (Tunis) 38 E e
Tungabhadra River 137 C e
Tung-chang 171 M e
Tung-chau 170 ins. A
Tungri, people 39 H h
Tung-tshu 170 ins. A
Tunguses, people
Tunguska River, Lower
Tunguska River, Upper
Tunis 53 D c
Tunis, bay of 34 ins. A
Tunis, French dependency 174 D a
Tunis, reg. 54 F f
Tunis, state 77 F e
Tunjá 214 B b
Tunsberg 58 F b
Tupiza 214 C e
Turan, khan 92 G b
Turcilingians, people
Turcomans, people 170 G e
Turdetani, or Turdetanians, people 38 A e
Turduli, people 38 B e
Turenne 61 D d
Turenne, castle 76 D d
Turenne, viscty. 78 B f
Turenum (Trani) 31 F a
Turfan
Turholz, mon. 94 C a
Turicum (Zurich) 39 J j
Turin 90 H h
Turin, univ. 100 G e
Türkheim 126 E b
Türkheim, imp. cy. 122 D d
Turkestan, reg. 170 H d
Turkestan, E., reg. 170 I e
Turkish (Ottoman) Empire, 1451—1481 93
Turkish (Ottoman) Empire, 1481—1683 124
Turkish (Ottoman) Empire, since 1683 164
Turkmanchai 170 F e
Turkomans, people 77 L e
Turks, people 165 leg.
Turks Islands 213 E b
Turner's Falls, village 189 B c
Turnhout 117 C c
Turones, see Tours
Turones, people, in Gaul 38 C c
Turones, people, in Germany 38 E c
Turoqua 38 A d
Turriff
Turris Libisonis 38 D d
Tursan, viscty. 69 C e
Turtle Mountain, Ind. Res. 188 G a
Turukhansk 171 J b
Tusayan, reg. 100 C d
Tuscaloosa 211 H d
Tuscan Presidios, dist. 118 G e
Tuscan Street, in Rome 24 A
Tuscana 27 F e
Tuscany, gr. duchy 161 H f
Tuscany, dist. 64 B b
Tuscany and Umbria, West Rom. prov. 42 E e (2)
Tuscarawas River 188 J b
Tuscarora, Ind. Res. 188 J b
Tuscaroras 193 F d
Tuscaroras, tribe 188 J c
Tuscia, dist. 27 F d
Tusculum 35 ins. B
Tusculum, bp. 96 B b
Tuskegee 207 H d
Tutbury 118 D c
Tutbury, mon. 97 P i
Tutela, see Tudela
Tutikorin 170 I h
Tuttlingen 143 G j
Tutuila, isl. 199 ins. D
Tuxtla 213 C c
Tuy 82 A a
Tuy, bp. 94 A c
Tver 138 E d
Twann 91 P k
Twat, reg. 53 B d
Tweed River 49 E d
Tweeddale, dist.
Twickenham 75 I i
Twiel, castle 62 E e
Twillingate, isl. 212 J d
Two Sicilies, km., 12 cent. 72 C d
Two Sicilies, km., 15 cent. 90 E e
Tyana 20 F d
Tybee Island 193 ins. C
Tyburn 75 I h
Tycha, quarter in Syracuse 31 ins. B
Tykocin 159 L b
Tylus Island 19 H e
Tymphæa, dist. 10 C b
Tymphe, mt. 10 C b
Tymphrestus, mt. 10 C d
Tyndale, dist.
Tyndaris 30 E d
Tyne River 49 E d
Tynemouth, mon. 97 P f
Tynemouth, parl. bor. 163 M b
Typhrestus, mt. 10 C d
Tyra 35 K d
Tyras River 35 J d
Tyrconnel, cty. 127 I g
Tyre 6 C b
Tyre, Ladder of, cape 6 C b
Tyre, plan of 18 ins. B
Tyrissa 10 C b
Tyrnau 115 I d
Tyrol, castle 72 C b
Tyrol, cty. 79 G e
Tyrol, princ. cty. 150 F c
Tyrone, cty. 127 J g
Tyropœon Valley 6 ins. A
Tyrrhenian Sea 29 B d
Tyrus (Tyre), in Phœnicia 6 C b
Tyrus, in Laconia 15 C b
Tyrus, in Peræa 7 D e
Tzaritzyn 139 F f

Uaupes River 214 C b
Ubangi River 175 E d
Úbeda 82 B b
Uberaba 214 E d
Uberi, people 26 B a
Überlingen, imp. cy. 142 D e
Ubii, people 39 I h
Ubulla 99 M g
Ucaca 99 M c
Ucayali River 111 C c
Uceda 83 E c
Ucetium, see Uzès
Uclés 82 B b
Udaipur 137 B d
Udine 90 D a
Udine, bp. 95 E b
Ufa 139 I e
Uffnau, isl. 91 Q k
Uganda, prot. 175 G d
Ugernum, see Beaucaire
Uglitch
Ugrians, people
Uigurs, people
Uintah, Fort 210 C b
Uintah, Ind. Res. 188 D b
Uirats, people
Ujjain
Ukak 99 M c
Uker River 154 G b
Ukermark, dist 85 C b
Ukraine, reg. 139 D f
Ukrians, people 63 G b
Ulatha, dist. 6 D b
Uleåborg 138 C c
Uliarus (Oléron), isl. 38 B c
Uliassutai
Ulloa, route of, 1537 107 F e
Ulm 62 E d
Ulm, imp. cy. 143 I h
Ulpia (Sardica) 39 M l
Ulpia, Basilica, bldg. in Rome 24 B
Ulpia Traiana 39 M k
Ulpiana 39 M l
Ulrichen 91 Q l
Ulster, prov.
Ulu-kem River
Ulwar 137 C c
Ülzen, Hanse. cy. 99 ins. B
Umachiri 214 B d
Uman 139 D f
Uman, reg.
Umarkot 137 A c
Umatas 198 ins. C
Umatilla, Ind. Res. 188 C a
Umballa 137 C b
Umber, lake 27 G d
Umbilicus, loc. in Rome
Umbria, Aug. Reg. 27 G e
Umbria, dist., 15 cent. 90 D c
Umbrians, people 29 C c
Umbro (Ombrone) River 27 F e
Umeå 166 I c
Umpquas, tribe 188 B b
Umtata River 175 M m
Unalaska, isl. 198 ins. A
Uncompahgre Mountains 198 D c
Uncompahgre, Ind. Res. 188 E c
Unestrudis River, see Unstrut River
Ungarisch Altenburg 155 I e
Ungava, dist. 212 H c
Ungava Bay 212 I c
Unghvar 168 H b
Unimak, isl. 198 ins. A
Union, Fort, in New Mexico 210 D c
Union, Fort, in N. Dakota 210 E a
Union Islands 172 H a
Union Pacific Grant 210 D b
Uniontown 206 ins.
United Netherlands, country 122 C b
United States, 1783 196
United States, 1910 198, 199
Unna River 155 I f
Unstrut River 62 F c
Unter-Öwisheim 142 C b
Unterwalden, canton 91 Q l
Upi 4 G c
Upland (Chester, in Pa.) 192 ins.
Upminster 75 J h
Upolu, isl. 172 H b
Upper Alsace, landgr. 114 D e
Upper Argen River 143 I j
Upper Bavaria, dist. 122 F e
Upper Britain, prov. 38 B b (1)
Upper Burgundy, dist. 62 C e
Upper Burgundy, km. 56 D c
Upper Burma, prov. 171 K f
Upper California, prov. 190 B d
Upper Canada, prov. 212 G d
Upper Dacia, prov. 39 Mk (1a)
Upper Egypt, reg.
Upper Gelderland 117 E c
Upper Germany, prov.
Upper Gihon, well 6 ins. A
Upper Guinea, reg. 174 C d
Upper Libya, East Rom. prov. 43 Gg (1)
Upper Lorraine, duchy 62 C d
Upper Lusatia, dist. 80 ins.
Upper Lusatia, margr. 87 J c
Upper Mœsia, prov. 39 Ml (2a)
Upper Palatinate, dist. 79 G d
Upper Pannonia, prov. 34 H d
Upper Peru, reg. 214 C d
Upper Pimería, dist. 190 C e

Upper Silesia, dist. 72 D a
Upper Tunguska River
Upsala 88 G b
Upsala, univ. 100 I c
Ur (Mugheir) 4 G c
Urabá, Gulf of 105 E e
Urabá, reg. 105 E e
Urach 143 H h
Urach, castle 62 E d
Urach, cty. 143 H i
Urach, Hohen, ruin 143 H i
Ural Mountains 138 I c
Ural River 139 H e
Uralian Cossacks, people 139 H e
Uralsk 139 H e
Urba (Orbe) 39 I j
Urban VIII, Wall of Pope 96 A
Urbevetum, see Orvieto
Urbino 90 M j
Urbino, bp. 95 E c
Urbinum (Urbino) 27 G d
Urbs Salvia 27 H d
Urci
Urcinium 26 C e
Urés 213 B b
Urga 171 L d
Urgel 82 C a
Urgel, bp. 94 C c
Urgenj
Urgo, isl. 26 D d
Uri, canton 91 Q l
Uri, dist. 71 R k
Uria 31 G b
Uria, lake 10 C d
Urias Bay 30 E a
Uriconium (Wroxeter) 51 O h
Urium 30 E a
Urk, isl. 117 D b
Ursberg, mon. 95 E b
Urseren 91 Q l
Urspring, mon. 143 I i
Urubamba 214 B d
Urubamba River 111 C d
Uruguay, country 215 D f
Uruguay River 215 D e
Uruguayana 215 D e
Uruk (Warka) 4 G c
Urumiah
Urumiah, lake
Urumtsi
Uscosium 27 I f
Usedom 63 G b
Usellis 38 D e
Ush
Ushuaia 215 C h
Usipetes, people 38 D b
Usk River
Uskub 77 I d
Uspallata Pass 215 C f
Ussuri River
Ustica, isl. 30 C d
Ustrina 22 A
Ust Maiskaya 171 O b
Ust Sysolsk 167 P c
Ust-Urt, reg. 139 H g
Ust Yansk 171 O a
Ust Zylma 138 H b
Usuguaya 215 C h
Utah, state 210 C c
Utah, ter. 1850 202 C g
Utah, ter. 1861 203 P g
Utah Lake 190 C c
Ute, Ind. Res. 188 E c
Utelle 150 D e
Utes, tribe 188 C b
Utians, people 8 D c
Utica, in Afrika 38 D e
Utica, in New York 207 K b
Utii, people 35 N e
Utinum, see Udine
Utis River 27 F c
Utrecht, in the Netherlands 117 D b
Utrecht, bp. 95 D a
Utrecht, lordship 114 C b
Utrecht, in Transvaal 175 N l
Utrecht, New, in New York 189 ins. C
Uxbridge 75 I h
Uxellodunum
Uxentis, isl. 38 A c
Üxküll 80 I c
Uyuni 214 C e
Uzentum 31 H c
Uzès 76 F d
Uzès, bp. 94 C c
Uzgent
Uzi, people
Uznach, castle 91 Q k

Vaal River 175 M l
Vabres, bp. 94 C c
Vacalus River 39 H h
Vacapa 190 C f
Vaccæi, people 38 B d
Vaccanæ 35 ins. B
Vada Sabatia 26 C c
Vada Volaterrana 26 E d
Vadimonis, lake 27 G e
Vaduz 134 E e
Vaduz, castle 91 R k
Vaga 46 H f
Vaigatch, isl. 138 J a
Vaihingen 143 G h
Vaison, bp. 95 D c
Valais, dist. 91 P l
Valais, rep. 151 H g
Valangin, castle 91 O k
Valcour 157 ins.
Valdai 131 J b
Valdai Hills 167 L d
Val de Grâce, church in Paris 149 B
Valdivia 215 B f
Val d'Ossola 91 Q l
Valence 61 F d
Valence, bp. 94 C c
Valence, univ. 100 F f
Valencia, in Spain 82 B b
Valencia, abp. 94 B d
Valencia, emir. 83 E d
Valencia, km. 83 K h
Valencia, univ. 100 E g
Valencia, in Venezuela 214 C a
Valencia de Don Juan 82 A a
Valenciennes 117 B d
Valens, Aqueduct of 93 G e
Valentia, see Vibo
Valentia (Valence, in France) 38 D c
Valentia (Valencia, in Spain) 38 B e
Valentia, Rom. prov., in southern Scotland 38 B a (3)
Valentia (Wales), Rom. prov. 42 B c (2)
Valentia Island 166 C e
Valentianæ, see Valenciennes
Valentinois, cty. 76 F d
Valentinois, dist. 126 D d
Valenza 90 I h
Vale of the Camenæ (Muses), loc. in Rome 22 A
Valera de Abajo 82 B b
Valeria, Rom. prov. 42 E e (10)
Valeria ripensis, Rom. prov. 42 F d (14)
Valeria Way, in Italy, road 27 H e
Valerian Way, in Sicily, road 30 D d
Valerius Asiaticus, Gardens of 22 A
Vale Royal, mon. 97 O h
Val-ès-Dunes 65 F f
Valetium 31 H b
Valideh Bridge 93 G e (11)
Valkenburg 117 D d
Valladolid, in Michoacan, Mexico 213 ins.
Valladolid, in New Mexico 190 D d
Valladolid, in Spain 82 H e
Valladolid, bp. 94 B c
Valladolid, univ. 100 E f
Valladolid, in Yucatan, Mexico 213 D b
Vallæ 11 D b
Valle Crucis, mon. 97 N h
Val Leventina, valley 91 Q l
Valley 72 C b
Valley Forge 195 C c
Valley Gate 6 ins. A
Valley of the Sweet Waters
Vallombrosa 64 B b
Vallombrosa, mon. 95 E c
Valmont, mon. 94 C b
Valmy 134 C d
Valognes 76 C b
Valois, cty. 76 E b
Valois, duchy 84 E e
Valona, bp. 95 F c
Valparaiso 215 B f
Valromey 126 D d
Val Sainte, mon. 91 P l
Val-Secret, mon. 94 C b (V. S.)
Valsers, mon. 94 C b (Val.)
Valtellina, dist. 91 R l
Valvata 26 E d
Van 20 J c
Van, lake 99 L f
Van Buren 211 G c
Vancouver 212 C d
Vancouver, Fort 198 A a
Vancouver, isl. 186 G d
Vandalia 211 H c
Vandalia, proposed col. in U. S. 194 C c
Vandals, kingdom of the, 5 cent. 50 E e
Vandals, kingdom of the, 6 cent. 52 C c
Vandals, people 45 H b, C e, F e
Van Diemen Gulf 172 C b
Van Diemen's Land, isl. 172 D e
Vandili, people 38 F b
Vangrones, people 39 J i
Vannes 61 B c
Vannes, bp. 94 B b
Van Reenen's Pass 175 M l
Vanua Levu, isl. 172 H b
Vapincum, see Gap
Var, dept. 148 F f
Var (Vara) River 130 O k
Varallo 130 Q i
Varanger Fiord 167 L a
Varangians, people 45 J d
Varangians, route of the 59 I b
Vararis Æstuarium (Moray Firth) 38 B a
Varaville 65 F f
Varch Bosna 72 D c
Vardar River 119 I e
Varduli, people 38 B d
Varennes 134 C d
Varese 161 G e
Varia
Varini, people 38 E b
Varkenskill 192 D d
Varna 59 J e
Varnitza 131 I d
Varus (Var) River 26 A d
Vasa 138 B c
Vasates, see Bazas
Vasco da Gama, route of 108 Q i
109 W g
Vascones, people 38 B d
Vasio or Vasione, see Vaison
Vassy 114 C d
Vasvar 123 I e
Vatican, palace in Rome 22 A
Vatican Bridge 96 A
Vatrenus (Santerno) River 27 F c
Vaucelles 118 D d
Vauclair, mon. 94 C b
Vaucluse, dept. 148 F f
Vaucouleurs 69 J f
Vaud, dist. 91 O l
Vaudemont 86 E d
Vauluisant, mon. 94 C b
Vauxchamps 154 B d
Vazerol 91 R l
Veamini, people 26 A c
Vecht River 117 E b
Vectilii, Palace of the 22 A
Vectis, isl. (I. of Wight) 51 P i
Vediantii, people 26 A d
Vegia 27 J c
Veglia, bp. 95 E b

Veii 27 G e
Veile 158 E a
Vela, Cape de la 105 F d
Velabrum, quarter in Rome 24 A
Velay, cty. 61 E d
Veldenz 122 D d
Veldidena 38 E c
Veleia 26 D c
Veleiates, people 26 D c
Velencze 159 J e
Vélez 214 B b
Velez, Peñon de 130 C f
Veleze 165 B c
Vélez Málaga 82 B b
Velia, in Lucania 30 D b
Velia, quarter in Rome 24 A
Veliki Luki 138 D d
Velinus, lake 27 G e
Velitræ (Velletri) 35 ins. B
Velitræ, bp. 96 B b
Vellberg 143 I g
Velletri 90 D d
Velletry, bp. 96 B b
Vellinghausen 134 D c
Vellore 137 C f
Veltæ, people 38 G b
Veltlin, dist., see Valtellina 91 R l
Venafri, bp. 95 ins.
Venafrum (Venafro) 30 D a
Venaissin, cty. 69 F d
Venaissin, prov. 148 F f
Venango, Fort 192 A c
Vence, mon. 148 C c
Vendée, dept. 148 D e
Vendée, dist. 130 C d
Vendôme 69 H g
Vendôme, cty. 69 H g
Vendôme, Place, loc. in Paris 149 B
Venedæ, people 38 F b
Venedic Bay 38 F b
Venelli, people 38 B c
Veneris, Portus 26 D c
Venetes or Venetis, see Vannes
Veneti, people, in Brittany 38 B c
Veneti or Venetians, people, in Italy 27 F b
Venetia, see Venice
Venetia, dist. in Roman times 27 F b
Venetia, prov., 19 cent. 158 F f
Venetia and Istria, prov. 42 E d (1)
Venetia and Istria, reg. 38 E c (10)
Venetian Alps, mts. 27 H a
Venetian Republic, 11 cent. 64 B a
Venetian Republic, 14 cent. 79 H f
Venetian Republic, 15 cent. 90 C b
Venetian Republic, 16 cent. 118 G d
Venetian Republic, 18 cent. 131 F d
Venetus, lake 39 J j
Venezia, Piazza, loc. in Rome 22 A
Venezuela, Gulf of 105 F d
Venezuela, reg. 105 F d
Venezuela, rep. 214 C b
Venice 56 E c
Venice, abp. 95 E b
Venice, duchy 63 G f
Venise, Petite, loc. in Versailles 149 A
Venlo 117 E c
Venlo, Hanse. cy. 99 ins. B
Venonæ 51 P h
Venonetes, people 26 D a
Venosa 90 E d
Venostes, Venostæ, people 26 E a
Venta Belgarum (Winchester) 51 P i
Ventadour 69 E d
Ventadour, castle 76 E d
Ventadour, cty. 78 C f
Venta Icenorum (Castor near Norwich)
Venta Silurum (Cærwent) 51 O i
Ventersdorp 175 M l
Ventimiglia 90 A c
Ventimiglia, bp. 95 D e
Venus, Temple of, on Mt. Ægaleos 16 B a
Venus and Rome, Temple of 24 B
Venus Cloacina, Temple of 24 A (9)
Venus Erycina, Temple of 22 A
Venus Genetrix, Temple of
Venus Victrix, Temple of 22 A
Venusia 30 E b
Veprik 131 J c
Vera 82 B b
Vera Cruz, modern site of 106 D a
Vera Cruz, Villa Rica de la 106 D a
Vera Cruz, la Antigua 106 D a
Vera Cruz, state 213 ins.
Veragri, people 26 B a
Veragua, reg. 105 D e
Veramin
Verbanus (Maggiore), lake 26 C a
Vercellæ (Vercelli) 26 C b
Vercelli 90 I h
Vercelli, bp. 95 D b
Vercelli, univ. 100 G e
Vercheres 189 B b
Verd, Cape 174 B c
Verden 62 E b
Verden, bp. 95 D a
Verden, princ. 122 E b
Verdun 62 C d
Verdun, bp. 78 D d
Verelå 131 I a
Veretum 31 H c
Vereya 153 P f
Vergil's Grave 31 ins. A
Veria 165 C c
Veringen 143 H i
Verkhoyansk 171 O b
Vermandois, cty. 61 E b
Vermilion Lake, Ind. Res. 188 H a
Vermont, dist. 189 B c
Vermont, state 199 K b
Verneuil 69 H f
Verneuil, castle 76 D b
Verni 170 I d
Vernio 90 L i
Vernon, in British Columbia 212 D c
Vernon, in France 69 H f
Vernon, Mount, town in Virginia 193 F b
Verodunum, see Verdun
Veroli, bp. 95 E c
Verona 26 F b
Verona, bp. 93 E b
Verona, march 72 C b
Verona and Aquileia, march 64 B a
Verrazano, route of 108 M d
Versailles 126 C b
Versailles, in 1789, plan 149 A
Versailles, Old 149 A
Versecz 168 G d
Verteræ 51 O g
Vertus 76 F b
Veruela, mon. 94 B c
Verulæ 30 C a
Verulam (Ferryland) 212 J d
Verulamium (Saint Albans, in England) 51 P i
Vervins 114 B d
Vesontio, see Visontio
Vesoul 122 D e
Vespasian, Forum of 24 B
Vespasian, Temple of
Vespucci, route of 105 G d, 108 L k
Vesta, Grove of 24 A
Vesta, Temple of 24 A
Vestals, House of the 24 A
Vestini, people 27 H e
Vesubia River 26 B d
Vesulus, mt. 26 A c
Vesunna (Périgueux) 38 C c
Vesuvius, mt. 30 D b
Veszprim
Veszprim, bp.
Vettona 27 G d
Vèttones, people 38 A d
Vetulonium 26 E e
Veurne (Furnes)
Vexin, dist. 69 H f
Vézelay 69 I g
Vézelay, mon. 94 C b
Via Æmilia (Æmilian Way), road 26 E c
Via Æmilia Scauri (Æmilian Way of Scaurus), road 26 D c
Via Antiana (Antian Way), road 35 ins. B
Via Appia (Appian Way), road 31 F b
Via Appia vetus (Old Appian Way), road 35 ins. B
Via Aurelia (Aurelian Way), road 26 E d
Via Cassia (Cassian Way), road 27 F e
Via Claudia Augusta (Claudian Augustan Way), road 27 G b
Via Claudia Valeria (Claudian Valerian Way), road 27 H e
Via Clodia (Clodian Way), road 27 F e
Via di Ripetta, street in Rome 22 A
Via Dolorosa, in Jerusalem 68 ins. B
Viadua (Oder) River 38 F b
Via Flaminia (Flaminian Way), road 27 G e
Via Flaminia vetus (Old Flaminian Way), road 27 G e
Via Flavia (Flavian Way), road 27 H b
Via Julia Augusta (Julian Augustan Way), road 26 B d
Via Labicana (Labican Way), road 35 ins. B
Via Lata, Aug. Reg. of Rome 22 A
Via lata (Broad Way), street in Rome 22 A
Via Latina (Latin Way), road 30 B a
Viale Aventino, street in Rome 22 A
Viale Giulio Cesare, street in Rome 22 A
Via mala, pass 150 E c
Via Merulana, street in Rome 22 A
Viana 214 E c
Via Nomentana (Nomentan Way), road 35 ins. B
Via Ostiensis (Ostian Way), road 35 ins. B
Via Popilia (Popilian Way), road 31 F d
Via Portuensis (Port Way), road 35 ins. B
Via Postumia (Postumian Way, in Liguria), road 26 C c
Via Postumia (Postumian Way, in Venetia), road 27 G b
Via Prænestina (Prænestine Way), road 35 ins. B
Via Sacra (Sacred Way), street in Rome 23 A, B
Via Salaria (Salarian Way), road 27 H e
Via Severiana (Severian Way), road 35 ins. B
Viasma or Vyasma 138 D d
Via Tiberina (Tiberine Way), road 35 ins. B
Via Tiburtina (Tiburtian Way), road 35 ins. B
Viatka or Vyatka 138 G d
Viatka, dist. 71 P b
Via Traiana (Trajan's Way), road 30 E a
Via Triumphalis (Triumphal Way), road 35 ins. B
Via Valeria (Valerian Way, in Italy), road 27 H e
Via Valeria (Valerian Way, in Sicily), road 30 D d
Vibii, Forum 26 B c
Vibinum 30 E a
Vibo, Gulf of 31 F d
Vibo Valentia 31 F d
Viborg, in Denmark 88 C c
Viborg, in Finland 138 C c
Vic 76 E d
Vicenza 90 J h
Vicenza, univ. 100 H e (Vic.)
Vicetia (Vicenza) 26 F b
Vich 82 C a
Vich, bp. 94 C c
Vicinonia River, see Vilaine River
Vicksburg 208 B c
Vico, lake 96 B a
Victoria, in Alberta 212 D c
Victoria, in Brazil 214 F e
Victoria, in Vancouver 198 A a

Victoria, state . . . 172 D d
Victoria Desert, Great . . . 172 B c
Victoria Falls . . . 175 F f
Victoria Land . . . 186 I a
Victoria Nyanza, lake . . . 175 G e
Victoria River . . . 172 B b
Victoria Strait . . . 212 E b
Victoriæ, Clivus, loc. in Rome 24 A
Victrix Julia Tarraconensis(Tarragona) . . . 38 C d
Victumulæ . . . 26 C b
Vicus Augustanus . . . 35 ins. B
Vicus Aurelii . . . 39 J i
Vicus Iulius . . . 39 J i
Vicus Jugarius, street in Rome 24 A
Vicus Tuscus, street in Rome 24 A
Vidin . . . 164 C b
Vidrus (Vecht) River . . . 39 I g
Viejo, el . . . 213 D c
Vielsalm . . . 117 D d
Vienna (Vienne), in France . . 38 C c
Vienna . . . 63 I d
Vienna, univ. . . . 100 I e
Vienne, in France . . . 69 F d
Vienne, abp. . . . 95 D b
Vienne, dept. . . . 148 E e
Vienne River . . . 69 D c
Viennensis, Rom. prov. . . . 42 D e (1)
Viennois, Dauphiny of, dist. . . 76 F d
Viennois, dist. . . . 126 D d
Vieques, isl. . . . 199 ins. G
Viersen . . . 117 E c
Vierwaldstätter See, see Lucerne, lake . . . 91 Q l
Vierzon . . . 69 I g
Vieux-Amis . . .
Vigan . . . 199 ins. H
Vigas, las . . . 201 H g
Vigenna, see Vienne
Vigevano . . . 90 B b
Vigo . . . 130 B e
Vijayanagar, Kingdom of . . . 112 A b
Viktring, mon. . . . 95 E b
Vilaine River . . . 148 D e
Vilcobamba . . . 214 B d
Vilija River . . . 159 M a
Vilini River . . .
Vilkomir . . . 159 M a
Villa Albani, loc. in Rome . . . 96 A
Villa Bella . . . 214 D d
Villa Borghese, loc. in Rome . 96 A
Villach . . . 63 G e
Villa Encarnación . . . 215 D e
Villa Farnesina, loc. in Rome . 96 A
Villafranca . . . 158 F f
Villagos . . .
Villa Ludovisi, loc. in Rome . 96 A
Villa Madama, loc. in Rome . . 96 A
Villa Nova, in Santa Catharina 215 E e
Villa Nueva, in Arg. Rep. . . . 215 C f
Villa Publica, loc. in Rome . . 24 A
Villa Rica, in Paraguay . . . 215 D e
Villa Rica de la Vera Cruz . .
Villa rica la Vieja . . .
Villars, in Provence . . . 126 E e
Villars-sur-Ecot . . . 143 ins. F
Villa Umberto I, loc. in Rome 22 A
Villaviciosa, in Asturias . . . 83 J g
Villaviciosa, in Castile . . . 130 C e
Villa Viçoza, in Brazil . . . 108 N i
Villefranche . . . 76 E d
Villegaignon Island . . . 108 M j
Villemur . . . 76 D e
Villena, marq. . . . 83 K h
Villeneuve . . . 126 B d
Villingen . . . 142 B d
Vilna . . . 138 C e
Vilvorde . . . 117 C d
Vimeiro . . . 130 B f
Viminacium . . . 39 M l
Viminal, quarter in Rome . . . 96 A
Viminal Gate . . . 22 A
Viminal Hill . . . 22 A
Vincennes . . .
Vinciacus, see Vinchy
Vinchy . . . 55 P i
Vindava, see Windau
Vindelicia, dist. . . . 38 E c
Vindhya Mountains . . . 137 C d
Vindilis, isl. . . . 38 B c
Vindobona (Vienna in Austria) 38 F c
Vindocinum, see Vendôme
Vindogladia . . .
Vindonissa (Windisch) . . . 39 J j
Vinegar Hill . . . 127 K i
Vinnitsa . . . 139 C f
Vinovia (Binchester) . . . 51 P g
Vintium . . . 26 B d
Vintodurnum, see Winterthur
Vipsanian Portico . . . 22 A
Virballen . . . 159 L a
Virère, Woods of . . .
Virgin Aqueduct . . . 35 ins. B (2)
Virginia City . . . 210 B c
Virginia, col. . . . 193 E c
Virginia, reg. . . .
Virginia, state, 1788 . . . 202 I c
Virginia, state, 1863 . . . 203 V h
Virginia Military Lands . . . 196 ins. B
Virginia, West, state . . . 203 V h
Virginia Yazoo Company . . . 196 A d
Virgin Islands . . . 105 H c
Virgin River . . . 210 C c
Virgin's Well . . . 6 ins. A
Viriballum, prom. . . . 26 C e
Virneburg . . . 122 D c
Viroconium (Wroxeter) . . .
Virodunum (Verdun) . . . 39 H i
Viromandis, see Saint-Quentin
Virton . . . 117 D e
Virtue, Temple of . . . 22 A
Viru . . . 111 B c
Virunum . . . 39 E c
Visa . . . 165 E c
Visconti, Dom. of the . . . 78 F f
Visconti, Milanese under the . 90
Visé . . . 117 D d
Visentium . . . 27 F e
Visontio (Besançon) . . . 39 H j
Visp . . . 91 P l
Vistula River . . . 159 J b
Visurgis (Weser) River . . . 38 D b
Vita . . . 42 E f
Vitebsk . . . 138 D d
Viterbo . . . 90 D c
Viterbo, bp. . . . 95 E c
Vith, Sankt . . . 117 E d
Viti Levu, isl. . . . 172 G b
Vitim River . . .
Vitodurum . . . 39 J j
Vitoria . . . 82 B a
Vitricium . . . 26 B b
Vitry . . .
Vittorio Emanuele, Corso, street in Rome . . . 22 A
Vittorio Emanuele, Piazza, loc. in Rome . . . 22 A
Vivarais, dist. . . . 76 F d
Vivarium, see Viviers
Vivienne, Rue, street in Paris . 149 B
Viviers . . . 78 D f
Viviers, bp. . . . 94 C c
Viviers, cty. . . . 69 F d
Viviscus . . . 26 A a
Vizagapatam . . . 137 D e
Vizakna . . . 159 L f
Vizcaya, dist., see also Biscay . 83 K g
Vizéu . . . 82 A a
Vizéu, bp. . . . 94 A c
Vizianagram . . . 137 D e
Vlaardingen . . . 62 C c
Vladikavkas . . . 167 O g
Vladimir . . . 138 F d
Vladimir Volynsk . . . 139 B e
Vladivostok . . . 171 O d
Vlieland, isl. . . . 117 C a
Vlissingen (Flushing), in Holland . . . 117 B c
Vlissingen (Flushing), in New York . . . 189 ins. C
Vöcklabruck . . . 123 G d
Voclade, see Vouillé
Vocontii, people . . . 38 D d
Vogtland, dist. . . . 85 G e
Vogules, people . . .
Volane River . . . 27 F c
Volaterræ . . . 26 E d
Volcæ Arecomici, people . . . 38 C d
Volcæ Tectosages, people . . . 38 C d
Volcei . . . 30 E b
Volcera . . . 27 I b
Volci . . . 27 F e
Volerius River . . . 26 D e
Volga River . . . 139 G f
Volhynia, dist. . . . 139 C e
Volkerode, mon. . . . 95 E a
Volkhov River . . . 88 N b
Volkovisk . . . 155 M b
Vollenhove . . . 117 D b
Vollmaringen . . . 143 G h
Volo . . . 164 C c
Vologda . . . 138 E d
Vologesia . . . 20 K f
Volsci, people . . . 30 C a
Volsiniensis, lake . . . 27 F e
Volsinii novi . . . 27 G e
Volsinii veteres . . . 27 G e
Volta . . . 161 H e
Volta River . . . 128 ins. D
Volterra . . . 90 L j
Volterra, bp. . . . 95 E c
Voltri . . . 150 E d
Volturara, bp. . . . 95 F c
Volturnum . . . 30 C b
Volturnus (Volturno) River . . . 30 D a
Vomanus River . . . 27 I e
Von der Leyen, princ. . . . 154 E d
Vonitsa . . . 131 H f
Voorne, East, isl. . . . 117 B c
Voorne, South, isl. . . . 117 C c
Voorne, West, isl. . . . 117 B c
Vorarlberg, dist. . . . 114 E e
Vorder-Rhein, see Hither Rhine River . . . 91 R l
Voronezh . . . 139 E e
Voronezh, gov. . . . 131 K c
Voronov . . . 153 P f
Vorsfelde . . . 85 B b
Vorskla River . . . 92 D c
Vosges, dept. . . . 148 F e
Vosges Mountains . . . 38 D c
Vosolvia . . . 39 I h
Vossem . . . 122 C c
Votyaks, people . . . 138 H d
Vouillé . . . 50 D c
Voullon . . . 50 D c
Vratza . . . 165 C b
Vredeland . . . 189 ins. C
Vriesendael . . . 192 D c
Vryburg . . . 175 F g
Vryheid . . . 175 N l
Vuelta, Cabo de la, cape . . . 111 A b
Vulcan Island . . . 30 E d
Vulcaniæ (Æolian, Lipari) Islands 30 E d
Vultur, mt. . . . 30 E b
Vyasma or Viasma . . . 138 D d
Vyatka or Viatka . . . 138 G d
Vychegda River . . .

Waadt, dist., see Vaud . . . 91 O l
Waag River . . . 63 J d
Waal River . . . 117 D c
Wabash River . . . 191 H d
Wacos, tribe . . . 188 G d
Wadai, sultanate . . . 174 E c
Wadan . . . 174 B b
Wadelai . . . 175 G d
Wadi Natrun, reg. . . . 150 B a
Wadstena . . . 88 F b
Wady Halfa . . .
Wagadugu . . . 174 C c
Waghäusel . . . 158 E d

Wagnelée . . . 156 A a
Wagner, Battery, fort . . . 208 E c
Wagram . . . 155 I d
Wagrians, people . . . 62 F a
Wahlstatt . . . 155 I c
Wahlstatt, mon. . . . 72 D a
Wahlwies . . . 62 E e
Waialua . . . 198 ins. B
Waiblingen . . . 143 H h
Waibstadt . . . 142 C b
Waidhofen . . . 115 H e
Waikato River . . . 172 G d
Wailuku . . . 198 ins. B
Waimanalo . . . 198 ins. B
Waimea . . . 198 ins. B
Wain . . . 143 J i
Wain, lordship . . . 143 J i
Wainganga River . . . 137 C d
Waitangi . . . 172 H e
Waitara . . . 172 G d
Waitzen . . . 159 J e
Waitzen, bp. . . . 95 F b
Wakefield, in England . . . 127 X m
Wakefield, parl. bor. . . . 163 M d
Wakefield, in Miss. . . . 196 B d
Wake Island . . . 179 H f
Walata . . . 174 C c
Walbeck . . . 62 F b
Walcheren, isl. . . . 117 B c
Walck . . . 131 I b
Waldangeloch . . . 143 G g
Waldburg . . . 143 I j
Waldburg, cty. . . . 143 I j
Waldeck, cty. . . . 114 E c
Waldeck, dist. . . . 86 G c
Waldeck, princ. . . . 134 E c
Walden, mon. . . . 97 R i
Waldenburg . . . 143 I g
Waldkirch . . . 142 A d
Waldsassen, mon. . . . 95 E b
Waldsee . . . 143 I j
Waldshut . . . 142 B e
Waldstein, castle . . . 123 H c
Waldstetten . . . 143 I h
Wales, dist. . . .
Wales, march . . .
Wales, princ. about 1300 . . .
Wales, princ. 17 cent. . . . 127 V n
Wales, North, dist. . . .
Wales, West, dist. . . .
Walfisch Bay . . . 175 E g
Walhain . . . 156 B a
Walkenried . . . 122 F c
Walkenried, mon. . . . 95 E a
Walker Pass . . . 210 B c
Walker River, Ind. Res. . . . 188 C c
Walkers . . . 196 B c
Wallachia, dist. . . . 77 I d
Wallachia, princ. . . . 119 I e
Wallachia, Great, dist. . . . 89 C b
Wallachia, Little, dist. . . . 89 B b
Wallachian Plain . . . 2 G d
Wallachian Thessaly, princ. . . 89 B c
Walla Walla, Fort . . . 198 B a
Walla, Wallas, tribe . . . 188 C a
Wall Brook, in London . . . 75 G g
Wallenstein, route of . . . 121 D c
Wallerstein . . . 143 J h
Wallhausen . . . 63 F c
Wallingford
Wallingford, castle . . .
Wallingford, parl. bor. . . 163 M f (Wall.)
Wallis, dist., see Valais . . . 91 P l
Walloons, people . . . 184 D b
Wallnut Hills, village . . . 208 B c
Wallnut Hills, Fort . . . 196 A d
Walsall, parl. bor. . . . 163 M e
Walsingham, Cape . . . 212 I b
Walsingham, mon. . . . 97 S i
Walsleben . . . 63 F b
Waltham, mon. . . . 97 R j
Waltham Abbey . . . 75 J h
Walton . . . 75 I i
Wampanoags, tribe . . . 189 C d
Wandewash or Wandiwash . . 137 C f
Wanganui . . . 172 G d
Wangen, imp. cy. . . . 143 I j
Wangenies . . . 156 B b
Wantage . . .
Wappingers, tribe . . . 188 L b
Warangal . . .
Warasdin . . . 159 I e
Warberg, in Sweden . . . 88 E c
Warberg, Hanse. for. cy. . . . 98 F b
Warburg, Hanse. cy. in Germany . . . 99 ins. B
Warden, mon. . . . 97 Q i
Wardour Castle . . . 127 W o
Warego River . . . 172 D c
Wareham, in England . . . 127 W p
Wareham, castle . . . 65 E e
Wareham, barl. bor. . . . 163 L g
Wareham, in Mass. . . . 207 L b
Warekauri Islands . . . 172 H e
Waren . . . 79 H b
Waren, princ. . . . 79 H b
Wargla, oasis . . . 2 E e
Warka . . . 159 K c
Warley . . . 75 J h
Warm Spring, Ind. Res. . . . 188 B b
Warnabians, people . . . 63 F b
Warneton . . . 117 A d
Warns, people . . . 50 F b
Warnstedt . . . 62 F c
Warren . . . 189 ins. A
Warrenton . . . 208 B c
Warrington . . . 127 W m
Warrington, parl. bor. . . 163 L d (Warr.)
Warsaw . . . 79 L b
Warsaw, duchy . . . 155 K b
Warsaw, gr. duchy . . . 152 D c
Warta River, see Warthe River
Wartau, castle . . . 91 R k
Wartburg, castle . . . 62 F c
Wartenberg, in Silesia . . . 123 I c
Wartenburg, in Saxony . . . 154 G c
Warthausen . . . 143 I i
Warthe . . . 63 I c
Warthe River . . . 63 I b
Warwick, in England . . . 127 X n
Warwick, castle . . . 65 F d
Warwick, cty. . . .
Warwick, parl. bor. . . . 163 M e
Warwick, shire
Warwick, in Rhode Island . . . 189 ins. A
Warwick Lane, street in London . . . 75 G g (32)
Wasatch Mountains . . . 187 H e
Wash, The, bay . . . 49 G e
Washington, in District of Columbia . . . 208 ins.
Washington, in Miss. . . . 196 A d
Washington, in Pa. . . . 211 I b
Washington, Fort, in Maryland 200 L i
Washington, Fort, in New York 195 D c
Washington, Fort, in Ohio . . . 196 ins. B
Washington, route of . . .
Washington, proposed state . .
Washington, state . . . 210 A a
Washington, ter. 1853 . . . 202 A f
Washington, ter. 1859 . . . 203 O f
Washington, ter. 1863 . . . 203 N f
Washita, River . . . 199 G d
Washita Fort . . . 210 F d
Wasit . . . 99 M g
Wassenberg . . . 72 B a
Wasseralfingen . . . 143 J h
Watauga . . . 191 I d
Watauga Association . . . 194 C c
Watauga River . . . 196 ins. A
Watauga Settlements . . . 196 ins. A
Watchet, parl. bor. . . .
Wateree River . . . 193 D d
Waterford, in Ireland . . .
Waterford, bp. . . . 97 D d
Waterford, cty. . . . 127 J i
Waterford, in Pa. . . . 192 A c
Water Gate . . . 6 ins. A
Waterloo . . .
Watertown . . . 189 ins. B
Watling's Island . . . 105 ins.
Watling Street, road in England . . . 51 P h
Watling Street, in London . . . 75 G g
Watson, Fort . . . 195 A g
Wattignies . . . 134 B c
Waverley, mon. . . . 97 Q j
Wavre . . . 156 B a
Waxhaw Creek . . . 195 A f
Wayne, Fort . . . 196 B b
Wayne's Treaty Line . . . 196 ins. B
Ways . . . 156 A a
Weald, The, forest . . . 49 F f
Weare, parl. bor. . . .
Wearmouth . . .
Wearmouth, mon. . . . 97 P g
Wedmore . . .
Weehawken . . . 192 D c
Wehlau . . . 123 K a
Weibertreu, ruin . . . 143 H g
Weichsel River, see Vistula River
Weiden . . . 123 G d
Wei-hai-wei . . . 171 N e
Weikersheim . . . 143 I f
Weilburg . . . 114 E c
Weilburg, castle . . . 62 E c
Weil der Stadt, imp. cy. . . . 143 G h
Weiler . . . 143 H g
Weilheim . . . 143 I h
Weiltingen . . . 143 J g
Weimar . . . 85 F e
Weinfelden . . . 142 D e
Weingarten, ab. . . . 143 I j
Weingarten, mon. . . . 95 D b
Weinheim . . . 142 C a
Weinsberg . . . 143 H g
Weinsberg, lordship . . . 143 H g
Weisse Elster River . . . 63 G c
Weissenau, ab. . . . 143 I j
Weissenburg, imp. cy., in Alsace 78 E d
Weissenburg, mon. . . . 95 D b
Weissenburg, imp. cy., in Bavaria . . . 79 G d
Weissenburg, castle, in Switzerland . . . 91 P l
Weissenburg, in Transylvania .
Weissenfels . . . 135 G c
Weissenhorn . . . 143 J i
Weissenstein . . . 143 I h
Weisser Berg, mt. . . . 123 H c
Weisses Meer, see Kara Sea . . 170 H a
Weisskirchen . . . 159 K f
Weisweil . . . 142 A d
Welbeck, mon. . . . 97 P h
Weldon . . . 208 E b
Weld Springs, village . . . 172 B c
Welehrad, mon. . . . 95 F b
Welfesholz . . . 63 F c
Welland River . . . 127 Y n
Well Gate . . . 6 ins. A
Wellington . . . 172 G e
Wellington Island . . . 215 B g
Wells, in England . . .
Wells, bp. . . . 97 O j
Wells, parl. bor. . . . 163 L f
Wells, in New Hampshire . . . 189 C c
Wels, in Austria . . . 63 G d
Welsh, people . . .
Wels Mountains . . .
Welzheim . . . 143 I h
Welzheim, lordship . . . 143 I h
Wen-chau . . . 171 N f
Wenden . . . 88 K c
Wendish March, dist. . . . 77 I f
Wendover, parl. bor. . . . 163 N f (We.)
Wends, people, in Austria . . . 54 G d
Wends, people, in Germany . . 46 I c
Wener, lake . . . 88 E b
Wenersborg . . . 88 F b
Wennington . . . 75 J h
Weobley, parl. bor. . . . 163 L e

Werben . . . . 63 F b
Werden, mon. . . . . 95 D a
Werdenberg, castle . . . . . . 91 R k
Werl . . . . 62 D c
Werla, castle . . . . 62 F b
Werra River . . . . 79 G c
Werschitz . . . . 159 K f
Wertheim . . . . 142 D a
Werwick . . . . 117 A d
Wesel . . . . 114 D c
Wesel, Hanse. cy. . . . . . . 99 ins. B
Wesen . . . . 91 R k
Weser River . . . . 62 E b
Wessagussett . . . . 189 ins. B
Wessex, km. . . . .
Wessobrunn, mon. . . . . 95 E b
Westacre, mon. . . . . 97 R i
West Africa, French, col. . . . 174 C c
West Africa, Portuguese, col. . 175 E f
West Bromwich . . . . 162 D e
Westbury, parl. bor. . . . . . . 163 L f
Westchester . . . . 189 ins. C
West Cornwall, parl. dist. . . . 163 I g
West Cumberland, parl. dist. . 163 K c
West Dereham, mon. . . . . . . 97 R i
Westerås . . . . 88 G b
Westerham . . . . 75 J i
Westerly . . . . 189 ins. A
Western, Fort . . . . 189 D b
Western Australia, state . . . . 172 C c
Western Ghats, mts. . . . . . . 112 A b
Western Plain . . . . 187 I d
Western Reserve of Connecticut, dist. . . . . 196 ins. B
West Fiord . . . . 166 H b
West Florida, col. . . . . 194 B d
West Frankish Kingdom . . . . 56 B c
West Franconia, duchy . . . . . 62 E d
West Friesland, dist. . . . . . 117 C b
West Galicia, dist. . . . . . . 139 B e
West Gloucester, parl. dist. . 163 L f
West Göthland, dist. . . . . .
West Goths, Kingdom of the, 486 . . . . 50 D d
West Goths, Kingdom of the, 6 cent. 52
West Goths, people . . . . . . 45 I c, D d
West Indies, reg. . . . 107, 108 E-O, a-l
West Indies, isl. . . . . 187 L f
West Kent, parl. dist. . . . . . 163 O f
Westland, dist. . . . . 172 F e
West Love, parl. bor. . . . . . 163 J g
West Marches, dist., in England
West March, dist., in Scotland
West Meath, cty. . . . . 127 J h
Westminster, in England . . . . 65 F e
Westminster, mon. . . . . 97 Q j
Westminster, parl. bor. 163 N f (Westm.)
Westminster, in Maryland . . . 208 ins.
Westminster, New, in British Columbia . . . . 212 C d
Westminster Hall, in London . 75 G g
Westmoreland, cty. . . . .
Westmoreland, parl. dist. . . .
Westmoreland, shire . . . . . .
West New Jersey, col. . . . . . 192 D d
West Norfolk, parl. dist. . . . 163 O e
Westover . . . . 193 ins. A
Westphalia, dist. . . . . 62 D b c
Westphalia, duchy . . . . 78 E c
Westphalia, km. . . . . 154 E c
Westphalia, prov. . . . . 158 E c
Westphalians, people . . . . . 55 Q i
West Point . . . . 195 D c
Westport . . . . 210 F c
West Prussia, dist. . . . . 135 I b
West Prussia, prov. . . . . . . 159 I b
West Riding, parl dist. . . . . 163 M d
West Roman Empire . . . . . 42 A-F e
West Saxons, people . . . . .
West Somerset, parl. dist. . . . 163 K f
West Suffolk, parl. dist. . . . . 163 O e
West Surrey, parl. dist. . . . . 163 N f
West Sussex, parl dist. . . . . 163 N g
Westsylvania, proposed state in U S. . . . . 195 A d
West Turkistan, Plains of . . . 3 K d
West Virginia, state . . . . . . 211 I c
West Voorne, isl. . . . . 117 B c
West Wales, dist. . . . .
West Worcester, parl. dist. . . 163 L e
Wethersfield, in Connecticut . 189 B d
Wethersfield, in England . . . . 185 G f
Wetter, lake . . . . 88 F b
Wettin, castle . . . . 63 F c
Wettin, cty. . . . . 85 F e
Wettin Lands 85
Wettingen, mon. . . . . 95 D b
Wetzlar . . . . 62 E c
Wetzlar, imp. cy. . . . . 78 F c
Wexford . . . .
Wexford, cty. . . . . 127 K i
Weybridge . . . . 75 I i
Weymouth, in England . . . . 84 B d
Weymouth, parl. bor. . . . . . . 163 L g
Weymuoth, in Mass. . . . . . . 189 ins. B
Wey River, in Hereford . . . . 127 W n
Wey River, in Surrey . . . . . . 75 H i
Wezet . . . . 117 D d
Whalley, mon. . . . . 97 O h
Wheeling . . . . 196 C b
Wherwell, ab. . . . . 100 A a
Whitby . . . .
Whitby, mon. . . . . 97 Q g
Whitby, parl. bor. . . . . 163 N c
Whitchurch, parl. bor. . . . . . 163 M f
White Chapel, loc. near. London 75 I h
White Earth, Ind. Res. . . . . . 188 G a
White Friars, mon. . . . . 75 G g
Whitehall, loc. in London . . . 75 G g
Whitehall, in New York . . . . 195 E b
Whitehaven, parl. bor. . . . . . 163 K c
White Horde, people . . . . . .
White Horse, village . . . . . . 212 ins.
White Mountain, in Bohemia . . 123 H c
White Mountain, Ind. Res. . . . 188 D d
White Mountains, in N. Hampshire . . . . 189 C b
White Nile River . . . . 174 G c
White Pass . . . . 212 ins.
White Plains, town . . . . 195 D c
White River, in Arkansas . . . 191 G d
White River, in Indiana . . . . 208 C b
White River, in S. Dakota . . . 198 E b
White Russia, reg. . . . . 138 C e
White Russians, people . . . . 138 C e
White Sea . . . . 138 E b
Whithorn, bp. . . . . 97 I e
Whitney, mt. . . . . 210 B c
Whorekill (Lewes, in Delaware) 192 D d
Whydah . . . . 174 D d
Wiblingen, ab. in Wurtemberg . 143 I i
Wiblingen, mon. . . . . 143 J i
Wichita . . . . 210 F c
Wichitas, tribe . . . . 188 G d
Wicklow . . . . 127 K i
Wicklow, cty. . . . . 127 K i
Widdern . . . . 143 H g
Widin, see Vidin
Wieblingen, in Baden . . . . . 142 C b
Wieliczka . . . . 115 I d
Wielun . . . .
Wien, see Vienna in Austria
Wiener Neustadt . . . . 115 H e
Wieprz River . . . . 159 L c
Wieringen, isl. . . . . 117 D b
Wieselburg . . . . 159 I e
Wiesensteig . . . . 143 I h
Wiesensteig, lordship . . . . . 143 I h
Wiese River . . . . 142 A e
Wiesloch . . . . 142 C b
Wigan . . . . 127 W m
Wigan, parl. bor. . . . . 163 L d
Wight, Isle of . . . . 49 F f
Wight, Isle of, parl. dist. . . . 163 M g
Wigmore, mon. . . . . 97 O i
Wigtown . . . .
Wigtown, cty. . . . .
Wigtown, dist. . . . .
Wi-ju . . . . 171 N e
Wildbad . . . . 143 G h
Wildberg, in Wurtemberg . . . 143 G h
Wildberg, castle, in Austria . . 79 I d
Wildenstein . . . . 143 J g
Wilderness, battle . . . . . 208 E b (Wil.)
Wildeshausen . . . . 62 E b
Wildhaus . . . . 91 R k
Wilhelmshaven . . . . 158 D b
Wilhelmstein, Fort . . . . 134 E b
Wilhelmsthal . . . . 134 E c
Wilkesbarre . . . . 195 D c
Wilkinson, route of . . . . . . 200 C d
Willamette River . . . . 198 A b
William, Fort (Calcutta) . . . . 137 E d
William, Fort, in Florida . . . . 193 D f
William, Fort (Portland) . . . . 210 A a
William, Fort, in Ontario . . . . 212 F d
William Henry, Fort . . . . . . 192 D b
William of Rubruck, route of .
Williams, Fort, in New York . 192 D b
Williamsburg . . . . 193 ins. A
Williamsport . . . . 208 ins.
Willoughby, route of . . . . . . 108 R a
Willow Brook . . . . 6 ins. B
Wills Creek, Fort . . . . 192 B d
Wilmington, in Delaware . . . 192 D d
Wilmington, in N. Carolina . . 193 F d
Wilsaetas, people . . . .
Wilsnack . . . . 87 H b
Wilson's Creek, battle . . . . . 208 B b
Wilson's Promontory . . . . . . 172 D d
Wilten . . . . 63 F e
Wilton . . . .
Wilton, mon. . . . . 97 O j
Wilton, parl. bor. . . . . 163 M f
Wiltshire, cty. . . . .
Wiltwyck . . . . 192 D c
Wiltz . . . . 117 D e
Wilzi or Wilzians, people . . . 63 G b
Wimbledon . . . . 75 I i
Wimmera River . . . . 172 D d
Wimmis, castle . . . . 91 P l
Wimpfen . . . . 62 E d
Wimpfen, imp. cy. . . . . 142 D b
Winburg . . . . 175 M l
Wincanton . . . . 127 W o
Winceby . . . . 127 Y m
Winchcombe, mon. . . . . 97 P j
Winchelsea, parl. bor. . . . . . 163 O g
Winchester, in England . . . .
Winchester, bp. . . . . 97 P j
Winchester, castle . . . . 65 F e
Winchester, college . . . . . . 100 A a
Winchester, deanery . . . . . . 100 A a
Winchester, hospitals . . . . . 100 A a
Winchester, mon. . . . . 100 A a
Winchester, parl. bor. . 163 M f (Winch.)
Winchester, in Virginia . . . . 193 E b
Windau, Hanse. cy. . . . . . . 99 H b
Windhoek, or Windhuk . . . . 175 E g
Wind River . . . . 210 D b
Wind River, Ind. Res. . . . . . 188 E b
Windsheim . . . . 114 F d
Windsor, in Canada . . . . 212 G d
Windsor, in Connecticut . . . . 189 B d
Windsor, in England . . . . . . 75 H i
Windsor, castle . . . .
Windsor, New, in Maryland . . 208 ins.
Windward Channel . . . . 213 E c
Windward Islands . . . . 213 F c
Winibigoshish, Ind. Res. . . . 188 H a
Winnebago, Fort . . . . 211 H b
Winnebago, Ind. Res. . . . . . 188 G b
Winnebagos, tribe . . . . 188 I b
Winnenden . . . . 143 H h
Winnepesaukee, lake . . . . . . 189 C c
Winnington Bridge . . . . 127 W m
Winnipeg . . . . 212 F d
Winnipeg, lake . . . . 212 F c
Winnipegosis, lake . . . . 186 I c
Winnsboro . . . . 195 A f
Winschoten . . . . 117 E a

Winterburg 142 ins. A
Winterstetten 143 I i
Winterthur 91 Q k
Wintney, priory 100 B a
Winton 172 D c
Winwaedsfield
Wirtemberg, ruin 143 H h
Wirzaburg, see Würzburg
Wisbech, parl. bor. 163 O e
Wisby 88 H c
Wisby, Hanse. cy. 98 G b
Wischehrad
Wisconsin, state 211 G b
Wisconsin, ter. 1836 202 F f
Wisconsin, ter. 1838 202 G f
Wisconsin River 199 H b
Wisera River, see Weser River
Wismar 80 B e
Wismar, Hanse. cy. 99 ins. B
Witham, mon. 97 O j
Witney, parl. bor.
Wittelsbach, castle 72 C b
Wittenberg 72 C a
Wittenberg, univ. 100 H d
Wittstock 123 G b
Witu 175 H e
Witwaters Rand, mts. 175 M l
Wloclawek 159 J b
Wloclawek, bp. 95 F a
Włodawa 155 L c
Woburn 189 ins. B
Woburn, mon. 97 Q j
Wogastisburg 55 R j
Wohlau 115 I c
Wohlau, princ. 115 I c
Woiwodina, dist. 159 J f
Wola 135 K b
Wolfach 142 B d
Wolfegg 143 I j
Wolfenbüttel 79 G b
Wolfenbüttel, duchy 122 E c
Wolfsegg 123 G d
Wolgast 63 G a
Wolgast, duchy 115 G b
Wolgast, Hanse. cy. 99 ins. B
Wollaston, Mount, village 189 C c
Wollaston Lake 186 I c
Wollaston Land 212 D b
Wollin 63 H b
Wolmirstedt 85 B b
Wolvega 117 D b
Wolverhampton, parl. bor. 163 L e (Wolv.)
Women's Tower, loc. in Jerusalem 6 ins. A
Won-san 171 N e
Woods, Lake of the 191 G b
Wood Street, in London 75 G g
Woodstock 127 X o
Woodstock, New 163 M f (New Wood.)
Woolwich 75 J i
Wootton Bassett, parl. bor. 163 M f (W. B.)
Worcester, in England
Worcester, bp. 97 O i
Worcester, cty.
Worcester, parl. bor. 163 L e (Worc.)
Worcester, shire
Worcester, in Mass. 189 C c
Wörgl 154 G e
Worksop, mon. 97 P h
Workum 117 D b
Wormatia, see Worms, on the Rhine River
Worms, on the Rhine River 62 E d
Worms, bp. 95 D b
Worms, imp. cy. 78 F d
Worms (Bormio), on the Adda 122 F e
Worndorf 142 C e
Wörnitz River 143 J g
Worringen 78 E c
Wrangell 198 ins. A
Wrangell, Fort 212 ins.
Wrangell, mt. 186 E b
Wreschen 159 I b
Wrexham parl. bor. 163 K d
Wrightstown 192 D c
Wrightsville 208 ins.
Wroxeter 51 O h
Wu-chau 171 M f
Wu-hu 171 M e
Wurm River 143 G h
Wurtemberg, castle 62 E d
Wurtemberg, cty. 78 F d
Wurtemberg, elect. 151 H g
Wurtemberg, km. 151 K j
Wurzach 143 I j
Würzburg 62 E d
Würzburg, bp. 95 D b
Würzburg, gr. duchy 154 E d
Würzburg, elect. 151 K j
Würzburg, univ. 100 G e
Wurzen 85 G e
Wu-sing 170 ins. A
Wutach River 142 B e
Wyandots, tribe 188 J b
Wychwood 49 F f
Wye River 49 E e
Wyk, in Holland 117 C b
Wyk by Duurstede 117 D b
Wymondham, mon. 97 S i
Wyoming 196 D b
Wyoming, state 210 D b
Wyoming, ter. 203 Q g
Wyoming Valley 195 C c
Wyre, Forest of 49 E e
Wyschehrad, castle

Xaltocan 106 A a
Xaltocan, lake 106 B a
Xanten 62 D c
Xanthus 20 C d
Xanthus River 20 C d
Xaragua, reg. 105 F c
Xauxa (Jauja) 111 B d
Xerxes Canal 11 E b
Xerxes, route of fleet of 13 D a
Xico 106 B a
Xingu River 214 D c
Xions 159 I b
Xochicalco 106 A b
Xochimilco 106 A a
Xuala 191 I d
Xyniæ 11 D c
Xynias, lake 11 D c
Xypete 16 B b
Xystus 6 ins. A

Yablonoi Mountains 171 M c
Yacki
Yadkin River 195 A e
Yakima, Ind. Res. 188 B a
Yakutat Bay 198 ins. A
Yakutsk 171 N b
Yalta 164 K f
Ya-lu River 171 N d
Yama 119 J b
Yamasees, tribe 188 J d
Yamburg 119 K b
Yanaon 137 D e
Yandabo
Yang-tse-kiang, R.
Yang-tun
Yangui
Yankton, Ind. Res. 188 G b
Yap, isl. 179 E g
Yapura River 214 C c
Yaqui, Rio, R. 190 C f
Yaquimi 190 D f
Yarkand
Yarm, parl. bor.
Yarmouth, in England 65 G d
Yarmouth, Hanse. for. cy. 98 ins. A
Yarmouth, parl. bor. 163 M g
Yarmouth, in Mass. 189 C d
Yarmouth, in Nova Scotia 212 I d
Yarmouth River 6 D c
Yaroslavl 138 E d
Yarrawonga 172 D d
Yass 172 D d
Yatwegs, people 71 K c
Yauco 199 ins. G
Yautepec, R. 106 B b
Yazoo Company 196 A d
Yazoo River 208 B c
Yedi Kouleh, castle 93 G e
Yedisan, reg. 139 C f
Yedo 171 P e
Yeletz 139 E e
Yellow Sea 171 N e
Yellowstone National Park 210 C b
Yellowstone River 210 D a
Yelnia 153 O g
Yemamah, el
Yemen, reg. 170 F g
Yenikale 164 F a
Yenisei River
Yeniseisk 171 K c
Yeni Shehr, quarter in Constantinople 93 G e
Yeovil 127 W p
Yeu, isl. 84 B f
Yezd
Yezo, isl. 171 P d
Yildiz Kiosk 93 G e
Ylst 117 D b
Yokohama 171 P e
Yola 174 E d
Yonkers 192 E c
Yonne, dept. 148 E e
Yonne River 62 B e
York (Toronto), in Canada 194 D b
York, in England
York, abp. 97 N g
York, castle 65 F d
York, cty.
York, Hanse. for. cy. 98 ins. A
York, in New Hampshire 189 C c
York, in Pa. 208 ins.
York, in Western Australia 172 A d
York, Cape 172 D b
York, Fort, in Sumatra 136 O e
York, Vale of 49 F d
York County 193 ins. A
York Factory, post 212 F c
York River 193 ins. A
York Town (Yorktown) 193 ins. A
York Wolds, dist. 49 F d
Yorkist estates 84
Yorkshire Coalfield 162 E d
Yosemite Valley 210 A c
Yoshino
Youghal
Youghiogheny River 192 B c
Ypres 117 A d
Ypres, Hanse. for. cy. 99 ins. B
Yssel River 117 E b
Ysselstein 117 C b
Yucatan, pen. 105 C c
Yucatan, state 213 D b
Yucatan Strait 187 K f
Yukon, ter. 212 B b
Yukon River 186 D b
Yuma 210 C d
Yuma, Ind. Res. 188 C d
Yumas, tribe 188 D d
Yü-mon-kwan, pass 92 J c
Yun-nan, prov. 171 K f
Yun-nan, reg. 92 J e
Yun-nan-fu 171 L f
Yungay 214 B c
Yung-ning, in Kwang-si 171 M f
Yung-ning-fu, in Yun-nan
Yung-ting 170 ins. A
Yuste, mon., see San Gerónimo de Yuste
Yverdon 91 O l
Yvetot 126 B b
Yvoix 117 D e

Zaandam 122 C b
Zabatus River 20 J d
Zabeda 6 E a
Zabern 114 D d

Zabern, castle . . . 62 D d
Zacatecas . . . 213 B b
Zacatecas, state . . . 213 B b
Zacatula . . . 213 ins.
Zacharias, Tomb of . . . 68 ins. B
Zacynthus, in Greece . . . 14 A b
Zacynthus, isl. . . . 14 A b
Zacynthus, in Spain . . . 12 C c
Zadracarta . . . 19 H c
Zafa, reg. . . .
Zafra . . . 82 A b
Zagazig . . . 174 J i
Zagrab . . .
Zahara . . . 83 J h
Zähringen, castle . . . 142 A d
Zaitun (Tsuen-chau-fu) . . .
Zalaca . . . 82 A b
Zalmon Mountains . . . 6 F c
Zama regia . . . 38 D e
Zamboanga . . . 199 ins. H
Zambesi River . . . 175 G f
Zamora, in Mexico . . . 213 ins.
Zamora, in Spain . . . 82 A a
Zamora, bp. . . . 94 A c
Zamosc . . . 139 B e
Zampa, reg. . . .
Zancle (Messina) . . . 30 E d
Zandvliet . . . 117 C c
Zane's Trace, road . . . 196 ins. B
Zanesville . . . 196 C c
Zante, isl. . . . 89 H g
Zanzibar . . . 175 H e
Zanzibar, isl. . . . 175 H e
Zaporogian Cossacks . . . 139 D f
Zara . . . 90 E b
Zara, abp. . . . 95 E c
Zaradrus River . . . 19 L d
Zarax . . . 15 D c
Zarax, mt. . . . 15 D c
Zardandan, reg. . . .
Zarephath (Sarepta) . . . 6 C b
Zaretra . . . 11 F d
Zariaspa . . . 19 K c
Zarnow . . . 123 K c
Zea Port . . . 16 D c
Zealand Island . . . 154 F a
Zealand, New, col. . . . 172 F d
Zebid . . .
Zebulon, Plain of . . . 6 C c
Zebulon, tribe . . . 7 ins. D
Zeeland, cty. . . . 117 B c
Zeeland, dist. . . . 78 C c
Zehdenick, mon. . . . 80 ins.
Zehngerichtebund (League of Ten Jurisdictions), dist. . . . 91 R l
Zeil, castle . . . 143 I j
Zeila . . . 109 V g
Zeirids, people . . . 66 H f
Zeithain . . . 135 G c
Zeitz . . . 63 G c
Zeitz, march . . . 63 G c
Zela . . . 20 F b
Zelea . . .
Zell, on the Harmersbach, imp. cy. . . . 142 B d
Zell, on the Moselle R. . . . 142 ins. A
Zell, on the Wiese R. . . . 142 A e
Zell, on the Ziller R. . . . 154 G e
Zemaun Shah, Dom. of . . .
Zengg . . . 72 D c
Zengg, bp. . . . 95 F b
Zengid Atabeks, people . . . 71 O f
Zenobia . . . 20 H e
Zenta . . . 131 G d
Zephyrium, prom. . . . 31 F d
Zerbst . . . 63 G c
Zerdan . . . 68 C b
Zerenj . . .
Zermatt . . . 91 P l
Zeugitana, reg. . . . 38 D e
Zeugma . . . 20 G d
Zeus, Altar of . . .
Zeus, Temple of . . .
Zeus Soter, Temple of . . . 16 D c (1)
Zevenaar . . . 117 E c
Zhagubitza . . .
Zianids, dynasty . . . 77 E e
Zichi, or Zichians, people . . . 35 L e
Zichia, reg. . . . 99 K e
Zidon . . . 6 C a
Zierikzee . . . 78 C c
Zierikzee, Hanse. cy. . . . 99 ins. B
Zigana . . . 20 H b
Zilis . . . 12 B c
Ziller Tal, valley in Tyrol . . . 114 F e
Zillerthal, in Silesia . . . 159 H c
Zinder . . . 174 D c
Zinjar . . .
Zinna, mon. . . . 80 ins.
Zion, cy., see Jerusalem
Zion, Gate of . . . 68 ins. B
Zion, mt. . . . 68 ins. B
Zion, quarter in Jerusalem . . . 6 ins. A
Ziph . . . 7 C f
Zips, dist. . . . 80 G g
Ziskaberg, mt. . . . 87 J c
Zitácuaro . . . 213 ins.
Zittau, in Bohemia . . . 79 I c
Zittau, in Lusatia . . . 115 H c
Zituni . . . 89 H g
Znaym . . .
Zoar . . . 7 C f
Zollern, castle . . . 62 E d
Zollern, cty. . . . 86 G d
Zollverein, German, (Customs-Union) . . . 160 D c
Zolyom . . .
Zombor . . . 159 J f
Zor (Tyre) . . . 6 C b
Zorah . . . 7 B e
Zorndorf . . . 135 H b
Zoroa . . . 6 E c
Zoster, prom. . . . 15 D b
Zschillen, mon. . . . 80 ins.
Zsibo . . . 159 L e
Zsibo Pass . . . 129 H c
Zug . . . 91 Q k
Zug, canton . . . 91 Q k
Zug, lake . . . 91 Q k
Zuider Zee, bay . . . 117 D b
Züllichau . . . 123 H b
Zülpich . . . 62 D c
Zultepec . . . 106 B a
Zululand, reg. . . . 175 N l
Zumpango . . . 106 A a
Zumpango, lake of . . . 106 A a
Zungaria, reg. . . .
Zungeru . . . 174 D d
Zuñi . . . 190 D d
Zuñis, tribe . . . 188 E c
Zurich . . . 91 Q k
Zurich, canton . . . 91 Q k
Zurich, lake of . . . 91 Q k
Zurich, mon. . . . 95 D b
Zurichgau, dist. . . . 62 E e
Zurita . . . 82 H e
Zusmarshausen . . . 122 F d
Zutfen, Hanse. cy. . . . 99 ins. B
Zutphen . . . 117 E b
Zutphen, cty. . . . 117 E b
Zwaanendael . . . 192 D d
Zweibrücken . . . 86 F d
Zweibrücken, princ. . . . 134 D d
Zwettl, mon. . . . 95 F b
Zwickau . . . 85 G e
Zwiefalten, ab . . . 143 H i
Zwiefalten, mon. . . . 143 H i
Zwingenberg . . . 142 C a
Zwinguri, Fort . . . 91 Q l
Zwittau . . . 168 E b
Zwolle . . . 117 E b
Zwolle, Hanse. cy. . . . 99 ins. B
Zwornik . . . 119 H e

INDEX-SUPPLEMENT

Aalst (Alost) 86 D c
Aarhus 88 D c
Abadeh 168K F c
Abash, reg. 104B D f
Abbadan, isl. 168K E d
Abdon 6 C b
Abel ha Sittim 7 D e
Abel Mehola 7 D d
Abercorn, bp. 60 C b
Aberdeen 128 F c
Aberdeen, cty. 128 F c
Aberffraw 60 G c
Abergavenny 74 J h
Aberystwith 74 J g
Abitibi, lake 191 I b
Abitibi River 191 I a
Abitibis, Fort des 191 J b
Abkhasia, auton. rep. 168G M/N g
Abrettene, reg. 9 F e
Abrittus 39 N l
Abrushum, R. 168K G b
Abulliond Geul 168J A a
Abus Aestuarium 51 Q h
Abusir, Pyramids of 4 ins.
Abydus 9 D d
Academy of Science, bldg. in Athens 23 D
Academy Street, in Athens 23 D
Acarnanians, people 8 N h
Accra 128C ins. D
Achaeans (Achaians), people 8 N h
Achaia, Proconsulate of 43 G f
Achilles, Burial mound of 9 A b
Achilleum 9 A b
Achonry 74 B a
Acilius, Compitum of 24 B
Acre 168J B c
Acton Burnell 74 K g
Adabazar 168J B a
Adalia, Gulf of 168J B b
Adam's Peak 137 D g
Addis Ababa 174 G d
Aden 104B E f
Ad Fines, near Florencia 27 F d
Ad Fines, near Volaterrae 26 E d
Adida 7 B e
Adonis River 6 D a
Adramyttium 9 D e
Adramyttium, Gulf of 9 D e
Adranos River 168J A b
Adyge Cherkises, auton. area 168F leg.
Adyge Cherkises, people 168J C a
Aegaei Mountains 14 ins.
Aegospotami River 9 D d
Aegusae Islands 30 B d
Aena 7 D g
Aenianians, people 8 N h
Aenus 9 D d
Aeolians, people 14 leg.
Aerarium, bldg. in Rome 24 A (15)
Aesepus River 9 E e
Aethiopia, reg., Egyptian emp. 4 F d
Aetolians, people 8 N h
Afghan Dominions 137 A b
Afiun Karahissar 164 E c
Afrau 174 Q n
Africa, Proconsulate of 42 D f
African Sea 29 B f
Afso 174 Q n
Agdir, reg. 45 F a
Agora (Lysimachia) 9 D d
Agrae Hills 23 D
Agreda 83 K g
Agrianes River 9 D c
Aguas Blancas 216 ins.
Aguatulco 107 E d
Agylla 27 G f
Ahaggar, reg. 174 D b
Ahaus 78 E b
Ahram 168K F d
Aianteum 9 B a
Aigues-Mortes 102 G g
Ain-Aicha 174 P n
Ain-Defali 174 P n
Ain-Tab 168J C b
Airds Moss 128 D e
Aire River, in France 104A C c
Airobol 165 E c
Aisma 168L D c
Ajax, Burial mound of 9 B b
Ajdir 174 Q n
Ajlun 168J C c
Ajudia 128C N e
Akershuus (Christiania) 88 D b
Akhsi 104B H c
Ak Mechet 168G L f
Akrabatta 7 C d
Akshi-Kioi 9 B b
Ak-su 104B I c
Ala 154 F f
Ala Kul 104B I c
Alans, people in Russia 45 M d
Alashia (Cyprus) 4 F c
Alba Julia (Karlsburg) 159 L e
Albanians, people, about 900 57 G-H e
Albanians, people, in 1929 168H E d
Albarracin Mountains 82 B a
Albreda 136 I d (A.)
Alcacer-el-Kebir 174 O n
Alcimus, prom. 16 D c
Alclyde 60 B b
Alcoraz 82 H e
Aldan River 104C M b
Aldborough (Isurium) 51 P g
Aleppo (Haleb) 68 C b
Alesund 181B B a
Alexander's Port 19 K f
Alexandria Troas 9 D e
Alexandropol (Leninakan) 168J D a
Alexandrovsk (Caspian sea) 168G P g
Alford 128 F c
Alhucemas Bay 174 Q n
Aller 60 H d
Alma Ata (Verni) 170 I d
Almenara 83 K h
Almonacid 153 D c
Almoravids, Dom. of the 66 E g
Alnwick 74 L d
Alopeconnesus 9 D d
Alpis Iulia 27 I b
Altai Mountains 104B I c
Altenberg (in Saxony) 87 I c
Altendorf (Stará Ves) 79 L d
Altis, loc. in Olympia 9 H f
Altkirch 91 P k
Alto Adige, reg. 168H ins.
Altsohl (Svolen) 79 K d
Alt-Zella, mon. 85 G e
Alula 182G G f
Amadia 168J D b
Amalion, bldg. in Athens 23 D
Amance 104A D c
Amara 168K E c
Amardus (Kizil Uzen) River 44 G c
Ambly 104A C b
Amboina, isl. 128C ins. C.
Ambrones 38 D a
Amecameca 106 B a
Amerongen 168D B c
Amjhera 104B R i
Ammon, dist. 7 D e
Amol, on Caspian Sea 104B F d
Amol, on the Amu-Daria R. 104B G d
Amor, dist. 4 F c
Amoun Derness, dist. 60 H c
Ampelus, in Crete 14 ins.
Amphipyrgos, prom. 10 B c
Amsterdam, isl. 128C M g
Amsterdam (Carmentine) 128C ins. D
Amu-Daria River 104B G d
Amur River 104C M b
Anaforta 168L D c
Anapa 139 E g
Anavio 51 P h
Anchedive Island 104B R j
Anchialus 39 N l
Ancient Prytaneum, in Athens 23 D (10)
Ancient Wall of Athens 23 D
Ancyle, deme 23 D
Andaman (Angaman) Islands 104C J f
Andaraba 104B G d
Andijan 104B H c
Angaman (Andaman) Islands 104C J f
Angara River 104C K b
Anglo-Norman Colonies & Earldoms 70 E c
Anglo-Saxons, people, about 900 57 C c
Angus, dist. 128 F d
Anim 7 C f
Annaghdown, bp. 97 B c
Annam 171 L g
Annan 128 E f
Annandale, dist 128 E e
Annopol 103 O c
Año Nuevo 181 U l
Anshan, dist. 4 G c
Antakia (Antioch) 168J C b
Antandrus 9 D e
Antioch, princ. in 1265 89 E c
Antofagasta, prov. 216 ins.
Antoninus and Faustina, Temple of 24 B (22)
Anzac Cove 168L D c
Apán 106 B a
Aphek, near Gebal 6 D a
Aphek, near Joppa 7 B d
Aphnitis Lake 9 E d
Aphrodisias 9 D d
Aphroditopolis 4 F d
Apollonia, in Cyrenaica 35 I g
Apollonia, in Guinea 128C ins. D
Apollonia, in Mysia 9 F d
Apollo Patroos, in Athens 23 D (5)
Apremont 104A C b
Apremont-Dun, seign. 104A C b
Apsinthii, people 9 D d
Aptera 14 ins.
Apuli, people 29 D d
Aquae, in Britain 51 P h

Aquae Flaviae 38 A d
Aquae Tarbellicae 38 B d
Aqueduct of Hadrian, in Athens 23 D
Aqueduct of Pisistratus, in Athens 23 D
Arabian Sea 104 B G f
Arabia Sebba, reg. 104 B E f
Arabistan, reg. 168 K E c
Arabs, people 168 L K i
Aracan, reg. 171 K e-f
Aragon, march 45 D d (Ar)
Aragon River 82 B a
Aramatha 6 E c
Aramu, people 4 F c
Aranjuez 130 C e
Ararat, mt. 168 J D b
Aras River 139 G h
Arbedo 86 G e
Arbela (Beth Arbeel) 6 D c
Arbil 99 L f
Arbocala 38 A d
Arcadians, people 8 N i
Arcadians, people 14 leg.
Archelais, in Palestine 7 C e
Archelaus, Dominions of 7
Arches, near Épinal 104 A D c
Arcis-sur-Aube 104 A B c
Arctonnesus, isl. 9 E d
Arda, R. 168 L E f
Ardabil 139 G h
Ardahan 139 F g
Ardasa 168 J C a
Ardstraw 74 C a
Arganthonius, mt. 9 F d
Argennum, prom. 9 D e
Argentaria 39 I i
Argentorate (Strasburg) 39 I i
Arghana Maden 168 J D b
Argob, reg. 6 D c
Argonne Forest 168 C C c
Arguin, isl. 128 B H d
Argyll and Tarbet, cty. 128 C d
Aribi, people 5 C b
Arica, reg. 216 ins.
Arisba, in Lesbos 9 D e
Arisbe, in Troas 9 D d
Arklow 74 C b
Arlberg Pass 87 H e
Armagaon 128 B ins. B
Armagh 74 C a
Armalec 104 B I c
Armenia, auton. rep. 168 G N-O g
Armenia, Lesser, km., in 1265 89 D c
Armenia, Lesser, km., in 1355 89 J g
Armenian Christians 168 L leg.
Armenians, people 168 L L h
Ar Moab 7 D f
Aror 53 I d
Arpad (Tel-Erfâd) 4 F c
Arran, isl. 128 C e
Arrancy 104 A C b
Arrö, isl. 87 H a
Arsakion, bldg. in Athens 23 D
Arsila 174 O n
Artace 9 E d
Artemea 9 E d
Artynia Lake 9 F d
Arve River, in Savoy 91 O l
Arx, in Munychia 16 D c
Ascalon 7 B e
Ascania Lake 9 G d
Asch 79 H c
Ashburton 74 J i
Ashdown 60 I d
Ashdown, dist. 60 D d
Asia, Proconsulate of 43 H f
Asia, Rom. prov. under Trajan 20 C c (I)
Asiago 168 H ins.
Askabad 104 B F d
Asmak River 9 B b
Asolo near Feltre 87 H f
Aspara 104 B H c
Aspinwall (Colón) 214 A b
Assiniboine River 190 E a
Assus 9 D e
Assyrian Empire 5
Assyrian trade-routes 44 leg.
Astacus, in Bithynia 9 G d
Astacus, Bay of 9 G d
Astae, people 9 F c
Astaroth 6 E c
Astrabad 104 B F d
Astrabad, reg. 139 H h
Astyra 9 D e
Åsunden, lake 88 E c
Atalaya 106 C a
Atarneus 9 D e
Athena Street, in Athens 23 D
Athene, Altar of 23 C
Athene Hygiaea, in Athens 23 C (4)
Athenry 74 B b
Athlone 74 C b
Atholl, dist. 128 E d
Athyras River 9 F c
Atrek River 139 I h
Augustobriga 38 A e
Augustus, Arch of 24 B (18)
Auldearn 128 E c
Aulon, str., on Andros I. 15 E b
Auschwitz (Oswiecim) 87 L c
Aust 60 C d
Austeravia, isl. 38 D b
Austerfield 60 D c
Austria, rep. 168 F H-I f
Ava 104 C J e
Ava, reg. 104 C J e
Avaris 4 ins.
Avars, people, in Hungary 45 H c
Avars, people, on the Don R. 45 M c
Avignon, abp. 94 C c (A.)
Avioth 104 A C b (Av.)
Avon River 60 D c
Awanui 179 I k
Awarua 179 H l
Axbridge 60 H d
Axim 128 C ins. D
Axos (Oaxus) 14 ins.
Ayana, reg. 109 V g
Aylesborough = Aylesb. 60 D d
Ayotzingo 106 B a
Ayr 128 D e
Ayr River 128 D e
Ayyub, Mosque of 93 G e
Ayyub, quarter 93 G e
Azcopatzalco 106 A a
Azerbaijan, auton. rep. 168 G O g
Azerbaijan, reg. 67 P f
Aziziyah 168 J A b
Azjer 168 K F d

Baal Hazor 7 C e
Baal Meon 7 D e
Baal Salisa 7 C d
Baba Eski 168 L F f
Babilu (Babylon) 4 G c
Babylon (Cairo) 99 J h
Babylonian trade-routes 44 leg.
Bacanore 104 B R j
Baccanae 35 ins. B
Bacharach 102 H c
Bactrus River 19 K c
Badakshan, reg. 104 B H d
Badenoch, dist. 128 D c
Bafk 168 K G c
Baghché 168 J C b
Bagistana (Behistun) 5 D b
Bahrein, isl. 104 B F e
Baikal, lake 104 C K b
Bairnsdale 172 D d
Baither 7 C e
Bakchiserai 139 D g
Bakewell 60 I c
Bakhtegan (Niriz), lake 168 K F d
Bakkar 104 B G e
Baku, Sea of 99 N f
Balasore 137 E d
Balaton, lake (Platten-See) 87 K e
Balga, castle 87 M a
Balkash, lake 104 B H c
Balkh 104 B G d
Ballarat 172 D d
Ballyk 9 B b
Bam 168 K G d
Bambilonia (Cairo) 99 J h
Bamborough 60 D b
Bamian 104 B G d
Bampur 168 K H d
Banana 182 CC h
Banda Islands 104 C M h
Banff, cty. 128 E c
Bangor, in Wales 60 G c
Banjaluka (Banialuka) 159 I f
Banjarmasin, reg. 104 C L h
Bankot 137 B e
Bannaventa 51 P h
Baňská Bystrica (Neusohl) 103 N d
Baňská Štiavnica (Schemnitz) 103 N d
Bar (Antivari) abp. 95 F c
Baramahal, reg. 137 C f
Barberini, Palazzo, bldg. in Rome 22 A
Barcelona, march 45 E d (B)
Barchin 104 B G c
Barda'a 99 M f
Bardney, abbey 74 M f
Bardo, in Posen 159 J b
Bardo, in Tunis 174 E a
Bardonis, mt. 26 D c
Barfurush 168 K F b
Bargu, reg. 104 C L b
Bar Harbor 181 U c
Barkhalikend 104 B H c
Barkul 104 C J c
Baroch 104 B R i
Barra, isl. (Calabria) 31 H b
Barra, isl. (Hebrides) 128 A c
Barrow-in-Furness 162 C c
Baselus (Besor) River 7 B f
Bashkir, auton. rep. 168 G Q e
Bashmakli 168 L E f
Basileus, Stoa 23 D (3)
Basilica Argentaria, bldg. in Rome 24 A
Basilica Fulvia, bldg. in Rome 24 A
Basilica Opimia, bldg. in Rome 24 A (6)
Basilica Porcia, bldg. in Rome 24 A (5)
Basing 60 I d
Bassae 14 B b
Batanga, Great- 174 E d
Batavia 128 C N f
Bateia 9 B b
Batel 174 Q n
Bath, in England 60 H d
Battas, people 104 C J g
Battle, abbey 74 N i
Batum 139 F g
Bauchi 174 E c
Bauske 88 K c
Bayazid 168 J D b
Beaufort, near Stenay 104 A C b
Beaumont, near Sedan 158 D d
Beaumont-en-Argonne 104 A B b
Beaune-la-Rolande 158 B d
Bedford, in England 60 I c
Bedmar 83 K h
Bedr 53 F d
Bedwin (Bedwyn) 74 L h
Bedwyn (Bedwin), Great-, parl. bor. 163 M f
Beer Elim 7 D e
Behistun (Bagistana) 5 D b
Beibahan 168 K F c
Belbeis 150 B a

Belleau Wood 168 C B c
Bellefontaine 104 A C b
Bellenz (Bellinzona) 91 R l
Benbecula, isl. 128 A c
Bencoolen (Benkulen) 104 C K h
Benešov (Beneschau) 135 H d
Benevento, march 45 H d (Be)
Benfleet 60 J d
Bengala, reg. 104 B I e
Benjamin Constant 181 U h
Bennamarim 7 D f
Bensington 60 D d
Beograd (Belgrade) 89 B b
Berar, prov., 18 cent. 137 D d
Beraun River 135 G d
Berbice 128 B ins. A
Bere, castle 74 J g
Bere Alston. parl. bor. 163 J g (B.A.)
Bereku 128 C ins. D
Berenice, in Egypt 4 F d
Berga, in Macedonia 11 E b
Bergreichenstein 103 K d
Bergulae 9 E c
Berkeley, castle 74 K h
Berlin, Treaty of 168 L leg.
Bermudas, isl. 128 B E d
Bernau 103 K b
Bernicia, dist. 60 C b
Berwick 128 G e
Berwick, cty. 128 F e
Besace, La- 104 A B b (L.B.)
Besbicus, isl. 9 F d
Besika Bay 9 A b
Besika Tepe 9 A b
Besztercze (Bistritz) 159 M e
Beszterczebanya (Neusohl) 159 J d
Beth Anoth 7 C e
Beth Arbeel 6 D c
Beth Emek 6 C c
Beth Gamul 7 D f
Beth Garma 99 L f
Beth Hagla 7 C e
Beth Maacha 6 D b
Bethramphtha 7 D e
Beth Rehob 6 D b
Beth Thappuah 7 C e
Betifuli 27 H f
Beuthen, castle, in Brandenburg 85 C b
Beyshehr 168 J B b
Bezek 7 C d
Bharatpur (Bhurtpore) 137 C c
Biana 104 B H e
Bias River 14 B c
Bidar 104 B R j
Biel 91 P k
Bielaia River 99 O c
Bielostok (Bialystok) 168 G J e
Bielsko (Bielitz) 155 J d
Bièvres 104 A C b (Bi.)
Bihach (Bihač) 87 J f
Bilin 82 J c
Bilin, castle 79 H c
Bilma, reg. 174 E c
Bima, isl. 128 C ins. C
Bimlipatam 104 B S j
Birjan 168 K G c
Birkenhead 162 C d
Birket el Karun (Qurun), lake 174 J j
Birmingport 181 S d
Birze 138 B d
Bisanthe 9 E c
Bishbalk (Urumtsi) 104 B I c
Bissao 181 Z f
Bistonis Lake 9 C c
Bistriţa (Bistritz) 159 M e
Bithynia and Pontus, Rom. prov. 20 D b (II)
Bitolj (Monastir) 165 B c
Bit-Yakin, reg. 5 D b
Blackpool 162 C d
Black Sea Basin 168 J B b
Blackwater River, in Ireland 74 B b
Blagny 104 A C b
Blagoveschensk 171 N c
Blair Atholl 128 E d
Blancheville 104 A C c
Blatobulgium 51 O g
Bleiberg 103 K e
Blemmyes, people 4 F d
Bletchingley 74 M h
Bne Barak 7 B d
Boa Vista do Rio Branco 181 U g
Bocca do Acre 181 U h
Bochum 168 E E b
Bodensee (Lake of Constance) 103 I e
Bodmin 74 I i
Boeotians, people 14 leg.
Boer Republics, the 175 N m
Boghaz-koi 4 F c
Bogou, reg. 174 C c
Bohun, dist. 74 J h
Bokhara 104 B G d
Bolerium, prom. 38 A b
Bolinas 180 O d
Bolingbroke 74 M f
Bolzano (Bozen) 103 J e
Bomba 174 F a
Bonin Islands 171 P f
Borgholm 88 G c
Borgo (di Valsugana) 168 H ins.
Borissow 153 N g
Bosham 60 I d
Bosnia, reg. 56 F d
Bosra 168 J C c
Botanical Garden, in Athens 23 D
Bothwell 128 E e
Boulevard des Italiens, in Paris 149 B
Bourbon, isl. 128 C K g
Bourdon 104 A C c
Bouresches 184 ins.
Bourgneuf, Bay of 102 C e
Bournemouth 162 E g
Bovianum vetus 30 D a
Bozanti 168 J B b
Brabant, duchy, 13 cent. 104 A B a
Bradford, battle 60 C d
Brahmanabad 53 I d
Brancepeth 74 L e
Branchidarum, Oppidum 19 K c
Bränkyrka 88 G b
Braşov, Brassó (Kronstadt) 159 M f
Bratislava (Presburg) 103 M d
Bravonium 51 O h
Brazhimov 71 P b
Breadalbane, dist. 128 D d
Brechin 128 F d
Brecknock, dist. 60 C c
Brecon 74 J h
Bremenium 51 O g
Bremetennacum 51 O h
Bressanone (Brixen) 168 H ins.
Brest-Kujawsk 88 H e
Brest-Litowsk 155 L b
Breux 104 A C b (Br.)
Briantica, reg. 13 D a
Bribiesca 83 K g
Bridport, English bor. 60 H d
Briey 168 E A c
Brigantes, people in England 51 O g
Brigobanne 39 J j
British North Borneo, col. 171 L h
Brixen (Bressanone) 168 H ins.
Brixillum 26 E c
Brno (Brünn) 87 K d
Brocavum 51 O g
Brocomagus 39 I i
Broumov (Braunau, in Bohemia) 135 I c
Brunanburh 60 H b
Bruneck (Brunico) 168 H ins.
Bruntál = Freudental 72 D b
Bruttii, people 29 E e
Bruyères, near Épinal 104 A D c
Bryges, people 10 C b
Brzesc (Brest Kujawsk) 135 J b
Brześć (Brest-Litowsk) 159 L b
Buccaneers, headquaters of the 128 B ins A
Buchan, dist. 128 F c
Buckingham, English bor. 60 I d
Budějovice (Budweis) 87 J d
Budorum, pen. 16 A b
Budva (Budua), bp. 95 F c
Buenos Aires 215 D f
Buenos Aires, audiencia 215 ins.
Buenos Aires, viceroyalty 215 ins.
Builth 74 J g
Bukharest, Treaty of 168 L leg.
Bulair (Playari) 168 L D c
Buleuterium, in Athens 23 D (8)
Buleuterium, in Olympia 9 H f (1)
Bulgaria, Khanate of 55 I e
Bulgaria, km. in 1929 168 G J-K g
Bulgarians, people, about 500 57 I d
Bulgarians, people in 1929 168 H F-G d; G c
Bulgars, people on the Upper Volga 59 N b
Bulgurlu 168 J B b
Bunarbashi 9 B b
Bunarbashi Brook, canal 9 A b
Bungay, castle 74 O g
Burdur 168 J B b
Burgas 168 L F e
Burgas, Gulf of 168 L F e
Burgenland, prov. 168 D D d
Burhanpur 128 B ins. B
Burma, reg. 104 C J e
Burtas, people 59 M c
Buryato Mongolia, Autonomous Socialist Soviet Republic 171 L c
Bury Saint Edmunds (Venta Icenorum) 51 Q h
Bury Saint Edmunds, abbey 74 N g
Bute, cty. 128 C e
Butifilis 104 B S j
Butler, fam. 74 C b
Butuntum 31 F a
Bydgoszcz (Bromberg) 87 K b
Byzantium 9 F c
Byzdry (Peisern) 79 J b
Cabyle 39 N l
Caconda 128 C I f
Caeni, people 9 D c
Caerleon, castle 74 J h
Caerphilly, castle 74 J h
Caesao 26 A c
Caesar, Statue of 24 B (23)
Café Corazza, in Paris 149 B
Cahul 139 C f
Caicus River 9 E e
Cailac 92 H c
Cairo, Calif. of 66 H g; 67 K h
Caistor (St. Edmund) 51 Q h
Caithness, dist. 128 E b
Calchedon 9 G d
Caledonia, reg. 128 B ins. A
Caledonia Bay 128 B ins. A (C. B.)
Caleta Buena 216 ins.
Caleta Colosa 216 ins.
Caleta Patillos 216 ins.
Caleti, people 38 C c
Calgary (Fort La Jonquière) 190 C a
Califate, The, emp. about 750 53
Calleva Atrebatum (Silchester) 51 P i
Calliupolis 9 D d
Calmar, Union of 77 leg.
Calpán, Ranchos de 106 B a
Calven, Pass 91 S l
Calydnae Islands 9 A b

Camanu, reg. 5 C b
Cambalec (Peking) 104 C L d
Cambambe, reg. 128 C I f
Cambodia, reg. 104 C K f
Cambrai (Cambray) 62 B c
Cambridge, in England 60 J c
Camerons, fam. 128 C d
Campbells, fam. 128 C d
Campo Formio 153 G c
Campo Militare, loc. in Rome 22 A
Camulodunum (Colchester) 51 Q i
Canary Islands 128 B H d
Canbalec (Peking) 103 L d
Canberra 172 D d
Candia 168 J A b
Cannes 157 B d
Canovium 51 O h
Cansay 92 M d
Canterbury, in England (Durovernum 51 Q i
Canterbury, bp. 60 E d
Cantigny 168 C B c
Cantwara, people 51 S k
Cape Breton Island 212 I d
Cape Cod 181 U c
Cape Three Points 128 C ins. D
Caporetto 168 B F b
Cappadocia, Rom. prov. under Trajan 20 G c (IV)
Capuchins, The, ch. in Paris 149 B
Capuchins, The, mon. 149 B
Caracarum (Karakorum) 104 C K c
Carbisdale 128 D c
Carcer (Prison), in Rome 24 A (4)
Cardia 9 D d
Cardiff, castle 74 J h
Cardigan, dist. 60 G c
Carduniash, reg. 5 D b
Caresus River 9 E d
Carians, people 8 Q i
Carian Tributary 13 K f (IV)
Carlisle, in England 60 C b
Carlow 74 C b
Carmarthen, castle 74 I h
Carmelites, The, mon. in Paris 149 B
Carmentine 128 C ins. D
Carnarvon, castle 74 I f
Carpintería 216 G i
Carrick, dist. 128 D e
Carrion River 83 E c
Carthaginian trade-routes 44 leg.
Cascaes 83 J h
Casimirs (Kazimierz) 103 O c
Cassaba 168 J A b
Castellorizzo, isl. 168 J A b
Castel Sant' Elmo 153 G d
Castilla 216 ins.
Castlekevin 74 C b
Castleroe 74 C a
Castor and Pollux, Temple of 24 A (21)
Catalauni 38 C c
Cataonia, reg. 20 F d
Cathedral (Metropolitan Church), in Athens 23 D
Catterick, mon. 60 D b
Caucasian Gates, Pass 18 F b
Caucasian peoples 168 L L g
Cauvery River 137 C f
Cavour, Piazza, loc. in Rome 22 A
Cavour, Ponte, loc. in Rome 22 A
Cavour, Via, street in Rome 22 A
Caystrus 20 D c
Céa River 83 D c
Cebrene 9 D e
Cecryphalea, isl. 15 D b
Cedrius, mt. 14 ins.
Celestins, The, mon. in Paris 149 B
Celje (Cilli) 159 H e
Celtae, people 29 C a
B b
Celts, people, about 900 57 B d/c
Cembalo 99 J e
Cemetery, in Athens 23 D
Central Australia, state 172 C c
Central Black Earth, economic reg. 168 F leg
Central Industrial, economic reg. 168 F leg.
Cephisia Street, in Athens 23 D
Ceramus 13 K f
Cerata, mt. 16 A a
Ceraunii Mountains, in Epirus 17 A a
Ceraunii Mountains, in Italy 27 H e
Ceres, Temple of, in Athens 23 D
Ceressus 11 E d
Ceriadac, deme 23 D
Cernauţi (Czernowitz) 168 G K f
Česká Skalice (Skalitz) 159 I c
České Budějovice (Budweis) 103 L c
Cetinje 165 A b
Ceuta 174 P n
Chagatai, Khanate of 92 leg.
Chahar, reg. 171 M d
Chalcedon 9 G d
Chalco, lake 106 B a
Chaldea, in the Middle Ages 99 M g
Chaldeans, people 168 L L h
Chalish (Karashar) 104 C I c
Chalti 168 J A b
Chalybon 20 G d
Chamonix 91 O m
Champagne, cty., 13 cent. 104 A A c
Champe, reg. 104 C K f
Champigny 158 B d
Chanak Kale 168 L D c
Chanchalacas, R. 106 D a
Chanderi 104 B H e
Changanor 104 C L c
Changchun 179 D c
Chantraines 104 A C c
Chaones (Chaoni), people 8 M g
Chapultepec 106 A a
Charadra River 16 B a
Charax(-Spasinu) 44 F c
Charikar 104 B G d
Charkov (Kharkov) 139 E e
Charleville (Ardennes) 168 C C c
Charmouth 60 H d
Charny 104 A C b
Charshembe 168 J C a
Chatalja 168 L G f
Châtenois 104 A C c
Chatham 162 G f
Chatyn Deirmeni 9 A b
Chaul 104 B R j
Chaumont-devant-Damvillers 104 A C b
Cheb (Eger) 87 I c
Cheboksara 168 G O d
Chebreiss 150 B a
Chechen, auton. area 168 G O g (2), leg.
Chechen, isl. 168 G O g
Chelm 159 L c
Chełmno (Kulm) 135 J b
Chełmno (Kulm), bp. 95 F a
Chelmża (Kulmsee), seat of bishopric 95 F a
Chelsea 60 D d
Chemin des Dames 168 C B c
Chemmis 4 F d
Cheng-tu-fu 104 C K d
Chen-si 104 C J c
Chequamegon, Fort 191 G b
Cheragan Palace 93 G e
Cherekli 168 J B a
Cherkasy 139 D f
Chernigov 71 M c
Chernoi-Yar 139 G f
Cherso, isl. 161 J e
Chersonesus, in Crete 14 ins.
Chertsey, mon 60 D d
Chesme 165 E d
Chester, battle 60 C c
Chester, castle 60 H c
Chester, County Palatine of 74 K f
Chester, Palatine Earldom of 65 E d
Chichester, Engl. bor. 60 I d
Chico Viejo 106 D a
Chigrin 139 D f
Chilen-fu 104 C L d
Chillaw 104 B R k
Chilternsaete, people 60 D d
Chimkent 170 H d
Chin, Sea of 104 C M e
China, Republic of 171 J M e
Chintabor (Goa) 104 B R j
Chiny 104 A C b
Chiny, cty. 104 A C b
Chipangu, emp. (Japan) 104 C O d
Chippenham 60 H d
Chirbury 60 H c
Chisholms, fam. 128 C c
Chisinau (Kishinev) 168 G K f
Chitor 92 H e
Chivril 168 J A b
Chocim 139 C f
Chojnice (Konitz) 135 I b
Chomutov (Komotau) 87 I c
Chorillos 216 F g
Chorlu 168 L F f
Chorum 168 J B a
Choshi 179 E d
Christchurch, parl. bor. 163 M g (Chr.)
Christiania (Akershuus) 88 D b
Christiansborg 128 C ins. D
Chrysopolis 9 G c
Chuguiev 139 E f
Chullu 44 B c
Churche, people 92 M c
Chu River 104 B G c
Chuvash, auton. rep. 168 G O d
Ciando (Shangtu) 104 C L c
Cibalae 39 F c
Cicones, people 9 C c
Cieszyn (Teschen) 159 J d
Cilicia, Rom. prov. under Trajan 20 F d (VI)
Cilician and Syrian Gates, pass 20 G d
Cilician Gates, pass 20 F d
Cilli, County of 87 J c
Cimbri, people 38 D a
Cimmerians, people 5 C a
Cimolus 15 E c
Circassia, reg. 164 F b
Cius 9 G d
Cius, Bay of 9 F d
Clackmannan, cty. 128 E d
Clanoventa 51 O g
Clare, dist. in Wales 74 J h
Clausentum (Southampton) 51 P i
Claverhouse 128 F d
Cleon, Wall of, in Athens 23 D
Cleveland, dist. in England 60 I b
Cleven (Chiavenna) 91 R l
Clitheroe 74 K f
Clonmel 74 C b
Cloppenburg 78 F b
Cluj (Klausenburg) 159 L e
Clun, castle 74 K g
Cluse, La 158 D e
Clydesdale, dist. 128 E e
Clysma 4 ins.
Coatlichán 106 B a
Cobh (Queenstown) 168 F D e
Coburg (Koburg) 79 G c
Coccium 51 O h
Cockermouth, castle 74 J e
Coelaletae, people 9 C c
Coelesyria, reg. 20 G f
Coilon (Quilon) 104 B H g
Colchester (Camulodunum) 51 Q i
Colchester, abbey 74 N h
Coleroon River 137 D f
Colisée, The, bldg. in Paris 149 B
Coll, isl. 128 B d

Collaguasi 216 ins.
Collège des Quatre Nations, bldg. in Paris 149 B
Collège Mazarin, bldg. in Paris 149 B
Collioure 83 L g
Collytus, deme 23 D
Colombey 158 D d
Colonae 9 D e
Colonia do Sacramento 128B F f
Colonia Falisca 27 G e
Colonus Agoraeus, deme 23 D
Colonus Hippius, deme 23 D
Cclumbum 104B R k
Comedae, people 19 L c
Commenda 128C ins. D
Compitum of Acilius 24 B
Compludo 83 K g
Compostela, Santiago de 82 A a
Compostela, Santiago de, abp. 94 A c
Conchi 216 ins.
Conchi, Land of 92 H b
Concord, Temple of 24 A (7)
Conde, Fort (Mobile) 191 H e
Connaught, prov. 74 B b
Consabura 38 B e
Constanța (Kustenje) 165 F a
Constantine, Statue of 24 B (15)
Constantinople, Treaty of 168L leg.
Conway 74 J f
Conway River 60 G c
Cophas 19 J e
Coptos 4 F d
Corameran River 104C K c
Corbilo (Nantes) 44 A b
Corbridge 60 H b
Cordeliers, The, mon. in Paris 149 B
Cordova, in Alaska 180 M a
Coreae 7 C d
Cork 74 B c
Coron (Koroni) 89 H g
Coronel 168A F f
Corpilii, people 9 C c
Corrib, Lough, lake 127 H h
Corso d'Italia, street in Rome 22 A
Cortina (d'Ampezzo) 168H ins.
Cortona, in Etruria 27 G d
Cortona, in Spain 38 C d
Cosmin 104C J f
Côte Lorraine 168C C c
Courland, bp. 88 J c
Courons, people 57 H b
Cours de la reine, in Paris 149 B
Coventry, abbey 74 L g
Coyoacán 106 A a
Cranganur (Cranganore) 137 C f
Cravant 86 D e
Crediton 60 C d
Crediton, bp. 97 N k
Cricklade, bor. 60 H d
Crimea, auton. rep. 168G L f
Croats, people in 1929 168H E c
Cromarty 128 D c
Cromarty, cty. 128 C b
Cronos Hill 9 H f
Crowland, mon. 60 I c
Cuantitlán 106 A a
Cuiavia (Kujavia), dist. 79 K b
Culloden Moor 128 D c
Cumania, reg. 99 J d
Cumans, people, in Turkestan 53 H b
Cumberland, dist. in England 60 H b
Cumuhi (Cummuhi), reg. 5 C b
Cumukh 99 M e
Cunetio 51 P i
Cunningham, dist. 128 D e
Cunus aureus 26 D a
Cupar 128 E d
Curia Julia 24 B
Cusus River, near Brigetio 39 F c
Cusus River, near Lauriacum 39 E c
Cuyavia, reg. 87 L b
Cybistra 20 F d
Cydamus 44 C c
Cynia, lake 10 C d
Cynkali 104B R k
Cypsela 9 D d
Cyrenaica, dist. 174 F a
Cyzicus 9 E d
Czechoslovakia, rep. 168G H/J f
Częstochowa 135 J c

Dabrath 6 C c
Dagasira 19 I e
Daghestan, auton. rep. 168G O g
Dahshur, Pyramids of 4 ins.
Daibul 104B G e
Dai'am 99 N f
Dalarne (Dalecarlia), dist. 88 F a
Dalriada, dist. 60 F b
Dalwhinnie 128 D d
Damascus, Kingdom of 5 C b
Damghan 104B F d
Damme, near Bruges 102 F c
Danelagh (Danelaw), The 60 leg.
Danishmend, reg. 67 N f
Danish Mercia 60 I c
Dannaba 7 D f
Dannewerk, wall 55 Q i
Darab 168K F d
Dardania, reg. 17 B a
Dardanus 9 D d
Darien Colony 128B ins. A
Dascylium 9 F d
Daulatabad 104B R j
Dauphin, Fort 190 E a
Dawston (Degsastan) 60 C b
Deal 154 A c
Debir 7 B f
Dęblin (Ivangorod) 159 K c
Debreczén 159 K e
Decapolis, dist. 7 leg.
Děčín (Tetschen) 135 H c
De Clare, earldom 70 E c (De C.)
De Courcy, earldom 70 E c (De Co.)
Deddington, castle 74 L h
Dedeagach 164 D b
Deer 128 F c
Deerhurst 60 H d
Dee River, in Wales 60 C c
Dee River, in Kirkcudbright 128 D f
Dee River, in Aberdeen 128 F c
Degsastan (Dawston) 60 C b
Deheubarth, dist. 60 G c
Dei Consentes, Portico of the 24 B (7)
Deira, dist. 60 D b
Deir-ez-Zor 168J D b
Dej (Dees) 159 L e
De Lacy, earldom 70 E c (De L.)
Delcus 9 F c
Delhi, Empire of the Sultans of 104B H e
Deligun Buldagha 92 L b
Delta, reg. 4 F c (I)
Demonnesi Islands 9 F d
Demarchia, bldg. in Athens 23 D
Denbigh, castle 74 J f
Denisli 168J A b
Deogir, reg. 104B R i
Deorham (Dyrham) 60 C d
Derat 168J C c
Derbent 139 G g
Derby, danish borough 60 I c
Derby, cty. 74 L f
Derna 174 F a
Deshima, isl. 128C O d
Desmond, dist. 74 B c
Deutschendorf 80 G g
Develtum 39 N l
Deveron River 128 F c
Devon, dist. 60 C d
De Vries, route of 128C P c
Dhafar 104B F f
Dhar 104B R i
Dhibat al Mahal, isl. 104B H g
Diagorgan 99 M f
Diala River 168K E c
Didyma 13 E c
Dieppe, near Verdun 104A C b
Dieuze 102 H d
Dindymus, mt. near Cyzicus 9 E d
Dinefwr 60 G d
Dinhaba 7 D f
Diomea, deme 23 D
Dionysium, Lenaeum and, in Athens 23 D (12)
Dirk Hartog, isl. 128C N g
Disna 88 M d
Disna River 88 L d
Dium, prom. 14 ins.
Dividing Range, Great 172 D c
Divonum 38 C d
Divrik (Divirigi) 99 K f
Divus Julius, Temple of 24 B (17)
Divus Romulus, Temple of 24 B (21)
Dixcove 128 C ins. D
Dixmude 168C B b
Dnieper River 139 D f
Doblen 88 J c
Doboj 87 L f
Dobruja, reg. 89 C b
Dodecanesia, isl. 165 E e
Dodekaschoenos, reg 4 F d (IV)
Dofar 104B F f
Dogger Bank 168A J b (II leg.)
Doliones, people 9 E d
Doljani (Dolyani), bp 95 F c
Dolonci, people 9 D d
Domašov (Domstadtl) 135 I d
Domeyko 216 ins.
Dominion of the Hammadites 66 G g
Dominion of the Karakhitai 92 H c
Dominions of Timur 92 leg.
Dompaire 104A D c
Dondra Head 137 D g
Don River, Scotland 128 F c
Doorn 168D B c
Doornik (Tournai) 86 D c
Dorchester 74 K i
Dore 60 I c
Dorestad 45 F b
Doria, Piazza, loc. in Rome 22 A
Dorians, people 14 leg.
Doriscus 9 D d
Dornoch 128 E c
Dorpat, bp. 88 L b
Dorset, cty. 74 K i
Dosab 168K H d
Douaumont 168C C c
Douglas, in Scotland 128 E e
Dover 60 J d
Downpatrick 74 D a
Downton 74 L h
Drač = Durazzo
Drepanum, in Asia Minor 9 G d
Drewenz River 135 J b
Dregoviches, people 57 H-I c
Drevlians, people 57 I c
Drissa River 88 M d
Drogheda 74 C b
Droi, people 17 C a
Droitwich 74 K g
Drumclog 128 D e
Dubica (Dubitza) 164 B b
Dublin 60 F c
Dubrovnik (Ragusa) 89 A b
Dubrovnik (Ragusa), abp. 95 F c
Dukha, people 5 C b
Dulyebs, people 57 H c
Dumbarton 128 D e
Dumbarton, cty. 128 D d
Dumbrek, R. 9 B b
Dumfries 128 E e
Dumfries, cty. 128 E e
Dun (-sur-Meuse) 104A C b
Dunajec River 135 K d
Dunbar 128 F e
Dunblane 128 D d

Dunblane, bp. 97 J c
Dundalk 74 C b
Dundee 128 F d
Dundram, castle 74 C a
Dunfermline 128 E d
Dungarvan 74 C b
Dunkeld 128 E d
Dunnottar Castle 128 F d
Dunwich 74 O g
Dunwich, bp. 60 E c
Duos Lucos, Inter, loc. in Rome 24 A
Duressi = Durazzo
Durham, Palatinate of 74 L e
Düren 168 E B b
Dürnstein 155 H d
Durobrivae, near Lindum 51 P h
Durobrivae, near Londinium 51 Q i
Durocobrivae 51 P i
Dur-Samand, reg. 104 B R j
Dutch, people in 1929 168 H C b
Dutch East Indies, col. 179 B/E h
Duzje 168 J B a
Dvina, Gulf of 167 G M b
Dvina River 167 N c
Dwara-Samudra 104 B R j
Dyfed, dist. 60 B d
Dyrham (Deorham) 60 C d

Earn River 128 D d
East Africa, British = Kenya, col. and prot. 175 G d
East Africa, German, Brit. Mand. 175 G e
East Africa, Portuguese = Mozambique 175 G g
East Anglia, km. 60 J c
Eastbourne 162 G g
East Götland, dist. 88 F b
East-Kirghiz, economic reg. 170 leg.
East March, dist. 128 F e
East Scheldt, R. 168 C B b
East Sea 99 G b
Ebora 38 A e
Echmiadzin 139 F g
Echo Hall, in Olympia 9 H f
École Militaire, in Paris 149 B
Écuries, in Paris = 1 149 B
Eddisbury 60 H c
Edelsland, reg. 128 C N g
Edgcott 84 C c
Edinburgh 128 E e
Edinburgh, cty. 128 E e
Edington 60 H d
Edirne (Adrianople) 93 C b
Eendrachtsland, reg. 128 C N g
Eger (Erlau) 79 L e
Eger (Erlau), bp. 95 G b
Egesta 30 B e
Eggenburg 87 J d
Egherdir 168 J B b
Eglaim 7 D f
Egnatian Way 10 A a
D b
Egremont, castle 74 J e
Egrigaia 104 C K d
Egyptian Empire 4
Eichstätt 79 G d
Eichstätt, bp. 79 G d
Eiderstedt, reg. 86 G a
Eifel, mts. 168 C D b
Eigg, isl. 128 B d
Eisenerz 103 L e
Ekhmim 4 F d
Elaeus, in Thrace 9 D d
El-Arish, in Egypt 67 M g
El-Arish, in Morocco 174 O n
Elbasan 165 A c
El Caney 213 E b
(E. C.)
Elde River 134 F b
Eleans, people 8 N i
Eleutherius, Port of 93 G e
Elfsborg 88 E c
El Gezira, reg. 174 G c
Elgin 128 E c
Elgin and Forres, cty. 128 E c
El Hasa, reg. 104 B E e
Elizabetpol 139 G g
El-Jauf 168 J C c
El Kab 4 F d
El Katif 104 B E e
El Katr, reg. 168 K F d
Ellandun 60 I d
Elmedsaete, people 60 D c
Elmham 60 E c
Elmina (São Jorge da Mina) 128 B H e
Elsinore (Helsingör) 103 K a
El Toco 216 ins.
Ely, mon., in England 60 E c
Ely (Hili), in India 104 B R j
Ely, Isle of, dist. 74 N g
El Yemamah 104 B E e
Embabeh 150 B a
Emmerich 168 E B b
Empinghan 74 M g
Empire of the Great Khan 92 leg.
Empire of the Sultans of Delhi 104 B H e
Emporium, loc. in Piraeus 16 D c
Enaghdun, bp. 74 B b
English Marches, dis 74 K d
English Pale, The, dist. 74 C b
Enncakrounos, in Athens 23 D (11)
Enneapylon (Pelasgikon) in Athens 23 C
Entebbe 174 G d
Enzeli 168 G O h
Eord(ai)i, people 10 B a
Epamanduodurum 39 I j
Ephron (Ephrem) 7 C e
Epirots, people 8 N h
Eppan 72 C b
Equins 104 B H c
Erbil (Arbil) 99 M f
Ercavica 38 B d
Eregli (in Cilicia) 168 J B b
Eregli (Heraclea) 168 J B a
Eressus (Eresus) 9 C e
Ergene, riv. 168 L F f
Ergines River 9 D c
Erginul, Erginur 104 C K d
Eridanus, River, in Athens 23 D
Erivan 139 F g
Erne, Lough-, lake 127 J g
Er Riad 104 B E e
Ersekujvar (Neuhäusel) 135 J e
Esbus 7 D e
Esdrelon 6 C c
Esebon 7 D e
Eskdale, dist. 128 E e
Esla River 83 D c
Essek (Osjek) 77 H c
Essequibo 128 B ins. A
Esthaol 7 C e
Estonia, rep. 168 G J/K d
Estrella Mountains 82 A b
Esztergóm (Gran) 59 H d
Esztergóm (Gran), abp. 95 F b
Etaples 86 C c
Etea 14 ins.
Ether (Jattir) 7 C f
Ethiopia (Abyssinia), reg. 174 G d
Etropolje 165 C b
Etrusci, people 29 B c
Etsch River = Adige River 90 C b
Eudoses, people 38 D a
Euesperides = Hesperis 44 D c
Eule, in Bohemia 103 L d
Eupen 168 E A b
Eureka 180 O c
Euripides Street, in Athens 23 D
Europus, in Syria 20 G d
Evangelismos, bldg. in Athens 23 D
Ewst River 88 L c
Eynsham 60 D d
Eyoub (Ayyub), mosque 93 G e
Eyoub (Ayyub), quarter 93 G e

Fairbanks 180 M a
Fair Island 128 ins.
Faith, Temple of 24 A (1)
Faknur 104 B R j
Falkenstein, castle, in Swabia 62 E d
Falkenstein, castle, on the Selke R. 85 F e
Falkirk 128 E e
Fansur 104 C J g
Fao 168 K E c
Farah 104 B G d
Far-Eastern, economic reg. 170 leg.
Far Eastern Region 171 N Q c
Far Eastern Republic 171 O P c
Farquharsons, fam. 128 E d
Fars, reg. 104 B F e
Farther India, reg. 104 C J e
Faucigny, reg. 91 O m
Faucilles, Monts 168 C C c
Faustina, Temple of Antoninus and 24 B (22)
Federal Democratic Republic Transcaucasia 1917—1918 168 G N/O g
Federal Territory = F. T. 172 D d
Federated Malay States = F. M. S. 171 L h
Fehértemplon (Weisskirchen) 159 K f
Fehmarn, isl. 134 F a
Felden 79 H d
Fellin 88 K b
Ferentis 27 G e
Ferghana, reg. 104 B H c
Ferlech 104 C J g
Fern Pass 87 H e
Ferrières, near Joinville 104 A C c
Ferrol 83 J g
Feron'an Grove 35 ins. B
Ferrybridge 74 L f
Fetlar, isl. 128 ins.
Fez, reg., 14 cent. 77 C f
Fidei (Faith), Temple 24 A (1)
Findhorn River 128 E c
Fines, Ad, near Volaterrae 26 E d
Finland, rep. 168 G K b/c
Finmark, reg. 138 B b
Finns proper, people 57 H-I a
Firando (Hirado), isl. 128 C O d
Firebr 104 B G d
Firth of Clyde 128 C e
Firth of Forth 128 F d
Firth of Lorne 128 C d
Fismes 168 C B c
Fitzgerald, fam. 74 B b
Flandrina 104 B R j
Flaviae, Aquae 38 A d
Flemings, people in 1929 168 H B b
Flevum 38 C b
Flodden Field 128 F e
Florent 104 A B b
Flushing 168 C B b
Foča 87 L g
Focsani (Fokshani) 153 J c
Fojnica 103 M g
Fons, Gate of, in Rome 24 A
Fonseca Bay 213 D c
Fontanafredda 150 G c
Forbes, fam. 128 F c
Forfar, cty. 128 F d
Formartin, dist. 128 F c
Fornham 65 G d
Fort Albany 128 B D c
Fort Amsterdam 128 B E c
Fort Bliss 180 Q d
Fort Chequamegon 191 G b
Fort Condé (Mobile) 191 H e
Fort Dauphin, in Canada 190 E a
Fort Dauphin, in Madagascar 128 C K g

Fort de la Reine . . . . . . 190 F a
Fort des Abitibis . . . . . . 191 J b
Fort des Miamis . . . . . . 191 H c
Fort Edward . . . . 191 K c
Fort Garry (Winnipeg) . . 212 F d
Fort Gibbon . . . . 180 L a
Fort Hollandia . . . . 136 I d
Forth River . . . . 128 D d
Fort James, in Gambia . 128 B H e
Fort Jemseg . . . . 191 L b
Fort La Tourette . . . . . . 191 H a
Fort Meductic . . . . 191 L b
Fort Miami . . . . 191 H c
Fort Michipicoten . . . . . 191 H b
Fort Nachouac . . . . 191 L b
Fort Perrot . . . . 191 G c
Fort Pickawillany . . . . . 191 I c
Fort Radisson . . . . 191 G b
Fortrose, bp. . . . . 97 I b
Fort Rouge . . . . 190 F b
Fort Rupert . . . . 128 B E c
Fort Saint Antoine . . . . 191 G c
Fort Saint Croix . . . . . . 191 G b
Fort Saint Jean . . . . 191 L b
Fort Saint Joseph, L. Huron 191 I c
Fort Saint Louis, Alabama R. . . . . 191 H e
Fort Saint Nicholas . . . . 191 G c
Fort Saint Pierre, in Mississippi . . . . 191 G e
Fort Sauvage . . . . 191 I b
Fort Sill . . . . 180 R d
Fort Tadoussac . . . . 191 K b
Fort Trempealeau . . . . . 191 G c
Fortune, Temple of . . . . . 24 A
Fort Victoria . . . . 137 B e
Fort York (Bencoolen) . 128 C ins. C
Fort Zelandia . . . . 128 C O d
Forum Fulvii . . . . 26 C b
Forum Piscarium (Fish-market), in Rome . . . . 24 A
Foula, isl. . . . . 128 ins.
Fountain Gate, in Rome . . 24 A
Fraserburgh . . . . 128 G c
Frazers, fam. . . . . 128 D c
Fredrikshamn . . . . 138 C c
Freistadt, in Austria . . . . . 79 I d
Freiwaldau (Frývaldov) . . 103 M c
French River . . . . 191 I b
Freudental (Bruntál) . . . . . 72 D b
Friesians, people in 1929 168 H C b
Friuli (Furlans), people in 1929 . . . . 168 H D c
Frouard . . . . 104 A D c
Frunse . . . . 170 I d
Fugui (Fu-chau) . . . . . 104 C L e
Fulford . . . . 65 F d
Fulginiae (Foligno) . . . . . 27 G e
Fulham . . . . 60 I d
Fulvian Way . . . . 26 C c
Fünen (Fyen or Fyn), isl. . . 88 D d
Furness, dist. . . . . 60 H b
Fustat . . . . 53 F c
Fuzo (Fu-chau) . . . . . . 104 C L e
Fyn (Fünen), isl. . . . . 88 D d
Fyvie . . . . 128 F c

Gadara, in Gilead . . . . . . 7 D d
Gadara, in Jair . . . . 6 D c
Gaina, reg. . . . . 51 R k
Galatia, Rom. prov. under Trajan . . . . 20 E c (III)
Galava . . . . 51 O g
Galich . . . . 138 F d
Galinds, people . . . . 57 H c
Galli, people . . . . 29 A b
Gallinazos . . . . 216 ins.
Gallipoli, pen. . . . . 168 L D c
Galloway, dist. . . . . 60 G b
Galway . . . . 74 B b
Gambia, reg. . . . . 128 B H e
Gambrium . . . . 9 E e
Gambron . . . . 128 C K d
Gandia . . . . 88 K h
Ganfu . . . . 104 C M d
Ganja (Gandja) . . . . 139 G g
Ganus . . . . 9 E d
Garamantes, people . . . . . 34 G h
Garanbi . . . . 179 D e
Garde Meuble, bldg. in Paris 149 B
Garde Meuble, bldg. in Versailles . . . . 149 A
Gardinas (Grodno) . . . . 168 G J e
Gargamish . . . . 5 C b
Gargara . . . . 9 D e
Gariannonum . . . . 51 Q h
Garibaldi, Monument of, in Rome . . . . 22 A
Garioch, dist. . . . . 128 F c
Garma, Beth . . . . 99 L f
Garry, Fort (Winnipeg) . . 212 F d
Gata Mountains . . . . 82 A a
Gath Hepher . . . . 6 C c
Gaulanitis, reg. . . . . 6 D c
Gävle (Gefle) . . . . 88 G a
Gaza, in Judaea . . . . 7 A e
Gaza, in Sogdiana . . . . . . 19 K b
Gebalene . . . . 7 C g
Gebel Silsileh . . . . 4 F d
Gedor, in Gilead . . . . 7 D d
Gedor, in Jair . . . . 6 D c
Gelsenkirchen . . . . 168 E B b
Gemauerthof . . . . 138 B d
Gembes . . . . 104 A C a
Gemina, Legio VII . . . . . 38 A d
Gemona . . . . 154 G e
Genevois, reg. . . . . 91 O m
Georgia, auton. rep. . . . 168 G N g
Gerbéviller . . . . 104 A D c
Gerenia (Pylus) . . . . 14 B c
Gerlos Pass . . . . 87 H e
German East Africa, Late, Brit. Mand. . . . . 175 G e
Germania Inferior . . . . . . 39 H h
Germania Magna, reg. . . . . 38 D b
Germania Superior . . . . . 39 H j
German Ocean . . . . 98 D b
German Republic on Volga . . . . 168 G O e
German South-West Africa, Late . . . . 175 E g
Germany, rep. . . . . 166 H e
Germe . . . . 9 E e
Gérouville . . . . 104 A C b
Gersif . . . . 174 Q n
Gerstungen . . . . 62 E c
Gesoriacum (Boulogne) . . . 38 C b
Gex . . . . 86 F e
Ghat . . . . 174 E b
Ghel (Ghelan), Sea of . . . . 99 M-N e
Gheluvelt . . . . 168 C B b
Gheria . . . . 137 B e
Gherla (Szamos-Ujvar) . . 159 L e
Ghiseh (Ghizeh) . . . . 150 B a
Giants, Stoa of the, in Athens 23 D (2)
Gibeah of Benjamin . . . . . 7 C e
Gibeah of Saul . . . . 7 C e
Gilbert, route of . . . . . . 108 L c
Gilead . . . . 7 D d
Gilead, reg. . . . . 7 D d
Gilgal, near Jericho . . . . . 7 C e
Gilgal, near Joppa . . . . . . 7 B d
Gilgal, near Ramathaim . . . 7 C d
Gilgal, near Shechem . . . . 7 C d
Gilgenburg . . . . 87 M b
Gilyan, reg. . . . . 139 G h
Gilyan, Sea of . . . . 99 N e
Gimso . . . . 7 B e
Ginaea . . . . 7 C d
Girba, isl. . . . . 44 C c
Giurgiu (Giurgevo) . . . . 165 D a
Giza (Ghizeh) . . . . 174 J j
Gjatsk . . . . 153 O f
Glamorgan, dist. . . . . 60 C d
Glasgow . . . . 128 D e
Glastonbury, ab. . . . . 74 K h
Glastonbury, mon. . . . . . . 60 H d
Glencoe, in Scotland . . . 128 C d
Glengarry . . . . 128 C c
Glenluce . . . . 128 D f
Glen Shiel . . . . 128 C c
Gloucester, in England . . . 60 H d
Gloucester, abbey . . . . . . 74 K h
Gloucester, cty. . . . . 74 K h
Glubokoie . . . . 153 N f
Glurns . . . . 91 S l
Gmünd, in Carinthia . . . . 87 I e
Gnesen (Gniezno) . . . . . . 63 I b
Gnesen (Gniezno), abp. . . . 95 F e
Gobelins, The, bldg. in Paris 149 B
Göding (Hodonin) . . . . . . 87 K d
Godmanham . . . . 60 D c
Gokcha, lake . . . . 168 K E a
Goldap . . . . 155 L a
Golden Mile-stone, in Rome 24 B (9)
Goldingen . . . . 88 J c
Gollub . . . . 87 L b
Golzow . . . . 85 C b
Gomer (Cimmerians), people 5 C a
Gomera, bay . . . . 174 P n
Gomera, (Peñon de Velez) 136 I c (P.)
Goplo, lake . . . . 88 H e
Gorales, people in 1929 . 168 H E c
Gordons, fam. . . . . 128 D e
Goree, isl. . . . . 128 B H e
Gorizia (Görz) . . . . 103 K f
Gormaz, San Estéban de . . 82 B a
Gortscha (Koritza) . . . . . 165 B c
Gortyn . . . . 14 ins.
Gorze . . . . 78 E d
Göta River . . . . 88 E b
Göteborg (Gothenburg) . . . 88 E c
Gothia (Crimea) . . . . 99 J d
Gotland, isl. . . . . 88 H c
Götland, East, dist. . . . . . 88 F b
Götland, West, dist. . . . . . 88 E b
Goulfeï . . . . 174 E c
Gower, dist. . . . . 60 G d
Gradisca . . . . 154 G f
Graecostasis, in Rome . . . 24 A (9)
Gran (Esztergom) . . . . 79 K e
Grand Arsenal, bldg. in Paris . . . . 149 B
Grand-Failly . . . . 104 A C b
Grand Morin, R. . . . . . 168 C B c
Grandpré, in France . . 104 A B b
Grandpré, cty. . . . . . . 104 A B b
Granicus River . . . . 9 E d
Grants, fam. . . . . 128 E c
Grappa, Monte . . . . 168 B F b
Graslitz . . . . 79 H c
Graupen . . . . 79 H c
Gravelotte . . . . 158 C d
Grave of Adam, mt. . . . 104 B I g
Grave of Saint Thomas . 104 B I f
Gray League . . . . 91 R l
Great Batanga . . . . 174 E d
Great Bedwin, parl. bor. . 163 M f
Great Belchen, mt. . . . . 168 C D c
Great Canal, in China . . 104 C L d
Great Desert . . . . 104 C K c
Great Dividing Range . . . 172 D c
Greater (Black) Sea . . . . . 99 J e
Greater Zap River . . . . 168 J D b
Great Gymnasium, in Olympia 9 H f
Great Hungary, reg. . . . . . 92 E b
Great Khan, Empire of the 92 leg.
Great Salt Desert . . . . 168 K F c
Great Wall, in China . . 104 C K d
Greece, rep. . . . . 168 G J h
Greek Orthodox . . . . . 168 L N g leg.
Greek trade-routes . . . . . . 44 leg.
Greencastle, in Ireland . . . 74 D a
Greencastle, in Pa. . . . . . 208 ins.
Greenland, reg. . . . . . . 128 B F
Greenwich, East, in Rhode Island . . . . 189 ins. A
Grenada, isl. . . . . 136 ins. A
Grimsby . . . . 74 M f

Grimsel Pass . . . . 91 Q l
Grójec . . . . 135 K c
Grosser Belchen, mt. . . 168 C D c
Gross Friedrichsburg . . 128 B H e
Grozka (Grocka) . . . . . . 139 B g
Grozny . . . . 168 K E a
Grudziądz (Graudenz) . . . 135 J b
Grünberg, castle in Bohemia 87 I d
Guadalaviar River . . . . . . 82 B a
Guadalcanal . . . . 83 J h
Guadarrama Mountains . . . 82 B a
Guaira, La . . . . 214 C a
Guaranis, reg. . . . . 128 B F g
Guiana, reg. . . . . 128 B F e
Guichet de Marigny, in Paris . . . . 149 B (3)
Gümürdjina . . . . 168 L E f
Güns (Köszeg) . . . . 115 I e
Güssing, castle . . . . 79 J e
Gwent, dist. . . . . 60 C d
Gwynedd, ter. . . . . 60 C c
Györ (Raab) . . . . 87 K e
Györ (Raab), bp. . . . . 95 F b
Gyrwe, people . . . . 60 D c

Habayes, Les . . . . 104 A C b
Habitancum . . . . 51 O g
Haddington, cty. . . . . 128 F e
Hadersleben (Haderslev) . . 88 C d
Hadid . . . . 7 B e
Hadrian, Aqueduct of, in Athens . . . . 23 D
Hadrianopolis, quarter in Athens . . . . 23 D
Hadrianutherae . . . . 9 E e
Hafir . . . . 53 G d
Hafisfiord . . . . 45 F a
Hagia Triada . . . . 4 B b
Haidar Pasha . . . . 168 J A a
Haifa . . . . 150 B a
Haji Chefan . . . . 168 L B b
Hala-l-Bedr . . . . 4 F d
Haleb (Aleppo) . . . . 4 F c
Halhul . . . . 7 C e
Halidon Hill . . . . 74 K d
Halil-Eli . . . . 9 B b
Hallein . . . . 79 H e
Hallstadt, near Bamberg . . 55 R j
Hallstatt, near Salzburg . . 103 K e
Halonnesos, isl. . . . . 9 C e
Halwan, near Babylon . . . . 5 D b
Halwan, near Bagdad . . . . 99 M g
Hamadan . . . . 53 G c
Hamar, in Iraq . . . . . . 168 K E c
Hamar, in Norway . . . . . 131 F a
Hami . . . . 104 C J c
Hamilton in Scotland . . . 128 D e
Hamm . . . . 168 E B b
Hammadites, Dom. of the . 66 G g
Hang-chau-fu . . . . 104 C L e
Hanifa, people . . . . 53 G d
Hankau . . . . 171 M e
Hanoi (Kesho) . . . . 104 C K e
Hansi . . . . 104 B H e
Hapharaim . . . . 6 C c
Harah (Herat) . . . . 104 B G d
Hardegg . . . . 72 D b
Hardt Mountains . . . . . 168 C D c
Harlech . . . . 74 I g
Harmakut, mts. . . . . . . 104 B I e
Harpessus River . . . . 9 C c
Harplea . . . . 14 C c
Hartmannsweiler Kopf . . 168 C D c
Hasa, El-, reg. . . . . 104 B E e
Hastings . . . . 60 J d
Haunts of the Buccaneers 128 B ins. A
Hay . . . . 74 K g
Haye Sainte, La . . . . . . 156 A a
Heathfield . . . . 60 D c
Heavenfield . . . . 60 D b
Hecanas (Magesaete), people 60 C c
Hedon . . . . 74 M f
Hejaz, reg. . . . . 170 E f

Hekatompedon (Temple of Athena), in Athens . . . . 23 C (1)
Helicon Mons, in Attica . . 23 D
Helif . . . . 168 J D b
Helles, cape . . . . 168 L D c
Hellespont (Dardanelles), str. 9 D d
Hellespontine Phrygia, satr. . 17 E b
Hellespontine Tributary . . . 13 K d (II)
Helmsdale . . . . 128 E b
Hendrica, dist. . . . . 60 D d
Hephaestia . . . . 9 C e
Heptanomis, reg. . . . . 4 F d (II)
Heraclea (Perinthus) . . . . . 9 E d
Heracleum, in Crete . . . . . 14 ins.
Heraeum, in Olympia . . . . 9 H f (7)
Heraeum, in Thrace . . . . . 9 E c
Herat . . . . 104 B G d
Hercules Custos, Temple of 22 A
Hercules Invictus, Temple of 24 A
Hercules Pompejanus, Temple of . . . . 24 B
Hereford, Palatine earldom . 65 E d
Hereros, people . . . . 175 E f
Heri-Rud, R. . . . . 168 K H c
Herkend, Sea of . . . . . 104 B I f
Hermandad, Santa . . . . . . 83 L h leg.
Hermes Street, in Athens . 23 D
Hermopolis, in Egypt . . . . . 4 F d
Hermupolis, in Greece . . 165 D e
Herod Antipas, Principality of 7
Herodes Atticus, Exedra of 9 H f (6)
Herodes Atticus, Tomb of . 23 D
Herstal . . . . 104 A C a
Hertford . . . . 60 D d
Hertogenbosch . . . . . . 168 E A b
Hestiaeotis, dist. . . . . 10 C c
Hexamilion . . . . 9 D d
Hexham, mon. . . . . 60 C b
Hielmar (Hjälmar), lake . . . 88 F b
Hieraconpolis . . . . 4 F d
Hierapolis, in Asia Minor . 20 C d
Hili (Ely) . . . . 104 B R j
Hilmend, lake . . . . 168 K H c
Himyar, people . . . . 53 G e
Hind . . . . 104 B R j
Hindenburg Line . . . . . 168 C leg.
Hindukush Mountains . . 104 B G d
Hippodrome, in Olympia . . 9 H f
Hirado (Firando), isl. . . . 128 C O d
Hispaniola, reg. . . . . . . 128 B ins. A
Hissar, in Turkestan . . . 104 B G d
Hissarlik . . . . 9 A b
Hittites, Kingdom of the . . 4 F c
Hixton Down . . . . 60 G d
Hjälmar (Hielmar), lake . . . 88 F b
Hoang-ho, R. . . . . 104 C L d
Hodonin (Göding) . . . . . . 87 K d
Hohenzieritz . . . . 154 G b
Holderness, dist. . . . . 60 I c
Holland, dist. in England . 60 I c
Holland, dist. in Friesland . 62 C b
Holme . . . . 60 I c
Holme Saint Benet, abbey . 74 O g
Holwan (Halwan) . . . . 53 G c
Holy Brotherhood . . . . . . 83 L h leg.
Holyhead . . . . 60 G c
Hooghly . . . . 137 E d
Hooghly River . . . . 137 E d
Hope (Spes), Temple of . . 24 A
Hôpital Saint-Louis, in Paris 149 B
Hořice (Horschitz) . . . . . . 87 J c
Horonaim . . . . 7 D f
Horsham . . . . 74 M h
Horsham, parl. bor. . . . . 163 N f
Hôtel de Cluny, bldg. in Paris 149 B
Hôtel de Soubise, in Paris . 149 B
Hôtel Rambouillet, in Paris 149 B
House of Parliament, in Athens . . . . 23 D
Hoy, isl. . . . . 128 E b
Hradec Kralove (Königgrätz) . . . . 87 J c

Hradec Kralove (Königgrätz), bp. . . . . 95 F a
Hradisch (Hradiště) . . . . . 87 K d
Hsiang-yang . . . . 104 C L d
Hudson, route of . . . . . 128 B D c
Hudson Bay Company . 128 B D c
Hudson Bay Territory . . . 133 L e
Huexotzingo . . . . 106 B a
Hueyotlipán . . . . 106 B a
Hulagu (Dominion of the Ilkhans) . . . . 92 leg.
Humaytá, in Brazil . . . . 181 U h
Hungarian Altenburg . . . 155 I e
Hungarians, people, on the Theiss R. . . . . 45 I c
Hungary, rep. . . . . 168 G I-J f
Huningue (Hüningen) . . . 157 B c
Hunkiar Iskelessi . . . . . 164 D b
Huns, people, in Hungary . 45 I c
Huns, people, on the Dnieper R. . . . . 45 K c
Huns, people, on the Ural R. 45 N c
Hunsrück, mts. . . . . . . 168 C D c
Huntingdon, Dan. bor. . . . 60 I c
Huntingdon, cty. . . . . 74 M g
Hu-peh, reg. . . . . 171 M e
Hushi (Huşi, Hush) . . . . 131 I d
Huzuli, people in 1929 . 168 H F c
Hvar (Lesina), isl. . . . . . . 90 F c
Hwang-Ho (Hoang-ho), R. . 92 M d
Hwicce, people . . . . 51 R k
Hyères . . . . 78 E g
Hyettus . . . . 11 E d
Hyogo (Hiogo, Kobe) . . . 171 O e
Hythe . . . . 74 O h

Iaca . . . . 38 B d
Iacetani, people . . . . 38 B d
Ibelim . . . . 68 ins. A
Ibir-Sibir, reg. . . . . . . 104 B G b
Iça River . . . . 214 C c
Ida Mountains, in Troas . . 9 D e
Idle River . . . . 60 D c
Idomene, in Epirus . . . . . 10 C c
Idomene, in Macedonia . . . 17 C a
Idria . . . . 103 L e
Iglau, in Moravia (Jihlava) . 79 I d
Iglau, in Zips (Igló, Spišská Nová Ves) . . . . 80 G g
Igló = Neudorf, in Zips . . 87 M d
Ilchester, bor. . . . . 74 K h
Ilebo . . . . 175 F e
Ile (Isle) Bourbon . . . . 128 C K g
Ilipa . . . . 38 A e
Ilium (Troy) . . . . 9 B b
Ilkhans of Persia, Dominion of the . . . . 92 leg.
Ilkley . . . . 51 P h
Illyrii, people . . . . 29 D b
17 B a
Ilus, Burial mound of . . . 9 A b
Imbros . . . . 9 C d
Imbros, isl. . . . . 9 C d
Imeritia, reg. . . . . 139 F g
Imil . . . . 104 B I c
Inauen River . . . . 174 P n
Incurables, The, bldg. in Paris . . . . 149 B
India, Farther, reg. . . . 104 C J e
Indian Islands, Sea of the 104 C K g
Indragiri . . . . 128 C ins. C
Ineboli . . . . 168 J B a
Ingushetiya, auton. area 168 F leg.
Inner Ceramicus, deme . . . 23 D
Inner Tibet reg. . . . . 171 K e
Insulae Nudorum (Nicobar Islands) . . . . 104 C J g
Insular Tributary . . . . 13 J e (V)
Intercontinental Railway . 215 leg.
Inverary . . . . 128 C d
Inverlochy . . . . 128 C d
Inverness . . . . 128 D c
Inverness, cty. . . . . 128 B c

Iona, mon. 60 F a
Ionians, people 14 leg.
Ionian Tributary 3 K f (III)
Ipoly (Eipel) River 159 J d
Ipswich, in England 60 J c
Iraq, reg. 67 P g
Irawadi River 104C J f
Irina Lagoon 19 K f
Irish Free State 168F D e
Iron Gate (Eiserntor Pass) 159 L f
Irtish River 104B H b
Isauria, reg. 20 E d
Isburus River 30 C e
Isfahan (Ispahan) 168K F c
Ishim River 104B G b
Isle (Ile) Bourbon 128C K g
Isle of France, march 45 E c (F)
Isles in the Midst of the Sea 4 E c
Ismarus, mt. 9 C d
Isnik Geul 168L G f
Isonzo River 135 G f
Isparta 168J B b
Issyk Kul 104B H c
Ištip 165 C c
Istri, people 29 C b
Itonian Gate 23 D
Itter, castle 79 H e
Ivanjica 165 B b
Ivanovo Voznesensk 167 N d
Iwaki 179 F d
Ixhuacán 106 C a
Ixtacmaxtitlán 106 C a
Izborsk 88 L c
Izhevsk 168G P d
Iztapalapa 106 A a

Jabal Shammar 170 E-F f
Jabesh, in Gilead 7 D d
Jablonne (Gabel) 159 H c
Jacatra 128C N f
Jacobabad 170 H f
Jacobites, people 168L L h
Jacob's well 7 C d
Jaffna (Jaffnapatam) 104B S k
Jahaz 7 D e
Jaice (Jajce) 90 F b
Jaik (Ural) River 53 H a
Jair, reg. 6 D c
Jaluit, isl. 179 H g
Jambi 128C ins. C
Jandishapur 99 M g
Janina (Jannina or Yanina) 89 B c
Janoha 7 C d
Janus, in Rome 24 A (13)
Japanese Mandate 179 G g
Japan Sea 104C N c
Jardin duLuxembourg, inParis 149 B
Jaroměř 87 J c
Jaszo, mon. 80 G g
Jats, people 128B ins. B
Jattir (Ether) 7 C f
Java, Lesser, reg. 104C K h
Jazoros 7 D e
Jedburgh 128 F e
Jedlinsk (Yedlinsk) 155 K c
Jedlnia 87 M c
Jehud 7 B d
Jelairs, people 104C L b
Jemseg, Fort 191 L b
Jenghiz Khan, Dominions of 92 leg.
Jenil River 82 B b
Jerablus 168J C b
Jesana 7 C e
Jews, people 168L K i
Jeziret-ibn-Omar 168J D b
Jibleam 7 D d
Jičin (Gitschin) 159 H c
Jidda 168J C e
Jihlava (Iglau) 87 J d
Jilove (Eule) 103 L d
Jogbeha 7 D d
John of Pian de Carpine, Route of 104B leg.

Jordan River, Source of 6 D b
Joscelin, Lordship of 68 C b
Josefov (Josefstadt) 159 I c
Jucar River 82 B b
Judaea, Rom. prov. 7 leg.
Julianehaab 181 W a
Julias (Beth Haran) 7 D e
Jullin 103 L b
Jumna River 137 D c
Juno, Temple of (on Forum Holitorium) 24 A
Junonia Falisca, Colonia 27 G e
Jupiter Custos, Temple of 24 A (2)
Jupiter Eleutherus, Stoa of 23 D (4)
Jura, isl. 128 C e
Jurjan 104B F d
Jutes, people, in Britain 51 R k
Jutes, people, in Denmark 42 D b
Juturna, Lake of 24 A (20)

Kaarta, reg. 174 B c
Kabardia, dist. 139 F g
Kabardino-Balgar, auton. area 168F leg.
Kadah 104C K g
Kafche-kue, reg. 104C K e
Kafirs, people 109 T k
Kai-fong-fu 104C L d
Kail 104B R k
Kaili 104C L h
Kaindu 104C K e
Kaisarieh 89 K g
Kakh 168K G c
Kakun 150 B a
Kalaat Sherghat 168J D b
Kalat 170 H f
Kalgoorlie 172 B c d
Kalhat 104B F e
Kalifati 9 A b
Kalinga, reg. 104B S j
Kallirrhoe 7 D e
Kalmar (Calmar) 88 G c
Kalmyk, auton. area 168G O f
Kamchatka, pen. 171 Q c
Kamenets Podolsk 139 C f
Kamexu (Kan-chau-fu) 104C K d
Kammer 79 H e
Kamon 6 D c
Kamrup, reg. 104C J e
Kan-chau-fu 104C K d
Kandahar 104B G d
Kane 104B E f
Kanklis, reg. 104B F c
Kansan 104C K d
Kaoli, reg. (Korea) 104C M d
Kao-tai 104C K d
Kaphtor (Crete) 4 E c
Karabagh, reg. 139 G h
Karabigha 168L F f
Karachal, mts. 104B H d
Karachaevo Cherkises, auton. area 168F leg.
Karagach 168L F f
Karajan 104C K e
Karajan, reg. 104C K e
Kara-Kalpak, Autonomous Socialist Soviet Area 170 H d
Karakhitai, Dominion of the 92 I c
Karakhitai, reg. 104B H c
Karakhoja 104C J c
Karakorum 104C K c
Kara Korum Mountains 170 I e
Karashar 104C I c
Kara Su River 168J D a
Karatepe 168K E b
Kardis 138 C d
Karelia, auton. rep. 168G L/M c
Karelians, people 57 J a
Karlovac (Karlstadt) 159 H f
Karlovci (Carlowitz, Karlowitz) 159 J f
Karlovy Vary (Carlsbad) 158 G c
Karlskrona 168F I d

Karnaim 6 E c
Karnata, reg. 104B R j
Karun, R. 168K E c
Karun, Birket el, lake 174 J j
Kaschau (Košice) 79 L d
Kashan 104B F d
Kashgar 104B H d
Kashimghar 104B H d
Kashmir (Keshimur), reg. 104B H d
Käsmark (Kešmarok) 79 L d
Kašperşké Hory (Bergreichenstein) 103 K d
Kasrkand 168K H d
Kassa (Kaschau) 87 M d
Kassala 174 G c
Kassim Pasha, quarter 93 G e
Kassubs, people in 1929 168H E b
Kastelorizo, isl. 168J A b
Katanga 175 F f
Katia (Katieh) 168J B c
Katif, El- 104B E e
Kaunas (Kovno) 168G K d
Kavak, near Constantinople 168L G f
Kavak, near Gallipoli 68L D c
Kaveri (Cauvery) River 137 C f
Kavsa 168J C a
Kayalik 104B I c
Kazakskaia, Autonomous Socialist Soviet Republic 170G I d
Kazerun 104B F e
Kazimierz 103 P c
Kazvin 168G P h
Kedemoth 7 D e
Kelkid Irmak 168J C a
Kelso 128 F e
Kelyub 150 B a
Kemkemjuts, people 104C J b
Kemmel, mt. 168C B b
Kempsford 60 I d
Kenchak 104B H c
Kenilworth, castle 74 L g
Kennedys, fam. 128 D e
Kentyre (Kintyre), dist. 128 C e
Kenya, col. 174 G d
Kepoi (Gardens), in Athens 23 D
Keraits, people 104C K c
Kerch 89 E a
Kerkhah, R. 168K E c
Kerman 104B F d
Kerman, reg. 53 H d
Kermanshah 168K E c
Kert River 174 Q n
Kerulen River 104C L c
Kesh 92 G d
Keshan 168L F f
Keshimur (Kashmir), reg. 104B H d
Kesho 104C K e
Kesmacoran, reg. 104B G e
Kesmark (Kežmarok) 103 O d
Kesteven, dist. 60 I c
Keuprikeui 168J A a
Khabiri, people 4 F c
Khaf 168K H c
Khaibar 53 F d
Khalkas, people 104C K c
Khalman (Haleb) 5 C b
Khamil (Hami) 104C J c
Khanate of Chagatai 104B G-I c
Khanate of Persia 104B F d
Khanate of the Crimea 139 E f
Khanate of the Golden Horde 99 K d
Khanbaliq (Peking) 104C L d
Khanfu 104C M p
Khanikin 168K E c
Khansa 104C M d
Khanu 168K G d
Kharesm 53 I b
Kharesm (Khiva), reg. 53 H b
Kharesm, Sea of (Aral Sea) 104B F c
Kharluks, people 104B H c
Kharput 168J C b
Khatanga River 104C K a

Khatti 4 F c
Khatti (Hittites), people 5 C b
Kheir 168K F d
Kheta, people 4 F c
Khilakhu (Cilicia), reg. 5 C b
Khilikhi (Cilicians), people 4 F c
Khingan-Mountains 104C L c
Khiva, reg. 104B F c
Khmer, reg. 104C K f
Khoi 168K E b
Khojend 170 H d
Khokand 104B H c
Khoper River 139 F e
Khorab 175 E f
Khotan 104B H d
Khumdan 104C K d
Khur 168K F c
Khuram 104B G d
Khurma, near Basra 168K E c
Khurma, near Mecca 170 E f
Khusistan (Khuzistan), reg. 53 G c
Khwarazm (Khiva), reg. 104B F c
Kiangning-fu 104C L d
Kia-yu-kwan 104C J d
Kidwelly 74 I h
Kiel Canal 168D B c
Kien-chang-fu 104C L e
Kiev, in 864 45 K b
Kifane 174 Q n
Kij Mekran, reg. 104B G e
Kilid-Bahr 168L D c
Killiecrankie Pass 128 E d
Kilmallock 74 B b
Kinana, people 53 F d
Kincardine, cty. 128 F d
Kin Dynasty 92 K d
King's Stoa, in Athens 23 D (3)
Kingsze 92 M d
Kinross, cty. 128 E d
Kinsale 74 B c
Kintyre (Kentyre), dist. 128 C e
Kipschak, khan. 99 L d
Kirchholm 88 K c
Kirghiz, people on the Yenisei R. 104C I b
Kirghiz, Autonomous Socialist Soviet Republic 170 I d
Kiriath Arba 7 C e
Kirioth 7 D e
Kirkagach 168J A b
Kirkcudbright 128 D f
Kirkcudbright, cty. 128 D e
Kirk-Kilisse 168L F f
Kirkuk 168J D b
Kirkwall 128 F b
Kish 4 G c
Kishinev 139 C f
Kishm, isl. 104B F e
Kittim, people 4 F c
Kizil Uzen, R. 168K E b
Kizlya 168K E a
Klaipeda (Memel) 168G J d
Klatovy (Klattau) 135 G d
Klek 157 D d
Klepsydra, Spring of 23 C
Kliszow (Klissow) 135 K c
Ključ 87 K f
Klosterzeven 134 E b
Knights of the Sword 80 I b
Koburg 79 G c
Kobylka 135 K b
Kochak Bay 168G P g
Kočevje (Gottschee) 168 D d
Koil 104B H e
Koja Chai, R. 168L D c
Kokenhusen 88 K c
Koko-Nor, lake 104C J d
Kolachel 104B R k
Kolozsvár (Klausenburg, Cluj) 159 L e
Kolymsk, Nizhne- 171 R b
Komarom (Komárno, Komorn) 159 J e
Komotau (Chomutov) 87 I c
Kong, reg. 174 C d
Konia (Konieh, Iconium) 89 J g
Königgrätz, bp. 95 F a
Konitza 165 B c
Konkan, reg. 104B R j
Konkan-tana 104B R j
Konstantsa (Constantsa) 168G K g
Koporye 88 M b
Kora 137 D c
Korčula (Curzola), bp. 95 F c
Korčula (Curzola), isl. 90 F c
Koreish, people 53 G d
Koritza 165 B c
Körmöczbanya (Kremnitz) 159 J d
Koroni (Coron) 89 H g
Kors, people 57 H b
Korusko 4 F d
Košice (Kaschau) 79 L d
Kosmidion, quarter 93 G e
Köszeg (Güns) 135 I e
Kotor (Cattaro) 89 A b
Kotor (Cattaro) abp. 95 F c
Kotrobah (Sokotra). isl. 104B F f
Kotylaion (Cotylaeum), mt. 11 E d
Koura (Kura) River 168G O g
Koweit (Kuwait) 168K E d
Kowel 159 M c
Koźmin (Koschmin) 159 I c
Krajina, dist. 168D C a
Kraków (Cracow) 87 L c
Krasnodar 168J C a
Krasnokokshaisk 168G O d
Kratovo 165 C b
Kremenchug 139 D e
Kremnitz (Kremnica) 79 K d
Kremsier (Kroměříž) 87 K d
Krithia 168L D c
Kriviches, people 57 I-J b
Krnov (Jägerndorf) 135 I c
Kroja (Kruja) 89 G f
Kroměříž (Kremsier) 87 K d
Kronstadt, in Transylvania (Braşov, Brassó) 159 M e
Krumlov (Krumau) 135 H d
Krupanj 103 N f
Ksar-el-Kebir 174 O n
Książ (Xions) 159 I b
Kuba, in Daghestan 139 G g
Kublai Khan, Empire of the 92 leg.
Kucha 104B I c
Kuchan 168K G b
Küchük Derbend 168L E f
Küchük-Kainarji 139 C g
Kuen-lun Mountains 104B I d
Kufa 53 G c
Kughi 104B G e
Kujavia (Cuyavia), dist. 79 K b
Kulevcha 164 D b
Kulja 104B I c
Kulpa River 87 J f
Kum 168K F c
Kum-Kale 168L D c
Kum Kioi 9 A b
Kummeh 4 F d
Kunduz 104B G d
Kupferberg 79 I c
Kuprikeui 168B L c
Kur (Kura) River 43 L e
Kuraiat 104B F e
Kurds, people 168L L h
Kurna 168K E c
Kurnegalle 104B S k
Kustenje (Constanța) 165 F a
Kutaia 165 F d
Kut-el-Amara 168K E c
Kuti, people 4 G c
Kutná Hora (Kuttenberg) 135 H d
Kuwait (Koweit) 168K E d
Kuyavia (Cuyavia), reg. 87 L b
Kwei-lin-fu 104C L e
Kyakhta 171 L c
Kyle, dist. 60 B b
Kyll River 104A D b
Kyūshū, isl. 171 O e

La Bassée 168C B b
La Besace 104A B b (L.B.)
La Central 216 ins.
Lacetani, people 38 C d
La Cluse 158 D e
Laconians, people 8 O i
Lac Saint Joseph 191 G a
Lactodorum 51 P h
Ladins, people in 1929 168H D c
Lagosta, isl. 161 K f
Lagunas 216 ins.
Lahari 104B G e
Laighin (Leinster), dist. 60 A c
Laing's Nek 175 N l
Laknaoti 104C I e
Lametz 104A B b
Lamzai (Yang-chau-fu) 104C M d
Lanark 128 E e
Lanark, cty. 128 E e
Lancaster, in England 74 K e
Lancaster, County Palatine of 74 K f
Lan-chau-fu 104C K d
Land of Conchi 92 G b
Lands of the Generality, dist. 134 C c
Lanercost mon. 97 O g
La Neuveville-devant-Nancy 104A D c
La Neuveville-lès-Raon 104A D c
La Neuville-au-Pont 104A B b
Langa 83 E c
Langeais 86 C e
Langres, Plateau of 168C C d
Lang-son 171 L f
Lankavi-Island 104C J g
Lanzarote, route of 108 O e
Lapis Niger, in Rome 24 A (11)
La Plata, reg. 128B F g
Lapsaki 168L D c
Larache 174 O n
Laranda (Karaman) 20 E d
Lasa 7 D e
Lastingham 60 D b
Las Vírgenes, Cape 108 K e
Latakia 168J C b
Latin America 180 Q f-U k
La Tourette, Fort 191 H a
Latvia, rep. 168G J-K d
Latvis, people 57 I b
Lauderdale, dist. 128 F e
Laugona (Lahn) River 39 J h
Laun 87 I c
Lau River 174 P n
Lauro 38 B e
Lausanne, Treaty of 168L leg.
Lavatrae 51 P g
Laxenburg, castle 79 J d
Lebecii (Libici), people 26 C b
Le Cateau 168C B b
Ledre 45 G a
Ledstone (Loides) 60 D c
Leepaja (Liebau) 168G J d
Leganes 83 K g
Legiolium 51 P h
Legio VII Gemina 38 A d
Leibnitz 87 J e
Leicester (Ratae) 51 P h
Leicester, bp. 60 D c
Leicester, cty. 74 L g
Leicester, danish borough 60 I c
Leighton Buzzard 60 I d
Leinster (Laighin), dist. 60 A c
Leinster, prov. 74 C b
Leipzig 63 G c
Leipzig, univ. 100 H d
Leith 128 E d
Leitomischl (Litomyšl) 79 J d
Leitomischl, bp. 95 F b
Leix, dist. 74 C b
Le Maire, route of 128B E h

Le Marais, quarter in Paris 149 B
Lemba 7 D e
Lenaeum and Dionysium, in Athens 23 D (12)
Lena-Transbaikal, economic reg. 170 leg.
Lenczica 87 L b
Leninakan (Alexandropol) 168 J D a
Leningrad (Petrograd, St. Petersburg) 168 G L d
Leninsk 170 H e
Lenkoran 139 G h
Lennox, dist. 128 D d
Lenzin 104 C L d
Leonidaeum, in Olympia 9 H f
Le Pas 180 Q b
Lerma 83 K g
Lerwick 128 ins.
Les Habayes 104 A C b
Lesser Armenia, km. in Cilicia 89 D c
Lesser Java, reg. 104 C K h
Lesser Phrygia, reg. 9 E d
Lesser Zab, R. 168 J D b
Leszno (Lissa) 135 I c
Létanne 104 A C b (Lé.)
Leucas (Leukas), isl. 10 B d
Leucas (Santa Maura) 10 B d
Leucates, prom. 10 B d
Leucos Limen 4 F d
Leuchtenburg, castle 79 H d
Leutschau (Levoča) 79 L d
Lewes, engl. bor. 60 J d
Lewes, castle 74 M i
Lewis, isl. 128 B b
Liang-chau 92 K d
Liao-ho, R. 171 M d
Liao-tung, pen. 171 N d
Libba 7 D e
Liberec = Reichenberg, in Bohemia 135 H c
Liberta, Piazza della, loc. in Rome 22 A
Library, in Athens 23 D
Liburni, people 27 I c
Lichtenberg, castle 78 E d
Lidisdale, dist. 128 F e
Liechtenstein, castle 91 R k
Lienz 79 H e
Ligures, people 29 A b
Lijdzaamheid 128 C ins. D
Limerick 74 B b
Limnae, in Thrac. Cherson. 9 D d
Limonum 38 C c
Lin-ching 104 C L d
Lincoln, bp. in England 60 D c
Lincoln, cty. 74 M f
Lincoln, danish borough 60 I c
Lindisfarne, bp. 60 D b
Lindiswara, reg. 51 R k
Lindsays, fam. 128 E d, F e
Lindsey, dist. 60 D c
Lingah 168 K F d
Linlithgow 128 E d
Linlithgow, cty. 128 E c
Lin-tsing-chau 104 C L d
Liptau (Liptó, Liptov) 87 L d
Lipotvár (Leopoldstadt) 159 I d
Lisht, Pyramids of 4 ins.
Lissa (Leszno) 115 I c
Lita (Litani) River 6 C b
Lithuania, rep. 168 G J d
Lithuanians, people in 1829 168 H F a
Litoměřice (Leitmeritz) 135 H c
Litomyšl (Leitomischl) 87 K d
Litomyšl (Leitomischl), bp. 95 F b
Littau (Litove) 72 D b
Little Entente 168 F leg.
Litvas, people 57 H c, J b
Livia and Tiberius, Possessions of 7
Livias 7 D e
Ljubljana (Laibach) 135 H f
Ljungby 88 G c
Llandovery 74 J h
Llan Elwy (Saint Asaph) 60 H c
Llanos 106 C a
Lleyn, dist. 60 G c
Llobregat River 82 C a
Loanda 128 C I f
Lob 104 C I c
Locac, reg. 104 C K g
Lochaber, dist. 128 C d
Loch Leven 128 E d
Loch Linnhe 128 C d
Loch Ness, lake 128 D c
Lochstädt 87 L a
Loch Tay 128 D d
Locrians, people 8 O h
Löcse (Leutschau) 87 M d
Lodomeria, reg. 139 B f
Loides (Ledstone) 60 D c
Lomża (Lomzha) 159 L b
London, in England 60 I d
London, abbey 74 N h
London, Treaty of 168 L leg.
Long (Makra) Stoa 23 D
Loos 168 C B b
Loreto 103 K g
Lorne, dist. 128 C d
Lothian, dist. 60 H b
Lough Rea, lake 127 J h
Lourenço Marques 175 G g
Lovosice (Lobositz) 135 G c
Lower Egypt, reg. 4 F c (1)
Lower Lorraine, duchy, 13 cent. 104 A A a
Lower Nairi Sea 5 D b
Lower Tunguska River 104 C J a
Lower Volga, economic reg. 168 F leg.
Low Germans, people in 1929 168 H C—E b
Lo-yang 104 C L d
Loznica 165 A a
Lubango 175 E f
Lubawa (Löbau) 155 J b
Lucani, people 29 D d
Luck 139 C e
Lucuci, bp. 99 K d
Lud (Lydians), people 4 E c
Ludgershall 74 L h
Ludgershall, parl. bor. 163 M f
Ludsen 88 L c
Lueitha 7 D f
Luga River 88 M b
Lugoj (Lugos) 168 H d
Luhith 7 D f
Lule Burgas 168 L F f
Luna, in Spain 83 K g
Lunda, reg. 175 F e
Lundenburg (Břeclav) 168 E b
Lungara, Via della, loc. in Rome 22 A
Luris, people 168 L M i
Lussin, isl. 161 J e
Luxemburg, cty., 13 cent. 104 A D b
Luziensteig, Pass 91 R k
Lwów (Lemberg) 159 L d
Lycaonia, dist. 20 E c
Lycia and Pamphylia, Rom. prov. 20 D d (V)
Lycopolis 4 F d
Lydian Empire 8 Q h
Lynn Regis 74 N g
Lyons, univ. 100 F e
Lysanias, Principality of 7
Lysimachia, on the Propontis 9 D d
Ma'bar, reg. 104 B R j
Macallisters, fam. 128 C e
Macassar 128 C ins. C
Mac Carthy, fam. 74 B c
Macdonalds, fam. 128 A c C e
Macdona lds of Clanranald fam. 128 C d
Macdonalds of Glencoe, fam. 128 C d
Macdonalds of Glengarry, fam. 128 C c
Macdonalds of Keppoch, fam. 128 D d
Macedonians, people 8 N g
Macestus River 9 F e
Macgregors, fam. 128 D d
Machin 139 C f
Maciejowice 135 K c
Macina, reg. 174 C c
Macintoshes, fam. 128 D c
Mackays, fam. 128 D b
Mackenzies, fam. 128 C c
Maclachlans, fam. 128 C d
Macleans, fam. 128 B d
Macleods, fam. 128 B c
Mac Mahon, fam. 74 C a
Mac Murrough, fam. 74 C b
Macnabs, fam. 128 D d
Macneills, fam. 128 A d
Macphersons, fam. 128 D d
Mačva, reg. 87 L f
Madain 53 G c
Madrigal 83 J g
Madytus 9 D d
Magesaete (Hecanas), people 60 C c
Magharis 168 L D c
Magnae 51 O h
Magnetes, people 8 O h
Maguire, fam. 74 C a
Magyars, people, on the Dnieper R. 45 K c
Magyars, people, on the Theiss R. 45 I c
Magyars, people, south of the Don R. 45 L c
Magyars, people in 1929 168 H E-F c
Mahdchin (Canton) 104 C L e
Mahrattas, people 128 B ins. B
Maidan-i-Naphtun 168 K E c
Maidos 168 L D c
Maikop 168 J C a
Mailapur 104 B S j
Maimachin 171 L d
Mainland, isl., Orkney Isl. 128 E a
Mainland, isl., Shetland Isl. 128 ins.
Mairie, in Paris 149 B
Majdan 103 M t
Makatea, isl. 180 M i
Makhach Kala (Petrovsk) 168 G O g
Makra (Long) Stoa 23 D
Malatia (Malatiyeh) 168 J C b
Malborgeth 154 G e
Malea, prom. in Lesbos 9 D e
Malene 13 E b
Malians, people 8 O h
Malines 81 M g
Malmesbury, bor. 74 K h
Malmesbury, mon. 60 D d
Malpas 74 K f
Malton, castle 74 M e
Mamre 7 C e
Mangaseya 128 C M b
Manias Geul 168 L F f
Manresa 83 L g
Mansura, in India 104 B G e
Mar, dist. 128 F c
Marabout 150 A a
Marais, Le, quarter in Paris 149 B
Marburg, in Hesse 122 E c
Marburg, in Styria (Maribor) 168 D c
Marcher Earldoms 74 J g
Marco Polo, Route of 104 B leg.
Marea 4 ins.
Mare Majus 99 J e
Mare Maurum 99 K e
Maresa 7 B e
Mari, auton. area 168 G O d
Mariana, in Corsica 26 D e
Mariana, in Spain 38 B e
Maribor (Marburg, in Styria) 168 D c

Marienburg castle, in Livonia 88 L c
Marion 181 T c
Maritsa (Maritza) River 139 C g
Marlow 74 M h
Marmarice (Marmaris) 165 F e
Marne-Rhine Canal 168 E B c
Maronea 9 C d
Maronites, people 168 L K i
Maros Vasarhely (Osorhej) 168 I c
Marquette and Jolliet 128 C leg.
Marshall, dist. in Wales 74 I h
Mars-la-Tour 158 C d
Martaban 104 C J f
Martinsberg, mon. 80 E h
Marton, battle 60 I d
Marville 104 A C b (Ma.)
Marylebone, parl. bor. 163 N f (Maryleb.)
Maserfield (Oswestry) 60 C c
Mask, Lough-, lake 127 H h
Masphate 7 D d
Massawah 174 G c
Mastusia, prom. 9 D d
Masurian Lakes 168 B H a
Masurs, people in 1929 168 H F b
Matadi 175 E e
Mater Matuta, Temple of 24 A
Mathons 104 A C c
Matthane 7 D e
Mauerbach, mon. 79 J d
Mauritania, reg. 174 B c
Maurits-tad (Pernambuco) 128 B G f
Mauthausen 155 H d
Mawarannahr, reg. 53 I b
Maybole 128 D e
Meath (Midhe), dist. 60 A c
Medaba 7 D e
Medeshampsted, mon. 60 D c
Mediaş (Mediasch, Medgyes) 159 M e
Medina 53 G d
Medina de Rioseco 83 J g
Medjidia 165 F a
Meduacus 27 G b
Meductic, Fort 191 L b
Meenen (Menin) 134 B c
Megaron, in Olympia 9 H f
Meknes 174 P n
Melas, gulf 9 D d
Melcombe Regis, bor. 74 K i
Meliapur 104 B S j
Melibar, reg. 104 B R j
Melinde (Malindi) 128 C K f
Melrose 46 F b
Melrose, mon. 60 C b
Memel River 88 J d
Menado 128 C ins. C
Mendeli 168 K E c
Mendereh, R. 168 L D d
Menderes River (Maeander R.) 89 I g
Menderes River (Scamander R.) 9 B b
Meng-tse 171 L f
Menin (Meenen) 134 B c
Menteith, dist. 128 D d
Menzala, lake 174 K i
Menzies, fam. 128 D d
Meonwara, people 60 D d
Merano (Meran) 103 J e
Merchant Adventurers, seats 88 B-De (M. a.)
Mercia, Duchy of 60 leg.
Mercia, km. 60 D c
Merians, people 59 M b
Merkits, people 104 C K b
Mernis, dist. 128 F d
Meroë 4 F e
Mers (Merse), dist. 128 F e
Mersina 168 J B b
Meserib 168 J C c
Meshed, in Iraq 104 B E d
Meshed, in Khorasan 104 B F d
Meshra-Klila 174 Q n
Meskene 168 J C b
Messenians, people 8 N i
Messines Ridge 168 C B b (M.)
Mesta, R. 168 L E f
Mestre 103 K f
Methurides Islands 16 A b
Methymna 9 D e
Metronia Gate, in Rome 22 A
Metropolitan Church, in Athens 23 D
Metroum, in Olympia 9 H f (4)
Metroum, in Athens 23 D (6)
Metsovon (Metzovon) 165 B d
Meurthe River 104 A D c
Mezen River 138 G c
Mezre 168 J C c
Miami, Fort (on L. Erie) 196 ins. B
Miami, Fort (on Maumee R.) 191 H c
Miamis, Fort des (on L. Michigan) 191 H c
Mianeh 99 M f
Michael, Saint, parl. bor. 163 I g
Michelau, reg. 87 L b
Michipicoten, Fort 191 H b
Middel Zee (Zuider Zee) 102 G b
Middle Angles, people 60 D c
Middle Egypt, reg. 4 F d (II)
Middle Empire see Khanate of Chagatai 104 B G-I c
Middle Germans, people in 1929 168 H C c-E b
Middleham 74 L e
Middle India, reg. 104 B E f
Middle March 128 E e
Middlesex, parl. dist. 163 N f (Midd.)
Middle Volga, economic reg. 168 F leg.
Midhe (Meath), dist. 60 A c
Midhurst, bor. 74 M i
Mien 104 C J e
Mikhailovsk 170 G d
Mikulov (Nikolsburg) 135 I d
Milassa (Milas) 168 J A b
Milborne Port, parl. bor. 163 L g (Milb.)
Milden (Moudon) 86 F e
Miletopolis 9 F d
Milford, castle 74 H h
Milos, isl. 165 D e
Milton, in Kent 60 J d
Ming Dynasty, in China 92 K e
Mingio (Ning-po) 104 C M e
Minibar, reg. 104 B R k
Ministero della Guerra, bldg. in Rome 22 A
Minoa, on Siphnus I. 15 E c
Minoa, pen. 16 A b
Minster, mon. 60 E d
Miraflores, in Chile 216 ins.
Mirapolis 104 B S j
Misco River 27 H d
Missinaibi River 191 I b
Mitanni, dist. 4 F c
Miteretane Sea 98 D f
Mitrovica Kosovska 165 B b
Mitrovica (Sremska) 87 L f
Mittenwald 103 J e
Mitylene, on Lesbos I. 9 D e
Mitylene (Lesbos), isl. 168 J A b
Mixquic 106 B a
Mizpa, in Gilead 7 D d
Mlada Boleslav (Jung-Bunzlau) 135 H c
Mobar, reg. 104 B R j
Modena, univ. 100 H f (M.)
Modon (Methoni) 89 H g
Modruš (Modrush), bp. 95 F b
Moffat 128 E e
Mogaung 104 C J e
Mohilev 153 O g
Moidart 128 C d
Mojaisk 153 P f
Molat (Meleda), isl. 90 F c
Moldavia, auton. rep. 168 G K f
Molossians, people 8 N h
Money changers, Arch of the 24 B
Mongol Baltic trade-route 98 leg.
Mongol Dynasty, in China 92 L d
Mongols, people 104 C L c
Monjuich 83 L g
Monmouth, castle in England 74 K h
Monomotapa, reg. 109 T i
Monserrat 83 L g
Monte Caseros 216 H i
Montecatini 79 G g
Montfaucon (en-Argonne), mon. 95 D b
Montfaucon, near Château-Thierry 184 ins.
Montfort (-l'Amaury) 76 D b
Montfort, near Langres 104 A C c
Montmélian 86 F f
Montpellier, bp. 94 C c
Monts Faucilles 168 C C c
Monzon 83 L g
Morava (March), R. 168 D D d
Moray, dist. 128 D c
Mordvins, people, about 900. 57 L c
Morena Mountains 82 A b
Moresnet 168 E A b
Morges 91 O l
Morhange 168 C D c
Moridunum 51 O i
Morin, Grand, R. 168 C B c
Morlaks, people in 1929 168 H E d
Mortimer, dist. 74 J g
Moson (Wieselburg) 159 I e
Mossi, reg. 174 C c
Mosychlos 9 C e
Motho 7 D f
Moudon 91 O l
Mountain Territory 168 K E a
Mount Kemmel 168 C B b
Mouree 128 C ins. D
Mucheon Come 7 D f
Mudania 168 G K g
Mukačevo (Munkács) 168 H b
Mulehet, reg. 104 B F d
Mul-Java (Malacca), pen. 104 C K f
Mülheim (on the Ruhr) 168 E B b
Mull, isl. 128 C d
Mumford 128 C ins. D
München-Gladbach 168 E B b
Municipal Theatre, in Athens 23 D
Munster, prov. in Ireland 74 B b
Murad Su, R. 168 J D b
Murano 103 K f
Murghab (Pasargadae) 19 H d
Murghab, R. 168 K H b
Murmansk 182 E E a
Muromans, people 59 M b
Murrays, fam. 128 D b
Mürz River 87 J e
Murzuk 174 E b
Musa Keui 168 L B a
Muscat 104 B F e
Mush 168 J D b
Mussur (Egypt), emp. 5 C c
Mustafa Pasha 168 J A a
Mutatili (Mutapili) 104 B S j
Mygdones, people 9 G d
Mynyw (St. Davids), bp. 60 B d
Myoshormos 4 F d
Myrina, in Lemnos 9 C e
Myrina, in Lydia 17 E b
Myrlea 9 F d
Myrtilis 38 A e
Mysians, people 8 Q a

Nablus 150 C h
Nachouac, Fort 191 L b
Nacrasa 9 E e
Nador 174 Q n
Nagy Szeben (Hermannstadt) 159 M f
Nagy Szombat (Tyrnau) 155 I d
Naharini, dist. 4 F c
Naimans, people 104 C J c

Nairi, dist. 4 G c
Nairi Sea, Lower 5 D b
Nairi Sea, Upper 5 D b
Nairn, cty. 128 E c
Nakhichevan 99 M f
Nakhichevan, auton. rep. 168 G O h
Nang chang-fu 104 C L e
Nandurbar 104 B R i
Nanking 104 C L d
Narenta River 103 M g
Narvik 168 F I b
Nasamones, people 18 B d
Nascivan 99 M f
Nassau, on Gold Coast 128 C ins. D
Natuna, isl. 104 C K g
Naupactus (Naupaktos) 10 C d
Nauru Island 179 H g
Navalia (Shipyards), loc. 24 B
Navarre, march 45 D d (N)
Naworth 74 K d
Naxus (Naxos), in Sicily 30 E e
Nazionale, Via, street in Rome 22 A
Neandria 9 D e
Neath, castle 74 J h
Nechtansmere 60 C a
Necuveran Islands 104 C J g
Negeb, reg. 7 B f
Negumbo 128 B ins. B
Nehawend 53 G c
Nejd, reg. 53 G d
Nejed (Nejd), Sultanate of 170 F f
Nejef (Meshed). in Iraq 99 L g
Nekheb 4 F d
Nekhen 4 F d
Nemea River 15 C b
Německý Brod (Deutsch-Brod) 87 J d
Nenagh 74 B b
Nepomuk 79 H d
Neptune, Temple of, on Sunium Prom. 16 C b
Nerchinsk 171 M c
Neuberg, in Styria 79 I e
Neudorf (Spišska Nová Ves, Igló) 79 L d
Neuhaus, castle in Bohemia 79 I d
Neuhausen, in Livonia 88 L c
Neuilly (near Paris) 168 D A d
Neuilly, Treaty of 168 L leg.
Neuilly Wood 168 C B c
Neusatz (Novi Sad, Ujvidék) 159 J f
Neusiedl, lake 103 M e
Neutra (Nitra. Nyitra) 79 K d
Neuve Chapelle 168 C B b
Neuveville-devant-Nancy, La 104 A D c
Neuveville-lès-Raon, La 104 A D c
Nevada Mountains 82 B b
Neva River 88 N b
Neville's Cross 74 L e
Neviodunum 27 J b
New Albion, reg. 107 E d
New Bern 193 F d
New Britain, reg. 136 Q-S d
Newcastle, in Leinster 74 C b
Newcastle, in Ulster 74 C a
New Castile, reg. 108 J i
New Edinburgh 128 B ins. A (N. E.)
New England, reg. 128 B E c
Newfoundland, isl. 186 N d
New Galicia, prov. 190 E g
New Guinea, Territory 179 F h
Newport, in Monmouth 162 D f
New Republic 175 N l (N.R.)
New Shops, bldg. in Rome 24 A (17)
New Zealand, Dominion of 172 F d
New Zealand (Statenland) 128 C Q h
Nganking 104 C L d
Nicobar Islands 104 C J g
Nicomedia (Ismid) 168 J B a
Nicoverra Islands 104 C J g
Nidisdale, dist. 128 E e
Nied River 104 A D b
Nijmegen (Nymegen, Nimwegen) 117 D c
Nijmegen (Nymegen, Nimwegen), Hans. cy. 99 ins. B
Nikh 168 K H c
Nikopoli 165 D b
Nilawar 104 B S j
Nimrim 7 D f
Nimwegen, Nimeguen see Nymegen (Nijmegen)
Nin (Nona) bp. 95 F c
Ning-hia 104 C K d
Ning-po 104 C M e
Ninua 5 D b
Niriz 168 K F d
Niriz (Bakhtegan), lake 168 K F d
Niš (Nish) 165 B b
Nishapur 104 B F d
Nisibin 168 G N h
Nisibin, metropol. 99 L f
Nitra (Neutra) 79 K d
Nizhne Kolymsk 171 R b
Nizhne Udinsk 179 A b
Nizhni Kamchatka 128 C Q c
Nizhni-Novgorod 138 F d
Noain 83 K g
No-Amon (Thebes) 4 F d
Nogent (-sur-Marne) 158 B d
Nogent (-sur-Seine) 69 I f
Nordstrand, isl. 86 G a
Norfolk, dist. 60 E c
Norfolk, cty. in England 74 N g
Norham 74 K d
Northallerton, parl. bor. 163 M c
North Australia, state 172 C b
North Caucasus, economic reg. 168 F leg.
Northeast, economic reg. 168 F leg.
Northern Ireland, reg. 184 B b
Northern Long Wall, in Athens 23 D
North Folk (East Angles), people 51 S k
North Osset, auton. area 168 F leg.
North Osset Territory 168 J D a
North Riding, dist. 60 I b
North Sporades, isl. 165 C d
North Uist, isl. 128 A c
Northumberland, duchy 60 H b
Northumbria, km. 60 C b
Northwest, economic reg. 168 F leg.
Northwestern Greeks, people 14 leg.
Norumbega, reg. 108 K c
Nosairians, people 168 L K h
Nossibé 175 H f
Noteborg 138 D d
Notley, mon. 127 P h
Nottingham, danish borough 60 I c
Nottingham, cty. 74 L g
Nová Ves (Neudorf) 79 L d
Nové Město (Neustadt, in Moravia) 135 I d
Novgorod, about 840 45 K a
Novi Pazar 165 B b
Novi Sad (Neusatz, Ujvidék) 159 J f
Novo-Cherkask 139 F f
Novorossisk 168 J C a
Nowe Miasto 155 K c
Nowy Port (Neufahrwasser) 168 D D c
Nowy Sącz (Neu Sandec) 135 K d
Nowy Targ (Neumarkt, in Galicia) 135 K d
Nubia, reg. 4 F e
Nukha 168 K E a
Nutmeg Islands 128 C ins. C
Nyborg 88 D d
Nyeman River 168 G J d
Nyitra (Neutra) 155 J d
Nyitra (Neutra), bp. 95 F b
Nymburk (Nimburg) 135 H c
Nymegen (Nijmegen) 55 Q i
Nyon 91 O l
Oakley 60 J d
Oaxus 14 ins.
Oberhausen 168 E B b
Oberland, reg., in Berne 91 P l
Obi River 104 B G a
O'Brien, fam. 74 B b
Observatory, bldg. in Athens 23 D
Ocean Island 179 H h
Ochakov 139 D f
O'Connel, fam. 74 A c
O'Connor, fam. 74 B b
Odar (Oder), R. 168 D D c
Ödemish 168 J A b
O'Dempsy, fam. 74 C b
Odeum of Herodes Atticus, in Athens 23 C
Odiham, castle 74 M h
O'Dogherty, fam. 74 C a
O'Donnel, fam. 74 C a
O'Donoughue, fam. 74 B b
O'Dwyer, fam. 74 C b
Oeum, in Attica 16 B a
Oeum, in Lacedaemonia 14 C b
O'Farrel (Ferral), fam. 74 C b
Offaly, cty. 74 C b
Offa's Dyke 60 C c
O'Flaherty, fam. 74 B b
O'Hara, fam. 74 B a
Ohrid (Okhrida) 165 B c
Ohud, mt. 53 F d
Oikanga 182 E E a
Oirat, Autonomous Socialist Soviet Area 170 J c
Okas 53 F d
O'Kelly, fam. 74 B b
Okhrida (Ohrid) 89 B b
Olbia (Astacus) 9 G d
Old Babylonian Empire 4
Old Calabar 136 J d
Oldenburg, in Holstein, bp. 95 E a
Old Sarum, bp. 97 P j
Old Shops, bldg. in Rome 24 A (16)
Oliva, in Spain 83 K h
Olomouc (Olmütz) 87 K d
Olomouc (Olmütz), bp. 95 F b
Olovo 103 N f
Oltu (Aluta), R. 168 I d
Olvera 83 J h
Olympene, reg. 9 F e
Olympia, Plan of 9 H f
Olympus, mt., in Lesbos 9 D e
Olympus Mysius, mt. 9 G d
O'Malley, fam. 74 B b
Oman, Gulf of 104 B F e
Oman, reg. 104 B F e
Oman, Sea of 104 B G f
Omiš (Almissa), bp. 95 F c
O'More, fam. 74 C b
Onchestus 11 E d
O'Neill, fam. 74 C a
Onon Kerule 92 L b
Onon River 92 L c
Opava (Troppau) 159 I d
Ophrynium 9 B a
Oppidum Branchidarum 19 K c
Oradea Mare (Grosswardein) 159 K e
Orange in Afrika, Guinea Coast 128 C ins. D
Orăștie (Broos) 159 L f
Ordovices, people 51 N h
O'Reilly, fam. 74 C b
Orford 74 O g
Orkhon River 104 C K c
Ormuz, Gulf of 168 K G d
Ormuz, isl. 104 B F e
Ormuz, km. 104 B F e
Ormuz, Strait of 168 K G d
Ornas (Otrar) 104 B G c
Ornas (Tana) 99 K d
Ornes 104 A C b
Oropesa 83 L g

O'Rourke, fam. 74 B a
Orphan Asylum in Athens 23 D
Ortenburg, castle 79 H d
Ortiz de Retes, route of 110 FF h
Ösel, bp. 88 I b
Osezaki 179 D d
O'Shaughnessy, fam. 74 B b
Osiek, near Thorn 159 J b
Osjek (Essek) 159 J f
Oslo 46 I a
Osmanie 168 J C b
Osorhej (Maros Vasarhely) 168 I c
Osseg (Osiek, near Thorn) 159 J b
Ossetes, people 67 O e
Ossory, dist. 74 C b
Ostrołęka (Ostrolenka) 135 K b
Ostyaks, people 138 K c
O'Sullivan, fam. 74 B c
Oswestry (Maserfield) 60 C c
Oswiecim 87 L c
Otford 60 E d
Otočac (Otoschatz), bp. 95 F c
O'Toole, fam. 74 C b
Otrar 104 B G c
Otterburn 74 K d
Ottoman Empire, 1451-1481 93
Ottoman Empire, 1481-1683 128A
Ottoman Empire, 1683-1913 164
Ottoman Empire till 1920, 1922 168 J B b
Oudle, mon. 60 D c
Oulu Kishla 168 J C b
Ourcq River 168 C B c
Our River 104 A D a
Outer Ceramicus, deme 23 D
Outer Tibet, reg. 170 J e
Oxus River 19 J c
Oxyrhynchus 4 F d
Oxyrhynchus, patr. 43 I h
Oykell River 128 D b

Pactye 9 D d
Padang 168 A O e
Padstow, mon. 60 G d
Pagan 104 C J e
Pagi Islands 104 C J h
Palace Garden, in Athens 23 D
Palace of the Crown Prince, in Athens 23 D
Palaeo-Kastro (Besika Tepe) 9 A b
Palaeo-Kastro (Ophrynium) 9 B a
Palaestra 9 H f
Palam 104 B H e
Palazzo Barberini, bldg. in Rome 22 A
Palazzo Senatore, bldg. in Rome 22 A
Palembang 128 C ins. C
Palermo, univ. 100 H g
Palmaria, isl., in Liguria 26 D d
Palmaria, isl., Pontiae Isls. 30 B b
Palmyrene, reg. 20 H e
Palo Alto, in California 180 O d
Palo Alto, in Texas 201 F d
Pampa Central 216 ins.
Panactum 16 A a
Pan-American-Railway 215 leg.
Pancrazio, Porta San, loc. in Rome 22 A
Panderma 168 J A a
Panormus in Achaia 14 B a
Panoramus, port, in Tenos I. 15 F b
Panthéon, ch. in Paris 149 B
Papremis 4 ins.
Papua, Territory of 172 D a
Parganas, 24 (Twenty four) 137 E d
Parisi, people in Roman Britain 51 P h
Parium 9 E d
Parrett River 60 C d
Partition of Guiana and the Westindies 128 B ins. A
Pashat 104 B H d
Passarowitz (Požarevac) 131 H e
Passavant (-sur-Aisne) 104 A B c
Passchendaele Ridge 168 C B b (P.)
Patani 104 C K g
Patroclus, Burial mound of 9 A b
Pattan 104 B R i
Patzinaks, people 47 M-O d
Pechelbronn 168 E B c
Pechenga 168 G L b
Pécs (Fünfkirchen) 159 J e
Pécs (Fünfkirchen), bp. 95 F b
Pécs (Fünfkirchen), univ. 100 J c
Pecsaete, people 60 D c
Peebles, cty. 128 E e
Pegu 104 C J f
Pegu, reg. 104 C J f
Peisern (Pyzdry) 79 J b
Peking 104 C L d
Pelagonia (Heraclea) 10 C a
Pelagonia, dist. 10 C a
Pelasgikon, in Athens 23 C
Pelopium 9 H f (5)
Penjdeh 168 K H b
Penjhir 104 B G d
Penner River 137 C f
Peñon de Velez, bay 174 P n
Penselwood, battle 60 C d
Pentan, reg. 104 C K g
Pentland Firth 128 E b
Penzance 102 B c
Peraeum 15 C a
Percote 9 D d
Pereiaslav 139 D e
Pereiaslavl-Saleski 138 E d
Pergamum 9 E e
Perinthus 9 E d
Perperene 9 D e
Perrhaebians (Perrhaebi), people 8 N h
Perrot, Fort 191 G c
Persepolis, ruin 168 K F d
Persia, khan. 104 B F d
Persia, reg. 53 G-I c
Persia, Sea of 99 M h
Persian Gates 19 H e
Perth, in Scotland 128 E d
Perth, cty. 128 D d
Petapoli 128 B ins. B
Peterborough, abbey 74 M g
Peterborough (Medeshampsted), mon. 60 D c
Peterborough, Soke (Abbey) of 74 M g
Peterhead 128 G c
Petersfield, bor. 74 M h
Pétervárad (Peterwardein) 159 J f
Petitjean 174 P n
Petrikau (Piotrkov) 79 K c
Petrograd (Leningrad, St. Petersburg) 168 D G b
Petrovaradin (Peterwardein) 87 L f
Pettau, March of 72 D b
Pevensey 60 E d
Pfirt 91 P k
Phabra, isl. 16 B b
Phalasarna 14 ins.
Phaleric Wall, in Athens 23 D
Pharaton 7 C d
Pharygae 16 F e
Phelleus, mt. 16 B a
Pherae in Messenia 14 C b
Pherae in Thessaly 11 D c
Philaedae 16 C b
Philiphaugh 128 F e
Philippeum, in Olympia 9 H f (8)
Philippus, Principality of 7
Phinopolis 9 G c
Phocians, people 8 O h
Phoenician trade-routes 44 leg.
Phreattys 16 D c
Phrygian Empire 8 Q h
Phrygian Kingdom 5 B b
Piazza Cavour, loc. in Rome 22 A
Piazza Colonna, loc. in Rome 22 A
Piazza Dante, loc. in Rome 22 A
Piazza della Libertà, loc. in Rome 22 A
Piazza del Popolo, loc. in Rome 22 A
Piazza di San Pietro, loc. in Rome 22 A
Piazza Doria, loc. in Rome 22 A
Piazza Navona, loc. in Rome 22 A
Piazza Risorgimento, loc. in Rome 22 A
Piazza Venezia, loc. in Rome 22 A
Piazza Vittorio Emanuele, loc. in Rome 22 A
Pica 216 ins.
Pickawillany, Fort 191 I c
Pictones (Pictavi), people 38 B c
Picts, people, 8 cent. 60 B a, b
Picts and Scots, Kingdom of 60 G a
Pietro in Montorio, San, ch. in Rome 22 A
Piety (Pietas), Temple of 24 A
Pindasus, mt. 9 E e
Ping-yang, in China 104 C L d
Pinkie 128 F e
Piraeus Street, in Athens 23 D
Pirate Cove 180 L b
Pireathon 7 C d
Pisagua 216 ins.
Pistoia 90 L j
Pisuerga River 83 E c
Pityonnesus, isl. 15 D b
Pizzo 161 K h
Place de l'Opéra, in Paris 149 B (2)
Place of Concord, loc. in Athens 23 D
Place of Constitution, in Athens 23 D
Place Royale, in Paris 149 B
Plana 103 O g
Pläswitz 155 I c
Plateau of Langres 168 C C d
Platten See (L. Balaton) 87 K e
Playari (Bulair) 168 L D c
Pleasant Island 179 H g
Plöcken Pass 79 H e
Plovdiv (Philippopolis) 93 C b
Plympton, bor. 74 I i
Plzeň (Pilsen) 103 K d
Poemanenum 9 F e
Poikile, Stoa-, in Athens 23 D (1)
Pointe (Point) de Galle 137 C g
Pointe Noire 182 C C h
Pokrovsk 168 G O e
Poland, rep. 168 G J e
Polangen 88 I d
Polesie, reg. 55 J c
Poles, people in 1929 168 H E—F b
Polianovka 138 D d
Policlinic, bldg. in Rome 22 A
Polish Corridor 168 D D c (P. C.)
Polock (Polotsk) 71 M b
Polock, princ. 71 L b
Polumbum 104 B H g
Pomaks, people in 1929 168 H F d
Pomerania-Stettin, duchy 79 H b
Pomerania-Wolgast, duchy 79 I b
Pomesania, bp. 95 F a
Pomfret, mon. 97 P h
Pommat (Formazza) 168 H C c
Pompey 104 A D c
Ponape, isl. 168 A R d
Poniec (Punitz) 135 I c
Pontafel 79 H e
Ponta Grossa 215 E e
Pont-à-Mousson 104 A D c
Pont de Grammont, in Paris 149 B
Ponteamas 104 C K t
Ponte Cavour, loc. in Rome 22 A
Ponte Garibaldi, loc. in Rome 22 A
Ponte Sisto, loc. in Rome 22 A
Ponte Umberto I, loc. in Rome 22 A

Ponte Vittorio Emanuele, loc. in Rome 22 A
Pontia, isl. 30 B b
Pont Marie, in Paris 149 B
Pont-Saint-Vincent 104A D c
Pontus, reg. under Trajan 20 G b
Poopo, lake 216 ins.
Porchester, bor. 60 I d
Pordenone 154 G e
Porolissa 44 D b
Porrentruy 91 P k
Porta del Popolo, loc. in Rome 22 A
Porta Flumentana, in Rome 24 A
Port Alfred 175 M m
Porta Maggiore, loc. in Rome 22 A
Porta Pia, loc. in Rome 22 A
Porta Portese, loc. in Rome 22 A
Porta San Giovanni, loc. in Rome 22 A
Porta San Lorenzo, loc. in Rome 22 A
Porta San Sebastiano, loc. in Rome 22 A
Port Desire 108 K l
Portendik 136 I d
Porte Saint-Antoine, in Paris 149 B
Porte Saint-Bernard, in Paris 149 B
Port Harcourt 174 D d
Port Moresby 179 F i
Port Nelson 180 R b
Porto Belgrano 181 U k
Porto Rose 168D D e
Porto Velho 181 V i
Port Royal (Kingston) in Jamaica 128B ins. A
Portus, loc. near ancient Troy 9 A a
Portus Lemanae 51 Q i
Port Vila 179 H i
Posidium, prom., Propontis 9 F d
Postumia (Adelsberg) 159 H t
Powis (Powys), dist. 60 H c
Poyang Lake 104C L e
Požarevac (Passarowitz 139 B g
Požega (Pozsega), in Slavonia 159 I f
Požega (Pozhega), in Servia 87 L g
Poznań (Posen) 66 J c
Poznań (Posen), bp. 95 F a
Pozo Almonte 216 ins.
Pozsony (Presburg, Bratislava) 79 K d
Pozsony (Presburg), univ. 100 I e
Prachatice (Prachatitz) 87 I d
Praesus 14 ins.
Praha (Prague) 87 J c
Praha (Prague), abp. 95 E b
Praïa 181 Y f
Predil, Fort 154 G e
Predil Pass 79 H e
Presburg (Pozsony, Bratislava) 87 K d
Prestonpans 128 F e
Priapus 9 E d
Přibyslav (Pribislau) 87 J d
Prinkipo (Princes) Islands 168L G f
Pripet River 55 J c
Prison (Carcer), in Rome 24 A (4)
Priština 165 B b
Prizren 165 B b
Proconnesus 9 E d
Proëdria, in Olympia 9 H f
Prome 104C J f
Pronectus 9 G d
Propontis (Sea of Marmora) 9 E d
Propylaeum, in Olympia 9 H f (11)
Providence Islands 128B ins. A
Pruntrut (Porrentruy) 91 P k
Prusa 9 G d
Prussi (Prussians), people 57 H c
Prymnessus 20 D c
Prytaneum, in Olympia 9 H f(9)
Prytaneum, Ancient, in Athens 23 D (10)
Psillium 9 G c
Pszczyna (Pless) 135 J d
Ptuj (Pettau) 103 L e
Pudefitani 104B R j
Puerto Escocés 128C leg.
Pulicat 104B S j
Pulo Condore Island 171 L h
Punt, reg. 4 F e
Puschlav (Poschiavo) 91 S l
Puszta, reg. 103 O e
Putlam 104B S k
Putumayo River 214 B c
Pyhrn Pass 87 J e
Pylus vetus 14 B b
Pyrgi 27 F f
Pyrgus 14 B b
Pyrrha 9 D e

Qemt (Egypt), emp. 4 F d
Quai Dauphin, in Paris 149 B
Quai des Théatines, in Paris 149B (Q. d. Th.)
Quai d'Orsay, in Paris 149 B
Quais, isl. 104B F e
Qu'Appelle River 190 E a
Quengian 104C K d
Quiahuiztlán 106 D a
Quilon 104B R k
Quiros, route of 128C P f
Qurun, Birket el, lake 174 J j

Raab (Györ), in Hungary 72 D b
Raabs, in Austria 72 D b
Rabaul 179 G h
Rabbit Islands 168L D d
Raby 74 L e
Racconigi 161 F e
Racionsh 87 L b
Raciawice 135 K c
Radcot Bridge 74 L h
Radimiches, people 57 J c
Radisson, Fort 191 G b
Radstädter Tauern, pass 87 I e
Radziejow 79 K b
Raeti, poeple 29 B a
Ragnit 103 P a
Rai (Ragy) 99 N f
Rakow (Annopol) 103 P c
Ramoth 6 E c
Ramsbury, bp. 60 I d
Ranchos de Calpán 106 B a
Ras (Novi Pazar) 89 G f
Ras-el-Ain 168J C b
Ratnapura 104B S k
Rauden, mon. 80 F f
Ravendan 68 C b
Rawitsch (Rawicz) 155 I c
Rayak 168J C c
Rea, Lough, lake 127 J h
Reading, in England 60 I d
Recklinghausen 168E B b
Reculver, mon. 60 E d
Redesdale, march 74 K d
Red Tower (Rotenturm Pass) 159 M f
Reged, dist. 60 C b
Reghinul Săsesc (Szasz-Regen) 159 M e
Regia, bldg. in Rome 24 A (18)
Reichenstein 87 K c
Reigate, castle 74 M h
Reikiavik 166 A c
Reine, Fort de la 190 F a
Remeth 7 C d
Renfrew, cty. 128 D e
Repgow 85 G e
Rephaim 7 C e
Reppichau 85 G e
Repton 60 I c
Resengo 104C K h
Resion, Gate of 93 G e
Resvojo, R 168L F e
Rethondes 168C B c
Retz, in Austria 87 J d
Retz, in France, seign. 76 C c
Rhaedestus 9 E d
Rhaeto-Romanians, people in 1929 168H C c
Rhebus 9 G c
Rhegion, Gate of 93 G e
Rhesus River 9 D d
Rethondes 168C B c
Rhizarion, bldg. in Athens 23 D
Rhodius-River 9 D d
Rhoeteum 9 B b
Rhoeteum, prom. 9 B a
Rhone-Rhine Canal 168E B c
Rhuddlan 74 J f
Rhyndacus River 9 F e
Riadh 104B E e
Riberalta 181 U i
Richmond, castle near York 74 L e
Riff, the, reg. 174 P n
Rimnik 139 C f
Rio do Padrào 108 R h
Ripen (Ribe) 88 C d
Risan (Risano), bp. 95 F c
Risorgimento, Piazza, loc. in Rome 22 A
River-gate, in Rome 24 A
Riyadh 170 F f
Road to Marathon, street in Athens 23 D
Robertsons, fam. 128 D d
Rochefort, near Langres 104A C c
Rohitsch (Rogatec) 79 I e
Romagne 104A C b
Roman Baths, in Athens 23 D
Roman Empire, under Diocletian 34, 35
Roman (Romanula) Gate 24 A
Roman Market, in Athens 23 D
Roman trade-routes 44 leg.
Roman Wall, in England 60 C b
Rome-Ostia Railway Station 22 A
Romney 74 N i
Romulus, Grave of 24 A (11)
Ronas Peninsula 128 ins.
Roncal 83 K g
Roosebeke 78 C c
Roratonga, isl. 180 L j
Ros (Rurik), House of 138 leg.
Roscrea 74 C b
Rosenau 80 G g
Rosenberg, castle 79 I d
Rositten 88 L c
Ross and Cromarty, cty. 128 D c
Rossieny 88 J d
Rostra, loc. in Rome 24 A (10)
Rostra Julia 24 B (17)
Roubaix 168C B b
Rouge, Fort 190 F b
Rousay 128 E a
Rovno 168 J a
Roxburgh 128 F e
Roxburgh, cty. 128 F e
Royal Palace, in Athens 23 D
Royal Palace, Ancient, in Athens 23 C (2)
Royal Stables, in Athens 23 D
Ruanda, reg. 175 F e
Rubruquis, Route of 104B leg.
Rudeshur, R. 168K F b
Rudnik 103 O f
Rue de Grenelle, street in Paris 149 B
Rue de Sèvres, street in Paris 149 B
Rue de Vaugirard, street in Paris 149 B
Rue du Bac, street in Paris 149 B
Rue Montmartre, in Paris 149 B
Rugians or Rugii, people 16 H b, G c
Ruhrort 168E B b
Ruhr Valley 168D B c (R. V.)
Rullion Green, battle 128 E e
Rum, isl. 128 B d

Rumania, princ. till 1881 . 164 Cb-Da
Rumania, km. 1882 . . . . . 164 Cb-Da
Rumania, km. 1918 . . . . 168 G J-K f
Rumanians, poeple . . . . 168 H F-G c
Rupert's Land . . . . 212 E-I c
Rupt . . . . 104 A C b
Rurik, House of . . . . . . 138 leg.
Rus'chuk . . . . 165 E b
Russia in Europe, 1300—1796 138—139
Russia (R.S.F.S.R.) . . . 168 F leg.
Russian River . . . . 190 A d
Russian Socialist Federal Soviet Republic . . . . 168 G L-R d
Ruthenia, dist. . . . . . . 168 D E d
Ruthenians, people in 1929 168 H F-G c
Ruthin, castle . . . . 74 J f
Ruza . . . . 138 E d

Saalabbin . . . . 7 B e
Saar Basin . . . . 168 E B c
Saargemünd (Sarreguemines) . . . . 168 E B c
Saaz (Žatec) . . . . 87 I c
Sabina, Santa-, ch. in Rome 22 A
Sabini, people, north-east of Rome . . . . 27 G e
Sabzawar . . . . 92 F d
Sachion (Sha-chau) . . . . 104 C J c
Sächsisch Reen (Szasz-Regen) . . . . 159 M e
Sacred Road, to Eleusis . . 23 D
Saffi . . . . 174 C a
Saffron Walden . . . . 127 Z o
Sagitaria (Tahiti) . . . . . 128 B A f
Saida (Sidon) . . . . 168 J C c
Saint Albans, mon., in England . . . . 60 D d
Saint Andrews, in Scotland 128 F d
Saint-Antoine, Fort . . . . 191 G c
Saint Asaph (Llan Elwy), bp. 60 H c
Saint-Aubin du Cormier . . 86 B d
Saint Bartholomew, isl. . 128 B ins. A
Saint Charles, in Quebec 191 K b
Saint Croix, in Quebec . 191 K b
Saint Croix, Fort, in Wisconsin . . . . 191 G b
Saint David, castle . . . . . 74 H h
Saint Davids (Mynyw), bp. . 60 B d
Saint Demetrius . . . . 9 A b
Saint Domingue, col. . . 128 B E e
Saint Eustache, ch. in Paris 149 B
Saint Eustatius, isl. . . . . 213 F c
Saint Fr. Xavier . . . . 191 H c
Saint Germain l'Auxerrois, in Paris . . . . 149 B
Saint Gotthard, mon. . . . . 80 E h
Saint Jean, Fort . . . . . . 191 L b
Saint Joseph, Fort (L. Huron) 191 I c
Saint Joseph, Fort (L. Michigan) . . . . 191 H c
Saint Joseph, Lac- . . . . . 191 G a
Saint-Julien-sur-Rognon . 104 A C c
Saint Louis, in Gambia . 128 B H e
Saint Louis (São Luiz do Maranhão) . . . . 128 B F f
Saint Louis, ch. in Paris . 149 B
Saint Louis, Fort in Alabama . . . . 191 H e
Saint Marcel, ch. in Paris 149 B
Saint Martin, ch. in Jerusalem . . . . 68 ins. B (10)
Saint Martin, ch. in Paris 149 B
Saint Medard, ch. in Paris 149 B
Saint Michael, parl. bor. . 163 I g
Saint-Mihiel . . . . 168 E A c
Saint Naoum . . . . 168 D E e
Saint Nicholas, Fort . . . 191 G c
Saint Osyth, mon. . . . . . 127 Q h
Saint Paul, Pribilof Isl. . . 180 K b
Saint Peter's Railway Station, in Rome . . . . 22 A
Saint Pierre, Fort (Rainy L.) 191 G b
Saint Pierre, Fort (Yazoo R.) 191 G e
Saint (San) Sebastian . . 128 C ins. D
Saint Sulpice, ch., in Paris 149 B
Saint Thaddeus . . . . 99 L f
Saint Thomas, Grave of 104 B I f
Saint Thomé, Jesuit mission . . . . 128 B ins. A
Sairam . . . . 104 B G c
Sakkara, Pyramids of . . . . 4 ins.
Sala . . . . 44 A c
Salacia . . . . 38 A e
Salahiyeh . . . . 150 B a
Salbai . . . . 137 C c
Salbke . . . . 85 F d
Salces . . . . 83 L g
Salinas . . . . 181 W h
Salsette Island . . . . 137 B e
Saltash, parl. bor. . . . . . 163 J g
Salwin River . . . . 104 C J e
Samaga . . . . 7 D e
Samara River . . . . 139 H e
Samarra . . . . 168 B L e
Sambhal . . . . 104 B H e
Sambhal, reg. . . . . 104 B H e
Samir . . . . 7 B f
Samland, dist. . . . . 87 M a
Samnites, people . . . . 29 D d
Samothrace . . . . 9 C d
Samothrace, isl. . . . . 9 C d
Samoyeds, people, in Asia 104 C J a
Samoyeds, people, in Europe 138 H b
Sana . . . . 104 B E f
San Clemente, in Spain . . 83 K h
Sanday, isl. . . . . 128 F a
Sandjy, Sea of . . . . . . 104 C L f
Sandu . . . . 104 C L c
Sandwich, in England . . . . 74 O h
Sandy Sea, desert . . . . 104 B F d
San Estéban de Gormaz . . 82 B a
Sanf, reg. . . . . 104 C K f
San Gerónimo, near Córdova 83 J h
San Giovanni in Laterano, ch. in Rome . . . . 22 A
Sangpo, R. . . . . 104 B I e
Sangüesa . . . . 83 K g
San Juan Hill . . . . 213 E b (S. J.)
Sankt Andrä . . . . 87 J e
Sankt Andreas (Sassandra) 128 B H e
Sankt Eustatius, isl. . . . . 213 F c
Sankt Martin, isl. . . . . . . 213 F c
Sankt Veit, in Carinthia . . 87 J e
San men Bay . . . . 171 N f
Sanoah . . . . 7 B f
San Pietro in Montorio, ch. in Rome . . . . 22 A
Sanquhar . . . . 128 D e
San Stefano, Treaty of . 168 L leg.
Santa Cruz (Saint Croix), isl, West Indies . . . . . 105 H c
Santa Hermandad . . . . . . 83 L h leg.
Santa (Saint) Lucia, isl. . 213 F c
Santa Maura (Leucas), isl. . 10 B d
Santa Sabina, ch. in Rome 22 A
Santiago de Compostela . . 82 A a
Santiago de Compostela, abp. . . . . 94 A c
Santi Quaranta . . . . 164 B b
Santo (San) Stefano . . . . 164 D b
São Agostinho, Capo . . . 108 N h
São Jorge da Mina (Elmina) 128 B H e
São Roque, cape . . . . . . 214 F c
São Salvador (Bahia) . . . 108 N i
São Thomé, Cape . . . . . 108 M j
Sapaei, people . . . . 9 C c
Sapera . . . . 104 B R i
Saphir . . . . 7 B e
Sapolye . . . . 88 M b
Sarai, Sea of . . . . 99 N f
Sarakhs . . . . 104 B G d
Sarepta, in Phoenicia . . . . 6 C b
Sarepta, in Russia . . . . . 139 F f
Sargasso Sea . . . . 108 K e
Sari . . . . 104 B F d
Sari Bair . . . . 168 L D c
Sari Kamish . . . . 168 J D a
Sarkel . . . . 45 L c
Saros, Gulf of . . . . . . 168 L D c
Saros Islands . . . . 168 L D c
Sarpedonium, prom. . . . . . 9 C d
Sarrebourg (Saarburg) . . 168 E B c
Sarum, Old, bp. . . . . 97 P j
Saseno, isl. . . . . 168 F I g
Sassandra (Sankt Andreas) 128 B H e
Sassanids, Dominion of the, 8 cent. . . . . 53 G c
Satganw . . . . 104 B I e
Satu Mare (Szatmar Nemeti) 80 H h
Saturn, Temple of . . . . . . 24 A (15)
Sauer, R. . . . . 168 E B c
Sauerland, dist. . . . . . . 168 E B b
Saulces-Montclin . . . . 104 A B b
Saulxerotte . . . . 104 A C c
Sauvage, Fort . . . . 191 I b
Sauville . . . . 104 A B b
Savah . . . . 104 B F d
Saverne (Zabern) . . . . . . 134 D d
Savigliano . . . . 150 D d
Saxons, people in France . 45 D c
Sayville . . . . 168 A F c
Scalae Gemoniae, loc. in Rome . . . . 24 A (3)
Scalanova . . . . 168 J A b
Scalloway . . . . 128 ins.
Scamander River . . . . 9 B b
Scandian Islands . . . . 38 E a
Scatinavia (Scandinavia) . . 38 E a
Scepsis . . . . 9 D e
Schauenburg, castle in Baden . . . . 142 B c
Schaumburg, castle in Lippe 72 B a
Schaunberg, castle in Austria 79 H d
Schaunberg (Schaumberg), cty. . . . . 79 H d
Scheggia Pass . . . . 27 G d
Schemnitz (Baňská Štiavnica, Selmeczbánya) . . . . 79 K d
Schneeberg (in Saxony) . . 87 I c
Schouten, route of . . . . 128 B F h
Schwarzawa River . . . . . 135 I d
Schyl (Jiu), R. . . . . 168 H d
Sciri, people . . . . 39 G b
Sciron, loc. in Athens . . . 23 D
Sciron River . . . . 23 D
Scodra (Scutari), bp. . . . . 94 F c
Scone . . . . 60 H a
Scotch Harbor . . . . 128 C leg.
Scotra (Sokotra), isl. . . 104 B F f
Scots, people, about 900 . . 57 B c-b
Scotts, fam. . . . . 128 E e
Sea of Chin . . . . 104 C L e
Sea of England . . . . 98 D b
Sea of Herkend . . . . . 104 B I f
Sea of Kharezm (Aral Sea) 104 B F c
Sea of Oman . . . . 104 B G f
Sea of Persia and the Indies . . . . 104 B F e
Sea of Sandjy . . . . 104 C L f
Sea of the Indian Islands 104 C K g
Sea of the Indies . . . . 104 B G f
Sebatum . . . . 27 F a
Sebu River . . . . 174 P n
Secondi . . . . 128 C ins. D
Sedd-el-Bahr . . . . 168 L D c
Sefid Rud=Amardus River 44 G c
Segeberg, castle . . . . 88 D e
Segesvar (Schässburg, Sighişoara) . . . . 168 I c
Segobriga, near Saguntum . 38 B e
Segobriga, near Toletum . . 38 B e
Segodunum . . . . 38 C d
Segor (Zoar) . . . . 7 C f
Segura River . . . . 82 B b
Segu Sikoro . . . . 174 C c
Sehwan . . . . 104 B G e
Seihun River . . . . 168 J C b
Seilan (Ceylon), isl. . . . 104 B S k
Seille River . . . . 104 A D c

Seistan, reg. 104 B G d
Selenga River 104 C K c
Selestat (Schlettstadt) 134 D d
Selke River 85 F e
Selkirk 128 F e
Selkirk, cty. 128 E e
Selmeczbánya (Schemnitz) 87 L d
Selsey, bp. 60 D d
Seluan 174 Q n
Selymbria 9 F c
Selymbria, Gate of 93 G e
Semender 45 N d
Semigallia, dist. 88 K c
Semigallians, people 57 I b
Semiscant (Samarkand) 104 B G d
Semlin (Zemun) 87 M f
Semnan 168 K F b
Semneh 4 F d
Senaculum, bldg. in Rome 24 A (8)
Senatorio, Palazzo, bldg. in Rome 22 A
Senj (Zengg) 72 D c
Senj (Zengg), bp. 95 F b
Senjirli 4 F c
Sennabris 6 D c
Senussi, people 174 F b
Septimius Severus, Arch of 24 B (11)
Seraijik 168 L D d
Serampur 128 B ins. B
Serbs, people in 1929 168 H E d
Sergin 168 L F f
Serre River 104 A A b
Serrhium, prom. 9 C d
Sestus 9 D d
Sevastopol (Cherson) 89 J f
Severians, people about 900 57 J c, I e
Sèvres 168 D A d
Sèvres, Treaty of 168 L leg.
Sézanne 104 A A c
Shabatz (Šabac) 87 L f
Sha-chau 104 C J c
Shadwan Island 150 B b
Shaftesbury 74 K i
Shaftesbury, mon. 97 O k
Shaliyat (Calicut) 104 B R j
Shamaiten (Samogitia), reg. 88 J d
Shamir (Van) 99 L f
Shangtu 104 C L c
Shatt-el-Arab, R. 168 K E d
Sheffield, castle 74 L f
Shemak (Shemakha) 99 M e
Sheppey, Isle of 60 E d
Sherborne, bp. 60 C d
Sheriffmuir 128 E d
Sheshauen 174 P n
Shiahs, sect 168 L N g, leg.
Shiblak 9 B b
Shilka River 104 C L b
Shipyards, loc. in Rome 24 B
Shiraz 104 B F e
Shirvan, reg. 139 G g
Shkodra (Scutari), in Servia 89 A b
Shoreham 74 M i
Shrewsbury in England 65 E d
Shrewsbury, abbey 74 K g
Shrewsbury, Palatine earldom 65 E d
Shropshire, cty. 74 K g
Shusha 168 K E b
Shushtar (Shuster) 99 M g
Šibenik (Sebenico) 87 J g
Šibenik (Sebenico), bp. 95 F c
Siberian, economic reg. 170 leg.
Sibir 104 B G b
Sibiu (Hermannstadt) 159 M f
Sicelia, hill in Athens 23 D
Sidini, people 38 E b
Sidnacaester, bp. 60 D c
Sieg River 134 D c
Sierra Gorda 216 ins.
Sierra Leone, reg. 128 B H e
Siewierz 79 K c
Sigeum 9 A b
Sighişoara (Schässburg) 159 M e
Sigrium, prom. 9 C e
Sikhs, people 137 B b
Si-kiang, R. 104 C K e
Sikkim 171 J f
Silberberg 103 M c
Silchester 51 P i
Silet 174 D b
Silian (Ceylon). isl. 104 B S k
Silivri, Gate of 93 G e
Siljan, lake 88 F a
Silk-Route 104 B leg.
Sillein (Zsolna, Žilina) 155 J d
Sillerie 191 K b
Sil River 82 A a
Silsileh, Gebel 4 F d
Simoeis River (Dumbrek R.) 9 B b
Sin 104 C L d
Sin-al-Sin (Canton) 104 C L e
Sinclayrs, fam. 128 E b
Sine 168 L D d
Si-ngan-fu 104 C K d
Si-ning-fu 104 C K d
Sinkalan (Canton) 104 C L e
Sinob (Sinope) 89 K f
Sinti, people 17 C a
Sinub (Sinope) 168 J C a
Siraf 104 B F e
Siugui 104 C M d
Sivas 89 K g
Siwa Oasis 174 F b
Skara 46 I b
Skias (Tholos), in Athens 23 D (7)
Skofja Loka (Bischoflack) 135 H e
Skoplje (Uskub) 89 H f
Skradin (Scardona), bp. 95 F c
Skutari 168 G K g
Slack 60 C c
Sleat Sound 128 C c
Slesvik 78 F a
Slesvik, Duchy of 78 F a
Slesvik (Schleswig), March of 62 E 1
Sligo, castle 74 B a
Slovenes, poeple, about 900 57 I-J b
Slovenes, people in 1929 168 H Dc, Gd
Sochaczew (Sokhaczew) 135 K b
Södermanland, dist. 88 G b
Soer 104 B F e
Sofala 128 C J g
Sofia, Treaty of 168 L leg.
Söke 168 J A b
Solangas, people 92 M c
Sole Bay 125 D b
Solingen 102 H c
Solon Street in Athens 23 D
Solovyeva 153 O g
Solvychegodsk 138 G c
Solway Firth 60 C b
Soma 165 E d
Somnath 104 B R i
Songhar 104 B R i
Songko River 171 L f
Sorbiodunum (Salisbury) 51 P i
Sous, Wadi 174 C a
Southampton in England 60 I d
Southern Country (Negeb) 7 B f
Southern Long Wall in Athens 23 D
Southern Sung Dynasty 92 K e
South Folk (East Angles), people 51 S k
South Mining, economic reg. 168 F leg.
South Osset, auton. area 168 F leg.
South Osset, Territory 168 J D a
Southport 162 C d
South Sea Islands, Japan. Mand. 179 G f
South Uist, isl. 128 A c
Southwark, bor. 60 I d
Southwest, economic reg. 168 F leg.
Spa 168 F G e
Spanish Main (Tierra Firme) 128 B ins. A
Spes (Hope), Temple of 24 A
Spey (Spay) River 128 E c
Spichern 158 D d
Spišská Stará Ves (Altendorf) 79 L d
Spišská Nová Ves (Igló, Neudorf) 87 M d
Spithead 127 X p
Spits (Zips), dist. 168 D E d
Split (Spalato) 89 A b
Split (Spalato), abp. 95 F c
Spoleto, march 45 G d (Sp)
Spring Gate 93 G e
Srebrenica 103 N f
Srebrenik 87 L f
Sredetz (Sofia) 89 B b
Środa (Schroda) 159 I b
Stadium, in Athens 23 D
Stadium, in Olympia 9 H f
Stadium, street in Athens 23 D
Stafford, bor. in England 60 H c
Stamford, in England, danish borough 60 I c
Stamford, mon. 60 D c
Stanimaka 165 D c
Stanislawow (Stanislau) 159 M d
Stará Ves (Spišská-, Altendorf) 79 L d
Stargard, in Holstein 103 J a
Stargardt (in Pomerelia) 87 L b
Starhemberg, castle, near Wels 79 H d
Starhemberg, castle, near Wiener Neustadt 123 I e
Stari Grad (Cittavecchia), bp. 95 F c
Statenland (New Zealand) 128 C Q h
State Treasury, in Rome 24 B (8)
Stato degli Presidii 151 I h
Stefano Rotondo, Santo, ch. in Rome 22 A
Stentoris Lake 9 D d
Stewarts, fam. 128 C d
Štiavnica (Baňská-, Schemnitz) 79 K d
Štip (Ištip) 165 C c
Stirling 128 D d
Stirling, cty. 128 D d
Stoa, on the Acropolis of Athens 23 C
Stoa Basileios, in Athens 23 D (3)
Stoa of Attalus 23 D
Stoa of Eumenes, in Athens 23 C
Stoa of Hadrian 23 D
Stoa of Jupiter Eleutherus 23 D (4)
Stoa of the Giants, in Athens 23 D (2)
Stoa Poikile, in Athens 23 D (1)
Stockbridge, parl. bor. 163 M f
Stockerau 87 K d
Stolberg (in Harz) 87 H c
Stolpe River 135 I a
Strasburg, near Thorn 87 L b
Strathclyde, dist. 60 B b
Strathclyde, km. 60 G b
Strathearn, dist. 128 D d
Strathmore, dist 128 E d
Strathnaver, dist. 128 D b
Streaneshalch (Whitby), mon. 60 D b
Street of Tombs, in Athens 23 D
Stříbro (Mies) 103 K d
Stroganov, Colony of 138 I d
Stryme 9 C d
Stuhm 87 L b
Styr River 168 I a
Suamians, people 57 H-I a
Suardones, people 38 E b
Subeitala 53 C c
Subotica (Szabadka, Maria-Theresiopel) 168 F c
Succur (Su-chau) 104 C J c
Su-chau (Siugui) 104 C M d
Suedia 168 J C b
Suffolk, dist. 60 E c
Sugd, reg. 92 G c
Sui-chau-fu 104 C K e
Suiones (Sueones), people 34 G b

Suiyan 171 M d
Suk-el Arba 174 O n
Sukhum-kaleh 164 G b
Sukkot 7 D d
Suleimanieh 168 K E b
Sulu, isl. 104 C M g
Sumatia 14 C b
Sumbal 104 B H e
Sumbal, reg. 104 B H e
Sumbawa, isl. 128 C ins. C
Šumen (Shumla) 165 E b
Sunarganw 104 C J e
Sungari River 104 C M c
Sung Dynasty 92 K d
Sung Dynasty, Southern 92 K e
Sungerlu 168 J B a
Sunian Gate, in Athens 23 D
Sunium, prom. 15 E b
Sunnites, sect 168 L leg.
Sunzumata 104 C L d
Surrounding Sea 104 C L g
Sutherland, cty. 128 D b
Sutherland, dist. 127 P f
Suthrige (Surrey), dist. 60 D d
Suvla Bay 168 L D c
Suvla Burun 168 L D c
Suwali 104 B R i
Svensksund 138 C c
Sverdlovsk (Ekaterinburg) 168 G R d
Svienta River 88 K d
Svitary (Zwittau, in Moravia) 168 E b
Swanage 60 I d
Swansea, castle, in Wales 74 J h
Swansea, in Mass. 189 ins. A
Sweden and Norway, km. 1815—1905 157 B a
Swenet (Syene) 4 F d
Swiecie (Schwetz) 135 J b
Syra, isl. 165 D e
Syra Orda 104 C K c
Syrian Gate 20 G d
Syrmia, dist. 87 L f
Szabadka (Maria Theresiopel) 159 J e
Szaszvaros (Broos) 159 L f
Szatmar Nemeti (Satu Mare) 80 H h
Szegedin (Szeged) 79 L e
Székesfehérvár (Stuhlweissenburg) 159 J e
Szendrö 87 M d
Szombathely (Steinamanger) 159 I e

Taanath-Shiloh 7 C d
Tabal, people 5 C b
Tabernae novae, bldg. in Rome 24 A (17)
Tabernae veteres, bldg. in Rome 24 A (16)
Tachau (Tachov) 87 I d
Tacna, prov. 216 ins.
Tacuba 106 A a
Tadoussac, Fort 191 K b
Tagong 104 C J e
Tahiti (Sagitaria), isl. 128 B A f
Taif 53 G d
Taifur Keui 168 L D c
Tain 128 D c
Tai-yuen-fu 104 C L d
Tajik, Autonomous Socialist Soviet Area 170 H e
Talas 104 B H c
Talay River 104 C K e
Ta-li-fu 104 C K e
Talish, reg. 164 H c
Tallinn (Reval) 168 D E b
Tamerlane (Timur), Dom. of 92 leg.
Tamworth, bp. 60 D c
Tanatus Island 51 Q i
Tanganyika Territory (Late German East Africa) 175 G e
Tangut 104 C J c
Tangut, reg. 104 C J d
Tannu-Tubin, rep. 170/171 K c
Tantamquerry 128 C ins. D
Taoce 19 H e
Tapiau 87 M a
Tarabulus (Tripoli) 168 J C c
Tarapacá, prov. 216 ins.
Tarbellicae, Aquae 38 B d
Targovicz (Targovitza 139 D f
Târgu Murtşului (Maros Vasarhely) 159 M e
Tarim River 104 B H d
Tarsi, people 104 B I c
Tarsius River 9 E e
Tartar, auton. rep. 168 G P d
Tartessus River 44 A c
Tartkul 170 H d
Tartu (Dorpat) 168 D F b
Tashkent 104 B G c
Tasman, route of 128 C O f
Tasmania (Van Diemen's Land) 128 C P h
Tasmanland, reg. 128 C O f
Tatar Dynasty in China 92 L d
Tatars, people in Azerbaijan 168 L M g
Tatars, people in eastern Asia 104 C L c
Tatars, people in Dobruja 168 H G d
Tauchira 44 D c
Taungu 104 C J f
Taungu, reg. 104 C J f
Taurirt 174 Q n
Tavoy 104 C J f
Tavoy, reg. 104 C J f
Tawalisi, people 104 C L g
Taydo (Peking) 104 C L c
Taza 174 P n
Tebez 7 C d
Tecoac 106 C a
Tegyra 11 E d
Tehennu, people 4 E c
Tejend, R. 168 K H b
Tekrit 168 J D c
Tel (Tell) el Kebir 174 J J i
Telingana, reg. 104 B R j
Tell el Amarna 4 F d
Tellenae 35 ins. B
Temesvar (Temisoara) 103 O f
Templin 87 I b
Tempsford 60 I c
Tenasserim 104 C J f
Tenduc, people 104 C L c
Tepeyac 106 A a
Teplice (Teplitz, in Bohemia) 159 G c
Teptunis 4 ins.
Teruentum 27 I f
Tešanj 87 K f
Teschen (czech Těšín) 79 K d
Teschen, (Těsín) princ. 79 K d
Teschen (polish Cieszyn) 168 F b
Tesmelucán 106 B a
Téte 182 E E i
Tettenhall 60 H c
Teuthrania, reg. 9 E e
Teutonic Order, 13 cent. 47 K c
Texcoco 106 B a
Texcoce, lake 106 B a
Thaema 44 E d
Thaenae 44 C c
Thana 104 B R j
Thebais, reg. 4 F d (III)
Theocoleum in Olympia 9 H f
Theodosius, Port of 93 G e
The Riff, reg. 174 P n
Thesmotheteum, in Athens 23 D (9)
Thesprots (Thesprotians), people 8 N h
Thessalians, people 14 leg.
Thimnath Serah 7 C e
Thirsk, castle 74 L e
Thisb(a)e 11 D d
Thisbe 7 D d
Thogarma, reg. 5 D b
Tholos (Skias), in Athens 23 D (7)
Thomar 83 J h
Thomond, km. 74 B b
Thonne le Thil 104 A C b (Th.)
Thonon 91 O l
Thourout, fair 99 ins.
Thracian Bosporus, str. 9 G c
Thracian Tributary 13 J d (I)
Thracians, people 8 P g
Thrasyllus, Monument of 23 C (10)
Three Points, cape 128 C ins. D
Thriasian Gate, in Athens 23 D
Thriplow (Triploe) Heath 127 Z n
Thsenthung (Tsuen-chau-fu) 104 C L e
Thule (Shetland) Islands 34 D a
Thuria 14 C b
Thuringia, state 168 D C c
Thurso 128 E b
Thymbra 9 B b
Thymbrius River 9 B b
Thyni, people 9 G d
Thyrea 14 C b
Tian-shan Mountains 104 B H d
Tiberius, Arch of, on the Forum 24 B (14)
Tibet, reg. 104 B I d
Tibet, Inner, reg. 171 K e
Tibet, Outer, reg. 170 J e
Tichiussa 17 E c
Tigranocerta 20 I c
Tihany, mon. 80 E h
Timişoara (Temesvar) 103 O f
Timna 7 C e
Timur, Dominions of 92 leg.
Tinnevelly 137 C g
Tintagel 74 I i
Tione 168 H ins.
Tippermuir 128 E d
Tiraspol 168 G K f
Tireboli 168 J C a
Tiree, isl. 128 A d
Tirmidh 104 B G d
Tirnovo (Tirnova) 93 C b
Tityrus, mt. 15 D d
Tivertzes, people 57 I d
Tobol River 104 B G b
Tokaj (Tokay) 87 M d
Tokat 168 J C a
Toledo, univ. 100 E g
Toledo Mountains 82 B b
Tönsberg 58 F b
Tor (Sinai Penins.) 150 B b
Torcy 168 C B c
Tordesillas 83 J g (Tordes.)
Torksey 60 I c
Torre (Tor), mon. 97 N k
Torrelobaton (Torrelob.) 83 J g
Torres, route of 128 C P f
Toruń (Thorn) 135 J b
Toski 174 G b
Touapse 182 E E c
Tougurt 174 D a
Tovačov (Tobitschau) 159 I d
Towcester 60 I c
Tozan, people 104 C K d
Tralee 74 B b
Tramin. castle 79 G e
Tranquebar 128 B ins. B
Transcaucasia, rep. 168 G N-O g
Transcaucasian Socialist Federal Soviet Republic (T.S.F.S.R.) 168 F leg.
Trans-Jordan, reg. 168 J C c
Transoxiana, reg. 53 I c
Transvaal (South African Republic) 175 M l
Trastevere Railway Station, in Rome 22 A
Traun River 135 G d
Trave River 134 F a
Treasuries in Olympia 9 H f
Trebbin, castle 85 C b
Trebiae 27 G e
Trebinje (Trebinye), bp. 94 F c

Trebitsch (Trebič) 87 J d
Tregony, bor. 74 I i
Trempealeau, Fort 191 G c
Trenčin (Trencsén, Trentschin) 63 J d
Trentino, reg. 168H ins.
Trikkala 89 B c
Trimontium 51 O g
Trincomali (Trincomalee) 137 D g
Trinovantes, people 51 Q i
Triocala 30 C e
Triploe (Thriplow) Heath 127 Z n
Tripods, Street of the, in Athens 23 C
Tripolitania, dist. 174 E a
Tripolitsa, in Greece 165 C e
Tritaea, in Achaia 14 B b
Trnava (Tyrnau, Nagyszombat) 79 J d
Trnova (Tirnova) 93 C b
Troas, reg. 9 D e
Trocnov (Troznow) 87 J d
Trogir (Traú), bp. 95 F c
Troian Plain 9 A b
Troitskaia 138 E d
Troki 88 K d
Tropaeum Augusti 26 B d
Troy in Asia Minor 9 B b
Troyland, reg. 9 D e
Trucial Oman, reg. 168K F d
Truns 91 R l
Truro, mon. 97 L k
Trutnov (Trautenau) 135 H c
Tsaribrod 168G J g
Tsaritsyn 139 F f
Tsarskoe Selo 138 D d (T.S.)
Tscherlitz (Echallens) 91 O l
Tsi-ning-chau 104C L d
Tsuen-chau-fu 104C L e
Tuapse 168J C a
Tuaregs, people 174 D b
Tuat 174 C b
Tüffer 72 D b
Tulcea (Tulcha) 165 F a
Tun 168K G c
Tunguska River, Lower- 104C J a
Tunguska River, Upper- 104C J b
Turaba 170 F f
Turan, reg., in India 53 I d
Turcoman Socialist Soviet Republic 168F leg.
Turfan 104C I c
Turkestan, economic reg. 170 leg.
Turkestan, East, reg. 170 I e
Turkey, Republic, 1923 168J B b
Turkish (Ottoman) Empire, 1683—1913 164
Turkish (Ottoman) Empire, till 1920, 1922 168J B b
Turkoman Socialist Soviet Republic 170 G d-e
Turks, people, 8 cent. 53 H b
Turks, people, 14 cent. 89 J g
Turks, people, in 1913 165 leg.
Turriff 128 F c
Tus 99 L g
Tutbury, castle 74 L g
Tuticorin 170 I h
Tuxtepec 216 D d
Tuz Geul 168J B b
Tuz-Khurmati 168J D c
Tuzla 108 N f
Tweeddale, dist. 128 E e
Twyneham 60 I d
Tyche, Temple of 23 D
Tyrconell, ter. 74 B a
Tyre 168J C c
Tyria 168J A b
Tyrnau (Trnava, Nagyszombat) 79 J d
Tzompantzinco 106 B a
Udgir 137 C e
Uglich 138 E d
Ugrians, people 104B G a
Uigurs, people 104C I c
Uirats, people 104C J b
Uist, North and South, isl. 128 A c
Ujda 174 Q n
Ujek-Tepe 9 A b
Ujiji 175 F e
Ujjain 104B R i
Ujvidék (Neusatz, Novi Sad) 168 F d
Ukrainian Socialist Soviet Republic (U.S.S.R.) 168F leg.
Uladh (Ulster), dist. 60 A b
Ulala 170 J c
Ulan-Butor-Khoto (Urga) 171 L d
Ulcinj (Dulcigno) 165 A e
Ulcinj, (Dulcigno), bp. 95 F c
Uliasutai 171 K d
Uliches, people 57 J d
Ulster (Uladh), dist. 60 A b
Ulster, prov. 74 C a
Ulu-kem River 104C J b
Uman reg. 104C J e
Umberto I, Ponte-, loc. in Rome 22 A
Umbilicus, in Rome 24 B (10)
Umbri, people 29 C c
Ume River 98 G a
Una River 87 K f
Unie, isl. 168F H g
Unghvár (Užhorod) 168 H b
Union of South Africa 175 F g
Union of Soviet Socialist Republics (Russia) 168G L-R d
Université, quarter in Paris 149 B
University, in Athens 23 D
University Street, in Athens 23 D
Unst, isl. 128 ins.
Upland, dist., in Sweden 88 G a
Upper Egypt, reg. 4 F d (III)
Upper Germans, people in 1929 168H C-E c
Upper (Gray) League 91 Q l
Upper Lorraine, duchy, 13 cent. 104A C c
Upper Nairi Sea 5 D b
Upper Silesia, reg. 168D D c
Upper Tunguska River 104C J b
Uppsala (Upsala) 88 G b
Ural, economic reg. 170 leg.
Uratu, dist. 4 G c
Urci 38 B e
Urci. bp. 42 B f
Urfa 168J C b
Urgenj 104B F c
Urmia 168K E b
Urmia, Lake 99 M f
Ursha 168L D c
Urumtsi 104B J c
Urundi, reg. 175 F e
Ush 104B H c
Usk, castle 74 K h
Usk, R. 60 H d
Uskub (Skoplje) 89 H f
Üsküdar 168L F f
Ussa River 138 J b
Ussuri River 104C N c
Ústí (Aussig) 135 G c
Uvejek 9 A b
Uxellodunum, in Britain 51 O g
Uxellodunum, in Gaul 38 ins.
Uzbek Socialist Soviet Republic 170 H d
Uzes, people, on the Dnieper R. 99 J d
Uzes, people, on the Ural R. 53 H b
Uzgend 104B H c
Užhorod (Unghvár) 168 H b

Vaçcanae (Baccanae) 35 ins. B
Vács (Waitzen) 87 L e
Vács (Waitzen), bp. 95 F b
Vadstena (Wadstena) 88 F b
Valencia Island, in Ireland 168F C e
Vallay of Salt 7 B f
Valley of the Sweet Waters of Europe 93 G e
Val Pusteria 168 H ins.
Valona (Avlona) 164 B b
Val Venosta (Vintschgau), reg. 87 H e
Väner (Wener), lake 88 E b
Vangui (Yang-chau-fu) 104C M d
Varad, Nagy-(Grosswardein, Oradea Mare) 168 G c
Värälä 138 C c
Varberg (Warberg) 88 E c
Varini, people 38 D a
Värmland (Vermland), reg. 45 G a
Varvakion, bldg. in Athens 23 D
Västerås (Westerås) 88 G b
Vätter (Wetter), lake 88 F b
Vaudemont 104A D c
Vaudemont, cty., 13 cent. 104A D c
Vaux (-devant-Damloup) 168C C c
Vaux-lès-Laferté 104A C b (V.l. L.)
Vaux-lès-Mouzon 104A C b (V.l.M.)
Vechta 78 F b
Veldes 79 I e
Veles 165 B c
Venta Icenorum (Caistor, Bury St. Edmunds) 51 Q h
Venus, Temple of, near Ardea 35 ins. B
Venus Cloacina, Temple of 24A (14)
Venus Genetrix, Temple of 24B (24)
Venzone 154 G e
Veps, people 59 L b
Veramin 104B F d
Verbas River 87 K f
Verneuil (near Évreux) 69 H f
Verneuil (near Montmédy) 104A C b (Ve.)
Versecz (Werschetz, Vršac) 168 G d
Vesle River 104A B b
Vespasian, Temple of 24 B (6)
Vesta, Temple of 24 A (19)
Veszprem 87 K e
Veszprem, bp. 95 F b
Veurne see Furnes 134 B c
Via Appia Nuova, street in Rome 22 A
Via Cavour, street in Rome 22 A
Via della Lungara, loc. in Rome 22 A
Via di Porta San Sebastiano, in Rome 22 A
Viale Ardeatino, in Rome 22 A
Viale Ostiense, in Rome 22 A
Via Nazionale, street in Rome 22 A
Via Nomentana, street in Rome 22 A
Viatka 138 G d
Viatka River 138 G d
Viatka-Vetluga, economic reg. 168F leg.
Via Venti Settembre, street in Rome 22 A
Viazma 138 D d
Viborg (Wiborg) 88 C c
Vieille Rue du Temple, street in Paris 149 B
Vielun (Wielun) 79 K c
Vienna, in Austria 63 I d
Vigneul-sous-Montmédy 104A C b (Vi)
Vijayadurg 137 B e
Vijayanagar, reg. 92 H f
Viking raids 45 E b
Világos 139 B f
Viliui River 104C L a
Viliya (Wiliya) River 88 K d
Villa Cisneros 181 Z e
Villafranca (Villefranche) 102 H g
Villa Hayes 216 H h
Villalar 83 J g (Villal.)
Villanueva, in Spain 83 K g
Villa Medici, bldg. in Rome 22 A
Villareal 83 K h
Villa Rica de Vera Cruz 106 D a

Villa Rica la Vieja . . . . 106 D a
Villa Viçosa (Portugal) . . . 83 J h
Ville, quarter in Paris . . 149 B
Villefranche (-de-Rouergue) 76 E d
Villefranche (-sur-Mer) . . 102 H g
Villers-lès-Mangiennes . 104A C b
Vilmanstrand . . . . 138 C c
Vilnius (Vilna) . . . . . . 168D F c
Vimy Ridge, mt. . . . . . 168C B b
Vincennes, in France . . . . 86 D d
Vincennes, Fort-(Indiana) . 191 H d
Vintschgau (Val Venosta), reg. 87 H e
Virbalis (Virballen) . . . . 159 L a
Virginia, reg. . . . . 191 I e-L b
Virocônium (Wroxeter) . . . 51 O h
Virzjärv (Wirzjärw), lake . . 88 K b
Vis (Lissa), isl. . . . . 90 F c
Visborg (Wisborg), castle . 88 H c
Visby (Wisby) . . . . 88 H c
Višegrad, in Bosnia . . . . . 87 L g
Visegrad, castle in Hungary 87 L e
Visoko . . . . 89 A b
Vitim River . . . . 104C L b
Vitry (-le-François) . . . . . 154 C d
Vitry (-en-Perthois) . . . 104A B c
Vittorio Emanuele, Ponte, loc. in Rome . . . . 22 A
Vittório Véneto . . . . . . 168B F b
Viza . . . . 165 E c
Vltava (Moldau), R. . . . 168D C d
Voguls, people . . . . 138 J c
Voivodina, reg. . . . . 159 J f
Vordernberg . . . . 79 I e
Vordingborg . . . . 87 H a
Voreda . . . . 51 O g
Vosprus . . . . 99 K d
Votiak, auton. area . . . 168G P d
Vots, people . . . . 57 I b
Vrana . . . . 87 J g
Vratza (Vraca) . . . . 165 C b
Vrbas River . . . . 161 K e
Vredenburg . . . . 128C ins. D
Vrhbosna (Sarajevo) . . . . . 87 L g
Vršac (Versecz, Werschetz) 168 G d
Vychegda River . . . . . . 138 G c
Vyschegrad (Wyszegrad), castle (near Bromberg) . . 79 K b
Vyšehrad (Wyschehrad), castle (near Prague) . . . 79 I d
Vytegra . . . . 182E E a

Wadgaon . . . . 137 B e
Wadi Halfa . . . . 174 G b
Wadi Sous . . . . 174 C a
Wagon Road (Hamaxitos) . 23 D
Wahabis, people . . . . . . 170 F f
Waldenburg, in Saxony . . . 79 H c
Waldenburg, in Wurtemberg 143 I g
Wales, princ. 8 cent. . . . . 60 C c
Wales, princ. 11 cent. . . . 65 E d
Wales, princ., 1200-1450 . . 74 I g
Wales in 1832 163
Wales, North-, dist. . . . . . 60 H c
Wallingford . . . . 60 I d
Walloons, people in 1929 168H B b
Walvis (Walfish) Bay . . . 175 E g
Wanborough . . . . 60 D d
Wantage . . . . 60 I d
Warangal . . . . 104B R j
Ware . . . . 127 Z o
Warga River . . . . 174 P n
Warszawa (Warsaw) . . . . . 87 M b
Wartenberg, castle, in Bohemia . . . . 79 I c
Washington, routes of . . . 195 C d
Wassulu, reg. . . . . 174 C d
Watchet, borough . . . . . . 60 H d
Waterford, in Ireland . . . . 74 C b
Waterloo . . . . 156 A a
Wawat, reg. . . . . 4 F d
Wedmore . . . . 60 H d
Weissenstein, castle, in Esthonia . . . . 88 K b
Weitenstein, castle . . . . . . 79 I e
Weitra . . . . 79 I d
Wells, in England . . . . . . 74 K h
Welsh Marcher Earldoms 70 F c (W.M.E.)
Welsh Mountains . . . . 2 D c
Welshpool . . . . 74 J g
Welsh Principalities . . 70 F c (W. P.)
Wends, people in 1929 . 168H D b
Wenlock, mon. . . . . 60 C c
Werdenfelds, castle . . . . . 79 G e
Werfen . . . . 87 I e
Werschetz (Versecz, Vršac) 168 G d
Weset . . . . 4 F d
Wessex, Kingdom of . . . . . 60 leg.
West, economic reg. . . . . 168 F leg.
Westerna, dist. . . . . 60 C c
Western Euphrates River . . 18 E c
Western Samoa, Territory of 172 H b
Westerwald, mts. . . . . . 168C D b
West Götland, dist. . . . . . 88 E b
West Hartlepool . . . . 162 E c
West Kirghiz, economic reg. . . . . 170 G d leg. (B)
Westmanland, dist. . . . . . . 88 F b
West March, dist. . . . . . . 128 E e
Westminster, abbey . . . . . . 74 M h
Westmorland, dist. . . . . . . 60 H b
Westmorland, cty. . . . . 74 K e
Westmorland, parl. dist. . . 163 L c
Westray, isl. . . . . 128 E a
West Riding, dist. . . . . . . 60 I c
West Samoa, Territory . . . 180 J i
West Saxons, people . . . . . 60 C-D d
West Scheldt, R. . . . . . 168C B b
West Sea (North Sea) . . . . 98 D c
West Wales, dist. . . . . . . 60 B d
Wexford . . . . 74 C b
Wezzan . . . . 174 P n
Whalsay, isl. . . . . 128 ins.
Wharfe River . . . . 60 D c
Whitby (Streaneshalch), mon. 60 D b
Whiterne (Whithorn), bp. . . 60 B b
White Russian Socialist Soviet Republic (W. R. S. S. R) . 168 F leg.
Whithorn . . . . 128 D f
Whithorn (Whiterne), bp. . . 60 B b
Wick . . . . 128 E b
Wicklow, castle . . . . 74 C b
Wied, castle . . . . 78 E c
Wiek, dist. . . . . 88 J b
Wieringen . . . . 168D A c
Wigmore, castle . . . . 74 K g
Wigtown . . . . 128 D f
Wigtown, cty. . . . . 128 D f
Wilimow . . . . 87 J d
Wiliya (Viliya) River . . . . 138 C e
William of Rubruck, Route of . . . . 104B leg.
Willis Islets . . . . 179 F i
Wilno (Vilna) . . . . 159 M a
Wilton, battle . . . . 60 I d
Winchester in England (Venta Belgarum) . . . . 51 P i
Windau River . . . . 88 J c
Winds (Slovenes), people . 56 E c
Wing . . . . 60 I d
Winnebah . . . . 128C ins. D
Winnipeg River . . . . 190 F a
Winwaedsfield, battle . . . . 60 D c
Wirzjärw, lake . . . . 88 K b
Wisborg (Visborg), castle . 88 H c
Wislica . . . . 87 M c
Witbois, people . . . . 175 E g
Witham, borough . . . . 60 J d
Witteland, reg. . . . . . . 128C N g
Wittgenstein, castle . . . . . 86 G c
Wkra River . . . . 135 K b
Woëvre Plain . . . . 168C C c
Wolkowysk . . . . 155 M b
Wollin, bp. . . . . 95 E a
Wolmar . . . . 88 K c
Wolodomir . . . . 99 H c
Wolyn, dist. . . . . 139 C e
Woodstock, borough . . . . 74 L h
Worcester, bp. in England . 60 C c
Wormser Joch, pass (Stelvio Pass) . . . . 86 H e
Wörth . . . . 158 D d
Wrath, cape . . . . 128 C b
Wreocensaete, people . . . 60 C c
Wycombe . . . . 74 M h
Wye River . . . . 60 C c
Wyschehrad (Vyšehrad), castle . . . . 79 I d
Wyszegrad (Vyschegrad), castle . . . . 79 K b
Wytschaete Ridge . . . . . 168C B b (W.)

Xavier, Saint Fr(ancis) . . . 191 H c
Xochimilco, lake . . . . 106 A a
Xocotla . . . . 106 C a
Xoïs . . . . 4 ins.

Yachi . . . . 104C K e
Yakut, economic reg. . . . 171 O b (G)
Yakutat . . . . 180 N b
Yakutsk, Autonomous Socialist Soviet Republic . 171 M/P b
Yala Geul . . . . 168L D c
Yamburg . . . . 88 M b
Yamurtalik . . . . 168J C b
Yandabu . . . . 171 K f
Yang-chau-fu . . . . 104C M d
Yang-tse-kiang, R. . . . . 104C K e
Yang-tsun . . . . 170 ins. A
Yanina (Janina) . . . . 89 B c
Yarkand . . . . 104B H d
Yarmouth, (I. of Wight) . . . 74 L i
Yarmouth, Great- (Norfolk) . 65 G d
Yarmouth, Great-, parl. bor. 163 P e
Yatnan (Cyprus), isl. . . . . . 5 C b
Yatreb (Medina) . . . . 53 G d
Yatvegs, people . . . . 71 K c
Yazvings, people . . . . . . 57 H c
Yedlinsk (Jedlinsk) . . . . . 155 K c
Yell, isl. . . . . 128 ins.
Yemama, reg. . . . . 53 G d
Yemamah, El- . . . . 104B E e
Yenihan . . . . 168J C b
Yeni Kioi . . . . 9 A b
Yenisei River . . . . 104C I a
Yeni-Shehr . . . . 9 A b
Yerkessi . . . . 9 A b
Yezd . . . . 170 G e
Yezdi Chast . . . . 168K F d
York, in England . . . . . . 60 D b
York, abbey . . . . 74 M f
York, Kingdom of . . . . . 60 I b
Yoshino . . . . 104C N d
Yozgad . . . . 168J B b
Ypiranga . . . . 215 D e
Yrac, reg. . . . . 99 K f
Yser River . . . . 168C B b
Ystad . . . . 103 K a
Yttingaford . . . . 60 I d
Yuan Dynasty . . . . 92 K e
Yu-ché, people . . . . 104C M c
Yugoslavia, km. . . . . . . 168F I-J g
Yung-ning-fu . . . . 104C K e

Zab River . . . . 53 G c
Zadar (Zara) . . . . 168 D d
Zafarin Islands . . . . 174 Q n
Zagreb (Zagrab, Agram) . . . 79 J f
Zagreb (Agram), bp. . . . . . 95 F b
Zagros Mountains . . . . . 168K D b-E c
Žagubica . . . . 165 B a
Zaiton (Tsuen-chau-fu) . 104C L e
Zaječa . . . . 103 N f
Zamość . . . . 155 L c
Zampa, reg. . . . . 104C K f
Zappeion, bldg. in Athens . 23 D
Zardandan, reg. . . . . . . 104C J e
Zarev . . . . 139 G f
Zary, abp. . . . . 99 M d
Zarnowitz . . . . 87 L a

Žatec (Saaz) . . . . 87 I c
Zator . . . . 87 L d
Zebid . . . . 104 B E f
Zeebrugge . . . . 168 C B b
Zeitun . . . . 168 K F c
Zeitz, bp. (Naumburg-) . . . 95 E a
Zeklers, people in 1929 . 168 H G c
Zelea . . . . 9 E d
Zemun (Semlin, Zimony) . 168 G d
Zenda Rud, R. . . . . . . 168 K F c
Zengg (Senj) . . . . 168 D d
Žepče . . . . 87 L f
Zephat . . . . 6 C c
Zephyrium, prom., in Crete 14 ins.
Zerenj . . . . 104 B G d
Zeus, Temple of, in Olympia 9 H f (2)
Zhagubitza (Žagubica) . . 165 B a
Zhaia . . . . 104 B F f
Zhitomir . . . . 139 C e
Ziegenhain . . . . 78 F c
Ziklag . . . . 7 B f
Zile . . . . 168 J C a
Zimony (Zemun, Semlin) 168 G d
Zinjar . . . . 77 M e
Zipangu, emp. (Japan) . 104 C O d
Zips, County of . . . . 87 M d
Zircz, mon. . . . . 80 E h
Ziza . . . . 7 D e
Znaim (Znojmo) . . . . 87 K d
Zolyom (Zvolen, Altsohl) 159 J d
Zone of the Straits . . . 168 D F e
Zsolna (Sillein) . . . . 155 J d
Zubeir. . . . . 168 K E c
Zuhab . . . . 99 M g
Zvornik (Zwornik) . . . . . 87 L f
Zwettl . . . . 87 J d